W9-BZO-601

International Directory of
COMPANY
HISTORIES

International Directory of
COMPANY
HISTORIES

VOLUME 100

Editor

Tina Grant

ST. JAMES PRESS
A part of Gale, Cengage Learning

GALE
CENGAGE Learning™

Detroit • New York • San Francisco • New Haven, Conn • Waterville, Maine • London

GALE
CENGAGE Learning™

International Directory of Company Histories, Volume 100

Tina Grant, Editor

Project Editor: Miranda H. Ferrara

Editorial: Virgil Burton, Donna Craft, Louise Gagné, Peggy Geeseman, Julie Gough, Linda Hall, Sonya Hill, Keith Jones, Daniel King, Lynn Pearce, Holly Selden, Justine Ventimiglia

Production Technology Specialist: Mike Weaver

Imaging and Multimedia: John Watkins

Composition and Electronic Prepress: Gary Leach, Evi Seoud

Manufacturing: Rhonda Dover

Product Manager: Jenai Mynatt

For product information and technology assistance, contact us at **Gale Customer Support, 1-800-877-4253.**
For permission to use material from this text or product, submit all requests online at **www.cengage.com/permissions.**
Further permissions questions can be emailed to **permissionrequest@cengage.com**

Gale
27500 Drake Rd.
Farmington Hills, MI, 48331-3535

LIBRARY OF CONGRESS CATALOG NUMBER 89-190943
ISBN-13: 978-1-55862-634-8
ISBN-10: 1-55862-634-4

This title is also available as an e-book
ISBN-13: 978-1-55862-763-5   ISBN-10: 1-55862-763-4
Contact your Gale, a part of Cengage Learning sales representative for ordering information.

BRITISH LIBRARY CATALOGUING IN PUBLICATION DATA
International directory of company histories, Vol. 100
Tina Grant
33.87409

Printed in the United States of America
1 2 3 4 5 6 7 13 12 11 10 09

Contents

Preface

The St. James Press series *The International Directory of Company Histories* (*IDCH*) is intended for reference use by students, business people, librarians, historians, economists, investors, job candidates, and others who seek to learn more about the historical development of the world's most important companies. To date, *IDCH* has covered more than 10,000 companies in 100 volumes.

INCLUSION CRITERIA

Most companies chosen for inclusion in *IDCH* have achieved a minimum of US$25 million in annual sales and are leading influences in their industries or geographical locations. Companies may be publicly held, private, or nonprofit. State-owned companies that are important in their industries and that may operate much like public or private companies also are included. Wholly owned subsidiaries and divisions are profiled if they meet the requirements for inclusion. Entries on companies that have had major changes since they were last profiled may be selected for updating.

The *IDCH* series highlights 25% private and nonprofit companies, and features updated entries on approximately 35 companies per volume.

ENTRY FORMAT

Each entry begins with the company's legal name; the address of its headquarters; its telephone, toll-free, and fax numbers; and its web site. A statement of public, private, state, or parent ownership follows. A company with a legal name in both English and the language of its headquarters country is listed by the English name, with the native-language name in parentheses.

The company's founding or earliest incorporation date, the number of employees, and the most recent available sales figures follow. Sales figures are given in local currencies with equivalents in U.S. dollars. For some private companies, sales figures are estimates and indicated by the abbreviation *est.* The entry lists the exchanges on which the company's stock is traded and its ticker symbol, as well as the company's NAICS codes.

Entries generally contain a *Company Perspectives* box which provides a short summary of the company's mission, goals, and ideals; a *Key Dates* box highlighting milestones in the company's history; lists of *Principal Subsidiaries, Principal Divisions, Principal Operating Units, Principal Competitors*; and articles for *Further Reading*.

American spelling is used throughout *IDCH*, and the word "billion" is used in its U.S. sense of one thousand million.

SOURCES

Entries have been compiled from publicly accessible sources both in print and on the Internet such as general and academic periodicals, books, and annual reports, as well as material supplied by the companies themselves.

CUMULATIVE INDEXES

IDCH contains three indexes: the **Cumulative Index to Companies**, which provides an alphabetical index to companies profiled in the *IDCH* series, the **Index to Industries**, which allows researchers to locate companies by their principal industry, and the **Geographic Index**, which lists companies alphabetically by the country of their headquarters. The indexes are cumulative and specific instructions for using them are found immediately preceding each index.

SPECIAL TO THIS VOLUME

This 100th volume of *IDCH* contains the first entry for the country of Paraguay (Banco Central del Paraguay).

SUGGESTIONS WELCOME

Comments and suggestions from users of *IDCH* on any aspect of the product as well as suggestions for companies to be included or updated are cordially invited. Please write:

The Editor
International Directory of Company Histories
St. James Press
Gale, Cengage Learning
27500 Drake Rd.
Farmington Hills, Michigan 48331-3535

St. James Press does not endorse any of the companies or products mentioned in this series. Companies appearing in the *International Directory of Company Histories* were selected without reference to their wishes and have in no way endorsed their entries.

Notes on Contributors

Gerald E. Brennan
Writer and musician based in Germany.

M. L. Cohen
Novelist, business writer, and researcher living in Paris.

Ed Dinger
Writer and editor based in Bronx, New York.

Heidi Feldman
Writer and editor based in California.

Paul R. Greenland
Illinois-based writer and researcher; author of three books and former senior editor of a national business magazine; contributor to *The Encyclopedia of Chicago History*, *The Encyclopedia of Religion*, and the *Encyclopedia of American Industries*.

Robert Halasz
Former editor in chief of *World Progress* and *Funk & Wagnalls New Encyclopedia Yearbook*; author, *The U.S. Marines* (Millbrook Press, 1993).

Evelyn Hauser
Researcher, writer and marketing specialist based in Germany.

Frederick C. Ingram
Writer based in South Carolina.

Micah L. Issitt
Philadelphia-based writer, historian, ecologist and humorist.

Carrie Rothburd
Writer and editor specializing in corporate profiles, academic texts, and academic journal articles.

Christina M. Stansell
Writer and editor based in Louisville, Kentucky.

A. Woodward
Wisconsin-based writer.

List of Abbreviations

¥ Japanese yen
£ United Kingdom pound
$ United States dollar

A

AB Aktiebolag (Finland, Sweden)
AB Oy Aktiebolag Osakeyhtiot (Finland)
A.E. Anonimos Eteria (Greece)
AED Emirati dirham
AG Aktiengesellschaft (Austria, Germany, Switzerland, Liechtenstein)
aG auf Gegenseitigkeit (Austria, Germany)
A.m.b.a. Andelsselskab med begraenset ansvar (Denmark)
A.O. Anonim Ortaklari/Ortakligi (Turkey)
ApS Amparteselskab (Denmark)
ARS Argentine peso
A.S. Anonim Sirketi (Turkey)
A/S Aksjeselskap (Norway)
A/S Aktieselskab (Denmark, Sweden)
Ay Avoinyhtio (Finland)
ATS Austrian shilling
AUD Australian dollar
ApS Amparteselskab (Denmark)
Ay Avoinyhtio (Finland)

B

B.A. Buttengewone Aansprakeiijkheid (Netherlands)
BEF Belgian franc

BHD Bahraini dinar
Bhd. Berhad (Malaysia, Brunei)
BND Brunei dollar
BRL Brazilian real
B.V. Besloten Vennootschap (Belgium, Netherlands)

C

C.A. Compania Anonima (Ecuador, Venezuela)
CAD Canadian dollar
C. de R.L. Compania de Responsabilidad Limitada (Spain)
CEO Chief Executive Officer
CFO Chief Financial Officer
CHF Swiss franc
Cia. Companhia (Brazil, Portugal)
Cia. Compania (Latin America [except Brazil], Spain)
Cia. Compagnia (Italy)
Cie. Compagnie (Belgium, France, Luxembourg, Netherlands)
CIO Chief Information Officer
CLP Chilean peso
CNY Chinese yuan
Co. Company
COO Chief Operating Officer
Coop. Cooperative
COP Colombian peso
Corp. Corporation
C. por A. Compania por Acciones (Dominican Republic)
CPT Cuideachta Phoibi Theoranta

(Republic of Ireland)
CRL Companhia a Responsabilidao Limitida (Portugal, Spain)
C.V. Commanditaire Vennootschap (Netherlands, Belgium)
CZK Czech koruna

D

D&B Dunn & Bradstreet
DEM German deutsche mark
Div. Division (United States)
DKK Danish krone
DZD Algerian dinar

E

EC Exempt Company (Arab countries)
Edms. Bpk. Eiendoms Beperk (South Africa)
EEK Estonian Kroon
eG eingetragene Genossenschaft (Germany)
EGMBH Eingetragene Genossenschaft mit beschraenkter Haftung (Austria, Germany)
EGP Egyptian pound
Ek For Ekonomisk Forening (Sweden)
EP Empresa Portuguesa (Portugal)
E.P.E. Etema Pemorismenis Evthynis (Greece)
ESOP Employee Stock Options and Ownership
ESP Spanish peseta

xi

Et(s). Etablissement(s) (Belgium, France, Luxembourg)
eV eingetragener Verein (Germany)
EUR euro

F
FIM Finnish markka
FRF French franc

G
G.I.E. Groupement d'Interet Economique (France)
gGmbH gemeinnutzige Gesellschaft mit beschraenkter Haftung (Austria, Germany, Switzerland)
G.I.E. Groupement d'Interet Economique (France)
GmbH Gesellschaft mit beschraenkter Haftung (Austria, Germany, Switzerland)
GRD Greek drachma
GWA Gewerbte Amt (Austria, Germany)

H
HB Handelsbolag (Sweden)
HF Hlutafelag (Iceland)
HKD Hong Kong dollar
HUF Hungarian forint

I
IDR Indonesian rupiah
IEP Irish pound
ILS new Israeli shekel
Inc. Incorporated (United States, Canada)
INR Indian rupee
IPO Initial Public Offering
I/S Interesentselskap (Norway)
I/S Interessentselskab (Denmark)
ISK Icelandic krona
ITL Italian lira

J
JMD Jamaican dollar
JOD Jordanian dinar

K
KB Kommanditbolag (Sweden)
KES Kenyan schilling
Kft Korlatolt Felelossegu Tarsasag (Hungary)
KG Kommanditgesellschaft (Austria, Germany, Switzerland)

KGaA Kommanditgesellschaft auf Aktien (Austria, Germany, Switzerland)
KK Kabushiki Kaisha (Japan)
KPW North Korean won
KRW South Korean won
K/S Kommanditselskab (Denmark)
K/S Kommandittselskap (Norway)
KWD Kuwaiti dinar
Ky Kommandiitiyhtio (Finland)

L
LBO Leveraged Buyout
Lda. Limitada (Spain)
L.L.C. Limited Liability Company (Arab countries, Egypt, Greece, United States)
L.L.P. Limited Liability Partnership (United States)
L.P. Limited Partnership (Canada, South Africa, United Kingdom, United States)
Ltd. Limited
Ltda. Limitada (Brazil, Portugal)
Ltee. Limitee (Canada, France)
LUF Luxembourg franc

M
mbH mit beschraenkter Haftung (Austria, Germany)
Mij. Maatschappij (Netherlands)
MUR Mauritian rupee
MXN Mexican peso
MYR Malaysian ringgit

N
N.A. National Association (United States)
NGN Nigerian naira
NLG Netherlands guilder
NOK Norwegian krone
N.V. Naamloze Vennootschap (Belgium, Netherlands)
NZD New Zealand dollar

O
OAO Otkrytoe Aktsionernoe Obshchestve (Russia)
OHG Offene Handelsgesellschaft (Austria, Germany, Switzerland)
OMR Omani rial
OOO Obschestvo s Ogranichennoi Otvetstvennostiu (Russia)
OOUR Osnova Organizacija

Udruzenog Rada (Yugoslavia)
Oy Osakeyhtî (Finland)

P
P.C. Private Corp. (United States)
PEN Peruvian Nuevo Sol
PHP Philippine peso
PKR Pakistani rupee
P/L Part Lag (Norway)
PLC Public Limited Co. (United Kingdom, Ireland)
P.L.L.C. Professional Limited Liability Corporation (United States)
PLN Polish zloty
P.T. Perusahaan/Perseroan Terbatas (Indonesia)
PTE Portuguese escudo
Pte. Private (Singapore)
Pty. Proprietary (Australia, South Africa, United Kingdom)
Pvt. Private (India, Zimbabwe)
PVBA Personen Vennootschap met Beperkte Aansprakelijkheid (Belgium)
PYG Paraguay guarani

Q
QAR Qatar riyal

R
REIT Real Estate Investment Trust
RMB Chinese renminbi
Rt Reszvenytarsasag (Hungary)
RUB Russian ruble

S
S.A. Société Anonyme (Arab countries, Belgium, France, Jordan, Luxembourg, Switzerland)
S.A. Sociedad Anónima (Latin America [except Brazil], Spain, Mexico)
S.A. Sociedades Anônimas (Brazil, Portugal)
SAA Societe Anonyme Arabienne (Arab countries)
S.A.B. de C.V. Sociedad Anónima Bursátil de Capital Variable (Mexico)
S.A.C. Sociedad Anonima Comercial (Latin America [except Brazil])
S.A.C.I. Sociedad Anonima Comercial e Industrial (Latin America [except Brazil])

S.A.C.I.y.F. Sociedad Anonima Comercial e Industrial y Financiera (Latin America [except Brazil])

S.A. de C.V. Sociedad Anonima de Capital Variable (Mexico)

SAK Societe Anonyme Kuweitienne (Arab countries)

SAL Societe Anonyme Libanaise (Arab countries)

SAO Societe Anonyme Omanienne (Arab countries)

SAQ Societe Anonyme Qatarienne (Arab countries)

SAR Saudi riyal

S.A.R.L. Sociedade Anonima de Responsabilidade Limitada (Brazil, Portugal)

S.A.R.L. Société à Responsabilité Limitée (France, Belgium, Luxembourg)

S.A.S. Societá in Accomandita Semplice (Italy)

S.A.S. Societe Anonyme Syrienne (Arab countries)

S.C. Societe en Commandite (Belgium, France, Luxembourg)

S.C.A. Societe Cooperativa Agricole (France, Italy, Luxembourg)

S.C.I. Sociedad Cooperativa Ilimitada (Spain)

S.C.L. Sociedad Cooperativa Limitada (Spain)

S.C.R.L. Societe Cooperative a Responsabilite Limitee (Belgium)

Sdn. Bhd. Sendirian Berhad (Malaysia)

SEK Swedish krona

SGD Singapore dollar

S.L. Sociedad Limitada (Latin America [except Brazil], Portugal, Spain)

S/L Salgslag (Norway)

S.N.C. Société en Nom Collectif (France)

Soc. Sociedad (Latin America [except Brazil], Spain)

Soc. Sociedade (Brazil, Portugal)

Soc. Societa (Italy)

S.p.A. Società per Azioni (Italy)

Sp. z.o.o. Spólka z ograniczona odpowiedzialnoscia (Poland)

S.R.L. Sociedad de Responsabilidad Limitada (Spain, Mexico, Latin America [except Brazil])

S.R.L. Società a Responsabilità Limitata (Italy)

S.R.O. Spolecnost s Rucenim Omezenym (Czechoslovakia

S.S.K. Sherkate Sahami Khass (Iran)

Ste. Societe (France, Belgium, Luxembourg, Switzerland)

Ste. Cve. Societe Cooperative (Belgium)

S.V. Samemwerkende Vennootschap (Belgium)

S.Z.R.L. Societe Zairoise a Responsabilite Limitee (Zaire)

T

THB Thai baht

TND Tunisian dinar

TRL Turkish lira

TWD new Taiwan dollar

U

U.A. Uitgesloten Aansporakeiijkheid (Netherlands)

u.p.a. utan personligt ansvar (Sweden)

V

VAG Verein der Arbeitgeber (Austria, Germany)

VEB Venezuelan bolivar

VERTR Vertriebs (Austria, Germany)

VND Vietnamese dong

V.O.f. Vennootschap onder firma (Netherlands)

VVAG Versicherungsverein auf Gegenseitigkeit (Austria, Germany)

W–Z

WA Wettelika Aansprakalikhaed (Netherlands)

WLL With Limited Liability (Bahrain, Kuwait, Qatar, Saudi Arabia)

YK Yugen Kaisha (Japan)

ZAO Zakrytoe Aktsionernoe Obshchestve (Russia)

ZAR South African rand

ZMK Zambian kwacha

ZWD Zimbabwean dollar

ABARTA, Inc.

———■———

1000 Gamma Drive, Suite 500
Pittsburgh, Pennsylvania 15238-2927
U.S.A.
Telephone: (412) 963-6226
Fax: (412) 968-1084
Web site: http://www.abarta.com

■ ■ ■

Private Company
Incorporated: 1972
Employees: 2,500
Revenues: $189 million (2007)
NAICS: 551112 Offices of Other Holding Companies;
312111 Soft Drink Manufacturers; 511110
Newspaper Publishers; 211111 Crude Petroleum
and Natural Gas Extraction; 311412 Frozen
Specialty Food Manufacturing

Through a diverse list of subsidiaries ABARTA, Inc., has interests in four major businesses; soft-drink manufacturing, newspaper publishing, oil and gas exploration, and ethnic frozen food. From its establishment in Pittsburgh, Pennsylvania, in 1933, the company expanded through strategic acquisitions to operate in six divisions spread throughout the northeast and across the United States. A third-generation, family-owned business, ABARTA was ranked in 2008 as the eighth largest independent Coca-Cola bottler in the United States, commanding annual revenues exceeding $180 million.

FOUNDATIONS: 1933–64

Pittsburgh native Rolland Adams founded the company that would later become ABARTA, Inc., in 1933 when he decided to invest in a struggling newspaper, the *Bethlehem Globe,* headquartered in Bethlehem, Pennsylvania. Adams, who was working as a bank examiner, teamed with a group of investment partners to purchase the *Globe,* but later bought out his partners to assume sole ownership of the newspaper.

Under Adams' leadership, the struggling newspaper slowly grew and, in 1951, Adams expanded his company with the purchase of the *Atlantic City Press,* which was established in 1895 in Atlantic City, New Jersey. Along with *Atlantic City Press* Adams also gained the *Press-Union* newspaper, which had been a subsidiary of *Atlantic City Press* since 1905. Adams decided to discontinue the *Press-Union* but expanded the reach of the *Atlantic City Press* with new offices in Cape May and Cumberland counties a few years after he assumed ownership.

In 1953 Adams used some of the revenues derived from his publishing enterprises to purchase partial interest in Coca-Cola bottling companies in Bethlehem and Pittsburgh, Pennsylvania. Between 1953 and 1963 Adams made arrangements to pass his various assets on to his extended family, which included his three daughters, Ann, Marcia, and Mimi, and their husbands. In 1963 Adams purchased 90 percent interest in the bottling operations in both Pittsburgh and Bethlehem. In addition, the company also purchased controlling interest in the Lehigh Valley Coca-Cola Company.

Adams' three sons-in-law, John Bitzer Jr., George Roehr, and Don Taylor, organized a holding company, which they called ABARTA, Inc., an acronym that blends the first letters of each of their last names, "B," "R," and "T," with an "A" for each of the three Adams sisters. Under the ABARTA banner Bitzer, Roehr, and Taylor purchased the remaining 10 percent interest in the Pittsburgh and Bethlehem Coca-Cola operations and, in 1964, purchased control of the *Atlantic City Press,* while Adams remained chief executive of the *Bethlehem Globe.*

THE FIRST ABARTA: 1965–72

After transferring his press businesses to his sons-in-law, Adams concentrated on other duties, including working as a trustee of his alma mater, Dickinson College, in Carlisle, Pennsylvania. Adams and his wife, Pauline S. Hornbach, donated $250,000 to Dickinson College to pay for the establishment of a new hall, named Adams Hall in his honor, to be one of the college's first women's dormitories. In 1966 Adams was granted an honorary doctor of laws degree for his achievements.

When Pauline Hornbach died in 1969 her interest in the company, which she shared with her husband, passed to her daughters, who inherited the *Bethlehem Globe* and the remaining 90 percent interest in the family's Coca-Cola bottling franchises. The following year Adams retired and passed complete control of the company to his daughters and sons-in-law.

Over the next few years ABARTA expanded its newspaper operations. In 1970 the company opened a production plant in Pleasantville, New Jersey, and the following year changed the name of the company from the *Atlantic City Press* to the *Press* in an effort to demonstrate the company's commitment to the entire region. The company also expanded its beverage division with the purchase of Cleveland Coca-Cola in 1971. This had been privately owned by members of the Mashburn family since 1930.

Ownership of the various companies was split among the family members. In 1972 the family dissolved the original ABARTA, Inc., and formed a new company with the same name as a holding company for all the family's business interests. Under the new ABARTA banner, the company consolidated all their various business interests under a single accounting system, while each company remained separate from a managerial standpoint.

SECOND-GENERATION LEADERSHIP: 1972–96

For the next several years ABARTA's publication division was the fastest-growing segment of the company's businesses. George Roehr, who was an expert in electronic systems management, personally saw the transition to electronic typesetting in 1975. The *Press* opened a Trenton, New Jersey, bureau in 1973 another division in Ocean County in 1975.

In 1974 ABARTA opened Summit Solutions as the company's bulk product purchasing division. Initially founded to serve as the purchasing company for ABARTA's various subsidiaries, it was soon expanded to offer bulk purchasing and material acquisition services to companies outside the ABARTA banner. Summit Solutions purchases raw materials, packaging, telecommunications equipment, computers, software, insurance packages and a variety of other materials and offers supplies to companies at a reduced cost and without the effort of finding suppliers.

From the mid-1970s ABARTA began expanding its bottling division. In 1975 ABARTA purchased 50 percent interest in New York Coca-Cola bottling. Two years later the company expanded its Cleveland operations with a new bottling plant in Carnegie, Ohio, and also purchased a Canada Dry bottling operation in the same region.

In 1979, the same year that founder Rolland Adams died, ABARTA entered a new industry, when they founded ABARTA Oil & Gas, Inc. ABARTA began this venture by making small investments in existing operations. The company remained a passive participant in this industry, however, while maintaining its twin focus in publishing and bottling. In 1980 ABARTA acquired full interest in New York Coca-Cola, buying out former partner Akron Coca-Cola.

KEY DATES

■

1933: The company is established by founder Rolland Adams.

1951: Adams purchases the *Atlantic City Press*.

1953: Adams begins acquiring minority interest in soft-drink bottling operations.

1963: Adams acquires 90 percent of Bethlehem and Pittsburgh Coca-Cola bottling operations.

1971: The company purchases Cleveland Coca-Cola.

1972: ABARTA is established as a holding company.

1974: ABARTA forms Summit Solutions as its purchasing division.

1975: The company purchases 50 percent of New York Coca-Cola.

1979: ABARTA Oil & Gas is formed.

1981: The company purchases a controlling interest in Buffalo Coca-Cola.

1993: A controlling interest in Coatesville Coca-Cola is acquired.

1998: ABARTA transfers ownership to third-generation family ownership.

2007: ABARTA purchases a controlling interest in Kahiki Foods, Inc.

By 1983 growth in the company's publishing business forced the company to double its publishing capacity. In 1987 ABARTA purchased new headquarters for its press division with a $3.2 million dollar building in Pleasantville, New Jersey. The former headquarters in Atlantic City was donated to Atlantic City Medical Center as the proposed site of a new facility.

In 1990 the company also converted from letterpress to Flexographic printing at a cost of nearly $12 million. While it was a major expenditure, the switch to Flexographic printing allowed the newspaper to print in full color. ABARTA also invested $400,000 to revamp newspaper production facilities and expand operations to allow for a larger staff.

By the late 1980s ABARTA's Oil & Gas division was becoming a more significant focus for the company. When the federal government began offering Section 29 tax credits for companies engaged in oil and natural gas drilling and exploration, ABARTA increased its investment in the industry, partnering with companies that had the capability to initiate new drilling operations. In 1993 ABARTA Oil & Gas conducted its first acquisition, purchasing 23 wells in Pike County, Kentucky.

This was the first of five acquisitions over the course of the next three years. The company also continued to invest in drilling new wells on existing properties.

While ABARTA Oil & Gas expanded, the company sold less profitable portions of other divisions in an effort to increase profitability and streamline operations. The company sold the *Bethlehem-Globe Times* in 1991 to concentrate on its other businesses and, in 1993, purchased controlling interest in Coatesville Coca-Cola. With the purchase of the Coatesville bottling operations, ABARTA combined its Lehigh Valley and Coatesville plants into a single unit, which was called ABARTA Beverage East.

ABARTA'S THIRD GENERATION

In 1996 the board of directors appointed John F. Bitzer III to serve as president and CEO when his father, John Bitzer Jr., retired from the company. As the company entered its third generation of family ownership, publishing and bottling remained the company's core focus industries, while ABARTA Oil & Gas was one of the company's fastest-growing divisions. In 1998 this division began to invest in private endeavors for the first time in the company's history, with the goal of becoming a full-service energy supply and extraction company. At the time, ABARTA held interests in more than 700 oil wells in Kentucky.

Based on a companywide feasibility study conducted in 1995, ABARTA decided to revise its financial principles. Instead of allowing each company to handle its financial planning and operations separately, the company designed a new subsidiary to handle finances for the company's entire beverage division. Shared Financial Services, Inc., was launched in 1998.

ABARTA conducted a major renovation of its South Jersey Publishing division in 2000, at a cost of more than $3.5 million. This included a new fiber-optic computer network, new HVAC systems, and a new web development department. In addition the company redesigned the entire format of the newspaper to achieve a more modern look. Later that year, ABARTA was presented with a leadership award by People Do Matter, an arm of the Pittsburgh Human Resources Association, in conjunction with Allegheny Community College.

In 2007 the board of directors at ABARTA decided to take the company in a new direction with the purchase of 90 percent interest in Kahiki Foods, a manufacturer of Asian, frozen food for the U.S. consumer market. Kahiki Food was established by founder Michael Tsao, owner of Kahiki Restaurant in Columbus, Ohio, as a way to sell his Asian food recipes to the public. With a manufacturing operation in Gahanna, Ohio, Kahiki produced more than 70 products for the retail grocery market. Kahiki foods grew more than 20 percent in 2005 and 2006, before the decision was made to sell the company to ABARTA.

SEVENTY-FIVE YEARS OF FAMILY COMPANY GROWTH

In 2008, 75 years after company founder Rolland Adams invested in his first newspaper, ABARTA operated a diverse list of subsidiary companies in four industry categories: newspaper publishing, where the company began; soft-drink manufacturing; oil and natural gas exploration; and its newest division, ethnic frozen foods. ABARTA's purchasing division, Summit Solutions, while one of the company's smallest operating divisions, also contributed to the company's growth as more than 50 percent of the company's clients were from outside the ABARTA family.

The ABARTA Beverage Group owned and operated four bottling companies in Cleveland, Ohio; Buffalo, New York; Lehigh Valley, Pennsylvania; and Coatesville, Pennsylvania. With combined sales of more than 16 million cases per year, ABARTA was the eighth largest independent bottler in the country and the company's most profitable single division. By 2008 the company's Oil & Gas Division owned an interest in 1,200 natural gas and oil wells across the country. The division had maintained an average of 20 percent profit growth per year since its inception. ABARTA Oil & Gas had expanded from its initial Kentucky fields to include operations in Pennsylvania, Ohio, West Virginia, Virginia, Louisiana, Kentucky, and Texas.

Micah Issitt

PRINCIPAL SUBSIDIARIES

Kahiki Foods, Inc.; South Jersey Publishing Company; Abarta Media Group, Inc.; Summit Solutions, Inc.; Abarta Oil & Gas, Inc.; Shared Financial Services, Inc.; Abarta Beverage Group, Inc.

PRINCIPAL OPERATING UNITS

Beverages; Frozen Food; Newspaper Publishing; Gas Exploration and Development.

PRINCIPAL COMPETITORS

Coca-Cola Enterprises Inc.; Con Agra Foods Inc.; New Jersey Media Group, Inc.

FURTHER READING

"ABARTA Oil & Gas Purchases 400 Wells from Meridian Exploration," *Pittsburgh Business Times,* October 27, 1998.

Bradshaw, H. H., Pete Bradshaw, and William Winston, *4x4 Leadership and the Purpose of the Firm,* Philadelphia: Haworth Press, 1998.

Clemens, John K., and Douglas F. Mayer, *The Classic Touch: Lessons in Leadership from Homer to Hemingway,* New York: McGraw-Hill Professional Publishers, 1999.

"Cooking Up a Profitable Strategy: Kahiki's New Owners Continue to Simplify Operations, Implement Cost-Savings Programs and Change the Gahanna Company's Manufacturing Methods," *Columbus Dispatch,* August 8, 2007.

"George L. Roehr Dead; Principal at Newspaper," *New York Times,* September 16, 1983, p. 43.

"Kahiki Foods Acquisition Complete," *Business First* (Columbus), June 26, 2007.

Lukasick, Jeanne, "Basically Abarta: How One Coke Bottler Applies Business Basics to Stimulate Growth in Its Low-Share Markets," *Beverage World,* October 1985, p. 94.

"Rolland Adams, Owner-Publisher of Newspaper in Bethlehem, Pa.," *New York Times,* September 3, 1979, p. D6.

Schnuer, Jenna, "Abarta Goes Where the Action Is," *Folio: The Magazine for Magazine Management,* May 1, 1996, p. 19.

Allgemeiner Deutscher Automobil-Club e.V.

Am Westpark 8
Munich, D-81373
Germany
Telephone: (49 89) 7676-0
Fax: (49 89) 7676-2500
Web site: http://www.adac.de

Not-For-Profit Association
Incorporated: 1903 as Deutsche Motorradfahrer-
    Vereinigung (DMV)
Employees: 7,900
Sales: EUR 610 million ($850 million) (2007)
NAICS: 813990 Other Similar Organizations (Except
    Business, Professional, Labor, and Political
    Organizations)

■ ■ ■

Allgemeiner Deutscher Automobil-Club e.V. (ADAC) is Germany's equivalent of the AAA. With over 16 million members, ADAC is the largest automobile club in Europe that helps motorists with information and advice, roadside assistance and technical services, insurance, and financing. ADAC's not-for-profit arm ADAC-Luftrettung runs air rescue service centers in Germany that provide medical and transportation services to victims of traffic accidents.

ADAC Service runs the popular Street Watch roadside assistance service that helps motorists fix technical problems on the spot. ADAC TruckService offers technical services to trucking companies and bus service providers. The club's three insurance subsidiaries, ADAC Autoversicherung, ADAC Rechtsschutz Versicherungs-AG, and ADAC-Schutzbrief Versicherungs-AG provide auto insurance, legal protection insurance, travel insurance, and other insurance products to its members. ADAC also offers rental cars at discounted rates, credit cards, and car loans to club members. ADAC Verlag publishes the monthly club magazine *ADACmotorwelt* as well as other periodicals and travel guides.

BUILDING GERMANY'S LARGEST CLUB FOR MOTORISTS

In May 1903, 25 motorcycle enthusiasts met in Stuttgart, Germany, to establish an association for the growing number of motorcycle riders in the country. There were several regional clubs for automobile lovers in Germany, but none existed for owners of motorized bicycles. The purpose of the new association was to promote motorcycling and to lobby for the interests of motorcyclists. The initiator, Emil Schmolz, who ran a car dealership in Stuttgart, became the first chairman of the German Association of Motorcyclists—Deutsche Motorradfahrer-Vereinigung (DMV). Nikolaus Hort, a newspaper editor in Stuttgart, became its first managing director. In 1905 Schmolz was succeeded by Josef Bruckmayer, the former chair of a local association for motorcyclists in Munich.

For an annual fee of six reichsmark, the price of about 13 pounds of meat or 265 pounds of potatoes, DMV members received a club magazine, attractive insurance rates, and access to the club's expanding network of gas stations offering oil and gasoline at

COMPANY PERSPECTIVES
■

We will do everything so that, while on the road, whenever people have questions concerning their mobility, they think of ADAC—their ADAC.

discounted prices. The number of DMV members grew much more quickly than expected—to 3,300 in 1904. The most prominent member was Prince Heinrich of Prussia, a brother of the German emperor and king of Prussia, Wilhelm II. By the end of 1905 DMV membership passed the 10,000 mark—more than all members of other motorist associations in Germany combined.

In 1906 DMV entered an agreement with Kaiserlicher Automobil-Club (KAC), Germany's prestigious Imperial Club for automobile owners. DMV agreed to limit its activities to motorcyclists and owners of small automobiles and to leave negotiations with public authorities to KAC. Organizing motorcycle and automobile races had become one of DMV's main activities to publicize the motorized life. As more owners of small automobiles joined DMV, the club's name was changed to Deutsche Motorfahrer-Vereinigung—German Motor Car Driver Association—in 1907.

When gasoline prices rocketed upward in 1907, DMV negotiated a price cap for their gasoline with a major German oil company and intensified efforts to tighten its own distribution network. In 1908 the club started paying for "border cards" for its members, which enabled motorists to enter another country without having to pay the regular customs fees. The new service proved especially popular among automobile owners.

NEW FOCUS ON AUTOMOBILE OWNERS

By 1911 about 70 percent of DMV members were automobile owners. To reflect this change, the club was renamed Allgemeiner Deutscher Automobilclub (ADAC)—General German Automobile Club—in 1911. Although ADAC aimed at addressing the owners of other motorized vehicles such as motorcycles, motor boats, and airplanes as well, automobile owners soon became the club's main focus. In 1910 ADAC began to fight the additional fees that a number of cities in Bavaria had begun to charge motorists for driving on their paved roads. The club organized protest marches, filed official complaints with city governments and published lists of Bavarian cities using the practice until

a national law was passed in 1913 that declared the so-called pavement toll illegal.

Long before the introduction of uniform traffic signs ADAC started putting up their own signs that said, for example, "Please drive on the right" or "Please drive slowly," in 1912. The necessary funds were raised by putting advertising on the signs as well. In the same year the club canceled the agreement with KAC that limited ADAC membership to owners of smaller cars. When ADAC celebrated its 10th anniversary in 1913, it was by far Germany's largest motorist club, numbering more than 20,000 members.

World War I put a sudden end to many of ADAC's activities, particularly motor sports competitions. As desire to help the war effort swept over the German people, more than 1,000 volunteers registered at the club's Munich office in August 1914, following the ADAC president's call to join a motor driver volunteer corps to support the German military. Another ADAC initiative was FAK, a transportation service between depots, field hospitals, and train stations. ADAC also received permission from the Austria-Hungarian War Ministry to collect so-called gifts of love, such as sausage, chocolate, and cigarettes, for soldiers on the front in Austria-Hungary and to send them there free of charge.

However, the initial war euphoria in Germany was soon replaced by grief over lost loved ones and, finally, over the lost war. World War I took a heavy toll on ADAC's membership, cutting it in half compared to 1914. However, after the ban on private motor vehicles was lifted in Germany in 1920, ADAC quickly reached prewar membership levels—despite significantly higher membership dues.

OFFERING TRAVEL
OPPORTUNITIES AND
ADDRESSING SECURITY ISSUES

In 1924 the club organized its first members' trip to Italy. About 80 ADAC members drove from Munich to Naples and attended the famous Targa Florio automobile race on Sicily. Four years later, some 130 ADAC members traveled to the United States by ship where they made a 2,175-mile trip from the East Coast to the Midwest where they met with members of American motor clubs and visited the Ford Motor Company in Detroit. In 1929 ADAC established Reise- und Wirtschaftsdienst GmbH, a travel agency and the club's first subsidiary. Organizing automobile and motorcycle races remained an important club activity during the 1920s as well. Favorite locations for the popular races were the Avus race track in Berlin and the

KEY DATES

1903: Deutsche Motorradfahrer-Vereinigung (DMV) is founded in Stuttgart.

1905: DMV headquarters are moved to Munich.

1911: The association is renamed Allgemeiner Deutscher Automobilclub (ADAC).

1925: Club magazine *ADAC-Motorwelt* is published for the first time.

1933: The DDAC established by the Nazis becomes Germany's only civil motor club.

1946: The club is reestablished after World War II under its old name.

1950: A new ADAC charter is passed.

1954: The popular roadside assistance service ADAC Strassenwacht is launched.

1958: Publishing subsidiary ADAC Verlag is founded.

1970: ADAC introduces a helicopter rescue service.

1972: Insurance subsidiary ADAC-Schutzbrief Versicherungs-AG is established.

1977: Legal protection insurance branch ADAC-Rechtsschutz Versicherungs-AG is founded.

1990: ADAC in East Germany merges with ADAC in West Germany.

1997: A new technical testing center is opened in Landsberg am Lech.

2002: The club offers its members exclusive auto insurance policies.

2003: Financial products subsidiary ADAC Finanzdienste GmbH is founded.

newly built Nürburgring with two race tracks near Adenau in the southern Eifel region.

In October 1925, following a leaflet campaign in Nuremberg accusing Josef Bruckmayer of financial irregularities, ADAC's president of 20 years resigned from his post. In the same year ADAC ceased publication of its 22-year-old monthly member publication *Motorfahrer*. It was replaced by *ADAC-Motorwelt*—ADAC Motor World—a monthly popular magazine with a beautifully illustrated four-color cover, featuring entertaining stories and anecdotes about cars and motorcycles, information on the club's latest events, and news from ADAC's regional and local chapters.

Another new club publication, *ADAC-Sport,* a newspaper covering motor sports news, technical and legal issues, was published only in 1925 and 1926. ADAC also published *Deutsches Autorecht*, German Automobile Law, covering legal issues involving motor vehicles. A supplement to *ADAC-Sport* at first, it became one of ADAC's regular monthly periodicals after 1926.

As traffic on Germany's roads increased, driver security became an important issue. In 1927 the government introduced uniform traffic signs for the entire German Empire. In the following year, ADAC launched an on-the-road patrol that patrolled major German cross-country roads to help motorists who were having technical problems, modeled after similar services by the large English and American auto clubs.

In 1930 the club began setting up emergency telephones along selected cross-country roads in Bavaria. The telephones were located in small roadside huts that also contained a first-aid kit and multilingual instructions on first-aid measures as well as on fixing technical problems in an emergency. Qualified help from ADAC arrived shortly after an emergency call was placed. The idea was consequently adopted in all of Germany. In 1933 ADAC compiled a list of ADAC-approved experts for members seeking professional advice after an accident, when needing repairs done, or when planning to purchase a vehicle.

REBUILDING AFTER WARTIME

By the early 1930s ADAC's membership had grown to over 100,000, making it the world's third largest automobile club. However, when the Nazis came to power under Adolf Hitler in 1933, they replaced the existing clubs for motorists in Germany by the newly founded Der Deutsche Automobilclub (DDAC). After the beginning of World War II in 1939, DDAC's regional offices were closed. No motorist club would exist until the war was over.

At a constitutive meeting in Munich in December 1946 ADAC was reborn as a new association under its old name. By 1949, the year when two separate German states were established, ADAC was active again in the three western German zones that became the Federal Republic of Germany. In 1948, after the Bavarian government returned the club's former property in Munich's Königinstrasse, ADAC moved back into its prewar headquarters. In 1951, only five years after its new formation, the club's membership was back at 100,000, the level of 1933.

After ADAC had been rebuilt, the club resumed its prewar activities: publishing the monthly magazine *Motorwelt,* organizing motor sports competitions, supporting members who were traveling abroad, and publishing up-to-date road maps. In 1950 ADAC's administrative board passed a new charter. A major success of the early 1950s happened in 1951 when the federal government of West Germany dropped its plans to introduce tolls on the *Autobahn* after massive protests by ADAC. However, the most important event in the club's postwar history was the relaunch of ADAC's roadside assistance service in 1954.

As the number of motorized vehicles on Germany's roads soared in the 1950s, safety on the road became one of ADAC's foremost concerns. In 1954, a fleet of 60 experienced auto technicians on bright yellow motorcycles with side cars started patrolling the streets, looking for stranded vehicles. Officially named ADAC Straßenwacht—ADAC Street Watch—it soon became known under its unofficial but popular name Yellow Angels. ADAC's street watchers performed every service imaginable, from restarting a dead engine, to hauling a broken-down vehicle to the next garage—all free of charge.

SERVICES IN THE SIXTIES AND SEVENTIES

In 1963 the Yellow Angels crew, which had grown fivefold within a decade, switched from motorcycles to Volkswagen Bugs. The service became so popular that some inventive criminals tried to imitate it in the 1970s. Dressed in imitation of the popular Yellow Angels outfit and driving the familiar yellow Volkswagen Bugs, they approached drivers who needed help and later presented them with enormous bills for towing their broken-down vehicles, which, they told their victims, would be reimbursed by ADAC.

In the late 1950s the club had established Street Watch base stations in large German cities. These offered additional driver safety and security services until they were closed in the 1990s. In addition to its Street Watch service, ADAC launched a number of services designed to prevent breakdowns and traffic accidents before they even happened. In 1962 ADAC's local chapter in Saarbrücken began to test vehicle lighting during the less busy fall and winter months.

Later in the decade ADAC Street Watch started offering mobile check-ups for club members' vehicles, including brake and speedometer tests, and tire inspections to pinpoint potential problem areas. The service was later expanded to testing starter systems, engine function, and emissions. ADAC's mobile check-up service became so popular that the club replaced the tents with custom-built testing trucks. As the number of motorized travelers abroad increased sharply, the club also initiated a towing service for broken-down vehicles in foreign countries. The thorough knowledge collected by the Yellow Angels was assembled in ADAC's *Pannen-statistik,* a summary of the most common problems of various vehicle makes, which was published by the club.

In 1968 the club launched a test project in Bavaria to rescue traffic accident victims by helicopter to speed the time until they received professional medical care. Two years later ADAC's first rescue helicopter went into service. After the club overcame initial problems—mainly securing financing—the service, which was supported by the private foundation Björn-Steiger-Stiftung, the Red Cross, government agencies, and health insurers, among others, evolved as one of the world's most tightly-knit air rescue networks.

Alarmed by the large number of fatal accidents—over 20,000 per year in the early 1970s—ADAC intensified its activities to make driving safer. Initiatives in the 1970s included promoting the use of safety belts, developing reflective traffic signs that were more visible at night, and introducing safe driving training courses for young and less experienced drivers. By the end of the 1970s the number of ADAC members had reached about five million.

PROTECTING THE ENVIRONMENT AND OFFERING SERVICES IN A REUNITED GERMANY

In the 1980s, rising concerns about the increasing pollution of the environment and its effects on human health and—ultimately—on life on earth, led to strict regulations in Germany, limiting the emissions of carbon monoxide, hydrocarbon, and nitrogen oxide released into the air by motor vehicles. To meet these new standards, non-diesel motor vehicles had to be equipped with three-way catalytic converters by 1986. In addition, lead-free gasoline, which was basically compatible with older engines as well, was introduced.

To promote the new technologies, ADAC launched a pilot project in Berlin where 15 cars of the Street Watch fleet were equipped with the new catalytic converters in 1983. In 1984 the club magazine *ADAC-Motorwelt* began featuring news and reports on the environment on a full page and published a map with the gas stations offering lead-free gasoline. In 1993 ADAC began publishing test reports on the impact of different car models on the environment such as emissions, fuel economy, and recyclable parts, to help environmentally conscious auto buyers find the right brand.

Meanwhile, the reunification of the two German states in October 1990 presented a historic opportunity to win new members. In 1988 ADAC had signed an agreement with East German authorities that allowed the club to extend its Street Watch service to the transit highways in East Germany between West Germany and West Berlin. According to the agreement, ADAC provided the vehicles, while the drivers were from East Germany and were trained by ADAC.

After the Berlin Wall came down in November 1989, a large number of East German tourists traveled to West Germany. To help them find their way around, ADAC distributed complimentary road maps and opened mobile information booths at the border. In spring 1990 a new automobile club named "ADAC in der DDR" was founded in East Germany with support from ADAC. Only a few months later, on October 3, 1990, the day East and West Germany were united, "ADAC in der DDR" was merged with the West German ADAC. By the end of that year the number of club members passed the ten million mark.

EXPANDING CONSUMER INFORMATION SERVICES AND INSURANCE OPTIONS

Providing consumers with qualified information on the growing variety of motor vehicles and related products and services became an important club activity in the 1990s. In 1997 ADAC's brand-new technical center opened in Landsberg am Lech, about 35 miles west of Munich. Equipped with state-of-the-art technology, ADAC's engineers started testing a broad variety of vehicles—from motorcycles to bicycles, from cars to trailers—as well as related products such as children's seats, helmets, snow chains, and detergents. Most importantly, the center began publishing the test results for the car models they had reviewed. In 1999 the center also started performing standardized crash tests.

After the turn of the millennium ADAC added a number of insurance and financial products to its existing range. As early as in the 1970s the club had ventured into the insurance market as an active player, after having brokered products from other insurers for many decades. In 1972 ADAC's first insurance subsidiary, ADAC-Schutzbrief Versicherungs-AG, was founded. It offered different travel insurance products, mainly the so-called *Schutzbrief*, a comprehensive policy for motor vehicle owners covering breakdowns, accidents and theft. Five years later the club founded a second insurance subsidiary, ADAC-Rechtsschutz Versicherungs-AG, which provided legal protection coverage for motorists.

In the early 1990s ADAC started brokering auto insurance policies from a handful of German insurers. However, when they started competing with ADAC by introducing their own *Schutzbrief* policies—ADAC's core insurance business—the club decided to end the cooperation. Instead, ADAC launched its own exclusive auto insurance policies for ADAC members in cooperation with two insurers, Deutscher Herold and Kravag in 2002. Finally, in 2007 ADAC started competing openly with other auto insurers by offering two different auto insurance plans through the newly founded insurance subsidiary ADAC-Autoversicherung AG, a joint venture with Frankfurt-based Zurich Group Germany in which ADAC held 49 percent.

BEYOND INSURANCE INTO GENERAL FINANCIAL SERVICES

In addition, the club introduced a variety of financial services, including auto loans and credit cards, through ADAC Finanzdienste GmbH, which was founded in 2003. While ADAC increased its activities in these traditionally commercial markets, critics questioned the club's nonprofit status, granting it major tax breaks without having to adhere to the more stringent accounting and publicity requirements that public companies of the same size had to follow.

In 2003, the year of ADAC's 100th anniversary, the club had more than 14 million members. Looking ahead in *100 Jahre ADAC,* the club's president, Peter Meyer, was confident that ADAC would remain the number one provider of services for Germany's motorists—despite sharply increasing costs for its roadside assistance programs and growing competition from auto manufacturers, insurance companies, and commercial service providers. Four years later the number of ADAC members passed the 16-million mark. In 2007, Meyer announced the club's next goals: Joining the league of Germany's top 20 insurers and winning two million additional members by 2010.

Evelyn Hauser

PRINCIPAL SUBSIDIARIES

ADAC Beteiligungs- und Wirtschaftsdienst GmbH; ADAC Autoversicherung AG (49%); ADAC-Rechtsschutz Versicherungs-AG; ADAC-Schutzbrief Versicherungs-AG; ARISA Assurances S.A. (Luxembourg); ADAC Finanzdienste GmbH; ADAC Autovermietung GmbH; ADAC Verlag GmbH; AD Clubreisen GmbH; ADAC Touring GmbH; ADAC Service GmbH; ADAC TruckService GmbH & Co. KG; Dienstleistungs-Center Halle GmbH; ADAC-Luftrettung GmbH; Aero-Dienst GmbH & Co. KG; Elbe Helicopter GmbH & Co. KG; ADAC Luftfahrt Technik GmbH; ACTA Assistance S.A. (France; 22%); ARC Transistance S.A. (Belgium; 35%); GKS Gesellschaft für Kommunikationsservice mbH; ADAC Stiftung "Gelber Engel" GmbH; ADAC Stiftung Sport.

PRINCIPAL COMPETITORS

Automobilclub von Deutschland e.V. (AvD); Auto Club Europa e.V. (ACE); ACV Automobil-Club Verkehr Bundesrepublik Deutschland; HUK-COBURG Haftpflicht-Unterstützungs-Kasse Kraftfahrender Beamter Deutschlands a. G. in Coburg, Allianz Deutschland AG.

FURTHER READING

Hutcheon, Paul, "'Mean Scots' Butt of German Insurer's Humour," *Sunday Herald,* March 30, 2008, p. 7.

100 Jahre ADAC. Bilder, Storys, Hintergründe, Munich, Germany: ADAC e. V., 2003, 194 p.

Petersdorff, Winand von, "Der Konzern der Gelben Engel," *Frankfurter Allgemeine Sonntagszeitung,* December 14, 2003, p. 35.

Thomas, Peter, "100 Jahre ADAC: Vom Motorclub zum Moilitätsdienstleister," *Frankfurter Allgemeine Zeitung,* February 15, 2003, p. 49.

Uniewski, Herbert, and Jörg Schmitt, "Crash-Tour in die Krise," *Stern,* July 15, 1999, p. 110.

Andin International, Inc.

—————■—————

609 Greenwich Street
New York, New York 10014
U.S.A.
Telephone: (212) 886-6000
Fax: (212) 866-6006
Web site: http://www.andin.com

Private Company
Incorporated: 1981
Employees: 500
Sales: $200 million (2007 est.)
NAICS: 339911 Jewelry (Including Precious Metal)
  Manufacturing

■ ■ ■

Andin International, Inc., is a privately held design, manufacturing, and wholesale jewelry company based in New York City. It supplies moderately priced private-label gold, diamond, and gemstone jewelry to high-volume retailers such as J.C. Penney, Macy's, QVC, Sears, and Zale Corporation. Manufacturing is done in plants in China, the Dominican Republic, India, Israel, and Thailand. Andin also owns and operates the web site Jewelry.com, a marketing platform that helps to provide consumers, especially men, with the kind of information they need in making jewelry-purchasing decisions. While the site does not directly sell jewelry, users shopping for particular items are directed to member retailers' web sites or helped to find the nearest store carrying the item.

Member retailers include Gordon's Jewelers, Helzberg Diamonds, J.C. Penney, Kay Jewelers, Macy's, Sears, and Zale. Andin benefits from Jewelry.com traffic because the site drives wholesale orders for its jewelry sold under the label of its retailer customers. The company claims that Jewelry.com receives more than 43 million unique visitors each year and boasts a database of 2.2 million registered users. Andin is involved in branded jewelry through sister company Aya International LLC. An Andin subsidiary until 2004, it offers jewelry designs by Andin's cofounder Aya Azrielant.

COMPANY FOUNDED: 1981

Andin was founded by Israelis Aya Azrielant and her husband, Ofer Azrielant. She was the daughter of a violin maker and was raised on a kibbutz in Israel. She studied literature, fine arts, and film making at Haifa University and met Ofer, a documentary filmmaker who did not have a degree, while the two were working on a documentary for Israel TV in Tel Aviv in the early 1970s. They married and to make ends meet in-between film projects began selling costume jewelry for Ofer's brother. In the mid-1970s they decided to open a jewelry store with the brother, despite a lack of experience in jewelry and retailing. "My wife and I thought we would go into the jewelry business for a few years, make a million dollars, then go back to making movies," Ofer Azrielant told the *New York Times* in 1990.

The jewelry store venture was a success that grew into a chain of stores in Israel. The Azrielant brothers had a falling out, however, and in 1981 Ofer and Aya Azrielant left the business and decided to move with

COMPANY PERSPECTIVES

Andin designs, manufactures, distributes and markets fine jewelry, catering predominantly to volume retailers. Andin strives to achieve the most successful styling, the highest conformity to quality standards and the best value. We work as a team, staying close to our customers, close to the marketplace and ahead of the competition.

their daughter to the United States, to New York, and start a jewelry company. They brought with them $250,000 in savings and a lone craftsman. In New York they studied the field and recognized that independents commanded the largest share of the marketplace. They also spotted an opening in mass-market fine jewelry, a niche that they believed was underserved between expensive jewelry and costume jewelry. "There was Tiffany and Bulgari at the high end," Aya Azrielant explained to *Working Woman* in a 1995 profile, "but at the low end, we saw garbage. We wanted to make jewelry with fine workmanship that retailed for $99 to $199." They borrowed $50,000 to start Andin International to manufacture private-label 14-karat gold and gem-set jewelry, setting up shop in the heart of Manhattan's midtown diamond district on 45th Street. While he concentrated on sales, she established the manufacturing operations.

The Azrielants also had help in diamonds from an unlikely source, Michael Roach, a Princeton University graduate who had studied with Tibetan monks to become a Buddhist monk. Because diamonds held a great deal of significance for Buddhists, he wanted to be involved with the stones, and after meeting Ofer Azrielant in 1981 he became involved in the launch of the company, learning how to appraise diamonds and to sell them. As head of the diamond division he was responsible for the hiring. Roach eventually left Andin to become a noted Buddhist teacher and founded Diamond Mountain University, an Arizona Tibetan Buddhist seminary.

SALES REACH $4 MILLION IN SECOND YEAR

The Azrielants' timing proved fortuitous, because at the time of Andin's founding, department stores in the United States—such as Abraham & Straus, J.C. Penney, Macy's, and Sears—were eager to participate in the fine jewelry market. Andin made it easy for them to do so,

not only providing the jewelry but also the display cases and camera-ready print ads. According to *Working Woman,* Andin "pioneered the production of small ads stuffed inside department-store bills." The retailers were geared to moving merchandise, and in Andin's first full year in business, 1982, sales reached $1 million. A year later that figure increased to $4 million.

Because of Andin's rapid growth, the company added to its quarters on 45th Street to accommodate the 300 people it employed by the mid-1980s. The space, spread across several floors in three buildings on 45th Street, was unwieldy and inefficient, forcing the Azrielants to look for a place to expand. Ofer Azrielant explained to the *New York Times,* "The options facing us were: move to New Jersey or Rhode Island, where we had looked at factory space; move offshore to Israel, Hong Kong or perhaps Bangkok, or find a building in New York and convert it to our needs." They decided to stay in New York City, their decision influenced by the financial assistance they received, including a $10 million loan through a tax-exempt bond and an $800,000 federal Urban Development Action Grant.

In 1988 Andin acquired a nine-story, 120,000-square-foot warehouse in Greenwich Village, occupying 75,000 square feet of it when it opened in 1990. The building cost $8.2 million, but the renovation cost another $12 million, which included new elevators and a state-of-the-art security system that was able to measure the amount of gold in an employee's body, such as gold crowns. The information was placed on bar-coded ID tags and employees had to pass through metal detectors to make sure that number remained constant as workers came and went each day. Such precautions were not just academic. In 1982, when Aya Azrielant was away from the business on a two-week maternity leave, she returned to find that an employee theft problem had developed. Almost the entire shop was fired and security measures were implemented before the issue was adequately under control.

OUTLET STORE OPENS

After ten years in business Andin was generating sales of more than $100 million. The company's success spawned competition, forcing Andin to remain cost-efficient and on the lookout for an edge. As much as possible the company saved scrap materials. The wash water of workers who were exposed to gold dust in the grinding and polishing of jewelry was recovered and processed for reuse. To sell merchandise overruns, Andin opened an outlet store in a Gurney, Illinois, outlet mall in 1992. Aya Azrielant also spotted a new opportunity in the early 1990s in higher-priced, more profitable jewelry using an electroforming process that created lightweight gold shells, especially well suited for making large earrings that did not hurt earlobes.

While attending an international jewelry fair in Basel, Switzerland, she had come across electroform technology, a well-established process that had not been applied to jewelry. Unlike cast jewelry that relied on liquid metal and molds, this method applied gold electrostatically over a base metal shape. A chemical process then dissolved the underlying metal, leaving behind a hollow and seamless 18-karat gold shell that was receptive to further design. Andin acquired an Israeli electroform lab, Jotaly Ltd., for $500,000, and spent another $1.5 million converting it into a jewelry manufacturing operation.

Andin began producing electroform earrings, but Aya Azrielant had bigger plans for the technology, using it to launch a moderately priced designer jewelry label under her own name. The Aya Azrielant Collection debuted in the spring of 1992. In addition to earrings, it would grow to include necklaces, pins, rings, and bracelets, and would be carried by higher-end department stores, including Bloomingdale's and Saks Fifth Avenue, as well as stores in Paris and Tokyo. The line also came with specially designed showcases and fixtures.

While much of the jewelry industry suffered through lean times in the early 1990s, when a downturn in the economy crippled sales, Andin prospered with its lower priced private-label cast jewelry and designer electroform jewelry. Annual sales reached $150 million by the mid-1990s, with Aya focusing on her designer collection and Ofer on the private-label business. The Azrielants were doing so well they bought back the 11-unit Israeli Jewelry Exchange retail chain from Ofer's brother. By the mid-1990s they also operated three Manhattan Diamond Stores in outlet malls; these were sold in 1996.

Andin found it difficult to grow beyond the $150 million level, however. Because the department stores sold the private-label jewelry under their own names, they had no motivation to be loyal to the company beyond price. As a result, foreign competitors with the advantage of low cost labor were often able to undercut Andin and take away business. In May 1997 the Azrielants agreed to sell Andin to Mt. Vernon, New York-based Michael Anthony Jewelers Inc. for $70 million, which included the assumption of $45 million in debt. Focusing on 14-karat gold jewelry and watches, Michael Anthony generated $150 million in annual sales. The combined company was slated to become one of the world's largest manufacturers of gold jewelry, but the sale never closed. In July the two parties called off the deal.

JEWELRY.COM ACQUIRED

To gain a competitive edge, in 2000 Andin acquired the rights to the Jewelry.com name from Miadora.com, one of the victims of the dot-com bust of that year. A number of start-ups had believed that the Internet was ideally suited to merchandise jewelry. However, at the first hint of trouble, the venture capitalists that funded the start-ups pulled their support and most of the jewelry sites folded. The Jewelry.com name remained valuable, but rather than using it in another attempt to retail jewelry, Andin relaunched the site in November 2001 as an informational resource for consumers that in effect created a virtual marketing arm for the customers of its private-label wares and retailers that carried the Aya Azrielant Collection. In this way, Andin could develop customer loyalty that was not based on price alone and thus drive its core business. The site essentially advertised items Andin produced, providing retail partners with an inducement to carry those pieces.

Jewelry.com targeted men because they typically bought jewelry as presents for women but were far from confident in their choices. Jewelry.com provided basic information about jewelry to help them overcome their fears. Moreover, the site promoted its six retail partners, which included some of the United States' largest and most trusted merchandisers, offering further reassurance: J.C. Penney, Macy's, Sears, Service Merchandise, the Kay division of Sterling, and the Zales division of Zale Corporation. Users of Jewelry.com could preshop at home and then visit a local branch of the retailer to view any merchandise that piqued their interest. They could either make a purchase online or in person.

DESIGN LABEL SPUN OFF IN 2004

Jewelry.com added coupons and special offers for consumers and began tracking jewelry sales for retail partners. Service Merchandise dropped out as a partner after going out of business in early 2002. Kay would also leave, but in September 2003 Aurafin/Oro America agreed to become a retail partner. While Jewelry.com was an important component, the private-label manufacturing operation remained the core of Andin. In 2004 the designer label split off as Aya International LLC, which opened its own office on Fifth Avenue in New York City. Andin then focused its attention on better serving its private-label customers. The company had an especially good relationship with J.C. Penney. In 2006 Andin was named Vendor of the Year, Jewelry Division, for helping to introduce "circle" pendants. Andin then played a key role in the J.C. Penney launch of a 14-karat gold line called "Classique" and a sales push for colored diamonds. For these efforts, Andin was again named J.C. Penney's Vendor of the Year in 2008. Private-label jewelry remained a highly competitive, price-sensitive business, but Andin appeared to be nimble enough to hold its own in the years to come.

Ed Dinger

PRINCIPAL SUBSIDIARIES

Jewelry.com.

PRINCIPAL COMPETITORS

Tiffany & Co.; Blue Nile Inc.; Solomon Brothers Fine Jewelry.

FURTHER READING

Bamford, Janet, "Good As Gold," *Working Woman,* May 1, 1995.

Beres, Glen A., "Jewelry.com: Targets Male Shoppers via Volume Retailer," *JCK's High Volume Jeweler,* January 2002, p. 17.

Lebow, Joan, "Precious Gems and High Rents," *Crain's New York Business,* June 13, 1988, p. 1.

Lyons, Richard D., "A Manhattan Warehouse Is Salvaged," *New York Times,* February 14, 1990, p. D22.

Manjeet, Kripalani, "Easy on the Earlobe," *Forbes,* September 13, 1993, p. 104.

Newman, Jill, "Aya Azrielant Writes Her Own Name in Gold," *Women's Wear Daily,* October 16, 1992, p. 17.

Angelini SpA

Viale Amelia, 70
Rome, 00181
Italy
Telephone: (39 06) 78053-1
Fax: (39 071) 2900020
Web site: http://www.angelinipharma.com

Private Company
Incorporated: 1940 as Aziende Chimiche Riunite Angelini Francesco (ACRAF)
Employees: 2,500
Sales: EUR 1 billion ($1.3 billion) (2007 est.)
NAICS: 325412 Pharmaceutical Preparation Manufacturing; 325411 Medicinal and Botanical Manufacturing

■ ■ ■

Angelini SpA is an Italian holding company operating primarily in the pharmaceuticals, parapharmaceuticals, and health aids sectors. The Rome-based company develops, manufactures, and distributes both branded and generic prescription drugs, as well as over-the-counter (OTC) medicines and mass market and parapharmaceutical products such as mouthwash, personal hygiene, and cosmetics. Angelini's largest operation is its ACRAF (Aziende Chimiche Riunite Angelini Francesco) pharmaceuticals unit, which is one of the top five pharmaceuticals companies in Italy. Through ACRAF, the company focuses on the pain relief, gynecology, antibiotics, cold and flu, pediatrics, neuropsychiatry, and ophthalmology sectors. Major products including Ox-

olamina, a cough suppressant; the anti-inflammatory Benzydamine; Prulifloxacin, an antibacterial agent; Trazodone, an antidepressant; and Dapriprazole, for the treatment of glaucoma.

Angelini's OTC brands include Moment, Tantum Verde, and Amuchina. The company also produces a variety of generic preparations for cardiovascular, anti-inflammatory, antibacterial, gastrointestinal, and other applications. Angelini produces a range of fine chemicals as well. Through its Fater joint venture partnership with Procter & Gamble (P&G), Angelini is also the leading producer of disposable diapers, tampons, and sanitary napkins in Italy, marketing under the Pampers and Lines brands. Beyond Italy, Angelini has operations in Portugal and Spain, and markets its products to more than 60 countries. Other holdings in the Angelini group include the Borgo Tre Rose hotel complex; the Idesa perfume, cosmetics, and related products group in Spain; and wine producer Tenimenti Angelini. The company reported sales of approximately EUR 1 billion ($1.3 billion) in 2007. Angelini remains a family-owned company, led by Francesco Angelini, grandson of the founder.

VITAMIN SUCCESS FOLLOWING WORLD WAR II

Angelini had its start as a small Ancona-based pharmaceuticals laboratory founded by Francesco Angelini in 1919. Angelini's business grew strongly over the next two decades. Angelini responded to the surge in demand for Italian-based pharmaceuticals by creating a new company, called Aziende Chimiche Riunite Ange-

COMPANY PERSPECTIVES

The reputation of Angelini's pharmaceuticals and parapharmaceuticals is supported by its capacity to manage complex sales networks through a range of diverse channels which promote widespread distribution and high levels of customer service. Angelini pursues its mission with knowledge and skill, a close focus on ethics, and respect for the individual, the environment and the community in which the Angelini Group operates. It is due in no small way to the values that inspire its corporate philosophy that Angelini is synonymous with guaranteed quality and safety, both to health professionals and to the general public.

lini Francesco, or ACRAF in 1940. World War II provided another growth opportunity for the company, after Italy's alliance with Germany cut off the country's supply of medicines and other pharmaceutical products from other Western markets.

The shortage of food both during and especially following the war had a major impact on the Italian population, with large numbers of people suffering from anemia. Recognizing an opportunity, ACRAF began importing and marketing vitamin B12 under the Dobetin brand name. The success of this venture gave the company the financial backing to expand its own industrial operations.

As part of this effort, the company moved its headquarters to Rome at the beginning of the 1950s. ACRAF then launched its first research efforts. These resulted in a number of successes by the end of the decade, notably with the launch of Tachipirina, a pediatric flu formula based on acetaminophen. Introduced in 1958, Tachipirina became a major new product for the company, becoming the most-prescribed children's medicine in Italy, a position it continued to hold into the next century. The success of Tachipirina was such that it grew into one of the three largest-selling of all pharmaceutical products in Italy. By then, Francesco Angelini had been joined by his son, Igino, who took over as head of the company after his father's death in 1964.

Angelini extended into two other operational areas in the late 1950s. The first of these was the production of fine chemicals, starting in 1957 from the company's Rome-based facilities. By the mid-1960s, the company's fine chemicals development had grown sufficiently to require its own dedicated facility. The company built a new factory in Aprilia, in the Latina province, which took over all of the group's fine chemicals production in 1967.

Angelini added another major product line at the end of the 1950s, when it launched a new company, Fater, and opened a factory in Pescara for the production of washable linen bands for use as diapers and sanitary napkins. Created in 1958, Fater soon became a major player in these segments in Italy. This became especially true after 1964, when Fater became the first in the country to introduce new disposable diapers. For this, the company adopted a new brand name, Lines, which was evocative of the original linen material used by the company.

By the end of the 1960s, Fater had launched production of disposable sanitary napkins. Lines became the dominant brand in Italy in this category as well. Fater's success in the disposable market led the company to invest in developing its own production equipment. In 1975, Angelini established its own production subsidiary, Fameccanica. That company became one of the first in Italy to incorporate CAD (computer-aided design) programming into its design and engineering and production processes.

RESEARCH AND DEVELOPMENT SUCCESS

In the meantime, Angelini's research efforts had resulted in the development of the company's first active molecules in 1964. The company's first success in this area came with its discovery of Benzidamina, an anti-inflammatory, which the company patented and then incorporated into a range of mouthwashes, tablets, and other presentations used for the treatment of oropharyngeal pain, including gingivitis, stomatitis, and dental interventions. The Benzidamina products were also launched as an OTC brand, Tantum Verde. By the mid-1970s, ACRAF boasted a catalog of several successful molecules, including the anti-glaucoma treatment Dapiprazolo; Trazodone, an antidepressant; and Oxolamina, a cough suppressant.

Angelini also began developing an international presence in the late 1970s. For this, the company bought three Spanish companies, Farma Lepori, L. Lepori, and Laboratorios Ausonia, in 1979. The first two were pharmaceuticals producers, while the third produced talcum powder and other infant care products. The entry into Spain also enabled the company to extend its production and marketing interests into Portugal, where it grew into one of that market's top 20 pharmaceuticals group, and one of the top companies

KEY DATES

■

1919: Francesco Angelini founds a company in Ancona, Italy, producing pharmaceuticals products.

1940: Angelini incorporates the company as Aziende Chimiche Riunite Angelini Francesco (ACRAF).

1958: Angelini creates subsidiary Fater, which launches production of diapers and sanitary napkins.

1964: The company patents its first molecule developed in-house, Benzidamina.

1979: Angelini extends its operations into Spain and Portugal through the acquisitions of three Spanish companies.

1985: Angelini launches the highly successful over-the-counter (OTC) pain reliever, Moment.

1992: Angelini agrees to merge Fater into a joint venture with Procter & Gamble.

2000: Company acquires Helsinn and Helfarma in Portugal and Amuchina in Italy; forms generics distribution partnership with Hexal in Germany.

2004: Angelini Acraf acquires nearly 10 percent of Elder Pharma in India.

2007: Angelini acquires CSC Pharmaceuticals Handel in Austria.

selling OTC medicines. Leading the move into the Iberian region was Francesco Angelini, son of Igino and grandson of the company's founder.

OTC medicines became a prominent part of the portfolio of the Angelini group starting especially from the mid-1980s. In 1985, the company decided to market ibuprofen for the Italian market, packaging its preparation under the Moment brand. For this launch, the company broke out of its traditional marketing focus on the healthcare professionals segment to launch its first consumer-oriented advertising campaign. Moment quickly became a best-selling pain-reliever brand in Italy. By the beginning of the 21st century, Angelini claimed the number two position in the OTC market in Italy.

Angelini also continued to invest in its own research and development program. This led to the establishment of a new research and development center at Santa Palomba, outside of Rome, in 1987, specializing in research into anti-inflammatories and pain relievers. By the beginning of the new century, the focus of the Santa Palomba center settled on two areas of research. On the one hand, the company sought to develop new and more effective forms of acetaminophen, and on the other hand, the facility sought to develop molecules to treat neuropathic pain.

DIVERSIFICATION

Other areas of the group's operations were also expanding in the 1990s. Francesco Angelini had returned to Italy to head the family's Fater operation. Under his direction, Fater and its Lines brand quickly took the leadership in the Italian diaper and sanitary products market. An important milestone for Fater came in the early 1990s, when the company agreed to form a joint venture partnership with P&G, owner of the Pampers diaper brand. The two companies agreed to merge their Italian diaper and sanitary napkins businesses under Fater in 1992. Pampers then became Fater's main brand, after Fater agreed to transfer the license to its Lines diapers brand to a third party to satisfy antitrust authorities. By 1993, Angelini and P&G had solidified their partnership, establishing a joint venture to take over the operations of Fameccanica as well.

Francesco Angelini had by then taken over as head of the company, following his father's death in 1993. The new head of the family empire led the group on a still wider diversification plan through the 1990s. For this, Angelini indulged his interests in a variety of areas, including wine making, edible oil product, and deli meats. In the mid-1990s, the group also entered the agri-foods business, buying seed producer Isea. In another extension, the company added a real estate component, which began operating a hotel complex, Borgo Tre Rose, situated in one of its vineyards.

In the new century, Angelini's operational structure was adjusted accordingly. The group created a new holding company, Finaf SpA, which became the oversight body providing central coordination for all of the company's operations. Another holding company was established to provide support services for the group's Iberian operations. The company's operations were then separated into three core divisions: Pharmaceuticals; Consumer Packaged Goods; and Machinery.

EUROPEAN OTC SUPPLIER IN THE 21ST CENTURY

The pharmaceuticals and parapharmaceuticals sectors remained the central focus of the company's operations. The company launched a series of acquisitions and partnerships, starting with the purchase of Genoa-based Amuchina, which produced sanitizers and disinfectants under the Amuchina brand, in 2000. Next, the Angelini group expanded its Iberian operations, buying two Portuguese companies, Helsinn Produtos Farmaceuticos and Helfarma Produtos Farmaceuticos. The latter acquisition also provided the company with the introduction into a new operational area, the production of generic medicines. By the end of 2000, Angelini had further established itself in that sector, setting up a generics production and distribution alliance with Germany's Hexal. In the following year, the company joined with another German partner, Phoenix Group, to acquire Sicily-based pharmaceuticals and parapharmaceuticals wholesaler Grossfarma Distribuzione.

Angelini continued to expand through the first decade of the 21st century. Angelini acquired Italian parapharmaceuticals group Farmamed, one of the Italian market leaders in that category. The following year, the company extended its reach into the fast-growing market for plant-based food supplements and health aids, acquiring Body Spring. Also in 2003, the company set up its own Italian generics business, Angenerico. That subsidiary was then joined with the former Helfarma operations in Portugal.

Angelini's fast-growing generics business led it to India, home of one of the world's largest generic drugs industries. In 2004, Angelini, through its Angelini Acraf subsidiary, invested in Elder Pharma, one of the top 50 Indian pharmaceuticals groups, buying just under 10 percent of the Mumbai-based company's shares. In 2008, Angelini raised its investment in Elder to nearly 13.5 percent.

By this time, the company had also acquired Austria's CSC Pharmaceuticals Handel GmbH. The two companies had been in a strategic partnership since 1998. The acquisition gave Angelini control of CSC's extensive pharmaceuticals distribution network throughout the Central and Eastern European region. The Angelini group had grown into one of the top five Italian pharmaceutical companies and one of the largest family-owned pharmaceuticals companies in Europe.

M. L. Cohen

PRINCIPAL SUBSIDIARIES

Acraf S.p.A.; Angelini Farmacêutica, Lda (Portugal); Angelini Farmaceutica, S.A.; Angelini Immobiliare S.p.A.; Angenerico S.p.A.; Angenérico, Produtos Farmacêuticos Genéricos, Lda (Portugal); Borgo Tre Rose S.p.A.; CSC Pharmaceuticals (Romania); Doctor Active; Fameccanica.Data S.p.A. (50%); Fater S.p.A. (50%); Finaf S.p.A.; Idesa S.A. (50%); Rega Farma-Promoçao de Produtos Farmacêuticos, S.A. (Portugal); Tenimenti Angelini S.p.A.

PRINCIPAL COMPETITORS

Novartis Italia Group; Chiesi Farmaceutici S.p.A.; Bayer S.p.A.; Beiersdorf S.p.A.; Inbios S.R.L.; Rohm and Haas Italia S.R.L.; Alfa Wassermann S.p.A.; Europharma 2000; Amgen-Dompe S.p.A.

FURTHER READING

"Bindarit Angelini Provides Development Update," *R&D Focus Drug News,* July 16, 2007.

Bouda, Francis J., "Winners and Losers: A Mixed Bag for the Disposable Diaper Industry," *Nonwovens Industry,* January 1991, p. 36.

Frosecchi, Walter, "Angelini Partnering Opportunity," *R&D Focus Drug News,* July 16, 2007.

"Helsinn and Angelini Enter Deal," *Pharma Marketletter,* July 11, 2005.

"Italian Company Raises Stake in Elder," *India Business Insight,* March 23, 2007.

"An Italian Multinational," *RI,* February 2006.

"Takeover of Grossfarma by Angelini and Phoenix Cleared," *European Report,* September 5, 2001, p. 343.

Anheuser-Busch InBev

———■———

One Busch Plaza
St. Louis, Missouri 63118
U.S.A.
Telephone: (314) 577-2000
Toll Free: (800) 342-5283
Fax: (314) 577-2900
Web site: http://www.anheuser-busch.com

Wholly Owned Subsidiary of InBev S.A.
Incorporated: 1860 as E. Anheuser & Company
Employees: 30,000
Sales: $16.7 billion (2007)
NAICS: 312120 Breweries; 3324310 Metal Can Manufacturing; 713110 Amusement and Theme Parks; 233110 Land Subdivision and Land Development

■ ■ ■

Anheuser-Busch InBev, is the largest brewer in the world, producing more than 100 million barrels of beer each year. The company's primary brands, Budweiser, Bud Light, Michelob, and Busch, are market leaders, enabling the massive St. Louis enterprise to claim nearly 50 percent of the U.S. beer market. The company competes globally, with its share of the world beer market at 11.5 percent. It owns 50 percent of the Mexican brewer Grupo Modelo, and has a significant share in the leading Chinese beer Tsingtao. Anheuser-Busch is a major aluminum recycler and has extensive bottling and packaging operations as well. Anheuser-Busch also operates nine theme parks, including Busch

Gardens and Sea World properties at several locations. The Busch family owns less than 2 percent of the company, although many Busch family members, including the founder's great-grandson August Busch IV, are involved in running the company. In 2008, the company was acquired by Belgian-Brazilian beer conglomerate InBev for $52 billion thus ending a long legacy of family ownership. Thereafter the company's name was changed to Anheuser-Busch InBev and its world headquarters were moved to Belgium, although its North American headquarters remained in St. Louis, Missouri, where the company was founded.

19TH-CENTURY ORIGINS

Until 2008 Anheuser-Busch had been overseen by a member of its founding family since 1860, when Eberhard Anheuser, a prosperous soap manufacturer in St. Louis, bought a failing brewery from Bavarian immigrant George Schneider. The brewery's cool underground caverns near the Mississippi River were conducive to good brewing, and Anheuser was determined to turn the business around, but he lacked experience in the industry. In 1864, he hired his son-in-law, Adolphus Busch, a German immigrant schooled in the art of brewing, as his general manager. Together, Anheuser and Busch approached the enterprise with an aggressive business strategy and knowledge in quality brewing, two factors that have informed Anheuser-Busch's history ever since.

According to a popular company legend, Adolphus Busch obtained the recipe for his beer during a visit to a German monastery. There, monks provided him with a

COMPANY PERSPECTIVES

Anheuser-Busch's passion for beer and commitment to quality have allowed the company to offer a diverse range of beers and beverages, loved by consumers across the United States and the world. This includes the world's largest selling beers, Bud Light and Budweiser.

recipe and some of their brewer's yeast, the secret of their excellent beer. That recipe became the basis of Anheuser-Busch beers, and the original strain of yeast, allegedly preserved for years in Adolphus's ice cream freezer, remained in use for many years. Although fictitious, the story highlighted two important philosophies at Anheuser-Busch: only the finest "European" ingredients were to be used and the basic recipe would remain essentially unchanged.

Anheuser and Busch increased the rejuvenated brewery's capacity from 3,000 to 8,000 barrels per year and began to expand their sales effort into Texas and Louisiana, as well as their home state of Missouri. The beverage became increasingly popular, as cowboys reportedly deserted their beloved red-eye whiskey for the light Bohemian beer, which became known as Budweiser in 1876, when the company purchased the rights to the name from the Bohemian brewer of "Budweis."

Budweiser's formula was enhanced by innovations in the brewing industry, particularly as pasteurization allowed for longer preservation periods. Moreover, newly invented refrigerated railroad cars permitted the transport of beer across state borders, and the bottling of beer allowed for easier distribution throughout the country. Regional brewers lost their advantage to large breweries such as Anheuser, which had found the means to supply beer to every state in the union. Despite the growth of its market, however, Anheuser still referred to itself as a "regional brewery"—an institution that understood the distinct needs and tastes of local people.

In 1879, the company became known as Anheuser-Busch. Anheuser died the following year, and Busch took over operations. The company continued to prosper, and its workforce increased. During his tenure, Busch initiated the concept of considering employees members of a family, cared for and nurtured by the company and expected to remain loyal to the company for a lifetime. Anheuser-Busch considered this unique relationship between employer and employee, intimate and cooperative, vital to producing an outstanding product.

In the 1890s, Pabst, a competitor, was the best-selling beer in the United States. Busch and his "family" thwarted the competition, however, with the introduction of Michelob in 1896. Forceful and frequent advertising promoted Budweiser and Michelob as the most popular beers in the country, and this goal was realized in 1901, when Anheuser-Busch became the leading national brewery.

DIVERSIFICATION AND WAR YEARS

Busch died in 1913, and his son, August A. Busch, Sr., took over; the younger Busch soon focused on diversifying the company's interests. Toward this end, Busch patented the first diesel engine, which was installed in the brewery to increase production. With the onset of World War I, Busch founded a subsidiary to produce the engines for Navy submarines. In addition, the Anheuser-Busch family purchased sufficient war bonds to finance two bombers—each named "Miss Budweiser."

After the war, in November 1918, President Woodrow Wilson signed the bill that instituted Prohibition. During this forced hiatus, Anheuser-Busch diversified into related fields. Malt syrup was canned and sold to people who required malt for their homemade brews. A refrigeration car company was established to transport perishables. Bevo, a soft drink made from ingredients similar to those found in beer, was a great success for three years; it later failed when Prohibition laws concerning the use of yeast forced the company to change ingredients. Nevertheless, Anheuser-Busch began a trend toward diversification that would thereafter characterize the history of the company.

When Prohibition ended, the company experienced an unforeseen problem: People had become used to the sweet taste of the soft drinks and homemade brews that were available during Prohibition. They were not willing to return to the more bitter commercial beer. In response, many brewers changed their formulas to achieve a sweeter taste. However, Anheuser-Busch refused to alter the formula for best-selling Budweiser. This decision was endorsed by Dr. Robert Gall, the company's post-Prohibition brewmaster. Instead, the company initiated a major advertising campaign, challenging consumers to a "five-day test." Busch predicted that after five days of drinking Budweiser the consumer would not drink a sweet beer again. The advertising campaign was successful and established a trend for future consumer appeals. In 1936, the company began offering its beer in cans.

KEY DATES

1860: St. Louis soap merchant Eberhard Anheuser acquires the Bavarian Brewery.

1864: Adolphus Busch begins working at the brewery.

1876: Budweiser brand is introduced.

1896: Michelob is introduced.

1936: Budweiser is packaged in cans for the first time.

1955: The Busch brand is launched.

1959: Company's first amusement park, Busch Gardens, opens in Tampa, Florida.

1964: Annual production reaches ten million barrels.

1981: Budweiser is introduced in Japan.

1982: Bud Light is introduced.

1989: Anheuser-Busch purchases Sea World.

1997: Worldwide annual production surpasses 100 million barrels.

2006: August Busch IV becomes CEO.

2008: Company is acquired by Belgium-based InBev.

During World War II, the company, led by Adolphus Busch III, again made substantial contributions to the war effort. Anheuser-Busch supplied the military with ammunition hoists, which were in production at a new company subsidiary. Moreover, the distribution of Budweiser beer was withdrawn from the Pacific Coast to supply the government with additional freight cars for war essentials, and spent grain was sold to financially troubled wartime farmers for poultry and livestock food. These patriotic actions elevated sales and advanced Anheuser-Busch's image as a patriotic company.

Between 1935 and 1950, the demand for Anheuser-Busch beer consistently exceeded the supply. In 1941, three million barrels of beer were produced, a figure that doubled by 1950. After the death of Adolphus Busch III in 1946, the company temporarily relinquished its lead in the industry. However, with the succession of his brother, August "Gussie" Busch, Jr., the company became the nation's top brewer once again.

POST–WORLD WAR II EXPANSION

August Busch, Jr., continued the practice of aggressive advertising established by his brother and father, which had involved the distribution of pocket knives and gold pieces, advertisements featuring reproductions of patriotic art such as "Custer's Last Stand," and the 1933 introduction of the famous Clydesdale horses, which remained popular into the 21st century. Under August Busch, Anheuser-Busch became the first brewery to sponsor a radio network. Positive consumer response prompted William Bien, the vice-president of marketing, to design a legendary advertising campaign: "Pick-a-pair-of-six-packs." The campaign cost $2.5 million for two months, but was the most successful promotion in the history of the beer industry to date.

Despite its successful promotions, Anheuser-Busch entered a close competition at the beginning of the 1950s with Carling beer. During this time, a holiday was declared in Newark, New Jersey, in honor of the opening of a new Anheuser-Busch factory in that city. The new facility and new equipment necessitated a price hike, however, and Carling profited when its economical beer attracted customers put off by Anheuser-Busch's higher prices. In response, Busch introduced a new, low-priced lager beer and also pursued aggressive advertising promotions. In 1953, Anheuser-Busch bought the St. Louis Cardinals baseball team, targeting sports fans as a new category of consumers. Ultimately, the company was successful in rebuffing Carling's challenge.

Another brewery soon attempted to displace Anheuser-Busch from its number one market ranking. Decreasing the price of its beer in the 1960s, the Schlitz brewery hoped to force Anheuser-Busch into a price war. August Busch, Jr., remained confident that consumers would recognize Anheuser-Busch beer as superior in quality. Public opinion, however, was never tested, as Schlitz committed several marketing and advertising mistakes, and Anheuser-Busch retained its ranking.

NEW GENERATION AT THE HELM

During this time, August Busch III began his career at his father's company. After attending college for two years in Arizona and undergoing instruction in the art of brewing at a school in Chicago, Busch III started in an entry-level position at the company. In 1979, he took over as CEO, vowing to uphold Adolphus Busch's philosophy that natural ingredients be used to distinguish the company's fine brewing from the lower-quality brewing of other beers.

The Miller Brewing Company challenged this philosophy during the 1970s and 1980s. Miller introduced a light, low-calorie beer in 1974, which became the best-selling beer for a few months. Although Anheuser-Busch soon edged back into the top ranking, it remained closely followed by the Miller brewery. In response to Miller's challenge, Anheuser-Busch introduced two light beers in 1977, Natural Light and Michelob Light, and the popular Budweiser Light was introduced soon thereafter.

Under Busch III, the company developed a unique strategy for dealing with competition that included introducing new brands, increasing the advertising budget, and expanding its breweries. Moreover, Busch III refocused the company's marketing practices to target more specific groups of consumers. He hired a team of 100 college graduates to promote the sale of Anheuser-Busch beers on college campuses. He also oversaw the development of new advertisements designed to appeal to the working class. In the process, the company's marketing budget quadrupled, and sales increased.

Busch III also adopted a "management control system" that increased the efficiency of the company, redefining it as a modern corporation rather than a small family business. The new management system emphasized planning, teamwork, and communications, controls that, ironically, were intended to promote Anheuser-Busch's image as a regional brewery producing different beers to satisfy individual tastes. Anheuser-Busch continued to rank first in the brewing industry into the 1980s. By 1980, sales had reached 50 million barrels, increasing to 86.8 million barrels by 1992. Although competition with Miller remained intense, the Budweiser brand outsold its next four competitors combined.

OTHER OPERATIONS

Anheuser-Busch initially espoused an acquisition policy of purchasing companies that would enhance its brewing operations. These included malt plants in Wisconsin and Minnesota; beer can factories in Florida and Ohio; and yeast plants in Missouri, New Jersey, California, and Florida. The St. Louis Refrigerator Car Company inspected and maintained the 880 refrigerated railroad cars used to transport the company's beer across the country. Manufacturers Railway shipped Anheuser-Busch beer after it was manufactured at the brewery with help from the malt and yeast subsidiaries.

Other subsidiaries, however, were soon established that were not directly related to the beer industry. Campbell-Taggart, Inc., the second largest bakery in the United States, was acquired in 1982, associating Anheuser-Busch's name with the food industry. In the 1980s, 6.7 percent of Anheuser-Busch's operating income was spent on food products. Another acquisition, Eagle Snacks, Inc., distributed food products nationally to bars, taverns, and convenience stores. Despite intense competition from Frito-Lay and Planters Peanuts, Eagle Snacks enhanced Anheuser-Busch's beer business by targeting consumers likely to purchase beer to complement their food products.

Anheuser-Busch also developed and acquired theme parks, forming the Busch Entertainment Corporation in 1979. The first Busch Gardens amusement park had opened 20 years earlier in Tampa, Florida, and featured a 300-acre park boasting one of the world's largest collections of wildlife under private ownership to date. Another tourist attraction, "The Old Country," in Williamsburg, Virginia, was modeled after villages in 17th-century Europe. Anheuser-Busch also acquired the eight-park Sea World chain of mostly aquatic theme parks in 1989 for $1.3 billion. Although these entertainment parks were not particularly profitable, they helped expose Anheuser-Busch's name to a new target group—a younger generation and their parents—and enhanced the company's reputation for contributing to the public welfare. Anheuser-Busch's ownership of the St. Louis Cardinals served a similar function.

Anheuser-Busch also devoted considerable energy to nurturing its foreign market. The corporation formed Anheuser-Busch International, Inc., in 1981 to expand its presence in the global beer market through joint ventures, licensing agreements, and equity investments in foreign brewers. The corporation's timing in this venture proved fortuitous: the fall of trade barriers and conversion of formerly communist and socialist governments to free enterprise systems opened a wealth of opportunity for Anheuser-Busch. By 1993, the company's beers were offered in 21 European countries and ranked as the second most popular lager beer in the Republic of Ireland and the United Kingdom. Budweiser was introduced to Japan in 1981 and stood as that country's leading import by the early 1990s because of successful promotion to the young adult market. With a 9 percent market share worldwide, Anheuser-Busch had the largest export volume of any American brewer in 1993, accounting for more than 45 percent of U.S. beer exports.

ADJUSTING TO A NEW MARKETPLACE

During the early 1990s, Anheuser-Busch was compelled to face the declining—and more discerning—use of alcoholic beverages among Americans. The company had introduced LA, the first low alcohol beer, in 1984, but this product did not prove widely successful. LA was replaced by O'Doul's in 1990, however, which soon became the nation's most popular non-alcohol brew. Moreover, as Americans' tastes grew more refined and microbreweries made unprecedented inroads into the modern beer industry, Anheuser-Busch sought to enhance the appeal of its brew. The company introduced eight new beers between 1984 and 1991. By 1993, Anheuser-Busch offered 19 beer brands, three of which were imports. Anheuser-Busch's Bud Dry and Ice Draft from Budweiser appealed to premium beer drinkers. New brand introductions did not seem to detract from Budweiser's brand power; the new variations captured 17 percent of the market, while Bud only lost half a share point.

As the decade progressed, so too did the growth of the craft-brewing industry. This soon forced the nation's three largest brewers to take heed of the beer industry's upstarts. Anheuser-Busch's closest rivals, Adolph Coors Company and Miller Brewing Company, introduced a host of new brands during the mid-1990s as a riposte. Anheuser-Busch followed suit, but to a much lesser extent. Anheuser-Busch pursued a more conservative strategy that proved to be a prudent approach later in the decade. By then, many of the specialty brands introduced by the big breweries were confirmed failures. Bill Weintraub, the senior vice-president of Adolph Coors, noted as much. "I think they've (Anheuser-Busch) understood that supporting their core brands is a smarter way to build brands over the long term," he conceded in the May 5, 1997, issue of *Brandweek*. Although Anheuser-Busch invested substantially in the craft-brewing phenomenon—including signing a distribution and equity partnership agreement in 1994 with Red Hook Brewery, a leading craft brewer—the company's primary focus was on its core brands.

DIVESTITURES AND NEW VENTURES

Amid a flurry of new beer brands introduced during the mid-1990s, Anheuser-Busch scaled back its operations, divesting properties while other large brewers expanded their portfolios. In 1995, the company announced it was severing its ties with Eagle Snacks, Inc., after 17 years of losses. Concurrently, Anheuser-Busch announced it was divesting itself of the St. Louis Cardinals and Busch Memorial Stadium properties. In 1994, the baseball franchise posted a loss of $12 million. Eagle Snacks too racked up $25 million in losses. The divestitures were made so that the company could direct more of its attention and resources to beer and theme parks, the two principal areas of Anheuser-Busch's focus for the future.

Of particular importance was injecting new life in the company's all-important Budweiser brand. The flagship brand was suffering from stagnant sales growth as the company entered the mid-1990s. Internationally, the company was realizing encouraging growth, thanks in large part to investments such as the 50 percent of Grupo Modelo (brewer of Corona beer) acquired in

1993 and the majority stake purchased in the Chinese brewer Budweiser Wuhan International Brewing Company, in 1995. Domestically, however, the brand's sales had flattened. The task of spurring Budweiser sales fell to August Busch IV, whom many regarded as the next in line to lead the family business; in 1997, August Busch III had announced his intention to retire in 2003.

Under the 30-year-old's direction, a revamped marketing plan was developed that aimed at winning over younger consumers, who had gravitated to imports and microbrews. "There was a culture weaved into the Budweiser brand," the younger Busch explained to *Fortune* on January 13, 1997. "No one wanted to change it." August Busch IV spearheaded the widely popular "talking frogs" advertising campaign for Budweiser and the successful "I Love You Man" advertising campaign for Bud Light, both of which were credited with lifting sales. In 1997, two years after the irreverent, youth-oriented advertising campaigns were launched, annual worldwide beer volume (including the interests Anheuser-Busch held in other breweries) surpassed 100 million barrels for the first time, as Budweiser sales moved measurably upward.

At the end of the 1990s, Anheuser-Busch's dominance of the U.S. beer industry testified to the prolific growth of the company during the 20th century. By 1999, the company's share of the U.S. beer market had risen to 47.5 percent, fueling confidence that August Busch III's goal of capturing 60 percent of the market by the middle of the next decade could be achieved.

SEISMIC SHIFTS

The company continued to garner praise from industry experts into the early years of the new century. August Busch III retired in 2002 although he remained chairman of the board. The chief executive position then went to Patrick Stokes, who had been president of the company's domestic brewing division. August Busch IV took Stokes's old job. In 2002, Anheuser-Busch had a record-breaking year, shipping 101.8 million barrels of beer. Sales and earnings were good, and the company was lauded for its strong marketing. It had introduced two new products, Michelob Ultra and Bacardi Silver, which had performed well. The company held out well against its domestic competitors, while it also grew its international sales. By 2002, it marketed in some 80 countries around the world. A profile of Anheuser-Busch in *Beverage Industry* (January 2003) quoted analysts with nothing but confidence about the company's future. "They're so unbelievably focused," said one market watcher. Another said, "The continued growth of Anheuser-Busch is very clear. ... They're having their way with the market."

However, all this quickly changed. Three years later, industry pundits grew concerned that drinkers were turning away from beer, in favor of wine and spirits. Although Anheuser-Busch dwarfed its nearest competitors, it still had to fend off marketing attacks from Miller and Coors that might drain market share from its brands. August Busch IV became CEO of Anheuser-Busch at the end of 2006. He faced new challenges that may not have been apparent at the start of the decade. In 2001, wine and liquor accounted for 42 percent of the overall liquor market. By 2006, that figure had grown to 45 percent and was likely to continue upward. Furthermore, many competitors in the market had consolidated, especially in markets outside the United States. In 2002, Miller Brewing was acquired by South African Breweries. This meant the competitive landscape was shifting, and the company needed to be prepared. Rumors swirled that Anheuser-Busch was to be acquired as microbreweries and foreign competitors chipped away at a flattening domestic beer market.

August Busch IV mused on the troubling trends facing the company mid-decade. He had long been credited with the company's winning advertising campaigns. Then at the helm, he oversaw inroads into new media. He also introduced new products and made an acquisition. In 2006, the company bought the Rolling Rock brand for $82 million from the Belgian brewer InBev. Looking at the popularity of liquor and cocktails, Anheuser-Busch brought out a few new lines. A two-bottle combination of liquors called Jekyll and Hyde was introduced in 2007. The company also brought out a line of two-ounce flavored, caffeinated malt drinks, playing on the popularity of energy drinks among young people.

The company also branched into marketing on the Internet with the introduction of BudTV. This was a proprietary channel resembling the popular YouTube site. It featured videos produced exclusively for the site, and designed to appeal to young drinkers. Anheuser-Busch also brought out high-end brands, such as Michelob AmberBock. AmberBock came in a distinctively shaped bottle, and bars were to stock special gold-rimmed glasses just for this beverage.

ACQUISITION BY INBEV

While the company had developed a variety of strategies to face down the changing conditions in its industry, it may have been too late. Sales of beer in the United States continued to fall as drinkers switched to other beverages. *Business Week* (March 19, 2007) called it "a

gradual un-beering of America." Globally, brewers continued to consolidate, creating new, larger competitors. At the beginning of 2008, the two companies that held the number two and three spots in the U.S. beer market, Miller and Coors, merged their domestic operations. Anheuser-Busch still held 49 percent of the U.S. beer market, but its nearest competitor would then have about 28 percent. The combined MillerCoors had its major namesake brands Miller and Coors, plus significant microbrew brands such as Blue Moon and Leinenkugel's. The new company also had some well-known import brands, among them Foster's and Peroni.

Anheuser-Busch hoped to gain an advantage while Miller and Coors struggled to align their management and merge their distribution chains. However, the ground quickly shifted when Anheuser-Busch itself became the target of takeover efforts by InBev S.A. InBev was the product of a merger in 2004 between the Brazilian company AmBev and the Belgian Interbrew. InBev was a globally dominant beer company, with substantial brands all across Europe, South America, and Asia. It employed 89,000 people and sold in as many as 130 countries. InBev had sold its Rolling Rock brand to Anheuser-Busch just two years earlier, and takeover talk had come up at that time. Then InBev made a hostile bid for Anheuser-Busch in July 2008. The bid was eventually termed "friendly" when the offer was increased and was approved by the board. The deal closed at the end of 2008. A year that had started with three domestic brewers battling over a flat market ended with two much bigger competitors. The newly merged Anheuser-Busch InBev would make one in four beers sold around the world. While its world headquarters were moved to Belgium, the company kept its St. Louis base to oversee North American operations.

Updated, Jeffrey L. Covell; A. Woodward

PRINCIPAL SUBSIDIARIES

Anheuser-Busch, Inc.; Anheuser-Busch International, Inc.; Busch Entertainment Corporation; Manufacturers Railway Company; St. Louis Refrigerator Car Company; Busch Properties, Inc.; Metal Container Corporation; Anheuser-Busch Recycling Corporation; Precision Printing & Packaging, Inc.; Grupo Modelo, S.A.B. de C.V. (50%); Harbin Brewery Group Ltd.; Crown Beers India Ltd.

PRINCIPAL COMPETITORS

MillerCoors; Heineken N.V.; Asahi Breweries, Ltd.

FURTHER READING

Arndorfer, James B., "Is He Busch League?" *Advertising Age*, June 27, 2005, pp. 1, 53.

"August Busch III Retires," *Beverage Industry,* July 2002, p. 10.

Baron, Stanley Wade, *Brewed in America: A History of Beer and Ale in the U.S.,* New York: Arno Press, 1972.

Brown, Heidi, "The Son Finally Rises," *Forbes,* March 12, 2007, pp. 74–79.

Bruss, Jill, "Still the King of Beers," *Beverage Industry,* January 2003, pp. 22–26.

Delaney, Lawrence, Jr., "Beer Brawl," *World Trade,* March 1993.

Fine, Jon, "A Small Drop in Bud's Barrel," *Business Week,* March 19, 2007, p. 30.

Foust, Dean, Jack Ewing, and Geri Smith, "Looks Like a Beer Brawl," *Business Week,* July 28, 2008, pp. 52–53.

The History of Anheuser-Busch Companies—A Fact Sheet, St. Louis: Anheuser-Busch Companies, Inc., 1992.

Khermouch, Gerry, "Tapped Out Brewery," *Brandweek,* May 5, 1997, p. 42.

Kratz, Ellen Florian, "The Beer King Gets a New CEO," *Fortune,* October 30, 2006, p. 198.

Krebs, Roland, *Making Friends Is Our Business: 100 Years of Anheuser-Busch,* St. Louis: Cuneo Press, 1953.

Lubove, Seth, "Unfinished Business," *Forbes,* December 10, 1990, pp. 170, 172.

Melcher, Richard A., "How Eagle Became Extinct," *Business Week,* March 4, 1996, p. 68.

Mullman, Jeremy, "A-B Primes Marketing Pump, Looks to Take Advantage of Turmoil in '08," *Advertising Age,* January 7, 2008, pp. 3, 23.

Sellers, Patricia, "Bud-Weis-Heir," *Fortune,* January 13, 1997, p. 90.

Theodore, Sarah, "Beer Has Big Changes on Tap," *Beverage Industry,* September 2008, pp. 24–31.

Wallace, Paul, "US Brewer Gets a Taste of Globalisation as In-Bev Swoops," *Euroweek,* September 28, 2008, p. 28.

Wells, Melanie, "Are Dynasties Dying?" *Forbes,* March 6, 2000, p. 126.

Annin & Co.

105 Eisenhower Parkway
Roseland, New Jersey 07068
U.S.A.
Telephone: (973) 228-9400
Fax: (973) 228-4905
Web site: http://www.annin.com

Private Company
Incorporated: 1847
Employees: 400
Sales: $173 million (2006)
NAICS: 315999 Other Apparel Accessories and Other
    Apparel Manufacturing

■ ■ ■

Annin & Co., a private company based in Roseland, New Jersey, is the United States' oldest and largest manufacturer of flags. Annin's specialty is the United States flag, including outdoor flags with brass grommets for attaching to flagpoles or with sleeves for hanging as banners, and parade flags fitted with sleeves for use with handheld flagpoles. Annin offers other U.S. flags as well, ranging in size from small handheld flags stapled to a stick to the largest American flag ever made, 104 feet by 235 feet, now held by the Smithsonian Institution.

Annin-made U.S. flags draped the coffin of President Abraham Lincoln, were raised by Marines on Iwo Jima's Mt. Suribachi, were planted on the surface of the moon by U.S. astronauts, and were hoisted above the ruins of the World Trade Center by New York firefighters. In addition, Annin produces flags for all 50 states and U.S. territories, Canadian provinces, all branches of the U.S. armed forces, the member countries of the United Nations, and altogether more than 200 international flags.

Annin also makes historical flags, golf flags, fishing and boating flags, religious flags, and novelty flags and banners. Annin also produces patriotic decorations, bunting, and fans. Standard American flags are distributed to chain stores, while the rest of the Annin inventory is sold through a network of about 2,000 independent flag shops. Flag manufacturing is conducted at plants in Coshocton, Ohio; South Boston, Virginia; and Verona and Bloomfield, New Jersey. Subsidiary Star Fields, LLC, produces embroidered star fields at its plant in Cobbs Creek, Virginia. A silk-screening plant is operated in Palm Bay, Florida, and embroidery is conducted at an Orange, New Jersey, plant. Annin is owned by descendants of the company's founders; three sixth-generation family members are active in management.

19TH-CENTURY ORIGINS

The Annin family history is very much an American story. The forefathers came to North America in the 1700s from Scotland well before the United States was created, fighting in the French and Indian War and the Revolutionary War. The family became involved in flag-making around 1820 when Alexander Annin, a ship chandler with a sail-making shop on the docks of New York City, began sewing flags for ships. As was always the case for flag makers, the sale of U.S. flags spiked

COMPANY PERSPECTIVES

Our mission at Annin & Co. is to be the world's premier manufacturer and distributor of flag products while maximizing the value delivered to our customers, our employees and our shareholders.

during time of war, and this was true for Annin in 1846 when the two-year Mexican War began and Annin-made flags were carried by U.S. armies in battles in New Mexico and California. A year later Annin's sons, Edward and Benjamin, established Annin & Co. to focus solely on flags, producing their products in a large Fifth Avenue factory.

The company quickly established itself as a leader in its field, as demonstrated by the selection of an Annin flag to wave over the laying of the cornerstone of the Washington Monument in 1848, and the presence of Annin flags at the inauguration of Zachary Taylor as president of the United States in 1849—the start of a custom that would see an Annin flag at each inauguration ever since. Annin's prominence grew further in 1851 when its flags were flown at the first International Exhibition. Annin flags flew at scores of World's Fairs and major expositions from that point on. The company also maintained a good business supplying flags for yachts. Annin flags have been carried by all defenders of the prestigious America's Cup yacht race.

Sales of U.S. flags soared during the Civil War in the 1860s, when for the first time a large number of Americans began buying flags to display at their homes. According to company lore Annin flags were also connected with both sides of the Civil War, at least indirectly. An Annin-made flag was certainly used to adorn the coffin of President Lincoln following his assassination, but one of Annin's presidents, Louis Annin Ames, nephew of the founders and grandson of Alexander Annin, was known to tell a story about an unusual order for a flag he took during his youth in the final decades of the 1800s. According to a *New York Times* account, "His customer was an elderly, distinguished-looking woman. As she spoke, she removed a diamond brooch from her dress, stuck the pin end into her hand and, as the blood came forth, said, 'I want you to make me a Confederate battle flag with the red the exact color of this blood.' The woman was the widow of Jefferson Davis [president of the Confederacy]."

AMES NAMED PRESIDENT: 1909

Ames took over as president of Annin & Co. in 1909, the same year that Commander Robert E. Peary carried an Annin-made U.S. flag on his expedition to the North Pole. A year later the company moved its headquarters to a building at 5th Avenue and 16th Street, which would become known as "Old Glory Corner." In 1915 Ames designed the municipal flag of the city of New York. It was Ames who began the company's exodus to New Jersey, building a state-of-the-industry plant in Verona in 1916, which included die-cutters to stamp out stars and help automate flag production. In all he would head Annin & Co. for more than four decades, including the times of patriotic fervor that accompanied World War I and led to booming flag sales.

Business declined dramatically a decade later when the stock market crash of 1929 precipitated the Great Depression of the 1930s. After Franklin Roosevelt was elected president in 1932 and instituted the National Recovery Administration (NRA), the cornerstone agency of his "New Deal" program to improve the economy, Annin enjoyed some success in selling copies of flags bearing the NRA insignia. It was not enough, however, to keep the business from sinking into debt. Fearing that creditors might enter judgments against the company in 1936, an election year when demand for flags and banners would normally increase and require all the working capital Annin had at its disposal to take full advantage of sales opportunities, Annin filed for bankruptcy protection.

The U.S. economy did not fully recover until the United States became involved in World War II and military spending spurred industry to new heights. Again, wartime drove flag sales and Annin enjoyed another growth spurt. Within months of the U.S. entry into the war in December 1941, Annin reported a 100 percent increase in demand for flags. The company also had to contend with shortages because many materials, including brass and cotton, were commandeered for military use.

Brass, which had been used to make grommets, was replaced by plastic, but a large quantity of cotton, about 25 million yards, was set aside by the government for use by flag companies. Much of that cotton would be used by Annin to make U.S. flags carried into combat, including the one raised on Mt. Suribachi on Iwo Jima, which was central in one of the most enduring iconic images of World War II. Following the war and the establishment of the United Nations in New York City, Annin also became the official provider of member nation flags that are flown outside the United Nations' building.

KEY DATES

1847: Annin & Co. is established in New York City.
1910: Headquarters moves to "Old Glory Corner," Fifth Avenue and 16th Street.
1916: The company's Verona, New Jersey, plant opens.
1952: Digby W. Chandler becomes the first nonfamily member to serve as president.
1975: The Colonial Flag Company is acquired.
1988: George H. W. Bush makes a presidential campaign visit to the Bloomfield, New Jersey, plant.
1998: The Dettra Flag Company is acquired.
2001: Joe LaPaglia is named president.
2006: C&P Embroidery is acquired.

NEW LEADERSHIP, NEW FLAG DESIGNS

Louis Ames retired in 1951 and a year later Digby W. Chandler was elected president of the company, the first non-descendant of Alexander Annin to hold the post. He himself was already of retirement age, having joined Annin in 1906 as an artists' assistant. He worked his way up through the ranks, along the way serving as artist, designer, salesman, vice-president, and general manager before heading the firm. He was a noted vexilogist (an expert on the study of flags). Several years after taking over the leadership of Annin, Chandler submitted the winning design for the 50-star U.S. flag that was needed when Hawaii was admitted as the 50th state.

The addition of Alaska and Hawaii into the Union created a number of problems for flag makers like Annin during the 1950s. In anticipation of Alaska and Hawaii becoming states, designs for both the 49-star and 50-star flag were enlisted from flag manufacturers by the government. Since 1818 the law called for adding a star to the flag on the next Fourth of July after a new state was admitted to the Union. The country had grown to 48 states in 1912 with the admission of Arizona, and the flag had remained unchanged with 48 stars for more than four decades.

With uncertainty about when Alaska and Hawaii would be added, Annin had to deal with difficult inventory issues, unsure how many 48-star flags to produce. There was still a demand for these flags because the life span of outdoor flags, due to the elements, was brief,

limited to just a handful of months, and they would have to be replaced. Although both Alaska and Hawaii joined the United States in 1959, Hawaii was not admitted until August of that year, resulting in the use of 49-star flag for one year until July 4, 1960, when the 50th star, and Chandler's design, could legally be implemented. Once the 50-star flag was made available, Annin enjoyed one of its strongest periods of growth as flag sales soared.

The Annin tradition continued to grow in the 1960s. In 1963 Annin expanded its presence in New Jersey, acquiring a 55,000-square-foot building in Bloomfield. In that same year, the National Geographic Society expedition that climbed Mt. Everest planted a Annin U.S. flag on the summit. At the end of the decade another Annin flag made an even longer trip, when it was taken to the moon by the astronauts of *Apollo 11* and left on the surface. In the meantime, Chandler died in October 1967 and the presidency of Annin & Co. was passed onto the fourth generation of the Annin family, to Carter Randolph Beard Jr., whose mother Edith was the daughter of Louis Annin Ames.

BICENTENNIAL CELEBRATION DRIVES SALES

The unpopular Vietnam war hurt U.S. flag sales in the late 1960s and early 1970s, leading to some consolidation in the flag industry. In 1975 Annin acquired Colonial Flag Company of Coshocton, Ohio, picking up another plant. The downturn in sales was reversed with the Bicentennial celebration of 1976, however. Not only was there increased demand for typical 50-star flags, they was a great deal of interest in older versions of the flag, in particular the first official American national flag, the Betsy Ross flag with its circle of 13 stars on a field of blue with 13 red and white stripes, and the Bennington flag, another Revolutionary War–era flag, which included a "76" inside a horseshoe of stars.

Other top sellers included the Gadsden flag, used by the Continental fleet and notable for its rattlesnake warning "Don't tread on me"; the Bunker Hill flag; and the Star-Spangled Banner flag with its 15 stars and 15 red and white stripes. Due to Bicentennial demand, Annin doubled sales during the 1975 to 1976 period.

Sales returned to a more predictable pace after the celebration, but there would be another spike preceding the presidential election of 1988, when candidate George H. W. Bush made patriotism and the Pledge of Allegiance the cornerstone of his campaign against Michael Dukakis. Not only did demand for U.S. flags increase, but Bush made an appearance at Annin's

Bloomfield, New Jersey, factory. While the company received some positive publicity as a result, it also drew the attention of reporters, who presented a picture of life in a flag-making plant that included many older women workers, low wages, and a building that lacked air conditioning.

Annin, which traditionally tried to remain above politics, also had to defend allowing one candidate to take advantage of its facilities. Moreover, Bush made a point of saying that business was booming at Annin, creating some friction with union workers who were negotiating a new contract. Tensions between workers and management soured in the aftermath of Bush's visit, as reported by the *Boston Globe* in a follow-up story in 1989 that quoted workers complaining of worsening conditions and harassment by management.

DETTRA FLAG COMPANY
ACQUIRED: 1998

The Persian Gulf War of 1991 once again resulted in soaring flag sales, spurred by the rise in patriotism, and Annin struggled to keep up with demand. In fact, sales during and after Desert Storm surpassed other peak periods, such as the unveiling of the 50-star flag and the Bicentennial. As usual, soon after the war came to a close flag sales returned to a more normal level, growing at an annual rate of about 10 percent.

One increasing source of income during the 1990s resulted from the growing popularity of seasonal banners displayed on residential flagpoles to commemorate holidays and other events. Annin also grew revenues in 1998 when it acquired its chief rival, Dettra Flag Company, based in Oaks, Pennsylvania, near Philadelphia. Dettra's history dated to 1901 when it won a contract from the Wrigley company to produce carnival and exposition flags.

A new president, Joe LaPaglia, took charge of Annin in January 2001, having joined the company the previous year to help eliminate redundancies inherited in the Dettra acquisition. Randolph Beard remained Annin's chairman. After taking the helm, LaPaglia faced other challenges. The terrorist attacks of September 11, 2001, resulted in another outpouring of patriotic spirit that drove the sale of U.S. flags for Annin.

Flag-buying season normally runs between Memorial Day and Labor Day, and peaks on the Fourth of July, so that inventories were quickly depleted in the days after the attacks, forcing the Annin plants to operate double shifts six days a week to keep up with demand. At one point, the company was turning out 50,000 flags a week. By the end of 2001 the company exceeded projected sales by 40 percent, or about $20 million. It was not until March 2002 that demand fell off enough to allow Annin to fill back orders for the larger flags used by schools and businesses.

In the weeks following the terrorist attacks on the United States on September 11, Annin negotiated a $1.62 million loan from the U.S. Department of Agriculture to expand its Coshocton, Ohio, plant and double production of U.S. flags. The older Oaks, Pennsylvania, plant was closed later in the decade. Annin grew further in 2006 when its subsidiary Star Fields, LLC, acquired D&P Embroidery, which supplied embroidered star fields to U.S. flag makers, picking up D&P's Cobbs Creek, Virginia, plant. As a result, Annin ensured a steady flow of domestically produced star fields for flag production. Because of popular desire to purchase U.S. flags made in America, Annin was only marginally threatened by foreign imports, and as the market leader it was ensured a steady business for years to come.

Ed Dinger

PRINCIPAL SUBSIDIARIES

Star Fields, LLC.

PRINCIPAL COMPETITORS

C.F. Flag Co.; J.C. Schultz Enterprises, Inc.; Valley Forge Flag Company.

FURTHER READING

Alters, Diane, "Bush Wraps Himself in Many Flags at Factory," *Boston Globe,* September 21, 1988, p. 12.

Briggs, Rosland, and Henry J. Holcomb, "N.J. Flag-Maker to Buy Pa. Rival," *Philadelphia Inquirer,* March 28, 1998, p. D1.

Dawkins, Walter, "History-Spangled Banner," *Hackensack (N.J.) Record,* June 14, 2007, p. L01.

"Demand for Flags Called 'Terrific,'" *New York Times,* August 2, 1942.

"Digby Chandler, Flagmaker, Dies," *New York Times,* October 8, 1967.

Kleinfield, N. R., "Annin, Top U.S. Flagmaker, Found Bicentennial 'Sweet,'" *New York Times,* December 31, 1977.

Lissner, Will, "Flag-Making Industry Is Upset by Alaska's Impending Statehood," *New York Times,* July 2, 1958.

"Louis A. Ames Dead; Maker of Flags, 86," *New York Times,* November 29, 1952.

"Old Old Glories Fly for Bicentennial," *New York Times,* July 5, 1975.

"13 Stripes, 50 Stars, 800 Tired Workers," *New York Times,*
March 10, 2002, p. BU2.

Thomas, Jerry, "In N.J., Old Glory Can't Pay the Bills," *Boston*
Globe, July 8, 1989, p. 3.

"Verona Plant Has Reason to Wave Flag," *New York Times,*
December 17, 1972.

Arçelik A.S.

Karaagac Caddesi, No. 2-6
Suetluece, Beyolu
Istanbul, 34445
Turkey
Telephone: (90 212) 314 34 34
Fax: (90 212) 314 34 63
Web site: http://www.arcelikas.com

Public Company
Incorporated: 1955
Employees: 11,079
Sales: EUR 3.72 billion ($5.62 billion) (2007)
Stock Exchanges: Istanbul
Ticker Symbol: ARCLK
NAICS: 335222 Household Refrigerator and Home and
    Farm Freezer Manufacturing; 335211 Electric
    Houseware and Fan Manufacturing; 335224
    Household Laundry Equipment Manufacturing;
    335228 Other Household Appliance Manufacturing

■ ■ ■

Arçelik A.S. is one of Europe's largest and fastest-growing manufacturers of home appliances, with a focus on the white goods categories. The Istanbul, Turkey-based company is also that country's largest home appliance maker, commanding more than 50 percent of the total white goods market there. The company holds the seventh-place position in Europe, and ranks in the top 15 in the world. Arçelik markets a collection of international and local brands. Beko is the group's flagship international brand, traditionally positioned at entry-level market segments. The company targets the midrange market through its ownership of the Grundig brand.

The company's third international brand, Blomberg, targets the mid-to-high end appliance bracket. All three brands are also used at the local level, both in Turkey and in other markets, to differentiate the company's product lines. Other local brands include Leisure and Flavel, which target the high-end market in the United Kingdom; Arctic, the leading home appliance brand in Romania; Austria's Elektra Bregenz; and the low-end Altus brand, primarily used for alternative distribution channels, such as supermarkets.

In addition to its own production, Arçelik acts as a distributor for a number of international brands, such as Sony electronics goods and Vodafone mobile telephone services. In terms of product segment, refrigerator sales are the group's largest white goods category, generating 46 percent of its annual turnover of nearly EUR 3.75 billion ($5.6 billion) in 2007. Washing machines add 26 percent, ovens add 14 percent, dishwashers produce 12 percent, and tumble dryers generate 2 percent. Turkey remains the company's main market, at 50 percent of sales. The rest of Europe accounts for 41 percent of the group's sales. The North African and Middle East regions account for most of the remaining revenues. However, in 2008, the group announced plans to enter the Chinese and other Asian markets. Arçelik is a public company listed on the Istanbul Stock Exchange. The company remains majority controlled by the Koç Group, Turkey's largest conglomerate. Rahmi M. Koç is the group's chairman and A. Gunduz Ozdem is the company's general manager.

COMPANY PERSPECTIVES

The company's mission, in line with values, goals and strategies of Koç Group, is to develop, produce, present and service products which meet our customers' needs beyond their expectations, ease home life, are easily purchased and used, and are reliable; and to grow and develop continuously in the target markets with shareholders' satisfaction by providing customer loyalty and satisfaction using resources effectively.

ORIGINS OF AN INDUSTRIAL LEADER IN TURKEY

Arçelik's origins began with the entrepreneurial Koç family, which was already established in business at the turn of the 20th century. In 1926, Vehbi Koç, then 25 years old, took over the family company and renamed it as Koçzade Ahmet Vehbi. Over the next decade, Koç developed a variety of business interests, later building Turkey's largest and most diversified conglomerate.

Koç's interests turned to industrial development during the 1950s and he became one of the first in the private sector to invest in manufacturing. The family's initial target was the office furniture sector, and Koç founded Arçelik for this purpose, opening a factory in Sütlüce. Yet the family quickly recognized an opportunity to invest in the durable goods market, specifically home appliance manufacturing. Koç went in search of a technological partner with home appliance manufacturing expertise.

Arçelik was unable to convince any of the major European white goods producers to back its project, however; the Turkish home appliance market appeared too tiny to be profitable. At last Arçelik turned to Israel-based Amcor, which agreed to license part of its product range.

Arçelik introduced its first appliance, a washing machine, in 1959. The machine was not only Arçelik's first product, it was also the first washing machine to be designed and produced in Turkey. This early entry enabled Arçelik quickly to capture a leading share of the domestic home appliance market. The success of the washing machine launch was soon matched by the debut of the company's next, and ultimately largest product line, refrigerators. Introduced in 1960, Arçelik's refrigerator was, once again, the first such appliance to be domestically designed and produced.

Arçelik's initial production of refrigerators barely reached 1,500 units its first year. Nonetheless, demand for Arçelik's products rose steadily through the decade. In order to meet demand the company transferred its production lines to a new, larger factory in Çayirove in 1968. By the middle of the next decade the company's once again extended its production capacity, opening a dedicated factory for refrigerator production in Eskisehir in 1975.

GE TECHNOLOGY IN THE SEVENTIES

Arçelik's growth was aided in part by favorable policies put into place by the Turkish government. With high import tariffs in place to protect domestic producers, Arçelik enjoyed a keen pricing advantage over imported brands. At the same time Arçelik's membership in the Koç group proved an extremely important factor in the company's growth. By then the Koç group had begun to branch out into a number of other areas in both manufacturing and retail.

Koç's manufacturing operations came to include the home electronics and appliance company Beko, as well as Ardem ovens. At the same time, Koç had put into place three retail operations, under the Beko, Atilimi, and Aygaz names, which together represented a national network of more than 3,500 stores by the early 1990s. In this way Arçelik enjoyed the benefits of its parent company's powerful distribution network. The presence of other manufacturing operations in the Koç group provided another advantage in that Arçelik was able easily to extend the range of products marketed under its brand name by relabeling products manufactured by its sister companies. Arçelik also began importing other goods, such as irons, small appliances, and kitchen utensils, which were also marketed under its brand name. By the end of the 1980s rebranded Koç group products represented more than 20 percent of the company's sales, while third-party goods accounted for 7 percent.

The rapid growth of the Turkish white goods market in the 1970s in the meantime had attracted the attention of the major international players. The presence of high import tariffs, however, made the forming of local partnerships a more profitable alternative for these companies. As a result Arçelik was able to form a technological partnership with General Electric (GE). This enabled the company to introduce its first automatic washing machine in 1975. The partnership with GE later resulted in the launch of a new product line for Arçelik, as the company introduced its first dishwasher in 1985.

KEY DATES

1955: Koç Group establishes an office furniture manufacturing business, Arçelik.

1959: Arçelik targets the home appliance market, launching its first washing machine.

1975: As part of a licensing agreement with General Electric, Arçelik launches its first automatic washing machine.

1991: Arçelik establishes a research and development center to gain technological independence.

1999: Koç Group merges most of its home appliance marketing and manufacturing operations into Arçelik.

2001: Arçelik takes over Koç's Beko brand.

2002: Arçelik gains international scale through the acquisition of Blomberg (Germany), Elektra Bregenz and Tirolia (Austria), Flavel and Leisure (U.K.) and Arctic (Romania).

2004: Arçelik forms a joint venture to acquire Grundig Multimedia, and takes full control of that company in 2007.

2008: Arçelik establishes a washing machine factory in China.

NEW PARTNERS IN THE EIGHTIES

The success of the GE partnership led Arçelik to seek new technology transfer agreements in the 1980s. In 1987, for example, the company joined with Bosch-Siemens to develop refrigerators based on the German appliance giant's designs. That year Arçelik also teamed up with Sahuurink in the Netherlands to produce a range of clothes dryers. Another partnership, with Italy's Bimak, allowed the company to introduce a line of irons.

Other partnerships followed into the early 1990s. The group reached a second license agreement with Bosch-Siemens in 1990, to produce dishwashers. In 1992 the company reached the first of two licensing agreements with Sanyo, focusing on the Japanese company's vacuum cleaner and electric motor designs. The second agreement, involving refrigerators, followed in 1994.

By then, however, Arçelik had made the decision to invest in developing its own technology. In 1991 the company set up a research and development (R&D) center. The investment quickly paid off, as the company

became one of the first to introduce an ozone-friendly refrigerator in 1994. The strength of Arçelik's R&D team not only reduced the company's reliance on licensed technologies, it enabled the company to eliminate its licensing program altogether. The last of the company's licensing agreements ran out in 2000.

Part of Arçelik's decision to invest in its own technology came from the group's rapidly growing export business. By the early 1990s the company was exporting more than 25 percent of its production—and exports accounted for an equivalent proportion of its revenues. By 1994 exports absorbed 46 percent of the group's production, representing 43 percent of its turnover.

Developing export sales became even more important for the company because the Turkish government, in its efforts to align itself with the European Union, began lowering its import tariffs. As a result Arçelik's market share—which reached 72 percent in the dishwasher segment and 54 percent in refrigerators in the mid-1990s—was expected to decline into the turn of the century. In order to develop its export sales, Arçelik borrowed the easier-to-pronounce brand name of its sister company Beko.

MERGING FOR STRENGTH AT THE TURN OF THE 21ST CENTURY

Arçelik had continued to build up its manufacturing capacity through the 1990s. The company opened a new dishwasher factory in Ankara in 1993. This was followed by the establishment of a Cayirova factory producing air conditioners in 1996. The expansion of the group's production capacity helped support its international growth. Through the decade the company established the Beko brand as a major name in the European white goods market. Lower wage costs in Turkey, where workers earned less than 10 percent than what was paid in Germany, for example, allowed Arçelik to position itself as a strong player in the lower-priced appliance segments.

The growing importance of international sales, as well as the need to protect its market share at home, encouraged the Koç group to restructure its home appliance marketing and manufacturing operations at the end of the 1990s. This process began in 1999 when Arçelik acquired the Ardem Cooking and Heating Appliance business. Soon afterward other Koç operations, including Türk Elektrik Endüstrisi A.S., Atilim A.S., and Gelisim A.S., were merged into Arçelik as well. The restructuring of the Koç group's appliances operations was largely completed by 2001, when Arçelik acquired the Beko sales and marketing division as well. Arçelik, listed on the Istanbul stock exchange, emerged as Turkey's largest industrial company.

The company began looking to establish a strong international presence. For this the company targeted the acquisition of complementary brands, both to extend its reach into new products and pricing segments, and to add to its geographic reach. The group's acquisition program also gave it a number of new local and international brands.

In 2002 the company acquired Germany's mid-to-high-end appliance brand Blomberg, its Austrian counterparts Elektra Bregenz and Tirolia, and the high-end U.K. home appliance brands Leisure and Flavel. These were shortly followed by the purchase of Arctic, in Romania. That company dominated the Romanian home appliance market, with a market share of more than 90 percent in some product categories.

GAINING A TECHNOLOGY EDGE

Arçelik, which had been developing a strong computer engineering technology component since the early 1990s, debuted its first "smart products" in 2003. Through the middle of the decade, the company emerged at the cutting edge of appliance technology in the European market. The company's product line grew to include low-energy refrigerators, the world's fastest washing machine—capable of completing a load of laundry in less than half an hour—and, in 2007, the "Tech-Touch" dishwasher. This machine was capable of analyzing the soil levels of a dish load, and adjusting the cleaning cycle accordingly.

By then Arçelik had acquired control of another major European brand. In 2004, the company teamed up with the United Kingdom's Alba to acquire Grundig Multimedia BV, one of the oldest European home electronics brands. By the end of 2007, however, Arçelik had decided to buy out its partner, taking full control of the Grundig brand. This became the group's third major international brand, alongside Beko and Blomberg.

Arçelik's strong growth had by then placed it in the top ten manufacturers in the European home appliance market, and among the top 15 home appliance companies worldwide. The company began to seek new market expansion opportunities. In 2005 the company entered Russia, establishing a factory to produce refrigerators and washing machines for that market. Its success in Russia led the company to target an entry into China as well. In July 2007 the company bought Changzhou Casa-Shinco, which was subsequently renamed Beko Electrical Appliances Co. The new subsidiary's washing machine factory launched production at the end of the year, with an initial capacity of 200,000 units per year. Arçelik had become one of Turkey's industrial flagships for the 21st century.

M. L. Cohen

PRINCIPAL SUBSIDIARIES

Arcelitalia SRL (Italy); Archin Limited (Hong Kong); ArcticPro SRL (Romania); Ardutch B.V. (Netherlands); Beko Cesko (Czech Republic); Beko Deutschland GmbH; Beko Electronics España S.L.; Beko Elektronik Llc (Russia); Beko Elektronik A.fi.; Beko France S.A.; Beko Plc. (U.K.); Beko S.A. (Poland); Beko Shanghai Trading Company Ltd. (China); Changzhou Beko Electrical Appliances Co. Ltd. (China); Elektra Bregenz AG (Austria); Raupach Wollert GmbH (Germany).

PRINCIPAL COMPETITORS

Siemens AG; Whirlpool Corp.; AB Electrolux; BSH Bosch und Siemens Hausgeraete GmbH; GE Appliances; Indesit Company S.p.A.; Fagor Electrodomesticos Soc Cooperative Ltda.; Candy S.p.A.

FURTHER READING

"Arçelik Acquisitions," *Appliance Design,* March 2008, p. 12.

"Arçelik Aims for Russian Share," *Appliance Design,* August 2005, p. 8.

"Arçelik to Market Sony Products in Turkey," *Economist Intelligence Unit,* June 15, 2004.

"Arçelik Wins Court Battle for Brand Control," *IPR Strategic Business Information Database,* May 9, 2002.

"Koç Merger to Make It European Giant," *IPR Strategic Business Information Database,* November 4, 1999.

Marsh, Peter, "Arçelik Seeks to Double Sales in Five Years," *Financial Times,* October 5, 2004, p. 30.

Remick, Norman C., Jr., "Arçelik in Pursuit of North Africa," *Appliance Manufacturer,* February 1997, p. G11.

"White Goods Firm Makes Its Move in Europe," *Economist Intelligence Unit,* December 23, 2002.

Arkema S.A.

420 rue d'Estienne d'Orves
Colombes, F-92705
France
Telephone: (33 01 49) 00 80 80
Fax: (33 01 49) 00 83 96
Web site: http://www.arkemagroup.com

Public Company
Incorporated: 1971 as Aquitaine Total Organico (ATO)
Employees: 15,000
Sales: EUR 5.68 billion ($8.73 billion) (2007)
Stock Exchanges: Paris
Ticker Symbol: AKE.PA
NAICS: 325188 All Other Inorganic Chemical Manufacturing; 325131 Inorganic Dye and Pigment Manufacturing; 325211 Plastics Material and Resin Manufacturing; 325311 Nitrogenous Fertilizer Manufacturing

■ ■ ■

Arkema S.A. is one of the top ten European chemicals companies. Created in 2004 as part of the restructuring of French petroleum giant Total's chemicals operations, Arkema focuses on three core areas: Vinyl Products, Industrial Chemicals, and Performance Products. The Vinyl Products division, which generated 25 percent of the company's EUR 5.68 billion ($8.73 billion) revenues in 2007, operates through four primary business units. These are Chlorine/Caustic Soda; PVC; Vinyl Compounds; and Pipes and Profiles. The division's brands include Lacovyl, used for the produc-

tion of packaging for cosmetic and pharmaceuticals products; Nakan, used in the production of medical equipment, coatings for instrument panels, and so on; and Lucobay, for window and shutter manufacturing.

The Industrial Chemicals division is Arkema's largest, accounting for 41 percent of sales. This division produces a wide range of chemical intermediates, including acrylics, thiochemicals, fluorochemicals, hydrogen peroxide, polyamides, slush moulding compounds, and PMMA (polymethyl methacrylate). Brands include Plexiglas and Altuglas (the U.S. and European brands, respectively); Albone, used in pulp and textile bleaching and water treatment; Aquakeep, a highly absorbent substance used in the production of disposable diapers; and Forane, used as a coolant in refrigeration and air conditioning systems.

The third division, Performance Products, adds 30 percent to the group's annual revenues, and includes such brands as Rilsan high-performance polyamides; Pebax Polyether Block Amides, used in the production of sneakers, toys, and watches, as well as in the automotive industry; and Orgasol, used to produce powdered cosmetics, among other applications. Arkema is a globally operating company, with nearly 90 production facilities in 40 countries. Europe remains the company's primary market, generating 60 percent of its turnover. North America adds 22 percent, while Asia, the focus of the group's growth strategy after about 2005, accounted for 13 percent of its 2007 sales. Arkema was formally spun off from Total in 2006, when it listed its shares on the Euronext Paris Stock Exchange. Leading the company is Thierry Le Henaff, as CEO and chairman.

COMPANY PERSPECTIVES

■

Strategy: To turn Arkema, a global chemical company and France's leading chemicals producer, into a growing industrial group, competitive and value-creating over the long term, with leading rankings in most of its activities. Three major strategic vectors: growth through innovation; increasing pace of development in Asia; improved competitiveness ... bolstered by a dynamic management of the business portfolio.

CHEMICALS PARTNERSHIP IN 1971

Although Arkema was not officially created until 2004, the company's operations stemmed from the first efforts by France's petroleum giants, Total and Elf, to enter the chemicals markets. Total, founded in 1924 as Compagnie Française des Pétroles (CFP), founded its first petrochemicals operations in the 1950s. The company had also backed the creation of Société Nationale des Pétroles d'Aquitaine (SNPA), in 1941, in partnership with the French government and others. That company was initially meant to explore for oil and gas reserves in France's Aquitaine region, and was also conceived as a petrochemicals producer. France's defeat in World War II put these operations, on hold, however.

Following the war, SNPA discovered the Lacq gas field in France's southwest in 1951. With reserves of 250 billion cubic meters, the Lacq field proved to be one of the largest ever found in France. It also proved a strong source of the highly toxic hydrogen sulfate and other substances. This enabled SNPA to develop a strong degree of expertise in handling sulfurous natural gas, as well as in extracting and refining the sulfates. While sulfates became a major French export product, SNPA also developed a close working relationship with France's industrial chemicals sector.

Demand for petrochemicals rose swiftly during the 1960s, especially with the rapid development of new plastics and other petroleum-based substances. These included acrylics, polyvinyl chloride (PVC), and polymethyl methacrylate (PMMA), more widely known as Plexiglas (in North America) or Altuglas (in Europe), among many others. By then, SNPA had become part of Elf, created in 1967 during the nationalization of most of France's oil and petrochemicals sector. CFP in the meantime had become better known under its retail brand, Total, introduced in 1961.

The swift rise in demand for petrochemical products caught France's two major oil companies, Total and Elf, somewhat by surprise. Chemicals had remained a mere sideline for the core businesses of both companies, and as such had been somewhat overlooked. In order to respond to the surge in demand, the companies decided to work together, merging their chemicals businesses into the single Aquitaine Total Organico (ATO) in 1971.

BECOMING ATOCHEM IN 1983

The move proved especially important as the effects of the Arab oil embargo of 1973 and the resulting surge in raw materials costs profoundly affected the petrochemicals industry. The creation of ATO helped buffer the rising prices at the chemicals operations at both Total and Elf. In 1973, the companies deepened their chemicals partnership, forming a new joint venture company, ATO Chimie. The relationship between the two companies—and archrivals—remained rocky through the decade. At the encouragement of the French government, ATO Chimie agreed to take over the chlorochemicals assets from Rhône-Poulenc, forming a second chemicals company, Chloé Chimie, in 1979. The Elf-Total partnership owned 80.5 percent of Chloé Chimie.

The deepening recession, oil crisis, and the rising cost of raw materials led Total to abandon its chemicals operations. In 1983, the company sold out its stake in ATO Chimie to Elf. Following that purchase, Elf reorganized its chemicals holdings, including ATO Chimie, Chloé, and majority control of Ugine Kuhlmann, a chemicals company created in 1971. The new company was called Atochem, and was considered the centerpiece of the French petrochemicals industry. By then, Atochem held major positions in the global chemicals sector as well, with operations spanning most of the world's major petroleum and industrial markets.

Although Elf had engaged in a widespread diversification effort in the late 1970s and 1980s, chemicals became an increasingly important part of its operations. The company's acquisition of Texas Gulf in the early 1980s enabled it to become the world's number one sulfur producer. The group added to its U.S. presence during the decade through Atochem's takeover of Thurmit Chemicals. In 1989, Atochem moved into the performance chemicals market as well, and over the next decade developed into one of the world's leading producers of polyamides, PVDF (polyvinylidene fluoride), organic peroxides, and other chemicals used for such varied purposes as anti-corrosion coatings and automotive fuels, the production

KEY DATES

1971: Total and Elf merge their chemicals operations to form Aquitaine Total Organico (ATO).

1973: Total and Elf deepen their chemicals partnership, forming ATO Chimie.

1979: ATO Chimie takes over the chlorochemicals assets from Rhône-Poulenc, forming a second chemicals company, Chloé Chimie.

1983: Total sells its shares in ATO Chimie to Elf; Elf reorganizes its chemicals holdings, forming Atochem.

1990: The French government restructures chemicals industry; Atochem acquires organic peroxides operations of Montedison of Italy.

1998: Elf acquires control of Plexiglas from Rohm & Haas.

1999: Total merges with Fina, then takes over Elf, forming Total Fina Elf, which merges all of its chemicals operations into Atofina one year later.

2004: Total restructures its chemicals operations, creating Arkema for its vinyl, industrial chemicals, and performance chemicals operations.

2006: Arkema completes its spinoff from Total with a listing on the Euronext Paris Stock Exchange.

2007: Arkema makes its first acquisition, of Coatex.

2008: The company launches construction of a new plant to produce polyvinylidine fluoride, in Changshu, China.

of athletic shoes, toys, and automotive components, and in the manufacture of cosmetics.

ATOFINA IN 2000

Elf's investment in the chemicals sector made it the strongest petrochemicals player among the world's major oil groups. At the beginning of the 1990s, however, the French government pushed through a new restructuring of the country's chemicals industry. As part of that process, Atochem became the central force in the country's production of styrenics, fertilizers, acrylics, and petrochemicals, in part by taking over the base chemicals operations of Orkem, a Total subsidiary, in 1990. In exchange, Total acquired Atochem's resins and paints operations, including paint subsidiary La Seigneurie. Also that year, Atochem boosted its performance chemicals division through the purchase of the organic peroxides operations of Italy's Montedison.

The shakeup of the petrochemicals sector came in advance of the French government's privatization program. Total was first to emerge from under government control, listing its stock on the New York Stock Exchange in 1991. The government's direct stake in the company was then reduced to just 5.4 percent.

Elf's turn came three years later, as the government reduced its share of the oil and chemicals giant to just 16 percent. By then, Elf had renamed its Atochem subsidiary as Elf Atochem. The name change proved only temporary, however. Through the decade Total had surged ahead, leaping from being the second largest oil group in France to the third largest in all of Europe. This position was consolidated through its $13 billion merger with Belgium's Petrofina in 1999, creating Total Fina. The merger also brought the company Petrofina's substantial chemicals interests. Petrofina's own chemicals interests dated from the 1920s; in the 1950s, the company became one of the first to recognize the importance of plastics, and ultimately emerged into a major producer of polypropylene, polyethylene, and polystyrene. Petrofina had also developed its own international network of chemicals companies, starting with the acquisition in 1954 of U.S.-based Cosden Chemicals.

Barely had Total Fina taken on its new name when the company launched a hostile takeover offer for Elf. While Elf fought back with a counteroffer, Total Fina won the day, paying $54 million to acquire its French rival. The newly reformed Total Fina Elf became the world's fourth largest oil company in 2000. The integration of the operations of the three companies led to the creation of a new dedicated chemicals unit, Atofina, in 2000. By then, one of Atofina's largest operations was its PMMA (polymethyl methacrylate) production, better known under the Plexiglas and Altuglas names in North America and Europe, respectively. Atofina already controlled Altuglas. In 1998, Elf acquired Plexiglas, which had operated as a separate company since World War II, from owner Rohm & Haas.

INDEPENDENCE IN THE 21ST CENTURY

Chemicals had become a small and somewhat underserved part of the larger gas and petroleum group, which later shortened its name again to Total. Into the first decade of the 21st century, Total decided to launch a reorganization of its chemicals operations, creating three new chemicals business units. The first of these was

Total Petrochemicals, which took over the group's petrochemicals, polyolefins, fertilizers, and styrenics operations. The second unit grouped together a number of specialty chemicals operations, such as the Bostik adhesives group; Atotech, focused on electroplating; and Hutchinson, a producer of rubber products. While these units were expected to remain within the Total fold—and replace Atofina altogether—the third business unit was destined to become an independent company.

By 2004, Total had created Arkema, which then took over a diversified range of 14 business units grouped under three primary divisions: Industrial Chemicals; Performance Chemicals; and Vinyl Products. The new company, with more than EUR 5 billion ($5.2 billion) in turnover, then ranked in the top 20 of Europe's chemicals companies. Taking charge of the company was Thierry Le Henaff, 41 years old at the time, who had spent about 15 years working at Total.

Le Henaff launched a "fine-tuning" of Arkema, leading a restructuring of the group's extensive operations ahead of its spinoff as an independent company, slated for 2006. Over the next two years, the group worked at improving its operating efficiencies, shutting down a number of under-performing plants and transferring production to more modern and efficient facilities. In the end, the restructuring led to the loss of some 1,000 jobs. The restructuring effort, which lasted into 2008, included the sale of a number of the group's business units, including its U.S.-based specialty amines operations in 2007, among others.

By 2006, the restructuring process had advanced sufficiently, and in that year Total spun off Arkema as a separate company, with a listing on the Euronext Paris Stock Exchange. By then, the company had begun to put into place a major part of its future growth strategy—the expansion of its Asian operations, especially those in China. The company expected to double the share of its turnover generated from Asian markets, from 13 percent in 2007, by 2010. For this, the company launched a major investment effort, which included the construction of a $10 million organic peroxide factory in Changshu, with a total production capacity of 3,000 metric tons per year. That site was completed in 2005. The company also launched the expansion of a number of other facilities in China and elsewhere. In the United States, for example, the company spent $45 million to upgrade its Calvert City, Kentucky, refrigerant plant in 2006.

By mid-2007, Arkema had marked a milestone in its restructuring program by launching its first acquisition, of France-based Coatex, a producer of acrylic-based specialty polymers. The purchase was expected to add EUR 150 million ($200 million) to Arkema's sales, which neared EUR 5.7 billion by the end of the year.

At the same time, Arkema confirmed its intention to expand the share of the Asian region in its overall turnover and production. The company's focus fell especially on China, particularly on the region around Changshu, where it continued to invest in expanding its five existing plants. In 2008, the company also launched construction of a new plant to produce polyvinylidine fluoride, marketed as Kynar, in Changshu. That facility was expected to be operational by 2010. Meanwhile, the group had formed a 60-40 joint venture with Japan's Daikin Industries to build a refrigerant hydrofluorocarbon (HFC) plant in Changshu, which came onstream in 2008. These growth moves fit in with Arkema's strategy to claim a place among the world's top chemicals companies in the 21st century.

M. L. Cohen

PRINCIPAL SUBSIDIARIES

Arkema (China) Investment Company Ltd.; Arkema France S.A.; Arkema GmbH (Germany); Arkema Inc. (United States); Arkema Peroxides India Private Ltd.; Arkema Quimica Ltda. (Brazil); Arkema Quimica S.A. (Spain); Arkema S.A. (Colombia); Arkema S.R.L. (Italy).

PRINCIPAL COMPETITORS

BP PLC; Elf Aquitaine S.A.; BASF SE; China National Chemical Corp.; Repsol YPF S.A.; Dow Chemical Co.; Sanofi-Aventis; LyondellBasell Industries; Novartis International AG; Belaruskaliy Production Amalgamation; SABIC; E.I. du Pont de Nemours and Co.; Polski Koncern Naftowy Orlen S.A.

FURTHER READING

Alperowicz, Natasha, "Arkema Outlines Indian, Chinese Investments," *Chemical Week*, March 17, 2008, p. 21.

"Arkema Divests US Amines Unit." *ICIS Chemical Business*, May 7, 2007.

"Arkema Reaffirms Ambition to Develop Technical Polymers Activity in Asia," *China Chemical Reporter*, May 6, 2008, p. 11.

"Arkema to Seek Acquisitions," *Chemical Week*, June 20, 2007, p. 5.

Baker, John, "Entering the Fray," *ECN-European Chemical News*, October 11, 2004, p. 20.

———, "Totally Independent at Last," *ICIS Chemical Business*, May 22, 2006, p. 18.

Chang, Joseph, "Arkema Looks to Build Growth in 2006–07," *Chemical Market Reporter,* April 17, 2006, p. 15.

Davis, Nigel, "Arkema Looks to Bright Future," *ICIS Chemical Business,* February 27, 2006, p. 18.

Esposito, Frank, "Arkema Boosting Kynar Capacity in North America," *Plastics News,* October 20, 2008, p. 1.

———, "Looking Back Through Plexiglas," *Plastics News,* September 15, 2008, p. 1.

Hilgers, Lauren, "Arkema Adding Nylon Capacity at Changshu Site," *Plastics News,* May 12, 2008, p. 11.

Robinson, Simon, "Arkema: Organic Growth Is Key to Independence," *ICIS Chemical Business,* April 17, 2006, p. 10.

Viswanathan, Prema, "Arkema to Up Presence in Asia," *Asian Chemical News,* June 20, 2005, p. 9.

Walsh, Kerri, "Arkema Returns to Black," *Chemical Week,* March 21, 2007, p. 21.

Wood, Andrew, "Arkema off to a Good Start," *Chemical Week,* October 11, 2006, p. 23.

Young, Ian, "Arkema Finalizes Preparations for Spinning out of Total," *Chemical Week,* April 12, 2006, p. 11.

Atwood Oceanics, Inc.

———— ■ ————

15835 Park Ten Place Drive
Houston, Texas 77084
U.S.A.
Telephone: (281) 749-7800
Fax: (281) 492-7871
Web site: http://www.atwd.com

■ ■ ■

Public Company
Incorporated: 1968
Employees: 900
Sales: $403 million (2007)
Stock Exchanges: New York
Ticker Symbol: ATW
NAICS: 213111 Drilling Oil and Gas Wells

Atwood Oceanics, Inc., is an international offshore drilling and completion contractor operating a fleet of eight mobile drilling units, over the years serving such major oil companies as BP, Chevron, ExxonMobil, Marathon, Phillips, Shell, and Texaco. The Atwood fleet includes one submersible, four semisubmersibles, one semisubmersible self-erecting tender-assist rig, and two cantilever jack-up rigs. Four units operate in Southeast Asia, including Malaysia, Thailand, and Vietnam; one in the Northwest Shelf of Australia; two in the Mediterranean region; and a single unit operating in the United States in the Gulf of Mexico. A ninth rig, a jack-up, is scheduled for delivery in late 2008. Atwood is a New York Stock Exchange–listed company based in Houston. It also operates subsidiaries located in Australia and Malaysia, while Atwood Oceanics Pacific Ltd. is incorporated in the Cayman Islands. Liaison offices are maintained in Egypt, Singapore, and the United Kingdom.

COMPANY FOUNDING

Atwood Oceanics was founded by John Horton Atwood, who was born in Wisconsin in 1923. After graduating from high school, where he was a standout athlete, lettering in baseball, football, and basketball, Atwood enrolled at the University of Wisconsin to study engineering and play football. World War II interrupted his education, however. He enlisted in the U.S. Marine Corps and became a radio operator, taking part in a pair of landings in the Marshall Islands in the Pacific. He was seriously wounded, receiving shrapnel in his neck and shoulder, some of which would never be removed and would trouble him for the rest of his life. Nevertheless, after being discharged from the Marines after the war, he was able to resume his athletic career at Purdue University, where he played football and baseball for one year while studying mechanical engineering. He took time off to play semiprofessional football and in 1948 signed with the New York Giants, playing one season in the National Football League as a running back and cornerback. Because of football he was only able to attend Purdue during the spring semester. He finally graduated with honors in mechanical engineering in 1951.

Atwood went to work for Standard Oil of Ohio. He moved to Houston in 1957 to work for Union Oil Company of California and its eastern subsidiary,

Global Marine Exploration. In 1960 he became the manager of the unit, and in 1964 he and three colleagues established a subsidiary called Global Marine, Inc., an offshore drilling contractor. After taking the company public on the New York Stock Exchange, Atwood resigned in 1968 to strike out on his own in offshore drilling. In October 1968 Atwood incorporated Atwood Oceanics, Inc. Two years later the company was operational in the Gulf of Mexico, and in 1972 Atwood took the company public. In that same year, subsidiary Atwood Oceanics Australia Pty. Ltd. launched operations in Australia. A Civil War buff, Atwood enjoyed giving the company drill ships Civil War–related names, such as Shiloh and Fredericksburg. Traces of this inclination were still evident in the names of the company's later Richmond and Vicksburg units.

CHANGES IN LEADERSHIP

Atwood performed well in the early 1970s. Revenues grew from $156.8 million in fiscal 1973 to $46.7 million in fiscal 1975. Net income during this period increased from $2.96 million to $4.28 million. In 1976 John Atwood resigned as chairman, chief executive officer, and president. He continued to provide consulting services to Atwood Oceanics and offshore rig management services to other companies for another 15 years. He retired in 1991 and lived until 2008, when he passed away at the age of 85 in his Houston home.

John Atwood was succeeded by John J. Macan. During his tenure, sales fell to $44.4 million in fiscal 1978 and the company posted a loss of $6.9 million. A year later the company rebounded when revenues improved to $58.7 million and the company turned a profit of $4.7 million. Sales dipped to $54.5 million in fiscal 1980, although net income jumped to $15.7 million due to the sale of the Fredericksburg. In November 1980, two months after the fiscal year came to a close, there was a change in administration. The board elected N. George Belury to replace Macan as chairman and

CEO. Macan then resigned his remaining post and was replaced as president by Robert E. Turrentine, an 18-year veteran of the offshore drilling business.

Although the 1980s were a particularly difficult period for the energy industry, especially later in the decade, Atwood fared better than most. It added several rigs to its fleet: the Hunter in 1981, the Eagle and Richmond in 1982, and the Falcon in 1983. By 1985 when the market for offshore drilling services began to erode, the company had ten drilling vessels at its disposal. In early 1986 just six were in operation, but they generated enough income to keep the company in a break-even position. Unlike its competitors, however, Atwood was not saddled with much long-term debt. The company was still able to turn a profit in fiscal 1989 before industry conditions finally caught up to Atwood.

NEW CEO: 1993

Atwood began the 1990s by recording $53.4 million in sales and a net loss of $2.1 million. Sales improved to $54.5 million in fiscal 1991, but the loss increased to $7 million. Fiscal 1992 was an even worse year, as revenues slipped to $44.8 million and Atwood lost nearly $20.1 million. That proved to be the bottom of the cycle, although not because market conditions had improved or day rates for the use of Atwood equipment had increased. Rather, Atwood was able to increase the utilization of its fleet. With 88 percent utilization in fiscal 1993, revenues rebounded to $51.8 million and the loss narrowed to $1.8 million. In fiscal 1994 the utilization rate improved to 99 percent and Atwood returned to profitability for the first time in five years, netting $6.2 million on sales of $66 million.

There were also changes in the top ranks during the early 1990s. John R. Irwin was named CEO in 1993. A petroleum engineer with 30 years of international experience, he had joined the company in 1979 as operations manager and was appointed executive vice-president in 1988. He became a director and president of the company in 1992. Day rates began to improve in fiscal 1995, and despite a low fleet utilization rate, Atwood was able to increase revenues to $72.2 million and net income to more than $7 million.

The trend continued in fiscal 1996 when Atwood recorded revenues of $79.5 million and net income of $11.4 million. The company took advantage of its momentum on several fronts in fiscal 1997. A $125 million revolving credit facility was arranged, which could then be used in a rig upgrading program. During the year major upgrades were made to the Atwood Hunter and Atwood Southern Cross, and plans were drawn up

KEY DATES

1968: John Horton Atwood founds offshore drilling rig company.
1970: Drilling operations commence.
1972: Company is taken public.
1976: Atwood leaves company.
1989: Company shows a profit for the last time before five-year downturn.
1997: Company listed on New York Stock Exchange.
2003: Delivery taken on Atwood Beacon.
2008: Atwood signs contract to build 10,000-foot water capable drilling rig.

for work on other units. Atwood also gained a listing on the New York Stock Exchange in August 1997. A two-for-one stock split was then declared in November of that year as a dividend for shareholders. When fiscal 1997 came to a close at the end of September 1997, Atwood posted revenues of $89.1 million and net income of $15.6 million.

ADDITIONAL FLEET UPGRADES

Two further upgrades to the fleet were completed in the first quarter of fiscal 1999. The Atwood Falcon then possessed a 3,500-foot water depth capability and was immediately put to work in Southeast Asia under a three-year contract. The Vicksburg unit underwent an even more extensive upgrade, completely refurbished and dispatched to India on a one-year contract. All told, the four upgrades completed over the previous two years came at a cost of $160 million. A third drilling unit, a self-contained platform rig managed on a project basis, was also upgraded during this time. The improved fleet could command higher day rates and negotiate longer-term contracts, so that when market conditions began to soften at the end of the year, Atwood was well insulated from the impact.

Much of the company's success was due to a strategy of mixing long-term contracts to provide downside protection with short-term contracts that permitted Atwood to take advantage of any improvements in market conditions while avoiding the risk of chasing the highest day rates. A further advantage to this approach was that the rigs were used consistently, keeping them in better mechanical condition and the rig crew in higher morale.

The company enjoyed the best year in its history to date in fiscal 1998, when revenues soared to $151.8 million and net income totaled $39.4 million. It was also able to hold onto most of these gains in fiscal 1999, even though that was not a good year for the offshore drilling market and several rigs in the fleet were idle for periods of time. The Seahawk rig was out of operation for most of the year, in a shipyard in Malaysia undergoing an upgrade and refurbishment; this work was part of a four-year contract extension that called for the operator to pay about $20 million of the $22 million project. Revenues fell slightly to $150 million and net income totaled $27.7 million.

FURTHER UPGRADES IN THE 21ST CENTURY

Atwood invested another $40 million on fleet upgrades in fiscal 2000. In addition to the work done on Seahawk, the Atwood Eagle was upgraded to 3,300-foot water depth. Atwood also spent $4.5 million to acquire the semisubmersible Ocean Scout, which was renamed the Seascout. To continue funding these upgrades, Atwood increased it credit facility to $150 million in June 2000. The company's hedging strategy also paid dividends in fiscal 2000. Despite revenues that decreased 10 percent to $134.5 million, the company was able to net $23.1 million.

Fleet upgrades continued in the new century, as Atwood positioned itself to take advantage of long-term growth expected in deepwater drilling. The Atwood Hunter and Atwood Eagle were in the shipyard in fiscal 2001 and additional enhancements were made to both of them beyond the original plan, taking full advantage of the downtime. Atwood Hunter was upgraded to a 5,000-foot water depth at a cost of about $45 million. The work on the Atwood Eagle cost $90 million and increased the rig's water depth to 5,000 feet. Additionally in fiscal 2001, Atwood signed a $125 million contract to build an ultrapremium jack-up in Singapore, slated to be ready in June 2002 and to take the Atwood Beacon name. Despite having some of its units out of operation during fiscal 2001, Atwood was able to increase revenues to $147.5 million and net income to $27.2 million.

After a ninth consecutive profitable year in fiscal 2002, netting $28.3 million on revenues of $149.2 million, Atwood recorded a loss of $12.8 million on revenues of $144.8 million in fiscal 2003 when the drilling industry experienced a significant downturn. Nevertheless, the company was well positioned for future success. Further work on the Atwood Eagle was completed during the year and the company took possession of the Atwood Beacon, which was completed in

2003 on time and within budget, thus completing a $460 million capital program that began in fiscal 1997.

RETURNING TO PROFITABILITY

As market conditions improved, Atwood quickly returned to profitability in fiscal 2004, netting $7.6 million on revenues of $163.5 million. The company also made a successful stock offering to pay down debt. Oil and gas prices soared and demand for drilling rigs increased, beginning a string of record results. Revenues improved to $176.2 million in fiscal 2005 and surged to $276.6 million in 2006 and $403 million in fiscal 2007. Net income during this period increased from $26 million in fiscal 2005 to $86.1 million in fiscal 2006 to more than $139 million in fiscal 2007. Some of the improvements in 2007 were the result of a $50 million investment in upgrades to three rigs in fiscal 2006, allowing these units to command even higher rates. In addition, work began on a new ultrapremium jack-up, the Atwood Aurora, which was slated for delivery in the autumn of 2008.

With revenues and earnings in fiscal 2008 well ahead of the pace set the previous year through three quarters, Atwood elected to take advantage of a strong balance sheet and a market that was not expected to soften for years to come. In July 2008 the company announced that it was building a new semisubmersible drilling rig at a cost between $750 million and $775 million. Capable of drilling in waters 10,000 feet deep,

it was scheduled for delivery in early 2011 and was under contract with Chevron Australia.

Ed Dinger

PRINCIPAL SUBSIDIARIES

Atwood Oceanics Management, L.P.; Atwood Oceanics Australia Pty. Ltd.; Atwood Oceanics Pacific Ltd.

PRINCIPAL COMPETITORS

Diamond Offshore Drilling, Inc.; Pride International, Inc.; Transocean Inc.

FURTHER READING

Abram, Lynwood, "Atwood Was War Vet, Pro Ballplayer, Offshore Executive," *Houston Chronicle,* July 18, 2008, p. 4.

"Atwood Oceanics Inc.," *Oil & Gas Investor,* January 1999, p. 4.

"Atwood Oceanics Inc.," *Oil & Gas Investor,* October 1999, p. 2.

"Atwood Oceanics Inc.," *Oil & Gas Investor,* October 2001, p. 4.

Shook, Barbara, "Atwood Expects to Survive, but Not Improve," *Houston Chronicle,* February 14, 1986, p. 4.

Sullivan, John A., "John Atwood, Founder of Atwood Oceanics, Dies at Age 85," *Oil & Gas Investor,* July 18, 2008.

Azelis Group

Via Leonardo da Vinci, 43
Trezzano sul Naviglio, 20090
Italy
Telephone: (39 02) 48 479 1
Fax: (39 02) 48 479 290
Web site: http://www.azelis.com

Private Company
Incorporated: 2001
Employees: 1,100
Sales: EUR 1.09 billion ($1.3 billion) (2007 est.)
NAICS: 424690 Other Chemical and Allied Products
  Merchant Wholesalers

■ ■ ■

Azelis Group is one of the largest and fastest-growing chemical distribution companies in Europe. Based in Trezzano, Italy, Azelis operates as a Europe-wide federation of largely local distribution companies in more than 25 countries. The company trades in coatings, including resins, additives, pigments, elastomers, and polymers; food and health ingredients, including flavorings, blenders, acidifiers, preservatives, and other basic and general food ingredients; pharma, ranging from active principal ingredients and finished products to veterinary products; plastics, supplying polymers as well as plastic pigments and additives; composites, with resins, catalyst inhibitors, foams, films, and reinforcements; rubber, including natural and synthetic rubber, additives, and fillers; and animal nutrition, supplying both additives and finished products. In addition, the company's Chemical Industries division provides formulation, basic chemistry, and synthesis services.

Azelis Group's holdings include Arnaud, a leader in France with operations spanning most of Central and Eastern Europe; Sibeco in the Benelux; Heinz Schlegel and Meister in Switzerland; Kraemer & Martin in Germany; Impex Quimica in Spain; and Brøste in the Nordic region. The company also operates offices in China, and is in the process of acquiring full control of India's Marigold International. CEO Udo Wenzel has been the chief architect of the group's growth since its formation in 2001. The company remains private, with investment group 3i controlling 57 percent of its shares. The group's partners—including Wenzel and some 100 managers of the companies acquired by Azelis—own the rest of the group's shares. Azelis produced revenues of more than EUR 1 billion ($1.4 billion) in 2008, with plans to double that figure by as early as 2012.

BACKGROUND FOR A EUROPEAN DISTRIBUTION LEADER

Although components of the Azelis Group were rooted in the 19th century, the company itself was very much a 21st-century creation, created in 2001 by the merger of Italy's Novorchem and France's Arnaud. Novorchem was the younger group, founded in 1998 by Udo Wenzel. A German native, Wenzel moved to Italy in his early twenties, earning his bachelor's degree. Wenzel then went on to take a Ph.D. in economics from the University of Zurich. Wenzel's first experience in the chemical industry was with the Hoechst Company, and by the early 1990s he had become managing director of that company's Trevira, Italy, branch.

COMPANY PERSPECTIVES

Azelis is a leading distributor of specialty chemicals, polymers and related services and our purpose is to grow business for our Principals and ourselves by satisfying the varying requirements of our customers. For our employees we will provide a stimulating and challenging work environment, providing encouragement and opportunities to develop and help to achieve their full potential and high levels of job satisfaction. For Principals we provide expert knowledge of and access to European markets serving the following industries: Food & Health, Pharma, Personal Care, Animal Nutrition, Plastics, Composites, Rubber, Coatings and Chemical Industries. For customers we provide a local, tailored service and supply the products they require when they require them, supported by high levels of technical and customer service. Our values underpin the way we do business and are shared across the whole of the Azelis Group. They are embodied in the way we behave and interact with our business partners. They represent our attitudes and the ways in which we believe we can add most value to our Principals and Customers.

After a stint with Alitalia, Wenzel joined Organa in 1997. Organa was then a small chemicals distributor in Italy half-owned by his father-in-law. In addition to sales of branded bulk chemicals, Organa held the exclusive license to distribute the Henkel brand of swimming pool and automotive care products. Wenzel's prior experience in the chemicals industry had given him insight into the shifting trends in the chemicals distribution market. In particular, Wenzel identified a need to create a group capable of providing distribution services across Europe. As he told *ICIS Chemical Business,* "I saw major changes in the distribution industry and it was luck that I had the opportunity through Organa to seize the challenge."

Wenzel founded his own company in 1998, called Novorchem Distribuzione, which then acquired Organa. By then, Organa had grown through a merger with another group, Chemplast. This extended the newly created Novorchem's reach into the paints, inks, polyurethanes, and adhesives markets. Through Novorchem, Wenzel quickly carried out the first phase of his development plan, completing a series of acquisitions to create a nationally operating chemicals distribution

group. In February 1999, Novorchem acquired Novaria Chemicals, focused on surface treatment products, as well as plastics and industrial chemicals. By December, the company had added operations in the food sector through its takeover of Giulio Gross, a company formed in 1953.

By 2000, Novorchem's holdings included Tradex Colori, the leading Italian distributor of resins, fibers, and additives for the textiles industry, founded in 1946. Another acquisition, of ChemVerga, gave the company a position in the market for adhesives and coatings. ChemVerga, founded in 1970, had roots as a distribution agent in the 1930s.

By the dawn of the 21st century, Novorchem had become a major chemicals distributor in Italy and already exhibited a number of the organizational features of the future Azelis group. Perhaps the most important of these was Wenzel's vision of a federation of partnership companies. To implement this, Wenzel kept the management teams of the companies acquired by the group in place, and allowed them a high degree of independence in their operations. Wenzel hoped thus to maintain the entrepreneurial spirit of the group's component companies, while also developing and exploiting the synergies among them.

MERGER WITH ARNAUD IN 2001

Wenzel's company exhibited a willingness to turn to private equity to fuel its growth. By 2001, Wenzel had brought in its first investors, selling a majority stake in Novorchem to Schroder Ventures (later Permira). Backed by Schroder, Wenzel's attention turned to the next phase of his growth strategy. With its Italian distribution network largely completed, the company then sought to develop its operations in the international market.

This goal led the company to neighboring France. Novorchem's timing was fortuitous, as one of that country's major chemicals distribution groups had just then come up for sale. Groupe Arnaud had been founded by Augustin Arnaud in 1908. Arnaud recognized that the explosive growth of France's industrial sector at the beginning of the 20th century had created a demand for raw materials, and the new chemicals products being developed at the time. Arnaud decided to position himself as an importer and distributor of these raw materials. The company soon became a major supplier to French industry.

Arnaud's son joined the company in 1935 and later became its leader. In the 1950s, the younger Arnaud developed a new business model built around developing specialized distribution units. These were then

```
┌─────────────────────────────────────────────┐
│                                             │
│              KEY DATES                       │
│                  ■                           │
│ ─────────────────────────────────────────── │
│ 1908: Augustin Arnaud founds a chemicals     │
│       distribution business in France.       │
│ 1998: Udo Wenzel founds Novorchem Distribuzi-│
│       one in Italy and acquires its first    │
│       company, Organa.                       │
│ 2001: Schroder Ventures acquires majority    │
│       shares of Novorchem and Arnaud and     │
│       merges them to form Azelis, under      │
│       Wenzel's leadership.                   │
│ 2002: Azelis launches pan-European expansion │
│       strategy, acquiring Chance & Hunt in   │
│       the United Kingdom.                     │
│ 2007: Azelis makes first acquisition outside │
│       of Europe, acquiring 49 percent of     │
│       India's Marigold International.         │
└─────────────────────────────────────────────┘
```

staffed with trained sales engineers, who worked directly with customers to implement the increasingly technologically advanced materials coming onto the market. As these units grew, Arnaud created a number of specialized subsidiaries, including Promecome and Comaip. Promecome, for example, specialized in the distribution of raw materials and components for France's fast-growing semiconductor and electronics industries. Another Arnaud operation was SCPO (Société Chalonnaise de Peroxydes Organiques), a joint venture created in partnership with Air Liquide and Peroxid Chemie in 1962.

The new approach was highly successful, and enabled Arnaud to grow into the leading French chemicals distributor over the next decades. By the early 1990s, Arnaud had begun looking toward its own international expansion. The collapse of the Soviet Union and the emergence of free market economies in Eastern and Central Europe provided the group with the target for foreign expansion. Arnaud first moved into Poland, establishing a subsidiary there in 1995. The company added operations in the Czech Republic in 1997. Romania followed in 1998, and a year later the company added Slovenia and Ukraine as well.

Throughout these decades of steady growth, Arnaud had remained under the leadership of Pierre Arnaud. His death at the dawn of the new century left the family-owned company without leadership. This led the Arnaud company to seek a new major investor in the company. At the same time, the availability of Arnaud represented an important opportunity for Udo Wenzel's own aspirations for Novorchem. In 2001, therefore, Schroder Ventures acquired a majority stake in Groupe Arnaud.

BECOMING A 21ST CENTURY LEADER

Following the Arnaud acquisition, Wenzel created a new company, Azelis, as the holding company for both Groupe Arnaud and the former Novorchem companies. These were then regrouped into a new company, Azelis Italy. Wenzel then went in search of the next piece of Azelis's European puzzle. Azelis, backed by Schroder Ventures, established a clear objective of becoming one of the top three chemicals distributors in Europe.

The United Kingdom provided the company with its next opportunity. Azelis quickly found its new target, with the purchase of the United Kingdom's Chance & Hunt in 2002. That company, with a history reaching back to 1825, had evolved into the distribution operations of British chemicals giant ICI. In 1999, Chance & Hunt was spun off from that company in a management buyout, led by Peter Fields. As a new major partner in the Azelis Group, Fields took up the position of group COO.

Azelis completed its coverage of the major European markets in 2003, buying Germany's Kraemer & Martin GmbH that year. That company, founded in 1936, had become a major player in the German market, with diversified distribution operations for pharmaceuticals, food and health, the chemical industry, and animal nutrition sectors.

The addition of Chance & Hunt helped boost Azelis's revenues past EUR 450 million ($470 million) by the end of 2003. By then, Azelis had found a new source of equity investment, when the newly renamed Permira (formerly Schroder Ventures) sold its stake in the company to Electra Partners. That company, which promised to spend nearly $50 million on further acquisitions, paid EUR 135 million to acquire 57 percent of Azelis. Electra's goal was to double Azelis's revenues before seeking its own exit, possibly through a public offering.

The year 2004 marked a significant milestone in Azelis's growth, as the company completed a number of major acquisitions. These included the United Kingdom's Pan Polymers, Belgium's Sibeco, and the Central and Eastern European distribution operations of the United Kingdom's CMS Chemicals. By the end of the year, the company had established itself in Spain as well, buying that company's Impex Quimica.

FURTHER EXPANSION

Azelis remained on the lookout for new expansion opportunities amid the fast-consolidating European chemicals distribution market. The company moved into the Scandinavian and Nordic markets in 2006, through its takeover of Sweden's Brøste group of companies. Originally founded in 1915 as a producer and distributor of salt, Brøste had launched the distribution of performance chemicals in the 1950s. By the end of the century, the company had become a leader in its markets, through its subsidiaries in Denmark, Finland, Norway, and other Nordic region markets. Also in 2005, Azelis added coverage in Ireland, buying that country's Brown & Gillmer. That company, created in 1846, helped boost Azelis's animal nutrition business.

After 2005, Azelis continued to plug the remaining gaps in both its geographic coverage and its range of chemicals products. The company added new acquisitions in Germany, particularly with the goal of solidifying its position in the plastics, coatings, and chemicals markets in that country. In 2007, Azelis added a major position in the U.K. fertilizer sector, through its takeover of the U.K. process chemicals operations of Finland's Kemira GrowHow. In Switzerland, the group acquired two Basel-region companies, Heinz Schlegel and Meister, which also enabled Azelis to enter the Austrian market.

Through 2007, Azelis completed several more important acquisitions. These included S. Black in the United Kingdom. That company, founded in 1968, had built up a leading position in the European personal care, food, and healthcare markets. The year 2007 also marked Azelis's first move beyond Europe. While the company had established an office in Shanghai, its Chinese business focused on sourcing products for the European market. The company's acquisition of a 49 percent stake in Marigold International, however, gave the company a direct entry into the polymer and chemicals distribution market in India. The company expected to acquire full control of Marigold as early as 2009.

By 2008, Azelis had become one of Europe's top three chemicals distribution companies. Azelis had by then succeeded in boosting its total revenues past EUR 1 billion ($1.4 billion). By then, too, Azelis had found a new source of investment capital, when 3i acquired Electra's stake in the company in 2006. The group's new majority shareholder shared Udo Wenzel's ambitions for the company, including the goal of doubling its revenues again by 2012.

M. L. Cohen

PRINCIPAL SUBSIDIARIES

Impex Quimica S.A. (Spain); Azelis Italia (Italy); Brøste (Denmark); Arnaud (France); Tara Kymya (Turkey); Azelis Plastics UK; Marigold International (India); Azelis Rus (Russia); Azelis Shanghai.

PRINCIPAL COMPETITORS

Univar N.V.; Brenntag AG; Agravis Raiffeisen AG; GEA Group AG; Bolton Group B.V.; Solvay Chemicals International S.A./NV.

FURTHER READING

"Arnaud, Novorchem Merge," *ECN-European Chemical News*, August 20, 2001, p. 17.

"Azelis Gains Foothold in Spain," *Pharma Marketletter*, October 11, 2004.

"Azelis Maintains Fast Track," *Chemical Week*, April 7, 2008, p. 31.

"Azelis Makes More Acquisitions," *Chemical Week*, June 23, 2004, p. 7.

"Azelis Subsidiary Buys UK Fertilizer Plants," *Chemical Week*, August 1, 2007, p. 5.

"A Born Entrepreneur," *ICIS Chemical Business*, November 7, 2005.

Burridge, Elaine, "Azelis Buys Pan-European Coverage," *ICIS Chemical Business*, August 20, 2007.

———, "Azelis in European Expansion," *ECN-European Chemical News*, October 24, 2005, p. 14.

———, "Azelis Targets European Buys," *ICIS Chemical Business*, October 16, 2006, p. 32.

———, "Growing Up Fast," *ICIS Chemical Business*, October 29, 2007.

"Electra Partners Buys Azelis," *Acquisitions Monthly*, December 2003, p. 52.

Pitman, Simon, "S. Black Eyes Ingredients Expansion Through Azelis Merger," *Food Navigator.com*, October 24, 2007.

Robinson, Simon, "Azelis Merges Belgian Firms into Benelux Unit," *ICIS Chemical Business*, July 31, 2006, p. 8.

Baldwin Richardson Foods Company

20201 South LaGrange Road, Suite 200
Frankfort, Illinois 60423
U.S.A.
Telephone: (815) 464-9994
Toll Free: (866) 644-2732
Fax: (815) 464-9995
Web site: http://www.brfoods.com

Private Company
Incorporated: 1997
Employees: 200
Sales: $122 million (2007)
NAICS: 311520 Ice Cream and Frozen Dessert Manufacturing; 311423 Dried and Dehydrated Food Manufacturing

■ ■ ■

Baldwin Richardson Foods Company is a private company based in the Chicago suburb of Frankfort, Illinois, its business divided among four units. The Retail brands unit is comprised of Baldwin Ice Cream, a premium ice cream line with about 20 flavors; the seven varieties of Mrs. Richardson's Dessert Toppings; and Nance's Mustards & Condiments, which include honey mustard, hot mustard, sharp and creamy mustard, as well as corn relish, corn sauce, and mild and hot chicken wing sauce. Baldwin Richardson's Liquid Ingredients & Sauces unit develops, processes, and packages a wide variety of ingredients used by food manufacturers, including bakery fillings, icings, ice cream variegates, shelf-stable cheese sauces, shelf-stable

yogurt and cream, syrups, ethnic and fusion sauces, and extreme flavors. The Foodservice Distributor unit offers Nance's Mustards & Condiments and Mrs. Richardson's dessert toppings, shake bases, pancake and waffles syrups, and beverage syrups that range in size from 1.75-ounce packets to gallon jugs. Major customers include McDonald's Corporation, Kellogg Company, General Mills, and Frito Lay-Quaker Oats. Baldwin Richardson also maintains a Private Label unit to act as a contract manufacturer of toppings, sauces, and other products for retail, foodservice, and industrial customers.

Although most of the company's products are manufactured at a plant in Macedon, New York, Baldwin Ice Cream is produced on a contract basis by a Dean Foods operation in Belvidere, Illinois. A distribution warehouse is maintained in East Williamson, New York. Owned by its chief executive officer, Eric G. Johnson, Baldwin Richardson is one of the largest African American–owned food suppliers in the United States.

BALDWIN ICE CREAM FOUNDED: 1921

The assets of Baldwin Richardson were assembled by Eric Johnson, using Baldwin Ice Cream as the core. Baldwin Ice Cream was founded in Chicago in April 1921 by seven African American postal workers who pooled their money to open an ice cream parlor at 5316 South State Street called the Seven Links Ice Cream Co. It quickly developed a loyal following in the African American community. During the 1930s the business

COMPANY PERSPECTIVES

We offer products that are steeped in old world quality. Whether describing the 1921 roots of the rich taste of Baldwin Ice Cream, the old fashioned fountain syrups and sundae toppings formulated by Richardson Foods in 1916 or Nance's mustards and wing sauces developed in 1925, you can be sure you're getting nothing but the finest tastes from Baldwin Richardson Foods.

was reorganized as the Service Links Ice Cream Co., and in 1946 one of the cofounders, Kit Baldwin, bought out his partner and renamed it Baldwin Ice Cream.

Baldwin was a 1911 graduate of the Tuskegee Institute. He moved to Chicago in 1919 where he found a job in the post office and remained employed for 22 years, working nights in order to run the ice cream shop during the day. The parlor and its ice cream was so popular that customers began asking for Baldwin Ice Cream at their local grocery stores to save a trip, and in the 1950s Chicago grocery store chains began to carry Baldwin ice cream in their stores located in African American neighborhoods, establishing a wholesale business.

Kit Baldwin died of a heart attack while on his way to a Tuskegee reunion in June 1962. He had become a respected leader of Chicago's African American business community and three times served as president of the Chicago Negro Chamber of Commerce. The business he left was generating about $400,000 in annual sales. Its next owner, an African American judge and minister, Archibald Carey, ran the company for five years, and when his health began to fail he sought another African American to buy the business. He turned to Joseph Robichaux, the only African American he knew who was involved in the dairy business.

BALDWIN ICE CREAM SOLD: 1967

Robichaux was a vice-president at the Wanzer Dairy Company Co. He agreed to buy Baldwin Ice Cream for $25,000 in 1967, primarily because he wanted it as a family venture. He dispatched his wife, Jolyn, to oversee business and he stopped by each afternoon to check on things. She was college educated, having attended Fisk University in Nashville before completing a degree in education at Chicago State College in 1961, along the way working as a court reporter and a medical assistant.

After college she worked for five years at the Betty Crocker Company.

After her husband bought Baldwin Ice Cream, she was little more than an observer at the company, which included three retail stores, but she soon realized that they were making more money from grocery store sales than the ice cream parlors and urged her husband to concentrate on the wholesale operation. He did not follow her advice, instead opening five more stores. In April 1971 he died suddenly from leukemia.

Jolyn Robichaux had to consider whether to sell Baldwin Ice Cream or hire someone to run it for her. She decided that because she would have to work closely with anyone she hired for at least a year to make them familiar with both the company and the market, she would become the boss herself. Her 14-year-old daughter, Glaze, also agreed to help raise her brother and assume the housekeeping responsibilities.

Once in charge, Robichaux was free to pursue her idea of growing the wholesale business. It was no small task, however. Baldwin Ice Cream had no salespeople, and the brand had not followed African Americans to the supermarkets in the new communities where they moved during the 1960s. Moreover, stores could not be certain of what flavors would be available at any given time, and delivery schedules were nonexistent, as drivers covered their territories as whim dictated.

Soon after the death of her husband, Robichaux began paying visits to the headquarters of the area grocery chains to make her pitch on why they should carry her products in more of their stores. She was given a chance to plead her case, primarily because she was a curiosity—not only an African American owner but a woman as well. Her message was simple: She pledged to grow retail sales of Baldwin ice cream by 50 percent in six months, at which point she would return for further discussion.

She then returned home and began to shake up her operation, firing people as needed, establishing job descriptions and delivery routes, buying new uniforms, implementing better accounting procedures, and establishing sales goals. Robichaux was fortunate to receive much needed help from the Department of Commerce's Talent Assistance Program that teamed successful executives with minority business owners. Leonard Abrahamson, an electronics manufacturing executive, became her mentor and helped nurture her business skills.

BALDWIN ICE CREAM SALES REACH $1 MILLION: 1975

Six months after making her promises to the chains, Robichaux made her return visits, and indeed sales had

KEY DATES

∎

1921: Seven Links Ice Cream Co. is established in Chicago.
1946: Kit Baldwin acquires the business and renames it the Baldwin Ice Cream Co.
1962: Kit Baldwin dies.
1967: Joseph Robichaux acquires Baldwin Ice Cream.
1971: Jolyn Robichaux takes control following her husband's death.
1985: Jolyn Robichaux is named National Minority Entrepreneur of the Year.
1992: Eric Johnson acquires Baldwin Ice Cream.
1997: Richard Foods is acquired and the company is renamed Baldwin Richardson Foods Co.
2005: The J.M. Smucker industrial bakery ingredients business is acquired.

increased more than 50 percent. She presented a list of stores that she wanted to carry Baldwin Ice Cream, and then persuaded individual store managers to free up space in their freezer cases for the product. Gradually Baldwin's coverage into the southern Chicago suburbs increased and then gained a foothold in the northern suburbs as well. Sales reached $1 million by 1975.

Still eager to gain more knowledge about the business, she traveled to Penn State University that year to enroll in the school's highly respected three-week ice cream technology course. Robichaux expanded into northwest Indiana and in 1983 sales topped $4 million. Also in 1983 she won the ice cream concession rights at O'Hare Airport, where she opened five stores. Her efforts received recognition in 1985 when she was named National Minority Entrepreneur of the Year.

Robichaux continued to push grocery chains to carry Baldwin Ice Cream beyond the Chicago area, and finally in 1989 she succeeded when Jewel, Dominick's, Omni, and Cub Foods agreed to sell the product throughout the Midwest and elsewhere. Later in the year production was moved from Wanzer Dairies to Borden Inc.'s Meadow Gold plant in Des Moines, Iowa. The Kroger supermarket chain then took Baldwin brand ice cream to markets in Alabama, Arkansas, Mississippi, and Tennessee. In the meantime, Robichaux began exiting the retail business, which at its peak included 15 shops. The original parlor closed at the end of 1990, a clear disappointment to the local community, but from a business point of view it was no longer profitable to keep.

Because her children were not interested in running Baldwin Ice Cream, Robichaux, who was over 70 years of age, decided to sell the business in the fall of 1992 in order to retire and devote her time to travel, painting, and writing the history of Baldwin Ice Cream. She found a suitable buyer in Eric Johnson and agreed to sell the business after meeting with him in June 1992, impressed by his marketing skills and confident that he was the right person to lead the company into the future.

JOHNSON BUSINESS LEGACY

Eric Johnson's family were another African American success story. In the 1950s his father used a $250 loan to establish Johnson Products Co., producing ethnic hair-care products. The younger Johnson began working part-time for the family business when he was just eight years old, his first assignment to fill shampoo bottles on the assembly lines. He told his father, "We're going to give people their money's worth." He overfilled them, however, preventing the bottles from being capped and was soon reassigned to the task of wiping off jars. He would go on to learn all aspects of the company, becoming a salesman during his summer vacations while in high school, and managing his own sales territory during college.

Johnson earned an undergraduate degree in finance and management from Babson College, and went to work as a personal-care products salesman for Procter & Gamble, although he intended to return to the family business, harboring a long-held dream of one day serving as president. He then furthered his education by earning a master's of business administration degree from the University of Chicago. In 1977 he rejoined Johnson Products, which was experiencing greater competition in the ethnic hair-care market after having the field to itself for 20 years.

By 1988 the company was losing money, and a year later he became chief executive after his father resigned as part of a divorce settlement that resulted in his mother gaining majority control. Eric Johnson then led a turnaround and spent four years at the helm of Johnson Products, but he and his mother eventually had a falling out over the future direction of the business, including a possible sale to a larger company. Johnson was offered a severance package of about $500,000 and agreed to leave in March 1992, a decision made easier because Johnson had grown weary of the personal-care products business.

ERIC JOHNSON ACQUIRES BALDWIN ICE CREAM

Johnson used his severance money to establish Tri-Star Industries and become involved in film production and real estate investments. He then used Tri-Star to acquire Baldwin Ice Cream, which he believed had a good deal of untapped potential because it had never been backed with any degree of advertising or promotion. "Clearly, what was selling the product was in the package," he told *Dairy Foods*. Although not familiar with the dairy industry, he knew supermarket distribution and was confident he could grow Baldwin Ice Cream.

On taking over, Johnson quickly made his mark. He completed the phaseout of retail operations, closing the last store in November 1992. He also increased the butterfat content of Baldwin ice cream from 12 percent to 13 percent and incorporated natural ingredients and flavorings to label the product as a premium ice cream. As a result, Baldwin was able in many cases to be the only premium ice cream available in half gallons in supermarket freezers.

He also negotiated a joint venture with Chicago-based Dean Foods to produce the products at the Dean's Belvidere, Illinois, plant. The alliance with Dean was also beneficial because the company operated 22 dairies and would be in a position to support the possible national distribution of Baldwin Ice Cream.

By 1997 Johnson had increased Baldwin's sales to $9.2 million. He then learned of an opportunity to greatly accelerate the growth of the company. A banker he was working with to identify business opportunities told him that Quaker Oats Co. was looking to sell Richardson Foods Co., its Liquid Products Division, which included Mrs. Richardson's dessert toppings and Nance's mustard and condiment products. Because Richardson's flagship products were ice cream toppings, it appeared to be a natural fit for an ice cream company like Baldwin.

Richardson had been established in the early decades of the 1900s in Rochester, New York, by pharmacist Alick Richardson and his brother Dirbin, who developed syrups for medicines that proved so flavorful that they were carbonated into drinks and led to the creation of dessert toppings. The business grew into Richardson Foods, based in Macedon, New York, and acquired by Quaker Oats in 1986. The Nance brand was also well established. It was founded in 1925 in upstate New York by Nance Delmarle, who created mustard products in her kitchen and began selling them in local grocery stores. Other products followed and eventually the brand became part of Richardson Foods to increase production to meet a widening demand.

RICHARDSON FOODS ACQUIRED: 1997

While Johnson did not offer the highest bid for Richardson Foods, he was the only one who indicated he wanted to keep the business intact and he was able to purchase the business for a reported $30 million. Richardson brought with it nearly $50 million in revenues, and the acquisition opened cross-marketing opportunities and access to new markets, especially in the foodservice industry. Two of Richardson's customers were McDonald's Corp. and Sysco Corp., a major distributor of food products to restaurants and institutions.

Under Quaker Oats' ownership, the Mrs. Richardson unit was valued because of its McDonald's business. Johnson, on the other hand, was just as interested in the branded retail products that had been neglected for years. He immediately began repackaging Mrs. Richardson's toppings and Nance's mustard, adorning them with new labels to improve shelf brand recognition. The combined company took the name Baldwin Richardson Foods Co. and enjoyed a steady increase in sales into the new century.

Business improved further in 2001 when the company reached an agreement with the Kellogg Company to become the sole supplier of fruit fillings for the Nutri-Grain cereal bar business, adding about $7 million in sales in 2002, when total revenues increased 12.7 percent to $69.9 million. A year later the Kellogg deal contributed about $16 million to the top line.

J.M. SMUCKER ASSETS ADDED: 2005

The next major deal for Baldwin Richardson came in 2005 when it acquired the industrial bakery ingredients business, primarily bakery fillings, of the J.M. Smucker Company. Not only did Baldwin Richardson add new products to its portfolio, it picked up new customer relationships as well. As a result, by 2008 annual sales topped $120 million, and there was every reason to expect that the company was positioned to enjoy even greater success in the coming years.

Ed Dinger

PRINCIPAL BRANDS

Baldwin Ice Cream; Mrs. Richardson's Toppings; Nance's Mustards & Condiments.

PRINCIPAL COMPETITORS

McCormick & Company, Incorporated; MGP Ingredients, Inc.; Tate & Lyle PLC.

FURTHER READING

Bilovsky, Frank, "Eric Johnson's Sweet Deal," *Rochester Democrat and Chronicle,* January 10, 1999, p. 1E.

Chao, Mary, "A Business Owner with a Taste for Success," *Rochester Business Journal,* March 12, 1999, p. 10.

Chavez, Donna M., "A Scoop of Sweet Success," *Chicago Tribune,* May 8, 1994, p. 1.

Glanton, A. Dahleen, "An Old Tradition, a New Success," *Chicago Tribune,* May 17, 1991, p. 1.

Gorman, John, "Ice Cream Exec Melts Resistance," *Chicago Tribune,* October 28, 1985, p. 21.

Gottesman, Andrew, "One for the Books, Jolyn Robichaux Had to Sell Herself Before Ice Cream," *Chicago Tribune,* p. 12.

Harris, Joyce M., "Family Dream Alive and Growing," *Chicago Sun-Times,* September 2, 1985, p. 39.

"Johnson: A CEO Again," *Black Enterprise,* December 1992, p. 17.

Lowe, Frederick H., "Eric Johnson Buys Baldwin Ice Cream," *Chicago Sun-Times,* September 10, 1992, p. 60.

Reiter, Jeff, "Evolution of a Brand," *Dairy Foods,* October 1993.

Waters, Jennifer, "Taking It from the Top-pings," *Crain's Chicago Business,* October 13, 1997, p. 4.

Banco Central del Paraguay

Federación Rosa y Cabo 1° Marecos
P.O. Box 861
Asunción,
Paraguay
Telephone: (595 21) 608-011
Fax: (595 21) 619-2637
Web site: http://www.bcp.gov.py

State-Owned Company
Founded: 1952
Employees: 1,192
Total Assets: PYG 12.37 trillion ($2.03 billion) (2005 est.)
NAICS: 521110 Monetary Authorities, Central Banks

■ ■ ■

The Banco Central del Paraguay (BCP), or Central Bank of Paraguay, is a government-owned institution that, like the central banks of other nations, serves as the government's banker, issuing the national currency and regulating the nation's financial institutions. Among its other functions are to accumulate and administer foreign monetary reserves and to maintain the value of the currency against other currencies by selling its foreign reserves when necessary. The BCP affects the money supply, mainly to cover government deficits, by issuing bills daily at maturities ranging from 35 to 360 days and call money with maturities from one to 15 days. It also, less often, issues long term bonds.

The BCP supervises the nation's banks, setting minimum capital requirements, requiring them to maintain a fixed ratio of reserves to deposits in both domestic and foreign currency, and acting as a clearinghouse for payments between banks. It also supervises, through the Superintendency of Banks (an institution that is part of the BCP), finance companies, savings and loan associations, exchange houses, warehouses, and public entities in Paraguay. The BCP also acts as agent and financial assessor for the government of Paraguay and other public bodies.

In theory, the Banco Central del Paraguay is independent of the government. However, its president and the other members of its board of directors are nominated by the president of the republic and confirmed by the congress, and its budget is part of the national budget. Furthermore, at least half—and perhaps 70 percent—of the nation's gross domestic product is outside the formal economy, and therefore outside its supervision. Paraguay has long served as a center for goods smuggled between its larger neighbors—Argentina and Brazil—and is perceived as one of the two most corrupt countries in South America by the organization Transparency International.

TRANSITION TO A SOUND CURRENCY

Although the first central bank in Latin America dates from 1886, Paraguay lagged far behind the growing consensus that a single institution was needed to serve as the issuer of paper money. It was not until 1907 that a so-called bank of the republic was established and not until 1944 that a law assigned to this institution the exclusive emission of paper money and coinage, plus the direction and administration of the nation's money, credit, and exchange. The BCP was established in 1952.

The first president of the BCP was Epifanio Méndez Fleites, previously chief of police in Asunción, Paraguay's capital. A populist, he controlled development loans and favored an easy money policy. According to an International Monetary Fund (IMF) study, in 1955 alone the BCP almost doubled the amount of credit available and the bulk of the loans went to contractors buying apartment houses on speculation. Foreign currency earned from exports had to be exchanged for Paraguay's greatly overvalued currency, the *guaraní*. The BCP then sold the foreign currency at much higher black market rates. This practice discouraged exports (or at least reported exports) and resulted in severe deficits in the balance of payments that made it difficult to pay for essential imports to keep the economy running.

Méndez Fleites helped General Alfredo Stroessner to seize the presidency in 1955 through a military coup. However, the general—who would rule Paraguay for the next 34 years—regarded Méndez Fleites as a dangerous rival and ousted him from his post before the end of the year. Stroessner feared inflation as a potentially destabilizing factor for any regime. Gustavo Storm, the new BCP president, secured an emergency loan from the IMF and adopted a frugal policy, imposing a lid on wage hikes and loans to businessmen.

The *guaraní* was allowed to find its own level in unrestricted currency trading until 1959, when it was fixed at 126 to the U.S. dollar—a rate preserved until 1982. Maintenance of law and order and of a stable currency usually headed the list of accomplishments that Stroessner laid out in his annual state-of-the-union addresses to Paraguay's congress.

During the 1960s Paraguay, supported by the United States, obtained badly needed development loans from such institutions as the IMF, the World Bank, and the Inter-American Development Bank. Inflation remained at minimal levels. Even so, prices were low for the nation's primarily agricultural exports, resulting in

trade deficits and a growing foreign debt. Writing in the *Financial Times* in 1968, a special correspondent who had just been in Asunción called the government "neither efficient nor honest. Paraguay is the staging point, for example, of smuggling operations in much of South America, and it is all done with the connivance of Government officials."

The decade of the 1970s was Paraguay's most prosperous up to that time. A unique bonanza was the building of the world's largest hydroelectric power installation to date, on the border with Brazil. Completed at a cost of more than $20 billion—mostly financed by Brazil—the Itaipú project enabled construction to rival agriculture as the chief reported economic sector in Paraguay, and for the government to sell most of the nation's half-share of the electricity generated. Paraguay enjoyed double digit growth each year between 1977 and 1980. During this period the BCP had high foreign reserves, and the IMF even accepted the *guaraní*, dubbed "the little dollar" in Paraguay, for use in its transactions.

SMUGGLING AND CORRUPTION

This period of prosperity came to a grinding halt in the early 1980s, when high interest rates and a consequent world recession created a financial crisis throughout Latin America. Paraguay's foreign debt began to spiral out of control after the *guaraní* was devalued in 1982. By mid-1986 the BCP was more than $250 million in arrears on debt payments. Inflation ranged between 30 and 45 percent in 1985. By the end of 1986 there was a different currency rate for exports, private sector imports, public sector oil and agricultural imports, and repayment of the public sector foreign debt. The free market exchange rate for *guaraní* per dollar was more than twice as high as the highest official rate. Bankers and economists said that the multiple exchange rates had produced a number of ills, including huge currency frauds.

The BCP again had to suspend some interest payments on its debt in 1987. Reporting for the *Financial Times* late in the year, Tim Coone wrote that officially sanctioned contraband equaled official trade and was draining the nation's foreign exchange reserves. "The level of corruption of government and army officials is now so endemic that it has ceased to be scandalous," he maintained. Not only luxury goods such as Scotch whiskey and branded perfumes and illegal ones such as cocaine and stolen cars made their way through the country to and from Argentina and Brazil, but even such traditional Paraguayan exports such as soybeans, cotton, cattle, and timber.

KEY DATES

1952: Establishment of Banco Central del Paraguay (BCP).
1959: The value of Paraguay's currency is fixed by the BCP at a level preserved until 1982.
1986: The BCP is more than $250 million in arrears on payments on its foreign debt.
1995: The BCP spends at least $175 million to bail out three failing banks and their depositors.
1998: The number of failed Paraguayan financial institutions since 1995 has reached 40.
2006: A former president of Paraguay is sentenced to six years in jail for diverting BCP funds.

Stroessner's dictatorship finally came to an end in 1989 by means of a military coup, but the nation's economic problems remained. Roger Cohen, a *Wall Street Journal* reporter, wrote from Asunción that the central bank, "Sprawling over 25 acres ... is larger than the U.S. Treasury, but with almost no money in its vaults. Here, Cesar Romeo Acosta, the former bank governor who was arrested as he tried to flee with his pockets bulging with dollars, presided over some astonishing horse-trading." Exporters smuggled their goods out to keep the authorities from exchanging their foreign currency earnings for the overvalued national currency at the BCP's official rate. Importers, on the other hand, prized the *guaraní* because they could use it at the official overvalued rate to buy dollars cheaply, ostensibly to pay for imported goods but in reality to fulfill bogus contracts.

MISMANAGEMENT AND FINANCIAL INSTITUTION FAILURES

The new government relieved the situation to some degree by introducing a unified floating exchange rate, which resulted in a major, although temporary, increase in official exports. Smuggling remained at high levels, however, and Paraguay suffered both from recessions in Argentina and Brazil and an inflation rate of 45 percent. In 1991 it requested an 18-month standby loan from the IMF—the first since Stroessner's early years in power—but this was not granted.

A run on three weak Paraguayan banks in 1995 resulted in the BCP spending at least $175 million, or about 15 percent of its reserves, to keep them from failing and depositors from losing their money. David Pill-

ing of the *Financial Times* wrote that lax controls on banking "are evident through a web of unregistered 'black' accounts, where high interest rates are offered and few questions asked. Much of the money disappearing into these accounts is believed to be funneled abroad or recycled through phantom companies."

Pilling also reported that $4.5 million was missing from the BCP and that all the directors of the central bank had been dismissed. (It was discovered the next year that the metal bars guarding the bank vaults could be unscrewed and removed.) According to the *Economist,* the BCP's treasurer was found to be lending $3 million of the bank's funds. By late 1996, four banks and 16 savings and loan associations had gone out of business. The number of failed Paraguayan financial institutions had reached 40 by late 1998. In every instance, investigators found mismanagement, fraud, or inadvisable lending practices, according to a high BCP official.

SCANDALS IN THE 21ST CENTURY

By late 2002 Paraguay was again in economic crisis because Argentina was in deep recession after defaulting on its debts and devaluing its currency. The finance minister and BCP president had resigned simultaneously, and the *guaraní* had dropped 30 percent in value since the beginning of the year. The national prosecutor for economic crimes had charged President Luis González Macchi with diverting $16 million from the central bank in 2000 to Citibank's New York headquarters, where the sum was earning high interest. Four former BCP officials went to jail in 2004 for their parts in the affair. In 2006 González Macchi was sentenced to six years in prison. In a nationally televised hearing, the judges said his actions had led to thousands of account holders losing their savings.

A new president of Paraguay, Nicomar Duarte Frutos, dedicated to rooting out corruption, took office in 2003. The government reached a settlement with domestic bondholders who had lost $138 million in defaulted dollar-denominated notes and secured a $76.3 million standby loan from the IMF. It also sought to put the country's financial house in order by auditing the activities of five ministries, representing one-third of the budget, every three months, and possibly privatizing some state-run companies.

Some of the banking reforms that Duarte sought came up against opposition in the congress. A goal of his administration—and that of the central bank—was to place Paraguay's financial cooperatives under the supervision of the Superintendency of Banks, a BCP agency. These cooperatives, whose finances, like the banks, were in disarray, accounted for one-fifth of the nation's private sector financial system. Instead, the recalcitrant legislators created a new body, composed of members who worked for the cooperatives and were appointed by them.

The BCP suffered another blow to its reputation in 2005, when BCP President Gabriel González resigned after firing bullets at protestors demonstrating outside his house. Former bank employees had been picketing his home for three months to protest the imminent bankruptcy of the banks' pension funds and to demand that the central bank make good the funds' losses. He was replaced by Mónica Pérez, an IMF economist with a doctorate from a German university. However, three BCP directors resigned in 2006, leaving the board without a quorum and Pérez as virtually the sole decision maker. Citizens' groups claimed her administration of the bank was therefore illegal, and she resigned in early 2007.

The resignation of Pérez came soon after the IMF urged the central bank to be more vigilant in fighting inflation, which reached 12.5 percent in 2006, higher than that of any other South American nation except Venezuela. The BCP had been accused of expanding the money supply at Duarte's request. During the waning days of Pérez's presidency it was discovered that $2.5 million worth of *guaraní* notes had disappeared while being sent to Paraguay from the plant in Europe where they had been printed.

Germán Rojas, the head of Paraguay's development bank, replaced Pérez as president of the BCP. Paraguay's finances improved in 2007–08, and the *guaraní* appreciated considerably against the dollar—16 percent in the first half of 2008 alone—because of a sharp rise of soybean prices. This caused problems for exporters, who pressed the BCP to restrain the rise of the national currency.

The 2008 election brought to power, for the first time in 61 years, a president of Paraguay who was not a member of the ruling Colorado party. Fernando Lugo Méndez, the new president, was considered a leftist and populist whose economic priorities would be different than the previous business oriented administrations. Under the circumstances, it was possible that the independence of the BCP might be tested by a part of the political spectrum not previously influential.

Robert Halasz

FURTHER READING

Cohen, Roger, "Paraguay Faces Questions After the Coup," *Wall Street Journal*, February 16, 1989, p. A10.

Coone, Tim, "Contraband Keeps Paraguay Afloat," *Financial Times*, December 16, 1987, p. 4.

Derham, Michael Thomas, "Against All Odds," *LatinFinance*, March 2005, pp. 51–53.

"Former Paraguay President Jailed," *BBC News*, June 6, 2006.

Freer, Jim, "Another Crisis," *Latin Trade*, October 1998, p. 15.

Lamb, Christina, "Paraguay Finds Old Habits Die Hard," *Financial Times*, May 9, 1991, p. 3.

Lewis, Paul H., *Paraguay Under Stroessner*, Chapel Hill: University of North Carolina Press, 1980, pp. 152–55.

Monahan, Jane, "Paraguay on the Right Path to Modern Policies," *Banker*, July 2005, pp. 134–35.

"Paraguay Devalued," *Financial Times*, September 24, 1986, p. 6.

Pilling, David, "Bringing Reality to Shoppers' Paradise," *Financial Times*, July 11, 1995, p. 3.

Rohter, Larry, "Troubles Push Paraguay Close to Bankruptcy," *New York Times*, November 29, 2002, p. C3.

"Shaky Times for the Central Bank," *Latin America Monitor*, April 2007, pp. 1, 7.

Smith, Tony, "Contraband Is Big Business in Paraguay," *New York Times*, June 10, 2003, pp. W1, W7.

"A Tale of Lost Paraguayos," *Economist*, November 23, 1996.

"Tough Choice Facing Rulers in Paraguay," *Globe and Mail* (Toronto), May 29, 1986, p. B24.

"Tough Times for the Little Dollar," *Financial Times*, January 30, 1968, p. 7.

Bank Austria AG

Schottengasse 6-8
Vienna, A-1010
Austria
Telephone: (43 5) 05 05 25
Fax: (43 5) 05 05 56155
Web site: http://www.bankaustria.at

Wholly Owned Subsidiary of UniCredit S.p.A.
Employees: 58,000
Total Assets: EUR 209.17 billion ($308.07 billion) (2007 est.)
NAICS: 522110 Commercial Banking; 522210 Credit Card Issuing; 522190 Other Depository Credit Intermediation

■ ■ ■

Bank Austria AG is Austria's largest banking group serving nearly 21 million customers throughout 2,800 branches in 21 countries. During 2007, the company served approximately 82 percent of large corporations, 62 percent of medium-sized businesses, and 45 percent of small businesses in its home country. Italy's Uni-Credit S.p.A.—one of the top ten banking institutions in the world—acquired a 95 percent stake in Bank Austria in 2005 as part of its acquisition of Germany's HVB Group. UniCredit purchased nearly all of the remaining shares of the company in 2008. As a subsidiary of UniCredit, Bank Austria operates as a leading financial institution throughout Central and Eastern Europe.

FOUNDATIONS AND DEVELOPMENT

Bank Austria was created in 1991, when Zentral-sparkasse und Kommerzialbank Wien (Z-Bank) absorbed Osterreichische Länderbank (OLB or Länderbank). OLB was the older of the two banking groups. It was founded in November 1880 as k.k. privilegierte Osterreichische Länderbank, a subsidiary of France's Société de L'Union Genérale. Länderbank was spun off from the parent company in 1882, and opened its first branch bank in Paris in 1882. The Austrian bank later established branch locations in Prague; London; Bolzano, Italy; and Pilsen, Czech Republic.

Over the course of its development, Länderbank came to emphasize commercial and retail banking as well as securities trading. The establishment came under state control in 1946, and although privatization began in 1956, the federal government still owned a controlling stake in Länderbank through 1990. By that time, OLB was the nation's fourth largest financial institution, with 4,200 employees, 1.1 million accounts, 140 domestic offices, and 24 foreign offices.

Although younger, Z-Bank had grown to become the larger of the two merged banks. It had been founded in 1905 by a resolution of the Vienna City Council and opened its headquarters branch there in 1907. Over the course of its first quarter-century in business, the institution built 23 offices throughout Vienna and captured one-fifth of the capital city's savings accounts. Z-Bank was transformed into a joint stock company in 1990, with 90 percent of its shares held by the city of Vienna's AV-Z trust and the remaining 10 percent in the hands of institutional investors. Its liabilities continued to be guaranteed by the city of Vienna even after the merger with Länderbank.

By the time of the merger, Z-Bank was Austria's largest savings bank, and Europe's seventh largest financial institution overall. In addition to its nearly 1,300 offices in Austria, the bank had branches in Milan, London, Tokyo, Frankfurt, Moscow, Paris, and Prague.

BANKING CONSOLIDATION IN AUSTRIA IN 1991

The 1991 union of these two massive banks was perceived as a first step to relieving what *Euromoney* called an "over-banked, over-branched, and over-staffed" Austrian banking industry. Under the chairmanship of René Alfons Haiden, it took five difficult years to consolidate and rationalize the two banks' operations. Dozens of branches were shuttered, and group employment was reduced by nearly 11 percent, from 9,929 in 1991 to 8,867 by the end of 1996. Productivity (in terms of pretax net per employee) doubled during the period, from ATS 292,000 to ATS 586,000. Assets increased 44 percent to ATS 742 billion, and operating profit jumped 80 percent to ATS 5.2 billion. During that time, however, Bank Austria's return on equity fluctuated between 4 percent and 7 percent, and its share price reflected that vacillation. Nevertheless, the merger was, according to the *Economist,* "widely seen as a success."

Having advanced through Z-Bank and served as deputy chairman of Bank Austria from 1991, Gerhard Randa became chairman of the group in 1995. Nicknamed "Rambo" by his colleagues in the Viennese banking community, the Harley-Davidson aficionado was known as an aggressive deal maker. One large deal was the 1994 acquisition of third-ranking GiroCredit Bank Aktiengesellschaft der Sparkassen. Although the two institutions were considered a logical fit, Bank

Austria divested its holdings in GiroCredit in 1997. Although acquisitions took center stage during Randa's tenure, he continued to emphasize efficiency, telling *Euromoney* in a June 1996 interview, "The key element to our strategy is productivity."

UNION WITH CREDITANSTALT: 1997

The ongoing restructuring of Austria's banking industry also entailed privatization of long-held government positions in key banks. In 1997 Bank Austria beat Italian, German, American, and domestic rivals with an ATS 17.2 billion ($1.5 billion) bid to acquire the federal government's 70 percent stake in the Creditanstalt-Bankverein. Known as Austria's most worldly bank, Creditanstalt was founded by the wealthy Rothschild family and later ranked among Europe's largest banks. It was at one time so influential that some historians assert that its 1931 crash triggered the Great Depression.

The merger agreement kept the venerable bank in Austrian hands, but came with some strings attached. For example, the government-brokered deal required that Creditanstalt "remain a separate legal operating entity for five years and that no targeted staff reductions may be undertaken by Bank Austria." This factor seemed to preclude many potential cost savings and economies. As the *Economist* pointed out in May 1997, "Instead of weeding out wasteful duplication, the two banks will continue to compete, even where they have branches side by side." *Institutional Investor*'s Giles Peel noted that the deal, which was supposed to have privatized Creditanstalt, "effectively postponed the long-awaited privatization" by merely transferring ownership of Austria's best-known bank from the federal government to the municipal government of Vienna, which still indirectly owned 45 percent of Bank Austria. (In fact, the federal government continued to own 19 percent of Bank Austria through the end of 1997.)

Early in 1997, Austria's coalition government outlined a privatization program through which the city of Vienna's Anteilsverwaltung Zentralsparkasse (AV-Z) foundation would reduce its 45 percent stake in Bank Austria to less than 25 percent within five years. Progress toward that goal was hindered that June, when the bank revealed that minority stakeholder Westdeutsche Landesbank Girozentrale (WestLB) of Germany, which already owned just over 10 percent of Bank Austria, enjoyed right of first refusal over any shares divested by AV-Z before the end of 2001. Analysts observed that this factor would likely prevent AV-Z from selling any equity to preclude the German bank from becoming the majority owner of Austria's flagship bank.

KEY DATES

1880: Osterreichische Länderbank (OLB) is founded as a subsidiary of France's Société de L'Union Genérale.

1905: Zentralsparkasse und Kommerzialbank Wien (Z-Bank) is formed.

1991: Bank Austria is created by the union of Z-Bank and OLB.

1997: The company buys the Creditanstalt-Bankverein shares from the Republic of Austria.

2000: Bank Austria merges with Bayerische Hypo- und Vereinsbank (HVB) AG.

2002: Bank Austria and Creditanstalt merge to form Bank Austria Creditanstalt AG (BA-CA).

2005: UniCredit S.p.A. acquires HVB.

2008: UniCredit acquires nearly all remaining shares of BA-CA; the company drops the Creditanstalt portion of its name.

Randa also quickly sidestepped the government's requirement that Creditanstalt remain independent by integrating international operations as well as the two institutions' investment banking subsidiaries. He also expected to achieve some economies by unifying back office operations. Thus, while the Creditanstalt name and legal entity persisted, many operations were merged.

Chairman Randa's strategy for the future targeted expansion into Eastern and Central Europe and Asia. Hoping to apply Bank Austria's extensive privatization and initial public offering experience (the institution had participated in the launches of British Petroleum, British Telecom, Wellcome, adidas, and many Austrian firms) in former communist countries, Randa established operations in Slovenia, the Czech Republic, Hungary, Poland, Russia, and Croatia. By mid-1997, Bank Austria was the leading foreign bank throughout Eastern and Central Europe.

MOVING INTO THE 21ST CENTURY

Changes were on the horizon for Bank Austria as the company entered the early years of the new millennium. During 2000, the company merged with Germany's Bayerische Hypo-und Vereinsbank AG (HVB). The deal—the first of its kind in postwar Austrian banking history—created the third largest banking institution in Europe and gave HVB access to Bank Austria's profit-

able Central and Eastern European (CEE) operations.

Shortly after the HVB merger, in 2002, Bank Austria merged its operations with Creditanstalt to form Bank Austria Creditanstalt AG (BA-CA). The company went public on the Vienna Stock Exchange on July 9, 2003, and then made history as the first foreign company to list on Poland's Warsaw Stock Exchange in October of that same year.

The most significant change during this period, however, came in 2005 when HVB agreed to be acquired by Italy's UniCredit S.p.A. in Europe's largest cross-border banking deal at the time. The union, completed in November of that year, was highly beneficial for BA-CA. Indeed, the bank would become the only financial institution to have operations in every East European country after the merger. In fact, its assets in the CEE region would grow from EUR 36 billion to EUR 70 billion.

In January 2007, UniCredit purchased HVB's 77.53 percent holding in BA-CA in a EUR 12.5 billion cash deal. UniCredit owned 94.98 percent of BA-CA after the purchase. BA-CA then gained control of HVB's holdings in Estonia, Latvia, and Lithuania, as well as Russian International Moscow Bank, which was eventually renamed ZAO UniCredit Bank. BA-CA acquired controlling interest in Ukrainian Ukrsotsbank in January 2008.

By this time, UniCredit was focused on unifying its holdings under the UniCredit name. As such, HVB Bank Hungary, HVB Serbia, and HVB Latvia adopted the UniCredit name. During this rebranding effort, it began what Europeans called a "squeeze-out" to acquire nearly all remaining shares of BA-CA. BA-CA stopped trading on the Vienna and Warsaw stock exchanges in 2008. The company dropped the CA portion of its name later that year. Known simply as Bank Austria, the company held the leading position in its home country and as a subsidiary of UniCredit, was part of one of the largest banking concerns in the world.

April Dougal Gasbarre
Updated, Christina M. Stansell

PRINCIPAL SUBSIDIARIES

Asset Management GmbH; AWT International Trade AG; BA-CA Administration Service GmbH; Bank Austria Creditantalt Leasing GmbH (99.98%); Bank Austria Creditanstalt Real Invest GmbH (94.95%); Bank Austria Creditanstalt Wohnbaubank AG; Bank Austria Trade Services Gesellschaft m.b. H.; BANKPRI-VAT AG; CABET-Holding-AG; card complete Service

Bank AG (50.1%); Domus Bistro GmbH; Domus Clean Reinigungs GmbH; Domus Facility Management GmbH; Lassallestrasse Bau-; Planungs-; Errichtungs-und Verwertungsgesellschaft m.b.H. (99%); Pioneer Investments Austria GmbH; Schoellerbank AG; UniCredit CA IB Beteiligungs AG; UniCredit CA IB AG; WAVE Solutions Information Technology GmbH.

PRINCIPAL COMPETITORS

Erste Bank der oesterreichischen Sparkassen AG; Investkredit Bank AG; Raiffeisen Zentralbank Österreich AG.

FURTHER READING

"Bank Austria," *Banker,* May 1995, pp. 4–5.

"Bank Austria: A Bank for Europe," *Euromoney,* July 1997, pp. 88–91.

"Bank Austria: A Wealth of Experience in Privatization," *Euromoney,* June 1996, p. 27.

"Bank Austria Creditanstalt Seen Planning Further Acquisition in Poland," *Interfax Poland Weekly Business Report,* December 22, 2003.

"Bank Austria: Number One in the Domestic Market," *Euromoney,* June 1996, pp. 24–25.

"Bank Austria Takes the Stage," *Banker,* November 1991, pp. 8–9.

"Best Firm in Austria," *Euromoney,* September 1994, pp. 46–47.

"CA and BA Fusion in Its Final Stages," *Austria Today,* August 8, 2002.

"Deals in the Balance," *Euromoney,* September 1997, pp. 409–10.

Frey, Eric, "All Eyes Turn to Growing Profits in Eastern Europe," *Financial Times,* October 25, 2005.

Hall, William, "The Waltz Stops Here," *Banker,* February 1997, pp. 37–39.

King, Paul, "Banking Tangles Begin to Unravel," *Euromoney,* January 1993, pp. 56–58.

——, "Take Your Partners," *Euromoney,* January 1992, pp. 29–33.

"A Long Way from America: Creditanstalt's Flawed Renaissance," *Economist,* May 17, 1997, pp. 84–85.

"Never Did Run Smooth—European Bank Mergers," *Economist,* November 12, 2005.

Peel, Giles, "Banking: Can Randa Make It Work?" *Institutional Investor,* September 1997, p. 29.

"A Powerhouse in Austria," *Euromoney,* September 1994, pp. 44–45.

"Red Faces in Vienna," *Banker,* June 1993, p. 4.

Shirreff, David, and John McGrath, "Death of a Bank," *Euromoney,* March 1997, pp. 44–50.

"Speed and Secrecy the Keys to Merger," *European Banker,* October 23, 2000.

"Strategic Alliances: An Interview with Gerhard Randa, Chairmam," *Euromoney,* June 1996, pp. 25–26.

"Warsaw Bourse Suspends Trade in Bank Austria Shares," *Global Banking News,* May 22, 2008.

Berwind Corporation

———— ■ ————

3000 Centre Square West
1500 Market Street
Philadelphia, Pennsylvania 19102
U.S.A.
Telephone: (215) 563-2800
Fax: (215) 575-2314
Web site: http://www.berwind.com

Private Company
Incorporated: 1886 as Berwind-White Coal Mining
    Company
Employees: 3,500
Sales: $1.71 billion (2006 est.)
NAICS: 551112 Offices of Other Holding Companies

■ ■ ■

Berwind Corporation is an investment management company owned by the fifth generation of one of Philadelphia, Pennsylvania's, most prominent Main Line families, the Berwinds, who built their fortune in the 1800s in coal and rail investments. Among Berwind's operating companies is Berwind Natural Resources Corporation (BNRC), a vestige of the family's past. Although the Berwinds have not been directly involved in coal mining since the early 1960s, BNRC owns about 400 million tons of coal reserves in the Appalachian Mountains of Pennsylvania, Kentucky, Virginia, and West Virginia, which the company leases and sells. BNRC also owns more than 150 million board feet of standing timber and controls more than 25 billion cubic feet of natural gas through working interests and royalty agreements.

The balance of Berwind's investment portfolio includes manufacturing and service companies in the automotive, pharmaceutical, specialty chemical, and office and craft industries. All are leaders within their niche markets. Operating companies include Colorcon, maker of pharmaceutical and candy coatings; Elmer's Products, Inc., maker of adhesives and a variety of craft, hobby, educational, office, and home repair products; CRC Industries, Inc., maker of maintenance and repairs specialty chemicals used in the automotive aftermarket, aviation, marine, electrical, and industrial markets; ECCO Group, offering amber warning lights, backup alarms, and related products for emergency services and other vehicles; National Pen Co., producer of promotional pens and other items; and Eagle Pack Pet Foods, manufacturer of superpremium natural and holistic pet foods.

A cash buyer, Berwind owns 100 percent of its operating companies and takes a long-term view on investments. Berwind prefers companies that generate annual sales between $200 million and $400 million. While Berwind grants a great deal of autonomy to the managers of the individual companies, encouraging them to exhibit an entrepreneurial spirit, it provides the necessary funding and other support to help grow the businesses.

ORIGINS IN COAL MINING

The Berwind family got its start in the United States in the 1840s when John E. Berwind and wife Augusta

COMPANY PERSPECTIVES

Berwind is a fifth-generation, family-owned investment management company with a distinguished history and a bias towards action.

Guldenferring moved from Prussia to Philadelphia, where he opened a music shop and began to turn out violins. He later worked as a cabinetmaker in a piano factory and did well enough to provide a good education for his five sons. One son, Charles F. Berwind, first became involved with the coal trade when he went to work as an office boy for the Powelton Coal and Iron Company. He was just 21 when he was named vice-president and became a partner in the firm. He then became partner in a coal firm called Berwind & Bradley and White & Lingle.

In the meantime, Berwind's brother, Edward J. Berwind, received an appointment from President Abraham Lincoln to the U.S. Naval Academy in 1865. Four years later he was commissioned as an ensign and served in the Navy until 1872 when he was discharged due to physical disability caused in the line of duty. He went to work for the Pennsylvania Railroad and then joined his brother and Judge Allison White in 1874 to form a bituminous coal company called Berwind, White and Company, the success of which was largely due to his ability to win contracts supplying coal to New York steamship companies and skill in acquiring coal mines in Pennsylvania, West Virginia, and Kentucky. In January 1886 the business was reorganized as the Berwind-White Coal Mining Company, with Edward serving as president, a post he would hold until 1930.

During his long tenure as Berwind-White's chief executive, Edward Berwind worked closely with J.P. Morgan and Company to achieve vertical integration in coal as had been done in steel and other industries during this time. As a result, Berwind gained interests in railroads, steamships, docks, lumber, and banks operating in the coalfields. He also became involved in the construction of the New York subway system, an outgrowth of Berwind-White supplying coal to the city surface transit system. Berwind became the chief executive of the Interborough Rapid Transit system (I.R.T). Along the way, Edward Berwind gained a reputation for avoiding publicity, hard work, and ruthlessness. He was reportedly hated by labor in the United States for refusing to bargain with workers, his mines being the last in the coal fields to unionize.

BECOMING DIVERSIFIED

In addition to Charles Berwind, two other brothers, John and Harry, became partners in Berwind-White. In 1930 Edward Berwind turned over the presidency of the company to Charles E. Dunlap and became chairman of the board. He left no children, but his nephews assumed prominent positions in Berwind-White. When Edward died in 1936 he made his sister, Julia A. Berwind, the principal legatee of his estate. After the death of his wife in 1922, Julia had served as his hostess at a family estate in Newport, Rhode Island. She lived until 1961, passing away at the age of 95 with no immediate survivors.

A year after the death of Julia Berwind, a new generation of the Berwind family under the leadership of Charles G. Berwind, Jr., decided to exit the coal mining industry, instead leasing the mines and collecting royalties on reserves, and using the cash flow to diversify and invest in non-coal assets through a new corporate entity, the Berwind Group. In addition to natural resources, the company became involved in such business areas as industrial products, real estate, pharmaceutical, and healthcare. In 1990 Berwind Group added a fifth major business area, forming Berwind Financial Group to provide investment banking services to both large and middle-market corporate clients and to make merchant banking investments. By this stage Berwind Group controlled 30 subsidiaries located in 17 countries.

During the three decades between the Berwind family's change of direction and the formation of Berwind Financial Group, several of Berwind's operational companies were acquired. The oldest investment was Colorcon, acquired in 1978 for $15 million, laying a foundation for Berwind Pharmaceutical Services. Colorcon started out in the early 20th century providing ink to the printing industry, shifting by mid-century to the production of inks and coatings for the pharmaceutical industry, used for labeling as well as to make pills easier to swallow and digest, and to provide temporary protection to allow the gradual "time-release" of medication. Colorcon also began serving the food industry, using its technology to make candy coatings, cake icings, and gum.

The next portfolio company to be added was CRC Industries, Inc., in 1981. The business was started in a Philadelphia garage in 1958 as Corrosion Reaction Consultants, Inc., by Charles J. Webb II, who had previously done well in the wool industry. He learned of a new multipurpose lubricant sold on the West Coast and secured an agreement to distribute it in the eastern half of the United States. Webb sold the anticorrosion product under the name CRC Corrosion Inhibitor and in the 1960s branched out by having the product

KEY DATES

1874: Berwind, White and Company formed.
1886: Business reorganized as Berwind-White Coal Mining Company.
1962: Berwind family exits coal mining industry in favor of diversified investments.
1978: Colorcon acquired.
1981: CRC Industries, Inc., acquired.
2003: Elmer's Products, Inc., acquired.
2004: National Pen Co. acquired.
2007: ECCO Group and Eagle Pack Pet Foods acquired.

reformulated to tap into specific markets: automotive, aviation, electrical, industrial, and marine.

Webb also began distributing his products in Europe and in 1967 established CRC Chemicals Europe as an import operation. Two years later CRC Australia followed. The European operation opened a manufacturing plant in Zele, Belgium, in 1975. With Berwind's financial backing starting in the 1980s, the unit grew through the acquisition of specialty chemical companies, including the German firm of Kontakt Chemie in 1984; the French concern Siceront KF in 1993; and another French company, Ets. Robert, in 1998. A fourth CRC operating unit was added in Asia in 1999.

ABANDONING LEVERAGED BUYOUTS

During the 1990s Berwind Financial Group became involved in leveraged buyouts, completing about a dozen acquisitions within the decade. A downturn in the economy at the start of the new century led to problems for some of the private capital group's holdings. Clinipad Corporation, a maker of sterile medical supplies, for example, was closed in 2000, and in January 2001, Classic Kitchen was forced to file for Chapter 11 bankruptcy protection. Moreover, the competition in leveraged buyouts had become too competitive, with too much money chasing too few opportunities, making deals cost prohibitive. By June 2001, the Berwind family announced that it would abandon the leveraged acquisitions field. A few months later, in October 2001, Berwind Financial was sold to the brokerage firm of Boenning & Scattergood Inc. The Berwind family elected to contract out its investment management business to SEI Investments, which in 2002 also took over Berwind's trust business.

The cash-only, 100 percent ownership philosophy of Berwind Corporation took further shape in the early years of the new century with the acquisition of Hunt Corp., a Philadelphia-based office products company whose best-known products were Boston pencil sharpeners and X-Acto knives. Hunt established a consumer products unit for Berwind, and Hunt in 2003 was folded into another Berwind acquisition, Columbus, Ohio-based Elmer's Products Inc., maker of Elmer's Glue. The Borden Inc. food company had first introduced the product in 1947 as Cascorez Glue. Elmer's became a stand-alone company, purchased by Berwind from Kohlberg Kravis Roberts & Company.

The next Berwind portfolio company to be added was National Pen Co., acquired in 2004. San Diego–area based National Pen sold custom imprinted promotional products such as pens and mugs, produced in plants located in San Diego County, Tennessee, Ireland, and Tijuana, Mexico. The company had been established in the Bronx, New York, as Modern Mold and Tool by machinist Al Liquori to provide plastic parts for writing instruments companies. In 1960 the company began to focus on ballpoint pens, and six years later turned its attention to personalized writing instruments, launching National Pen. In 1982 it acquired its chief rival, U.S. Pencil and Stationery Company, as well as a Canadian mail-order company, Perfect Pen & Stationery Co., Ltd. As a result, National Pen became one of the largest advertising specialty products manufacturers in the United States and forged licensing deals with such major companies as the Walt Disney Company, the National Football League, Major League Baseball, the National Basketball Association, McDonald's, AT&T, and Exxon. By the time Berwind acquired it, National Pen was generating $160 million in annual sales. With the deep pockets of Berwind to back it, National Pen hoped to complete acquisitions in the promotional products industry to solidify its position in its field.

ACQUISITIONS CONTINUE

Another Berwind operating company, Boise, Idaho-based ECCO Group, was added in 2007. A manufacturer of backup alarms and warning lights, ECCO Group was formed in 2005, but its roots could be dated to 1972, when Electronics Control Co. was founded in Boise by Carl Peterson. A year earlier the U.S. Occupational Safety and Health Administration (OSHA) mandated the use of backup warning alarms for all vehicles that operated off public roads. To take advantage of this new market, Peterson's company began marketing a few simple backup alarms. Over the years the company's slate of products broadened through internal development and acquisitions to include amber warning lights, strobe lights, rotating lights, light bars, and sirens. ECCO Group was established in 2005 to help support the international expansion of the business. Again, Berwind looked to grow the business further through the kind of support it could provide to ECCO's management.

Another 2007 acquisition was Eagle Pack Pet Foods, manufacturer of holistic, superpremium, and natural pet food. The company was established in 1970 and a decade later became a pioneer in holistic pet nutrition, developing pet foods that were antibiotic-free, used grains that were herbicide-free, and had nutritional supplements added. A year after purchasing Eagle, Berwind grew the business further by paying $400 million for Wellness Pet Food, adding the All Wellness and Old Mother Hubbard brands and $150 million in annual sales.

In 2008 Berwind also provided financial backing to some of its other holdings. Colorcon broke ground on a new global headquarters, expected to open in 2009. In addition, Berwind invested in CRC Industries by acquiring Indianapolis-based Specialty Coating Systems, which specialized in parylene conformal coating. There was every reason to expect that Berwind would continue to take a long-term view toward its operating companies and would continue to seek further investment opportunities.

Ed Dinger

PRINCIPAL SUBSIDIARIES

Berwind Natural Resources Corporation; Colorcon; CRC Industries, Inc.; ECCO Group; National Pen Co.; Eagle Pack Pet Foods.

PRINCIPAL COMPETITORS

Apollo Advisors, L.P.; Bruckmann, Rosser, Sherrill & Co., L.L.C.; The Jordan Company, L.P.

FURTHER READING

"Berwind-White Coal Shifts Its Officers," *New York Times,* January 5, 1930.

"E. J. Berwind Dies; Coal Operator, 88," *New York Times,* August 19, 1936.

Gotlieb, Andy, "Berwind Family in $83 Million Fight," *Philadelphia Business Journal,* December 18, 2000.

———, "Berwind Pulling Out of Buyouts," *Philadelphia Business Journal,* June 8, 2001, p. 1.

Holman, Kelly, "Berwind Bags Hunt for $112 M," *Daily Deal,* November 13, 2002.

———, "Berwind Group Halts Buyout Activities," *Daily Deal,* June 11, 2001.

Ingham, John N., *Biographical Dictionary of American Business Leaders: Vol. 2, H–M,* Westport, Conn.: Greenwood Publishing Group, 1983.

"J. E. Berwind Dies of Heart Attack," *New York Times,* May 24, 1928.

Betsey Johnson Inc.

—————— ■ ——————

498 7th Avenue, 21st Floor
New York, New York 10018-6798
U.S.A.
Telephone: (212) 244-0843
Toll Free: (800) 407-6001
Fax: (212) 244-0855
Web site: http://www.betseyjohnson.com

Private Company
Founded: 1978
Employees: 310
Sales: $100 million (2007 est.)
NAICS: 448120 Women's Clothing Stores; 315232 Women's and Girls' Cut and Sew Blouse and Shirt Manufacturing; 315233 Women's and Girls' Cut and Sew Dress Manufacturing; 315234 Women's and Girls' Cut and Sew Suit, Coat, Tailored Jacket, and Skirt Manufacturing

■ ■ ■

Betsey Johnson Inc. is a fashion label founded in 1978 by Betsey Johnson and her business partner Chantal Bacon. On its web site, the company describes its "trademark look" as "sexy silhouettes, hippie inspired flowing fabrics, whimsical detailing and, most importantly, a fabulous fit." Johnson adds: "Like red lipstick on the mouth, my products wake up and brighten and bring the wearer to life ... drawing attention to her beauty and specialness ... her moods and movements ... her dreams and fantasies." Known as fashion's "wild child" with an effusive personality and a penchant for turning cartwheels at the finale of her runway shows, Betsey Johnson built an empire around her own creative vision of fashion and fun for women and girls. After 30 years of operations, in 2008 the business included over 50 stores around the world, including locations throughout the United States and in Canada, England, and Japan. In addition to Betsey Johnson stores, the designer merchandise is also available at over 600 specialty stores and high-end department stores in the United States, Europe, and Asia.

BETSEY JOHNSON: BIRTH OF A DESIGNER

The story of the Betsey Johnson company is inseparable from the biography of the charismatic founder and entrepreneur for whom it is named. Born in Connecticut, Betsey Johnson first tasted the joy of fashion when she studied dance as a child (including ballet, acrobatics, and tap). Johnson's childhood dance teacher exposed her to design by allowing Johnson to create her own costumes, and her mother helped her sew dance costumes for her dolls. Later, she attended Syracuse University, where she was a fine arts major and cheerleader with aspirations of becoming a dancer or illustrator.

In 1964, Johnson received her entrée to New York's fashion scene when she won *Mademoiselle* magazine's Guest Editor Contest. *Mademoiselle* editor Betsy Blackwell noted Johnson's budding talent for illustration and gave her assignments that helped her land freelance jobs. She went on to a choice position as top fashion designer at the cutting-edge Paraphernalia clothing boutique, home to renowned young London mod fashion designers including Mary Quant.

In New York, Johnson quickly became immersed in the Andy Warhol–influenced pop-art social circle that included the rock band The Velvet Underground—whose founding member John Cale prominently sported Johnson's designs (Johnson and Cale were married briefly)—and actress/socialite Edie Sedgwick, who was Johnson's house model. At Paraphernalia, Johnson honed her ability to quickly move a concept from design sketch to in-store product, developing a flair for sexy styles, flowing fabrics, and vibrant colors. She quickly attracted a following among celebrities, including Brigitte Bardot, Julie Christie, and Twiggy, and earned laudatory writeups in *Life* magazine and *Vogue*.

In 1969, Johnson opened her first clothing store, a boutique called Betsey Bunki Nini. She also began working for Alvin Duskin in San Francisco, commuting between New York and the West Coast. In the 1970s Johnson held a number of freelance positions, and she became creative maven of the junior Alley Cat clothing label, a leading producer of styles associated with rock music as well as the bohemian/ethnic look. Johnson's fresh vision was acknowledged when she became the youngest designer ever to receive the Coty Award, which she shared with Halston, in 1972. *Newsweek* named her "the most important young designer in America" that year.

BETSEY JOHNSON INC.: THE FIRST DECADE

With a decade of experience and accolades under her belt, in 1978 Johnson branched out on her own, founding the Betsey Johnson label with business partner and Parisian-born former model Chantal Bacon. Johnson and Bacon were both heavily involved in the New York rock nightlife scene and shared a circle of high-profile friends.

The two had met when Bacon worked for Betsey Johnson's Kids, a division of Shutterbug, in 1975. They launched their clothing line with $200,000, earned through a combination of family and bank loans and stock earnings from a Bayer Aspirin TV commercial that Johnson had filmed. Johnson became the label's public spokesperson and directed creative design of stores and clothing, while Bacon managed the retail business, sales, merchandising, and production aspects.

The first Betsey Johnson store, which opened in New York's trendy Soho neighborhood in 1979, actually resulted from a near disaster. Bacon and Johnson inaccurately gauged the level of consumer interest in their quirky, punk-music and pop-art-influenced line. In order to determine the necessary level of product for the second season, they assumed that at least five women in each state would buy each outfit. They nearly went out of business due to overproduction of merchandise that was too adventurous for department stores, including Lycra hot-pink and black striped clothes. "We had a lot of crazy stuff and didn't know how to get rid of it," Johnson told *Women's Wear Daily* in 1985, continuing, "so we opened a store."

The stand-alone store fared well. By 1985 Johnson and Bacon owned and operated three stores in New York City, with stores contributing 20 percent of the company's total volume of $10 million according to the September 18, 1985, *Women's Wear Daily*. Soon thereafter, Betsey Johnson became one of the first designers to open a store on Melrose Avenue in Los Angeles in the 1980s, contributing to a trend that transformed that street into a shopping mecca. Other stores opened in Miami, San Francisco, Los Angeles, and Santa Monica.

The Beverly Center store in Beverly Hills, California, piloted the company's mall strategy, which was to place stand-alone Betsey Johnson stores only in strategically selected top fashion malls. As the first mall-based store, the Beverly Center boutique sported Betsey Johnson stores' signature black-and-white checkerboard floor, pink décor, and murals. Betsey Johnson clothes also were offered in the junior and contemporary areas of high-end department and specialty stores including Bloomingdale's, Burdine's, Nordstrom, and Marshall Field's.

POISED FOR EXPANSION AFTER A DECADE OF GROWTH

By its tenth anniversary in 1988, the company had left behind its somewhat rocky beginning and could celebrate a decade of largely steady growth. Betsey Johnson Inc. was positioned to become a major player

KEY DATES

1972: Betsey Johnson is the youngest designer ever to receive the Coty Award.

1978: Betsey Johnson founds her eponymous fashion label with business partner Chantal Bacon.

1979: The first Betsey Johnson store opens in New York's Soho district.

1990: Betsey Johnson receives the Tommy Award.

1995: Twenty-one Betsey Johnson stores operate in the United States.

1997: Sales reach $38 million.

1998: The London store is opened.

1999: The company opens a store in Vancouver; Betsey Johnson receives the Timeless Talent Award from Council of Fashion Designers of America.

2000: Sales reach between $40 million and $50 million.

2002: Betsey Johnson is inducted into New York's Fashion Walk of Fame.

2003: The Toronto store opens.

2005: Forty-five Betsey Johnson stores operate worldwide.

2006: A store opens in Japan; the Betseyville line is introduced.

2007: Company sells a majority interest to Castanea Partners.

in fashion design, with a wholesale business of between $8 million and $9 million and retail business of $5 million, according to the September 7, 1988, *Women's Wear Daily.*

In the 1990s, Betsey Johnson, at the time in her mid-50s and a major player in the fashion industry, set her sights on expanding, building, stabilizing, and diversifying her company. By 1995 there were 21 Betsey Johnson stores throughout the United States, and the designer opened a new showroom on Seventh Avenue in New York City, more than doubling the size of her previous showroom at 12,000 square feet. In 1997, according to *Women's Wear Daily,* the company's sales had grown to $38 million, with $20 million coming from stores.

Seeking a new and marketable "look," Betsey Johnson stores served as testing grounds for brand-building initiatives including jeans, handbags, and accessories. The increased volume of new product lines

necessitated the doubling of the Seventh Avenue showroom to 30,000 square feet. The company also transitioned its styles from "juniors" to "contemporary." Cute dresses gave way to brocade jackets and pants, and the designer launched the Ultra line of designer-priced clothing, ranging from $300 to $600 wholesale. The Ultra line was sold in Betsey Johnson stores as well as in the upscale Fred Segal and Linda Dressner venues; high-visibility customers included rock star Courtney Love and actress and comedian Sandra Bernhard.

In 1997, a new prototype store was launched on Wooster Street, featuring a more sophisticated style—English cabbage wallpaper, antiques, and painting instead of the more familiar pink neon and mural-based décor. Another prototype store was launched on Melrose Avenue in Los Angeles in 1999, with a minimalist aluminum-and-silver décor.

INTERNATIONAL GROWTH AND LICENSING AGREEMENTS

Beginning in the late 1990s, the company set its sights on international markets, opening stores in London (1998), Vancouver (1999), Toronto (2003), and Japan (2006). Betsey Johnson clothes had been sold directly to the Japanese market beginning in about 1986 or 1987, and the company had signed an exclusive distribution agreement with the Japanese Seibu company in 1992. In the late 1990s the company signed with the Japanese Elite Co., Ltd., to produce a handbag line to be sold in stores in Japan, and the company expanded its European presence in Italy, France, England, and Spain through a distribution agreement.

In 2002, the company signed an agreement with Centro Tessiles, which would distribute Betsey Johnson products in six showrooms in Europe, including France, Spain, Italy, England, Germany, and the Benelux nations of Belgium, the Netherlands, and Luxembourg. By 2005 there were 44 Betsey Johnson stores worldwide, including three outside the United States and a franchised store in Dubai. In 2006 the company increased its presence in Japan when it signed a five-year distribution agreement with Tokyo-based U International Office Co. Ltd. for a variety of products, with plans to open ten stores in Japan over a three-year period.

In the early 2000s, Betsey Johnson aggressively pursued licensing agreements to diversify her product lines. While she was very selective about partnerships—she had been in business for 24 years before she signed her first licensing agreement—the licensing strategy enabled her to add new wares including shoes, lingerie, handbags, belts, cold-weather accessories, eyewear, watches, jewelry, swimwear, legwear, children's sportswear, and perfume. Wholesale business increased 100 percent in 2000 with expected sales of $40 million to $50 million, according to *Women's Wear Daily*. By 2005 the aggressive licensing campaign brought the company's expected retail volume to $120 million, with retail excluding licensed categories comprising $50 million to $60 million of that total.

Amid a business climate of consolidation and mergers in 2000, Betsey Johnson Inc. remained independent. In January 2000 *Women's Wear Daily* reported that Johnson had looked into selling or merging the company but ultimately decided to withstand the pressure and continue her majority ownership and the family-type business atmosphere that had driven the company for over two decades.

ADDING CREATIVITY BACK INTO GROWTH

The 1990s had been about growing the company, and to some extent, ever since the disastrous overproduction of the second season, Betsey Johnson had always walked a fine line between her creative exuberance and the compromises required by marketable merchandise. When Betsey Johnson clothing began to take on a more mature look in the 1990s, the designer retained her more offbeat creations for runway shows, keeping those items separate from store merchandise. "We were focused on making everything so salable," she stated in the May 3, 2000, *Women's Wear Daily*. She added, "But it's like turning off my light switch."

In 2000, Johnson turned her creative light switch back on with a strategic compromise: store merchandise would include 20 "totally extreme" runway items, including hot pants and motorcycle jackets. Later that year, Johnson spiced up her runway show by using Playboy bunnies as models, complete with designer rabbit ears and cotton tails.

To free her time for creative design work, Johnson began delegating more administrative work to her staff, which included 45 employees in the wholesale division. In particular, Mandy Black, age 24, the firm's design director and Betsey Johnson line manager, and Johnson's daughter Lulu Johnson, the company's design-assistant and Ultra line manager, began to take on more responsibilities.

Looking for an inspiring change of scenery to nurture her creative juices, Johnson headed for Mexico after a 2003 fashion show. There, she found her muse. She bought a four-room hotel in the small Mexican town of Zihuatanejo on the Pacific Coast, and transformed it into a vacation home-away-from-home called "Betseyville." Invigorated by her new surroundings, Johnson designed a new "Betseyville" line of casual sportswear, including rock-influenced T-shirts, skirts, and jackets. A Betseyville line of handbag and leather accessories followed in 2006. In 2004, enamored with her rejuvenating sojourns in Mexico for work and relaxation, Johnson bought another house there, which she named "Villa Betsey." Villa Betsey became her main retreat and creative oasis, while Betseyville is available to the public for vacation rentals.

LEADERSHIP, ADVOCACY, AND AWARDS

Johnson discovered a lump in her breast after having a ruptured implant removed in 2000, and it turned out to be breast cancer. Following treatment, as a survivor of the disease, Johnson worked as an advocate in the fight against breast cancer, serving as honorary chairperson for Fashion Targets Breast Cancer (2003) and co-designing a T-shirt for the Courage Nights events (2004). In 2004 the National Breast Cancer Coalition recognized Johnson with an award for her work as an advocate for the crusade against breast cancer.

Betsey Johnson received numerous other awards for her vision and talent as a designer. The American Printed Fabrics Council celebrated Johnson's use of American-made prints in her designs with a Tommy Award in 1990; perhaps due to her distaste for a period when she traveled to Hong Kong ten times a year as a freelance designer in the 1970s, Johnson made a practice of sourcing all her fabrics and production in the United States. In 1999 the Council of Fashion Designers of America created the Timeless Talent Award especially for Johnson. In 2002 Johnson was inducted into the Fashion Walk of Fame on Seventh Avenue in New York City, where a bronze and granite plaque featuring a Betsey Johnson sketch, signature, and biography is embedded in the sidewalk. In 2005 Johnson received Lifetime Achievement Awards from the Accessories Council and the National Association of Women Business Owners. Johnson received Designer of the Year awards at the 28th Annual American Apparel & Footwear Association American Image Awards in 2006, and at the annual Fashion Accessories Benefit Ball in 2007.

FUTURE DIRECTIONS

In 2007, after looking for a buyer for over a year, Betsey Johnson sold a majority interest of her company to Castanea Partners, a Boston-based private-equity firm run by a former CEO of Neiman Marcus Group. While the terms were not made public, the August 24, 2007, *New York Post* reported that the price was probably around $50 million. The company's annual sales, according to the *New York Post,* were around $100 million, including licensing income.

Approaching 30 years in business, Johnson had reinvented her label numerous times, always retaining her unique and individualistic stamp. The company had grown and expanded rapidly, through aggressive campaigns to build licensing and distribution channels. With the support of a solid partnership with Castanea Partners, Johnson and her partner Chantal Bacon sought a new level of growth opportunities. The company's goal was to add 10 to 12 stores a year to the existing 51 stores, as well as expand licensed products and global presence. Johnson also planned to add products in categories including children's wear and bridal.

While the *New York Post* cited Betsey Johnson's "idiosyncratic behavior" as one reason it took so long to find a buyer, as the company celebrated its 30th anniversary in 2008, all signs seemed to indicate continued prosperity and health for the Betsey Johnson empire. A bevy of special releases were created in all product categories, and Betsey Johnson stores proudly featured a hand-drawn self-portrait of their namesake, drawn especially for the 30th anniversary season. Despite the new relationship with Castanea Partners, thus far Betsey Johnson Inc. appeared to retain its spotlight on just one businesswoman and her unique creative vision: Betsey Johnson.

Heidi Feldman

PRINCIPAL COMPETITORS

Diane Von Furstenberg; Tory Burch; Behnaz Sarafpour.

FURTHER READING

"Bacon Says Johnson Not for Sale," *Women's Wear Daily,* November 15, 2000, p. 2.

"Betsey Johnson Inks Deal with Seibu in Japan," *Women's Wear Daily,* September 9, 1992, p. 12.

Bloomfield, Judy, "Happy Partners Bacon & Johnson," *Women's Wear Daily,* September 7, 1988, p. S24.

"Boneparth, Johnson to Headline AAFA Awards," *Women's Wear Daily,* February 14, 2006, p. 28.

Daria, Irene, "Fashion's Independent Spirits," *Women's Wear Daily,* September 18, 1985, p. S92.

Davis, Alisha, "Newsmakers," *Newsweek,* October 2, 2000, p. 80.

DeCarlo, Lauren, "Betsey's Growth Spurt," *Women's Wear Daily,* June 9, 2005, p. 12.

———, "Honoring Betsey Johnson," *Women's Wear Daily,* March 17, 2005, p. 16.

D'Innocenzio, Anne, "Betsey Johnson: All Grown Up," *Women's Wear Daily,* December 17, 1997, p. 9.

———, "Betsey Johnson's New Chapter," *Women's Wear Daily,* May 3, 2000, p. 8.

Greenberg, Julee, "Betsey Johnson Signs Europe Deal," *Women's Wear Daily,* March 14, 2002, p. 10.

———, "Contemporary Retail's Movement," *Women's Wear Daily,* July 5, 2007, p. 15.

Heintz, Nadine, "We Love Her for Her Stylish Life," *Inc. Magazine,* April 2004, p. 124.

Hirshlag, Jennifer, "The Lady of the House: Betsey Johnson Proves Her Brand to Be a Timeless Treasure with Accessories," *Women's Wear Daily,* January 3, 2006, p. 165.

"In Brief," *Women's Wear Daily,* March 30, 2006, p. 3.

"Johnson's Mall Strategy," *Women's Wear Daily,* July 31, 1995, p. 24.

Kapner, Suzanne, "Firm Buys Big Stake in Betsey Johnson," *New York Post,* August 24, 2007.

Lockwood, Lisa, "Betsey in a Cartwheel: Johnson Sells Majority to Castanea Equity Firm," *Women's Wear Daily,* August 23, 2007, pp. 1–12.

Mistry, Meenal, "Happy Birthday, Sweet 60," *Women's Wear Daily,* August 8, 2002, p. 4.

Scardino, Emily, "Good Taste: Betsey Johnson," *Footwear News,* August 1, 2005, pp. 86–87.

Socha, Miles, "Resisting the Urge to Merge," *Women's Wear Daily,* January 3, 2000, p. 10.

"Tommys Set for Johnson and Roberts," *Women's Wear Daily,* October 15, 1990, p. 14.

"Welcome to Betseyville," *Women's Wear Daily,* March 13, 2003, p. 10.

Williamson, Rusty, "Leaping Leopards: Betsey Johnson Jumps into Handbags with a New License," *Women's Wear Daily,* August 2, 2006, p. 51S.

Bill & Melinda Gates Foundation

———————■———————

P.O. Box 23350
Seattle, Washington 98102
U.S.A.
Telephone: (206) 709-3100
Fax: (206) 709-3252
Web site: http://www.gatesfoundation.org

Nonprofit Foundation
Incorporated: 1994 as the William H. Gates Foundation
Employees: 626
Total Assets: $35.9 billion (2008 est.)
NAICS: 813211 Grantmaking Foundations

■ ■ ■

The Bill & Melinda Gates Foundation (Gates Foundation) is the world's largest charitable foundation. Its assets of approximately $36 billion dwarf most other foundations, including such well-known giants as the Ford Foundation, the Carnegie Corporation, and the Rockefeller Foundation. The Gates Foundation gives away more than $2 billion annually. By 2008, the foundation had given away $16.75 billion over its life span thus far. The foundation funds initiatives in all 50 states in the United States and in some 100 countries worldwide. Its overarching philanthropic goals are to promote education and health for the world's underprivileged.

The Gates Foundation funds a variety of health initiatives in the developing world, such as the search for vaccines for AIDS and malaria. Its educational initiatives include a minority scholarship program and a campaign to provide computers to needy public libraries across the United States and Canada. The Gates Foundation's assets were initially provided by Bill Gates, founder of the computer software firm Microsoft, and his wife Melinda French Gates. In 2006, billionaire investor and CEO of Berkshire Hathaway Corporation Warren Buffett added much of his own fortune to the Bill & Melinda Gates Foundation, essentially doubling its assets. Top executives at the Gates Foundation include Bill Gates's father, William H. Gates, Sr., and Jeff Raikes, a longtime Microsoft executive.

FUNDING A FOUNDATION WITH THE MICROSOFT FORTUNE

The enormous endowment of the Bill & Melinda Gates Foundation derived from the fortune of the computer magnate Bill Gates, perhaps Harvard University's most successful dropout. Gates left Harvard when he was only 19 and founded a computer software company in 1975 with a longtime friend, Paul Allen. Their company, Microsoft, was chosen by IBM in 1980 to write the operating system for the computer maker's new personal computers. Microsoft's operating system, called MS-DOS, became the standard operating system used on all IBM-compatible personal computers. Microsoft reaped vast amounts of money from the licensing of its system. In 1986, Microsoft went public. Gates's stake in the hugely profitable company made him a billionaire, and he was soon touted as the world's richest man. The company continued to grow and expand into the 1990s, as it developed or acquired many new software products. Microsoft was the world's leading software company, an

COMPANY PERSPECTIVES

Guided by the belief that every life has equal value, the Bill & Melinda Gates Foundation works to help all people lead healthy, productive lives. In developing countries, we focus on improving people's health and giving them the chance to lift themselves out of hunger and extreme poverty. In the United States, we seek to ensure that all people—especially those with the fewest resources—have access to the opportunities they need to succeed in school and life. Based in Seattle, the foundation is led by CEO Jeff Raikes and co-chair William H. Gates Sr., under the direction of Bill and Melinda Gates and Warren Buffett.

indomitable competitor in the booming software industry. Gates's fortune was estimated at around $65 billion at the end of the 20th century.

Microsoft generated great wealth, not only for Gates and cofounder Allen, but also for scores of executives whose stock in the company made them rich. Many Microsoft executives were young, and they found themselves able to retire comfortably by age 40. According to a July 24, 2000, article in *Time,* dozens of Microsoft millionaires set up charitable foundations in the 1990s. "The status symbol of the '80s was a BMW. The status symbol of this decade is having your own foundation named after you," claimed a Microsoft employee quoted in the article.

Gates himself became one of the richest men on the planet while he was still in his 30s. Gates was instrumental in the running of his company and seemed to have no plans to step back from the extraordinary business he had founded in his teens. However, Microsoft's competitive clout in the 1990s brought it much criticism. Antitrust allegations soured a major acquisition the company planned to make in 1995, and in 1998 the U.S. Justice Department filed a far-reaching antitrust suit against Microsoft. Gates was also at times reviled as the personification of a company perceived by some as greedy and rapacious. He was called a miser, for holding on to his personal fortune. Microsoft had initiated a giving program as early as 1983, which at first focused on funding computer and science education scholarships. Gates arranged for charitable giving of his own wealth in the mid-1990s, when he announced that he intended to give away most of his money before his death.

Gates established a foundation for the charitable disbursement of much of his wealth in 1994, shortly after his marriage to Melinda French. This was known as the William H. Gates Foundation, and it was run by Gates's father, a Seattle lawyer, initially from the basement of his home. Gates's marriage to Melinda French appeared to spur the billionaire to find a way to give back some of his money. French grew up in Texas and studied computer science, engineering, and business at Duke University before joining Microsoft in 1987. While working as project manager at Microsoft, she also volunteered her time at a Seattle high school. On the eve of the marriage of French and Gates, Gates's mother read the couple a letter that seemed to prod them to consider what to do with their plenty. As paraphrased in an article in the *New York Times Magazine* (April 16, 2000), it read, "From those who are given great resources, great things are expected." The magazine also went on to claim that French was the instigator in the move toward building the Gates Foundation.

LIBRARY INITIATIVE ADDED

The William H. Gates Foundation began with an endowment of $106 million. Gates's father, who had retired from his law firm, volunteered to run the organization. Although he was active in local charity works, Gates, Sr., had no actual background in running a foundation. Although Gates was urged to hire someone with a professional background in charitable giving, the Gates Foundation continued to be overseen by Gates, Sr., Bill, and Melinda, and beginning in 1997, former Microsoft Corporation executive Patty Stonesifer. Over its first several years, Bill and Melinda Gates added about $2 billion to the foundation. Some of its first projects were geared to the Seattle and Pacific Northwest area. The Gates Foundation contributed $2 million to the Seattle Area YMCA, $20 million to the Seattle Public Library, and $1 million to the Tacoma Art Museum. Aside from programs that benefited the Northwest, the Gates Foundation also began to target educational programs and issues of global health.

In 1997 a separate charitable program, targeting $200 million for the Gates Library Foundation, was endowed. The object of this charity was to overcome the "digital divide," whereby wealthier people had access to technology and information and poorer people did not. The Library Foundation planned to bring computers to poor and underserved public libraries across the country. The Library Foundation not only provided the computers, but also furnished Internet access and gave training and technical support to librarians. While a very small staff ran both Gates Foundations, the library initiative required hundreds of paid technicians to do the installa-

KEY DATES

1994: William H. Gates Foundation is founded.
1997: Gates Library Foundation is founded.
1999: All Gates foundations are folded into one organization.
2000: First Millennium Scholars are chosen.
2006: Warren Buffett announces gift of much of his fortune to Gates Foundation.

tion and training across the United States and Canada. Patty Stonesifer, an old friend and coworker of Bill and Melinda, ran the library program. Over the next three years, the library initiative installed more than 22,000 computers in roughly 4,500 libraries in the United States. An additional 1,400 libraries in Canada were provided with some 4,000 computers.

HEALTHCARE EMPHASIS

Gates and his wife both had a consuming interest in computers and technology, given their work for Microsoft. A program such as the library initiative seemed a natural place to spend a fortune made in software. However, they became aware that simply giving people technology was not always effective charity. Gates recounted to the *New York Times Magazine* a trip he took to South Africa in the mid-1990s. Inhabitants of a poor ghetto eagerly showed the Microsoft billionaire the town's only computer. Gates noticed that the town also had only a single electrical outlet. Gates told the magazine, "I looked around and thought, 'Hmmm, computers may not be the highest priority in this particular place.'"

Gates and his family members began researching other areas where the Gates Foundation might make a difference. In the late 1990s, the Gates Foundation began funding a variety of healthcare programs designed to improve conditions in the developing world. This was an area where money was lacking, due to market forces. Pharmaceutical companies had little incentive to spend research and development funds on third world diseases such as malaria. Despite the vast numbers of people affected by malaria (about 200 million yearly in the late 1990s), drug companies could not expect to make a profit from customers in the world's poorest nations. Thus the amount spent on vaccine development was fairly low. Worldwide spending on malaria vaccine research in the mid-1990s was about $60 million.

In 1999 the Gates Foundation funded a $50 million Malaria Vaccine Initiative, making it the single biggest backer of malaria research. The Gates Foundation also funded a $100 million Children's Vaccine Program. This was to distribute vaccines in the third world that were already commonly in use in the developed world. The vaccine program would buy and distribute vaccines for common childhood diseases such as tetanus, polio, whooping cough, diphtheria, and measles in countries where existing healthcare programs were inadequate.

The Gates Foundation also funded research on a vaccine for AIDS. Of AIDS sufferers, 70 percent were in sub-Saharan Africa, in poor countries where drug companies did not expect much return on their research investment. At the international AIDS conference in 1998, the Gates Foundation announced an initial gift of $1.5 million for its International AIDS Vaccine Initiative. The Gates gift promptly attracted other donations, one from the British government and one from the Elton John Foundation. The Gates Foundation increased its AIDS vaccine funding to $25 million the next year. The AIDS initiative targeted promising research, and helped drug manufacturers speed the work to clinical trials. In exchange for funding research, the Gates Foundation expected the pharmaceutical companies to provide resulting drugs or vaccine at low cost to developing countries.

ADDITIONAL INITIATIVES IN HEALTHCARE AND EDUCATION

The AIDS Vaccine Initiative left the drug companies free to charge what they wanted for their new products in the United States, where there was some hope of profit. AIDS researchers agreed that the search for a vaccine seemed very difficult because of the peculiar nature of the AIDS virus. The Gates Foundation was able to provide money to researchers much more quickly than other organizations such as the National Institutes of Health, and therefore gave needed momentum to a difficult project. The Gates Foundation gave money to other, similar healthcare projects as well. It funded work to detect and cure cervical cancer in 1999, giving $50 million to an existing network of care providers in Africa. The foundation's total spending on global health initiatives was estimated at around $400 million annually by 2000.

The Gates Foundation also was interested in helping disadvantaged students in the United States and elsewhere gain access to quality education. In February 1999 a new foundation, the Gates Learning Foundation, was endowed. Like the Gates Library Foundation, the Learning Foundation aimed to bridge the "digital divide," providing access to technology for people who otherwise might not be exposed to it. With $1 billion, the foundation announced that it would provide college scholarships to 20,000 minority students over the next two decades. The foundation ran its Millennium Scholars Program through the United Negro College Fund, the Hispanic Scholarship Fund, and the American Indian College Fund. To be eligible, students had to be enrolled in a four-year college program and studying within certain specified fields. The winners received a grant to cover the difference between their financial aid package and the actual cost of their college education, including housing and books. The first winners for the program were picked in 2000. That year, the foundation also announced a similar scholarship program to pay for graduate study at the University of Cambridge in England. The $210 million fund was intended primarily for students from developing countries.

CONSOLIDATION INTO ONE FOUNDATION

By 1999, the Gates fortune was spread between three foundations: the William H. Gates Foundation, begun in 1994, the Gates Library Foundation, and the Gates Learning Foundation. These three had overlapping goals of providing opportunities for healthcare and education. In August 1999, the three foundations were folded into one, under the name the Bill & Melinda Gates Foundation. The foundation moved into a new building in Seattle, leaving the elder Mr. Gates's basement at last. Gates and his wife also stepped up the rate they gave to their foundation, infusing quarterly chunks of $5 billion and $6 billion at a time. In October 1999 the foundation had assets of $17.1 billion, which made it the richest endowed foundation in the world to date. A year later, its endowment had reached $21.8 billion. According to *Time* magazine (July 24, 2000), Bill Gates had given "more money away faster than anyone else in history." Its largest programs were the $1 billion Millennium Scholarship Program, the $750 million grant to the Global Alliance for Vaccines and Immunization, and $350 million earmarked for teachers and schools in the United States for a variety of educational improvements.

Even its smaller grants were substantial, such as the $50 million for malaria vaccine research, another $50 million for groups working for the worldwide eradication of polio, and $25 million for a group fighting tuberculosis worldwide. Most of the Gates Foundation's projects were long-term, with results not expected for years, or even decades. By 2001 it was still too early to see concrete results; yet in the few short years of its existence, the Gates Foundation had made a marked impact, putting millions of dollars into areas that might otherwise have received little attention.

RAPID GROWTH IN THE 21ST CENTURY

The foundation continued to give away money in unprecedented amounts in the early years of the 21st century. It was the single biggest private donor to education in the United States, and its spending on global health initiatives outpaced even that of the World Health Organization. The foundation clung to broad goals, backing programs that had visionary sweep. For example, the foundation was interested in charter schools, and in 2001 it picked an innovative charter school in Minnesota and gave it $4.3 million to replicate its pattern at 15 other schools. Systemic change was the goal, and the Gates Foundation was well positioned to promote a large agenda. In public health, the foundation outspent entire governments.

As its interests grew more complex, the foundation was reorganized. Early in the new century, the foundation hired top experts to oversee grants in specific areas. Simple proposals that had been reviewed by Bill Gates, Sr., and Patty Stonesifer gave way to more structured projects overseen by a professional staff. Although the number of employees grew, both Bill and Melinda Gates remained extremely hands-on in the running of the foundation.

In 2006, Bill Gates announced that he would retire from his role as primary software architect at Microsoft in two years, to devote most of his time to his philanthropy. He had already stepped back from being CEO six years earlier although he continued to serve as chairman of the company. His interest in the scientific and medical work of the foundation was intense, and as early as 2004, Gates began discussing ways to shift his focus from his company to the charity.

WARREN BUFFETT'S GIFT

While Gates was extricating himself from Microsoft, his friend Warren Buffett was also looking for a way to give away his own huge fortune. Buffett was the founder of the investment firm Berkshire Hathaway, and was considered the world's second richest man, behind Gates. The two met in 1991, and had similar concerns with the impact their wealth could make on the world's poor. Although Buffett had his own family foundation, and had vowed to pass on his money only after he died, he changed his mind. In 2006, Buffett announced that he would give about $30 billion to the Bill & Melinda Gates Foundation. He respected the work the foundation had been doing, and it was simpler to add his money to the existing foundation, rather than try to duplicate its work.

The Buffett gift increased the assets of the Gates Foundation considerably. The amount the foundation needed to give away each year also almost doubled. The sudden influx of money meant the Gates Foundation needed to double its staff and find larger headquarters. While the goals of the foundation were not altered, the organization had to develop a more professional infrastructure. The foundation increased its spending on its library initiative, dedicating some $30 million for public libraries to upgrade their computer equipment. This brought the foundation's total investment in computer accessibility through libraries to $325 million. This was a continuation of work the foundation started in the 1990s. The foundation also developed a new focus on outreach. In order to publicize its programs, it sometimes involved celebrities such as Oprah Winfrey, as well as government spokespeople or church leaders. The foundation realized that outreach, marketing, and public relations could be just as crucial to a program's success as its actual application.

The foundation appointed a new CEO, Jeff Raikes, in 2007. The following year, as promised, Gates retired from the day-to-day operations of Microsoft. Also in 2008, the foundation broke ground on a new headquarters in Seattle. The new campus spread over 12 acres, with two office buildings, a visitors' center, and an entrance pavilion. Cost of the new headquarters was to run to $500 million. Meanwhile, the foundation continued to fund new initiatives, including a major push into solving world agriculture problems. Mid-decade the foundation donated $900 million toward helping small farmers increase output and adapt crops to local conditions. In 2008, the foundation announced a major new agriculture program run in tandem with the Howard G. Buffett Foundation. Howard Buffett was one of Warren Buffett's sons. This program, called Purchase for Progress, helped small farmers find better distribution for their crops. All in all, with the Warren Buffett gift added to its substantial assets, the Bill & Melinda Gates Foundation looked forward to more groundbreaking work in philanthropy in years to come.

A. Woodward

PRINCIPAL COMPETITORS

The Wellcome Trust; David and Lucile Packard Foundation; Carnegie Corp. of New York.

FURTHER READING

"The Art of Giving," *Business Week,* October 25, 1999, p. 80.

"Bill Gates's Other Chief Executive," *Economist,* January 20, 2007, p. 77.

Cantrell, John, "Father Gives Best," *Town & Country,* December 1999, p. 210.

Coeyman, Marjorie, "From the Foundation Up," *Christian Science Monitor,* April 3, 2001, p. 15.

Cohen, John, "Gates Foundation Rearranges Public Health Universe," *Science,* March 15, 2002, p. 2000.

"Fitting the Bill?" *Global Agenda,* June 7, 2008, p. 20.

"Giving Billions Isn't Easy," *Time,* July 24, 2000, pp. 52, 53.

Guth, Robert A., "Gates Foundation Seeks Out Nontypical Research to Fund," *Wall Street Journal,* October 23, 2008, p. A4.

Guth, Robert A., and Roger Thurow, "Weaving Africa's Breadbasket," *Wall Street Journal,* September 25, 2008, p. A18.

Hardy, Quentin, "The World's Richest Donors," *Forbes,* May 1, 2000, p. 114.

Heim, Kristi, "Gates Foundation's Step to New Campus," *Seattle Times,* July 23, 2008, p. B1.

Lewin, Tamar, "Gates Foundation Names 4,100 Minority Scholarships in 2-Decade Program," *New York Times,* June 9, 2000, p. C10.

Loomis, Carol J., "Warren Buffett Gives It Away," *Fortune,* July 20, 2006, pp. 56–69.

Maich, Steve, "The Gospel According to Bill," *Maclean's,* July 21, 2008, pp. 36–40.

Oder, Norman, "Gates Offers New Grant Program," *Library Journal,* February 15, 2007, p. 1.

Reis, George R., "U.S. Philanthropy Boosted by High-Tech Billions," *Fund Raising Management,* August 1999, p. 5.

Schlender, Brent, "Bill Gates Reboots," *Fortune,* July 10, 2006, pp. 72–76.

———, "Gates After Microsoft," *Fortune,* July 7, 2008, pp. 110–16.

Strouse, Jean, "How to Give Away $21.8 Billion," *New York Times Magazine,* April 16, 2000.

Tice, Carol, "Gates Fund Earning Nonprofits' Respect," *Puget Sound Business Journal,* February 16, 2001, p. 13.

Waldhole, Michael, "Group Pledges $150 Million in Bid to Boost Children's Vaccinations," *Wall Street Journal,* September 21, 2000, p. B2.

Billerud AB

—■—

Box 703
Solna, S-169 27
Sweden
Telephone: (46 08) 553 335 00
Fax: (46 08) 553 335 80
Web site: http://www.billerud.com

Public Company
Incorporated: AssiDomän Karlsborg AB
Employees: 2,364
Sales: SEK 7.76 billion ($1.2 billion) (2007)
Stock Exchanges: Stockholm
Ticker Symbol: BILL
NAICS: 322110 Pulp Mills; 322121 Paper (Except
   Newsprint) Mills

■ ■ ■

Billerud AB is a major Swedish producer of paper for the packaging industry. The Solna-based company operates in three primary markets: Packaging and Specialty Paper; Packaging Boards; and Market Pulp. The Packaging and Specialty Paper division is Billerud's largest, producing sack and kraft papers for the food packing, industrial packaging, and sack solutions markets. This division produces nearly 550,000 metric tons per year. In 2007 the division generated 51 percent of Billerud's total revenues of SEK 7.76 billion ($1.2 billion). Packaging Boards division produces fluting and liners used in fresh foods packaging to transport fruits and vegetables, as well as for shipping consumer goods, beverages, and the like. This division added 30 percent

of the group's 2007 turnover, with a production capacity of 530,000 metric tons per year. The Market Pulp division produces long-fiber market pulp used for the production of tissues, packaging paper, and writing paper. This division accounted for 19 percent of Billerud's sales, with a total capacity of 350,000 metric tons. Billerud's industrial operations include three pulp and paper mills in Sweden, and a paper mill in the United Kingdom. Billerud is listed on the Stockholm Stock Exchange, and is led by CEO and president, Per Lindberg.

PULP MILL IN 1883

The modern Billerud was created in 2001 through the merger of two paper mills owned by AssiDomän and a third by Stora Enso. The Billerud name, however, had long held a prominent place in the Swedish pulp and paper industry, stemming from the late 19th century. The earliest association between the name Billerud and the Swedish paper industry stemmed from a sulfite pulp mill founded by V. Follin in the town of Säffle, in the Värmland region of Sweden in 1883. The pulp mill took its name from the name of the property on which it was located, Billerud. Production began the following year.

The Billerud company soon began expanding, through the buying of a number of other mills in the Värmland region including Stömne Bruks AB in 1899. Into the turn of the 20th century the company's acquisitions included Slottsbrons Sulfit in 1904 and Nors Jernbruks the following year. By the beginning of World War I Billerud had completed several more acquisitions, including Hillringsbergs AB, adding a sawmill and two pulp mills in 1907, and Stömne Sulfitfabrik in 1910. The purchase of Rämen-Lilhendahl in 1915 added two more pulp mills as well as a new sawmill.

By 1920 Billerud counted nearly 30 sawmills, pulp mills, and other factories, including Bosjö Bruk, a pulp mill originally founded in 1637 and acquired by Billerud in 1920. Toward the end of the 1920s the company came under the control of Christian Storjohan, a prominent Swedish businessman. Under his leadership, Billerud continued its expansion, opening a new paper mill in Gruvön in 1931. This mill, which was expanded in 1937, later became one of the founding businesses of the modern Billerud. Another important acquisition during this period was that of Lier, Varald & Bogen, in Norway, which transformed Billerud into a major Scandinavian forest holder.

Billerud continued its growth through the post–World War II era. Acquisitions remained an important part of the group's growth through the 1950s, with a number of notable additions including Barkens Sagverks in 1953, Upperuds Trämassefabrik in 1954, and Hellfors Bruks in 1958. The last not only added nearly 115,000 hectares of forests to Billerud's extensive holdings, it also added sulfite, sulfate, and pulp mills, and a paper mill.

PAPER SACK INVESTMENTS IN THE SIXTIES

Billerud carried out an international expansion effort during the 1960s, entering Portugal, then Scotland in 1964. The Scottish entry, carried out through the purchase of Robert L. Fleming Ltd., was particularly significant for the later Billerud, as it led the company into the production of paper sacks. Billerud stepped up this area of business the following year, acquiring a stake in Belgium paper bag producer Manusack S.A., before acquiring full control in 1974. By then the company had also added wallpaper components including France's Cartonneries Meniguat, in 1968, and Sweden's

Svenska Wellpappfabriken. Another major international move came in the early 1970s, when Billerud launched a joint venture with Brazil's Aracruz Cellulose to establish the world's largest eucalpytus-based paper mill.

Billerud had also taken a place at the forefront of pulp and paper technology during this period. In 1964 the company's Gruvön mill became the first in the sector to introduce computer control in its production systems, helping to establish a standard in the international paper industry. Into the early 1970s the Gruvön operation took the lead in addressing the environmental concerns raised by the paper production process. In 1971 the mill became one of the first to incorporate the use of oxygen in its bleaching process. This new technology permitted a major reduction in the use of chlorine in paper production. Further advancements in technology allowed the company to abandon the use of chlorine entirely in 1991.

In 1978 Billerud moved into the global big leagues, completing a merger with the packaging and forestry operations of Swedish company Uddeholm, which also had extensive steel interests. Uddeholm's forestry business had originally been established in Skoghall in 1855. Over the next century, Uddeholm had developed its own extensive forest holdings in Sweden, as well as strong operations both in pulp and in paper production.

The combined company, named Billerud Uddeholm, became the fifth largest forest company in Sweden, and one of its largest specialty producers of packaging papers and cartons. The company also boasted an extensive industrial base in Sweden and in Western Europe. In addition to its industrial operations, which included four paper mills and four paper bag factories, Billerud oversaw forest holdings of more than 600,000 hectares. Through its Gruvön mill, Billerud had also become the first in the industry to introduce the production of white top liner for cardboard packaging products.

SUCCESS INVITES TAKEOVER ACTIONS AND MERGERS

With these holdings Billerud Uddeholm, which maintained a public listing on the Stockholm Stock Exchange, became extremely attractive to its larger competitors. The company found itself the object of a takeover offer by Stora Kopparbergs, controlled by the Wallenberg family. Uddeholm agreed to sell its controlling stake to Stora in 1984. The acquisition, which cost Stora SEK 3.6 billion, catapulted Stora into the lead position of the Swedish forestry sector. The addition of Billerud, which became known as Stora Billerud, also helped balance Stora's own paper operations, which had

KEY DATES

1883: The Billerud company is founded as a sulfite pulp mill in Säffle, Sweden.
1931: Billerud builds the Gruvon paper mill.
1937: The Swedish Forestry Service acquires the Karlsborg sulfate pulp mill, originally founded in 1912.
1943: The Karlsborg mill becomes part of new ASSI forest products company.
1978: Billerud merges with the pulp and paper operations of the Uddeholm group.
1984: Billerud is acquired by Stora.
1994: AssiDomän acquires the Skärblacka paper mill, originally founded in 1872.
2000: Stora Enso and AssiDomän agree to merge the Gruvön, Skärblacka, and Karlsborg mills into a new company, Billerud.
2001: Billerud goes public with a listing on the Stockholm Stock Exchange.
2004: Billerud acquires Henry Cooke of England.
2008: Billerud acquires BAC Sag & Vyvleri of Sweden and 70% of Cebeco Mediena of Lithuania.

focused on the production of newsprint and writing paper and the like.

The Billerud name gradually faded amid Stora's own drive to become one of Europe's leading forestry and pulp and paper majors. In 1989 much of Billerud's former operations was spun off to form the Nordic Papers Group. Nonetheless, the Gruvön plant remained a central part of the group's packaging operations as Stora itself evolved into Stora Enso in the late 1990s. The merger of Stora with Finland's Enso in 1999 created the leading forest products group in Europe, and one of the top five worldwide.

The merger also brought with it a restructuring of Stora Enso's operations at the beginning of the 2000s. As part of that process Stora Enso began to focus its paper production on newsprint and magazine and fine paper, and packaging board. Each of these were areas in which Stora Enso ranked among the top three worldwide. This refocusing effort led the company to spin off its Gruvön business.

In 2000 Stora Enso had announced its agreement to merge the Gruvön plant with two paper mills held by AssiDomän, Skärblacka, and Karlsborg. The three operations were then incorporated into a new company, which carried the revived Billerud name.

SKÄRBLACKA AND KARLSBORG HISTORY

Both the Skärblacka and Karlsborg mills had long been mainstays in the Swedish pulp and paper industry. Skärblacka was the older of the two, having been constructed in 1872 in the Östergötland region. After fire destroyed the original mill in 1903, the company recovered, commissioning a new mill by 1905. The Skärblacka works developed its own power plant, which became a factor in its takeover by Fiskeby Fabriks in 1917.

By 1942 the Skärblacka mill had come under the control of Swedish cooperative giant Kooperativa Forbunder, also known as KF. Under KF, Skärblacka mill became a major producer of packaging paper, in part to support KF's own consumer goods manufacturing operations. The Skärblacka business grew in 1953 through a partnership with the nearby Ljusfors paper mill in 1953. This partnership eventually led to a merger of the two businesses into the larger Skärblacka company.

Still a subsidiary of Fiskeby Fabriks, Skärblacka's ownership changed hands again in 1985, when Holmens Bruk acquired Fiskeby, and then again in 1989, after another company, MoDo, acquired Holmens Bruk. MoDo then sold the Skärblacka works to AssiDomän in 1994.

Skärblacka joined AssiDomän's own paper production operation, centered on the Karlsborg mill. That mill had originally been established as a sulfate pulp mill in 1912. However, the plant proved financially unviable, and was forced to close in 1918. Yet a little more than a decade later, the mill was reopened, supported by a local initiative. The new company was given the name of Kalix Träinindustri.

The Kalix business came under the control of the Swedish Forestry Service in 1937. In 1943 the Forestry Service created a new industrial holding company, ASSI. The new operation then took over the Karlsborg mill. As part of ASSI, the Karlsborg plant extended its operations into paper production, following the inauguration of its first paper machine in 1953.

A second paper machine was added in 1957. The Karlsborg site was further expanded at the end of the 1970s, with a launch of a modernization program. By the beginning of the 1990s the site no longer used chlorine bleaching in its production process.

GOING PUBLIC IN 2001

The newly configured Billerud defined itself as a specialty packaging products group focused on niche markets where it held leading positions. The company was the largest European producer of white bag paper, with a 49 percent share of the market, and white kraft-liner, with a 50 percent share. The company also claimed the lead with a 26 percent share of the European monoglazed (MG) paper market, a 33 percent share of the Scandinavian fluting market, and a second place position with 29 percent of the machine finished (MF) paper segment. The company's total production capacity neared 1.3 million tons per year of pulp and paper, generating revenues of SEK 6.2 billion ($620 million).

Billerud was taken public in 2001, allowing Assi-Domän to sell off its holding in the company, while Stora Enso reduced its own position to just 30 percent. With its sales rising in the early 2000s, the company launched an investment program at its Gruvön and Skärblacka facilities, worth more than SEK 315 million ($31 million). That effort enabled the company to boost its sack and kraft paper production by an additional 13,000 metric tons per year.

The company completed another major expansion at the beginning of the following year, when it paid £17.5 million ($39 million) to acquire Milnthorpe, England-based Henry Cooke from South Africa's Barloworld. The purchase gave Billerud expanded packaging paper operations, with an addition capacity of 45,000 metric tons per year. Cooke also brought the company its specialty production of medical and flexible packaging, and an added £30 million ($60 million) in annual revenues.

NICHE FOCUS IN THE 21ST CENTURY

Billerud's investments continued into the second half of the decade, despite the difficult market conditions facing the paper and packaging industries at the time. In 2006 the company made a major SEK 1.05 billion ($105 million) energy efficiency upgrade, including rebuilding the company's bark boilers. The investment was expected to generate cost efficiencies both by reducing the group's fuel consumption and through the sale of excess electricity. By the end of 2006 Billerud had announced a new investment plan to spend SEK 370 million ($37 million) on upgrades to its paper production lines at its Gruvön and Skärblacka sites.

Billerud's investments also included a strong product development program. The company launched its Billerud Flute brand in 2005, featuring lower weight and increased strength. The company also released a new grade of liquid board, used in the production of fluid-grade packaging for milk, juice, and other liquids. Another area of company interest was the fashion industry, particularly the development of specialty packaging and papers for carrier bags for the designer segment. In 2007 Billerud inaugurated a specialized "Box Lab" to boost its research efforts on developing new packaging technologies for perishable foods.

In 2008 Billerud took steps to ensure its raw materials supply. In March of that year the company reached an agreement with Banverket, the Swedish railroad service, to acquire 10,000 cubic meters of forest along the Haparanda railroad line in north Sweden. The company then purchased a 70 percent stake in Cebeco Mediena, a pulpwood trading company based in Lithuania. This purchase was followed in August 2008 by the acquisition of BAC Sag & Hyvleri, a Sweden-based timber company based in the Norrbotten region. The new Billerud looked forward to a future focused on the niche packaging market.

M. L. Cohen

PRINCIPAL SUBSIDIARIES

Billerud (Shanghai) Rep. Office; Billerud Benelux B.V. (Netherlands); Billerud France S.A.S.; Billerud GmbH (Germany); Billerud Ibérica S.L. (Spain); Billerud S.r.l. (Italy); Billerud Sales Ltd U.K.

PRINCIPAL COMPETITORS

RGM International Private Ltd.; Vietnam Paper Corp.; Baykalsk Pulp and Paper Mill Joint Stock Co.; Marubeni Corp.; International Paper Co.; Votorantim Participacoes S.A.; Kertas Leces, PT; Anglo American PLC; Stora Enso AB; Svenska Cellulosa AB; Weyerhaeuser Co.; UPM-Kymmene Corporation.

FURTHER READING

"Acquisitions: Not Many on the Trail but Billerud Goes for Cooke," *Printing World,* November 25, 2004, p. 41.

Ayshford, Hilary, "Board Level," *Packaging Week,* January 31, 1990, p. S17.

"Billerud AB Invests SEK370m at Skarblacka and Gruvon Mills in Sweden," *Nordic Business Report,* December 7, 2006.

"Billerud AB Shuts Down Paper Machine at Gruvon Mill," *Nordic Business Report,* October 1, 2008.

"Billerud Hopes Box Lab Will Bear Fruit," *Packaging Today International,* August 2007, p. 9.

"Billerud Moves a Step Closer to Cooke Deal," *Printing World,* January 8, 2004, p. 30.

Fales, Gregg, "Billerud to Be Reborn," *PIMA's North American Papermaker,* December 2000, p. 17.

Pitt, Philip, "All Aboard for the Right Pack," *Packaging Week,* February 25, 1993, p. 33.

"Swedish Packaging Paper Company Billerud AB Strengthens Raw Materials Acquisition in Northern Sweden," *Nordic Business Report,* August 20, 2008.

"Swedish Packaging Paper Group Billerud AB Signs Major Wood Deal with Swedish Rail Administration," *Nordic Business Report,* March 10, 2008.

"Three Mills Merger for Swedish Giants," *Printing World,* November 6, 2000, p. 8.

Bryce Corporation

———————————————————————————■———————————————————————————

4505 Old Lamar Avenue
Memphis, Tennessee 38118-7033
U.S.A.
Telephone: (901) 369-4400
Toll Free: (800) 238-7277
Web site: http://www.brycecorp.com

Private Company
Incorporated: 1969
Employees: 1,100
Sales: $350 million (2007 est.)
NAICS: 322223 Plastics, Foil, and Coated Paper Bag
Manufacturing; 322221 Coated and Laminated
Packaging Paper and Plastics Film Manufacturing;
325520 Adhesive and Sealant Manufacturing

■ ■ ■

Bryce Corporation is a private company based in Memphis, Tennessee, involved in the flexible packaging industry, producing products that offer custom combinations of polypropylene, polyethylene, and polyester laminations, as well as waxed paper and other materials to provide a moisture and oxygen barrier and ensure freshness in food products. The Bryce Company subsidiary supplies customers in the food industry, especially in the salty snack category, including potato chips and pretzels, but also for candy, cookies, and baked goods, and specialty foods, such as beef jerky and sunflower seeds. Bryce also offers plastic-film laminated packaging for pet foods and treats, and provides packaging solutions for household products, including wet and dry wipes. Customers include the likes of Pepsico's Frito-Lay operation, Kraft Nabisco, and the Kellogg Company. Another Bryce Corporation subsidiary, Cyber Graphics, is a full-range prepress operation, involved in package design, product photography, production art, color separation, and other operations.

The company maintains plants in Memphis; Searcy, Kansas; and Shannon, Mississippi. Distribution centers are also located in Searcy and Memphis as well as in rural Pennsylvania. In addition, Bryce owns a stake in a joint venture called Johnson Bryce Inc., a Memphis minority-owned flexographic printing company, serving such customers as Frito-Lay, General Mills, Mars, Procter & Gamble, Pepsico's Gatorade, and Hewlett-Packard. Bryce Corporation is family owned and headed by the third generation of the Bryce family.

LINEAGE DATES TO 1922

Although Bryce Corporation was founded nearly half a century later, the company traces its heritage to 1922, when William H. Bryce, Sr., helped save the small Dallas, Texas-based Dixie Wax Paper Company by making advances in waxing technology that resulted in the invention of "Brad-Tite" waxed paper. Bryce then established a Dixie Wax Paper operation in Memphis in 1927. In the meantime, new opportunities for the waxed paper industry emerged in salty snacks, potato chips in particular. For most of the 19th century, potato chips were only to be found in restaurants, but late in the century grocery stores began carrying the popular item, leading to the opening of potato chip factories and the rise of the snack food industry.

At first, chips were packed at the store in paper bags, but the grease seeped through and the product did not remain fresh and crisp for very long. In 1926 Laura Scudder ironed together sheets of waxed paper to create the first potato chip bag. This was the first major step in modern snack food packaging. Dixie Wax Paper made a significant improvement to the waxed bag in 1933, introducing the first "preprint waxed bag," Dixie's Fresheen, which featured a glassine coating that greatly improved the shelf life of potato chips.

Bryce's son, William H. Bryce, Jr., joined his father at Dixie Wax Paper in Memphis after serving in the Navy during World War II and the Korean War. In 1957 they left Dixie Wax Paper and formed Bryce Packaging Corporation. Four years later the business was sold to the Riegel Paper Corporation for about $600,000 in cash. At the same time, Riegel acquired a minority stake in Dixie Wax Paper and its Dallas and Memphis operations. The younger Bryce stayed on to work for Riegel, and then in 1969 left to form Bryce Corporation, setting up shop in a leased Memphis warehouse. His former boss, William M. Riegel, would join him and become chairman of the board at Bryce Corp.

ADVANCES IN SNACK FOOD PACKAGING

William Bryce, Jr., played an important role in the snack food packaging industry. At the time Bryce Corp. was founded, flexible packaging relied on waxed paper and cellophane. Bryce became an advocate of polypropylene in snack food packaging and pioneered extrusion lamination, leading to modern plastic packaging that included polyethylene and polyester formulations that greatly improved product freshness and longevity.

To keep pace with demand for its packaging products, Bryce Corp. opened a plant in Searcy, Arkansas, in 1976. A new Memphis plant followed in 1981. The extra production capacity would lead to diversification beyond salty snack packaging in the mid-

1980s, when Bryce Corp. began providing packaging for confectionery, cookie, and baked goods. By this time the third generation of the Bryce family was involved in the business. William H. Bryce III came to work for his father in 1975, but health problems would not permit him to take on as much responsibility as his younger brothers, Thomas J. and John D. Bryce. As a freshman at Davidson College, William Bryce III suffered a brain tumor that would hinder him until his death in 2004 at the age of 54.

At the end of the 1980s and start of the 1990s, Bryce Corp. began branching out in a number of directions. The Coating Technologies unit was formed to produce thermal laminating films and equipment, allowing customers to produce their own laminated items, including book covers, menus, point-of-purchase displays, and identification cards. A joint venture, Bryce-Toga USA, was launched in 1989 with São Paulo-based Toga Embalagens, Brazil's largest food packaging company. Operating out of Memphis, Bryce-Toga supplemented Bryce's capabilities in grocery products packaging, including nuts, chocolate bars and other candy, frozen foods, and nonfood items such as film.

JOHNSON BRYCE ESTABLISHED: 1992

In 1992 Johnson Bryce Inc. was founded. The joint venture grew out of efforts by one of Bryce's main customers, Frito-Lay, which in the mid-1980s launched an effort to do business with minority-owned suppliers. Because there were no minority-owned companies with which to do business, Frito-Lay decided to take the initiative and help develop some. In 1988 the company backed African American Robert Johnson, a former Sears executive, and his daughter, who had worked in marketing for New England Bell. They originally established a packaging venture in Atlanta, but lacked the necessary equipment and expertise to keep up with changes in packaging materials. Frito-Lay then brought Bryce Corp. into the picture because of its experience and access to high-tech equipment, and the business was reorganized in Memphis.

The Johnsons brought with them a six-color printing press salvaged from the original operation and Bryce contributed the other machinery needed to complete a packaging manufacturing system. Johnson Bryce shared space in the 18,000-square-foot building that housed the Bryce Toga operation. In the first year of operation Johnson Bryce turned out one billion bags that supplied 32 Frito-Lay plants, generating about $15 million for the joint venture, which was 51 percent owned by the Johnson family with the balance owned by the Bryce

```
┌─────────────────────────────────────────┐
│                                         │
│            KEY DATES                    │
│                 ■                       │
│  ─────────────────────────────────      │
│                                         │
│  1957: William H. Bryce, Sr., and       │
│        William H. Bryce, Jr., found     │
│        Bryce Packaging Corporation.     │
│  1961: Riegel Paper Corporation         │
│        acquires Bryce Packaging.        │
│  1969: William H. Bryce, Jr., starts    │
│        Bryce Corporation.               │
│  1989: Bryce-Toga USA formed.           │
│  1992: Johnson Bryce Inc. formed.       │
│  1993: William Bryce, Jr., retires;     │
│        Cyber Graphics launched.         │
│  1997: Interest acquired in German      │
│        company, Holderfer               │
│        Kunstsoffwerk.                   │
│  2004: Johnson Bryce moves into new     │
│        plant.                           │
│  2005: Bryce begins using seven-color   │
│        technology.                      │
│                                         │
└─────────────────────────────────────────┘
```

family. In 1996 the company moved to a new 50,000-square-foot facility in Memphis.

At the start of 1993 there was a changeover at the top ranks of Bryce Corp. William Bryce, Jr., retired as chief executive officer and William Riegel retired as chairman. Thomas Bryce then became chairman at the age of 38, and his brother, John, one year younger, was named president. The two of them also served as co-CEOs until 1997, when Thomas Bryce became the lone CEO while retaining the chairmanship. Their father, as well as Riegel, remained on the board of directors. William Bryce, Jr., remained on the board until his death in 2003. He left the next generation a company that had sales of some $200 million, providing Bryce Corp. with a 30 percent share of the U.S. market in snack food packaging.

The company grew even larger later in 1993 with the acquisition of Buffalo, New York-based Transparent Bag Corporation, a polyethylene film and bag manufacturer that generated annual revenues of $5 million. In October 1993, the Bryce family was reunited with the remnants of Dixie Wax Paper Company, then known as Dixico Inc. The company, which continued to maintain plants in Dallas and Memphis, was acquired from Bell Packaging Corp. of Dallas. Although Dixico was struggling financially, it brought another $50 million in sales to the balance sheet, specialized packaging technology, and such valuable customers as Nabisco and Keebler. Furthermore, the Cyber Graphics subsidiary was founded that same year, in the summer of 1993, and Bryce-Toga broke ground on a new 100,000-square-

foot plant in Shannon, Mississippi, near Tupelo. The plant opened in 1998.

REORGANIZATION EFFORT IN 1995

After taking stock of its new operation, Bryce Corp. undertook a reorganization effort in 1995. The Dixico plant in Dallas was closed, as was the Buffalo plant of Transparent Bag Corp. Equipment from these operations was transferred to the Memphis plants. Within the Memphis operations, about 50 workers were transferred to the newer plant to accommodate the plant consolidations. When the changes were complete, the company was able to continue growing its product offering. In 1996 the company unveiled an innovative extrusion laminate process that, combined with oxygen barrier technology, allowed it to enter the small-bag pet food and pet treats market with a new easy-open packaging product.

Bryce Corp. also harbored international aspirations. The Bryce International LLC division took a major step in this effort in 1997 when it acquired a majority interest in a German packaging company, Holderfer Kunstsoffwerk, owned by the Kobusch family. The business operated in both Europe and Asia, not only providing Bryce with entry into these markets but also into such new areas as meat, fish, cheese, and liquids. Based in Holdorf, Germany, the new venture assumed the name Kobusch Bryce GmbH, and included an interest in TigerPack Limited, a consumer packaging company based in Shanghai that served Asia.

NEW DEVELOPMENTS IN THE 21ST CENTURY

At the start of the new century, Bryce Corp. expanded its technical capabilities to include film metalizing, in this way eliminating the problem of oils from products such as potato chips seeping into metal laminates and distorting the surface look of the package. As a result, the shelf appeal of the products was improved. Bryce then commercialized the extrusion lamination method with a cold seal process. This combination allowed substrates (such as metal and plastic films, with their individual strengths) to be joined, and the package could be sealed with little or no heat pressure to prevent damage to the contents. In 2003 the company developed slit scoring to improve easy-open packaging with a directional tear feature. Also in that year, Cyber Graphics introduced the In The Round digital photopolymer system, using a round plate to print on a press-ready sleeve to provide faster, high-quality printing.

Johnson Bryce underwent some changes as well in the early years of the new century. It joined forces in 2000 with another minority-owned company, Atlanta-based Film Fabricators Inc., after the two companies teamed up to win a $100 million contract from Procter & Gamble Company (P&G), which like Frito-Lay had made an effort to develop minority suppliers. Founded in 1985 by CEO Woody Hall, Film Fabricators was a longtime P&G supplier, focusing on the Pampers disposable diapers business, which then became the focal point of the new Hall-Bryce Alliance. In 2004 Johnson Bryce moved to a new location in Memphis where it could add new capabilities and refocus on adhesive lamination and surface print applications. Well into his 60s, Robert Johnson sold his stake in the joint venture to Ron Purifoy in January 2007.

In the meantime the innovative spirit at Bryce Corporation continued to thrive. In 2005 the company became one of the first in the flexible packaging industry to use seven-color print technology. With printing becoming increasingly important to the business, the Mississippi plant was expanded in 2007 to add printing equipment. The future appeared bright for the company, with a fourth generation of the Bryce family preparing to take control of the business one day.

Ed Dinger

PRINCIPAL SUBSIDIARIES

Bryce Company; Bryce International Company; Kobusch Bryce GmbH (Germany); Cyber Graphics.

PRINCIPAL COMPETITORS

Bemis Flexible Packaging; Sealed Air Corporation; Reynolds Flexible Packaging.

FURTHER READING

Barton, Christopher, "Johnson Bryce Merger Brings $100 Million Job," *Commercial Appeal,* November 1, 2000, p. C1.

"Bryce Bags Recognition for Packaging," *Commercial Appeal,* June 11, 1991, p. B7.

Campbell, Laurel, "Bryce Brothers Take Charge," *Commercial Appeal,* January 9, 1993, p. B4.

———, "Bryce Corp. Prepares for Dixico Purchase," *Commercial Appeal,* September 24, 1992, p. B3.

Flamm, David, "Black, White Owners of Firm Show Profits Can Be Made in the Bag," *Commercial Appeal,* April 8, 1993, p. B3.

VanValkenburgh, Joan, "Bryce Packaging Expands Overseas," *Commercial Appeal,* April 18, 1997, p. B8.

———, "Bryce Set to Shift Some Jobs," *Commercial Appeal,* July 12, 1995, p. B8.

Watson, Mark, "Mr. Bryce Considered Employees to Be Family," *Commercial Appeal,* August 26, 2003, p. B3.

Buckhead Life Restaurant Group, Inc.

265 Pharr Road
Atlanta, Georgia 30305-2241
U.S.A.
Telephone: (404) 237-2060
Fax: (404) 237-2160
Web site: http://www.buckheadrestaurants.com

Private Company
Incorporated: 1979
Employees: 1,400
Sales: $70 million (2007 est.)
NAICS: 722110 Full-Service Restaurants

■ ■ ■

Buckhead Life Restaurant Group, Inc. (BLRG), is a privately held Atlanta, Georgia-based company that operates a dozen mostly upscale restaurants in Atlanta, primarily located in the trendy Buckhead neighborhood. BLRG restaurants cover a wide variety of styles and cuisines. Pano's and Paul's, the company's oldest property, is a white-cloth restaurant perennially ranked among Atlanta's best. Other upscale restaurants in the group include 103 West, catering mostly to a business clientele; and the Buckhead Diner, offering quality comfort food, such as berry-scented pan-fried chicken with Yukon whipped potatoes, homemade potato chips, and white-chocolate banana-cream pie.

More casual eateries include the Atlanta Fish Market, specializing in seafood; Bluepointe, offering modern American cuisine with Asian accents; and Chops, a steak house that on its lower level includes the

Lobster Bar seafood restaurant. To cover other cuisines, BLRG offers Kyma, a white-cloth Greek restaurant; Nava, an upscale Southwestern eatery featuring a menu with both Latin and Native American influences; Pricci, a stylish Italian restaurant; and another Italian restaurant, Veni Vidi Vici, located in midtown Atlanta and close to the local theater and cultural scene.

In addition, BLRG operates the Buckhead Bread Company, originally established to supply BLRG restaurants with baked goods, which was expanded to include the Corner Café, offering baked goods to the public while also offering a breakfast, lunch, brunch, and catering menu. BLRG expanded beyond the Atlanta market with the opening of the Chops Lobster Bar in Boca Raton, Florida, in 2008. BLRG is primarily owned by president Pano Karatassos, an award-winning restaurateur, and his family. Each restaurant has an equity partner, with Karatassos holding a controlling interest.

GROWING INTO A RESTAURANT CAREER

Pano Karatassos grew up in the food industry in Savannah, Georgia. His father, who was born in Greece, ran a food import business, Pano's Food Shop, and a café, P&K Delicatessen, serving Savannah's Greek and Jewish community. "Being immigrants," Karatassos told *Nation's Restaurant News,* "our parents could keep an eye on us if we worked in the business. They didn't know what babysitters were back then." While his friends may have dreamed of becoming doctors or lawyers, Karatassos planned on a restaurant career.

COMPANY PERSPECTIVES

Running a restaurant is not one big thing. It is a thousand little things.

At the same time, he was also determined not to take over the family businesses, inspired by his father's insistence that, "The key is waiting." Instead he decided to leave town and strike out on his own. In the late 1950s Karatassos joined the Navy, serving almost four years as a cook and baker. After his discharge he enrolled at the Culinary Institute of America, graduating in 1960. He then returned to Savannah to start his career, again eschewing the family businesses, and serving instead as executive chef at the Hilton Savannah DeSoto.

Sensing that he needed more training, Karatassos gave up his post and took a major pay cut to become an apprentice for renowned chef Hermann Rusch at the Greenbrier Hotel, the highly regarded resort in White Sulfur Springs, West Virginia. With Rusch as his mentor, Karatassos was then able to find work in resort hotels in Switzerland, including the Gstaad Palace hotel and Montreaux Palace hotel. In the United States Karatassos also worked at Palm Beach Everglades Club in Palm Beach, Florida, and the Hotel Corp. of America in Washington, D.C. While he was in Washington in 1968, Karatassos met Paul Albrecht, his future partner, the "Paul" of Pano's and Paul's.

Raised in Munich, Germany, Albrecht trained in Europe, graduating from Munich's Hotel and Restaurant School, before coming to the United States, where Karatassos took him under his wing. "Not only was he my first friend in this country," Albrecht recalled in an interview with the *Atlanta Journal-Constitution,* "he showed me the ropes of American culinary dining." In 1969 the two friends joined the staff at the Lodge of the Four Seasons in Lake Ozark, Missouri, with Karatassos serving as food and beverage manager and Albrecht as executive chef.

PANO'S AND PAUL'S OPENS

Karatassos and Albrecht decided in the late 1970s to open a restaurant together and began considering Sun Belt cities in which to locate, finally settling on Atlanta because, as Karatassos explained to the *Atlanta Journal-Constitution,* it was "the most success-oriented city in the South." At the time, Atlanta had a poor reputation as a restaurant town, boasting few notable examples of

fine dining. Karatassos and Albrecht looked to the affluent Buckhead district, taking a lease on a space in a West Paces Ferry Road shopping center in November 1978.

Following renovations, they opened the 160-seat Pano's and Paul's in January 1979 to critical acclaim. For several years every night was as crowded as a typical Saturday night for most restaurants. The décor was that of a 1920's Parisian club, a romantic atmosphere created by intimate booths and velvet drapes. In spite of the white-linen nature of the restaurant, the menu was hardly intimidating, a mix of American and continental fare, including fried onion rings, trout with fried capers and garlic mayonnaise, and the signature item, batter-fried cold water lobster tail with honey mustard and chutney sauce.

The second restaurant Karatassos and Albrecht opened, under the auspices of the Buckhead Life Restaurant Group, Inc., holding company they formed, came in 1981 when the owners of the Lenox Square Mall offered them an excellent deal on space. The result was the Fish Market, whose ornate décor—marble walls and antique furnishings—overshadowed its mall locale. Quickly earning a reputation as Atlanta's best seafood restaurant, it sat 128 and the menu featured a broad range of fresh fish, which were openly displayed to customers who could make their own selections. In order to ensure a supply of fresh fish for both the Fish Market and other BLRG restaurants to follow, Karatassos established a wholesale fish operation at this time.

103 WEST OPENS

A third BLRG restaurant followed just one year later with the opening of 103 West. Also boasting a luxurious décor, 103 West offered a French-influenced menu of American cuisine. Not only did it seat 225 in the main dining room, 103 West offered private dining facilities that would become a mainstay for private banquets. It quickly became the highest-volume property for BLRG. For the fourth BLRG restaurant, which opened in 1985, Karatassos turned to Northern Italian cuisine. Capriccio Ristorante was a 127-seat affair whose décor was reminiscent of an Italian garden, complete with marble columns and statues of the Greek gods.

After successfully launching four upscale restaurants, Karatassos looked to expand his customer base by creating a high-volume restaurant. The result was the November 1987 opening of the Buckhead Diner, the "Orient Express of diners," as Karatassos described it, replete with plenty of neon, stainless-steel, and mahogany. The trade publication *Restaurant/Hotel Design International* granted its top design award to the

KEY DATES

1979: Pano's & Paul's opens in Atlanta's Buckhead district.
1981: The Fish Market opens.
1982: The company opens 103 West.
1987: The Buckhead Diner opens.
1989: New York–style steak house, Chops, is added.
1993: The Fish Market is relocated and renamed the Atlanta Fish Market.
1994: The Lobster Bar is added to Chops.
1996: Nava opens, featuring an upscale Southwestern menu.
2001: Greek restaurant Kyma opens.
2008: The company expands to Boca Raton, Florida, with Chops Lobster Bar.

establishment. Less pricey than its compatriots, the Buckhead Diner and its unique mix of stylish comfort foods generated enough sales to supplant 103 West as the highest-volume restaurant in the BLRG stable.

To close the 1980s, Karatassos tried his hand at the classic New York steak house, launching Chops in August 1989. He also upgraded 103 West, with interior renovations, improvements to the kitchen, and changes to the menu, undertaken by Belgian master chef Eddie Van Maele.

ECONOMIC DOWNTURN HALTS EXPANSION

The economy turned sour at the start of the 1990s, and BLRG put a halt to expansion for a few years. Business did not stand still, however. In 1991 Capriccio was revamped as Pricci, a Tuscan-style trattoria. With an average dinner check of $28 this was more in keeping with the times than the $45 average check of Capriccio's. As part of the redesign, the dining room was also enlarged to 170 seats and a corporate bakery was added to supply bread to all of the BLRG restaurants. A retail counter was also opened and quickly developed a following.

In 1993 Fish Market was relocated and renamed Atlanta Fish Market. That year BLRG also made its debut in midtown Atlanta, taking over Veni Vidi Vici, a three-year-old restaurant inspired by Italian cookbook author Marcella Hazan. The original restaurant struggled and after it was forced to close in 1992 because it could no longer pay its rent, BLRG took over. After a complete revamp of its operations, Veni Vidi

Vici reopened in January 1993.

Buckhead Bread Company was launched in 1994 to build on the success of the retail counter at the Pricci corporate bakery, as well as the growing business serving area coffeehouses. When it outgrew its space it was relocated elsewhere in Buckhead, where the Corner Café was also added. Just two years later a new 17,000-square-foot warehouse was needed to support the wholesale business.

Another change to the BLRG slate of restaurants came in 1996, when the space below Chops became available. The Lobster Bar was added as a complementary operation. When more space became available in the building that housed Chops and The Lobster Bar, and Karatassos took advantage of the opportunity to open the company's tenth operation. The result was the opening of Nava, a restaurant featuring Southwestern cuisine, in 1996. The new 120-seat restaurant, along with the wholesale bakery and seafood businesses and the business brought in by the Olympics held in Atlanta that year, helped BLRG increase revenues from $35 million in 1995 to $46 million in 1996.

END OF A PARTNERSHIP

Karatassos and Albrecht parted ways in 1998 after 30 years of working together. According to all reports, the parting was amicable—although Karatassos had developed a reputation for being a perfectionist. Albrecht indicated that he wanted to move to Destin, Florida, an area he enjoyed, to open a new restaurant and banquet-catering business. He remained a co-owner of Pano's & Paul's, however, which around this time received a much needed upgrading.

While Karatassos' longtime business partner may have made his departure, Karatassos' children were becoming involved in BLRG. Like his father, Pano Jr. was a graduate of the Culinary Institute of America and an aspiring chef; brother Niko would gravitate to the front of the house and corporate responsibilities; and their sister Ann would manage the executive payroll. Karatassos himself did not lack energy, either, still willing and able to work double shifts most days of the week, handling corporate affairs during the days and making the rounds of the restaurants, as needed, at night.

In 1999 Karatassos opened Bluepointe, a seafood restaurant. In that same year, BLRG branched out into a new direction, teaming up with Chicago-based Levy Restaurants to provide catering to the 20,000-seat Phillips Arena, serving about 1,800 people in the club section and a comparable number in the 90 corporate suites.

EXPANSION BEYOND ATLANTA

Because of his Greek heritage, Karatassos harbored a long-held dream to open a restaurant featuring Greek cuisine. That dream came true in 2001 with Kyma, an upscale seafood restaurant and ouzo bar. Another goal was to expand BLRG beyond Atlanta and perhaps nationally, focusing on the Chops and Atlanta Fish Market brands. Karatassos considered such growing Southeastern markets as Charlotte and Raleigh, in North Carolina, and Nashville, Tennessee, but instead took the first step in Boca Raton, Florida. In 2007 BLRG acquired Pete's Restaurant and, after some remodeling and development, opened Chops Lobster Bar in 2008.

In the meantime, BLRG's flagship restaurant, Pano's and Paul's, by that point an Atlanta institution, was set to relocate after turning 30 years old in early 2009. It was slated to open elsewhere in the Buckhead district, where it would likely continue its history of success.

Ed Dinger

PRINCIPAL SUBSIDIARIES

103 West; Bluepointe; Buckhead Bread Company & Corner Café; Chops; Chops Lobster Bar; Kyma; Nava; Panos & Paul's; Veni Vidi Vici.

PRINCIPAL COMPETITORS

Club Management Enterprises, L.L.C.; McCormick & Schmick's Seafood Restaurants, Inc.; Morton's Restaurant Group, Inc.

FURTHER READING

Cobb, Catherine R., "Karatassos Grows Company Nationally on His Own Terms," *Nation's Restaurant News*, June 25, 2007, p. 46.

———, "Pano Karatassos," *Nation's Restaurant News*, May 19, 2008, p. 124.

Crabb, Cheryl, "Pano Fishes in Suburbs," *Atlanta Business Journal*, January 3, 1997, p. 1A.

D'Ambrosio, Elizabeth, "Casual with Class: Buckhead Life Restaurant Group," *Restaurant Business*, September 20, 1988, p. 260.

Hayes, Jack, "Buckhead Life Restaurant Group," *Nation's Restaurant News*, January 30, 2006, p. 14.

———, "From Capriccio Emerges Pricci" *Nation's Restaurant News*, February 4, 1991.

———, "Karatassos' Buckhead Life Group to Expand Outside of Atlanta," *Nation's Restaurant News*, May 21, 2001, p. 6.

———, "Pano & Paul Part Company, End 30-Year Relationship," *Nation's Restaurant News*, August 17, 1998, p. 1.

Hutchcraft, Chuck, "A Family Life," *Restaurants & Institutions*, May 1, 2001, p. 125.

Kessler, John, "Paul's Gone, but Pano Carries on Regal Touch," *Atlanta Journal-Constitution*, November 27, 1998, p. Q1.

Maloof, Denise N., "Karatassos Helps Atlanta Become Known as a Restaurant Town," *Atlanta Journal-Constitution*, August 17, 1994, p. B8.

Walker, Tom, "Appetite for Success," *Atlanta Journal-Constitution*, July 27, 1989, p. B1.

Wolson, Shelley, "Sixth Sense," *Restaurant Business*, May 1, 1992, p. 126.

Cass Information Systems Inc.

13001 Hollenberg Drive
Bridgeton, Missouri 63044
U.S.A.
Telephone: (314) 506-5500
Fax: (314) 506-5955
Web site: http://www.cassinfo.com

Public Company
Incorporated: 1984
Employees: 659
Sales: $97.55 million (2007)
Stock Exchanges: NASDAQ
Ticker Symbol: CASS
NAICS: 518210 Data Processing, Hosting, and Related
     Services

■ ■ ■

Headquartered in Bridgeton, Missouri, Cass Information Systems Inc. is a leading payment and information
processing services provider. The company offers freight
invoice payment, audit, and rating services through its
Transportation Information Services unit. In addition,
its Utility Information Services unit is a leading provider
of energy-related information. Finally, the Telecom
Information Services unit of Cass Information Systems
provides expense management services. The company's
Cass Commercial Bank subsidiary provides commercial
banking services to privately owned firms within the
industries it serves, as well as to churches and ministries.

ORIGINS IN CASS AVENUE BANK

Although Cass Information Systems was incorporated in
1984, the company's roots date back to 1906, when
several businessmen established Cass Avenue Bank in St.
Louis, Missouri. Located in a rented storefront at 1462
Cass Avenue, the bank initially provided both retail and
commercial banking services. Over time, it focused
more on commercial services as the neighborhood surrounding the bank changed.

Cass Avenue Bank prospered during its early years.
In May 1927 the institution relocated to a building at
13th and Cass Avenue, from which it would operate
until 1974. Cass Avenue Bank became a trust company
in 1929, subsequently adopting the name Cass Bank &
Trust Co. The organization survived the stock market
crash of 1929, the Great Depression during the 1930s,
and the challenges of World War II.

The 1950s were a pivotal decade for Cass Bank &
Trust. It was during this time period that the institution
began to evolve from a community bank into a diversified financial services provider serving other area
businesses. In particular, Cass began serving the
transportation industry, which was flourishing in the
geographic area that surrounded the bank.

During 1956, its 50th anniversary year, Cass
introduced its Freight Payment Plan, which helped
trucking companies deal with complicated billing
requirements enforced by the Interstate Commerce
Commission (ICC). The plan initially required carriers
and shippers to each maintain accounts at the bank, and
allowed carriers' invoices to be paid like checks, drawn
against shippers' accounts.

In 1957 Cass removed the requirement that carriers maintain accounts at the bank. Instead, they could simply submit invoices to Cass, which would draw funds from the shipper's account and send a check to the carrier. This change allowed Cass to begin marketing itself to carriers nationwide, which was realized by the adoption of a national sales strategy in 1966. Cass eventually removed the requirement that shippers maintain accounts at the bank, and by 1967 the organization was competing against some of the nation's leading banks in the provision of this service.

In addition to freight payment, Cass also offered payroll processing services to companies in the St. Louis area. The organization was among the first U.S. banks to use computers for processing payroll checks. By 1967, Cass's Automated Payroll Plan had approximately 350 customers.

In the beginning, Cass's freight payment service was a manual one. As the service grew and was marketed nationally, the need for a more computerized approach was identified. Computerized reporting, which allowed Cass to generate more detailed reports, was added in 1970.

In 1971, a second Cass Bank & Trust Co. location was established in downtown St. Louis. Midway through the decade, the organization faced a number of challenges as its payment service grew, including duplicate invoicing on the part of carriers. Cass saw the need for a comprehensive transportation and freight accounting system to automate the payment process. In 1977 Larry Collett—who eventually became chairman and CEO of Cass Information Systems—was hired to develop the new system, which was introduced the following year.

In addition to the introduction of new systems and technology, the organization's business structure evolved as well. In 1980 the Cass Transportation Services unit was formed to separate transportation from commercial banking and payroll processing.

FORMATION OF CASS INFORMATION SERVICES INC.

The separation of banking operations from freight bill payment was taken a step further in 1984, when the organization formed Cass Information Systems Inc. Along with subsidiary Cass Bank & Trust Co. (which changed its name to Cass Commercial Bank in 1998), the new enterprise was owned by a holding company named Cass Commercial Corp.

The formation of Cass Information Systems allowed for the addition of new payable and transportation-related services. The shift came at a time when many industry banks were shedding their freight payment operations due to the growing complexity of the shipping industry. This spelled opportunity for Cass Information Systems, which began growing via acquisitions. In time, freight payment services were acquired from Bank of America, National Bank of Detroit, AmSouth, and others.

An auditing business named Traffic Associates Inc. was acquired in 1986. Two years later, Cass acquired Columbus, Ohio-based Comtrac Information Systems Inc. in a deal with the First National Bank of Chicago. The acquisition of Comtrac allowed Cass to offer freight rating services, and led to the establishment of Cass Rating Systems. Comtrac's facilities were converted into a freight payment services processing center.

During the late 1980s, the increasing number of companies that chose to outsource their freight payment function furthered growth. Cass Information Systems ended the decade by earning $3.62 million on revenues of $23.11 million in 1989. The company's earnings represented 67 percent of Cass Commercial's $5.39 million in earnings. The previous year, Cass Information had contributed $3.22 million to Cass Commercial's earnings of $4.91 million.

The company ushered in the 1990s with an important leadership change. In addition to heading Cass Information Systems, Larry Collett was named president and CEO of holding company Cass Commercial Corp. in 1990, succeeding Harry Krieg. By August 1990, Cass Information counted a number of major companies among its customer base, including Sears, Dow Chemical, and M&M Mars.

A major, but short-lived, change followed in 1991, when Cass Information Systems changed its name to Cass Logistics Inc. as part of an effort to provide a broader range of transportation-related information

```
┌─────────────────────────────────────────┐
│                                          │
│              KEY DATES                   │
│                   ■                      │
│  ─────────────────────────────────────   │
│  1906:  Cass Avenue Bank is formed in    │
│         St. Louis, Missouri.             │
│  1929:  Cass Avenue Bank becomes Cass    │
│         Bank & Trust Co.                 │
│  1956:  The company introduces its       │
│         Freight Payment Plan and         │
│         celebrates 50 years of           │
│         operations.                      │
│  1984:  Cass Information Systems Inc.     │
│         is formed.                       │
│  1991:  Cass Information Systems changes  │
│         its name to Cass Logistics Inc.  │
│  1994:  Another name change occurs when  │
│         Cass Logistics reverts back to   │
│         Cass Information Systems Inc.     │
│  1996:  Parent Cass Commercial Corp.     │
│         begins trading on the NASDAQ.    │
│  1998:  Cass Bank & Trust Co. changes    │
│         its name to Cass Commercial Bank.│
│  2000:  Cass Commercial Corp. changes    │
│         its name to Cass Information      │
│         Systems Inc.                     │
│  2001:  Company relocates to new         │
│         headquarters facility in the     │
│         northeast suburbs of Columbus,   │
│         Ohio.                            │
│                                          │
└─────────────────────────────────────────┘
```

services. Cass Logistics ended 1991 with revenues of $26 million. By 1992 the company had an estimated 26 percent share of the freight payment market, and was processing approximately 18 million transactions per year, worth $4 billion.

In June 1992, Larry Collett assumed the additional role of chairman at Cass Commercial Corp., succeeding Harry Krieg. That year, the workforce at Cass Logistics included 450 people. Of these, 290 were based at the company's headquarters. It also was in 1992 that plans were formed to move the company's headquarters to a building in Bridgeton, Missouri, which had been home to Hewlett-Packard. In addition to working with about 22,000 carriers, the company's customer base had expanded to include more *Fortune* 500 firms, such as Nabisco, Nestlé, Hershey, and Monsanto.

When regulatory and technical roadblocks hindered efforts to implement the company's broader logistics services strategy, Cass Logistics changed its name back to Cass Information Systems Inc. in 1994. In June of that year, the company acquired a major competitor, snapping up the First National Bank of Boston's Freight Management Division for $1.25 million. On July 1, 1996, parent Cass Commercial Corp. began trading on the NASDAQ National Market under the symbol

CASS. This milestone was achieved during the company's 90th anniversary year.

FOCUS ON ENERGY

As Cass Information Systems headed into the second half of the decade, it was serving more than 2,000 customers, including 109 *Fortune* 500 enterprises. In addition, the company was processing about 20 million invoices per year, with a collective value of approximately $6 billion. As rising energy costs came to the forefront, Cass capitalized on the situation and developed the Utility Payable Division in 1998. Cass sought to use its technology to help companies with multiple locations in different geographic regions, and served by multiple utilities, to determine how much they were spending on energy and negotiate better rates.

The utility business of Cass Information Systems was especially important in the wake of deregulation, which allowed the purchase of energy nationwide, as opposed to buying it only from a local utility. Initial customers for this service included The Gap, The Limited, Church's Chicken, Popeye's Chicken & Biscuits, America's Favorite Chicken, and CVS Revco.

As the 1990s came to a close, Cass Information Systems was embracing the Internet as a key element of its product mix. Accordingly, the company moved its services onto a web-based platform in 1999, making access easier for customers. Cass bought back 120,000 shares of its common stock in August, and ended the year by revealing plans to buy back up to 200,000 additional shares in 2000.

Cass ushered in the new millennium with a major change, as Cass Commercial Corp. changed its name to Cass Information Systems Inc. in January 2000. This was a reflection of the former subsidiary's importance to the larger business. Significant growth began to occur within Cass's Utility Payable Division during the early years of the new century. In August 2000, the Utility Navigator division of White Plains, New York-based InSITE Services Inc. was acquired, expanding the company's capabilities in utility processing systems and services.

One year later, Cass's utilities arm, then known as its Utility Information Systems Division, was processing some 2.5 million invoices annually, worth $2 billion. At that time, the company relocated to a new, expanded headquarters facility in the northeast suburbs of Columbus, Ohio. Spanning 45,500 square feet, the new facility included a state-of-the-art data processing center and a wide range of new equipment.

PREPARING FOR THE FUTURE

Beyond advances in its utilities business, 2001 also was an important year at Cass Information Systems on the new product side. That year, the company unveiled a new Transportation/Financial Analysis reporting system. Cass called the new Internet-based product, which gave customers unprecedented tools for data analysis and decision making, the most significant introduction in the company's history to date.

Heading into the middle of the decade, growth continued at Cass Information Systems. In 2004 the company acquired Greenville, South Carolina-based ProfitLab Inc., a management and consulting firm serving the telecommunications industry.

In December 2005, Cass sold the business assets of its Government e-Management Solutions Inc. subsidiary, a software firm serving the government sector, to Ottawa, Ontario, Canada-based N. Harris Computer Corp. for $7 million. Heading into 2006, Cass Information Systems was processing more than $15 billion in invoices per year. By this time the company had processing centers located in St. Louis; Boston; Greenville, South Carolina; and Columbus, Ohio.

In April, Chief Financial Officer Eric Brunngraber, who had joined the company in 1979, was named to the new position of president and chief operating officer. Three months later, Cass was added to the Russell 2000 Index, which ranked the largest U.S. stocks based on market capitalization. In August, Cass acquired Wellington, Kansas-based NTransit Inc.'s auditing services, bolstering its offerings in the area of transportation information services.

Heading into 2008, Cass was benefiting from strong growth within its utility services arm. Strong performance in this area helped push the company's revenue up 8 percent in 2007, from $82.1 million in 2006 to $88.7 million. Net income for the year surged 18 percent, rising from $15.1 million to $17.8 million. A leadership change occurred in July 2008, when Eric Brunngraber was promoted to CEO, succeeding a retiring Larry Collett, who remained chairman. Brunngraber led Cass Information Systems toward the 21st century's second decade in a strong position. From its small start in the freight payment field during the 1950s, the company had evolved into an industry leader that made approximately $22 billion in payments for its clients each year.

Paul R. Greenland

PRINCIPAL SUBSIDIARIES

Cass Commercial Bank.

PRINCIPAL OPERATING UNITS

Telecom Information Services; Transportation Information Services; Utility Information Services.

PRINCIPAL COMPETITORS

C.H. Robinson Worldwide Inc.; Data2Logistics; U.S. Bancorp.

FURTHER READING

"Cass Commercial Corp. Becomes Cass Information Systems, Inc.; Parent Merges with Its Fast-Growing Technology Subsidiary," *Business Wire,* January 16, 2001.

"Cass Commercial Corporation to Begin Trading July 1 on NASDAQ National Market," *PR Newswire,* July 1, 1996.

"Cass Information Systems Inc. Releases Major Internet Reporting Service; New System Is 'Most Significant' Product Release in CIS History," *Business Wire,* May 17, 2001.

Donaldson, Rob, "Collett Replaces Krieg as Cass Commercial Chairman," *St. Louis Business Journal,* June 15, 1992.

"Dramatic Growth in Utility Information Systems Division Spurs Move of Cass Information Systems to Larger Headquarters in Columbus, Ohio," *Business Wire,* August 1, 2001.

The History of Cass, St. Louis, Mo.: G. Bradley Publishing Inc., 2006.

Manning, Margie, "Cass Banks on Utilities, Freight," *St. Louis Business Journal,* February 9, 1998.

Miller, Patricia, "Cass Carves Niche Handling Freight Bills for Companies," *St. Louis Business Journal,* March 23, 1992.

Sahm, Cathy, "Collett Wearing Two Hats, CEO of Cass Commercial," *St. Louis Business Journal,* August 20, 1990.

Ce De Candy Inc.

———— ■ ————

1091 Lousons Road
Union, New Jersey 07083-5029
U.S.A.
Telephone: (908) 964-0660
Fax: (908) 964-0911
Web site: http://www.smarties.com

Private Company
Incorporated: 1949
Employees: 250
Sales: $30 million (2007 est.)
NAICS: 311330 Confectionery Manufacturing from
　　Purchased Chocolate

■ ■ ■

Ce De Candy Inc. is a privately held candy manufacturer based in Union, New Jersey, best known for the Smarties brand of small, round, artificially fruit-flavored tablets packaged in cellophane rolls. In Canada and about 17 other countries they are sold as Rockets because of a trademark conflict with Nestlé. The busiest times of the year are centered around the Easter, Valentine's Day, and Halloween holidays. All told, Ce De Candy turns out 2.5 billion rolls of Smarties each year, and claims that if the discs were laid end to end they would stretch around the earth more than three times. Core customers for Smarties are older than the five- to nine-year-old demographic that might be expected, with marketing studies revealing that 12- to 18-year-olds are in fact the primary consumers.

Other Ce De products include Bubble Gum Smarties, Tropical Smarties, Easter Smarties, X-Treme Sour Smarties, Smarties Parties, Smarties Mega Lollies, Smarties Double Lollies, Smarties Pops, Love Hearts, Candy Money, and Candy Lipsticks. Manufacturing plants are operated in Union, New Jersey, and Newmarket, Ontario, Canada, where a sales office is also maintained. The Canadian plant supplies about 40 percent of the Smarties sold in the United States, especially during Halloween. Wholesale customers include big-box merchandisers Wal-Mart and Target, warehouse clubs Costco and BJ's, drugstore chains such as Rite Aid and Walgreens, as well as convenience stores and dollar outlet stores. Ce De Candy is owned and operated by the Dee family.

ORIGINS

Ce De Candy was founded by Edward Dee, who was born in England and whose family was involved in the candy business. In 1933 his family had joined forces with Matlow Brothers, which had been established in London five years earlier to make table jelly and jelly candies, to share a small factory. Dee's father and uncle, with cousins Alfred and Maurice Matlow, worked for the new company that resulted from this partnership, named Swizzels Limited. It focused on the production of fizzy sweets in compressed tablet form, called Fizzers, which became very popular in England at the time.

Due to World War II and the bombing of London, Matlow Brothers and Swizzels relocated their operations to a former textile mill in Derbyshire. Gradually the two companies would merge their operations, eventually becoming a single entity, Swizzels Matlow Ltd. Following the war, the company looked to expand to other countries. Thus, Edward Dee and Maurice Matlow were dispatched in 1949 to the United States to establish an operation in New Jersey. Dee, around 24 years of age, decided he was better off striking out on his own, however, and soon left.

Dee launched his own candy company, Ce De Candy, renting a small garage in Bloomfield, New Jersey, and outfitting it with a small disc press and a wrapping machine. Here he developed a product similar to Fizzers. He eliminated the bicarbonate, which gave Fizzers its fizz, and instead of sugar relied on dextrose to create a small disc-shaped candy that he wrapped in cellophane. For the name of his product he chose Smarties, which was also the name Rowntree and Macintosh in England was using for a shell-encased chocolate candy similar to M&Ms that it sold in England and Canada. Unfortunately for Rowntree and Macintosh, the company failed to trademark the Smarties name in the United States. The memorable name would give Ce De Candy an edge in the fight with Swizzels Matlow in the candy wafer niche.

The eight original colors of Smarties were red, yellow, orange, green, purple, pink, light brown, and dark brown. They were sold in bulk in display boxes, retailing for one cent per roll. Edward Dee added other products in the 1950s, including candy necklaces, sold 48 to a display box, with 12 boxes in each case. They retailed for five cents, as did boxes of Popeye Candy Cigarettes, which featured the likeness of the popular Popeye cartoon character. The company would also offer wearable candy rings, candy lipsticks, Moondrops (essentially large Smarties with a candy coating), Big Ben Hard Candy Rolls, and lollipops, as well as plastic jet planes sold in display boxes suitable for the display cases of candy stores and other retailers. Ce De Candy was the first to sell candy necklaces in the United States, originally imported from Holland. Because they were such a generic product, and not protected by trademark like Smarties, candy contractors in the Far East soon imitated them. The quality of the imitations was poor, however, and Ce De Candy continued to rely on its Dutch supplier for many years.

MOVING INTO NEW QUARTERS

After about three years operating out of a garage, Ce De Candy moved its operations to a small factory in Elizabeth, New Jersey, which it shared with a biscuit company. In 1963 the business had grown enough that it moved to a newly constructed building in Union, New Jersey. The company rented the facility for the next 30 years before finally purchasing it. In the late 1960s Ce De Candy opened a factory in downtown Toronto to supply the Canadian market.

The move to Canada also eliminated the nettlesome problem of the volatile value of the U.S. dollar. This was an issue because in Canada business was only done through a single distributor who was quoted a price at the beginning of the year that remained steady for the next 12 months. By operating in Canada, Ce De Candy could do business in Canadian dollars and eliminate a good deal of uncertainty in its finances. Also in the 1960s Edward Dee established Northern Expediting Corp. to buy mill rolls of cellophane for Smarties wrappers. The company also supplied other candy makers, and in the beginning this income helped to subsidize the operations of Ce De Candy.

Like many candy companies, Ce De Candy over the years introduced items that enjoyed short-term success and were pulled from the market after their popularity faded. For a time the company sold what it called Spare Tires, large dextrose rings in Smartie colors. Around 1980 it sold Sweet Feet, feet-shaped, wine gum candy, marketed as "The Only feet you can eat." They were similar to the gummy candies of a later year. Ce De Candy was also ahead of the times in the 1980s when it began selling Mega-Sour candy rolls through the convenience store channel. The product was pulled because Americans were not accustomed to sour candy, although that would later change and the sour category would become a staple of the candy industry.

The flagship Smarties product, in the meantime, maintained its place as a perennial favorite, one of the top-selling non-chocolate candies in the United States. Although the taste would remain the same, the look evolved due to changing government regulations on chemicals and additives. Thus, the Smarties of the 1950s were brighter in shade and over the years became more pastel in color. In addition, the brand was gradually extended to include a host of new flavors, such as tropical fruits and extremely sour flavors, as well as Easter colors and a bubble gum variety.

THE NEXT GENERATION JOINS THE COMPANY

Edward Dee's sons became involved in Ce De Candy in the 1970s. Jonathan Dee joined the company in 1974

```
┌─────────────────────────────────────────────┐
│                                               │
│              KEY DATES                         │
│                   ▪                            │
│  ─────────────────────────────────────────    │
│                                               │
│  1933: Dee family cofounds Swizzels Limited in │
│        England.                                │
│  1949: Edward Dee starts Ce De Candy in Bloom- │
│        field, New Jersey, garage to produce    │
│        Smarties candy.                         │
│  1963: Company moves to Union, New Jersey.     │
│  1991: Smarties and Mr. T. team up for youth-  │
│        oriented charitable efforts.            │
│  1996: Swizzels Matlow sells its U.S. operation│
│        to the Dee family.                      │
│  2004: Company launches get-out-the-vote       │
│        initiative.                             │
│  2005: Mega Smarties introduced.               │
│                                               │
└─────────────────────────────────────────────┘
```

and by the end of the decade replaced his father as president. Edward Dee would remain chairman, a title he would continue to hold well into the next century. Also in the 1970s Michael Dee began working for Ce De Candy, although he would come and go over the years. A third brother, Joel, was also employed by the company, but he eventually left to start a Dee family-owned organic and natural foods business in California called Edward & Sons.

The Canadian operation vacated its century-old Toronto building in the early 1990s and moved to the Toronto suburbs, establishing a sales and production facility in Newmarket. The downtown five-story Toronto property was then taken over by developers who gutted it to create a residential loft property called the Candy Factory. Another major change to the Ce De Candy operations came in 1996 when after nearly five decades of competition the partners who owned Swizzels sold the U.S. operation to the Dee family. In reality it was more of an accommodation, with Ce De Candy agreeing to stay out of Europe and Swizzels Matlow agreeing to stay out of the United States. Ce De Candy not only solidified its place in the North American market but also picked up a manufacturing plant in Charleston, South Carolina, from Swizzels Matlow.

Other changes were also taking place in the industry and within the company. The days of corner stores peddling penny candies were long gone, and with their passing, Ce De Candy's customer base consolidated into a few large customers, mostly major chain stores. Promotional efforts took on greater importance as a result. In 1991 the company teamed up with one of the era's most popular celebrities with children, Mr. T., the action hero of television and film.

Together they raised money for the Children's Defense Fund, and established Crusade for Kids, a program that promoted candy, such as Smarties, as an alternative to drugs. Also during his visits to city schools, Mr. T. urged young people to stay in school. A company-sponsored essay contest also offered scholarships to deserving students.

CHANGES IN PACKAGING

Although the look of Smarties changed over the years, the wrapper had remained consistent. In the late 1990s, however, Northern Expediting decided to switch from cellophane to polyvinyl chloride (PVC), which was less expensive per square inch. Just two years later, however, the company concluded that in this case the old ways were best, and whatever savings that may have been realized in the switch to PVC were lost due to mis-wraps and machine downtime, attributable in large part to static buildup caused by PVC, which affected the ability of wrapped candy to be carried by conveyors and properly drop into hoppers. Machine operators also had to contend with frequent, unpleasant electric shocks. Cellophane, on the other hand, did not have static buildup problems and if it failed to run properly it was generally the fault of the machine. Moreover, cellophane was suited to all of the different generations of the twist-wrap machines used by Ce De Candy and Northern Expediting. Thus, after two years of using PVC, the companies returned to cellophane.

The switch was made in time for Ce De Candy to celebrate its 50th anniversary by sprucing up its packaging with a move from one color to four. Northern Expediting wanted to make use of an Aquaflex press that was underutilized and could be dedicated to the task every day, but it had difficulty keeping four-color jobs in register. The press was retrofitted with improved heaters and ultraviolet dryers and other problems were addressed until it was turning out the celebratory wrappers at a fast and consistent pace, thus providing Northern Expediting with a profitable piece of equipment for ongoing use.

By the start of the new century, Edward Dee had turned over complete control of the business to his sons, with Jonathan Dee serving as president and Michael Dee as vice-president, although he retained the title of chairman. It was not a seamless transition, however, as the elder Dee explained to the *Star-Ledger* of Newark, New Jersey. "Even though you say they're in charge, it's very difficult when you would see something that you didn't like, not to say anything," he said, adding, "But you have to do it, because you read about all these companies where the original founder doesn't want to let go of the reins and if the kids are capable, they go somewhere else. So I didn't want to have that and we didn't."

What Dee left his offspring was a stable company generating sales in excess of $50 million a year. The third generation of the Dee family was also involved, with Edward Dee's granddaughters, Sarah and Jessica, working for the family business as well and preparing to one day take charge. In addition, Ce De Candy enjoyed an extremely low rate of turnover, resulting in a workforce that included many people with tenures of 20 to 25 years, and an enhanced family atmosphere.

ADDING NEW PRODUCTS IN THE 21ST CENTURY

Both the Union and Newmarket plants were expanded, allowing Ce De Candy to sell the South Carolina plant in 2004. Although the company's core business remained traditional Smarties, it continued to add new products in the new century. In 2005 it unveiled three new products: Mega Smarties, larger versions of the original Smarties; Bubblegum Smarties, offering discs of bubble gum instead of flavored sugar; and Mega Smarties Sweet and Sour Gummies, large sugar-coated, pastel-colored gummies. The company also continued to offer candy necklaces, but over the years had grown disenchanted with its Dutch supplier, the ownership of which had changed hands numerous times. In 2008 Ce De Candy took its formula to a new contract manufacturer and new candy necklaces became available shortly before Halloween of that year.

In the 21st century, Ce De Candy also continued to tie Smarties to worthwhile community efforts, as the company had previously done in the early 1990s with Mr. T. At this time it focused on encouraging young people to vote. In 2004 it teamed up with the nonprofit "Rock the Vote" organization and MTV, and launched a "Smarties Vote" initiative, which including Smarties packaged in rolls with "Rock the Vote" printed on the side, and T-shirts declaring "Don't Be Stupid: Smarties Vote."

With the new century also came fresh challenges. In early 2006 the Food and Drug Administration announced new bioterrorism regulations that had to be in place within six months. These regulations called for a system that was able to track raw materials from the time of arrival until a finished product reached the customer. Ce De Candy implemented a tracking system that not only allowed it to comply with the new regulations, but also improved productivity and the accuracy of the manufacturing processes. There was every reason to expect that this innovative spirit, coupled with a respect for tradition, would allow Ce De Candy to continue to make a profitable business out of the manufacture and sale of small pressed discs of flavored dextrose.

Ed Dinger

PRINCIPAL COMPETITORS

Nestlé USA Inc.; New England Confectionery Company.

FURTHER READING

Burrows, Kate, "Family-Focused," *US Business Review,* February 2006, p. 78.

"Cellophane Brings Trouble-Free Wrapping for Smarties," *Candy Industry,* June 2000, p. 76.

"How I Passed Control to My Sons," *Newark (N.J.) Star-Ledger,* June 16, 2006, p. 50.

Schiavo, Brian, "Getting Smart with Traceability," *Food Logistics,* April 2007, p. 44.

Tarbous, Ken, "New Jersey-based Maker of Smarties Candy Battles Imitators," *East Brunswick (N.J.) Home News Tribune,* October 3, 2004.

Cerebos Gregg's Ltd.

———— ■ ————

291 East Tamaki Road
East Tamaki
Auckland,
New Zealand
Telephone: (64 09) 274 2777
Fax: (64 09) 274 2775
Web site: http://www.cerebos.co.nz

Wholly Owned Subsidiary of Cerebos Pacific Ltd.
Incorporated: 1984
Employees: 440
Sales: NZD 546.52 million ($423.1 million) (2007 est.)
NAICS: 311230 Breakfast Cereal Manufacturing; 311421 Fruit and Vegetable Canning; 311423 Dried and Dehydrated Food Manufacturing

■ ■ ■

Cerebos Gregg's Ltd. is the New Zealand arm of Singapore-based foods group Cerebos Pacific. Based in Auckland, Cerebos Gregg's oversees one of New Zealand's leading brand families. The company's brands include flagship brand Gregg's, producer of a wide range of foods such as sauces and gravies, herbs and spices, pastes and meal preparation products, and desserts and coffees. Other brands include Raro powdered fruit-flavored drinks; Bisto, a line of instant gravy mixes; and Whitlocks sauces and chutneys. Coffee and tea are an important part of the Cerebos Gregg's business. The company not only produces coffees, it also sells its coffees directly to consumers, through the 50-café Robert Harris Tea and Coffee chain, as well as Auckland's

Atomic Coffee café and the Wellington-based Caffe L'affare. Both of these products are also sold through retail and restaurant and catering channels. The company operates several factories in New Zealand, both directly and through its subsidiaries. While Cerebos Gregg's operates as an independent business, it is part of the larger Cerebos Australia and New Zealand division of Cerebos Pacific with sister company Cerebos Australia. In 2007, Cerebos Gregg's posted revenues of $423 million. George Crocker is the company's chief executive officer.

ORIGINS IN THE 19TH CENTURY

Both the Cerebos and the Gregg's names had their origins in the 19th century. The Cerebos business was the more international of the two, tracing its own history to England in the 1820s. During that period, H. W. Brand, who served as the royal chef to King George IV, concocted a chicken-based beverage meant to stimulate the king's fragile health. After leaving the king's service, Brand set up his own business, and began selling Brand's Essence of Chicken as a health remedy. Brand's wife sold the business to John James Mason in 1893; four years later, Mason brought in a partner, Thomas Dence. The company then took on the name of Brand & Co. Ltd. The Dence family emerged as the controlling force in the company throughout the first half of the next century.

Brand & Co. began extending its product line at the beginning of the 20th century. The company added a variety of other meat-based "essences," including veal, mutton, and beef. The company also marketed a product known as "Meat Juice." While continuing to

COMPANY PERSPECTIVES

When opportunity knocks, it's a chance for people to use their talents to create rewarding outcomes. At Cerebos, we recognise that helping people to pursue opportunities can improve job satisfaction and boost productivity. We encourage our employees to seek out what they see as opportunities and identify them to others who can help them achieve their goals. In other words, it's OK to put your hand up for something around here. The opportunities we actively encourage include, internal promotion, experience in different areas of the business, professional training and personal development, and an environment where "having a go" is supported. Cerebos is a growing business with exciting plans for accelerated growth. We have both the backing of a multi-national organisation and the freedom to act with a great deal of autonomy. We call it the best of both worlds.

target the invalid market for these products, the company also expanded its food production into a variety of other areas. By the late 1920s, the Brand & Co. brand family included a wide range of puddings, sauces, pickles and condiments, sandwich pastes, and picnic foods. This period also saw the debut of the A1 brand. In the late 1920s, the company added a French subsidiary as well.

Brand & Co. went public in 1949. While advances in medicine and pharmaceuticals marginalized the company's "foods for invalids" product lines, the company successfully expanded its food production into other areas, such as baby foods and meat and fish pastes. Brand's Essence of Chicken nonetheless remained an important part of the company's offering, particularly in the Asian regions, into the 21st century. By the 1950s, the strength of both the Brand and A1 brand names made the company an attractive buyout target. This was accomplished in 1959, when Cerebos offered £3 million to take over the company's operations.

ORIGINS OF THE CEREBOS BRAND

Cerebos itself had by then grown into an internationally operating food group. Cerebos originated in France in 1892. A French scientist had developed a method of producing a free-flowing table salt through the addition of calcium phosphate to ordinary salt. The new product was given the name Cerebos, incorporating *Ceres,* the name of a Roman goddess, and *os,* French for bone, because of the importance of both calcium and phosphate for strong bone growth. Cerebos initially was manufactured at a factory in Paris.

By 1894, the Cerebos brand had reached Great Britain, where a new company was established, Cerebos Ltd. That company became responsible both for the original Parisian factory and British operations. At the beginning of the 20th century, Cerebos acquired a United Kingdom-based salt works in Greatham. By 1919, the company had expanded its U.K. sale operations, acquiring the Middlewich Salt Company Ltd. Cerebos's international expansion was facilitated by the British Empire's wide reach. Canada became a major market for the company at the dawn of the 20th century as well. At first, Cerebos exported its U.K. production to that market; in 1920, however, the company decided to build a dedicated production facility in Toronto.

Cerebos began introducing other products starting in the 1920s. One of its most successful product launches was the Bisto brand of instant gravies. Developed in 1908 by two British housewives, the Bisto brand quickly grew into a highly popular timesaving product. Under Cerebos, sales of Bisto grew so strongly that by 1930 they far outweighed its Cerebos salt sales. By then, the company had added a number of other products. In Paris, for example, the company launched production of mustard, among other condiments. Further expansion came in 1939, when the company acquired the pepper and spice business of John Crampton & Co.

The post–World War II era was a time of rapid expansion for the company. Cerebos began adding a number of foreign manufacturing and sales subsidiaries. The company entered the New Zealand market starting in the late 1940s, with the purchase of a stake in Dominion Salt Ltd. in 1948. By 1953, the company had established a dedicated New Zealand subsidiary to oversee its growing business there. In 1961, Cerebos New Zealand acquired Whittome Stevenson & Co. That purchase added new manufacturing capacity for the company's New Zealand operations, enabling Cerebos to begin manufacturing directly for the New Zealand market. In 1967, Whittome Stevenson changed its name to Cerebos Foods (New Zealand).

Cerebos itself became the object of a takeover offer at the end of the 1960s. Struggling to maintain profitability after a decade of rapid growth, Cerebos agreed to a £61 million takeover by bakery products group Rank Hovis McDougall (RHM) in 1968. Under new ownership, Cerebos Foods (New Zealand) continued its own

```
┌─────────────────────────────────────────────┐
│                                               │
│              KEY DATES                        │
│                  ■                            │
│ ─────────────────────────────────────────    │
│                                               │
│  1861:  William Gregg establishes a merchant  │
│         and coffee roasting business in       │
│         Dunedin, New Zealand.                 │
│  1894:  Cerebos, a producer of free-flowing   │
│         salt, is created.                     │
│  1953:  Cerebos establishes a New Zealand     │
│         subsidiary.                           │
│  1961:  Cerebos New Zealand acquires          │
│         Whittome Stevenson & Co.              │
│  1964:  Gregg's Ltd. is formed as a holding   │
│         company for Gregg's food and          │
│         beverage operations.                  │
│  1967:  Whittome Stevenson changes its name   │
│         to Cerebos Foods (New Zealand).       │
│  1984:  Gregg's merges with Cerebos New       │
│         Zealand and goes public as Cerebos    │
│         Gregg's.                              │
│  1990:  Cerebos Gregg's acquires Robert       │
│         Harris Tea & Coffee Specialists       │
│         Limited.                              │
│  2000:  Cerebos Gregg's and sister company    │
│         Cerebos Australia join forces with    │
│         Cerebos Pacific organization, forming │
│         a new division, Cerebos Australia     │
│         and New Zealand.                      │
│  2006:  Cerebos Gregg's acquires Caffe        │
│         L'affare chain and restaurant.        │
│                                               │
└─────────────────────────────────────────────┘
```

growth. In 1969, for example, the company formed a table salt packing joint venture, Cerebos-Skellerup, to produce packaged salt for the New Zealand market. The company then moved its operations to larger facilities in East Tamaki. Cerebos Foods also grew through its share of the Dominion Salt operations, which set up a subsidiary on New Zealand's North Island in 1972. The following year, the new business built a salt refinery complex, featuring both solar and vacuum drying methods, at Mt. Manganui.

FORMING CEREBOS GREGG'S IN 1984

In the early 1980s RHM restructured its operations, setting up a new dedicated company to oversee Cerebos's Asian operations, Cerebos Pacific, in 1981. Cerebos Pacific at first was set up as a management vehicle for Cerebos's operations in Australia, New Zealand, Malaysia, Thailand, Taiwan, and elsewhere. By 1982, Cerebos Pacific had gone public, and had acquired all of RHM's operations in the Southeast Asian and Australasian markets. RHM nonetheless remained majority shareholder in Cerebos Pacific through the end of the decade.

Cerebos New Zealand operated more or less independently in its own market. The financial clout of its parent company enabled it to expand its presence in New Zealand. In 1984, the company acquired rival Gregg's Ltd. and went public as Cerebos Gregg's Ltd.

Gregg's was one of the largest and best-known food brands in New Zealand. The company stemmed from a merchant and coffee-roasting business set up by William Gregg in Dunedin in 1861. Gregg had emigrated from Northern Ireland to Australia in the early 1850s, joining the gold rush to the Ballarat gold fields. A gold strike in Dunedin, however, encouraged Gregg to move to New Zealand at the beginning of the 1860s. Gregg soon abandoned the search for gold in favor of his growing food business, which expanded to include spices and general merchandise. Gregg later moved into the food import and export market as well.

Gregg's then launched its own food manufacturing operations, selling its coffees and other products under its own name. In the 1920s, Gregg's had outgrown its original status as a family-owned concern, and incorporated as a limited liability company. This led to a move to consolidate all of the company's operations into a single factory in Dunedin in 1925. The new facility also enabled the company to extend its product lines. In the 1930s, for example, the company added salad dressing mixes and custards, among other products.

The post–World War II era saw Gregg's emerge as a major New Zealand foods group. The company proved itself as something of an innovator. In 1955, the company launched a new instant pudding that became a hit among New Zealanders. At the same time, the group began developing what became a world first—instant coffee—introduced in the early 1960s. Gregg's also added a new fruit canning operation, Island Foods, based in the Cook Islands, in 1961. That company added its line of canned pineapple and citrus fruits. From that facility, Gregg's launched a new brand, Raro, a powdered fruit-flavored drink. In 1964, the company restructured its operations, setting up Gregg's Ltd. as the holding company for W. Gregg's and Island Foods.

A PERIOD OF GROWTH

Following the merger and its subsequent public offering, Cerebos Gregg's began developing its international sales as well. This led the company to establish a new export subsidiary in 1985. The company also stepped up its stake in the Dominion Salt Group, gaining control of 50 percent of that company's shares. Cerebos Gregg's also underwent a change in ownership, after Japan's Suntory group acquired RHM's stake in Cerebos Pacific in 1990. Cerebos Gregg's listing was subsequently removed from the New Zealand stock exchange, and Cerebos Gregg's became a 100 percent subsidiary of Cerebos Pacific.

Acquisitions helped support the company's growth into the 1990s, starting with the purchases of Food System NZ and Natural Nectar, both in 1986. At the same time, Cerebos Gregg's boosted its coffee operations. For a start, the company launched a new foil-pack instant coffee, known as Red Ribbon Roast. This brand was extended to include granulated coffee in 1991, followed by instant decaffeinated coffee in 1992. The granulated coffee was rebranded as Gregg's Rich Roast in the middle of the decade, and was then joined by a new freeze-dried coffee, Gregg's Café Gold, in 1995. Another extension of the Gregg's coffee range came in 2001, with the launch of the Gregg's Distinction instant coffee brand.

While coffee helped fuel the Gregg's brand, it was also helping to fuel the growth of Cerebos Gregg's. In 1990, the company acquired Robert Harris Tea & Coffee Specialists Limited. A native New Zealander, Robert Harris had been introduced to European-style roast coffee while serving in the New Zealand army in Italy during World War II. Harris returned to New Zealand with the project of developing his own roast coffee blend adapted to the New Zealand palate. By 1972, Harris had succeeded in developing his recipe, and he set up for business that year. Harris established his own café-style coffee shop, which grew to include its own food and snacks menu.

FUELED BY COFFEE IN THE 21ST CENTURY

Under Cerebos Gregg's, the Robert Harris café chain expanded strongly through the 1990s and into the new century. By about 2005, the Robert Harris chain had grown to 50 locations throughout New Zealand, and had also developed into a strong coffee and tea retail brand in its own right.

Cerebos Gregg's continued to invest in the New Zealand beverage market through the 1990s. The company created a joint venture with Rio Beverages in 1997, transferring part of its own fruit juice production to the new operation. The participation of Cerebos Gregg's in the joint venture proved short-lived, however, and the company sold its stake in Rio Beverages to Coca-Cola in 2002. During this period, the company shed a number of other brands in its family, including Sancho, sold in 1999, and Horleys, sold in 2001.

Cerebos Gregg's and sister company Cerebos Australia joined forces with the Cerebos Pacific organization, forming a new division, Cerebos Australia and New Zealand, in 2000. Nonetheless, both companies continued to operate independently in their own markets.

Cerebos Gregg's launched a number of new products during the decade, including a popular line of flavored and spicy pastes. The company put its instant beverage technology to work in other areas, launching the Slushy Powdered Beverage line in 2002, followed by the Wacko brand of powdered soft drinks in 2003.

Coffee continued to fuel part of the group's growth. In 2002, the company introduced a new retail coffee line, Robert Harris Premium. The company also sought new coffee brands, which led to the acquisition of Auckland's Atomic Café in 2005. Founded in 1992, Atomic Café had grown into one of New Zealand's leading organic and fair-trade coffee brands.

This acquisition was complemented in 2006 by the purchase of Wellington-based Caffe L'affare. Founded as a coffee shop in the 1990s, the company had begun supplying the national restaurant and catering market by the end of the decade. By 2001, Caffe L'affare had launched retail supermarket sales as well. The addition of Caffe L'affare enabled Cerebos Gregg's to extend its coffee operations into the fresh ground and premium ranges. Backed by the international operations of parent Cerebos Pacific, Cerebos Gregg's remained one of the leading food groups in New Zealand in the 21st century.

M. L. Cohen

PRINCIPAL SUBSIDIARIES

Atomic Coffee Roasters Ltd.; Caffe L'affare Limited; Dominion Salt Limited; Robert Harris Tea & Coffee Specialists Limited.

PRINCIPAL COMPETITORS

Goodman Fielder Proprietary Ltd.; Frucor Beverages Ltd.; Coca-Cola Amatil (NZ) Ltd.; Heinz Wattie's Ltd.; Manildra Group of Cos.; Kellogg (Australia) Pty. Ltd.; Sanitarium Health Food Co.; Just Water International Ltd.

FURTHER READING

"Cerebos Consolidates Foodservice Brands," *Hospitality,* March 19, 2004.

"Cerebos Gregg's Buys Caffe L'Affare," *Australasian Business Intelligence,* November 4, 2006.

"Cerebos Gregg's: Growth Through Innovation," *Australasian Business Intelligence,* October 4, 2005.

"Cerebos Secures L'Affare Brand, Restaurant," *Australasian Business Intelligence,* October 3, 2006.

The Cheesecake Factory Inc.

26901 Malibu Hills Road
Calabasas Hills, California 91301
U.S.A.
Telephone: (818) 871-3000
Fax: (818) 871-3001
Web site: http://thecheesecakefactory.com

Public Company
Incorporated: 1978
Employees: 29,400
Sales: $1.5 billion (2007)
Stock Exchanges: NASDAQ
Ticker Symbol: CAKE
NAICS: 722110 Full-Service Restaurants

■ ■ ■

The Cheesecake Factory Inc. runs 144 casual dining and upscale casual restaurants in 35 states that offer about 200 menu items ranging from sandwiches and salads to steaks and seafood, and cheesecake, which comes in about 40 varieties. Each restaurant has a unique design, but all are opulent and feature Las Vegas–style glitz. In addition to its flagship concept, the company operates 13 Grand Lux Cafés, and one RockSugar Pan Asian Kitchen. It has two bakery production facilities, one in California and one in North Carolina, which produce over 60 varieties of quality cheesecakes and other baked products. Additionally, the company licenses two bakery café outlets to another foodservice operator under The Cheesecake Factory Bakery Café trademark and sells its

cheesecakes online and to grocery stores and foodservice operators.

EARLY HISTORY AND GROWTH

Cheesecake first appeared in Greece at least 2,000 years ago and was originally made with cottage cheese. By the 1950s, when Evelyn Overton began making cheesecake in her basement in Detroit, cream cheese was the main ingredient. Evelyn's cheesecakes proved so popular with her friends and at bake sales that she and her husband, Oscar, started a bakery business. In 1972, the Overtons moved to the Woodland Hills suburb of Los Angeles and built a wholesale bakery, producing cheesecakes and other desserts for local restaurants.

In 1975, the bakery outgrew its quarters and moved into a larger facility in Woodland Hills, and David Overton, the Overtons' son, relocated to Los Angeles to work for the business full-time. In 1978, with backing from his parents, Overton opened a 100-seat restaurant and wholesale bakery in Beverly Hills featuring ten flavors of the Overtons' cheesecakes on its one-page menu. "We were completely naive about food service," Overton told Milford Prewitt in a 1995 article in *Nation's Restaurant News.* "We simply wanted to open a restaurant that would showcase our cheesecakes. At that time, most restaurateurs were using every excuse to explain why they could not carry our product, including expenses."

Evelyn's cheesecakes proved popular with California diners, and in 1983, Overton opened a second restaurant, in Marina del Rey. By 1987, the Beverly Hills shop was grossing $3 million a year, even without a bar area, with diners spending an average of $8 for dinner. The Marina del Rey location had a bar and combined indoor and outdoor seating for 250 people. With average checks of $11, that location grossed over $8 million in 1987. In fact, annual sales were increasing by 15 percent a year, and Overton opened a third restaurant, in Redondo Beach, south of Los Angeles. The company spent $2 million renovating the location into a 21,000-square-foot, 300-seat restaurant. The new unit was located on the waterfront at King's Harbor, a popular tourist destination.

EMPHASIS ON DESSERTS

The chain's one-page menu had expanded, offering items ranging from pizza to meatloaf to omelets to chicken tacos to baby back pork ribs. In the Marina del Rey kitchen, three prep cooks worked full-time, and separate lines handled broiling, sautéing, frying, and the oyster bar. However, the specialty of the house continued to be cheesecake—including fresh banana cream, southern pecan, Craig's crazy carrot cake, and brownie fudge—with 42 varieties baked at the company's facility in Woodland Hills.

Despite diets and health consciousness, 70 to 80 percent of the Cheesecake Factory customers ordered dessert. In a 1987 *Restaurant Business* article, Marina del Rey general manager Douglas Zeif told Dolores Long, "Dessert sales boost our check average by about 15 percent. We're just the opposite of most other dinner houses that don't promote desserts because they're anxious to turn the tables. But we want everybody eating cheesecake; the profit margin on this item is between 65 and 70 percent for us." The Cheesecake Factory's success directly contrasted with the country's eating habits. According to MRCA Information Services, which monitored in-home and away-from-home eating patterns, the total consumption of cheesecake in the United States fell a huge 27 percent between 1987 and 1988, with the big loser being the "plain" cheesecake.

To encourage diners in health-conscious California to order cheesecake, work shifts received incentives for the most cheesecake orders, especially for seasonal or special flavors, as well as for daily specials and new menu items. While the company introduced new flavors of cheesecake, strawberry was the favorite, followed by white chocolate raspberry truffle, chocolate mousse, white chocolate macadamia, and chocolate chip.

Although it concentrated on its restaurants, the company also sold a limited number of cheesecake flavors (chocolate chip, lemon twist) at the retail level. Customers included major restaurant chains in Southern California, such grocery store chains as Kroger's and Dominick's Finer Foods in Chicago, and food warehouse companies, such as the Price Club in San Diego.

EXPANDING BEYOND SOUTHERN CALIFORNIA

Overton began the decade by opening his fourth restaurant, at the Warner Center in Woodland Hills, California. In 1991, the chain took its successful concept across the continent, to Washington, D.C., for its first restaurant outside Southern California. The new location, in the fashionable Chevy Chase section of the District, followed the formula Overton described to Michael Hartnett in a 1993 *Restaurant Business* article: "Scour large metropolitan areas to find 'trophy sites' offering high visibility, easy access, and close proximity to traffic-builders like shopping centers and tourist attractions." Overton built his restaurants to seat between 250 and 750 people and designed them to fit the individual site, incorporating the view if there was one, or, if there was not, adding architectural features, such as sweeping staircases and dramatic lighting. The average cost for a new location, not counting the land, was $250 to $350 per square foot.

In 1992, Overton and his mother incorporated the company and took it public in September. The Cheesecake Factory's stock closed that first day at a price of a little over $18 a share. The company's profits that year were $4.7 million on sales of $51.9 million. Restaurant sales accounted for $42.8 million (82.5 percent of sales) and the wholesale bakery for $9.1 million. Annual sales at the five restaurants averaged $8.6 million, on an average check of $13.57.

In 1993 two more restaurants were opened in California (on the water in Newport Beach and in Brentwood) and, in November, the second unit outside of California was opened, in the Atlanta, Georgia, suburb of Buckhead. By opening three or four units a year, Overton hoped to generate sales increases of 25 percent per year, but easily surpassed this figure. The three new restaurants contributed to 1993 revenues of

KEY DATES

1972: Evelyn and Oscar Overton build a wholesale bakery in Los Angeles.

1975: The bakery moves to a larger facility and David Overton joins the business full-time.

1978: David Overton opens a restaurant and wholesale bakery in Beverly Hills, California.

1983: Overton opens a second restaurant, in Marina del Rey, California.

1988: The company opens a third restaurant in Redondo Beach, California.

1991: The chain takes its concept to Washington, D.C., to open the first restaurant outside of Southern California.

1992: The company incorporates and goes public.

1993: The company opens two more restaurants in California and one in Georgia.

1995: Gerald Deitchle succeeds William Kling as chief financial officer and senior vice-president; the company moves to new corporate headquarters in Calabasas, California.

1996: Evelyn Overton dies.

1998: The first Cheesecake Factory Express opens at the interactive DisneyQuest recreation center in Orlando, Florida.

1999: The Grand Lux Café opens in the Venetian Resort in Las Vegas, Nevada; the company partners with Nabisco on a dual-branded Oreo cookie cheesecake sandwich sold through vending machines.

2001: The second and third Grand Lux Café locations open.

2006: The company opens a second bakery facility in North Carolina.

2008: The company opens its first RockSugar Pan Asian concept restaurant.

nual food trips Overton made with his staff to New York and Boston. The list of offerings included pasta, burritos and fajitas, steaks, seafood, ribs, pizza, burgers, omelets, salads, sandwiches, and vegetarian dishes. In addition to cheesecakes, dessert options ranged from hot fudge sundaes to fresh fruit to cakes to apple dumplings.

It could not be determined how much the Cheesecake Factory's growth contributed to the comeback of cheesecake, but MRCA Information Services reported a 4.9 percent increase in consumption between 1988 and 1993. Furthermore, in its "1993 Menu Census," *Restaurants & Institutions* magazine found that cheesecake was the most offered dessert on the menus of local fast-food, family-style or white tablecloth restaurants, and local bakery/cafés. Cheesecake was on the menu of 64 percent of the restaurants in the country; apple pie appeared on the menu of 61.5 percent.

The survey also found that cheesecake was the fifth best-selling menu item. It was outranked only by french fries, two chicken dishes, and pizza, with pizza beating cheesecake by only one percentage point. Further, the popularity of cheesecake was not limited to restaurant diners. The 1993 Retail Bakery Study conducted by *Bakery Production and Marketing* reported that 54 percent of retail bakers across the country offered cheesecake, and in-store bakers reported increased sales of prepackaged, frozen cheesecakes. *Bakery* estimated that sales of cheesecake products in the United States totaled $430 million, more than $30 million higher than in 1988.

Overton continued to open new restaurants, financing the growth in part from the sale of 1.1 million shares of common stock. By early 1995, the chain numbered 11 units, with new stores in Bethesda, Maryland, a Washington suburb; and two restaurants in Florida, in the Miami suburbs of Coconut Grove and in Boca Raton. Restaurant sales for 1994 grew 31 percent to $73 million, and the Cheesecake Factory was number 25 in *Restaurant Business*'s top 50 growth chains, ranked by percentage increase in system units. Earnings for the year increased 53 percent, to $7.2 million.

$67 million, an increase of 30 percent. In its first ten days of operations, the 12,000-square-foot Atlanta location had sales of $322,000.

THE COMEBACK OF CHEESECAKE

Top menu items for the chain were pasta dishes, followed by Cajun Jambalaya and Spicy Cashew Chicken. The company changed the menu twice a year, in June and in December, with new items added from the an-

HIGH-VOLUME OPERATIONS

The chain's expansion saw no letup as three more restaurants opened within an 11-week period late in 1995: in Chicago at the John Hancock Center, at the Galleria in Houston, and at the Atrium in Chestnut Hill, a suburb of Boston. The Cheesecake Factory's average building costs of $3.5 million per unit were two to three times (or more) greater than those of competitors, such as Ruby Tuesday, Applebee's, Landry's

Seafood, Chili's, or Outback or Lone Star steakhouses. The company's new sites were running 14,000 to 24,000 square feet with seating for 400 to 700; competitors' sites were typically 5,000 to 7,000 square feet and accommodated about 200 people. The Cheesecake Factory filled each seat an average of four times or more a day, and even its smaller units were doing well. Average sales per square foot were $800 to $900, much higher than comparable casual restaurant averages of $400 to $500.

The pre-opening costs for three big restaurants in different areas of the country combined with the expenses of training new staff had an impact on the company's bottom line in the last quarter of the year— for the first time, the company's net income did not grow. The pre-opening costs for the Chicago unit were estimated to be near $1 million, for example, but by its third month, that restaurant was generating about $1 million per month in sales. The Chestnut Hill restaurant, although open only a few weeks in December, generated more than half a million dollars in sales in 1995.

In a May 1995 article in *National Restaurant News,* Overton further described what he looked for when selecting sites. "What we like in a site is one that gives us 250,000 people in a five-mile radius, medium-to-high income, and we like opening near apartment dwellers rather than around home owners. Apartment dwellers go out more frequently. People who own homes tend not to go out as much." However, he went on to explain that by the end of the decade, his "trophy sites" would be harder to find, and that the company was therefore working on a smaller prototype, about 4,500 square feet in size.

One problem the company experienced mid-decade was producing enough bakery goods for its growing number of restaurants, along with its wholesale and mail-order business. To correct this, construction began on a new bakery facility, capable of producing 1,000 cheesecakes an hour using vats the size of hot tubs and customized machinery from Italy. The new facility was 45,000 square feet, replacing one that was only 14,000 square feet. The company's plans for expanding its retail distribution included selling its cheesecakes through Sam's Club and Price/Costco discount stores and additional supermarket chains. It also developed an Oreo cookie cheesecake sandwich with Nabisco that began selling in vending machines in 1999.

In July 1995, Overton selected Gerald Deitchle, a former executive at Long John Silver's Restaurants Inc., to be chief financial officer and senior vice-president. Deitchle succeeded William Kling, who retired. In November 1995, the Cheesecake Factory appeared on the 1995–96 list of the *Forbes* "200 Best Small Companies in America" for the first time, ranking number 79. By the end of the year, the Cheesecake Factory had moved from Woodland Hills to its new corporate headquarters in Calabasas Hills, California, hiring additional staff and beginning production at the new bakery facility. For the year, restaurant and bakery sales each increased 37 percent, and the company had revenues over $100 million for the first time, reaching $117 million. The chain's restaurants continued to average $8.6 million per unit per year, significantly higher than the $1.3 million considered good by competitors.

ADDING A SECOND BRAND

At the end of the year, the company raised its menu prices about 2.7 percent, the first significant price increase in three years. During 1996, three restaurants opened—in the Old Orchard Center in Skokie, Illinois, in Harborplace of Baltimore, Maryland, and in Illinois. These brought the total number of units to 17.

Founder Evelyn Overton died in 1996. Very protective of the Cheesecake Factory name and the concept, David Overton refused to franchise. Instead, his plans for the future were to accelerate the number of restaurant openings and develop new customers and distribution strategies. Thus, in 1997, the Cheesecake Factory contracted with Host Marriott Services to operate the Cheesecake Factory Bakery Café at a major mall in Ontario, California; at Reagan International Airport outside Washington, D.C.; and in a Norfolk, Virginia, mall. The following year, the company opened the Cheesecake Factory Express at the interactive DisneyQuest recreation center in Orlando, Florida. A second Express unit opened at DisneyQuest in Chicago in 1999.

The company remained a wizard of high-volume operations in mixed-retail settings. "I'm not sure any restaurant did $10 million in a mall before we did," Overton boasted in a 2000 *Nation's Restaurant News* article. However, although the chain's sales per square foot were four times the average of other casual dining establishments in the late 1990s, some analysts worried that the ongoing expense of building large, opulent restaurants would cut into the Cheesecake Factory's profits. To address Wall Street's concerns, between 1997 and 2000 the company invested in its corporate ranks and formalized its employee compensation program. Overton and his sister also sold off close to 80 percent of their stock in the company, leaving the family trust with about 1 percent ownership.

The company also created a second brand, the Grand Lux Café, a more upscale, 24-hour restaurant at the Venetian Resort in Las Vegas in 1999, to ensure deeper market penetration. Grand Lux's success was immediate; its sales the first year totaled $18 million, nearly twice the Cheesecake Factory's average. For the company as a whole that year, revenues were $348 million from the central bakery, 34 full-scale restaurants, two fast-food DisneyQuest centers, and royalties from the three-unit bakery café concept licensed to Host Marriott Services (the new HMS Host).

By 2000, the company had 36 full-scale locations and plans to triple that number by 2006. Throughout the next several years, the Cheesecake Factory reached for ten or more openings per year, and by 2003, that number had slightly more than doubled, while revenues had reached $773.8 million. Beginning in 2001, bakery production sold under the Dream Factory brand to other restaurants, including Barnes & Noble cafés, and in 2003, the company established a distribution relationship with SYSCO for its Dream Factory line. Overton was inducted into the MenuMasters Hall of Fame during this time.

STRATEGIES FOR GROWTH IN A TROUBLED ECONOMY

The Cheesecake Factory passed two milestones in 2006 with more than 100 stores and more than $1 billion in sales. The company opened a second bakery facility in North Carolina, which handled distribution throughout the eastern half of the United States. However, like many casual dining operations, the company was experiencing declines in sales, especially in states hit hardest by the housing slump, and in profits.

Share prices fell 18 percent because of rising food costs and the hesitance of people to dine out in difficult financial times. The company began to pursue other avenues of increasing income; it opened catering units at two of its restaurants, pushed its takeout menu, experimented with home delivery, raised prices, and tried in other ways to boost what each customer spent. It also cut the number of new openings almost in half from its planned 17 in 2008.

However, while analysts insisted that the company should focus on its loyal customers at its established restaurants, and while dealing with four high-level resignations, the company went ahead with a new concept, RockSugar Pan Asian Kitchen, featuring the cuisines of Thailand, Vietnam, East Asia, Malaysia, and Indonesia, in mid-2008. Whether the new restaurant would be able to generate greater appeal and greater revenues by blurring the line between the upscale and casual dining segments and attracting a younger, more stylish crowd than the Cheesecake's Factory's other chains was a question that time would answer.

Ellen D. Wernick
Updated, Carrie Rothburd

PRINCIPAL SUBSIDIARIES

The Cheesecake Factory Bakery Inc.; The Cheesecake Factory Restaurants Inc.; Grand Lux Café LLC.

PRINCIPAL COMPETITORS

Carlson Restaurants Worldwide Inc.; OSI Restaurant Partners LLC.

FURTHER READING

Claiborne, Craig, and Pierre Franey, "Naturalizing Cheesecake," *New York Times Magazine,* September 15, 1985, p. 77.

"Deitchle Named New CFO at Cheesecake Factory," *Nation's Restaurant News,* July 24, 1995, p. 12.

Hartnett, Michael, "What a Cakewalk," *Restaurant Business,* November 1, 1993, p. 74.

Hirsch, Jerry, "Firm's Menu Needs Price Hike, Experts Say: Cheesecake Factory Should Rely on Its Customer Base, Not a New Chain, for Growth," *Los Angeles Times,* May 26, 2008, p. 3.

Jennings, Lisa, "Cheesecake Factory Living Large with Oversized Growth," *Nation's Restaurant News,* December 19, 2005, p. 10.

Krumrei, Doug, "Smile, Say Cheeeeeeese Cake," *Bakery Production and Marketing,* November 24, 1994, p. 18.

Lang, Joan, "Desserts Help Sweeten Profits," *ID: The Voice of Foodservice Distribution,* March 1996, p. 95.

Long, Dolores, "Success Is Sweet for the Cheesecake Factory," *Restaurant Business,* May 1, 1987, p. 128.

Martin, Richard, "Cheesecake Factory Steps Up Growth Pace," *Nation's Restaurant News,* February 14, 1994, p. 3.

"Oh No, Not Again!" *Time,* June 17, 1996, p. 22.

Papiernik, Richard L., "Cheesecake Factory Has Big Design on Hefty Slice of Market," *Nation's Restaurant News,* August 14, 1995, p. 11.

———, "When You're at the Top, Be Sure to Watch for Slippery Slopes," *Nation's Restaurant News,* March 11, 1996, p. 11.

Prewitt, Milford, "Cheesecake Factory," *Nation's Restaurant News,* May 22, 1995, p. 106.

"Restaurant IPOs, Sweet and Sour," *Business Week,* April 15, 1996.

Romeo, Peter, "Top 50 Growth Chains," *Restaurant Business,* July 20, 1995, p. 66.

Schonfeld, Erick, "Say Cheese! This One's Good Enough to Eat," *Fortune,* April 1, 1996, p. 161.

"Slippery at the Top: The Best Small Companies in America," *Forbes,* November 6, 1995.

Spector, Amy, "The Cheesecake Factory," *Nation's Restaurant News,* August 14, 2000, p. 46.

Taylor, Jeffrey, "Mixing Success with a New Expansion Plan," *Investors Business Daily On-Line,* May 10, 1995.

Youn, Jacy L., "Precious & Few: The Cheesecake Factory," *Hawaii Business,* June 1, 2004, p. 27.

Clopay Corporation

———— ■ ————

8585 Duke Boulevard
Mason, Ohio 45040-3100
U.S.A.
Telephone: (513) 770-4800
Toll Free: (800) 282-2260
Fax: (513) 770-3558
Web site: http://www.clopay.com

Wholly Owned Subsidiary of Griffon Corporation
Incorporated: 1888 as Seinsheimer Paper Company
Employees: 3,000
Sales: $1.16 billion (2007)
NAICS: 321918 Other Millwork (Including Flooring);
326113 Unsupported Plastics Film and Sheet
(Except Packaging) Manufacturing

■ ■ ■

A subsidiary of Griffon Corporation, Clopay Corporation is a Mason, Ohio-based manufacturing company comprised of three business units. Clopay Building Products Company is the largest manufacturer of steel, wood, and aluminum residential garage doors in the United States, and also manufactures commercial overhead sectional doors, both insulated and uninsulated, for indoor and outdoor applications. The products are carried by leading home center retail chains, including The Home Depot, Inc., Menard's Inc., and Lowe's Companies, Inc. Clopay Plastics Products Company, more global in scope, produces specialty films, engineered laminations, and extrusion coatings to serve several markets: consumer goods, such as coffee filters

and disposable heating pads; healthcare, including gowns, shoe covers, and specialty drapes; hygiene, offering baby diapers and other products; protective apparel, including garments and shoe covers; graphic arts through the production of pressure sensitive adhesive labels; and industrial products, including house wraps and automotive headliners, air ducts, and caps. Manufacturing facilities for Clopay Plastics are located in Ohio, Kentucky, and Tennessee in the United States, and internationally in Germany and Brazil. Finally, Clopay Service Company sells and installs a variety of products—including garage doors, flooring, kitchen and bath cabinets, and manufactured fireplaces—in 24 markets in the United States through a network of distribution centers.

COMPANY FOUNDED: 1859

Clopay was launched as a paper jobbing business established by Bernard Seinsheimer in Cincinnati, Ohio, in 1859. The Seinsheimer Paper Company started out as a one-room operation but steadily grew as a distributor of wrapping paper, paper bags, and other paper products. The founder's son, A. H. Seinsheimer, joined the company in 1865 after serving in the Union army during the Civil War and eventually took over. Under the younger Seinsheimer, the business was incorporated as the Seinsheimer Paper Company in 1889, expanding its operations to include manufacturing and increasing its reach beyond Cincinnati to encompass the entire country. At the time of his death in September 1920, the company operated a pair of 100,000-square-foot plants located in Cincinnati and New Orleans, and maintained offices in a number of large cities. By this time his son, Louis A. Seinsheimer, had replaced him as president.

Seinsheimer Paper did not take the name Clopay Corporation until 1930, when it adopted the trade name of a cloth-paper material it developed. The name was coined by merging elements of the words "cloth" and "paper." The cloth-paper material was used to produce window shades, introduced in 1930. Given the onset of the Great Depression that would last the entire decade, the introduction of such a low-cost consumer product played an important role in keeping the company healthy during this difficult period. Military spending due to World War II lifted the United States out of the Depression, but unlike much of U.S. industry, Clopay did not profit very much from defense contracts because most of its plants were not adequate for such work.

Nevertheless, Clopay produced what it could in support of the war effort—laminated waterproof packaging materials, shell liners, airplane drop tanks, and blackout window shades developed for use on the home front. These shades were made from cellulose fibers, although they were still called paper shades, and following the war they became a major product for the company. To manufacture the shades a plant was acquired in 1946 from the Steel Materials Corporation in Cincinnati and converted. In the summer of 1946 the shades became available, making a major contribution to the $10.7 million in sales Clopay generated that year. Other important products at the time were garment bags and cardboard protectors for metal coat hangers sold to the dry cleaning industry. Clopay also began offering inexpensive venetian blinds that brought in nearly $500,000.

FOLDING DOORS ADDED: 1955

Clopay gained a listing on the New York Stock Exchange and continued to grow into the 1950s, taking advantage of its expertise in plasticized fiber used in making window shades to become more committed to the emerging plastics field. Clopay became involved in the plastic extrusion business on a trial basis in 1950 and quickly made a major commitment to plastics that

was deepened in 1955 with the acquisition of a manufacturing plant in Augusta, Georgia. The company became involved in the folding doors business also in that year, offering vinyl plastic versions.

Clopay looked to increase its folding door business in 1960 with the acquisition of Detroit-based Straits Products, Inc., making Clopay the country's only company offering a full line of folding doors. Four years later Clopay sold the architectural door division to focus on its consumer line of folding doors. Also in 1964, Clopay became involved in garage doors through the acquisition of Hialeah, Florida-based Baker-Aldor-Jones, which made aluminum, fiberglass, and steel doors. Clopay added to its garage door holdings in 1969, acquiring Russia, Ohio-based Francis Products, Inc., manufacturer of overhead doors and related products. Both companies continued to sell products under their own names until 1972, when both adopted the Clopay brand. More garage door manufacturing plants were also opened in Ludlow, Vermont, and Ada, Oklahoma, in 1977. In other parts of its business, Clopay in the 1970s opened a plant in Fresno, California, and established its first technical center, located in Cincinnati. In addition, Clopay expanded into Europe, in 1972 forming Associate Clopay Europe.

Sales were in the $50 million range in the early 1970s, but because of garage door sales, that number more than doubled to $103.3 million in 1981. A downturn in the building market due to a poor economy hurt door sales and overall profits. Household and plastics products, on the other hand, were doing quite well, including a new line of ready-made window blinds as well as disposable diapers and surgical drapes that found a new market in Japan. Clopay expanded its plastic film business in the early 1980s by adding capacity to both the Augusta and Fresno plants and opening a new plant in Nashville, Tennessee, in 1985. However, the execution of this expansion effort was not handled well, leading to a loss of $1.9 million on sales of $139 million, compared to a $2.5 million profit on sales of $134 million the previous year.

CLOPAY SOLD TO INSTRUMENTS SYSTEMS CORP.: 1986

In 1985 Clopay underwent changes in the management ranks. Chairman and CEO John D. Rauh was replaced by Robert B. Goergen, the chairman of Goergen & Sterling Inc., a New York equity investment and management services company, and a well-known turnaround specialist. He wasted little time in making Clopay an attractive acquisition target. The home and commercial products divisions were combined and all building products manufacturing was consolidated at

```
╔══════════════════════════════════════╗
║                                      ║
║            KEY DATES                 ║
║                 ■                    ║
║  ──────────────────────────────────  ║
║                                      ║
║  1859:  Bernard Seinsheimer opens paper jobbing
║         business in Cincinnati.
║  1889:  Business incorporated as Seinsheimer Paper
║         Company.
║  1930:  Company changes name to Clopay
║         Corporation.
║  1946:  Plant acquired from Steel Materials Corpora-
║         tion to produce paper shades.
║  1955:  Clopay becomes involved in folding door
║         business.
║  1964:  Garage doors added to product lines.
║  1986:  Clopay sold to Instrument Systems Corp.
║  1989:  Window shade business divested.
║  1995:  Instrument Systems changes name to Griffon
║         Corporation.
║  1996:  Finotech joint venture formed in Germany.
║  2001:  Stake acquired in Clopay do Brasil.
║  2002:  Headquarters moved to Mason, Ohio.
║  2005:  Clopay acquires remaining interests in Fino-
║         tech and Clopay do Brasil.
╚══════════════════════════════════════╝
```

the Russia, Ohio, plant. Less than a year after taking charge Goergen engineered a sale to a Cincinnati investment firm, Volco Inc. Another company, Jericho, New York-based Instrument Systems Corp., made a higher offer, however, prompting a bidding war. In the end, Instrument Systems won out with a $22.70 a share tender offer, or about $37 million.

Instrument Systems Corp. was started as Waldorf Controls Corporation in College Point, Long Island, in 1959 but quickly assumed the Instrument Systems name. Serving the military market, the company manufactured electronic and electromechanical products. Under the leadership of Edward J. Garrett and two brothers, the company grew into a conglomerate in the 1960s, housing 18 subsidiaries involved in the manufacture of such products as car batteries, outdoor furniture, giftware, plastic packaging, calculators, and sheet-metal building products. A semiconductor division followed in 1970. The rest of the decade was not kind to Instrument Systems, which was hit hard by this recessionary era. Moreover, Garrett underwent heart surgery and emerged, according to some, a different person, firing his brothers and 33 other executives in December 1978. The recession of the early 1980s also adversely impacted the company, and Instrument Systems did not begin to recover until after Garrett died in 1982 and

was succeeded by his son-in-law, Harvey Blau. Increased military spending by the Reagan administration helped revive the company's fortunes, so that Instrument Systems was able to outbid Volco for Clopay. Instruments Systems assumed a new name, Griffon Corporation, in 1995.

The largest part of Instrument Systems in the late 1980s was its telephonics division, which produced such items as communications and radio control systems for the Navy. With the end of the Cold War and cutbacks in defense spending in the early 1990s, telephonics would become secondary to Clopay. In fiscal 1991, for example, Clopay contributed 70 percent of the parent company's $52 million income on sales of $565 million.

Under new ownership, Clopay narrowed its focus somewhat, paying more attention to its garage door business. An authorized dealer network for doors was established in 1988, while a year later the Clopay Window Fashions subsidiary, which produced stock blinds and roller shades, was sold to a competitor, Kirsch. In that same year, Clopay introduced a new line of insulated residential and commercial doors. The company then became a leader in the residential garage door market in 1992 after acquiring Wisconsin-based Ideal Door Co. and Phoenix Door Co. for $15 million, as well as Automatic Door Company. They became part of Clopay Building Products, a name the garage door unit took in 1992. Brand awareness was then bolstered by the launch of a print and television advertising campaign.

The business grew further in 1995 with the acquisition of Orlando, Florida-based Atlas Roll-Lite Door, which served the self-storage market as well as offering sectional garage doors, rolling steel doors, grilles, and counter shutters. Annual sales for Clopay Building Products then reached $300 million. The addition of Atlas also led to a reorganization of the unit, which in 1996 was split between three divisions: residential products, commercial products, and storage products.

GERMAN JOINT VENTURE
FORMED: 1996

While Clopay Building Products focused on the domestic market, Clopay Plastic Products, in the meantime, looked overseas for further growth. In 1996 a joint venture called Finotech was formed with Corvin GmbH, a German manufacturer of nonwovens (fabrics neither woven nor knit, such as felt). Finotech, 60 percent owned by Clopay, manufactured specialty plastic film and laminate products in Europe that were marketed there as well as in the Middle East and South African markets. Clopay then acquired another German company in 1998, paying about $30 million for Bohme

Verpackungsfolien GmbH, which served the hygienic market with specialty plastic packaging and films.

In the late 1990s, Clopay began scouting for a new location where it could combine its corporate headquarters with a new technical center. After years of being headquartered in downtown Cincinnati the company had run out of room and was unable to find suitable accommodations in that city. Clopay considered sites in Kentucky, going so far as to apply for tax incentives in late 1998. The company also looked at possible sites in Boone County, Ohio. Finally, in December 2000, Clopay agreed to move its operations to a 20-acre campus in Mason, Ohio, located about 15 miles north of Cincinnati. The new 46,000-square-foot headquarters and 80,000-square-foot technical center opened in 2002.

Clopay Building Products took advantage of a robust economy and building boom in the late 1990s to grow even further through acquisition. Holmes-Hally Industries Inc. of Los Angeles was acquired in September 1997, a deal that brought with it Tempe, Arizona-based Anozira Door Systems and Auburn, Washington-based Holmes Door. Moreover, the deal made Clopay Building Products North America's largest manufacturer of residential doors. The self-storage products no longer fit in with Clopay's long-range plans, and in 1999 the Roll-Lite line of these products was sold and Clopay concentrated on its rolling and sectional door products.

Clopay continued to add door products in the new century, while also selling the Atlas door assets in 2002 to The Chamberlain Group, Inc. In 2000 Clopay introduced the Holmes Garage Door, a line of steel doors sold through retail home centers and lumberyards. A line of mesh and screen security doors was added in 2004, and a year later the Avante Collection was unveiled, featuring glass and aluminum and an upscale look. In 2006 stylish wooden doors supplemented Clopay's product lines with a more vintage look, available in cedar, hemlock, and redwood. The company also added sliding doors to complement its overhead and sheet roll-up doors, and expanded its production capacity in 2006 with the acquisition of a vacant plant in Troy, Ohio. In addition to new designs, Clopay Building Products also incorporated new materials and constructions. In 2007 the company added three-layer sandwich construction options that incorporated a thermal break to improve energy efficiency.

INTERNATIONAL EXPANSION IN THE 21ST CENTURY

Clopay Plastics Products Company made further inroads overseas in the early years of the new century, acquiring a stake in Clopay do Brasil in 2001 to manufacture plastic hygienic and specialty films. In 2005 Clopay acquired the rest of the business and also acquired the remaining 40 percent stake of Finotech. In 2006 Clopay reorganized its European operations, merging Clopay Aschersleben and Böhme Clopay to create Clopay Europe. On other fronts, the plastics unit became a global printer in 2003 by establishing Advanced Printing Nashville and Advanced Printing Aschersleben GmbH in Germany. A year later it emerged as the world's largest producer of microporous breathable films. To maintain its competitive edge, Clopay Plastics Company opened a new research and development technical center in 2004.

In fiscal 2006 garage doors accounted for $549.7 million and installation services another $338.7 million of Griffon's $1.64 billion in revenues. Specialty plastic films contributed another $381.4 million. A severe drop in new home construction that began in 2006 resulted in a sharp decline in revenues for Clopay Building Products, with garage door sales falling to $479.5 million and installation services to $275.6 million. The company responded by cutting costs, closing the Tempe plant and moving these operations to Troy. Clopay also looked to achieve some diversity by acquiring Cabinet West Distributors, Inc., a Las Vegas-based residential cabinet installation company operating in southern Nevada. Clopay Plastics Products helped to make up some of the losses incurred by Clopay Building Products, growing sales to $406.6 million in 2007. To ensure that both units were well funded to sustain and grow their operations into the future, Griffon in 2008 arranged a five-year $100 million revolving credit facility.

Ed Dinger

PRINCIPAL SUBSIDIARIES

Clopay Building Products Company; Clopay do Brasil; Clopay Plastic Products Company; Clopay Service Company; Finotech.

PRINCIPAL COMPETITORS

Hoermann Gadco LLC; NCI Building Systems, Inc.; Overhead Door Corporation.

FURTHER READING

Bolton, Douglas, "Clopay Fortunes Up," *Cincinnati Post*, October 13, 1992, p. 5C.

Buckhout, Wayne, "Depression in Building Hurts Clopay," *Cincinnati Enquirer*, May 7, 1982, p. C5.

Cincinnati: A Guide to the Queen City and Its Neighbors, Cincinnati: Wiesenhart Press, 1943.

"Clopay, New Exchange Listing, Extends Paper Specialty Line," *Barron's National Business and Financial Weekly,* January 12, 1948, p. 34.

"The Clopay Store," *Cincinnati Enquirer,* July 10, 1988, p. 1g.

"Clopay's Strategy for Future," *Cincinnati Post,* January 8, 1985, p. 9C.

Felds, Gregg, "Clopay Planning Divestitures, Layoffs," *Cincinnati Enquirer,* October 31, 1985, p. D9.

Hemmer, Andy, "Garage-Door Maker Clopay Plans Move from City," *Business Courier Serving Cincinnati–Northern Kentucky,* January 15, 1999, p. 3.

Jankowski, David, "Clopay's Goergen Has Golden Touch," *Cincinnati Business Courier,* May 19, 1986, p. 1.

Larkin, Patrick, "Clopay Reorganizes into 3 Divisions," *Cincinnati Post,* May 15, 1996, p. 7B.

Memoirs of the Miami Valley, Chicago: Robert O. Law Company, 1920.

Smith, Sarah S., "Clopay Invests $30 Million in German Firm," *Plastics News,* July 6, 1998, p. 1.

Stammen, Ken, "Clopay Corp. Relocating to Warren," *Cincinnati Post,* December 1, 2000, p. 10C.

CMS Energy Corporation

1 Energy Plaza
Jackson, Michigan 49201
U.S.A.
Telephone: (517) 788-0550
Fax: (517) 788-1859
Web site: http://www.cmsenergy.com

Public Company
Incorporated: 1987
Employees: 7,898
Sales: $6.5 billion (2007)
Stock Exchanges: New York
Ticker Symbol: CMS
NAICS: 221112 Fossil Fuel Electric Power Generation; 221122 Electric Power Distribution; 221210 Natural Gas Distribution

∎∎∎

CMS Energy Corporation is the parent company for Consumers Energy Company, an electric and natural gas utility serving nearly 6.5 million customers in Michigan. Consumers Energy is the second largest utility in Michigan, operating 12 coal-fired and two oil-fired generating plants, 13 hydroelectric facilities, a pumped storage generating plant, and several combustion-turbine facilities. CMS Energy launched a major restructuring effort in 2001. It sold off its international investments, overcame a electricity trading scandal, exited the wholesale energy trading market, and revamped its strategy to focus mainly on its Consumers Energy subsidiary.

EARLY HISTORY

CMS Energy's main subsidiary, Consumers Energy Company, holds an important place in the history of the power industry in the United States. Founded as Consumers Power in 1910 through a merger of a variety of gas, electric, and electric trolley companies, the company was at the forefront of the development of the large utilities that marked the business world of the dawn of the twentieth century. By the 1960s, Consumers Power had established itself as an old, dependable, solid utility company. As the largest utility in Michigan, the company had paid regular and substantial dividends for some 50 years.

Although when Consumers was founded, hydro power had been the main energy source in Michigan, by the 1950s coal-powered turbines were delivering 80 percent of the state's power. It was Consumers Power's efforts to develop alternate sources of electric power that would land the company on the verge of bankruptcy and would lead to the founding of CMS Energy.

The period after World War II was one of optimism for American industry and science; nuclear power appeared poised to become the pollution-free, inexpensive energy source of the future. Consumers Power was quick to jump on the nuclear bandwagon, building first an experimental nuclear plant at Big Rock, Michigan, and then the much larger commercial Palisades plant. In spite of technical difficulties in the operation of the Big Rock plant and serious cost overruns in the construction of Palisades, in 1970 Consumers embarked on the construction of a third nuclear reactor at Midland, Michigan. The Midland facility was originally scheduled

COMPANY PERSPECTIVES

We believe these principles are essential to achieving success for our employees, our customers, our neighbors, our shareholders and our Company. Safety: We put safety first in everything we do. Integrity: We conduct our business with honesty and fairness. Commitment: We keep the promises we make. Dedication: We strive to exceed the expectations of our customers and our other stakeholders. Intensity: We set challenging goals and apply creativity, teamwork and perseverance to achieve them. Diversity: We cherish our differences and treat everyone with respect and dignity. Cooperation: We nurture a positive, constructive work environment by supporting each other, treating each other with respect and celebrating our successes. Outreach: We improve the quality of life in our communities through leadership and volunteerism. Communication: We understand the importance of sharing information with our employees, customers and shareholders. Stewardship: We take pride in protecting precious natural resources including water, land and air.

to open in 1975 at a cost of about $500 million. Nine years and $3.5 billion later, Consumers Power pulled the plug on the still unfinished plant.

The Midland debacle plunged Consumers Power into a state of crisis. Stock prices plummeted from a high of $55 before Midland to only $5.00 a share in 1985. Income, which had been dwindling, fell to a net loss of $270 million. Financial analysts were suggesting that bankruptcy might be the most attractive option for the beleaguered utility. To make matters worse, Dow Chemical had made massive investments in the ill-fated plant in an agreement to buy excess steam to be used in its chemical processing.

The giant chemical company sued Consumers Power, alleging mismanagement and a cover-up on the part of the utility. The Michigan Public Service Commission, the regulatory agency that oversees utility rates, authorized an emergency $99 million rate increase fearing that bankruptcy of Michigan's largest utility would wreak havoc with the suffering Michigan economy. The commission was reluctant, however, to let rate payers bear the full burden of the Midland fiasco, and Consumers was faced with the need for massive reorganization to deal with its huge debt burden.

In 1985, Consumers Power hired William T. McCormick, Jr., to head the reorganization of the troubled company. McCormick, who held a doctorate in nuclear physics from Massachusetts Institute of Technology, had extensive experience dealing with regulators and politicians from years spent as a lobbyist in Washington. This experience would be crucial in the new CEO's handling of the Consumers Power reorganization.

CMS ENERGY FORMED IN 1987

McCormick's first move was to create a holding company for Consumers Power. In May 1987, shareholders of Consumers Power approved a reorganization plan in which shares of Consumers common stock were converted into shares of CMS Energy Corporation common stock, and Consumers Power became a subsidiary of the new energy company.

The creation of CMS Energy offered several advantages to the utility. Charges of mismanagement had severely damaged the reputation of the 75-year-old firm, and McCormick felt that starting afresh with a new name and management team could only improve investor confidence. More importantly, the new energy corporation could expand into nonregulated energy related ventures without putting its regulated utility business at risk. McCormick moved quickly to cut costs and free up cash to retire preference stock and to refinance the company's crippling debt load. By 1987, the new management had succeeded in paying off or refinancing some $3 billion in debt, reducing CMS's fixed charges by $67 million.

It was McCormick's solution for the Midland plant fiasco that would prompt both the most plaudits and the most controversy for the newly born energy corporation. It was clear that it would be impossible to salvage the nuclear capacity of the project but even with the new cost-cutting plan and rate hikes it would be equally unrealistic to expect to recover from the burden of taking the $3.6 billion loss that abandoning the project would entail.

"Some people jumped all over us for suggesting anything other than abandoning the plant," McCormick stated in a 1988 article in *Forbes*, "but we projected we would need additional capacity by the early 1990s when we could get the cogeneration plant into operation, and everyone realized that it would be senseless to throw these usable assets away." Under McCormick's plan the nonnuclear facilities of the plant would be converted to a gas-fired 1,370 megawatt cogeneration plant, salvaging about $1.5 billion worth of existing facilities. Of course completing the conversion would cost an additional $500 million but McCormick had a solution for raising these funds.

KEY DATES

1910: Consumers Power Company is formed.
1987: CMS Energy Corporation is created as a holding company for Consumers Power.
1997: Consumers Power changes its name to Consumers Energy Company.
1999: CMS acquires Panhandle Eastern Pipeline Co.
2001: The company launches a major restructuring effort that includes a massive asset reduction program.
2003: Natural gas transmission assets including Panhandle Eastern Pipeline are sold.

MIDLAND COGENERATION CONTROVERSY

McCormick managed to convince Dow Chemical that they should once more join forces and operate the new Midland project as a joint venture. The cogeneration plant would provide steam for Dow's processing needs and electricity to be sold to CMS's subsidiary, Consumers Power. Dow Chemical, along with a number of smaller companies with a vested interest in the survival of the plant, was to control 51 percent of the newly formed Midland Cogeneration Venture. CMS Energy, in turn, swapped $1.5 billion of abandoned Midland assets for a 49 percent interest in the cogeneration facility plus $1.2 billion in notes. CMS's equity in the venture was deliberately kept below 50 percent so that the new power plant would be governed by the federal Public Utilities Regulatory Policy Act (PURPA), which gave independent power producers certain advantages in selling power to utilities provided they were not more than 50 percent owned by a public utility.

Under PURPA, public utilities were required to buy power from the independents for the avoided cost of producing this power by the utility itself, which would usually entail a higher price than would be attainable on the wholesale market. Part of the agreement between CMS and its Midland partners specified that Consumers would buy the bulk of Midland's power at this higher PURPA rate, thereby securing a market for the cogeneration project's energy. More importantly, McCormick planned to use the cash generated by the notes to fund CMS's investment in its nonregulated energy business.

By 1987, with reduced costs and the noncash credits from Midland, CMS's earnings rebounded to $262 million. Investors, charmed by McCormick's innovative ideas and persuasive rhetoric, returned to the

CMS fold and stock prices once again rose to almost $40 by 1989. However, not everyone was happy with the new plans for Midland. Regulators who had already bailed out the company by agreeing to large rate hikes were angered that the cash from the Midland deal was to be used to grow CMS through diversification rather than to be passed on to subsidiary Consumers Power and its customers.

CMS's use of PURPA to allow Consumers to pay higher-than-market rates for the cogeneration plant's energy also came under fire by the Michigan Public Service Commission, which would agree to let Consumers pass on the higher PURPA costs to its customers for only about half of the energy that Consumers had agreed to buy from the Midland venture. To make matters worse, an industrial coalition calling itself ABATE was also determined to block the higher rates and appealed in federal court to strip Midland of its qualification to operate under PURPA.

After seven years of lawsuits, countersuits, and appeals by CMS, its partners in the Midland Cogeneration Venture, ABATE, the Michigan Public Service Commission, and the Michigan Attorney General, many of the issues surrounding the Midland plant still remained unresolved. The Michigan Public Service Commission's limits on recoverable costs, as well as rulings reducing recoverable write-offs of the abandoned nuclear facilities at Midland, saw CMS posting substantial losses for three years in a row from 1990 through 1992. With shrunken dividends and an uncertain future investors once again shied away from CMS stock and share price dropped to only $15.

In 1993, CMS Energy finally reached an agreement with the Michigan Public Service Commission that would allow Consumers to recover from its rates 915 of the 1,240 megawatts of energy the company had agreed to buy annually from the Midland partnership. This compromise, although it remained under appeal by ABATE, finally allowed CMS to emerge from the Midland quagmire and to once again become a profitable enterprise. Record electric sales by Consumers, as well as a boom in foreign independent power production, boosted CMS's revenues to $3.6 billion in 1994. The resolution of a host of regulatory issues allowed net income to return to $179 million although this was still short of pre-1990 levels.

GROWTH THROUGH DIVERSIFICATION

In spite of the troubles with the Midland venture, CMS Energy stuck to their plan of diversification, albeit at a slower pace than McCormick would have liked had the cash from Midland been forthcoming. In the 1960s, Consumers Power had created a subsidiary, the Nomeco Oil and Gas Company, to manage the development of oil and gas reserves needed to operate Consumers' utility business. With only eight employees, Nomeco was originally intended only to build domestic reserves of oil and gas for the company's use and was not envisioned as a revenue producer.

As part of McCormick's new vision for the company, CMS expanded the mandate of this subsidiary to include significant independent production of oil and gas to be sold on the open market for immediate earnings. By the early 1990s the subsidiary had producing wells in the United States, Australia, Colombia, Equatorial Guinea, and New Zealand with proven reserves of 60 million net equivalent barrels and almost 100 employees. As the resolution of Midland related disputes began to free up cash in the mid-1990s, CMS was able to further expand its oil and gas production, acquiring four gas and oil production companies in Michigan, Africa, and Colombia, and beginning production in the huge oilfields of Ecuador. By 1995 proven reserves had almost doubled to 113 million barrels, and revenue from Nomeco was close to $90 million.

In the late 1980s, CMS formed two subsidiaries, CMS Gas Marketing and CMS Gas Transmission and Storage, to take advantage of Consumers Power's expertise in gas procurement and handling. These service-based companies were one of the early successes of CMS's program of expansion, making a respectable $4 million in net income on revenues of $42 million by 1991. The opening of the Grands Lacs Market Center in St. Clair, Michigan, in 1994 was an important step for CMS as it would provide a major storage and exchange point for buyers and sellers through the United States and Canada. CMS's gas service companies would continue to contribute substantially to CMS's recovery in the mid-1990s, with revenues reaching $145 million by 1994.

One of McCormick's most ambitious plans for CMS Energy was the development of its independent power production business. McCormick believed that the power industry in the United States was moving inexorably toward less regulation and more competition, and he was determined to put CMS Energy at the forefront of this movement. A subsidiary, CMS Generation, was founded in 1986 with the aim of furthering the independent power production business.

CMS's cash flow problems of the late 1980s and early 1990s severely restricted the growth of this business sector, however, as the heavy investment needed to acquire or build new plants was simply not available. To make matters worse, one of the few investments the new subsidiary was able to make was Oxford Energy Co., a tire burning power plant that went bankrupt in 1992, costing CMS $31 million. It was not until 1993 that CMS Generation was able to produce even modest revenues for its parent company, with its acquisition of a New York waste wood burning electricity plant as well as its first foreign plant in Argentina. It would be this foreign investment that would finally pay off for CMS's independent power unit.

Growth in the domestic independent power production sector was much slower than analysts such as McCormick had predicted, with 1994 estimates coming in at only about 1 percent annually through the year 2020. International markets, however, surged in the mid-1990s. Many countries in Latin America, Asia, and Eastern Europe were faced with power shortages yet could not afford to expand and run their own generating systems. Governments began to look at large American and European power companies as potential partners in building their power infrastructures. With limited competition in these markets, returns on investment could be up to double those in the domestic power market.

In 1994, CMS entered this market on a large scale, founding new joint projects in Argentina, the Philippines, India, and Morocco. Revenues doubled from the previous year and, even more importantly, high rates of return meant that net income from these operations quadrupled from 1993. At $20 million, this income represented the largest contribution to CMS's bottom line from the company's nonutility businesses.

The year 1994 was also an important year on the domestic front for CMS Generation as they began the process of acquiring HYDRA-CO, the independent power subsidiary of Niagara Mohawk Power, although earnings from this acquisition would not be incorporated into CMS finances until the following year. The addition of HYDRA-CO's plants would bring CMS Generation's total number of U.S. plants to 25, making CMS one of the nation's top five independent power producers. Consumers Power changed its name to Consumers Energy Company in 1997 to reflect its diversified holdings. In spite of the serious problems of the 1980s and early 1990s, CMS seemed poised to emerge as an important player on the international energy scene.

Indeed, the company's diversification efforts continued well into the late 1990s. Investments were made in power facilities in Morocco, Australia, and Brazil. It also expanded into Ghana and India. In 1999, it purchased Panhandle Eastern Pipeline Co. and various other companies from Duke Energy Corporation in a $2.2 billion deal. The purchase included 10,400 miles of natural gas pipeline that extended from the Texas Gulf Coast to Michigan and from Kansas and Oklahoma to Michigan. Overall, CMS's assets grew to $4.1 billion in 1999.

CHANGES IN THE 21ST CENTURY

While CMS Energy spent most of the latter half of the 1990s aggressively pursuing expansion, it was forced to retool its strategy during the early years of the new millennium. With profits waning, the company announced plans to focus on its North American operations while selling off unprofitable businesses and investments. CMS posted a loss of $545 million in 2001, due mainly to restructuring charges that included the sale of investments in Argentina, Australia, Brazil, Equatorial New Guinea, India, the Philippines, and Thailand. At the same time, Consumers Energy's Palisades nuclear plant shut down for over seven months that year for repair, forcing the company to buy its power from other sources.

At the same time, CMS Energy became embroiled in a public scandal during 2002 when the U.S. Securities and Exchange Commission, the Commodity Futures Trading Commission, and the Federal Energy Regulatory Commission began investigating reports of "round-trip" electricity trades—these trades involved companies that sold and purchased natural gas and electricity in an even swap, which artificially inflated revenue but had no impact on profits. Chairman and CEO William McCormick resigned as a result of CMS Energy's involvement in such trades, leaving Kenneth Whipple at the helm.

With losses in 2002 reaching $620 million, Whipple faced an uphill battle. The company continued to revamp its business structure, opting to shutter its exploration and production operations. During 2003, it sold its natural gas transmission assets including the Panhandle Eastern pipeline for $1.8 billion. The company also restructured its CMS Marketing, Services, and Trading subsidiary while exiting the wholesale energy trading business. This subsidiary was renamed CMS Energy Resource Management. David Joos, the company's president and chief operating officer, took over as CEO in October 2004 while Whipple remained chairman.

By 2005, the company had shed over $4 billion in assets in just four years. Consumers Energy sold its stake in the Midland Cogeneration Venture in 2006. CMS also continued to whittle away its international ventures and by 2007, completed its asset reduction program. It also sold the Palisades nuclear plant in a $380 million deal. Losses for the year totaled $227 million.

From 1998 to 2008, CMS Energy posted losses of $660 million. Nevertheless, the company's management team believed CMS had completed a successful transition and was on track for success in the years to come. The company was heavily focused at this time on renewable energy sources, expecting its supply to the public to increase to 10 percent by 2015. Most of its renewable energy was expected to come from wind turbines.

Hilary Gopnik
Updated, Christina M. Stansell

PRINCIPAL SUBSIDIARIES

Consumers Energy Company; CMS Enterprises Company; EnerBank USA.

PRINCIPAL COMPETITORS

American Electric Power Company Inc.; DTE Energy Company; Xcel Energy Inc.

FURTHER READING

Bush, George, *Future Builders: The Story of Michigan's Consumers Power Company,* New York: McGraw-Hill, 1973.

Carlson, Paul, "CMS Net Loss Surges 152% to $227 Million with Charges in 'Successful Transition Year,'" *Electric Utility Week,* February 25, 2008.

"CMS Closes $2.2 Billion Deal," *Oil Daily,* March 30, 1999.

Cook, James, "So Near, but Maybe Not So Far," *Forbes,* September 19, 1988, pp. 128–30.

Egan, John, "Out of the Briar Patch," *Financial World,* October 29, 1991, p. 26.

Lane, Amy, "CMS Board: 'Buck Stops Here,'" *Crain's Detroit Business,* May 27, 2002.

———, "CMS Energy's CEO Cites Successes, Challenges on His 2nd Anniversary," *Crain's Detroit Business,* May 3, 2004.

———, "CMS Selloff Nears End," *Crain's Detroit Business,* May 16, 2005.

———, "CMS Unplugged," *Crain's Detroit Business,* July 1, 2002.

Maher, Tani, "Power Games," *Financial World,* October 3, 1989, pp. 30–31.

Mitchell, Russell, "Dow and Consumers Power Are Lovey-Dovey Again," *Business Week,* October 27, 1986, p. 90.

———, "The $4 Billion White Elephant on Bill McCormick's Back," *Business Week,* June 9, 1986, p. 64.

Norman, James R., "Reined In," *Forbes,* August 16, 1993, p. 70.

Tice, David W., "Less There Than Meets the Eye: A Hard Look at CMS Energy's Financials and Earnings," *Barron's,* October 16, 1989, pp. 15, 20–24.

——, "Risky Venture: A Utility's Cogeneration Project Still Has Woes Aplenty," *Barron's,* October 21, 1991, pp. 24, 38.

"US FTC Formally Clears Southern's Buy of CMS Gas Pipeline Assets," *Platts Oilgram News,* July 23, 2003.

Whitman, Martin J., "Virtues of Bankruptcy: For Nuclear Utilities, There May Be Many," *Barron's,* May 6, 1985, pp. 16–18, 43–45.

Woodruff, David, "Plugging into the Power Surge Abroad," *Business Week,* August 15, 1994, pp. 100, 102.

Colorado Boxed Beef Company

302 Progress Road
Auburndale, Florida 33823-2711
U.S.A.
Telephone: (863) 967-0636
Toll Free: (800) 955-0636
Fax: (863) 965-2222
Web site: http://www.coloradoboxedbeef.com

Private Company
Incorporated: 1975
Employees: 475
Sales: $629 million (2007)
NAICS: 424470 Meat and Meat Products Merchant Wholesalers; 414460 Fish and Seafood Merchant Wholesalers

■ ■ ■

Colorado Boxed Beef Company (CBBC) is an Auburndale, Florida-based distributor of beef, pork, lamb veal, seafood, lunch meat, and cheese as well as other fresh, frozen, and dry products. The company serves such channels as independent and chain supermarkets, foodservice distributors, restaurant chains, military bases, cruise lines, and amusement parks. Company brands include Angus Ranch Brand, Bridgewater Farms, Cedar Creek, and New Generation, a line of irradiated products. Business is conducted through several operating divisions. CBBC Sales Division sells meats and seafood as well as groceries, dry goods, and paper goods to retailer and foodservice distributors in the southeastern United States. Based in Georgia, The Great

Fish Company distributes packaged, retail-ready frozen seafood throughout the United States and Mexico. Operating out of Port Everglades, Florida, CBBC Cruise Line Division serves cruise ships operating in Florida, and through an alliance with InterSupply Shipstores B.V., the company also supplies cruise ships sailing from ports in Rotterdam, Netherlands. Facilities in Blaine, Washington, and Los Angeles also allow the division to do business with seasonal cruise lines.

A refrigerated-frozen distributor, Prefco Distribution, LLC serves independent grocery stores and restaurants in southwest Texas, supplying them with meats, seafood, cheeses, and other products. Colorado Boxed Beef International Division procures beef, pork, poultry, seafood, vegetable, and other products from more than 200 suppliers around the world. Finally, Alterman Transportation Group, also based in Auburndale, Florida, is a less-than-a-truckload refrigerated trucking company operating all along the East and parts of the Midwest and Southeast. CBBC does not maintain its own slaughter facility, thus relying each day on the shipment of fresh and frozen raw product for processing. CBBC is a family owned company, operated by second-generation members of the Saterbo family.

COMPANY FOUNDED: 1975

CBBC was founded in 1975 by Richard Dean "Dick" Saterbo and his wife Edith. Born in Austin, Minnesota, in 1929, Dick Saterbo earned a degree from an area junior college in 1949 and a year later began his career in the meat distribution industry, working as a salesman for Hormel Company in Austin. He then resumed his education, enrolling at Baylor University, where he graduated in 1954.

Returning to Austin, Saterbo became the manager for the foodservice division at Hormel, a post he held until 1967, when he became the national sales manager at Chicago's B&B Packing Company. In 1972 he moved to Bartow, Florida, to become brand manager for B&B. In 1975 he struck out on his own, establishing Colorado Boxed Beef with his wife and a partner in Winter Haven, Florida. Dick Saterbo served as president of the new concern.

The idea of boxed beef was relatively new. Until the 1970s packers shipped beef as partial carcasses. New technology allowed the beef to be cut into portions, sealed in vacuum packs ready for retail sale, and shipped in cardboard boxes—hence, the "boxed beef" tag. Although the business was located in Florida, it took the name Colorado Boxed Beef because Saterbo's 50-50 partner at the time was a Colorado beef supplier. CBBC reboxed his beef for distribution in the Florida market, operating out of a 3,000-square-foot warehouse in Winterhaven with just four employees. The company made its first shipment of fresh boxed beef in October 1975, altogether shipping 29,000 pounds in the first week of operation.

MOVE TO AUBURNDALE: 1982

CBBC enjoyed steady growth so that in 1982 the Saterbos were able to buy out their partner. By this time the company employed 40 people and was shipping about 500,000 pounds of beef. The company also established its own packing plant in Auburndale, Florida, where the company made its home in 1982, and although the beef was bought from the Midwest, Colorado was retained in the company name. In addition to beef, CBBC began to carry other products, adding pork, lamb, veal, poultry, and seafood as well as frozen vegetables and deli items. In 1983 CBBC suffered a setback when fire destroyed a

warehouse. One night later, however, the company was once again making shipments to customers.

The expanded product lines allowed CBBC in 1986 to begin serving the cruise line industry in Florida. By this time, three of the four sons of Dick and Edith Saterbo—Bryan, Steve, and John Saterbo—were involved in the business. In 1989 Edith Saterbo retired, around the same time that Dick Saterbo was diagnosed with cancer. Two years later, in August 1991, he passed away at the age of 62 in the Winter Haven Hospital. His wife would survive him until 2007.

Following the death of their father, Bryan, Steve, and John Saterbo took control of CBBC, each becoming a senior vice-president. Steve headed marketing and finance, John was in charge of sales and purchasing, and Bryan was responsible for operations. Bryan Saterbo would eventually take the title of chief executive officer. The brothers continued what their parents had begun, expanding the company's product lines, distribution channels, and markets served. By the end of 1995 CBBC was generating annual revenues of more than $210 million.

NEW PROCESSING PLANT OPENS: 1996

In 1996 CBBC opened a new 25,000-square-foot processing plant in Auburndale. This facility allowed the company to become one of the first packers to offer modified atmosphere packaging (MAP), resulting in case-ready ground beef portions and patties with an extended shelf life. The facility also processed steaks and pork chops. It enjoyed strong growth, so that in just four years, the amount of MAP processing increased from about 20,000 pounds of product a week to as much as 600,000 pounds a week. Steak processing also increased from 10,000 pounds per week to 150,000 pounds.

To expand, CBBC established a number of subsidiaries, including Colorado Custom Distribution, The Great Fish Company, and Gulf State Logistics. It also grew through acquisition. In 1997 it paid $14 million for Atlanta Provision Company, a meat and seafood distributor that had been a direct competitor in the Florida and Georgia markets. The two companies were a good fit. Although lacking in logistics, Atlanta Provision was strong in marketing and customer service. CBBC was not only able to incorporate those strengths, it added size and new customers and bolstered its dominant position in the southeast region.

RECALL HITS COMPANY: 1998

In 1998 CBBC had to deal with a product recall. In November that year the Florida Department of

KEY DATES

1975: Richard and Edith Saterbo start the Colorado Boxed Beef Company (CBBC) in Winter Haven, Florida.

1982: The company moves to Auburndale, Florida.

1986: CBBC begins serving cruise ships.

1991: Richard Saterbo dies and his sons assume control of the company.

1996: A new processing plant opens in Auburndale.

2000: The New Generation line of irradiated products introduced.

2003: Alterman Transport Lines, Inc., is acquired.

2004: PREFCO Corporation is acquired.

2007: Edith Saterbo dies.

Agriculture found a sample of CBBC beef from a retail store that tested positive for *E. coli* contamination. The state did not retest the sample, as was normally done, and did not notify CBBC of the test results for 20 days. CBBC immediately issued a voluntary recall of 359,000 pounds of ground beef and ground beef products, covering brand names Colorado Gold, 200 Percent, and Winn Dixie. The products had been sold to stores in Florida, Georgia, North Carolina, and South Carolina, as well as to the Jacksonville Naval Air Station in Florida. It was this experience that spurred CBBC to pursue the irradiation of its meat products to kill harmful bacteria. Since 1993, in fact, the company had been irradiating poultry, produce, spices, and food packaging.

In 2000 CBBC began working with Plant City, Florida-based Food Technology Service Inc., an irradiation processor, the first in the country to have a food irradiation facility to serve manufacturers, retailers, processors, and distributors. In December 1999 the two companies launched the New Generation brand of irradiated fresh and frozen ground beef portions and patties and chicken breasts and tenders, the first such product line to be offered in the United States. New Generation became available to foodservice and retail customers in 2000 following a 60-day waiting period mandated by the U.S. Food and Drug Administration.

While supermarket customers were interested in the food safety aspect of New Generation products, the company was worried that the public would not be comfortable with the idea of irradiation. Moreover, there were concerns about taste and the slightly higher cost of the products. As a result, no one was clamoring to be the first retailer to embrace irradiation. Most were eager, however, to be second. On the other hand, no restaurant chains, institutional food service companies, or cruise lines expressed any interest at all in New Generation products.

In June 2000 the New Generation products began to be carried by a handful of Florida grocers: Wyndle's Foodland in Plant City, Florida; Mac's Meat, in Winter Haven; and Stuart Fine Foods, in Stuart, Florida. Of the chain retailers, only Wal-Mart was to test New Generation in 55 of its Florida Supercenters. All told CBBC spent about $100,000 to develop the brand, which the company never expected to be more than a niche product. The forward thinking CBBC did receive some industry recognition, however. In 2000 it was named Processor of the Year by the *National Provisioner* trade publication.

ALTERMAN TRANSPORT LINES ACQUIRED: 2003

In early 2003 CBBC added a transportation unit, acquiring Alterman Transport Lines, Inc., out of bankruptcy. The less-than-a-truckload refrigerated motor carrier had been founded in Miami in 1938 by Sidney Alterman with a single truck. He grew it into a national enterprise with terminals across the country. Before his death in 2000 the company began sustaining operating losses, unable to contend with falling revenues and the rising cost of fuel, driver salaries, and health and liability insurance. His son, Rick Alterman, was unsuccessful in finding a buyer for the business, and in late 2002 began the process of liquidating the assets. CBBC then stepped in to purchase the company, which it renamed Alterman Transportation Group and moved to Auburndale. Improvements were made to the operation, including a 2004 arrangement with Sunco Carriers of Lakeland, Florida, that addressed the lack of backhaul freight to Florida.

In 2003 CBBC also decided to divest some assets. In March of that year it sold its specialty meat-cutting division and an affiliated broadline foodservice operation, J&B Foodservice, to Buckhead Beef of Atlanta, a subsidiary of Houston-based SYSCO Corporation. Together these units generated about $76 million in annual sales. CBBC retained its retail boxed beef and custom distribution businesses, cruise lines segment, and New Generation division, which combined accounted for about $450 million in annual sales.

CBBC further grew its transportation assets and geographic reach in 2004 with the acquisition of the distribution division of Houston-based PREFCO Corporation, a refrigerated-frozen distribution company that supplied independent restaurants and grocery stores in southwest Texas with boxed beef and other meats, seafood, cheese, and other products. The deal brought with it a fleet of refrigerated trucks and a full-service cold storage facility. PREFCO was well established in Texas. It was founded in 1941 by Hans and Erna Pauly as Pauly Packing Company, also known as Blue Ribbon Packing Company, a regional packer with its own slaughter facilities. A second generation of the family closed the packing plant and in 1986 formed PREFCO.

In the new century, CBBC continued to add to its product lines. It also expanded its footprint, so that by 2006 it was able to serve every city in Florida, Alabama, Georgia, North Carolina, South Carolina, Tennessee, and Texas. In 2007 revenues totaled $629 million, and there was every reason to expect that number to grow higher in the years to come.

Ed Dinger

PRINCIPAL SUBSIDIARIES

The Great Fish Company; Prefco Distribution LLC.

PRINCIPAL DIVISIONS

CBBC Sales; CBBC Cruise Line; Colorado Boxed Beef International; Alterman Transportation Group.

PRINCIPAL COMPETITORS

Harker's Distribution, Inc.; Sherwood Food Distributors; SYSCO Corporation.

FURTHER READING

Albright, Mark, "Florida Meatpacker Discussed Irradiation Issue," *St. Petersburg Times,* April 17, 2000, p. 8E.

"Colorado Boxed Beef," *F&D Reports,* September 26, 20006.

Fritz, John, "Consumers Told to Check Beef," *Florida Times-Union,* November 26, 1998, p. A1.

Galosich, Allison, "Trailblazers," *National Provisioner,* June 2000, p. 26.

———, "Triple Threat," *National Provisioner,* June 2000, p. 38.

"Sysco Agrees to Buy Meat-Cutting Assets from Colorado Boxed Beef," *Houston Business Journal,* March 31, 2003.

Compañia Sud Americana de Vapores S.A.

Plaza Sotomayor 50
Valparaíso,
Chile
Telephone: (56 32) 220-3000
Toll Free: (800) 804-9391
Fax: (56 32) 220-3333
Web site: http://www.csav.com

Public Company
Founded: 1872
Employees: 7,321
Sales: $4.15 billion (2007)
Stock Exchanges: Santiago
Ticker Symbol: VAPORES
NAICS: 483111 Deep Sea Freight Transportation;
488390 Other Support Activities for Water
Transportation

■ ■ ■

Compañia Sud Americana de Vapores (CSAV), a
Chilean company, is the largest maritime shipping firm
in Latin America and is one of the oldest existing shipping firms in the world. It operates on all inhabited
continents of the world except Australia, transporting
large numbers of containers and a wide variety of
conventional cargo. To do so, CSAV, or Vapores, has
specially designed vessels for bulk cargo, frozen cargo,
vehicles, and forestry products. The company has also
introduced intermodal services, which combine different
means of transport, as well as complementary services
such as port storage.

THE EARLY YEARS

Compañia Sud Americana de Vapores (CSAV), or in
English, South American Steamship Company, was
founded in 1872 from the merger of Compañia Nacional de Vapores, founded in 1864, and Compañia Chilena de Vapores, founded in 1870, with the latter
absorbing the former to establish the only remaining
shipping firm of any importance in Chile. The Lyon
family was the largest shareholder, and Alfredo Lyon
Santamaría was the first general manager. He was succeeded by his brother Horacio.

Originally CSAV operated only along Chile's long
Pacific Ocean coastline, where its vessels were the sole
link to remote regions of the country, but in 1873 it
established service to Callao, Peru, the port for Lima,
and extended it to Panama the following year. The
Chilean government granted the company a subsidy of
CLP 100,000 a year for a period of ten years, with the
condition that it serve certain routes. Since Chile had
no official merchant marine body, in this way Vapores
became, in effect, the national flag carrier on the high
seas.

After ten years, the subsidy rose to CLP 125,000.
In return, the company agreed to such conditions as
continuing to serve Callao and intermediate ports from
Valparaíso; continuing service to the far south Chilean
ports twice a month; carrying government mail and
important government officials for free, plus military
personnel at half price; and providing Chilean warships
with coal, where available, at cost, plus making its own
vessels available to the navy in case of war.

COMPANY PERSPECTIVES

The company's philosophy is principally to attain a superior level of service quality for its customers, by offering timely and efficient measures for helping them improve their foreign trade operations by making available to them all its installations, technology and services, and ensuring them of reliable carriage of their products to and from the principal areas of the world.

The government subsidy allowed CSAV to survive and prosper. Even so, the Panama service ended after only a year because of heavy losses. By the end of 1876 Vapores had 17 ships—all but one built in Great Britain or Germany rather than Chile—compared to five at its inception four years earlier. In 1879 some of the company's ships were pressed into service for transporting troops and stores in a war against Peru and Bolivia. One of them was captured and burned by the Peruvians; after the war it was restored in Chile by public subscription.

The subsidy was extended and increased in 1883, and once more in 1887 when CSAV promised, among other things, to restore service to Panama, which it did the following year. A short time later, the company established regular service to Central America, in conjunction with the British-based Pacific Steam Navigation Company. By 1892 Vapores had reached Acapulco, and a few years later, San Francisco, but service to the latter ended in 1914 because of heavy competition from European steamship lines. However, the opening of the Panama Canal at this time allowed the company to reach New York, and the outbreak of World War I in that year meant that for several years it faced no competition from European shipping companies. In the United States, Vapores was commonly called simply the Chilean Line.

ESTABLISHING SERVICE TO EUROPE

CSAV established service to Europe in 1921. Its New York route was suspended in 1931 because of declining traffic in the depths of the Great Depression. This service was resumed in 1939, following the loss of the cross-Atlantic trade with Europe due to the outbreak of World War II. In 1943 Vapores sold the United States three of its ships in exchange for the right to buy four new cargo vessels of the C-2 type for the same price as

U.S. companies. By this time the company had created a commercial bank that at the end of 1944 became the Banco Sud Americano.

CSAV resumed European service in 1950, with ships leaving New York to call at ports in Great Britain, France, Belgium, the Netherlands, and Germany. During this period the holds of some company ships were converted to refrigerated chambers that took on board South American fruit for sale in the United States and Europe. This traffic would make Vapores a leader in the shipment of refrigerated products. In 1961 the company formed what became its principal subsidiary, Sudamericana Agencias Aéreas y Marítimas S.A. (SAAM), for air and shipping agency business.

By the 1960s CSAV was controlled by Chile's Vial and MacAuliffe families, who were its leading shareholders and also those of Banco Sud Americano. Closely allied, sometimes by marriage, was the Claro family, which came into prominence after brothers Raúl and Luis Claro founded an electrical utility in 1904.

Ricardo Claro Valdés joined with Javier Vial Castillo and Fernando Larraín Peña at the end of the 1960s to create what became Grupo B.H.C., the second largest business group in Chile. Among its holdings was a 3 percent stake in CSAV. After this group fell victim to an economic crisis in the early 1980s, Claro was able to construct a diversified business group of his own, including Vapores, in which he held a dominant stake through Marítima de Investimientos, S.A. Claro became president of CSAV in 1988.

A sore point among opponents of the military dictatorship of General Augusto Pinochet in the 1970s and 1980s was the alleged detention and torture of leftists on CSAV ships immediately after the military coup of 1973 that brought Pinochet to power. Claro himself served as an economics adviser to the government in this period.

ENTERING NEW MARKETS

Passenger steamship service having long ended, CSAV was best known in the United States for its role in the fruit trade. In 1989 it had a fleet of 52 owned and chartered ships and was carrying more than half of Chile's fruit shipments to the United States on special reefers (refrigerated ships). During the peak of the fruit shipping season, Vapores made weekly stops in Philadelphia and also called at West Coast ports. By 1991, however, it held only one-third of this market, having lost much business to Nippon Yusen Kabushke Kaisha of Japan (the NYK Line). CSAV was also losing business to NYK in fruit shipments to European ports, especially Rotterdam.

KEY DATES

1872: Compañia Sud Americana de Vapores (CSAV) is founded from the merger of two shipping firms.

1876: Vapores has 17 ships in service.

1900: CSAV has regular service to Central America and stops in Acapulco and San Francisco.

1914: Opening of the Panama Canal allows the company to establish a New York route.

1950: Service to Europe, initiated in 1921 but interrupted by World War II, is restored.

1989: CSAV's fleet of owned and leased ships has reached 52.

2000: Acquisition of Norasia Lines Ltd. puts Vapores into the China trade.

2003: CSAV orders 22 new containerships at a cost of $1 billion.

In other respects, CSAV was doing much better. It had upgraded its container ship capacity, improved its services to Atlantic and Gulf of Mexico ports in the United States, and opened new routes in Southeast Asia, in addition to the ones already in service in the Far East. In 1996 Vapores and Kristian Gerhard Jebsen Skipsreden A/S of Norway agreed to jointly operate seven dual-purpose vessels carrying oil and its byproducts and bulk products between the principal Atlantic markets. Three years later, the company acquired majority holdings in Brazil's Companhia Libra de Navegação and Uruguay's Montemar Marítima S.A., which were engaged in container shipping. CSAV had already joined Libra and another company in a vessel sharing arrangement linking the Atlantic ports of the United States to the Caribbean and the Atlantic ports of South America.

In 2000 CSAV acquired the principal assets of the Maltese shipping company Norasia Lines Ltd., including Hong Kong-based Norasia China Ltd., with operations in various Chinese cities. This acquisition, along with the previous ones, made Vapores one of the world's top 20 shipping companies at that time and a truly global player. Also that year, the company introduced a container service linking Asia, Central and South America, and the port of Vancouver/Fraser, British Columbia, from where eastbound cargo would move primarily by railway to Toronto, Montreal, and other cities. The new service would operate alongside an existing one stopping in the port of Los Angeles/Long Beach.

In 2003 CSAV signed the largest shipbuilding contract in its history, which called for the construction of 22 containerships at a cost of about $1 billion. Delivery was completed in 2006.

FACING COMPETITION

Norasia had made China the principal customer of CSAV by 2004, when it began offering services to India, where it established 14 offices. Claro called his company Chile's most global business, with four regional agencies and 276 worldwide. By this time it had 90 ships plying the shipping lanes to five continents. In 2007 some 90 percent of its revenues came from outside Chile.

CSAV was not universally prized by investors, however. In 2003 the powerful Matte group sold its 6 percent stake in the company, and in 2005 AntarChile S.A., the holding company for the Angelini group and the biggest single enterprise in Chile, sold its 18.4 percent stake on the Santiago stock market through four brokerage houses for almost $305 million. By 2006 Vapores was warning that its excellent results in 2004 and 2005 could not be repeated because of overcapacity in the container shipping business and increasing fuel prices. The company fell into the red that year, losing $58.2 million after earning a profit of $132 million the previous year. CSAV returned to the black in 2007, earning $116.3 million. Claro's company, Marítima de Inversiones, S.A., held 45 percent of the shares.

Competition was indeed severe in the maritime trade, with companies willing to cut their rates in order to retain business. Foreign shipping lines that came calling in Chile included Maersk Sealand, MSC Ship Management (Hong Kong) Ltd., and China Shipping Container Line Co. Ltd., one of the six largest in the world. Some of the merchant ships plying the world's seas were more than twice as large as those of CSAV, allowing economies of scale and lower cost of services. Vapores suffered a blow when it lost to Hamburg Süd the contract to carry copper from Corporación Nacional del Cobre de Chile (Codelco)—the world's leading producer of the metal—to Asia, a contract it had held for a decade.

Another problem was piracy. Claro said that CSAV was suffering an average of one assault on its ships per month, mainly in the ports of Guayalquil, Ecuador, and Rio de Janeiro and Santos, Brazil. In the latter case a Vapores ship was boarded by machine gun-wielding pirates who opened a container of frozen chickens.

CSAV was engaged in container shipping, carrying liquid and solid bulk cargo, refrigerated (reefer) cargo, forestry products, and vehicles, either directly or through subsidiaries such as Libra, Libra Uruguay, and

Norasia, which were involved in container shipping. The most important segment of business for CSAV was container transport. SAAM was providing harbor services and land logistics in different ports of Latin America. Intermodal services combining different means of transport had been introduced by the company, as well as complementary services such as port storage and services.

How CSAV would deal with an unfavorable economic climate was not clear in 2008. Chilean market analysts complained that the company was customarily tight lipped and offered very little information beyond that required by law as a publicly traded company. According to one report, rates had fallen by 40 percent because of the need to fill ships previously ordered in the maritime industry and coming on line at this time. In late 2007 CSAV acquired a $675 million credit to buy more containerships, and in early 2008 shareholders voted to increase the company's capital by $200 million. The ships were expected to be of greater size than before and more efficient in consuming fuel.

Robert Halasz

PRINCIPAL SUBSIDIARIES

Corvina Shipping Co. S.A. (Panama); CSAV Agency, LLC (United States); CSAV GmbH (Germany); CSAV Group (China) Shipping Co. Ltd. (China); CSAV Inversiones Navieras S.A.; Empresa de Transporte Sudamericana Austral Ltda.; Inversiones Nuevo Tiempo S.A. (Panama); Inversiones Plan Futuro S.A. (Panama); Odjfell y Vapores S.A. (51%); Norgistic (China) Ltd. (China); Sudamericana, Agencias Aéreas y Marítimas S.A.; Tollo Shipping Co. S.A. (Panama).

PRINCIPAL DIVISIONS

Administration and Finance; Asia Region; Cargo Services and Intermodal; Chartering Bulk Cargo and Automobiles; East Coast South America Lines; Libra and Libra Uruguay Lines; Marketing and Business; Reefers; Ship Management; West Coast South American Lines.

PRINCIPAL COMPETITORS

China Shipping Container Lines Co. Ltd.; Compañia Chilena de Navegación Interoceánica; Maersk Sealand; MSC Ship Management (Hong Kong) Ltd; Nippon Yosen Kabashiki Kaisha (NYK).

FURTHER READING

Aldunate Montes, Felipe, "Timón a Oriente," *AméricaEconomía,* July 9–29, 2004, pp. 32–33.

Anderson, Steve, "Rivalry Intensifies for Chile's Fruit Business," *Journal of Commerce,* June 18, 1991, p. 6C.

Bate, Alison, "CSAV to Call in Asia, Canada, Latin America," *Journal of Commerce,* March 2, 2000, p. 12.

Bay-Schmith C., Jocelyn, "Navieras sacan sus garras" *El Mercurio,* April 26, 2006.

"Chilean Line Ships to Extend Service," *New York Times,* April 3, 1950, p. 39.

"La conquista de los mares," *Capital,* April 21–May 5, 2006, pp. 80–81.

Dahse, Fernando, *El mapa de la extrema riqueza,* Santiago: Editorial Acancagua, 1979, p. 41.

Eguiguren Rozas, Enrique, and Manuel Grez Matte, *La Marine Mercante y su Importancia en la Economia Nacional,* Santiago: University of Chile, 1946, pp. 85–93.

Fazio Rigazzi, Hugo, *Mapa actual de la extrema riqueza en Chile,* Santiago: LOM ARCIS, 1997, pp. 329–31.

———, *Mapa de la extrema riqueza al año 2005,* Santiago: LOM Ediciones, 2005, pp. 256–57.

Hall, Kevin G., "CSAV to Join Vessel-Sharing Latin Service," *Journal of Commerce,* June 24, 1998, p. 10A.

Vega, Francisca, "Mar tormentoso," *AméricaEconomía,* April 1, 2008, pp. 41–42.

Vélez, Claudio, *Historia de la Marina Mercante de Chile,* Santiago: University of Chile, 1961.

Zeitlin, Maurice, and Richard Earl Ratcliff, *Landlords & Capitalists: The Dominant Class of Chile,* Princeton, N.J.: Princeton University Press, 1988, pp. 64–66, 123.

Countrywide Financial

—·—

4500 Park Granada
Calabasas, California 91302
U.S.A.
Telephone: (818) 225-3000
Toll Free: (800) 796-8448
Fax: (818) 225-4051
Web site: http://www.countrywide.com

Wholly Owned Subsidiary of Bank of America Corporation
Incorporated: 1969
Employees: 50,600
Sales: $25.1 million (2007)
NAICS: 522110 Commercial Banking, 522291 Consumer Lending, 522292 Real Estate Credit, 522310 Mortgage and Nonmortgage Loan Brokers, 524126 Direct Property and Casualty Insurance Carriers, 524210 Insurance Agencies and Brokerages

■ ■ ■

Countrywide Financial does business in the area of mortgage lending, including mortgage banking, banking and mortgage warehouse lending, dealing in securities, and insurance underwriting. Countrywide writes, sells, and services single-family home mortgages and was the largest lender by loan volume among independent residential mortgage lending firms in the United States when it was purchased by Bank of America in 2008. The company also offers home equity loans, commercial mortgages, and subprime mortgages. Its capital markets segment buys and sells mortgages and offers asset management and brokerage services. Countrywide sells life, property/casualty, and reinsurance products, and licenses proprietary technology to mortgage lenders in the United Kingdom. The company has 660 branches in the United States and administrative and loan servicing operations in India.

A NEW LENDER GOES PUBLIC

Countrywide was founded in 1969 by David Loeb, a New Yorker who had moved to Virginia to expand his fledgling mortgage banking business, United Mortgage Servicing, and his top-notch young salesman, Angelo Mozilo, a native of the Bronx, who began processing loans at the age of 16. After Loeb was forced to relinquish his original 50 percent stake in United due to pressure from corporate raiders, the two set out to build a new mortgage company they ambitiously named Countrywide. They opened their first office in Anaheim, California. While Mozilo, known for his self-confidence and survival instincts, served as the loan officer, Loeb, whose strength was in holding down costs, performed the underwriting duties from an office in New York City.

In an attempt to speed their progress toward becoming a nationwide company, the partners quickly went public—an unusual move in the industry. Their stock offering, however, proved initially to be a mistake; in exchange for a smaller portion of ownership and an assortment of lawyers, directors, and shareholders to answer to, the founders received only a small portion of new capital, $800,000, not enough to see the company through its first years. To keep Countrywide afloat,

COMPANY PERSPECTIVES

∎

Countrywide Financial is proud to have become a wholly owned subsidiary of Bank of America Corporation. We have become America's leading home loan provider and we know with this position comes great responsibility to our communities and our customers. We are committed to responsible lending practices, meaningful community development initiatives and providing a broad suite of products. Combining the two companies will create unique opportunities that will build stronger customer relationships and deliver solutions that are more responsive to customers' needs.

Mozilo hit the streets of Los Angeles selling loans, while his wife and their three children stayed with relatives back East. Loeb, meanwhile, closed the New York office and moved to Los Angeles.

During the early 1970s, the company managed to stay in business despite the onset of inflation and high interest rates. By 1974, the firm had expanded to eight branch offices, but it was nowhere near realizing its dream of becoming a nationwide company, and furthermore, it was barely making enough money to survive. It appeared that while the firm's eight offices were doing quite well, Countrywide itself, which bore nearly all the risks of the operation, was not.

Realizing that a drastic change had to be made for the company to prosper, Loeb developed a radical idea: Fire all of the salespeople and rebuild the corporation under a new philosophy. Like other mortgage companies, Countrywide employed a highly paid, commissioned sales force. This conventional approach, Loeb reasoned, placed more emphasis on the sales team than on the product itself, and Countrywide's "product," he maintained, should be its price—the combination of interest rates and points that would provide the home buyer with the best value. In order to achieve this goal, Loeb planned to convert the branch offices into uniform loan processors, with the central office taking care of sales by mailing out notices to realtors.

OFFERING AN ATTRACTIVE PRODUCT

Although Mozilo, who had developed a reputation for forming close relationships with employees, initially balked at such draconian measures, he eventually came to accept his partner's "product driven" philosophy. "Interest rates are the very fiber of what this country is all about," he stated in *Mortgage Banking*. "The success or failure of capitalism rides with interest rates—it's where the tar hits the road." Rather than making the change gradually, Mozilo agreed to fire 92 of the company's 95 employees and shut down all of the branch offices at once, retaining the services of only a single secretary to help him and Loeb put together the first mailings to realtors.

The product that Countrywide made available was attractive. Not only were their interest rates lower than the competition's, but they also offered an unprecedented guarantee to lock in the rate quoted at the time of origination through the 60 to 90 days it would take to close a transaction on a home. Nevertheless, few realtors were impressed; Mozilo was again forced to work making personal sales calls to keep the company afloat. This time his job was to convince realtors that they could benefit from his company's new idea.

Mozilo finally persuaded enough realtors to necessitate the reopening of the first Countrywide branch office in Whittier, California. The office was so successful that it nearly collapsed from the volume of new loans to be processed. New offices were soon needed to handle the ever-increasing demand. Although Countrywide handled a large amount of loans, it was able to maintain its high standards for approval because its loan processors were no longer motivated to take a chance on a questionable loan just to get a sales commission. Despite the ominous presence of stagflation and 17.5 percent interest rates strangling the real estate market, Countrywide rebuilt itself into a profitable company by 1978.

A STANDARDIZED APPROACH PAYS OFF

While discounted prices created the demand that fueled the company's early growth, uniformity was the key to maintaining effective management. Each new Countrywide office that opened shared the characteristics of its predecessors: a shopping center or Main Street storefront, approximately 1,000 square feet of office space with a private area for meetings with applicants, and no more than two full-time employees. While a few offices were decorated with elegant furnishings, most conformed to the standard, no-frills company look. By standardizing everything from loan processing to floor coverings, Countrywide was able to keep costs down and improve efficiency. Not only did this strategy boost loan quality, it lowered the cost of loan originations below the 1 percent allowed by the Federal Hous-

KEY DATES

1969: David Loeb and Angelo Mozilo found
Countrywide in Anaheim, California.

1974: The company fires all but three employees,
shuts down its branch offices, and
restructures.

1988: The company founds a new subsidiary,
Countrywide Servicing Exchange, to act as a
broker for buyers and sellers of servicing
rights.

1990: The company introduces its own state-of-the-
art loan origination service, EDGE.

1992: The company launches the "House America"
program.

2003: David Loeb dies at the age of 79.

2006: The company enters the U.K. market and
also moves into banking, opening small bank
offices at home.

2008: Bank of America purchases Countrywide.

ing Administration (FHA). Other mortgage bankers, in contrast, were losing money on originations and had to raise servicing fees to make up the difference.

Countrywide's unconventional discounting and standardization policies were not the only factors that contributed to its rise to the top of the mortgage banking industry. The ability to skillfully read—or some would say fortuitously guess—when interest rates would fall also played a major role. In the early 1980s, while rates were still high, the company began selling its servicing business to maintain profitability. While critics believed such a move was the equivalent of trading in valuable assets for short-term gain, Mozilo, who expected the record-high rates to fall, reasoned that what appeared to be assets would quickly become liabilities once rates fell and throngs of homeowners began refinancing their homes.

Mozilo's gamble paid off. Interest rates plummeted, creating a boom in the refinancing business. Countrywide, having gained wider access to capital markets through its growing profitability, was prepared to meet the new demand, and, with the lowest originating fees and interest rates in the industry, Countrywide was able to take full advantage. By the mid-1980s, the company had expanded to 104 offices in 26 states, providing itself with the facilities to make the most of the boom years of 1984 and 1986. The firm also increased its loan production by initiating a registry

program, agreeing to sell mortgages originated by small savings and loan associations and guaranteeing a loan rate to mortgage applicants. As a result of such strategies and market conditions, the company was able to process more than $3.2 billion in originations by the middle of the decade.

In the midst of the boom in loan originations, Countrywide realized that such favorable conditions would not last forever. A plan for maintaining profitability when interest rates rose had to be developed; otherwise, the completion of a natural business cycle would seriously threaten the company. Again, the company chose the unconventional route. Just as it had earlier sold off many of its loan servicing contracts to raise capital, it decided at this time to build that business to buffer changes in the market. The balanced strategy, which the company called the "macro hedge," helped to make the company's bottom line less sensitive to changes in interest rates. By holding on to the servicing rights of its loans and aggressively purchasing the rights to service mortgages originated by other lenders, the company was able to sustain earnings when a rise in interest rates caused a decline in loan originations. As the decade progressed, the company's servicing portfolio played an increasingly important role, reaching the $1 billion mark in 1984, only to increase tenfold over the next four years. In 1988, the company founded a new subsidiary, Countrywide Servicing Exchange, to act as a broker for buyers and sellers of servicing rights.

BENEFITING FROM TECHNOLOGY

While Countrywide grew steadily through its first two decades, it was at the beginning of the next decade that revenues and profits began to soar. One of the principal factors behind the upsurge was the unforeseen collapse of the savings and loan industry, the chief rival of the mortgage banks. Most mortgage banks, however, were unable to keep up with the demand that rushed their way because they depended on commercial banks, which had tightened their purse strings as a result of the savings and loan scandal, for the money they lent out. While most mortgage banks were set back by the limits of the commercial banks' willingness to lend, Countrywide had no such problem. One of the few public companies in the industry, it already had access to capital. With a proven track record of efficient management and favorable market conditions, Countrywide was a safe bet for investors, who eagerly put up $409 million for new issues of stock between 1987 and 1992.

Countrywide was able to handle the wave of new business without being overwhelmed largely because of its early commitment to technology in the 1970s. Having invested heavily in computerized loan processing at a time when other mortgage bankers were not buying technology, the company further stood out from the competition through its ability to accommodate the surge of new employees and offices needed to handle the added demand. With a solid technological infrastructure in place, the cost and time needed to train new loan production employees was reduced, making it easier for the company to maintain profitability despite fluctuations in the market. During refinancing booms, for instance, the company was able to hire temporary employees to meet the immediate demand, sometimes letting them go when conditions changed.

In addition to giving Countrywide the flexibility to meet the ever changing demands of the volatile housing market, technological innovation enabled the company to reduce the time and cost associated with loan processing and funding. In 1990, for instance, the company introduced its own state-of-the-art loan origination service, EDGE, which was designed to reduce the risks of deficient loans and guarantee pricing. The system was able to significantly reduce origination and processing costs, while accelerating funding time to fewer than 30 days on conventional loans, by enabling loan representatives to enter customer information only once. Common information could then be copied to other files automatically; figures such as loan rates and discount points could be downloaded as well. EDGE then printed out completed legal copies of all documents on a laser printer, eliminating the need for preprinted loan forms and saving the company $1 million a year.

EMERGING AS THE NATION'S TOP MORTGAGE BANKER

By 1992 Countrywide began to realize the full benefits of the strategy it conceived in the 1970s and refined over the next two decades. Largely as a result of its continued commitment to technology, its balanced marketing strategy, and its unmatched aggressive pricing, the company emerged as the nation's top mortgage banker. Taking full advantage of a 19-year low in interest rates, Countrywide originated more than $30 billion in mortgages, moving past such perennial powers as Prudential Insurance Co. and Norwest Corp., while enjoying $246 million in total revenue and profits of $60.2 million—a 170 percent jump from the previous year.

In an attempt to further reduce origination costs and extend its lead over the competition, Countrywide made another landmark advance in the field of artificial-intelligence underwriting systems the following year, through its introduction of the Countrywide Loan

Underwriting Expert System (CLUES). The state-of-the-art system was developed to expedite loan processing by handling most routine cases automatically. Able not only to approve an application—in less than a minute in routine cases—but also to underwrite all types of mortgage loans, the system helped Countrywide's underwriters spend more time on difficult or exceptional cases. With CLUES handling more than 7,000 loans per month, nearly 85 percent, underwriters were able to increase production and attract more customers.

As Countrywide entered the mid-1990s, it directed much of its attention to a market that had been underserved traditionally by banks and mortgage companies alike: the low- and moderate-income population. In 1992, the company launched the House America program, to attend to this need. Designed to make the "American Dream" of home ownership a reality for those who lacked the finances, the credit history, or the stable employment necessary to qualify for a loan an opportunity to do so, House America represented an unprecedented move in the industry. Under the flexible underwriting program, customers were approved for mortgages with a down payment of as low as 3 percent of the sale price. The program, the company pointed out, provided financial counseling and education to thousands, helping individuals with high student loan payments and unstable employment alike to find ways to better manage their money. Countrywide supported its commitment to this goal by pledging to sell $5 billion in House America–type loans to the nation's two largest mortgage lenders, the Federal National Mortgage Association (Fannie Mae) and the Federal Home Loan Mortgage Corporation (Freddie Mac), both of which were established by Congress to ensure that lenders would have a constant source of money for mortgages.

According to Mozilo, House America, as its mission statement read, was designed for the purpose of creating an "equality paradigm ... which will positively impact the revitalization of local communities and economies through home ownership." Accordingly, Countrywide took unprecedented measures to give minority populations greater access to loans. The company's field officers, in fact, did not have the authority to deny loans to minority applicants; officials from central headquarters, including Mozilo, first reviewed the applications.

While Countrywide's commitment to equal housing drew praise from some, it was also intended to bolster profits. With the nation's population growth occurring fastest among immigrant populations, minority and low-income groups represented an area of great potential to the company. The company predicted annual earnings of more than $300 million by the end of the decade. According to a *USA Today* survey, only 43 percent of African American and 40 percent of Hispanic families at the time—compared to 70 percent of white families—owned their own home.

DIVERSIFICATION IN THE 21ST CENTURY

By 2002, Countrywide's financial success was apparent in several newly formed and purchased business segments. While mortgage lending still accounted for about 70 percent of its revenues, the company hoped to diversify and lessen that amount. According to Mozilo in a 2002 *Los Angeles Daily News* article, as Countrywide took "its place among the elite financial services providers," it changed its name to Countrywide Financial Corporation to reflect its new identity as a financial services group. In 2003, Countrywide's banking operation experienced a boost in assets, as did its insurance segment.

When David Loeb died at the age of 79 in 2003, Countrywide was the second largest home loan provider behind Wells Fargo and ahead of Washington Mutual. There were more than 500 branch offices of Countywide Home Loans across the nation, and the company was active in banking, insurance, capital markets, loan closing services, and global marketing. In fact, the volume of Countrywide's loan-servicing portfolio had grown 48 percent from $421 billion to $621 billion between October 2002 and October 2003. Between 1995 and 2005, earnings from banking increased to 26 percent of revenues. In 2005, the company made a push into the commercial insurance brokerage business, offering auto, life and disability, and health insurance to individuals, and made plans to get into directors and officers liability insurance.

THE MORTGAGE CRISIS

In 2004, Countrywide was the largest mortgage originator in the United States with $353 billion in home loans. However, the picture began to change as the American economy began to struggle. The refinancing boom was drawing to a close that year, and mortgage lenders, including Countrywide, were laying off workers nationwide. Nevertheless, Countrywide began to focus on an expansion plan both nationally and globally during this time. In 2006, it entered the United Kingdom and also moved into banking, opening small bank offices staffed by two people, where consumers could open deposit-based accounts and other investments, such as certificates of deposit, money markets, and savings accounts with high interest rates. By the end of 2006, Countrywide had 89 bank locations in 14 states, up from six in 2002.

By 2007, however, it had become clear that the economy was nearing recession, and many critics were accusing the mortgage lending industry of playing a major role in the downfall, as they had extended loans and were collecting interest and fees from people who had no adequate means to repay them. Loan defaults and foreclosures soared, and Countrywide found itself without a market. The company experienced its first quarterly loss in 25 years, of $1.2 billion. By December of that year, with mortgage originations 57 percent lower than the year before, the company was planning to cut around 10,000 jobs. In January 2008, Bank of America stepped in and purchased the struggling Countrywide at a bargain price of a little over $4 billion. With the future of the housing market still uncertain and the economy poised for a possible tailspin, Countrywide's future was uncertain. In August 2008 the company reported that it was facing over 30 lawsuits, including class-action suits alleging securities fraud and charges of "predatory lending." While Countrywide's existence seemed tenuous at best, Bank of America remained optimistic that it could absorb the debt and turn things around.

Jason Gallman
Updated, Carrie Rothburd

PRINCIPAL SUBSIDIARIES

Balboa Insurance Group, Inc.; Balboa Life & Casualty LLC; Calabasas Commerce Center II Association; Countrywide Capital Markets, Inc.; Countrywide KB Home Loans, LLC; Directnet Insurance Agency, Inc.; Effinity Financial Corporation; GHL Mortgage Services Limited; LandSafe Appraisal Services, Inc.; Meritplan Insurance Company; Newport Insurance Company; Newport Management Corporation; Recon Trust Company; The Countrywide Foundation; Trusite Real Estate Services, Inc.

PRINCIPAL COMPETITORS

Citigroup; Fannie Mae; C-BASS; CTX Mortgage; DHI Mortgage; GMAC-RFC; HSBC Finance; Wachovia Corporation; Washington Mutual; Freddie Mac; JP Morgan Chase.

FURTHER READING

Barrett, Amy, "Countrywide's Home Sweet Loans," *Business Week,* September 14, 1992.

"CFC: Wholesale Down but Brokers Still Key," *Origination News,* December 2007, p. 1.

Cocheo, Steve, "Mortgage Machine," *American Banking Association Banking Journal,* October 1995.

Collett, Wayne C., "Homeward Bound," *Mortgage Banking,* January 1995, pp. 1–6.

Cziborr, Chris, "Countrywide Launching Insurance Unit in Irvine," *Orange County Business Journal,* March 7, 2005, p. 3.

Darlin, Damon, "Desensitizing," *Forbes,* September 14, 1996, pp. 60–61.

Hill, Christian, and Jim Carlton, "Countrywide Credit Takes Mortgage Market by Storm," *Wall Street Journal,* September 4, 1992.

Kulkosky, Edward, "Mozilo's Countrywide Still in the Fast Lane," *American Banker,* June 11, 1993.

Magnet, Myron, "Countrywide Credit Industries: Be Ready to Push Your Luck," *Fortune,* April 4, 1994.

Pondel, Evan, "Countrywide Goes for New Identity; Name Emphasizes Financial Services," *Los Angeles Daily News,* November 12, 2002, p. B1.

Wilcox, Gregory J., "BOFA, Troubled Lender Seal Deal; Countrywide: California Layoffs Anticipated in $4.1 Billion Buyout," *Los Angeles Daily News,* January 12, 2008, A1.

———, "Countrywide Suffers First Loss in a Quarter Century; Lender $1.2 Billion in Red," *Los Angeles Daily News,* October 27, 2007, p. N1.

Willette, Anne, "New Rules Help More People Qualify," *USA Today,* November 15, 1994.

Dale and Thomas Popcorn LLC

———■———

1 Cedar Lane
Englewood, New Jersey 07631
U.S.A.
Toll Free: (800) 767-2676
Fax: (201) 645-4848
Web site: http://www.daleandthomaspopcorn.com

Private Company
Incorporated: 2002
Employees: 250
Sales: $40.8 million (2007 est.)
NAICS: 311423 Dried and Dehydrated Food Manufacturing

■ ■ ■

Dale and Thomas Popcorn LLC is a maker of gourmet popcorn (kosher certified) that hopes to be to popcorn what Starbucks is to coffee. The company sells online, through catalogs, and in about 15 company-owned retail shops located in New Jersey, New York, Florida, Massachusetts, and Michigan. The company has long harbored plans to open franchised shops as well. Employing a popcorn chef trained at the Culinary Institute of America and relying on the best popping corn available from Indiana, Dale and Thomas offers a wide array of exotic popcorn combinations, including such sweet varieties as Chocolate and Peanut Butter Drizzlecorn, Cinnamon Crème Drizzlecorn, Frosted Gingerbread, Chocolate Chunk N'Caramel, Peanut Butter & White Chocolate Drizzlecorn, and Sweet Georgia Pecan. Other flavors include Country Smokehouse

Cheddar, Blue Ribbon Chili & Sour Cream, and an Italian collection of three flavors: Veneto, Roma, and Umbria.

In addition, the company offers Popsters, whole caramel popcorn kernels dipped in either peanut butter, milk chocolate, or dark chocolate, and Pop Truffles, similar to Popsters but available in six flavors, such as espresso and dark chocolate raspberry. The shops sell popcorn by the bag, where customers can add mix-ins, similar to Cold Stone Creamery. For take-out as well as online and catalog sales, ready-made Dale and Thomas Popcorn is also available in medium and large tins, offering three different sections and flavors; variety packs; gift tins, tubs, and crates; and sampler gift boxes. Dale and Thomas also offers a business gift program; a Popcorn of the Month club with 3-, 6-, and 12-month subscriptions; and the PopClub frequent buyer program. Aside from gourmet flavors, Dale and Thomas offers a wholesale brand of popcorn labeled Popcorn, Indiana, and a retail product, Movie Theater Popcorn, which the company maintains captures the taste of actual movie theater popcorn in a bag. Dale and Thomas is a private company based in Englewood, New Jersey. The "Thomas" in the name is basketball star Isiah Thomas, a major investor. Warren Struhl, chief executive officer and cofounder, is the majority shareholder.

ENTREPRENEURIAL ORIGINS

Dale and Thomas was cofounded in 2002 by entrepreneurs Warren Struhl and Richard Demb. It was Struhl who supplied the idea of creating a national, premium popcorn brand. After Struhl graduated from Tulane University in 1984, he moved to Chicago and went to work for JMB Realty. Chicago was known for its street popcorn, and Struhl soon became a steady customer. In recalling those days, he told the *Record* of Bergen County, New Jersey, "I used to live in Chicago and ate popcorn from a popcorn cart every day for lunch. I always thought there was an opportunity to open stores and create the first retail brand, just like Starbucks did with coffee." He filed away that idea, however, and in 1987 started up another business, PaperDirect, Inc., a catalog company that sold specialty computer papers, which he grew to annual revenues of $100 million before selling the business to a *Fortune* 500 company in 1993. Struhl would then become an investor in retail, catalog, and consumer products. He started another company, Genesis Direct, a catalog direct marketer that did not fare as well as PaperDirect and declared bankruptcy in 1999. Later that same year he started another company, Awards.com, in Lyndhurst, New Jersey, to sell trophies, promotional items, and corporate gifts.

Although he remained involved in Awards.com, Struhl returned to his idea of starting a chain of premium popcorn stores. He teamed up with Richard Demb in 2002 and together they began brainstorming about Struhl's idea. They decided to create a fictional town called Popcorn, Indiana. A few minutes of online research soon revealed that there was an actual small town in Indiana called Popcorn, population around 50, located some 70 miles southwest of Indianapolis, prompting Struhl and Demb to fly to Indiana to pay a visit. There they met Popcorn's mayor, Dale Humphrey, a third-generation Popcorn resident and former popcorn farmer who had since turned to raising cattle.

Humphrey charmed them with stories about his neighbors and Indiana's relationship to popcorn. It turned out that, due to its climate and fertile soil, Indiana was in fact the popcorn capital of the United States, responsible for nearly 30 percent of the country's crop. The largest producer of popcorn, Weaver Popcorn Co., dedicated to selling movie theater popcorn and other concession businesses, was based in the northern part of the state, as were Orville Redenbacher and a number of other brands. In southern Indiana, Princeton Farms Popcorn was a major brand.

FIRST TAKE-OUT SHOP OPENS IN INDIANA

Impressed with Humphrey, Struhl and Demb hired him as a consultant and together they developed a company under the name Popcorn, Indiana, which in 2002 began marketing gourmet popcorn online. The company's headquarters was established in Englewood, New Jersey, where Struhl was a resident, along with a plant that popped the corn that was sold online. It then supplied popcorn, toppings, and mix-ins to a Popcorn, Indiana, take-out shop the company opened in New York City at Broadway and 63rd Street, the décor affecting a small-town look inspired by Humphrey. The partners soon found that they were not the only people enamored with popcorn. Not only were customers enthusiastic about the product; people who would be key to the company's growth soon introduced themselves.

One was Ed Doyle, a 1990 graduate of the Culinary Institute of America, who had been enjoying success in a restaurant career, serving as an executive chef at Boston hotels, but was looking to make his mark in some other way. While snacking on popcorn, he became inspired to create gourmet popcorn recipes that were a step above the caramel and cheese-flavored popcorn generally available. He began concocting his own flavors and when he learned about Popcorn, Indiana, he contacted Struhl and Demb and was hired as the company's popcorn chef, in charge of a test kitchen to develop new products.

Another person who took notice of Popcorn, Indiana, was Isiah Thomas, president of the New York Knicks basketball team and later the coach. On his way to work at Madison Square Garden in 2003, he stopped by the popcorn shop and immediately associated the snack with his childhood. "All of my fond memories come from everyone sitting around, telling stories and sharing a bowl of popcorn," he told *Time* magazine. Interested in becoming involved with the company, he had an associate contact Struhl and Demb, who initially thought they were receiving a prank phone call. Instead, they soon found themselves having lunch with Thomas at a midtown restaurant and telling him their ideas about carving out a niche in the premium end of the popcorn business.

It was Thomas who astutely remarked that what they were really selling was not popcorn but memories, the associations that people like Thomas and his family

KEY DATES

2002: Company founded as Popcorn, Indiana.
2004: Company renamed Dale and Thomas Popcorn, LLC, following involvement of Isiah Thomas.
2005: Holiday demand forces two-week moratorium on Internet sales.
2007: Goldman Sachs invests in company.

in Chicago had with popcorn. With Thomas clearly in tune with the business, and a former Indiana University basketball player as well, he was an obvious fit for the company. In 2004 he became a major investor and celebrity promoter, and Popcorn, Indiana, was recast as Dale and Thomas Popcorn, with Thomas's last name joined with Humphrey's first name, a tribute to the latter's influence and an appropriately folksy name in the vein of Ben & Jerry's. Humphrey was never more than a consultant to the company and he passed away in 2007. The management team was also bolstered with talent, including franchising head David Orwasher, known for opening the first 750 Starbucks stores on the East Coast, and another Starbucks executive, Stuart Fields, to serve as chief operating officer.

DEAL WITH MUSICLAND

After generating sales of $1 million in the company's first year, Dale and Thomas enjoyed steady growth, building its catalog and web business while opening new stores that were a step up from the original take-out shop. The new shops were between 600 and 1,200 square feet in size and featured seating and a popcorn bar where customers could choose their popcorn flavors and mix-ins. Sales topped $5 million in 2004. A boon to business came when the product was named one of Oprah Winfrey's "favorite things" in her *O* magazine. In 2005 NBC's *Today Show* also raved about Dale and Thomas Popcorn.

Also in 2005, the company struck a deal with Musicland, owners of the Sam Goody, Suncoast, and Media Play chains, to open stand-alone Dale and Thomas stores in the greater New York City area or popcorn outlets inside Sam Goody and Suncoast stores. There was the potential for Musicland to build as many as 200 stores, 50 in Manhattan. Another deal reached in 2005 was with Allied Office Products, which agreed to offer Dale and Thomas popcorn to its 15,000 customers. The popcorn was so popular that during the 2005 holiday

season the company had to stop taking orders online for two weeks.

To keep up with demand, Dale and Thomas moved its manufacturing operations in 2006 to a temporary site to allow its old factory to be expanded. By the spring of 2007 the renovated facility was supplying 12 Dale and Thomas company-owned stores, and management indicated that it planned to open as many as 400 more stores over the next three years. Aside from customers, Wall Street also took notice of the company and the possibility that Dale and Thomas could evolve into a major premium brand. Investment bank Goldman Sachs invested in the venture to help fund the store expansion plans.

LOOKING TO THE FUTURE

The Dale and Thomas brand continued to increase its exposure. In an effort to build sales for the Super Bowl in 2008, the company hired former National Football League quarterback and television sports commentator Troy Aikman and announcer Joe Buck to collaborate with Popcorn Chef Doyle on two new limited edition flavors marketed for the big game, which over the years had evolved into a major food holiday. The two flavors that resulted were Halftime Chili & Sour Cream, and Dark Fudge Drizzlecorn.

Although Dale and Thomas generated sales of $40 million in 2007, it remained unprofitable and, according to *Forbes,* continued to have problems in product delivery and customer service. "Opening new stores," maintained *Forbes,* "has taken more time and money than Struhl anticipated. He once planned to have 1,000 stores, something that looks like a long shot now. He hopes signing up franchises will help." To make matters worse for Dale and Thomas, the benefit of being associated with Isiah Thomas lost much of its luster, forcing the company to play down his involvement. In 2007 Thomas and the Knicks lost a sexual harassment lawsuit aimed at him and he was fired as the Knicks coach and president. In 2008 he received more unwanted publicity when the police were summoned to his house and he was taken to the hospital with what authorities ruled was an accidental overdose of prescription drugs. By telling the press that it was his 17-year-old daughter who was the actual victim, Thomas only drew more attention from New York tabloids. Despite all of these difficulties, Struhl hoped to turn a profit in 2008. "When you move this quickly," he told *Forbes,* "you always hit potholes." Whether the venture would prove successful in the future was yet to be determined.

Ed Dinger

PRINCIPAL COMPETITORS

CaramelCrisp LLC; The Popcorn Factory; Popcorn Palace.

FURTHER READING

Coudret, Rebecca, "Company with Hoosier Ties Seeks the Newest in Upscale Snacking, and It's Not Your Father's Popcorn," *Evansville Courier & Press,* April 25, 2007, p. D1.

Dunaief, Daniel, "Popcorn Company Aims for Recognition, Expansion," *New York Daily News,* February 7, 2005.

Keaton, Joanne, "Hoosier Snacks," *Indiana Business Magazine,* February 1992, p. 80.

Passy, Charles, "Dale and Thomas Popcorn Is a Hit," *Cos News Service,* November 28, 2007.

Randall, David K., "Dandy Corn," *Forbes,* March 10, 2008, p. 70.

Sayre, Carolyn, "Pass the Popcorn," *Time,* March 12, 2007, p. G4.

Verdon, Joan, "Kernel of an Idea Is Off and Poppin'," *Record* (Bergen County, N.J.), November 19, 2004, p. B1.

Deluxe Entertainment
Services Group, Inc.

—■—

1377 North Serrano Avenue
Los Angeles, California 90027
U.S.A.
Telephone: (323) 960-3600
Fax: (323) 960-7016
Web site: http://www.bydeluxe.com

Wholly Owned Subsidiary of MacAndrews & Forbes Holdings, Inc.
Founded: 1915 as the camera and film department of Fox Film Corporation
Employees: 1,200
Sales: $900 million (2007 est.)
NAICS: 512191 Teleproduction and Other Postproduction Services; 512199 Other Motion Picture and Video Industries; 334612 Prerecorded Compact Disc (Except Software), Tape, and Record Reproducing; 512120 Motion Picture and Video Distribution

■ ■ ■

Deluxe Entertainment Services Group, Inc., is a leading provider of postproduction, manufacturing, asset management, and distribution services to the film industry. The firm's various units perform digital postproduction and mastering services including film-to-video and video-to-film transfer; author DVDs; manage digital and other assets; restore older films; create subtitles and foreign-language release versions; distribute promotional materials; and manufacture and distribute film and digital cinema prints. Deluxe has offices in the United States, Canada, Spain, Italy, and the United Kingdom, and its clients include such major names as 20th Century Fox, Paramount, Sony, MGM, and New Line.

BEGINNINGS: 1915

The roots of Deluxe date to 1915, when film exhibitor/distributor William Fox founded the Fox Film Corporation in Fort Lee, New Jersey, to produce motion pictures. To organize the necessary equipment, and to manufacture film prints for distribution, the new company created a film and camera unit headed by Alan Freedman. This operation was expanded in 1919 when Fox opened a studio in Hollywood, California, where a new film processing and printing laboratory was built on the south side of the company's studio lot. At the same time, the firm added facilities in New York, where it was headquartered.

At this time movies were still silent, with live accompaniment supplied by musicians in theaters. Efforts to create a synchronized soundtrack were ongoing, however, and in 1926 Fox bought the patents of a sound-on-film process (later known as Movietone) developed by Case Research Labs in Auburn, New York, as well as those of a German firm, Tri-Ergon. In 1927 Fox rival Warner Brothers released *The Jazz Singer*, the first feature film to contain recorded dialogue via synchronized phonograph discs, and Fox soon began to produce sound films of its own. The difficulty of maintaining strict synchronization between a film (which might have to be spliced and thus shortened) and disc (which could also skip) quickly became apparent to both exhibitors and audiences, and Movietone was soon chosen as the standard of the industry.

Soon after, Fox introduced a new widescreen process, Grandeur, which used 70mm-wide film that yielded a sharper image and better sound. Theater owners who had just invested in sound equipment balked at installing the necessary projectors and larger screens, however, and it was quickly abandoned.

Although the profits of Fox and other movie companies had boomed with the introduction of sound, in 1930 William Fox was forced out of the company that bore his name after he overextended himself in attempts to take over Metro-Goldwyn-Mayer and a theater chain. Control would subsequently be held by a group of financiers.

DE LUXE LABORATORIES, INC., CREATED: 1932

In 1932 Fox Film laboratories head Alan Freedman founded an affiliate company called De Luxe Laboratories, Inc., which would operate Fox's lab on West 55th Street in New York. It was then considered the largest film processing facility in the world, with capacity of half a billion feet per year and the ability to print the theatrical standard 35mm gauge as well as 16mm and color film.

In 1935 Fox and 20th Century Pictures merged to form 20th Century-Fox, with 20th Century head Darryl F. Zanuck taking charge of the studio. During World War II, production was curtailed in an effort to conserve film stock, with Fox cutting back from about 50 to just over 30 features per year, and following strict government rules about printing only a minimal number of "takes."

At the start of the 1950s the industry shifted to nonflammable safety film from the highly flammable nitrate-based stock heretofore used, making film process-

ing, distribution, and projection considerably safer. In 1953 American movie studios, threatened by the surging popularity of television, tried to boost attendance by introducing a range of new formats including 3-D and widescreen films. The latter were achieved by several technical methods, with Fox/De Luxe using an anamorphic lens that "squeezed" the wide image to fit standard 35mm film. Named CinemaScope, the process soon became an industry standard.

The company also developed a new audio technology, in which magnetic stripes were overlaid on a film print to provide four separate channels of sound. The greater expense of making such prints, and the reluctance of exhibitors to invest in additional equipment, led filmmakers to abandon the process for all but the most prestigious releases.

In 1953 De Luxe Laboratories signed a long-term agreement with Technicolor Motion Picture Corporation to process Technicolor dye transfer prints at its New York facility. At this time the firm was still headed by its original president, Alan Freedman.

DELUXE WINS FIRST OSCAR: 1961

In 1961 Deluxe (as the name was then rendered) was honored with an Academy Award for technical achievement. The Oscar was won for a process the firm's engineers had developed for recomposing CinemaScope films for conventional (non-squeezed) film formats.

In 1972 the company began to manufacture videocassettes. At this time few consumers owned home video equipment, but the move would prove fortuitous a few years later when the popularity of VHS tapes took off. In 1978 Deluxe named Burton "Bud" Stone president. Stone's father had been chief engineer of Consolidated Film Labs in New Jersey, and the younger Stone had worked as an assistant film editor and in sales and marketing for several New York labs. He had also founded Allservice Film Laboratories in 1963, and in 1971 was named to head Precision Film Labs, an affiliate of Deluxe.

In 1983 Fox sued rival studio Columbia for $120 million for breach of contract after the latter firm canceled its film-processing contract with Deluxe because Fox chairman Marvin Davis had borrowed a copy of the still-unreleased Columbia feature *The Toy* to show his family. The suit was settled in January 1986 with Columbia agreeing to resume using Deluxe Laboratories for its movie and TV printing services.

In the spring of 1990 financially strapped 20th Century Fox owner Rupert Murdoch's News Corp. an-

KEY DATES

1915: Fox Film Corp. founded in Fort Lee, New Jersey.

1919: Fox builds additional labs in Hollywood and New York.

1926: Fox buys patent for sound-on-film process, dubs it Movietone.

1932: De Luxe Laboratories, Inc., formed.

1935: Fox merges with 20th Century to form 20th Century-Fox, headed by Darryl Zanuck.

1953: Fox/De Luxe introduces widescreen CinemaScope process.

1961: Firm, by this time known as Deluxe, wins first technical Academy Award.

1972: Deluxe begins manufacturing videocassettes.

1990: Deluxe Labs purchased by Rank Organisation plc for $150 million.

1998: Company renamed Deluxe Entertainment Services Group.

2004: Firm gains control of EFILM; acquires Matsushita Electric's Digital Video Compression Center.

2006: MacAndrews & Forbes Holdings buys Deluxe from Rank for $750 million; company renamed Deluxe Entertainment Services Group, Inc.

nounced it would sell Deluxe Laboratories to the Rank Organisation plc. The $150 million deal was opposed by the U.S. Justice Department because Rank also owned The Film House Group of Toronto, Canada, giving it the second and third largest film processing labs in North America and about half of the $140 million market. A federal judge denied the request for an injunction, however, and at year's end the sale was completed.

The company's new owner was a London-based conglomerate with interests in gambling, hotels, film studios, theaters, and other ventures. In addition to The Film House, Rank also owned Rank Film Laboratories, Ltd., of Denham, England, and a video duplication unit, which would be folded into Deluxe. During the late 1980s and early 1990s Deluxe undertook a $20 million equipment upgrade that allowed for faster print production and greater capacity. In 1994 Cyril Drabinsky was named president of the company, taking the place of the retiring Bud Stone. Two years later the firm duplicated its one-billionth videocassette.

DELUXE ENTERTAINMENT SERVICES FORMED: 1998

In May 1998 the Rank unveiled a new name for its Film and Entertainment Services Division at the Cannes Film Festival. The Deluxe Entertainment Services Group would take the renowned laboratory's name, reflecting the prominence of the brand within the industry. Rank's other film and video units were also renamed, with Rank Film Laboratories, Ltd., of Denham, England, becoming Deluxe Laboratories Ltd.; Rank Video Services America of Deerfield, Illinois, and Los Angeles renamed Deluxe Video Services; Rank Video Services Europe of London becoming Deluxe Video Services Ltd.; and Pinewood Studios Ltd. taking the name Deluxe at Pinewood Studios Ltd. Deluxe Laboratories, Inc., of Los Angeles and Deluxe Laboratories Ltd. of Canada (the former Film House) made up the rest of the firm's operations.

The company's video unit was by this time shipping tapes and DVDs directly to large retailers such as Wal-Mart and Kmart, bypassing middlemen and helping increase revenues. The firm had earlier dabbled in rack-jobbing (distributing videos to stores on displays that the company owned) and shipping by truck through respective Pittsburgh and Detroit subsidiaries, but neither venture had been successful. Its video duplicating and distribution operations at this time were centered in a 535,000-square-foot facility in Pleasant Prairie, Wisconsin.

In 1999 Deluxe acquired a London-based DVD authoring unit, Electric Switch, and in 2000 bought a DVD manufacturing plant in Carson, California, from Pioneer Video Manufacturing. The year also saw the acquisition of Vision Entertainment, an asset management firm, and the investment of $10 million in a postproduction facility in Israel. Deluxe by then reportedly had 45 percent of the postproduction market in the United States, and revenues of $1.7 billion. During 2000, owner Rank also sold Pinewood Studios to an investor consortium.

In late 2001 Deluxe Laboratories partnered with Post Logic Studios to offer digital film print services. Post Logic would perform mastering duties, while Deluxe would make the prints. The firm then had the capacity to print four billion feet of film per year, copy one million videotapes per day, and make eight million DVDs per month.

STAKE IN EFILM PURCHASED: 2002

In the summer of 2002 Deluxe bought a 20 percent stake in EFILM, LLC, which had been acquired by

Panavision not long before. The nine-year-old EFILM provided digital laboratory services including high-resolution film scanning and mastering. EFILM would subsequently expand its 5,000-square-foot operation to 30,000 square feet. Its clients were a "Who's Who" of Hollywood and independent film studios.

The year 2002 also saw Deluxe buy an 80 percent stake in the North American and European DVD production operations of Taiwan-based optical disc firm Ritek, which would be called Deluxe Global Media Services; add laboratories in Toronto and Rome; and expand postproduction services in Toronto. Other activities included the purchase of Capital FX of London and the rebranding of Electric Switch as Deluxe Digital Studios. The company had also formed a unit called Deluxe Digital Media Asset Management, and during the year it bought Vision Entertainment of California, which warehoused and distributed materials for clients such as MGM Home Entertainment.

In 2003 Deluxe formed a joint venture with QC Corp. to operate a DVD-manufacturing facility in Canada, and bought Sonic Foundry's Media Services Division and the European operations of Disctronics, which could replicate 1.5 million optical discs per day. The firm also purchased distribution services firm ETS to expand its theatrical print distribution, and introduced a new anti-piracy watermarking technology called FCT (forensic coding technology).

Acquisitions in 2004 included Matsushita Electric's Digital Video Compression Center, which helped make Deluxe's DVD compression, encoding, and authoring capabilities the largest in the world at that time; and Softitler, an international subtitling company. Deluxe also bought the remaining 80 percent stake in EFILM from Panavision to become that firm's sole owner. EFILM was then considered the industry's premiere digital film company, having produced digital negatives for titles such as *The Passion of the Christ* and *Spiderman II*. Another new unit, Deluxe Media Management, was founded to handle storage and distribution of promotional items such as posters and large displays for studios. The firm was then processing close to five billion feet of movie film per year, and had 27 facilities in operation worldwide.

The industry was moving rapidly from film-based to digital postproduction, with a digital intermediate (DI) created instead of a film negative for more than half of U.S. major studio feature films. A DI could come from either a digitally-scanned shot-on-film production, or from one recorded digitally. The resulting data file could then be manipulated to correct colors, hide unwanted bits of scenery, and more. A completed DI could be converted to film for release prints or copied for the growing number of theaters using digital cinema projection systems, as well as serving as the basis for DVD masters. While this process had been used for special-effects sequences that were converted to film and spliced into a negative, the shift to a full DI for a feature film was a major step forward.

The vast amount of data storage required for such films (and to back them up for safekeeping) kept the firm in a constant process of adding capacity. In the industry's 2K standard, 2,048 lines of horizontal and 1,556 lines of vertical resolution were achieved, with a single image taking up 12MB. A film shot at 24 frames per second might typically be 175,000 frames long, thus requiring approximately 2,000 gigabytes of data storage. Newer films were using the even higher-resolution 4K standard, which required as much as four times the information. Deluxe's digital asset management services included storing and maintaining these massive—and extremely valuable—files for its clients, and the company also archived film prints, paper materials, and even props.

RANK SELLS FIRM TO MACANDREWS & FORBES: 2006

In December 2005 Rank announced that it would sell Deluxe to a unit of MacAndrews & Forbes Holdings, Inc., for $750 million, and the deal was completed early the following year. The company's new owner, led by financier Ronald Perelman, had a diverse portfolio of holdings that included consumer goods, gaming, financial services, security, defense, medical, and biotechnology companies, as well as movie industry rental giant Panavision. The deal did not include DVD replication unit Deluxe Media Services, which was later sold to Digital Audio Disk Corporation. In early 2006 Deluxe also opened an EFILM Digital Laboratory at George Lucas's Industrial Light & Magic facility in San Francisco.

In March 2007 Deluxe signed a worldwide print services agreement with Twentieth Century Fox. The firm would produce both film prints and digital cinema copies, and perform delivery and other logistics services. It was the first major deal of its type involving digital film to be signed in Hollywood, and brought the company full circle to its roots as part of Fox Film Corp. Meanwhile, the firm's busy EFILM unit had opened a new 8,000-square-foot facility in Hollywood to focus on producing preview "trailers."

During 2007 MacAndrews & Forbes Holdings completed a $610 recapitalization of Deluxe, which was arranged by Credit Suisse Group. It would include a $157 million dividend to MacAndrews & Forbes, which had originally invested $155 million in the company. In early 2008 Deluxe added a laboratory in Hollywood on the site of its original 1919 plant there. The three-story, 35,000-square-foot facility would enable it to increase film-printing capacity by 30 percent. The firm had also added new operations in New York and Vancouver, the latter by purchasing a postproduction business from Rainmaker Entertainment for $14 million, and was making plans to move its Toronto operations into a new 80,000-square-foot space.

Nearing the end of its first century in business, Deluxe Entertainment Services Group, Inc., had firmly established itself as one of the world's leading film and digital video service providers. The company was smoothly transitioning from film-based to digital media as the industry moved closer to a fully digital content delivery system, and its future looked bright.

Frank Uhle

PRINCIPAL SUBSIDIARIES

Deluxe Laboratories, Inc.; Deluxe Digital Media; Deluxe Digital Studios; Deluxe Media Management; EFILM Digital Labs; Deluxe MediaVu; Deluxe Consulting Group; CIS Hollywood; Deluxe Film Services; Deluxe Film Rejuvenation; Deluxe Laboratories, Inc. (Canada); Deluxe The Lab (Canada); Deluxe Film Services Ltd. (Canada); Deluxe Postproduction (Canada); Softitler Canada, Inc. (Canada); Deluxe Laboratories, Ltd. (United Kingdom); Deluxe Digital Studios (United Kingdom); Deluxe Digital London (United Kingdom); Deluxe Labs Italia (Italy); Carme 1-3 (Italy); Fotofilm Deluxe Madrid (Spain).

PRINCIPAL COMPETITORS

Technicolor, Inc.; Ascent Media Group, Inc.; Eastman Kodak Co.; Fotokem Industries, Inc.; Pacific Title and Art Studio; Modern Videofilm, Inc.

FURTHER READING

"Convergence Sets the Stage for Deluxe Acquisitions," *DCD Business Report*, August 16, 2004.

Crabtree, Sheigh, "Deluxe Laboratories and Post Logic Studios Have Formed an Alliance to Offer Clients Digital Intermediate," *Hollywood Reporter*, December 7, 2001, p. 74.

——, "Deluxe Labs Wades into Digital," *Hollywood Reporter*, July 8, 2002, p. 6.

——, "Deluxe to Start S.F. EFILM Ops," *Hollywood Reporter*, December 8, 2005.

"Deluxe Acquires Authoring Pioneer DVCC," *Medialine*, August 1, 2004, p. 9.

"Deluxe Lab's Bud Stone Dies at 80," *Daily Variety*, April 21, 2008.

"Fox Film, Coca-Cola Unit Settle Suit Over a Contract," *Wall Street Journal*, January 10, 1986.

"Fox Sells Laboratories," *Wall Street Journal*, April 4, 1932, p. 7.

Giardina, Carolyn, "Fox Processes Deluxe Labs Deal," *Hollywood Reporter*, March 13, 2007.

——, "Movin' on Up to a Deluxe H'wood Lab," *Hollywood Reporter*, March 7, 2008.

Goldstein, Seth, "A Renamed Deluxe Video Has Big Plans," *Billboard*, June 6, 1998.

——, "Vid Duplicators Take on Distribution," *Billboard*, October 31, 1998.

Graser, Mark, "Deluxe Reeling in Film; Processor Poised to Take on Technicolor," *Daily Variety*, August 9, 2004.

Holman, Kelly, "Deluxe Dividend for Owner," *Daily Deal*, May 4, 2007.

Hope, Michelle, "EFILM Relies on SANs and SATA," *InfoStor*, September 1, 2004, p. 32.

Kollewe, Julia, "Rank Completes Break-Up with Pounds 430M Sale of Deluxe Film Arm," *Independent*, December 29, 2005.

Levy, Sasha, "Deluxe Laboratories Sets Israel Production Facility," *Hollywood Reporter*, April 11, 2000, p. 12.

McKernan, Brian, "EFILM's DI Directions," *Digital Cinema*, June 1, 2004, p. 12.

"News Corp. Completes Sale of Unit to Rank Organisation," *Dow Jones News Service*, December 17, 1990.

Parisi, Paula, "Stone Steps Aside at Deluxe," *Hollywood Reporter*, December 14, 1994, p. 6.

"Rank Gets the Deluxe Treatment," *One to One*, July 1, 1998, p. 12.

Solomon, Aubrey, *Twentieth Century-Fox: A Corporate and Financial History*, Metuchen, N.J., and London: Scarecrow Press, 1988.

Winter, Mark, "The (Virtual) Show Must Go On," *Optimize*, February 1, 2005, p. 61.

The Columbus Dispatch

Dispatch Printing Company

———— ▪ ————

34 South 3rd Street
Columbus, Ohio 43215-4201
U.S.A.
Telephone: (614) 461-5000
Toll Free: (800) 282-0263
Fax: (614) 461-6087
Web site: http://www.dispatch.com

Private Company
Incorporated: 1871
Employees: 2,100
Sales: $488 million (2007 est.)
NAICS: 511110 Newspaper Publishers; 515112 Radio
    Stations; 515120 Television Broadcasting

■ ■ ■

The Dispatch Printing Company is a private company owned by the Wolfe family of Columbus, Ohio, and is best known as the publisher of the *Columbus Dispatch* daily and Sunday newspapers. Although Dispatch Printing is primarily a media company, it houses a wide scope of Wolfe family business interests. At one time Dispatch Printing included Ohio Partners Ltd., a venture capital company; The Capital Ltd., a real estate business; Dispatch Consumer Services Inc., a direct-marketing company and publisher of weekly suburban newspapers; Wolfe Enterprises Inc., a community relations company; and Wolfe Aviation, an aeronautical services company. Aside from the *Columbus Dispatch,* the company's print properties include the "This Week" chain of about two dozen weekly community

newspapers; *Columbus Parent,* a free monthly parenting magazine; *Alive!,* a weekly arts, entertainment, and dining publication; and *Fronteras,* a Spanish-language weekly publication.

The Dispatch Broadcast Group includes two television stations, located in Columbus and Indianapolis; a 24-hour cable television news channel, Ohio News Network, and the Sky Trak Weather network in Indianapolis; two Columbus radio stations; the Ohio News Network–Radio; and Radio Sound Network, provider of satellite services to radio broadcasters. In addition, Dispatch Printing operates a number of web sites, many of which draw on the company's other media properties for content. As circulation numbers and ad revenues for the *Columbus Dispatch* have declined in recent years, an increasing emphasis has been placed on convergence among Dispatch Printing's media operations.

DISPATCH PRINTING FOUNDED: 1871

In June 1871, the Dispatch Printing Company was founded to establish an evening newspaper in Columbus, the *Daily Dispatch,* which later took the name the *Evening Dispatch.* The ten incorporators were mostly printers and included William Trevitt Jr., Samuel Bradford, Timothy McMahon, James O'Donnell, Peter C. Johnson, L. P. Stephens, John M. Webb, J. S. B. Given, C. M. Morris, and Willoughby Webb. Other than Webb, who would become editor, each man paid $100 to create a capital pool of $900. Trevitt supplied the printing press. In addition, the stockholders agreed

COMPANY PERSPECTIVES

Both the print and online arms of Ohio's Greatest Home Newspaper are committed to providing the most accurate, timely and in-depth news and information to the Columbus metropolitan area. Every day, we strive to reflect the spirit of the community with a commitment to excellence that not only extends to the writing, editing and photography of our products, but also to their readability and design.

to work for the publication for ten weeks with their salary deferred to a later date. The first issue, a mere four pages in size, appeared on July 1, 1871. Cost on the street was three cents, but most of the copies were delivered free to a list of 1,000 names that had been previously canvassed by another paper that was never published. The *Dispatch* secured the list and delivered the paper to these people on a trial basis in a move that paid off: More than 800 became regular subscribers.

After ten weeks the stockholders began drawing one-quarter of their salary, the balance credited on the books in the form of stock. The cash amount would increased to 50 percent the second year, and 75 percent the third. The *Dispatch* merged with the *Daily Statesman* in June 1872. In the summer of 1874 the *Dispatch* was sold for $10,500 to Captain John H. Putnam and Doctor G. A. Doren, who would not run the paper for very long. In January 1876 they sold the business to William D. Brickell, a printer by trade, and Captain L. D. Myers, the latter of whom served as editor. Myers retired in 1882 and Brickell bought him out to become the sole owner. During his tenure, the *Dispatch* added a Sunday edition in late 1899.

WOLFE BROTHERS ACQUIRE DISPATCH PRINTING: 1905

Brickell sold the *Dispatch* to Congressman J. J. Gill of Steubenville, Ohio, in 1903. Due to poor health, however, Gill was soon looking for a buyer. In August 1905 brothers Robert and Harry Wolfe acquired the paper. They were originally from Cumberland, Ohio, the sons of shoemaker Andrew Jackson Wolfe, and were raised in modest circumstances with limited education.

Robert, 12 years older than his brother, was not content with his lot, however. "I was born to a condition to which I would not submit," he once said. "I changed it." At 14 he drove a canal boat as a teenager

between Cumberland, Maryland, and in Georgetown, Washington, D.C., then became an ordinary seaman on a schooner plying the coastal waters. For a time he found himself in New York City, where he sold copies of the *New York Sun* during the tenure of editor Charles A. Dana, an experience that began a fascination with the newspaper business.

Wolfe return to the sea, traveling to Cuba, worked as a tie cutter in the swamps of Louisiana, and punched cattle in Texas before coming to Columbus in 1888, where his family had moved the previous year. At the age of 28 he entered the shoe business, cofounding H.C. Godman Shoe Company and becoming a traveling salesman. He also indulged his interest in newspapers: In 1889 and 1890, Wolfe wrote a popular column of local happenings for the *Columbus Sunday Capital.*

In 1890 his 18-year-old brother, Harry, joined Godman as a shoemaker, and soon the Wolfes began turning out shoes on the side. In 1893 they incorporated Wolfe Brothers Shoe Company. The business prospered, leading to the start of a chain of retail stores under the Wear-U-Well banner.

Like his brother, Harry Wolfe had also sold newspapers, providing his first source of income when he was ten years old. With the profits of their shoe businesses, they were in a position to rejoin the newspaper field at a much elevated level. First, in 1902 they acquired the *Ohio State Journal*, Columbus's oldest newspaper, established in 1811 as the *Western Intelligencer.* Then, in 1905, the Wolfe Brothers acquired the *Evening Dispatch* which had emerged as the city's leading afternoon paper. Applying their business experience, they turned the *Evening Dispatch* into a very profitable business while continuing to make a fortune making and selling shoes, and engaging in banking as well. In 1925 the Wolfe family established a securities brokerage, the Ohio Company, which became part of Dispatching Printing.

The Wolfe brothers were also very much involved in Republican politics, and used their wealth and the power of their newspapers to become influential voices in the state. The family estate, known as the Wigwam, became a meeting place for Ohio politicians, some of whom would play national roles, including Warren Harding, Calvin Coolidge, and Herbert Hoover.

ROBERT WOLFE DIES IN FALL: 1927

In November 1925 Dispatch Printing opened a new printing plant, capable of printing 100,000 32-page papers every hour. They were delivered by a fleet of 17 trucks to distribution points and substations, received

KEY DATES

1871: The Dispatch Printing Company is founded to publish *Daily Dispatch,* a Columbus, Ohio, evening newspaper.
1899: The Sunday edition is founded.
1905: Robert and Harry Wolfe acquire the company.
1927: Robert Wolfe dies.
1933: Radio station WBNS is established.
1949: WBNS television station goes on the air.
1959: A joint-operating agreement is reached with the *Citizen-Journal* morning newspaper.
1974: Indianapolis television station WTHR is acquired.
1986: The *Citizen-Journal* folds, allowing the *Dispatch* to become only morning newspaper of Columbus.
1988: Consumer News Services Inc. is formed.
1993: The Ohio News Network is launched.
2005: The weekly newspaper, *Alive!,* begins publication.

for delivery by about 500 carriers. The 1920s would also bring one of paper's most famous writers, James Thurber, an Ohio State University graduate who would later make a bigger splash in New York City with his writings and cartoons that appeared in the *New Yorker* magazine. The decade also brought tragedy to the *Dispatch.* On January 13, 1927, Robert Wolfe fell to his death from a casement window on the fifth floor of the Dispatch Building. He was 66 years old.

Replacing his brother as publisher, Harry Wolfe carried on the task of growing Dispatch Printing, as did his three sons and Robert's son, 34-year-old Edgar Thurston Wolfe. The five family members would have an equal voice in the running of the various Wolfe enterprises. Following the stock market crash of 1929, they had to contend with the impact of the Great Depression that encompassed all of the 1930s. Although the price of the *Dispatch* was lowered to just a penny for the daily edition, the paper managed to avoid cutting its workforce.

The *Ohio State Journal,* on the other hand, was forced to cease publishing its Sunday edition in 1932, leading to its sister paper picking up some of the features and a two-year Sunday hybrid called the *Sunday Journal-Dispatch.* Despite tough times, Dispatch Printing delved into other media in 1931, launching a radio

station under the call letters WBNS, which stood for Wolfe Banking Newspapers & Shoes.

The company kept its thumb on the pulse of other technological developments as well. In 1935 the *Dispatch* published its first photo transmitted by wire, and in 1941 the paper took part in a demonstration of facsimile technology, faxing, when a section of the paper was sent by telephone lines to remote printers located in home and businesses. Because the United States was soon involved in World War II, this work was discontinued.

Harry Wolfe died of kidney disease in January 1946. His nephew, Edgar Wolfe, became the dominant player in family affairs and the publisher of the *Dispatch* and the *Ohio State Journal.* During his tenure, *Dispatch Printing* became involved in television, acquiring a license and establishing WBNS-TV (channel 10), which went on the air in 1949. In February 1957, Edgar Wolfe died from cancer at the age of 63. One cousin, Robert Huston Wolfe, succeeded him as publisher of the *Dispatch,* while another cousin, Preston Beebe Wolfe, was named president of Dispatch Printing.

OHIO STATE JOURNAL MERGES WITH COLUMBUS CITIZEN: 1959

In 1959 the Wolfe family merged the *Ohio State Journal* with the *Columbus Citizen,* established in 1899, to form the a morning newspaper called the *Citizen-Journal.* It was printed under a joint-operating agreement with *Dispatch Printing,* which called for the *Dispatch* to be responsible for production, advertising, and distribution. It would also provide newsroom space for the *Citizen-Journal.* For the next quarter-century the two dailies would peacefully coexist.

To handle the production needs of two newspapers, Dispatch Printing enlarged its plant in 1965 to add more presses. A year earlier the *Dispatch* had turned to computers to help increase productivity. Although radio and television were important components of Dispatch Printing, the newspapers remained the flagship business. When the *Dispatch* celebrated its centennial in 1971, daily circulation totaled more than 172,000 while Sunday circulation topped 330,000. Twenty-five years earlier those circulation figures were 146,000 and 173,000 respectively. During this time, Dispatch Printing also added to its other holdings. In 1974 it acquired an Indianapolis television station, WLWI, which two years later would change its call letters to WTHR.

In addition to serving as president of Dispatch Printing, Preston Wolfe succeeded his brother as publisher of the *Dispatch.* In 1973 Preston Wolfe turned over both posts to Edgar Wolfe Jr. His time at the top would be brief, however. In January 1975 he and four others were traveling by private airplane to attend the annual Alfalfa Club dinner as guests of Ohio Senator Robert Taft Jr., when outside Washington, D.C., their twin engine plane, troubled by rain and fog, struck a broadcast tower several miles from the airport. It exploded and crashed on the American University campus, killing all five passengers.

John F. Wolfe, a cousin of Edgar Wolfe Jr., took over as publisher of the *Dispatch,*, but it was Edgar's brother, John W. "J. W." Wolfe, who as chairman of Dispatch Printing "called the shots," in the words of John Wicklein, writing in *American Journalism Review.* He added that J. W. "made the newspaper a plaything of his political and personal desires," this from a man "who almost never set foot in the newsroom." According to Wicklein, J. W. was a private, quick-tempered man who abhorred publicity.

From his bank offices across the street from the *Dispatch,* he issued directives to his cousin or directly to an editor on the slant he wanted taken on sensitive stores, or stories to avoid altogether. "To journalism professors, competing reporters and some of its own staff, the paper under J. W.'s tutelage was vapid and dishonorable—shamelessly boosting Ohio State and its Big Ten Buckeyes, ducking controversial coverage and aggressively supporting Republican candidates in its news columns and editorials," wrote Wicklein.

DISPATCH BECOMES MORNING PAPER: 1986

Under J. W.'s control, the *Dispatch* found itself in an afternoon time slot that was no longer advantageous, one occupied by the *Citizen-Journal,* part of the Scripps-Howard chain. In 1983 Dispatch Printing announced that it did not plan to renew its joint-operating agreement with the *Citizen-Journal.* As a result the *Citizen-Journal* was forced to fold in 1985 and the *Dispatch* became a morning publication and Columbus became a one-newspaper town. To keep pace with a media world in which newspapers faced increasing competition, Dispatch Printing began construction on a new, modern $128 million printing plant, capable of producing magazine-quality color pictures, and able to accommodate later deadlines as well as earlier deliveries. When the facility opened in 1990, the newspaper was redesigned to include full color on every front section.

While metropolitan daily newspapers faced an increasing level of competition from television, and later the Internet, in the 1990s, one area of journalism was doing well: the free community weekly newspaper, a primary source of local information. The Columbus area

was served by Suburban News Publications, but in 1988 Dispatch Printing took steps to break into this coveted niche, launching Consumer News Services Inc. to acquire a pair of advertising shoppers. A year later they were converted to community newspapers under the "This Week" banner, and in 1990 Consumer News began launching other weeklies. Suburban News was not happy about this development, accusing Dispatch Printing of attempting to monopolize area advertising dollars, and lobbying state and federal authorities to investigate the matter. The U.S. Department of Justice did look, but by the end of 1991 the agency indicated that it would not interfere with Dispatch Printing's entry into the community newspaper field.

ONN LAUNCHED: 1993

The early 1990s also saw Dispatch Printing expand its other media holdings. In 1993 the company's Dispatch Broadcast Group launched the Ohio News Network (ONN), an independent 24-hour cable news service. In subsequent years Dispatch Printing would feud with Ohio cable television companies over carrying ONN and under what terms, using popular WBNS-TV as a bargaining chip, withholding the channel from cable systems as part of the negotiations.

In 1994 J. W. Wolfe died, leading to significant changes at the *Dispatch.* In the months after his death, a new editor, Michael F. Curtin, was installed, and he began an effort to improve the journalistic quality of the newspaper. In 1999 he was named president and brought in Ben Marrison from the *Cleveland Plain Dealer,* head of that paper's statehouse bureau. Marrison soon took over as editor, allowing Curtin to focus on other aspects of Dispatch Printing. Marrison focused on improving the quality of writing at the *Dispatch* while emphasizing greater coverage of the growing Columbus suburbs.

Despite the editorial improvements, the *Dispatch,* like newspapers across the country, had to contend with declining readership and advertising revenues. In 2002 the *Dispatch* underwent a major redesign as the paper adopted the 50-inch web width that had become the industry standard. Dispatch Printing also pursue a convergence policy, looking to leverage the assets of all of its media assets by developing working relationships to share and develop content. The web sites of ONN, WBNS, and WTHR were brought together in 2004 to create Ohio's largest online news platform.

Dispatch Printing also looked to exploit niche opportunities as they arose. To serve Ohio's growing Latino community, a Spanish-language weekly newspaper, *Fronteras,* was introduced, and in 2005

Alive!, a free weekly covering arts, entertainment, and dining was added as well. With the *Dispatch* continuing to lose advertising revenues and forced to make job cuts in 2007 and 2008 to lower overhead costs, the continued convergence of media properties was clearly the future strategy for Dispatch Printing.

Ed Dinger

PRINCIPAL SUBSIDIARIES

Dispatch Broadcast Group; Consumer News Services Inc; Wolfe Aviation; Wolfe Enterprises Inc.

PRINCIPAL COMPETITORS

Block Communications, Inc.; Cm Media Inc.; Gannett Co., Inc.

FURTHER READING

Albrecht, Robert, "New Century Bring Challenges, Triumphs," *Columbus Dispatch,* June 30, 1996, p. C3.

Hudson, Eileen Davis, "Columbus," *Mediaweek,* March 20, 2000, p. 22.

———, "Columbus, Ohio," *Mediaweek,* February 2, 2004, p. 12.

Jackson, William, "Blood Tells in Wolfe Family Empire," *Business First-Columbus,* June 20, 1994, p. 1.

Jackson, William, Stephen Lilly, Rob Messinger, and Carrie Shook, "Media Baron Leaves Behind Vast Estate," *Business First-Columbus,* June 20, 1994, p. 1.

Lee, Alfred E., *History of the City of Columbus, Capital of Ohio,* New York: Munsell & Co., 1892.

Lilly, Stephen, "Justice Department Investigates Dispatch," *Business First-Columbus,* July 30, 1990, p. 1.

"Ohio Publisher and Four Others Die in Washington Plane Crash," *New York Times,* January 26, 1975.

Price, Rita, "Technology Changes the Face—and Pace—of the Paper," *Columbus Dispatch,* June 30, 1996, p. 8.

"Robert F. Wolfe Dies in Fall from Window," *New York Times,* January 14, 1927.

Stratton, Lee, "Competition Plays an 'Extra' Role," *Columbus Dispatch,* June 30, 1996, p. 6.

Tebben, Gerald, "Columbus—and the Paper—Prosper in Postwar Years," *Columbus Dispatch,* June 30, 1996, p. 7.

Wicklein, John, "Hello, Columbus," *American Journalism Review,* June 2000, p. 46.

Elliott-Lewis Corporation

▪

2900 Black Lake Place
Philadelphia, Pennsylvania 19154
U.S.A.
Telephone: (215) 698-4400
Fax: (215) 398-4465
Web site: http://www.elliottlewis.com

Private Company
Incorporated: 1905 as Elliott-Lewis Electric Company
Employees: 550
Sales: $47.1 billion (2007 est.)
NAICS: 238220 Plumbing, Heating, and Air Conditioning Contractors

■ ■ ■

Elliott-Lewis Corporation, Inc. (ELCO), is a full-service mechanical construction and maintenance company specializing in heating, ventilating, and air conditioning (HVAC), but also working in plumbing, building automation, wastewater, and data management. Elliott-Lewis was founded in Philadelphia, Pennsylvania, and over more than a century grew to become one of the largest mechanical construction and HVAC companies in the Delaware Valley, serving clients in Pennsylvania, New Jersey, Delaware, Washington, D.C., and a few locations in southeast Florida. ELCO earns annual revenues in excess of $47 million and employs more than 500 full-time employees working at eight locations and seven subsidiary companies.

THE EARLY YEARS

Thomas H. Lewis, Sr., and his partner Frank R. Elliott started Elliott-Lewis Electric Company (ELCO) in 1905. The two men, both in their early twenties, had practical experience as electricians and invested their own capital, a total of $10,000, to purchase a workspace at 1008 Race Street in Philadelphia, Pennsylvania. Over the decade that followed, Lewis and Elliott expanded into the appliance sales and rental business, offering refrigerators, ovens, and a variety of other home appliances.

In 1932, ELCO became one of the first companies to sell General Motors' new line of oil-burning heating equipment. Although the 1930s and early 1940s were a difficult time for many independent companies, the decision Lewis and Elliott made to invest in the new technology allowed their company to endure through the worst of the financial crisis. By 1934, ELCO was one of the largest suppliers of oil heating in the Philadelphia area. That same year, General Motors introduced their first commercial cooling unit and Elliott-Lewis again invested in the emerging technology, becoming the first HVAC supplier in the region.

The period from 1942 to the early 1950s was difficult for Elliott-Lewis, largely due to changing market conditions brought about by World War II. The Elliott family sold their shares to the Lewis family in the 1950s as Thomas Lewis, Jr., son of the founder, began taking over management of the company. Despite reduced revenues, Elliott-Lewis expanded to Atlantic City, New Jersey, in 1945 in an effort to enlarge their client base. In 1965, ELCO moved into a new, 52,000-square-foot facility at 2301 Cherry Street in Philadelphia and opened HVAC subsidiaries in New Jersey and Pennsylvania. Thomas Lewis, Sr., died in 1967, at age 82, leaving his son Thomas Lewis, Jr., as CEO and president.

In 1973, Elliott-Lewis abandoned the appliance supply business and began concentrating on large-scale HVAC projects. By 1975, Elliott-Lewis was bringing in annual revenues in excess of $10 million, employed 138 full-time staff members, and was firmly established as one of Philadelphia's leading corporations. By 1980, ELCO was again expanding its list of services. In addition to HVAC installation and maintenance, the company began working in refrigeration, plumbing, wastewater collection and processing, and mechanical construction. ELCO's staff not only offered installation but also offered to repair and maintain systems installed by other companies.

In 1986, ELCO purchased Modern Air Conditioning, Inc., in southwest Florida and expanded into a new market. Soon after, ELCO purchased R.L. Anderson, Inc., a Florida company that offered full-service facilities management, including HVAC, plumbing, and electrical services. Although still centered in the Northeast and the Delaware Valley, the company's expansion into Florida allowed them to reap revenues from a strong HVAC market and revenues increased significantly over the following decade.

NEW LEADERSHIP

In 1987, after the retirement of Thomas Lewis, Jr., William R. Sautter, a Philadelphia native who joined the firm in 1971 as a controller, was promoted to president. That same year, Sautter opened the Sautter Crane

Rental subsidiary, which rented boom trucks to local construction companies. Increasingly, ELCO concentrated on mechanical construction, and expansion into that market, such as through Sautter Crane, helped the company to become more self-sufficient with regard to construction projects.

In the 1990s, Elliott-Lewis handled many of the most lucrative contracts in the Philadelphia area, including the Philadelphia International Airport, which the company gained as a client in 1990. Three years later, ELCO gained another high-profile client when they became the maintenance management company for the Philadelphia Convention Center. Thus established as a company with the capability to handle large projects, other high-profile clients followed, including Temple University and Tastykake Bakery Co.

ELCO also added information management to its list of facilities management services. The newly formed Information Technology Unit (ITU) installed telephone, data, and security systems, and ELCO hired a staff of individuals to provide expert service in handling data for their clients. The ITU was another step in ELCO's goal to become a full-service provider for their clients and to remain up to date in terms of technology.

In 1998, FirstEnergy Corporation, a subsidiary of Enron Corporation, acquired Elliott-Lewis. Although the purchase price was not released, the acquisition was part of a major campaign to purchase mechanical construction and energy management firms, estimated at more than $250 million in investment. At the time of the purchase, the members of the Lewis family had been preparing to purchase controlling interests in the company from various investors and sell it to the next generation of family members, but, instead, it passed out of family hands.

COMPANY GROWS UNDER
FIRSTENERGY

In 2001 ELCO won its first contract to handle maintenance for the U.S. Department of Defense, which included maintaining military bases in northeast Pennsylvania. Over the next several years, ELCO won additional Department of Defense contracts in New Jersey, New York, and Washington, D.C. By 2006, Department of Defense contracts constituted more than 15 percent of the company's annual revenues.

While ELCO was gaining ground with new contracts, the company suffered a significant setback when they lost the maintenance contract for the Philadelphia International Airport. The four-year, $50 million contract, which included landscaping, elevator and escalator maintenance, and a variety of other

KEY DATES

1905: Company founded by Thomas H. Lewis and Frank R. Elliott.

1932: Elliott-Lewis (ELCO) begins selling oil heating equipment.

1934: Company begins selling commercial cooling equipment.

1945: Company expands to Atlantic City, New Jersey.

1965: Company opens heating, ventilating, and air conditioning (HVAC) subsidiaries in New Jersey and Pennsylvania.

1973: ELCO ceases distribution of appliances.

1986: Company acquires subsidiary in Southeast Florida.

1987: Company opens Sautter Crane Rental subsidiary.

1990: ELCO becomes facilities manager for Philadelphia International Airport.

1993: Company wins contract for maintenance of Philadelphia Convention Center.

1998: Company acquired by FirstEnergy.

2001: Company gains first Department of Defense contracts.

2005: FirstEnergy sells controlling stock to management company headed by William R. Sautter.

services, was given to a newly formed company, Philadelphia Airport Services, which submitted a bid of $2 million less than ELCO's initial bid.

ELCO sued the city to prevent the loss of their contract, complaining that city procurement officers gave "special treatment" to Philadelphia Airport Services because the company had close ties to government employees. It was revealed that U.S. Facilities, the parent company of Philadelphia Airport Services, was partially owned by former City Controller Thomas A. Leonard and Willie Johnson, a prominent local business owner with links to former mayor John Street's campaign. In addition, Philadelphia Airport Services hired Milton Street, the brother of the former mayor, as a consultant with a monthly stipend of $30,000. Records later showed that U.S. Facilities had donated more than $30,000 to Mayor John Street's campaign.

In 2003 the media revealed that Philadelphia Airport Services was planning to award a $1.2 million subcontract to manage baggage conveyance systems to Notlim Management Services, Inc., a company headed

by Milton Street, triggering a strong public reaction. When the links between Milton Street and Philadelphia Airport Services were revealed, Mayor Street put a stop to the Notlim Management Services contract, despite its having been approved by airport management.

While the airport contract was a major loss for ELCO, the firm remained strong and continued to win lucrative new contracts. It was announced in 2003 that ELCO would be the new facilities management provider for Cleveland Browns Stadium, the $280 million stadium built in 1999 for the NFL Cleveland Browns. The contract included a variety of services, from landscaping, plumbing, and electrical, to HVAC and data management.

COMPANY AVOIDS COLLAPSE

In 2004, FirstEnergy, which was shaken by the fall of their parent company Enron, decided to streamline their operations to focus on the utility business. Sautter and a group of partners invested their own capital to prevent the company's closure. The following year, as the four-year Philadelphia International Airport contract came to a close, ELCO submitted a new bid to manage airport maintenance.

In 2005 it was revealed that ELCO's airport bid of $14.9 million was lower than the $17.2 million bid of its rival, Philadelphia Airport Services. Despite ELCO's lower bid, the contract with Philadelphia Airport Services was extended for several months while city and airport officials debated both contracts. The controversial connections between Philadelphia Airport Services and Mayor Street's family again became the subject of media and public scrutiny. As a result of an ongoing Federal Bureau of Investigation investigation into the events surrounding the 2001 bidding process, Milton Street was indicted for failure to pay taxes on $2 million in income for his consulting work with Philadelphia Airport Services.

City officials claimed that the delay was due to dissatisfaction with ELCO's minority participation goal. In ELCO's initial bid, the company proposed hiring 22 minority contractors to handle less than 22 percent of the work. After several months of delays, it was announced that ELCO would be awarded the $56 million contract as of March 1, 2005. As part of the new bid, ELCO agreed to award $3.6 million per year to 12 local minority- and female-owned firms, equaling more than 25 percent of the annual contract revenues.

In 2008, ELCO was one of the largest facilities maintenance companies in the Delaware Valley and handled contracts in excess of $47 million annually. Although HVAC remained a major focus for the company, ELCO's experience and expertise in facilities management and construction allowed them to grow significantly in the early 21st century. With a client list that included many of Philadelphia's largest businesses, and seven subsidiary companies, Elliott-Lewis Corporation showed little sign of slowing down.

Micah Issitt

PRINCIPAL SUBSIDIARIES

A.A. Duckett, Inc.; Cooling Construction Company; Sautter Crane Rental, Inc.; Welsch-Wayman, Inc.; Air Systems, Inc.; Modern Air Conditioning, Inc.; R.L. Anderson, Inc.

PRINCIPAL COMPETITORS

Sauer Inc.; John J. Kirlin Inc.; PPL Energy Services Holdings, LLC; HEC/Denron Plumbing & HVAC Inc.; Joule Industrial Contractors; PSEG Energy Technologies; EMCOR Group Inc.; John W. Danforth Co.

FURTHER READING

"Company Occupies 52,000 SqFt Townhouse at 2301 Cherry Street," *Philadelphia Evening Bulletin,* August 13, 1965.

"Elliott Lewis Given Permission to Occupy Building in Atlantic City," *Philadelphia Evening Bulletin,* March 24, 1945.

"Elliott-Lewis to Operate, Maintain Stadium," *Contractor,* January 2003, p. 54.

Gelbart, Marcia, "Airport Contract Not Yet Resolved," *Philadelphia Inquirer,* December 30, 2005.

———, "Airport Contract to Change Hands," *Philadelphia Inquirer,* December 22, 2006.

———, "Two Firms Vie for Lucrative Airport Contract," *Philadelphia Inquirer,* August 30, 2005.

Key, Peter, "Elliott-Lewis Gets First of 3 Possible Contract Renewals," *Philadelphia Business Journal,* May 19, 2006.

Mader, Robert P., "FirstEnergy Buys Elliott-Lewis," *Contractor,* July 1998, p. 7.

Prokop, Trudy, "Future Looks Good to Elliott Lewis," *Philadelphia Evening Bulletin,* January 20, 1975.

"T. H. Lewis, Sr., Is Dead at 82; Founded Firm," *Philadelphia Evening Bulletin,* January 30, 1967.

"Thomas Lewis, Sr., Elected President and CEO of Elliott-Lewis," *Philadelphia Evening Bulletin,* May 18, 1967.

ElringKlinger AG

Max-Eyth-Strasse 2
Dettingen an der Erms, D-72581
Germany
Telephone: (49 7123) 724-0
Fax: (49 7123) 724-9006
Web site: http://www.elringklinger.de

Public Company
Incorporated: 1879 as Paul Lechler
Employees: 3,602 (2007)
Sales: EUR 607.8 million ($838 million) (2007)
Stock Exchanges: Frankfurt am Main Stuttgart
Ticker Symbol: ZIL
NAICS: 339991 Gasket, Packing, and Sealing Device
   Manufacturing; 336399 All Other Motor Vehicle
   Parts Manufacturing; 336312 Gasoline Engine and
   Engine Parts Manufacturing; 421120 Motor Vehicle
   Supplies and New Parts Wholesalers; 325211
   Plastics Material and Resin Manufacturing

■ ■ ■

ElringKlinger AG is the world's leading supplier of
cylinder-head gaskets for diesel engines, and supplies
specialty gaskets, power train and exhaust system shielding parts, and cover modules to many of the world's
largest auto manufacturers. Automotive spare parts,
which are distributed worldwide under the Elring brand
name, account for about 15 percent of total sales. The
company's high-performance plastics subsidiary Elring-
Klinger Kunststofftechnik, which contributes roughly 10
percent to ElringKlinger's total revenues,

engineers and manufactures various products for
industrial use, such as bellows, hoses, diaphragms, heating elements, insulation parts, valves for industrial and
medical technology applications as well as rings, seals
and packaging for the food industry. In addition, the
company offers engineering and engine testing and
simulation services via its subsidiary ElringKlinger
Motortechnik. Based in Dettingen an der Erms,
Germany, the publicly traded company, in which the
Lechler family owns a 55 percent majority share, has additional production facilities in Western Europe, North
and South America, South Africa, and Asia. Elring-
Klinger owns a 50 percent stake in Japanese automotive
gasket manufacturer Marusan Corporation.

SELLING GASKETS FOR
AUTOMOBILES IS EARLY SUCCESS

In 1879 Paul Lechler, a well-to-do businessman, decided
to start a technical goods wholesale business in Stuttgart,
Germany. The 30-year-old entrepreneur was able to
combine his creativity with practical thinking, and his
dynamism with a fine sense for business opportunities.
Located near Stuttgart's main train station, Lechler's
import, export, and wholesale trade firm took off
quickly. Starting out with trading technical oils and
other chemicals and raw materials, he was able to
establish sales offices in all of the region's major cities as
well as in most large cities throughout Germany within
four years.

By 1883 Lechler was shipping his goods to
Switzerland, France, England, Italy, the Netherlands,
and the United States. At the end of the 1880s Lechler's

COMPANY PERSPECTIVES

What really makes things move? Enhancing mobility. Environmentally friendly, economical, efficient. Setting standards with innovative technologies. For today and tomorrow. Thinking ahead to overcome former boundaries. Taking responsibility for increased sustainability. Acting with determination to reach new goals. This is what moves us. We develop solutions for the future that move us all forward and that no one can live without.

product line included wood impregnation materials, special paint coatings for drinking water containers, water pumps, nozzles, sealing materials, and gaskets. In 1889 Lechler received a German patent for the copper-asbestos ring gasket he had invented. They were licensed to gasket manufacturers at first and remained in the company's product line for over a century.

Until the end of the 19th century the copper-asbestos gaskets Lechler sold to his growing clientele were mainly used in steam engines. However, a new market began to emerge around the turn of the 20th century when a growing number of German companies started manufacturing automobiles. Lechler began to promote the copper-asbestos gaskets he had local suppliers manufacture as the perfect gaskets for use in automobiles—strong enough to withstand high temperatures and pressure. As the number of German automakers rose, the demand for automotive gaskets grew very rapidly in the first decade of the 20th century.

One of Lechler's first major customers was Daimler predecessor Daimler-Motoren-Gesellschaft. As standards for the quality of gaskets used in automobiles became stricter, Lechler switched suppliers and started purchasing his merchandise from manufacturers in France. In order to best serve his automotive industry customers, Lechler established a separate division for automotive gaskets within his enterprise. Another division continued to sell gaskets for other uses, such as in locomotives and machinery. By 1914 Lechler's company had evolved as the main supplier of copper-asbestos gaskets to German automakers. Before long the company founders discontinued their attempts to enter additional promising markets, such as manufacturing ball bearings and spark plugs, and focused on the growing market for automotive gaskets.

FROM WHOLESALE TRADE TO INDUSTRIAL MANUFACTURING

The outbreak of World War I in 1914 suddenly cut the company off from its gasket suppliers in France. In this politically and economically unpredictable situation, the company's management made a far-reaching strategic decision—to launch its own gasket production. The first gasket manufacturing workshop was established in Stuttgart in the same year, followed by a second one in 1917.

As the war progressed, it became increasingly difficult to secure the necessary raw materials, mainly asbestos, that were needed for making the asbestos-cardboard commonly used in gaskets at the time. Mixing the asbestos powder with rock powder or other substitutes resulted in asbestos-cardboard of substandard quality that, for example, was inadequate for use in airplanes. Finally, the company located a Swiss supplier of asbestos in Poschiavo, near the Italian border. A second supplier of asbestos was found in Rottenburg, Germany. The Swiss connection ended during the 1920s. Deutsche Asbestwerke in Rottenburg, however, became one of Lechler's major suppliers for many years.

After he returned from military service in 1919, Paul Lechler's son, Paul Lechler Jr., succeeded the company founder—who was by then in his seventies—and became managing partner. A new piece of company property was purchased that year in Cannstatt, a small town just outside of Stuttgart, where a factory for the industrial production of gaskets was built. By 1921, the number of workers at the factory had grown to 60 and Lechler's gasket business had become the company's strongest sales generator. Since product quality depended mainly on the quality of the tools with which they were manufactured, Lechler added a tool-making division to the site. However, since the company's shipping department was still located in a different part of town, the factory's daily output had to be brought there by a horse-drawn carriage.

The rapidly advancing devaluation of the German currency after the end of World War I put an enormous burden on the economy and doing business became increasingly difficult. Lechler decided to continue producing and selling his goods to his customers—not, however, without first overcoming major challenges. Production was cut back as demand slowed down, making layoffs unavoidable. In the early 1920s, at the height of the hyperinflation, invoices had to be paid immediately to prevent the amount payable from increasing rapidly. Checks had to be cashed just as quickly. Therefore, apprentices transported money to and from

KEY DATES

1879: Entrepreneur Paul Lechler starts a technical goods wholesale business.

1900: Lechler begins selling gaskets to the emerging German automotive industry.

1914: The company starts its own gasket production.

1924: Lechler begins with the serial production of cylinder-head gaskets.

1927: Joint sales firm Diring Dichtungsring-Ges. mbH is founded.

1961: The company's gasket division is spun off into Lechler Dichtungswerke KG.

1972: Elring Dichtungswerke acquires German gasket manufacturer Röthlingshöfer; plastics products manufacturer Carl Huth + Söhne is taken over.

1977: The company acquires French shaft seal ring manufacturer Procal.

1978: Spanish gasket manufacturer Guaco S.A. is taken over.

1993: Gasket production joint venture Changchun Elring Gaskets is established in China.

1994: ElringKlinger is formed by the merger of Elring with Richard Klinger's automotive division.

2002: ElringKlinger shares are publicly traded at the stock exchanges in Frankfurt am Main and Stuttgart.

2007: An automotive components production subsidiary is set up in India.

2008: ElringKlinger acquires Swiss heat shield manufacturer Sevex and opens a plastics production subsidiary in China.

the bank in backpacks and workers were paid on a daily basis.

Since Lechler sold his products in about 20 different countries, keeping track of the currency exchange rates was another major task. After a new currency was introduced in November 1923, Lechler's first balance sheet after the end of the inflation revealed that company losses had been rather modest. On the other hand, Lechler had rescued the relationships with important customers, such as the automakers Opel and Adler.

DEVELOPMENTS IN TECHNOLOGY AND MARKETING

In the 1920s a major technical development reshaped the market for automotive gaskets. While the very first generations of automobiles used flathead engines primarily, newer internal combustion engines consisted of a cylinder block and a number of cylinder heads, which had to be sealed by a new kind of gasket. This principle soon became the norm and Lechler launched his first assembly line for copper-asbestos cylinder-head gaskets for the Opel "Leapfrog" model in 1924.

The proliferation of new car models from many different manufacturers in the 1920s presented gasket producers with a problem. For every new type of gasket, new tools had to be custom made, which was quite expensive. On the other hand, older models had to remain in the company's catalog to supply the market with spare parts. Whenever a new batch of gaskets was to be produced, tools had to be switched before the production process could continue.

To solve this problem Lechler and three other southern German gasket manufacturers founded Diring Dichtungsring-Gesellschaft, a joint gasket marketing and sales firm, in 1927. The four companies agreed to market their products exclusively via Diring and to divide the business for metal-asbestos gaskets among their plants based on their share in Diring, which was determined by each company's total sales. As the company with the biggest revenues, Lechler held 47 percent in Diring and Lechler's director of gasket production became one of Diring's CEOs. For metal-asbestos gasket orders which had been filled, shareholders were paid fixed prices based on the size and complexity of the product. All other gasket orders were given to the shareholder with the lowest bid.

From its start in a Stuttgart office, Diring's business volume grew fairly quickly. In addition to lowering costs by allowing each company to focus its expertise on just part of the vast range of gaskets, the combined power of the four companies resulted in a much stronger market position for Diring. Moreover, Diring was perfectly set up to expand their shareholders' activities in the growing automotive spare parts market. Diring's success in that area attracted other manufacturers of sealing materials, such as compressed cork, who signed exclusive distribution agreements for their products with the sales firm. Diring systematically expanded its product line and, in addition to sealing materials, included the products from Lechler's two other divisions as well: sealing materials, undercoating, and aluminum paint, among others, from the company's chemical products unit; and car wash jets from Lechler's apparatus engineering division.

INTERNATIONAL GROWTH THROUGH MARKETING AGREEMENTS

Diring's efforts to expand its reach beyond Germany resulted in the foundation of a subsidiary in France, where high customs fees made imports very expensive. However, the establishment of a production facility in the country was halted when Curty, the leading French gasket manufacturer, reached an agreement with Diring that allowed the company to market Curty's product range through its new sales office in France. At the same time, Curty agreed to stop its exports to other countries except for the French colonies. Similar agreements were reached with the largest American gasket manufacturer, Chicago-based Victor, and with England's market leader Payen in the early 1930s.

In its first full tax year, 1928, Diring grossed 3.6 million reichsmark (RM). The economic depression that followed, however, cut the company's sales by more than 40 percent, reaching a low of RM 2.1 million in 1932. With the beginning of the Nazi era in Germany, Diring's sales picked up again, reaching RM 8.4 million in 1939. The driving force behind this upswing was the rising demand from German automakers.

However, as Adolf Hitler's Wehrmacht marched into Poland on September 1, 1939, the German war industry took precedence over everything else. As the war progressed, Lechler's workers were drawn into the military and replaced by prisoners of war and forced laborers. Under the directives governing the state-controlled war economy, Lechler was required to make patented technologies available to its direct competitors and to issue, with one of them, a combined product catalog. During the bombing raids on Stuttgart of 1943 and 1944, Lechler's headquarters and administrative offices were almost completely destroyed, while the company's production facilities suffered less severe damage.

Diring's revenues recovered slowly after the war, because only three of Germany's largest carmakers were allowed to produce automobiles, and then only a very limited number of vehicles for the Allied occupation forces. Until the currency reform in 1948 and the foundation of the Federal Republic of Germany in western Germany the next year, Lechler completed a number of Diring-orders for gaskets used in trucks and jeeps of the American and French military administrations. However, fueled by the postwar reconstruction boom in Germany, Diring's business began to soar again and sales grew sevenfold between 1946 and 1955, reaching DEM 22 million by the end of that period.

By 1960 Diring grossed more than DEM 35 million. Yet, the foundation of the initial agreement between the Diring shareholders was crumbling. The biggest problem was that over time member companies had developed different types of gaskets for the same purpose, resulting in competing products. Some companies had specialized in certain product areas, but were not allowed to become their sole manufacturer because of the shareholder agreement. After lengthy negotiations the shareholders decided to end their partnership and canceled their shareholder agreement in 1960. Three years later Diring was dissolved.

REORGANIZATION AND EXPANSION OF THE PRODUCT RANGE

Lechler soon underwent a series of organizational changes which resulted in the company's gasket division becoming an independent enterprise. In 1951 the company founder's grandson, Klaus Lechler, had become a partner in the company, which was then transformed into a general partnership. A decade later, on April 1, 1961, Paul Lechler OHG was split into three independent companies. The technical chemicals division became Lechler Bautenschutz Chemie KG; the apparatus engineering division was renamed Lechler Apparatebau KG; and the gasket division was spun off into Lechler Dichtungswerke KG. Induva Industrie-Verwaltungs-AG became the parent company of the three subsidiaries while Paul Lechler OHG remained as the ultimate holding company.

When one of the company founder's great-grandsons and Klaus Lechler's nephew, Walter Herwarth Lechler, became a limited partner in Lechler Dichtungswerke in 1962, it was transformed into a limited partnership. After the sales firm Diring was shut down in 1963, 260 former Diring employees returned to Lechler. In 1964 Lechler Dichtungswerke was renamed Lechler Diring Dichtungswerke and established its own gasket sales department.

Also in 1964 Lechler Diring Dichtungswerke began to move operations to a new location in Dettingen an der Erms, about 15 miles south of Stuttgart, where new headquarters, production facilities, and warehouses were built. In 1968 warehousing and shipping divisions were moved to Dettingen and the production in Bad Cannstatt was closed down in 1971. The company was renamed two more times—Lechler Elring Dichtungswerke KG in 1965 and Elring Dichtungswerke KG in 1971. After Lechler had sold its technical chemicals subsidiary in 1975, Elring Dichtungswerke KG merged with Induva to become Elring Dichtungswerke GmbH in 1978.

After Diring ceased to exist, Elring focused on expanding its product range to include those automotive gaskets that had been manufactured by other Diring shareholders and began to look for related products to broaden the company's range. In 1964 the company acquired a share from leading French gasket manufacturer Cefilac-Curty in Procal, a manufacturing venture for shaft seal rings—ring-shaped rubber gaskets—in Langres, France. In 1966 Elring offered Procal shaft seal rings in addition to its flat gasket range and landed a large order from a German automaker that same year.

ACQUISITIONS IN THE SEVENTIES

By 1970 one-quarter of Procal's output was being sold to German customers. In 1972 Elring Dichtungswerke acquired one of the company's former suppliers, German gasket manufacturer Röthlingshöfer based in Langenzenn near Nuremberg. The new production subsidiary specialized in solid metal gaskets and parts, heat shields for temperature-sensitive engine modules, and combination rubber-metal pieces. Also in 1972 Elring acquired Carl Huth + Söhne, a manufacturer of products made from the synthetic fluoropolymer polytetrafluoroethylene (PTFE) for the chemical, electrical and electronics, and construction equipment industry based in Bietigheim about 15 miles north of Stuttgart. PTFE fibers were used as a substitute for high-quality asbestos fibers in a broad variety of industrial settings.

While Elring's initial intention was to use Huth's know-how for developing new solutions for gaskets, the lion's share of Huth's revenues continued to come from customers outside the automotive industry. Hence, the company took over the marketing and distribution for Elring's industrial product lines as well. In 1977 Elring took over the remaining shares in Procal which became a legally independent subsidiary. Because the market for sealing solutions for moving parts was much larger than that for flat gaskets, the importance of Procal for Elring increased continuously. In 1979 Carl Huth was fully integrated into Elring. Three years later Elring established its in-house plastics division.

FOCUS ON AUTOMOTIVE GASKETS DRIVES R&D AND FOREIGN EXPANSION

Gaskets were considered a low-tech mass product by many. However, manufacturing them required increasing customization as newer engines were designed and other applications progressed. In addition the mass use of cylinder-head gaskets in motor vehicles placed much higher demands on their stability, durability, and flexibility, because they had to withstand hot gases and oil, as well as extremely high pressures. To meet these demands, Lechler put together a small research and development (R&D) department for cylinder-head gaskets in the mid-1930s. This grew steadily after the war and was moved to Elring's brand-new R&D center in Dettingen in 1972. Rapid technological progress in the auto industry continued in the following decades and working closely with car manufacturers in developing new products became a critical success factor.

In addition to massive investments in R&D activities, Elring began to expand abroad in the 1960s. German motor vehicle manufacturers had started setting up factories in Western Europe in the 1960s and Elring followed suit. In 1966 Elring acquired Indupack, a Danish manufacturer of gaskets for the Volkswagen "Bug" automobile. In the same year Elring sealed a license agreement with Spanish manufacturer Guma for automotive gaskets. Twelve years later the company acquired a majority stake in sister company Guaco, gaining a brand-new cylinder had gasket manufacturing plant that was renamed Elring Española.

In the mid-1960s Elring also began to explore market opportunities in Eastern European countries. The company manufactured cylinder head gaskets for the Eastern German vehicle manufacturer VEB Nordhausen in the 1960s. It also established two sales subsidiaries in then-Yugoslavia and granted the Yugoslavian manufacturer Jugoazbest licenses for a variety of gaskets in the 1970s. Elring also entered large technology transfer projects with customers in Turkey and in the Soviet Union in the late 1970s and early 1980s, which included the planning and setup of complete gasket manufacturing plants. Similar projects were realized in Romania and Hungary by Elring subsidiary Procal.

In 1981 Elring established a business division geared solely at the rapidly consolidating automotive market. Two years later the company founded ElringGaskets (PTY) Ltd. in Johannesburg, South Africa, after Daimler-Benz transferred its diesel engine production for commercial vehicles to a state-owned manufacturer. During the 1980s Elring also established a foothold in Asia by acquiring a minority share in Marusan, a Japanese gasket producer.

MERGER ACCELERATES GLOBALIZATION, GOING PUBLIC PROVIDES FUNDING FOR FURTHER EXPANSION

After the disintegration of the communist bloc in the early 1990s the consolidation of the auto industry continued on a global level. To remain competitive in such a business environment, Elring set its sights on further international expansion. The company entered additional production joint ventures in Asia, including South Korea and China, and merged with the automotive division of Richard Klinger GmbH in 1994.

Grown out of an engineering office for gaskets founded by Richard Klinger in Vienna in 1885, the firm had evolved into a major manufacturer of cylinder-head gaskets during the 20th century. At the time of the merger Klinger owned manufacturing plants in Italy and the United Kingdom and a joint venture in Mexico which was taken over completely later in the decade. Following the merger the company was renamed Elring-Klinger GmbH. In 1997 ElringKlinger also established a strong presence in the United States. That year the company's automotive shielding parts plant opened in Livonia, Michigan. In the same year ElringKlinger set up two new subsidiaries, one near São Paulo in Brazil and one near Milan in Italy.

To secure the necessary funding for a new round of global expansion, the company was transformed into a public corporation. On October 30, 2000, the merger of ElringKlinger GmbH with parent company ZWL Grundbesitz- und Beteiligungs-AG created the new ElringKlinger AG. Just over one year later the company's shares were listed at the stock exchanges in Frankfurt/Main and Stuttgart for the first time. Roughly 63 percent of the share capital remained in the hands of Lechler family shareholders.

The 2000 acquisition of Versatech Sealing Systems, a Canadian manufacturer of multilayer steel gaskets, oil pans, sealing and cam covers, and rocker cover sealing systems, further strengthened ElringKlinger's market position in North America. Winning large gasket orders for General Motors' V-8 engines for pickup trucks helped the company gain market position in the United States and Canada, where the company had made significant investments since 1995, and where cylinder-head gasket production began in 2001.

The growing popularity of diesel engines in Europe and the United States, a niche in which ElringKlinger had achieved market and technology leadership for cylinder-head gaskets, gave the company an additional boost in the early 2000s. By 2004, ElringKlinger's 125th anniversary, the company clearly dominated the market for diesel engine seals with an 80 percent share in Europe and was approaching an estimated 25 percent share in the North American market for cylinder-head gaskets. In that year the company took a major step into another global automotive hub—Japan—by setting up a sales and engineering joint venture with Tokyo-based

Marusan Corporation. In 2008 the company raised its stake in Marusan to 50 percent.

ADDING HIGH-PERFORMANCE PLASTIC PARTS AND AUTOMOTIVE TESTING SERVICES FOR FUTURE GROWTH

To secure future growth, ElringKlinger began to expand into additional markets in the 1990s. In 1993 the company formed a new business branch specializing in thermal and acoustic shielding parts. Four years later the company started up ElringKlinger Motortechnik, an engineering and engine testing and simulation services subsidiary for the automotive industry. Serial production of cylinder-head cover modules began in Dettingen an der Erms in 1999. Two years later ElringKlinger started up an engine cover production in Spain. In 2007 the company set up an automotive components production subsidiary in India. In the year after, ElringKlinger acquired Swiss heat shield manufacturer Sevex AG.

The company's plastics technology branch, which had been transformed in 1996 into the independent subsidiary ElringKlinger Kunststofftechnik, played a crucial role in ElringKlinger's diversification strategy. In 1997 ElringKlinger Kunststofftechnik established a special branch for elastomer technology and modules that developed high-performance plastics compounds for various industrial applications. Based on the company's own brand of the PTFE compound, ElringKlinger Kunststofftechnik engineered and manufactured composites that permanently bonded PTFE with metals and other plastics and were very resistant to wear, pressure, and temperature.

In addition to automotive parts and modules, the company made bellows, hoses, diaphragms, heating elements, insulation parts, and valves for industrial and medical technology applications as well as rings, seals, and packaging for the food industry. The 2001 merger of ElringKlinger Kunststofftechnik with German plastics processing specialist Venus GmbH based in Heidenheim significantly strengthened the company's market position. By 2007, the company's plastics subsidiary contributed roughly 10 percent to ElringKlinger's total revenues.

Evelyn Hauser

PRINCIPAL SUBSIDIARIES

ElringKlinger Kunststofftechnik GmbH (74.5%); Elring Klinger Motortechnik GmbH (92.86%); ElringKlinger Logistic Service GmbH (76%); Elring Klinger (Great

Britain) Ltd.; Elring Parts Ltd. (United Kingdom); Elring Klinger S.p.A. (Italy); ElringKlinger Sealing Systems, S.L. (Spain; 90%); Elring Klinger S.A. (Spain; 51%); ElringKlinger México, S.A. de C.V.; EKASER, S.A. de C.V. (Mexico); Elring Klinger do Brasil Ltda; Elringklinger of North America, Inc. (United States; 60%); ElringKlinger Sealing Systems (USA), Inc.; ElringKlinger Sealing Systems Inc. (Canada); ElringKlinger Automotive Components (India) Pvt. Ltd.; Changchun ElringKlinger Ltd. (China; 78%); ElringKlinger Engineered Plastics (Qingdao) Commercial (China; 74.5%); Elring Gaskets (Pty) Ltd. (South Africa; 51%); ElringKlinger Korea Co., Ltd. (South Korea; 50%); ElringKlinger Marusan Corporation (Japan; 50%); Marusan Corporation (Japan; 50%); Technik-Park Heliport Kft. (Hungary).

PRINCIPAL COMPETITORS

Freudenberg & Co. Kommanditgesellschaft; Dana Holding Corporation; Federal-Mogul Corporation.

FURTHER READING

Begin, Sherri, "High Expectations; ElringKlinger Wants to Dominate MLS Market," *Rubber & Plastics News,* September 17, 2001, p. 4.

De Saint-Seine, Sylviane, "Diesel Boom Creates Two Winners," *Automotive News Europe,* June 16, 2003, p. 37.

"ElringKlinger Acquires Large Order from U.S. Truck and Engine Manufacturer," *OTS Originaltextservice,* August 23, 2006.

"ElringKlinger AG," *Rubber World,* December 2000, p. 11.

"ElringKlinger Buys Out Spanish Shareholders," *European Rubber Journal,* March 1, 2008, p. 2.

"ElringKlinger Lifts Stake in Marusan Corporation to 50%," *OTS Originaltextservice,* May 2, 2008.

"ElringKlinger Opens Indian Unit," *Rubber & Plastics News,* April 21, 2008, p. 4.

Floerecke, Klaus-Dieter, "ElringKlinger Looks to Expand Externally," *Rubber & Plastics News,* January 9, 2006, p. 18.

———, "We Are Champions of German Industry," *Automotive News German Auto Industry Newsletter,* July 16, 2007.

Hocker, Klaus, "Step by Step; From a Seal Manufacturer to a Systems Supplier: Application for a Twin-Piston Pump in the Medical Sector," *Process Worldwide,* October 28, 2002, p. 48.

Warth, Hermann, *Geschichte eines schwäbischen Unternehmens: 100 Jahre Elring-Dichtungen,* Fellbach, Germany: Elring Dichtungswerke GmbH, 1987, 114 p.

Wolf, Stefan, "Wertschöpfung der Zulieferer gewinnt an Bedeutung," *Börsen-Zeitung,* October 7, 2006, p. B7.

Evialis S.A.

BP 234, Talhouet
Vannes, F-56006 Cedex
France
Telephone: (33 02 97) 48 54 54
Fax: (33 02 97) 48 54 00
Web site: http://www.evialis.com

Public Company
Incorporated: 1962 as Guyomarc'h S.A.
Employees: 3,366
Sales: EUR 759 million ($1.12 billion) (2007)
Stock Exchanges: Euronext Paris
Ticker Symbol: GYO
NAICS: 311119 Other Animal Food Manufacturing;
325412 Pharmaceutical Preparation Manufacturing

∎∎∎

Evialis S.A. is a leading France-based specialist in the animal health and nutrition sector. The company operates through three core divisions: Evialis Nutrition, Evialis Premix and Specialties, and Evialis Health. The Nutrition division, which incorporates the company's production of compound feed, is by far the company's largest, generating 84 percent of total revenues of EUR 759 million ($1.12 billion) in 2007. This division oversees nearly 50 manufacturing plants around the world, producing a full range of animal feeds, including fish feed, and produces more than 2,400 metric tons per year. The Premix division adds 12 percent to sales, and provides a range of premixes (which incorporate vitamins and trace minerals, etc.) from 13 factories. The

Health division, which generates 4 percent of group sales, is France's leading producer of medicated premixes, and operates three manufacturing sites.

Established in 1954, Evialis has been present on the international market since the late 1960s. International sales account for 26 percent of the company's total turnover. The group is present in nearly all of the top ten feed markets, with a substantial presence in Asia, notably in Vietnam and China. Evialis's strategy calls for further expansion on a global level. Following the integration of majority shareholder InVivo's animal health and nutrition operations, Evialis's revenues are expected to reach EUR 1.5 billion by 2009. Evialis is listed on the Euronext Paris stock exchange and is led by CEO Pierre Lefebvre.

FOUNDATION IN FEED

The post–World War II period saw a dramatic shift in France's agricultural sector, as the government encouraged the country's wholesale transition to industrial farming techniques. These policies had a dramatic impact, not only on production levels, but also on the nature of farming itself. Perhaps no other region in France was as affected by the adoption of industrial farming methods as the Brittany region, particularly its livestock production. By the end of the 1950s, the region's animal population had soared. Brittany soon emerged as the country's major livestock supplier. The massive increases in livestock populations were coupled with increasingly intensive ranching methods. Before long, the region had adopted the factory farming methods pioneered in the United States, under which animals were no longer allowed to range or graze freely. This resulted in new opportunities for the animal feed sector.

Among the first of the new entrants into the feed industry was Jean Guyomarc'h, who founded a small feed business in Vannes in 1954. That small, family-owned business quickly grew into a major feed producer in the Brittany region. By the beginning of the 1960s, Guyomarc'h had targeted further growth through vertical integration. For this, the company targeted the fast-growing market for poultry products, stimulated in large part through the rapid growth of the self-service supermarket format in France at that time. Poultry, particularly chicken, was chosen since chickens were relatively easy to slaughter, process and package, and separate and sell in parts.

In 1960, Guyomarc'h added its own poultry farms, complete with slaughtering facilities. The company quickly added its own line of prepared and ready-to-eat foods as well. At the same time, the waste byproducts provided a new source of added protein for the group's feed production.

INTERNATIONAL EXPANSION

Guyomarc'h's success in France led the company to seek expansion elsewhere. The group's first move was to Spain, where it set up a subsidiary manufacturing premix in Madrid in 1968. The rapid growth of chicken production in Brazil led the company to establish operations there as well, through the acquisition of Socil in 1974. Guyomarc'h extended its reach to a third continent two years later when it established Sipra (Société Ivoirienne de Production Animale) in the Ivory Coast. A second Spanish subsidiary followed in 1978, with the purchase of Agrotesca, based in Corogne, in the Galicia region. This purchase enabled the company to add compound feed production to complement its Spanish premix business. The company then added

operations in Southeast Asia, opening a subsidiary in Indonesia in 1982.

In the late 1980s, Guyomarc'h reorganized its operations. As part of this effort, the company created a new subsidiary, called Guyomarc'h Nutrition Animale, or Guyomarc'h NA, for all of its animal feeds and nutrition businesses. This reorganization was completed in 1988. Guyomarc'h NA continued its expansion in the French feeds sector. In 1990, Guyomarc'h NA acquired one of its major rivals, Cofna, which boosted the company into the leadership ranks on a national level. Soon after the Cofna purchase, Guyomarc'h found a new financial partner in the form of Paribas Affaires Industrielles, the future BNP Paribas, which acquired a majority stake in the company, through its subsidiary NHG, which then became NHG Guyomarc'h.

The backing of Paribas enabled Guyomarc'h NA to grow strongly through the decade. Acquisitions played a major role in the company's growth at this time. In 1992, the company bought Delatzur, a specialist in compound feeds production. The following year, Guyomarc'h NA added two more companies, Rental and Rouergue Aliments. New acquisitions followed in 1995, with the purchase of compound feed producer Novaliment, and in 1996 with the purchase of Oftel, another compound feed producer.

By then, Guyomarc'h's parent NHG had launched a restructuring of its holdings. This led to the spinoff of Guyomarc'h's food production into a new dedicated company, SAGAL SAS, in 1994. Guyomarc'h NA in the meantime had continued to seek new horizons. The company added its first operations in Eastern Europe in 1993. By 1995, the company had also entered China, through a partnership with Shandong Province to establish a premix production joint venture.

BECOMING EVIALIS IN THE 21ST CENTURY

Guyomarc'h NA went public in 1997, listing its shares on the Paris Stock Exchange. The offering came in support of the group's increasingly ambitious expansion plans. In that year, the company increased its presence in Eastern Europe, acquiring premix producer Ilpasz, based in Poland. The company reinforced its presence in that market the following year, buying Paszutil there. Also in 1999, the company made another major international move, buying Cargill's Brazil-based compound feed operations. This helped increase the company's total facilities in that country, the world's third largest feed market, to five in the early years of the new century.

Guyomarc'h entered a number of other international markets in the late 1990s. The company

KEY DATES

1954: Jean Guyomarc'h founds an animal feed business in Vannes, France.

1960: Guyomarc'h diversifies into poultry farming, becoming a vertically integrated feed-to-food group.

1968: The company moves into the international market, establishing a subsidiary in Madrid, Spain.

1988: Guyomarc'h regroups all of its feed, premix, and animal health operations into a new subsidiary, Guyomarc'h Nutrition Animale.

1990: Paribas, through subsidiary NGH, acquires controlling stake in Guyomarc'h.

1994: NGH spins off Guyomarc'h's food business as SAGAL SAS.

1997: Guyomarc'h NA goes public on the Paris Stock Exchange.

2001: The company changes its name to Evialis as part of a new globalization strategy for the 21st century.

2008: InVivo acquires a majority stake in Evialis, merges its animal health and nutrition operations into Evialis.

established its first operations in India and in Vietnam in 1998. The latter quickly grew to become one of the company's most important individual markets. In support of its growth there, the company bought a new feed factory in South Vietnam in 2001, and then added a third facility in Ho Chi Minh City in 2003.

The company also added several more components to its French network. These included Mesny, a compound feed producer acquired in 1997; Jolivet, based in the west of France in 1998; Aliments Cavaignac and SN2A, both compound feed producers in 1999; and animal health laboratory Franvet, in 2000. By the end of 2000, the group had added two more French feed producers, Gheerbrandt and UAR, as well as Portuguese premix specialist Iberil & Zoon.

Entering the new century, Guyomarc'h NA developed a new strategy, based on establishing itself as one of the leading global feed players. Toward this end, in 2001 the company decided to change its name, adopting the more universal-sounding name Evialis. At the same time, the company restructured its operations into three core divisions, Evialis Nutrition, Evialis Premix and Specialities, and Evialis Health. The company

also began rebranding its operations and products under the Evialis name, a process that would continue through much of the decade.

CRITICAL MASS IN THE GLOBAL MARKET

Evialis's international strategy was based on the company achieving critical mass by establishing a presence in most of the world's major feed markets. Toward this end, the group acquired Italy's IZA in 2001, and then entered the South Africa market, buying Coprex that year. Evialis soon solidified its South African presence, adding feed producer Progress Feed in 2003, followed by Monti Feeds in 2005.

The company also sought to boost its presence in the booming Chinese market, establishing a new premix facility in the city of Qindao, in Shandong Province, in 2004. In that year the group also consolidated its Polish operations into a single company, creating Evialis Polska. By 2006, the group had reinforced its Eastern European presence through the purchase of Agricola, based in Romania.

Evialis also developed a number of partnerships. The most prominent of these was the creation of Nutréa, a joint venture with Unicopa, which became the leading animal nutrition player in the West France region. Evialis's share of that company, with eight factories and an annual production of 1.5 million metric tons, stood at 34 percent. Other shareholdings acquired during the decade included a majority stake in Bern-Aqua, based in Belgium, and 80 percent of Zoofort, based in Mato Grosso, Brazil.

In 2007, the company acquired Trouw Nutrition France, formerly part of Nutreco Holding of the Netherlands. The group also sought to fill the remaining gaps in its international profile. This led the company to Russia, where it acquired Rossovit, a premix producer, that same year. By April 2008, the company had plugged another major hole in its global network, buying up a 70 percent stake in one of Mexico's largest feed producers, Malta Cleyton. Soon after, Evialis raised its Brazilian profile as well, through its agreement to take over the operations of Cargill Animal Nutrition in Brazil. The deal, which included four factories, as well as the Brazilian rights to the Purina brand name, boosted Evialis to the lead in that market.

By then, Evialis had strengthened its position in the French market as well. At the beginning of 2008, the company gained a new majority shareholder, in the form of InVivo, a union of farm cooperatives active in the feed, seeds, and agribusiness sectors. InVivo's investment in Evialis proved to be only the first step toward the development of a partnership between the two companies. By July 2008, InVivo had agreed to merge its own feed, premix, and animal health operations into Evialis.

The merger was expected to transform Evialis, doubling the company in size. The incorporation of In-Vivo's operations was expected to add sixteen new factories, and boost the company's presence to nearly 65 markets worldwide. At the same time, turnover from international operations was expected to rise to 40 percent, compared to just 26 percent the year before. The merger was also expected to give Evialis a more balanced revenue portrait, with feed contributing just 65 percent of sales, compared to 80 percent in 2007. As the new powerhouse in the French animal health and nutrition market, Evialis was setting its sights on gaining a place among the sector's global leaders in the 21st century.

M. L. Cohen

PRINCIPAL SUBSIDIARIES

Agro Management Services SNC; Alissea SAS; Bernaqua SA (Belgium); Evialis Galicia SA (Spain); Evialis India Ltd; Evialis Polska Sp Zoo (Polen); Guyokrma Spol Sro (Czech Republic); Guyomarc'h Vcn Ltd (Vietnam); Guyomarc'h Vietnam Ltd (Vietnam); Iberica De Nutricion Animal Sl (Spain); Iberil SA (Portugal); Npna SAS; Ona SAS; SAfe SAS; SAntamix Iberica Sl (Spain); Sfna SAS; Shandong Guyomarc'h Animal Nutrition Feed Additive Ltd (China); SNC Fabricants Associes; Vitargos-Rossovit SArl (Russia); Wirifa SAkti Pt—Ji. (Indonesia).

PRINCIPAL COMPETITORS

Cargill Inc.; Archer Daniels Midland Co.; Eli Lilly and Co.; Edison S.p.A.; ConAgra Foods Inc.; National Foods Holdings Ltd.; Murphy-Brown L.L.C.; Land O'Lakes Inc.; Proagro C.A; Kerry Group PLC; AGRAVIS Raiffeisen AG; Nutreco Holding N.V.; Union InVivo; Terrena S.C.A.

FURTHER READING

Best, Peter, "Evialis Reveals Growing Global Ambitions," *Food Industry Network,* October 1, 2006.

"Evialis Sees Profits Rocket," *Europe Intelligence Wire,* September 26, 2008.

"InVivo and Evialis Plan to Merge All of Their Feed, Premix & Health Activities," *PR Newswire,* July 1, 2008.

Lundeen, Tim, "Evialis Buys Brazilian Cargill Business," *Feedstuffs,* June 23, 2008, p. 24.

——, "Global Feed Compounder Grows," *Feedstuffs,* April 7, 2008, p. 21.

"Nutreco Holding NV Mergers with Evialis Group," *Feedstuffs,* January 8, 2007, p. 7.

"Socil Guyomarc'h Acquires Agribands," *South American Business Information,* January 8, 2002.

Family Sports Concepts, Inc.

5510 West LaSalle Street, Suite 200
Tampa, Florida 33607
U.S.A.
Telephone: (813) 226-2333
Toll Free: (800) 728-8878
Fax: (813) 226-0030
Web site: http://www.beefobradys.com

Private Company
Incorporated: 1998
Employees: 7,000
Sales: $225 million (2007)
NAICS: 722110 Full-Service Restaurants

■ ■ ■

Based in Tampa, Florida, Family Sports Concepts, Inc., is a private company that franchises the Beef O'Brady's chain of casual family sports restaurants. Comprised of more than 260 locations in about 21 southeastern and midwestern states, the chain focuses on smaller communities and shopping centers anchored by grocery stores. Beef's, as the restaurant is informally called, has carved out a niche in the sports bar segment by appealing to families. Since the beginning it has generally eschewed hard liquor, selling only beer and wine, and closing early, around 11:00 P.M. The restaurants keep prices in check by serving food in plastic baskets and offering a limited menu, which includes Beef's signature hot wings, hamburgers, other sandwiches, wraps, soups and salads, fish and chips, chicken fingers, and a single dessert item: Chocolate Eruption Cake. Beef's is known

for its community involvement, especially the financial support of local youth sports leagues and high school sports. Many participants visit Beef's after their games, and the restaurants' bevy of televisions show live professional and collegiate sports year-round. All Beef's restaurants are franchised operations. Family Sports Concepts offers a full range of support to its owner-operators, including help with financing, site selection, construction, and a nine-week training program. The company charges a $35,000 franchise fee, $5,000 grand opening fee, and a 4 percent royalty. An advertising fund accounts for another 1.5 percent.

FOUNDER MOVES TO FLORIDA

The Beef O'Brady's chain was founded by Jim Mellody, a Pennsylvania native who had worked in the insurance field and grew tired of the cold weather of the Northeast when he threw out his back shoveling snow. He was in his early 30s when he moved his family to Tampa, Florida, in 1971. With his wife's cousin he opened a pizzeria near the University of Tampa. The next 15 years were a struggle for Mellody as he strove to make a living in the restaurant field. Working 80-hour weeks, he tried opening pizzerias and Italian restaurants in both Tampa and Brandon, Florida. One of his failed ventures, Great Milano, became his nickname.

In 1985 the "Great Milano" was working for a food distributor in the Tampa area and one of his customers was Mrs. G's Sandwich Shop. Mellody decided to buy the 1,250-square-foot, one-room place and turn it into a neighborhood pub that served steak and potatoes. For a name he combined "beef," for the steaks he planned as his signature menu item, and his mother's maiden name, O'Brady, to coin Beef O'Brady's.

Almost immediately Mellody plugged in a television so he and his patrons could watch sports. During the major league baseball season in 1987, a local Brandon youth, Jody Reed, was called up by the Boston Red Sox, creating a great deal of interest in Red Sox games. Mellody bought a satellite dish to receive the games and thus quickly established Beef's as a sports bar.

What actually did not work out was his idea to serve steak as a signature dish. His customers were more interested in finger food, such as hamburgers and French fries. A friend from upstate New York came to visit and told Mellody about the Buffalo wing craze, and Mellody decided to concoct his own hot wing sauce to bring the item to his customers, more as a come-on than a moneymaker. "I was running these $70 ads in the paper," he recalled in an interview with *Nation's Restaurant News,* "and drawing maybe three or four people—so I bought $70 worth of wings and put a sign out front saying 'Free chicken wings.'" He began drawing a crowd and soon chicken wings became Beef's signature item.

EXPANSION BEGINS

Beef's was a popular spot for sports fans. When the beauty salon next door closed, Mellody acquired it and added a second room to Beef's. He also put up two more satellite dishes and additional televisions to increase his sports trade.

Mellody also began seeing an increase in families eating at Beef's. To accommodate the younger children, he installed video games. Soon the sports pub became known as a family sports pub. Mellody embraced the format, refusing to add dart boards and pool tables, eschewing hard liquor, and setting the closing hours at 11:00 P.M., although he could be flexible on this point. When Mellody began building a rapport with local sports teams, the pub was filled with high school football coaches and players after their games on Friday

nights. "They'd be hanging around and talking football all night," he recalled, speaking with *Nation's Restaurant News.* "I'd just throw them the keys and trust them to lock up on their way home. They'd stay there until four or five in the morning—going over every play."

Mellody's family sports pub idea provided so popular that he opened another Beef's in Plant City, Florida, followed by stores in Bloomingdale, Lakeland, and Apollo Beach. Some of his customers also grew interested in operating a Beef's, and they began filling in the central west coast Florida region with licensed stores. By 1996 Mellody owned six Beef's and another 22 stores operated on license, together generating more than $15 million in annual sales.

Mellody was interested in expanding the chain further, possibly out of state, but realized that he did not possess the necessary business experience, nor had he set up an organization capable of achieving that goal. Through a mutual friend, Outback Steakhouse cofounder Robert Basham, he met Chuck Winship, who was highly qualified to spearhead an expansion effort.

FAMILY SPORTS CONCEPTS IS FORMED

Before his tenure at Outback, Basham had worked with Winship at Sunstate Franchise Company, Ltd., operators of Chili's Grill & Bar franchised operations. As president of Sunstate, Winship grew the number of units to 30. After Sunstate was sold to Brinker International Inc., Winship was looking for an investment opportunity and through Basham became familiar with Beef O'Brady's. Winship and Sunstate's founder, Gene Kippers, formed Family Sports Concepts Inc. on January 1, 1998 and acquired the rights to the Beef O'Brady's chain. Although they planned to grow Beef's through franchising, they allowed the 20 licensed operators to continue their handshake deals or to become franchisees and grow with the support of the parent company. Family Sports also agreed to abide by Mellody's principles, refraining from the sale of hard liquor and requiring franchisees to participate in their communities.

As president of Family Sports, Winship assembled a strong management team, including Nick Vojnovic as vice president of training and franchising and Ken Hall, a *Tampa Tribune* newspaper executive, to head marketing. He also expanded the menu to help increase average per unit sales and updated the décor. Because of cash flow constraints, however, the company was too quick to sell five-unit franchise agreements, leading to problems with operators who may not have completed the training program, made poor real estate decisions, or

KEY DATES

1985: Jim Mellody opens the first Beef O'Brady's in Brandon, Florida.
1998: Family Sports Concepts, Inc., is formed to acquire the Beef O'Brady brand.
2002: Mellody dies.
2004: Beef O'Brady chains enters Arkansas, Illinois, Kentucky, Ohio, and Texas.
2007: Levine Leichtman Capital Partners invest in company.
2008: First hotel unit opens.

simply lacked the ability to properly run their businesses. As a result, the chain grew in fits and starts, with new openings offset by the closure of some units.

Beef's grew by three stores in 1999, followed by 17 in 2000, and 16 in 2001. Eventually, Family Sports was in a position to insist that franchisees have a successful restaurant in operation before opening a second. Only franchisees with considerable restaurant experience and available capital would be considered for multi-unit deals.

MULTI-STATE EXPANSION IN 21ST CENTURY

By January 2002 the Beef's chain totaled 65 units in Florida, Alabama, Georgia, and Kentucky. Systemwide annual sales were in the $50 million range. Jim Mellody owned a stake in ten of the restaurants, but his association with Beef's would end in 2002. His health failed quickly and in November of that year he succumbed to cancer at the age of 63. He left behind a restaurant chain with about 85 units. During his final year, Beef's entered South Carolina and North Carolina, focusing on the suburban Charlotte, Hickory, and Raleigh markets, and was on the verge of cracking the 100-unit threshold.

To facilitate further growth, despite difficult economic conditions that hindered other restaurant chains, Family Sports bolstered its management ranks in 2003 by adding three new positions: chief operating officer, chief financial officer, and vice president of franchise development and operations. Also, to drive growth Beef's developed a marketing program it called "Way of Life." It became mandatory for franchisees to use the program to facilitate the requirement that they become involved in their communities. Moreover, as Beef's moved into new markets, an emphasis was placed on franchisees who were well suited to follow the program, with preference given to people who already had deep ties to the communities in which they operated.

EXPANDING BEYOND THE SOUTH

One of the new markets targeted, northeast Ohio, was far removed from the sunshine of Florida, but the Beef O'Brady's name was already familiar to that area's baseball fans, because the Cleveland Indians held their spring training in Winter Haven, Florida, where a Beef's restaurant often played host to team radio broadcasts. The entry into Ohio in 2004 was part of a push into America's heartland to markets in Ohio, Kentucky, and Arkansas.

Playing a key role in Beef's expansion was Vojnovic, who had been named chief operating officer, also succeeding Winship as president in January 2005. Vojnovic's ties to the restaurant trade were deep. His mother's parents had operated a pair of fine-dining restaurants in Belgrade, Yugoslavia: the Continental Café downtown and Restaurant Dedinge near the king's palace. During World War II the Nazis seized the establishments, and following the war the Communists took over as the country came under the dominance of the Soviet Union.

The family immigrated to the United States, where Vojnovic was born and began his own restaurant career at the age of 12 in Monroeville, Pennsylvania, earning $1.25 an hour as a dishwasher at an Italian restaurant. Later he enrolled in Cornell University's acclaimed hospitality program, graduating in 1981. He changed jobs at a fast pace over the years, eventually connecting with Winship and Knippers at Sunsrate. When they formed Family Sports, they made a point of bringing in Vojnovic, who because of family reasons was willing to stay put with a company. His skill, enthusiasm, and honesty made him popular with franchisees and played an important part in the growth of the Beef's chain.

After entering Illinois and Texas in 2004, Beef's ventured into Minnesota, Tennessee, Virginia, Maryland, Indiana, and Wisconsin in 2005, when the Beef's chain numbered 180 units in 17 states. Systemwide sales increased from $110 million in 2004 to about $142.2 million in 2005, due not only to the addition of new stores but also to average annual unit sales jumping from $900,000 to $1 million. This surge was the result of changes to the menu, the addition of four new chicken wing flavors, wraps, salads, basket meals, and a half-pound steak burger. The company had also rolled out a new ad campaign employing the theme, "What's a Family Sports Pub?"

MID-DECADE DEVELOPMENTS

In 2005 Family Sports implemented a five-year plan that imposed a limit of one unit on most franchisees until they had established a successful business. The company also elected to focus more on filling in existing territories rather than entering new states. The Beef's chain expanded at a steady pace, topping the 200-unit mark in 2006 when systemwide sales increased to $181 million. To help fuel further growth, Family Sports received an infusion of cash from Beverly Hills, California-based Levine Leichtman Capital Partners in 2007.

It was not a particularly good time for the casual dining sector, which had to deal with higher labor costs due to an increase in the minimum wage and high energy costs that impacted food costs. Because a large number of Beef's units were located in Florida, insurance rates also increased because of hurricanes. To make matters worse, customers were hurt by economic conditions as well, resulting in flat sales. Nevertheless, Beef's continued to grow, aided in part by changes to its menu. Ribs were added to improve its standing against such competitors as Applebee's and Chili's, and a smaller-portion menu offered at a lower price was also made available. A wine-based margarita was also tested to help offset the chain's lack of liquor, which caused "veto votes" among some groups of diners who wanted to have more drink options.

FIRST HOTEL UNIT OPENS

Another reason that Beef's was able to weather tough economic conditions was its flexible format, which could range widely in size, allowing franchisees to take over vacated properties and save money on existing setups and equipment. Beef's was also a good candidate for hybrid locations, such as the University of South Florida campus and Tradewinds Island Grand Resort on St. Pete Beach. In September 2008, the first Beef's opened in a hotel, the Best Western Hotel and Conference Canter in Brandon, Florida. It was also the first Beef's in the chain to offer banquet facilities, and the first in the Tampa Bay area to serve liquor, perhaps a harbinger of things to come chainwide. Management hoped to grow the chain to 450 units by 2010 and increase sales to about $450 million.

Ed Dinger

PRINCIPAL SUBSIDIARIES

FSC Franchise Company LLC.

PRINCIPAL COMPETITORS

Applebee's International, Inc.; Brinker International, Inc.; Buffalo Wild Wings, Inc.

FURTHER READING

Cebrzynski, Gregg, "Beef O'Brady's Aims to Hold 'Third Place' Reflects Trend Toward Lifestyle Marketing," *Nation's Restaurant News,* October 23, 2006, p. 4.

———, "Beef O'Brady's Credits New Ad Strategy for Sales Gains," *Nation's Restaurant News,* November 14, 2005, p. 18.

———, "Beef O'Brady's Franchisees Commit to a Certain 'Way of Life,'" *Nation's Restaurant News,* August 9, 2004, p. 14.

Coomes, Steve, "Nick Vojnovic," *Nation's Restaurant News,* October 1, 2007, p. 80.

Hayes, Jack, "Regional Powerhouse Chains: Beef O'Brady's Family Sports Pubs," *Nation's Restaurant News,* January 28, 2002, p. 20.

Jackovics, Ted, "Community Mourns Beef O'Brady's Founder," *Tampa Tribune,* November 24, 2002.

Norris, Maya, "Beefing Up," *Chain Leader,* September 2005, p. 57.

Sandler, Michael, "Beef O'Brady's Chain Founder Dies at Age 63," *St. Petersburg Times,* November 25, 2002, p. 3B.

"Taking Wing," *Tampa Tribune,* December 14, 1998, p. 8.

Ferolito, Vultaggio & Sons

---

5 Dakota Drive, Suite 205
Lake Success, New York 11042
U.S.A.
Telephone: (516) 812-0300
Toll Free: (800) 832-3775
Fax: (516) 326-4988
Web site: http://www.drinkarizona.com/

Private Company
Founded: 1971
Employees: 100
Sales: $600 million (2006 est.)
NAICS: 312111 Beverages, Fruit and Vegetable Drinks, Cocktails and Ades, Manufacturing; 312120 Breweries

■ ■ ■

Ferolito, Vultaggio & Sons, maker of the widely popular AriZona Iced Tea, produces teas, juice drinks, energy drinks, powdered tea mixes, and fruit smoothies and is a leader in its industry. Offering alternatives to traditional colas and other carbonated drinks, the company was founded in Brooklyn by Don Vultaggio and John Ferolito andin the early 2000s remains a privately held and family-run U.S. business. Ferolito, Vultaggio & Sons (FV&S) has distinguished itself for its nontraditional approach to both product development and advertising. Their products, remarkable for their oversized bottles and cans that feature brightly colored graphics, are available nationwide in supermarkets and convenience stores.

The company's AriZona Iced Tea is the leading ready-to-drink tea in the country.

ORIGINS IN A VOLKSWAGEN BUS

John Ferolito and Don Vultaggio went into business together in the early 1970s, soon after graduating from high school. While they held delivery jobs at a brewery and beer distributorship, they decided to team up, part-time, to form their own business on the side. Together, the Brooklyn natives purchased a used Volkswagen bus for a couple hundred dollars, ripped the seats out of the back, and proceeded to work delivering reduced price beer and soda to Brooklyn homes and grocery stores.

This venture soon became full-time work, and the men purchased a used truck to make wholesale deliveries. Their territory centered on such neighborhoods as Crown Heights and Bedford-Stuyvesant, known as tough, high crime areas that other union drivers tended to avoid. Vultaggio and Ferolito were eventually successful enough to acquire a small fleet of trucks, though they were still second-tier distributors flogging beer at cut rate prices.

Not satisfied with their role as distributor, the pair soon decided they'd rather make their mark with their own product. They established the Hornell Brewing Company in the mid-1980s to oversee this new venture; it would eventually become a division of FV&S. The first product FV&S tried, and ultimately failed, to market was Spence & Wesley, a flavored seltzer water named for Vultaggio's sons.

FROM DISTRIBUTORSHIP TO MALT LIQUOR MAKER

The partners achieved a higher profile with their next product, a malt liquor with a high alcohol content, named Midnight Dragon. Ferolito and Vultaggio made the product available at a very low price and promoted it vigorously, reportedly targeting the streets of Manhattan's and Brooklyn's black and Hispanic neighborhoods in particular, every night for a year, shaking hands with passersby and thanking owners of small stores for their orders. Citing FV&S's approach as one example, one *Wall Street Journal* reporter made the accusation that companies employing such tactics "play a part in the cycle of poor nutrition that is approaching crisis levels in the inner city."

FV&S also publicized the brew with suggestive point-of-sale posters, notably one displaying a woman clad in red lingerie, sipping the brew through a straw, with the accompanying tagline, "I could suck on this all night." This ad was withdrawn following protests by the National Organization for Women, although Ferolito was said to have told the *Wall Street Journal* in 1989: "Real men like sex and sex sells beer. I'm not interested in wimps and achievers who want to suck on a lime and drink Corona." Although available only in the New York City metropolitan area at the time, Midnight Dragon had estimated sales of one million cases in 1988. The following year FV&S formed a joint venture with a Cincinnati brewer to introduce Midnight Dragon to other major U.S. markets and to handle additional marketing and production.

FV&S next launched a new brand of malt liquor it called Crazy Horse, named after the Sioux leader, with a label that bore a drawing of an Indian in a feathered headdress. Produced through an agreement with G.

Heileman Brewing Co. and sold in 40-ounce bottles, the beer was marketed in New York City and five states.

The brand soon drew a wealth of negative attention. In 1992 the U.S. Surgeon General called the brand name "an insensitive and malicious marketing ploy" aimed at Native Americans, who had long been experiencing a high rate of alcoholism and alcohol-related illness. The U.S. Bureau of Alcohol, Tobacco and Firearms, which had approved the product only two months earlier, then reversed itself, citing technical violations that it said, with the clear glass, 40-ounce bottle and dark color of the beverage, "all combine to create the misleading impression that the product is a bottle of whisky."

Congress passed measures in 1992 essentially banning the product, but in 1993 a federal judge overturned the act on First Amendment grounds. In 1997 FV&S was still fighting legislation that banned Crazy Horse in some states, as well as contending with an organized boycott of AriZona teas. Annual sales of the brew had dropped by that time from a peak of three million to some 240,000 cases, according to Vultaggio. When G. Heileman went bankrupt and its assets were sold to another bottler and distributor, SBC Holdings, that company issued an official apology to the Sioux people. Lawsuits against Hornell and FV&S dragged on but were eventually settled in 2004. The name of the brand was changed to Crazy Stallion.

ENTERING THE ICED TEA MARKET

Hornell Brewing was earning annual revenues of about $10 million when in 1992 FV&S launched the product that was to make its fortune—AriZona Iced Tea. Some 200 ready-to-drink teas had been introduced in the previous two years, produced by such industry giants as Lipton and Snapple, but AriZona stood out for its pastel colored packaging, vaguely reminiscent of Native American artwork, and its jumbo 24-ounce can. "You know how much time you have at the cooler when the consumer's thirsty?" Vultaggio asked a reporter rhetorically. He answered, "A split second. Make it easy and they'll buy it." The six foot eight inch tall cofounder credited the can's creation to "my partner, myself, my wife, and a gal in South Jersey who does our mechanicals."

The brand name, Vultaggio said, came to him when he was standing in front of a map in his office and asking himself "Where is hot?" and "What sounds good?" The idea for the product, he confessed, was inspired by rival Snapple Beverage Corp., which was also founded in Brooklyn. "We had been beer guys all our lives and we

KEY DATES

1971: John Ferolito and Don Vultaggio found beverage distributor.
1980s: Ferolito and Vultaggio establish the Hornell Brewing Company.
1992: Ferolito, Vultaggio & Sons launch AriZona brand iced tea.
2002: Company forms an International Division to launch AriZona brand overseas.

only knew beer," Vultaggio told a *Beverage World* reporter, noting "Iced tea was foreign to us." Nevertheless, he and Ferolito thought they could do whatever the three founders of Snapple had done.

Vultaggio relayed that his company paid more for extra tea flavoring and higher grade sweeteners but marketed 24-ounce AriZona for the same 99 cents as the 16-ounce bottle of Snapple's iced tea. Later, AriZona would preprint "99 cents" on its bottles to avoid retail markup. Production was handled by the same Cincinnati company that made Midnight Dragon, Hudepohl-Schoenling Brewing Co. Over 700,000 cases were sold by the end of 1992, and *Fortune* magazine named AriZona one of the hottest products of 1993.

The product's success was also reportedly inspired by the partners' experience selling in urban neighborhoods. "We learned a lot working up and down the street," Ferolito told a *Brandweek* reporter. "Party King was a popular soft drink that taught us pretty colors worked in the inner city. Sweetness worked too; that's why Nehi was a success." Twenty-four-ounce beer cans were already available in these markets.

Ferolito and Vultaggio knew all about the beverage wholesaling game after more than 20 years in the business. They ordered wholesalers—mostly large beer distributors of Budweiser and Miller—to repack their products into "rainbow cases" that would provide small retailers with an assortment of the four AriZona Iced Tea flavors—lemon, diet lemon, raspberry, and tropical—even if the retailer ordered only one case. The multiethnic FV&S sales team was told to get the product placed in all its existing beer accounts. The company resisted paying "slotting allowances" to supermarkets. "I don't like retail chains," Ferolito said in 1994. "They're a pool of sharks that you can't sell your products to like a human being." By late 1997, however, FV&S would give in, routinely paying slotting fees to chain stores.

SUCCESS AND EXPANSION

By mid-1993 the four AriZona teas each were available in 7.7- and 16-ounce sizes as well as in the big can, in more than 30 states. FV&S sold more than ten million cases of AriZona in 1993; 80 percent of the sales were in only four markets: New York, New Jersey, Miami, and Detroit. AriZona had seemingly come from nowhere to take fourth place among ready-to-drink teas in the United States.

The point man for the expansion of FV&S products was Michael Schott, who was minority owner and vice-president of Hudepohl-Schoenling when that company had contracted to produce and distribute Midnight Dragon. Schott was running a Detroit beer wholesaling operation when FV&S introduced AriZona Iced Tea. He brought it to Detroit and took it to the top there in its first year, moving 900,000 cases of the beverage in 1993. FV&S then hired Schott as its chief operating officer and charged him with making the drink national. Before the end of 1994 AriZona Iced Tea was being sold in all 50 states, with estimated sales of $300 million a year, compared to an estimated $10 million to $20 million in 1992 and an estimated $130 million in 1993. Ferolito and Vultaggio each pocketed $30 million in after-tax profits in 1994.

By the end of 1993, FV&S had also begun making AriZona Iced Tea available in a proprietary 20-ounce long-neck, widemouth bottle (produced by Anchor Glass) that proved even more popular than the big can. Packaging innovations continued, as they began offering the beverage in milk style wax cartons, large aseptic packs, and even in powdered form. Moreover, the AriZona design was licensed for lollipops and freeze pops, beach towels, shirts, and other goods.

In early 1994 FV&S widened the beverage line by introducing AriZona Cowboy Cocktails, a juice-based drink in such flavors as Mucho Mango and Strawberry Punch, with Kiwi Strawberry and Pina Colada added later. Soon the company was also putting out lemonade and a nonfat, chocolate flavored drink. During this time Canadian distribution was also achieved through an agreement with Molson Breweries.

By this time FV&S was seeking to move from its overcrowded 6,000-square-foot Brooklyn warehouse, where, Vultaggio said, "we have been burglarized about 20 times and the roof is impossible to repair." In the fall of 1994 the company began its move to a corporate office park in Lake Success on Long Island, although the sales staff would remain at the Brooklyn site. During this period the partners decided against taking FV&S public and also reportedly turned down an offer of about $400 million for the company from Heileman.

FV&S began 1995 by introducing its iced tea in a fifth flavor—ginseng—in 20-ounce, cobalt blue bottles. Later in the year the company introduced the first of what became its Soda Shop line of carbonated soft drinks—Chocolate Cola, Diet Chocolate Cola, Vanilla Cola, Chocolate Covered Cherry Cola, and Root Beer Float—under the AriZona name. The root beer drink included milk and cream, which, according to Vultaggio, was unprecedented in a carbonated beverage. These drinks were marketed in a thicker 19-ounce bottle to accommodate the carbonation, and with labels featuring the distinctive AriZona package graphics. FV&S's estimated sales of $285 million in 1995 included 20.3 million cases of AriZona Iced Tea. Earnings were said to be $45 million before taxes. (A later estimate put 1995 sales at $355 million.)

THE GOING GETS TOUGHER

In 1996 FV&S introduced Mississippi Mud, a black and tan beer that was a blend of English porter and continental pilsner. The first alcoholic beverage since Crazy Stallion to be marketed by the company, the brew came in a 32-ounce glass jug inspired by the rustic clay whiskey drinking vessel John Wayne hoisted in the film *The Alamo*. Despite the broadened scope of its product line, or perhaps because of it, AriZona's sales slipped to an estimated $337.3 million in 1996. Moreover, its share of the iced tea market fell to 9.6 percent, compared to 10.7 percent in 1994. FV&S's totals would have looked worse, according to a *Newsday* article, if the company had not raised prices sharply and introduced new superpremium-priced flavors.

By the spring of 1997 Schott and several FV&S sales and marketing executives had departed, forcing Vultaggio to assume the position of sales manager himself. One job that demanded action was to smooth the ruffled feathers of some of the company's 500 distributors, who were angered by what they considered broken promises and strong arm tactics. At least five distributors had filed lawsuits against FV&S, charging that the company had breached contracts for distribution rights. In early 1997 the company shifted its business in many markets from beer wholesalers to soft drink bottlers, thereby, according to one account, throwing its distribution system into chaos.

As a result, FV&S next began shipping its goods directly to major national retail chains, paying local distributors a per-case fee of about $1.50 for circumventing the wholesale end of the business. The company also switched from 24-unit to 12-unit cases for some of its higher priced packages, thereby enabling retailers to invest less money in AriZona inventory while continuing to stock a variety of flavors. Some warehouse

club stores had been reluctant to spend $300 to $400 to stock the brand, and some suspected that the 24-unit cases were so heavy that clerks might avoid restocking shelves.

By this time the partners were reportedly reconsidering their determination to hold the annual advertising budget to $1 million, trivial compared to Snapple's $33 million and Lipton's $17 million in 1996. The company had sponsored the Schwinn Cycling & Fitness racing series and other bicycling events in major metropolitan areas in 1996 but dropped this promotional effort, which included AriZona uniforms, posters, and banners, after a single year.

Despite earlier urgings from Schott, and even at one point from Ferolito, Vultaggio had in 1995 vetoed a plan to hire an advertising agency from more than a half-dozen interviewed. Beverage industry consultants considered the rejection a mistake. "AriZona had a great burst in the beginning because of the packaging, but the consumer is tired of that," said one, adding, "If you don't spend money to promote your brand, you will fall to the earth and crash."

By this time Strawberry Punch, tropical-flavored tea, and the carbonated line of beverages all had failed—the latter, according to a distributor, because FV&S failed to get the message out that AriZona had such drinks, while marketing them in bottles similar in size and appearance to that of the teas and juices. "I saw people shaking it up in the store, thinking it was tea," Vultaggio said.

ONGOING INNOVATIONS

Still, the company continued to innovate and remained competitive. By the spring of 1997 AriZona's new Green Tea with Ginseng and Honey had become one of FV&S's biggest hits. It also introduced an egg cream called Lite Chocolate Fudge Float and added to its line a Herbal Tea the ingredients of which included chamomile, ginseng, bee pollen, and honey. While some AriZona products maintained the original southwestern motif in their packaging, others seemed to take reflect designs of the Far East or recalled American artwork of the 19th century. Still others had a ceramic appearance "like they were handpainted in Tuscany," according to Vultaggio. FV&S also added a line of diet teas, a proprietary 16-ounce bottle, and a squeezable plastic sports bottle made to look like a metal can. The product line extended to nearly 50 stock keeping units in late 1997.

In the fall of 1998 FV&S test marketed Blue Luna iced coffee, its first nonalcoholic beverage line not under the AriZona brand name. Introduced in Café Latte and

Lite Café Mocha flavors and sweetened with the newly approved product Splenda, Blue Luna came in elaborate 12.5-ounce bottles shaped like double handled Roman jugs. The company also designed a Total Extreme Sport beverage, through the AriZona line, with a 24-ounce plastic bottle that used a thermal barrier to preserve coolness and a dual-flow spout for control. Earlier in the year, FV&S had commissioned pop artist Peter Max to create a limited-edition series of 16-ounce bottles for its core Lemon Tea line. In 1998, the company won 11 awards for its innovative and aesthetically pleasing packaging designs.

In 1999, the company launched its web site, and it offered its first non-beverage product, a Salsa N'Chips snack item, through the Blue Luna Café line. By this time, the company's $500 million AriZona brand included seven flavored teas, seven juice drinks, two nonalcoholic colada mixes, four diet teas, and a carbonated soft drink. While the company had stalled its introduction of new entries in the AriZona line for a short time, the year 1999 saw the introduction of a new Blue Luna coffee line, Crazy Carrot (a 25 percent juice mélange), and a new Orangeade.

BACK ON TOP

At century's end, things were looking up again, and the company led the market in distinctive new products in the New Age beverage niche. Still, industry observers seemed to agree that FV&S's unique, award winning packaging designs had contributed in large part to the company's sales and success, and some expressed concern over the company's meager advertising budget and strains on relations with its distributor network.

Ferolito and Vultaggio, however, disagreed. Rather than engaging in expensive advertising and research campaigns, the company preferred to invest in high quality ingredients for its beverages. Don Vultaggio, dubbed "the blue collar anti-CEO" in a 2006 issue of *Time,* proudly touted his "rubbish marketing approach" to research and development. The company saved the expense of focus groups and marketing firms by simply looking in garbage cans to see what types of drinks people were buying. Vultaggio found, for example, that resealable bottles were preferable to cans (enabling consumers to retain beverage freshness) when he noticed, on a scavenging trip, that empty bottles tossed out of car windows and left on the sides of New York highways tended to have caps on. As for product design, his inspiration for the original AriZona bottle had reportedly been a bottle of his wife's perfume, and he also borrowed ideas from movies, television, and other food categories.

The 21st century brought the company several years of double-digit growth. With so-called New Age products and healthful products gaining widespread popularity, FV&S gave soda companies some serious competition. Its teas, sports drinks, and bottled waters catered to the country's new concern for obesity and health problems related to drinking too much soda. While many of its competitors (including Lipton, Snapple, and Nestea) had been acquired by larger companies by this time, the AriZona brand remained private and independent.

The company's commitment to innovative packaging led to its introducing the first plastic bottle in the industry to duplicate glass containers for "hot fill" use, meaning they could be safely filled with hot liquids. The new 42-ounce polyethylene terephthalate (PET) bottle was used for AriZona original lemon tea, green tea with ginseng and honey, Asian plum green tea, and AriZona RxStress caffeine-free tea. Other new items included: Kahlua Iced Coffee, developed with Allied Domecq (2001); powdered teas, lemonades, and vitamin herbal sodas (2002); infused waters, dairy-based Cappuccino Shakes, No Carb Green Teas, AriZona Botanically Brewed Teas, and Extreme Rx Energy Shot Energy Drinks (2003); AriZona Decaf Diet GreenTea, sweetened with Splenda (2005), and black and white tea (2007).

The company positioned its successful AriZona brand for launch in the international market in 2002, hiring Alberto Uribe as president of the new International Division. Uribe came to FV&S with experience as an executive for PepsiCo International.

In 2004, AriZona iced tea was the top ready-to-drink tea in the nation, surpassing competitors Lipton and Snapple in what had become a $3.5 billion market category. The next year, AriZona led the iced tea market with a 32.3 percent market share in supermarkets, convenience stores, and drugstores. Annual sales in 2005 in major retail distribution channels exceeded $417 million, and total sales were over $600 million, according to the April 10, 2006, issue of *Time.* Dominated by the success of its AriZona brand, the company's innovative packaging, as well as its quirky research and marketing strategies seemed to align perfectly with consumer beverage preferences in the early 2000s.

Robert Halasz
Updated, Heidi Feldman

PRINCIPAL SUBSIDIARIES

Arizona Tea Company; Hornell Brewing Company.

PRINCIPAL COMPETITORS

PepsiCo Inc.; The Coca-Cola Company; Snapple Beverage Corporation.

FURTHER READING

"AriZona Starts PET Evolution," *Packaging Digest,* October 2001, p. 32.

Berkowitz, Harry, "Half Empty or Half Full?" *Newsday,* April 7, 1997, pp. C7, C9–C10.

Bird, Laura, "U.S. Moves Against Label of a New Brew," *Wall Street Journal,* April 24, 1992, p. B4.

Christy, Nick, "The Call from Ferolito, Vultaggio & Sons: Here Comes the Jug, Here Comes the Mug," *Beverage World,* October 31, 1996, p. 17.

Collins, Glenn, "A Feisty Brand's Newest Frontier: Premium Colas," *New York Times,* October 28, 1995, p. 35.

Dwyer, Steve, "Innovative to a 'Tea,'" *Prepared Foods,* April 1999, p. 12.

"Ferolito Vultaggio & Sons," *Beverage Industry,* November 2002, p. 21.

"Ferolito Vultaggio & Sons," *Dairy Foods,* August 2001, p. 23.

Freedman, Alix M., "Poor Selection," *Wall Street Journal,* December 20, 1990, p. A1.

Gregory, Sean, "Raising Arizona," *Time,* April 10, 2006, p. A11.

Khermouch, Gerry, "Arizona Accelerates New Products," *Brandweek,* June 7, 1999, p. 6.

———, "Between Coke and a Hard Place," *Brandweek,* June 22, 1998, pp. 36, 38.

———, "Grand Can Yen," *Brandweek,* November 7, 1994, pp. 23–24, 26–29.

———, "Still Winging It," *Brandweek,* October 27, 1997, pp. 38, 40.

Mallia, Joseph, "Lake Success Beverage Maker Hit for $1M," *Newsday,* February 12, 2008.

Prince, Greg W., "Tall Order," *Beverage World,* June 1994, p. 22.

Roth, Daniel, "Just Call Us Cockroaches," *Forbes,* August 26, 1996, p. 58.

Theodore, Sarah, "Arizona Enjoys Its Place in the Sun," *Beverage Industry,* July 2004, p. 40.

"Vultaggio, AriZona Never Take a Holiday from Package Design," *Beverage World,* August 15, 1997, p. 24.

Frontera Foods, Inc.

---

449 North Clark Street, Suite 205
Chicago, Illinois 60610-4500
U.S.A.
Telephone: (312) 661-1434
Fax: (312) 661-1830
Web site: http://www.fronterakitchens.com

Private Company
Incorporated: 1995
Employees: 122
Sales: $20 million (2007 est.)
NAICS: 311423 Dried and Dehydrated Food
Manufacturing

■ ■ ■

Based in Chicago, Frontera Foods, Inc., is the food marketing and distribution company of award-winning chef Rick Bayless, specializing in authentic Mexican cuisine. Ownership is split equally between Bayless, who serves as chief executive officer, and Manuel Valdez, the private company's president. Frontera Foods operates as a separate entity from Bayless's Chicago full-service restaurants, Frontera Grill and Topolobampo, but maintains its headquarters above the adjacent restaurants. The company operates a quick-serve concept, Frontera Fresco, located in four Macy's department stores, including the Chicago flagship location.

Frontera products, containing no preservatives or additives, are inspired by the restaurant and reformulated for home use. Retail products available in grocery stores and online include Gourmet Mexican

Salsa, Salpica Salsa, Frontera Classic Salsas, Gourmet Mexican Soup, barbecue and grill sauces, cocktail and Ceviche sauces, hot sauces, guacamole mix, chili mix, organic tortilla chips, stone-fired pizza with a Mexican flair, and the Mexican Pantry line of taco sauce, cooking sauce, enchilada sauce, and fajita marinade. The products are packaged in gift sets and are available for purchase on a wholesale basis. Frontera Foods also produces Bayless's television cooking program, *Mexico— One Plate at a Time,* which airs on public television stations and is sold on DVD by the company.

FROM OKLAHOMA CITY TO CHICAGO

A fourth-generation member of a family involved in the restaurant and grocery industries, Rick Bayless was born in 1953 in Oklahoma City, Oklahoma, where his family operated a barbecue place. He developed an interest in Mexican food when he first visited Mexico at the age of 14. He enrolled at the University of Oklahoma, earning a degree in Spanish language and literature and Latin American culture. He then received a master's degree in linguistics from the University of Michigan and in 1980 began doctoral work in anthropological linguistics at the school. Over the next five years he and his wife, Deann Groen, visited every state in the Mexican Republic, but instead of focusing on linguistics Bayless took note of the differences of regional flavors and gathered recipes. The couple then used this material to write a book, *Authentic Mexican: Regional Cooking from the Heart of Mexico,* which was published by William Morrow in 1987.

The book was very well received, and Bayless used its publication as a stepping-stone to open a storefront restaurant in the River North district of Chicago, where he and his wife settled after returning from Mexico to teach Mexican cooking. They served as restaurant consultants while he also hosted a public television cooking show, *Cooking Mexican.* They had considered both Los Angeles and New York, but chose Chicago because much of her family lived there.

Bayless's restaurant took the name Frontera Grill and offered contemporary regional Mexican cuisine. Even as the 65-seat, reasonably priced restaurant worked out problems with some of the dishes and service, it received rave reviews and became very successful. In 1988 Rick Bayless was named Best New Chef by *Food and Wine* magazine.

Bayless decided to open a fine-dining companion and acquiring the adjacent storefront to open a 45-seat upscale eatery called Topolobampo, which shared the same entrance and bar. While entrees at Frontera Grill ranged from $8 to $15, entrees at Topolobampo were priced from $15 to $20. "There is still that public sentiment that Mexican food is something you eat while you are getting drunk on margaritas," he explained to *Nation's Restaurant News,* continuing, "I want to show the world that it's not second-class food."

Bayless was also devoted to proving that authentic Mexican could be very healthful. As much as possible he relied on organic, locally grown produce and meat, poultry, and dairy products that were free of antibiotics or steroids. He even refused to offer takeout sales because of a lack of environmentally friendly packaging.

BAYLESS IS NAMED BEST AMERICAN CHEF

More personal accolades were to follow for Bayless. In 1991 he was named Best American Chef in the Midwest by the James Beard Foundation, and in 1995 he won National Chef of the Year honors from the Foundation. Winning the top award surprised Bayless. "I didn't expect it at all," he told *Nation's Restaurant News,* noting, "It had never gone to anyone who does something outside of the classical mode and never to someone do-

ing real ethnic food or to anyone in the Midwest." Not only did the award drive further business to his restaurants, it also provided Bayless with a platform to enter the retail food market, which would take the name Frontera Foods to build on the brand of his signature restaurant, the goal to bring authentic Mexican food to the home.

Bayless's partner in Frontera Foods, Manuel Valdez, had been a regular customer at Frontera Grill. He suggested that Bayless consider selling some of his products to the public, and after getting to know one another, they began considering a business partnership. Boasting a Cuban heritage, Valdez grew up in Chicago where his parents operated a bodega. He earned an M.B.A. from Northwestern University. Although he had wanted to launch businesses related to microbrewing or artisanal cheese, he instead went to work as a marketing manager for Kraft Foods Inc., where according to *Forbes,* he worked on "nonartisanal Velveeta and Kraft Singles."

In late 1995 Bayless and Valdez formed a food marketing and distribution company under the Frontera Foods banner. Despite the advice of their attorneys that one of them needed to have majority control, they agreed to a 50-50 split. While Bayless's reputation was a key element of the company's potential success, he also knew that Valdez would have to be the one whose focus was solely on the venture. "It was very clear there was no way to determine which of those things was more valuable," he told *Forbes.*

FRONTERA FOOD PRODUCTS DEBUT

Bayless and Valdez devoted the next year to getting Frontera Foods off the ground. They decided the first product line was to be salsa. After requesting 20 ideas Valdez received five salsas from Bayless, who had reviewed the recipes used in his restaurants. He settled on salsas that were unique to the marketplace, but Valdez believed they were too foreign to the tongues of most U.S. consumers, and he asked for something milder, a roasted tomato salsa. Bayless compromised with a salsa based on a mild dried red chili, which became the basis for a line of fire-roasted salsas.

The partners had to decide how they were going to bottle the salsas. Rather than do it themselves, they decided to work with a manufacturer who could do it less expensively and make sure the products were properly packaged and labeled. Most co-packers were geared toward mass production, however, so Frontera Foods spent six months looking for a manufacturer who could make custom, homemade products using raw ingredients. Once Houston's Riba Foods Inc. had been

```
┌─────────────────────────────────────────────┐
│                                               │
│              KEY DATES                        │
│         ───────────────■───────────────       │
│                                               │
│   1987:  Rick Bayless opens Frontera Grill.   │
│   1995:  Rick Bayless and Manuel Valdez form  │
│          Frontera Foods.                      │
│   1996:  Frontera Foods offers its first      │
│          products.                            │
│   2000:  Bayless starts a cooking show on PBS │
│          called *Cooking Mexican.*            │
│   2005:  The Frontera Fresco quick-service    │
│          restaurant opens.                    │
│                                               │
└─────────────────────────────────────────────┘
```

selected, more months passed as the recipes were properly formulated. Jean Marie Brownson, former test kitchen director of the *Chicago Tribune*'s food department, was hired to test every batch of salsa to ensure quality.

Finally, in the summer of 1996, the Frontera Foods line of salsas hit the market. They performed well, especially through such upscale channels as Crate & Barrel and Whole Foods supermarkets, and department stores such as Neiman Marcus, Bloomingdale's, and Marshall Field's. Providing an added boost to the Frontera name was a second cookbook, *Rick Bayless's Mexican Kitchen,* written with his wife and published in 1996.

In the summer of 1997 a pair of hot sauces were added to Frontera Foods' slate of products. Although improved production and distribution allowed the company to lower its price from $5.99 per bottle to $3.99, the company planned to remain in the high-end of the market. As for developing new products, Bayless decided what he would like to see as a consumer in a certain category, and then worked with the manufacturer to create a product that met his satisfaction. Grilling sauces and cooking salsas were added in 1999. A third Bayless book, *Salsas That Cook,* published in 1999, helped to support the launch of the new products.

NEW COOKING SHOW PREMIERES

Bayless continued to build his profile, and Frontera Foods expanded into television production in May 2000 with the debut of the 26-part cooking show *Mexico— One Plate at a Time* on PBS. Rather than taping all his shows in a studio, Bayless took his audience on location in Mexico to show roadside food stands as well as large regional markets. Bayless occasionally had to contend with heckling children and vendors who could not

understand why their businesses were being disrupted. Recipes were also demonstrated in scenes shot from Bayless's Chicago kitchen. The program proved popular, leading to multiple 13-part seasons, which are sold on DVD by Frontera Foods. Essentially, television is considered a break-even business for Frontera Foods, its main value being to drive product sales.

In the 21st century Frontera Foods continued to add new products, including a line of frozen pizzas. While at first blush pizza did not seem an appropriate category to pursue, it was in keeping with Bayless's experience in Mexico. He had once lived above a pizzeria in Mexico City and was very familiar with the unique flavors the shop had to offer, including chorizo, poblano chilies, and roasted peppers. He shared a Mexican pizza with Valdez and the partners decided to try marketing a line of frozen pizzas. This proved highly successful, soon accounting for 25 percent of Frontera Foods' sales.

The company also attempted to venture both down-market and up-market from the Frontera brand. Valdez suggested that Frontera Foods try Southwestern-style salsas. Bayless did not want to compromise the Frontera brand with such Americanized fare, so the partners agreed to start a downscale "fun" brand called Salpica, priced about 20 percent less than Frontera. On the other end of the spectrum, the company launched the Topolo brand, in keeping with the higher-end Topolobampo restaurant. The 14-item line was unveiled in 2002 and was sold exclusively through kitchenware retailer Williams-Sonoma.

Neither Salpica and Topolo performed well enough, however, and both were eventually dropped in favor of focusing on the main Frontera brand, which continued to expand its product lines. In the summer of 2003, for example, a line of bite-sized tortilla chips were introduced in a variety of flavors, including Roasted Tomato Cilantro, Stone Ground Blue, and Garlic Jalapeno and Chipotle Sesame.

FRONTERA FRESCO OPENS

Valdez urged Bayless to expand his restaurant business through Frontera Foods by considering the creation of a quick-service concept. Bayless refused to open something as mundane as a taqueria, and when Valdez suggested a restaurant that served tortas, essentially a sandwich, his partner rejected that as well. Instead they began building a menu for a food-court concept. They agreed on tamales, quesadillas, and huaraches, a open-faced flatbread sandwich. Tortas would eventually be added as well as a taqueria salad, soup, guacamole and chips, and desserts.

In the final months of 2005 they opened a food-court kiosk at Chicago's Marshall Field's department store under the Frontera Fresco name. A year later, due to the sale of the department store chain, Marshall Field's became a Macy's store. To maintain a high-quality image, the menu was kept limited and the dishes prepared in view of customers. Once Bayless and Valdez were comfortable with the operation, they looked to expand the concept. They opened new locations in Macy's department stores in Skokie, Illinois, and San Francisco and Costa Mesa, California.

Although he was slow to expand his restaurant and retail foods business, Bayless was dedicated to his mission of championing authentic Mexican cuisine to an American audience. The sixth season of *Mexico—One Plate at a Time* began airing in April 2008, and later in the year a seventh season was completed. With this kind of media support for Bayless and the Frontera brand, there was every reason to expect that Frontera Foods would continue to enjoy steady growth in its high-end niche of Mexican food products for years to come.

Ed Dinger

PRINCIPAL SUBSIDIARIES

Frontera Media Productions.

PRINCIPAL COMPETITORS

Amy's Kitchen, Inc.; Riba Foods, Inc.; Santa Barbara Salsa.

FURTHER READING

Borden, Jeff, "Frontera Chef Savors Success Sparked by Hot Ethnic Market," *Crain's Chicago Business,* October 20, 1997, p. 6.

Buchthal, Kristina, "Frontera's New Frontier," *Restaurants & Institutions,* February 15, 2006, p. 49.

Camp, Paul A., "Frontera Grill—Now That's Mexican," *Chicago Tribune,* April 24, 1987, p. 29.

Cassell, Deborah, "The Poblano Chili," *Snack Food & Wholesale Bakery,* August 2007, p. T-8.

Dando, Pat, "Celebrity Chef Creates Retail Success," *Stagnito's New Products Magazine,* July 2003, p. 18.

Lambert, Emily, "The Odd Couple (Partners at Frontera Foods)," *Forbes,* September 4, 2006, p. 73.

Sheridan, Margaret, "Name Games," *Restaurants & Institutions,* August 15, 1999, p. 58.

Toops, Diana, "A Love Affair with Mexican Food," *Food Processing,* May 2002, p. 52.

Walkup, Carolyn, "Rick Bayless: Winning Awards, Accolades and Appetites," *Nation's Restaurant News,* June 26, 1995, p. 29.

———, "Success Is in the Bag: Chef-Owners Wrap Their Efforts into Gourmet Retail," *Nation's Restaurant News,* May 5, 1997, p. 92.

Galtronics Ltd.

———————— ■ ————————

P.O. Box 1589, Industrial Zone
Upper Tiberias, 14115
Israel
Telephone: (972 04) 673 9777
Fax: (972 04) 813 5620
Web site: http://www.galtronics.com

Private Company
Incorporated: 1978
Employees: 450
Sales: $1.39 billion (2007)
NAICS: 334419 Other Electronic Component
    Manufacturing

■ ■ ■

Israeli-based Galtronics Ltd. is one of the world's leading specialists in the design and manufacture of antennas for wireless communications. The company develops and produces a range of antennas for mobile telephones, portable computers, Wi-fi and wireless networking components, two-way radios, and telematics applications such as GPS navigation systems. Operating design and production facilities at its Tiberias base, in 2006 the company added a manufacturing facility in China with a production capacity of more than 250 million antennas per year. The company also operates a small design office in South Korea. Galtronics is a private company owned by founder Ken Crowell and is led by CEO Michael Elliott. Moreover, the company is literally on a mission, being a pioneering member of the so-called Business as Mission evangelical Christian movement,

which seeks to proselytize through industrial and other business initiatives.

SEEKING A WAY INTO ISRAEL

In the early 1960s Ken Crowell worked as an engineer at Aerojet General in California's Sierra Nevada region, while his wife Margie operated a religious bookstore from the couple's home. Both Crowells were active in a local evangelical church. A meeting with a visiting missionary convinced the Crowells to enter this field as well, and by 1963 the couple had moved to Portland, Oregon, where they enrolled in the Multnomah School of the Bible.

The Six-Day War in Israel in 1967 had a major impact on the Crowells. By the time of their graduation in 1968, they had become determined to move to Israel, to develop their missionary activities there. Yet, the anti-Jewish implications of the evangelical movement left Israel remained highly resistant to attempts by non-Jews to proselytize the community there. As such, the Crowells were ineligible to receive a clergy visa from the Israeli government, which were given out only to recognized and mainstream religious organizations.

The Crowells nonetheless sought a means to establish themselves in Israel. An opportunity came in 1968 when Crowell took a job with Motorola to join that company's Israel-based research and development (R&D) team. Motorola had been one of the first Western companies to invest in the young Israeli state, establishing its R&D operations there in 1964. Motorola Israel also became Motorola's first wholly owned international subsidiary. This branch quickly became the heart of Motorola's R&D effort, and is credited with being the first in the world to develop cellular telephone technology.

Crowell spent three years working in Israel before returning to the United States for a position at Motorola's Florida office. While working for Motorola in the United States, Crowell, joined by his wife, continued his missionary and proselytizing efforts. Nonetheless, the Crowells remained determined to return to Israel and to establish missionary activities there.

ON A BUSINESS MISSION

With his entry into the country under his missionary guise barred, Crowell needed to find an alternative entry. The struggles of the Israeli economy, hard hit by an Arab League boycott, provided Crowell with the inspiration he required. If the country refused missionary activities, it nonetheless had become an important center for high-technology industries. Crowell understood that he could more easily return to the country as a businessman.

Crowell's years with Motorola provided him with the product he needed. While the company's cellular telephone development took place in Israel, the country lacked a local supplier of radio antennas. Crowell, then in his mid-40s, approached Motorola with a plan to found a business focused on developing and manufacturing UHF-VHF antennas. Motorola agreed to back the effort, and was to remain a major customer for Crowell into the 21st century.

Crowell next presented the Israeli consulate in Florida with his plan to found a business in the country. Although Crowell's evangelical faith and messianic leanings failed to impress, his business plan remained attractive to Israel, which was in need of foreign investment, exports, and foreign currency exchange. The Israeli government agreed to help Crowell establish his business, providing him with assistance through the Investment Authority, and streamlining the application process. By November 1978 the Crowells had returned to Israel to found their company.

Crowell settled on Tiberias, in the Galilee Valley, for the headquarters of the new company, which he named Galtronics. The choice of Tiberias was made for a number of reasons, including the lack of an existing industrial infrastructure there, as well as the presence of a small messianic movement. The high rate of unemployment among this population provided Galtronics with a ready workforce.

RELIGIOUS AND CULTURAL CONFLICT

Galtronics soon found itself in conflict with the Israeli Orthodox community, particularly the militant group Yad L'Achim, which had led the resistance against proselytizing activities in the country since the 1950s. Backlash against the proselytizing movement had been building in the country in the late 1970s, ultimately leading to the passage of legislation in 1977 banning certain forms of missionary activities, especially those that promised material rewards.

The legislation, which outlawed the distribution of gifts and other types of remuneration during proselytizing activities, provided criminal penalties—including up to five years imprisonment. At the same, the legislation was given a broad interpretation in which the handing out of pamphlets or lunch or other invitations were considered as remuneration. While the legislation remained in effect through the turn of the century, however, it was rarely enforced.

Nonetheless, Galtronics quickly found itself the targets of Yad L'Achim criticism, which launched a campaign to expose the company's missionary intentions. The Crowells did little to dispel the organization's charges; indeed, the couple founded their own church, called the Peniel Fellowship, soon after their arrival in Israel. At first operating from the Crowells' own home, the Peniel Fellowship moved into its own quarters in 1982.

Over the next decades the company spawned a number of other missionary operations, such as Galadon, created in 1985, to distribute "communion juice" manufactured in Israel. Another company, Galcom, developed a "fixed-tuned" radio, one tuned to a specific radio station broadcasting religious content. The expansion of the company's range of operations led to the establishment of a dedicated administrative, management, lobbying, and marketing wing, Gal Group, in 1987. On a more cultural level, the company added the multimedia theater Galilee Experience in 1990, a music production and distribution arm, Galilee of the Nations

KEY DATES

1978: Ken Crowell founds Galtronics in Tiberias to produce antennas for Motorola two-way radio handsets.
1991: Galtronics adds a production and marketing facility in Livingstone, Scotland.
1998: Galtronics' revenues near $100 million.
2006: Galtronics opens manufacturing facility in Wuxi, China.
2007: Galtronics reports revenues of $1.7 billion.

Music, in 1999, and Megavoice, a distributor of evangelical audio products, in 2000.

Ironically Galtronics' secular operations soon overshadowed its religious origins, as the company became a focal point for antenna R&D during the 1980s. The company's close partnership with Motorola was the central factor in Galtronics' growing success.

INTERNATIONAL EXPANSION

Galtronics initially focused on producing and refining antennas for Motorola's two-way radio designs. The U.S. company's expansion into cellular telephone development provided Galtronics with the opportunity to expand its own R&D technologies. By the early 1990s Galtronics had taken a place at the leading edge of advanced antenna design. The company contributed a number of milestones to the cellular telephone market, including the invention of the first swivel dipole antenna. Galtronics was also the first to incorporate the use of polyurethane over-molding for radio antennas.

Perhaps the group's most significant invention was its "Stubby" antenna, which, at just one inch in length, paved the way toward dramatic reduction in the size of mobile handsets. By 1990 the company's sales had topped $6.2 million. Nearly all of the group's sales went to the export market, and principally the United States, the United Kingdom, and Japan.

The outbreak of the first Persian Gulf War provided a new growth opportunity for Galtronics, as Motorola received the order to supply two-way radios and mobile handsets to the U.S. troops. Galtronics was forced to expand its production to meet the new demand. At the same time, Motorola, concerned by the instability of the Middle East region, asked Galtronics to add a second production facility elsewhere.

For this, Galtronics chose Scotland, where it spent $5 million to open a factory in Livingstone. The choice

of Scotland also served as part of the group's strategy to expand its reach into the European market, which had begun to see the stirrings of interest in the cellular telephone market. The move quickly paid off, as the company received a first contract for $1 million from a Finnish high-technology group. This placed Galtronics in position to profit from the extraordinary rise of Finland's Nokia as it became a world-leading mobile telephone handset provider. In the 1990s Galtronics also began sourcing production capacity from China.

Galtronics' growth took off during that decade. By 1994 the company's total sales had reached $30 million—doubling revenues from the year before. Exports continued to represent the group's primary market, accounting for some 99 percent of the company's revenues. By then Galtronics had expanded its customer base to include most of the cellular telephone industry's major players, including Ericsson, Nokia, AEG, Uniden, and TCM.

SHIFTING MANUFACTURING TO CHINA IN THE 21ST CENTURY

By 1998 Galtronics' sales had topped $70 million, as the cellular telephone industry was poised to enter into a new and dramatic growth phase at the turn of the century. Galtronics resisted advice calling for the company to go public to raise the investment capital needed to meet the coming demand for its products. Instead, the company brought in a group of investors rooted in the evangelical movement. This relationship proved short-lived, however, as the company and its investors disagreed on financial strategy. While the investment group sought short-term profits, Galtronics' clung to its roots as a "tentmaker" (that is, a business established to provide financial support for missionary activities).

In the end the partnership was disbanded and full control of the company reverted to the Crowells. Approaching his mid-70s, Crowell continued to provide the group's leadership during the first years of the new century. In 2007, however, Crowell at last passed the company's reins to Michael Elliott, who became the company's CEO.

During the early 2000s Galtronics found itself as the idol of the Business as Mission movement. Its status as a pioneer and its success in developing its operations from its Israeli base brought accolades in the missionary community for what many considered the most admired "kingdom" company.

Into the later years of the first decade of the 2000s Galtronics remained at the lead of its niche category, boasting sales of more than one billion antennas. Galtronics had successfully diversified its target markets as well, adding wireless antenna products for the computer, mobile computing, and networking sectors. At the same time Galtronics remained at the forefront of antenna technology. In 2008 the company revealed its new multiband Stilt technology, which it claimed would have "game-changing" status. Indeed, the new technology allowed the company to reduce the size of its antennas to a thickness of just a few microns.

Galtronics had also boosted its R&D and manufacturing capacity. The company added a 40-member team of design engineers in South Korea. In 2006 the company moved directly into China, establishing its own factory in Wuxi, in order to produce high-volume, low-cost antennas. With more than 10,000 square meters of production space at the outset, the Wuxi site was capable of supplying more than 250,000 million antennas per year. The increase in capacity soon paid off for the group, which saw its total sales rise to $1.7 billion by that year. Galtronics had at least succeeded in its mission to become a major force in the global antenna market.

M. L. Cohen

PRINCIPAL SUBSIDIARIES

Galtronics China.

PRINCIPAL COMPETITORS

China Electronics Corporation; Siemens AG; Hitachi Ltd.; LG Group; Nokia Corporation; Technitrol Delaware Inc.; Teac Corporation; NEC Corporation; Denso Corporation.

FURTHER READING

"Antenna Manufacturer Reports Rapidly Expanding Sales, Exports," *Israel Business,* June 1991, p. 6.

"Antenova Wins Million Antenna Contract with Major Handset Maker," *Electronics Weekly,* May 12, 2004, p. 1.

"Galtronics Receives Standards Certificates," *Israel Business Today,* June 10, 1994, p. 14.

"Galtronics Tunes In to Exports," *Israel Business Today,* January 21, 1994, p. 13.

Goheen, William, *The Galtronic's Story,* New York: Wipf & Stock Publishers, 2004.

Maxwell, Joe, "The Mission of Business," *Christianity Today,* November 2007, p. 24.

"Wireless Network Group to Expand Galtronics Product Offerings," *PR Newswire,* October 1, 2001.

Gaylord Bros., Inc.

7282 William Barry Boulevard
North Syracuse, New York 13212-3347
U.S.A.
Telephone: (315) 457-5070
Toll Free: (800) 448-6160
Fax: (800) 272-3412
Web site: http://www.gaylordmart.com

Subsidiary of Demco, Inc.
Incorporated: 1896
Employees: 135
Sales: $30 million (2007 est.)
NAICS: 322130 Paperboard Mills; 323118 Blankbook,
    Loose-Leaf Binder, and Device Manufacturing

■ ■ ■

Gaylord Bros., Inc., is an independently operated subsidiary of Demco, Inc. Both are direct marketers of library supplies and services, but Gaylord focuses more on university libraries and libraries run by corporations, museums, and government institutions. Based in the Syracuse, New York, area, Gaylord distributes book trucks, step stools and ladders, book jackets, labels, book repair supplies, archival products, library signage items, media storage supplies, security systems, audiovisual carts, exhibit cases and display panels, library furniture for adults and children, computer furniture, and communal space furniture. Library supplies account for 40 percent of sales, library furniture another 40 percent, and the remaining 20 percent comes from the sale of archival supplies.

Most sales are drawn from a main reference catalog, produced in-house and mailed at the beginning of the year. The company also does a number of smaller targeted mailings throughout the year to highlight different parts of its product offerings to specific customers. The Gaylord International Division also serves libraries and archives around the world, offering free library design assistance. Gaylord manufactures about 40 percent of the products its sells.

LATE 19TH-CENTURY ORIGINS

Gaylord Bros. was founded in Syracuse, New York, in the late 1800s by a pair of young brothers: Henry Jay Gaylord, who according to his obituary was about 21 at the time of the founding of the business, and Willis E. Gaylord. They worked together in a local bank, one of their jobs being to repair torn currency. Not satisfied with the usual method of currency repair, which involved the use of straight pins, they developed a new method using gummed mending tissue. After they received help from a chemist on the proper adhesive to use and managed to obtain credit from a paper mill, they went into business in September 1896. They produced three inch by four inch sheets of their mending tissue, which were packaged in bundles of 24, and made systematic mailings to banks across the country, accompanied by a promotional circular and a self-addressed, stamped envelope. Banks were asked to return the package if uninterested or make remittance in the form of $0.20 in stamps. Within days the brothers received their first bit of income, $.35 from the Bowery Savings Bank of New York. About one-third of the mailing resulted in sales, an extremely high success rate for a

COMPANY PERSPECTIVES

Gaylord Bros. was founded on essential values that we continually strive to uphold today. It is in these values that our outstanding tradition of trust is born. Trust in the quality of our products, trust in our innovative solutions and trust in our years of expertise.

direct-marketing operation, and another third of the recipients were kind enough to return the merchandise.

The involvement of Gaylord Bros. with the library market was purely happenstance. A librarian who came across the currency mending tissue recognized that it could also be used to repair torn book pages. Gaylord Bros. was asked to supply the tissue in one and one-half inch by eight and one-half inch strips. Sensing a new opportunity, the brothers expanded their mailings to include public libraries. After an order was placed by a superintendent of schools, they realized there was also a promising school market for their product. They then expanded their product line to include a gummed mending cloth for binding, developed with the Nashua Gummed and Coated Paper Company at the behest of a librarian requesting a stronger book mending product. A few years later they expanded beyond mending products and became increasingly committed to the library market when they introduced, again to satisfy a customer request, the pamphlet binder, which would become a perennial bestseller.

FOCUSING ON LIBRARY SUPPLIES

For seven years the Gaylords worked out of a small cellar workshop where they conducted their experiments, prepared the products, and kept the accounts. Finally in February 1903 they were able to move out and set up shop in the Third National Bank Building in Syracuse. By the end of the decade business was steady enough that the brothers were able to quit their bank jobs. They also elected to drop bank supplies and focus solely on developing and selling library supplies. The double-stitched binder and multibinder were introduced in 1909. Three years later the first folded and sealed book pockets were offered. In 1922 reinforced book pockets were added.

Experiencing steady growth, Gaylord Bros. moved into a three-story building in 1922. Just eight years later the company constructed the first building of its own, located on Gilford Street in Syracuse. That extra

manufacturing space would be needed to produce a new product introduced that year, the Model C Book Charger, an electric stamping machine that printed due dates on circulation cards. It was the first device of its kind and proved to be a major source of revenue for Gaylord Bros. Decades later this simple circulation control product would evolve into a computerized circulation system. Before then, however, the company branched into more mundane product areas, including library furniture. In the early 1940s Gaylord Bros. introduced the sloped-shelf book truck for transporting and shelving books without the fear of the books toppling off the cart.

Willis Gaylord passed away and Henry Gaylord carried on as president of the company until his death at the age of 82 in 1955. The business passed out of family control in 1974 when it was sold to the Croydon Company. It was a period of change on all fronts for the company. Gaylord in 1970 secured the exclusive rights to the Se-lin method of spine label adhesion, developed several years earlier by the Battelle Institute. Gaylord made improvements to the product, which developed into a top-selling line. More and more, however, library automation systems played an important role for Gaylord.

COMPUTERIZED CIRCULATION SYSTEM INTRODUCED

In 1974 Gaylord formed the GIS Library Systems division to offer a computerized circulation system to replace the old manual card catalog and stamped card method of tracking books. The initial product, Gaylord System 100, introduced in 1975, combined a computer located at a library for online transactions with a computer maintained at Gaylord's offices where overnight batch processing was conducted. The division, which became known as Gaylord Information Systems, regularly upgraded its product lines, introducing the GS 300 and GS 400 systems. In 1984 the GS 3000 Catalog Management System became one of the first online catalog systems. In that same year the division unveiled the Gaylord School Library Management System, a product that combined an online catalog and circulation module that could be run on personal computers.

Gaylord turned to the bibliographic services field through the acquisition of the MiniMARC system, which stored MARC (machine-readable-cataloging) records on videodiscs. After some improvements this product was renamed the SuperCAT cataloging support system, introduced in July 1988. Libraries could then use MARC records stored on CD-ROM discs for card cataloging purposes. Next, Gaylord Information launched Galaxy, a fully integrated automation system

```
┌─────────────────────────────────────────────┐
│                                               │
│              KEY DATES                        │
│                    ■                          │
│                                               │
│  1896:  Company founded by Henry and Willis Gay-  │
│         lord to produce currency mending materials. │
│  1903:  The brothers are able to leave their cellar │
│         workshop for space in bank building.   │
│  1930:  Company constructs own building.       │
│  1955:  Henry Gaylord dies.                    │
│  1974:  Croydon Company acquires Gaylord.      │
│  1975:  Gaylord System 100 computerized circulation │
│         system introduced.                     │
│  1997:  Polaris Integrated Library System introduced. │
│  2003:  Demco Inc. acquires Gaylord name and   │
│         library supply business.               │
│  2005:  Gaylord moves to smaller facility.     │
│                                               │
└─────────────────────────────────────────────┘
```

geared toward small and medium-sized libraries but which also found customers in medical and academic libraries. Galaxy, which ran on minicomputers, remained popular through much of the 1990s, but eventually the system's VAX/VMS computer platform became outmoded.

In January 1997 Gaylord introduced the Polaris Integrated Library System, a client-server system that made use of the popular Microsoft Windows operating system and was scalable to meet the needs of both small and large public libraries. Moreover, it allowed access to the catalog and other materials over the Internet. In 2001 Polaris was enhanced further through an alliance with Baker & Taylor, a major distributor of books, videos, and music. A new interface allowed Polaris customers to order books through Baker & Taylor and have the items automatically integrated into the library's circulation database.

Also in the mid-1990s, Gaylord became involved in the security software business, offering several products. The company's Full Armor software product created password locks to prevent unauthorized access to programs and possible damage. The InCase BASIC product was a data-entry program used to quickly document security incidents such as thefts and accidents. The material could then be speedily retrieved through key word searches and a report could be printed. To keep track of the many keys a library dispensed, Gaylord offered Key-Z, a system to keep tabs on who had possession of keys to every door in the library. Another product, Found-In, tracked lost and found items as well as items confiscated or held for safekeeping. The new security line also helped libraries monitor their parking

lots through the Park-It product, which made parking assignments, maintained records of vehicle owners, and could also report violations.

CONTINUED EMPHASIS ON TRADITIONAL PRODUCTS

Library automation systems did not eliminate the need for traditional library products, however. In the 1970s Gaylord ramped up production of book pockets by acquiring and modifying a machine that made seed packets. The company continued to make improvements to everyday items such as book trucks and library furniture. Danish designer Jens Risom was hired to help in the development of the Informa line of furniture Gaylord introduced in 1986. A premium furniture line was unveiled in 1992, followed in 1998 by the launch of the St. Croix value line of furniture. Furthermore, Gaylord did not lose sight of its roots in book mending and preservation products. When the Library of Congress warned of the dangers to preservation caused by acid-based products, Gaylord developed a line of acid-free archival products, first offered in the 1992 Archival Catalog.

By the late 1980s Gaylord served about 70,000 libraries across the United States. In addition to its Syracuse-area headquarters, where the computer software systems were developed, Gaylord maintained a plant in Sanford, North Carolina, for making furniture; a Los Angeles, California, plant that produced shelving and other hardware; and a Germantown, Maryland, plant where other products were manufactured.

DEMCO ACQUIRES GAYLORD NAME

Gaylord experienced some problems remaining competitive in the 1990s, as demonstrated by efforts in the middle of the decade to receive breaks on utilities and state funds to help retrain workers. In both cases, the company maintained that it might have to move hundreds of jobs from New York State to other locations. In November 2002 Gaylord hired New York-based investment bank Jordan, Edmiston Group to help facilitate a sale. There was one ardent suitor, Madison, Wisconsin-based Demco, a longtime competitor, who had been interested in acquiring Gaylord for many years and had became more assertive in the fall of 2001.

Demco had been established in Wisconsin in 1905 as the library division of Democrat Printing Company, initially dedicated to printing forms for the University of Wisconsin–Madison. In 1925 Norman D. Bassett acquired Demco Library Supplies. To better serve his library customers, Bassett added a variety of products to Demco's mail-order catalog, including catalog cards and mending supplies, as well as library research and product locator services. In 1968 Demo Library Supplies became Demco, Inc., under new owner John Wall. Demco offered many of the same products and services as Gaylord, but focused on grade school and public libraries rather than Gaylord's primary niche, university and museum libraries. Where they primarily competed was in the public library market. Overall they were a good fit.

In May 2003 Croydon agreed to sell the Gaylord Direct operations, which included library supplies and furnishings, along with the Gaylord name, to Demco. Croydon retained Gaylord Information Systems, which was subsequently renamed GIS Information Systems and in 2005 became Polaris Library Systems to take advantage of its flagship brand.

Although owned by Demco, Gaylord continued to operate as a separate enterprise and direct it own affairs, albeit under the leadership of a new president, Guy Marhewka, who brought with him an extensive background in the direct marketing of industrial products. No longer needing as much space, Gaylord exchanged its 205,000-square-foot facility for a 72,200-square-foot site in the Cicero community in North Syracuse in 2005. Under Marhewka's leadership, Gaylord enjoyed three consecutive years of sales growth in the single digits, a marked improvement over the sales

losses incurred before his arrival. By 2008 sales were in the $30 million range, spurred in large measure by the sale of archival products. As a result, Gaylord placed increasing emphasis on museum sales.

Ed Dinger

PRINCIPAL DIVISIONS

Gaylord International.

PRINCIPAL COMPETITORS

Brodart Co.; Highsmith Inc.

FURTHER READING

Breeding, Marshall, "1986 to 2005: The Polaris Story," *Smart Libraries Newsletter,* July 2005.

Buchel, John, "100 Years of Serving Libraries," *Wisconsin State Journal,* September 3, 2005, p. D10.

Dickinson, Casey J., "GIS Brings Libraries to the Cutting Edge," *CNY Business Journal,* December 24, 2004.

Kriss, Erik, "Company Threatens to Pull Jobs from County," *Syracuse Herald-Journal,* October 4, 1995, p. D1.

Moriarty, Rick, "Competitor Buys Gaylord Bros.," *Syracuse Post-Standard,* May 20, 2003, p. C1.

Mulder, James T., "Gaylord Demands Lower Rates," *Syracuse Herald-Journal,* January 27, 1995, p. B5.

Palmateer, Paige, "Gaylord Brothers, a Full-Service Operation," *Business Journal—Central New York,* August 25, 2006.

Gibson Guitar Corporation

—■—

309 Plus Park Boulevard
Nashville, Tennessee 37217
U.S.A.
Telephone: (615) 871-4500
Toll Free: (800) 444-2766
Fax: (615) 889-5509
Web site: http://www.gibson.com

Private Company
Incorporated: 1902 as the Gibson Mandolin-Guitar
    Manufacturing Company
Employees: 1,000
Sales: $252.4 million (2007 est.)
NAICS: 339992 Musical Instruments (Except Toy)
    Manufacturing

■ ■ ■

Gibson Guitar Corporation, one of the world's foremost manufacturers of fretted instruments, has enjoyed the respect of musicians for most of its long history. Its instruments have been used by some of the best guitarists known, including Chet Atkins, the Everly Brothers, Chuck Berry, Eric Clapton, Jimmy Page, B. B. King, Frank Zappa, and Joe Walsh. The company fell from its status as a premier guitar maker to near bankruptcy in the 1980s but was brought back to solvency and its former respect by new owners, Henry Juszkiewicz and David Berryman. Although best known for its acoustic and electric guitars, by the mid-1990s the company also produced bass guitars, mandolins, synthesizers, drums, amplifiers, and various accessories for its instruments. In

the 21st century the company was a pioneer in new ventures merging high technology with traditional instruments.

EARLY HISTORY

Orville Gibson, the company's namesake, was making his living as a salesman and clerk when he bought a small workshop in Kalamazoo, Michigan, in the 1880s to build mandolins. At the time, most mandolins were made by bending and forming the wood into shape. However, Gibson believed that this technique stressed the wood and resulted in inferior vibrating characteristics. He therefore developed a new technique based on violin construction that involved carving the front, back, and sides of the mandolin rather than bending the wood into shape. Gibson created the first arch-top acoustic mandolins using this technique, although he received only one patent for his designs for a mandolin in 1898. Gibson began applying his techniques to the construction of guitars, banjos, and lutes as well.

Gibson soon earned a reputation as a maker of high-quality, custom stringed instruments. By 1896 Gibson was making instruments full time. By early in the 20th century demand for Gibson's instruments outpaced his ability to meet it. In response Gibson entered into an agreement with five Kalamazoo financiers to form the Gibson Mandolin-Guitar Manufacturing Company in 1902. According to the contract, O. H. Gibson was not a major stockholder; instead, he was given a few shares of stock and a lump sum of $2,500 for his patent and the right to use his

COMPANY PERSPECTIVES

Gibson is known worldwide for producing classic models in every major style of fretted instrument, including acoustic and electric guitars, mandolins, and banjos. Gibson's HD.6X-PRO Digital Guitar and the Gibson Robot Guitar represent the biggest advances in electric guitar design in over 70 years. Founded in 1894 in Kalamazoo, Michigan, and headquartered in Nashville since 1984, Gibson Guitar Corp.'s family of brands includes Epiphone, Dobro, Maestro, Kramer, Steinberger, Tobias, Echoplex, Electar, Flatiron, Gibson Baldwin Music Education, Slingerland, Valley Arts, Maestro, Oberheim, Sunshine Piano, Take Anywhere Technology, Baldwin, J&C Fischer, Chickering, Hamilton, and Wurlitzer.

including the two-footed, intonation-adjustable bridge, the f-hole design, and narrow pegheads.

EARLY INNOVATIONS IN GUITAR DESIGN

Guitars slowly increased in popularity in the 1920s, and Gibson responded by introducing several new models. Its first modern guitar, part of the company's Style 5 series in the Master Line Master Tone line, was introduced in 1922. One of the best known of Gibson's early acoustic guitars, the L-5 used Loar's innovations to build a specific pitch into the sound box, a radical concept at the time. Another unusual design, the flat-top guitar, had been produced by the company as early as 1918; however, it did not begin serious production of a flat-top model until 1926. In addition to several flat-top models, Gibson began production of an economy series, the Kalamazoo line, in 1929.

Despite the Depression the market for guitars expanded rapidly in the 1930s. As in the past Gibson promptly followed the trend, shifting the focus of their production and advertising from mandolins and banjos to guitars. Not only did they expand their line of arch-top f-hole guitars and flat-top guitars, the company also pioneered new designs. In 1934 it created its legendary Super 400. An 18-inch wide archtop, this guitar pushed the edges of guitar design in size and established higher standards for craftsmanship and decoration. Other new guitar designs included the Jumbo, a 16-inch-wide flat-top, and a Premier version of the L-5, which featured a modern-style, rounded cutaway.

Gibson's expansion stalled during World War II for several reasons. Materials that met the company's standards were hard to come by, so rather than lower the quality of their instruments Gibson discontinued several models, including the L-5 and Super 400. Other models continued to be made but at a radically slower rate. In addition, the company shifted production from musical instruments to parts useful in the war effort. In 1944, as the war neared its conclusion, the Chicago Musical Instrument (CMI) Company acquired Gibson and prepared the company to meet the pent-up demand for guitars when the war ended.

POSTWAR BOOM

The postwar period saw phenomenal expansion for Gibson, much of it due to the vision and leadership of Ted McCarty. McCarty joined Gibson in 1948 and served as company president from 1950 to 1966. During his tenure company sales grew from less than a million dollars a year to $15 million a year, its workforce grew

name. Gibson sold his stock in July 1903 but remained at the company until 1904, consulting and training employees on his construction techniques. Thereafter, he received a monthly pension until he died in 1918.

From its inception, the company focused on innovation and the production of high-quality instruments, goals it became known for over the next half-century. During the company's first few years production manager Sylvo Reams improved upon Gibson's already popular instruments, refining his construction techniques and using higher-quality materials and finishes. The product line began with six guitar models (three archtops with oval soundholes and three with round soundholes) and four harp guitars. Within the company's first decade, it had been granted patents for the elevated pickguard, the intonation-adjustable bridge, and the harp guitar and had introduced one of the first production guitars with a cutaway.

Despite these early innovations in fretted instrument design, the company made few changes to its guitar line in the 1910s. Instead, it concentrated on its mandolins, a far more popular instrument at the time and one that made up most of Gibson's sales. Through either luck or foresight, Gibson began making banjos in 1917, positioning the company to take advantage of the sudden popularity of this instrument in the early 1920s. Lloyd Loar, a well-known mandolinist and composer, added his talents as an acoustics engineer and musician to Gibson's engineering and research and development teams. He made significant contributions to the company's Master Line Master Tone instruments,

KEY DATES

1894: The earliest documented Gibson instrument is created.
1902: The Gibson Mandolin-Guitar Manufacturing Company is incorporated.
1917: The Gibson company begins manufacturing banjos.
1918: Founder Orville Gibson dies.
1935: Gibson introduces an electric guitar.
1944: The Chicago Musical Instrument Company acquires Gibson.
1950: Ted McCarty becomes president of the company.
1952: Gibson introduces the Les Paul guitar model.
1957: Chicago Musical Instrument Company acquires Gibson's former rival, Epiphone.
1983: Gibson is offered for sale by its new owner, Rooney Pace and Piezo Electric Product, Inc.
1984: Gibson closes its Kalamazoo factory.
1986: Henry Juszkiewicz and David Berryman buy Gibson for $5 million.
1987: Gibson acquires the Steinberger and Flatiron Mandolin Company.
1993: Gibson acquires the Original Musical Instrument Company; sales reach $70 million.
1994: Gibson celebrates its 100th anniversary.
1997: A Nashville retail and factory center opens.
2001: Gibson acquires Baldwin Piano & Organ Co.
2003: Gibson introduces its digital guitar; the Gibson Foundation is launched.
2005: Gibson guitars are featured in the Guitar Hero video game.
2007: Gibson introduces a self-tuning guitar.

from 150 employees to 1,200, and its profits multiplied 15 times. McCarty also led CMI to purchase rival Epiphone in 1957, giving Gibson greater control of the market.

Underlying Gibson's vast success during this period was McCarty's ability to lead the company to fruitful innovations. Under McCarty, Gibson finally committed the company to the electric guitar market, having missed the mark with their early efforts in the area. Gibson had introduced an electric guitar in 1935, the aluminum-bodied Electric Hawaiian Guitar. The large, hollow-body guitar used a magnetic pickup that needed thousands of wire windings. However, when Grammy Award–winning guitarist and inventor Les Paul, who

had been endorsing Gibson guitars since 1928, approached the company with a solid-body electric guitar in 1941, Gibson rejected the idea outright. Paul continued to try to convince Gibson throughout the 1940s but met with little success until McCarty was at the helm. By that time, Leo Fender had developed his own highly successful solid-body electric guitar, the Fender Telecaster.

Although Gibson had missed the chance to take the pioneering role in electric guitars, McCarty made sure they did not lag in subsequent improvements to the design. The Les Paul model debuted in 1952, and Gibson continued to refine the design for decades. Also under McCarty's leadership, Gibson designers introduced the humbucking pickup, the first semi-solid guitar, and the distinctive reverse-body Firebirds. McCarty personally contributed several groundbreaking changes, including the stop tailpiece and the Tune-O-Matic bridge. Other important models were introduced during this period, such as the first thinline archtop, the Byrdland, and the commercially unsuccessful but subsequently influential solid bodies known as the Flying V, Explorer, and Moderne.

Although electric guitars played an increasing role in Gibson's sales in the 1960s, the company continued to introduce new acoustic models as well. The Hummingbird, Dove, and Everly Brothers models debuted at that time, as did several artist models, including the Johnny Smith and Trini Lopez. However, after McCarty left in 1966 the company released few new models, suffering from the loss of McCarty's perceptive assessments of the market.

DECLINING SALES

In 1969 CMI merged with ECL, an Ecuadoran brewery, and the following year the two companies formed Norlin. Norlin combined Gibson guitars with Moog synthesizers and Lowrey organs and pianos to form a music division. Gibson suffered under the new management. Although a few new models were introduced in the 1970s, such as the short-lived Mark series acoustics and the Marauder, S-1, and RD electrics, they were not successful. The company managed to maintain sales through most of the 1970s, but the long-term effects of absentee corporate management could be seen when sales steadily declined in the 1980s.

Although the guitar market in general suffered during the 1980s, Gibson exacerbated the problem by allowing its quality to slip and by abandoning their popular guitar models in favor of poorly conceived new models. "Corporate bean counters from thousands of miles away started dictating to the sales department that the old stuff was stale, and that what they needed was new, new, new," Matt Umanov, a New York guitar retailer, told the *New York Times* in 1994. "That led to all kinds of stupid design changes."

In 1983 Norlin was taken over by Rooney Pace and Piezo Electric Product, Inc., and the new owners promptly put the Gibson music division up for sale. New owners did not materialize, and Gibson's bad times continued. In 1984 the company closed its Kalamazoo factory. Several new models were introduced and met with such a terrible response that they were discontinued almost immediately. Severe cuts in staff and the closing of all divisions but one line of guitars did not stem Gibson's losses. Finally, the company was purchased for $5 million by enthusiastic new owners Henry Juszkiewicz and David Berryman in 1986.

TURNAROUND UNDER NEW OWNERS

Juszkiewicz, who took over as company chairman, was eminently suitable to reverse the company's fortunes. A longtime Gibson guitar enthusiast, he had played guitar professionally in high school and college. Juszkiewicz explained in the June 23, 1997, *Industry Week,* "I'm a guitar player and looked at Gibson as the ultimate instrument, something to be revered. I thought the brand was a pot of gold." In addition to a musical sensibility and an appreciation for the company's products, Juszkiewicz brought an M.B.A. from Harvard and some tough business experience to bear on Gibson's problems. He set—and achieved—a growth goal of 30 percent each year, and he declared that Gibson would become the largest music company in the world.

Juszkiewicz and Berryman began by firing 30 of Gibson's 250 employees, including all of the company's top management. They then began a series of acquisitions, enabling the company to compete in expanded market sectors and to bring talented craftspeople on board. Acquisitions included: Steinberger, a manufacturer of high-tech electric guitars and basses (1987); the Flatiron Mandolin Company (1987); Oberheim Corporation, a synthesizer manufacturer (1990); Tobias, maker of handtooled professional quality basses (1990); the Original Musical Instrument Company (O.M.I.), originator of the Dobro resonator guitar (1993); the Slingerland Drum Company (1995); Baldwin Piano & Organ Co. (2001); and the third largest Chinese piano maker, Northeast Piano Co., Ltd. (2006).

Reissues of classic guitar models also played an important role in refreshing the company's reputation. To re-create popular models, such as the Advanced Jumbo and the J-200, the company retooled its factories and dismantled old sound pickups to study their design. In addition to reviving the classic Gibson acoustic and electric guitar models, the partners reestablished the company's amplifier division and expanded its line of accessories to include strings, picks, straps, pickups, and the Gibson Tourwear clothing line.

RAISING PRICES TO BOOST SALES AND REPUTATION

In a surprising move, Gibson raised its prices to boost sales. Company research had determined that the public was eager to pay more for the finest instruments bearing the trusted Gibson name (in 1997, Gibson guitars sold from $700 to over $20,000). Meanwhile, Gibson revived its lower-priced, Korean-built Epiphone line of guitars marketed to younger players. Epiphone production had been moved to Asia in the 1970s, and in late 1995 Gibson returned Epiphone to the United States, moving it into its own facility in Nashville.

The company also made strong efforts to win back the loyalty of successful musicians. Much of the old Gibson aura could be attributed to famous musicians playing their guitars, such as Chuck Berry and his Gibson ES-350T. The company created a new operation to custom craft and hand tool instruments for celebrities. In addition, Gibson began wooing endorsements from well-known musicians by providing their guitars. Famous musicians who renewed or began endorsing Gibson included Chet Atkins, Steve Miller, and B. B. King. Many other musicians joined the ranks of Gibson guitar users, such as Emmylou Harris, Pete Townshend, Travis Tritt, Johnny Cash, Neil Young, Peter Frampton, and Paul McCartney.

Reflecting a new focus on consumers versus manufacturers and dealers, Gibson began to buy ads in magazines such as *Esquire, GQ,* and the *New Yorker,* minimizing its advertising in trade publications like *Guitar Player.* In the 1990s, the company increased its sponsorship of live music events, most notably the Gibson Guitar Festival in Newport, Rhode Island. In 2005, the Universal Amphitheatre in Los Angeles was renamed "The Gibson Amphitheatre at Universal Citywalk" as the result of a joint partnership with Gibson, Universal Studios, and House of Blues Concerts. Beginning in 1997, the company also targeted consumers through new factory-museum retail complexes in Nashville and Memphis, Tennessee. Factories were open for tours, allowing the public to view Gibson's bluegrass instruments in various phases of construction, so that customers theoretically could buy guitars and then watch them being made.

STABILITY RESTORED AND GROWTH RENEWED

The changes instituted by Juszkiewicz and Berryman turned the company around. Juszkiewicz told the *New York Times* in 1994 that since 1986 Gibson had achieved a compound annual growth rate in sales of 30 percent. Starting with annual sales below $10 million in 1986, the company reached an estimated $70 million in sales by 1993. By 1996, the company's status and solubility was restored, with sales of $150 million. By 1997, the company operated eleven factories and employed 1,000 people—four times the number of employees it had when Juszkiewicz took over the company in 1986.

One sour spot in Gibson's otherwise brilliant renaissance was the company's relationships with guitar retailers. Retailers disliked Gibson's price increases, and complained about communication problems. Gibson filed several trademark infringement lawsuits against retailers in the first decade of the 2000s, alleging that they sold guitars under other names that were copies of Gibsons.

Gibson's successful rejuvenation was the result of excellent new leadership as well as other factors. While the company's new management implemented much-needed changes to bring about seemingly miraculous growth, the turnaround undoubtedly was aided by an explosion in the guitar market that coincided with Gibson's rebirth. Two of Gibson's key market sectors—baby boomers and generation-Xers—began buying large numbers of guitars in the 1990s and first decade of the 2000s, fueled in part by the popularity of such television programs as *American Idol* and the film *School of Rock* (in which comedian Jack Black plays a Gibson guitar). However, when asked to comment on the "chicken or egg" situation, Juszkiewicz proclaimed confidently in the March 1997 *Sales & Marketing Management:* "We *caused* the boom in the guitar market."

CELEBRATING A CENTURY

Gibson celebrated its 100th anniversary in 1994. Although the company proper was founded in 1902, Gibson Guitar has long cited 1894 as the earliest confirmable date of a Gibson instrument. An engraving on a mandolin states, "Made by O. H. Gibson, 1894," although Orville Gibson was known to have made instruments before that date. The company used the anniversary as the theme of a major international promotion. Gibson offered a special commemorative line of guitars releasing a different electric and acoustic model each month in 1994 in limited runs of 100. A

concert in Tokyo by the heavy-metal group the Scorpions launched a series of national and international concerts and exhibits. A White House salute to Gibson, hosted by President Bill Clinton and First Lady Hillary Rodham Clinton, highlighted the year's activities.

With Gibson exhibiting serious expansion goals, there was some speculation that the company might make a public offering of stock to gain additional cash for acquisitions. "On the one hand it's appealing because it would be a quick way to do it," Juszkiewicz reflected in an interview with the *New York Times* in 1994, continuing, "But then I don't know if I could operate the way I want having to answer to other people." Gibson remained privately owned, with Juszkiewicz at the helm.

INNOVATIONS FOR THE 21ST CENTURY

In the late 1990s, Juszkiewicz knew that computer technology would drive future growth in the music industry. To take advantage of this new direction, Gibson acquired Opcode Systems, a music production software and hardware manufacturer, in 1998. In 2003, Gibson introduced its landmark digital guitar and it opened Gibson Audio to design and develop audio products that merge cutting edge technology with traditional consumer electronics.

In 2004, Gibson Audio introduced the high fidelity Wurlitzer Digital Jukebox, which enabled users to store 1,000 CDs as Windows Media files and featured a wireless touchscreen remote control; in 2006, Gibson acquired Deutsche Wurlitzer. In 2007, Gibson launched a revolutionary self-tuning electric guitar, powered by robotics technology and capable of adjusting its own pitch in about two seconds according to six types of tuning systems. The first model sold out in a single weekend, and two new models were offered in 2008 to accommodate demand.

Gibson partnered with RedOctane to feature its guitar models in the Guitar Hero rock guitar video game in 2005. Game players could choose from several Gibson electric guitars as they "performed" songs by Ozzy Osbourne, David Bowie, Boston, The Ramones, and others in their own virtual rock bands. Guitar Hero sales exceeded $1 billion in just 26 months. However, in 2008, Gibson and Activision (the company that purchased RedOctane in 2006) entered into a dispute regarding Gibson's 1999 patent for the technology used in the game. Gibson also reached out to the children's music market when it teamed up with Tiger Electronics in 2007 to launch the Power Tour Electric Guitar, a follow-the-lights play-it-yourself guitar loaded with twelve classic rock songs.

In 2003 the company launched The Gibson Foundation as its charitable arm. Company sales had soared to over $250 million. In 2005, the new Gibson Baldwin Music Education began to offer more affordable music instrument lines and donated portions of proceeds to music education. In 2008 Gibson and TC Group (a maker of high-end professional audio products) initially announced a merger, but plans were shelved when the two companies could not resolve several issues within the prescribed timetable for merger negotiations. A resoundingly successful future seemed more than likely for Gibson, given the company's dramatic renaissance and sustained growth over the previous two decades.

Susan W. Brown
Updated, Heidi Feldman

PRINCIPAL SUBSIDIARIES

The Original Musical Instrument; Epiphone; Oberheim Electronics; Steinberger; Slingerland; Tobias; Baldwin Piano & Organ Co.; Northeast Piano Co., Ltd.; Flatiron Mandolin Company; Deutsche Wurlitzer.

PRINCIPAL COMPETITORS

Fender Musical Instruments Corporation; C.F. Martin & Co.; Yamaha Corporation.

FURTHER READING

Brewer, Geoffrey, "The Front Man," *Sales & Marketing Management,* March 1997, pp. 36–43.

Carter, Walter, et al., *Gibson Guitars: 100 Years of an American Icon,* Los Angeles: General Publishing Group, 1994.

"Gibson Acquires Deutsche Wurlitzer," *Music Trades,* August 2006, p. 29.

"Gibson Acquires Opcode Systems," *Music Trades,* July 1998, p. 38.

"Gibson Foundation Launched," *Music Trades,* August 2003, p. 63.

"Gibson Guitar Announces Launch of Gibson Les Paul Robot LP Studio Ltd. and Gibson Robot SG Special Ltd. Models," *PR Newswire,* April 7, 2008.

"Gibson Guitar Announces Launch of the Gibson Baldwin Music Education Division," *Mix,* May 13, 2005.

"Gibson Guitar Won a Trademark Infringement Case Last Week in U.S. District Court in Nashville, Tenn., Against Guitar Maker Paul Reed Smith," *Brandweek,* March 15, 2004, p. 8.

"Gibson to Enter Consumer Electronics," *Music Trades,* November 2003, p. 45.

Gill, Chris, "Gibson's Century of Excellence," *Guitar Player,* September 1994, pp. 33–36.

Hallam, Kristen, "Gibson Guitar Corp. to Strum Up Bluegrass Museum in Nashville, Tennessee," *Knight-Ridder/Tribune Business News,* March 24, 1997.

"An Industry First … Gibson to Open Factory Inside Shopping Mall," *Music Trades,* December 1999, p. 39.

"Innovation and Quality: Gibson's Manufacturing Strategy," *Music Trades,* August 1986.

"Joe Perry and Gibson Guitar Launch New Signature Model at House of Blues in Boston," *PR Newswire,* May 15, 2003.

Kageyama, Yuri, "New Guitar Can Do Own Tuning," *Houston Chronicle,* December 4, 2007, p. 8.

Lambert, Mel, "Gibson and TC to Merge," *Pro Sound News Europe,* February 2008, p. 3.

"The Leo Award," *Guitar Player,* January 1993, p. 52.

McCraw, Jim, "The Gibson Guitar," *Popular Mechanics,* December 1995, pp. 64–67, 122.

Miller, Bryan, "Saving Gibson Guitars from the Musical Scrap Heap," *New York Times,* March 13, 1994, p. 7F.

"Nashville, Tenn.-based Gibson Guitar Makes Comeback Fueled by Nostalgia," *Atlanta Journal-Constitution,* November 30, 2003.

"RedOctane Signs Deal with Gibson Guitar for New Video Game Launch," *PR Newswire,* August 30, 2005.

"The Sale of Gibson," *Guitar Player,* January 1987, p. 12.

Sporich, Ben, "Gibson Picks on Activision's Ax: Patent at Issue in 'Guitar Hero' Dispute," *Los Angeles Business Journal,* March 31, 2008, p. 1.

Stevens, Tim, "The Guitar Man," *Industry Week,* June 23, 1997, pp. 12–17.

"TC Group, Gibson Discontinue Merger Talks," *Mix,* April 10, 2008.

"U.S. Music Instrument Maker Acquires Chinese Piano Firm," *AsiaPulse News,* December 18, 2006.

"Universal Amphitheatre Takes Gibson's Name," *Mix,* April 18, 2005.

Waddell, Ray, "Guitar Festival Gibson's First Title Sponsorship," *Amusement Business,* June 22, 1998, p. 6.

Walsh, Christopher, "Gibson Creates Digital Jukebox," *Billboard,* January 10, 2004, p. 8.

Watson, Bruce, "How to Take on an Ailing Company—and Make It Hum," *Smithsonian,* July 1996, pp. 53–62.

Gilmore Entertainment Group L.L.C.

8901-A Business 17N
Myrtle Beach, South Carolina 29572-0014
U.S.A.
Telephone: (843) 913-1400
Toll Free: (800) 843-6779
Fax: (843) 913-1441
Web site: http://www.gilmoreentertainment.com

Private Company
Founded: 1986 as Calvin Gilmore Productions Ltd.
Employees: 255
Sales: $32 million (2006 est.)
NAICS: 711310 Promoters of Performing Arts, Sports, and Similar Events with Facilities

■ ■ ■

Gilmore Entertainment Group L.L.C. is a private company based in Myrtle Beach, South Carolina, owned and headed by Calvin Gilmore, who also serves as producer, director, and entertainer. The company's main business is the operation of the 2,200-seat Carolina Opry Theater in Myrtle Beach, home to the *Carolina Opry* country music-oriented variety show, the annual *Carolina Opry Christmas* special, and *Good Vibrations,* featuring pop music of the 1960s through the 1980s. The theater also houses the corporate office of Gilmore Entrainment.

A sideline to the Carolina Opry is Candock Recording Studio, which produces music products for sale at the theater and online, and provides recording services to entertainers such as the Gatlin Brothers, Kenny Rogers, and the Beach Boys. Another Gilmore Entertainment venture is *Spotlight Magazine,* an advertising-supported playbill magazine for theaters in Myrtle Beach as well as in Branson, Missouri, a popular country music destination. In addition to the Carolina Opry, Gilmore Entertainment mounts outside productions for a variety of venues, including cruise ships and casinos.

FOUNDER TRIES NASHVILLE: 1967

Calvin Gilmore grew up on a small family farm started by his grandfather in the Ozark Mountains of Missouri, where he developed a love of music at the church his family had founded and grew determined to become a professional musician. He was just 20 when he began performing at night in restaurants and clubs in Kansas City while working at Hallmark Cards in the mailroom during the day. The young singer-songwriter then began touring with his guitar on the Midwest club and lounge circuit. In 1967 he traveled to the center of country music, Nashville, Tennessee.

Gilmore was talented enough to receive encouragement from a local label that advised him to produce a quality demo tape. To raise the money needed for studio time and other expenses, Gilmore turned to real estate sales in the Lake of the Ozarks resort area. He proved to be a natural salesman and was so successful that about a year later he bought the business. He also married and began raising a family. Although he retained his love for music, the need to support his family and an unwillingness to be separated from them in order to lead the road life of a musician led Gilmore to focus on his real estate company.

Once Gilmore was financially secure, however, an urge resurfaced in him in the early 1980s to perform again. To satisfy that desire without having to travel, he began nurturing the idea of producing a country music variety show at a resort area that would be likely to supply a ready audience of tourists. He recalled passing through Myrtle Beach, South Carolina—a family resort town that had begun to take shape in the early 1900s—during his time in college. In the 1920s came the opening of the first golf course, and 30 years after that a golf boom would come to Myrtle Beach.

Eventually the area—consisting of the Myrtle Beach metropolitan area and the 60-mile-long Grand Strand complex of beach towns and barrier islands—would boast well over 100 golf courses, which became the chief attraction of the area. Gilmore paid a visit in 1984, telling *Amusement Business* in a 1994 interview, "I saw lines at the restaurants and a lack of nightly entertainment." The community did boast something of a "beach music" scene, but there was clearly an opening for a country music venue and Gilmore decided he would commit all of his resources to creating one.

CAROLINA OPRY OPENS: 1986

Gilmore, his wife, and two young children moved to Surfside Beach in 1986. There on the southern end of the Grand Strand he bought an old nightclub, renovated it, and bestowed upon it the name The Carolina Opry, which he operated under the auspices of Calvin Gilmore Productions. The 1,000-seat theater held its first country music variety show on May 2, 1986. It was not an immediate success, drawing average houses, but Gilmore grew the business with brochures, radio and television advertising, and through strong word-of-mouth, and soon the show became a regular sellout.

Although winter was the off-season for Myrtle Beach, Gilmore was able to bring in revenue by mounting his first *Christmas Special* in 1986. It ran for eight days and most of the ten performances were sold out. That initial success led to more elaborate productions and extended runs, so that in time the Christmas show would run from early November through New Year's Eve, and play a major role in developing an off-season market for the Myrtle Beach area.

In 1987 Gilmore was able to leverage the size of his audience to sell advertising for a show bill, which in 1987 was launched as *Oprybill,* initially 16 pages in length with Calvin Gilmore's wife, Janis, serving as publisher. The name was later changed to *Spotlight Magazine,* and the publication peaked at 64 pages, half of which were advertising, before settling in at 48 pages. In 1992 the publishing operation expanded to Branson, Missouri, where it beat out New York City's well-established *Playbill* to provide show bills for 13 top theaters in the area. Despite some success in landing national subscribers, *Spotlight* left the national market after two years to focus its efforts on the Gilmore productions in South Carolina.

DIXIE JUBILEE OPENS: 1989

There was enough business in the Myrtle Beach area that Gilmore built a second theater in North Myrtle Beach, the 1,000-seat Dixie Jubilee. It opened in September 1989, offering a variety show similar to the *Carolina Opry*. Although two weeks later Hurricane Hugo struck the area, the new venue built an audience as well, and soon it too began selling out. Gilmore selected the talent and produced and directed both shows, which featured old guard country music and contemporary country, as well as rock and blues. Gilmore took special pride in discovering and nurturing new talent, and in 1990 he established Candock Recording Studio as a way to help showcase some of the emerging artists in the area and create retail products to sell at the theaters' gift shops. The facilities would take on outside work as well.

In 1991 ground was broken on an even larger theater in Myrtle Beach, located between the Surfside Beach venue and Dixie Jubilee at the intersection of Business 17 and Bypass 17 on a 23-acre parcel of land Gilmore shared with entertainer Dolly Parton. They hoped to create synergy by locating their venues next to one another. Dolly Parton's Dixie Stampede, an 80,000-square-foot showhouse, offered a Civil War re-creation as well as a rodeo in two nightly shows that altogether served 2,000 dinners each night to patrons divided into "Yankee" and "Rebel" sections. Gilmore, for his part, opened a new $6 million 2,200-seat Carolina Opry Theater in June 1992 to serve as the new home of the *Carolina Opry*. At the same time, the Surfside facility debuted a new production, *Southern Country Nights,* again following a variety format.

Nevertheless, the three Gilmore sites developed their own character and following. All were adept at catering to their patrons, in particular the motorcoach group sales business that was a major key to profits. At most performances the Carolina Opry Theater accommodated as many as 20 motorcoach groups (and even more during Christmas specials), and the other two theaters each hosted 14 motorcoach groups. A greeter welcomed each bus and passengers were given some orientation. To help passengers, many of them elderly with special needs, the buses parked next to a ramp to provide easy entrance into the theater, where the greeter led them to reserved seating. Staff members were also available to purchase snacks and souvenirs for patrons unable to make the trip to the snack bar or gift shop. Following the show, a member of the Opry cast paid a visit to the buses to meet with passengers and sign autographs. To keep the tour bus operators happy, the theaters also provided complimentary passes to the drivers and escorts.

In the meantime, as the business branched out, Gilmore formed an Advisory Board of Directors to help direct growth. In 1991 Gilmore's longtime friend David J. Olive was hired as vice-president and he helped open the Carolina Opry Theater. He then became president of Calvin Gilmore Productions in December 1993. Although an insurance man by trade, Olive shared Gilmore's passion for music, having served as part-time music director at the church where he, his wife, and the Gilmores were members. Olive and Gilmore also formed a Gospel group, Lighthouse, where they performed together.

THE FAMILY CHANNEL ACQUIRES MAJORITY STAKE: 1993

It was also in December 1993 that Gilmore sold an 80 percent controlling interest in Calvin Gilmore Productions to The Family Channel Television Network. For some time he had been interested in aligning the theaters with a television network. After holding discus-

sions with several of them, Gilmore settled on The Family Channel, which was received by more than 95 percent of all cable homes. As a result, he had access to the capital needed for national expansion, the MTM Records label, and global television exposure. With the backing of The Family Channel, Gilmore hoped to expand into television, movies, and syndication. In 1994 The Family Channel began taping and broadcasting *Country Music Spotlight* from the Carolina Opry Theater. A televised special, *Great American Music: A Salute to Fast Cars,* was also taped at the theater and broadcast nationally.

Gilmore planned to add more production venues across the country, identifying 15 markets for future development. In keeping with this plan, a fourth theater was built in Charleston, South Carolina, the 928-seat Charleston Music Hall, and in September 1995 a new show was launched, *The Serenade Show,* a Broadway-influenced production. The success Gilmore had enjoyed in Myrtle Beach, however, was not matched in Charleston, and *The Serenade Show* was canceled in 1999. Calvin Gilmore Productions retained the lease for several more years, and in 2008 the company returned with a musical revue it had originally produced for the American Music Theatre in Lancaster, Pennsylvania.

After Rupert Murdoch's News Corporation, owner of Fox Television Network, acquired The Family Channel in 1997, Calvin Gilmore arranged to reacquire most of the assets he had sold four years earlier. The new company, Gilmore Entertainment Group L.L.C., then facing increasing entertainment competition all along the Grand Strand, scaled back its ambitions, in some ways a victim of its own success. In 1998 the company consolidated its three shows at the Carolina Opry Theater, which became its sole venue, although it would regularly mount outside productions for cruise ships, casinos, and other locales, charging a flat fee plus production expenses.

Despite new musical attractions in Myrtle Beach, Calvin Gilmore remained the undisputed country music impresario of the area. He continued to direct and produce the new Carolina Opry Theater shows, where he also became a favorite performer. His musical career reached a peak in 2003 when he was invited to perform at the legendary Grand Ole Opry in Nashville. Gilmore would make repeat performances on its stage and turn out albums of gospel and original music as well.

GOOD VIBRATIONS SHOW OPENS: 2004

In the new century, Gilmore Entertainment sought to stay abreast of the interests of its audience. In 2004 the company became involved in the field of tribute music, producing a show called *Tribute! The Concert,* featuring a rotating lineup of country music tribute artists. The show was performed in the former Dixie Jubilee Theater, which Gilmore has since sold to the Disney Company. The company also ventured beyond country music in 2004, creating a new show to alternate with the *Carolina Opry* called *Good Vibrations,* appealing to baby boomers by featuring pop music of the 1960s, 1970s, and 1980s.

In 2008 Gilmore Entertainment considered taking over production responsibilities for the 1,500-seat Roanoke Rapids Theatre in North Carolina. It had been built by the city of Roanoke Rapids in 2006 at the cost of $21.5 million in an attempt to boost tourism through an arrangement with Dolly Parton's brother, Randy Parton, to serve as the headline act in a five-year contract. Called the Randy Parton Theater, it opened in the summer of 2007 but failed to draw as well as had been hoped. Matters grew worse in December 2007 when city officials claimed that Parton had arrived drunk for a show. He was then banned from performing, his contract bought out, and his name stripped from the marquee.

In May 2008 a tentative agreement was reached between Gilmore Entertainment and the city to take over the management of the theater for a five-year term. The deal was not finalized, however. The letter expired on June 1, 2008, and was extended by another month, when the agreement again lapsed. Whether a contract would ever be completed remained an open question, but there was every reason to expect that Gilmore's flagship operation, the Carolina Opry Theater, would continue to flourish in the years to come.

Ed Dinger

PRINCIPAL SUBSIDIARIES

Calvin Gilmore Productions Ltd.; Candock Recording Studio; Spotlight Magazine.

PRINCIPAL COMPETITORS

Gaylord Entertainment; On Stage Entertainment, Inc.

FURTHER READING

Cox, Jonathan B., "Calvin Gilmore to Run Roanoke Rapids Theatre," *Raleigh (N.C.) News & Observer,* May 9, 2008.

Fleisher, Lisa, "Gilmore to Handle Theater in N.C.," *Myrtle Beach (S.C.) Sun News,* May 9, 2008.

Kimes, Kent, "Myrtle Beach, S.C.'s Planned Music Theater Could Set Off Area Turf War," *Myrtle Beach (S.C.) Sun News,* January 10, 2004.

Magenheim, Henry, "S.C. Country Music Attractions Redefine Tour Client Services," *Travel Weekly,* December 17, 1992, p. 28.

Waddell, Ray, "Gilmore Entertainment Company to Branch Out from Myrtle Beach," *Amusement Business,* January 10, 1994, p. 8.

Watson, Tom, "Achy Breaky Myrtle Beach: Country's Invasion Has Given Some Operators the Blues," *Restaurant Business,* February 10, 1995, p. 66.

Golden Neo-Life Diamite International, Inc.

3500 Gateway Boulevard
Fremont, California 94538-6584
U.S.A.
Telephone: (510) 651-0405
Toll Free: (800) 432-5842
Fax: (510) 657-7563
Web site: http://www.gnld.com

Private Company
Incorporated: 1958 as Neo-Life Company
Employees: 600
Sales: $757 million (2007)
NAICS: 325411 Medicinal and Botanical Manufacturing

■ ■ ■

Golden Neo-Life Diamite International, Inc. (GNLD), is a privately held company based in Fremont, California, that sells nutritional supplements, herbal products, weight loss products, skin cream, environmentally friendly cleaning products, and water treatment products. The company sells these wares through a network of independent distributors who purchase the products and sell them to their own customers.

To support distributors, GNLD offers training and marketing materials, including brochures, CDs, and DVDs; handles the accounting of commissions; and packs and ships customer orders. Emphasizing its role in healthy lifestyles, GNLD encourages its independent distributors to use the products and share the products with family and friends. The company maintains a 25,000-acre retreat in Northern California where distributors are brought in for training and recreation. GNLD operates in more than 50 countries, the bulk of its business done overseas, and it performs especially well in African nations and Eastern Europe.

ROOTS DATE TO 1958

GNLD is the result of a merger between three companies: Golden Products, Neo-Life Company, and Diamite Corporation. The oldest entity was Neo-Life, founded by Donald Pickett in 1958. According to *The Story of GNLD* and similar accounts written by James W. McAfee, a nutritionist and member of GNLD's Health Professionals Council, one of GNLD's signature products, Tre-en-en, was first marketed by Pickett himself.

McAfee traced the development of Tre-en-en to research performed at Hollywood Presbyterian Hospital in 1946 to measure the impact of nutrients in nourishing the glands. Coming to believe that modern refining techniques stripped many nutrients from grains, researchers reportedly developed a way to extract oils from wheat, rice, and soy, combining them into a supplement that took the name Tre-en-en, Greek for "three in one."

According to McAfee, the company's roots lay with a man he identifies only as Wally, a coal wholesaler from Portland who learned of the work being done in Southern California and moved there to enroll his wife, a sufferer of rheumatoid arthritis, in the research project. After adding Tre-en-en to her diet she went into

COMPANY PERSPECTIVES

GNLD realizes that for every person who wants to feel better and live a healthy life, questions come to mind as they stand before the wall of supplements at the local store. What should I be taking? Which product is the best? Fact is, you can get lost in a world of promises and labels that don't deliver what your body really needs. Nutrition has come a long way and for nearly 50 years, GNLD has established a reputation for setting the highest standard. Whether you have been guided to GNLD for a specific product, or you are here to discover Vitality in one easy-to-use system, we welcome you to the world's best blend of what nature and science can deliver. Good nutrition, done right, will deliver more energy and vitality to your life than anything you've ever tried before. GNLD takes the guesswork out of good nutrition!

remission. When the research project came to an end in 1958, the couple is said to have learned that the results would be written up and the supplement the researchers developed would be shelved. Wally asked the head researcher if he could have access to the product for the benefit of his family and others and was told, according to McAfee, "If you will take this supplement and share it with people you will be doing something sixteen times more important than we doctors do."

Charged with this mission, Wally and his wife tried to persuade physicians to buy Tre-en-en and met with no takers. So the couple turned to Donald Pickett, a professional salesman, who in 1958 formed Neo-Life Company, the name referring to the "new life" people could expect by using this supplement. Rather than selling directly to physicians, Pickett opted to sell directly to consumers, and he developed, according to McAfee, "a marketing program which rewarded people for taking the time to explain the difference between this supplement and the others found in health food stores and supermarket shelves."

Pickett added other nutritional products and the company grew. In 1976 Pickett, who was growing elderly, sold one-third of Neo-Life to brothers Jerry and Robert Brassfield, multi-level marketers who owned Golden Products and Diamite Corporation and were interested in becoming involved in the nutritional products business, as reported by Peter Delevett of the *Business Journal, Bay Area West,* in 1998.

According to GNLD literature, Jerry Brassfield had always been interested in nutrition because as a child he suffered from severe allergy and asthma problems: "Jerry's only relief came after his mother started adding quality nutritional products to his daily diet. Just a few short years later at the age of 19 Jerry discovered that sharing quality products person to person was the basis for a financially rewarding home based business."

GOLDEN PRODUCTS FORMED: 1970

In 1970 Jerry and Robert Brassfield started a company called Golden Products, which did not focus on nutritional supplements. Rather, it followed the lead of the preeminent company in the multi-level marketing industry, Amway Corporation, offering a line of home care products. In 1975 they formed another company, Diamite Corporation, to sell cubic zirconia jewelry and other inexpensive fashion jewelry via in-home parties.

According to Delevett, "Family-owned Neo-Life had trouble adjusting to an outside partner, and the Brassfields negotiated to buy out Mr. Pickett in 1983." The Brassfields then ran Golden Products, Diamite, and Neo-Life as separate enterprises. It was also in 1983 that Rudy Revak was named president of Diamite and dropped jewelry in favor of so-called contemporary-lifestyle products, primarily including nutritional supplements, but also skin-care cosmetics, home-care products, and water-filtration systems. Revak hired Willie Larkin II to handle marketing, and in 1986, under Larkin's leadership, the company began increasingly focusing sales efforts on the African American demographic. Black distributors would eventually account for around half of Diamite's revenues.

DIAMITE SUED: 1992

As the economy stalled in the early 1990s, interest in multi-level marketing companies increased, as a growing number of people looked to supplement their incomes. Diamite received unwanted publicity in 1992 when a California law firm, Lieff Cabraser and Heimann, filed a lawsuit in San Jose's U.S. District Court accusing the company of being a "classic pyramid scheme" that defrauded its independent distributors. The firm represented a single distributor, 56-year-old Daisy Daludado, but went to court seeking permission to expand the case into a class-action suit, thereby gaining a list of Diamite's distributors in order to send them a legal notice of the suit. Daludado claimed to have lost $7,500 on products she purchased for her inventory and to attend training seminars as far away as Florida, which she said offered more cheerleading than actual sales training.

KEY DATES

1958: Donald Pickett founds Neo-Life Company.
1970: Jerry and Robert Brassfield start Golden Products.
1975: The Brassfields establish Diamite Corporation.
1976: The Brassfields acquire a stake in Neo-Life.
1983: The Brassfields buy out the Pickett family.
1998: Three companies are combined to create Golden Neo-Life Diamite International, Inc.
2005: Roget Uys is named chief executive.

She claimed that when it became apparent that she would not buy more products or refer more friends as distributors, Diamite "abandoned" her. The lawsuit also maintained that Diamite products were priced higher than similar products found in stores and that some of the health and diet aids were not effective. Moreover, the suit contended, "The true objective of Diamite's marketing scheme is to perpetrate an endless chain of distributors"—a chain that would collapse when distributors could no longer find new participants in the program. Such a contention was what separated an illegal pyramid scheme from a legitimate multi-level marketing business.

DIAMITE SETTLES SUIT: 1993

Diamite disputed Daludado's claims and described the effort as a nuisance suit, calling it a "form of legalized extortion." There were no other complaints on file against Diamite, either on the state or federal level. Diamite offered to refund Daludado's money, less a 10 percent handling charge, to settle the case. She refused, and the matter proceeded.

Lieff Cabraser succeeded in making it a class-action suit. In April 1993 the matter was finally settled when Diamite agreed to set up a cash refund plan for distributors, allowing anyone involved in the marketing program within the previous four years to receive a 90 percent reimbursement on their unsold inventory, or 20 percent of their business expenses. Diamite considered the case meritless and did not admit to any wrongdoing under the terms of the agreement.

In the mid-1990s, the Brassfield-controlled companies intensified their efforts to grow internationally but encountered a number of problems. According to the *Business Journal,* "overseas distributors grew confused by the different names and products, some of

which competed with one another. Separate corporate identities also increased the hassles of dealing with regulators in other countries." In 1996 the Brassfields began to consolidate their operations, bringing together the different products, marketing plans, staffs, distributors, and company cultures into a single entity, Golden Neo-Life Diamite International, Inc.

The transition was completed in 1998 and the company moved forward as a single enterprise. About three-quarters of GNLD's sales came from nutritional supplements; with the aging of the U.S. population, and malnutrition in many parts of the world, such products were the company's primary focus going forward.

While the companies comprising GNLD were coming together, GNLD made a major push into Africa, especially Uganda, Kenya, and other countries in East Africa. The products reportedly did especially well among the upper classes, who increasingly embraced herbal medicine and homeopathy and recognized the link between diet and disease. Other operations would open in Botswana, Cameroon, Ghana, Lesotho, Mozambique, Namibia, Nigeria, South Africa, Swaziland, and Tanzania. Aside from these developing countries, GNLD also did well in Eastern Europe and the former satellite states of the Soviet Union where capitalism was taking shape, establishing distributor networks in such countries as Bosnia and Herzegovina, Croatia, Estonia, Hungary, Latvia, Lithuania, Romania, and Slovenia.

NEW OFFICERS: 2005

By the start of the 21st century GNLD had increased worldwide sales to the $300 million range and was aiming to become a $1 billion company in the near future. Although Jerry Brassfield remained very much involved in the company, changes were made in the upper ranks of management in 2005. Dan Laws, a former public accountant who joined GNLD as an auditor in 1975 and later became chief financial officer, took over as chief operating officer, responsible for the company's global operations as well as finance. A new president and chief executive officer, Roget Uys, was also brought in. Given the importance of the African market, it was fitting that Uys was a native of South Africa. He had been involved with GNLD since 1989. GNLD celebrated its 50th anniversary in 2008. It had enjoyed a prosperous run by focusing on the direct marketing of nutritional products; whether that formula would continue to succeed for another 50 years remained to be seen.

Ed Dinger

PRINCIPAL SUBSIDIARIES

GNLD International, LLC.

PRINCIPAL COMPETITORS

Alticor, Inc.; AMS Health Sciences, Inc.; Nu Skin Enterprises, Inc.

FURTHER READING

Bailey, Brandon, "'Pyramid Scheme' Alleged in Milpitas," *San Jose Mercury News,* July 5, 1992, p. 1B.

Brown, Caryne, "Door-to-Door Selling Grows Up," *Black Enterprise,* December 1992.

Delevett, Peter, "GNLD Thrives in Den of Techies," *Business Journal, Bay Area West,* April 27, 1998, p. 1.

"The Golden Lesson," *Africa News Service,* March 25, 2002.

McAfee, James W., *The Story of GNLD,* James W. McAfee, 2006.

Romano, Bill, "Milpitas Firm Settles Suit, Ending 2-Year Court Rift with Distributors," *San Jose Mercury News,* April 14, 1993, p. 2B.

"Shrewd Business in Food Supplements," *Africa News Service,* March 28, 2007.

Griffith Laboratories Inc.

1 Griffith Center
Alsip, Illinois 60803
U.S.A.
Telephone: (708) 371-0900
Toll Free: (800) 346-4743
Fax: (708) 389-4055
Web site: http://www.griffithlaboratories.com

Private Company
Incorporated: 1919
Employees: 2,500
Sales: $520.4 million (2007 est.)
NAICS: 311423 Dried and Dehydrated Food Manufacturing

■ ■ ■

Based in Alsip, Illinois, Griffith Laboratories Inc. is a leading manufacturer of products for restaurants, food processors, grocery stores, and other food industry operators worldwide. The company makes items such as coating systems, crumbs, dough blends, dry mixes, flavors, food bases, sauces, and seasoning blends. Its offerings ultimately end up in a variety of edible goods, such as ready-to-eat meals, processed meat, poultry, and snack foods.

FORMATIVE YEARS

The roots of Griffith Laboratories stretch back to 1919, when Enoch Luther Griffith established the company in Chicago with his two sons, Carroll L. Griffith and F.

Willard Griffith. Born in Winston-Salem, North Carolina, the founder had moved to the Chicago area in 1893, after growing up in southwest Missouri and Kansas. During its formative years, Griffith Laboratories focused on selling seasonings to sausage makers, approaching them with sales kits that included product samples. The company went on to develop meat seasonings that were tailored to specific regional tastes.

Almost from the very beginning, Griffith Laboratories was very much influenced by the international scene. During its first decade, the company started importing Prague Salt from Germany, where the compound had been developed to quick-cure meats. International expansion occurred when Toronto, Ontario-based Griffith Laboratories Ltd. was established in 1927. Breakthroughs that year included the introduction of liquid seasonings.

In 1929 Griffith Laboratories moved into a new facility in Chicago's central manufacturing district, north of the old Chicago Stockyards. Designed by A. Epstein, the building was located at 1415-31 West 37th Street. It also was in 1929 that the company hired a scientist named Lloyd Augustus Hall. The fact that Hall was of African American heritage was evidence of the company's progressiveness during an era when racial discrimination was rampant. Hall went on to become Griffith Laboratories' scientific director and to author more than 40 scientific papers. In 1956, he received the Honor Scroll Award from the Chicago chapter of the American Institute of Chemists.

Despite the dire economic challenges of the Great Depression, Griffith Laboratories continued to develop

COMPANY PERSPECTIVES

■

Our focus, knowledge and commitment to the food industry allow us to offer our customers the expertise and consumer-preferred products they need and want. We look forward to continuing to shape the future of food.

innovative products and equipment. Examples included an improved version of Prague Salt called Prague Powder, as well as the Prague Pickle Scale, the Ham Press, and Big Boy Pumps.

EARLY GROWTH AND EXPANSION

Physical expansion also occurred at Griffith Laboratories during the 1930s. The company developed its Research and Experimental Kitchen in 1937, and in June 1938 announced plans for a two-story addition to its facility on West 37th Street. The $35,000 project expanded the facility's overall size to 66,000 square feet.

Griffith Laboratories capped off the 1930s with a plan to increase awareness of its brand among consumers. This was accomplished via the introduction of a spice set in 1939. Sold at retailers such as Marshall Field's and Macy's, the set included 12 spices, which were prepared using a proprietary purifying method, in white glass jars with an accompanying storage rack. The spices eventually became commonplace in U.S. kitchens, and their containers went on to become collectible items.

In 1940 Griffith Laboratories named Oren Arbogast as its advertising agency. Along with companies in virtually every industry, the organization was affected by World War II. Wartime production led to the development of new products, including cold pack beef and gravy, which the U.S. Army used for rations. After the war, the product was marketed to the general public. The increased focus on testing and experimentation at this time set the stage for future product expansion. During the late 1940s, new products that resulted from the work of the company's testing kitchen included an antioxidant named G-4, as well as dry soluble seasonings.

In January 1946, Griffith Laboratories bade farewell to its founder, Enoch L. Griffith, who died in Coral Gables, Florida, at the age of 78. At the time of his death, Griffith was chairman and president of Griffith

Laboratories Inc., which then had operations in Chicago and Newark, New Jersey, as well as president of the company's Canadian operation, Toronto, Ontario-based Griffith Laboratories Ltd.

International growth continued at Griffith Laboratories during the 1950s and included the establishment of operations in Mexico in 1954. During this decade, the company also opened new spice extraction plants in the United States and Canada. In Canada, which was home to a burgeoning fish industry, Griffith Laboratories began marketing batters and breadings.

FACING CHALLENGES

On September 1, 1955, two of Griffith Laboratories' facilities suffered approximately $250,000 in damage in what was described as Chicago's worst fire in 21 years. The incident, which required the resources of about half of the city's firefighters, reportedly began when an explosion occurred on the loading dock off of Griffith Laboratories' spice extraction building. It resulted in a blaze that caused more than $1 million in total damages, including the destruction of the nearby Carr-Consolidated Biscuit Co. More than 40 people were injured while trying to escape the fire, and three lost their lives.

Midway through the 1950s, the nation's economic prosperity resulted in increased demand for fine meat products. This was good news for Griffith Laboratories and other spice companies whose products were used to season sausage and a variety of other smoked and cured meats. Product breakthroughs during the 1950s included the introduction of Griffith Laboratories' line of Mince Master equipment, which was considered a major advancement in the sausage-making field. When the government imposed pretesting regulations in 1958 for the use of chemicals in food, the company developed the testing and research that was needed for companies to secure Food and Drug Administration (FDA) approval.

During the mid-1960s, company leadership was provided by Carroll Griffith. In 1966 he faced a life-threatening situation when armed robbers invaded his Hinsdale, Illinois, home. Fortunately, Griffith was unscathed during the incident. However, the robbers stole $15,000 in valuables, including a $10,000, four-carat diamond ring.

During the 1960s Carroll Griffith's son, Dean, established a plant in Bleiswijk, Holland, which was the company's first in Europe. The move was made in response to a growing demand for locally produced products. A number of breakthroughs occurred on the product front throughout the decade. These included

KEY DATES

1919: Enoch Luther Griffith establishes the company in Chicago with his two sons, Carroll L. Griffith and F. Willard Griffith.

1927: International expansion begins when Toronto, Ontario-based Griffith Laboratories Ltd. is established.

1929: Griffith Laboratories moves into a new facility in Chicago's central manufacturing district.

1946: Enoch Griffith dies in Coral Gables, Florida, at age 78.

1955: Two of Griffith Laboratories' Chicago facilities suffer fire damage.

1998: The company opens its new Culinary Center.

2007: Griffith Laboratories' global workforce includes 2,500 people.

the development of a powdered soy protein concentrate. In order to bolster the nutrition and structure of meat patties, the company created a granulated version of the concentrate that was dubbed Patti Pro. Additionally, Griffith Laboratories received approval from the government to offer a natural smoke flavoring in 1964.

Griffith Laboratories dealt with a number of changes during the early 1970s. In mid-1971 the company sought an extension from Chicago's Department of Environmental Control to gain more time to comply with the city's requirements for pollution abatement equipment. In December 1972, Griffith Laboratories experienced a setback when the FDA allegedly discovered cockroaches and other insects in mustard flower, green onions, and yeast during an inspection of the company's Chicago facilities.

Following accusations by the office of the United States Attorneys, which claimed the company sold contaminated spices, in February 1973 Federal District Court Judge Thomas R. McMillen fined the company $4,900 for allowing its ingredients to become contaminated. In addition, then Executive Vice-President Dean Griffith was fined $500 for the incident. Despite this setback, the company continued to achieve strong international growth. Throughout the 1970s Griffith Laboratories formed new operations in the United Kingdom, Australia, Belgium, Colombia, Costa Rica, Japan, New Zealand, the Philippines, and Thailand.

DEVELOPING OPERATIONAL SOPHISTICATION

During the early 1980s, Griffith Laboratories made a significant information technology investment at its Chicago facility, purchasing a DPS 7/45 computer system from Honeywell Inc., which was worth approximately $703,000. This was but one example of the many technology investments the company had made. In fact, by the mid-1980s Griffith Laboratories had established an extensive Factory Management System at its facilities in Union, New Jersey; Union City, California; Alsip, Illinois; and Lithonia, Georgia. The system was used by approximately 600 employees, and included a shop floor data collection system that was comprised of a variety of Honeywell components.

During the 1980s Griffith Laboratories ranked as one of the largest food ingredient and seasoning companies. Midway through the decade, the company marketed approximately 15,000 types of ingredients and seasonings. Its customer base included some 8,000 different food manufacturers, restaurants, distributors, and other organizations. The depth of Griffith Laboratories' product line could be seen by looking at barbecued potato chips, for which it had 38 different recipes alone.

Heading into the late 1980s, Griffith Laboratories used dot matrix printers to generate labels for some 6,000 different food products. The printers replaced a thermal printing system the company had previously used to make labels. They allowed Griffith Laboratories to print larger runs of labels in less time and enabled the company to be more responsive to labeling requirements established by the FDA.

A number of important developments occurred during the early 1990s. In late 1991, Griffith Laboratories acquired Custom Food Products Inc. Custom Food Products manufactured products such as sauces, soup bases, and gravies. Following the deal, Custom Food Products continued to operate as an independent company. It also was around this time that a new facility was established in São Paulo, Brazil.

In 1993, a major expansion occurred at the company's breading plant in the United Kingdom, which doubled in size. That year, several key leadership changes occurred. In April, Alan H. Hawley, who had served as president and CEO of Griffith Laboratories Canada, was named CEO of the company's operations in the Pacific Rim. In addition, L. Dick Buell, who had served as president and CEO of Griffith Laboratories U.S.A., was named president and CEO of the company's operations in North America.

As evidence of Griffith Laboratories' sophisticated operations, during the mid-1990s it implemented full-text indexing and retrieval technology for use in its research and development and shipping departments. One advantage of the new technology was that the company's scientists gained an effective system for sharing knowledge. Tools such as these were especially important as Griffith Laboratories continued to become a more global enterprise. One example of this was the establishment of a new company in Seoul, South Korea, in 1996.

On the product development front, Griffith Laboratories unveiled its Gourmet Ethnic line of seasonings. The new product range could be used for both meat and non-meat products, and included Caribbean, Italian, French, Mexican, and Asian seasonings. In addition to sausages, the seasonings could be used in burgers, pizza toppings, ground meat, meatloaf, and more.

In October 1998, a major development unfolded when Griffith Laboratories opened its new Culinary Center. The facility, which was based at the company's Illinois headquarters, provided scientists and customers with educational opportunities in the culinary arts. In addition to a fully equipped kitchen, the center included a library, as well as meeting and presentation areas.

PREPARING FOR THE 21ST CENTURY

Griffith Laboratories ended the 1990s by announcing plans to spin off its Griffith Micro Science International subsidiary, a medical and laboratory equipment business. At this time, Griffith Laboratories' annual sales were estimated at approximately $417 million. By the dawn of the new millennium, Griffith Laboratories had approximately 170 patents to its name. Global expansion continued in 2000 via the formation of a joint venture in Thailand. By mid-2001, the company's international footprint spanned 14 countries, and included 20 facilities.

In mid-2002, Griffith Laboratories changed its leadership structure when Mark A. Duffy was named president in charge of the company's domestic operations. Early the following year, a new corporate logo was unveiled, which depicted the international aspect of Griffith Laboratories' operations. It was also in 2003 that Griffith Laboratories was recognized by Yum! Brands Inc. with STAR Awards for International Food Supplier of the Year and Global Supplier of the Year.

As Griffith Laboratories grew in size, the company continued to rely on technology to manage its operations. One example of this was the implementation of new software for labor reporting and time-and-attendance functions in early 2004. In 2007 the company's Custom Culinary Inc. business acquired Avon, Ohio-based DM Foods, which supplied foodservice operations and restaurants with culinary flavor systems and sauces. By this time, Griffith Laboratories' global workforce had grown to include 2,500 people. That year, the company's web site was enhanced to include versions in Chinese, Spanish, French, Italian, and German.

Developments continued as Griffith Laboratories headed into the end of the decade. In 2007 Chris Savage was named president of the company's operations in Canada and Jennifer Convery was appointed general manager of Griffith Laboratories U.S.A. As of late 2008, Griffith Laboratories remained a family-owned enterprise. Chairman Dean Griffith represented a third generation of family leadership. He was joined in the corporate suite by President and CEO Hervé de la Vauvre. Moving forward into the 21st century's second decade, Griffith Laboratories appeared to be well positioned for continued leadership within its industry.

Paul R. Greenland

PRINCIPAL SUBSIDIARIES

Custom Culinary Inc.; Griffith Laboratories U.S.A. Inc.; Griffith Laboratories Ltd.; Griffith Laboratories Pvt Ltd.; Griffith Laboratories s.r.l.; Griffith Laboratories Worldwide; Griffith Laboratories Zhongshan Co. Ltd.; Laboratories Griffith de México.

PRINCIPAL COMPETITORS

BakeMark USA LLC; Danisco A/S; Tate & Lyle plc.

FURTHER READING

"Enoch L. Griffith: Headed Research Chemists Firm in Food-Processing Work," *New York Times,* February 1, 1946.

O'Donnell, Claudia D., "Center Furthers Culinary Art & Science," *Prepared Foods,* October 1998.

"Q&A with Mark Duffy: President of Griffith Laboratories—USA and Custom Culinary," *Snack Food & Wholesale Bakery,* September 2005.

"Two Employees Missing After Bakery Blaze," *Chicago Daily Tribune,* September 3, 1955.

Groupe Caisse d'Epargne

—————— ■ ——————

77 Boulevard Saint Jacques
Paris, F-75673 Cedex 13
France
Telephone: (33 1 58) 40 41 42
Fax: (33 1 58) 40 48 00
Web site: http://www.caisse-epargne.fr

Cooperative Bank
Founded: 1818
Employees: 55,800
Total Assets: EUR 483 billion ($712 billion) (2007)
NAICS: 522120 Savings Institutions

■ ■ ■

Groupe Caisse d'Epargne (GCE) is one of France's largest banks, offering a full range of retail banking services and products to the private, commercial, and public sectors. GCE is the holding company overseeing the group's operations, which include Caisse Nationale des Caisses d'Epargne (CNCE), the central coordinating body and banker for the Caisses d'Epargne, a nationally operating network of 411 locally based, cooperative savings banks. Other parts of the GCE group include Crédit Foncier, one of France's leading specialist real estate finance banks; Banque Palatine, focused on the corporate banking sector; nearly 35 percent of Natixis, a major provider of wholesale banking, asset management, securities, and related services; Nexity, one of France's largest real estate companies; insurance services through Ecureil Assurances; and Financière Océor, which oversees GCE's international holdings and investments, including its banking operations in France's overseas territories. The company also holds majority control of Banque BCP, operating in France and Luxembourg; and CIH, in Morocco.

GCE produced a net income of EUR 9.8 billion ($12 billion) in 2007. Commercial banking accounted for 70 percent of this total, while Wholesale Banking & Financial Services added 15 percent. Insurance and Real Estate accounted for 10 and 5 percent, respectively. In 2008, GCE announced its intention to merge CNCE with smaller rival Banque Fédérale des Banques Populaires, the central institution for the Banque Populaire banking group. The merger, to be completed near the end of 2009, was expected to create France's second largest banking group (behind Crédit Agricole), with a total income of EUR 17.5 billion ($24 billion) and total savings and deposits of EUR 480 billion. The combined group would also boast more than 100,000 employees, and 8,200 branches, although the company was expected to maintain separate Caisse d'Epargne and Banque Populaire banking networks. The combined company would also control nearly 70 percent of Natixis. GCE lost its chairman and chief executive officer after a trading scandal resulted in a EUR 600 million loss in October 2008.

FRENCH SAVINGS PIONEER

Groupe Caisse d'Epargne stemmed from a movement initiated by French aristocrats in the early 19th century to encourage savings among the French population as a means of alleviating poverty and improving the quality of life of the population. One of the first efforts in this

COMPANY PERSPECTIVES

From its very origins, the French savings bank movement has always wanted to play an active role in developing a market economy with a responsible, human face. As such, its determination to ensure a long-term reconciliation between economic efficiency, social justice and environmental precaution is the quintessence of the market position adopted by Groupe Caisse d'Epargne. Ambition, Trust and Commitment are the key corporate values of Groupe Caisse d'Epargne. They can be traced back to the very origins of the Group, and coincide perfectly with the aspirations expressed by its customers, employees and cooperative shareholders.

direction came in 1787, with the formation of the Compagnie Royale d'Assurances sur la Vie, under the direction of banker Étienne Delessert. That company was granted a monopoly for providing life insurance and related services to the French population.

The company did not survive the French revolution. In 1818, however, Delessert's son, Benjamin Delessert, revived his father's ideals. Joining with the Duke François de La Rochefoucauld-Laincourt, Delessert founded a new institution, the Caisse d'Epargne. The Caisse d'Epargne was meant to serve as an instrument to promote financial responsibility, in an effort to reduce individual exposure in times of financial crisis, and to improve the social welfare. As Delessert was quoted as saying: "Let us try to get people to understand the benefits, one could almost say the miracles, of saving."

The Caisse d'Epargne was established following the mutual—or cooperative—model, in which customers were also shareholders in the institution. The Caisse d'Epargne also introduced the savings book, which provided a tangible record of customers' savings deposits, accounts, and the interest received. The first Caisse d'Epargne, located in Paris, soon inspired others to form their own local Caisses d'Epargne. By the early 1830s, there were 27 Caisses in operation in France.

An important milestone in the development of the Caisse d'Epargne network came in 1829. In that year, the Caisses were permitted to open accounts at the Royal Treasury. Thus, the Caisses deposited their customers' savings at the Royal Treasury, which guaranteed a fixed interest rate on deposits. Soon after, in 1835, the French government adopted formal legislation recognizing the Caisses d'Epargne as "private institutions of public utility." Then, in 1837, the French government offered to transfer the management of the Caisses' funds to the government-owned Caisse des Dépôts, providing further protection to savers' deposits.

CONTRIBUTING TO THE NATIONAL SOCIAL WELFARE

These actions led to an upsurge not only in the number of customers, but also in the number of Caisses that appeared in France over the next several decades. Between 1835 and 1839, the total number of Caisses d'Epargne surged to 284. The growing number of locally owned and operated Caisses—which ultimately neared 600 into the 20th century—as well as the increasing wealth they governed, led the French government to make compulsory the transfer of their funds management to the Caisse des Dépôts in 1852. In return, each Caisse d'Epargne was provided with separate reserve and guarantee funds.

Toward the end of the century, pressure began to build calling for the government to allow the Caisses to regain control over the management of their funds. This debate ultimately ended with the passage of new legislation in 1895, which stated that the deposits generated through the Caisse d'Epargne network were to be considered as state funds. The legislation also provided for the creation of a third "personal wealth" fund for each Caisse, containing surplus revenues. These included donations, bequests, and subsidies, as well as the net interest generated by the Caisse after transferring part of the interest payments from the Treasury to its customers.

The creation of the new reserve fund allowed the Caisses to participate in financing the local social infrastructure, such as the construction of low-cost housing, operation of public baths, the creation of public vegetable gardens, and similar projects. Over time, the Caisses became important members of the local and national social welfare sector, supporting charities, public assistance programs, and related activities.

The Caisses, however, remained limited by law to their savings operations, and were restricted from entering other banking sectors, such as mortgages and lending. The limitation not only restricted the group's range of action, it also limited its appeal to French savers, who increasingly brought their business to competing, full-fledged banks. The group's Alsace and Moselle members, however, gained some degree of lending experience, as those regions found themselves within

KEY DATES

1818: Benjamin Delessert leads the creation of the first Caisse d'Epargne in Paris.

1835: The French government adopts legislation recognizing the Caisses d'Epargne as "private institutions of public utility."

1950: The Minjoz Act permits the Caisse d'Epargne to begin providing lending services.

1984: The French government passes a new Banking Act, which officially grants banking status to the Caisses d'Epargne.

1999: Groupe Caisse d'Epargne (GCE) is formed; acquires Crédit Foncier de France.

2002: GCE forms Eulia in partnership with the Caisse des Dépôts.

2003: GCE acquires Banque Sanpaolo, which is later renamed Banque Palatine.

2006: GCE and Banque Populaire combine their corporate and investment banking operations into a new joint venture, Natixis.

2008: CGE and Banque Populaire announce their agreement to merge their central coordinating bodies.

Germany's borders from 1870 until the end of World War I, and again during World War II. The Caisses d'Epargne in both regions were allowed to continue their lending operations even after the regions returned to French control.

ADDING LENDING AND OTHER SERVICES

This provided the Caisse d'Epargne network with a certain degree of leverage during the postwar reconstruction of France. The need to rebuild large parts of France's infrastructure placed heavy demands on the available lending pool. The Caisse d'Epargne lobbied to gain the right to utilize their deposits held by the Caisse des Dépôts to provide lending products and services. The group was aided by Jean Minjoz, who had become a member of the board of directors at the Caisse d'Epargne in Besançon in 1946. The following year, Minjoz, who was also the deputy to the French Parliament for the Doubs region, championed new legislation governing the Caisse d'Epargne network.

Passed in 1950, the Minjoz Act, as it was called, enabled the Caisses d'Epargne to provide lending services for the first time. As a continued precaution, however, the Caisses could not grant loans directly, but instead transferred loan applications for treatment by the Caisse des Dépôts. The amount of loans permitted by the group as a whole remained limited to just 10 percent of its total deposits at the Caisse des Dépôts.

The Caisse d'Epargne group nevertheless relied on what was essentially a single product, its savings passbook, until the mid-1960s. During that decade, the French government carried out a major reform of the country's banking system. The Caisses d'Epargne were then permitted to expand their range of products and services for the first time, and to compete head-to-head with the country's banks.

The group, eager to retain customer loyalty, launched a series of new products during the 1960s and into the 1970s. These included the Livret Epargne-Logement (the housing passbook), introduced in 1965. The following year, the network added a mortgage product, Prêts Epargne-Logement. This was followed by investment vehicles, the SICAV and the Livret Porte-feuille, introduced in 1967. By the end of the decade, the Caisse d'Epargne had launched housing and savings bonds as well.

The next move toward full-fledged banking status came in 1972, when the group was authorized to market personal loans and mortgage products. The Caisses were also allowed to establish competitive interest rates. At the same time, the local Caisses were permitted to provide loans and mortgage products to customers from outside their savings customer base. The new rules also did away with the 10 percent quota established by the Minjoz Act. As a result, the local Caisses became important sources of financial support for their governments.

ACHIEVING FULL-FLEDGED BANKING STATUS

The Caisse d'Epargne achieved full-fledged banking status in the early 1980s. This came about starting in 1983, when new legislation converted the group's status to that of a non-profit-making credit institution. The new status granted the group the right to perform the full range of banking services. The following year, the French government passed a new Banking Act, which officially granted banking status to the Caisses d'Epargne. At that time, there were 464 local Caisses in operation.

In order to govern what had become a national banking network, Caisse d'Epargne established a new central body to oversee the group's operations. This body was called the Centre National des Caisses d'Epargne (CNCE). The CNCE then launched a major restructuring of the Caisse d'Epargne network, reducing the number of local Caisses to 186 by 1990, and again to just 35 by 1991. At the same time, the Caisse d'Epargne had begun marketing to the corporate market for the first time, following new legislation in 1987.

Initially limited to lending only to privately held companies, the Caisses were granted authorization to lend to public companies in 1999. That year also marked the clarification of Caisse d'Epargne's ownership structure. The group formally adopted cooperative banking status, transferring ownership to 451 local savings companies.

The new structure led to the next major phase in the development of the Caisse d'Epargne, which then reinvented itself as a multifaceted French financial powerhouse, known as Groupe Caisse d'Epargne (GCE). In 1999, the group acquired the Crédit Foncier de France (CFF), one of the government's primary public sector lending vehicles, originally established by decree by Louis-Napoleon Bonaparte in 1852. Under GCE, CFF grew strongly, acquiring real estate lending specialist Entenial in 2004. The following year, CFF merged with Entenial, as well as with A3C and Crédit Foncier Banque, and then changed its own status to that of banking institution.

BECOMING A 21ST CENTURY POWERHOUSE

In 2002, Caisse d'Epargne teamed up with the Caisse des Dépôts to create a new company, Eulia, which took over the investment banking, insurance, real estate, and related specialized financial services of both banks. Just two years later, the two groups restructured the partnership, as Caisse des Dépôts transferred its holding in Eulia, as well as its investment banking and asset management subsidiary CDC Ixis, to Groupe Caisse d'Epargne, which then achieved universal banking status.

The group filled a gap in its portfolio in 2003 when it acquired a majority stake in Banque Sanpaolo, which specialized in the small-to-medium business market. Originally founded in Turin, Italy, in 1563, Banque Sanpaolo changed its name to Banque Palatine in 2005. In 2006, GCE teamed up with small rival, Groupe Banque Populaire, another banking cooperative, to combine their corporate and investment banking operations into a new joint venture, Natixis. Floated on the Euronext Paris stock exchange soon after, Natixis quickly became one of France's largest companies to date in terms of its market capital, and also took a place among the leading European banks. The creation of the modern GCE continued into 2007, when the group

spun off its real estate operations as a new company, Nexity. That company too was taken public, becoming a leading French real estate player.

The chaos that struck the global financial markets in 2008 provided a new growth opportunity for GCE. While GCE had held merger talks with Banque Populaire, the prospect of receiving government approval had remained rather unlikely. In 2008, however, GCE and Banque Populaire announced their intention to merge their central coordinating bodies by the end of 2009. The combined company was then expected to become France's second largest banking institution, trailing only Crédit Agricole. With the French government desperate to shore up the country's increasingly fragile banking sector, the merger was quickly approved.

The willingness of the French government to maintain the stability of the country's financial sector was further in evidence given the financial scandal that hit GCE in October of that year, when it was revealed that reckless trading operations had resulted in the loss of more than EUR 600 million ($800 million). The scandal ended in the resignation of the company's chairman and chief executive officer, as well as its chief financial officer. Nevertheless, the scandal was not expected to derail the group's merger with Banque Populaire. When completed, GCE was expected to preside over a nationally operating network of more than 8,200 branches, which would retain their Caisse d'Epargne and Banque Populaire names, and total savings and deposits of more than EUR 480 billion. Groupe Caisse d'Epargne had become a French financial powerhouse for the 21st century.

M. L. Cohen

PRINCIPAL SUBSIDIARIES

Assurances IARD; Banque BCP; Banque Palatine; CEMM(6); CIH (Morocco); CNP; Coface; Crédit Foncier; Ecureuil; Financière Océor; Natixis; Natixis Financement; Natixis Garanties; Natixis Global Asset Management; Natixis Interépargne; Natixis Securities; Nexity.

PRINCIPAL COMPETITORS

HSBC Holdings plc; Fortis N.V.; Royal Bank of Scotland Group plc; Caisse Nationale des Caisses d'Epargne et de Prevoyance S.A.; Caja de Ahorros y Pensiones de Barcelona–La Caixa; Caja de Ahorros y Monte de Piedad de Madrid; Landesbank Berlin AG; Caisse d'Epargne et de Prevoyance Cote d'Azur S.A.; Cheltenham and Gloucester plc.

FURTHER READING

"Caisse d'Epargne Board Meets on Derivatives Losses," *Global Banking News,* October 20, 2008.

"Caisse d'Epargne Chiefs Step Down Following 600m-Euro Loss," *Europe Intelligence Wire,* October 20, 2008.

Crumley, Bruce, "Trying to Generate Interest," *Time International,* April 25, 2005, p. 14.

Daneshkhu, Scheherazade, "French Bank in $800m Scandal," *Financial Times,* October 18, 2008, p. 1.

"French Bank Chiefs Quit Hot Stocks," *International Herald Tribune,* October 21, 2008, p. 15.

Jolly, David, "A Crisis in Finance," *International Herald Tribune,* October 9, 2008, p. 12.

"Natixis Unit Rescued for $1.5 Billion," *International Herald Tribune,* November 23, 2007, p. 14.

Simmons, Jacqueline, and Gregory Viscusi, "2 Banks in France Near Deal," *International Herald Tribune,* March 13, 2006, p. 12.

Story, Louise, "Two French Banks Acquire Bond Insurance Company," *New York Times,* November 23, 2007, p. C2.

Heuliez

Groupe Henri Heuliez S.A.

Boulevard Georges Pompidou
Cerizay, F-79140
France
Telephone: (33 05 49) 81 33 11
Fax: (33 05 49) 81 30 50
Web site: http://www.heuliez.com

Private Company
Incorporated: 1920 as Carrosserie Heuliez
Employees: 1,600
Sales: EUR 180 million ($220 million) (2008 est.)
NAICS: 336399 All Other Motor Vehicle Parts Manufacturing; 336111 Automobile Manufacturing; 336211 Motor Vehicle Body Manufacturing; 551112 Offices of Other Holding Companies

∎∎∎

Groupe Henri Heuliez S.A. is one of the oldest automotive contractors in France. Based in Cerizay, in the west of France, the company serves as a major partner to the European automobile industry, providing turnkey services for the production of vehicles (systems that are so complete the client needs only to "turn the key" to operate), as well as vehicle components and systems, and "Body in White" modules (unpainted components awaiting stamping). Heuliez's production includes the retractable hardtop module for the Peugeot 206 Coupe Convertible, more than 350,000 of which have been sold since its introduction in 2000. The company has also produced more than 90,000 complete Opel Tigra TwinTop Roadsters since launching that vehicle's

production in 2004. Another successful line was the rear seat structure for the Renault Modus, introduced in 2007, and entirely engineered by Heuliez. Heuliez has announced plans to market a line of electric vehicles under its own name by 2010.

After a difficult financial period in the middle of the first decade of the 21st century, Heuliez brought in a new majority shareholder, in the form of India's Argentum Motors, which acquired a 60 percent stake in Heuliez in 2008. Argentum has promised to maintain Heuliez's design and engineering and assembly operations in France, while moving manufacturing to its lower-wage facilities in India. Following the investment, Heuliez adopted a new three-part company structure: Heuliez Electric; Heuliez Engineering and Design; and Heuliez Manufacturing. The Heuliez family remains a major shareholder in the company, and Paul Quéveau, great-grandson of the company's founder, is the company's CEO. According to Quéveau, the company's revenues reached EUR 180 million ($220 million) in 2008.

FROM COACHES TO CARS

The Heuliez family was involved in the coach-building industry as early as the start of the 19th century. Born in 1776, Louis Heulier (the family changed the spelling of its name after a clerk's calligraphy suggested a "z" instead of an "r" at the end) became a noted cartwright in Cerizay before his death in 1843. The Heuliez family continued to produce and repair carts, carriages, and wheelbarrows into the next century. Adolphe Heuliez, born in 1854, took over the family business at the

COMPANY PERSPECTIVES

One of the ace cards regarding our know-how is that we move a process team in with the product teams, from the very beginning of a project. Our design brings all the project players together in a single development scheme and in one place. This know-how extends to other automobile areas, in addition to engines and suspensions, developed by us with our partners. Heuliez has the experience and adjusts its product and process development to suit the manufacturing rates. We handle everything from very small runs (a few parts per day) to very high production rates (8,000 parts/day). Decision-making procedures are always fast and efficient because of our size and our concern to maintain flexibility and customer listening at all costs.

beginning of the 20th century, and maintained an active repair business. He was joined by his son Louis, born in 1887.

In 1920, the father-son team launched a new carriage-making business, Carrosserie Heuliez. That company specialized in producing horse-drawn carriages in the English style. Louis Heuliez became head of the company in 1922 and under his direction led the company into a new direction: the automotive industry. In 1923, Heuliez invented a new method of rubberizing tires that would revolutionize the French automotive industry. Heuliez called his invention the Elastic Rubber Tyre, and before long Heuliez began supplying the new tire type throughout France.

This success encouraged Heuliez to investigate other areas of the automotive sector. The company turned its carriage-making experience toward the market for automobile bodies, which at the time were still constructed on a wood frame. For this Heuliez teamed up with Peugeot, supplying the station wagon body for the Peugeot 177B in 1925. The success of this venture led to a long-term relationship between the two companies, which continued into the 21st century. By 1932, Heuliez had produced its first bus body, also based on a wood frame.

Heuliez became interested in American automotive construction methods, particularly their use of steel frames. By 1936, Heuliez had developed its own steel-based auto frame, which it launched under the Robustacier (literally, "strong steel") name. In the early 1930s,

Louis Heuliez's sons, twins Henri and Pierre, entered the family business. By the end of the decade, the company employed 60 people.

The brothers took over the company after their father's death in 1947. At the time, Heuliez was struggling for survival. Cerizay had been largely destroyed by the Nazis during the occupation, and the company's workforce had been cut in half. Nevertheless, the brothers were determined to rebuild the company, with Henri taking charge of its industrial operations and Pierre leading its engineering and design wing. Heuliez, which had continued to operate from a small workshop in the center of Cerizay, moved to new quarters on the outskirts of town. That site provided room for Heuliez's future expansion, as the original workshop grew from 1,000 square meters to more than 64,000 square meters by the end of the 1960s.

The need to rebuild Cerizay provided the company with a new direction. The Nazis had destroyed Cerizay's school, and the town turned to Heuliez to supply the school with new furniture. Heuliez applied its Robustacier technology to the production of desks and other school equipment. By 1952, the company decided to create a full-fledged company for this market. Before long, the Robustacier brand became the largest in France, supplying furniture to some 60 percent of the country's schools. Heuliez later spun off the furniture operation into a merger with Behin, creating Behin Robustacier in 1971.

NEW DIRECTIONS

Heuliez adopted new serial production techniques in 1953. This move not only allowed the company to increase the volume of its production but also to diversify its lines. The company added the production of light and medium weight truck bodies, as well as vans and ambulances, in the 1950s. By the end of the decade, the company had developed its first buses, in partnership with Citroën.

The introduction of press-molding equipment in 1961 permitted the company to begin developing and producing individual components for the automotive industry. At first, this production was limited to small and medium production runs. In 1965, however, the company added a new factory, in nearby Bressuire. There the company launched production of a number of components, such as doors for the new Peugeot 404 and seats for the Citroën 2CV.

The arrival of Gérard Quéveau into the business provided another new direction for the company. An engineer, Quéveau had completed an internship at Heuliez while a student in the 1950s. He then married

1920: Adolphe Heuliez founds a carriage-making business in Cerizay, France.

1922: Heuliez's son Louis takes over as head of the company and leads it into supplying bodies and components for the automotive sector.

1953: Heuliez launches serial production for the first time.

1961: Heuliez begins vehicle prototyping with a convertible concept car for Citroën.

1995: Heuliez receives a contract to produce a fleet of electric cars.

2000: The company's retractable hardtop system for convertibles is incorporated into the Peugeot 206 CC.

2004: Heuliez launches production of the complete Opel Tigra TwinTop; introduces its Cleanova electric power technology developed in partnership with Dassault.

2008: Heuliez sells a 60 percent stake to India's Argentum and announces plans to market its Friendly electric power cars by 2010.

into the family, and joined the company in 1961. Quéveau's influence led Heuliez into the development of prototype vehicles for the major automotive companies, starting with a convertible concept car for Citroën, a four-door version of the DS. While neither this vehicle, nor several other vehicles developed by Heuliez, became production models, the company had more success with the Simca 1100 convertible and the Simca 1501 coupe, both introduced in 1968 and both of which went into production the following year.

In 1970, the company restructured its various businesses under a holding company, Holding Henri Heuliez. By then the group had extended its operations, based at a newly built factory in Bourg-en-Bresse, in France's Ain department, to produce vans and truck cabins and sleeping cabins for the Paul Berliet company. Berliet later purchased the Bourg-en-Bresse factory from Heuliez in 1984. By this time, the company had added a joint venture with Germany's Webasto, launched in 1982, to create sunroofs.

Berliet, which soon became Renault Vehicles Industriel (RVI), and Heuliez found themselves as rivals in the mid-1970s. In 1975 Heuliez received an order to develop the bodies for the Mercedes O 305 bus. The design of the O 305 proved superior both in

performance and sound levels to its French counterparts, and began gaining a major share of the French bus market. Heuliez continued to develop for Mercedes, adding an articulated bus in 1979. In response to the gains made by Mercedes in France, RVI turned to the government, which pressured Heuliez into developing bodies for RVI's buses instead, starting in 1984. By the beginning of 1991, Heuliez had sold majority control of Heuliez Bus to RVI and Volvo Bus Corporation.

AUTOMOTIVE FOCUS

Led by Gérard Quéveau, Heuliez refocused itself around its core automotive sector operations in the 1990s. The company sold more of its operations, including its ambulance division, based in Saint Laurent sur Sevre since 1985, to GIFA in 1992. The following year, the company sold its part of the sunroof joint venture to Webasto.

In the meantime, the creation of the PSA automotive company, which regrouped the Peugeot and Citroën operations, provided the company with new sources of orders. In the early 1980s, the company was tapped to develop and produce the station wagon version of the Citroën BX, one of France's most popular vehicles in the late decades of the 20th century and considered by some to be one of the most comfortable cars ever designed. After the BX ceased production in 1992, Heuliez added new Citroën models, including the luxury-class XM, and from the mid-1990s, the Xantia.

Citroën's decision, made in 1998, to end production of the Xantia by 2002 forced Heuliez to seek to diversify its client base. The company added a contract to produce the Microcar Lyra. This was a "license-free" electric vehicle, a French peculiarity for those who were either too young or otherwise unable to obtain driving licenses, which had limited top speeds of around 30 miles per hour. Heuliez also was awarded a contract to produce minivan taxis powered by natural gas for the Malaysian market.

Heuliez had also been developing its expertise in the late 1990s and into the beginning of the new century in two more areas that were to prove important to the group over the next decade. Through the 1990s, Heuliez had been investing in new technologies that enabled it to introduce a retractable hardtop roofing system for convertible automobiles. The technology enabled the company to secure a major new order in 2000, to produce the roofing module for the new Peugeot 206 CC convertible introduced that year. The model proved a huge success, and through the middle of the decade Heuliez produced more than 350,000 modules.

The success of the 206 brought the company a major order from Opel. In 2004, Heuliez launched production of the complete Opel Tigra TwinTop, a two-seater roadster that featured Heuliez's retractable hardtop. Other orders followed, including rear seats for the Renault Modus and the Range Rover, front seats for certain Ford models, and the body for the Citroën C6.

ELECTRIC FUTURE IN THE 21ST CENTURY

Heuliez had by this time come under the direction of the next generation of the family, Paul Quéveau, son of Gérard Quéveau. Nevertheless, the Tigra TwinTop failed to excite the consumer public. By 2007, only 90,000 or so of the model had been sold, falling far short of initial projections and throwing Heuliez into financial disarray. By the end of the year, the company had gone bankrupt and had been forced to turn to its banks for protection, while it sought a new investor to ensure its survival.

The other major direction taken by Heuliez since the mid-1990s provided the company with hope for its future. Heuliez had begun exploring electric vehicle technologies as early as the beginning of the 1980s, when its bus division produced the first electric bus to appear on France's city streets. In the mid-1990s, Heuliez returned its focus to developing electric vehicles. In 1995, the company received the contract to produce a fleet of electric cars for PSA based on the Peugeot 106 and the Citroën Saxo models. While this production remained somewhat limited—to fewer than 6,500 vehicles up to 2003—it provided the company with valuable experience with electric-powered vehicles.

The increasing alarm over the destruction of the environment and the depletion of the world's fossil fuel sources heightened the demand for vehicles capable of operating on alternative fuel sources from around 2005. Heuliez stepped up to the challenge, forming an alliance with industrial and construction giant Dassault to develop a new generation of electric power trains. By 2004, the company had debuted its new technology, dubbed Cleanova, introducing its first prototypes that year.

Heuliez was also determined to develop its own automotive models. In 2008, the company unveiled two new automobile lines. The first, an electric-powered utility van called the Pelican, was slated to go into production by the end of the year, becoming the first vehicle in the company's history to sport the Heuliez brand name. While that vehicle was destined for the government and professional sector, Heuliez also introduced its own line of electric-powered automobiles, the Friendly, production of which was expected to begin in 2010.

In the meantime, Heuliez appeared to have found the investor to bring it out of bankruptcy and bankroll its future growth. In October 2008, the company signed an agreement transferring 60 percent of its stock to India's Argentum Motors. The deal called for Argentum to invest EUR 10 million ($12 million) into Heuliez immediately, with another EUR 10 million to follow over the next five years.

With new owners, Heuliez restructured its business into three components, Heuliez Electric, Heuliez Engineering and Design, and Heuliez Manufacturing. While the first two divisions were expected to maintain their operations in France, Heuliez Manufacturing was expected to transfer much of its manufacturing operations to India in order to take advantage of that country's lower wages.

The global economic collapse of late 2008 seemed to threaten the Argentum rescue of Heuliez, as the Indian company failed to pay the EUR 10 million it owed by the end of November 2008. However, both Argentum and Heuliez pointed to the turmoil in the financial markets as the cause of the delay, and Argentum reaffirmed its commitment to the Heuliez rescue. In the meantime, Heuliez continued working toward the launch of the Friendly, hoping that the electric vehicle would provide new power to its future.

M. L. Cohen

PRINCIPAL DIVISIONS

Heuliez Electric; Heuliez Engineering and Design; Heuliez Manufacturing.

PRINCIPAL COMPETITORS

Faurecia S.A.; Valeo S.A.; Automobiles Citroën S.A.; Groupe FMC France S.A.S.

FURTHER READING

"Argentum Acquires Controlling Stake in Heuliez," *Auto Business News,* August 18, 2008.

Armitage, Tom, "Heuliez Gives Chery a Piece of the Sky," *Automotive News Europe,* September 17, 2007, p. 16.

Ciferri, Luca, "Heuliez Expects Boom in Hardtop Market," *Automotive News,* July 17, 2006, p. 18A.

Engerbau, Philippe, "L'Indien Argentum Demande un Delai," *La Nouvelle Republique,* November 29, 2008.

Gay, Bertrand, "Heuliez Lancera un Vehicule Electrique en 2010," *Les Echos,* October 3, 2008.

McVeigh, Paul, "Argentum Motors Takes Control of Heuliez," *Automotive News Europe,* August 18, 2008, p. 4.

Morton, Ian, "Blue Skies Ahead for Convertible Market," *Automotive News Europe,* September 6, 2004, p. 23.

Murris, Christine, "Heuliez à l'Heure Indienne," *Valeurs Actuelles,* October 23, 2008.

"New Heuliez Competitive Car," *Interlink,* October 26, 2008.

Norrito, Gaspard, "Heuliez se Relance avec la Voiture Electrique," *Ouest-France,* October 1, 2008.

Oliveira, Paulo Soares de, "Car Building Is in Heuliez CEO Queveau's Blood," *Automotive News,* September 17, 2007, p. 11.

Saint-Seine, Sylviane de, "Heuliez Family Could Cede Control," *Automotive News Europe,* December 11, 2006, p. 1.

Snyder, Jesse, "Hey Macarena! Heuliez Shows Glass Roof that Fits in Trunk," *Automotive News Europe,* February 6, 2006, p. 18.

Wright, Rebecca, "Can Electric Cars Save Coachbuilders?" *Automotive News Europe,* May 12, 2008, p. 18.

Hay Group Holdings, Inc.

———————■———————

The Wanamaker Building
100 Penn Square East
Philadelphia, Pennsylvania 19107-3388
U.S.A.
Telephone: (215) 861-2000
Fax: (215) 861-2111
Web site: http://www.haygroup.com

Private Company
Incorporated: 1946
Employees: 2,800
Sales: $443 million (2008 est.)
NAICS: 541611 Business Management Consulting
  Services; 551112 Offices of Other Holding
  Companies

■ ■ ■

Hay Group Holdings, Inc., is the holding company for Hay Group and a group of management consulting companies that help clients develop business strategies, develop leadership, and implement effective employee evaluation and compensation programs. Among Hay Group's more than 7,000 clients are such industry giants as ABC India, Standard & Poor's, Wal-Mart, and the Arab African International Bank, as well as several not-for-profit and educational organizations. Hay developed the standards for evaluating public "admiration" for corporations and advises more than three-quarters of *Fortune* magazine's top 50 most-admired firms. Since opening its first international branch in 1963, Hay has expanded to operate 85 offices in 47 countries.

The Hay Group lists the design and analysis of organizations as its key area of expertise. In addition, the company has developed expertise in designing management and employee compensation packages and remunerations systems. The Hay Group's clients include chemical manufacturing and distribution firms, educational institutions, financial services companies, healthcare organizations, manufacturing firms, oil and gas companies, public and not-for-profit companies, and telecommunications companies.

FOUNDATIONS AND GROWTH

Edward N. Hay, then personnel manager for First Pennsylvania Bank of Philadelphia, founded the company that later became Hay Group, Inc., in 1943. Working from a small office space he rented from First Pennsylvania, Hay began consulting to emerging companies, helping them find ways to streamline and improve their hiring and employee management services.

As a former deputy administrator of the U.S. Office of Price Administration during World War II, Hay had developed expertise in employee evaluation and the development of pay scale systems, skills he marketed when he started his consulting business. His first major contract came in 1945 when General Foods, Inc., asked Hay to evaluate the company's management structure. Hay examined every aspect of the company's management system, which included 450 managers in various

COMPANY PERSPECTIVES

We believe that the key to business success is to ensure that employees are correctly motivated, rewarded and clearly aware of their contribution and the part it plays in business strategy. Our clients come to us for comprehensive services and support critical to their maximizing the performance of their people and turning their strategy into reality. Drawing on pioneering research and world-leading databases, we can help you ensure that your people are working in line with your strategy, in jobs that are appropriate to their skills. This will deliver results that both you and they can see and appreciate.

positions, and recommended unique methods for evaluating manager performance and establishing an equitable pay scale.

Word spread of Hay's successful work with his various clients and soon his services were in high demand. Hay's unusual but highly successful evaluation methods established him as a pioneer in business organization. In 1946 Hay incorporated his company as E.N. Hay & Associates and by 1949 Hay was billing over $100,000 annually from his clients.

Hay not only wanted to develop more effective methods to evaluate organizations but also wanted to make his methods available for general use in organizations. In the 1940s Hay purchased the rights to the publication *Personnel Journal,* which allowed him to publish his ideas on management consultation. In 1950 Hay began publishing *Men and Management,* a single-page newsletter containing updates in management evaluation techniques.

In 1949 Hay hired Dale Purves, an expert in upper-level management who was a fellow member of the War Labor Board during World War II. Before signing on with Hay, Purves worked as general manager for La Consolidae, a Mexican steel manufacturing company. Purves and Hay developed the "Hay Guide Charts," a new method of organizational evaluation that was popularized through publications in *Personnel.* Using the Guide Charts, Hay and Purves developed what they called the "Chart-Profile Method of Job Evaluation." The Chart-Profile Method places focus on evaluating each job with regard to the goals of the company and the intended function of the position in question.

INTRODUCING PSYCHOLOGY-BASED ANALYSES

Hay's general principles were developed over more than 60 years into a point/value system of analysis based on three factors: accountability, know-how, and problem solving. By evaluating positions, rather than employees, Hay allowed businesses to compare pay rates among companies offering similar positions, thereby setting industry standards and allowing companies to develop competitive strategies for recruitment. Another important factor in developing Hay's unique system was the integration of psychological analysis into the job evaluation process. Hay hired Milton L. Rock, a local Philadelphian with a Ph.D. in psychology, to help develop psychological assessment processes for the company's evaluation programs.

In 1954 Hay introduced the Hay Compensation Survey Comparisons, which drew information from eight corporations to begin the process of building a comparative database of employee compensation. Within three years Hay Group was billing more than $500,000 annually and rapidly becoming one of the most respected management-consulting firms in the nation. Edward Hay died in 1958 at age 67, and management of the company shifted into a partnership with co-managers Milton Rock and Dale Purves.

EXPANSION AND INTERNATIONAL GROWTH

Under the leadership of Rock and Purves, Hay Group expanded outside Philadelphia for the first time with the establishment of a district office in Toronto, Canada, in 1960. The strategic move to Canada also provided Hay Group with access to an untapped Canadian market. Revenues continued to grow and, three years later, the company established its first international office in London, England, a country with a rapidly expanding consultation market. Hay's Guide Chart Method was soon gaining an international reputation as one of the most effective systems in play. In 1965 the company posted over $1 million in billed revenues annually and opened their second U.S. office in San Francisco, California.

After the death of Dale Purves in 1966 Rock was left as the sole managing partner. Rock grew the company through strategic acquisitions and aggressive expansion of international operations. In 1968 Hay acquired Chicago-based Marketing Management, Inc., and that same year opened a new office in Chicago. In 1970 the Hay Group was reporting more than $5 million in revenues and, within four years, billing would triple to exceed $15 million.

KEY DATES

1943: Edward N. Hay and Associates is founded in Philadelphia.

1945: The company wins its first major contract with General Foods.

1946: The company is incorporated as E.N. Hay & Associates.

1950: Hay begins publishing *Men and Management* newsletter.

1954: Hay initiates the first Compensation Survey Comparisons.

1958: Hay becomes a partnership under Milt Rock and Dale Purves.

1960: Hay opens an office in Canada to expand client base.

1963: Hay opens its first overseas office in London.

1965: Annual billing for the company exceeds $1 million.

1968: Hay acquires Chicago-based Marketing-Management, Inc.

1970: Billing surpasses $5 million.

1974: Hay acquires Huggins & Co, Inc., and enters actuarial services.

1980: Hay enters the communications business with three new subsidiary companies.

1984: Saatchi & Saatchi Company, PLC, acquires the Hay Group; annual billing passes $100 million.

1985: Hay combines operations with McBer & Company.

1990: Internal management conducts a buyout; Hay becomes a private company again.

1998: Hay opens new world headquarters in Philadelphia.

1999: *Working with Emotional Intelligence* is published by the company.

2003: Hay celebrates 60 years in business.

During the 1970s, Hay Group expended a significant amount of revenue to develop their psychological evaluation and behavioral sciences departments. This began in 1971 when Hay created the Management Climate Analysis practice, combining behavioral and psychological studies to gain a better understanding of both working conditions and efficiency. Hay entered the benefits and actuarial business in 1974 with the purchase of Huggins & Co., Inc. The new subsidiary was renamed Hay Huggins Co. The

company specialized in compensation and benefits consulting, actuarial management, and industrial management. Hay then expanded operations at Hay Huggins Co. to include consultations for mergers and start-ups.

Hay Group's international expansion continued in Europe, including the establishment of new offices in Italy and France. Hay underwent a major expansion in 1979 with the acquisition of Italian corporation ISSO, a company providing management training consultation and training programs for upper management. Hay France acquired Gamma International, a company involved in the design and development of management information systems. The purchase of Gamma International was important in that it allowed Hay to expand into the software production business.

In 1980 Hay entered another facet of the consulting business with the establishment of three new communications subsidiaries: Hay Communications Limited, Information for Industry, Inc., and Pentacle. Hay Group's new communications subsidiaries placed the company in prime position to advertise their services across industry lines and provided another avenue for future growth.

ACQUISITION BY SAATCHI & SAATCHI

In 1984 London-based Saatchi & Saatchi, PLC, at the time Europe's largest advertising agency and the parent company of U.S.-based Saatchi & Saatchi Compton, acquired Hay Group in a deal estimated at $125 million. At the time of the buyout Hay Group operated 94 offices in 27 countries. Milt Rock remained on staff as chairman of the newly named Saatchi Consulting. That same year the Saatchi Company announced billing in excess of $100 million. Hay Group was the third U.S. company acquired by Saatchi & Saatchi since 1982, a group which also included the former Compton Advertising Company.

The following year Saatchi & Saatchi decided to combine Hay with Boston-based McBer & Company, a human resources firm that specialized in management planning and analysis. McBer & Company was responsible for developing several unique measures of business climate analysis. These were combined with Hay Group's tools and services over the next several years.

Milt Rock retired in 1985, after overseeing the early stages of the merger with McBer & Company, and was replaced by Charles Fiero as CEO. Within a year, Robert Rock succeeded Fiero as CEO and the following year Chris Matthews was appointed to the position, replacing Rock. Matthews had joined the company in 1975 and worked in a variety of positions in upper management before the board of directors appointed him chief executive.

In 1989 Saatchi & Saatchi sold controlling shares of Gamma International S.A., for a reported price of $12.4 million. The following year a group of managers and Hay's 135 partners partnered with an outside investor group to acquire controlling stock of Hay Group from Saatchi & Saatchi for a reported price of $80 million and a $10 million dollar subordinated note. Saatchi had been attempting to divest itself of its various consulting companies for most of the year and chose to accept the investment group's offer after a previous offer of $120 million fell through. The decision to sell was motivated by more than $11 million in losses over the previous fiscal year, which forced the company to reduce its operations to 80 offices in 29 countries.

REBUILDING AND RESTRUCTURING

Despite losses, Hay Group was billing for more than $200 million in 1990. The following year Hay published a new book, *The Hay Group Guide to Executive Compensation.* Reviews were mixed but the book helped Hay to garner additional attention for its publishing and management expertise businesses. Also in 1991 Hay became involved in a debate over whether Canadian subsidies were harming U.S. alfalfa exports to Asia. Studies released over the next few months supported Hay Group's position in the conflict.

In 1997 Hay Group debuted their Seven Lever Integrated Change Management Model. According to the model, each of the Seven Levers—values and culture, core processes, individual and team competence, leadership, organization, team and job design, reward and recognition, management processes and systems—must be aligned according to the strategic goals of the organization or the desired result of the change the organization is attempting to implement. Also that year the Hay Group conducted its first annual survey of "The World's Most Admired Companies" for *Fortune* magazine. Over the next decade, Hay Group's survey of admiration would become one of the best-known company products and a trusted measure of public image in business. In 2002 Hay Group would add another list, "America's most Admired Companies," to their annual surveys for *Fortune.*

In 1998 Hay Group opened a new worldwide headquarters in Philadelphia, Pennsylvania, where the company was founded. In 1999 author Daniel Goleman published the book *Working with Emotional Intelligence*

using research collected by the Hay Group. Over the next few years the concept of "Emotional Intelligence" would become a popular topic in discussions of business efficacy.

By 2000, Hay Group had returned to profitability and growth. Growth was recorded in the logistics-to-recruitment, personnel, and commercial divisions. Analysis of the Hay Group's success indicated that the company's ability to capitalize on industry trends, such as adapting to increased outsourcing in the public and private sectors, contributed to their success in increasing profit margins. The personnel portion of Hay's business was its most profitable, accounting for more than 40 percent of the company's total profits. Hay Group also tapped into emerging trends with strong investment into the Internet industry and teamed with Internet research companies to produce a strong information technology development area.

Hay Group celebrated its 60th year in business in 2003 with a growth strategy that included a focus on international expansion. By the following year, with new offices opened in Johannesburg, South Africa; New Delhi, India; and Tel Aviv, Israel, the company had offices in 43 countries. In India, Hay won an 18-month contract to conduct a comprehensive survey of Indian CEOs. In 2008 Hay Group was a global leader in management consulting. With more than 85 offices in 47 countries, the company was also strategically placed for international growth. Amid widespread recession during this time, Hay Group would likely be called upon to help its clients rethink growth strategies and implement reasonable reactions to tough economic times.

Micah Issitt

PRINCIPAL SUBSIDIARIES

Hay Group Investment Holding B.V.; Hay Acquisition Company, Inc.; Hay Interim, Inc.; McBer and Company, Inc.

PRINCIPAL COMPETITORS

Watson Wyatt, Inc.; Mercer LLC; Towers Perrin.

FURTHER READING

Avakian, Laura, "The Hay Group Guide to Executive Compensation," *Physician Executive,* September–October 1991, pp. 47+.

"Dale Purves Dead; Industry Adviser, 64," *New York Times,* May 15, 1966, p. 88.

Davis, Riccardo A., "Hay Group Management Buys Consulting Unit from Parent," *Philadelphia Business Journal,* June 11, 1990.

Dougherty, Philip H., "Advertising: Saatchi & Saatchi Acquires Hay Group," *New York Times,* November 14, 1984.

Goleman, Daniel, Richard E. Boyatzis, and Annie McKee, *Primal Leadership: Realizing the Power of Emotional Intel-* *ligence,* Cambridge, Mass.: Harvard Business Press, 2002.

Heracleous, Loizos, *Strategy and Organization: Realizing Strategic Management,* Cambridge, U.K.: Cambridge University Press, 2003.

Tyson, Shaun, *Essentials of Human Resource Management,* Boston, Mass.: Butterworth-Heinemann, 2006.

Herman Goldner
Company, Inc.

———■———

7777 **Brewster Avenue**
Philadelphia, Pennsylvania 19153
U.S.A.
Telephone: (215) 365-5400
Fax: (215) 492-6274
Web site: http://www.goldner.com

Private Company
Incorporated: 1919
Employees: 225
Sales: $80 million (2007 est.)
NAICS: 423710 Hardware and Plumbing and Heating Equipment and Supplies Merchant Wholesalers; 423720 Plumbing and Heating Equipment and Supplies (Hydronics) Merchant Wholesalers; 238220 Plumbing, Heating, and Air-Conditioning Contractors

■ ■ ■

Headquartered in Philadelphia, Pennsylvania, Herman Goldner Company, Inc., is one of the largest mechanical construction and maintenance companies in the northeastern United States. Over more than a century, the Goldner Company has assisted in the construction and facilities maintenance of several of the most prominent building projects in the Philadelphia area, including the city's sports complexes, hospitals, and educational institutions. With revenues exceeding $70 million annually and contracts shared with dozens of local construction firms, Goldner has become an anchor in the Philadelphia community and one of the city's dominant construction corporations.

BASEMENT BEGINNINGS

Herman J. Goldner, founder of Herman Goldner Company, Inc., started his mechanical services company in the basement of his family home on Hancock Street in Philadelphia, Pennsylvania, in 1887. Using a horse-drawn cart, Goldner helped customers install plumbing and electrical services in their homes. The company was incorporated in Pennsylvania in 1919. In 1924, Goldner occupied a building at 425 West Lehigh Avenue, which would remain the company's headquarters until 1964.

After Herman J. Goldner's death in 1929, control of the company passed to his eldest son, Roy J. Goldner, who led the company through the difficult economic crisis of the Depression Era. The 1930s and 1940s were a difficult time for most companies in the Philadelphia area, as the economy suffered from the effects of the Great Depression and World War II, and many of Goldner's competitors were forced to close. Goldner was able to survive by expanding services and capitalizing on innovative developments in heating and plumbing technology.

Upon the death of Roy Goldner in 1943, control of the company passed to Herman W. Goldner, youngest son of the founder, who had been part of the company since 1929 and served in a variety of positions including vice-president and treasurer. It was under the leadership of Herman W. Goldner that the company became one of the leading mechanical construction firms in Philadelphia. With large-scale projects across the city,

COMPANY PERSPECTIVES

Meeting the needs of our customers is paramount within our organization. Our experienced team of Account Executives, Project Managers, Engineers and Skilled Tradesmen offer our clients quality, cost-effective solutions.

Goldner became a full-service mechanical construction company handling plumbing, wastewater collection, and HVAC (heating, ventilating, and air conditioning). After the death of Herman W. Goldner in 1959, the presidency passed to David R. Super, who managed the company until his retirement in 1964, when the presidency passed to Herman E. Goldner, grandson of the founder.

In 1964, Goldner moved from its main office on Lehigh Avenue to a new facility at 133 Hunting Park Avenue. The Goldner family had been living outside the Philadelphia area since Herman E. Goldner moved his family out of the city in 1959 upon his return from a term of military service. As the company was outgrowing its facilities, Goldner and the other board members were considering leaving the city. In an effort to keep the company in the city and preserve employment opportunities for local laborers, the Philadelphia Industrial Development Corporation (PIDC) helped Goldner to obtain a low-interest mortgage for their new Hunting Park headquarters.

Business increased sharply in the 1960s and 1970s, reaching more than $20 million annually by 1976. As the company grew, they expanded into new areas, beginning with a branch headquarters in New Castle, Delaware, in 1970, which was intended to become the central location for the company's petrochemical and refinery divisions.

A PERIOD OF GROWTH AND EXPANSION

By 1979, the company had again expanded beyond the capacity of their Hunting Park facility and again considered leaving the metropolitan area. The PIDC intervened to keep Goldner in the city, offering to help the company obtain new headquarters at 7777 Brewster Avenue at a price of $59,000 for a property estimated at a market value of $310,000. The PIDC also agreed to contribute 40 percent of the construction costs, estimated at $1.25 million, for a new 100,000-square-foot facility.

In 1987 Goldner celebrated its 100th anniversary with a fourth generation of the Goldner family working for the company, as Herman W. Goldner began in the company's special projects division. The company was one of the ten largest contractors in the region and had successfully adjusted to new technological advancements in the industry. Strong financial growth continued throughout the 1980s and into the next decade.

In 1994, Spectrum Arena Limited Partnership engaged Goldner as a subcontractor to complete the HVAC system during the construction of the First Union Center. For the construction of the HVAC system, Goldner worked with a partner, Heat Transfer Technology (HTT), which in turn hired Cimco Corp. and Klenzoid Inc. to manufacture the equipment needed for the HVAC system. When the HVAC system was put into operation, it malfunctioned and resulted in a complete system failure. Goldner blamed the malfunction on Cimco Corp.'s use of steel piping, rather than copper, and on faulty construction by engineers at Klenzoid Inc. Goldner and HTT sued Klenzoid and Cimco for a breach of contract but were forced, in the meantime, to correct the problems with the HVAC system at a substantial loss in profit.

In 1995, the presidency shifted to Gerard C. Goldner, while Herman E. Goldner remained CEO. That same year, the company expanded its Brewster location with the construction of a 10,000-square-foot technical center, which became the headquarters for the company's computer-aided drafting and information technology divisions. Goldner also invested heavily in an effort to stay ahead of emerging technology, and developed a division to handle computer automation for clients, running various facilities within a building from a central control center.

ENTERING THE 21ST CENTURY

By 2000, Herman Goldner was the fourth largest contractor in the Northeast, with sales of over $85 million annually, and the 36th largest mechanical construction firm in the nation. That same year, Gerard C. Goldner was named CEO, as Stephen J. Williams, who worked as a division manager and later vice-president, became president and chief operating officer. Also that year, Goldner was hired to manage the air conditioning at the Republican National Convention held at the First Union Center in Philadelphia. Because of the television and electrical equipment needed for the convention, over 6,000 tons of additional cooling equipment was installed in the convention area.

In 2001, under the leadership of Williams, the company began streamlining its operations toward

KEY DATES

1887: Herman J. Goldner starts mechanical services company in the basement of his family home.

1919: Company is incorporated in Pennsylvania.

1929: After Herman J. Goldner's death, his eldest son, Roy J. Goldner, assumes control of the company.

1943: Control of the company passes to Herman W. Goldner, youngest son of the founder.

1959: Davis R. Super becomes company president.

1964: Herman E. Goldner, grandson of the founder, assumes the company presidency; company moves to new headquarters on Hunting Park Avenue.

1970: Company opens branch headquarters in Delaware.

1979: Company moves to new facility at Brewster Avenue.

1987: Company celebrates its 100th anniversary.

1995: Company expands with construction of a new technical center.

2000: Gerard C. Goldner becomes CEO.

2008: Gerald Goldner retires, and Herman W. Goldner, representing the fourth generation of family leadership, becomes CEO and president.

mechanical construction and away from industrial supply, which had become one of the company's focus areas in the 1970s and 1980s. In July 2001, the company sold the industrial supply division to Deacon Industrial Supply, while another division handling valve actuation was sold to Chalmers and Kubeck, Inc. That same year, Goldner completed one of the largest mechanical construction projects in the company's history at the Kimmel Center for the Performing Arts. The project involved the installation of air units, two cooling towers, three boilers, and all the connected ducts and structural modifications.

While the residential HVAC industry thrived in the early years of the new century due to rising temperatures during the summer months and economic growth in the middle class, the commercial HVAC market suffered. The recession of 2001 brought about a 14 percent reduction in the number of commercial and industrial HVAC system installations. In 2002, the number of large tonnage liquid chillers, machines generally used to cool large-scale building projects such as skyscrapers and stadiums, fell over 20 percent.

While residential and light commercial units were expected to drive another banner year, the outlook for nonresidential large-unit air conditioners and heat pumps was more guarded. While many industry observers believed commercial and industrial markets would recover somewhat, they acknowledged that their improvement would depend on how much the economy rebounded from the recession of 2001 that claimed millions of jobs and derailed office and industrial construction.

CHANGING FOCUS TO REMAIN PROFITABLE

Although Goldner experienced the effects of a declining HVAC market, a diverse list of services and prominent clients in the Philadelphia area allowed the company to maintain strong profit margins. Goldner also capitalized on a nationwide trend in renovation for educational institutions. According to industry analysis, higher education organizations across the country spent more than $60 billion between 2001 and 2005 for renovations. Goldner was awarded a major project to work on, the Swarthmore College Science Center, which included the installation of a comprehensive HVAC system, water management facilities, and a steam absorption chiller.

Other major projects beginning in 2002 included new construction on the Wachovia Center, a sports complex in Philadelphia and home of the Philadelphia Flyers professional ice hockey team. Goldner installed a water chilling and boiler system in the newly remodeled Wachovia Center.

Goldner engaged in a program to increase the environmental friendliness of its products in the early years of the new century. The program was partially in response to proposed Senate legislation calling for the total in renewable energy to reach 10 percent by 2020. By 2003, Goldner had installed more than 100 centrifugal chiller units and more than 1,000 geothermal heat pumps for commercial and industrial projects.

In 2003, Goldner secured a long-term service agreement with the city of Philadelphia to provide facilities management services for the Philadelphia Tri-Plex, a group of government buildings including the Criminal Justice Complex, Municipal Services Building, and the One Parkway Building. The services offered included HVAC installation and maintenance and building automation services. In addition, Goldner was asked to install York and Carrier gas-fired absorption chillers in the Tri-Plex.

Responding to public demands for improved air quality standards during this time, Goldner debuted CrispAir Duct Mounted Sanitizer units as a new product offering for the company's clients. The CrispAir units used ultraviolet light to sanitize the air pumped into a room and were shown in tests to significantly reduce the amount of mold, mildew, and other airborne bacteria present in circulated air. Goldner became the sole distributor of the new technology in the Philadelphia area to date.

LOOKING TO THE FUTURE

Goldner participated in the 2003 Philadelphia Cool Challenge, helping to provide free air conditioning to elderly, low-income households in Philadelphia and the surrounding areas. Over the course of the program, the foundation raised more than $55,000 and provided air conditioning to more than 300 homes in the region.

One of the largest projects in the first decade of the 2000s was a contract for a new pharmaceutical manufacturing facility for the Merck Pharmaceutical Company in West Point, Pennsylvania. The project was one of Goldner's first that focused on high purity stainless steel piping, a product line that had become a focus for the Goldner company in the several years prior to the contract. The project was also a major challenge for Goldner's design division, which produced over 1,600 isometric drawings of the facilities prior to the beginning of installation.

In 2005, the company worked on Citizens Bank Park, installing and servicing the ballpark's HVAC and automation services, and also won a contract to install a new boiler for the Lincoln Financial Field, the stadium used by the Philadelphia Eagles of the National Football League. That year Goldner also completed a project to replace six cooling units at King of Prussia Mall, in King of Prussia, Pennsylvania. Between 2005 and 2006,

Goldner replaced eight cooling towers in downtown Philadelphia.

In June 2008, Herman W. Goldner IV became the fourth generation of the Goldner family to serve as CEO of the company. From 1887 to 2008, the Herman Goldner Company had grown from a one-person operation to become one of the largest and most respected mechanical construction firms in the Philadelphia area. In addition to HVAC and construction, Goldner offered plumbing and electrical work and automated systems installation and maintenance and sanitary systems processing. With revenues exceeding $70 million annually and prominent long-term projects in place, Goldner was looking forward to growth in the future.

Micah Issitt

PRINCIPAL COMPETITORS

Sauer Inc.; John J. Kirlin Inc.; PPL Energy Services Holdings, LLC; HEC/Denron Plumbing & Hvac Inc.; Joule Industrial Contractors; PSEG Energy Technologies; EMCOR Group Inc.; John W. Danforth Co.

FURTHER READING

"FYI," *Air Conditioning, Heating & Refrigeration News*, September 18, 2000.

Gillespie, John T., "Firm to Stay in City with Offer of Cheap Land," *Evening Bulletin*, January 17, 1978.

"Goldner Wins Award for SAP Headquarters," *Contractor*, September 2000.

"Herman W. Goldner," *New York Times*, June 16, 1959, p. 35.

Mader, Robert P., "Goldner Goes to Bat for Phillies," *Contractor*, August 2003.

O'Connor, Marjie, "Deacon Industrial Supply Purchases Goldner Industrial Division Assets," *Supply House Times*, January 1, 2001.

Hero Group

Niederlenzer Kirchweg 6
Lenzburg, CH-5600
Switzerland
Telephone: (41 62) 885-5111
Fax: (41 62) 885-5430
Web site: http://www.hero-group.ch

Private Company
Incorporated: 1886 as Conservenfabrik Henckell &
   Zeiler
Employees: 3,500
Sales: CHF 1.9 billion ($1.6 billion) (2007)
NAICS: 311421 Fruit and Vegetable Canning; 311422
   Specialty Canning; 31123 Breakfast Cereal
   Manufacturing; 311411 Frozen Fruit, Juice, and
   Vegetable Manufacturing

■ ■ ■

Hero Group is a leading European manufacturer of
branded consumer food products, including baby food,
fruit jams and spreads, fruit-based chilled beverages,
baking aids and decorating products, and cereal bars.
The company's major brands are Hero in Switzerland;
Schwartau in Germany; Organix and Juvela in the
United Kingdom; Frio in the Netherlands; Casa de Mateus in Portugal; Semper in Sweden; Småfolk in
Norway; Sunar in the Czech Republic and Slovakia; Vitrac in Egypt; and Ülker Hero in Turkey.

Hero's subsidiary Beech-Nut Nutrition is the
second largest branded baby food manufacturer in the
United States. Its other American brands include Cake

Mate, Paas, Pumpkin Masters, and Houston Harvest.
About two-fifths of Hero's revenues stem from infant
nutrition products, and about one-third is generated by
fruit-based products. Headquartered in Lenzburg,
Switzerland, Hero has major subsidiaries in many
Western European countries as well as in Poland, the
Czech Republic, Slovakia, Turkey, Egypt, Japan, Russia,
and Ukraine. Non-European sales account for approximately one-quarter of total revenues. The company
is owned by German entrepreneur Arend Oetker.

SMALL CANNING FACTORY
BECOMES PUBLIC CORPORATION

In 1886 two former classmates from Hanover, Gustav
Henckell and Gustav Zeiler, established a canned fruit
and vegetable company in Lenzburg, a Swiss city about
halfway between Basel and Zurich. The company was
called Conservenfabrik Henckell & Zeiler. Henckell, a
traveling salesman for a Munich-based canned food
firm, and Zeiler, an experienced gardener and fruit
farmer, purchased or leased several pieces of fertile farm
land around Lenzburg, an area that was well protected
from frost and extreme weather by the surrounding
mountains.

Henckell & Zeiler started growing strawberries,
green peas, and green beans because they were not available on the market in the quality and quantities needed.
In the first half of 1886, a small canning factory was set
up in Lenzburg that soon began putting out strawberry
jam, canned green peas, and green beans. A first large
order for about 11,000 pounds of canned vegetables was
received by Zurich-based Thayssen & Cie in the same
year.

COMPANY PERSPECTIVES

We strive to be the most innovative nutrition company in our core categories, serving our demanding consumers worldwide. *Mission Statement.* We develop, innovate continually and remain dedicated to products of superior quality in order to exceed our consumers' changing and increasing expectations. *Our Values.* Honesty and fairness are essential to the way we do business. We are a family company that keeps its promises. We do what we say we will do and will conduct ourselves in accordance with our code of ethics.

Soon it became obvious that Henckell & Zeiler's initial capital deposit was not sufficient to sustain the business. In December 1886 a third investor was found in local businessman Carl Roth. In 1888, Roth became a shareholder as well, and the company was renamed Henckell, Zeiler & Roth. When Zeiler died unexpectedly in 1889, Henckell and Roth remained as shareholders, and the company name was changed to Henckell & Roth. Henckell was responsible for production and sales, while Roth handled the finances. In 1898 the company was converted to a public corporation and renamed Conservenfabrik Lenzburg, vormals Henckell & Roth AG.

BRANDED PRODUCTS AND RAPID EXPANSION SPUR DYNAMIC GROWTH

A period of dynamic growth for the company ensued. The share capital of CHF 600,000, 15 times the amount of the company's initial share capital, enabled Conservenfabrik Lenzburg to expand rapidly. A first major step in that direction was a merger with Switzerland's oldest canned vegetables manufacturer Conservenfabrik Frauenfeld in 1906. Founded in 1868, Burkhardt-Gänsli was based in Frauenfeld, northeast of Zurich, and it added spinach, carrots, Spanish salsify, and other canned vegetables to the company's product range. Frauenfeld's director, Hans Wälli, joined Conservenfabrik Lenzburg as managing director.

In 1910 the company introduced a brand name that would become one of Switzerland's best-known brands for canned vegetables and fruit jam: Hero, a word that incorporated H and R, representing Henckell and Roth. A new and unique logo was created, featuring

three tin cans. As the demand for Conservenfabrik Lenzburg's products soared, particularly among urban consumers, the company invested in additional production capacity. By 1912 Conservenfabrik Lenzburg was selling more than 30 different fruit jams under the Hero label to individual consumers as well as to commercial customers.

Between 1912 and 1939 Conservenfabrik Lenzburg added to its operations five more factories in Switzerland. One acquisition, completed in 1917, was of Wurst- und Fleischwarenfabrik Lenzburg, a manufacturer of fresh and canned meat products and, in fact, Switzerland's first producer of canned meat products. Also during this time a new canned food subsidiary was set up in Hallau, about 20 miles north of Zurich.

In the mid-1920s Hero took over two more Swiss canned food manufacturers, Conservenfabrik Saxon, 50 miles south of Bern, and Conservenfabrik Seetal AG located in Seon, south of Lenzburg. Another important step toward a more diversified product range was taken in 1933 when Hero launched Parmadoro, a variety of canned tomato-based products. Three years later Conservenfabrik Seetal successfully introduced canned ravioli under the name Super Raviolini alla Milanese. Canned ravioli and other pasta products would remain in Hero's product range although they would never achieve the same market share as the company's main products: fruit jams and canned vegetables.

INTERNATIONAL EXPANSION, GENERATION CHANGE, AND WORLD WARS

Beginning in 1912, Hero went to great lengths to conquer new geographic markets. Soon the company shipped its products to far-away lands such as China and South America. At the same time, Hero began to establish production subsidiaries abroad. The first one, Conserves Lenzbourg, was set up in Lyon, France, in 1912. Two years later, a second business venture abroad was established with one of Hero's longtime suppliers, the Dutch fruit and vegetable trading firm A.G.T. Jansen & Zoon. Located in Breda, a very fertile region of the Netherlands, N.V. Hero Conserven at first supplied various fruits and vegetables to Hero.

World War I interrupted the company's expansion abroad. During the war, Conserves Lenzbourg in Lyon was sequestered by the French. International expansion resumed in the 1920s. In 1920, additional land was bought near Breda, where a new canning factory was built. Two years later Hero took over Spanish fruit producer Champagne Frères Ltd. in Alcantarilla, about

KEY DATES

1886: Gustav Henckell and Gustav Zeiler establish a canned food company in Lenzburg.
1898: The company goes public.
1906: Wälli/Sultzberger, Switzerland's oldest canned food manufacturer, merges with Hero.
1910: Hero is introduced as a brand name.
1936: Hero subsidiary Conservenfabrik Seetal successfully launches canned ravioli as an Italian delicacy.
1949: A canned food joint venture is set up in Brazil.
1967: Hero acquires a majority stake in Italian canned food manufacturer Lido.
1987: The company takes over Swiss pasta manufacturers Robert Ernst, Adolf Montag, and Gebr. Weilenmann.
1995: Hero is acquired by the German Schwartau group and is grouped with Schwartau's non-German subsidiaries.
2003: Arend Oetker acquires Hero's publicly traded shares and takes the company private.
2004: Hero enters the baby food business.

25 miles north of the Mediterranean port of Cartagena. Champagne Frères mainly produced canned fruits including peaches, apricots, oranges, pears, and cherries.

Meanwhile, the output of Hero's Swiss farming operations was no longer sufficient to meet demand. Therefore, the company began to contract with local farmers who were willing to follow the company's quality guidelines. During the 1930s, a growing number of farmers around Lenzburg supplied Hero with apples, plums, berries, cherries, and various vegetables. By 1936, the company's 50th year in business, Hero's domestic workforce had grown to about 400 employees. During the harvest season, which lasted from June until September, more than 600 additional workers were employed at the company's main factories in Lenzburg, Frauenfeld, and Hallau. In addition to a broad variety of fruit jams, canned fruit and vegetables, and canned meat products, the company manufactured fruit-based syrups and specialties for commercial bakeries and confectioners. All in all, the company offered 270 different products in packaging sizes ranging from small cans and jars for consumers to large wooden barrels for commercial customers.

During the first decades of the 20th century, the next generation of family managers and shareholders joined the enterprise. After company founder Gustav Henckell married the widow of his deceased business partner Gustav Zeiler in 1897, his stepson, Gustav Ferdinand Zeiler, a mechanical engineer, had become a proxy in his father's company in 1912. In 1925 Zeiler became head of Hero's administrative board of directors.

In addition to his responsibilities at Hero, Zeiler established a second company for the production of inexpensive and light cardboard packaging for transporting tin cans, which were then sold to Hero as well as to other canned food manufacturers. In 1927, Eduard Wälli, the son of Hans Wälli, became managing director of Hero's French subsidiary in Lyon. In 1940 he succeeded his father as a member of Hero's administrative board of directors. Carl Roth's son Karl Roth was managing director of Hero's Dutch subsidiary until he fled the Nazis at the beginning of World War II and later became director of finances at Gustav F. Zeiler's packaging company.

World War II suddenly halted the company's growth. One major problem for the company was the increasing scarcity of two essential products: metal and sugar. To solve the first problem, Hero distributed pamphlets to Swiss households, asking the women of the house to immediately return empty tin cans to the company in exchange for a modest compensation. In response to the sugar shortage, Hero created a new line of fruit jams containing more fruit and less sugar. Maxi Fruit, with half the sugar of standard fruit jams, would become one of Hero's bestsellers.

During the 1940s Hero shuttered three of its factories in Switzerland. The company's production subsidiary Helvetia in Gross Gerau, Germany, was sold and Conservenfabrik Saxon was closed down. Restructuring, however, a new canned food company, Conservas Alimentacias Hero S.A., was founded in Brazil in 1949. Three years later Hero, which held a minority stake in the new venture, signed a license agreement with Conservas Alimentacias that allowed the company to market its products (fruit jams, canned fruit, tomato paste, and ravioli) under the Hero brand name. By the end of the 1940s, the founders of the original company had all died and new leadership was in place.

MECHANIZATION, CONVENIENCE, AND COMMERCIAL CLIENTELE

The postwar era was the age of mechanization at Hero. In 1946 a cutting machine for beans and a large mechanical pressure-cooking facility (the first of its kind in Switzerland) were installed at the Frauenfeld branch. One year later the company began to raise a kind of pea that could be harvested mechanically. In the early 1950s Hero developed and patented an automated hydrostatic cooker for vegetables. In the middle of the decade, Hero pioneered the mechanized farming of other vegetable crops such as green beans and spinach. Another major technical innovation was launched in the mid-1970s, when Hero became the first Swiss firm to package its preserved fruit and vegetable products in tin cans with a bright white coating inside, said to help preserve flavor and appearance. Also toward that end, the company switched from soldering of the cans to electrical welding.

The 1950s also saw Hero gain a growing share in the market for prepared foods. After the relaunch of canned ravioli in 1948, the company invested heavily in marketing to establish the product in the Swiss market. In the early 1950s the company mailed flyers to all households in larger Swiss cities containing recipes for different ready-to-serve meals using Hero canned ravioli. Retailers were asked to build "ravioli pyramids" in their stores to promote sales. Aided by Swiss consumers' growing curiosity for international food, Hero's canned ravioli became a bestseller. One of the company's largest customers for the Italian specialty was the Swiss army, which by the end of the 20th century would be purchasing almost 100 tons per year. As the trend toward convenience food intensified in the 1970s, Hero added ready-to-eat salads and salad dressings as well as ready-made fried potatoes and other potato dishes to its product range.

Hero further expanded by acquiring other food manufacturers and by targeting commercial customers in order to boost sales. In 1967 the company acquired a majority stake in Italian canned food manufacturer Lido in northern Italian Verona. The company was later renamed Hero Italia. In 1981 Hero acquired the ravioli brand Roco and in 1987 took over three Swiss pasta product manufacturers. In 1982 the company set up a new industrial product division for customers in the hospitality and food production industries. Seven years later Hero closed down the canning factory in St. Gallen, which had been taken over in 1965, but continued to market its product line under the moderately priced St. Gallen brand.

RESTRUCTURINGS

As the consolidation of the global food industry accelerated in the late 1980s, Hero struggled to keep up. The company had achieved strong market positions in its core product areas in Switzerland, the Netherlands, France, and Spain but lacked the capital needed for substantial further growth. Therefore, Hero became an ideal takeover candidate for large globally positioned corporations in the food sector. When the Jacobs Suchard group attempted an unfriendly takeover in 1987, two Hero top managers, Rudolf Stump and Felix Dony, rescued the company's independence through a management-led buyout. However, paying the enormous interests on the borrowed funds became a serious financial burden for the new shareholders and the company.

A new chapter in Hero's history began in 1995 when the company was acquired by the German Schwartauer Werke, a private company owned by the German entrepreneur Arend Oetker, a great-grandson of August Oetker, who was the founder of one of Germany's largest food companies, the Bielefeld-based Oetker-Group. After taking over Schwartauer Marmeladenfabrik, which his mother had inherited, as managing partner in 1968, Oetker transformed the mid-sized traditional fruit jam factory into a diversified food products and fruit juice manufacturer.

In 1995 the Oetker-controlled subsidiary Schwartau International GmbH acquired FIM AG, the holding company that held Stump and Dony's combined share capital of 40 percent in Hero, which represented 54 percent of the voting rights. The acquisition of additional shares from other Hero investors raised Schwartau's share in Hero to 50.1 percent of the share capital and 61 percent of the voting rights. At the time of the takeover, Hero was grossing about CHF 1.2 billion generated by 20 production plants in seven European countries. To help Oetker finance the deal, Hero acquired Schwartau's fruit-based products for bakeries, baking aids, and decoration subsidiaries in the Netherlands, the United Kingdom, Poland, France, the United States, and Puerto Rico—a significant boost for Hero's total sales. Hero's subsidiaries were reorganized under the new Hero Holding and staffed with new management.

The addition of Schwartau's international business significantly strengthened Hero's presence in Europe and the United States and created opportunities for cooperation in the areas of purchasing and marketing for both Hero and Schwartau. However, this was only the first step in a series of financial and legal transactions between the two companies. In spring 2002 Oetker-owned Hero Holding, FIM AG, acquired a 51 percent stake in the branded products division of Schwartauer Werke—which had been separated from its industrial division—including Schwartauer brand fruit jams and baking products and Corny brand cereal bars, adding another CHF 420 million to Hero's total sales.

To help finance the deal, Hero sold its Dutch industrial baking products branch worth an estimated CHF 70 million. Following the partial reverse takeover in 2002, Arend Oetker acquired in 2003 the remaining 26 percent of Hero shares held by other investors.

That year the company was delisted from public trading. Hero management declared that taking the company private was a reaction to Hero's continued success in the market in competition with large multinational corporations not having been rewarded by other investors, reflected in weak share prices and trading at the Swiss stock exchanges. However, the German news weekly *Focus* speculated that it was the last step of a well-conceived plan to give Oetker's enterprise and heirs a significant tax break under Swiss tax law.

INNOVATIVE FRUIT-BASED PRODUCTS AND BABY FOOD

In the 1990s Hero had to face increasingly fierce competition in its traditional product areas from large multinational corporations. At the same time, while sales of store brands at large retail chains soared, manufacturers such as Hero were left with shrinking profit margins. To significantly improve the company's profitability, Hero began to withdraw from low-margin activities and to focus on brand-name products. In 1996 the company sold its store-brand soft-drink manufacturing subsidiary in the United Kingdom.

Later in the decade Hero also sold fruit-based beverage subsidiary Klindworth, French fruit juice subsidiary Rea, and the money-losing German fruit juice subsidiary Lindavia Fruchtsaft AG. A century-long era ended in 2005 when Hero gave up the production of canned fruit compotes in Lenzburg. The company also sold its meat products and dry pasta products divisions, as well as the British baking products brand Super Cook. Hero's branded fruit jam division, on the other hand, was significantly strengthened when the company took over Egyptian market leader Vitrac and Portuguese jam manufacturer Casa de Mateus in 2002. The company's German subsidiary Schwartau sustained its position as market leader in Germany with its premium brands Schwartau Extra and Mövenpick against strong competition from store brands and discount stores.

Hero then focused on two promising growth markets: baby food and health-enhancing fruit and cereal products. In addition to significant growth through acquisitions in these areas, the company invested heavily in the development of new products. Hero's buying spree began in 2004 when the company acquired three baby food brands—Galactina, Adapta, and Céralino—from Warner AG, a Bern-based

manufacturer of pharmaceuticals; Sunar brand in the Czech Republic and Slovakia from American food giant Heinz; and the infant biscuits branch from joint venture partner Ülker Gida in Turkey.

In 2005 Hero took over Beech-Nut Nutrition Corporation, America's second largest manufacturer of baby food. One year later Hero acquired the leading Swedish baby food producer Semper AB, which boasted a 60 percent market share in Sweden and a strong foothold in other Scandinavian countries and Russia. In 2007 Hero took over two Western European manufacturers of milk products for infants, the Swedish Götene Ingredients AB and the Dutch Friesland Foods B.V., and bought the Juvela line of gluten-free food products from Dutch food company Royal Numico. The following year the company acquired U.K.-based Organix Brands Ltd., a manufacturer of additive-free baby foods.

Beginning in the early 2000s, Hero also successfully introduced a number of new, innovative products. In 2005 the company launched Fruit 2 Day, a chilled fresh fruit puree with fruit chunks that was billed as a convenient and healthful alternative to one daily serving of fresh fruit. One year later Hero subsidiary Schwartau introduced Samt, a creamy fruit jam with no seeds. In 2007 Schwartau launched a line of smoothies under the Pur Pur brand name as well as Frutissima, a chilled fruit jam. Schwartau cereal product innovations included KnusBits, crunchy cereal balls in a resealable container, and a salty low-fat cereal snack called Corny Pepp.

In 2008 Hero entered a strategic joint venture with WhiteWave Foods Co., a subsidiary of Dean Foods Co., one of the largest foods company in the United States. Based in Broomfield, Colorado, the new 50/50 business venture was set up to produce a line of chilled fruit products, including Fruit 2 Day, for U.S. consumers through distribution to American food retail chains via Dean Foods' nationwide comprehensive distribution network. By 2008, health-enhancing food products were accounting for more than half of Hero's annual sales. The company's goal was to raise that percentage to 75 percent by 2010. With roughly one-quarter of the total stemming from markets outside Western Europe, Hero aimed for continued growth in the United States, the Middle East, Russia, Africa, and Asia.

Evelyn Hauser

PRINCIPAL SUBSIDIARIES

Hero Switzerland; Schwartauer Werke GmbH & Co. KGaA (Germany); Cap'Fruit S.A. (France); Hero France SAS (France); Hero España S.A. (Spain); Hero Italia

SpA (Italy); Hero Portugal Lda; Hero Nederland BV (Netherlands); OY Semper AB (Finland); Semper AB (Sweden); Småfolk (Norway); Organix Ltd (United Kingdom); Beech-Nut Nutrition Corporation (United States); Signature Brands LLC (United States); Hero USA; Hero Polska Sp. z o.o. (Poland); Hero Czech s.r.o. (Czech Republic); Hero Slovakia s.r.o.; Hero Gida San.ve Tic. AS (Turkey); Hero Nutritional Food Industries SAE (Vitrac) (Egypt); Hero Japan Co., Ltd.; Hero Rus (Russia); Hero UA (Ukraine).

PRINCIPAL COMPETITORS

Del Monte Foods Company; H.J. Heinz Company; Nestlé S.A.; Groupe Danone; Andros France SNC; Zentis GmbH & Co. KG; HiPP GmbH & Co. Vertrieb KG; Innocent Drinks; Royal Numico N.V.

FURTHER READING

Bulkeley, Andrew, "Swiss Food Concern to Go Private," *Daily Deal,* March 22, 2003.

Diakantonis, Demitri, "Dean Foods Forms JV with Hero," *Daily Deal,* November 5, 2008.

Harrington, Ben, "Food: German Billionaire Scoops Up Organix Baby Foods," *Daily Telegraph,* February 28, 2008, p. 1.

"Hero Goes East," *Lebensmittel Zeitung,* September 13, 1996, p. 34.

"Hero Group to Form Subsidiary for Expansion on Russian Food Market by July 1," *Russia & CIS Business and Financial Newswire,* May 14, 2008.

Homer, Eric, "Switzerland's Hero Group Hungry for $100 million via Deutsche Bank," *Private Placement Letter,* July 28, 2003.

Qualität bleibt zeitlos: Hero geht ins zweite Jahrhundert. Lenzburg, Switzerland: Hero, 1986, 29 p.

Horizon Food Group, Inc.

———————— ■ ————————

Three Embarcadero Center, Suite 2360
San Francisco, California 94111-4026
U.S.A.
Telephone: (415) 394-9700
Fax: (415) 788-2030
Web site: http://www.horizonfoodgroup.com

Private Company
Incorporated: 1996
Employees: 350
Sales: $70 million (2007 est.)
NAICS: 311813 Frozen Bakery Product Manufacturing

■ ■ ■

Horizon Food Group, Inc., is a unit of San Francisco investment firm Horizon Holdings LLC, comprised of three snack food companies: Horizon Snack Foods, Inc., formerly Cutie Pie Corporation; Ne-Mo's Bakery, Inc.; and La Tempesta Bakery Confections, Inc. Horizon Snack Food is one of the largest snack pie makers in the United States and also offers 3-ounce honey buns. In addition to retail products sold under the Cutie Pie and Home Run Pie labels, the company produces pies under private labels. Available in apple, berry, cherry, chocolate, and lemon flavors, the snack pies are produced in turnover style and are available in 2-ounce and 4.5-ounce versions. The company's foodservice business is primarily devoted to schools, but products are also sold to other institutions, as well as bakery and fast-food customers. The freeze/thaw fruit turnovers are available in 2-ounce, 3-ounce, and 3.75-ounce sizes, suitable for breakfast, lunch, and snack programs.

Ne-Mo's offers individually wrapped, single-portion baked goods, primarily sold in convenience stores and delis, but also available in vending machines and some fast-food restaurants. Products include cakes and breads, such as banana bread and lemon bread, Danish pastries, cinnamon rolls, muffins, coffee cake, cake slices, iced cake squares, and Bundt-style cakes. More upscale in focus is Horizon's La Tempesta Bakery Confections, Inc., subsidiary, which offers biscotti, a traditional low-fat Italian cookie; biscotti caramel clusters; amaretti (an Italian almond cookie similar to a macaroon); and a line of Italian-inspired cookies sold under the Indulgent label.

The men behind the creation of Horizon Food Group are the managing partners of Horizon Holdings: Philip S. Estes and James M. Shorin. Although they serve as co-chairmen of portfolio companies, they are known for giving managers of acquired companies a free hand in running their businesses, while helping them grow by using their expertise to make add-on acquisitions, install better financial controls, and refine marketing plans. All Horizon Food Group companies share some administrative functions, providing additional cost savings. Horizon Holdings is owned by Estes, Shorin, and the wealthy individuals and family trusts they represent.

HORIZON HOLDINGS FOUNDED: 1989

Both 30 years old at the time, Estes and Shorin founded Horizon Holdings LLC in 1989 to acquire small companies in mature industries. Business was not Estes'

COMPANY PERSPECTIVES

Horizon has led the acquisition of numerous food and beverage companies that have been merged together to form the Horizon Food Group, Inc.

first area of interest. Rather, he received a degree in petroleum geology from the University of Oklahoma and took a master's degree in the subject from Stanford University before changing course and earning a master's of business administration from Harvard Business School. He went to work for Drexel Burnham Lambert as an investment banker, helping small to mid-sized companies arrange financing, primarily through the high-yield or "junk bond" markets. After four years with Drexel, Estes struck out on his own. His departure, he maintained, was not related to the problems that led to the eventual demise of the venerable Wall Street investment bank.

Estes' partner, James Shorin, was a certified public account who earned his undergraduate degree at Duke University, followed by a law degree from Stanford University and a master's of business administration from the University of Chicago. Before joining Estes, he worked as a consultant with Bain & Company, one of the top management consulting firms in the country. At Bain he gained experience in the type of work he would do for Horizon Holdings, helping companies develop and implement post-acquisition strategies, and improve their operations and marketing. He also worked in a wide variety of industries during his time at Bain, including cruise lines, healthcare, manufacturing, real estate, savings and loan, and semiconductor.

After establishing Horizon Holdings and raising about $5 million, Estes and Shorin began looking for investment opportunities, but unlike other venture capitalists located in the San Francisco area, they had no interest in high-technology start-ups. Rather, they were looking to invest in basic manufacturing and distribution companies in mature industries, with annual revenues that ranged from $5 million to about $70 million. In the spring of 1990 the firm was reported by *Arizona Business Gazette* to be "negotiating for control of a Southern California company that makes foods for institutional buyers, including hotels and hospitals." It was also interested in an "East Coast metal bender that makes consumer products."

A year later Horizon Food Group began to take shape when Estes and Shorin acquired Portland,

Oregon-based Coffee Bean International (CBI). CBI was a coffee roaster, a two-man operation established in a small town in Oregon in 1972. With the popularity of the Starbucks coffeehouse chain that spurred an interest in gourmet coffees, CBI was well positioned to serve the many independent coffee retailers that cropped up across the country in the 1980s and early 1990s. With Horizon's help, CBI would expand beyond specialty retailing to include foodservice customers.

CUTIE PIE ACQUIRED, HORIZON FOOD GROUP FORMED

Horizon's next major food industry acquisition came in 1996 with the addition of Cutie Pie Corporation. The company was well established in its market place, founded in 1956 in Salt Lake City, Utah. At that time it produced fresh and raw pies, serving bakeries, grocery stores, and restaurant customers. To accommodate growing demand, the company began producing frozen pies that could be shipped long distances and then thawed for sale. The company became involved in the private-label pie business in 1993 when it began producing pies for the Albertson's supermarket chain. The Home Run Pie label had been added a year earlier through the acquisition of the California Pie Company, which had been established in Dublin, California, in 1982, and later moved to Livermore, California. Home Run Pies were distributed to grocery stores throughout the western United States.

As a part of Cutie Pie, California Pie expanded its markets to include schools, fast-food restaurants, and military bases. The California Pie facilities were then devoted to the production of fresh pies, while the Salt Lake City facility turned out frozen pies. In 1994 Cutie Pie targeted the school market, establishing a Food Service Division that developed a product lower in fat and higher in fruit and fruit juice content to meet standards set by the National School Lunch Program. Once the new pies qualified, Cutie Pie and Home Run Pies were distributed to school lunch programs in all 50 U.S. states.

Cutie Pie's revenues were then in the $15 million to $20 million range and the company was profitable and enjoying steady growth. The management team was eager to take Cutie Pie to the next level, to make it a national player in the snack pie sector, but lacked the money needed to purchase new equipment and strengthen the infrastructure. Not only would it be difficult to find a lender, the company was reluctant to take on debt. Cutie Pie would have to find a partner with the kind of financial wherewithal needed to grow the business. Through personal connections Cutie Pie and Horizon Holdings were introduced. Once the

KEY DATES

1989: Horizon Holdings LLC formed.
1991: Coffee Bean International, Inc., acquired.
1996: Cutie Pie Corporation acquired; Horizon Food Group formed.
1997: La Tempesta acquired.
1999: Ne-Mo's Bakery acquired.
2004: Coffee Bean International sold.

managers at Cutie Pie were reassured that Estes and Shorin were not venture capitalists looking to sell a property for a profit as soon as possible, a deal was struck and Cutie Pie became a portfolio company of Horizon Holdings.

With the addition of Cutie Pie, Horizon Holdings formed Horizon Food Group in 1996. The following year, Estes and Shorin added to the CBI component with the acquisition of La Tempesta, a natural combination since biscotti was a traditional dipping cookie preferred by many coffee drinkers. La Tempesta was founded in San Francisco in 1983 by Bonnie Tempesta, a first generation Italian American. Newly divorced and a single mother, Tempesta was employed at a chocolate shop and served espresso and cappuccino. Because the shop owner was looking for homemade Italian biscotti to sell, Tempesta began producing the cookie using an aunt's recipe. Her baking started out as a sideline that she carried out using her home oven during her days off. She made about $40 a week but realized that the product was popular and she could earn more money if she could turn out more cookies. Thus, after a year of part-time baking, she quit her job and established La Tempesta Bakery Confections with Aurora Marcheschi.

NE-MO'S BAKERY ACQUIRED

Horizon Food Group completed another major acquisition in July 1999, picking up Carlsbad, California-based Ne-Mo's Bakery. The company had been founded by 22-year-old Ed Smith and his wife, Mary, in 1975. He had grown up in a Chicago suburb and as a teenager became involved in the restaurant business, eventually working as a chef. After he and his wife moved to San Diego in 1972, he was unable to land a restaurant job and instead went to work as a dishwasher at DeMar Cheese Cakes in Encinitas, California. He soon became a baker but very quickly was out of work when the business shut down. His wife pregnant with their first child, Smith decided to make cheesecake at home for sale to local restaurants, preparing the batter in a five-gallon plastic bathtub the couple had purchased in anticipation of the baby. For the name of their new business they drew on their nicknames, Ned and Mona, to coin Ne-Mo's Bakery.

Although the business started off modestly, Smith was able to move his operation to a commercial facility in Escondido, California, in 1976. He decided to expand the business into the snack cake business because he believed there was an opening in the market, dominated by Hostess and Dolly Madison, for higher-quality, fresh-baked items. Smith used a family recipe to bake carrot cake that he began supplying to a local 7-Eleven store. Ne-Mo also began growing its product line beyond carrot cake to include other breads and cakes. They grew so popular that 7-Eleven signed Ne-Mo to a national distribution deal before the end of the 1970s, as did the Circle K convenience store chain. Ne-Mo was able to ride the wave of expansion in convenience stores, and as demand grew for the baked goods, the company eventually moved into a 40,000-square-foot plant in Escondido in 1979. It would later add another 20,000 square feet. Ne-Mo did not, however, take short cuts, remaining committed to baking from scratch.

Smith continued to produce high-end goods sold under the Ne-Mo name and created another source of revenue by beginning to bake private-label goods for fast-food restaurant chains, including Carl's Jr., Jack-in-the-Box, and Taco Bell. By the mid-1990s, Ne-Mo's products numbered about 80, generating annual sales of $25 million. To fuel further growth, Smith sold the business to Horizon Food Group, but as was the case with previous acquisitions, Smith stayed on to run the business he founded. For Horizon, Ne-Mo's was a good fit because its products complemented the pies and cookies offered by the other Horizon portfolio companies, and it brought sales connections to a host of new channels, including convenience stores and fast-food chains, as well as vending machines and fund-raising ventures.

Horizon Food Group expanded in other ways in 1999 to support its subsidiaries. A second pie line was added to Cutie Pie's Livermore facility that could produce more fresh and frozen pies. A Cutie Pie competitor, Houston, Texas-based Huffman Bakery, was also acquired and its operation was used to supply fresh pies to the Texas market. Around the same time, one of Cutie Pie's independent fresh pie distributors in California was acquired, and Horizon Transportation Group was formed to facilitate the shipping and distribution of Cutie Pie products across the country through independent truck operators.

CUTIE PIE CORPORATION BECOMES HORIZON SNACK FOODS

Cutie Pie added a new product in 1999, a glazed honey bun, which necessitated a name change in 2000, when Cutie Pie Corporation became Horizon Snack Foods. The unit continued to expand in the new century. By 2002 it had entered ten new states in the Northeast and South. To appeal more to the convenience store market, the company introduced a line of pies in 2003 that at 4.5 ounces were larger than its traditional products. Also in 2003 the Cutie Pie label was brought back, the company taking advantage of its brand awareness. By this point, coffee was no longer considered to be a good fit with snack cookies, breads, cakes, and pies, and CBI, the original member of Horizon Food Group, was deemed expendable. In April 2004 CBI was divested. The other Horizon Food Group companies continued to prosper despite the popularity of the Atkins diet and other diets that limited the intake of carbohydrates. In 2007 Horizon Food Group posted sales of nearly $70 million. It was still very much a small company, but it was profitable and continued to enjoy steady growth. Its owners, Horizon Holdings, remained interested in further acquisitions in the specialty food and sweet snack industries.

Ed Dinger

PRINCIPAL SUBSIDIARIES

Horizon Snack Foods, Inc.; La Tempesta Bakery Confections, Inc.; Ne-Mo's Bakery, Inc.

PRINCIPAL COMPETITORS

Entenmann's Inc.; Interstate Bakeries Incorporated; Tasty Baking Company.

FURTHER READING

Bratt, L. Erik, "A Recipe for Success," *San Diego Union-Tribune,* October 7, 1995, p. C1.

Edwards, John, "Twosome Typify a New Breed of Venture Capitalist," *Arizona Business Gazette,* May 11, 1990, p. 3.

Lee, Ellen, "Pies Hit Home Run in Tri-Valley," *Pleasanton (Calif.) Valley Times,* April 13, 2001, p. D2.

Malovany, Dan, "New Horizons," *Snack Food & Wholesale Bakery,* April 2000.

"Sweet Success," *San Diego Union-Tribune,* June 27, 2004, p. N4.

Human Factors International

Human Factors
International Inc.

410 West Lowe
Fairfield, Iowa 52556
U.S.A.
Telephone: (641) 472-4480
Toll Free: (800) 242-4480
Fax: (641) 472-5412
Web site: http://www.humanfactors.com

Private Company
Incorporated: 1981
Employees: 260
Sales: $28 million (2008 est.)
NAICS: 511210 Software Publishers

■ ■ ■

Human Factors International Inc. (HFI) is a leading user-centered design firm that helps companies create software applications and web sites that are intuitive and easy to use. HFI offers usability consulting services that focus on elements such as site architecture and navigation, design/graphic production, and usability testing. The company also provides the training and products its clients need to attain, maximize, and maintain usability with their systems.

HFI serves a large customer base from a range of industries, including aerospace, automotive, telecommunications, government, financial services, healthcare, shipping, travel and hospitality, energy, computers, and software development. HFI's clients include many *Fortune* 500 enterprises and government agencies, such as Boeing, the Centers for Disease Control and Preven-

tion, Dell Computer, Ernst & Young, the Library of Congress, the Social Security Administration, Sprint, Sun Microsystems, United Health Care, and Verizon Wireless.

In addition to the company's headquarters in Fairfield, Iowa, HFI has domestic offices in San Francisco, New York, Minneapolis, Chicago, Boston, and Baltimore. Internationally, the company has operations in China, India, and the United Kingdom.

COMPANY ORIGINS

HFI's origins can be traced back to 1981, when Dr. Eric Schaffer cofounded a company named Human Performance Associates Inc. As a graduate student, Schaffer was influenced by his professor, Dr. Bob Bailey, a scientist with a profoundly pragmatic viewpoint. One of Bailey's friends was Ted Lesher, a businessman and real-estate salesman who played a role in convincing Dr. Bailey that selling "human performance engineering" (a systematic problem-solving approach) to AT&T could be a lucrative endeavor.

In 1981, while working on contract at Bell Labs, Schaffer received an invitation to participate in a new consulting venture with Lesher and Bailey. According to Schaffer, months of strategic planning meetings followed the invitation. Many of the meetings were held at a Kentucky Fried Chicken restaurant in Mendham, New Jersey, near the homes of Bailey and Lesher, while others occurred in the basement of Schaffer's home in nearby Boonton Township.

"While starting the company, we struggled hard with our future business model," Schaffer explained in a

COMPANY PERSPECTIVES

Since 1981 we have focused on human factors-based usability, whether it applies to software development, creating digital experiences or creating new products. HFI is the largest company in the field by a factor of more than five.

November 2008 interview with the author. "We discussed ideas that are just now starting to come to pass in the field—like the concept of 'certification,' and software products to support the design process. Ultimately, we built the company on a contracting model; delivering 'human performance engineering staff' to AT&T."

Working for AT&T accounted for the bulk of Human Performance Associates' business. In 1982 the firm was asked to create a course for IBM, which Schaffer and his colleagues were allowed to develop into a new product they could market at a later time. Named "How to Design Effective CRT Screens," the two-day course focused on designing screens for mainframe computers. "I typed the visuals on pages of paper, and then photographed them to make 35mm slides," Schaffer recalled, adding, "While the slides were difficult to manage, it was years before we switched to overhead projectors."

CHALLENGES TO A FLEDGLING COMPANY

After AT&T operated as a regulated monopoly for many years, growing antitrust concerns and a long court battle eventually led the company to divest its operations, and in 1984 it was divided into eight smaller companies. This presented major challenges for Human Performance Associates, which relied upon AT&T for the bulk of its work. The company quickly began looking for other sources of business, which it found within the insurance industry.

During the mid-1980s, consistency was a major design-related challenge for Human Performance Associates' clients. According to Schaffer, the problem came to the forefront while he was working with Met Life. This discovery resulted in the development of the company's first template-based screen design standard. At this time, Ted Lesher was serving as Human Performance Associates' president, and Schaffer headed the company's technical staff—a role he embraced and would fill for

many years. Sales continued to grow throughout the 1980s, eventually reaching about $2.5 million.

In 1988 Schaffer decided to leave the East Coast and move to Iowa. Convinced that the business could not succeed with operations based in the rural state of Iowa, Lesher refused to relocate operations. This ultimately resulted in a decision to split up the company. Following what Schaffer described as a very difficult struggle, Lesher retained rights to the company name, as well as a good portion of its assets. Two years after the split, Human Performance Associates fell into bankruptcy.

NEW COMPANY IS BORN

In late 1988 Schaffer established Human Factors International (HFI), with operations based in an Iowa farmhouse. "We built out a very pleasant office space and had about a dozen chickens outside (until the local fox visited)," he recalled in the aforementioned interview. "David Ballou and Dr. John Sorflaten were the technical staff, and Don Langstaff was president. We had a nice pond for occasional fishing and swimming. Needless to say, we were never bored."

A noteworthy development took place in 1989 when Jay More joined HFI as head of sales and marketing. More, who later became company president, brought a new level of sophistication to HFI's marketing initiatives, and focused on developing and strengthening the organization's brand. Nearly two decades later his initial work remained at the heart of HFI's positioning.

Dr. Susan Weinschenk, a colleague and friend of Schaffer's who had continued working for Human Performance Associates, encouraged him to take flying lessons. By 1990, he had become a licensed pilot. A Cessna 182RG put the company within easy reach of customers throughout the United States, and Schaffer used the aircraft to further HFI's national growth, performing the bulk of its consulting and training work.

One constant in the technology industry is change. By 1991 the movement away from text-based mainframe computer interfaces to graphical user interfaces (GUIs), which took advantage of computers' growing graphical capabilities, was underway. This shift initially had a negative impact on HFI's business. Many observers argued that, because of the inherent user-friendliness of GUIs, the company's services would be rendered obsolete. However, the greater degrees of freedom associated with GUIs were accompanied by greater opportunities for user error. This situation ultimately led HFI to convert its existing mainframe course into a new one named "How to Develop Effective Graphical User Interfaces."

KEY DATES

1981: Dr. Eric Schaffer cofounds Human Performance Associates Inc.

1988: Following the division of Human Performance Associates, Schaffer establishes Human Factors International (HFI).

1991: The company's focus shifts away from text-based interfaces for mainframe computers and toward graphical user interfaces (GUIs).

1999: HFI's services are in high demand for web sites created by Internet and e-commerce start-ups.

2006: HFI (Shanghai) Software Consulting is established.

2008: HFI Labs is formed to support the company's research and development activities; the company is named to *Inc.*'s list of fastest-growing private U.S. companies.

INTERNET REVOLUTION

HFI's revised course ultimately led to a flurry of new business. However, GUI-related work began to level off during the late 1990s. At the same time, the Internet exploded in popularity. This development had a major impact on HFI. The company began marketing its services via e-mail, and developed its first web site, which had the name "HFI Design Magic."

The Internet boom continued through the end of the decade, and by 1999 HFI was consumed with work in this area. The company's annual sales increased to approximately $12 million as its services were in high demand among Internet and e-commerce start-ups, which sought to maximize the usability of their web sites.

In 1999 several large companies expressed an interest in acquiring HFI. Among them was a leading Indian systems integrator. After traveling to Bangalore and meeting with executives from this company, Schaffer decided not to pursue the deal. However, the trip was beneficial because he saw an opportunity to begin doing business from India. Along with Jay More, who was named company president in 1999, Schaffer began laying the necessary groundwork to bring this opportunity to fruition.

HFI soon began working with Apala Lahiri Chavan and her small design firm, ZindaGUI Pvt Ltd., and hiring Indian staff members. A partnership was later formed with TATA Infotech, in which HFI supplied designs that were coded by Indian systems integrators. This allowed the company to provide customers with an end-to-end solution and market its services aggressively.

GLOBAL EXPANSION

Building upon its international expansion in India, during the early 2000s HFI expanded its global operations to include the United Kingdom and China. The technology industry suffered greatly in the wake of the dot-com collapse of the early 2000s. However, HFI was largely spared from the turmoil. In addition to its work on web sites, the company also was doing human factors work for companies such as Northrop-Grumman and Lockheed.

By 2001 HFI had a workforce of about 100 people, including 42 usability experts. That year, the company introduced a Web cast and white paper series called the Usability Broadcast Network. It also unveiled a usability resource named Usability Central, which offered customers design tools, templates, and guidelines in one location. In addition, HFI began offering a course called "The Science and Art of Effective Web Design."

In 2002 HFI launched its Certified Usability Analyst (CUA) training program. By 2003 the company's non-Web human factors projects had grown to include interactive voice response (IVR) architecture and design for Konica-Phillips; the development and design of an on-demand video catalog interface for Scientific Atlanta; IVR navigation, architecture and scripting for Gateway Computers; electronic book interface designs for Everybook Inc.; in-flight touch screen flight management systems for commercial airlines; and the development of integrated flat-panel touch screen management systems for 911 emergency services call centers for Plant Equipment Inc.

In 2003 Schaffer's friend and former colleague Susan Weinschenk joined HFI. That year, the company developed the Schaffer-Weinschenk Method. Based upon principles from human-computer interaction, ergonomics, psychology, and marketing, the method became the only ISO-certifiable process for user-centered design.

Developments continued at HFI during the middle years of the first decade of the 2000s. In 2004 Schaffer published "Institutionalization of Usability: A Step-by-Step Guide," adding to the numerous resources his company had introduced throughout the years. By 2005 HFI had taught more than 2,000 courses and worked on more than 2,500 projects.

In addition to its Fairfield, Iowa, headquarters, HFI's geographic footprint had expanded considerably by the middle of the first decade of the 2000s. Domestically, regional offices had been established in Boston, Baltimore, New York, and San Francisco. On the international front, locations were in place in India (Bangalore, Mumbai, and Pondicherry), as well as London and Singapore.

HFI's international growth came at a good time, given that there was a significant international shortage of usability professionals. Global growth continued in 2006, when HFI established a new operation in China named HFI (Shanghai) Software Consulting.

BEYOND USABILITY

During the later years of the first decade of the 2000s, HFI was firmly established within its industry. The company continued to serve as a major educational resource for the approximately 2,000 individuals who had received CUA certification worldwide. This was enhanced by the introduction of an online community in 2008 called CUA Central. Another noteworthy development was the formation of HFI Labs, which supported the company's ongoing research and development activities in the area of user experience methods and techniques.

In 2008 HFI was named to *Inc.* magazine's list of the nation's 5,000 fastest-growing private companies. The honor came at a time when HFI's annual sales had increased 105 percent over a three-year period. In September 2008 Schaffer introduced a new approach called PET Design, which focused on the creation of more effective web sites and stronger customer interactions by looking beyond usability and also considering the elements of persuasion, emotion, and trust. Begun as a training program, PET Design was expected to serve as the basis for a new consulting practice within the organization.

Heading toward the 21st century's second decade, HFI was on strong footing. From its mainframe computer origins at AT&T, the company had evolved into the largest usability and user-experience design firm in the world and seemed well positioned for continued success.

Paul R. Greenland

PRINCIPAL SUBSIDIARIES

HFI-Asia; Human Factors Europe Ltd.

PRINCIPAL COMPETITORS

Avenue A Razorfish; Digitas Inc.; The Nielsen Norman Group.

FURTHER READING

Rogers, Amy, "The Human Factor—Engineers Focus on Site Usability," *Computer Reseller News,* August 28, 2000.

Schaffer, Eric, "A Better Way for Web Designs," *Information-Week,* May 1, 2000.

"World's Largest Usability Company Opens First China Office," *China Business News,* September 14, 2006.

JBS S.A.

Av. Marginal Dreita do Tietê 500
São Paulo, São Paulo 05118-100
Brazil
Telephone: (55 11) 3144-4000
Fax: (55 11) 3144-4279
Web site: http://www.jbs.com.br

Public Company
Incorporated: 2006
Employees: 39,275
Sales: BRL 14.73 billion ($7.75 billion) (2007)
Stock Exchanges: São Paulo
Ticker Symbol: JBSS
NAICS: 112111 Beef Cattle Ranching and Farming;
112112 Cattle Feedlots; 311611 Animal (Except
Poultry) Slaughtering; 311612 Meat Processed from
Carcasses; 311613 Rendering Meat By-Products
Processing

■ ■ ■

JBS S.A., once merely an obscure regional Brazilian meatpacker, has become, mainly through acquisitions, the world's largest exporter of beef, with productive capacity in the main beef producing countries in the world. Its holdings include Swift & Company, which makes it also the third largest pork producer and processor in the United States. JBS's high risk acquisitions policy is based on the ability of developing countries to pay for its protein and involves assumption of a large burden of debt. The family-controlled company is led

by three brothers dubbed *caubóis* (cowboys) by one Brazilian business publication.

A HALF-CENTURY IN THE BEEF BUSINESS

José Batista Sobrinho, also known as Zé Mineiro, started his business career in Anápolis, Goiás, where he bought cattle for resale to meatpacking plants. Feeling that he was underpaid, he opened a butcher shop there in 1953, slaughtering one cow each day, and also became the beef supplier for other butchers in the city. With the planned construction nearby of a new federal capital, to be named Brasília, Zé saw an opportunity to expand the business. In 1957 he established one of the first slaughterhouses in the region. He and five employees began slaughtering 25 to 30 cattle a day to supply beef to the construction companies building the future capital.

In 1962 Zé leased a slaughterhouse in Luziâna, not far from Brasília, and increased his output to about 55 animals a day. He then began selling the meat to the newly established butchers in the city. Seven years later, Formosa Industrial Slaughterhouse was acquired. Further investment tripled capacity there to 120 head of cattle per day. Also in 1969, Zé's company became Friboi Ltda.

Brazil had the world's fourth largest stock of cattle, but much of the 105 million head was not of good quality. There were almost no feedlots; instead herds grazed on generally poor pastureland and were prone to hoof-and-mouth disease. As a result, the average steer was not slaughtered until reaching about five years of age, which limited production. The Brazilian government, however, was helping to finance ranching in states such as Goiás, which were well north of the historic heart of the beef industry, Rio Grande do Sul, the nation's southernmost state. Government was also aiding meatpackers to expand and modernize the nation's 30 or so plants as a means of promoting exports and feeding the many Brazilians who were migrating to the cities and earning wages that allowed them to eat beef for the first time.

As late as 1979, Brazil was a net importer of meat. To ensure that enough meat reached the public at home, the government purchased a considerable amount in some years and paid for them to be kept in cold storage by firms such as Friboi. In 1979, however, all restrictions on meat sales, including taxes, were eliminated. As a parallel measure, all subsidies were also removed, including payments for storage. The subsequent world recession of the early 1980s reduced the typical Brazilian's earnings by more than 25 percent and per-capita consumption of meat by about the same amount, resulting in considerable excess capacity and lower earnings for meatpackers.

By the middle of the decade, however, demand had risen dramatically within the country as economic recovery reached levels that again allowed citizens to make beef a regular part of their food purchases. By 1986 Brazil was importing so much beef that in October of that year the government banned export sales and even ordered federal police to confiscate cattle from ranches throughout the country for slaughter. Suppliers had been withholding cattle from the market in hopes of winning higher prices than those offered by the government. Some rich cattlemen even bought back animals they had sold for slaughter during this time.

Even in the 1990s, cattle raising in Brazil was still described as almost medieval. The herds were said to be raised without even minimal sanitary conditions. More than 60 percent of the cattle sold to the large meatpackers came from small- and medium-sized ranchers who gave them the least care. An estimated 40 percent of the meat supply was believed to be sold illegally. Processors were traditionally family-owned and run without professional executives or technical experts.

Friboi continued to grow amid the vicissitudes of its economic sector. Zé stepped down from active management of the company in 1994, when the eldest of his three sons, José Batista Júnior, succeeded him as chief executive. The company's growth continued under Júnior, with 12 acquisitions made between 1993 and 2005, in the course of which it became the largest meatpacker in Brazil. Friboi began exporting fresh meat in 1997. A truck fleet was established in 2000 to carry 42 animals in each vehicle.

RISE TO THE TOP

In 2004 Friboi moved its headquarters to an old meatpacking plant in São Paulo. During the year the company made its largest purchase to that time and its first one outside of Brazil, buying Swift Armour S.A., the largest beef producer and exporter in Argentina but a company that was financially troubled, at auction for only $200 million. (Friboi had, in 2000, purchased Swift Armour's operations in Brazil.) The acquisition of this company made Friboi the leading meatpacker in Latin America.

The company suffered a misstep in 2005, however, when a federation of Brazilian cattle ranchers filed suit against a group of meatpackers, including Friboi, claiming that the group had acted illegally to keep prices for cattle low. Friboi reached a settlement with the government before four other firms were convicted and fined heavily for taking part in what was found to be a cartel. Júnior resigned as chairman and chief executive officer of Friboi in order to run for governor of Goiás. He was succeeded by his brother Joesley. The company became a corporation in 2006, when it changed its name to JBS, made up of the initials of founder José Batista Sobrinho.

The new corporation was ready to put the past behind it and grow still further. To do so, it had restructured its operations so that the quality of its product would not be in doubt. Furthermore, it had opened its books so that investors would be willing to provide the funds needed to help the company become an international player in a globalized economy. JBS became the first Brazilian meatpacker to go public, selling 49 percent of its shares on the São Paulo exchange in March 2007.

Armed with BRL 1.4 billion (about $735 million) from the stock offering, and aided by a currency appreciating against the dollar, JBS purchased Colorado-based Swift & Company in May 2007 for about $225

KEY DATES

1953: José Batista Sobrinho opens a butcher shop in the Brazilian state of Goiás.

1957: Batista opens one of the first slaughterhouses in the region.

1969: Company is renamed Friboi Ltda.

1993: Friboi completes the first of several acquisitions that makes it Brazil's leading meatpacker.

2004: Purchase of Argentina's Swift Armour makes Friboi Latin America's largest meatpacker.

2006: Friboi changes its name to JBS in honor of its founder and becomes a corporation.

2007: JBS makes its initial public offering of stock, the first Brazilian meatpacker to do so; JBS becomes the world's largest beef processor by buying Swift & Co.

million in cash and assumption of $1.16 billion in debt, thereby transforming itself into the world's largest beef processor and the world's second largest meat exporter. Swift's annual sales were five times that of JBS. Besides the U.S. operation, which consisted of four beef plants and the processing of pork and lamb as well, Swift had an Australian division that was that nation's largest beef processor and exporter. It became a part of JBS subsidiary Australia Meat Holdings Pty Ltd.

The Batistas intended to transform the company into a platform for worldwide export, especially to China. Although JBS had found major markets in Europe and the Middle East, most East Asian countries had refused to accept Argentine or Brazilian beef because of outbreaks of foot-and-mouth disease. Fresh meat from Argentina and Brazil also was banned from the NAFTA countries (Canada, Mexico, and the United States) for the same reason. By purchasing Swift, JBS was opening the way to selling its beef in these markets, although Japan and South Korea remained off limits because of pressure from their own ranchers and fears of mad cow disease.

However, Swift was losing money and had experienced a federal raid of its plants in six U.S. states, during which more than 1,000 of its workers were found to be illegal immigrants. Only days after the announcement of its sale, the Moody's bond rating service lowered its classification for JBS. To fortify its own finances, JBS turned to the Brazilian government, selling its development bank, BNDES, a 13 percent stake in the company for BRL 1.85 billion (about $950 million).

Renamed JBS USA Inc., the new acquisition added a second shift at its main plant, in Greeley, Colorado, hiring 1,300 new workers. The expansion of operations was costly, even though the company saved $35 million through economies such as eliminating managerial positions. Despite rising revenues, the beef division lost $101 million in the last quarter of 2007, offsetting higher profits in the pork division and the Australian beef division. The loss was attributed in part to higher cattle prices that were coupled with lower prices for beef carcasses, as well as higher prices for diesel fuel, which added to transport costs. Joesley Batista took the blame, saying the company's expansion of production to gain market share had raised demand, and hence prices, for cattle, and had lowered beef prices by augmenting supply.

FURTHER ACQUISITIONS IN 2008

This setback did not dissuade JBS from a dizzying round of new purchases in early 2008. First, the company entered into an agreement with Cremonini S.p.A. to purchase half of Inalca S.p.A., the leading Italian beef processor, for EUR 225 million ($330 million). This acquisition constituted an opportunity to access new markets in Europe and Russia and to benefit from Inalca's widely recognized state-of-the-art production techniques and added value products. Soon after, JBS acquired Tasman Group, proprietor of six Australian slaughterhouses for cattle, calves, sheep, and hogs, and a feedlot for cattle and sheep. The purchase price, which included assumption of debt, was AUS 160 million (about $150 million).

In the United States, JBS purchased Smithfield Beef Group Inc. (the beef packing unit of Smithfield Foods Inc.), consisting of four slaughter plants, a cattle feedlot, and refrigerated transportation vehicles, for $565 million in cash. It followed up this transaction by acquiring National Beef Packaging Company LLC, the fourth largest U.S. beef processor, with six slaughter and processing plants, for $970 million in cash, stock, and assumption of debt and other liabilities. The purchase included a large number of vehicles for the transportation of livestock and refrigerated transportation of carcasses.

These acquisitions made JBS, in theory, the largest beef processor and cattle feedlot operator in the United States, subject to approval of the antitrust division of the U.S. Department of Justice. Critics of the company, however, including members of Congress, argued that JBS had the potential to both depress cattle prices and raise beef prices because its purchases would have a chilling effect on competition within the $30 billion per year U.S. cattle market. The attorney general of Texas argued that three of the five largest U.S. processors, JBS, Tyson Foods, Inc, and Cargill Inc., would control more than 80 percent of capacity for processing beef. In October 2008 the Justice Department and 13 states filed a federal lawsuit to void the National Beef Packing purchase.

The Smithfield acquisition was not challenged. Renamed JBS Packerland, with JBS Five Rivers for its feedlot subsidiary, it was the largest beef slaughtering company in the United States and the third largest U.S. pork producer. Parent JBS was the largest beef producer in the world in terms of slaughtering, production, and exporting capacity. By this time, however, some industry analysts had begun to suspect that the expansion of JBS was unsustainable. The company had lost money in 2007 and the first half of 2008. As fears of a global recession grew, they questioned whether pressed consumers, especially in developing countries, would be willing to pay for beef rather than lower priced chicken or pork. However, the company's losses in the first two quarters of the year were more than compensated for by a $694 million profit in the third quarter. JBS USA accounted for 43 percent of total revenues in that quarter.

Although Joesley Batista was the chief executive of JBS, Júnior, the eldest of Zé's three sons, was considered the architect of the company's acquisition strategy, which had begun when it was still known as Friboi. He and Wesley—the third son—were based in Colorado, where Júnior acted as the company's deal maker and Wesley as director of its operations in the United States. All three had elected to forgo college in order to work their way up the company ladder. They were said to stay in touch by telephone almost every day. The three and their father, now in his mid-70s, also reviewed business matters each Sunday by conference call or, if all were in Brazil, at Zé's home outside São Paulo or the family ranch, accessible by private jet. Two family-owned entities held 50.1 percent of JBS's common stock in late 2008. BNDES held 13 percent, pension funds held 14 percent, and public shareholders held 21 percent.

Robert Halasz

PRINCIPAL SUBSIDIARIES

Australian Meat Holdings Pty Ltd. (Australia); Inalca S.p.A. (Italy; 50%); JBS Packerland (United States); JBS USA Inc. (United States); Swift Armour S.A. (Argentina).

PRINCIPAL DIVISIONS

Argentina Food; Australia Food; Brazil Food; Transportation; USA Food.

PRINCIPAL COMPETITORS

Bertin Ltda.; Cargill Inc.; Marfrig Frigofóricos e Comércio de Alimentos S.A.; Tyson Foods, Inc.

FURTHER READING

"Brazil Takes Bigger Slice of Meat Market," *Financial Times,* November 1, 1984, p. 32.

Carmagos, Daniella, "A saga global dos caubóis de Anápolis," *Exame,* March 26, 2008, pp.104–06.

Carvalho, Denise, "Antes da bolsa, muito trabalho," *Exame,* March 14, 2007, pp. 56–57.

Dunn, Sharon, "High Costs Blamed for JBS' Loss," *Greeley Tribune,* April 1, 2008.

Etter, Lauren, and John Lyon, "Brazilian Beef Clan Goes Global As Troubles Hit Market," *Wall Street Journal,* August 1, 2008, pp. A1, A10.

Ishmael, Wes, "Money Talks," *Beef,* June 2008, p. 8.

Jackson, Bill, "JBS Eyes Foreign Markets," *Greeley Tribune,* April 13, 2008.

———, "Swift Gaining Competitive Edge Under New Ownership," *Greeley Tribune,* November 9, 2007.

Maidenberg, H. J., "Brazil Begins Modernizing Beef Industry," *New York Times,* April 5, 1972, pp. 63, 69.

Miller, Ben, "JBS Suffers Indigestion," *LatinFinance,* June 2008, pp. 21–22.

Peck, Clint, "Swift Buyout Good for Cattlemen," *Beef,* July 2007, p. 34.

Salomão, Alexa, and Daniella Camargos, "Nasce uma multinacional," *Exame,* June 6, 2007, pp. 120–23.

Sternstein, Aliya, "Brazilian Beef Processor Rustles Up Cattle Industry," *CQ Weekly,* March 31, 2008, pp. 813–14.

Wagtyl, Stefan, "Brazil to Take on Rebel Ranchers," *Financial Times,* October 10, 1986, p. 48.

Wilke, John R., and Lauren Etter, "Brazilian Beef Purchase Is Challenged by the U.S." *Wall Street Journal,* October 21, 2008, p. A6.

JM Smith Corporation

---■---

101 West Saint John Street, Suite 305
Spartanburg, South Carolina 29306-5150
U.S.A.
Telephone: (864) 542-9419
Toll Free: (800) 845-7558
Fax: (864) 582-6585
Web site: http://www.smithdrug.com

Private Company
Incorporated: 1944 as Smith Drug Company
Employees: 970
Sales: $2 billion (2007 est.)
NAICS: 424210 Drugs and Druggists' Sundries
Merchant Wholesalers; 518210 Data Processing,
Hosting, and Related Services

■ ■ ■

Based in Spartanburg, South Carolina, JM Smith Corporation is the holding company for Smith Drug Company, QS/1 Data Systems, Integral Solutions Group, and Smith Premier Services. Smith Drug is a wholesale drug company serving more than 1,000 independent pharmacies in South Carolina, North Carolina, Alabama, Arkansas, Florida, Georgia, Kentucky, Louisiana, Missouri, Oklahoma, Tennessee, Texas, and Virginia. In addition to pharmaceutical drugs, the company supplies its customers with home medical equipment and health and beauty aids. QS/1 Data Systems, which grew out of the computerization of Smith Drug, provides pharmacy software and the hardware to run it to more than 8,000 pharmacies in the United States and Canada as well as Pacific Rim countries. Through CornerDrugstore.com, QS/1 also helps independent pharmacies to create an online presence, or bolster the services of an existing web site.

Another unit, Smith Premier Services, offers insurance companies and employers pharmacy benefit management services and a prescription benefit plan under the Premier Pharmacy Plan banner, working through more than 57,000 pharmacies. A fourth JM Smith subsidiary, Integral Solutions Group, expands the company's reach beyond the pharmacy field, providing design, installation, integration, and maintenance services for communication networks to a wide range of healthcare companies and other industrial sectors as well as governmental entities.

FOUNDER OPENS FIRST PHARMACY IN NORTH CAROLINA

The founder of JM Smith was James M. Smith, who in 1925 opened a pharmacy, Smith Drug Store, in Asheville, North Carolina. He then took on business partners to become involved in another 16 pharmacies that opened in North Carolina, South Carolina, and Georgia by the 1940s. To supply these stores he established a warehouse and distribution operation. Realizing that other independent pharmacies could benefit from the purchasing power and merchandising services provided by this unit, he decided to sell his pharmacy interests and in 1944 formed Smith Drug Company in Spartanburg, South Carolina, to serve as a wholesaler, initially to Spartanburg-area pharmacies and hospitals. Soon he was joined by his two sons, James

(Jim) Smith Jr. and Henry Dale Smith. They both became registered pharmacists, although Jim Smith was also interested in electrical engineering, having earned a degree in that field from the Massachusetts Institute of Technology.

James Smith looked for other opportunities in the wholesale drug business. Visiting relatives in Springfield, Illinois, he recognized an opening for a wholesale business in that area and began laying the groundwork for a new company. His sudden death in 1951 put a temporary hold on those plans, however. Jim Smith became the company president but was not enamored with the administrative responsibilities and turned over the lead role to his brother Henry, who then assumed the presidency. In 1953 Henry left Smith Drug to rekindle the wholesale business James Smith had envisioned in Springfield, and at the start of 1954 H.D. Smith Wholesale Drug Company opened its doors.

While his brother was growing a thriving wholesale business in Illinois, Jim Smith took the reins of Smith Drug and used his engineering background to make his mark on the company. He began to computerize the operation in 1959 when he automated the company's payroll. He also made sure to provide excess computing capacity to allow for some experimentation. A few years later he formed Smith Data Processing to develop software for other companies and to serve as an area computer service bureau. JM Smith Corporation was also formed to act as the holding company for Smith Drug and Smith Data Processing.

Out of Smith Data Processing grew QS/1 Data Systems. In 1977 Smith and some of his programmers undertook the task of creating pharmacy management software. The result was the QS/1 Pharmacy System. QS stood for "quantum sufficient," or a "sufficient amount," while the number 1 referred to the IBM Series 1 computer for which the software was initially designed. The system handled a variety of applications, including the maintenance of customer records, government record compliance, and the printing of prescription bottle labels. It was an expensive program, however, and out of the price range of many small pharmacies. As a result, a stripped-down version became available in 1987 in the $10,000 price range. A year later QS/1 expanded beyond the pharmacy industry, adapting its programming to serve a new market: dentists.

JIM SMITH DIES

Jim Smith died in 1985 and his brother Henry and son "Jimmy" Smith took over JM Smith, with Henry Dale Smith becoming chairman and chief executive officer while Jimmy Smith, who was in his mid-20s, was named president. JM Smith was still comprised of two subsidiaries, but that would change in 1990 when the president of Smith Data Processing, Glenn Hammett, announced his retirement. Moreover, the QS/1 business had begun to take off. It was by this time the largest part of JM Smith and was broken out as a separate company. William R. Cobb was named president. He had joined Smith Data Processing and worked with Jim Smith on the original development team for QS/1 Pharmacy System. He then became vice-president in 1986, responsible for product development and hardware selection.

Other management changes would soon take place as well at JM Smith. In early 1992 Bill Shelley, the longtime president and a 39-year veteran of the company, retired as president of Smith Drug. Also in 1992 Henry Dale Smith's son, Dale Smith, was named vice-chairman, a newly created position. A year later Jimmy Smith, who disagreed with his uncle on how to run the business, elected to resign. He told Spartanburg's *Herald-Journal* that with the promotion of his cousin, he was no longer in line to become chair of JM Smith: "It was clear that my future was not there. I finally came to the realization that it was no longer my dad's company, it was my uncle's company." Nevertheless, he insisted that he was not forced out, and remained a company stockholder; several years later, Dale Smith would become chief executive of H.D. Smith Wholesale Drug Company and a nonfamily member would take charge of JM Smith.

Much of the growth of JM Smith in the 1990s was tied to QS/1. After Cobb had taken over the division, it experienced declining sales of its flagship system, prompting a search for new services. Computer systems were designed for home medical equipment providers as well as institutional pharmacies. To help keep track of inventory, replenish supplies, and change prices automatically, point-of-sale systems were developed. QS/1 also added hardware maintenance and training and began offering forms and other supplies.

KEY DATES

1925: James M. Smith opens pharmacy in Asheville, North Carolina.
1944: Smith Drug Company founded in Spartanburg, South Carolina, as drug wholesaler.
1951: James Smith dies; sons Jim and Henry Dale Smith take charge.
1954: H.D. Smith Wholesale Drug Company opens in Springfield, Illinois.
1977: QS/1 Data Systems formed.
1985: Jim Smith dies; brother becomes chairman and chief executive.
1997: Smith Premier Services formed.
1998: Henry Dale Smith retires.
2002: CornerDrugstore.com acquired.
2004: Integral Solutions Group formed.
2008: Digital-DNS acquired.

The 1990s saw steadily increasing healthcare costs, forcing many employers providing healthcare to their workforce to seek ways to keep overhead in check. One area of concern was prescription drug coverage. In 1997 JM Smith launched Smith Premier Services as a pharmacy benefit management unit to help employers and insurance carriers control their prescription drug costs. A major component was the Premier Pharmacy Plan, a prescription drug benefit card accepted by a network of pharmacies that would grow to more than 55,000 in the United States and Puerto Rico. Smith Premier used QS/1 technology to help control costs by use of point-of-sale systems to make pharmacy claims more efficient. Personal service and thorough account management were other keys to success of Smith Premier, which experienced a slow start but began to hit its stride after two years. Sales offices were opened in Atlanta; Charlotte, North Carolina; Nashville, Tennessee; and Baltimore.

STRONG GROWTH AND EXPANSION

In February 1998 Henry Dale Smith retired. Succeeding him as chair and CEO was William R. Cobb. He took over a company that was becoming better known for information technology (IT) than the wholesale drug business. Although it received less attention than its high-tech sister companies, Smith Drug was actually enjoying strong growth. In the early 1990s it served about 200 accounts. A decade later that number had grown to about 800 in nine southeastern states, and annual sales topped $1 billion despite the proliferation of drugstore chains.

To help offset the power of the chains, Smith Drug and Georgia's Academy of Independent Pharmacy (AIP) formed an alliance to improve the volume buying power of both organizations. Smith Drug also greatly expanded its presence in Georgia, where previously it had served about 50 pharmacies. The wholesaler could then tap into AIP's membership pool of 500 pharmacies. Other alliances followed in the new century. In 2001 a contract was signed with Innovatix, a national group purchasing organization in the alternate care marketplace, to supply its 2,300 members with generic and brand-name pharmaceuticals and medical and surgical supplies. Innovatix members included physician groups, long-term care facilities, and health maintenance organizations.

To better serve its growing roster of customers, Smith Drug opened a new 250,000-square-foot distribution center in 2004 in Fairforest, South Carolina, replacing a 50-year-old facility that through five expansions had grown to 100,000 square feet. Work was also begun on a 100,000-square-foot distribution facility in Paragould, Arkansas, to better serve that part of the country. It opened in 2005.

High technology was not limited to QS/1 and Smith Premier. Smith Drug replaced its old paper-based picking system, labor intensive and prone to errors, with a new voice-directed picking system, Vocollect's Voice-Directed Distribution product. It was introduced first in South Carolina and later in Arkansas. Orders entered into the computer system of Smith Drug were turned into voice commands by Vocollect's voice interface software. Employees were then directed by voice to pick up items. The system, programmed to recognize the voices of the employees, received voice confirmation that the items were picked. Not only was Smith Drug able to achieve a 20 percent increase in productivity, it saved money on overtime that was no longer needed, resulting in a six-month return on the investment. Furthermore, the reduction in errors helped in retaining current customers and adding new ones.

ACQUISITIONS IN THE 21ST CENTURY

JM Smith's other companies expanded their operations as well in the new century. In 2002 the pharmaceutical web site CornerDrugstore.com was acquired and folded into QS/1. Founded by the National Community Pharmacists Association, CornerDrugstore.com had been established to create an online network of independent pharmacies, allowing them to fill customers' prescriptions and sell over-the-counter products online and provide relevant information. The company brought with it more than 800 independent and regional chain pharmacy customers.

In 2004 JM Smith acquired Integral Technical Services Inc., a 17-year-old Greenville, South Carolina-based fiber optics and high-end cabling company that served customers in healthcare, education, financial services, and manufacturing. The business was then combined with Smith Data Processing and the IT and network departments of QS/1 to form Integral Solutions Group, which became the fourth company of JM Smith. The addition of Integral Technical helped the new unit to take JM Smith into new service areas and a broader range of customers.

Through a network of 16 offices in the United States, the subsidiary offered network design, integration, installation, and maintenance to customers in the healthcare, hospitality, education, entertainment, financial, manufacturing, and government sectors. Beyond just voice, data, and video, the company was able to manage building systems, such as security, fire control, lighting, and heating and air conditioning, combining them to lower cabling costs and ongoing operating costs. The company also continued to provide medical and government forms and medicine vial labels. The subsidiary grew further in 2008 with the acquisition of another Greenville-based company, Digital-DNS, a network services company that brought with it a computer network monitoring system that filled out the service offerings of Integral Solutions. Overall, JM Smith was more diversified than ever and well positioned for ongoing prosperity.

Ed Dinger

PRINCIPAL SUBSIDIARIES

Integral Solutions Group; QS/1 Data Systems; Smith Drug Company; Smith Premier Services.

PRINCIPAL COMPETITORS

Cardinal Pharmaceutical Distribution; Kinray Inc.; McKesson Corporation.

FURTHER READING

Anderson, Trevor, "Integral Solutions Group Acquires Greenville Tech Firm," *Spartanburg (S.C.) Herald-Journal,* August 6, 2008, p. C4.

"Consumer Centric: Four Healthcare-Related Companies Comprise JM Smith Corp., Making It a Total Solution Provider for Customers Throughout the United States," *US Business Review,* March 200, p. 90.

"JM Smith Corporation," *South Carolina Business Journal,* January 1, 1989, p. 11.

Winston, Chris, "Spartanburg, S.C., Pharmacy Supplier Is Quiet Privately Held Powerhouse," *Spartanburg (S.C.) Herald-Journal,* October 17, 2004.

Jysk Holding A/S

Sødalsparken 18
Brabrand, DK-8220
Denmark
Telephone: (45 89) 39 75 00
Fax: (45 89) 39 75 01
Web site: http://www.jysk.com

Private Company
Incorporated: 1979 as Jysk Sengetøjslager
Employees: 14,000
Sales: DKK 6.3 billion ($2.5 billion) (2007)
NAICS: 442110 Furniture Stores; 423210 Furniture
   Merchant Wholesalers; 442291 Window Treatment
   Stores

■ ■ ■

Jysk Holding A/S is the "other" Scandinavian flatpack furniture giant. Founded in 1979, the Brabrand, Denmark-based company has grown into one of Europe's leading home furnishing companies. Jysk oversees nearly 1,500 stores in 32 countries. Jysk focuses on the low-price sector, especially the bed and bedding segment. The company is Europe's largest seller of mattresses. Most of the company's stores operate under the JYSK name, pronounced as "yoo-sk" and taken from the name of a Danish dialect. Jysk's core operations remain the Northern and Central European regions, which are informally grouped by the company as Jysk Nordic. These operations, which cover Scandinavia, the Netherlands, the United Kingdom, Poland, Hungary, the Czech Republic, Slovakia, and Slovenia, represent

nearly 500 company-owned stores. The group's German and Austrian business, which operate stores under the Dänisches Bettenlager and Betternwelt names, are grouped into a separate company, while the French and Swiss Jysk businesses are grouped directly under the holding company.

Jysk also operates a small chain of Inspiration furnishing stores in New Jersey in the United States. While much of the company's growth has come from its own expansion, Jysk has long operated a franchise network, which has helped it penetrate a number of markets, including Canada, the United Arab Emirates, and Iceland. The company has plans to enter Russia in 2009, and China in 2010. By then the company expects to have more than 2,000 stores worldwide. Jysk remains 100 percent owned by its founder and chairman Lars Larsen and generates total sales of approximately $3.7 billion each year. Jan Bogh is the group's managing director.

ORIGINS IN 1979

In the late 1970s Lars Larsen worked at a draper's shop, but dreamed of founding his own home furnishings store. The Danish retail market at the time remained highly fragment, dominated by small, independent stores that emphasized the quality of their goods over pricing. Larsen, however, recognized opportunity in building a large-volume operation targeting the discount sector. By developing purchasing strength through high volume, Larsen sought to pass on pricing benefits to his customers.

Larsen at first focused his retail concept on the bedding and bed linen market, emphasizing products such as eiderdowns, comforters, quilts and the like—a particularly important product category for the Nordic climate in Denmark. Larsen began developing relationships with suppliers willing to back the young business. His breakthrough came when he managed to convince a branch of the Norresundby Bank to provide financial backing.

Larsen chose the name Jysk Sengetøjslager for his store. Jysk was the name of the dialect spoken in Jutland, the largest region of Denmark. According to the company's web site, the word *jysk* carried other connotations as well, such as "modesty, thoroughness and honesty." Larsen opened his first store in Aarhus in 1979. The shop was small, featuring a self-service, no-frills design with goods displayed in the boxes from which they were received from the manufacturers.

Larsen himself starred in the company's advertising campaign, introducing himself to Danish consumers with the now-famous tagline: "Hello, my name is Lars Larsen and I have a good deal for you." The company's initial focus on bedding was further reinforced by adopting a goose into the company's logo. Later advertising campaigns featured the "goose on the loose" tagline.

The success of the store enabled Larsen to roll out the Jysk concept into other Danish markets. The company also expanded its product range to add furniture and other home furnishings. Jysk's rapid expansion enabled it to head off challenges posed in particular by another fast-growing furniture group, Sweden's Ikea.

The two companies came to resemble each other quite closely, particularly with their focus on the so-called flatpack segment, in which customers were required to assemble their own furniture. This permitted furniture to be packed flat in their cartons and in store warehouses, maximizing the use of space. Despite competition from the rival Scandinavian furniture group, Jysk was able to differentiate itself. Jysk stores tended to be smaller. The company also managed to offer lower prices, in part by turning away from Ikea's preference for using known designers.

GOING INTERNATIONAL IN 1984

Rapid growth in Denmark quickly encouraged Larsen to target expansion on an international level. The company's first move came in 1984, when it opened its first store in Germany. This store took on the name of Dänisches Bettenlager—a name the company would maintain for the German market into the later years of the first decade of the 2000s. While the German operations were conducted under Jysk's direct control, the company also put into place a franchising model. The company's first franchise store opened in Greenland that year.

The move into franchising often took the form of long-term partnerships. Such was the case with the company's entry into the small Faroe Islands, with its population of just 50,000. Larsen's initial franchise partner reneged on their deal, leaving with Larsen with several containers of unsold product that had been destined for the Faroe Islands store. In 1984, however, Larsen met Jakup Jacobsen, who was then working as a fisherman, in one of the Jysk stores. Jacobsen convinced Larsen to give him the Faroe Island franchise—which quickly became one the company's most active. Jacobsen soon became Jysk's primary franchisee, opening his next store in Iceland in 1988. Over the next two decades Jacobsen expanded his own Jysk empire to more than 60 stores, including control of the Canadian, Estonian, Latvian, and Lithuanian markets.

Jysk itself was moving forward with its goal to become a leading European furniture retailer. Norway became the group's next market, with its first store opened in Stavanger in 1989. The company next entered enemy territory, as it were, when it opened its first store in Ikea's home turf, in Malmö, Sweden, in 1991. By then the company had developed a second store format, called Jysk Bäddlager. At the same time, the company also began adapting its format for an entry into the U.S. market. This move came 1992, when the company opened its first store in New Jersey. For its U.S. entry, the company added a new store name, Bed n' Linen. The group's U.S. business was later expanded into a second format, Linen n' Furniture, and by 1995 the company's U.S. operations included four stores. However, the group's U.S. expansion appeared to stop there, as Jysk's U.S. presence remained focused on its four New Jersey locations, renamed as Inspiration, into the end of the first decade of the 2000s.

NEW NAME IN 2001

By 1995 Jysk boasted more than 500 stores in its network. The group filled in a gap in its Scandinavian coverage the following year, with the opening of its first store in Finland, in Turku. Jacobsen next led the expansion of the group's franchise business, with the opening of its first Canadian store, in Coquitlam, British Columbia, in 1996. In that year, also, the first franchise store opened in Latvia.

Not all of the company's efforts were equally successful. The company attempted to expand its brand into the travel market, setting up its own tourism agency selling holiday packages through its furniture stores. Customers failed to warm to the concept, however, and Jysk was forced to abandon these operations.

Jysk returned its focus to expanding its international presence at the start of the 21st century. Jysk entered Austria in 2000, opening its first store there in Vocklabruck. This expansion came through the group's German subsidiary, and the Dänisches Bettenlager brand was extended to the Austrian market. Also in that year, the company moved into the Polish market, with a first store in Gdansk.

In 2001, Jysk changed its name, dropping the Sengetøjslager to become simply Jysk A/S. Larsen was also joined at the head of the company by Jan Bogh, who took over as the group's managing director. The company then began rebranding its operations in Denmark, Sweden, and Finland, converting all of its stores in these markets to the Jysk name. The following year the group's Norwegian stores adopted the simplified name as well. By 2004 all of the company's stores, with the exception of its German and Austrian businesses, had changed their name to Jysk.

By then the company had added a number of new markets, including the Czech Republic in 2003 and Hungary in 2005. The group's franchise operations all grew significantly during this period, with new stores in Estonia, Lithuania, Bulgaria, Moscow, and Kiev opening by 2006. In the meantime, the group's Canadian operations had become one of its fastest growing, with 33 stores operating there by 2007. That year the company's franchise partnerships had extended its reach into the United Arab Emirates as well, with a first store opened in Dubai.

HEADING TO CHINA BY 2010

Jysk continued to fill in gaps in its geographic portfolio. In 2006 the company opened four stores in the Netherlands, as well as its first two stores in Switzerland and a store in Slovakia. Jysk then moved into France, with a store opening in Corbeil-Essonnes, near Paris, in 2007.

At the beginning of 2008, the group plugged another major hole in its geographic coverage: the United Kingdom. The group established a headquarters for that market in Manchester, then promptly opened its first two stores in Mansfield and Lincoln by April of that year. Jysk U.K. appeared to be among the most ambitious of the company's foreign subsidiaries. Despite the gloomy economic period, the company announced plans to open as many as 25 new stores per year in the United Kingdom, with plans to boost its presence in the market to as many as 500 locations. The company backed these expansion plans with a $100 million in funding.

Europe continued to play a central role in Jysk's growth strategy. The company added operations in Macedonia, Romania, and Slovenia in 2007 and 2008. The company then announced its plan to enter the Russian market directly in 2009. This expansion was to be followed by a more ambitious move, as the company announced its intention to open its first stores in mainland China by 2010. At that time, the group expected to increase its total store network to more than 2,000 stores, compared with nearly 1,500 at the end of 2008. With sales of $2.5 billion in that year, Jysk had established itself as a major player in the world's home furnishings market.

M. L. Cohen

PRINCIPAL SUBSIDIARIES

JYSK A/S; JYSK AB (Sweden); JYSK AS (Norway); JYSK B.V. (Netherlands); JYSK d.o.o (Slovenia); JYSK Kft (Hungary); JYSK Limited (United Kingdom); JYSK

OY (Finland); JYSK s.r.o (Czech Republic); JYSK s.r.o (Slovakia); JYSK Sp. z o.o (Poland).

PRINCIPAL COMPETITORS

PPR S.A.; Delta Corporation Ltd.; Mohamed Mahmoud Sons Group; IKEA North America; Steinhoff International Holdings Ltd.; Conforama Holding S.A.; Ikea Deutschland GmbH and Company KG; Pelhams Ltd.; Hoeffner Moebelgesellschaft GmbH and Company KG; Blokker B.V.

FURTHER READING

Bruno, Joe Bel, "Jysk, Danish Retail Giant, to Open Sainte-Foy, QC Store on October 18th," *America's Intelligence Wire,* October 2, 2008.

Buckland, Danny, and Steve Hawkes, "Furniture Chain Targets IKEA's in Price War," *Times Online,* April 1, 2008.

Cooper, Matt, "Jysk to Open New Store in Niagara Falls," *America's Intelligence Wire,* August 6, 2008.

Duxbury, Nick, "A Wild Goose Chase?" *Property Week,* June 27, 2008, p. S11.

Godfrey, Ron, "JYSK Boss Hails Customer Care Strategy," *Press,* June 12, 2008.

"Jysk Settles into U.K. with Two Stores," *Property Week,* February 1, 2008, p. 7.

Slaughter, Powell, "Danish Retailer Paints a Target on Ikea," *Home Furnishing Business,* April 3, 2008.

Todd, Lisa, "Ikea Watch Out, There's a Jysk About," *Sunday Mirror,* April 6, 2008, p. 28.

Knauf Gips KG

Am Bahnhof 7
Iphofen, D-97346
Germany
Telephone: (49 9323) 31-0
Fax: (49 9323) 31-277
Web site: http://www.knauf.com

Private Company
Incorporated: 1933 as Rheinische Gipsindustrie und Bergwerksunternehmen OHG
Employees: 22,000 (2007)
Sales: EUR 5.5 billion ($7.6 billion) (2007)
NAICS: 327420 Gypsum Product Manufacturing; 327999 All Other Miscellaneous Nonmetallic Mineral Product Manufacturing; 326140 Polystyrene Foam Product Manufacturing; 333911 Pump and Pumping Equipment Manufacturing

■ ■ ■

Knauf Gips KG is one of the world's largest manufacturers of gypsum-based construction materials and products. Operating about 60 quarries and mines around the globe, Knauf Gips is also a large gypsum mining company. Headquartered in Iphofen in northern Bavaria, Knauf has over 150 manufacturing plants in many Western and Eastern European countries, including Russia, Ukraine, and Turkey, as well as in North and South America, Indonesia, and China. The company's range of gypsum-based products includes gypsum plasters for interior and exterior use, plasterboard, and gypsum fiber boards for walls and floors. Knauf also makes a complete product range for drywall construction and interior finishing for the construction trade and the home improvement market. In addition, Knauf produces lime and cement plasters, glass wool and other insulation materials, cardboard, molded polystyrene used in packaging, and injection molded parts for the automotive and consumer electronics industries.

The company's mechanical engineering division makes control consoles, switching cabinets, machine coverings, and other components. Knauf USG Systems, a joint venture with American USG, makes glass fiber-reinforced cement panels for use indoors and outdoors. Another subsidiary, Knauf AMF, manufactures modular ceiling systems based on mineral fiber panels. Roughly four-fifths of Knauf's sales are generated outside of Germany. The private company is owned and managed by the Knauf family. Managing partners are the cousins Nikolaus and Baldwin Knauf, the oldest sons of the two brothers, Alfons and Karl Knauf, who founded the company during the Great Depression.

RESEARCH LEADS TO GYPSUM MINING OPERATION

Alfons and Karl Knauf spent many of their teenage years in Wellen, a small town on the river Mosel on the Luxembourg border. The Saar region had a long tradition in mining and the two brothers decided to become mining engineers. During their college years they developed a special interest in gypsum, one of the most important minerals for construction materials. Alfons and Karl studied the different kinds of gypsum in col-

COMPANY PERSPECTIVES

The Knauf philosophy stems from the model on which the company is based: we are a family company. The family includes our employees and our customers and consumers. Our strength comes from the earth. So ecology and economy are inseparable as far as we are concerned. And we demonstrate this. We act on it. Our focus is on our customers. They are the meaning and purpose of our thoughts and actions. It is us who make the market. We plan innovations to meet tomorrow's requirements. We are the market leaders. This implies an obligation to assume responsibility for the public and the environment. The high quality of our products enhances and creates an atmosphere of well-being for people.

lege and spent their semester breaks exploring the quality of the gypsum rock deposits in their home region.

Next, Alfons Knauf asked a friend who was working at a university to locate all gypsum rock deposits elsewhere in Germany on the geological maps he had access to and to collect as much additional information on the deposits as possible. Based on that research, Alfons Knauf rode across Germany on a motorcycle and visited the most promising sites, where he collected additional probes and information on existing mining operations.

When 26-year-old Alfons Knauf graduated from the Berlin Technical College in 1932, Germany was experiencing a severe economic, political, and social crisis. The chances of finding a civil service position looked slim. Hence, the Knauf brothers decided to found their own gypsum mining enterprise. Their research had shown that a deposit in Schengen, Luxembourg, contained high-quality gypsum rock. Lengthy negotiations with the owner of the land resulted in an agreement that allowed the Knaufs to mine the gypsum in exchange for a mining fee. A similar agreement was signed with the city of Schengen.

Hand drills were acquired, railroad tracks were laid, mining workers were hired, and a small office space was found at the Oudill-Gloden Café and Restaurant in Schengen. On October 4, 1932, the first shipment of raw gypsum rocks was delivered by boat to a cement factory in Oberhausen, a city in the heart of the highly industrialized Ruhr region.

GROWING A BUSINESS IN PLASTER PRODUCTS

The next year, the Knauf brothers acquired a small lime works in Perl, a German town in the upper Mosel region, after they had received a mining permit for the nearby gypsum rock deposits. Named Rheinische Gipsindustrie und Bergwerksunternehmen OHG, the Knauf brothers' first factory started producing plaster of paris and building plaster in a variety qualities as well as floor panels made from plaster and coconut fibers.

For deliveries inside the region, the Knaufs purchased a large truck and founded a separate trucking business. However, most of Rheinische Gipsindustrie's output was shipped by boat down the Mosel River to the large cement factories along the Rhine and Ruhr—for a good reason. Buying from the Knauf brothers saved them a good deal of money because shipping their product by boat cost less than a quarter compared to shipping it by train from other suppliers.

This competitive advantage helped the Knauf brothers win new customers, but it had a downside as well. The water levels of the Mosel fluctuated significantly depending on the season. The rather primitive boats sometimes had to wait for days, or even weeks, until the river carried enough water, and their freight did not always arrive at its final destination. To ensure that they could guarantee reliable deliveries, in 1935 the Knauf brothers started leasing storage space in close proximity to their main customers.

The thriving business with cement manufacturers along the Rhine and Ruhr generated a constant stream of revenues that enabled the Knauf brothers to expand their enterprise. The re-integration of the Saar region into the German Empire in 1935 and the economic boom that followed in the second half of the 1930s under the Nazis, particularly with the construction of the *Autobahn,* but also the construction of bunker systems and other military installations, gave the construction industry a major boost.

As rising demand for their plaster products reached the capacity of the existing plant, Alfons and Karl Knauf started looking for additional mining and production locations. Prior to the beginning of World War II, the Knauf brothers acquired a second plaster production in Siersburg and two nearby gypsum quarries and two additional gypsum quarries, one in Hüttenheim near Iphofen in Franconia and one in Stadtoldendorf south of Hannover. In 1938 the Knauf brothers renamed their company Gebr. Knauf, Westdeutsche Gipswerke. By that time their operations produced 28,000 tons of plaster annually—almost as much as the largest German plaster manufacturer.

KEY DATES

■

1932: Alfons and Karl Knauf start a gypsum mining operation.

1938: The company is renamed Gebr. Knauf, Westdeutsche Gipswerke.

1947: Fränkische Gipswerke GmbH is founded in Iphofen.

1958: Gebr. Knauf builds its first gypsum plaster board factory in Iphofen.

1960: Alfons Knauf's patented *Rostbandverfahren* technology increases plaster of Paris output by a factor of seven.

1962: The company's first factory for processing synthetic gypsum is built in Castrop-Rauxel.

1970: Knauf's first subsidiary abroad is founded in Austria; Knauf acquires a majority stake in Dortmund-based Deutsche Perlite GmbH.

1972: Gebr. Knauf Saar-Gipswerke is merged with Gebr. Knauf Westdeutsche Gipswerke.

1974: Knauf spins off its engineering division and launches its first home improvement product line.

1978: The company acquires a production facility for glass wool in the United States.

1979: Knauf takes over drywall construction products manufacturer Richter System GmbH & Co.

1993: Knauf expands into Russia.

1995: A plasterboard joint venture is established in China.

2002: The company builds an insulation materials production plant in California.

2003: The company is renamed Knauf Gips KG.

WARTIME DISRUPTION AND POSTWAR RECONSTRUCTION

Shortly after the beginning of World War II in September 1939, the western Saar region became one of the war's first battlefields. In their temporary domiciles in Iphofen and Stadtoldendorf, the Knauf brothers learned about the destruction of their Perl plant in 1940. Although the Knaufs were able to move back into their homes after Adolf Hitler's victory over France, factory reconstruction went slowly due to the growing difficulties of obtaining the necessary machinery and supplies during the war. The truck fleet was seized by the *Wehrmacht*, and the drivers were drafted into the military. In 1943 Gebr. Knauf leased an additional plaster manufacturing plant in Markt Einersheim northwest of Hüttenheim. Toward the end of the war, the Knaufs once more moved away from the Saar to Iphofen.

After the war ended in 1945 all operations of Gebr. Knauf that were located in the French-, British-, and American-occupied zones were overseen and managed by trustees appointed by the Allied forces' administrations. In 1947 Karl Knauf founded a new company, Fränkische Gipswerke GmbH, to regain a foothold in the market. Fränkische Gipswerke was based in a warehouse complex at Iphofen's train station that was used as a workshop, garage, storage space, office, and home for Karl Knauf's family.

In 1948 Gebr. Knauf's subsidiaries in the British and American zones were returned to their owners. Three years later the Knaufs regained control over their operations in the Saar, which were by then named Saar-Gipswerke GmbH. In the years following the foundation of the Federal Republic of Germany in 1949 in West Germany, the Knauf enterprise began to thrive, driven by the enormous demand for construction materials, including plaster, in postwar Germany.

COMPETITIVE ADVANTAGE THROUGH INNOVATION

Securing additional sources of raw material supply became an ongoing task for Knauf. In the 1950s and 1960s the company acquired a number of smaller plaster manufacturers and systematically developed new gypsum deposits in southern and northern Germany. New heavy machinery made it possible to extract the gypsum through surface mining in the 1960s. However, it was the Knauf brothers' focus on developing their own technical and product innovations that laid the foundation for the company's dynamic growth in the next decades.

Convinced that only the quick transition to industrial production methods could satisfy the huge demand, Karl Knauf decided to use rotary kilns for plaster manufacturing—something unheard of in southern Germany. After the initial skepticism of the company's customers had been overcome, demand for Knauf's "rotary kiln plaster" rose quickly, so that an additional rotary kiln was installed in 1953. Five years later, under the brand name Perllitin, Knauf started manufacturing brushable gypsum varieties in several colors for use in interior wall design.

The company also introduced plaster in small tubes for patching small cracks or holes in walls and ceilings. It became a bestseller. After intensive research and development, Knauf built its first gypsum plasterboard factory in Iphofen in 1958. In the following decades gypsum plasterboard, or drywall, evolved as one of Knauf's main products.

A number of gypsum quarries in Franconia contained significant amounts of anhydrite, a grayish mineral that could be transformed to gypsum by mixing it with water. Karl Knauf planned to use it for a plaster floor mixture and his chief chemist, Bruno Wandser, developed and patented a chemical substance which was needed in order for the anhydrite floor to harden. Additional intensive testing yielded a concrete-like material that proved to be ideal for building supportive structures in underground coal mines and Knauf started supplying the so-called mining anhydrite to coal mines in the Saar, Ruhr, and Eiffel regions.

REPLACING LIME PLASTER WITH GYPSUM

In the late 1950s Knauf's laboratories followed up with another innovation—a building plaster based on plaster of Paris. The idea behind it was to replace the commonly used lime plaster with a gypsum-based product. At the heart of the four different varieties of Knauf's ready-to-use dry plaster mixes was a so-called delayer, a proprietary ingredient that slowed the hardening of the wet plaster while it was applied to a surface. This special property allowed users to work on larger surface areas at a time and to smoothen them consistently before the plaster hardened.

A major invention followed in 1960 with the so-called *Rostbandverfahren,* a new technology for producing plaster of Paris developed and patented by Alfons Knauf that boosted the output of Knauf's Siersburg plant by a factor of seven. To sell the resulting enormous volumes of plaster of Paris, the company expanded its sales efforts to all of Germany. Looking for new ways to expand the market for plaster, Alfons Knauf envisioned a wall plaster that could be applied mechanically instead of by hand. In 1965 his engineers came up with Maschinenputz MP 75, a so-called machine plaster. Along with the plaster, Knauf developed the machine as well—a combined plaster mixer and conveyor named Gipsomat. Manufactured under a license from Knauf by German machine tool firm Putzmeister, the Gipsomat was a combination of a mixer and an applicator and became a bestseller.

Early in the 1960s Knauf began to explore a new potential raw material source—so-called industrial gypsum. Initial tests had shown that the plaster made from the synthetic material, a side product of many industrial processes, did not harden like plaster made from natural gypsum. After many experiments, Knauf's laboratory developed a process that modified the crystalline structure of the synthetic material and the necessary technology for mass production. In 1962 the company built a new plaster factory for processing industrial gypsum in Castrop-Rauxel. In the following years Knauf continued to work closely with manufacturers producing industrial gypsum as a side product and refined the company's processing technologies.

DIVERSIFICATION AND EXPANSION FOLLOW REORGANIZATION

By the late 1960s the enterprise of the two Knauf brothers consisted of two rather different companies. Gebr. Knauf Saar-Gipswerke, based in Siersburg, manufactured mainly building plaster, which was marketed directly to the construction trade. Iphofen-based Gebr. Knauf Westdeutsche Gipswerke produced primarily plaster of paris and gypsum plaster board and distributed its product lines via construction wholesalers. To streamline the organization, the Knaufs decided to unite the two separate administrative organizations and to merge the two companies. Beginning in 1967, company headquarters were located in Iphofen.

Two years later, Alfons Knauf's oldest son, Nikolaus, and Karl Knauf's oldest son, Baldwin, became managing partners. Their brothers and sisters, most of whom were already actively involved in the management of the family business, became limited partners. Nikolaus, a mining engineer, managed the company's technical division with his uncle Karl. Baldwin, who had a degree in business administration, together with his uncle Alfons were responsible for administration and sales.

In 1972 Gebr. Knauf Saar-Gipswerke was officially merged with Gebr. Knauf Westdeutsche Gipswerke. By that time Gebr. Knauf had about 14 production subsidiaries in Germany and the company's workforce had grown to roughly 2,000. Until their death in the early 1980s, the two company founders, Alfons and Karl Knauf, continued to support their sons in steering the family business.

The year 1970 was an important historical milestone for Knauf. In that year the company took its first steps into two new directions that led to the continual growth of the enterprise in the following decades—diversification and expansion abroad. Starting out in Weissenbach, Austria, in 1970, Knauf built plaster and gypsum wallboard factories in many countries around the world.

GLOBAL EXPANSION IN THE SEVENTIES AND EIGHTIES

In the 1970s and 1980s the company set up subsidiaries in Belgium, the Netherlands, Italy, Greece, Switzerland, and France. Diversification began in 1970 when Knauf acquired a majority stake in Dortmund-based Deutsche Perlite GmbH. If sandy, corn-sized perlite, a volcanic glass, was exposed to a high temperature, it expanded to 15 times its original size—similar to popcorn. The resulting perlite granulate was an ideal material for use in construction for thermal and sound insulation. In later years Knauf would develop other perlite-based products such as waterproof cement boards marketed under the Aquapanel brand, and perlite dry bulk levelers.

In 1974 Knauf launched its first product line for the home improvement retail market, which was developed by Knauf's Bauprodukte division. In 1979 Knauf acquired Richer System GmbH & Co., a manufacturer of drywall construction products, including metal rails, corner protection rails, and punched and galvanized metal parts for drywall construction. Three years later Knauf took over lime plaster manufacturer Koch Kalk und Bau GmbH. The company was later transformed into Knauf Marmorit, which by 2008 operated eight production sites for cement and lime plaster for external use as well as heat insulation products.

When the economic recession following the oil price rise in 1973 slowed Knauf's expansion, the company spun off its engineering division into a new subsidiary, Knauf Engineering, in 1974. Instead of building new plaster factories for Knauf, its engineers built them for other clients. In the 1970s Knauf Engineering planned and built complete plaster factories in many countries, including Iran, Algeria, Egypt, Pakistan, Yugoslavia, the Soviet Union, Thailand, and China.

Another area Knauf Engineering focused on was the development of technologies and equipment for processing so-called FGD-gypsum. A new law in Germany in 1983 ushered in the new age of synthetic gypsum. According to the law, coal-fired power plants had to be equipped with flue gas desulfurization (FGD) technology. Large amounts of natural gypsum rock were used in the process, which in turn produced large amounts of synthetic gypsum or FGD-gypsum.

In the 1980s Knauf Engineering realized more than a dozen FGD-gypsum processing facilities for large electric utility companies in Germany and abroad. FGD-gypsum also evolved as a major raw material for Knauf's plaster production, which made the company less dependent on the location of natural gypsum deposits. Thanks to the contacts Knauf Engineering had

built, Knauf signed long-term agreements for the delivery of FGD-gypsum with many large power plant operators around the world.

NEW FOREIGN SUBSIDIARIES AND GLOBAL ACQUISITIONS

When Knauf started expanding globally in the 1990s, Knauf Engineering returned to its original activity—building new plants for Knauf. However, according to company estimates, about one-fourth of the world's production capacities for gypsum-based products were set up by Knauf Engineering. A second Knauf engineering subsidiary, PFT Putz- und Fördertechnik, successfully developed and marketed mixing pumps and conveyor technologies for applying building plaster. PFT founded foreign subsidiaries in many countries in Western Europe, the United Kingdom, Turkey, Poland, and the United States.

In 1978 Knauf again ventured into new territory when it acquired a production facility for glass wool in the United States in Shelbyville, Indiana, from Certain Teed Corp. When the demand for glass-wool-based insulation products increased, Knauf built a second plant in Lanett, Alabama, in 1987. Three years later the company acquired Southern Ohio Foam, a manufacturer of thermal insulation products and packaging materials made from polystyrene foam.

In 2002 Knauf invested over $150 million in a state-of-the-art production plant for insulation materials in Shasta Lake, California. By then Knauf's North American subsidiary generated $400 million in annual sales. After the turn of the new millennium Knauf acquired ten glass wool and mineral wool producers in Europe and established additional capacities in Eastern Europe and Russia. Knauf also ventured into the production of injection molded parts made from polystyrene foam for the automotive and consumer electronics industries.

In the 1990s Knauf expanded into other western European countries. In Scandinavia the company acquired gypsum product manufacturers in Denmark, Finland, and Norway. Knauf also established a production subsidiary in Turkey. After the opening of the Iron Curtain in 1989 Knauf focused its geographic expansion efforts on Central and Eastern Europe. New production plants and sales offices were established in East Germany, Hungary, the Czech Republic, Poland, Croatia, Macedonia, Bulgaria, and the Baltic states.

GROWING THE BUSINESS IN RUSSIA AND CHINA

However, Knauf's most important investment abroad was the establishment of a number of large factories in

Russia beginning in 1993. These were located near the metropolitan areas of Moscow and St. Petersburg as well as in Krasnodar in southern Russia by the Black Sea and the joint venture OAO Knauf Gips in Novomoskovsk, Russia's largest gypsum mining operation, in the Tula region. Knauf also ventured into Moldavia, Kazakhstan, and Ukraine.

As early as the 1970s Knauf took its first steps to conquer another potentially vast market—China. After first contacts were established, the company's engineering units built two large plaster factories and one gypsum panel plant in China. In 1995 Knauf established the company's first joint venture, Knauf Plasterboard (Wuhu) Co. Ltd., in the country. Two additional drywall productions were set up north of Hong Kong and near Tianjin, China's third largest city, in the late 1990s. Finally, Knauf moved into South America where it established production sites in Brazil and Argentina. By 2008 Knauf operated more than 150 manufacturing plants and about 60 gypsum quarries and mines around the globe.

SUCCESS THROUGH CUSTOMER EDUCATION

One of Knauf's success recipes over the years had been to set up training centers at many of the company's subsidiaries where wholesalers and retailers were informed in seminars on Knauf's products in great detail, and where tens of thousands of craftspeople in the various construction trades received practical training in how to work with the company's products. Most importantly, this strategy created lasting personal relationships between Knauf's salespeople and technical personnel and their customers and helped a great deal in obtaining critical information for the company's market research.

Early in the 21st century, with approximately 1.1 billion tons of gypsum stone reserves, there seemed to be no shortage of raw material supplies for Knauf. In terms of global demand, the company's strategic focus moved away from the stagnating German market toward the promising growth markets in Central and Eastern Europe as well as in Asia and the Middle East.

Evelyn Hauser

PRINCIPAL SUBSIDIARIES

Knauf Bauprodukte GmbH; Knauf Perlite GmbH; Knauf PFT GmbH & Co. KG; Richter System GmbH & Co. KG; Knauf USG Systems GmbH; Knauf AMF GmbH & Co. KG; Knauf Dämmstoffe GmbH; Knauf Marmorit GmbH; Knauf Integral KG; Knauf La Rhénane SA (France); Knauf Insulation (Belgium); Knauf N. et B. Knauf et Cie. S.C.S. (Belgium); ISO-LAVA G.C.V. (Belgium); Knauf GmbH Sucursal en Espana (Spain); Knauf UK GmbH (United Kingdom); Danogips A/S (Denmark); Knauf Oy (Finland); NOR-GIPS AS (Norway); Knauf Insulation Ltd. (United Kingdom); Knauf di Lothar Knauf s.a.s. (Italy); Knauf Gypsopiia A.B.E.E. (Greece); Knauf Ges. m.b.H (Austria); Knauf Praha spol. s.r.o. (Czech Republic); Knauf Sp. z.o.o. (Poland); Knauf Insulation (Czech Republic); Knauf Riga SIA (Latvia); Knauf d.o.o., Croatia; Knauf Radika AD, Mazedonia; Knauf GUS (CIS) (Russia); Knauf Gips Kyiv TOO (Ukraine); Knauf Gips Kaptschagaj OAO (Kazakhstan); TEPE Knauf A.S. (Turkey); Knauf Morocco; Knauf Plâtres Tunisiens (Tunisia); Knauf Plasterboard (China); PT Knauf Gypsum Indonesia; Knauf Insulation (United States); Knauf do Brasil Ltda.; Knauf ISOPOR Ltda. (Brazil); Yesos Knauf GmbH Sucursal Argentina.

PRINCIPAL COMPETITORS

Lafarge S.A.; Compagnie de Saint-Gobain; BPB plc; Saint-Gobain Rigips GmbH.

FURTHER READING

"German Knauf Gips Plans to Buy Austrian Heraklith," *APA-Economic News Service,* August 1, 2005.

"Knauf Grows Abroad," *Europe Intelligence Wire,* February 18, 2005.

"Knauf Launches Plant in Kazakhstan," *Central Asia & Caucasus Business Report,* November 29, 2004.

"Knauf Postpones Investment into Ukraine until 2012," *Ukraine Business Weekly,* July 28, 2008.

"Knauf to Invest over 100 mln Euros in Development in Russia," *Russia & CIS Business & Investment Weekly,* August 26, 2006.

"Knauf to Set up Gypsum Board Plant in RAK FTZ," *MENA English (Middle East and North Africa Financial Network),* March 23, 2008.

Komina, Natalya, "Knauf Fosters Growth Areas in Russian Industry," *RusData DiaLine-BizEkon News,* March 19, 1997.

Kullrich, Antje, "Der stille Billigflieger," *Börsen-Zeitung,* January 30, 2008, p. 7.

Rödiger, Werner, et al., *Wachsen und Werden: Biografie der Unternehmerfamilie Knauf,* Iphofen, Germany: Knauf Gips KG, 2003, 416 p.

Kronos, Inc.

---

297 Billerica Road
Chelmsford, Massachusetts 01824
U.S.A.
Telephone: (978) 250-9800
Toll Free: (800) 225-1561
Fax: (978) 367-5900
Web site: http://www.kronos.com

Private Company
Incorporated: 1977
Employees: 3,400
Sales: $662 million (2007 est.)
NAICS: 511210 Software Publishers

■ ■ ■

Kronos, Inc., is a leading provider of human capital management (HCM) software and services. Clients in over 60 countries use Kronos's products to manage their workforce, reduce costs, increase worker productivity, and improve employee satisfaction. The company serves a broad range of industry and its customers include IKEA Systems B.V., Waste Management Inc., Volkswagen de Mexico S.A. de C.V., and the U.S. Department of Homeland Security. Kronos, which has experienced robust growth since the 1990s, was taken private in 2007 by Hellman & Friedman Capital Partners LLC. Kronos claims that 30 million people use its products each day.

DEVELOPMENT AND EARLY YEARS

Kronos (the Greek word for "time") was founded in 1977 by Mark S. Ain, a computer science and engineering graduate of the Massachusetts Institute of Technology, with an M.B.A. from the University of Rochester. His prior work experience consisted of stints at Esso International, Digital Equipment Corp., and a Concord, New Hampshire, consulting firm. Working out of his home in Newton, Massachusetts, Ain and inventor Larry Baxter had been planning since 1974 to introduce a microprocessor based product for a technologically backward industry. Ain and his partner considered 150 possible products and narrowed this field to 12 before choosing the time clock business, which had remained essentially unchanged since 1888. In place of the standard electromechanical time clock, used for payroll purposes, Baxter devised an electronic time clock. The year 1978 was devoted to funding the endeavor, and the Kronos electronic time clock was introduced in December 1979. The first one in the United States, it sold for under $1,000, compared to about $400 for electromechanical time clocks.

Electromechanical time clocks, some still in operation after 40 years, recorded only the hour and minute that workers punched in and out, leaving to clerks the tedious and error prone task of totaling the numbers every week or two. By contrast, electronic clocks delivered a total each day, printed on the time card, and could be linked to other computers to total the numbers for the payroll period electronically. Nevertheless, developing their clock took Ain and Baxter nearly three

---

COMPANY PERSPECTIVES

Kronos' vision is to be universally recognized as experts who empower organizations to effectively manage their workforce.

---

years instead of the six months they expected, mainly because the software had to accommodate hundreds of different corporate policies on such matters as how overtime was calculated and how late a worker would be permitted to punch in before being docked.

Kronos's first customer was a small copy shop on Broadway in New York City, so small, Ain recalled to a *Boston Globe* reporter, "that the only place for the clock was in the restroom." Another early customer, he added, was a frustrated convenience dairy owner in a tough section of Brooklyn who "called and said that he was about to use an ax on 'the clock' or on one of our servicemen," and whose second clock caught on fire. Business was so poor that on three occasions Ain told his employees not to cash the paychecks he distributed. In the fall of 1980, however, the company received $500,000 in venture capital investment. By 1981 Kronos had sales of about $2 million a year, and in 1984, when sales reached $9 million, the company was making a modest profit and was able to move to Waltham from leased quarters in Cambridge near Harvard University's business school.

A PERIOD OF GROWTH BUT NO PROFITS

By mid-1985 Kronos's models had advanced considerably in sophistication. They could be programmed to keep workers from clocking in (by magnetic ID card at that time) too early or out too late and thus earning unauthorized overtime. They could break down labor costs by worker, department, overtime hours, and shifts, and calculate labor costs every day to keep them from outstripping sales. The company's clientele included restaurants, retailers such as Montgomery Ward (its biggest customer in 1986), hospitals, factories, and even brokerage houses and law firms. The Marriott hotel chain was installing $4 million worth of Kronos's most advanced system, one linked to an IBM computer, in all 150 of its hotels and was expecting to save at least $6.5 million a year, mostly in labor expenses.

In 1987 Kronos introduced its Jobkeeper Central system, which automated a company's production data, recording such items as billable time, job status, and

production efficiency. Another system introduced in this period was Timekeeper Central, which fed the data from time clocks to a mainframe computer that calculated a company's pay rates and work rules for the payroll program. This enabled managers to track their employees at any moment and avoid overtime by scheduling first the ones who had not worked a full week. By early 1987 Kronos had installed nearly 30,000 time clocks in about 25,000 companies.

Company revenue came to $17 million in fiscal 1986 (the year ended September 30, 1986). This represented a compounded annual growth rate of more than 60 percent since the first 1979 shipment. However, Ain pointed out that Kronos had received $6 million in venture capital and $1.5 million and $2.5 million from a private equity placement. The company, he told the *Boston Globe,* "has only been at the break even point for the last three years or so. We're now transitioning to profitability, looking to go public a year from now."

This assessment was rather optimistic if, as a *Forbes* article reported, Kronos had accumulated losses of $2 million by 1987. During that year Ain raised $3 million more by another private stock placement but chose not to take the company public. When the stock market crashed in October 1987, Ain's irritated backers believed the company had missed its chance to raise as much as $50 million from the sale of stock.

During fiscal 1987 Kronos's revenues grew to $20.3 million, but the company lost $176,000. At this point disgruntled board members, including investors from Drexel Burnham's venture capital unit and New England Capital, pressured Ain into hiring Yagiv Kadar, a Boston paper company executive, as chief operating officer. Kadar immediately fired 15 longtime employees hired by Ain and made the underperforming sales staff meet quotas 60 percent higher than before.

THE PATH TO PUBLIC OWNERSHIP

Kronos had net income of $316,000 on revenues of $25.9 million in fiscal 1988; net income of $1.4 million on revenues of $32.9 million in 1989; net income of $1.5 million on revenues of $39.6 million in 1990; and net income of $2.3 million on revenues of $47.8 million in 1991. In June 1992 the company made its initial public stock offering, raising $9.9 million. Ain again was in full control of his company as president, chairman, and chief executive officer. Clients included such corporate giants as General Motors, Nabisco Brands, American Express, Coca-Cola, and Sony Pictures. One customer said Kronos products had paid for themselves

KEY DATES

1977: Mark S. Ain establishes Kronos.
1979: The Kronos electronic time clock makes its debut.
1987: By this time, Kronos has installed nearly 30,000 time clocks in about 25,000 companies.
1992: Kronos goes public.
1995: Revenues surpass $100 million; the company expands into Mexico.
1998: Cost Systems Group Inc. is acquired.
2001: Gerber Distributing Company is purchased; Workforce Central 4 is launched as Kronos's first entirely web-based suite.
2006: Unicru Inc. is acquired; the company expands into China and Singapore.
2007: Kronos is taken private by Hellman & Friedman Capital Partners LLC.

within six months. About 25,000 units were being shipped annually.

Originally offered for $12 a share, Kronos stock traded as high as $24 in 1992. The underwriter estimated that Kronos had great potential for growth because only an estimated 15 percent of the 650,000 U.S. businesses with 25 or more hourly employees were operating with computerized time clocks. The company posted revenues of $58.1 million (about 10 percent from international operations) and net income of $3.6 million in fiscal 1992. Ain told a *Wall Street Journal* reporter that sales had remained strong despite the recession of the early 1990s because "We tend to get big orders when a company gets in trouble, because that's when they want to control costs. We received four or five big orders the last two years from companies that had just filed bankruptcy."

During fiscal 1993 Kronos earned $4.1 million on net revenues of $67.1 million. Its biggest client at this time was NationsBank, with whom it had signed a multiyear deal worth $5 million to $6 million. Kronos also had won a $3.2 million contract in 1992 with the Chicago Board of Education to install equipment tracking staff attendance, labor costs, and bus movements. Its Timekeeper systems were selling for between $1,300 and $250,000, depending on how many employees a company had and the type of operating system being used. Applying similar technology, new company products also were tracking inventories and managing

shipping and receiving. Customers at that time included General Electric, Pillsbury, and Sears stores.

Kronos made several acquisitions in 1993 and 1994. These included the technology and certain assets of Computer Recovery, Inc., a time accounting software-development concern; ShopTrac Data Collection Systems, a manufacturer of software; all the territories covered by Bay Area Realtime Systems, Inc.; all the territories covered by Midwest Time Accounting Systems, Inc.; certain territories covered by Interboro Systems Corp.; and all of the Southern California territories covered by Compu-Cash Corp. Kronos moved its manufacturing facility from Lowell, Massachusetts, to Chelmsford, Massachusetts, in 1994.

Kronos had net revenues of $92.9 million in fiscal 1994 and $120.4 million in fiscal 1995. Net income came to $4.9 million and $8.4 million, respectively. In fiscal 1996 the results were even better: $148 million and $11.4 million, respectively. In January 1995 the company adopted a shareholder rights plan to defend against a hostile takeover. Shares of its common stock traded for as high as $50 during the year. Ain held 6.4 percent of the stock in 1995; institutions held 83 percent of the company's common stock in 1996. Kronos had no long term debt in June 1996.

EXPANDING PRODUCT LINE

Among the major systems offered by Kronos in 1995 were Timekeeper Central, Timekeeper/AS, ShopTrac Data Collection, and Workforce Management. The Timekeeper systems automatically calculated data on employee hours and then consolidated that information into a number of standard labor management reports. The ShopTrac Data Collection System captured labor and material data for manufacturers to provide real-time information on cost, location, and completion time. This included time and attendance data to provide information for the basis of managing labor resources. The Workforce Management System, developed for the retail and hospitality markets, consisted of several integrated modules that generated the correct staffing level required for the expected level of business, then combined these data with detailed employee information to produce a complete, detailed work schedule. This information was then integrated with the Timekeeper Central System to enable management to compare actual labor costs to budgeted costs.

Optional software modules offered by Kronos included Scheduling, which assisted in creating employee schedules; CardSaver, which recorded employees' in-and-out data for wage and hour inquiries;

Accruals, which calculated each employee's available benefit time; and Attendance Tracker, which recorded and documented employee absences. It also offered the Archive Program, automatically performing long term record keeping. These modules and the program were all designed to expand and enhance the range of functions performed by Kronos's time and attendance and shop floor data collection systems. The company also was marketing standard "off-the-shelf" interface software, including Time Bank (purchased from a third party), Kronos Database Poster (an interface from Timekeeper Central to industry-standard X-Base databases), and DKC/Datalink, an interface between Datakeeper Central and popular material requirements planning (MRP) systems.

Kronos's Datakeeper Central System was collecting and formatting data and transmitting them to MRP and other related applications or host systems. Its Time-Maker System was designed to give smaller businesses the advantage of automated time and attendance data. Gatekeeper was being used to control employee access to a facility. Kronos TeleTime System allowed customer telephones to serve as data input devices. The company also was marketing ACES and ACES PLUS, obtained from a third party, to read data from forms and transmit those data to a time and attendance database.

INTERNATIONAL GROWTH

Kronos also was manufacturing a complete family of intelligent data collection terminals to collect and verify data and communicate these data to a computer for use with the company's application software. Some of these terminals—wall-mounted, desk-mounted, and hand-held—were designed to operate in harsh environments. It was also marketing a number of accessories to its products, including badges, badge making equipment, time cards, bar code labels, and modems.

Kronos's extensive service and support organization accounted for 27 percent of its net revenues in fiscal 1995. This organization relocated from corporate headquarters in Waltham to a new Customer Support Center in Chelmsford during 1996. The company had 21 direct sales and support offices in the United States in 1995. It also had two such offices in Canada and one in Great Britain, and the company also expanded into Mexico that year. In addition to about 50 independent dealers in the United States actively selling and supporting Kronos's products, the company also had such dealers in Argentina, Australia, Canada, Guam, Guatemala, Hong Kong, Jamaica, Mexico, Netherlands Antilles, Panama, Puerto Rico, Singapore, South Africa, Venezuela, and the West Indies. In 1996 it opened subsidiaries in Australia and South Africa. Kronos also

had a joint marketing agreement, established in 1993, with ADP, Inc., under which this company marketed Total Time, a proprietary version of Kronos's PC-based time and attendance software, with data collection terminals manufactured by Kronos.

Kronos was leasing its headquarters in Waltham and its manufacturing facility in Chelmsford in fiscal 1995. In November of the calendar year the company signed a ten-year agreement allowing it to lease another facility in Chelmsford and simultaneously relocated its manufacturing operations to the new facility. Kronos also was leasing 46 sales and support offices in North America and Europe during 1995.

Kronos secured a contract from the state of New York in 1997, which granted the company license to sell its products to all of the state's government organizations including agencies, departments, commissions, counties, cities, towns, villages, and community colleges. The company also continued to grow by making strategic acquisitions. During 1998, the company bought Cost Systems Group Inc., manufacturer of a labor productivity management software package under the name Visionware. It also purchased three of its dealers including Maine-based Higgins Office Products, Canada's MITS Computers Systems Ltd., and Interboro Systems Corp., which served the New York and New Jersey markets.

MOVING INTO THE 21ST CENTURY

The company entered the new millennium on solid ground. Kronos's headquarters were moved to Chelmsford in 2000. The company acquired Denniston & Denniston Inc. the following year and also added Gerber Distributing Company to its arsenal. The latter was the largest dealer acquisition in its history to date. Kronos then went on to purchase SimplexGrinnell LP's Workforce Solutions Division in 2002. Two years later, the company acquired 3i Systems, whose customer base included federal government agencies. It bought Canada-based AD OPT Technologies, an advanced workforce planning and scheduling solutions provider, that same year.

On the product front, the company launched Workforce Central 4, a web-based suite of labor management solutions as well as its first PDA-based solution in 2001. It moved into the human resources management sector the following year through an agreement to license the source code of Best Software's web-based Abra Enterprise product line. During 2004, it launched Workforce Central 5, which offered absence management capabilities for the first time.

Kronos's revenues surpassed $500 million in 2005 and the company reported its 100th consecutive quarter of revenue growth that year. In addition, company founder Mark Ain assumed the executive chairmanship role while his brother, Aron, took over as chief executive officer. The company continued with its growth plans and over the next two years expanded into China, Singapore, India, and Western Europe.

In addition to expanding abroad, Kronos looked to new markets for additional growth. Its expansion strategy became well known during 2006 when the company bought talent acquisition and management firm Unicru Inc. in a $150 million deal. As an August 2006 *Workforce Management* article put it, "Thanks partly to its recent acquisition of hourly workforce specialist Unicru, Kronos is in the midst of a rebirth that could transform the firm from a trusty provider of time-and-attendance applications to a dominant player in the human resources software arena." Indeed, Kronos's management team had set a lofty goal for the company—to be the first company focused on HCM to secure $1 billion in sales.

Private equity firm Hellman & Friedman Capital Partners LLC made a $1.74 billion buyout offer for Kronos in early 2007. The deal was completed in June of that year and Kronos began operating as a private company. Returning to the private sector would allow the firm to invest in new technology as well as domestic and international expansion without having each move scrutinized by Wall Street investors. At the same time, Hellman & Friedman would provide the necessary funds to fuel Kronos's growth. While only time would tell if Kronos would meet its $1 billion sales goal, broth-ers Mark and Aron believed the company was on track for success in the years to come.

Robert Halasz
Updated, Christina M. Stansell

PRINCIPAL COMPETITORS

Ceridian Corporation; Oracle Corporation; SAP AG.

FURTHER READING

Bulkeley, William M., "Kronos Corp. Expects to Report Decline in Net for Quarter, Rise for Full Year," *Wall Street Journal,* October 23, 1992.

Bushnell, Davis, "Your Time, His Clock," *Boston Globe,* March 23, 1987, pp. 37–38.

Frauenheim, Ed, "Kronos Enjoys Its Private Life, Expands Abroad," *Workforce Management,* July 23, 2007.

———, "The (Would-Be) King of HR Software," *Workforce Management,* August 14, 2006.

Jereski, Laura, "'I'm a Bad Manager,'" *Forbes,* February 8, 1988, pp. 134–35.

"Kronos Acquires Two of Its Former Dealers for Frontline Labor Management," *Business Wire,* November 8, 1999.

"Kronos Acquires Visionware Product Suite," *Software Industry Report,* March 16, 1998.

Newport, John Paul, Jr., "Timing Is All," *Fortune,* June 24, 1985, pp. 67–68.

Oliveri, David, "Kronos Carries the Time Clock into the Future," *Boston Business Journal,* September 21, 1992, p. 7.

Strohler, Steven R., "City Payroll Unit Will Get Privatized," *Crain's Chicago Business,* June 14, 1993, p. 35.

Weiner, Elizabeth, "Time Clocks Catch Up with the Computer Age," *Business Week,* November 26, 1984, p. 178H.

Weisman, Robert, "Kronos Agrees to $1.74b Buyout," *Boston Globe,* March 24, 2007.

KTM Power Sports AG

Postfach 91, Stallhofner Strasse 3
Mattighofen, A-5230
Austria
Telephone: (43 07742) 60 00 0
Fax: (43 07742) 60 00 303
Web site: http://www.ktm.com

Public Company
Incorporated: 1934 as Kraftfahrzeuge Trunkenpolz Mattighofen
Employees: 1,625
Sales: EUR 605 million ($741.1 million) (2007)
Stock Exchanges: Vienna
Ticker Symbol: KTM
NAICS: 336991 Motorcycle, Bicycle, and Parts Manufacturing

■ ■ ■

KTM Power Sports AG is Austria's only motorcycle manufacturer, and the second largest in Europe, behind BMW. Long a niche producer focused on the high-performance off-road racing sector, KTM has developed a full range of both race-ready on-road and off-road vehicles, as well as street motorcycles, quads, and all-terrain vehicles (ATVs). KTM's motorcycle operations include the Husaberg sport-racing brand. In 2008, the company also launched its first sports car, the X-Bow. KTM sold more than 92,000 motorcycles in its 2007–08 fiscal year, for total revenues of EUR 605 million ($741 million). The company's largest product group remains off-road motorcycles, at 44 percent of sales, while on-road motorcycles add 31 percent, and minicycles generate an additional 2 percent. A significant proportion—19 percent—of KTM's revenues is generated through sales of branded accessories, clothing, and similar merchandise.

Europe remains KTM's largest market, at 65 percent of sales, while the North American market accounts for 24 percent of its turnover. Altogether, KTM operates sales subsidiaries in 19 countries, with joint venture distribution partnerships in Argentina, Dubai, Greece, New Zealand, and South Africa. The company's penetration of Asian markets was expected to grow following the launch of a development and distribution partnership with India's Bajaj Auto Ltd. to develop engines for use in both companies' motorcycles. KTM is listed on the Vienna Stock Exchange, and led by CEO Stefan Pierer.

ORIGINS IN METALWORKING SHOP

KTM Power Sports originated as a small metalworking shop in Mattighofen, in Upper Austria, in 1934. Founded by Hans Trunkenpolz, the company, Kraftfahrzeuge Trunkenpolz Mattighofen, quickly developed a strong business repairing motorcycles. By 1937, motorcycles had become something of a specialty, as Trunkenpolz added sales of DKW motorcycles as well. Over the next decade, Trunkenpolz expanded the shop to include auto repairs, and by the 1950s the business had grown into one of the largest motorcycle and auto repair centers in the region.

COMPANY PERSPECTIVES

We have further developed from an off-road motorcycle manufacturer to an innovative producer of street motorcycles, ATVs and a premium sports car. This development has been promoted by focusing on technology, innovation, creativity and design. Having clearly positioned KTM as a manufacturer of race-ready vehicles, we paved the way for opening up and establishing niche markets at the international level, such as the Supermoto segment. Launching our ATV and unveiling our first KTM X-Bow premium sports car also marked initial inroads into the four-wheel segment. In line with our Ready to Race corporate philosophy, the riding and driving experience so typical for KTM is also guaranteed with our new four-wheel products. To ensure sustainable development, we aim to continue concentrating on strategic growth and expanding the entire product range in the future, in particular Husaberg motorcycles.

Trunkenpolz by then was determined to build his own motorcycle designs. In 1951, the company launched the development of its first motorcycle design, the R100, featuring a "98 cm3" engine. Trunkenpolz quickly attracted the attention of an investor, Ernst Kronreif, and in 1953 the pair decided to go into business together, creating a new company, Kronreif & Trunkenpolz, Mattighofen—the origin of the KTM brand name. The company opened its first factory in Mattighofen, and began serial production of the R100. At first, the company's 20 employees produced just three motorcycles each day.

KTM won its first race that year, taking the first, second, and third places at Gaisberg. This marked the beginning of one of the most illustrious motorcycle racing names in the second half of the 20th century. By 1954, KTM had won its first Austrian national championship in the 125 cc category. That win provided strong backing for the launch of the group's KTM Tourist motorcycle, introduced in 1955.

Crisis struck the European motorcycle industry in the late 1950s with the arrival of the first Japanese motorcycles to the continent. The new models, available at lower prices but boasting advanced technology, nearly wiped out much of Europe's motorcycle manufacturing sector, which found their production facilities outmoded and their motorcycle models unable to compete with the sleeker, sportier, and generally more reliable Japanese counterparts.

KTM was swept up in the crisis, and by 1959 the company was forced to shut down its own motorcycle production. Instead, the company turned to new markets, such as scooters, mopeds, and bicycles. The company launched its first scooter, the Ponny, and its first moped in 1959. Another moped, the Comet, introduced in 1963, became a bestseller for the company, with more than 10,000 sold by 1966. In the meantime, the company also added its first bicycles, in 1964.

ENTERING THE U.S. MARKET

Motorcycles nevertheless remained the lifeblood of the company. KTM reentered the market in 1964, developing a new model for the grueling Six Days competition. That circuit later brought KTM to the United States. In 1968, the company reached an agreement with Jack Penton to produce a new motorcycle specifically for the U.S. market. Penton imported KTM's motorcycles, which were sold as the Penton Six Days.

Penton played an important role in pioneering the U.S. dirt bike market through the 1970s. Meanwhile, KTM continued to win races, building a strong brand name. The popularity of the KTM brand in the United States led the company to establish a dedicated subsidiary there in 1978. KTM America Inc., based in Lorain, Ohio, also added its own production facilities, launching a 50 cc dirt bike for the U.S. market.

KTM also made the decision to bring more of its component manufacturing in-house. Prior to the 1970s, KTM's motorcycles were based on third-party engines, especially the Sachs engine. In 1970, however, the company decided to develop its own engines. Also in that year, KTM debuted a new 250 cc bike. The new model helped establish KTM as one of the major players on the international off-road racing circuit. KTM was aided in this by its association with Russia's Gennadij Moisseev. The Russian racer had been racing for another manufacturer in the early 1970s. When Moisseev's motorcycle did not arrive in time for a race, KTM offered to lend him one of their 250 cc models. Impressed by the bike, Moisseev then agreed to race for KTM, winning a number of championships, including the 250 cc Motocross World Championship in 1974.

KTM continued to develop its technological base as well. In 1975, the company debuted its first 125 cc engine designed in-house. The company then launched its first water-cooled 125 cc bike in 1981. This was followed by the introduction of a new rear suspension system, dubbed "Pro Level." in 1982, as well as a water-cooled four-stroke engine. The company had also changed its name, becoming KTM Motor Fahrzeugbau KG in 1980.

The company's water-cooling technologies enabled it to launch production of its own radiators starting in 1984. KTM's radiators soon attracted attention from other manufacturers, and the company added an original equipment manufacturer operation during this time. The success of its radiator sales provided the financial support for a new expansion phase for the company.

BANKRUPTCY AND RESCUE

By 1986, the company had become the first in the industry to equip its off-road bikes with both front and rear-wheel disc brakes. In 1987, KTM launched serial production of its four-stroke engine. The success of its motorcycle models encouraged the company to focus more on this market, and the company began shedding its other products, including scooters in 1988.

The unexpected death of founder Hans Trunkenpolz in 1989 caught the company off guard. The company unraveled soon after. KTM went in search of a new investor, and a majority stake was sold to GIT Trust Holding that year. By 1991, however, the company had foundered against the global recession.

KTM was forced into bankruptcy that year. The company was then split up into its four primary components: motorcycles, bicycles, radiators, and tooling.

The rescue of the KTM brand came in 1992 when the motorcycle operations were acquired through a management buyout led by Cross Holding AG. That company had been founded as an investment group in 1987 by Stefan Pierer and Rudolf Knuenz. Pierer himself stepped up as KTM's new chief executive officer and set out to rebuild the company as a major European motorcycle manufacturer under the name KTM Sportsmotorcycle GmbH.

Pierer pared down KTM's production operations, introducing a leaner, more efficient operating structure. The company then targeted expansion into a new direction, the Hard Enduro category, and launched a new generation of motorcycle designs. The company also added a new branch to its racing activities, entering—and winning—the Rally Circuit. Racing was to play an increasingly important role in KTM's success through the 1990s and into the new century, as the company's motorcycles became some of the most winning in the world.

At the same time, KTM began broadening its production scope. While the motocross and dirt bikes were to remain a company mainstay, KTM began to develop vehicles for on-road racing and recreational use. This effort was launched in 1994, with the introduction of the on-road Duke series. By 1997, KTM had introduced the road-ready LC4 Supermoto, as well as its first cruising motorcycle, the LC4 Adventure. KTM also added a second strong name to its off-road racing stable, buying Sweden's Husaberg AB in 1995. By this time, KTM's own production had once again topped 12,000 motorcycles per year.

NEW CATEGORIES IN THE 21ST CENTURY

KTM began beefing up its marketing efforts in the second half of the 1990s. For this, the company raised capital through a public offering on the Vienna Stock Exchange in 1996, at that time taking the name of KTM Motorradholding AG. The company then opened the first in a string of international sales subsidiaries, in Germany and Switzerland. By the middle of the next decade, KTM had established a direct presence in 19 foreign markets, as well as joint venture partnerships in five more.

At the beginning of the new century, KTM expanded its production capacity, refurbishing its existing plants, and then opening a new engine assembly facility in Munderfing in 2002. The company's sales were also growing strongly. By 2003, the group topped 70,000 motorcycles for the first time, recording total sales of EUR 376 million. By 2006, the number had climbed past 84,000, and then reached 92,000 in 2007.

By this time, KTM had begun to seek further extensions to its product line. In 2005, the company entered into a partnership with U.S.-based Polaris to develop its own line of racing-ready ATVs. The initial agreement, which gave Polaris a 25 percent stake in KTM, provided Polaris with the option to acquire KTM over time. Before the end of 2006, however, Pierer and Knuenz announced their decision to maintain control of KTM. Instead, the partners restructured Cross Holding, shedding its other investments to focus solely on KTM. Cross Holding then changed its name, becoming KTM Power Sports AG.

Part of the impetus for this decision by Pierer and Knuenz stemmed from their enthusiasm for KTM's newest direction: development of a sports car. For this, KTM teamed up with Audi to develop a rear-wheel drive, high-performance road vehicle, dubbed the X-Bow. By 2008, KTM had become convinced of the feasibility of the project, and launched series production of the vehicle at a dedicated factory in Graz. By July 2008, the company had begun delivering the first X-Bows to its customers.

While Europe, followed by North America, remained KTM's most important market, the company also began seeking to broaden its horizons. Toward this end, the company formed two important joint ventures in 2007. The first was with Bajaj Auto Ltd., one of India's leading motorcycle companies, to develop new motorcycle models together. The deal also gave KTM access to Bajaj's distribution network in India. Soon after, KTM reached a joint venture with Al Shafar, a leading industrial conglomerate based in Dubai, to distribute motorcycles, ATVs, and sports cars to the United Arab Emirates.

KTM, which had been suffering from the weakening dollar, expected its sales to be hit by the global economic decline of 2008. Nonetheless, the company had firmly established itself as Europe's second largest motorcycle manufacturer and one of the foremost names in the worldwide power sports sector in general.

M. L. Cohen

PRINCIPAL SUBSIDIARIES

KTM-Sportmotorcycle AG; KTM North America, Inc.; KTM-Sportmotorcycle GmbH; KTM-FABAG; KTM-Sportmotorcycle UK Ltd.; KTM-Sportmotorcycle Espana S.L. (Spain); KTM-Sportmotorcycle France SAS; KTM-Motorsports, Inc. (United States); KTM-Sportmotorcycle Italia s.r.l. (Italy); KTM-Sportmotorcycle Nederland B.V. (Netherlands); KTM-Sportmotorcycle Scandinavia AB (Sweden); KTM-Sportmotorcycle Japan K.K.; KTM-Sportmotorcycle Belgium S.A.; KTM Canada Inc.; KTM-Racing AG; KTM Hungária Kft. (Hungary); KTM-Sportcar GmbH; KTM Nordic Oy; KTM Sportmotorcycle d.o.o.

PRINCIPAL COMPETITORS

Honda Motor Company Ltd.; Bayerische Motoren Werke AG; Suzuki Motor Corporation; Kawasaki Heavy Industries Ltd.; Yamaha Motor Company Ltd.; Harley-Davidson Motor Co.; Hero Cycles Ltd.; Piaggio and C. S.p.A.

FURTHER READING

Ebert, Guido, "Bajaj Buys Stake in KTM," *Dealernews,* January 2008, p. 22.

———, "KTM Earnings Slashed by Weak Dollar," *Dealernews,* June 2008, p. 12.

———, "KTM Ends Possible Union with Polaris," *Powersports Business,* August 14, 2006, p. 1.

———, "KTM's Cross Sets Deadline for Buyback of Polaris Stock," *Powersports Business,* December 25, 2006, p. 11.

"Polaris Won't Acquire KTM Majority," *ATV Sport,* November 2006, p. 11.

La Seda de Barcelona S.A.

Passeig de Gracia 85
Barcelona, E-08008
Spain
Telephone: (34 93) 467 17 50
Fax: (34 93) 467 17 78
Web site: http://www.laseda.es

Public Company
Incorporated: 1925
Employees: 715
Sales: EUR 1.34 billion ($1.98 billion) (2007)
Stock Exchanges: Madrid
Ticker Symbol: SED
NAICS: 325221 Cellulosic Manmade Fiber Manufacturing; 221330 Steam and Air-Conditioning Supply; 325211 Plastics Material and Resin Manufacturing; 325212 Synthetic Rubber Manufacturing; 325222 Noncellulosic Organic Fiber Manufacturing

■ ■ ■

La Seda de Barcelona (LSB) is Europe's largest producer of PET (polyethylene terephthalate) and the third largest in the world. Founded in 1925 to produce artificial silk—*seda* means "silk" in Spanish—LSB has transformed itself into an integrated chemicals holding company, with operations including PET and PTA (purified terephthalic acid) production, chemicals, PET preforms, and PET recycling. PET production, conducted through the Artenius group of companies, is LSB's main operation, accounting for 50 percent of its revenues. The group operates factories in Spain,

Portugal, Turkey, Greece, Italy, and the United Kingdom, with a total production of approximately one million metric tons per year. LSB holds a 29 percent share of the European PET market, and controls 11 percent of the global market.

LSB has put into place a vertical integration strategy. The company is one of the world's leading producers of PTA, the purified terephthalic acid powder that is the main raw material for PET production. The company produces nearly 700,000 metric tons of PTA per year, for a 22 percent share of the European market, and a number three ranking. LSB is also integrated forward into the packaging sector, following the acquisition of the European PET and preforms operations of Australia's Amcor in 2007. While the integrated PET operations are the group's main focus, LSB also operates a chemicals division, producing ethylene oxide, glycols, polyols, and ethoxylates, among others. This division operates through subsidiary Industrias Químicas Asociadas (IQA). LSB is listed on the Madrid Stock Exchange and is led by CEO Joan Brat. The company's turnover reached EUR 1.34 billion ($1.98 billion) in 2007.

ORIGINS AS ARTIFICIAL SILK SUBSIDIARY

La Seda de Barcelona (LSB) was founded in 1925 as a subsidiary of Akzo, the Dutch chemical company, to produce viscous rayon. Also known as artificial silk, the new textile material provided the name for the company: *seda* is Spanish for "silk." As majority shareholder, Akzo not only helped fund LSB's expansion, it also helped the company in making technological advances. By the end of the 1950s, LSB had grown into Europe's leading producer of artificial and synthetic textile fibers. Akzo later reduced its stake in LSB, which went public with a listing on the Madrid Stock Exchange. Nonetheless, Akzo's shareholding remained at 57.5 percent through the 1980s.

During the 1960s, LSB consolidated this leadership position with an investment into polyester fibers and yarns. For this effort, the company established a new factory in El Prat de Llobregat. Spain's booming textiles and clothing sector provided a ready market for the company, which also generated a significant proportion of its revenues from other European markets. The company continued to seek new materials. This led to the acquisition of Perlofil in 1968, adding that company's polyamide production. Perlofil was then the largest producer of polyamide—also known as nylon—in Spain.

LSB's next extension was to have a greater impact on the company's profile into the beginning of the next century. In 1982, LSB launched a small operation for the production of polyethylene terephthalate, or PET. The new material was initially used in the production of textile fibers. However, scientists quickly developed new methods of working with PET, which presented a number of important advantages over other plastics. PET provided a greater transparency than other plastic compounds, such as polyvinyl chloride, or PVC, at greater consistency, in addition to stronger resistance at lighter weights. In addition, PET provided a strong fluid barrier, while remaining comparatively inert. Thus, PET was much less likely to leech toxic compounds. Furthermore, the production process for PET produced lower pollution levels than other plastics; its lighter weight also helped reduce transportation costs and the pollution resulting from its transport.

These qualities made PET an extremely attractive material for the food and beverage industries, which rapidly adopted PET packaging in the 1980s and 1990s. This was particularly true in the bottled water market, which boomed during the period as manufacturers discovered they could charge consumers as much as 3,000 times the price they paid for tap water. The high resistance level of PET also made the material an attractive choice in the soft-drink market. Here, too, manufacturers found a strong profit incentive. The higher resistance of PET allowed the manufacturers to develop ever-larger packaging sizes, with two-liter and even three-liter bottles becoming possible, and then quite common. Since water made up most of this additional volume, the larger sizes became a source of pure profit for soft-drink manufacturers.

STRUGGLING TO REMAIN PROFITABLE

PET remained only a small part of LSB's operations through the 1980s. The company's early investment in the material nonetheless represented a lifeline for the company as it struggled into the early 1990s. By 1990, LSB had grown to annual revenues of $230 million. However, the company struggled to maintain profitability, posting a loss that year of $25 million. LSB also carried a heavy debt burden of nearly $120 million.

Into 1991, as the world slipped into a new economic crisis, LSB's fortunes waned still further. By the end of that year, the company's losses had swollen to $50 million. Perhaps still more critical for the company was the loss of confidence of its majority shareholder, as Akzo (shortly to become Akzo Nobel) revamped its own synthetic fibers strategy. The weakness of the Spanish synthetic textiles market, which remained LSB's primary market, led Akzo to announce its decision to sell LSB in 1991. Part of Akzo's motivation was to stimulate the restructuring of the fragmented Spanish synthetic textiles sector, in general.

Akzo therefore went in search of a Spanish buyer for the company. The poor economic climate and the crisis in the Spanish textile sector, however, made the search difficult. Akzo at first entered negotiations with a Spanish investment consortium but was unable to reach a sales agreement. At last, in a rush to divest LSB, Akzo agreed to sell the company to Jacinto Soler Padro, a Spanish lawyer, for the symbolic price of one peseta. Padro in turn agreed to launch a buyout offer to LSB's minority shareholders.

The deal quickly turned sour, as both Akzo and Padro accused each other of reneging on the sale agreement. At the same time, Akzo found itself under

```
┌─────────────────────────────────────────────┐
│                                             │
│              KEY DATES                       │
│              ▬                               │
│                                             │
│  1925:  La Seda de Barcelona (LSB) is founded as a │
│         subsidiary of Akzo to produce artificial silk. │
│  1968:  LSB acquires nylon operations of Perlofil and │
│         becomes leading producer of synthetic fibers │
│         in Spain. │
│  1982:  LSB launches its first entry into PET │
│         (polyethylene terephthalate) production. │
│  1991:  LSB goes private. │
│  1995:  LSB acquires Industrias Químicas Asociadas, │
│         a leading producer of glycols, one of the main │
│         ingredients in PET. │
│  1996:  LSB shares are reinstated as the company │
│         develops its new strategic plan focusing on │
│         the PET and chemicals sectors. │
│  2003:  LSB adopts new strategic plan to become the │
│         European leader in the PET market. │
│  2007:  LSB acquires Selenis (Portugal and Italy) and │
│         PTA leader Advansa (Netherlands). │
│                                             │
└─────────────────────────────────────────────┘
```

legal attack from the unions and then from the Catalan government. Finally, the Spanish National Stock Market Commission refused to recognize the legitimacy of the sale to Padro. As a result, trading in LSB's shares was suspended and its management was forced to resign.

NEW MANAGEMENT AND NEW DIRECTIONS

LSB's management crisis was finally resolved in 1993, when a new management team, headed by chairman Rafael Español, took over the company's direction. Español pushed through a restructuring of LSB's operations, including shedding a number of jobs and redeveloping its production methods to respond more closely to the demand for its products. The company then carried out a restructuring, which created separate companies for each of its main business lines.

By 1995, Español's management team had decided upon a new direction for the company. The ongoing shift in the global textile sector to lower-priced markets in Eastern Europe and Asia had resulted in a major loss in competitiveness for LSB's synthetic textiles operations. On the other hand, LSB's smaller PET operation provided a more promising direction.

As part of its new focus on PET, LSB first boosted its chemicals operations. In 1995, the company bought Spain's Industrias Químicas Asociadas, a major producer

of ethylene oxide and other chemicals, especially glycols—one of the main ingredients in PET production. At the same time, LSB regrouped its polyester and PET production into a new company, Catalana de Polimers. The company then launched construction of a new PET factory. When the new facility opened in 1998, LSB emerged as one of Europe's largest PET manufacturers. The company also claimed the Spanish leadership for the production of polyester fibers.

The new direction inspired confidence with the National Stock Market Commission, which lifted the suspension of the company's shares in 1996. Also in that year, LSB spun off its polyamide and rayon operations into a new company, Poliseda y Viscoseda Barcelona. After shutting down the Viscoseda arm of the business, LSB sold the Poliseda operations to Merido Fibres, based in the Netherlands, in 2001.

TAKING THE EUROPEAN PET LEAD IN THE 21ST CENTURY

While building its PET operations in the late 1990s, LSB also made an attempt to expand into other areas, notably specialty chemicals. In support of this, the group carried out two significant acquisitions. The first of these was of a 55 percent stake in Hispano Quimico, acquired in 1998. That company produced chemicals for the paint, paper, textile, and leather industries. The following year, LSB joined with Uniroyal Chemical to buy General Quimica, part of Spain's Repsol. That company produced chemicals for textile and leather dyes, as well as rubber components and pesticides.

By 2003, however, LSB moved to refocus itself entirely on building an integrated PET operation. The company began divesting its noncore holdings, and, as part of the strategic plan put into place that year, targeted the European leadership in the PET sector. LSB was restructured into a holding company overseeing three companies, Industrias Químicas Asociadas, Catalana de Polimers, and Inquitex. The latter company, which incorporated LSB's textiles operations, was sold in 2006. LSB then launched a major investment program, converting its existing facilities to expand its PET capacity. At the El Prat de Llobregat factory, the group's production capacity was boosted to 190,000 tons per year in 2004.

LSB also sought acquisitions to meet its growth targets. After flirting with the possibilities of merging with one or another of its Iberian rivals, including Ercros in Spain and Selenis in Portugal, the company instead focused on developing its vertical integration capacity. This led to the 2006 purchase of Advansa, the Netherlands-based producer of purified terephthalic acid

(PTA), the main component of PET, owned by Turkey's Sabanci group. The addition of Advansa also boosted LSB's PET production, while introducing the company to the preform packaging sector. The deal instantly boosted LSB into the top ranks of European PTA producers, with an annual capacity of 750 tons, while adding an additional 320,000 tons of PET capacity.

LSB boosted its PET capacity again in 2007, buying the Spain-based PET operations of Eastman Chemical Iberia that year. The company also began negotiations to acquire Eastman's factories in the United Kingdom and the Netherlands. Soon after, LSB bought a 70 percent share of the industrial operations of Portugal's Selenis, a deal that included the Italian production facilities of Selenis. Following that purchase, LSB rebranded its PET operations under a new name, Artenius.

LSB celebrated a major step forward in its vertical integration program in July 2007, when the company agreed to acquire the entire European PET-based preform packaging wing of Australia's Amcor. However, LSB suffered a disappointment in 2008, when it failed in its attempt to acquire its chief Spanish rival, Iterquisa. While the two companies had initially reached an agreement, the softening economy at the beginning of 2008 made the purchase, slated to cost EUR 400 million ($600 million), unfeasible.

Concerns raised by the environmental impact of PET began to heighten toward the end of the decade. The recycling rate of PET-based bottles barely reached 15 percent, while the marketing efforts of the world's beverage industries, particularly the bottled water market, had increasingly convinced people to buy bottled water. In response, LSB stepped up its PET recycling program. The company merged the management of its four recycling facilities in Spain, Italy, and France, while increasing its own recycling capacity to 140,000 metric tons per year, with a goal of reaching 20 percent of its total PET capacity.

By 2008, La Seda de Barcelona held the clear European lead in PET production, with a 29 percent share of that market. The company's production capacity of some one billion metric tons also gave it the third place position at the global level, for an 11 percent market share. LSB had successfully transformed itself from a small local producer of artificial silk to a global contender in the world's PET market.

M. L. Cohen

PRINCIPAL SUBSIDIARIES

Artenius Hellas Holding, S.A.; Artenius Holding, B.V.; Artenius Italia, S.p.A; Artenius PET Packaging Belgium, N.V.; Artenius PET Packaging Deutschland, GmbH; Artenius PET Packaging Europe, Ltd.; Artenius PET Packaging France, S.A.S.; Artenius PET Packaging Iberia, S.A.; Artenius PET Packaging UK, Ltd.; Artenius Portugal, Industria de Polimeros, S.A.; Artenius Romania, SRL; Artenius Sines, S.A.; Industrias Químicas Asociadas LSB, S.L.U.; Recuperaciones de Plásticos Barcelona, S.L.

PRINCIPAL COMPETITORS

Rayonier Inc.; International Paper do Brasil Ltda.; Bayer Hispania S.A.; Travancore Rayons Ltd.; Indo Bharat Rayon, PT; Hilados Flexilon S.A.; Grupo Empresarial ENCE S.A.; Telares Los Andes S.A.; Cydsa SAB de C.V.; Mehler AG.

FURTHER READING

Alperowicz, Natasha, "La Seda Buys Sabanci PET Business, Reinforcing Top European Slot," *Chemical Week,* August 9, 2006, p. 14.

Bains, Elizabeth, "LSB in Talks to Buy Interquisa," *ICIS Chemical Business,* May 21, 2007.

Castano, Ivan, "Dividing the Cake," *ECN-European Chemical News,* February 16, 2004, p. 19.

———, "Spanish Merger?" *ECN-European Chemical News,* January 24, 2005, p. 18.

Jackson, Debbie, "Akzo Sells Spanish Fibers Firm for One Peseta," *Chemical Week,* August 7, 1991, p. 12.

"La Seda Acquires Firm," *Plastics News,* January 21, 2008, p. 15.

"La Seda Breaks Ground on Portuguese PTA Plant," *Chemical Week,* March 24, 2008, p. 29.

"La Seda Gains Advansa Operations," *Plastics News,* January 15, 2007, p. 10.

"La Seda Rebrands PTA PET as Artenius," *ICIS Chemical Business,* March 5, 2007.

"La Seda Shelves Purchase of Interquisa," *Chemical Week,* February 25, 2008, p. 5.

"La Seda to Merge with Indorama?" *Chemical Week,* July 28, 2008, p. 5.

Young, Ian, and Michelle Bryner, "La Seda and Indorama Drive PTA-PET Consolidation in Europe," *Chemical Week,* January 7, 2008, p. 15.

GROUPE LATECOERE

Latécoère S.A.

135 rue de Périole
Toulouse, F-31079 Cedex
France
Telephone: (33 05 61) 58 77 00
Fax: (33 05 61) 58 97 38
Web site: http://www.latecoere.fr

Public Company
Incorporated: 1917 as Société Industrielle d'Aviation Latécoère
Employees: 3,663
Sales: EUR 489.4 million ($718.9 million) (2007)
Stock Exchanges: Euronext Paris
Ticker Symbol: LAEP
NAICS: 336413 Other Aircraft Part and Auxiliary Equipment Manufacturing; 336411 Aircraft Manufacturing

■ ■ ■

Latécoère S.A., one of the most famous names in aviation history, has evolved into one of France's leading aircraft components manufacturers. The Toulouse-based company provides design and engineering, manufacturing, and assembly services to the aviation industry, focusing on aerostructures—doors and fuselage sections—and onboard wiring systems.

The Aerostructures division comprises the group's largest operation, representing 77 percent of its revenues of EUR 489 million ($718 million) in 2007. This division produces nose sections, upper shell and fuselage sections and panels, as well as passenger doors, emergency exit doors, and cargo and bay doors. The company's clients include Airbus, Dassault, Embraer, and Bombardier. The Onboard Wiring and Systems division adds 23 percent to sales, and includes the full onboard wiring of aircraft (such as the Falcon 7X from Dassault), as well as component systems including radionavigation harnesses, avionics bays, taxiing assistance systems, and passenger video systems. Engineering services accounts for the remaining 5 percent of the group's revenues.

Latécoère operates several facilities in the Toulouse region, including its factory in Périole. In the first decade of the 21st century, Latécoère also developed an international component to minimize the impact of fluctuations in international exchange rates. Accordingly, the company has established manufacturing subsidiaries in the Czech Republic, Brazil, and Tunisia. The company also operates subsidiaries and offices in Germany, Spain, and the United States. Latécoère is listed on the Euronext Paris stock exchange. The Latécoère family continues its involvement in the company, maintaining a 7.3 percent stake. Francois Bertrand is the group's president and CEO.

FROM ROLLING STOCK TO AVIATION

Pierre-Georges Latécoère's father had established a successful manufacturing business in Bagnères-de-Bigorre at the beginning of the 20th century. When Latécoère's father died in 1905, his mother maintained the business, which specialized in wood products. Latécoère, 22 years old at the time, completed his engineering degree at the prestigious École Centrale the following year, and then returned to Bagnères to take over the family business.

Latécoère quickly steered the company toward a new range of products, specifically rolling stock for France's fast-growing tramway and railroad system. By the beginning of World War I, Latécoère had established the company as a major partner to the railroad industry. This position was confirmed when the company received an order for 10,000 wagons from the Chemins du Fer du Midi. In order to fulfill that contract, Latécoère opened a second factory, in Toulouse.

World War I had a major impact on the future direction of the company. Pierre-Georges Latécoère attempted to join the army but was refused due to his poor vision. Instead, Latécoère entered the artillery section; after a few months, however, Latécoère's commander sent him back to his business, the better to apply his skills to supporting France's military effort. The Toulouse factory began turning out large caliber shells, while the Bagnères plant became a major supplier of rolling kitchens.

Before the war's end, Latécoère had determined the future of his company: aviation. By the end of 1917, Latécoère had won the company's first aircraft manufacturing contract, for the production of 1,000 Salmson 2A2 airplanes. Latécoère launched a new company, Société Industrielle d'Aviation Latécoère, which opened its own factory in Montaudran and built up a workforce of some 700. In just over half a year, the factory had completed some 800 airplanes, representing a production rate of six per day. The company soon completed the contract; by then, however, the war was over.

TAKING TO THE SKIES

Latécoère's involvement with aviation had only just begun. Before the end of the war, Latécoère had begun dreaming of creating a civil air service linking France with its colonies in North Africa and ultimately stretching to South America. Latécoère's vision was all the

more striking given that most aircraft of the day were unable to fly for very long distances without stopping. Nevertheless, Latécoère, joined by a number of prominent aviators, including Beppo de Massimi and others, persevered.

The Armistice was signed in November 1918. By December of that year, Latécoère himself had pioneered the company's first international flight, from Montaudran to Barcelona, inaugurating what came to be known as "The Line." By February of the following year, The Line had been extended to Alicante; one month later, two airplanes, led by Latécoère and Massimi, arrived in Rabat, Morocco. There, they delivered the morning's newspaper, as well as a bouquet of violets, to Marshal Lyautey, then the Resident General of Morocco.

Impressed, Lyautey used his influence to help push through the company's request to establish a dedicated airline. The company managed to overcome the initial reluctance of the French government. The prospect was a daunting one, as the company proposed at the beginning to complete transcontinental flights using single-engine, canvas-based aircraft. Nevertheless, the government agreed to support the newly founded Lignes Aeriennes Latécoère, supplying 14 Bréguet biplanes for the endeavor.

The new airline soon boasted many of the biggest names in French aviation history, including Daurat, Beatue, Vanier, Mermoz, and Saint-Exupéry. By the end of 1919, the company had established a weekly flight linking Toulouse and Casablanca. By September 1920, the airline had initiated daily flights, and began flying its first passengers as well.

The company opened up new lines in the 1920s, including a line linking Alicante to Oran and Algiers in Algeria. In 1923, the group opened up the Casablanca-Dakar leg. The company added regular service to Dakar two years later, and completed its first nonstop flight from Toulouse to Dakar in 1927. By then, Latécoère had also been opening up its South American service. The company's first flight there connected Rio de Janeiro with Buenos Aires in 1925. The opening of the Toulouse-Dakar line proved a crucial step in the company's South American ambitions, as the company completed the link to that continent before the end of the decade. Latécoère's South American flights were initially limited to its postal service. This success provided a new name for the airline, which became known as Compagnie Générale Aéropostale in 1927.

SEAPLANE MANUFACTURER

In support of the group's aviation operations, Latécoère continued to develop its manufacturing operations as

KEY DATES

1917: Pierre-Georges Latécoère founds Société Industrielle d'Aviation Latécoère to build airplanes.
1927: The company's airline service adopts the Aéropostale name.
1948: The company moves into missile development with the approval of the French government.
1961: Pierre-Jean Latécoère takes over as head of the company and begins to shift focus to components supplier.
1981: Pierre-Jean Latécoère retires.
1985: The company goes public, listing its stock on the Paris bourse's Secondary Market.
1989: Latécoère employees complete an employee buyout of the company.
1998: Latécoère returns to the stock market as Latécoère SA.
2008: The company fails in its plans to gain "super tier one" status through the acquisition of two manufacturing sites from Airbus.

well. For this, Latécoère launched a new company in 1921, Compagnie Générale d'Entreprises Aéronautiques, uniting a number of Toulouse-based companies active in the field. That company launched a number of successful aircraft designs during the 1920s, notably the Laté 17, a four-passenger plane introduced in 1924. The development of more modern aircraft types during the decade outpaced that business, however. By the end of the 1920s, the company had been sold.

Instead, Latécoère refocused his engineering and manufacturing interests around the development and construction of seaplanes, based at the Montaudran factory. The company's first seaplanes appeared in the mid-1920s, including an adaptation of the Laté 17. By 1929, the company had debuted the more robust Laté 32. For its transatlantic service, meanwhile, the company had developed the Laté 28, which featured seats for eight passengers, as well as onboard comforts such as a toilet. This design allowed the company to set a number of long-distance and speed records in the early 1930s. The Laté 28 also became the first plane to complete the southern transatlantic crossing in 1930.

Latécoère continued to develop its range of seaplanes through the 1930s. New success came with the Laté 300, which arrived in Saint-Louis, in Senegal, on New Year's Day of 1934 after a 23-hour flight covering nearly 3,900 kilometers and setting a new world record for distance. This success led to new military contracts, including the Laté 550 bomber and the Laté 301, a military version of the 300, launched in 1936.

Latécoère's designs not only grew more powerful during the 1930s, they also grew larger, and by the end of the decade the company was producing some of the world's largest seaplanes. This culminated with the creation of the 75-metric ton Laté 631. Developed at the company's newest factory, on the Rue de Périole in Toulouse in 1939, the six-engine plane became the largest seaplane to fly successfully.

ADAPTING IN THE POSTWAR ERA

France's defeat by Germany in 1940 placed much of Latécoère's fleet under German control. A number of the company's aircraft managed to avoid capture, however, and were put into service in support of the Royal Air Force. The Latécoère company's days appeared numbered, as the German firms Heinkel and Junkers sought to gain control of its works. Pierre-Georges Latécoère himself did not survive the war; he died in 1943.

The end of the war brought still more changes to the company. Latécoère lost control of Aéropostale airline, which was taken over by the French government and served as the basis for the national airline, Air France. The company continued to produce its flying boats into the 1950s. However, these operations were beset by a series of crashes. Furthermore, the introduction of jet engine technology during World War II, coupled with major improvements in the fuselage structures, had increasingly made the company's seaplanes obsolete. As the last technical obstacles for safe ground landings were removed, the era of the large flying boat came to a close.

Instead of fading away, however, the Latécoère company succeeded in adapting its operations to the new climate. The company made an initial attempt to redevelop itself as a modern aircraft builder, producing two fighter jets, as well as a civilian light jet, the Laté 870. These efforts were quickly abandoned, however. More successful was the company's move into missile development, beginning with the French government's approval in 1948. Over the next decade, the company developed a number of prototypes in cooperation with the French government and armed forces, and by 1961 the company had delivered its first 50 missiles.

That year also marked the arrival of a new generation of the Latécoère family into the company's direction. Pierre-Jean Latécoère, the only child of Pierre-

Georges, was born in 1932 and had studied chemistry and mathematics. The younger Latécoère's direction proved decisive for the company's survival, as the French aeronautics industry underwent a profound transition. The country's aviation and aerospace industries coalesced around the twin poles of Société Nationale de Construction Aéronautique du Sud Ouest (SNCASE, later known as Aérospatiale), for civilian aircraft; and Dassault, for military aircraft.

One of the results of the nationalization of the aviation industry was the creation of a new layer of subcontractors for the production of individual components and systems, and other services, such as engineering and design and assembly. Pierre-Jean Latécoère recognized the need to shift the company's focus to these new operations. Over the next two decades, Latécoère succeeded in establishing itself as a major partner to the country's aviation and aerospace industry. Among other projects, the company succeeded in winning the contract for developing the arms for the Arianne satellite. The company also developed human centrifuges for the European aerospace effort.

EMPLOYEE BUYOUT IN 1989

Pierre-Jean Latécoère retired in 1981, tapping François Junca as his successor. In 1985, the company went public, listing its stock on the Paris bourse's Secondary Market. The following year, Latécoère added a new wing to its operations, an Electricity and Electronics division. This operation then began developing software for the ATEC system under development at Aérospatiale. In 1989, Latécoère expanded its range of operations again, buying a 30 percent stake in Société Industrielle du Midi (Sidmi). That company specialized in providing assembly services for aircraft structures and systems. Production of these structures then became a major focus of the Latécoère group. By this time, Junca had led the company in an employee buyout, with 91 percent of the company's workforce taking part.

Through the 1990s, Latécoère targeted a move into the global aerospace and aviation markets. For this, the company targeted the development of partnerships with the world's major aircraft builders. France remained the group's core market, however, as it achieved a number of successes, including a contract to provide components for the Super Transporteur cargo plane under development by Airbus. A contract to provide the rear fuselage for Dassault's Falcon 50 EX helped boost the group's Aerostructures division, which became its largest market at the beginning of the new century.

Latécoère also produced a number of innovations during this time. These included the Landscape Video Camera System, which provided passengers a view of the aircraft. This system quickly proved popular among many of the world's passenger airlines. These successes also enabled the company to return to the stock market as Latécoère SA in 1998, with a renewed listing on the Paris Exchange. By then, the group's revenues had neared FRF 1 billion (approximately $150 million). More than two-thirds of this total was achieved in France, with 91 percent coming from the civil sector.

OUTSOURCING FOR SURVIVAL IN THE 21ST CENTURY

The company suffered through the slump in the global aviation industry following the September 11, 2001, terrorist attacks in the United States. Toward the middle of the decade, however, the company's fortunes were buoyed by a number of important contracts, most notably by the Airbus 380, Dassault Falcon 7X, and the Boeing 7E7. For the Airbus 380, the company also developed its External Taxi Aid Camera System (ETACS), starting in 2004.

By mid-decade, Latécoère had consolidated its operations around a dual core: Aerostructures, which represented more than three-fourths of its revenues; and Wiring Systems. A series of successful partnerships, with Airbus, Dassault, Bombardier, and others, had also enabled it to make a strong increase in turnover, to nearly EUR 500 million ($700 million) in 2007.

However, the weak dollar, which accounted for 80 percent of the group's revenues, forced it to take steps to reduce its exposure to exchange rate fluctuations. The company adopted a new policy of outsourcing part of its operations to lower-cost markets, establishing manufacturing and assembly subsidiaries in the Czech Republic, Tunisia, and Brazil.

In the second half of the decade, Latécoère was confronted with a new challenge. The European aviation industry had begun to adopt the new business model developed by its U.S. counterpart, in which the major companies began to shed their manufacturing components in order to refocus on aircraft design and engineering. This shift created a new layer of so-called super tier one manufacturers, which became the primary partners for the major aviation groups.

Latécoère then sought to establish itself among this top tier. In early 2008, the company became the preferred bidder for two of Airbus's production sites, in Méaulte and Saint Nazaire. The purchase would have more than doubled Latécoère's operations, and propelled it into the major ranks of aircraft components suppliers. However, Airbus was forced to abandoned its sell-off plans amid the global economic crisis that year. Instead,

Latécoère announced new cost-cutting efforts, including shifting more of its production to its foreign factories. The French aviation pioneer continued to seek new ways to spread its wings into the 21st century.

M. L. Cohen

PRINCIPAL SUBSIDIARIES

LATecis; LATecis Iberia (Spain); Latecoere Developpment; Latecoere do Brasil (Brazil); Latecoere Inc. (United States); LATelec; LATelec GmbH (Germany); Letov s.r.o. (Czech Republic); SEA LATelec (Tunisia).

PRINCIPAL COMPETITORS

Boeing Company; European Aeronautic Defence and Space Company EADS N.V.; Lockheed Martin Corporation; Airbus S.A.S.; Northrop Grumman Corporation; Mitsubishi Heavy Industries Ltd.; MAN AG; BAE Systems PLC; Raytheon Company; Finmeccanica S.p.A.; Safran S.A.; Liebherr International AG.

FURTHER READING

"AIDC and Latecoere Team to Bid for Airbus Contracts," *Flight International,* December 24, 1997, p. 6.

"EU Approves 14 Million EUR French Aid for Latecoere's Research Project," *TendersInfo,* July 19, 2008.

Hollinger, Peggy, "Latecoere Pulls Investment in Aircraft," *Financial Times,* July 3, 2008, p. 17.

"Interview with Francois Bertrand, Chairman of Latecoere," *Europe Intelligence Wire,* October 2, 2008.

Kelly, Emma, "Embraer Chooses Latecoere to Supply Fuselage for New Jet," *Flight International,* August 25, 1999, p. 14.

"Latecoere Announces Restructuring Measures," *Europe Intelligence Wire,* October 3, 2008.

"Latecoere Expects A380 and 7X Work Will Boost Turnover by 20%," *Flight International,* March 8, 2005.

"Latecoere Tightens Belt," *Europe Intelligence Wire,* October 3, 2008.

"Latecoere's Top-Tier Ambitions," *Interavia Business & Technology,* Autumn 2007, p. 11.

Sparaco, Pierre, "Globalization Model," *Aviation Week & Space Technology,* April 14, 2008, p. 76.

Loos & Dilworth, Inc.

———— ■ ————

61 East Green Lane
Bristol, Pennsylvania 19007-3411
U.S.A.
Telephone: (215) 785-3591
Toll Free: (800) 229-5667
Fax: (215) 785-3597
Web site: http://www.loosanddilworth.com

Private Company
Incorporated: 1893
Employees: 24
Sales: $143 million (2006 est.)
NAICS: 424690 Other Chemical and Allied Products
    Merchant Wholesalers

■ ■ ■

Based in Bristol, Pennsylvania, near Philadelphia, Loos & Dilworth, Inc., is a privately held oil and chemical distribution company that splits its business between the Chemical Division and Automotive Division. The Chemical Division is a niche market distributor serving customers around the world with adhesives and sealants; inks and coatings; soaps and detergents; fragrance and flavor chemicals; chemicals used in cosmetic and personal care products; tire and rubber elastomers; pharmaceutical and medical chemicals; asphalt and cement processing chemicals; specialty solvents; textile defoamers and wax emulsions; chemicals used in the electronics industry; and specialty surfactants. Suppliers include Eastman Chemical Resins, Inc., for resins and other products; Hercules Incorporated for resins and pa-

permaking chemicals; Croda Singapore Pte Ltd. for surfactants; Arkema Inc. for specialty polyolefins and hot melt adhesives; Dexco Polymers LP for styrenic block polymers; and Tosoh USA, Inc., for ethyleneamines.

The Automotive Division of Loos & Dilworth is more of a regional concern, focusing on the Philadelphia metropolitan market. A Laurel, Maryland-based subsidiary, Loos & Dilworth Co., Inc., supplies customers in the passenger car and light truck markets in Maryland, Virginia, and Washington, D.C. Both units distribute Valvoline brand motor oils, in bulk, drum, or package quantities; Valvoline wiper blades; the Valvoline Professional Series of oil treatments and system cleaners, radiator products, transmission products, brake fluids and flushes, power steering products, and heater and air conditioning products; and Valvoline's Pyroil value brand of fuel additives, power steering and brake fluids, sealers and conditioners, winter chemicals, spray lubricants, cleaners and degreasers, oil additives, and automotive refrigerants.

Other product lines carried by the Loos & Dilworth Automotive Division include the 76 Lubricants brand of synthetic oil, transmission fluid, and greases and gear oil; Meguiar's car products car cleaning and waxing products and accessories; Zerex antifreeze; Eagle One Car Care Products; Cabin Air Filters; Kendall Lubricants; Pit Stop Oil Filters; and Aviation Products. Customers for these automotive products include automotive repair shops, car dealerships, quick-lube shops, and tire dealers.

The company also helps customers devise programs to improve customer retention, create new revenue

Loos & Dilworth, Inc., is committed to providing quality brands at competitive prices with the highest level of service in the industry. We invest in our business to provide state of the art vehicles, bulk and package storage facilities, and the technology to allow our business to grow and operate at maximum efficiency. Our customers can enjoy one-stop-shopping, which along with the consultative program designs our sales staff can offer, allows our customers to focus on growing their businesses. Our commitment to our customers is: Our delivery will be as good as our promise. We will provide our customers with only the highest quality products which meet or exceed industry specifications.

streams, increase traffic, develop consumer rebate programs, implement warrant programs, and design consumer education and point-of-sale materials. Additional services offered by Loos & Dilworth include sales training, waste management assistance, equipment analysis and loan packages, technical and product information, help with lubrication equipment installations and repairs, and demographic studies and oil testing. Loos & Dilworth is owned by its president, Richard G. Campbell, who purchased the business from the Loos family.

FIRM FOUNDED: 1893

Loos & Dilworth, Inc., was founded in 1893 in Philadelphia, Pennsylvania, by Augustus Jacob Loos and John Dilworth. Dilworth stayed with the company only until around 1900, but because the two men remained close friends, Loos decided to keep Dilworth in the company name. Loos was born in Staten Island, New York, in 1853. At the age of 20 he enrolled at Cornell University, studying science but intending to become a journalist or literary writer. After graduation in 1877, in fact, he moved to New York City and took a staff position with the *New York Tribune*. When his father died, however, Loos left the newspaper and moved to Philadelphia, where he went to work for his father's employer, the Chester & Tidewater Oil Company. In 1886 he became manager of the concern, a position he held until teaming up with Dilworth to launch his own business. Loos also became well connected in the area's oil industry; he served as secretary of the Philadelphia

Oil Trade Association from 1892 to 1895, and later became president of the organization.

Loos & Dilworth set up shop in the old waterfront section of Philadelphia as a wholesaler of naval stores and industrial machine oils, acting as a chemical blending house. The primary customers for the oils were the area's fabric manufacturers. With Dilworth's departure, Loos carried on alone until his son, Paul R. Loos, a trained engineer with a degree from the University of Pennsylvania, joined the family business in 1918 when his father reached retirement age. Another son and Cornell graduate, Henry B. Loos, had gone into government service and was involved in ship construction during World War I. He was one of the victims of the great influenza epidemic that swept the world in 1918 and died as a result.

Augustus Loos died in 1926 at the age of 72. By this time Paul Loos had begun to take Loos & Dilworth into the oil and chemical products that would become the firm's mainstay. In the 1920s the company continued to deal in naval stores, including products derived from southern Georgia pine trees that were used to caulk wooden vessels, but increasingly the focus shifted to oils and chemicals. It was during this period, in 1925, that Loos & Dilworth became one of the country's first distributors of Hercules chemical products, focusing on resin chemicals.

In addition, as automobile ownership became more common and the demand for automotive products increased, Loos & Dilworth became a motor oil supplier in the 1920s. For many years the company distributed lubricants and other products that were produced by another Philadelphia-based company, Sun Refining and Marketing Company, part of Sun Oil Company, later known as Sunoco, Inc. The company survived the Great Depression that spanned the 1930s and when the economy was revived through military spending during World War II, Loos & Dilworth prospered even though the automotive market was hampered because wartime restrictions on gasoline and rubber limited driving. The company found a new use for its pine oil product, which was sold to military uniform manufacturers as a wool scour.

HARWOOD LOOS JOINS COMPANY: 1944

A third generation of the Loos family became involved in the business in 1944 when Paul's son, H. Howard (Harwood) Loos, went to work for the company as a field sales representative. The younger Loos was around 30 years of age at the time. He had previously worked in San Francisco as an aircraft mechanic for Boeing, and

<table>
<tr><td colspan="2" align="center">KEY DATES</td></tr>
<tr><td>1893:</td><td>Augustus Loos founds company with John Dilworth.</td></tr>
<tr><td>1918:</td><td>Paul Loos joins family business.</td></tr>
<tr><td>1926:</td><td>Augustus Loos dies.</td></tr>
<tr><td>1944:</td><td>Third generation becomes involved through Howard Loos.</td></tr>
<tr><td>1971:</td><td>Company moves from Philadelphia to Bristol, Pennsylvania.</td></tr>
<tr><td>1980:</td><td>Loos & Dilworth starts distributing Valvoline products.</td></tr>
<tr><td>1984:</td><td>Richard G. Campbell assumes control.</td></tr>
<tr><td>1997:</td><td>Maryland subsidiary formed.</td></tr>
<tr><td>2001:</td><td>ConocoPhillips products added.</td></tr>
</table>

then lived in Chicago and New York before returning home to Philadelphia in 1941. After learning the business through sales, he joined the management team and was groomed to succeed his father.

Under the leadership of Harwood Loos, Loos & Dilworth continued to grow in the postwar years. The city of Philadelphia, however, underwent some changes, and when the waterfront area became a less than desirable location, Loos & Dilworth left for the suburbs. In 1971 the company moved to a new location in Bristol, Pennsylvania, northeast of Philadelphia. It was an advantageous location because of its proximity to railroads and major highways, including the Pennsylvania Turnpike that connected to east-west routes and the New Jersey Turnpike that shared Interstate 95, running the length of the East Coast. The Bristol site also provided the firm with much needed space, not only for bulk storage but also for future expansion.

After many years of distributing Sunoco products, in 1980 Loos & Dilworth's main supplier of lubricant products became the Valvoline Oil Company. Valvoline's Zerex antifreeze product line was also added. By this time Loos was 65 years of age. Two years later he retired and then in June 1984 sold a stake in the business to Philadelphia entrepreneur Richard G. Campbell, who then became president and took control of Loos & Dilworth. Campbell carried on the tradition established by the Loos family and built upon it. In 1998 Loos commented, "It was comforting for me to turn over the company to a man of vision. Rick has done a wonderful job with the company my grandfather started." Loos lived until the age of 91, dying in July 2006.

GROWTH AND EXPANSION

Under Campbell's leadership, Loos & Dilworth expanded its reach south of the Philadelphia market through the acquisition of the assets of Capital Petroleum & Supply Inc., based in Capital Heights, Maryland. A subsidiary under the name Loos & Dilworth Co., Inc., was created and in July 1997 the unit's Capital Heights distribution facility was opened for business, supplying Valvoline motor oil and other chemicals to customers in Maryland, Virginia, and Washington, D.C. The main focus was servicing the passenger car and light truck market in this region.

In the late 1990s, Loos & Dilworth greatly expanded its product offerings. A month after the launch of the Maryland unit, the company added to its chemical product offerings in adhesives with hydrocarbon resins, random copolymers of ethylene, and other products. Also in August 1997 Loos & Dilworth began carrying three new Plastolyn products from Hercules Resins, low-molecular weight resins used in such products as rubber shoe soles. In the summer of 1998 the company forged a distribution agreement with Ivanhoe Industries, an Illinois-based manufacturer of food-grade kosher silicone antifoams and emulsifiers, used in food processing such as potato chip production, and fermentation, as well as in adhesives and wax coatings, and agriculture and water treatment applications.

Also in 1998, Loos & Dilworth became a distributor for Total Petroleum Inc. and its specialty solvents and mineral seal oil. These products were primarily sold to the adhesives, inks, lubricants, and soap industries. In 1999 Loos & Dilworth supplemented its product offerings to the personal care and cosmetic industries, adding two chemical families. One was fatty acid-based and conveyed hydrophobicity (or water repellency), while the other was water soluble and helped substances adhere to hair, nails, and skin.

NEW PRODUCT LINES FOR THE 21ST CENTURY

The addition of new products continued in the new century. In 2000 the company began distributing the Elf Atochem line of chlorotoluene derivatives, used in ultraviolet-cured coatings, inks, and resins, and bromine derivatives, used in adhesives, coatings, paints, and sealants. Loos & Dilworth supplied these chemicals to the adhesives and sealants, paint and coatings, ink, and flavor and fragrance markets. To make it easier for formulators and purchasing agents to place orders, Loos & Dilworth launched a new interactive web site to serve a variety of industries, including adhesives and sealants, inks and coatings, soaps and detergents, foods and beverages, cosmetics and personal care, and specialty solvents.

On the automotive side, Loos & Dilworth branched out beyond Sunoco products in 2001 when an agreement was reached with ConocoPhillips Company to distribute many of its brands, including the product lines of Kendall, Conoco, and 76 Lubricants. Loos & Dilworth also added the car care products of Meguiar's, Inc., an Irvine, California, manufacturer of consumer car wash detergents and degreasers, polishes and waxes, detailing products, wheel and tire products, and car interior care products.

The Chemical Division of Loos & Dilworth continued to add to its slate of niche products as well. In 2007, for example, it began carrying Westlake Chemical's Epolene polymers and a newly developed rosin amine surfactant, a film-forming product that acted as a corrosion inhibitor, from Croda International Plc, a United Kingdom-based manufacturer of specialty chemicals. In 2008 Loos & Dilworth began representing a family of light-colored terpene phenolic resins, developed for use with certain hot melts, solvent-based acrylic, and natural rubber-based pressure sensitive adhesives. While smaller than the two leading distributors that were the main competitors for the Chemical Division, Loos & Dilworth remained viable because of its attention to customer service, an approach that was shared by the Automotive Division and would likely help the company prosper well into the second century of its history.

Ed Dinger

PRINCIPAL SUBSIDIARIES

Loos & Dilworth Co., Inc.

PRINCIPAL COMPETITORS

Ashland Inc.; International Specialty Products, Inc.; Tennant Inks & Coatings Supplies Ltd.

FURTHER READING

"Augustus J. Loos," *Cornell Alumni News,* March 18, 1926, p. 299.

Holmes, Frank R., and Lewis A. Williams Jr., *Cornell University: A History,* New York: University Publishing Society, 1905.

Isenberg, Louis M., "H. Harwood Loos, Company President, 91," *Philadelphia Inquirer,* p. B10.

"L&D Opens Oil Distribution Facility," *Chemical Marketing Reporter,* July 15, 1997, p. 37.

"Loos & Dilworth Chosen" *Chemical Market Reporter,* June 29, 1998, p. 33.

Maui Land & Pineapple Company, Inc.

Maui Land & Pineapple Company, Inc.

120 Kane Street
Kahului, Hawaii 96732-6687
U.S.A.
Telephone: (808) 877-3351
Fax: (808) 871-0953
Web site: http://www.mauiland.com

Public Company
Incorporated: 1969
Employees: 1,000
Sales: $154.1 million (2007)
Stock Exchanges: New York
Ticker Symbol: MLP
NAICS: 111339 Other Noncitrus Fruit Farming;
    233110 Land Subdivision and Land Development;
    551112 Offices of Other Holding Companies

■ ■ ■

One of Hawaii's oldest and largest corporations, Maui Land & Pineapple Company, Inc. (ML&P), grows pineapple and develops and operates resort and commercial property on approximately 25,000 acres of land in Maui. ML&P conducts its business through two primary operating subsidiaries, Maui Pineapple Company, Ltd., and Kapalua Land Company, Ltd. The pineapple operations, situated on roughly 2,000 acres owned by the company, represent the company's original business, whose roots indirectly stretched to the first appearance of pineapple in Hawaii in 1813. The company exited the canning business in 2007 and focuses on growing fresh and organic pineapple under

the names Maui Gold and Hawaiian Gold. The real estate–related business of ML&P emerged during the 1960s, when the company began developing residential, commercial, and resort properties. It operates the Kapalua Resort as well as the Pu'u Kukui Watershed Preserve, the largest private nature reserve in Hawaii.

ORIGINS

The history of ML&P incorporated the history of the Baldwins, a family of New England Congregational missionaries who arrived on the Hawaiian Islands in 1836. Displaying considerably more prowess as land barons than as proselytizers, the Baldwins became one of the "Big Five" families who controlled Hawaii in the century before World War II, establishing a far-reaching business empire with holdings in agriculture, ranching, coffee, canning, and other activities. Their grasp on the Hawaiian economy was comprehensive, maintained by a labyrinthine network of businesses whose development spanned generations of Baldwins. One of these businesses spawned from the varied interests of the Baldwins was ML&P's earliest direct predecessor, the Keahua Ranch Co., which was incorporated in December 1909 to control a portion of the family's pineapple operations.

In 1929 the Keahua Ranch Co. was renamed the Haleakala Pineapple Co., Ltd., three years before the pineapple operations of Haleakala and Maui Agricultural Company were consolidated to create Maui Pineapple Company, Ltd. J. Walter Cameron, a descendant of the Baldwin family, was appointed manager of the new company, presiding over its

COMPANY PERSPECTIVES

Maui Land & Pineapple Company, Inc.'s (ML&P) vision is to create and manage holistic communities that integrate agriculture, wise stewardship of natural resources and eco-effective design principles to build a sustainable future for Maui. These holistic communities are intended to foster an authentic sense of place and a strong feeling of belonging, mutual obligation and respect. They are designed to value and protect the natural environment, while supporting the cultivation of fresh, healthy, homegrown foods that seek to contribute to Maui's economic health and agricultural character, thus reducing our dependence on imports.

ML&P's vision rests on a foundation of the four cornerstones underlying all holistic communities. These cornerstones are authenticity, inclusiveness, sustainability and ecosensitivity.

development for the next 30 years until a flurry of corporate maneuvers created the ML&P that emerged in the 1990s. In August 1962, Alexander & Baldwin, a principal Baldwin family concern, merged three of its pineapple operations, Baldwin Packers, Ltd., Maui Pineapple Company, Ltd., and the old Haleakala Pineapple Company, to create what four months later became simply the Maui Pineapple Company, Ltd. J. Walter Cameron was named president of the Alexander & Baldwin subsidiary, joined by his son, Colin Campbell Cameron, who was appointed general manager.

It was the younger Cameron who exerted the greatest influence over the company during the 20th century. A Maui native, Colin Cameron earned a master's degree in business administration at Harvard College, leaving the institution in 1953 to return to the pineapple operations on Maui. In 1964, Colin Cameron was promoted to general manager and executive vice-president when his father retired from day-to-day control over the company to become its chairman. Although the Camerons held prominent titles at Maui Pineapple, the fortunes of the company were not entirely under their control. Alexander & Baldwin held sway as the parent company of Maui Pineapple, having the final say in the decision making affecting its subsidiary.

It was a relationship that became strained during the 1960s and irrevocably damaged in 1967 when Alexander & Baldwin's new president, Stanley Powell, Jr., delivered an ultimatum. Powell wanted to centralize all

management decisions in Honolulu, which, in Colin Cameron's view, put him in an untenable position. Cameron believed the pineapple operations could not flourish if they were managed from afar. Further, he had tired of competing for attention with Alexander & Baldwin's other subsidiaries, which included sugar and shipping operations that were much larger and made much more money than Maui Pineapple. In response, Colin Cameron resigned in 1967, the same year his father retired as chairman. Both remained on the company's board of directors, however, and would return shortly to submit a proposal to Alexander & Baldwin.

A NEW BEGINNING IN 1969

In 1969 the Camerons made their bid for independence. They approached Alexander & Baldwin about purchasing Maui Pineapple Company and reached an agreement in July for a $20 million buyout of the enterprise. In September the Camerons changed the name of the company to Maui Land & Pineapple Company, Inc. Three months later, they took ML&P public. With J. Walter Cameron serving as chairman and Colin Cameron serving as president and chief executive officer, ML&P took its first steps unfettered by Alexander & Baldwin, beginning a new era as the 1970s began.

As the company set out on its own, it drew support from two primary business areas. One side of ML&P represented the most recent addition to the Cameron family's business activities, its importance reflected by the inclusion of the word "land" in the new corporate title. During the 1960s, Colin Cameron had spearheaded resort planning and development activities that had operated under the control of Maui Pineapple Company. Following the Camerons' purchase of Maui Pineapple Company, these real estate activities were organized into a new subsidiary incorporated in 1970 as Honolua Plantation Land Company, Inc.

Through Honolua Plantation, with Colin Cameron as its president, ML&P began building residential housing projects, beginning with a 174-unit, low- and moderate-cost housing project called Napilihau that began construction in 1972. By the time the Napilihau units were ready for occupancy in 1974, the Camerons had formed another real estate development subsidiary named Kapalua Land Company, Ltd. Following the 1975 incorporation of Kapalua Land, the Honolua Plantation subsidiary was responsible for the management and development of non-resort lands, while Kapalua Land oversaw the duties of resort development. Kapalua Land's resort development activities during the 1970s included the construction of an 18-hole golf

KEY DATES

1909: Keahua Ranch Co. is incorporated to control a portion of the Baldwin family's pineapple operations.

1929: Keahua Ranch is renamed the Haleakala Pineapple Co., Ltd.

1932: Haleakala and Maui Agricultural Company are consolidated to create Maui Pineapple Company, Ltd.

1962: Alexander & Baldwin merges three of its pineapple operations: Baldwin Packers, Ltd., Maui Pineapple Company, Ltd., and the old Haleakala Pineapple Company.

1969: The Cameron family buys the company; it goes public as Maui Land & Pineapple Company, Inc.

1975: Kapalua Land Company, Ltd., and Maui Pineapple Company, Ltd., are incorporated.

1978: The Kapalua Bay Hotel opens.

1992: The Ritz Carlton Kapalua opens.

1993: The company posts an $11 million loss.

2003: David C. Cole is named CEO.

2007: The company shutters its canning operations.

2008: ML&P lists on the New York Stock Exchange.

course, condominium complexes, and the 196-room Kapalua Bay Hotel, which opened in 1978. The other side of ML&P's business was its pineapple operations, representing the thread that connected the Cameron family–controlled company to the 1909 founding of the Keahua Ranch Co. In 1975 the pineapple operations were separated into their own subsidiary called Maui Pineapple Company, Ltd.

J. Walter Cameron's death in 1976 left Colin Cameron as the patriarch of the family and principal leader of ML&P. His father's legacy—a half century of stewarding the fortunes of the company's pineapple operations—would stand in contrast to his own, as Colin Cameron devoted the bulk of his energies to the development of ML&P's real estate activities, particularly during the late 1980s. The Kapalua Land subsidiary served as the hub of activity, presiding over the development of The Ironwoods, a 40-unit condominium project that was completed in 1980, and The Ridge, a 161-unit condominium project, also completed in 1980. The subsidiary also completed its second golf course, The Village Course, in 1980.

Financial pressure, attributable to the more than $50 million of debt that weighed ML&P down in 1984, forced Cameron to sell what was regarded as his masterpiece, the Kapalua Bay Hotel, in 1985. Despite the divestiture, Cameron, serving as chairman and acting president of Kapalua Land after the sale of the company's signature hotel property, pressed ahead with other real estate development projects. In 1985 the company acquired the Kaahumanu Shopping Center and broke ground the following year on the Pineapple Hill at Kapalua project, a single-family residential project. The Pineapple Hill at Kapalua development, comprising 99 lots, was completed in 1987 and was followed by the development of Kapalua Place, an eight-lot, single-family residential project, completed in 1989.

FACING CONTROVERSY AND COMPETITION

Against the backdrop of commercial and residential development projects, Cameron was busy working on what could be called his dream project. At roughly the same time as ML&P's formation, Cameron and his father had begun planning a large-scale hotel project that became known as the Kapalua project. They conducted an archaeological survey on an area in West Maui, later deciding on a beachfront plot known as the Honokahua site. Years of planning went into the project, time spent designing the hotel, having the zoning code changed to permit the construction of the hotel, and securing the financial backing to fund the project. By 1986, the final hurdles before beginning construction had been cleared. Ritz-Carlton had agreed to serve as the hotel operator and financing had been obtained from Japanese investors.

There was one nagging problem, however. The Honokahua site was discovered to be an ancient Hawaiian burial ground, the magnitude of which was not fully realized until late in the project's development. A thorough excavation of the site had unearthed 700 burials by 1988, including a variety of artifacts that were estimated to be 3,500 years old. By 1989, construction of the $100 million, 450-room Ritz-Carlton was a year behind schedule and Cameron found himself at the center of protests and heated debate. Kapalua Land was at risk of losing the financial backing for the project and suffering the departure of its Ritz-Carlton partners.

While Cameron's hotel project sat motionless, mired in controversy, ML&P was still able to fall back on its pineapple operations, which had recorded consecutive years of profitability that stretched from 1977 to the end of the 1980s. The company's Maui Pineapple Company subsidiary ranked as the largest producer of private-label pineapple in the United States, providing a steady stream of income that tempered the frustration stemming from the hobbled Kapalua hotel project. As ML&P exited the 1980s, however, its pineapple operations suffered a devastating setback that later resulted in the worst year ever recorded by ML&P or any of its predecessors. The first sign of trouble surfaced in 1989, when the Kapalua project was a year behind its construction schedule.

The source of the trouble was Thailand, which had begun gearing up for large-scale pineapple production in the late 1980s. As a pineapple-producing region, Thailand possessed ideal characteristics, including excellent growing conditions and laborers willing to work for low wages. The number of canning businesses in the country proliferated as a result, concurrent with increased production by ML&P and other U.S.-owned pineapple canning businesses. In 1989 the abundance of pineapple produced and canned led to an oversupply in global markets, resulting in Maui Pineapple Company's $3.9 million operating loss for the year, a year after the subsidiary had registered profits totaling $7.2 million.

MOUNTING PINEAPPLE CRISIS

By 1993, the situation had become disastrous. After ordering its workers to let 20,000 tons of pineapple rot in the fields rather than try to move the fruit onto the glutted world market, Maui Pineapple Company recorded $16.2 million in operating loss. ML&P, unable to offset the loss with its real estate activities, registered a net loss of $11 million on revenues of $131 million.

While the company reeled from its mounting pineapple losses, the ill-fated Kapalua project regained its footing, giving ML&P executives at least one positive development to which they could point during the early 1990s. The site of the resort had been relocated away from the burial ground and the hotel was slated to open in 1992. For Cameron, the grand opening of the long-planned-for hotel was a celebration that he never saw. In June 1992 Cameron was found unconscious in the ocean near his home on Maui, having died of a heart attack while swimming. The Ritz-Carlton hotel opened four months later.

Cameron's sudden death prematurely ushered in a new era of leadership. Mary Cameron Sanford, Colin Cameron's sister, was appointed chairman and Maui Pineapple Company's president, Joseph H. Hartley, was promoted to president and chief executive officer of ML&P. Together, the pair had to contend with the worst crisis in the company's history. The first order of business was to arrest the financial slide experienced by the company's pineapple business and to resolve the difficulties stemming from the market glut. Pineapple

harvesting and canning were trimmed by 25 percent in response to the surfeit of pineapple available and extensive efforts to reduce costs were initiated. Capital improvement spending was cut drastically, slashed from $8.2 million to $1.5 million over the course of the next two years. Executive salaries were reduced, wages were frozen, and employees were laid off. The company ended its 20-year practice of hiring offshore workers during the harvest season and a longstanding arrangement with Wailuku Agribusiness to farm 40,000 tons of pineapple for ML&P was abandoned.

By 1995, the sweeping measures had begun to yield positive results, aided substantially by the U.S. International Trade Commission's ruling that Thai pineapple canneries were guilty of selling their product in the United States at prices lower than the cost of production. As a result of the ruling, duties were imposed that averaged roughly 25 percent of Thai pineapple sale prices, which buoyed the market sufficiently to enable ML&P to raise its prices 23 percent.

A drought in 1996 inflicted another blow to ML&P's pineapple business, but after the temporary setback the company recorded encouraging success with its pineapple operations during the late 1990s. Pineapple sales registered their greatest upswing at the end of the decade, when, in sharp contrast to the early 1990s, there was a worldwide shortage of pineapple. At the decade's conclusion, a new generation of management took the helm at ML&P. Mary Sanford was appointed director emeritus, making room for the ascension of the next line of Camerons, Richard H. Cameron, Colin Cameron's son, who was selected as chairman in March 1999. As Richard Cameron faced the challenge of shepherding the family business into the next century, ML&P's legacy of perseverance bolstered belief in its ability to contend with the difficulties of the future.

MOVING INTO THE 21ST CENTURY

Nevertheless, problems continued into the early years of the new millennium. Intense competition threatened to derail the company's pineapple operations and a major retooling was in order. Significant change began to take place in 2003. ML&P hired David C. Cole, a former AOL executive and Hawaii native, to head its turnaround efforts. By this time, AOL founder Steve Case owned over 40 percent of the company. He turned to Cole, who had left AOL to start his own eco-friendly farm in Virginia, to shore up profits while maintaining the company's eco-friendly image.

ML&P's first order of business was to revamp its pineapple operations. By 2003, the global market for fresh pineapple was worth over $1 billion. It was the second fastest growing fruit in popularity in the United States—behind papayas—based on per capita consumption. Fresh Del Monte Produce Inc. controlled nearly 70 percent of the fresh pineapple market and ML&P began to slowly chip away at its market share by focusing on its own fresh pineapple. The company sold its Costa Rican subsidiary in order to focus on domestic production. It also began its slow exit from canning pineapple. In fact, the last remaining cannery at all in Hawaii closed its doors in June 2007.

The company also made changes in its real estate business. The Kapalua Bay Hotel on Maui closed in April 2006 to make way for new resort condominiums slated to open in 2009. The company recycled nearly 98 percent of the materials from the old property, using them in the creation of the new property. This sector of the company's business was threatened by the weakening U.S. economy and overall downturn in the real estate market. Higher energy costs also began to eat into company profits, forcing ML&P to announce the layoff of nearly 26 percent of its workforce in July 2008.

While the company faced stark challenges related to competition and the faltering economy, ML&P management believed it was well positioned to meet these challenges head on. It argued that its high-end resort property was somewhat resistant to the mortgage crisis happening in the United States and was fairly recession-proof. The company claimed that owners of $4 million vacation homes were unlikely to be harshly affected by economic downturns. The company remained focused on controlling costs in an effort to maintain its profitability. Its stock moved to the New York Stock Exchange in April 2008. It also partnered with Calavo Growers Inc. to market and distribute its Maui Gold pineapples in North America. Net income increased nearly 10 percent in 2007, reaching $8 million. While only time would tell if Cole's strategy would pay off in the long run, it appeared that the changes he implemented had indeed led to short-term profits.

Jeffrey L. Covell
Updated, Christina M. Stansell

PRINCIPAL SUBSIDIARIES

Honolua Plantation Land Company, Ltd.; Kapalua Advertising Company, Ltd.; Kapalua Bay Holdings, LLC (51%); Kapalua Land Company, Ltd.; Kapalua Realty Company, Ltd.; Kapalua Waste Treatment Company, Ltd.; Kapalua Water Company, Ltd.; Maui Pineapple Company, Ltd.

PRINCIPAL COMPETITORS

Alexander & Baldwin Inc.; Del Monte Fresh Produce Company; Dole Food Company Inc.; Four Seasons Hotels Inc.; Chiquita Brands International Inc.

FURTHER READING

Bartlett, Tony, "Kapalua Expands Resort with Hotel, Golf Course, More Acreage: Secluded Location Will House 550-Room Ritz-Carlton," *Travel Weekly*, December 13, 1990, p. 66.

Chang, Diane, "Paradise Lost," *Hawaii Business*, December 1991, p. 68.

Eagar, Harry, "Coping with 'Change,'" *Maui News*, June 8, 2008.

Frank, Robert, "Juicy Details," *Wall Street Journal*, October 7, 2003.

"Hawaii to Lose Its Last Pineapple Cannery," *Deseret Morning News*, May 7, 2007.

Ishikawa, Lisa, "Greener Acres?" *Hawaii Business*, May 1994, p. 12.

Jokiel, Lucy, "Colin Cameron's Toughest Decision," *Hawaii Business*, May 1989, p. 16.

Joyce, Amy, "Executive Cultivates Agriculture, Tech Skills," *Washington Post*, September 8, 2003.

Ma, Lybia, "Still on Track: The Group Dubbed 'Most Likely to Succeed' in 1987 Is Still Running Hard," *Hawaii Business*, May 1990, p. 77.

"Maui Land & Pineapple Laying Off 274 Workers," *Associated Press Newswires*, July 25, 2008.

"Maui Pine to Focus on Fresh Pineapples," *Associated Press Newswires*, April 23, 2003.

"Most of Kapalua Bay Hotel Recycled," *Associated Press Newswires*, November 14, 2006.

"Passing the Baton," *Hawaii Business*, May 1993, p. 9.

Yang, Catherine, "You've Got Pineapples," *Business Week*, September 22, 2003.

Max & Erma's Restaurants Inc.

4849 Evanswood Drive
Columbus, Ohio 43229
U.S.A.
Telephone: (614) 431-5800
Toll Free: (866) 629-3762
Fax: (614) 431-4100
Web site: http://www.maxandermas.com

Private Company
Incorporated: 1972
Employees: 5,126
Sales: $174.9 million (2007)
NAICS: 722110 Full-Service Restaurants

■ ■ ■

Headquartered in Columbus, Ohio, Max & Erma's Restaurants Inc. operates and franchises more than 100 casual, family-style restaurants in Ohio and about a dozen other U.S. states. The chain is known for its signature gourmet hamburgers, an all-you-can-eat sundae bar, and a variety of moderately priced menu items. About 25 percent of the chain's locations are franchises. Struggling in the early 2000s, as were many of its competitors in the casual dining sector, the company was taken private in 2008 by investor group G & R Acquisition Inc. Plans to turn the company's fortunes around focused on menu changes and restaurant redesign that would distinguish the company among its competitors, as well as financial measures to weather the economic downturns affecting restaurant sales in general.

1972 ORIGINS

Max & Erma's was founded by Barry Zacks, a graduate of Cornell University who returned to his hometown of Columbus, Ohio, to take a position at his family's footwear company, R.G. Barry Corporation. However, footwear did not hold the entrepreneur's interest for long. In 1972, the 36-year-old purchased a local bar and restaurant from longtime owners Max and Erma Visconik. Located in Columbus's historic German Village, the building had been constructed in 1889 by the Franklin Brewing Company. Known during Prohibition as Kaiser's Café, the pub had stayed afloat selling "near beer" and groceries during that time.

Zacks's revamp of the business targeted the mid-priced segment of the dine-out market with a particular emphasis on singles. He cultivated a fun atmosphere with a ubiquitous decor since characterized as the "garage-sale look," featuring moose-head trophies, nostalgic photos, and memorabilia as well as plenty of brass and Tiffany-style stained glass. Promotions were usually adult-oriented and sometimes raunchy. The "So Happy It's Thursday" (S-H-I-T) events of the early 1980s, for example, lampooned competitor T.G.I. Friday's salute to the beginning of the weekend.

Telephones at each table encouraged patrons to flirt with one another. Max & Erma's also earned a reputation for gigantic serving portions, a distinction founded on its signature Garbage Burger. This hand-pattied, ten-ounce behemoth with "the works" was credited as the original gourmet hamburger. Zacks was also cited as one of the progenitors of the salad bar and potato skins appetizer. With its modest prices and a strong emphasis

COMPANY PERSPECTIVES

We believe that a great experience starts with our food. That's why we use the freshest, highest quality ingredients in everything we serve. Freshness and quality are truly the foundations upon which Max & Erma's was built. We make every effort to do things the right way, not the easy way. We believe this dedication and passion is the reason we're better and the reason our guests return more often. Our market research tells us that our guests know what they are going to order before they get to our restaurant because they crave certain items, our signature dishes.

on bar beverages, Max & Erma's earned a reputation as a gathering place for singles.

LEADERSHIP ISSUES

The concept was a hit. By the time the chain went public in 1982, it boasted ten locations in Ohio, Michigan, Indiana, Kansas, Kentucky, and Pennsylvania, and annual revenues of over $12.5 million. However, this growth had masked a number of problems, not least of which was a lack of profitability. In a lengthy 1990 critique of the chain for *Restaurant Business*, Ralph Raffio asserted that the company had "not once [turned] a profit in its first 15 years of existence." (It had in fact recorded a $185,000 surplus in 1982, which had been accounted for as a 44-week year.) Raffio blamed flighty management and ill-conceived programs, criticizing "the time the dinner house chain's new drive-thru window had to be promptly shuttered because a well-done burger took 13 minutes to cook. Never mind that within two weeks of installing the drive-thru, a customer actually ran out of gas waiting for his order."

Critics—among them members of Max & Erma's own board of directors and executive team—cited poor site selection and an out-of-control menu as key obstacles to profitability. Some thought Barry Zacks's choices for new locations were too dependent on price instead of market and demographic characteristics. The company often entered new markets via the purchase of failed restaurants and converted them to the Max & Erma's theme, resulting in a hodgepodge of dissimilar storefronts, sometimes in less-than-ideal locations. Zacks would later acknowledge that this was a core shortcoming, telling *Business First-Columbus*'s Ann Hollifield that "The one thing I learned from Max & Erma's is the

most important thing is location, location, location, and the fourth one is location. I made those mistakes with Max & Erma's, and I don't want to make them again."

Notwithstanding award-winning menus, a slavish attention to food trends saw the chain adding 20 to 30 new items to the menu each year, giving it a 30-plus page menu by the mid-1980s. The eclectic lineup expanded from all-American burgers and appetizers to include everything from a raw bar to homemade pasta, a variety of ethnic dishes, and exotic sauces. Furthermore, each restaurant tailored its offerings to local tastes, making chainwide procurement next to impossible.

Most of the blame for these difficulties was placed squarely on the shoulders of Barry Zacks. Raffio boiled the chain's difficulties down to a single factor: the founder's "rambunctiousness." In July 1986, CFO William Niegsch told *Nation's Restaurant News* that "This company is a textbook case of being started by an entrepreneur … and now it's time for more professional management." It was one of the most discreet criticisms made of Zacks during this period.

Zacks stepped down that year and was replaced by Todd Barnum, who with three other top executives purchased the founder's remaining 20-plus percent stake in the chain. Zacks went from chairman and CEO to "Founder and Independent Businessman" in the 1986 annual report, and he remained on board for a while as a consultant. Zacks died from cancer four years later at the age of 54.

Barnum had been with the eatery since its inception, advancing to president in 1974. He expressed his confidence in the company's continuing viability in Raffio's 1990 article, asserting that "No matter how terrible things got financially for us, there were still a lot of people having a great time at our restaurants. The restaurant concept itself was never the problem. Executing it was."

ACHIEVING PROFITABILITY

Team Barnum proved that theory by turning a $300,000 profit for the company during his first full year at the helm. The new CEO used a variety of fairly simple strategies, focusing on the menu, marketing, operations, and remodeling. By eliminating low-sale, high-labor dishes, the company simplified its menu from 36 pages to six. It also shrank some of its "enormous portions" offering the six-ounce Erma burger as an alternative to the Garbage Burger, for example. The company hired a marketing executive to manage promotional campaigns via outdoor and events advertising, direct mail, and television. Market research helped the chain trace key demographic trends. For example, as

KEY DATES

1972: Barry Zacks purchases a bar and restaurant in Columbus, Ohio, from longtime owners Max and Erma Visconik.
1982: Max & Erma's holds its initial public offering.
1988: The company begins to franchise.
1997: The company opens the first Ironwood Café, followed by two more.
1998: The company closes the first Ironwood Café.
2000: The remaining Ironwood Café's are closed.
2008: A Pittsburgh-based investment group takes the company private.

Max & Erma's core baby-boomer clientele aged, married, and had children, the chain's emphasis shifted from singles to a more family-oriented clientele. A $2-million remodeling program updated equipment as well as decor.

These efforts began to bear fruit within months. Sales increased from $16.5 million in 1986 to a record $24.3 million in 1989, while net income increased from a deficit of $318 million to a record $1.2 million. The turnaround won praise from the likes of the *Wall Street Journal* and *Business Week,* and this positive press helped the relatively small company become one of the restaurant industry's most-watched growth stocks. Having stabilized the chain's finances, Barnum embarked on what he called a "modest, controlled expansion," concentrating primarily on existing markets.

GROWTH AND COMPETITION

The company adhered to this reasonable plan, adding only two units by the end of 1989 for a total of 13 locations, but enthusiasm took hold in 1990, when the chain added five new restaurants. This growth spurt proved poorly timed, however, with a national recession bruising the results of even the usually recession-resistant casual theme segment of the restaurant industry. With net income declining to less than $500,000 in 1991, Max & Erma's reined in growth to just one unit per year in 1991 and 1992. Net recovered to $1.1 million in the latter year, by which time the company had 20 locations clustered in the Midwest.

Max & Erma's pursued healthier expansion in the mid-1990s, increasing revenues and profits to record levels in 1996. The chain achieved this feat through continued reductions in operating costs, a strategic

menu revamp, and the introduction of a new restaurant prototype. In 1993, the company abandoned its traditional site selection strategy, which still focused on acquiring existing restaurant buildings and refurbishing them as Max & Erma's. Instead, the chain developed a stand-alone model that would provide a distinctive atmosphere and lower start-up costs. Participation in "restaurant parks" also proved a viable growth vehicle in some markets. These retail developments, often in suburban areas, combined several different (mostly casual) restaurants in one destination. After posting its fifth consecutive year of record revenues and earnings in 1997, the company also began to explore a new avenue for its business: airport eateries.

In an effort to increase individual dining tabs, the company introduced new, slightly more expensive menu items and began to push its long-neglected bar offerings. Sales grew from $43.5 million in 1993 to $79.9 million in 1996 while net income increased from $1.4 million to $2.2 million, capping five consecutive years of growth in both categories. From a well-established presence in Ohio, Michigan, Kentucky, and Pennsylvania, the company established itself in major markets of Illinois and North Carolina. By the end of 1996, the company had 40 units throughout the Midwest.

By 1999, during which period revenues reached $100.5 million, the company was aggressively pursuing growth. Up until then Max & Erma's had averaged fewer than two new restaurants a year since 1972; in 1999, it opened six new restaurants and planned for eight to ten per year during the next few years in Atlanta, Georgia; Columbus and Toledo, Ohio; Chicago, Illinois; the Carolinas; and West Virginia. The company also focused on franchises as a way to spread its name. Some of these franchised units opened in new markets, and three new units debuted in hotels not already providing their own foodservice.

However, as Carol Casper of *Restaurant Business* warned, casual-themed restaurants faced the prospect of becoming "victims of their own Success," as "hundreds of imitators and innovators flooded the market" at the turn of the century. Max & Erma's worked to differentiate itself from its competitors via an easily recognizable facade, a continuously evolving, value-oriented menu, a highly trained service staff, and a fun, yet family-oriented atmosphere. At the same time, the company was also trying to broaden and distinguish its fare. "We sense a sameness developing in all the chain restaurants and this 'ho-hum, we know what this is like' attitude among customers," Barnum explained in a 1999 *Columbus Dispatch* article. Max & Erma's rolled out 15 new menu items in 1997. It also embarked on a new gourmet pizza-and-pasta concept called Ironwood Café, a name that called to mind the hardwood that fueled the new restaurant's ovens.

TURBULENT TIMES IN THE RED

Unfortunately, the first Ironwood Café lasted only a year, spoiling Max & Erma's string of record-breaking sales. The company sold the remaining two Ironwood Cafés in 2000, and by 2001, Max & Erma's was focusing again on aggressive expansion plans for its then 60-plus-unit chain

In 2002, Max & Erma's opened six company-owned units, and franchisees opened three. In 2003, growth in numbers continued, but beginning in 2002 profits for the company began to wane. The reasons cited by industry observers were weak economic conditions in the Midwest, the company's base, and high gasoline prices, which led diners to stay at home. When Rob Lindeman, who had begun serving tables and bartending at Max & Erma's in Dayton in 1990, and who had supervised the company's franchising and marketing since 2003, became president of the company in late 2005, the company was operating in the red.

The company faced management challenges as well during this time. It was losing board members rapidly, due to death, retirement, and ouster. In 2006, Roger Blackwell, the company's largest shareholder, went to jail for insider trading charges involving another company. All of this left the company at times without enough non-management board members to comply with NASDAQ's requirements.

The close to 100 company-owned and franchised Max & Erma's restaurants continued to lose money in 2006 and 2007. "The last few years have been some of the most challenging we've ever had," Barnum confessed in a January 2007 *Columbia Dispatch* article. The company thus focused on claiming a larger share of the casual dining market. Abandoning its dark colors and cluttered interiors in favor of brighter, colorful interiors, it remodeled ten of its 100 units in 2007. "We realized we weren't as different as we used to be," confessed Lindeman (who became CEO when Barnum retired in late 2007) in a *Chain Leader* article that year. The company also restructured its operations and began to explore ways to bring a cash infusion into the company.

Max & Erma's also began to pursue franchising opportunities in the West and Southwest, hoping to increase its percentage of franchises from about 25 to 60 percent. The company rolled out a new prototype unit with patio and fireplace designed to appeal both to dining audiences and to prospective franchisers.

In 2008 Max & Erma's was acquired by Pittsburgh investor group G & R Acquisition and taken private.

Challenges remained primarily in increased food and gas costs and the fact that the neighborhood bar-and-grill industry was crowded and competitive. The company remained hopeful, however, for a turnaround facilitated by the infusion of cash from its new owner. Whether Max & Erma's famous burgers, supersized sundaes, and focus on fresh food could pull it into the black and ahead of its competitors was still an open question.

April Dougal Gasbarre
Updated, Carrie Rothburd

PRINCIPAL COMPETITORS

Applebee's International Inc.; Brinker International Inc.; Darden Restaurants Inc.; Carlson Restaurants Worldwide Inc.; Ruby Tuesday Inc.

FURTHER READING

Casper, Carol, "Small Is Beautiful: Max & Erma's Acts Like an Independent," *Restaurant Business,* September 1, 1996, pp. 98–99.

———, "Staying Power," *Restaurant Business,* September 1996, pp. 81–105.

Curet, Monique, "Struggling Chain; 'For Sale' One Option for Max & Erma's," *Columbus Dispatch,* September 20, 2007, p. 10C.

Farkas, David, "Disciplining the Menu: How a Process Helped Max & Erma's into the Black," *Restaurant Hospitality,* August 1990, p. 132.

Hollifield, Ann, "Max & Erma's Founder Launching a New Business," *Business First-Columbus,* December 29, 1986, p. 8.

Kapner, Suzanne, "Max & Erma's Retools Menus, Adopts New Strategy to Boost Profits," *Nation's Restaurant News,* May 20, 1996, p. 7.

"A Light Touch: Max & Erma's Ditches Dark Colors and Heavy Décor to Create a Female-Friendly Interior," *Chain Leader,* April 2007, p. 24.

"Max and Erma's Promotes S-H-I-T," *Restaurant Business,* January 1, 1983, pp. 162–63.

Nash, Bob, "Max & Erma's Bounces Back by Correcting Early Mistakes," *Business First-Columbus,* March 4, 1985, p. 12.

Prewitt, Milford, "Itty-Bitty Max & Erma's Gets Big-Time Press Attention," *Nation's Restaurant News,* January 22, 1990, p. 14.

Raffio, Ralph, "Can Max & Erma's Rebuilds," *Restaurant Business,* June 10, 1990, pp. 127–33.

Saunders, Amy, "Sale Provides Max & Erma's with a Lifeline," *Columbus Dispatch,* April 29, 2008, p. 1A.

"Scuttling a Trusty Formula Can Help Revive Growth," *Wall Street Journal,* November 27, 1990, p. B2.

Turnbull, Lornet, "Max & Erma's Chief Lays Out Chain's New Growth," *Columbus Dispatch,* April 9, 1999, p. 1C.

Walkup, Carolyn, "Max & Erma's Discovers Success in Slow Growth," *Nation's Restaurant News,* March 22, 1993, p. 16.

———, "Max & Erma's Zacks Drops Management Role," *Nation's Restaurant News,* July 7, 1986, pp. 1–2.

Meadowcraft, Inc.

———— ■ ————

4700 Pinson Valley Parkway
Birmingham, Alabama 35215
U.S.A.
Telephone: (205) 853-2220
Fax: (205) 854-4054
Web site: http://www.meadowcraft.com

Private Company
Incorporated: 1985
Employees: 2,000
Sales: $123 million (2001 est.)
NAICS: 337124 Metal Household Furniture Manu- facturing

■ ■ ■

Meadowcraft, Inc., is a leading domestic maker of casual outdoor furniture and the largest manufacturer of outdoor wrought iron furniture in the United States. Other Meadowcraft products, all of which are designed and distributed by the company, include a variety of wrought iron indoor furniture and both indoor and outdoor wrought iron accessories, outdoor cushions, and umbrellas. The company's products are sold by specialty furniture retailers throughout the United States. Meadowcraft was taken private by a group led by chairman Samuel R. Blount in 1999. Falling sales and profits forced the company to declare bankruptcy in 2002. Meadowcraft emerged from Chapter 11 the following year.

ORIGINS IN IRON WORKS

Meadowcraft traces its origins to the 1923 founding of the Birmingham Ornamental Iron Co., in Birmingham, Alabama, by B. M. Meadow. The fledgling operation began fashioning such ornamental iron products as decorative fencing and gates for Birmingham residences and businesses. Over the years, the company diversified its iron product offerings and its customer base, producing a variety of iron products for local business facilities.

During World War II, Birmingham Ornamental Iron (BOI) began manufacturing a line of metal furniture, in part to offset seasonal drops in revenues it experienced given its dependence on the construction industry. The company found a ready, if unlikely, customer in electronics giant Philco, which had been diversifying its interests during the war. From 1946 to 1948, Philco marketed and sold Meadowcraft furniture, named for the founder of BOI, but dropped the line when demand for Philco electronics products resumed following the war.

Following the loss of Philco as a customer for its furniture, BOI resumed its focus on the construction industry, producing stairs, railings, grillwork, metal signs, and a variety of metal products for use in local industrial facilities, including in regional plants for Ford Motor Co. and the Container Corp., as well as in the construction of Prudential Life Insurance Co. offices and the Georgia Tech library.

By the early 1950s, the company's furniture line was languishing and facing steep financial losses. Moreover, BOI had warehoused thousands of tons of metal for use in its furniture; further losses would ensue if that inventory had to be sold as scrap. The problem was met by the company's vice-president, general manager, and treasurer, William McTyeire Jr. An engineering graduate and enthusiastic salesperson as well, McTyeire decided to turn the furniture operations around.

MEADOWCRAFT FURNITURE TAKES OFF

McTyeire instituted a policy of commitment to quality in design and manufacture, as well as to dealer satisfaction. Among the qualities recommending Meadowcraft furniture were its ten-year rust-free guarantee and its availability in popular styles and colors. Moreover, to ensure a high quality product, the company invested in the latest and best manufacturing equipment. Maintaining, "the dealer is always right," McTyeire reportedly once accepted a return shipment of wrought iron furniture made by a competitor from a dissatisfied dealer who mistook the furniture for Meadowcraft. Rather than returning the shipment to the dealer, McTyeire saw to it that the pieces were refurbished and returned to the dealer, with an explanation, at no charge. Consequently, that dealer was duly impressed with Meadowcraft, as were many other dealers over the years.

McTyeire also spearheaded direct mail selling efforts aimed at leading furniture retailers across the country. The company spent heavily on advertising in general, overseeing print and radio promotions. Moreover, the company began offering Meadowcraft furniture for use on the sets of the country's most popular television programs. In the mid-1950s, the company received an important commission from television stars Desi Arnaz and Lucille Ball, who ordered over 500 pieces of Meadowcraft furniture for use at their new Palm Springs resort hotel.

By the late 1950s, the company was ranked third in the United States in wrought iron furniture sales and was first in the South. The iron works' sales surpassed $3 million in 1957, over one-third of which was generated by its Meadowcraft furniture line. Still, the iron works' primary business was in manufacturing the miscellaneous and ornamental metal products.

A NEW IDENTITY AS MEADOWCRAFT

By 1967, when the company was employing a workforce of 259 and the founder's descendant Evelyn Meadow was serving as chairman, BOI had grown into a collection of consolidated furniture and housewares makers, still based in Birmingham. In 1985, these manufacturers were incorporated as Meadowcraft, with Samuel R. Blount as the new concern's chairman. The popularity of Meadowcraft furniture was rekindled during this time, when retail giant Wal-Mart began offering outdoor furniture at its stores, including the company's lines of chairs, tables, and benches. The Meadowcraft products proved popular and regularly sold out.

When Bill McCanna took over the presidency of Meadowcraft in 1991, his focus was on quality control, particularly as it pertained to designing, producing, and shipping on a reliable, timely, and cost effective basis. McCanna, who came to Meadowcraft after two decades of running manufacturing plants for *Fortune* 500 companies, made modernizing the firm's distribution his first order of business. At the time, the company had been overseeing about ten warehouses scattered around Birmingham, with crews wandering around them searching for the furniture needed to fill orders. A new, better organized system would be in place by mid-decade.

Meadowcraft had net income of $2.2 million in fiscal 1991 (the year ended April 28, 1991) on $50.1 million in sales. In the early 1990s Meadowcraft's factory closeout sale at Wal-Mart's flagship store in Bentonville, Arkansas, reportedly sold more wrought iron furniture in 32 days than the Wal-Mart chain sometimes sold during an entire outdoor furniture selling season. For Wal-Mart "it was a real eye-opener," according to Blount, and impelled the giant chain to increase its orders from Meadowcraft. Meadowcraft added indoor wrought iron furniture to its products in the early 1990s. The company reported net income of $2.8 million in 1993 on net sales of $73.1 million. This increased to $6.4 million on net sales of $96.2 million in 1994 and $10 million on net sales of $120.8 million in 1995.

In 1994 Meadowcraft added a 660,000-square-foot manufacturing and distribution facility to its existing

KEY DATES

1923: Birmingham Ornamental Iron Co. is established.
1985: The company incorporates as Meadowcraft, Inc.; Samuel R. Blount is named chairman.
1997: Meadowcraft goes public.
1999: A group led by Blount takes the company private.
2002: The company declares bankruptcy.
2003: Meadowcraft emerges from Chapter 11.

operation in Wadley, Alabama. The company also completed a 500,000-square-foot distribution center on Birmingham's Carson Road in early 1995 and a 160,000-square-foot addition to that center later in the year. This facility was adjacent to the company's newest expansion, a 350,000-square-foot factory near company offices off Pinson Valley Parkway. A smaller factory/warehouse at the company's Selma, Alabama, plant was also under construction in 1995. The $30 million Pinson Valley plant, located in Valley East Industrial Park, was completed in late 1995. The company also was leasing a 240,000-square-foot plant and corporate headquarters on Meadowcraft Road and a 340,000-square-foot distribution center on Goodrich Drive. Both were about half a mile from the Carson Road/Pinson Valley facilities.

McCanna told a reporter in 1995, "We've probably added more square footage of manufacturing space over the past few years than any other company in Alabama." The expansion came in the face of caution among analysts about the furniture industry, but McCanna maintained that Meadowcraft's improved sales had come across the board. By this time, the company's outdoor furniture brands included Meadowcraft, Plantation Patterns, Arlington House, and Salterini. The new Interior Images line of upscale, iron indoor furniture for distribution in specialty stores also had shown strong sales, and Meadowcraft was about to introduce a lower priced line of indoor furniture for mass market merchants. The firm also was making bed frames, tables, plant stands, kitchen racks, and other home accessories. In fiscal 1997 it added wrought iron garden products as well.

A PERIOD OF EXPANSION

Meadowcraft's net income grew to $7.9 million on net sales of $117.4 million in 1996 and $15.9 million on

net sales of $141.9 million the following year. The company was a partnership 90 percent owned by Blount and other family members and 10 percent owned by McCanna in 1997, prior to making its initial public offering of common stock in November 1997. More than 3.2 million shares—about 17 percent of the company—were sold at $13 a share, raising $39 million, of which $32.7 million was paid to Blount and McCanna, who retained 73 percent and 8 percent of the company, respectively. The remainder of the amount was earmarked for capital investments. Another 500,000 shares were sold shortly after.

Meadowcraft began production in March 1998 at a new, 600,000-square-foot manufacturing/office/distribution center north of San Luis, Arizona, which became the largest manufacturing complex in Yuma County to date. A 175,000-square-foot plant across the border in San Luis, Mexico, purchased in October 1997, was turning out welded patio chairs, umbrella tables, and poolside tables. This unfinished furniture was then shipped to the Arizona plant to undergo a primer coat process to reduce corrosion, followed by an electrostatic dry paint process. A gas furnace then fused the paint to the metal. These new facilities were intended to reduce transportation costs for Meadowcraft's West Coast customers.

Meadowcraft begin production in early 1998 of outdoor tubular steel furniture in an idle Alabama manufacturing facility whose conversion was completed in December 1997. A 520,000-square-foot manufacturing/distribution/office facility was also completed in 1998, adding to the Carson Road complex in Birmingham. In addition, the company was expanding its Selma and Wadley facilities by about 70,000 and 10,000 square feet, respectively. Work on a second Pinson Valley warehouse also was under way in 1998.

Meadowcraft's net sales grew to $162.2 million in 1998 and its net income to $22.3 million. By this time it was commanding 23 percent of the $1.5 billion outdoor furniture market, according to McCanna. Advertising remained an important component of company success; Meadowcraft's products were being promoted by Paul Harvey on his daily news and commentary radio show.

With Meadowcraft's sales increasing so rapidly, production was at a record pace. A *Birmingham News* reporter who visited the new Carson Road plant in early 1998 described it as "a scene from America's industrial heyday." Whereas before 1991, workers had labored artisan-style over a particular chair, table, or bench from start to finish, the new plant was built in such a manner that the job would be broken down into segments, with workers organized into teams. The new factory was expected to turn out two million pieces of wrought iron furniture in 1998.

Meadowcraft was working closely with its mass market clients, building enough inventory between June and January to supply them for the February through May rush period for outdoor furniture. Orders were arriving electronically in selling season by means of a computer line. Computerized inventory tracking and shipping systems enabled line supervisors to ensure that all goods were sent out exactly as ordered. During the peak of the spring selling season as many as 150 trucks and trailers arrived at the loading docks. "They have as sophisticated of an operation as I have seen," said a securities analyst, who observed of Meadowcraft's main customer, "Wal-Mart has put people out of business [for not meeting delivery dates]. They can make your life hell."

A VARIETY OF PRODUCTS

Meadowcraft, in mid-1998, was offering consumers a wide variety of products in three markets: the outdoor mass market under the Plantation Patterns brand name; the outdoor specialty market under the Meadowcraft, Arlington House, and Salterini brand names; and the indoor specialty and mass markets under the Interior Images by Salterini and Home Collection from Plantation Patterns brand names, respectively.

Outdoor products sold through mass merchandisers under the Plantation Patterns name included dining groups composed of action chairs, stack chairs, dining tables, bistro groups, and accent tables; accessories such as chaises, gliders, baker's racks, and tea carts; cushions and umbrellas; and garden products. Outdoor products for the specialty market were similar. The company's outdoor furniture products came in a variety of styles and colors and were being sold at different prices to appeal to a range of consumers. The indoor collections, all in wrought iron, included occasional tables, dining groups, beds, and accent pieces. The garden products included shepherd hooks, trellises, arbors, and plant stands.

Meadowcraft was serving the outdoor mass market, including national chains, discount retailers, mass merchants, and home centers; the outdoor specialty market, including furniture stores, specialty stores, and garden shops; and the indoor market, including specialty furniture stores, mass merchandisers, and department stores. In fiscal 1998, the company sold products to more than 1,500 mass and specialty accounts, including nine of the top ten U.S. discount retailers/mass merchants and home centers. Typically, by early fall of each year, Meadowcraft received estimated

requirements from customers for about 70 percent of the sales that it would produce and ship during the following selling season.

In 1998, Meadowcraft was ranked first in terms of earnings and sales in *Business Week* magazine's June roster of "100 Hot Growth Companies." As the company name was becoming well known nationally, Meadowcraft chair and controlling stockholder, Samuel Blount, made a move to acquire all outstanding shares of Meadowcraft under the umbrella of his MWI Acquisition Co. in 1999. Meadowcraft returned to private ownership later that year after the $197 million deal was finalized. Also that year, Bill McCanna retired as the company's president and was replaced by Timothy Le Roy, formerly the company's vice-president of sales and marketing.

MOVING INTO THE 21ST CENTURY

While Meadowcraft enjoyed success during the late 1990s, the company began to face challenges in the early years of the new millennium. As the U.S. economy began to weaken, the company saw increased competition from less expensive imports made by Chinese manufacturers. To make matters worse, two of its largest customers—Kmart Corp. and Service Merchandise—had declared bankruptcy. The loss of sales from both companies contributed to an overall loss of $46 million in 2001.

Meadowcraft launched a major restructuring effort in response to industry conditions. With material costs on the rise, it looked for ways to trim operations. As part of this strategy, it shuttered its facilities in Yuma, Arizona, as well as its plant in Mexico. The company's debts were mounting, however, and in September 2002 the company filed for Chapter 11 bankruptcy protection. At the time of the filing, Meadowcraft owed more than $100 million to 200 different creditors.

Led by Chairman Blount and new President and CEO Jerry Camp, Meadowcraft worked diligently to emerge from Chapter 11. A U.S. Bankruptcy Court judge approved Meadowcraft's reorganization plan in September 2003, which allowed the company to move ahead with financing from commercial financier CIT Group Inc. By this time, demand for outdoor living space furniture and accessories was growing. In fact, the Hearth, Patio & Barbecue Association claimed that in 2005, the outdoor room market was worth $10 billion.

While many of its competitors went overseas to manufacture, Meadowcraft kept nearly 96 percent of its manufacturing operations in Alabama. The company focused heavily on serving its specialty retailers and its custom orders were made in 15 working days or less. The company's new mantra became "Put Pride in the Box," and it encouraged all of its employees to meet goals related to quality, delivery schedules, and customer service.

At the same time, Meadowcraft launched a green program designed to save energy and reduce its use of natural resources. During 2007, over 70 percent of product materials came from recycled goods. Nearly 90 percent of the steel and 80 percent of the corrugated paper the company consumed came from post-consumer-use goods. Meadowcraft claimed that through its recycling programs, it saved over 60,000 trees, 25,000 cubic yards of landfill, 14 million gallons of water, and 20 million kilowatt hours of energy per year.

Meadowcraft's plans for the future focused on maintaining its leading position as the number one manufacturer of outdoor iron furniture in the United States. However, it would continue to face challenges as the U.S. economy remained weak due to the housing and credit crisis plaguing the nation. As a business that relied on the strength of retailers, Meadowcraft remained subject not only to the whims of consumer demand but to trends in consumer spending as well.

Robert Halasz
Updated, Christina M. Stansell

PRINCIPAL COMPETITORS

Brown Jordan International Inc.; Pier 1 Imports Inc.; Windham Castings Inc.

FURTHER READING

"Business and Industry: Success Story," *South,* August 1, 1957, pp. 14–16.

Diel, Stan, "Meadowcraft Goes Public; Shares on NYSE," *Birmingham News,* November 26, 1997, p. 1C.

Hubbard, Russell, "Wrought-Iron Chain Link," *Birmingham News,* February 1, 1998, pp. 1D, 3D.

Ingram, Cinde W., "Meadowcraft Emerges from Chapter 11 with Continued Industry Support," *Casual Living,* October 2003.

———, "Meadowcraft Putting Pride into Product," *Casual Living,* October 1, 2007.

———, "Meadowcraft Restructures, Files Chapter 11," *Casual Living,* October 2002.

"Meadowcraft Accepts Sweetened Buyout Bid," *New York Times,* May 15, 1999.

Milazzo, Don, "Furniture Maker Expanding," *Birmingham Business Journal,* July 10, 1995, p. 10.

Normington, Mick, "Meadowcraft Expands with 400 New Workers," *Birmingham News,* September 8, 1995, pp. 1B, 5B.

Pressler, Margaret Webb, "Living It Up out Back," *Washington Post,* June 26, 2005.

Scott, L. E., "New Firms for Yuma County," *Arizona Business Gazette,* April 8, 1998, p. 1.

Thomas, Larry, "Wrought-Iron Producer Meadowcraft to Go Public," *Furniture Today,* August 18, 1997, pp. 2, 57.

Metavante Corporation

4900 West Brown Deer Road
Milwaukee, Wisconsin 53233
U.S.A.
Telephone: (414) 357-2290
Fax: (414) 357-9896
Web site: http://www.metavante.com

Wholly Owned Subsidiary of Metavante Technologies Inc.
Incorporated: 1964 as M&I Data Services Inc.
Employees: 5,500
Sales: $350.6 million (2007 est.)
NAICS: 518210 Data Processing, Hosting, and Related
Services

■ ■ ■

Milwaukee, Wisconsin-based Metavante Corporation is a leading provider of banking and payment technologies. A subsidiary of holding company Metavante Technologies Inc., the company's customer base includes approximately 8,000 financial services firms and businesses worldwide. After about 2005, Metavante claimed to have relationships with 97 of the nation's leading 100 banks. The company created the first operational check image exchange network in the United States, and operates the nation's second largest electronic bill payment platform.

Metavante's product and service range covers a wide variety of applications within the financial sector. The company organizes its offerings into 12 main categories of solutions: acquiring, banking, commercial treasury, e-banking, e-payment, healthcare payment, image, issu-

ing, payment network, risk and compliance, sales and service, and wealth management.

ORIGINS AND EARLY YEARS

Metavante Corp.'s roots date back to 1964, when the company was established as M&I Data Services Inc. During its formative years the enterprise was a subsidiary of Marshall & Ilsley Corp., and provided data processing services for M&I Bank correspondent banks. Three years after its formation, M&I Data Services achieved pioneer status when it initiated the nation's very first remote bank processing operation.

Developments continued during the 1970s. Midway through that decade, in 1976, M&I Data Services was involved in the first electronic funds transfer transaction over a Wisconsin automated teller machine (ATM) network. This ultimately led to the establishment of the first shared cash network in the United States.

Growth continued at M&I Data Services during the 1980s. By mid-1987, the company served a base of some 400 customers in 25 states. In July of that year, M&I Data Services revealed plans to acquire the Fort Lauderdale, Florida-based mortgage banking systems developer Software Development Corp. At this time, the company was led by President Dennis J. Kuester. M&I Data Services rounded out the 1980s with several important developments. The introduction of document composition software gave financial institutions the ability to enhance customer communications by providing them with customized statements.

In addition, Lexington, Kentucky-based Central

Bank and Trust Co. chose the company to provide balancing and settlement services, as well as ATM support and transaction authorizations for its regional Central Anyhour Teller system. It was in 1989 that M&I Data Services took steps to simplify its Extended Banking System software—which was used by large banks with deposits of more than $1 billion—so that it could be utilized by midsized banks.

EARLY GROWTH

The first half of the 1990s was especially busy for M&I Data Services. In 1990 the company generated almost 13 percent of its parent company's earnings. Late that year, it acquired the Baltimore, Maryland-based data center of Provident Bankshares Corp. and installed a new computer system, which enabled better support for Provident's system of 38 branches. This was followed by a five-year, $17 million deal with BankAmerica Corp. in 1991, which involved moving banks that BankAmerica had acquired to a common software platform.

By 1992 M&I Data Services was marketing products such as Reliance 2000, a database software package for mainframe computers. Developed in tandem with its Berkeley, California-based marketing partner Software Alliance Corp., the application was used by companies such as Chicago-based Northern Trust Corp. Early in the year, M&I Data Services formed a new Outsourcing Technology division to sell data processing services to larger banks. While the majority of the company's customers had assets in the neighborhood of $120 million to $3.3 billion, the new division was focused on banks with assets as high as $10 billion.

At this time, M&I Data Services was benefiting from consolidation within the banking industry, which led more banks to outsource portions of their operations. Midway through the year, Chase Bank of Arizona tapped M&I Data Services to handle its retail and back-office applications. Around the same time, construction was under way on an 18,450-square-foot, $1 million facility in Madison, Wisconsin, for the company's Micard Services division.

In 1993, M&I Data Services secured a number of new contracts. Early in the year, West Virginia-based One Valley Bancorp chose the company to handle its data processing and management information systems functions. In addition, Pikeville, Kentucky-based Pikeville National Corp. turned to M&I Data Services to consolidate its data processing operations. These customer acquisitions were followed by the addition of Racine, Wisconsin-based Johnson International Inc., which signed a six-year data processing contract with M&I Data Services.

In late 1993, two new personal computer-based software applications were introduced. These included a product named Executive Information System, a monitoring tool for senior bank managers, as well as an application called Salespartner that helped bank branch employees work more efficiently. On the leadership front, Joseph L. Delgadillo was named as president and chief operating officer of M&I Data Services in March 1993. About a year later, Chairman and CEO Dennis J. Kuester was named to parent Marshall & Ilsley's board of directors.

In late 1994 M&I Data Services revealed plans to acquire the Reliance 2000 division, which provided mainframe software to banks, from partner Software Alliance Corporation. In a pioneering move that set the stage for the electronic bill presentment and payment services that would emerge during the early years of the new century, M&I Data Services processed the first web-based banking transaction in 1995.

ACQUISITION ACTIVITY INCREASES

Acquisition activity heated up at M&I Data Services during the latter half of the 1990s, by which time its customer base had grown to include some 800 financial institutions. Midway through 1996, the company revealed plans to acquire the Bedford, New Hampshire-based software developer EastPoint Technology. The EastPoint Technology deal was completed in December, when M&I Data Services also agreed to acquire the item processing unit of Des Moines, Iowa-based Federal Home Bank. As part of the transaction, M&I Data Services secured four processing centers. Located in Des Moines; St. Louis and Kansas City, Missouri; and Minneapolis, Minnesota; the centers processed some 750,000 items per day, bolstering the check-processing capabilities of M&I Data Services. Additionally, the company saw its annual revenues increase approximately $8 million, and some 155 new bank customers joined its client base.

By mid-1997 M&I Data Services had achieved remarkable growth. The company's success had made a

```
┌─────────────────────────────────────────────┐
│                                               │
│              KEY DATES                        │
│                    ■                          │
│                                               │
│   1964:  The company is established as M&I     │
│          Data Services Inc., a subsidiary of   │
│          Marshall & Ils-ley Corp.              │
│   1967:  M&I Data Services initiates the       │
│          nation's first remote bank            │
│          processing operation.                 │
│   1976:  M&I Data Services is involved in the  │
│          first electronic funds transfer       │
│          transaction over a Wisconsin ATM      │
│          network.                              │
│   1995:  The company processes the first       │
│          web-based banking transaction.        │
│   2000:  M&I Data Services changes its name    │
│          to Metavante Corp.                    │
│   2007:  Marshall & Ilsley Corp. spins off     │
│          Metavante; a new holding company      │
│          named Metavante Technologies Inc. is  │
│          created, which begins trading on the  │
│          New York Stock Exchange.              │
│                                               │
└─────────────────────────────────────────────┘
```

major impact on its home state's economy. Since 1992, M&I Data Services had brought some 900 new technology-related jobs to Wisconsin. These employees were needed to help the company develop and market new products, such as a customer service software application called BankerInsight, which could be used by bank call centers and branches to cross-sell services.

As of early 1998, M&I Data Services had a base of 1,000 U.S. customers and 92 international customers. That year, the company teamed up with Marquette University in Wisconsin to offer a new MBA program for students interested in pursuing careers in the technology management field. In addition to classroom training, the program involved a five-month graduate assistantship at M&I Data Services. Heading toward the end of the decade, the financial services industry was experiencing growth in services related to Internet banking. By mid-1999 M&I Data Services had about 200 customers who relied upon its services to support operations in this area.

The industry also experienced growth in the credit card arena during the late 1990s. In September, M&I Data Services agreed to acquire Willowbrook, Illinois-based Cardpro Services Inc., which offered debit and credit card personalization services. Two months later, M&I Data Services began offering the Visa Business Check Card, allowing its bank customers to provide new financial tools to their small business customers. M&I Data Services ended the decade with revenues of

$583 million, 41 percent higher than 1998 levels of $413 million.

FOCUS ON THE INTERNET IN THE 21ST CENTURY

The dawn of the new millennium was accompanied by an explosion in e-commerce. Billing itself as the leading provider of e-banking solutions for the business market, M&I Data Services was well positioned to capitalize on the dot-com craze. Early in 2000, the company partnered with Biztro Inc. to offer e-banking services to the small business sector. Other significant developments followed. In March, M&I Data Services revealed plans to construct a 160,000-square-foot facility in Milwaukee's Park Place office complex, which would house approximately 1,000 employees. At this time, the company's national workforce included about 5,000 people, some 3,500 of whom worked in the Milwaukee area. The need for the new facility was driven by plans to add about 500 new jobs by the end of the year.

It also was in 2000 that M&I Data Services announced the relocation of its call center to a 100,000-square-foot building in Milwaukee's Schlitz Park. The move was prompted largely by growth within the company's e-banking and electronic bill payment segments.

A major change in the history of M&I Data Services unfolded when the company decided in 2000 to change its name to Metavante Corporation. According to the company, the new name incorporated "meta," to suggest bigger or newer, and "avant," to suggest the image of moving forward. The new name was accompanied by plans to spin Metavante off as a separate publicly traded company via an initial public offering (IPO) that hoped to generate up to $200 million. By gaining its independence and having its own stock, the company hoped to grow more easily via acquisitions. However, when the market for technology stocks weakened later that year, plans for the IPO were canceled. Despite this setback, Metavante continued to introduce new offerings, including a computerized stock trading service for trust departments.

Several key developments unfolded in 2001. In April, Metavante shuttered six regional offices and shaved 400 jobs from its payroll, most of which were related to traditional data processing services. Around the same time, the company furthered its growth via the acquisition of San Jose, California-based CyberBills Inc. In August, a new consulting arm named Metavante Wealth Management was formed, and the North American assets of Germany's Brokat Technologies were acquired in a $19.5 million deal. Growth in Metavante's electronic bill payment business occurred when the company snapped up most of the assets of Lawrenceville, New Jersey-based Paytrust Inc. Midway through the year, the Atlanta-based electronic bill payment technology firm Spectrum EBP was acquired.

On the leadership front, President and CEO Joseph Delgadillo was named chairman in 2003, and Frank R. Martire was named president and CEO. The changes occurred at a time when Metavante was growing rapidly via acquisitions and expanding into areas outside of banking.

EXPANDING BEYOND BANKING

In early 2004, Metavante added the Florida-based financial transaction software firm Kirchman Corp. to its list of acquisitions. A major $610 million cash deal unfolded in July of that year, when the company acquired electronic fund transfer and debit card payment processor NYCE Corp. Shortly thereafter, Addison, Texas-based financial technology firm Vectorsgi Inc. was acquired in a deal estimated at about $100 million. Metavante capped off the year with revenues of $971.9 million.

Early in 2005, the company announced the sale of its 401(k) administration business, which focused on small businesses, to Great-West Life & Annuity Insurance Co. and The Retirement Advantage. In a move aimed at bolstering the firm's employee healthcare business, which provided debit cards that workers used to access healthcare spending accounts, Waltham, Massachusetts-based Med-i-Bank was acquired midway through the year. Around the same time, the company paid $19.5 million for Herndon, Virginia-based Treev LLC, an electronic document storage firm. Metavante ended the year with the acquisition of Carrollton, Texas-based AdminiSource Corp., further expanding its healthcare payments business.

Acquisitions continued in 2006. That year, Metavante acquired VICOR in a move that strengthened its commercial treasury solutions offerings. However, despite its growth and strong financial performance, bad news for Metavante's workforce came late in the year, when the company eliminated 180 jobs.

Growth continued in 2007. In January, Metavante snapped up Franklin, Tennessee-based Valutec Card Solutions Inc., an in-store gift and loyalty card firm that catered to small and midsized businesses. In April, Marshall & Ilsley Corp. once again revealed plans to spin off Metavante. On October 25, shareholders gave their approval of the transaction, which was valued at $4.25 billion and involved the private equity firm Warburg Pincus LLC securing a 25 percent interest in the company.

A new holding company named Metavante Technologies Inc. was created as part of the deal, and it began trading on the New York Stock Exchange under the symbol MV on November 2, 2007.

After going public, Metavante continued on a growth path. This was evident in two deals that unfolded in January 2008. Metavante Technologies Ltd. was formed after the company acquired the London-based prepaid debit card services firm Nomad Payments Ltd. A few days later, San Diego, California-based Ben-Soft Inc. was acquired, furthering growth within Metavante's healthcare payments business.

On October 31, 2008, Metavante announced a significant leadership change when CEO Frank Martire was named chairman, succeeding Dennis Kuester, who remained a director. In addition, Chief Operating Officer Michael Hayford assumed the additional role of president. Moving forward, the company seemed well positioned for continued growth during the second decade of the 21st century.

Paul R. Greenland

PRINCIPAL DIVISIONS

Banking and Trust Solutions; Business Transformation Services; Commercial Treasury Solutions; Consulting and Professional Services; EFT Solutions; ePayment Solutions; Healthcare Payment Solutions; Image Solutions; Payment Network Solutions; Risk and Compliance Solutions.

PRINCIPAL COMPETITORS

BA Merchant Services LLC; First Data Corporation; Fiserv Inc.

FURTHER READING

Gores, Paul, "Failed Spinoff a Boon to M&I; Metavante Now Adds Some Real Change to Bottom Line," *Milwaukee Journal Sentinel,* July 15, 2001.

———, "M&I Bank Spinoff OK'd; Metavante Stock Will Begin Trading," *Milwaukee Journal Sentinel,* October 26, 2007.

———, "M&I Finds Market Too Shaky for IPO; Bank Holding Company Had Cut Metavante Price Twice," *Milwaukee Journal Sentinel,* November 2, 2000.

———, "Metavante to Acquire Texas Company; In Sixth Deal Announced in '05, Role in Health Care Payments Will Broaden," *Milwaukee Journal Sentinel,* November 23, 2005.

Schulhofer-Wohl, Sam, "Simply Choosing a Name Was Big Step for New Company," *Milwaukee Journal Sentinel,* July 14, 2000.

Strachman, Daniel, "M&I Data Takes Step to Buying Division from Software Alliance," *American Banker,* December 22, 1994.

Tyson, David O., "Marshall & Ilsley Firms Software Plans; Subsidiary Will Sell Mortgage Banking Systems Directly," *American Banker,* July 29, 1987.

Minera Escondida Ltda.

———————■———————

Avenida Americo Vespucci Sur 100
Santiago,
Chile
Telephone: (56 02) 330-5000
Fax: (56 02) 207-6520
Web site: http://www.escondida.cl

Private Company
Employees: 2,588
Sales: $10.12 billion (2007 est.)
NAICS: 212234 Copper Ore and Nickel Ore Mining;
    486990 All Other Pipeline Transportation

■ ■ ■

Minera Escondida Ltda. operates the largest and richest copper mine in the world, located in the Atacama Desert of northern Chile, about 100 miles southeast of Antofagasta. The Escondida mine yields more copper each year than any other. This mine also yields smaller but commercially viable amounts of gold and silver. It is owned by a consortium of three foreign companies that spent nearly $1 billion to bring the mine into production.

LAYING THE GROUNDWORK: 1981–90

La Escondida ("Hidden Mine") was unknown until a random drilling in 1981 found ore with an average copper content twice that of the largest existing mine in Chile—the nation that produces more copper than any other—and several times that of U.S. and Canadian copper mines. Reserves were estimated at 1.8 billion metric tons, which meant that the mine was expected to be worked well into the 21st century.

The discovery was made by a joint venture between Getty Oil Company and Utah International, Inc. By 1985 Getty had been taken over by Texaco Inc., and Utah International, formerly a subsidiary of General Electric Co., was owned by Broken Hill Proprietary Ltd. (BHP), Australia's largest corporation. In that year Utah International purchased Texaco's stake and began looking for partners. A consortium was formed, with BHP assuming 60 percent of Minera Escondida, London-based Rio Tinto-Zinc Corporation (RTZ) taking 30 percent, and JECO Corporation, a Japanese consortium of smelters dominated by Mitsubishi Corporation, holding the remaining 10 percent of the shares.

The project advanced slowly because of projected start up costs in the neighborhood of $1 billion. There were doubts that the price of copper would support a significant increase in output. However, the main problem may have been political: widespread international condemnation of the repressive military regime of General Augusto Pinochet and fears that a new government might reverse Pinochet's investment-friendly economic policies and nationalize the mine. Chile's chief copper producer, Corporación Nacional del Cobre de Chile (Codelco), was nationalized in the 1970s. Nevertheless, to many analysts, the attractions of Escondida—the mine's high average copper content and its projected low cost of production—outweighed the risks.

To raise some of the start up funds, the consortium

signed contracts to furnish 77 percent of Escondida's output over the first 12 years to smelters in Japan, Germany, and Finland. Government lending agencies in those countries lent the consortium about 60 percent of the money needed to put the mine into production. In all, it was the biggest single foreign investment in the history of Chile to date. The World Bank's International Finance Corporation purchased 2.5 percent of Minera Escondida's shares from BHP. Minera Escondida was granted a mining concession, valid indefinitely, from the Chilean government, and subject only to payment of annual fees.

EXCAVATION BEGINS: 1988

Onsite work began in 1988. Electric shovels created a hole 650 feet deep and nearly a mile wide, making Escondida an open pit copper mine second in size only to Chuqicamata, owned by Chile's state-run Codelco. A plant was completed in 1990 to crush copper sulfide ore and separate, by means of a flotation extraction process, 2,000 metric tons of concentrates a day—averaging 35 percent copper—from the unwanted material. Minera Escondida built transmission lines, connected to Chile's northern power grid, to provide power for its mine facilities. Electricity was purchased under contracts with local generating companies.

The concentrates were then mixed with water extracted from wells beneath the salt flats of the desert and pumped up to the mine, located 3,100 meters (about 10,000 feet) above sea level. This slurry was sent by a 165-kilometer (100 mile) pipeline to Minera Escondida's port facilities at Coloso, just south of Antofagasta. It then underwent a pressurized filtration process that reduced the humidity of the concentrates to 9 percent. The highly saline wastewater, once separated from the concentrates, was directed almost a mile out to sea, where the impact on marine life was said by the company to be minimal.

These facilities were completed by the end of 1990, six months ahead of schedule and $170 million below

the $1 billion earmarked for the project. Escondida's average copper content of 2.1 percent was extremely favorable compared to older, heavily exploited mines elsewhere. Its low cost of production owed much to a non-unionized workforce far leaner than that employed by state-owned Codelco.

During 1991, the first full year of operation for the Escondida mine, about 600,000 metric tons of copper concentrates were exported, where they were refined into the equivalent of about 250,000 metric tons of pure copper. The exported material not previously contracted for was committed to smelters in Spain, South Korea, and the Philippines.

INCREASING PRODUCTION

By 1993 Minera Escondida's owners were ready to spend an additional $284 million to increase production of copper from 390,000 tons in 1993 to 480,000 tons in 1995. Much of the added output was to come from a $164 million plant being constructed at Coloso, using hydrometallurgical technology patented by the company and developed in BHP's laboratories in California to produce copper cathodes—refined copper produced from electrolysis. This process employed ammonia to leach copper from the ore. The plant, however, funded from Minera Escondida's own cash flow, was closed in 1996 because production levels did not meet expectations and the costs incurred were too high. Instead, a facility with the capacity to produce 126,000 tons of copper cathodes a year from oxide ores by conventional leaching methods, solvent extraction, and electrowinning went into service in December 1998, at a cost of $451 million.

The Los Colorados flotation process concentration plant was also being expanded, and in 1997 Escondida became the most productive copper mine in the world to date. The amount of finished copper from its concentrates and from leaching reached a peak of about a million metric tons in 1999, but then dropped because of low prices for copper on the world market. This made it uneconomic for Escondida to operate at full capacity, and production of finished copper from the mine fell to less than 800,000 tons in 2002.

Chileans who had opposed turning over a national treasure for foreigners to exploit cited a study that claimed the government had lost between $125 million and $212 million a year between 1998 and 2002 because Minera Escondida had been sending almost all of its concentrates abroad rather than, like Codelco, refining a significant amount within Chile. The argument noted that Escondida's concentrates were mainly sold to a consortium of refiners represented among the

KEY DATES

1981: Random drilling yields discovery of what proves to be the world's largest copper mine to date, located in the Chilean desert.

1988: Excavation begins on open pit mine 650 feet deep and almost a mile across.

1990: Plant completed to separate concentrates from excavated ore.

1993: Expansion project begins to raise the plant's copper output using hydrometallurgical technology.

1997: Escondida becomes the most productive copper mine in the world to date.

1998: Facility completed to produce copper from conventional leaching methods.

1999: Mine reaches peak production of about one million metric tons of copper a year.

2002: Second concentrator plant, Laguna Seco, and a second pipeline open.

2004: The company's profits reach $1.73 billion.

2005: Production begins at second open pit mine, Escondida Norte.

2006: Minera Escondida opens a bioleaching facility and a water-desalinization plant; miners win significant gains after a 25-day strike.

2007: Production and profits reach record levels.

company's owners and that Escondida earned less money than Codelco per ton of copper produced. A rebuttal study pointed out that Escondida was also donating 1 percent of its pretax earnings for social and environmental projects.

MORE COPPER, BIGGER PROFITS IN THE 21ST CENTURY

In spite of the drop in production, in 2002 Minera Escondida launched an expansion project that consisted of a new concentrator plant, Laguna Seco, with the capacity to treat 110,000 metric tons—almost as much as Los Colorados—of copper ore per day; a second slurry pipeline to transport the concentrate to Coloso; and a tailings site where the residue—about three-quarters of the total—discarded by the concentrator plants would be deposited. The following year the company approved the creation of a second open pit mine, Escondida Norte, about three miles north of the original one, at a cost of $431 million. Ore first left this mine for processing in late 2005. The two mines were then moving a

million tons of material a day for further processing. In all, Minera Escondida spent $2.125 billion for four phases of expansion of the original project.

Minera Escondida's production of copper rose in 2003, but its profits remained below the 2000 peak of $459 million until 2003 because of lower production and the lower price being paid for the metal. However, a rise in the price of copper and an increase in production to nearly 1.2 million metric tons—22 percent of Chile's output—more than tripled profits to $1.73 billion in 2004. BHP, which had become BHP Billiton in 2001 because of a merger, was then the largest diversified natural resources company in the world, yet its share in the Escondida mine alone accounted for 15 percent of its profits in 2004. RTZ (later known as Rio Tinto plc) saw its profits rise 87 percent for the year.

Beginning in 2006, Minera Escondida began producing more copper cathodes by an alternative process involving the bioleaching of low grade copper sulfide ore. The process, like the one for the earlier leaching plant, involved heap leaching, solvent extraction, and electrowinning. However, the leaching of deposits in heaps occurred in this case by oxidization in the presence of bacteria in the open air at temperatures favorable for bacterial activity. The final cost of this facility was $988 million. By either conventional or bioleaching methods, the cathodes, weighing about 70 kilograms (about 155 pounds) each, consisted of almost pure copper and were being sold under the ESOX brand. Most of them were sold under annual contracts to rod producers, with the rest available on the spot market, where goods were made available for immediate delivery.

This leaching process also involved the establishment of a water-desalinization plant in Coloso, the largest such facility in Chile, in 2006 at a cost of about $160 million. This plant produced from seawater 525 liters (about 140 gallons) of industrial water per second for leaching the copper sulfides. Because the water was lifted from sea level to Escondida's altitude, the four pumping stations required costly power consumption that might make the project economically unsound if world copper prices were to fall. However, the price of copper reached record highs of more than $4 a pound during 2006. Copper cathode was being transported by a privately owned rail line to the government-operated port of Antofagasta or the privately owned port of Mejillones. Escondida itself was accessible by public road.

WORKERS STRIKE: 2006

Minera Escondida suffered a 25-day strike in 2006. Some 2,000 workers demanded that the company, greatly enriched by the high world price of copper, raise its wages and rejected three offers before accepting the fourth. The new contract, which according to officials made the miners the highest paid in South America, included a 5 percent increase in wages, a bonus of CLP 9 million ($16,600), and new education, healthcare, and housing benefits. Company officials estimated that Escondida had lost $200 million in profits because of the strike, which followed a shorter one in 2003. Minera Escondida reported that by the end of 2006 it had invested a total of $5.64 billion in Chile and that the company and its owners had contributed another $5.68 billion to the Chilean treasury in taxes and royalties.

Copper production from Escondida's mines reached a record 1.48 million metric tons in 2007. This was partly due to the start up of the bioleaching plant the previous year and improved daily yield in the concentrating plants. Concentrate accounted for 84 percent of production and cathodes for the remaining 16 percent. Minera Escondida's total sales reached $10.12 billion and profits $6.47 billion. The company announced that, during the first quarter of 2008, it earned $1.92 billion. With this result it exceeded Codelco's earnings for the first time. The state company's comparable net profit was $1.6 billion during this period.

Minera Escondida's record profits were based on copper selling, at times, for $4 a pound or more in the futures market during 2006–08, compared to only $1 a pound in 2003. The price rise up of the metal was attributed to a construction boom in Asia. However, by their nature, the prices of metals and other commodities in the futures market were speculative. Writing in *Forbes* in early 2008, A. Gary Shilling urged investors to sell commodities, especially copper. "The recession will col-lapse demand for copper," he maintained. "This substance has no OPEC propping it up. Go short. The long and deep recession I've been forecasting has commenced." Thus the financial health of Minera Escondida in the foreseeable future was likely to depend on the condition of the world economy.

Robert Halasz

PRINCIPAL COMPETITORS

Corporación Nacional del Cobre de Chile; Grupo Mexico, S.A.B. de C.V.; Phelps Dodge Corporation.

FURTHER READING

Crawford, Leslie, "All Systems Go for Chilean Copper Giant," *Financial Times,* December 12, 1990, p. 30.

———, "Chilean Copper Giant Inaugurated Today," *Financial Times,* March 14, 1991, p. 30.

Fazio Rigazzi, Hugo, *Mapa de la Extrema Riqueza al Año 2005,* Santiago: LON Ediciones, 2005, pp. 301–05.

Gooding, Kenneth, "Escondida Has Backing for $284m Expansion," *Financial Times,* May 28, 1993, p. 30.

Haflich, Frank, "Utah Int'l Seeks Escondida Funding," *American Metal Market,* July 29, 1986, pp. 1, 5.

Keegan, Rebecca Winters, "Copper and Robbery," *Time,* June 23, 2008, p. 115.

"Minera Escondida Levanta Mayor Planta Desalinizadora del Pais," *El Mercurio de Chile,* May 23, 2006.

Shilling, A. Gary, "Sell Commodities," *Forbes,* March 10, 2008, p. 110.

"Texaco Will Sell Copper Unit Stake," *New York Times,* August 21, 1985, p. D4.

"A Worrying Precedent," *Economist,* September 9, 2006, p. 40.

NBP

Narodowy Bank Polski

Narodowy Bank Polski

———————■———————

ul Swietokrzyska 11/21
Warsaw, 00-919
Poland
Telephone: (48 022) 653 1000
Fax: (48 022) 620 8518
Web site: http://www.nbp.pl

State-Owned Company
Incorporated: 1945
Employees: 4,481
Sales: $67.93 billion (2007)
NAICS: 521110 Monetary Authorities—Central Banks;
    522320 Financial Transactions Processing, Reserve,
    and Clearing House Activities

■ ■ ■

Narodowy Bank Polski (the National Bank of Poland, or NBP) is the central bank of Poland. The NBP oversees the country's monetary policies in order to maintain the stability of the zloty, the Polish currency, the stability and security of its financial system, and ultimately the stability of the country's economy as a whole. NBP has established a number of fiscal objectives, one of which is the goal of stabilizing the country's inflation rate at 2.5 percent.

NBP is also Poland's currency issuer, operates the Polish mint, and oversees the country's payment systems and official reserves. NBP also provides educational and informational services. Since Poland's admission into the European Union, NBP has also been charged with preparing the country for entry into the euro zone as well. The conversion to the euro was expected to take place before 2010. Sławomir Skrzypek has been president of the NBP since 2007.

CENTRAL BANK FOR A NEW NATION IN THE NINETEENTH CENTURY

Banks had been in operation in Poland since as early as the 15th century. Over the next centuries the region also developed its first currency, which was given the name of zloty. Yet the many political upheavals of the region and shifting geographic boundaries of the state left the country unable to develop a strong central bank to oversee its economic and financial policies.

The first attempt to establish a central bank came in the late 1820s, in the aftermath of the Napoleonic Wars. The creation of the short-lived autonomous Congress Kingdom of Poland and the relative political stability of the period encouraged the Ksawery Drucki Lubecki to lobby for the founding of a central bank. Lubecki was a member of a prominent princely family, descended from the house of Rurik, former rulers of Russia. Born in 1779, Lubecki had been a member of the provisional government established under Russian rule in the Duchy of Warsaw. During this time, from 1817 to 1821, Lubecki successfully negotiated treaties settling Poland's foreign debt. Nonetheless, Poland's financial system remained extremely fragile.

Following the creation of the Congress Kingdom in 1921, Lubecki became the Minister of the Treasury. Within three years Lubecki successfully balanced the kingdom's budget, collecting overdue taxes and pushing

COMPANY PERSPECTIVES

The National Bank of Poland is responsible for the stability of the national currency. Fulfilling this constitutional obligation, the NBP develops and implements the monetary policy strategy and the annual monetary policy guidelines. Through the management of the official reserves the NBP ensures the requisite level of the State's financial security.

through reforms to end abuses of the system. Lubecki then turned the excess budget toward building up the kingdom's industries, notably mining, steel production, and textiles. These efforts, which were meant to prove that the Congress Kingdom would not become a financial burden to Russia, were ultimately intended to preserve the kingdom's autonomy under czarist rule.

By the mid-1820s Lubecki had established the first of two state-operated banks, the Land Credit Society. This was followed in 1928 with the Bank Polski, or the Bank of Poland, backed by a royal decree from Czar Nicolai I. Bank Polski took control of the Polish mint, and began printing its first notes, the zloty, in 1830.

The November Uprising of that year ended the Bank Polski experiment. Following Poland's defeat the Kingdom of Poland was abolished and absorbed directly into the Russian empire. While Bank Polski continued to operate for some time, it lost its status as a central bank, and was placed under the authority of Russia's Treasury Ministry. Bank Polski's minting rights were taken away in 1832. Zlotys remained in circulation for some time, but were eventually captioned in Russian, while the ruble and kopeck, introduced into Poland in 1842, became the official currency. A decade after the creation of the Russian State Bank in 1860, Bank Polski lost its right to issue currency. By 1885 Bank Polski had been transformed into no more than a branch of the Russian State Bank, which then absorbed the Polish bank's assets by the middle of the next decade.

INDEPENDENT CENTRAL BANK IN 1924

The aftermath of World War I set the stage for a new attempt at creating a central bank in Poland, which became an independent nation in 1918. The new Polish government, led by Władysław Grabski, announced its determination to establish a new central bank, again named Bank Polski. The creation of Bank Polski was delayed for several years, however, as the Polish parliament proved unable to agree on a resolution. In the meantime, the country's currency and financial policy remained under the auspices of the Polish National Loan Office. That body had originally been set up in 1916, under Poland's occupation by Germany and Austria during World War I.

Nonetheless, the groundwork for the creation of the new Bank Polski had been laid, with legislation passed in 1919 calling for the issuing of new currency, once again named the zloty. In 1924 the Polish government finally reached an agreement on the form of the country's central bank. This led to the establishment of Bank Polski S.A., as a joint-stock company with state support and charged with carrying out the government's fiscal policy. While Bank Polski operated independently of the Polish government, the country's president was responsible for appointing the bank's chairman.

Bank Polski then began issuing currency based on the gold standard, replacing the heavily devalued Polish mark introduced by the National Load Office during the war. The new currency immediately faced a crisis, as a poor harvest and the collapse of the country's industrial sector severely weakened the zloty. With meager reserves of gold and foreign currency, Bank Polski was unable to defend the zloty against further deflation. Grabski was forced to resign, and the new government sparked a new inflationary period by issuing new currency and coins.

The zloty found stability only in 1927, following an industrial upswing and the support of international loans. Bank Polski continued to govern the country's fiscal policy through a period of relative stability for the next decade. The German invasion of Poland in 1939, and the country's subsequent division between Germany and the Soviet Union, represented a new crisis for the country's central bank. Bank Polski administrators fled the country, removing its gold reserves as well. Operations were established in London for the duration of the war, along with the Polish government in exile.

COMMUNIST-ERA MONOPOLY IN 1945

Following Poland's liberation by the Soviets, the country established a new government, the Polski Komitet Wyzwolenia Naraodowego (PKWN). Backed by the Red Army, the PKWN replaced the government-in-exile. In 1945 the PKWN established its own central bank, Narodowy Bank Polski, or the National Bank of Poland (NBP). The NBP was initially meant to be linked with Bank Polski. However, Moscow's assertion of control over Poland quickly doomed the former state bank.

KEY DATES

∎

1828: Ksawery Drucki Lubecki leads the creation of Bank Polski, the first central bank in Poland.

1885: Bank Polski is dissolved into the Russian State Bank.

1924: Following Poland's independence, the country establishes a new central bank, Bank Polski.

1945: Narodowy Bank Polski (the National Bank of Poland, or NBP) is created by the new Soviet-backed Polish government.

1987: As part of the reform of the Polish banking sector, NBP spins off its retail service operations; the following year, the NBP branch network is broken up into nine independent universal banks.

1993: NBP carries out a "shock therapy" reform of the Polish banking sector, resulting in the country's strong economic growth by the end of the decade.

2007: NBP appoints Sławomir Skrzypek as its new president.

Poland's gold reserves were returned to Poland by 1946. Soon afterward Bank Polski was dismantled and absorbed into the NBP. By then, the NBP had been granted the monopoly on minting and currency issuing, and began printing a new zloty for the postwar era.

Within the next decade NBP evolved into a Polish banking monopoly charged with carrying out the objectives of the Communist government's planned economy. In particular the NBP became the central lending body for the country's industrial reconstruction. At the same time NBP served as the country's savings bank monopoly, while overseeing the country's network of small cooperative banks as well. NBP established a national network of branch offices providing retail and commercial services. Each branch was also given oversight for the state enterprises operating in its region.

The NBP's role was largely limited to the domestic sector. Foreign trade transactions were handled by Bank Handlowy w Warszawie S.A., the country's oldest surviving bank, which had been established in 1870. Foreign currency operations were placed under the control of Bank Polska Kasa Opieki S.A., a bank originally created in 1929, then reactivated in 1954. A third bank, Bank Gospodarki Zywnosciowej, was created in 1975 to take over the coordination of the country's cooperative banks, which served primarily the rural agricultural and food sectors, as well as artisans and craftspeople in the cities.

NBP's role as an instrument of the government often meant that its fiscal policies were subordinated to political objectives. As a result, by the early 1980s the zloty held little value, even within Poland, and the U.S. dollar had become the country's de facto currency.

REFORM THE BANKING SECTOR IN 1989

Movement toward the reform of Poland's banking sector began even before the collapse of the Communist government. Faced with mounting financial and political pressures—including the rise of the Solidarity movement led by Lech Wałęsa—the Polish government launched an initial reform effort in the early 1980s. In 1982 the government passed new banking legislation permitting the creation of new banks in the country. Only two banks received licenses. Bank Rozwoju Eksportu started up operations in 1987, followed by Lódzki Bank Rozwoju S.A. in 1989.

By 1987 the NBP itself had been targeted for reform. The government split off the bank's retail service operations, creating a new state-owned bank, Powszechna Kasa Oczczednosci. However, further reform of the banking sector was to wait until the collapse of the Communist government in 1989. That year the new government passed the Banking Act of 1989, establishing a Western-style, two-tiered banking system. A more thorough restructuring of the NBP, designed to transform it into a pure central bank, was then put into place. NBP's 400 branch offices were reconfigured into nine universal state banks (a tenth would come into operation in 1993). These banks, which remained state-owned, took over the NBP's deposit-lending business.

The new legislation also permitted the creation of new mixed-capital banks. NBP was placed in charge of granting licenses, applying the rather liberal criteria established by the legislation. As a result, Poland witnessed an explosion of new banks. Between 1989 and 1991, more than 70 mixed capital banks had entered the Polish market. Many of the new banks were founded under the auspices of various government ministries. The legislation also permitted foreign ownership of domestic banks, and as a result a number of new banks were majority controlled by foreign banks.

REFORMING THE REFORM IN THE NINETIES

The liberalization of Poland's banking sector quickly foundered in the wake of scandals and a chaotic economic climate as the country transitioned to a free-market system. By 1991 the NBP's president and deputy president had both been forced to resign. In their place Lech Wałęńsa appointed a little-known professor of banking law, Hanna Gronkiewicz-Waltz, then 37 years old. Her appointment was initially rejected by the Polish parliament, which sought someone with more experience for the position. In the end, however, Gronkiewicz-Waltz received the appointment. She was charged with carrying out the "shock therapy" reform program stipulated by Treasury Minister, and future NBP president, Leszek Balcerowicz.

Gronkiewicz-Waltz quickly proved herself up to the task as she led the banking sector through a major restructuring. She instituted a new era of highly restrictive financial policy. A large number of banks, including many of the smaller cooperative banks that had gone bankrupt, were allowed to collapse. Other banks were forced to undergo a consolidation. During this period, the NBP also raised interest rates, despite the opposition of the Polish government. Indeed, the government rejected NBP's first three annual reports; the bank finally released its first annual report only in 1997. That year marked the introduction of new banking legislation, launching the privatization of the country's state-owned banks, a process overseen by NBP.

NBP's economic reform efforts bore fruit however. By the end of the 1990s, the Polish economy was flourishing, with annual growth rates of 6 percent by the turn of the century. The country had also become a major destination for foreign capital eager to invest in the Eastern European market. NBP's fiscal policies soon inspired its counterparts in other banks in the region, helping to prepare the next wave of expansion of the European Union (EU).

STEERING TOWARD ENTERING THE EU

Leszek Balcerowicz took charge of NBP in the early 2000s, and steered the country on a course to enter the euro zone as early as 2007. By 2004 Poland appeared on its way to meeting EU admission standards, with growth sustained at 6 percent per year and inflation rates down to 2.5 percent, despite a lingering budget deficit that had reached 7.5 percent of the country's gross domestic product.

In 2006, however, Balcerowicz found himself in conflict with the newly elected conservative government under the Law and Justice Party led by twin brothers Lech and Jarosław Kaczyński. That year the government created a new and highly controversial Financial Supervisory Commission, modeled after its counterpart in the United Kingdom and other European countries, which effectively transferred control over bank regulation in the country to the prime minister's office. In the end the conflict resulted in Balcerowicz's ouster in 2007, when he was replaced as NBP president by Sławomir Skrzypek.

In the meantime the country had been unable to reach its earlier goal of entry into the euro zone by 2007. With the country's inflation rate climbing—to 4.4 percent in the first half of 2008—amid the global economic turmoil, Poland's move toward the euro faced further delays. Nonetheless, the NBP had established itself as the centerpiece of the flourishing Polish economy in the early 21st century.

M. L. Cohen

PRINCIPAL COMPETITORS

Oesterreichische Nationalbank; Ceska narodni banka; National Bank of Ukraine; Banca Nationala a Romaniei; Magyar Nemzeti Bank; Narodna banka Srbije; Bulgarian National Bank; Hrvatska narodna banka.

FURTHER READING

Cienski, Jan, "Freedom of Polish Bank at Risk, Says Its Chief," *Financial Times,* September 7, 2008, p. 8.

————, "Warsaw Central Bank's Role to Be Reduced," *Financial Times,* July 22, 2006, p. 6.

"Hanna Gronkiewicz-Waltz," *Business Week,* June 12, 2000, p. 96.

"Leszek Balcerowicz, President, National Bank of Poland," *Business Week,* June 7, 2004.

"NBP Borrows Swiss Franc from Banks," *Europe Intelligence Wire,* November 18, 2008.

Oliver, Lee, and Chloe Hayward, "Market Unfazed by 'Surprise' Polish Rate Increase," *Euromoney,* July 2007.

"Poland's Central Bank Raises Interest Rates," *Global Banking News,* June 26, 2008.

"Polish Banking Scandal Leads to Tighter Rules," *Europe 2000,* October 1991, p. R213.

Reed, John, "Polish Banks Braced for Rush to Conversion," *Financial Times,* January 2, 2002, p. 2.

Stojaspal, Jan, "Hanna Gronkiewicz-Waltz: Bank President, 46," *Time International,* September 13, 1999, p. 34.

99¢ Only Stores

4000 Union Pacific Avenue
City of Commerce, California 90023
U.S.A.
Telephone: (323) 980-8145
Fax: (323) 980-8160
Web site: http://www.99only.com

Public Company
Incorporated: 1982
Employees: 10,000
Sales: $1.19 billion (2008)
Stock Exchanges: New York
Ticker Symbol: NDN
NAICS: 452990 All Other General Merchandise Stores

■ ■ ■

99¢ Only Stores operates more than 277 locations, with 193 in California, 48 in Texas, 24 in Arizona, and 12 in Nevada. Stores are designed to be full-service "destination" locations with merchandise that encompasses a wide array of name-brand closeout and regularly available consumable products, including food and beverages, such as produce, deli, and other basic grocery items, health and beauty care, and household supplies. 99¢ Only also operates a wholesale business named Bargain Wholesale, which distributes discounted merchandise to retailers, other distributors, and exporters. The chain is the smallest of the top-four dollar chains in the United States in revenue and store count, but the highest in sales per sellable square foot.

STORE ORIGINS

The founder of 99¢ Only, David Gold, most likely drew his inspiration for the deep-discount chain he created from an epiphany decades before he opened his first store. While Gold was working at a liquor store he co-owned with his brother-in-law, he reportedly noticed that bottles of wine priced at $0.99 sold better than bottles priced just a few pennies more. The allure, he knew, was more psychological than financial, a ploy on the minds of consumers that was universally effective. He vowed to open his own store one day that offered a full gamut of merchandise all priced under one dollar, but for years his entrepreneurial plan remained on the drawing board.

Before putting his plan into action, Gold, the son of Russian immigrants, established himself in a business that required many of the same talents he would need to make his dream a reality. Gold began as a wholesaler, starting his own operation in 1976 that purchased and sold name-brand, closeout merchandise. It was Gold's responsibility to locate the best bargains and then find retailers willing to purchase the merchandise, a task that he executed with skill. One of Gold's competitors would later note as much, remarking that Gold was "the best merchant I've ever seen."

Other observers directed more praise Gold's way, with one of his retail customers describing a particular talent that was indispensable in the discount business arena. "He has a retentive, calculator mind," the candy retailer explained, referring to Gold. "He will remember the price of something you showed him a year or two earlier, even if he didn't buy it." His native inclinations served him well in the wholesale business, but always in the back of Gold's mind was the desire to open his own "dollar store." It took until Gold was in his 50s to finally put his liquor-store observations to the test, but when he did take that first step, his seasoned experience as a bargain hunter garnered instant success.

"I talked about opening a store that would sell only name brands and everything for a dollar for 20 years before I did it," Gold said, explaining his latent foray into the retail world. "Finally my wife said, 'Why don't you just do it.'" Gold made his move in August 1982, when he opened his first 99¢ Only store in the Los Angeles area. Opening day was an unqualified success, with long lines of eager customers waiting to see what they could purchase for $0.99. News cameras appeared as well, arriving to record the event and feed the public's curiosity, which added to the spectacle of the grand opening.

RETHINKING THE DOLLAR STORE CONCEPT

The excitement generated by the first store opening set a precedent, demonstrating to Gold the importance of starting out with strong publicity. As other 99¢ Only stores opened in the wake of the first store's success, grand opening promotions served as an effective tactic to draw attention to a new location. One favorite grand opening gimmick used by Gold repeatedly was offering a 19-inch television for $0.99 to the first nine patrons at a new location. When news of the offer spread, it was not uncommon for people to stand outside the doors of a new 99¢ Only for as long as two days to secure one of the coveted first nine places in line.

The fascination surrounding Gold's dollar store concept, particularly as introduced into the sophisticated Los Angeles area, was difficult for some industry observ-

ers to comprehend. In fact, the concept had existed for decades before Gold opened his first 99¢ Only store. However, there were several unique characteristics of Gold's retail business that partly explained the attention it attracted. Perhaps most important, Gold filled his stores with name-brand merchandise, such as housewares and household staple items, rather than an eclectic assortment of odds and ends from obscure, or anonymous, manufacturers.

Moreover, the stores themselves were different from the typical deep-discount store. They were large—and would increase substantially in size as the concept flowered into a full-fledged chain—and brightly lit, with attractive interiors that belied the fact that every item was available for 99¢.

The manner in which the merchandise was displayed was different as well. Instead of lumping merchandise in bins, the store's inventory was displayed on color-coordinated shelving, with each color denoting a particular product category. The store's product mix was different too; instead of the trinkets that filled most dollar stores, 99¢ Only stores carried a substantial percentage (40 percent of product mix) of consumable items, such as packaged foods and beverages.

Further, company executives and store managers established a policy of carrying at least one item from each product category, striving to maintain a consistency of product availability. "They (99¢ Only customers) can't walk in and think 'maybe they've got toothpaste and maybe they don't,'" explained the company's chief financial officer, "because if that's the case then they're going to shop you like a treasure hunt."

POSITIONED AS A SHOPPING DESTINATION FOR BASIC GOODS

Thus, 99¢ Only Stores presented themselves as the equivalent of supermarkets, minus fresh produce, meats, and dairy goods, but with one enormous advantage: everything inside the store was priced 20 to 80 percent lower than similar items at conventional stores. The trick to filling stores with name-brand, staple items at dramatically lower prices was locating the wholesale bargains in the first place (a duty that fell to Gold as the company's chief buyer) and then possessing the purchasing power to acquire merchandise in large volumes, thereby reducing the price of the wholesale merchandise.

Gold was a proven bargain-hunter, and his purchasing power was augmented by keeping his wholesale business, Bargain Wholesale, running, which gave him the purchasing might to buy in great quantities. As the chain of retail stores grew larger, it developed its own ability to acquire in bulk, but with the wholesale opera-

KEY DATES

■

1976: David Gold starts his own wholesale operation, purchasing and selling name-brand, closeout merchandise.

1982: Gold opens his first 99¢ Only store in the Los Angeles area.

1996: The company holds its initial public offering and moves into a new 840,000-square-foot warehouse in the City of Commerce, near downtown Los Angeles.

1997: 99¢ Only acquires 48 percent of Minnesota-based Universal International, Inc.

1998: 99¢ Only acquires Universal International.

2000: Eric Schiffer, the founder's son-in-law, becomes president of the company.

2004: Schiffer succeeds Gold as CEO of the company; Jeffrey Gold becomes president.

tion always in support, the two entities formed a wonderful synergy that greatly enhanced Gold's ability to purchase in volume.

With a sound business strategy underpinning the success of the first 99¢ Only store, Gold moved methodically forward with his expansion plans. He gradually opened additional units, locating each within a 50-mile radius of downtown Los Angeles and selecting locations whose demographics conformed to his criteria. "We like to be where families are largest, because they buy the most consumables," Gold noted, explaining part of the company's site-selection process.

As expansion moved forward, Gold was careful not to accumulate any debt, and never did—even when the chain numbered more than two dozen units. As the chain grew, it developed a particular clientele, attracting middle-class patrons who frequented a 99¢ Only store more than once a week. This was another characteristic of the company's stores that strayed from convention, which dictated that dollar stores generally attracted poorer clientele who visited the stores once a month and purchased decorative or nonessential items.

Gold's customers used his stores as they used drugstores or supermarkets. Everyday, staple merchandise attracted a regular and loyal customer base, and it was this strength that encouraged Gold to go forward with his expansion plans. The recession of the early 1990s helping spur growth with consumers looking for a deal, and by the mid-1990s, he was ready to significantly increase his pace of expansion.

PUBLIC OFFERING FUELS EXPANSION AND ACQUISITION

By 1996, there were more than 30 99¢ Only stores scattered throughout the Los Angeles area, with annual sales topping $150 million. The company was debt-free, and Gold intended to keep it that way, but he also wanted to accelerate expansion; so in May 1996 he offered a piece of ownership in the company through an initial public offering (IPO) of stock. He sold one-third of the company to the public in the IPO, with Gold family members, who occupied most of the company's top executive posts, retaining ownership of the balance. With the proceeds raised through the IPO, Gold opened a number of new stores before the end of the year, giving the company a total of more than 40 stores as it entered 1997.

The growing chain was supported by the addition of a new 840,000-square-foot warehouse in the City of Commerce, near downtown Los Angeles, that served as the nerve center for the company's operation. From this warehouse, merchandise could be quickly shipped to each of the company's stores, all clustered around downtown Los Angeles. The logistical abilities of the warehouse would be taxed in 1997, as Gold established ten additional 99¢ Only stores during the year, giving him a total store count of 52 by year's end.

Aside from opening ten new units in 1997, company executives busied themselves during the year by completing an acquisition. In November 1997, 99¢ Only acquired 48 percent of Minnesota-based Universal International, Inc., for $4 million in cash and merchandise. Universal, for years a wholesaler, operated a chain of discount stores named Only Deals, 49 of which were scattered throughout eight upper-midwest states, with another eight stores in Texas. In 1998, 99¢ Only acquired the remainder of Universal International, a deal that would also give the company control over the 40 percent stake Universal held in Odd's-N-End's, a 22-store closeout retailer operating in upstate New York.

AIMING FOR CONTROLLED GROWTH AND NEW PRODUCT CATEGORIES

As details of the Universal International acquisition in 1999 were being released, 99¢ Only was posting record financial totals and attracting the attention of investors, who had nothing but praise to heap on the company. "Forget everything you know about 99 cent stores," one analyst remarked, adding that 99¢ Only Stores "has some of the characteristics of a drug store with the price point of a dollar store. It's big and clean and merchandised like a full-priced drug store ... and the lighting is good and people walk around the store to help you." Another analyst envisioned the proliferation of Gold's concept throughout the country, projecting that if 99¢ Only extended its presence into other major markets, there was room for 4,000 or more stores. Gold distanced himself from that claim, stating, "I don't think that far ahead. If you do," he warned, "you just get into dreaming."

With his mind focused on the near future, Gold set the pace for 99¢ Only's expansion into other states during the late 1990s. The company was gearing toward a 20 percent annual growth rate in terms of its physical expansion, with 12 new stores slated to open in 1998. In fact, sales rose from $150 million in 1995 to about $360 million in 1999, and by 1999 the company had 73 stores—all spacious with an average size of about 17,000 square feet. Most of the chain's products were "reorderables" and came from marketers such as Colgate-Palmolive, Procter & Gamble, Playtex, Keebler, Hershey, and Revlon with 10 percent of items private label and the remainder oddities; 40 percent of items for sale were consumables.

In 2000, the year during which Gold's son-in-law, Eric Schiffer, became president of the company, the chain added frozen and refrigerated items. In 2001, 99¢ Only Store's 112 stores in California, Nevada, and Arizona added body washes and decorative candles and a plant and gardening section that expanded in 2002. The following year with 145 stores, the recession-proof store added a "gourmet fancy food" section in its Sacramento store as revenues increased about 30 percent. Sales per store averaged $4.8 million in 2002 with the company's highest volume store in Beverly Hills, California, grossing at $9.9 million. Still the chain, whose revenues totaled $664 million, used no advertising agency, creating instead its own print and occasional outdoor and radio campaigns in-house and turning down 90 percent of the deals proffered it by merchants.

MOVING INTO TEXAS

In 2003, 99¢ Only prepared for its expansion into Texas with the purchase of the former Albertson's 740,000-square-foot distribution warehouse in Houston. That July, the company opened its first four stores in Houston; the number of stores in Texas increased to 18 in 2004 when the company also expanded to Dallas. Yet the chain that could boast close to $900 million in revenues, gross margins of 40 percent, and double-digit total sales growth struggled to make it in Texas.

"We underestimated the challenge of getting middle-income customers to visit the store for the first time, and I think that has translated as a shortfall for us. [Texas shoppers] are entrenched in a preconceived mind-set of what a dollar store is," Schiffer announced in a 2004 *Dallas Business Journal*. Well-heeled Texans seemed less drawn to the concept of deep-discount stores than their California or Nevada peers, and competition for those who were seeking a bargain proved much fiercer than expected in Texas with the presence of Dollar General, Dollar Tree, Sun 99 Cents Store, and 99 Cents & Up. By mid-2004, the company was slashing prices at its 23 Texas stores, widening the selection of products in an effort to be more competitive, and putting more money toward marketing stores through newspaper ads and direct mailing.

ROUGH TIMES AND TURN AROUND

The expansion into Texas marked the beginning of a rough stretch for 99¢ Only Stores. When Eric Schiffer moved from president to chief executive officer and chairman in October 2004, and Gold's son, Jeffrey, became president, shares of the company's stock had fallen by about 66 percent, and the company announced that it was trimming its annual unit growth rate from 30 to 15 or 20 percent. By 2005, however, the company had hit its stride again, leading the dollar store market with a 19 percent sales increase over 2003.

By 2007, when 99¢ Only Stores celebrated its 25th anniversary, the 255-store chain was reporting better results in Texas where it had more than 40 outlets, many of them new smaller-format stores. Then in 2008, in the midst of the nation's economic downturn, even as analysts were projecting that 99¢ Only Stores were more likely to profit from hard times than their larger competitors, the company took a drastic step. After two consecutive quarter losses, 99¢ Only Stores decided to leave Texas and focus on the California, Nevada, and Arizona stores that accounted for about 90 percent of its sales.

The "oldest single-price retail store" company also began offering variable pricing in 2007. It had previously played around with the quantity and size of goods in an attempt to offer a wider array of items—all under 99 cents—to customers. Finally in 2008 the company faced breaking its 99 cent price ceiling for the first time after announcing its second consecutive quarter of losses midyear. Benefits of the change would include a wider array of merchandise and the opportunity to become more of a one-stop shop. As the decade came to a close and $22.26 had the same buying power that 99 cents had had when the company began in 1982, 99¢ Only was hoping that the lure of the deep discount combined with added convenience would continue to attract customers of every socioeconomic level to its 279 locations.

Jeffrey L. Covell
Updated, Carrie Rothburd

PRINCIPAL SUBSIDIARIES

Bargain Wholesale; Universal International Inc.

PRINCIPAL COMPETITORS

Big Lots Inc.; Dollar General Corporation; Dollar Tree Inc.; Wal-Mart Stores Inc.

FURTHER READING

Brott, Tamar, "The Price Is Right; 99¢ Only Stores," *Los Angeles Magazine,* August 1, 2001, p. 42.

Daniels, Wade, "99¢ Flush with Cash, Poised for Slow Expansion," *Los Angeles Business Journal,* December 8, 1997, p. 28.

"David Gold," *Chain Store Age Executive,* December 1997, p. 128.

Facenda, Vanessa L., "More Bang for Less Than a Buck: The 'Less Than a Dollar' Store Is Perfecting the Art of Being a Value-Priced Convenience Store," *Retail Merchandising,* October 1, 2002, p. 36.

Ferguson, Tim W., "Frozen Peas, Half Off," *Forbes,* August 12, 1996, p. 88.

"99¢ Only Aims to Crack $1 Billion," *MMR,* May 3, 2004, p. 130.

"99¢ Only Is Not Your Average Dollar Store," *Retail Merchandiser,* July 1, 2003, p. 32.

Porter, Thyra, "99¢ Only Stores Broadening in Kitchen," *HFN—The Weekly Newspaper for the Home Furnishing Network,* March 23, 1998, p. 44.

Scally, Robert, "Brand Names Make Dollars and Sense for 99¢ Only," *Discount Store News,* March 17, 1997, p. 3.

———, "99¢ Only Prepares for Continued Growth," *Discount Store News,* May 25, 1998, p. 3.

———, "99¢ Only to Venture Out of LA to Eastern, Midwestern Markets," *Discount Store News,* March 9, 1998, p. 10.

Stanley, T. L., "Feature: Closeout Chic," *Brandweek,* August 9, 1999.

Zaragoza, Sandra, "99¢ Only Stores to Cut Texas Price Point," *Dallas Business Journal,* June 4, 2004, p. 5.

The O'Connell Companies Inc.

---

480 Hampden Street
Holyoke, Massachusetts 01040-3309
U.S.A.
Telephone: (413) 534-5667
Toll Free: (800) 255-0235
Fax: (413) 534-2902
Web site: http://www.oconnells.com

Private Company
Incorporated: 1926 as Daniel O'Connell's Sons Inc.
Employees: 730
Sales: $92.9 million (2007 est.)
NAICS: 236210 Industrial Building Construction; 236220 Commercial and Institution Building Construction; 561110 Office Administrative Services; 551112 Offices of Other Holding Companies

■ ■ ■

The O'Connell Companies Inc. is a privately held Holyoke, Massachusetts-based holding company for construction and real estate–related subsidiaries, most notably the original business, Daniel O'Connell's Sons Inc. This company is a construction management and project planning services company maintaining its main office in Holyoke and branch offices in Franklin, Massachusetts (near Boston), and New Haven, Connecticut. The company does a wide range of work in the New England market, including academic projects, such as classrooms, labs, and residential halls; corporate and institutional projects, including office buildings and the

Basketball Hall of Fame in Springfield, Massachusetts; hospitals and other healthcare projects; residential and hotel projects, including garages; museums, theaters, and other art projects; and utility and infrastructure projects, including bridges and dams.

O'Connell Companies operates in smaller markets through Western Builders, Inc., based in Granby, Massachusetts. Another subsidiary, O'Connell Development Group, pursues development opportunities for the construction units as well as outside firms. Out of the company's involvement in hydroelectric facilities grew O'Connell Energy Group, which develops, finances, builds, operates, and manages northeastern hydroelectric facilities and also offers energy management consulting services.

Another O'Connell company is the Appleton Corporation, a real estate management firm for apartment and condominium complexes, retirement communities, office buildings, retail centers, medical offices, and industrial-technology facilities. All told, the company manages a portfolio of about two million square feet. Appleton offers facilities management, accounting and financial, and security services. In addition, it provides resident services for elderly properties and communities. Originally formed to take care of O'Connell properties, Appleton does about one-third of its business with outside parties. Another example of the synergy created between the O'Connell subsidiaries is Appleton's use of O'Connell Energy to develop energy strategies for the facilities it manages.

Somewhat further afield is another subsidiary, New England Fertilizer Company, a North Quincy,

COMPANY PERSPECTIVES

DOC has deep roots in all types of construction. We take particular pride, however, in meeting the technical and logistical challenges of our assignments. We've gutted and rebuilt a four-lane bridge from the water up while traffic continued to travel across the bridge. We've quietly rebuilt a library around studying students and replaced load-bearing walls in a high-rise building while it remained occupied. Quite simply, we've faced every construction challenge imaginable, and succeeded.

Massachusetts-based biosolids management company, essentially converting sewage sludge into pelletized fertilizer. The company operates plants in North Andover and Quincy, Massachusetts; Palm Beach County, Florida; and Shakopee, Minnesota.

O'CONNELL FAMILY FLEES IRELAND

Like many families in Ireland in the 19th century, the O'Connells immigrated to the United States during the potato famine. According to the *Encyclopedia of Massachusetts* published in 1916, the original Daniel O'Connell, father of the man who would establish Daniel O'Connell's Sons, was born in 1799 and brought his family from County Kerry, Ireland, to Holyoke in 1847. He went to work as a laborer on the Holyoke dam and died just two years later due to a cholera epidemic, leaving six children. His namesake, also born in Ireland, worked as a water boy on the dam as well. He would eventually go to work for the city of Holyoke and rose through the ranks to become superintendent of streets.

In 1879, the story goes, a new mayor of Holyoke was elected and informed Daniel O'Connell that he was expected to fire three of his men to make way for three of the mayor's friends. Rather than comply and take on men who were not as qualified as those on his crew, O'Connell resigned, or was perhaps fired. According to family lore, the next day a man from the Whiting silk mill contacted O'Connell to confirm that his departure from city employment had been indeed the result of a principled stand. Word was passed to William Skinner, who owned the Skinner Silk Mills, and O'Connell was hired to pave the factory yards with cobblestone. Daniel O'Connell started his own construction business in 1879.

CONSTRUCTION COMPANY INCORPORATES

O'Connell quickly moved beyond paving and road jobs to take on a variety of other projects, including bridges, reservoirs, and buildings. O'Connell's sons also became involved in the business and following his death in 1916 they took charge. In 1926 they incorporated the company as Daniel O'Connell's Sons Inc. A third generation of the family took the helm in 1930 in the form of Daniel J. O'Connell. Unlike the company's founder, this Daniel O'Connell was well educated, graduating from Worcester Academy and earning a bachelor of science degree from the Massachusetts Institute of Technology in 1929.

Daniel J. O'Connell would also bring his sons Daniel, Franklin, and James J. into the family business, after taking them as youngsters to visit job sites. According to Franklin O'Connell in an interview with *Holyoke Magazine,* his father never pressured them to join him in the business: "My father always said, 'Don't feel you have to carry on the family tradition, but if you'd like to come to work here, there'll always be a place for you.'"

Under the leadership of Daniel J. O'Connell, the construction business continued to thrive and expanded in new directions, some of which had nothing to do with building or real estate. In 1947 he acquired a traprock mine from the Holyoke Street Railway and opened a quarry. The land also held obvious promise as a ski run, and around 1960, because he believed area children needed more winter activities, O'Connell opened the Mount Tom Ski Area. It became a well-known place for children to learn the basics of skiing and made O'Connell a much beloved figure in the community.

What was more important to the family business, of course, were the building projects undertaken during his tenure. Virtually every Catholic church in the region was built by Daniel O'Connell's Sons. In the late 1960s and early 1970s, the company constructed most of the new buildings at the University of Massachusetts campus at Amherst, as well as the buildings for the Greenfield Community College and Holyoke Community College, and Mercy Hospital in Springfield, Massachusetts.

APPLETON CORPORATION IS FORMED

In 1972 Appleton Corporation was created to manage properties developed by the O'Connell family. The initial focus was on residential properties, in particular some housing complexes for the elderly. (Daniel J.

KEY DATES

1879: Daniel O'Connell establishes a construction company.
1916: O'Connell dies.
1926: Daniel O'Connell's Sons is incorporated.
1972: Appleton Corporation is established.
1975: Western Builders Inc. is established.
1979: The O'Connell Companies Inc. is created as holding company.
1984: O'Connell Development Group is formed.
1989: O'Connell Energy Group grows out of O'Connell Development.
1995: Development of a new Basketball Hall of Fame begins.
2002: Hall of Fame opens.

O'Connell was known for his work with the elderly, leading to a 1973 honorary doctorate degree from St. Anselm's College in Manchester, New Hampshire, for his efforts.) Not only did the scope of properties increase to include retail sites and mixed-use facilities, Appleton later expanded its purview to the management of properties for third parties. Real estate consulting work would be added as well.

Next, in 1975, the O'Connell family started Western Builders, Inc., in Granby, Massachusetts, to focus on residential and nonresidential construction projects in smaller markets. To house these entities and Daniel O'Connell's Sons, The O'Connell Companies Inc. was established as a holding company in 1979. Serving as president was Robert Mahar, while O'Connell's son assumed other roles. Daniel J. O'Connell Jr. soon died, passing away in 1981. Franklin O'Connell served as vice-president and treasurer of Daniel O'Connell Sons and O'Connell Companies. His brother, James J., was an executive vice-president at O'Connell Companies, but his pride was Mount Tom Ski Area and the development for learn-to-ski programs for school children as well as the elderly and blind.

To generate more business in eastern Massachusetts and southern New Hampshire, Daniel O'Connell's Sons opened a permanent office in Boston in 1980. In 1983 Daniel J. O'Connell died, succumbing to cancer at the age of 76. As chairman of the board of the O'Connell Companies, he left behind the largest construction firm in western Massachusetts and one of the largest in the entire state. Mahar and the O'Connell family continued to grow O'Connell Companies in the 1980s. O'Connell

Development Group was established in 1984 to oversee the company's development activities as well as to take on outside clients. One area of emphasis was the development of hydroelectric facilities. This sector became large enough that a separate company, O'Connell Energy Group, was formed in 1989 to finance, build, and operate hydroelectric facilities in the New England states.

Also in the 1980s O'Connell Development and Dunn Associates of Boston formed New England Fertilizer Company to operate a plant to convert sewage sludge, which for years had been discharged into Boston Harbor at the rate of some 70 tons per day, into fertilizer pellets. The technology, available since the mid-1970s, heat-dried the sludge into a biosolid that was then granulated into pellets that were 60 percent organic matter and included slow-release calcium, iron, nitrogen, phosphorous, and sulfur. These were ideally suited for golf courses and large-scale agriculture use. In 1988 New England fertilizer won an eight-year contract to operate a temporary biosolids processing facility in Quincy, Massachusetts, serving sewage treatment plants on Deer Island and Nut Island. A permanent plant opened in Quincy in 1991.

NEW PRESIDENT NAMED IN 1993

The 1990s brought changes to the management ranks of O'Connell Companies. Mahar retired as president in 1993. He was replaced by Dennis A. Fitzpatrick, who in the 1980s had succeeded Mahar as president of Daniel O'Connell's Sons. James J. O'Connell died at the age of 50 in 1995. His widow, Mary Rose O'Connell, continued to run Mount Tom Ski Area until escalating debt forced the facility to be closed in 1998. Franklin O'Connell also owned a stake in Mount Tom, and when he died in 1998 at the age of 57 he left that interest in his will to a family friend, Joseph O'Donnell.

A year later he and Mary Rose O'Connell stirred controversy in the area when they attempted to increase the size of the quarry, comprised of 7.2 acres, on the nearly 400-acre footprint of the property. Many in the community objected to the expansion of excavation, which they contended would destroy wildlife and plants, pollute groundwater, and mar the general beauty of the mountain. The matter would not be settled until 2002 when Mary O'Connell and O'Donnell agreed to sell all but a 16-acre parcel of land, which included the quarry, for $3 million to a group of buyers intent on preserving the area, including the state Department of Environmental Management, the U.S. Fish & Wildlife Service, the greater Holyoke Boys & Girls Clubs, and the Non-profit Trustees of Reservations. The quarry would be allowed to operate for ten more years, or until two million tons of basalt was removed, at which point the quarry property could be acquired by the purchasing group at no additional cost.

Through the end of the century and into the new, development and construction remained the focus of O'Connell Companies, primarily in the 413 area code that covered all of western Massachusetts. Noteworthy projects in the 1990s included the Holyoke Crossing shopping mall and the reconstruction of the Memorial Bridge in Springfield. The latter came with a myriad of challenges. Not only did the bridge have to remain open throughout the job, but also the schedule demanded that O'Connell crews work through harsh winters, and when spring came they had to contend with flood waters. For its efforts, the company garnered its second prestigious Build America Award.

BASKETBALL HALL OF FAME OPENS: 2002

O'Connell Companies also made an extraordinary effort to develop a new Basketball Hall of Fame to ensure that the hall remained in Springfield. In 1995 the hall's board of trustees considered moving the museum to Disney World, in Orlando, Florida. Visitation at the hall had waned, but its loss would nevertheless be a serious blow to the community. O'Connell Companies then led the charge, without any promise of a payoff, to develop a new Naismith Memorial Basketball Hall of Fame that would also include an 18-acre riverfront retail and entertainment complex. O'Connell played a key role in cobbling together financing from federal, state, and private sources, and also designed a distinctive hall of fame building, anchored by a 90-foot dome. When the project finally came to fruition and the museum opened in 2002, the Appleton Corporation subsidiary took over management of the facility.

Also in the early 2000s, New England Fertilizer expanded beyond Quincy to other parts of the country. A new processing plant opened in Shakopee, Minnesota, in 2000. Two years later a facility opened in North Andover, Massachusetts. In 2004 the company won a contract to build and operate a biosolids processing plant in West Palm Beach, Florida. On the development and construction side of O'Connell Companies, the goal as the first decade of the new century came to an end was to expand and diversify the portfolio, emphasizing the residential sector, in particular low-income complexes. Moreover, O'Connell looked to make deeper inroads into the Worcester, Massachusetts market as well as communities in Northern Connecticut.

Ed Dinger

PRINCIPAL SUBSIDIARIES

Appleton Corporation; Daniel O'Connell's Sons Inc.; O'Connell Development Group; O'Connell Energy Group; Western Builders Inc.

PRINCIPAL COMPETITORS

Dimeo Construction Company; James J. Welch & Co., Inc.; Walsh Brothers, Inc.

FURTHER READING

"At 57, Franklin O'Connell Company," *Boston Herald*, July 25, 1998, p. 26.

"Builders," *Springfield (Mass.) Union-News*, May 2, 1996, p. 2.

"D. J. O'Connell Sr., 76, Contractor," *Boston Globe*, July 16, 1983.

"James O'Connell, 50, President of Mt. Tom," *Springfield (Mass.) Union-News*, November 20, 1995, p. B5.

Litchfield, Kathleen, "A Construction Model," *Springfield (Mass.) Union-News*, May 2, 1996, p. 6.

O'Brien, George, "Property Management Is a Data-Driven Business," *Business West*, March 31, 2008.

O'Quinn, Bea, "O'Connell's Perseverance Pays Off," *Springfield (Mass.) Union-News*, September 26, 2002, p. F8.

Plaisance, Mike, "Both Sides Invoke O'Connell Name in Quarry Debate," *Springfield (Mass.) Sunday Republican*, July 4, 1999, p. A11.

Otto Fuchs KG

Derschlager Strasse 26
Meinerzhagen, D-58540
Germany
Telephone: (49 2354) 73-0
Fax: (49 2354) 73-201
Web site: http://www.otto-fuchs.com

Private Company
Incorporated: 1910 as Metall- und Armaturenwerke
    GmbH
Employees: 7,500
Sales: EUR 2.5 billion ($3.4 billion) (2007)
NAICS: 331316 Aluminum Extruded Product
    Manufacturing; 332112 Nonferrous Forging;
    331421 Copper Rolling, Drawing, and Extruding;
    332321 Metal Window and Door Manufacturing

∎∎∎

Otto Fuchs KG is Europe's leading manufacturer of
forged light metal wheels and supplies chassis
components, drivetrain, and suspension parts to some of
the world's largest automakers. Otto Fuchs is also a supplier of finished forged and ring-rolled jet engine parts
as well as large forged structural parts to most of the
world's aircraft manufacturers. As well, the company
makes the forged preform of the combustion chamber
of the European booster rocket Ariane. The company
develops and produces standard and specialty alloys
from aluminum, magnesium, copper, titanium, and
nickel; manufactures bars, pipes, and profiles made of
aluminum, brass, and magnesium; and makes other

extrusion-pressed products in about 50 alloy
compositions. Otto Fuchs has production subsidiaries
and joint ventures in the United States, Hungary, and
South Africa. The company also makes light metal
profiles for windows, doors, and facades for Bielefeld-
based subsidiary Schüco International KG, the European
market leader in solar technologies for innovative building envelope designs and in window and facade systems
for the construction industry. The private company is
owned by third- and fourth-generation family members
of company founder Otto Fuchs.

CHANGE FROM BRASS TO
ALUMINUM PRODUCTS CREATES
FOUNDATION FOR GROWTH

In 1910 engineer Otto Fuchs and his uncle, Hugo vom
Hove, acquired the assets of Meinerzhagener Metall-
werke AG, a bankrupt brass foundry and brass products
manufacturer in Meinerzhagen, a small German city
about 60 miles south of Dortmund. Under Fuchs' early
leadership the company manufactured mainly brass
weights for scales that were sold throughout Germany.
The German Post Office was one of its main customers.
Otto Fuchs and his uncle soon expanded the foundry's
product line. In 1916 Otto Fuchs took over his uncle's
share in the company and renamed it Otto Fuchs.

During World War I the company manufactured
cast and extruded parts for industrial clients and the
German military. After the war ended in 1918 Otto
Fuchs grew continuously and manufactured parts
mainly for customers in the burgeoning electrical
industry, the railroad, and the emerging automobile

COMPANY PERSPECTIVES

Flights into space, worldwide transportation of people and goods, high-tech in machine tool engineering, making a mark on big cities with modern architecture. ... All of these places are where our company is represented with ideas, products and solutions. Imagination and the courage to think openly are the breeding grounds for extraordinary achievements with which we continuously develop new areas of business.

industry. By the mid-1920s Otto Fuchs was Germany's third largest producer of nonferrous extruded parts. However, the onset of the worldwide Great Depression at the end of the decade halted the company's growth and made massive layoffs unavoidable.

When the company founder passed away in 1931, his oldest son, Hans Joachim, took his place. The 28-year-old had studied business administration in Cologne and gathered practical experience in a metal trading firm before he joined the company in 1927. After his father's death Hans Joachim Fuchs became the personally liable partner and his brother Otto Eberhard and his sister Elisabeth became limited partners in the business. Otto Eberhard Fuchs, who had also studied business administration, was killed during World War II and his two daughters became limited partners.

In 1934 Hans Joachim Fuchs made a far-reaching strategic decision when he decided to manufacture products from aluminum and other light metals. With significant financial investments in expertise from chemicals firm IG Farben and in an additional extrusion press, the company entered another period of strong growth. As Adolf Hitler's Germany prepared for war in the second half of the 1930s, the demand for finished aluminum and other light metal products rose sharply. To keep up with it, Otto Fuchs built a new foundry and machining shop and invested in a huge hydraulic forging press with a press capacity of 8,000 metric tons, which was housed in a new building.

EXPANSION DRIVEN BY MILITARY NEEDS IN WORLD WAR II

The new equipment enabled the company to mass-produce large die-forged aluminum and magnesium parts of high quality for the German aerospace industry. By 1938 Otto Fuchs' workforce had grown to about

1,000. However, as the German war machine gained strength, the number of workers doubled once again in a short period. When there proved to be a lack of skilled workers available in the Meinerzhagen region, the company acquired a second location in Dülken near Viersen, about 45 miles west of Dusseldorf, where it concentrated its nonferrous metal activities.

Between 1942 and 1944 Otto Fuchs employed about 1,000 forced laborers, mainly from Russia. When the Allied troops began moving toward the lower Rhine region in the fall of 1944, raw materials, machine tools, and other equipment were moved back from Dülken to Meinerzhagen in 87 rail cars and 26 trucks. Despite such efforts to preserve the manufacturing capabilities that were essential to the Nazi war effort, both plants were so badly damaged during the last months of the war that production came to a standstill.

MAKING TITANIUM PARTS FOR AIRCRAFT AND ULTRALIGHT WHEELS FOR CARS

After the end of World War II the British occupation forces suspended Hans Joachim Fuchs from the management of his company, which was put in the hands of a trustee. Moreover, they put the company on the index of firms to be dismantled. Hans Joachim Fuchs did not give up trying to save the family company, however, and at the last minute he was able to convince the British to allow the company to survive intact.

To get the enterprise up and running once again, the forging and extrusion halls were transformed into a repair shop for railroad cars. Orders were sufficient to sustain a small workforce of 150 who went to work rebuilding the company's production facilities. With permission by the British military administration, Otto Fuchs began manufacturing much needed household goods of light metal such as pots, hooks, and hangers.

The currency reform in 1948 marked the turnaround for the war-damaged West German economy, which then entered the postwar reconstruction boom of the 1950s. Foreseeing the huge demand for his products, Hans Joachim Fuchs invested large sums in state-of-the-art manufacturing technology and new buildings. After receiving an engineering degree at Stuttgart University, his son Otto Rudolf joined the company in 1954 where he led the pressure-die-casting department that manufactured, among other products, the so-called Mercedes Stars for Mercedes Benz. Two years later Otto Rudolf Fuchs became managing director of the Dülken plant.

In the early 1950s the company continued to produce consumer goods made from light metals,

---

KEY DATES

■

1910: Otto Fuchs acquires a brass foundry and brass products manufacturing plant in Meinerzhagen, Germany.

1916: The company is renamed Otto Fuchs oHG.

1931: Hans Joachim Fuchs becomes personally liable managing partner.

1934: Otto Fuchs starts manufacturing products from aluminum and other light metals.

1964: The company sets up one of the world's largest forging presses; Otto Fuchs acquires Bielefeld-based Heinz Schürmann & Co.

1979: The company takes over aluminum forge Weber Metals in the United States.

1995: An aluminum wheel production joint venture is founded in Hungary.

1998: Otto Rudolf Fuchs, his two sons and half-sister Christiane Fuchs remain as family shareholders.

2005: A joint venture for the production of vehicle components is set up in South Africa.

2007: Otto Fuchs starts manufacturing forged and ring-rolled jet engine parts.

---

including ashtrays, tin boxes, aluminum pots, and portable stoves. At the same time, Otto Fuchs began to use titanium alloys for manufacturing parts for the aerospace industry. It was also in the 1950s when the company began to produce parts for gearboxes. At the end of the decade the company's workforce was back at over 2,000.

GROWTH AND EXPANSION IN THE SIXTIES AND SEVENTIES

In the first half of the 1960s, new production facilities were added continuously to the Meinerzhagen plant, where one of the world's largest forging presses with a pressing capacity of 30,000 metric tons was installed in 1964. By the middle of the decade, Otto Fuchs had become one of the largest manufacturers of nonferrous semifinished products in Europe. The company was approached by Stuttgart-based automaker Porsche about the development of a new kind of ultralight wheel with a modern design for the new Porsche 911 model, which was also to be used in racing cars. Within only a few months, Otto Fuchs engineers presented Porsche with an acceptable solution, which marked the company's entry into another growth market. Soon Otto Fuchs also

received orders from other German carmakers, including Mercedes Benz, BMW, Audi, and Volkswagen, for the company's forged light metal wheels.

The economic downturn following the oil crisis of 1973 interrupted the company's dynamic growth. As the German aerospace, auto, construction, electric, and machine tool industries struggled with rapidly increasing prices for mineral oil and oil-based raw materials, Otto Fuchs reduced its workforce and output. Three years later the German economy recovered from the crisis, putting the company back on the growth track. In 1974 Otto Rudolf Fuchs became the company's personally liable partner while his father became managing limited partner with full power of attorney.

ACQUISITION OF SCHÜCO LEADS TO NEW MARKETS

The acquisition of the Bielefeld-based firm Heinz Schürmann & Co. in 1964 was a major stepping-stone in the history of Otto Fuchs. Grown out of a craft business for rolling grilles for shop windows and shop window systems founded in 1951, Heinz Schürmann—or Schüco for short—had developed into a provider of complete window, door and facade systems made mostly of aluminum profiles in combination with light metals, steel and plastics, during the 1950s. By setting up a wholesale business in Bielefeld in addition to the craft business, Schüco aimed at providing a full line of aluminum products to the construction trade, from doorknobs to meter-long bars for facade construction. By the late 1950s the company had established additional subsidiaries in Frankfurt, Hamburg, and Dusseldorf, and had won a growing roster of loyal customers, such as locksmiths and metalworking shops. In the year before the takeover, Schüco's 150 employees generated DEM 20 million in annual sales.

After Schüco became part of the Otto Fuchs group, the company entered a period of dynamic growth. As architects began to design more buildings with large glass facades, the demand for Schüco's products rose steadily. The ongoing construction boom favored prefabricated systems solutions. Although there were some synergies between Otto Fuchs and Schüco—mainly, Otto Fuchs manufactured some of the aluminum products that Schüco marketed to its clientele—the latter remained an independent enterprise.

In the 1960s Schüco focused its efforts on establishing a number of branded product lines to distinguish itself from other competitors. Some of the company's first brands were "Allwetter" and "Alldoor" for window and door systems. In addition to expanding the company's product range by adding products from other manufacturers, Schüco began to develop its own products as well, setting up a factory for metal fittings in Borgholzhausen, northwest of Bielefeld. Moreover, the company started offering technical advisory services for architects, who were an important target group as opinion leaders and potential customers. When Schüco was experiencing difficulties finding shipping companies that were able to transport its six-meter-long light metal bars, the company set up its own delivery fleet.

SUBSIDIARY SCHÜCO BECOMES EUROPEAN MARKET LEADER

In the 1970s Schüco management set its sights on conquering new markets in Western Europe in order to be less dependent on the ups and downs of the German construction industry. A network of partner firms was established that covered most of Western Europe. Schüco licensees were also found in Saudi Arabia and Japan. To withstand the fierce competition of established aluminum product manufacturers, the company introduced a number of innovative products to the market, such as thermal insulation composite systems that resulted in lower energy consumption in buildings, and window frames made of plastics instead of aluminum.

Schüco also entered the market of facade construction, established one of Europe's biggest testing centers for windows and facades, and provided hardware and software to its customers in the construction trade that helped them find the right products to fit their needs and to simplify their ordering process. Investing in a state-of-the-art, high-rise warehouse with electronically controlled order picking and optimizing logistics helped the company to significantly shorten order fulfillment times. Schüco's efforts resulted in rapid growth during the 1970s. In the middle of the decade, the company employed about 1,200 workers and grossed DEM 190 million per year. Until the end of the 1970s, Schüco's total sales more than doubled, reaching DEM 200 million in 1980.

With the strategic focus on innovative aluminum-glass architecture such as curtain facades and atriums in large commercial construction objects, and on solar technology and winter gardens in the private construction market, Schüco's rapid growth continued throughout the 1980s—driven by intensified marketing efforts and a constant stream of innovations. Among the most noteworthy were complete systems for the construction of large atriums and of reflective glass facades, so-called structural glazing facades; ISKO-THERM, the first system for other manufacturers to put together thermal insulation aluminum profiles; and

new designs that helped prevent damage by physical objects and fire, or break-ins. To further expand Schüco's product range, Otto Fuchs management decided to acquire Carl Schnicks GmbH & Co., a German plastics processing firm in Haan near Düsseldorf, which enabled the company to manufacture extruded construction profiles made from plastic materials.

Schüco's sales organization was structured into three divisions, each one focusing on one important target group, including construction firms for aluminum and plastics products, and wholesalers of construction components. Each customer group was informed about new Schüco products at large international trade shows, and through educational seminars and videos. At the company's 50th anniversary in 2001, Schüco was Europe's market leader for window and facade systems, grossing over DEM 2 billion in that year.

ADDING AUTOMOTIVE CHASSIS COMPONENTS AND JET ENGINE PARTS

While the subsidiary Schüco had established a strong foothold in the European construction industry during the 1980s and 1990s, Otto Fuchs—in addition to manufacturing aluminum building products for Schüco—greatly expanded its activities in the automobile and aerospace sectors. High demand for forged light metal wheels from the auto industry was a major driver for Otto Fuchs' growth in the 1980s. After the recession of 1993 was overcome, more German automakers demanded that their suppliers' wheels be lightweight and less expensive. Otto Fuchs launched a new generation of forged light metal wheels that were mass-manufactured in a fully automated production process.

In 1995 the company set up two such production lines with an annual output of approximately one million wheels. This enormous capacity, however, was still not sufficient to satisfy market demand. Consequently, in 1995 Otto Fuchs, along with the American cast aluminum wheels manufacturer Superior Industries International Inc., set up Suoftec Kft., a 50-50 joint venture, to build an additional aluminum wheel production plant in Tatabánya near Budapest in Hungary. Two years later, production of lightweight forged wheels for Audi began, which had granted Suoftec a five-year contract for 700,000 wheels. Additional contracts were secured from Audi and Rover Group in the second half of the 1990s.

In 1979 Otto Fuchs took over Weber Metals Inc., a supplier of forgings to the American aviation and space industries based in Los Angeles, California, to gain market share in the United States. To reach that goal, the company, again, installed one of the world's largest forging presses with a pressing capacity of 35,000 metric tons at the American subsidiary. Within two years, Weber Metals' annual sales doubled and continued to grow, reaching $100 million in 1998. One of Weber's main customers was American aircraft manufacturer Boeing.

In Germany, Otto Fuchs invested heavily in the latest technologies and equipment, such as new extruding presses for the production of difficult to manufacture profiles for the aerospace industry, to stay ahead of the competition. The company also invested in the development of new, innovative materials, such as an aluminum alloy for aircraft brake systems that revealed its superior qualities to other such materials on the market at very high temperatures up to 400 degrees Fahrenheit.

LEADERSHIP CHANGES AT THE TOP

The late 1980s and 1990s brought about changes in the company's shareholder structure. For the first time in the company's history, two nonfamily managers became personally liable partners in the company in addition to Otto Fuchs in 1988. Four years later Hans Joachim Fuchs passed away and his son Otto Rudolf retired from active company management in 1993. In 1996 the next Fuchs family generation also received shares in the business, increasing the number of limited partners to 22.

Reaching decisions among shareholders, however, became much more difficult. After a split into two groups that were unable to reach agreements with each other, one group was bought out in 1998. In the end Otto Rudolf Fuchs and his two sons, Otto Heinrich and Ludwig, as well as his half-sister Christiane Fuchs were left as the remaining partners in the company.

After the turn of the 21st century Otto Fuchs further expanded its light metal product range for the automotive industry when the company started manufacturing aluminum profile floors for commercial vehicles and chassis components. In 2003 the company invested about EUR 20 million in an additional extruding press that was installed in a hall almost 400 feet long and about 175 feet wide and went onstream the following year. In 2005, a second joint venture for the production of suspension components, Foxtec Ikhwezi, was set up in East London, South Africa, with the South African firm Ikhwezi Investment Holding.

One year later the new plant started manufacturing forged suspension parts for Daimler's Mercedes C-Class model, which were delivered on a just-in-time basis to the automaker's nearby assembly line. Finally, beginning in 2006 Otto Fuchs won a new forged wheel contract for the new 911 Turbo model from Porsche—once the company's first customer in that area. By 2008, Otto Fuchs had become Europe's leading manufacturer of forged light metal wheels and chassis components.

Due to increasing market demand, Otto Fuchs' aerospace division enjoyed a healthy growth of 20 percent per annum in the middle of the first decade of the 2000s. To win additional business in that market the company began to produce parts for jet engines and made a significant investment in a new ring-rolling mill that enabled the company to manufacture large, seamless rings made of nickel or titanium up to about 6.6 feet in diameter and casings up to about three feet in height. Another major investment in new equipment made it possible for Otto Fuchs to finish these parts in-house through heat treatment, machining, and ultrasonic inspection, making the company a full-service supplier of finished ring-shaped jet engine parts to most of the world's aircraft manufacturers. By 2008, Otto Fuchs was still a family-owned business, but managed by a team of three nonfamily managers, with one of them being the personally liable partner.

Evelyn Hauser

PRINCIPAL SUBSIDIARIES

Schüco International KG; Weber Metals Inc. (United States); Suoftec Kft. (Hungary; 50%); Foxtec Ikhwezi (Pty) Ltd. (South Africa; 70%).

PRINCIPAL COMPETITORS

Hayes Lemmerz International, Inc.; Alcoa Inc.; mefro wheels GmbH; Borbet Leichtmetallräder GmbH; Ronal Group; Nippon Light Metal Company, Ltd.

FURTHER READING

"Al Alloy Has High Strength, Fatigue at High Temperatures," *Advanced Materials & Processes,* September 2003, p. 13.

"Hungary Forged Wheels Project Set," *American Metal Market,* September 4, 1995, p. 6.

Krieg, Holger, *Unsere Fabriksken,* Lüdenscheid, Germany: MSM Verlag, 2007, pp. 77–83.

"New Vehicle Component Plant to Open in East London," *Africa Monitoring: South Africa,* September 13, 2006.

100 Jahre Hans Joachim Fuchs, Meinerzhagen, Germany: Otto Fuchs KG, 2003, 19 p.

"Suoftec Profits Slip in 2006," *Europe Intelligence Wire,* March 21, 2007.

"Wheel Maker Expands in Europe," *Los Angeles Daily News,* April 6, 1999, p. B3.

Overland Storage Inc.

4820 Overland Avenue
San Diego, California 92123-1235
U.S.A.
Telephone: (858) 571-5555
Toll Free: (800) 729-8725
Fax: (858) 571-0982
Web site: http://www.overlandstorage.com

Public Company
Incorporated: 1980 as Overland Data Inc.
Employees: 397
Sales: $127.7 million (2008)
Stock Exchanges: NASDAQ
Ticker Symbol: OVRL
NAICS: 334112 Computer Storage Device Manufacturing; 334119 Other Computer Peripheral Equipment Manufacturing

■ ■ ■

Overland Storage Inc., formerly Overland Data Inc., is a leading provider of data protection appliances serving the needs of midrange and distributed enterprises. Its products are sold in the Americas, Europe, the Middle East, Africa, and the Asia Pacific. The company uses a tiered approach to help its customers save time and money by categorizing data based on how frequently it is accessed, and then choosing the most appropriate data storage products based on access needs.

The company manufactures products in three designated tiers of data storage: nearline data protection, disk-based backup and recovery, and tape automation.

Overland's award-winning products include NEO SERIES and ARCvault families of tape backup and archive appliances (for rarely accessed data), REO SERIES disk-based backup and recovery appliances with Virtual Tape Library (VTL) capabilities (for occasionally accessed data), ULTAMUS RAID family of nearline data protection appliances (for frequently accessed data), and Snap Server networked and desktop appliances. These products are sold through leading original equipment manufacturers (OEMs), commercial distributors, storage integrators, and value-added resellers. In 2008 Overland Storage claimed over 100,000 installations and a customer list including many of the world's most successful companies.

ORIGINS

Overland Data Inc., later renamed Overland Storage Inc., began operations in 1980, with the goal of developing data storage solutions that would be easy to use and affordable for companies worldwide. The company was cofounded by Martin D. Gray, who served as a director from the start. By the 1990s, Overland was acknowledged as a leader in tape solutions for end users, distributors, and OEMs in global industries. At that time, the company offered three technology choices: DLT (digital linear tape), 18- and 36-track, and 9-track. Clients included IBM Corporation. Scott McClendon became president and CEO in 1991.

In 1997 the company went public with an offering of 3 million shares at $10 per share, increasing an initial filing of 2.7 million shares. A class-action lawsuit alleged

COMPANY PERSPECTIVES

We are a global data protection company. We help mid-range and distributed enterprise customers reduce the backup window, improve data recovery speed, simplify short- and long-term data retention and make cost-effective disaster recovery a reality. Our affordable and reliable solutions ensure data is constantly protected, readily available, and always there.

that the company's initial public offering violated federal securities laws with misleading statements in the Prospectus; the suit was settled in 1999. Revenues for fiscal 1997 were $59.1 million, an increase of 25 percent over the previous fiscal year's $47.2 million.

Overland quickly established itself as a leader in the tape-based storage market. The company led the market in 1997 for growth in unit shipments of DLT-based automated tape libraries. By 1998, Overland had received seven major industry awards for its DLT Library Xpress data library—the first fully scalable automated library solution that enabled customers to adjust capacity and performance upward based on expanding data needs—with 5,000 units shipped and an amazing 1 percent annualized field failure rate.

Another DLT solution, the LoaderXpress auto-loader—an automated desktop solution that avoids single tape-loading by enabling PC servers to be backed up for up to two months without any operator intervention—earned two awards in 1998. That year, Overland introduced WebTLC, a software technology that enables Internet-based remote operation of tape libraries and autochargers. The company also developed its Variable Rate Randomizer (VR2) data-encoding technology, enabling customers to significantly increase the capacity and throughput of linear tape formats.

During the 1990s Overland established itself as an OEM for several industry leaders, including Siemens. In 1998 Bell Microproducts Inc. became the first national distributor for Overland's automated DLT storage solutions line, expanding its availability. The following year, Overland signed a distribution agreement with Ingram Micro Inc., the world's largest wholesale provider of technology products and services, for national distribution of the DLT LoaderXpress autoloader, DLT Minilibrary Xpress, and table top DLT4000 and DLT7000 drives.

NEW MARKETS, NEW TECHNOLOGIES

With its 20th anniversary approaching, Overland began broadening its product line and technology roster in 1999 to move into new market segments. Recognizing that tape technology would ultimately be relegated to archival storage only, the company acquired the optical storage robotics assets of a major CD robotics automation company. To reach the higher-end enterprise market, Overland unveiled new products including the scalable EnterpriseXpress family and SanPiper SCSI to fiber channel bridge for storage area networks.

The company expanded into the small business backup market through a joint development agreement with Tecmar Technologies, a leading provider of entry-level tape storage products for network storage users. The two companies worked together to design and manufacture high performance Travan (a) and Travan NS (a) tape drives, using Overland's VR2 technology. Overland also wooed customers with a pioneering and unique guarantee—the GUTS warranty programming. Under the GUTS warranty, all DLT products were guaranteed to deliver 99 percent uptime performance and 100 percent data recovery. In 1999 fiscal revenues increased 23 percent to $92.2 million, from $75.2 million in fiscal 1998.

In 2000 Overland acquired Tecmar's inventory, fixed assets, supplies, intellectual property, and trademarks. Overland continued to produce Tecmar tape drives for the small and midsize business markets, making them available to resellers through a full-featured Web store for Tecmar products. Embracing the Internet as a vehicle for growth, Overland was the first independent tape library manufacturer to offer tapes and accessories over the Web. The company also announced the launch of a business-to-business (B2B) e-commerce site and an Accessories online Web store, and it made its Sales and Marketing tools available to resellers on the Web.

AWARD-WINNING PRODUCTS AND A SOLID CUSTOMER LIST

By 2000 the company's list of OEM customers included Compaq, IBM, Fujitsu, Siemens Computers, and Groupe Bull, and its commercial distributors included Ingram Micro, Tech Data Corporation, and Bell Microproducts. The company also sold its product through storage integrators and value-added resellers. Revenues for 2000 increased 33 percent over the previous year, reaching $123 million, from $92.2 million in fiscal 1999. Net income, however, decreased from $4 million in 1999 to $2.1 million in fiscal 2000, due

KEY DATES

1980: Overland Data is incorporated.

1991: Scott McClendon becomes president and CEO.

1997: The company goes public.

2000: Overland acquires Tecmar Technologies and earns American Electronics Association's High Tech Award.

2002: A Singapore location opens to serve the Asia Pacific region; company is renamed Overland Storage Inc.

2003: Overland acquires Okapi Software.

2005: Overland acquires Zetta Systems and outsources its manufacturing operations with Sanmina SCI Corporation.

2006: Overland reinstates formerly outsourced manufacturing in San Diego.

2008: Overland acquires Snap Server.

primarily to losses at Tecmar, an underperforming subsidiary. Overland discontinued Tecmar's Ditto product line and downsized its Colorado-based Tecmar subsidiary, localizing some of its functions into Overland's San Diego facility.

In 2000 Overland received the American Electronics Association's High Tech Award, an honor recognizing San Diego–area tech firms demonstrating strong financial growth, product innovation, and civic leadership. In 2001 the company boasted 20 years of record revenues and a 28 percent annual compound growth rate. Over 40,000 automated tape libraries had been shipped worldwide, and the company had received 27 product awards, positioning Overland as an industry leader.

Overland's growth and expansion into new markets and technology offerings necessitated a new management strategy. The company hired Christopher Calisi, former CEO of eHelp Corporation and vice-president of the Communication Products division at Symantec, as its new president and CEO, retaining former president Scott McClendon as chairman of the board. In an interview in the April 2001 *Computer Technology Review,* Calisi stated, "My vision [for Overland] is growth, pure and simple."

As part of its planned expansion, the company constructed a new 158,000-square-foot facility at the Kearny Mesa Spectrum in San Diego, with more space for its engineering, operations, production, and

worldwide marketing and sales staffs. New directions in technology offerings included products based on super-drive technology and a partnership with Seagate's LTO Ultrium drive. In 2001, Overland introduced the NEO SERIES of scalable libraries.

OVERSEAS SITE ON HORIZON

Despite a seemingly bright future, the company's third quarter 2001 profits fell short of expectations due to slow customer orders. Overland responded by instituting a 10 percent across-the-board pay cut, eliminating executive bonuses, and laying off 26 full-time and 17 part-time employees, leaving the company with about 300 employees. When news of the layoffs was made public, Overland stock fell 33 percent to $5.50 per share, according to the *San Diego Business Journal* (April 30, 2001). However, Overland ended fiscal year 2001 with revenues of $155.7 million, reflecting an overall 27 percent revenue increase over fiscal 2000 revenues of $122.98 million.

After financials surpassed expectations in the first quarter of fiscal 2002, Overland announced the opening of a Singapore location to serve the Asia Pacific region. According to the November 19, 2001, *Business Wire,* international markets accounted for 40 percent of the company's revenues, and the midrange tape market was growing 30 percent annually in the Asia Pacific region. In calendar 2001, the company's shipments of DLT- and 8-millimeter-based tape libraries with fewer than 40 cartridges led the market in rapid growth.

NEW NAME, NEW DIRECTION

In 2002 Overland Data Inc. changed its name to Overland Storage Inc. to more accurately reflect its broader market focus. The company separated into two business units—tape and software—partnering with Astrum Software for two product families and with Prisa Networks for a third. After more than a year of development work, Overland shipped the first product in a new family of storage management software for mid-tier users. Despite a difficult economic environment, the company concluded 2002 with record revenues of $163.4 million, surpassing the previous year's $155.7 million revenues.

In 2003 Overland's Neo Series 2000—the newest member of the Neo Series tape library family for enterprise tape backup applications—received *Storage Magazine*/SearchStorage.com's Product of the Year award in the Backup/Hardware category. Overall, Overland's Neo technology held the distinguished privilege of having received more industry awards than any product by any other vendor.

Overland continued to move beyond tape technologies in 2003, expanding into the disk-based appliance market when it acquired Okapi Software, a year-old San Diego manufacturer of a backup accelerator appliance based on Serial ATA drives that backed up data from multiple local and remote servers and then exported data to tape for secondary backup. Okapi founder and CEO John Matze became Overland's CTO. Later that year, Matze was featured as one of *CRN* magazine's Top 25 Innovators. The company launched its new REO Series of disk-based backup and recovery applications. According to President and CEO Christopher Calisi, the R2000 was capable of reducing backup time by 80 percent or more for some customers.

PEAKS AND VALLEYS AHEAD

Overland seemed to be doing everything right, and the company received both awards and acclaim. In 2003, Overland was named to Deloitte & Touche's Technology Fast 50 Program for San Diego, which recognized fifty fastest-growing technology companies based on five years of annual revenues. The company also received an InfoWorld 100 Award for its creative use of technology in customer support systems. These awards were followed in 2004 by Overland's selection in the *San Diego Business Journal*'s Best Companies to Work for Awards, honoring nine outstanding San Diego companies. In 2004 Overland also led its industry in shipping units and terabytes of iSCSI-based Disk to Disk (D2D) backup products. Fiscal 2004 revenues were $238 million, an increase of 22 percent over the previous year.

In 2005, according to Freeman Reports' annual Tape Library Outlook (cited in the April 13, 2005, *PR Newswire*), Overland was either first or second in unit volume for every major tape technology. That year, the company's performance earned it a spot in the prestigious Network World 200 Issue of *Network World* magazine, an annual guide to the 200 biggest North American public companies in the network industry. Overland's REO 4000 appliance was named Disk Product of the Year in 2005 at the second annual Storage Awards (or Storries), surpassing products from competitors IBM, EMB, and HP. The company was the first to ship over 1,000 disk-based backup and recovery appliances in March 2005. The company claimed over 20,000 customers, including the American Medical Association, the BBC, Carnegie Mellon University, Continental Airlines, The Golf Channel, National Instruments, Oxford University, and Rand McNally.

Later the same year, however, after 25 years of untarnished industry leadership and annual revenue increases, Overland suffered a major setback when its longstanding and largest OEM customer, Hewlett-Packard Company, announced that it had selected another supplier for its next-generation midrange tape automation products. Shortly after Hewlett-Packard's announcement, Overland entered into discussions with Dell regarding an agreement to supply an ARCvault tape library under development. However, in 2006, after a year of work to tailor the library to Dell's requirements, Dell informed Overland that it would terminate the agreement.

In fiscal 2005 the company's revenues fell for the first time ever. The company earned $4.6 million on $236 million in total sales in fiscal 2005, compared with earnings of $10.6 million on $238 million total sales in fiscal 2004.

MORE CHALLENGES

During this difficult period, Overland fended off the unwanted advances of Advanced Digital Information Company (ADIC). In 2005 ADIC purchased a large number of Overland shares and issued a securities filing indicating its interest in buying Overland for $7.90 a share. On the day of ADIC's offer, Overland's stock price surged by 42 percent to $9.64. However, Overland rejected the offer and adopted a "poison pill" shareholders rights plan under which existing shareholders were granted the right to buy shares at a reduced price if another person or group were to acquire 15 percent of the company's shares. ADIC withdrew its offer.

As part of its strategy to expand beyond tape-based products, the company acquired Zetta Systems, a small storage provisioning software vendor, for $9 million in 2005. Overland incorporated Zetta's data protection software into the 2007 launch of its new ULTAMUS Pro storage appliance. However, the product was discontinued and the related development facility closed due to a lack of revenue generated by its release. This failure resulted in an impairment charge of $8.4 million in the first quarter of fiscal 2007. In May 2007 the company had suffered seven consecutive quarters of losses.

In fiscal year 2007 the company also suffered from problems related to outsourcing. In 2005 Overland had outsourced its manufacturing to Sanmina SCI Corporation in San Jose, seeking to enhance its competitiveness with increased cost savings. The company let go approximately 140 San Diego employees and incurred around $3 million of pretax charges in conjunction with the outsourcing. When quality declined and costs rose above expectations, resulting in fourth quarter losses of $5.7 million on revenue of $41.7 million, the company transferred all of its manufacturing back to San Diego in 2006.

During the critical period after the Hewlett-Packard announcement, Overland shuffled its senior management. Scott McClendon replaced Christopher Calisi as interim president and CEO in 2006, and in 2007, Vernon A. LoForti (former Overland CFO) became president and CEO. The board created a new strategy committee to work on plans for the company's uncertain financial future. The company reduced its global workforce in 2007 and 2008 by 14 percent and 13 percent, respectively.

MIXED OUTLOOK FOR THE FUTURE

Overland incurred operating losses for three straight fiscal years after the loss of business from Hewlett-Packard, ending fiscal 2008 with an accumulated deficit of $50.9 million. Net revenues in fiscal 2008 fell to $127.7 million, from $160.4 million in fiscal 2007. Overland executives weighed alternatives including divesting some current operations to focus on fewer opportunities. The company cut approximately $10 million from planned fiscal 2009 expenditures. In October 2008 the company received a NASDAQ Staff Deficiency Letter because its stock had fallen below the minimum requirement of $1 per share for inclusion on the NASDAQ Global Market for 30 consecutive business days. Overland's Board filed a proposal for shareholder approval to authorize a reverse stock split, hoping to increase the per share price of common stock.

Despite the company's financial difficulties, its technology had continued to receive acclaim. In 2007 Overland's NEO SERIES and ARCvault 24 tape libraries led the rankings in the product features category of the second annual Diogenes Labs-Storage magazine Quality Awards. Overland was also recognized as a Five-Star Partner—or one of North America's top information technology vendors—in CMP Media's *VARBusiness* magazine in March 2007.

In an effort to revitalize sales, in June 2008 Overland acquired Snap Server, enabling the company to enter the distributed network-attached storage market while adding to the company's short-term operating expenses. Under LoForti's strategy, Overland also transitioned from an emphasis on OEM customers to a "channel-centric" company. (Channels link vendors to their small- and medium-sized business customers.) While it appeared that Overland's leadership would make every effort to return the company to profitability,

the future looked uncertain for a company that had long been at the top of its game.

Heidi Feldman

PRINCIPAL SUBSIDIARIES

Overland Storage (Europe) Ltd.; Overland Storage SARL; Overland Storage GmbH; Zetta Systems, Inc.

PRINCIPAL COMPETITORS

Quantum Corporation; EMC Corporation; NetApp Inc.; Hewlett-Packard Company; IBM Corporation; Dell Inc.; DataDomain; FalconStor Software Inc.; Infortrend Corporation; Buffalo; LaCie Group S.A.; Sepaton Inc.

FURTHER READING

Allen, Mike, "Firm Courting Overland Decides to Back Away," *San Diego Business Journal,* November 28, 2005, p. 9.

———, "Overland Data Reports Cutbacks," *San Diego Business Journal,* April 30, 2001, p. 10.

———, "Overland Hires New CEO After Struggling Through Tough Fiscal Year," *San Diego Business Journal,* August 20, 2007, p. 8.

———, "Overland Loses More," *San Diego Business Journal,* May 7, 2007, p. 15.

———, "Overland Pulls Back," *San Diego Business Journal,* August 14, 2006, p. 41.

———, "Pesky Rumors of Overland Sale Won't Go Away," *San Diego Business Journal,* October 17, 2005, p. 12.

Biggar, Heidi, "Overland, ADIC Diversify Core Businesses," *InfoStar,* July 2002, p. 8.

Cecil, Mark, "Advanced May Ultimately Overlook Overland," *Mergers & Acquisitions Report,* October 24, 2005.

Fass, Ilona, "Spotlight on … Overland Data," *Computer Technology Review,* April 2001, p. 53.

Kovar, Joseph F., "Storage Is Prime Target—Slew of Acquisitions Highlight Growing Interest in Technology," *Computer Reseller News,* January 2000, p. 76.

"Overland Buys Okapi," *Client Server News,* June 30, 2003, p. 10.

"Overland Buys Zetta as Part of Ongoing Overhaul," *eWeek,* August 9, 2005.

"Overland Data" *San Diego Business Journal,* March 27, 2000.

"Overland Data Announces Initial Public Offering of 3 Million Shares of Common Stock," *Business Wire,* February 21, 1997.

"Overland Data Breaks New Ground," *Business Wire,* March 14, 2001.

"Overland Data Expands into Asia to Support Strong Growth and Worldwide Demand," *Business Wire,* November 19, 2001.

"Overland Storage: 25 Years of Leadership in Data Protection," *PR Newswire,* September 27, 2005.

"Overland Transfers Assembly Work to San Jose Firm," *San Diego Business Journal,* September 27, 2004, p. 16.

"Overland Unveils Internet Strategy, Launches B2B E-Commerce Site," *Business Wire,* April 18, 2000.

"2004 Best Companies to Work for Award Winners," *San Diego Business Journal,* Advertising Supplement, February 9, 2004, pp. A3, A6.

P.W. Minor and Son, Inc.

———————————— ■ ————————————

3 Treadeasy Avenue
Batavia, New York 14020-3009
U.S.A.
Telephone: (585) 343-1500
Web site: http://www.pwminor.com

Private Company
Incorporated: 1867 as Minor Brothers Boots and Shoes
Employees: 200
Sales: $25.2 million (2007)
NAICS: 316210 Footwear Manufacturing

■ ■ ■

P.W. Minor and Son, Inc., is a family-owned and operated shoe manufacturer based in Batavia, New York. While the vast majority of U.S. shoemakers have gone out of business due to foreign competition, Minor has carved out a niche producing specialized men's and women's footwear in a wide range of sizes and widths, targeting people suffering from diabetes, arthritis, and foot trauma, and others who are simply in the market for comfortable shoes. The shoes feature deep toe boxes as well as extra depth to accommodate special insoles and other orthotics, and can be adjusted for a better fit. People with diabetes, for example, have poor circulation and lack sensitivity to pain, requiring shoes with extra room to avoid the development of painful foot conditions. People with arthritic feet also require ample room as well as extra cushioning and shock absorption. Other conditions mitigated by Minor footwear include bunions, enlargements between the big toe and second

toe, requiring shoes with extra large shoe boxes; hammertoes, a condition often caused by poor fitting shoes that causes toes to bend downward; metatargalgia, a painful condition related to the imbalance of the metatarsal bones that support the body during walking; and plantar faciitis, an inflammation that causes pain under the heel when walking or running.

A key to Minor's success is the sense of style the company has brought to medical shoes, long known for being boxy and bland looking. Product lines include Smart Casual, Classic Casual, Dress Collection, Athletic Collection, Boot Collection, and the Medical Collection, which includes dress, casual, work, and athletics shoes, and boots. A network of qualified dealers sell Minor shoes and boots, many of them specializing in orthopedic footwear and keeping a Certified Pedorthist on staff to make sure customers' feet are accurately measured and the shoes properly fitted. Minor shoes are also available through a handful of online retail partners. Through the Treadeasy Foot Care division of subsidiary Prime Materials Corporation, P.W. Minor offers fitting and evaluation devices, casting products, shoe inserts, and heat-moldable inlays. Prime Materials is also a full-service foam converter for the footwear as well as aerospace, automotive, construction, and other industries.

POST–CIVIL WAR ROOTS

The man behind the "P.W." name was Peter Wycoff Minor, the son of a hardware store owner in Interlaken, New York, located in the Finger Lakes region between Syracuse and Binghamton. He and his brother, Abraham

Vorhees Minor, would become partners in the shoe manufacturing business. Both were young men when the Civil War began in 1861. According to a story told to the press by the great-grandson of A. V. Minor, company president Hank Minor, the two were foot solders who, during their long walk home following the Civil War, discussed their futures. One of them asked, "You want to go back into business with father?" The other replied, "Nope. Do you?" Perhaps inspired by aching feet from their journey, they decided to make shoes and boots.

Letters written in the 1950s by A. V. Minor's son, Halsey Parshall Minor, tell a different story, however. The two brothers enlisted in the army at the same time, but they wielded brass musical instruments instead of rifles. They played in a band for parade and drill, never traveling farther south than Elmira, New York. Other Minor brothers did see action, including Henry, who was captured by the Confederates and held captive in the infamous Libby Prison in Richmond, Virginia. P. W. and A. V. Minor traveled after the war to bring home their brother, who was in "wretched condition." It was perhaps then that they might have discussed their future plans, but it was unlikely they made the journey with their invalid brother on foot.

ENTERING THE SHOE BUSINESS IN 1867

Halsey Minor's letters contend that after the war they, in fact, first tried their hand at show business before turning to the shoe business. Their army band went to work with Stow Brothers circus, but flooding on the Wabash River hindered the movement of the show, which broke up in Covington, Indiana. It looked like a promising community, and P. W. Minor and his wife decided to settle here. They soon grew homesick, however, and returned to Interlaken, where, in the spring of 1867, P. W. Minor opened a general store with a man named Jim Benjamin. They were soon joined by A. V. Minor. They sold shoes at the store, which burned down later in the year. They reopened the store on the corner of Main Street and Cayuga Street, and in the rear

of the building, they began to make men's shoes and boots.

The shoe manufacturing business took the name Minor Brothers Boots and Shoes. A. V. Minor served as the salesman, traveling by horse and wagon once a week to take orders, while P. W. Minor served as superintendent of the small factory. The business did well enough that the factory was relocated to a larger, two-story building at the corner of Mechanic Street and Main. Here Minor Brothers began making ladies' shoes as well.

The business was then moved to Auburn, New York, and a new partner, Walter Ogden, was taken on as a partner. Later the factory returned to Interlaken, established in an empty skating rink on Cayuga Street. Ogden sold his interest and A. V. Minor left the business as well, purchasing the site at Main and Cayuga to open a grocery store, which Halsey Minor would one day buy and operate for half a century.

COMPANY MOVES TO BATAVIA, NEW YORK: 1921

The shoe company took the name P. W. Minor and Son. The factory remained in Interlaken until 1921 when the business was moved to Batavia, New York. The company began to struggle and was on the verge of collapse during the 1920s when A. V. Minor's son, Henry Minor Sr., stepped in to take charge and turn it around. He had been employed by a shoe manufacturer in Auburn and brought in a new group of people to run the business. He would also bring his children into the business.

Henry "Bud" Minor Jr. joined the company in the late 1940s. Soon his father retired, leaving him responsible for the business but greatly lacking in experience. A few months later the company was near ruin, the bank threatening to foreclose in six months. Bud Minor pleaded with the banks, which granted six additional months to stabilize the business. Over the next year he managed to save the company and keep it in the family.

By the 1960s Bud Minor was well seasoned in the shoe business. His company's focus was on traditional women's shoes, but it was becoming obvious that the economics of the industry were undergoing rapid change. It became increasingly difficult to manufacture in the United States and remain competitive with shoes produced overseas where inexpensive labor was abundant. Rather than shut the doors of the company or take production offshore, Bud Minor made the key decision to focus on therapeutic footwear, which was just beginning to develop as a niche. It was a switch that

KEY DATES

1867: The Minor Brothers Boots and Shoes company is established in Interlaken, New York.

1921: P.W. Minor & Son moves to Batavia, New York.

1972: The company's factory is relocated to a Batavia industrial park.

1977: A move to North Carolina is rejected.

1986: Henry Minor III joins the company.

2000: The Treadeasy Footcare Products Division is formed.

2001: The Prime Materials Corporation is created to acquire Treadeasy.

2006: The company's Smart Casual Collection for Women is introduced.

2008: The Smart Casual Collection for Men is added.

saved the family business. After losing money in the 1960s, the company would turn profitable and remain so, while thousands of U.S. shoe manufacturers fell by the wayside.

FACTORY MOVES TO INDUSTRIAL PARK: 1972

With business picking up, P.W. Minor moved its operations to an industrial park in Batavia in 1972. Five years later, the company was given an opportunity to relocate the business to North Carolina, where labor was cheaper and, at the time, the apparel industry was booming. The Minor family decided to remain in western New York, recognizing that the company's skilled workforce, although higher paid, was a key to the success of P.W. Minor. By the end of the 1970s, the company was generating annual sales of about $10 million.

Well into the 1980s, P.W. Minor, although finding a way to survive, was seen as little more than a little old ladies' shoe company. That would begin to change in 1986 when Henry "Hank" Minor III joined P.W. Minor after working at a Boston consulting firm for several years. He soon replaced his father as president. Improvements were made on a number of fronts.

Instead of uninspiring black-and-white catalogs, the company began producing color catalogs, professional slicks for newspaper ads, and point-of-purchase materials to help retailers sell P.W. Minor shoes. More

importantly, the company embraced contemporary styling to make the shoes more appealing to consumers, an increasing number of whom were buying the shoes for comfort and not by prescription. P.W. Minor also improved its relationship to retailers by maintaining a large stock of sizes and widths, becoming a highly reliable shoe source.

As a result P.W. Minor become one of the top brands of specialty shoe dealers and enjoyed an annual growth rate of 10 to 12 percent into the early 1990s. For its 125th anniversary, the company in 1992 introduced its first "dating" program, providing accounts with a 2 percent discount and 125 days to pay. A coupon program was also launched. Dealers could hand out as many coupons as desired and customers could complete them for entry in a monthly drawing in which several people won a new pair of P.W. Minor shoes.

REGULATORY CHANGES FAVOR P.W. MINOR

Another important factor in the growth of P.W. Minor in the 1990s was the graying of America. Baby boomers were entering the age range that could especially benefit from the therapeutic footwear offered by P.W. Minor, creating a quickly growing pool of potential new customers. Moreover, this generation was expected to live longer than previous ones and could be expected to experience more health problems and foot problems. Also of help to the business was the 1993 decision by the federal government to reimburse Medicare patients for the cost of therapeutic shoes related to severe diabetic foot disease.

Although other shoe manufacturers were tempted to venture into the therapeutic footwear business, P.W. Minor remained well positioned because potential rivals lacked the expertise needed to compete. In addition to that barrier, they would also have to be willing to carry about 140 sizes and widths for every shoe pattern and color to be a viable player in the field—a costly investment with no guarantee of acceptance by specialty retailers who had already built solid relationships with P.W. Minor and the other established therapeutic shoe companies.

By the late 1990s P.W. Minor was posting sales in the $20 million range and making inroads in global distribution. The company's primary product was its Xtra Depth line, accounting for about 80 of more than 100 styles. A half-inch to a quarter-inch deeper than most shoes, the Xtra Depth shoes were ideally suited for custom orthotics. P.W. Minor also offered the Thermold line, which, with the application of heat, could be molded to conform to deformities or adapt to other foot problems.

The company's five-year plan during this period was to add even more product lines in its therapeutic niche. In early 2000 P.W. Minor unveiled the Treadeasy Footcare Products Division, to become more of a total footcare products company. The new line included fitting and evaluation devices, casting products, fabrication and modification materials, shoe horns, and a variety of orthotics, geared toward specialty shoe stores as well as orthotic and prosthetic services centers, pedorthic labs, and repair shops. In 2001 P.W. Minor expanded the scope of this venture by establishing Prime Materials Corporation, which acquired Treadeasy, and made its foam converting services available to outside footwear companies and other industries.

SMART CASUAL LINE FOR WOMEN ADDED: 2006

P.W. Minor also added to its footwear styles, introducing the Xsensibles line of men's and women's footwear in 2000. Made mostly in Portugal, the Xsensibile collection offered a variety of leathers and colors, a further attempt to improve the style and look of orthopedic shoes. The Batavia factory continued to turn out about 1,000 pairs of shoes a day, the result of as many as 200 manufacturing steps, all completed under a single roof, unlike overseas operations when a single operation might be performed by an entire factory. Some of the steps still involved old-fashioned stamps and presses, but designs were being done on computers, and computer-guided cutting machines sliced sheets of leather and pelts.

To keep pace with the demands of its baby boomer customer base, the company's designers continued to look to improve the styling of the shoes. In 2006, the company introduced its Smart Casual Collection for women. Building on that success, a Smart Casual Collection for men was launched in the spring of 2008, followed by a line of men's upscale dress shoes. These new lines were expected to drive sales in the years to come, as would inroads into the global marketplace.

The company added new countries to its distribution on a regular basis. Its key international markets were found in Australia, Canada, and the United Kingdom. In 2008 Mike Minor, a fifth-generation member of the founding family who began working in the factory as a teenager, was preparing to lead the company into the future.

Ed Dinger

PRINCIPAL SUBSIDIARIES

Prime Materials Corporation.

PRINCIPAL COMPETITORS

Acor Orthopaedic, Inc.; Ecco Shoes International; Mephisto S.A.

FURTHER READING

Beardi, Cara, "Shoe Company in Batavia Is Operated 'Like a Family,'" *Buffalo News,* July 28, 1998, p. D3.

Blackwell, Jeffrey, "Shoemaker Fits Tight Niche," *Rochester Democrat and Chronicle,* February 22, 2002, p. 12D.

Hartley, Tom, "Stepping Boldly," *Business First of Buffalo,* June 1, 1998, p. 17.

"P.W. Minor Breaks Out of Pedorthic Box with More Fashionable Line," *Footwear News,* October 16, 2000, p. 25.

Rieger, Nancy, "Major Changes Keep Minor Ahead," *Footwear News,* June 1, 1992, p. 16.

Schneider-Levy, Barbara, "New Frontier," *Footwear News,* October 1, 2007, p. 14.

———, "Treading Forward," *Footwear News,* April 17, 2000, p. 17.

Palfinger AG

—————•—————

Franz-Wolfram-Scherer-Strasse 24
Bergheim-Salzburg, A-5101
Austria
Telephone: (43 0662) 46 84
Fax: (43 0662) 45 00 84
Web site: http://www.palfinger.com

Public Company
Incorporated: 1932
Employees: 4,377
Sales: EUR 800 million ($1 billion) (2008)
Stock Exchanges: Vienna
Ticker Symbol: PAL
NAICS: 333120 Construction Machinery Manufacturing; 333923 Overhead Traveling Crane, Hoist, and Monorail System Manufacturing

■ ■ ■

Palfinger AG is one of Europe's leading manufacturers of truck-mounted cranes and other equipment for lifting, loading, and handling materials. The Bergheim-Salzburg, Austria-based company has long been one of the world's largest producers of knuckle-boom cranes. The company claims a global market share of 30 percent in this category, which also accounts for the largest part of the group's turnover. Palfinger has also successfully diversified into other lifting and handling categories, notably through a string of acquisitions.

The company's other production units include tail-lifts from MBB (Germany), Omaha Standard (USA), and Ratcliff (UK); work platforms from Wumag and Bison (both Germany); Stepa farm and telescopic cranes (through Madal, in Brazil); and Crayler transportable forklifts. The company also produces bridge inspection units, as well as specialized handling and work equipment for the railroad industry. Palfinger has established a global presence, with sales and distribution partnerships in 130 countries, and factories in 14 countries. More than 90 percent of the group's revenues, expected to top EUR 800 million in 2008, were generated outside of Austria. Listed on the Vienna Stock Exchange, Palfinger remains majority controlled by the founding Palfinger family. Herbert Ortner is the group's chief executive officer.

ORIGINS IN FARM VEHICLES SERVICES

Richard Palfinger founded a business repairing farm vehicles in Austria in 1932. Palfinger's workshop provided both repair services and fitting services, adapting a variety of trailers, tippers, bodies, and other attachments for farm machinery of the period. These activities eventually led the company to begin designing its own attachments and farm equipment. The wholesale adoption of mechanized equipment by the agricultural sector during the 1950s represented an important opportunity for the Palfinger family, including eldest son Hubert, who had joined the family business. During this time, the company shifted the focus of its business from the repair and services side to the production side. After developing a number of its own agricultural equipment designs, Palfinger turned to what was to become the group's specialty. In 1959, Palfinger built its first crane.

Into the next decade, the company invested in

developing its expertise in crane construction, adding the first hydraulic systems. Hubert Palfinger then took over as head of the company, and led it in its new direction. In 1964, the company decided to focus on the truck-loaded hydraulic crane market. For this, Palfinger invested in new production facilities, and by 1966 the company had shifted its manufacturing from its former workshop method to serial production methods.

Hydraulic truck-loading cranes became especially popular in Europe. The narrow streets of the region's cities played a role in this preference, as the smaller vehicles provided lifting and handling capabilities in more confined spaces. The truck-loaded crane also permitted more efficient operations; the combination of flatbed and crane enabled a single vehicle both to transport and offload materials and merchandise. This type of vehicle also permitted a reduction in personnel.

Palfinger's designs quickly caught the attention of customers beyond Austria. The new production capacity enabled the company to fill its first international orders, to France and Switzerland, by 1966. In this way, the company overcame the drawbacks of the relatively small Austrian market. At the same time, Palfinger invested strongly in developing its own technology. The company's engineering and design efforts paid off as early as 1971, when Palfinger received two patents. The first was for its "hydraulic lift instantaneous control system" while the second was for its cylindrical design of the crane extension system.

MORE PATENTS AND NEW MARKETS

Other important patents followed. These included the patent in 1973 for the company's mast grab, which enabled Palfinger to market its cranes as multifunctional equipment. Even more important was Palfinger's patent for a foldable boom, awarded in 1976. The new design permitted cranes to achieve a far longer reach, as the booms were folded over the flatbed for easier transport. Knuckle-boom cranes then became a company specialty. By this time, Palfinger had moved to

new and larger production facilities in Bergheim-Salzburg, which also became the site of the group's headquarters. From there, Palfinger oversaw its continued engineering development effort. This resulted in the launch of a new patent in 1978. Palfinger's extension cylinder system helped establish an industry standard. Another company success was its design for underwater cranes, launched in 1980, for use in pipeline construction for the offshore oil industry.

Into the 1980s, the company also built up expertise in crane control and safety systems. In 1981, for example, Palfinger debuted its compensated overload safety system. Through the decade, the company also extended its range of products. In 1988, the group launched a new crane system, the Epsilon, specifically for use in forestry and recycling applications. The company added another specialized crane family, Stepa, which focused on the farm crane market, in 1990. This was followed by the launch of Palfinger Railway, which, as its name suggested, developed specialized cranes and other equipment for the railroad sector.

Palfinger's work on extending its product line and technical expertise also helped raise the group's international profile. Through the 1980s, Palfinger's foreign sales had grown strongly. By the end of the decade, more than 90 percent of Palfinger's revenues came from outside of Austria. By then, the company had established itself as the world's second largest manufacturer of truck-mounted cranes. Palfinger's reach extended to 70 countries.

INTERNATIONAL PRODUCTION

These came to include the North American market at the start of the 1990s. The company launched a Canadian subsidiary in 1990, opening a warehouse in North Tonawanda. This was complemented by the opening of a new 50,000-square-foot manufacturing-warehouse-office complex in Niagara Falls, Ontario. The new site, which included a 25,000-square-foot production facility, provided a boost to the company's North American presence. However, the region, with its wider streets and larger building lots, remained a more limited market for truck-loaded cranes than Palfinger's core European market.

Austria's position in the Central European region, and its constitutional neutrality, presented new market opportunities with the collapse of the Communist eastern bloc. In 1993, the company added its first manufacturing facilities in that region, with a factory in Maribor, in Slovenia. By 1995, the company had begun sourcing booms from Beta, based in Cherven Brjag, in Bulgaria. Palfinger later acquired control of Beta's fac-

KEY DATES

1932: Richard Palfinger establishes a repair workshop in Austria.

1959: Palfinger produces its first crane design.

1964: Palfinger shifts focus to the truck-loaded hydraulic crane market.

1976: Palfinger receives a patent for a foldable boom and becomes a knuckle-boom crane specialist.

1990: Palfinger establishes a North American subsidiary in Canada.

1999: Palfinger goes public; acquires French hook-loader leader Guima.

2005: Palfinger purchases Ratcliff Group's Tail Lifts factory in Welwyn, England.

2007: Palfinger acquires MBB Liftsystems, becoming a global tail-lift leader.

2008: Palfinger acquires Omaha Standard in the United States.

tory, which became the site of the group's crane boom production starting in 1999.

Palfinger remained at the forefront of crane technologies during the decade as well. In 1992, the company introduced a new, patented, sequential control system. The company also received a patent for its swing-up stabilizer design, as well as for a return oil utilization system for its loading cranes, introduced in 1992. Palfinger also invested in its programming capacity, launching among others the COSSAN system of weld analysis and optimization in 1996. Another technological breakthrough came in 1998, with the launch of the Palfinger Active Oscillation Suppression system. The following year, Palfinger debuted its patented hydraulic overload safety system.

While knuckle-boom cranes remained the company's flagship line through the beginning of the new century, Palfinger actively sought to diversify its handling equipment catalog. This effort took off in the 1990s. In 1996, the company added its first hook loaders, under the Palift name. This was followed by the company launch of the Crayler transportable forklift in 1997. These additions to Palfinger's product lines were backed up by the opening of a new factory, dedicated to the production of Epsilon cranes, in Elsbethen in 1999. Palfinger's strong growth during the 1990s also enabled it to claim the world leadership in the knuckle-boom crane segment, beating out longtime rival Hiab.

ACQUIRING SCALE IN THE 21ST CENTURY

Palfinger set into motion a new expansion phase at the end of the century. In 1999, Palfinger went public, listing its shares on the Vienna Stock Exchange. While the Palfinger family retained majority control of the group's shares (62% in 2008), the public offering provided the company with the capital needed for its new growth strategy. Much of this strategy was based on carrying out an ambitious acquisition program to reinforce the group's international production capacity, as well as provide new product extensions. For this the group turned first to France, where it bought Guima SA. That purchase gave the company control of the global number two producer of hook-loaders.

Next, Palfinger moved to the United States, where it acquired that country's Tiffin Loader Cranes, which had previously been Palfinger's exclusive U.S. dealer. This purchase provided the basis for the creation of a U.S. subsidiary, Palfinger USA Inc., in 2001. Also that year, Palfinger established a production presence in the South American market, acquiring Brazil's Madal SA. Madal specialized in producing hydraulic truck cranes and other farm-use hydraulic lifting equipment, claiming the South American leadership in this category with operations in ten countries.

The difficult economic climate at the beginning of the decade led to a restructuring of Palfinger's manufacturing operations. Into the middle of the decade, Palfinger shifted an increasing amount of its production out of higher-wage areas including Austria, France, and other Western European markets. Instead, the company invested in its foreign manufacturing capacity. The company acquired a second factory in Slovenia in 2001. Two years later, the group purchased a new plant in Tenevo, Bulgaria, to which it transferred production of its hydraulic cylinders in 2004. The company also began acquiring its structural steel supplier, PiR, based in Rijeka, Croatia, taking a 20 percent share in 2001. By 2007, the company had taken full control of PiR.

Palfinger also continued to carry out the second prong of its expansion strategy, adding new product lines. In 2000, Palfinger debuted its Mobiler container transfer system. This was followed by the introduction of a tail-lift system, Palgate, in 2001. In South America, the company expanded its range to include telescopic cranes. By 2003, the company had added its own line of lifting platforms, dubbed ACCESS.

The acquisition of Bison, based in Germany, in 2004, marked another major milestone for the company, adding not only that company's line of truck-mounted aerial work platforms but also boosting Palfinger's access to the significant German market. Palfinger returned to Germany in 2007, buying MBB Liftsystems AG, one of the world's largest manufacturers of tail-lift vehicles. By then, Palfinger's operations in that category included its purchase of Ratcliff Group's Tail Lifts factory in Welwyn, England, acquired in 2005.

Palfinger's acquisitions continued into 2008, and included Wumag GmbH, in Germany, a leading producer of truck-mounted work and access platforms in that market. By September of that year, Palfinger increased its U.S. presence as well, buying Omaha Standard, a leading producer of truck bodies and pickup tail lifts. At the same time, Palfinger had begun to seek new markets in the Asian region. The company established a Singapore-based subsidiary in 2006, and then opened an assembly facility in Shenzhen, China. In 2007, Palfinger entered India, launching a distribution joint venture to that market with Dubai-based Western Auto LLC. As one of the world's leading truck-mounted crane specialists, Palfinger had raised its expectations high for the 21st century.

M. L. Cohen

PRINCIPAL SUBSIDIARIES

Bison Palfinger GmbH; China Palfinger (Shenzhen) Ltd. (China); Croatia PiR metal d.o.o.; Guima Palfinger S.A.S. (France); Interlift Inc. (United States); Madal Palfinger S.A. (Brazil); MBB HUBFIX s.r.o. (Slovakia); MBB Inter S.A.S. (France); MBB Liftsystems AG; Palfinger Asia Pacific Pte Ltd (Singapore); Palfinger Europe GmbH; Palfinger France S.A.; Palfinger Gru Idrauliche S.r.l. (Italy); Palfinger Inc. (Canada); Palfinger Southern Africa (Pty) Ltd.; Palfinger USA, Inc.; Ratcliff Palfinger Ltd. (United Kingdom); Tiffin Loader Crane Company (United States).

PRINCIPAL COMPETITORS

Siemens AG; Caterpillar Inc.; APAC Inc.; MAN AG; Deere and Co.; Komatsu Ltd.; Konecranes PLC; Manitou BF S.A.; Bauer AG; CNH UK Ltd.; Imtech Deutschland GmbH and Company KG.

FURTHER READING

"Austrian Crane Maker to Open Falls Plant," *Business First of Buffalo,* September 24, 1990, p. 33.

Ebisch, Robert, "Will Knuckle Booms Ever Break into the USA?" *Cranes Today,* March 2008, p. 39.

Gale, Lindsay, "Catalyst for Change?" *Access International,* November–December 2004, p. 11.

Hayes, David, "Load Warriors," *Cranes Today,* August 2005, p. 28.

Keenan, John, "'Perfect Fit' Helps Seal Purchase," *Omaha World-Herald,* October 4, 2008.

Morais, Richard C., "Die Familie Firma," *Forbes,* July 21, 2008, p. 94.

North, Will, "Made in Bulgaria," *Cranes Today,* October 2007, p. 13.

"Palfinger Acquires Omaha Standard," *Trailer/Body Builders,* September 29, 2008.

"Palfinger Hits New Heights," *Cranes Today,* March 2004, p. 9.

"Palfinger Profits Continue to Rise," *Cranes Today,* June 2006, p. 9.

"Palfinger Signs Distribution JV in India," *Cranes Today,* October 2007, p. 13.

GIVENCHY PARIS

Parfums Givenchy S.A.

— ■ —

77 rue Anatole France
Levallois Perret, F-92532 Cedex
France
Telephone: (33 01 40) 89 60 00
Fax: (33 01 73) 02 61 21
Web site: http://www.parfums.givenchy.com

*Wholly Owned Subsidiary of LVMH Moët Hennessy Louis
    Vuitton S.A.*
Incorporated: 1957
Employees: 700
Sales: EUR 280 million ($340.6 million) (2007 est.)
NAICS: 325620 Toilet Preparation Manufacturing

■ ■ ■

Parfums Givenchy is one of the world's best-known
fragrance and cosmetic companies. The company also
boasts one of the greatest names in fashion history,
although Parfums Givenchy operates separately from the
Givenchy fashion house. Both companies are part of
luxury products group LVMH Moët Hennessy Louis
Vuitton. Parfums Givenchy develops, designs, and
markets its own line of both men's and women's
fragrances, including "Ange ou Démon," launched in
2007, "Very Irresistible Givenchi," and "Givenchy Pi
Neo," introduced in 2008. In celebration of the
company's 50th anniversary in 2007, Parfums Givenchy
also reissued a number of the most popular perfumes of
its past, including the iconic "L'Interdit," originally created for actress Audrey Hepburn in the 1950s. While
fragrances make up the largest part of Parfums

Givenchy's sales of approximately EUR 280 million
($340 million), the company has balanced its portfolio
with its own lines of cosmetics and skin care products.
Parfums Givenchy also lends its name to a number of
independently operating spas, which pay licensing fees
for the use of the Givenchy name and its products.
Alain Lorenzo is president of Parfums Givenchy.

FOUNDING A FRAGRANCE ICON

Hubert James Taffin de Givenchy was born in Beauvais
in 1927. In 1945, at the age of 17, Givenchy moved to
Paris, where he served in a series of apprenticeships and
assistant's positions to many of that city's noted designers of the time. After stints with Robert Piguet, Lucien
Lelong, and finally Elsa Schiaparelli, Givenchy decided
to go into business on his own, and founded his own
house in 1952.

The following year, however, marked a major moment in Givenchy's career. In that year, Givenchy met
legendary Spanish designer Cristóbal Balenciaga, who
became the younger Givenchy's mentor and close friend
until Balenciaga's death in 1972. Balenciaga was to
prove crucial in helping Givenchy make a number of
decisions that would catapult him into the center of the
Parisian—and world—fashion scene.

Another encounter in 1953 was to prove equally
important to Givenchy's career, both as a couturier and
in his entry into the designer fragrance market.
Givenchy had been given word that American director
Billy Wilder was sending over a "Miss Hepburn" for a
makeover during the shooting of the film *Sabrina*. The
young Givenchy was expecting to receive Hollywood

legend Katharine Hepburn in his studios. Instead, Givenchy received another Hepburn, who was soon to become a screen legend in her own right and who would play an important part in helping Givenchy himself achieve international fame.

Audrey Hepburn was at the time an up-and-coming actress, having just won the Oscar for best actress for her role in William Wyler's *Roman Holiday* the year before. The designer provided her with some fashions for her role in *Sabrina,* and Givenchy and Hepburn quickly became friends, with Hepburn becoming both Givenchy's muse and major ambassador for many years. The match between Hepburn and Givenchy's designs was said by some observers to have provided one of the most important influences on clothing fashions in the late 20th century.

Givenchy's fame soared with that of Hepburn, who wore the Parisian designer's clothing in many of her subsequent films, including *Love in the Afternoon* (Wilder, 1957), *Funny Face* (Donen, 1957), and *Breakfast at Tiffany's* (Edwards, 1961). Before long, Givenchy was approached by a number of pharmaceuticals groups seeking licenses to develop perfumes under his name. However, Balenciaga encouraged Givenchy to launch his own fragrance company instead.

Givenchy agreed, setting up a perfume division, which launched production at Balenciaga's Paris factory. Givenchy's brother was placed in charge of the group's perfumes operations, and Givenchy himself led the development of the company's fragrance collection, which debuted with "De" in 1957. While "De" was the first fragrance to be marketed by the company, Givenchy had also developed a second fragrance, a personal fragrance for Audrey Hepburn. When, in 1957, Givenchy revealed his plan to market that fragrance as well, Hepburn reportedly declared, "I forbid you." Inspired, Givenchy gave the name "L'Interdit" to the new fragrance.

Hepburn agreed to appear in the advertising campaign promoting the fragrance—marking the first time a fragrance group had teamed up a with a Hollywood star to endorse its perfumes. Unlike the many celebrities to follow this example, Hepburn took no fee for the endorsement. The success of "L'Interdit" gave Parfums Givenchy one of the world's best-selling designer fragrances. The company was especially successful in the United States, which came to represent a significant part of its sales.

LOOKING FOR A BUYER

Parfums Givenchy launched its first men's fragrances at the end of the 1950s, "Monsieur Givenchy" and "L'Eau de Vetyver." Both fragrances debuted in 1959, with the latter originally developed as Givenchy's own personal fragrance. The company's next major perfume launch came in 1970, with the release of the women's fragrance "Givenchy III," named for the address of the company's headquarters at 3 avenue George V in Paris.

The launch of Givenchy's first men's ready-to-wear collection, Gentleman Givenchy, in 1973 inspired the group's next fragrance launch. In 1975, the company introduced "Givenchy Gentleman" to complement the clothing line. The company closed out the decade with a new women's fragrance, introduced as "L'Eau de Givenchy" in 1980.

By then, Hubert Givenchy had begun looking for a buyer for the company's perfume division. In 1980, the company reached an agreement in principle to sell Parfums Givenchy to British conglomerate Beecham. However, the sale quickly met with resistance during a time when France had become increasingly jealous of allowing the icons of its cultural heritage to pass into foreign ownership.

At the insistence of French President Valerie Giscard d'Estaing, the sale to Beecham was canceled. Instead, the French government, through its IDI investment vehicle, agreed to purchase Parfums Givenchy. The acquisition provided the company with the time needed to find a new French home. This led the company to Veuve Cliquot, one of France's most venerable Champagne houses. In 1981, Veuve Cliquot agreed to pay FRF 160 million (approximately $30 million) to acquire IDI's 75 percent stake in Parfums Givenchy. Hubert Givenchy maintained a 25 percent share in the perfume company. As part of the sale agreement, Veuve Cliquot also received the right of first refusal, should Givenchy decide to sell the designer clothing house as well.

Veuve Cliquot's purchase of Parfums Givenchy became part of an ongoing trend in the French luxury

KEY DATES

1952: Hubert Givenchy founds his own fashion house in Paris.

1957: Givenchy forms Parfums Givenchy, which has its first success with "L'Interdit," designed for Audrey Hepburn.

1981: Champagne House Veuve Cliquot acquires control of Parfums Givenchy.

1988: Parfums Givenchy becomes part of the LVMH luxury products group.

1997: Parfums Givenchy becomes a centerpiece of LVMH's Perfumes & Cosmetics division.

2003: Liv Tyler becomes the face of the company's new perfume, "Very Irresistible Givenchy."

2007: Parfums Givenchy celebrates its 50th anniversary with the launch of the "Les Parfums Mythiques" collection.

goods sector, which saw the consolidation of many of the country's most prominent designer names and brands into an increasingly smaller number of diversified groups. One of the first to move in this direction had been rival Champagne house Moët et Chandon, which acquired the Christian Dior label in the early 1970s.

BECOMING PART OF LVMH MOËT HENNESSY LOUIS VUITTON

Parfums Givenchy grew strongly as part of Veuve Cliquot, in part by taking advantage of its new parent's strong international distribution network. The company also launched a highly successful product in 1984. The new perfume, "Ysatis," became one of its strongest sellers, particularly in the United States. By the mid-1980s, "Ysatis" accounted for nearly 78 percent of the group's U.S. volume. Its success also helped push the group's total revenues to $83 million at that time. The success of "Ysatis" also inspired Parfums Givenchy to create its first new men's fragrance since the mid-1970s. This resulted in the launch of the "Keryus" men's line, including an eau de toilette and an aftershave, in 1986.

The consolidation of the French luxury-goods sector took additional steps forward in the late 1980s. Veuve Cliquot raised its stake in Parfums Givenchy to nearly 100 percent by the middle of the decade. In 1987, Veuve Cliquot agreed to be acquired by the Louis Vuitton group in a deal worth nearly $800 million. By the following year, Louis Vuitton had itself been merged into the new French luxury goods powerhouse, LVMH Moët Hennessy Louis Vuitton. That company exercised its right to acquire the Givenchy design house in 1988. This marked a reunion of sorts between Givenchy and Parfums Givenchy, although the companies remained separate operations under the LVMH roof.

Parfums Givenchy achieved new success at the beginning of the 1990s, with the introduction of the "Amarige" fragrance line in 1991. The company next sought to extend its brand into new territory, the young women's (under 20 years) market, filling a longstanding gap in the group's portfolio with the launch of "Fleur d'Interdit." The new fragrance marked a departure from the group's more floral or woody scents, providing a "fruity floral" note designed to appeal to younger consumers. The new perfume was also at a lower price point within the Givenchy brand, allowing the company to compete with such youth-oriented rivals as Calvin Klein's CK One and Elizabeth Arden's Sunflowers. The growing purchasing power of this market segment into the 1990s made it a highly attractive one for the company. At the same time, the group hoped to develop a longer-term relationship with these customers as they matured.

Starting in the late 1980s, Parfums Givenchy began diversifying in order to reduce its reliance on the perfume sector, where sales typically occurred in the second half of the year. To develop a more balanced cash flow throughout the year, the company decided to launch its first cosmetics and skin care lines in 1989. By the middle of the 1990s, these products combined to generate some 20 percent of the company's total revenues, which reached a total of $260 million in volume in 1995.

The launch of the skin care and cosmetics lines also led the company into a new direction: spas. For this, the company licensed its name and products to third-party investors. The first Givenchy luxury spa opened in Versailles in 1992. By the end of the decade, new spas had opened in the United States, the United Kingdom, Egypt, and elsewhere, and toward the end of the next decade, there were seven Givenchy spas in operation around the world.

GOING GLOBAL

As part of the LVMH group, Parfums Givenchy was able to choose between remaining a relatively small niche player in the perfume market, or, backed by LVMH's financial, marketing, and distribution might, transform itself into a global fragrance player. In 1994, a new management team, led by a new company president, Alain Lorenzo, decided to take the latter route. By 1996, the company prepared a new fragrance, "Organza" and backed up its launch with its largest marketing effort to date, spending some $50 million to promote the brand.

The launch was accompanied by a changing of the guard at the Givenchy couture house as well. Hubert Givenchy retired in 1996, and the company brought in high-profile designer John Galliano. The excitement generated by Galliano's arrival spilled over into the Parfums Givenchy brand as well. The importance of brand and brand positioning was underscored when Parfums Givenchy successfully fought a court battle to maintain its policy of limited distribution. In this way, the company's products remained exclusive to higher-end retail channels.

By 1997, Parfums had become one of the centerpieces of the newly formed Perfumes & Cosmetics Group within LVMH, which boasted combined sales of more than $1.5 billion. The operations of the new division soon included control of the Sephora retail perfumery chain, providing a new and fast-growing outlet for Parfums Givenchy fragrances.

Givenchy launched several new fragrances toward the dawn of the new century, including the men's fragrance "Pi," introduced in 1999, and the women's fragrances "Oblique" and "Hot Couture." Throughout much of the 1990s, the company backed up its marketing with the use of a number of international supermodels, including future French first lady Carla Bruni, Laetitia Casta, Eva Herzigova, and Yasmeen Ghauri.

In the 21st century, however, Parfums Givenchy returned to its Hollywood beginnings. In 2003, the company tapped rising starlet Liv Tyler as the face for the launch of its latest perfume, "Very Irresistible Givenchy." The relationship between Givenchy and Tyler quickly deepened, as the company once again turned to Tyler to support the launch of a new cosmetics line, called "Givenchy Le Makeup," which debuted in 2004.

The company developed a new men's fragrance, "Very Irresistible Givenchy for Men," in 2005, followed by the debut of a new women's fragrance, "Ange ou Démon," in 2006. The advertising campaign for that fragrance featured Marie Steiss, daughter of then-French Prime Minister Dominique de Villepin. The company also debuted an extension of the popular "Amarige" line that year, called "Amarige Wedding."

Celebrating its 50th anniversary in 2007, Parfums Givenchy decided to revisit its own history, creating a new collection called "Les Parfums Mythiques," based on its past fragrance successes. The collection included re-creations of the original "L'Interdit," as well as "Vetyver," "Givenchy III," and seven others.

Parfums Givenchy also continued to look forward in the new century. In 2008, the group unveiled its latest men's fragrance, dubbed "Givenchy Pi Neo." For the launch of the new fragrance, the company recruited more star power, in the form of pop singer Justin Timberlake. Parfums Givenchy thus appeared to be poised to carry on its long tradition as one of the world's preeminent fragrance companies.

M. L. Cohen

PRINCIPAL SUBSIDIARIES

Givenchy Corp. (United States); Givenchy Japan KK; Givenchy S.A.; Koret Inc. (United States); Parfums Givenchy (Argentina); Parfums Givenchy Inc. (United States); Parfums Givenchy Italia S.R.L. (Italy); Parfums Givenchy KK (Japan); Parfums Givenchy Ltd. (United Kingdom); Parfums Givenchy Spain.

PRINCIPAL COMPETITORS

PPR S.A.; Christian Dior S.A; L'Oréal S.A.; Alliance Boots Holdings Ltd.; Gillette Co.; Coty Argentina S.A.; Estée Lauder Companies Inc.; Shiseido Company Ltd.; Liz Claiborne Inc.

FURTHER READING

Aktar, Alev, "Givenchy Takes Aim at Top Scent Ranks, Boosts Ad Budgets," *WWD*, December 13, 1996, p. 1.

Born, Pete, "Givenchy Widens Its Sights," *WWD*, June 24, 1994, p. 5.

Costello, Brid, "Givenchy's Irresistible Man," *WWD*, May 27, 2005, p. 7.

———, "A Vintage Year for Parfums Givenchy," *WWD*, September 16, 2005, p. 24.

"French Justice," *WWD*, December 20, 1996, p. 7.

Groves, Ellen, "For Its 50th, Givenchy to Relaunch 10 Scents," *WWD*, August 3, 2007, p. 8.

———, "Givenchy Plays a New Tune with Timberlake," *WWD*, February 22, 2008, p. 13.

———, "Givenchy Sets Ange ou Demon Launch," *WWD*, June 6, 2006, p. 13.

Milton, Tina, "New Story Begins at Givenchy with Launch of Ange ou Démon," *Duty Free News International*, July 1, 2006, p. 12.

Naughton, Julie, "A New Makeup for Givenchy in the US," *WWD*, July 2, 2004, p. 6.

"Reinoso's Reign," *Global Cosmetic Industry*, October 2004, p. 64.

Weil, Jennifer, and Julie Naughton, "Givenchy: Manning the Market," *WWD*, August 1, 2008, p. 4.

Peet's Coffee & Tea, Inc.

1400 Park Avenue
Emeryville, California 94608-3520
U.S.A.
Telephone: (510) 594-2100
Fax: (510) 594-2180
Web site: http://www.peets.com

Public Company
Incorporated: 1966
Employees: 3,678
Sales: $249.4 million (2007)
Stock Exchanges: NASDAQ
Ticker Symbol: PEET
NAICS: 311920 Coffee and Tea Manufacturing; 45299
   All Other Specialty Food Stores; 421990 Other
   Miscellaneous Durable Goods Wholesalers

■ ■ ■

Founded in Berkeley, California, in the mid-1960s, Peet's Coffee & Tea, Inc., encompasses nearly 180 retail stores in six states. The company also sells over 30 types of whole bean and ground coffee as well as tea through a mail-order program and on its web site, and through approximately 8,000 grocery outlets including Publix Super Markets Inc., Safeway Inc., Albertsons LLC, Ralph's Grocery Company, and Whole Foods Market Inc. Peet's focuses on offering fresh roasted whole bean coffee. Home delivery and grocery store clients receive roasted-to-order coffee directly from its new state-of-the-art roasting facility, which opened its doors in Alameda, California, in 2007.

THE FOUNDING OF PEET'S

Peet's Coffee & Tea came into being in 1966, when good coffee meant vacuum-packed percolator grind. For the preceding decade, national coffee brands had been debasing their product, incorporating an ever-higher proportion of inexpensive, tannic robusta coffee beans. Meanwhile, Alfred Peet, a Dutch immigrant with a passion for European-style dark roasts, had begun importing arabica coffee beans, which yield the strong, oily brews favored by Europeans, in the 1950s. Peet had grown up in the family's coffee and tea business in Alkmaar, Holland. After World War II, he worked in the tea trade in Indonesia.

In the mid-1960s in San Francisco, Alfred Peet began brewing his own blend of dark roast beans, which he sold at his first retail store at Walnut and Vine Streets in North Berkeley. Although some dismissed his dark-roasted coffee as tasting "burnt" the brew caught on with students, artists, writers, and musicians, and the outfit quickly became known as a small, premium purveyor of quality beans with a devoted group of followers, who accorded it cult-like status.

It would be five years before Peet's opened its second store in Menlo Park and nine more years before it opened its third outlet on Domingo Avenue in Berkeley in 1980. From the start, Peet's emphasized quality over quantity and the roasting of fine beans rather than the creation of coffee shops. In fact, Peet's deliberately focused on the sale of whole beans for home consumption and guaranteed delivery of its beans fresh from the roasting facility. Peet's was as happy to have its customers order its coffee by mail and brew their own morning cup at home as to have them come in and buy a cup of ready-made coffee. This commitment continued throughout the 1980s and 1990s. "I still consider us a specialty roaster more than a beverage bar," Jerry Baldwin, whose company took over ownership of Peet's from Alfred Peet in 1984, was quoted as saying in a 1999 *San Francisco Chronicle* article. Peet's coffee beans and teas were never vacuum-packed and were shipped within 24 hours of being roasted to order. In the store, coffee was made fresh every half hour, and no beans were allowed to stand for more than seven days.

PEET'S AND STARBUCKS

In 1984, the year espresso machines made their appearance, Jerry Baldwin bought Peet's, adding it to a portfolio that included Caravali, a wholesale coffee brand, and a small Seattle chain known as Starbucks. Inspired by Peet's, Baldwin and his two partners, Gordon Bowker and Zev Siegl, had pulled together $8,000 in cash and loans in 1971 to found Starbucks. That was when Baldwin first met Peet; in 1971, he and his partners traveled to Berkeley to learn about Peet's coffee before Alfred Peet would sell it to them for use at Starbucks. When they returned to Seattle, they served Peet's coffee for the next 18 months at their new store in the Pike Place Market. That store, just like Peet's, was designed to be more of a coffee and tea outlet than a café, and did not at the time offer espresso or muffins, or even any place to sit down. Coffee was poured free into porcelain cups for tasting, and while the customer paused to drink, Baldwin and his staff bombarded him or her with information about coffee. Sales of fresh-roasted beans and teas exceeded the owners' expectations that first year, totaling $49,000. In 1972, Starbucks opened its second store near the University of Washington, and a third store followed soon after.

In 1987, Baldwin sold Starbucks, which then had only six stores, to Howard Schultz, a former Peet's employee who had left Peet's in 1986 to start his own coffee company, Il Giornale. Baldwin's reason for selling Starbucks was that it would never be as good as Peet's. The deal included a noncompete agreement, which expired in 1992, the year that Starbucks went public and began its expansion worldwide.

The expansion of Peet's during the 1970s and 1980s was conservative by comparison. The company opened stores sporadically—one or two every year, all within northern California—and its marketing strategy was low-key. The decision to keep the company small and local was in part a conscious reflection of maintaining Alfred Peet's tradition. Baldwin emphasized quality over quantity and word-of-mouth publicity. Furthermore, Baldwin himself favored a small approach to business, based upon his own early dislike of the bureaucratic world. A native of San Francisco, Baldwin started out his work life as a bellhop and doing inventory for clothing stores. After completing a stint in the army, he took time off and traveled to Hawaii, and then went to work for Boeing in 1969 as a programmer for government contracts such as the Concorde. Eventually he left the corporate world to become an English teacher. However, while Baldwin admittedly did not like the corporate atmosphere for its bureaucracy, he acknowledged in a 1999 *Boston Globe* article that his time at Boeing gave him some idea of his capabilities.

ACCELERATING EXPANSION

The growth of Peet's picked up somewhat in 1994 after the company received a $6 million private placement from the San Francisco investment firm Hambrecht & Quist. The money allowed Peet's to open a 60,000-square-foot roastery in Emeryville, which had the capacity to supply 150 stores. Stores at this time and throughout the remainder of the 1990s averaged $1.2 million in sales annually. They cost about $350,000 to $400,000 to open, outfit, and decorate in the company's coffee-inspired colors, but each was run autonomously by its manager and reflected the style of the neighborhood in which it was located.

By 1996, sales at the approximately 30 Peet's stores, which by then sold coffee, tea, scones and muffins, and a variety of brewing accessories and equipment, totaled about $40 million. In comparison, Starbucks brought in $696.5 million from its more than 1,100 stores in the United States, Canada, Japan, and Singapore. The two regarded themselves as friendly competitors with distinct orientations. Then, in 1997, with the spread of coffee-shops still on the rise, Peet's caught the expansion bug.

KEY DATES

1966: Alfred Peet opens the first Peet's store in North Berkeley.

1971: Peet's opens its second store in Menlo Park; Jerry Baldwin and partners open the first Starbucks outlet in Seattle's Pike Place Market, selling Peet's coffee.

1980: Peet's opens a third store in Berkeley.

1984: Baldwin's group buys Peet's Coffee & Tea.

1987: Peet's owners sell the Starbucks chain to Howard Schultz.

1994: Peet's opens a 60,000-square-foot roastery in Emeryville.

1997: Peet's opens its first store outside northern California; Chris Mottern replaces Salkin as president and chief executive officer.

2001: Company goes public.

2002: Patrick O'Dea is named CEO.

2007: The company opens a new roasting facility in Alameda.

Plotting a national expansion that included opening ten to 15 new stores annually until there were several hundred Peet's stores across the country, Baldwin aimed to establish a national presence for his high-end company. "My goal is for Peet's to stay independent," he said in a 1999 *New York Times* article. "To do that, we're forced to grow. Peet's would be more vulnerable in a single market than in multiple markets." Expansion would also protect Peet's against a potential regional economic downturn.

New shops were planned to open primarily in cities where Peet's mail-order business already had a solid following. Although 45 percent of Peet's mail-order business came from Southern California, Peet's had a sizable clientele nationwide (an estimated $1 million in online sales alone in 1998), due in large part to the relocation of students and other Californians who missed their Peet's brew. Some in the business world expressed concern that the conservative Peet's could never catch up with Starbucks and faced a significant hurdle in finding affordable real estate in markets where the multitude of coffee and bagel chains had pushed prices up. Others expressed concerns about Baldwin's tightly controlling management style and the fact that, even as the company prepared for expansion, two top executives had recently left the company, and it was without a president and chief executive. In 1997, Chris Mottern replaced Samuel Salkin as president and chief executive officer.

Retired Alfred Peet himself was of the opinion that the move to expand should have occurred in the early 1990s when Starbucks began its successful growth campaign. However, Baldwin remained optimistic about carving out a market as the number two coffee chain with what he deemed the best products and execution in the industry. Peet's first growth move was to employ a Starbucks-type maneuver, opening its Pasadena store across from one of Starbucks' busiest shops in 1997, the first store outside of Northern California.

NATIONAL GROWTH

Even as Peet's looked to a national market, it remained insistent upon not becoming so large that individual stores lost their neighborhood feel or that the company replaced quality with consistency as some of its competitor chains had. Most employees were part-time, but all received benefits. In order to avoid problems with theft and poor performance, servers were interviewed twice, and all were offered stock options. Peet's also remained committed to putting money back into the communities it served both at home and overseas. The company supported Coffee Kids, an international nonprofit organization dedicated to improving the life of children and families in coffee-growing communities, and sponsored an annual seven-day bike ride to raise funds for HIV/AIDS-related medical care and public awareness. All stores upheld Peet's longtime tradition of serving drinks free on Christmas and the anniversary of its opening, a day when employees donated their tips to a local nonprofit organization and Peet's then matched the amount raised up to $1,000 per store. Customer loyalty was encouraged with programs such as "Peet's Customer of the Week" promotion, the winner of which received complimentary coffee.

By 1999, Peet's had closed nearly 50 stores, had expanded into the Chicago and Portland, Oregon, areas, and was set to enter the Boston market where heavy mail-order business had indicated the area was ripe for a new coffee establishment. "We believe that limited and selective additions of new store sites, rather than broad scale site development, will better support our brand position," the company said in a press release. Boston coffee drinkers had been introduced to Peet's in 1995 when Au Bon Pain began to serve Peet's coffee in its stores. Peet's discontinued supplying Au Bon Pain with its coffee in 1998 because, according to Peet's, coffee was kept on the burners too long. Starbucks, which had opened its first store in Boston in 1994, and bought out the Coffee Connection, a Boston institution, in 1995, welcomed the addition of Peet's. "It elevates awareness of coffee in the market, and that tends to be a positive thing," said Donna Peterson, marketing manager for the Starbucks New England region, in a 1999 *Boston Globe* article. Plans for the Boston market called for stores with a café atmosphere, including laptop plug-ins, and for a lighter roast to accommodate East Coast taste in coffee.

Peet's also adopted a more aggressive approach toward marketing its coffee on the West Coast in 1999. It partnered with Host Marriott to establish Peet's kiosks at the San Francisco International Airport. "The opening of these kiosks represents a wonderful opportunity to introduce Peet's to visitors to the Bay Area and to help build brand awareness in markets like Los Angeles and Chicago," Baldwin was quoted as saying in a 1999 company newswire. Other moves to update the company included providing high-speed Internet access for linking its 56 stores with corporate headquarters. In 2000, Peet's contracted with an online advertising agency to launch an interactive promotional campaign designed to raise coffee drinkers' awareness of the importance of freshness in quality coffee. This campaign led immediately to a significant increase in online revenue.

MOVING INTO THE 21ST CENTURY

With Americans buying 450 million cups of coffee a day and spending $18 billion a year on the beverage at the start of the 21st century, and coffee houses becoming increasingly popular meeting places, Peet's arranged for its January 2001 initial public offering of stock (IPO) of 3.3 million shares of common stock. The sale would lower Baldwin's share of the company from 31 percent to about 15 percent. Some thought it a bad time for an offering. In fact, Peet's posted a net loss of $2.5 million on total revenue of $39.2 million for the first six months of 2000, compared to a net gain of $100,000 on revenue of $31.2 million for the first six months of 1999. However, Baldwin insisted that Peet's would be able to ride the wave of coffee enthusiasm created by rival Starbucks and others. As Baldwin saw it, Peet's timing was perfect; Peet's would step in with its better product and reap the rewards of selling to an educated public ready to graduate to super-premium coffee.

Indeed, the IPO raised $17 million and allowed Peet's to continue its steady expansion. By 2002, the company was operating over 60 stores in four states. Peet's signed a deal with grocery chain Safeway Inc. in April of that year, and its coffee beans became available in Safeway stores across the East Coast as well as in many western markets, including Denver and Phoenix.

Patrick O'Dea was named CEO of the company in 2002 while Jean-Michel Valette was tapped as chairman in 2003 upon Mottern's retirement. With a new management team in place, Peet's stepped up its expansion efforts. In fact, by 2007 there were 120 stores and the company's coffee could be found in over 4,000 grocery stores across the nation. While the company pursued growth, it worked diligently to maintain its uniqueness in a coffee market saturated by Starbucks. When asked about this strategy in a September 2006 *Oakland Tribune* article, O'Dea replied, "The most important thing to us as we grow is to make sure that we stay true to the 40-year deeply seated culture of quality that emanates from this place." He went on to explain, "Our religion around coffee is: First, we are selective about the beans we buy and we pay whatever it takes to get the quality. Second, we only artisan roast by hand in small batches by trained masters. Our average roaster has been roasting over ten years, our master roaster over 25. It's as much of an art, like winemaking, as it is a science."

The company supported artisan roasting by opening a new $30 million state-of-the-art roasting facility in Alameda, California, in 2007. Founder Alfred Peet died that year and to honor his accomplishments, the company held a special event that allowed fans of Peet's to tour the new roasting facility in March 2008.

With sales and profits on the rise, it appeared as though Peet's strategy—especially its aggressive move to get its products on grocery store shelves—was paying off. Its competitors, meanwhile, were struggling. While Peet's saw profits growing from its successful wholesale business, the intense expansion of Starbucks caught up with it and that chain announced during 2008 that it would close nearly 600 locations and eliminate up to 12,000 jobs. Meanwhile, Peet's maintained its growth efforts. During 2008 the company signed a deal to supply bagged coffee to Florida-based Publix Super Markets Inc. All in all, the company expected to be in over 8,000 stores across the nation by the end of 2008.

Facing an uncertain economy and rising fuel costs, many U.S. consumers began to cut back on unnecessary spending—which included $3 to $4 specialty coffee drinks. Nevertheless, Peet's was able to post profits in 2008, as nearly 72 percent of its operating profit stemmed from coffee sales in grocery stores, its home delivery business, and from sales to the foodservice industry and business offices. With a solid strategy in place, Peet's appeared to be well positioned for growth in the years to come.

Carrie Rothburd
Updated, Christina M. Stansell

PRINCIPAL COMPETITORS

Green Mountain Coffee Roasters, Inc.; International Coffee & Tea LLC; Starbucks Corporation.

FURTHER READING

Baertlein, Lisa, "Peet's Eyes U.S. Grocery Growth as Starbucks Shuts Cafes," *Reuters News,* July 20, 2008.

Buchanan, Susan, "Coffee Retailers Endure Economic Storm," *Wall Street Journal,* July 28, 2008.

Donker, Anne, "On a Coffee Family Tree an Older Branch Sprouts Anew," *New York Times,* August 22, 1999, section 3, p. 4.

Dunlap, Kamika, "Peet's Piques Alamedans' Interest at Grand Opening," *Oakland Tribune,* March 9, 2008.

Emert, Carol, "A Wake-Up Call for Peet's," *San Francisco Chronicle,* April 30, 1997, p. B1.

Gaines, Judith, "Up the Latte of Success," *Boston Globe,* July 5, 2000, p. D1.

Gellene, Denise, "Another Cup of Coffee?" *Los Angeles Times,* February 20, 1997, p. D1.

Julian, Sheryl, "Peet's 'Cupper Brings His Brew to Town," *Boston Globe,* July 19, 1995, p. 73.

Mara, Janis, "Coffee Roasters Pushes Beyond Its 'Peetnik' Roots," *Oakland Tribune,* September 14, 2006.

Resende, Patricia, "Business People: Baldwin Aims to Restart a Coffee Legacy," *Boston Herald,* December 12, 1999, p. 46.

Shepherd, Lauren, "Peet's Moves East in Bid to Offer Premium Coffee at Grocery Stores Nationwide," *Associated Press Newswires,* March 21, 2008.

Torres, Blanca, "Peet's Gears Up to Expand Chain," *Oakland Tribune,* March 11, 2007.

The Penguin Group

80 Strand
London, WC2R 0RL
United Kingdom
Telephone: (44 20) 7010 3396
Fax: (44 20) 7010 6642
Web site: http://www.penguin.com

Division of Pearson plc
Incorporated: 1936 as Penguin Books Ltd.
Employees: 4,000 (est.)
Sales: £846 million ($1.7 billion) (2007 est.)
NAICS: 511130 Book Publishers

∎ ∎ ∎

The Penguin Group is one of the world's two largest English-language publishers. Active in the United Kingdom, many Commonwealth countries, and the United States, Penguin Group is either the largest or second largest publisher in all the markets in which it competes. Penguin revolutionized the publishing industry in the 1930s by perfecting the mass market paperback.

The famous Penguin colophon first appeared on reprints of popular hardcover books and classic works. The company soon began commissioning original works. It has published a voluminous roster of leading literary figures, as well as more commercially oriented writers.

The group evolved as the industry consolidated and grew more vertically integrated, with many traditional hardcover publishers handling their own paperback releases. In addition to the imprints with which it is most closely identified (Penguin, Puffin, and the Penguin Group), it is home to dozens of imprints including Viking, Plume, Berkley, and DK.

GETTING ONE'S FEET WET

Penguin's founder, Allen Lane, was born in Bristol in 1902. William E. Williams, Penguin's chief chronicler, records of Lane's school career: "He appears to have been an average pupil who showed no particular aptitude for anything." Outside of class, however, his business acuity manifested itself at an early age as he reportedly bribed choirboys with candy to do his gardening chores.

Lane entered the publishing trade at age 16 when he went to work for his uncle, John Lane, who had founded The Bodley Head in 1887. The Bodley Head was a very prestigious London press that had published the likes of Oscar Wilde, Anatole France, and Agatha Christie. John Lane impressed upon his apprentice the importance of careful attention to printing and layout. Lane also learned about shipping, distribution, sales, and marketing in his initial immersion in the industry.

A NEW IDEA IN PUBLISHING

John Lane died in 1925, and Allen took over leadership of the company. By the mid-1930s, however, Allen Lane's interests and goals in publishing had diverged significantly from those of The Bodley Head's business. Specifically, he perceived a market for low-cost paperbacks of higher-quality reading material than found in typical newsstand fare. With a start-up capital of just £100, Lane started his own venture, organizing a printing of the first Penguin books. According to company literature: "He wanted a 'dignified but flippant' symbol for his new business, and when his secretary suggested a Penguin, another employee was dispatched to London Zoo to do some sketches." The resulting logo would become one of the world's most recognizable into the next century. The Bodley Head agreed to distribute the books but stopped short of providing any financial backing as their own financial health was troubled.

The first ten Penguin titles, released on July 30, 1935, had all sold well for other publishers in hardback. Lane expected to expand their market by offering them at a greatly reduced price, only six pence, one-seventh the cost of a new hardback. The first group of works by writers including Agatha Christie, André Maurois, and Ernest Hemingway, included popular mysteries as well as more serious fare with the potential to become literary classics, something that might garner enduring sales. A second group of ten titles appeared in October 1935. With books by Dashiell Hammett, V. Sackville-West, and others, this group too aimed to please a diverse audience.

Lane faced enormous risks with the new venture; the size of the printing orders he needed to place to achieve the necessary economies of scale were enormous. Figuring he needed to sell 17,500 copies of a title to break even, he started by ordering 20,000 copies, but only binding half of them.

The literary establishment of the time scoffed at Lane's idea. One particularly vocal critic among writers was George Orwell, who was concerned about the potential for reduced royalties. Ironically, he would later become one of Penguin's bestselling backlist authors; the

firm had sold nearly seven million copies of his *Animal Farm* by the mid-1980s.

Penguin was not so much focused on the traditional bookstore customer, but on more casual readers at newsstands and department stores. It was a buyer for Woolworth's (reportedly at the urging of his wife) who gave Penguin its first big break.

The new books stood out from the beginning, thanks in part to their instantly recognizable design. Bands of color flanked the bold text titles on the cover; there were originally different colors for different genres (such as green mysteries, blue biographies, cerise travel writing, red plays) before Penguin settled exclusively on its trademark orange that had at first been reserved for fiction. Occasionally, as with an author such as James Thurber, a simple line drawing was added. At 7 1/8 inches by 4 3/8 inches, the books were proportioned for portability.

SPINOFFS

Penguin Books Ltd. became an independent company on January 1, 1936. The Bodley Head had continued to flounder and in fact went bankrupt within a year, leaving Penguin as its largest creditor. The rapidly growing Penguin company, on the other hand, acquired a new building in rural Harmondsworth by the end of 1937, after operating a makeshift distribution center in a crypt beneath London's Holy Trinity Church for several years.

A proliferation of new series soon followed. In May 1937 the company introduced its nonfiction Pelican Books beginning with George Bernard Shaw's *The Intelligent Woman's Guide to Socialism, Capitalism, Sovietism and Fascism*. Although mostly a reprint, a new section that Shaw penned on fascism represented the first original work commissioned by Penguin.

Also launched during this time was a series of mostly original, topical books called Penguin Specials, which took sales to new levels (as many as 250,000 copies for some titles). Geneviève Tabouis's *Blackmail or War?* sold a quarter of a million copies within three weeks. The more expensive King Penguin series, begun in 1939, added color illustrations. Other new lines appeared around the same time. The Puffin brand of picture books for children debuted in 1940. These were followed by story books and cut-out books.

WARTIME ACTIVITIES

During World War II, the press had to cope with trade route disruptions and materials shortages. However, its popularity gave it an edge when it came to paper rationing. Paid advertisements began to appear in the

```
┌─────────────────────────────────────────────┐
│                                               │
│               KEY DATES                       │
│                  ■                            │
│                                               │
│  1935:  Allen Lane publishes the first Penguin│
│         paperbacks.                           │
│  1946:  Penguin Classics series launched with │
│         a translation of *The Odyssey.*       │
│  1960:  Penguin triumphs in U.K. obscenity    │
│         trial over publishing *Lady           │
│         Chatterley's Lover.*                   │
│  1961:  Penguin Books Ltd.'s initial public   │
│         offering is 150 times oversubscribed. │
│  1970:  Pearson Longman acquires Penguin.     │
│  1975:  As the industry grows more vertically │
│         integrated, Penguin acquires Viking   │
│         Press, a leading hardcover publisher. │
│  1996:  Penguin buys another large U.S.       │
│         publisher, the Putnam Berkley Group.  │
│  2000:  Penguin acquires Britain's Dorling    │
│         Kindersley (DK).                       │
│  2008:  Penguin scores blockbuster success    │
│         with several titles repackaged as     │
│         trade paperbacks.                      │
│                                               │
└─────────────────────────────────────────────┘
```

books. During this time, Allen Lane's brother John, a marketing wizard, was killed in action in North Africa in 1942.

After the war there followed series devoted to Shakespeare, modern painters, musical scores, and British architecture, as well as several periodicals (*Science News* and *Penguin New Writing,* for example). The successful Penguin Classics series was launched soon after the war, beginning with Homer's *The Odyssey.* These were translations, academically sound but written in contemporary English.

As Williams later described, "for every civilized and balanced person there are Penguins to suit each mood and purpose." By 1951 there were 1,800 titles in all, and Penguin was probably the best-known publisher in Britain.

INTERNATIONAL INTERESTS

Penguin took overseas sales seriously, and it gained a leading edge among English-language publishers in many parts of the world. Penguin formed an American affiliate in 1939 but, after a series of disagreements with Lane, its local managers bought the business out in 1948. It continued to sport the Penguin logo for another three years until it adopted the New American Library name. (Penguin eventually acquired this unit and Dutton Books, in 1986.) By 1949 Penguin was

starting another U.S. operation, Penguin Books Inc., basing it in Baltimore. Several years earlier, it had set up an Australian subsidiary, Penguin Books Pty Ltd, near Melbourne.

According to *The Penguin Story* (1956), Penguin sold 2.6 million books outside of Britain in 1950, 380,000 of them in the United States. By 1955, total international sales had doubled, with the United States accounting for one-fifth of the total, or one million books. About 750,000 Penguins, printed in Britain, were sold through the Australian subsidiary. Penguins were also distributed in Europe, Canada, South Africa, and South America. India and West Africa were important emerging markets. By 1955, the world outside the United Kingdom accounted for a little more than half of Penguin's total annual sales of ten million books. (After selling imported books there for years, Penguin set up a publishing operation in India around 1985.)

HIGHER PROFILE

In 1960 Penguin became the first to publish the uncensored version of *Lady Chatterley's Lover* in the United Kingdom. (It had been released in the United States by another firm the previous year.) The controversial debut proved a test case for Britain's Obscene Publications Act of 1959. Penguin won the six-day trial, held in the legendary Old Bailey, and garnered tremendous publicity (and sales) in the process. Ironically, Allen Lane was not entirely opposed to censorship in certain cases. Several years later, he burned most of a printing of fairly tasteless Siné cartoons that his onetime heir apparent, Tony Godwin, had commissioned.

Penguin Books became a public company in 1961 with a listing on the London Stock Exchange. Its initial public offering was 150 times oversubscribed, meaning that there was demand for 150 times more shares; the company, therefore, could have priced the stock much higher. Penguin had grown significantly and maintained a workforce of about 500 in the mid-1960s.

Lane died on July 7, 1970, from colon cancer. A controlling stake in his highly prized business was subsequently acquired by Penguin's sometime distribution partner, Pearson Longman Ltd., itself the product of a 1968 merger between *Financial Times* owner Pearson and the venerable, family-owned book publisher Longman. The deal squelched a takeover bid by McGraw-Hill of the United States.

AN EVOLVING INDUSTRY

Penguin's global sales passed £40 million in 1974 as consolidation and vertical integration were quickly changing the industry. Other publishers' takeover of their own paperback businesses forced Penguin into hardbacks. In 1975 its U.S. subsidiary acquired Viking Press, a well-regarded literary publisher formed in 1925 by Harold Guinzburg.

In spite of the dismal performance of the British pound, Penguin survived a shakeout of U.K. publishers in the late 1970s. In the midst of it, Peter Mayer was brought over from the United States to lead the group beginning in 1978. Mayer had two decades of experience at American paperback houses Pocket Books and Avon Books. He is credited with restoring Penguin's fortunes, but, said some, at the cost of its unique identity, as hardback and paperback publishing became more closely integrated.

In 1981 Penguin had more than 1,000 employees globally and was producing 45 million books a year. By the time of the group's 50th anniversary in 1986, Penguin was producing 48 million mass-market paperbacks a year valued in excess of £50 million. It boasted 6,000 titles in print. Punished by unfavorable exchange rates, Penguin, like many other British publishers, shifted much of its printing outside the United Kingdom in the 1980s.

Acquisitions had continued in April 1985 when the group bought U.K. hardback publishers Michael Joseph and Hamish Hamilton, paperback publisher Sphere Books, and a distribution group named TBL from the Thomson Organisation for £11.5 million. The next year Penguin bought New American Library and Dutton Books. Dutton dated to the 1850s and was the home of such writers as Jorge Luis Borges and *Winnie the Pooh* author A. A. Milne; it ceased as a separate unit in 1989 and was absorbed by Penguin.

Penguin had also arranged to publish movie tie-ins, or special editions of books that had been adapted for the movies, including *Brideshead Revisited* and *A Passage to India*. The company started a books-on-tape unit in 1993.

THE PUTNAM PURCHASE

Penguin's U.S. business acquired Putnam Berkley Group Inc. in 1996 to form Penguin Putnam Inc. This new entity had combined U.S. sales estimated at $377 million and nearly 1,800 employees. Putnam was founded in 1848 by George Palmer Putnam. It had become one of the leading publishers of American letters, and its roster included Washington Irving, Nathaniel Hawthorne, and Edgar Allan Poe. From 1884 to 1936 Putnam had grown through several partnerships, and in 1936 a link with London's Coward-McCann gave it a presence in the United Kingdom. Two years before

Penguin's U.K. censorship test with *Lady Chatterley's Lover*, Putnam had faced one of its own in the United States with the 1958 publication of *Lolita*. Putnam bought U.S. paperback press Berkley Books in 1965 and the group itself had been acquired by media conglomerate MCA, Inc., in 1975.

Penguin's U.S. affiliate added The Avery Publishing Group in August 1999. Avery focused on health and fitness topics. Alpha Books, best known for its "Complete Idiot's Guide" series of instructional manuals, was transferred to Penguin from Pearson Education three years later. In the meantime, Penguin acquired Britain's Dorling Kindersley for $435 million in 2000. Better known by its "DK" imprint, the company had been launched in 1974 as a book packager and specialized in graphic-intensive nonfiction books for younger readers.

Even without the DK acquisition, total international revenues exceeded £750 million ($1 billion) in 2000. North America accounted for more than two-thirds the total. Front-list titles were as important as ever, with dozens of new books making the bestseller lists. The group was streamlining its distribution systems and venturing into eBooks.

The group continued to adapt its formats to suit current needs. It signed a new agreement to distribute thousands of eBook titles via a linkup with Ingram Digital. Penguin also found new ways to reinvigorate its original strength—paperbacks. The Associated Press in 2008 noted that the group's U.S. unit had successfully repackaged a number of hardcover books into huge success as trade paperbacks, in spite of a lackluster sales environment.

Frederick C. Ingram

PRINCIPAL SUBSIDIARIES

Penguin Publishing Company Ltd.; Penguin Group (USA) Inc.; Penguin Ireland; Penguin Group (Australia); Penguin Group (Canada); Penguin Books India Pvt. Ltd.; Penguin Group (New Zealand); Penguin South Africa.

PRINCIPAL COMPETITORS

Random House, Inc.; Verlagsgruppe Georg von Holtzbrinck GmbH; HarperCollins Publishers LLC; Simon & Schuster, Inc.

FURTHER READING

Alaton, Salem, "Penguin: 50 Years of the Curious Bird," *Globe & Mail* (Canada), July 6, 1985, p. E15.

Appleyard, Bryan, "In the Empire of the Birds," *Times* (London), September 5, 1985, p. 8.

Baines, Phil, *Penguin by Design: A Cover Story, 1935–2005,* New York: Penguin, 2005.

Block, Valerie, "Stepping Out of the Shadow," *Crain's New York Business,* February 11, 2002, p. 4.

Brady, James, "A Gentleman's Trade," *Advertising Age,* November 20, 1989, p. 24.

Brady, Rosemary, "Between Scylla and Charybdis," *Forbes,* November 8, 1982, pp. 230, 232.

"British Penguin to Acquire New American Library and E. P. Dutton," *Publishers Weekly,* October 10, 1986, pp. 18f.

Coleman, Terry, "Living to Tell the Tale—Penguin Books," *Guardian* (London), February 15, 1995, p. 2.

Feather, John, "Allen Lane's Idea," *A History of British Publishing,* London: Croom Helm, pp. 206–13.

Italie, Hillel, "Penguin Group (USA) Enjoys Run of Paperback Sensations," *Associated Press Newswires,* April 10, 2008.

Kirkpatrick, David D., "Penguin Group Hires Publisher Fired by Rival," *New York Times,* January 25, 2003, p. C1.

———, "President and Chief Leaves Penguin Putnam Books," *New York Times,* September 25, 2001, p. C16.

Lewis, Jeremy, *Penguin Special: The Life and Times of Allen Lane,* London and New York: Viking, 2005.

Penguins, a Retrospect, 1935–1951, Harmondsworth, U.K.: Penguin, 1952.

Petrikin, Chris, "Lynton Lights Successful Fire Under Penguin," *Variety,* September 29, 1997, pp. S47f.

Symons, Julian, "The Flight of the Penguin," *Sunday Times* (London), September 8, 1985.

Traut, Dennis, *Penguin's Penguins,* New York: Penguin, 1982.

Wavell, Stuart, "Publish and Be Damned? Penguin Books—Profile," *Sunday Times* (London), June 11, 1995.

Williams, William E., *Allen Lane: A Personal Portrait,* London: Bodley Head, 1973.

———, *The Penguin Story,* Harmondsworth, U.K.: Penguin, 1956.

Wise, Michael, "Appeal to Masses Puts Penguin Books Back in the Black," *Globe and Mail* (Canada), May 18, 1985, p. E15.

Yelaja, Prithi, "Build It and They Will Come," *Toronto Star,* April 12, 2008, p. E8.

The Pentland Group plc

8 Manchester Square
London, W1U 3PH
United Kingdom
Telephone: (44 20) 7535-3800
Fax: (44 20) 7535-3837
Web site: http://www.pentland.com

Private Company
Founded: 1936
Employees: 2,000
Sales: £940.9 million ($1.88 billion) (2007 est.)
NAICS: 422340 Footwear Wholesalers; 422320 Men's
and Boys' Clothing and Furnishings Wholesalers;
422330 Women's, Children's, and Infants' Clothing
and Accessories Wholesalers

■ ■ ■

The Pentland Group plc owns and licenses more than 12 well-known sports and leisure apparel brands, including Speedo swimsuits; Ellesse and Berghaus sportswear; Boxfresh streetwear; the Mitre soccer brand; and Kanga-Roos and Kickers footwear. The company also sells Red or Dead designer footwear and accessories, One True Saxon brand clothing, and is also the worldwide licensee for Ted Baker footwear. In addition, Pentland owns a majority stake in retailer JD Sports Fashion plc. Throughout its first 50 years in business, Pentland was a relatively obscure manufacturer of mostly private-label shoes sold in Great Britain. The company catapulted onto the global stage in the early 1980s via its role in the development and success of Reebok brand athletic

shoes. Pentland made a vital investment in the then-struggling U.S. licensee of the brand in the early 1980s and helped guide its explosive growth during the decade, later divesting its stake in the multibillion-dollar firm. Chairman R. Stephen Rubin took the company private in 1999 through family investment firm Robert Stephen Holdings plc.

FOUNDED IN 1932

Pentland's origins stretch back to 1932, when Berko and Minnie Rubin established the Liverpool Shoe Co. to sell footwear to Britain's retail chains. A 1973 article on the company credited the business's early success to its founders' "extraordinarily good sense of what would sell." From a base capital of £100, Liverpool Shoe incorporated in 1936 and purchased its first manufacturing operation, Merrywell Shoes, in 1946. Liverpool Shoe continued to grow via acquisition throughout the postwar era, purchasing both Dines Shoes Ltd. and Batson and Webster Ltd. in 1962 and John F. Kirby Ltd. in 1963 before going public in 1964. Although the shares were in high demand—the floatation was oversubscribed 97 times—the Rubin family retained a majority interest in the firm.

Liverpool Shoe was by this time manufacturing a wide variety of footwear, from formal to athletic, for men, women, and children. The company's "Beatle boots" were a big hit in the 1960s, and the 1965 acquisitions of Wareings Ltd. and Wesco Footwear Ltd. continued to boost the company's domestic manufacturing capabilities. However, the firm began to suffer under pressure from rising imports during the latter years of

> ## COMPANY PERSPECTIVES
>
> Our mission is to create a world class company, engaging world class people, developing world class brands, delivering world class financials.

the decade, incurring losses from 1967 to 1971. These difficulties were exacerbated by the untimely death of the founder in 1969 at the age of 56. Thirty-one-year-old son R. Stephen Rubin took the helm that year and undertook a restructuring and diversification in the hopes of revitalizing the business.

SECOND GENERATION BRINGS DIVERSIFICATION

Trained as a barrister, Rubin had started out at the family company in sales, but quickly proved himself a savvy investment manager. While continuing to support the shoe business, he began in the early 1970s to shape the company into something of a venture capital firm. Rubin acquired Pentland Maritime Shipbrokers Ltd. in 1971, and while the resulting amalgamation would never be known for its shipping interests, he changed the company name to Pentland Industries Ltd. two years later.

In 1973, Rubin launched Pentland Shipping Services Ltd. and Pentland Insurance Brokers Ltd. The company made its first venture capital–type investment in 1974, when it bought a 51 percent interest in Unican for a meager £51. The home-brewing and wine-making business took off, and in 1978 Pentland sold its stake to Robertson for a handsome £1 million. Pentland used the proceeds to launch its own line of skateboards, shoes, handbags, luggage, and sportswear under the Airborne brand in 1978.

In the meantime, Rubin had maintained Liverpool Shoe as a holding company for the growing conglomerate's footwear interests. Faced with a flood of cheap shoes from the Far East, he reluctantly slashed domestic production to a single plant and set up his own Hong Kong manufacturing operation in 1969. Pentland acquired Amalgamated Shoe Company and Priestly Footwear Ltd. in 1972, and by the end of the decade had purchased the U.K. license to the Pony footwear brand as well. Over the course of his first decade in the role of chairman, Stephen Rubin had succeeded in turning his birthright from a loss-plagued shoemaker into a budding conglomerate that by 1979 had over £25 million in annual sales and more than £1

million in pretax profits. It was only the beginning of a string of stunning successes.

THE REEBOK ACQUISITION

The most significant event of the 1980s, if not Pentland's entire history, started with the apparently inauspicious investment of £50,000 ($77,500) in Reebok USA Ltd. Inc. in 1981. In exchange for the capital infusion, Pentland received a 55.5 percent interest in the firm. Reebok USA was then the struggling North American licensee of J.W. Foster & Sons Inc. Established in 1895, the family-owned J.W. Foster—the world's oldest shoe company—was then hand-making expensive running shoes for world-class athletes. American Paul Fireman had first taken note of the company's Reebok brand shoes—named for an African gazelle—at a 1979 trade show, and garnered the North American rights to the trademark that same year. Acting as chairman of Reebok USA from 1981 to 1984, Stephen Rubin taught the company the secrets of East Asian sourcing and helped formulate a fresh, new marketing plan.

Late in 1982, the company launched the world's first shoe designed specifically for aerobic exercise. The shoes' bright colors and fashionable styling took the U.S. footwear market by storm. A particularly innovative feature was the use of garment or glove leather, which eliminated the need for a breaking-in period. Sales rose from $300,000 in 1980 to $66 million in 1984, the same year that Fireman and Pentland acquired Reebok International (and the worldwide rights to the Reebok brand) from the founding Foster family for $700,000. By 1986, Reebok's sales had rocketed to $919 million, giving it a leading 34 percent share of the American athletic footwear market.

When Reebok International went public in 1985, Pentland made $12.5 million on its sale of 14.8 percent of the company's total equity. The value of its remaining 40.7 percent stake continued to grow throughout the rest of the decade, exceeding a half billion U.S. dollars by the end of the 1980s. In addition to this astounding return on its initial investment, Pentland was by the mid-1980s earning "dividends"—its share of Reebok's profits—amounting to 80 percent of Pentland's after-tax profits. By 1990, Pentland's sales had multiplied nearly 30 times from 1979, to £743.45 million ($1.3 billion), and its after-tax net amounted to £29.91 million ($53.39 million).

GROWTH THROUGH ACQUISITION AND DIVESTMENT

Not content to simply sit back and enjoy the bountiful fruits of his Reebok investment, Rubin sought new

KEY DATES

1932: Berko and Minnie Rubin establish the Liverpool Shoe Co.
1946: The manufacturing operations of Merrywell Shoes are purchased.
1964: Liverpool Shoe goes public.
1971: Pentland Maritime Shipbrokers Ltd. is purchased.
1973: The Pentland Industries Ltd. name is adopted.
1981: The company invests in Reebok USA Ltd. Inc.
1989: The company changes its name to Pentland Group plc.
1990: Authentic Fitness Corporation, the North American licensee of the Speedo brand, is acquired; an 80 percent stake in Speedo (Europe) Ltd. is purchased.
1991: Pentland sells its stake in Reebok; Pony International Inc. is acquired.
1993: The Berghaus, Brasher, and Ellesse brands are added to Pentland's holdings.
1995: Mitre Sports International is acquired.
1999: Robert Stephen Holdings plc takes Pentland private.
2005: Pentland purchases a stake in retailer JD Sports Fashion plc.
2008: U.S. swimmer Michael Phelps makes Olympic history, winning a record eight gold medals while wearing a Speedo suit.

opportunities. Pentland used $700,000 of the proceeds of the 1985 Reebok offering to acquire a 51 percent stake in Boston-based Holmes Products Corporation, a manufacturer of household heating and air conditioning appliances. Aided by the launch of the "Heat Director"—promoted as "the first-ever oscillating fan heater"—Holmes's sales more than doubled to $12 million in 1985 and jumped to $30 million in 1986. Other late 1980s acquisitions added real estate management, ceramic tile distribution, and refrigeration interests to the group. In 1989, a reverse takeover joined Bertrams Investment Trust PLC as well as its stationery and greeting card business to the conglomerate. The company changed its name to Pentland Group plc that year.

In February 1991, Rubin began a two-stage divestment of Pentland's remaining 30.9 percent stake in Reebok, selling 18 percent of the equity back to Reebok for

$460 million. The remaining 12.9 percent went to an investment firm for $310 million that December. Although he was rather tight-lipped at the time, Rubin would later acknowledge that "certain political differences" with Paul Fireman had helped motivate the sale. The divestment reduced Pentland's year-over-year sales by more than half, to £340.1 million in 1991.

Rubin was not about to let the resulting bankroll sit idle in a vault. Although he would continue to dabble in a variety of consumer products, the chairman increasingly targeted acquisitions in the sporting goods industry. In 1990, he purchased a significant stake in Authentic Fitness Corporation, the North American licensee of the Speedo brand. Before the year was out, he acquired an 80 percent stake in Speedo (Europe) Ltd., adding complete ownership of Speedo International and Speedo Australia early in 1991.

One of the biggest names in swimwear, Speedo accounted for 65 percent of competitive (as opposed to the much larger fashion) swimsuits sold worldwide. In an effort to broaden the brand's appeal without losing its high-performance image, Pentland carefully expanded its scope to include gear for triathletes and beach wear. Speedo's status, and Pentland's piecemeal strategy of acquiring it, would become a model for the company's activities in the early 1990s.

GROWING ANOTHER SHOE BRAND

Building upon more than a decade of ownership of the U.K. Pony distributorship, Pentland purchased Pony International Inc., the global shoe and sportswear subsidiary of adidas AG, in July 1991. Two years later, Pentland took a controlling 80 percent stake in Pony USA, which was then generating about three-fourths of the brand's worldwide sales. (The remaining 20 percent was purchased in 1995.)

Rubin worked Pentland's marketing and distribution magic on the struggling organization, repositioning the brand as a performance shoe and increasing its advertising budget. He also boosted research and development and transferred Pony's production to Pentland's own East Asian sources. Rubin even made a stab at acquiring former Pony parent adidas AG in the ensuing year and a half, but abruptly pulled out of the deal with no comment late in 1992.

From 1992 through 1996, Pentland purchased controlling stakes in, or made outright purchases of, nine major sporting goods brands. In 1993, the company added the United Kingdom's Berghaus mountaineering apparel, footwear and accessories; Brasher hiking boots; and Ellesse, an Italian line of tennis and downhill ski apparel. (Pentland had been the Ellesse licensee in the United Kingdom since 1981.) Reusch, a German manufacturer of ski and goal-keeping gloves, was acquired in 1994, and another soccer-related company, ball maker Mitre International, came on board in 1995. Pentland also bought the global Lacoste license, with its famous crocodile; U.S. fashion footwear manufacturer Main Woods Inc.; and designer clothing labels Red or Dead and Moda Prima during this period.

In keeping with his 1997 self-characterization as "a long-term builder of brands," Rubin committed himself and his company to an emphasis on sporting goods, including apparel, equipment and footwear, as well as sporty clothing. The company divested all of its consumer products subsidiaries save Holmes Products, the air conditioning firm, but was merely waiting for "the right opportunity" to sell this company. Having assembled a group of "next generation" brands, Rubin began to set up the infrastructure necessary to support their continued expansion. From 1995 through mid-1997, he created joint ventures to distribute Pentland brand goods to South Korea, China, Vietnam, Singapore, Malaysia, Indonesia, Argentina, and India.

RESTRUCTURING TO INCREASE PROFITABILITY

Known—and sometimes criticized—for his cautious fiscal management, Rubin could not hope to duplicate the unbelievable, Reebok-fueled growth in sales and profits recorded in the 1980s. While Pentland's revenues more than doubled, from £326.5 million in 1992 to £889.6 million in 1996, pretax net increased only by about 9 percent, from £33.7 million to £36.6 million, during the period. As analyst Michael Costello had predicted to *Footwear News*'s James Fallon in 1992, "The value of major brands like Reebok and Nike could peak in 1996 or 1997 as their markets mature. What Pentland is doing is putting itself in a position for the next group of brand names to develop." In 1997, it appeared that Rubin had positioned his company well. Rubin's son, Andrew, took over as CEO in 1998.

Over the next several years, Pentland began a restructuring effort that included the selling of noncore assets to shore up profits. Believing private status would allow the company to better focus on its individual brands, the Rubin family investment arm—Robert Stephen Holdings (RSH) plc—made a move to take Pentland private in July 1999. Later that year RSH purchased the 37.7 percent of Pentland it did not already own.

MOVING INTO THE NEW MILLENNIUM

The Pentland Group entered the 2000s on solid ground. During 2000, its Speedo brand launched a new line of swimsuits under the Speedo Fastskin name. The suit was worn by 13 of the 15 world record breaking athletes in the 2000 Sydney Olympics. Speedo was also the most-worn brand among swimmers in the 2004 Athens Olympics. During the 2008 Beijing Olympics, swimmer Michael Phelps made Olympic history winning a record eight gold medals while wearing a Speedo suit.

In 2001 Pentland signed a deal to develop and market the Ted Baker line of footwear. It also purchased the remaining 25 percent of Brasher Boot Company Ltd. it did not already own. New state-of-the-art company headquarters opened in London in 2002.

Growth continued over the next several years. During 2004, Pentland became the licensee for the Airwalk brand of footwear and apparel in the United Kingdom and Ireland. It also purchased the remaining 5 percent of Red or Dead that year. British streetwear brand Boxfresh International Ltd. was acquired in 2005. In addition, the company began to develop its Clerk & Teller clothing brand. Pentland added the One True Saxon brand to its arsenal in 2006. The company moved into the retailing sector with its 2005 purchase of a majority stake in sports fashion and footwear retailer JD Sports Fashion plc.

Pentland also remained focus on its U.S. growth during this time period. It acquired a 50 percent interest in Atsco Brands, the U.S. distributor of the Ellesse and KangaRoos brands, in 2005. It also planned for additional expansion in the U.S. market in the years to come.

By this time, the company's acquisition strategy during the early years of the new century appeared to have paid off. Sales and profits were on the rise, leaving Pentland well positioned among its competitors. With the Rubin father and son duo at the helm, Pentland appeared to be on track for growth as a private brand management company. Chairman Rubin's comments in an April 2008 *Financial Times* article laid out the company's ownership status. "Our philosophy is to be a long-term family company that can be passed on to the next generation. We are more inclined to reinvest in the group than take money out for dividends."

April Dougal Gasbarre
Updated, Christina M. Stansell

PRINCIPAL COMPETITORS

L.L. Bean Inc.; The Timberland Company; V.F. Corp.

FURTHER READING

"Andrew Rubin," *Sporting Goods Business,* July 1994, p. 56.

Batchelor, Charles, "Best to Keep It in the Family," *Financial Times,* April 21, 2008.

"Brand Analysis—Pentland's Superbrand City," *Drapers Record,* November 9, 2002.

Fallon, James, "Pentland Confirms Plan to Take Reebok Public," *Footwear News,* May 13, 1985, pp. 1–2.

———, "Pentland Details Acquisition Strategy," *Footwear News,* May 28, 1990, p. 55.

———, "Pentland Directors Accept Bid of RSH to Take Company Private," *Women's Wear Daily,* September 8, 1999.

———, "Pentland Is Filthy Rich but Will Avoid the Cleaners," *Footwear News,* May 16, 1988, pp. 8–9.

———, "Pentland to Put 31.5% Reebok Stake on Block," *Footwear News,* June 18, 1990, pp. 2–3.

———, "Rubinesque: Pentland's Stephen Rubin Knows the Art of the Deal," *Footwear News,* January 27, 1992, pp. 36–37.

Forman, Ellen, "Pentland to Start Trading in U.S.," *Footwear News,* July 14, 1986, p. 35.

Kletter, Melanie, "Pentland Group Set for U.S. Expansion," *Women's Wear Daily,* October 21, 2005.

McEvoy, Christopher, "Stephen Rubin, Executive Chairman, Pentland Group," *Sporting Goods Business,* February 10, 1997, pp. 40–41.

"Political Football: Adidas," *Economist,* April 11, 1992, pp. 69–70.

Price Brown, Jessica, "Pentland Sales Defy Downturn," *Drapers,* August 9, 2008.

Seckler, Valerie, "El Greco, Pentland Join Forces," *Footwear News,* August 3, 1987, pp. 1–2.

———, "El Greco Went for $24.5 Million," *Footwear News,* September 28, 1987, pp. 2–3.

———, "Pentland Net Up 13.2% on 41.6% Higher Sales," *Footwear News,* March 21, 1988, p. 27.

———, "Reebok Looks at Possibility of Going Public," *Footwear News,* March 11, 1985, pp. 1–2.

———, "Warnaco-Authentic: What Went Wrong with Wachner's Deal," *Women's Wear Daily,* July 31, 1996, pp. 1–3.

Tedeschi, Mark, "Reebok Will Buy Back Most of Pentland Shares," *Footwear News,* February 25, 1991, pp. 2–3.

Tosh, Mark, "Rubin Sketches Plans for Pentland," *Footwear News,* September 9, 1991, p. 22.

Piaggio & C. S.p.A.

Via Rinaldo Piaggio 25
Pontedera, Pisa 56025
Italy
Telephone: (39 0587) 272 111
Fax: (39 0587) 272 344
Web site: http://www.piaggio.com

Public Company
Founded: 1884
Employees: 4,102
Sales: EUR 1.69 billion ($2.49 billion) (2007 est.)
Stock Exchanges: Borsa Italiana
Ticker Symbol: PIA
NAICS: 336991 Motorcycle, Bicycle, and Parts
  Manufacturing; 336112 Light Truck and Utility
  Vehicle Manufacturing

■ ■ ■

Piaggio & C. S.p.A. is a leading manufacturer of motor scooters, motorcycles, mopeds, and light vans and trucks. The company's most well-known product is the Vespa motor scooter, a model that became extremely popular in Europe after World War II. Americans were introduced to the Vespa when Audrey Hepburn and Gregory Peck rode on one in the 1953 film *Roman Holiday.* The company's other brands include Aprilia, Moto Guzzi, Derbi, Gilera, and Scarabeo. Under the leadership of Roberto Colaninno, Piaggio went public in 2006 and has increased its expansion efforts in North America, India, and China. Industrial group Immsi S.p.A. owns nearly 56 percent of Piaggio.

BEGINNINGS IN THE 19TH CENTURY

Piaggio & C. dates back to 1884, when Rinaldo Piaggio, son of a Genoa joiner, expanded his family's old woodshop in the town of Sestri Ponente into a steam-driven sawmill. Rinaldo was only 20 years old, but he demonstrated precocious business acumen. He set his new factory to produce fittings and furniture for ships, and courted the accounts of the local shipyards. Within 15 years, Piaggio's naval fittings shop had won a virtual monopoly over the northwest coast of Italy. All the shipyards turned to Piaggio for furnishings. The business continued to expand as contracts came in from other parts of Italy, and then from international shipbuilders. When the century turned, Piaggio was a well-known name abroad as well as in Italy. The cabins and saloons of more than 70 shipping lines were outfitted with Piaggio furnishings.

Rinaldo Piaggio, on the lookout to expand his factory in a new direction, began to solicit business from railways to build and outfit railway cars. The work was not too different from the complex woodworking required for naval fittings, but the factory had to be altered to accommodate sheet steel work. Within a few years, Piaggio had more jobs for railway cars than for ship fittings, and the company opened a new factory in the town of Finale Ligure. With the opening of the new factory in 1906, Piaggio was able to take on even more railway car business, and began to make other wheeled vehicles as well. Piaggio made trucks, trams, freight cars, and even luxury automobiles.

COMPANY PERSPECTIVES

Our mission is to create values for our shareholders, customers and employees, being a global player with top quality products, service and solutions for urban and out-of-town mobility that constantly adapt to evolving needs and lifestyles; to strengthen our position as a player contributing to social and economic development in our community and working to safeguard the environment and general wellbeing; and to be the world leader as regards "Made in Italy" light mobility, in terms of design, creativity and tradition, and internationally recognized as the reference company in Europe with a model based on quality, tradition and sustained value creation.

WARTIME PRODUCTION

During World War I, the two Piaggio factories were refitted to manufacture weapons. The factories also began to make motorboats and airplanes. The new factory at Finale Ligure manufactured boats, including an anti-submarine boat known as the MAS, which was instrumental in destroying the Austro-Hungarian submarine fleet. The older factory at Sestri Ponente principally repaired and maintained warplanes. However, both factories were soon converted to mass-produce airplanes. In 1917 Rinaldo Piaggio bought a new factory in Pisa and transferred the production of railway cars and wheeled vehicles there. Piaggio bought another factory, a car works in Pontedera, and began to build airplane engines there. Piaggio produced engines under license to more established manufacturers, and then began designing its own. Piaggio made the "P2," a single-engine fighter plane, beginning in 1923. Five years later, Piaggio equipped the Finale Ligure factory with a complete wind tunnel and hydrodynamic testing tank.

Piaggio had turned from motorboats to "flying boats"—high-speed planes that could take off from and land in water. In the 1920s and into World War II, the various Piaggio factories were turning out some of the most advanced flying boats in the world, as well as airplane engines, small planes, bombers, and passenger and cargo planes capable of transoceanic flights, in addition to railway cars and stainless steel locomotives. All these products contributed greatly to Italy's war effort; consequently, the factories were bomb targets. The Pontedera factory was completely destroyed in World War II, not only bombed by the Allies but also mined by the Germans as they retreated. When the war ended, Piaggio had virtually nothing left.

Founder Rinaldo Piaggio had died in 1938, and the job of postwar renewal fell to his two sons, Armando and Enrico. They split responsibility for the company's four factories. Armando took over the two older ones, Sestri Ponente and Finale Ligure, and Enrico took Pontedera and Pisa. It was Enrico who came up with the idea of making motor scooters.

POSTWAR SCOOTER SUCCESS

The scooter was not a new idea. Several manufacturers had made small, light motorcycles before, but they had not caught on. Enrico Piaggio decided that scooters would sell if they could be made right. A small, light, inexpensive vehicle might be all that many families could afford, so he envisioned a wide market for the scooter. He imagined it as something that women, as well as men, would ride. He thought further that it needed room for a spare wheel, which should be easy to change. Furthermore, if it was not to be just for sunny days, it should have some sort of mudguard to protect the rider's clothes from puddle splashes. With these general specifications, Enrico contacted one of the chief designers from Piaggio's prewar days, Corradino D'Ascanio.

D'Ascanio was a brilliant engineer who had created the first fully functional helicopter. D'Ascanio drew up plans for a scooter that had a pressed steel body with a shield-shaped front and a wide back housing for the engine and spare wheel. There was no chain linking the front and back wheels, as the rear wheel was powered by a direct drive. The platform seat was built to be comfortable for women in skirts. It took only five months to move from plans to development. Piaggio rebuilt the demolished Pontedera factory to mass-produce the scooter, and in 1946 the first model was offered for sale. This was the Vespa, Italian for "wasp" so named because of the thin-waisted shape of the vehicle.

The Vespa was an immediate success, and quickly became a symbol of postwar Italy. Enrico Piaggio had been correct in assuming that small, low-cost transport would sell well, but he could not have guessed the chic appeal of the little machine. In ten years, Piaggio had sold over one million Vespas. Audrey Hepburn and Gregory Peck rode one in the 1953 film *Roman Holiday*, and the Vespa gained immediate popularity. Although celebrities rode them, so did workers using them to get to their jobs, and families piled on them for weekend vacations. By 1956, there were 4,000 Vespa sales outlets in Italy, 8,000 in the rest of Europe, and another 2,000 in other parts of the world. The company also produced the Ape (Italian for "bee"), a three-wheeled version of

KEY DATES

1884: Rinaldo Piaggio expands his family's wood-shop into a steam-driven sawmill.
1906: A new factory opens and production of railway cars and other wheeled vehicles expands.
1917: Rinaldo Piaggio buys a new factory in Pisa; production of railway cars and wheeled vehicles is transferred to the new facility.
1946: The Vespa scooter is launched.
1953: Audrey Hepburn and Gregory Peck ride a Vespa in the film *Roman Holiday*.
1965: Enrico Piaggio dies suddenly; son-in-law Umberto Agnelli is named his successor.
1982: Piaggio stops exporting its scooters to the United States.
1988: Piaggio reorganizes its corporate structure, forming a sub-holding company under the main umbrella of Piaggio & C. S.p.A., called Piaggio Veicoli Europei S.p.A.
1999: Morgan Grenfell Private Equity Ltd. purchases 80 percent of Piaggio while Texas Pacific Group takes a 10 percent share.
2000: Vespa returns to the U.S. market.
2003: Roberto Colaninno and industrial holding group Immsi S.p.A. take control of Piaggio.
2006: Piaggio goes public.

the Vespa, and made Vespa models in a variety of engine sizes. Piaggio also briefly marketed a small car, but when Fiat came out with a similar one, Piaggio withdrew its model.

The two factories under the control of brother Armando Piaggio were making airplanes and engines, as they had through the war. The airplane division eventually split off from the scooter division in 1966, and operated as a completely separate entity. This division became known as Piaggio Aero Industries S.p.A. in 1998 after a group of investors led by the Di Mase and Ferrari families purchased the assets of the company.

The scooter business continued to thrive into the 1960s. It was the best-selling scooter in over a hundred countries, and was being built under license in several European countries and in Brazil and India. The Vespa still had its movie star cachet, especially as seen in *La Dolce Vita*, ridden by Marcello Mastroianni.

A CHANGING INDUSTRY

Enrico Piaggio died suddenly in 1965, at the age of 60. His successor was his son-in-law, Umberto Agnelli. Agnelli's family ran Fiat, the Italian car manufacturer and conglomerate, and Umberto later became managing director of that company. The scooter industry had dipped somewhat in the late 1950s, as wages rose and many consumers spent their money on cars instead of two-wheelers. However, the Vespa was still popular through the 1970s, especially among young people. Production remained high, although by the end of the 1970s the company was hampered by labor disputes. Strikes held down production to about three-quarters capacity in 1979; sales were nevertheless close to $500 million, and Piaggio turned a profit. Costs increased, as the company spent more on developing new models, and also spent money on acquisitions such as Gilera di Arcore, a leading Italian motorcycle manufacturer. Foreign sales still made up more than 40 percent of Piaggio's business.

One place the Vespa did not catch on was the United States. Piaggio sold its scooters there beginning in the 1950s under its own name and also through a Sears, Roebuck brand, the Allstate Crusaire. However, sales were never high, and in 1982 Piaggio stopped its U.S. exports because it was unable to comply with strict pollution control standards. Meanwhile, Piaggio was shipping roughly 17,000 scooters a year to Japan in the early 1980s. By the mid-1980s, Japanese manufacturers were exporting their own scooters. Kawasaki, Yamaha, Honda, and Suzuki all made significant inroads into European motorcycle and scooter markets in the 1980s, with serious repercussions for some of the older brands. The Japanese models were in many cases less expensive, lighter, and better made than the European vehicles they had copied, and many European makers suffered.

The Italian government, however, kept down the number of light motorcycles imported to Italy to protect its own industry, and the Japanese threat in fact solidified Piaggio. About half its sales were of its Vespa models, and half were mopeds. The company continued to invest heavily in its plants, and began to cooperate with other European companies to fight back against the Japanese imports. In 1981 Piaggio signed a deal with the French bicycle and moped maker Peugeot to develop a motorcycle, hoping to find a midrange niche between the low-cost Japanese models and the German luxury models.

Nevertheless, the shrinking European market for two-wheeled vehicles stalled Piaggio in the mid-1980s. The number of units sold in 1980 was 937,000 vehicles, while in 1984 it was only 553,000. Piaggio had a new managing director in 1984, Giorgio Brazzelli. Brazzelli took the view that the slump in sales was more or less permanent, and the company had to reduce its costs to make a profit. After barely breaking even for three years in a row, Piaggio finally had a healthy profit of ITL 17 billion ($11.05 million) on sales of ITL 663 billion in 1986. Much of the jump was attributable to greatly increased sales of components and parts.

REORGANIZATION BEGINS IN 1988

The company diversified further in the late 1980s, increasing its investments in automobile components and other industries related to vehicle manufacture. Piaggio also reorganized its corporate structure in 1988, forming a sub-holding company under the main umbrella of Piaggio & C. S.p.A., called Piaggio Veicoli Europei S.p.A. Piaggio Veicoli held all the core businesses related to the manufacture and sale of vehicles, including scooters, motorcycles, three-wheelers, and the light trucks the company was beginning to develop. Another division handled the manufacture of Piaggio's bicycle brands. A third major division was responsible for car and motorcycle components and the other miscellaneous ventures, such as industrial robots, that Piaggio had bought into.

In addition to diversification and reorganization, Piaggio aimed to make its business more international in the late 1980s, increasing its joint ventures with foreign companies. In 1989, Piaggio joined a West German engine component manufacturer, Kolbenschmid, in a joint venture to produce water pumps and oil pumps at plants in Italy and France. Then in 1991, Piaggio entered a joint venture with the Japanese firm Daihatsu Motor Co. Ltd. to develop light transport vehicles. Piaggio also attempted to expand its presence in mainland China by taking on a joint venture with a Hong Kong firm in 1993.

Despite all these changes, Piaggio had difficulty extricating itself from the troubles of its shrinking market. In the early 1990s, Piaggio's share of the European market for two-wheeled vehicles had fallen to about 28 percent, largely due to the success of Japanese imports. Piaggio still had almost half the market share where only low-priced scooters were concerned, but profits were low, and in 1993 the company lost ITL 91 billion ($60 million). In that year Piaggio got a new chairman, 29-year-old Giovanni Agnelli, son of the former chairman, Umberto Agnelli. Agnelli was the Piaggio heir and perhaps also in line for a position at his father's company, Fiat. He had been raised and educated in the United States, and had worked for IBM and in a Fiat subsidiary before taking over Piaggio. He found the company in disarray. Diversification into components had taken away the focus on Piaggio's core product,

motor scooters, and the company was only limping along, losing money.

Agnelli quickly sold unprofitable component businesses, and spent huge sums on the development of new scooter models. Agnelli guessed that the scooter might have a comeback in Europe, because auto traffic was getting increasingly congested. Piaggio came out with plastic-body models, which the Japanese companies had long favored, gave them stronger engines, and tried to recapture the star appeal the Vespa had enjoyed in the 1950s and 1960s. Whether due to transportation strikes, traffic jams, rising car and gas prices, or clever marketing, the scooter market indeed picked up. Between 1991 and 1996 sales of scooters in Europe more than doubled, and sales in Italy alone quadrupled. Piaggio's share of that growing market rose from about 25 percent to almost 50 percent.

BUILDING THE OVERSEAS MARKET

Aware that the boom in Europe might soon peak, Piaggio also built up its presence in overseas markets, particularly in India and China. These countries were in a similar position to Italy's just after the war, with a large population in need of basic transportation but not quite ready or able to afford a car. Piaggio's Indian subsidiary had sales of about $200 million annually in the mid-1990s and a respectable market share of around 15 percent. In China, sales were about $36 million in 1995, and all Piaggio's Asian subsidiaries were accounting for more than 30 percent of the company's total sales. Chairman Agnelli aimed to increase the amount of Piaggio's business in Asia over the next five years, hoping to have half the company's sales come from there by the end of the century.

Piaggio's turnaround demonstrated the strength of its basic product, the scooter. The company had lost considerable ground from the late 1970s on, when Japanese imports eroded its core European markets. However, the Vespa had very strong brand recognition because of its past. It managed to be classic without being outmoded, due in large part to the improvements carried out after 1993. Piaggio's management was able to foresee a renewed need for the scooter in Europe, and to move on to growing markets abroad. Piaggio's Chairman Agnelli saw the future of the company in its overseas markets, where there was still room for considerable expansion. Tragedy struck in late 1997, however, when 33-year-old Agnelli died after battling a rare form of intestinal cancer. His mother, Antonella Bechi Piaggio, died shortly thereafter.

During 1999, Morgan Grenfell Private Equity Ltd., the private equity group of Germany's Deutsche Bank

AG, purchased 80 percent of Piaggio while Texas Pacific Group took a 10 percent share. The remaining portion of the company remained in the Agnelli family.

PIAGGIO IN THE 21ST CENTURY

Piaggio made several moves during the early years of the new millennium to solidify its position as a leading manufacturer of two-wheeled motor vehicles. The Vespa returned to the U.S. market in 2000 and the company opened its first Vespa Boutique in Los Angeles. The company purchased Spanish motorcycle manufacturer Derbi-Nacional Motor S.A. the following year and its Gilera brand also began making a name for itself in the world of motorcycle racing.

Perhaps one of the biggest changes came in 2003 when Roberto Colaninno and industrial holding group Immsi S.p.A. took control of Piaggio. By this time the European scooter market, which had seen demand surge in 2000, was experiencing another slump. At the same time, the company was struggling under a large debt load and was facing employee unrest. Furthermore, its products often broke down within the first year of ownership. Piaggio was therefore forced to retool its strategy. The company began an aggressive cost-cutting effort, revamped its assembly lines, restored good relations with its employee unions, and also launched a new marketing campaign.

In April 2004, the company signed a deal with China's Zongshen Industrial Group to produce and market engines, vehicles, and components in Asia. Piaggio also completed its acquisition of faltering motorcycle manufacturer Aprilia S.p.A. Under the leadership of Colaninno, Piaggio set its sights on expanding in new markets across North America, India, and China. Plans were also set in motion in 2007 to build a new Vespa production facility in Vietnam.

Overall, management expected to see increased demand for the Vespa as fuel costs continued to rise and commuters looked for environmentally friendly modes of transportation. According to the company, certain Vespa models could get up to 70 miles per gallon. The company also claimed that if all Americans used one of Vespa's eco-friendly models, national fuel consumption could be reduced by 14 million gallons of gasoline per day and carbon dioxide emissions could fall as much as 324 million pounds per day.

Piaggio went public on the Italian stock exchange in July 2006. Sales in 2007 grew 5.3 percent over the previous year and the company's Vespa sales climbed by 17.1 percent during the same time period. With sales and profits on the rise, it appeared that Piaggio had

overcome the challenges of previous years and was on track for future growth.

A. Woodward
Updated, Christina M. Stansell

PRINCIPAL SUBSIDIARIES

Nacional Motor SA (Spain); Piaggio Vehicles Pvt. Ltd. (India); Moto Guzzi S.p.A.; Zongshen Piaggio Foshan Motorcycle Co. Ltd. (China; 32.5%); Piaggio Vespa B.V. (Netherlands); Piaggio Vietnam Co. Ltd.; Aprilia World Service B.V. (Netherlands); Piaggio Group Americas Inc. (United States).

PRINCIPAL COMPETITORS

BMW AG; Honda Motor Co. Ltd.; Yamaha Motor Co. Ltd.

FURTHER READING

Blum, Patrick, "Steyr Sells Moped Division to Piaggio," *Financial Times,* February 25, 1987, p. 27.

"The Bottom-Pinchers' Chariot," *Economist,* September 21, 1996, p. 64.

Buxton, James, "Piaggio Profits Trebled," *Financial Times,* May 22, 1981, p. 29.

Clark, Jennifer, "Piaggio Focuses on Long Term with Merger," *Wall Street Journal Europe,* December 31, 2004, p. M1.

Cornwell, Rupert, "Entering a Year of Promise," *Financial Times,* January 31, 1980, p. 23.

Dodsworth, Terry, "Peugeot and Piaggio to Co-operate on Motorcycles," *Financial Times,* September 13, 1980, p. 19.

"Generating a Buzz—Piaggio," *Economist,* July 15, 2006.

Larner, Monica, "The Ultimate Scooter Returns," *Business Week,* November 27, 2000.

O'Brian, Heather, "Colaninno in Piaggio Driver's Seat," *Daily Deal,* September 26, 2003.

Pollack, John, "Vespa Scooters Collide with Anti-Japan Charge," *Advertising Age,* June 22, 1992, p. 14.

"Significant Advance at Piaggio," *Financial Times,* June 23, 1986, p. 30.

Tagliabue, John, "Made in Italy (Mostly), Driven in the U.S. A.," *New York Times,* May 18, 2003.

———, "Sometimes Two Wheels Are Better Than Four," *New York Times,* August 17, 1996, pp. 33–34.

Vella, Matt, "Veni, Vidi, Vespa," *Business Week Online,* July 14, 2006.

Wallace, Charles P., "The Next Mr. Fiat?" *Fortune,* October 14, 1996, pp. 182–86.

Whittaker, Malcolm, "Vespa Scooter Style Icon to Stay European," *Reuters News,* October 21, 1999.

Wyles, John, "Piaggio and Kolbenschmid in Venture," *Financial Times,* June 21, 1989, p. 33.

Laboratoires Pierre Fabre S.A.

Le Carla Burlats
Castres, 81106 Cedex
France
Telephone: (33 5 63) 62 38 50
Fax: (33 5 63) 51 68 75
Web site: http://www.pierre-fabre.com

Private Company
Incorporated: 1961
Employees: 9,500
Sales: EUR 1.7 billion ($2.5 billion) (2007 est.)
NAICS: 325412 Pharmaceutical Preparation Manufacturing; 325620 Toilet Preparation Manufacturing

■ ■ ■

Laboratoires Pierre Fabre S.A. is one of France's largest independent pharmaceuticals groups. Based in Castres, in the French southwest, Fabre operates through three primary divisions: Medicines, Family Health, and Dermo-Cosmetics. The company's Medicines division focuses on the oncology, cardiovascular, gynecology, pneumology, psychiatric, and rheumatology segments. Much of the company's pharmaceutical research is directed toward plant-based substances. An example of this is the group's anti-cancer agent Navelbine (Vinorelbine), derived from the periwinkle plant and first launched in 1989. Other major compounds developed by the company include Tardyferon, Lercan, Optruma, Ixel, Cyclo 3, and Ossopan. The Medicines division generated approximately 32 percent of Pierre Fabre's 2007 revenues of EUR 1.7 billion ($2.5 billion). The larger Dermo-Cosmetics division, which accounts for more than 45 percent of group sales, includes the company's family of dermatological and cosmetic products. This division includes consumer brands such as Avene, Elancyl, Klorane, A-derma, and Galénic, as well as the dermatological brands Pierre Fabre Dermatology, Glytone, and Ducray.

The third division, Family Health, includes the company's range of over-the-counter (OTC) and self-medication products. The division's products include oral hygiene products; plant-based nutritional and health products; and products for the treatment of allergies, nicotine delivery, female health, analgesics, and skin care, among others. Pierre Fabre has long been an internationally operating company. Sales outside of France represent more than 46 percent of the group's total turnover. Pierre Fabre is a privately owned company. In 2008, founder Pierre Fabre, then 82 years old, transferred his 60 percent control of the company to his charitable foundation, the Pierre Fabre Foundation. At the same time, the company named Jean-Pierre Garnier, formerly CEO of GlaxoSmithKline, as the company's chief executive officer.

FROM PHARMACIST TO PHARMACEUTICALS

Pierre Fabre began his career as a pharmacist, with his own pharmacy in the small town of Castres, in France's southwest. In 1961, however, Fabre's interest in the potential medicinal properties of plants led him to launch his own pharmaceuticals production. Fabre's first product was a "veinotonic"—a treatment for veinous

COMPANY PERSPECTIVES

■

40 years of experience in the service of health. Our mission: Innovate for the well-being of all.

insufficiency—derived from butcher's-broom (*Ruscus aculeatus*). Fabre called the tonic Cyclo 3. From the outset, Fabre displayed an understanding of the importance of marketing and packaging in the health and beauty market. An important part of Cyclo 3's success was Fabre's decision to package the tonic in an innovative, easy-to-open single-dose glass vial.

Phytochemicals were to remain the major focus of the research and development efforts of the Medicines division of Laboratoires Pierre Fabre. Over the next decades, the company scored a number of notable successes in this effort. Among the most important discoveries made by the company was the development of an anti-cancer compound, Vinorelbine, derived from a periwinkle found in Madagascar. Launched in 1989 under the brand name Navelbine, the compound became the company's flagship pharmaceutical product. This was particularly true after the company received authorization to market Navelbine in the United States in the 1990s. The launch of Navelbine confirmed Laboratoires Pierre Fabre's position among the leading independent French pharmaceuticals companies.

By then, Fabre had also established itself as one of the country's leading suppliers of health and beauty products. This effort began in 1965, when Fabre acquired Klorane, a small Puteaux-based company that had achieved some success with its plant-based soaps. Under Fabre, Klorane's production was quickly expanded into shampoos. The launch of Klorane's Shampoo with Chamomile in 1966 represented a new success for the company, becoming one of its strongest sellers into the next century.

Klorane also developed a range of technical shampoos, such as Klorane Bébé, in 1967, which became a mainstay of French maternity wards. In 1968, the company launched a line of shampoo treatments for various hair conditions. Into the 1970s, the Klorane brand added its own line of pharmaceutical cosmetics. This was joined by a new cleanser, a cornflower-based makeup remover for women with sensitive eyes, in 1972. Under Fabre, Klorane's growth was swift; by the early 1970s, the Klorane brand claimed a 35 percent share of the French pharmaceutical cosmetics market.

INTERNATIONAL EXPANSION

By then, Fabre had also begun expanding into new areas. The company's success in France, where its products were largely carried through the pharmacy channel, encouraged the company to expand into neighboring markets. Starting in 1970, the company added subsidiaries in Spain, Italy, and Germany. Fabre continued expanding its range of operations as well. In 1969, the company acquired Ducray Laboratories, a company based in Vichy that specialized in medical and pharmaceutical products for the treatment of dermatological disorders and other skin conditions.

Supporting the group's expansion into the 1970s was the establishment of its first dedicated research and development laboratory, the Pierre Fabre Research Center, in Castres. Over the next decades, Pierre Fabre emerged as the major employer in Castres and the surrounding region. The company also became one of the area's largest property holders, acquiring a large number of historic buildings, mansions, and manor houses. These were then converted to house the various branches of the growing Pierre Fabre empire.

Among the new extensions of the Pierre Fabre group toward the end of the 1970s was the launch of the Galénic brand in 1977. Like other parts of Pierre Fabre's operations, Galénic focused on the use of plant-based substances. The new brand developed its own line of therapeutic skin care and health and beauty aids. Fabre grew again in 1980, acquiring the René Furterer brand of professional hair care products.

Founder Pierre Fabre in the meantime had been building up a wider range of investments, in part by rescuing a number of struggling businesses in the region around Castres. Thus, by the end of the century, Fabre's personal interests had extended into publishing and printing, with holdings including Éditions Privat in Toulouse; Société de l'Imprimerie Artistique in Lavaur; and a stake in Midi Libre, a daily newspaper published in Montpellier. Other holdings included the Castres rugby team; vineyards and orchards; and Sud Radio and Digivision, a television production studio, both based in Toulouse.

More directly related with Laboratoires Pierre Fabre was the company's acquisition of the Eaux d'Avene thermal spring and spa. The therapeutic properties of the Avene spring water had been recognized in the early 18th century, and the spring had been the site of a spa for the treatment of dermatological conditions since 1743. By the early 1960s, the spa had fallen into disuse.

The beginning of a new era for the Avene spring began in 1965, when Pierre Fabre purchased the spa and restored it, building a new hotel on the site. Ownership of the spa was transferred to Laboratoires Pierre Fabre in 1975. It was not until the mid-1980s, however, that the company decided to develop a line of skin and beauty products based around the therapeutic water of the Avene spring. This effort started in 1986, with the founding of a dedicated research and development center, Avene Laboratories. By 1989, the company was ready to launch the Avene skin care line.

The Avene brand quickly became a new success for the company, and soon established itself as a leader in the therapeutic skin care sector on a global level. Among the new and important markets for the company was Japan. Pierre Fabre's entry there had come in 1986, through a joint venture partnership created with Japanese cosmetics and perfume giant Shiseido. By the end of the decade, the company had added subsidiaries in Belgium and Switzerland as well. In 1989, the company moved into Portugal, buying two companies there, Robapharm and Lineapharm.

In 1990, Fabre boosted its international profile through the acquisition of U.S.-based Physicians Formula Cosmetics. That company, founded in the late 1930s, focused on the production of hypoallergenic cosmetics and skin care products. The addition of the mass market Physicians Formula brand represented Fabre's first extension beyond its core pharmacy and drugstore channel.

BRIEF PARTNERSHIPS

The launch of the Navelbine anti-cancer agent in 1989, and its authorization in the U.S. market several years later, had helped raise Pierre Fabre's pharmaceuticals profile to a global level as well. The company's strong research and development component, and its long-standing expertise in plant-based research, made it a sought-after partner by other pharmaceutical and research players at the beginning of the new century.

Fabre formed one of its first partnerships in 1999, with France's National Scientific Research Center (CNRS). Two years later, the company agreed to develop a cancer treatment research partnership with Celera Genomics. Also in 2001, the company formed a research partnership with Genfit, focusing on diabetes treatments. By 2003, the company had strengthened its U.S. presence as well, forming a development and distribution agreement with Cypress Bioscience for Pierre Fabre's milnacipran pain reliever used to treat fibromyalgia.

Pierre Fabre, in his late 70s by this time, had also been developing plans for his succession. This effort had begun in the early 1990s, when Pierre Fabre had reached a verbal alliance with his counterpart at Servier, then the third largest independent laboratory in France. The search for succession took on more earnestness in the late 1990s, as Fabre saw its profits collapse. In 1998, Fabre turned to outside help, bringing in Jean-Luc Belangeard, former head of Hoffmann-La Roche's diagnostic division, to lead the company.

Pierre Fabre also targeted new diversified growth. In 1998, the company acquired majority control of Dolisos, then the second largest producer of homeopathic products in the world, with a listing on the Paris stock exchange. However, Dolisos had been losing money through the 1990s, and quickly became a drag on Fabre's bottom line as well.

Fabre continued to seek new partners. The need to develop scale had become all the more urgent given the rapid consolidation of the global pharmaceuticals sector in the late 1990s. Fabre began merger discussions with bioMérieux, a company that specialized in diagnostic products, led by Fabre's friend Alain Mérieux. The two companies were said by some observers to have begun merger talks as early as the 1980s. In 2000, Fabre and bioMérieux agreed to a merger, forming France's second largest independent pharmaceuticals company.

However, the union between the two proved brief. Unable to agree on management styles, and with few similarities between the two companies, Fabre and Mérieux agreed to dissolve the merger. By 2003, Fabre had regained control of Laboratoires Pierre Fabre and its operations. Also in that year, the company decided to exit the U.S. mass market, selling 80 percent of its Physicians Formula subsidiary to investment group Summit Partners.

Meanwhile, Dolisos had failed in its attempt to turn around its Dolisos homeopathy wing. The company had begun looking for a buyer for its more than 65 percent stake in that operation by the beginning of the 21st century, nearly completing a sale to Merck in 2002. Instead, the company moved to buy out the remaining shares of Dolisos, succeeding in gaining control of nearly all of that company in 2004. This set the stage for the sale of Dolisos, which was delisted from the Paris bourse that year. By 2005, the company had reached an agreement to sell Dolisos to its chief rival, Laboratoires Boiron, in a share-swap deal valued at nearly EUR 33 million ($40 million).

THREE-PRONGED STRATEGY FOR THE FUTURE

Having shed its homeopathic division, Pierre Fabre then regrouped around a three-division strategy: Medicines, Family Health, and Dermo-Cosmetics. The company continued to invest in its growth by boosting its research and development component. In 2002, for example, the company founded its Skin and Superficial Epithelium Research Center in conjunction with St. Jacques Hospital in Toulouse. The company also completed the acquisition of U.S.-based Genesis, and its Wellskin and Glylone brands. This acquisition gave Fabre direct entry into a new sales channel, the offices of dermatologists. Genesis's distribution covered nearly half of that U.S. market.

Fabre continued to seek new growth opportunities into the second half of the decade. The company turned toward the South American market, where it acquired 70 percent of Darrow Laboratorios, based in Rio de Janeiro in Brazil, in 2006. The purchase gave Fabre an important presence in that national market—the 11th largest pharmaceuticals market, and seventh largest cosmetics market in the world.

Fabre also moved to strengthen its presence in Germany, where its subsidiary there remained heavily focused on Novalbine sales. However, Fabre's patent on that molecule had expired. Faced with the arrival of new generic forms of the drug, the company sought to expand its portfolio of products in Germany and elsewhere. As part of that effort, the company agreed to acquire the German operations of Zambon Laboratory in 2007.

Fabre also boosted its OTC operations that year, buying up the OTC business of Belgium's biopharma operations. The agreement gave Fabre control of the OTC portfolio in the Benelux markets, as well as in France, Switzerland, and Greece. The acquisition gave Fabre control of more than ten new drug brands, including Cicatryl ointment; the gastrointestinal treatment Carbolevure; Nceyrane, a disinfectant; and Toclase, a cough suppressant.

Fabre continued to seek new horizons in 2008. The company launched an oncology research partnership with India's Nicholas Piramal in January 2008. In October of that year, Fabre founded a new marketing unit, Pierre Fabre Podologie, to develop a closer distribution relationship with France's podologists (podiatrists). By this time, Pierre Fabre, then in his early eighties, had taken steps to preserve the independence of the group he had founded nearly 50 years before. In October 2008, Fabre turned over his controlling stake in the company to his charitable group, the Pierre Fabre Foundation. At the same time, Fabre named a new chief executive, Jean-Pierre Garnier, former head of GlaxoSmithKline, to take over as head of the company. From a small pharmacy in southwestern France, Pierre Fabre had built a major independent player in the global cosmetics and pharmaceuticals markets.

M. L. Cohen

PRINCIPAL SUBSIDIARIES

Pierre Fabre (Suisse) S.A.; Pierre Fabre Chine; Pierre Fabre Iberica S.A. (Spain); Pierre Fabre Inc. (United States); Pierre Fabre Ltd (United Kingdom); Pierre Fabre Pharma Canada Inc.; Pierre Fabre Pharma GmbH (Germany); Robapharm AG (Switzerland); S.A.S. Les Thermes; Sante Active Inc. (United States); Tema Medical (Pty) Ltd (South Africa).

PRINCIPAL COMPETITORS

RPG Enterprises; Nestlé S.A.; McKesson Corp.; Procter & Gamble Co.; Aventis S.A.; Johnson & Johnson; Bayer AG; Pfizer Inc.; Roche Holding AG; Sanofi-Aventis.

FURTHER READING

David, Christian, "Pierre Fabre, Le Seigneur du Midi," *L'Expansion,* September 1, 2002.

Delaroche, Philippe, "Pierre Fabre, Adepte du Marketing Global," *L'Expansion,* June 1, 2005.

Eisberg, Neil, "French Over-the-Counter (OTC) Pharma Concern Pierre Fabre (Castres) Has Acquired the OTC

Business of Belgian Biopharma Company UCB (Brussels) in France, the Benelux Countries, Switzerland and Greece," *Chemistry and Industry,* January 29, 2007, p. 14.

"Fabre Takes Full Control of Dolisos," *Nutraceuticals International,* January 2004.

Gallard, Philippe, "Quatorze Ans pour un Accord entre Fabre et bioMérieux," *L'Expansion,* September 28, 2000.

"Genfit, Pierre Fabre Renew Their Collaboration," *R&D Focus Drug News,* January 21, 2008.

Halpern, Nathalie, "Merieux and Fabre to Separate," *Financial Times,* January 25, 2002.

"Pierre Fabre Donates Equity Interest to Fabre Foundation,"

Household & Personal Products Industry, October 2008, p. 28.

"Pierre Fabre in US Sell-off," *Cosmetics International,* November 21, 2003, p. 9.

"Pierre Fabre Overhauls Ducray Brand," *Cosmetics International,* June 22, 2007, p. 4.

"Pierre Fabre Takes to Protect Independence," *Cosmetics International,* September 19, 2008, p. 4.

"Q&A Claire Salmon-Legagneur of Pierre Fabre Inc.," *Cosmetics International,* January 25, 2008, p. 14.

"Sante Active Inc., the U.S. Subsidiary of Laboratoires Pierre Fabre, France," *Global Cosmetic Industry,* May 2008, p. 12.

QSS Group, Inc.

———————————————■———————————————

4500 Forbes Boulevard, Suite 200
Lanham, Maryland 20706-6316
U.S.A.
Telephone: (301) 577-0700
Fax: (301) 918-4822
Web site: http://www.qssgroupinc.com

Wholly Owned Subsidiary of Perot Systems Corporation
Incorporated: 1994
Employees: 1,400
Sales: $260 million (2007 est.)
NAICS: 541511 Custom Computer Programming
Services; 518111 Internet Service Providers; 518210
Data Processing, Hosting, and Related Services;
541512 Computer Systems Design Services;
531513 Computer Facilities Management Services

■ ■ ■

QSS Group, Inc., is a Lanham, Maryland-based
information technology (IT) and engineering support
services company that serves federal government agencies, including Commerce, the Department of Defense,
Department of Homeland Security, Housing and Urban
Development, Human Services, the Intelligence Community, the National Aeronautics and Space Administration (NASA), Treasury Department, and the Executive
Office of the President. A subsidiary of Perot Systems
Corporation, QSS offers intelligence technology services,
including architecture development, system and security
engineering, program management, and help desk
services. QSS also offers IT enterprise solutions, including consulting, network design and other infrastructure
services, help desk and call center services, Web and
database design, software development life-cycle services
and support, and security and authorization services.

In addition, QSS provides science and engineering
services related to spacecraft development, mission
operations, surveillance and reconnaissance, ground
control systems, flight software, wind tunnel tests,
propulsion research, atmospheric and earth science,
space and solar physics, and computational sciences,
including intelligence systems, autonomy and robotics,
and modeling and simulation. QSS maintains operations in about 60 cities in the United States as well as
offices in England, France, Germany, and the
Netherlands.

ORIGINS

QSS Group was a very small operation, founded in
1988, when Frank F. Islam acquired it in 1994; QSS
dates its history to the latter year, when it began its
transformation from an unknown bit player to
celebrated success story, one that garnered Islam several
rewards for his entrepreneurship. Islam was born in Aligarh, in northern India, and began his college education
at Aligarh Muslim University before emigrating to the
United States in 1968 "in pursuit of hope, happiness
and dreams," as he recalled in a speech he gave at the
school in 2008. In the United States, Islam completed
his education, enrolling at the University of Colorado
and earning a bachelor of science degree in computer
sciences. He stayed in Boulder to earn a master's degree
in computer science as well as a second master's in applied mathematics.

Upon graduation in 1976, Islam moved to the Washington, D.C., area to begin his career at Computer Sciences Corporation (CSC), working as a software engineer on a contract basis at the Goddard Space Center, involved with orbit and altitude determination for the satellite that communicated with the space shuttle. He left for Hughes Aircraft in 1982. There Islam started out involved in software development, moved up to program manager, and graduated to the post of project manager. He was also involved in projects for the U.S. Navy, NASA, and the Federal Aviation Administration, providing him with experience serving federal government agencies.

While successful by the definition of many, Islam was reportedly not completely satisfied with his life at Hughes and harbored an urge to take on the challenge of starting his own business. Islam left Hughes and struck out on his own, planning to put to use the skills and insights he had developed from implementing and managing projects related to information technology and engineering services at CSC and Hughes. Although Islam acquired QSS in 1994, the company had actually originated in 1988 as Quality System Services. It was little more than a one-person shell company, but it possessed one important asset: certification from the Small Business Administration to do business with the federal government. In 1994, when the owner elected to go into the fax business, he sold Quality System Services to Islam. Not happy with the name, Islam changed it to QSS Group, Inc.

To buy Quality System and start his business, Islam mortgaged his house and then set up shop in College Park, Maryland. He told the *Daily Record* of Baltimore, "I started with no employees, no revenues, no place to sit, no computer and no copy machine." All he had was a phone. He had to rely on his wife, who worked at CSC, for his health insurance and income. He spent some time marketing himself but with no success, according to the *Daily Record*. "It was pretty bad," he admitted. "I began to doubt myself." Islam's luck changed later in 1994 when he landed his first

customer: NASA's Goddard Space Flight Center. QSS was hired to perform engineering and database services. The $200,000 NASA contract was less than Islam's accumulated debt of $250,000, but it was a beginning. Nevertheless, another year and a half would pass before he was able to draw a salary.

SECOND CONTRACT SECURED: 1995

Devoted to customer satisfaction, Islam and QSS performed well for NASA on the initial contract, which opened the door to a 1995 information technology contract with the Goddard Space Flight Center. For this contract QSS did development work on client/server applications. It also provided information technology security. QSS was by this time better established in its field, and revenues increased to $3.4 million in 1996. To maintain its edge, the company placed an emphasis on hiring the most qualified people available, a very high percentage of which held advanced degrees. They also shared Islam's commitment to quality work and meeting customer needs, as demonstrated by the high percentage of performance fees the company received on its government contracts. About half of these contracts were based on how well a vendor performed. QSS received on average about 95 percent of the potential payout on these contracts.

The Small Business Administration's 8(a) program that opened the way for minority-owned businesses to compete for federal contracts was a contributing factor in the QSS success story. The program had been established in 1969 to help minority business owners who had a net worth of less than $250,000, not including their equity in their home and business. There was no guarantee of winning federal contracts, but the door was opened, and Frank Islam as an Asian American qualified and took advantage of 8(a). The Washington, D.C., location of QSS was also important, because that was where the bulk of the customers were located. By fiscal 2000 QSS was the second largest 8(a) contractor in the United States, in that year receiving $66.6 million in business through the program. A year later Frank Islam was named the Minority Small Business Person of the Year for the Washington metropolitan area by the Small Business Administration. In 2002 NASA named QSS its Minority Contractor of the Year.

QSS ENTERS AEROSPACE ENGINEERING MARKET: 1998

The rapid growth of QSS in the late 1990s was noteworthy and resulted in other, mainstream awards

KEY DATES

1994: QSS Group is founded.
1997: Frank Islam is named Ernst & Young Entrepreneur of the Year.
1998: QSS enters aerospace engineering market.
2007: QSS sold to Perot Systems Government Services.

for Frank Islam. In 1997 he was named Ernst & Young Entrepreneur of the Year, at a time when his company was just beginning to surge. In 1998 QSS generated revenues of $16.5 million, (none of which yet came from the Department of Defense), or an 8,800 percent five-year growth rate. This performance provided QSS with a No. 11 ranking on the *Inc.* magazine list of the fastest-growing private companies. Furthermore, in 1998 QSS won a major engineering contract with NASA, giving the company entry into the aerospace engineering market and a host of new lucrative contract possibilities. The company also teamed up with much larger companies to win contracts. In 1999, for example, QSS joined forces with Raytheon Company and some small vendors to fulfill a five-year $33 million contract to maintain the space science data operations at the Goddard Space Flight Center.

The company was also entirely capable of winning sizable contracts on its own. In March 2001 it received a $180 million contract from NASA for engineering and scientific support. In July 2005 QSS won the largest contract in its history to date, worth a possible $300 million over five years. The contract called for QSS to provide support for the U.S. Coast Guard Operations Systems Center. By this time the Coast Guard had been folded into the operations of the Department of Homeland Security. Formed in the wake of the terrorist attacks of September 11, 2001, the new agency provided QSS with many new opportunities and helped QSS grow annual revenues to $300 million in 2006.

PEROT ACQUIRES QSS: 2007

In 2006 Islam was approached by Perot Systems Government Services, a division of Plano, Texas-based Perot Systems Corporation, about buying QSS. He agreed to sell the business for $250 million, and the deal was finalized in early 2007. It was the largest acquisition in Perot's history. Islam's reasons for selling QSS were manifold. First, the timing was right. The company was an attractive acquisition target, perhaps at the peak of its

value. As Islam explained in an interview he gave to the *ExecutiveBiz* newsletter, "We had successfully diversified the customer base so that we were not reliant upon any one significant contract or agency." Anther factor was the company's size. Islam characterized it as "big enough to have a significant impact on any company that might acquire us, without being so big as to pose an integration challenge." While Islam was reportedly content to continue running QSS for many years to come, he was also not averse to taking on a new challenge in life and was willing to sell at the right price. Hardly desperate to sell the business, Islam was able to command a premium for QSS, but more than that, he thought QSS "would be a good fit and that this would therefore provide a great opportunity for the employee population to continue to grow with the business."

After selling QSS, Islam, although wealthy, was not ready for retirement, despite years of 16-hour days and workweeks of six and seven days. He formed the Debbie and Frank Islam Foundation to provide scholarships for the arts and education around the world, including his native India. He also formed FI Investment Group and became chairman and CEO. Through the group's subsidiaries, Islam was able to act as a venture capitalist as well as acquire small companies to grow. The portfolio companies would soon include Viligar, an information services company; Millennium Scan, a healthcare company that provided noninvasive, full-body screening; and SouthPeak, an interactive video game publisher.

What made QSS attractive to Perot, according to *Defense Daily,* was that it strengthened "Perot's information technology capabilities, particularly in the areas of information assurance and applications development and management. It also expand[ed] its service offerings within the Departments of Defense and Homeland Security (DHS) and [gave] it new government-wide acquisition contracts." Perot Systems was established in Texas in 1988 by Ross Perot, who became better known to the world for running for president of the United States four years later, and, according to some analysts, essentially established the IT services industry.

Over the years, Perot Systems built up a roster of major corporate clients, and in 2002 acquired ADI Technology Corporation, a consulting and IT services provider for the federal government, which became the foundation for Perot Systems Government Services, Inc. The subsidiary grew further with the 2003 acquisition of Soza & Company, Ltd. Thus, the addition of QSS was part of an aggressive push by Perot into the public sector. As part of Perot, QSS entered a new phase of its history, and given the success of its new corporate parent, there was every reason to believe that it would continue to prosper despite the loss of its longtime chief executive.

Ed Dinger

PRINCIPAL OPERATING UNITS

Information Technology Enterprise Solutions; Science and Engineering Solutions; Intelligence Technology.

PRINCIPAL COMPETITORS

CACI International Inc.; Computer Sciences Corporation; Raytheon Company.

FURTHER READING

Ariano, Alexis, "Here's How MD. Entrepreneurs Came to Start Their Own Firms," *Baltimore (Md.) Daily Record,* January 6, 1999, p. 1A.

"Executive Spotlight with Frank Islam," *ExecutiveBiz,* June 14, 2007.

Hoover, Kent, "Favored Few Nab 8(a) Work," *Dallas Business Journal,* October 5, 2001, p.1.

"Living the American Dream—Frank Islam," *IndiaPost.com,* July 13, 2008.

"Perot Systems Agrees to Acquire Federal IT Services Provider QSS Group," *Defense Daily,* December 22, 2006.

R.R. Bowker LLC

———■———

630 Central Avenue
New Providence, New Jersey 07974
U.S.A.
Telephone: (908) 286-1090
Toll Free: (800) 526-9537
Fax: (908) 219-0098
Web site: http://www.bowker.com

Wholly Owned Subsidiary of Cambridge Information
    Group, Inc.
Incorporated: 1911
Employees: 230
Sales: $25.6 million (2008 est.)
NAICS: 511130 Book Publishers

■ ■ ■

R.R. Bowker LLC serves the publishing, bookselling, and library trades with bibliographic information and other data services. In addition to its flagship *Books in Print* reference source, the firm offers data tracking and ordering systems Pubnet, PubEasy, and PubTrack, as well as database access and enhancement products AquaBrowser and Syndetic Solutions. The firm has since 1968 assigned the International Standard Book Number (ISBN) with which each book published in the United States is cataloged. New Jersey-based Bowker also has operations in England and Australia.

BEGINNINGS

R.R. Bowker's origins can be traced to the late 1850s, when German immigrant Frederick Leypoldt founded a company to import and sell books. Leypoldt had arrived in New York in 1855 from Stuttgart and worked in a bookstore there for several years before leaving to start an import business in Philadelphia. When the Civil War began in 1861, foreign titles became difficult to obtain, and he soon turned to selling American books and publishing translations. In 1864 Leypoldt added a New York branch, which became his sole operation two years later when he formed a publishing partnership with Henry Holt.

Leypoldt was unhappy with the state of the book publishing industry, regarding it as beset by unfair pricing policies and poor copyright protection, and in 1868 he began publishing the monthly *Literary Bulletin,* a periodical that included news and editorials as well as a listing of available titles. After selling his share in the firm to Holt to concentrate on compiling bibliographic listings, he oversaw the 1870 publication of the *American Catalogue for 1869,* which collected the monthly title listings from what had become known as the *Trade Circular and Literary Bulletin.*

In early 1872 Leypoldt bought a 20-year-old trade newsletter called the *American Publishers' Circular and Literary Gazette,* which was merged into his own monthly to form the *Publishers' and Stationers' Weekly Trade Circular,* which offered both editorial content and lists of new titles. It was soon adopted as the official voice of the Publishers Board of Trade and the American Book Trade Association, and in 1873 its name was shortened to *Publishers Weekly.* That same year Leypoldt published the *Uniform Trade List Annual,* which compiled all the titles published in the United States.

Later known as the *Publishers' Trade List Annual,* it would become one of the firm's signature offerings.

One of the first contributors to *Publishers Weekly* was Richard Rogers Bowker, who had contributed a review of literature from 1871. Born in Salem, Massachusetts, in 1848, Bowker had attended the City College of New York before taking a job as literary editor of the *New York Evening Mail.* In 1875 he began working for the *New York Tribune* and was also named editor of *Publishers Weekly.* Bowker was a strong advocate for libraries, and in 1876 he joined with Leypoldt and Massachusetts-based librarian Melvil Dewey to lay plans for what would become the American Library Association. A publication called the *American Library Journal,* edited by Bowker, would serve as its house organ.

Growing out of a regular column in *Publishers Weekly, Library Journal* (as it later became known) was intended to serve librarians the way the former served booksellers, but the new magazine struggled to find subscribers and would lose money for many years. Leypoldt was reportedly not an especially good businessman, and in 1879 Bowker bought his interest in *Publishers Weekly* for $5,000, which was used to support work on the *American Catalogue* of books published up to 1876, which appeared in 1880. Leypoldt also was working on a growing list of other titles that included the *Index Medicus* for physicians.

BOWKER TAKES CONTROL OF THE FIRM IN 1884

After two years in London on assignment for *Harper's,* Bowker returned in 1884 following Leypoldt's unexpected death to publish and edit *Publishers Weekly.* He also continued Leypoldt's money-losing *American*

Catalogue, completing it and widening its scope. To streamline the business, some titles, including *Index Medicus,* were sold.

During these years Bowker advocated strongly for the passage of international copyright legislation, and his efforts bore fruit in 1891 when President Benjamin Harrison signed the first American copyright law. In 1911 Leypoldt's widow Augusta, who had worked with Bowker following her husband's death, agreed to become partners with him in the newly formed R.R. Bowker Company.

The firm continued to introduce new titles for the publishing industry such as the 1915 *American Booktrade Manual* (later the *American Book Trade Directory*), which listed and described book retailers, publishers, wholesalers, periodicals, and more. In 1921 the company began importing the *Reference Catalog of Current Literature* from English firm J. Whitaker & Sons, which would later take the title *British Books in Print,* and over time it added other English and European bibliographic titles. In 1932 Carolyn Ulrich, head of the New York Public Library's periodicals division, completed the first volume of a directory of magazines and journals for Bowker; this would become known as *Ulrich's International Periodicals Directory.*

In 1933 Richard Rogers Bowker died at the age of 85, and *Publishers Weekly* coeditor Frederic Melcher was named to head the firm. At this time *Publishers Weekly* had 2,000 subscribers while *Library Journal* had 4,500.

BOOKS IN PRINT DEBUTS IN 1948

New titles added in the coming years included the *Literary Market Place* (a publishing industry directory that listed agents, publishers, media outlets, distributors, and service firms), which was launched in 1940, and 1948's *Books in Print.* The latter, a title index to the *Publishers' Trade List Annual,* proved an immediate hit with librarians and booksellers and would go on to be one of the firm's most prominent offerings, and, along with *Publishers Weekly,* one of its most profitable. Bowker was moving forward with technology, using new cold type processes that had been developed by Frederic Melcher's son Daniel. In 1956 a new spinoff, the *Subject Guide to Books in Print,* was also introduced.

Changes were also taking place with *Library Journal.* In 1948 a new feature called "School Libraries" had been added, and this section became so popular that it evolved into a stand-alone magazine, *Junior Libraries,* in 1954. This would later be retitled *School Library Journal.*

In 1960 the monthly *American Book Publishing Record (ABPR)* was introduced, which gave full Library

```
┌─────────────────────────────────────────┐
│                                           │
│             KEY DATES                     │
│                ■                          │
│  ──────────────────────────────────────   │
│                                           │
│  1872:  Frederick Leypoldt introduces     │
│         *Publishers Weekly.*              │
│  1876:  Leypoldt, Melvil Dewey, and       │
│         Richard Rogers Bowker found       │
│         *Library Journal.*                │
│  1879:  Bowker buys *Publishers Weekly*   │
│         from Leypoldt.                    │
│  1911:  Leypoldt's widow and Bowker       │
│         found the R.R. Bowker Co.         │
│  1948:  *Books in Print* introduced as    │
│         index to *Publishers' Trade List  │
│         Annual.*                          │
│  1967:  Xerox buys Bowker for $90         │
│         million.                          │
│  1968:  Firm named official U.S. issuer   │
│         of ISBN numbers.                  │
│  1985:  Reed purchases company from       │
│         Xerox.                            │
│  1986:  First electronic version of       │
│         *Books in Print* appears on       │
│         CD-ROM.                           │
│  2001:  Cambridge Information Group        │
│         buys firm, sells directories to   │
│         Information Today.                 │
│  2007:  AquaBrowser producer Medialab     │
│         Solutions BV acquired.            │
│                                           │
└─────────────────────────────────────────┘
```

of Congress cataloging information for each title listed in *Publishers Weekly.* During the year Bowker also added a bibliography of Spanish-language books published in the Western Hemisphere called *Fichero Bibliografico Hispano-Americano.* Other titles documenting this sector of the marketplace ensued, such as *Libros en Venta,* a Spanish version of *Books in Print.*

In 1961 the firm took control of the Jaques Cattell Press, whose founder had died the previous year. Titles such as *American Men of Science,* which had been published in cooperation with Bowker for some time, would continue under the leadership of Cattell's widow Elizabeth.

In 1963 company president Frederic Melcher died, and his place was taken by his son Daniel. During his career the senior Melcher had left his mark on the world of libraries and publishing, with numerous accomplishments that included the founding of the prestigious Newbery and Caldecott Awards for children's books.

In 1964 new subsidiary Library Journal Cards, Inc., was founded to produce catalog cards and related materials that simplified the work of school library staff. On the technical front Bowker was increasingly relying on computers for use in typesetting, which sped up production and allowed for more manipulation of information into derivative products. The firm was also adding new titles for an global clients including the

International Literary Market Place and *International Book Trade Directory.*

SALE TO XEROX IN 1967

In December 1967 Bowker was merged into the Education Division of Xerox Corporation. The following year industry veteran George McCorkle was named president and Daniel Melcher became chairman, although he resigned a few months later, reportedly frustrated with the company's new direction.

Bowker was designated by the Library of Congress as the official issuer of ISBN numbers for books published in the United States in 1968. The ISBN system assigned a unique identification number to each title and was widely used in the book trades.

In the fall of 1977 the firm added another new magazine, *Bookviews,* which was targeted at book consumers, but it was not a success and soon was shuttered. Two years later Bowker began distributing the *Australian Books in Print* of D.W. Thorpe Pty. Ltd., and in 1983 a new bimonthly title, *Small Press,* was added to cover the output of the rapidly growing ranks of small publishing companies.

In 1984 the firm created an Electronic Publishing Division that began to offer dial-up access to *Books in Print* and also launched the Book Acquisition System, which allowed libraries and bookstores to order any title from a central database of 630,000 in-print books by entering an ISBN. The project was created in collaboration with distributor Baker & Taylor, which would supply price information, with Bowker forwarding orders to a publisher or wholesaler designated by the user.

In July 1984 the company bought software database and print listing products from PC Telemart, in a bid to produce reference materials for the computer industry. For the year Bowker had sales of $41.5 million and a profit of $7.8 million. Circulation of flagship title *Publishers Weekly* stood at 38,000, and the firm employed 340.

REED HOLDINGS ACQUIRES BOWKER IN 1985

With Xerox seeking to pay down its rising debt, in 1985 it sold Bowker to Reed Holdings, Inc., for $90 million. The firm's new owner was part of Reed International plc of the United Kingdom, which had interests in publishing, paint, and paper. Its U.S. operations included numerous business journals published by Cahners Magazines and several trade show units. Bowker magazine titles including *Publishers Weekly* and *Library Journal* were soon shifted into the Cahners portfolio.

In 1986 Bowker introduced CD-ROM versions of *Books in Print* and *Ulrich's*. Over the next several years they were joined by more than a dozen other titles including *Literary Market Place, American Book Trade Directory, Bowker Annual,* and the *Enviro/Energyline Abstracts* index to environmental/energy research and news. Some databases were available both on CD-ROM and via the Dialog database service.

In 1991 Bowker became part of Reed's new Reference Publishing Division, which also included Martindale-Hubbell, Marquis Who's Who, National Register Publishing Co., K.G. Saur, and D.W. Thorpe.

In 1993 the first global English-language CD-ROM version of *Books in Print* was introduced in partnership with fellow Reed units Thorpe and Saur, plus J. Whitaker & Sons of England, publisher of *Bookbank*. During the year the firm's parent, known as Reed Elsevier after a merger with Dutch publisher Elsevier NV, expanded Bowker's data unit into Reed Reference Electronic Publishing, which would handle all of the company's digital information projects.

In 1994 Bowker partnered with Online Computer Center Inc. (OCLC) to develop a joint book ordering and cataloging service for librarians. The firm also sold its *Environmental Abstracts* title to Congressional Information Service. In 1996 the company formed a joint venture with the American Booksellers Association, the Association of American Publishers, and the National Association of College Stores to upgrade ten-year-old online ordering system Pubnet, whose heart was *Books in Print*.

In the late 1990s Bowker's flagship *Books in Print* began facing unexpected competition from new free online information sources such as Amazon.com, and sales began to plummet. In 2000 the firm introduced the subscription-based online Booksinprint.com, which was enhanced with book reviews, tables of contents from Blackwell's, information about out-of-print books from Alibris, electronic titles from netLibrary, and direct online ordering via wholesaler Brodart. The cost was $2,500 per year for a single user and $750 for each additional one, although libraries could still purchase the less-expensive CD-ROM and print editions. Online versions of many other products were also created, including Globalbooksinprint.com, Ulrichsweb.com and Literarymarketplace.com, as well as a site called BookWire.com that offered industry news and other information.

PURCHASE BY CAMBRIDGE INFORMATION GROUP IN 2001

In February 2001 the firm sold its children's reference titles to Greenwood Publishing Group, and in August science and technology publisher Cambridge Information Group of Bethesda, Maryland, bought Bowker for a figure estimated at $20 million to 30 million. After acquiring the firm, Cambridge sold ten of its directory titles, including *Literary Market Place* and *American Men and Women of Science,* to Information Today, Inc., which would retain the Bowker name for *The Bowker Annual Library and Book Trade Almanac*. Reed's Cahners unit would continue to publish several former Bowker magazines including *Publishers Weekly* and *Library Journal*.

After the sale the company was reconfigured as R.R. Bowker LLC. Still headquartered in New Providence, New Jersey, it would also continue to operate U.K. and Australian subsidiaries. Bowker CEO Andrew Meyer subsequently retired, and general manager Michael Cairns was put in charge.

The firm's publications included the flagship *Books in Print* series and its offshoots; *Ulrich's Periodical Directory; Magazines for Libraries;* nearly a dozen journals and newsletters including *Business Information Review* and *Journal of Information Science;* and various other products and web sites. Bowker would also continue to be the official U.S. assigner of ISBNs. Sister unit Cambridge Scientific Abstracts became the home of its abstract and index series including *Information Science Abstracts* and *British Humanities Index*.

Still seeking to re-create itself in the digital information age, Bowker began to pursue a strategy of partnering with other companies. In early 2002, retail giant Barnes & Noble announced it would use *Books in Print* as its exclusive source of bibliographic information, with wholesaler Baker & Taylor agreeing to help expand the information it contained. In May Bowker became the sole owner of Pubnet, the joint-venture firm that was used by more than 3,000 U.S. booksellers to order directly from publishers. Other ventures of the year included the U.S. launch of the International Standard Music Number (ISMN) for sheet music, a partnership with ebrary to add searchable content to Booksinprint.com, and an expanded relationship with OCLC.

SIMBA INFORMATION ACQUIRED IN 2003

In the fall of 2003 Bowker acquired Primedia subsidiary Simba Information, Inc., a 15-year-old publisher of newsletters and analysis for the publishing and media industries. Other additions of the year included e-commerce service PubEasy, Childrensbooksinprint.com, and Spanishbooksinprint.com. In 2004 the firm bought college publishing information provider Monument Information Resources of New Jersey and Oregon-based Syndetic Solutions, which developed multimedia content for online library catalogs.

In 2005 an information gathering deal with Nielsen Bookdata of the United Kingdom lapsed and Bowker took over the creation and management of British bibliographic information for Globalbooksinprint.com. It included books, audiobooks, and videos, and was subsequently upgraded to integrate Spanish-language materials. Bowker also partnered with Ann Arbor, Michigan-based All Media Guide and wholesaler Ingram Book Group to enhance the content it provided. New products added during 2005 included *Ulrich's Resource Linker* and *Bowker's Book Analysis System,* in a partnership with H.W. Wilson.

In early 2006 the firm's *Ulrich's* line was transferred to Cambridge Scientific Abstracts, and in the fall the new *Resources for College Libraries* appeared in collaboration with the American Library Association's Association of College and Research Libraries. It had been assembled by some 500 bibliographers to identify core titles in a wide range of disciplines. A reader's advisory product, *Fiction Connection,* was added during the year as well, which was soon followed by a nonfiction version.

In early 2007 Bowker introduced PubTrack Consumer, which gave publishers information about consumer preferences and demographics. In May the firm partnered with Lulu.com to sell ISBNs to self-published authors, and in June it bought Medialab Solutions BV, creator of the AquaBrowser Library search platform, which was in use by some 60 million library patrons in the United States. and Europe. Medialab would remain headquartered in Amsterdam. In 2008 Bowker continued to add new products including a data warehousing service for publishers and a web site called MyIdentifiers.com.

In more than a century of service to the publishing, bookselling, and library communities, R.R. Bowker LLC had established itself as one of the world's leading bibliographic authorities. Challenged by changes wrought by the digital revolution, the firm was working to reinvent its products and services under the wing of new owner Cambridge Information Group.

Frank Uhle

PRINCIPAL SUBSIDIARIES

Bowker U.K. & International Ltd. (United Kingdom); Thorpe-Bowker (Australia); Syndetic Solutions, Inc.; Simba Information, Inc.; Medialab Solutions BV (Netherlands); Pubnet.

PRINCIPAL COMPETITORS

The H.W. Wilson Company; Cengage Learning; Greenwood Publishing Group; Neal-Schuman Publishers, Inc.; Information Today, Inc.; EBSCO Industries, Inc.; BPI Communications, Inc.

FURTHER READING

Casper, Scott E., et al., *A History of the Book in America: Volume III: The Industrial Book, 1840–1880,* Chapel Hill: University of North Carolina Press, 2007.

Hane, Paula J., "Reed Elsevier Sells Bowker to CSA, ITI," *Information Today,* October 1, 2001, p. 1.

Horwitz, Sari, "Xerox to Sell Publishing Subsidiaries," *Washington Post,* April 23, 1985.

McDermott, Irene E., "*Books in Print* Wrestles with Amazon," *Searcher,* July 1, 2001, p. 53.

Milliot, Jim, "Bowker Moves Forward Under New Ownership," *Publishers Weekly,* January 14, 2002, p. 11.

"Primedia Sells Simba Information to R.R. Bowker," *Business Publisher,* September 17, 2003, p. 2.

Quint, Barbara, "Bowker for Sale, All or in Parts," *Information Today,* April 2001, p. 8.

Rogers, Michael, "Bowker on the Rebound," *Library Journal,* April 1, 2006, p. 26.

"R.R. Bowker Acquires Syndetic Solutions," *Business Publisher,* September 30, 2004, p. 2.

Renaissance Learning, Inc.

2911 Peach Street
Wisconsin Rapids, Wisconsin 54494-1905
U.S.A.
Telephone: (715) 424-3636
Toll Free: (800) 656-6746
Fax: (715) 424-4242
Web site: http://www.renlearn.com

Public Company
Incorporated: 1986 as Advantage Learning Systems
Employees: 990
Sales: $108 million (2007)
Stock Exchanges: NASDAQ
Ticker Symbol: RLRN
NAICS: 511210 Software Publishers

■■■

Renaissance Learning, Inc., is the world's leading provider of computer-based reading, writing, and math assessment programs for kindergarten through 12th-grade students. Its software products are used in approximately 75,000 classrooms across North America. The company's principal product is a software program called Accelerated Reader, which was invented by founder Judith Paul for use by her own children. The software tracks students' reading ability and comprehension through computerized tests based on thousands of books. Students earn points based on the length and difficulty of the books they have mastered. The product is marketed directly to teachers. Renaissance Learning also offers Accelerated Math, STAR Reading, English in a

Flash, Read Now Power Up, and other language acquisition and reading intervention software, as well as classroom response system software. All are designed to allow teachers to track the progress of individual students, so that teachers can focus their classroom time more precisely on individual needs. The company also produces NEO laptops, priced competitively for school markets. Renaissance Learning is based in Wisconsin Rapids, Wisconsin. More than 70 percent of the company's stock is in the hands of founders Judith and Terrance Paul. Until 2000, the company was known as Advantage Learning Systems, Inc.

DEVELOPING A BUSINESS FROM A FAMILY PROJECT

Judith Paul came up with the idea for Renaissance Learning's key software product as a result of her dissatisfaction with the way her children were being motivated to read in school. Paul had a degree in education from the University of Illinois and was actively engaged with the educational careers of her four children in the mid-1980s. Her children's school offered prizes such as pizza to students who read a lot of books. However, the school program did not differentiate between students who read difficult, lengthy books and students who read as many easy books as they could simply to win the prize.

Teachers also did not have an accurate means to keep track of reading comprehension. Students could claim that they had read a book, and the teacher would not know if they actually had, or if they had understood it. Paul also was alarmed that many classic books that she had read in her own childhood were not being read

COMPANY PERSPECTIVES

Renaissance Learning is the world's leading provider of computer-based assessment technology for pre-K–12 schools. Adopted by more than 75,000 North American schools, Renaissance Learning's tools provide daily formative assessment and periodic progress-monitoring technology to enhance the curriculum, support differentiated instruction, and personalize practice in reading, writing and math. Our products help educators make the practice component of their existing curriculum more effective by providing tools to personalize practice and easily manage the daily activities for students of all ability levels. As a result, teachers using Renaissance Learning products accelerate learning, get more satisfaction from teaching, and achieve higher test scores on state and national tests.

at school, perhaps because they were too challenging. She therefore made up a program for her own children, which included a recommended reading list containing many classics of children's literature and a point system based on difficulty and length of each book. Her children earned points for books read, scoring higher for reading the more challenging ones. In addition, they did not receive their points until they passed a multiple-choice test about the book, which Paul designed.

Word of Paul's program spread to a nearby Catholic school, and teachers there offered to pay Judith Paul to let them adopt her system. Paul's husband Terrance, then president of Best Power Company in Necedah, Wisconsin, helped formalize his wife's reading program by translating it into computer software. In 1986, the Pauls founded a company they called Advantage Learning Systems to develop and market their reading software. The software eventually was named Accelerated Reader, and they marketed directly to teachers by mailing brochures to names on mailing lists they procured. The company's marketing material was heavy with testimonials from teachers who had liked the software. Sales also grew as word-of-mouth spread the virtues of Accelerated Reader. The company first operated out of the Pauls' home in Port Edwards, Wisconsin. Later Judith Paul ran it out of a building that had formerly housed a supermarket.

Advantage Learning operated differently from many other educational software companies by marketing directly to teachers. Most other firms sold to entire school districts, but Advantage Learning aimed at individual teachers, convincing them that they could keep track of the needs of individual students and spend their teaching time more wisely by using the reading software. The basic Accelerated Reader program sold for less than $400 and included testing and comprehension software for a list of 150 to 200 books. Teachers pleased with the success of the program persuaded other teachers to buy Accelerated Reader, and teachers with the basic package often moved on to buy software for more or different books. Buoyed by raves from satisfied teachers, Accelerated Reader found its way into classrooms all across the country. By 1992, Advantage Learning had annual sales of $3.2 million.

That year, Terrance Paul joined Advantage Learning full time. He had been involved in a difficult struggle with Best Power, a family-run company, over whether to take the firm public. Paul wanted to keep Best private, and he was finally let go with a $1 million settlement. He turned his energies to Advantage Learning and helped the company manage its rapid growth in the 1990s.

EMPHASIS ON TEACHER TRAINING

Advantage Learning quickly became a leading force in the educational software market as Accelerated Reader gained popularity. The number of computers in classrooms across the country grew, and pressure on schools and teachers to raise reading levels remained strong, so Accelerated Reader had a naturally expanding market. In the early 1990s, there were few other products that competed with it. Sales and income for the company increased decidedly, year by year. By 1993, Advantage Learning decided it needed to find a way to train teachers in how better to use its products. It launched a subsidiary company in Madison, Wisconsin, that year, called the Institute for Academic Excellence. (When the parent company's name was changed in 2000 to Renaissance Learning, the subsidiary changed its name to School Renaissance Institute.)

The subsidiary began with only three employees, whose job was to study the effectiveness of Advantage Learning's products. The Institute staff conducted research on Accelerated Reader and other software programs and contributed articles to education periodicals such as the *School Library Journal*. The institute recruited former teachers and school administrators and trained them to lead workshops in the use of Advantage Learning's software programs. Within four years, the Institute had around 85 employees, and it had trained tens of thousands of

---

KEY DATES

1986: Advantage Learning Systems founded by Judith and Terrance Paul.
1993: A subsidiary, Institute for Academic Excellence, launched.
1997: Company goes public.
2000: Name changed from Advantage Learning Systems to Renaissance Learning Systems.
2005: Computer company Alpha Smart, Inc., is acquired.

---

teachers at seminars across the United States. The seminars ran from one to three days, and the price ranged from slightly more than $100 to about $550. By 1996, the Institute for Academic Excellence accounted for more than 20 percent of the parent company's revenue.

Renaissance Learning also grew through acquisition. In 1996, it purchased a small publisher of math software in Vancouver, Washington, called IPS Publishing. The firm specialized in math assessment software. Advantage Learning planned to mimic its success with Accelerated Reader by putting out a math assessment package, so this acquisition fit in with its goals. The deal was estimated to have cost the company around $6 million.

GOING PUBLIC

Sales for 1996 rose to $22.4 million, up from $3.2 million just four years earlier. Net income in 1996 was $4.2 million, and the company's market still seemed to be expanding. By 1996, Accelerated Reader had found its way into approximately 26,000 schools, which represented 21 percent of all the kindergarten through 12th-grade schools in the United States. Accelerated Reader still accounted for almost 70 percent of Advantage Learning's sales. Satisfied customers continued to come back for more software; in 1996 alone nearly 80 percent of Advantage's new customers made subsequent purchases from the company.

Spending by schools on educational software continued to grow nationally, with estimates projecting 15 percent growth annually in the market in the years leading into the new millennium. Accelerated Reader thus seemed a secure mainstay for its makers. Advantage Learning also brought out new software. A new product, debuted in September 1996, was a reading assessment software program called STAR. This software allowed a teacher to assess a student's reading level in as little as

ten minutes. Teachers found this useful and time-saving, especially in cases where a new student started at school long before transcripts and past reading achievement scores arrived.

In 1997 the company decided to launch a public offering. It had a formidable track record, with sales and net income rising in double-digit increments yearly, and predictions of 40 percent annual growth over the next three to five years. Judith and Terrance Paul were still the only stockholders, and they planned the public offering in part to be able to pay themselves back money they had lent the company. The company also had incurred debt for construction. Furthermore, the company wanted cash to bring out new products. It planned to introduce its new Accelerated Math software in 1998, and it also considered putting out versions of its reading software in other languages and marketing its English-language products overseas. Being a public company was seen as an advantage when dealing with overseas markets, where education spending was likely to come under the purview of government ministries. The Pauls sold 20 percent of their company in the September 1997 public offering. The shares quickly rose from $16 to more than $26 a few weeks later.

COMPETITION GROWS

By 1998, Advantage Learning seemed to have convinced the stock market that it was a good bet. The company had revenues of $50 million, but market capitalization of more than 17 times that, or $862 million by the end of 1998. Investors perhaps understood that education software had a growing customer base as the use of computers in schools increased. Accelerated Reader boasted a market share of 30 percent of kindergarten through 12th-grade schools in the United States and Canada by 1998, and it was clearly a strong product.

However, being the leader in software was always a risky business, as computer products were easy to imitate. Scholastic Corporation began marketing a similar reading software tool, called Electronic Bookshelf, which threatened Accelerated Reader. Scholastic already held 10 percent of the total educational software market, and it reached students and teachers directly through its book clubs. Fear of Scholastic's encroachment apparently spooked investors, and the company's stock went through rapid swings in 1999. However, the company continued to exhibit a strong growth rate of more than 60 percent.

In addition, Accelerated Reader and Accelerated Math fit in with many people's ideas of the way to ensure that children became academically proficient: The software offered a form of quality control through its continuous testing. The need for more testing and more feedback seemed a given of mainstream educational debate, and the market for the company's products did not look like it would wither any time soon. The company continued to reap the benefit of word-of-mouth endorsements of its products, as well. The principal of a troubled school in Chicago was quoted in the March 22, 1999, issue of *Forbes* explaining how she promised her students she would kiss a pig if they racked up a certain point total on Accelerated Reader by the end of a year. Her students surpassed the goal she had set, she kissed the pig, and the school went off probation. Stories like this were great publicity for the company.

Nine new software products were introduced in 1999 and three new software firms were acquired. Sales in 1999 reached $83.6 million, with earnings of more than $17 million. By the end of 1999, the company had firmed up plans to use the Internet to sell its products. It began selling its quizzes over the Internet in November 1999 and began working on online versions of some of its educator training courses. In 2000, the company began offering software designed to help teachers prepare students for standardized tests. The software, called Surpass, first focused on the Texas Assessment of Academic Skills, and then expanded to cover major assessment tests in other states. Surpass was somewhat different from other test preparation software, in that it had students take tests on paper, just as they would for an actual statewide assessment test. The program was meant to tutor students in test-taking skills, not the math and reading skills the standardized tests assessed.

By 2000, when the name of the company was changed to Renaissance Learning Systems, the company found its various software programs in more than 50,000 schools. It had developed beyond its core product, Accelerated Reader, to offer a range of reading, math, and test-taking programs. Through its teacher training subsidiary, the company had trained more than 200,000 people since its inception. Growth had been strong ever since the firm began in Judith Paul's home, and market conditions seemed favorable to the company for some time to come. According to the November 2000 issue of *Kiplinger's Personal Finance,* industry analysts who followed the company's stock predicted the company would see long-term profit growth of 35 percent a year.

GROWTH SLOWS IN THE 21ST CENTURY

Education was a major theme in the 2000 presidential election, and it seemed probable that education spend-

ing on technology and software would continue to grow during the Bush administration. The picture continued bright for the company through 2001. For two years in a row, the company was more profitable than any of its competitors in the educational software niche, beating out other contenders such as Harcourt Education, Pearson Education, and the Minnesota-based newcomer Plato Learning. Renaissance hung on to profit margins above 30 percent through 2001. Chairman Terrance Paul initially had high hopes for new federal legislation that the Bush administration was quick to pass. The No Child Left Behind Act became law in January 2002. Paul assumed that the law's emphasis on testing and accountability would spell more opportunity for educational software. Although many schools were cutting back on their budgets in the early years of the new century as economic contraction hit them, Renaissance remained poised for growth.

The company made several changes to accommodate increasing opportunities. While the founding Pauls were cochairs of the board, the chief executive position had passed to Michael Baum. Baum stepped aside in 2002, and Terrance Paul again took the reins. Earnings growth was then projected at about 20 percent, rather than over 30 percent, as belt-tightening schools kept orders flat or shrinking.

Furthermore, the company had expected No Child Left Behind to make an impact on the educational software industry by 2002, but this had not happened. With its stock price falling on this bad news, Paul initiated a new strategy. The company focused its marketing on school districts, rather than on individual schools and teachers. By mid-2003, this new course seemed ironed out, and Paul again retired to his cochair role. John Hickey, who had been president and chief operating officer, then became CEO. When announcing Hickey's new position, Paul told *Electronic Education Report* that he and his wife were ready to "step back and hand off the baton to a younger, aggressive, yet experienced team." Renaissance was on its way to becoming a "much larger company," he told the industry news organ. The new team would take it to the next level.

COMPUTER COMPANY ACQUIRED

Sales peaked in 2003 at $130.5 million. The next year, sales were down almost 13 percent, to $114 million, and profit was also declining. Nevertheless, the company pursued its growth strategy, and in January 2005 purchased a small California-based computer company, Alpha Smart Inc. Renaissance paid $57 million for

Alpha Smart, which made portable computers or laptops for school children. This looked like a promising complement for Renaissance's software business. However, some of Alpha Smart's product lines were expensive to manufacture and thus had lower profit margins, and Renaissance phased these out. Furthermore, integrating the new company proved more difficult than expected. Earnings dropped almost 50 percent in the fourth quarter of fiscal 2005. John Hickey, the new president and CEO, resigned in January 2006, and Terrance Paul again stepped into the top job.

Renaissance streamlined some of its operations, increased its sales staff, and dedicated itself to a new focus on core products in order to get back on track. However, the growth that it had envisioned at the start of the decade still seemed to elude Renaissance. Its profit margins had been over 30 percent in the early years of the decade, and by the middle of the decade were about 20 percent. In 2007, two years after it had acquired Alpha Smart, Renaissance, according to some, had not not adequately integrated the laptop maker. Revenue and profits fell, and the company's stock price followed suit.

One issue that may have kept the company from fulfilling the promise of the early years of the 21st century was the effect of No Child Left Behind. Terrance Paul had assumed that the federal legislation would be a boon to Renaissance. Paradoxically, however, under the strictures of the new law, teachers may have found less use for Accelerated Reader. Renaissance's products were designed to give teachers a break while students read to themselves and tested themselves. This required what many teachers called a "free reading" period. Accelerated Reader also offered what the industry called "formative assessment," giving students feedback on how they were doing and how they might develop. Under No Child Left Behind, the emphasis was more on test-oriented assessment. This cultural shift seemed to have worked against Renaissance's core products, at least in the short term.

Despite these difficulties, there were signs of growth to come. By 2007, the company had an array of products, including reading, math, and writing software, a program for English-language learners, a reading intervention software package, and the NEO laptops. Renaissance was making inroads into the educational market in the United Kingdom. Also in 2007, the company saw its first quarterly growth since 2003. Revenue was up 10 percent for the first quarter of 2008, although worries about more state budget

cuts meant the company did not let itself get too optimistic.

A. Woodward

PRINCIPAL SUBSIDIARIES

AlphaSmart Direct, Inc.; Renaissance Learning UK; Advantage Learning Systems India Pvt. Ltd.

PRINCIPAL COMPETITORS

Pearson plc; Plato Learning, Inc.; Scientific Learning Corporation.

FURTHER READING
"Accelerated Reader Leads Renaissance to Q3 Growth," *Electronic Education Report,* November 21, 2007, p. 1.

"ALS Enters Test-Prep Market," *Heller Report on Educational Technology Markets,* July 2000, p. 7.

Bergquist, Lee, "Educational Software Maker Advantage Learning Systems Inc. Plans IPO," *Knight-Ridder/Tribune Business News,* March 4, 1997.

———, "Software Makes Mark in Classroom," *Milwaukee Journal,* November 16, 1997, pp. 1, 5.

Fitch, Stephane, "Back of the Class," *Forbes,* November 30, 1998, pp. 364–65.

Gertzen, Jason, "Software Firm's Shares Fall 13% on Slow Sales," *Milwaukee Journal Sentinel,* June 28, 2002, p. 6D.

Hajewski, Doris, "Renaissance Earnings Drop 46% in Fourth Quarter," *Milwaukee Journal Sentinel,* April 19, 2006, p. D3.

Mathews, Jay, "Heavy Reading Reaps Rewards," *Washington Post,* March 19, 2002, p. A11.

Newman, Judy, "Renaissance Sales, Profits Fall," *Wisconsin State Journal,* July 19, 2007, p. E1.

———, "Shareholders to Assess Wisconsin Educational-Software Firm's Performance," *Knight-Ridder/Tribune Business News,* April 18, 2000.

———, "Wisconsin Entrepreneur Motivates Students to Improve Reading Skills," *Knight-Ridder/Tribune Business News,* October 9, 1997.

———, "Wisconsin Rapids, Wis.-based Educational Software Firm's Stock Recovery," *Knight-Ridder/Tribune Business News,* July 2, 1999.

———, "Wisconsin Rapids, Wis.-based Software Maker Acquires Canadian Firm," *Knight-Ridder/Tribune Business News,* January 3, 2000.

"Renaissance Learning Leads the Education Software and Online Publishing Industry for Profitability in 2000," *Electronic Education Report,* April 25, 2001, p. 1.

"Renaissance Learning Plan Has Yet to Drive Sales or Profitability in 2006," *Electronic Education Report,* July 28, 2006, p. 1.

"Terrance Paul Turns Renaissance Learning Reins over to Hickey, Who Was Promoted to CEO," *Electronic Education Report,* August 1, 2003, p. 1.

Upbin, Bruce, "Instant Feedback in the Classroom," *Forbes,* March 22, 1999, pp. 68–72.

Wiser, Justin, "Investing 101: It's Academic," *Kiplinger's Personal Finance Magazine,* November 2000, p. 82.

Saxton Pierce Restaurant Corporation

8117 Preston Road
Dallas, Texas 75225-6332
U.S.A.
Telephone: (214) 373-3400
Fax: (214) 373-3403
Web site: http://www.saxtonpierce.com

Private Company
Incorporated: 1996
Employees: 750
Sales: $30.9 million (2007 est.)
NAICS: 722110 Full-Service Restaurants

■ ■ ■

Saxton Pierce Restaurant Corporation is a privately held company that serves as a major franchisee of McAlister's Deli, a fast-casual restaurant chain that focuses on sandwiches, soups, and salads. McAlister's has more than 250 units located in about 22 states. As the largest franchisee in the system, Saxton Pierce operates more than 40 units in Kansas, Mississippi, Missouri, Oklahoma, and Texas. An affiliated company, Bothwell-Saxton Restaurants, operates McAlister's Deli units in Oklahoma and Kansas. Another affiliate, a development company called SR Properties, LLC, develops small, upscale retail and office centers anchored by a McAlister's Deli. They range in size from 10,000 to 25,000 square feet, and are located in smaller markets in Mississippi, Oklahoma, and Texas. Maintaining its

headquarters in Dallas, Texas, Saxton Pierce is headed by Kelly G. Saxton.

KELLY SAXTON: ALL-AMERICAN FOOTBALL PLAYER

Born in Kansas, Kelly Saxton earned a degree in business administration from Missouri Southern State College, where he received a full scholarship to play on the college division football team. In 1980 and 1981 he earned All-American honors as a defensive tackle from the National Association of Intercollegiate Athletics. After graduating in 1982 he needed to find employment to support his wife and young son, and his father, Edwin "Gene" Saxton stepped in to help. The elder Saxton had developed a business, Docksil Sausage Company, which supplied pizza toppings to restaurants. Because he was on the verge of retirement and did not have to worry about any conflicts of interest, Gene Saxton took advantage of his relationship with the founder of the Ken's Pizza and Mazzio's Italian restaurant chain, Ken Selby, to set his son up in business.

Selby was a young high school chemistry teacher in 1961 when he took a job as a part-time pizza maker in a Tulsa, Oklahoma, pizza parlor. He soon opened his own shop, simply called The Pizza Parlor, and in 1965 quit teaching to devote himself to the restaurant business, opening a second store and adopting the name Ken's Pizza Parlor, which in time was shortened to Ken's Pizza. He also began franchising, and by 1975 he was operating a chain of about 100 company-owned and franchised stores. Late in the decade he decided to develop a new, more upscale Italian restaurant concept,

---

COMPANY PERSPECTIVES

Saxton Pierce is committed to serving customers great food and great service. These are the key ingredients for the high level of customer satisfaction at Saxton Pierce restaurants.

which he planned to call Maggio's, an allusion to the Italian American character of the same name in the novel *From Here to Eternity.* Because of trademark considerations, Maggio's was renamed Mazzio's Pizza, and made its debut in 1979. It quickly began to supplant Ken's Pizza as Selby's main brand.

Through his father, Kelly Saxton acquired a pair of franchised Ken's Pizza stores in the Jackson, Mississippi, metropolitan area, in the cities of Clinton and Pearl. Saxton's father also helped finance the deal and made available a corporate shell he had founded around 1970 called Gene Saxton Brokerage to serve as a holding company. It was this entity that would one day become Saxton Pierce Restaurant Corporation. "This is your opportunity," Saxton recalled his father telling him, according to the *Clarion-Ledger* of Jackson, Mississippi. "Make it work," he said.

The Ken's Pizza stores were converted to the Mazzio's format, and after two weeks of training, Kelly Saxton began his restaurant career in the early 1980s. Although years later he expressed mild regrets that he had not been more proactive in handling problems himself, rather than relying on the franchiser, he indeed made a success of the opportunity given to him. In his first year in operation, Saxton generated revenues of $400,000 from his two restaurants. He was doing well enough after three or four years that he opened a third Mazzio's restaurant in the Jackson area. Taking on partners, he was able to add more units in Jackson over the next several years. He also became involved in Kansas, taking advantage of a chance to open Mazzio's stores there as well. They did not perform as he had hoped, however, and were eventually sold.

MOVE INTO ARKANSAS: 1996

Saxton's next attempt to expand beyond Mississippi came in 1996 when he added six Mazzio's units located in Arkansas, owned by Jim Robertson, a former cook at a Ken's Pizza who would become the manager of the first Mazzio's Pizza. He became a franchisee in 1991.

After merging his stores with Saxton's operation, then doing business as Pizza Concepts, Inc., Robertson stayed on to serve as a key executive, taking charge of new store development, site acquisitions, new construction, and other responsibilities. Later in 1996, in October, Saxton also gained entry into the Texas market when he merged with the Mazzio's franchise operation owned by Travis N. Pierce, which included about 20 units. Pizza Concepts, Inc., then became Saxton Pierce Restaurant Corporation.

Although Saxton Pierce was doing well with the Mazzio's restaurants, as well as a few Ken's Pizza stores, by 1998 Mazzio's was a mature concept, one whose primary requirement was solid day-to-day operations. Kelly Saxton was more growth-oriented and looked for a fresh challenge and a new restaurant format to franchise. His next opportunity was so close that he almost overlooked it. He and his wife often ate at a Jackson chain restaurant called McAlister's Deli, and over lunch one day she asked him if he had ever considered becoming a McAlister's franchisee. Intrigued, Saxton spent the next year considering the idea, doing due diligence to make sure he was certain the McAlister's concept would have broader, more national appeal.

The man behind the creation of McAlister's was a dentist named Don Newcomb who had developed an interest in the restaurant business during his days as a teenage soda jerk in Ripley, Mississippi, in the 1950s. He became a successful dentist in Oxford, Mississippi, and invested in real estate as well as franchised restaurants for the Sonic and Danver's chains. Newcomb harbored a dream of starting his own restaurant, however, and in 1987 seized an opportunity when an old Oxford gas station was converted into a 1950s-style diner for the shooting of a movie, *The Heart of Dixie.* After the movie was completed, Newcomb purchased the property and turned it into an actual restaurant, originally calling it Chequers.

Because of possible problems with the Chequers name from the Checkers restaurant chain, Newcomb changed the name to McAlister's Gourmet Deli, drawing on his wife's maiden name. The unpretentious setup, relying on plastic ware and baskets, and good food, was especially attractive to college students. In 1992 a second store was opened in the college town of Hattiesburg, Mississippi, and Newcomb closed his dental practice to focus on growing his restaurant business. In 1993 McAlister's entered Tupelo, Mississippi, and a year later came to Jackson, another town with a large number of college students.

<table>
<tr><td colspan="2">

KEY DATES

■

</td></tr>
<tr><td>**1982:**</td><td>Kelly Saxton opens two Mazzio's Pizza restaurants in Jackson, Mississippi, area.</td></tr>
<tr><td>**1996:**</td><td>Pizza Concepts, Inc., merges with operations of Travis Pierce to create Saxton Pierce Restaurant Corporation.</td></tr>
<tr><td>**1998:**</td><td>Saxton Pierce opens first McAlister's Deli.</td></tr>
<tr><td>**2000:**</td><td>SR Properties is established as property development wing.</td></tr>
<tr><td>**2002:**</td><td>Travis Pierce bought out.</td></tr>
<tr><td>**2003:**</td><td>Saxton Pierce sells its Mazzio's units.</td></tr>
<tr><td>**2007:**</td><td>Oklahoma and Kansas McAlister's restaurants sold to Bothwell-Saxton Restaurants.</td></tr>
</table>

SAXTON PIERCE OPENS FIRST MCALISTER'S UNIT

It was also in 1994 that Newcomb began to franchise the McAlister's concept, bringing in executive talent to drive its growth. In 1998 Newcomb recruited Michael J. Stack to serve as chief executive officer, a man who had 35 years of restaurant experience, holding important posts at Pizza Hut, Western Sizzlin', and Host International/Marriott Corporation. Stack was so impressed with the McAlister's concept that he made a buyout offer, which Newcomb accepted, selling 70 percent of the business. Stack and his partner and chief operating officer, Phil Friedman, built up the infrastructure of McAlister's and shifted its franchising approach. Instead of accepting franchisees with no restaurant experience, they sought seasoned and successful franchise operators who were looking for a second concept. Saxton Pierce clearly fit that bill.

To serve as the point person on the McAlister's effort, Saxton hired Kirk Lanier. Also a customer of the first Jackson McAlister's, Lanier had gone to work for McAlister's in 1996 and became the general manager of the chain's seventh location and was then placed in charge of management development. Hence, he was the ideal person to help Saxton Pierce launch its new effort. Saxton Pierce opened its first McAlister's in Longview, Texas, in 1998. Soon after, a second store opened in Tyler, Texas. For the next three years, Saxton Pierce would continue to run its Ken's Pizza and Mazzio's stores while growing the McAlister's business.

In 2000 Saxton Pierce established SR Properties as a property development wing to establish small, upscale retail centers that had a McAlister's store as an anchor. Saxton Pierce was willing to open McAlister's units in existing shopping centers and at other locations, but SR Properties allowed Saxton Pierce to take advantage of opportunities as they arose. In some cases it was easier to find prime sites that were larger than the footprint required for a McAlister's. By having SR Properties acquire the larger parcel and develop a retail center on it, Saxton Pierce could ensure a good location for a McAlister's. Moreover, the company could bring their experience as retailers to bear on the development of the site, unlike developers who might want to skimp on parking, for example, to save on costs. SR Properties, on the other hand, focused on creating a retail environment that would benefit McAlister's and other retail tenants. The first centers were opened in Richland, Mississippi, and Athens, Texas.

MAZZIO'S UNITS SOLD: 2003

By the end of 2001, Saxton Pierce was operating 35 restaurants in three states generating $26.7 million in annual sales, including 28 Mazzio's restaurants, two Ken's Pizza restaurants, one Mazzio's Italian Eatery, and four McAlister's Delis. Kelly Saxton was then ready to focus all of his attention on McAlister's, and began taking steps to exit the Mazzio's business. He and other shareholders bought out Travis Pierce in June 2002. Because the company had established awareness as Saxton Pierce, the name was retained even though Pierce was no longer involved. A few days later, Saxton Pierce reached an agreement with McAlister's Management Corp. to open an additional 14 McAlister's stores. Over the next year Saxton Pierce opened ten more McAlister's. Early in 2003 Tommy Johnsey, vice-president of operations, asked Kelly Saxton if he would consider selling the Mazzio's side of the business. Saxton agreed, and in November 2003 Saxton Pierce sold its Mazzio's holdings to Johnsey and three other Saxton Pierce executives. They included Joey Sebren, director of the Mississippi Mazzio's operations; Lisa Rice, the company's director of marketing; and Randy Moyer, area director of the Texas stores. Together they had formed a company called Pinnacle Restaurant Corp., and with most of the financing provided or arranged by Kelly Saxton they were able to acquire the Mazzio's stores of Saxton Pierce.

With its focus solely on McAlister's Deli, Saxton picked up the pace of opening new stores, essentially one every 90 days. Because most of its activity was then in Texas, the company moved its headquarters from Ridgeland, Mississippi, to Dallas. The company also expanded aggressively in Oklahoma and in Kansas. In June 2007 these units were broken off into an affiliated company, Bothwell-Saxton Restaurants, a partnership with Craig Bothwell. A onetime dishwasher at a Ken's

Pizza Parlor in the 1960s, Bothwell had grown up through the ranks of Mazzio's Corp., eventually becoming chief operating officer and president. He retired in 2005 and became a McAlister's franchisee.

With Bothwell responsible for the units under the control of Bothwell-Saxton, Kelly Saxton oversaw the expansion of the chain under Saxton Pierce. He was assisted by his sons, who had been working in the company's restaurants since they were teenagers and were given ownership stakes in Saxton Pierce at this time. The eldest, Adam, was a graduate of Southern Methodist University and became director of development. Matthew Saxton, three years younger, graduated from the University of North Texas with a degree in hospitality management and was put in charge of project development for Saxton Pierce. By the fall of 2008, the company was operating more than 40 McAlister's restaurants, with half a dozen under construction in Texas and ready to open later in the year and into 2009. Although pleased with the McAlister's business, Kelly Saxton indicated in a November 2008 interview that he remained open to the idea of taking on a new restaurant concept should the opportunity arise, perhaps one that would work well in concert with a McAlister's in one ofd the retail centers developed by SR Properties.

PRINCIPAL COMPETITORS

Applebee's International, Inc.; The Quizno's Master LLC; Doctor's Associates Inc. (Subway).

FURTHER READING

Floyd, Nell Luter, "A New Menu in Metro Jackson," *Jackson (Miss.) Clarion-Ledger,* July 30, 2002, p. 1C.

Goldberg, Eddy, and Kerry Pipes, "Kelly Saxton Doesn't Just Talk the Talk About Employees," *Multi-Unit Franchisee,* March 13, 2007.

"Management Acquires Saxton Pierce," *Mississippi Business Journal,* June 17, 2002, p. 9.

Sebren, Joey, "Fresh Firm Rises from Restaurant Group," *Jackson (Miss.) Clarion-Ledger,* November 22, 2003, p. 1C.

Szabo, Joan, "Great Minds Think Like Family," *Area Developer,* September 1, 2005.

Schneidersöhne Deutsch-
land GmbH & Co. KG

---■---

Gehrnstrasse 7-11
Ettlingen, 76275
Germany
Telephone: (49 7243) 730
Fax: (49 7243) 73173
Web site: http://www.schneidersoehne.com

Private Company
Incorporated: 1922 as G. Schneider & Söhne GmbH
Employees: 1,359
Sales: EUR 846 million ($1.24 billion) (2007)
NAICS: 422110 Printing and Writing Paper

■ ■ ■

Schneidersöhne Deutschland GmbH & Co. KG is one of Europe's largest suppliers of paper. The company distributes over 8,000 types, including paper for print and images, paper for digital printing, pressure sensitive paper, paper for labeling, cardboard and packaging paper, recycled paper, paper for business uses, and envelopes and mailers. Schneidersöhne consists of three divisions. The Paper division supplies paper for graphical and advertising applications to the German printing industry. Business Paper, provides printer paper, copier paper, and other types for use in offices. Finally, Kuvert manufacturers a wide range of envelopes and mailers for business. The European printing industry comprises Schneidersöhne's primary customer base. Schneidersöhne has 12 distribution centers and five sales offices in Germany and is owned by Altor Equity Partners, a Swedish investment group.

ORIGINS IN FELT AND RAGS

The founder of Schneidersöhne, Gotlob Schneider, was born in 1857 in the town of Lauffen am Neckar in southern Germany. As a destitute 17-year-old, Schneider left his home and lived for a time in Ludwigshafen where he worked for a rag company. From there he moved to Ettlingen where he was hired by a paper-maker, Papierfabrik Buhl. Since rag was the essential raw material for rag paper, then used for German legal publications, Schneider's experience at the rag company served him well at Buhl. He advanced rapidly and before long he was promoted to the post of *Prokurist,* the second highest ranking position in the company. In April 1883 he married Emilie Rissel, the daughter of an Ettlingen businessman, and together they started a family, which by the turn of the 20th century consisted of six sons and two daughters.

In 1902 Schneider started his own felt business at home, while keeping his job at Buhl. He purchased the large lengths of old felt that had been used in the paper production at Buhl, and then Emilie and the children washed it in the Alb River. The clean felt sold locally to be used as blankets for cows. The fledgling enterprise was bolstered by its association with the import business run by Otto Rissel, Emilie Schneider's brother. With the customer contacts Rissel provided, the felt business was soon booming. In fact, Schneider and Rissel worked so closely that they kept joint books until 1908.

Given Schneider's experience at Papierfabrik Buhl, paper seemed a natural direction for expansion of the home enterprise. Paper sales grew quickly, but for the first few years, Schneider continued to work for Buhl.

By 1904 demand for paper in the region around Ettlingen was booming, and Schneider resigned from Buhl to devote himself full-time to his own company. He maintained his contact with Buhl, however, an association that would stand him in good stead when his customers requested specialty products which his own company could not provide. Schneider continued to use rooms at his brother-in-law's house to store his stock until 1911 when the company moved into a set of rooms all its own in Ettlingen.

GROWTH THROUGH ACQUISITION

The company prospered. In 1914 the onset of World War I presented economic hardship, but Schneider was able to weather it, selling a glossy wood-free paper. After the war ended, Schneider and his sons made the enterprise a partnership, G. Schneider & Söhne OHG–G. The new name reflected the growing responsibility the Schneider offspring were beginning to assume in the business and not always to the complete satisfaction of their father. According to one company story, for example, one Schneider son purchased a motorized truck for deliveries without consulting his father. Gotlob Schneider was reportedly furious when he found out; he believed that horse-drawn wagons were perfectly adequate.

The hyperinflation of 1923 affected Schneider & Söhne like all other businesses in Germany. Unlike many others, however, the company found opportunity in the crisis. With the government printing hundreds of thousands of new banknotes daily, sales of banknote paper went a long way to helping Schneider through the difficult economic times. It was around this time that the company began expanding within Germany. In 1922 it opened a sales office in Frankfurt am Main.

Two years later Schneider purchased Papierhandlung Steinberg, a paper company in Cologne, and added additional warehouse capacity there later that year. Most significantly, in 1924 Schneider & Söhne purchased Pa-pierfabrik Buhl, the company that had given Gotlob Schneider his start and which by that time had established a significant presence in Ettlingen. In 1926, the company made another major purchase in the city when it acquired the land and buildings of the Hansa Konservenfabrik, a bankrupt Ettlingen jam-maker. Schneider's headquarters were moved onto the site and would remain there into the 21st century.

During this time the Schneider sons began to take over responsibility for the various parts of the company. The company had grown large enough to warrant that its primary divisions become two independent companies, The felt division became Schneiderfilz GmbH, while the paper division became G. Schneider & Söhne, Papiergrosshandlung. Gotlob Schneider, by then in his seventies, retired from his business and passed it on to his sons. In 1930 he died, followed two years later by his wife Emilie, who had also been an integral part of the business. The management of the company was taken over by their son Siegfried.

THE DEPRESSION AND THE WAR YEARS

The Great Depression hit Germany hard, and G. Schneider & Söhne struggled as well. The company reported the first loss in company history in 1929. When the National Socialists under Adolf Hitler came to power there were initially few repercussions. Eventually, however, the firm's workers were required to join the German Labor Front, the organization the Nazis had set up to replace labor unions. Later, in the mid-1930s, the Nazi government took over control of the entire German paper-making industry. The company, however, managed to find a profitable new niche within the strict new regulatory environment by collecting and recycling old paper.

By 1936 the company had 142 employees working in the Ettlingen, Cologne, and Frankfurt facilities. A growth spurt was starting, and for the first time in its history Schneider & Söhne hired managers from outside the Schneider family. With the acquisition of Papiergrosshandlung Weil that same year, it acquired a site in Freiburg. Schneider took over another paper factory, Papierwarenfabrik A. Stork in Karlsruhe and the Geiger'sche Papierhandlung in Frankfurt in 1938. The company was renamed Papierschnieder GmbH in 1940. Around this time it expanded its line of paper to include paper and packaging for industrial uses.

In 1938, as the Nazis shifted to a wartime economy and raw material rationing was put into place, Schneider & Söhne notified its customers that the quality of its product would, of necessity, be lower. In 1939, as

KEY DATES

1902: Gotlob Schneider founds a felt company in Ettlingen.
1922: Company is reorganized as G. Schneider & Söhne GmbH.
1928: Paper and felt activities are split into separate businesses.
1956: Company headquarters are rebuilt in Ettlingen after the war.
1965: Reorganization as G. Schneider & Söhne GmbH & Co KG is complete.
1968: Much of main Ettlingen warehouse is destroyed by fire.
1986: Company formally adopts name Schneidersöhne
1996: Papierschneider GmbH is sold.
2005: Stora Enso acquires Schneidersöhne.
2008: Altor Equity Partners acquires Schneidersöhne from Stora Enso.

Germany began fortifying the nearby border with France, management decided the Ettlingen facilities were too close to the potential war zone and moved its paper warehouses to an unused textile factory in Ebingen, 100 miles inland. During the war years manpower became a problem. By the end of 1942 nearly every able-bodied man had been inducted into the military, and factories throughout Germany, including Schneider & Söhne's, were increasingly manned by forced laborers from countries the Nazis had invaded. Schneider's office work was done largely by German women.

As the war raged, and the Allied bombing raids on German cities increased, Schneider & Söhne's product inventory was moved away from Frankfurt and Cologne, two of cities targeted frequently by the Allies, and into storage facilities in the surrounding countryside. It was a critical decision; the Schneider & Söhne establishments in both cities were completely destroyed by war's end.

When the French army occupied Ettlingen on April 5, 1945, Siegfried Schneider and his 16-year-old son Dieter were arrested as war criminals. However, a Jewish employee whom the Schneiders had concealed from the Gestapo, as well as forced laborers who felt Schneider had treated them relatively well, came forward and spoke before the authorities on their behalf. As a result, two days following their arrest, Siegfried and Dieter Schneider were released. Siegfried Schneider was initially forbidden by the Allies from reclaiming ownership of

the firm. Again, however, the favorable testimony of former workers reportedly persuaded the occupation government to reconsider their decision. In January 1946, barely six months after the conclusion of hostilities, the company was returned in full to the Schneider family.

PROSPERITY AND GROWTH IN THE POSTWAR ERA

Life in the years immediately following World War II was marked by shortages. For many companies, as well as individuals, necessities for survival were obtainable only through barter on the black market. Schneider & Söhne, however, was in a good position because paper was one of the most sought after items for barter. The company underwent some organizational changes in the late 1940s. A subsidiary was founded in Saarbrücken in 1946, the facility in Freiburg was spun off into an independent subsidiary in 1948, and a year later an envelope factory was built near the company's headquarters in Ettlingen. Envelopes were a new product area for Schneider & Söhne, one that would eventually become one of the company's main divisions.

The 1950s were a period of increasing prosperity for Germans and German companies, a time known as the *Wirtschaftswunder* or the Economic Miracle. It was typified in the paper and print industry by the rise of the DRUPA, the annual trade show held by the industry in Düsseldorf. The company was growing quickly in the mid-1950s. It laid the cornerstone for a new complex of buildings on the site of its Ettlingen headquarters in 1956 and introduced the partial automation of its shipping department in 1958. A computerized bookkeeping system introduced in 1960 eventually evolved into a subsidiary software firm, OSC Organisations Software Consulting GmbH of Ettlingen.

In 1964 a facility was established in Hamburg to service the areas of the northern Federal Republic, a region in which the firm was growing rapidly. In this same period Schneider & Söhne began working closely with the Berlin papermaker Obst & Co., a cooperative relationship that led to the two companies sharing office facilities in the city. The setup became Schneider & Söhne's de facto Berlin branch, which was formalized in 1985 when Schneider acquired the partner firm. In 1965 Schneider & Söhne was reorganized, and it became G. Schneider & Söhne GmbH & Co KG. By that time it was known informally to most customers as Schneidersöhne, but the firm assumed that name officially only in 1986.

The German paper industry entered a downturn in the late 1960s. By the beginning of the 1970s, however,

Schneidersöhne was strong again, due in large part to an agreement with the Japanese paper company Jujo. Jujo licensed Schneidersöhne to sell a newly patented carbonless carbon paper (CCP), which made the old blue carbon paper obsolete. CCP was an instant bestseller; it boosted Schneidersöhne's revenues significantly and lifted it out of the crisis. As photocopiers grew more widespread and increased in sophistication in the 1970s, the firm developed popular paper particularly for these machines.

Schneidersöhne underwent further organizational changes in the 1980s. At the beginning of the decade the last of Gotlob Schneider's children died. After revising the company's partnership agreement, which was outdated, another reorganization took place. The company in Ettlingen was split into two separate organizations. The administration in Ettlingen became a holding company for the entire group while the distribution facilities was used simply as branch location.

ESTABLISHING AN INTERNATIONAL PRESENCE

By the start of the 1990s, Schneidersöhne was the paper distributor with the broadest distribution network and product range, represented by its three main divisions: Paper, Business Paper, and Envelopes (manufactured by its Kuvert division). It had opened new facilities in Nuremberg, Bremen, Osnabrück, Hannover, Kiel, Dortmund Stuttgart, and, following the fall of the Berlin Wall in 1989, centers in Dresden and Ronneburg in the former German Democratic Republic as well.

The firm adopted a new expansion strategy for East Germany, limiting itself to setting up either warehouses or sales offices there rather than full distribution facilities. The firm also established its first foreign subsidiaries during this time as well, in the Netherlands and Austria. After the fall of the Communist regimes behind the Iron Curtain, the company expanded into the countries of Eastern Europe, moving into the Czech Republic in 1991 and Hungary and Lithuania in 1997.

The so-called paperless office, which many industry observers predicted would result from the rise of the personal computer, had not materialized. In fact, the computerization of the workplace led to an unprecedented demand for paper, a demand that boosted Schneidersöhne's revenues significantly in the 1990s. The new income fueled further expansion. In 1998, for example, the firm acquired a large share in Lies Printservice, a manufacturer of supplies for the printing industry. It also established subsidiaries in

Germany, Belgium, Italy, and Switzerland.

By 2002 Schneidersöhne had become the largest paper manufacturer in Europe, with annual revenues of EUR 1.1 billion and approximately 2,150 employees. Companies in the printing industry formed its primary clientele. The company remained a private company, owned by descendants of the Schneider family, although its management had long since been in the hands of outsiders. In the early 2000s, however, company revenues began to decline, falling nearly EUR 100 million between 2002 and 2003. Moreover, the German *Kartellamt,* the country's antitrust authorities, accused Schneidersöhne and nine other firms in the German paper industry of price fixing and levied fines of more than EUR 57 million altogether. The charge was later upheld after industry appeals, although only about EUR 18 million in fines were levied.

NEW SCANDINAVIAN OWNERS

The Schneider family sold Schneidersöhne in 2005 to the Swedish-Finnish company Stora Enso, the world's largest producer of paper and cardboard. The family was paid EUR 450 million in cash for the company. Stora Enso, which distributed paper as well as manufactured it, integrated Schneidersöhne as a full subsidiary into the paper wholesaler Papyrus. Two Schneidersöhne executives, Christian Klaus Peter and Michael Schneider, remained with their company during the integration process. The acquisition made Stora Enso the world's second largest wholesaling concern in any industry. The year before the takeover revenues had dropped once again, and Schneidersöhne fared no better afterward. The first three quarters of 2006 were even worse than the year before.

When Stora Enso acquired Schneidersöhne, it was considered a stroke of good fortune that a strategic investor, a partner in the paper industry, had acquired it rather than a private equity house interested only in raking in profits. By 2008, however, the thinking had turned around completely. Schneidersöhne was a paper wholesaler that sold paper produced by a variety of manufacturers. Under its new parent, however, Schneidersöhne was made to focus on selling Stora Enso product. Schneidersöhne continued to stock paper from other producers, but its relation to its parent was challenging.

In April 2008 Stora Enso divested its entire distribution portfolio, selling Papyrus, and with it Schneidersöhne, which was responsible for about 45 percent of Papyrus's total revenues, to the Swedish investment group Altor Equity Partners. Schneidersöhne hoped that the acquisition by Altor would enable it to regain some of the independence of action that it lost in 2005.

Gerald E. Brennan

PRINCIPAL SUBSIDIARIES

Schneidersöhne Kuvert Verwaltungs-GmbH; Schneidersöhne Deutschland Verwaltungs-GmbH; Schneidersöhne Kuvert GmbH & Co. KG; Classen-Papier GmbH.

PRINCIPAL DIVISIONS

Paper; Business Paper; Kuvert Envelopes.

PRINCIPAL COMPETITORS

Carl Berberich GmbH; Igepa Group GmbH & Co. KG; Antalis GmbH; Xerox GmbH.

FURTHER READING

Lehmkühler, Sabine, *100 Jahre Schneidersöhne: People and Paper,* Schneidersöhne GmbH, 2002.

"Stora Enso Completes Acquisition of Schneidersohne Group," *Nordic Business Report,* September 1, 2005.

The Schwarz Group

Lidl Dienstleistung GmbH & Co. KG
Rötelstrasse 30
Neckarsulm, 74166
Germany
Telephone: (49 7132) 30 6060
Web site: http://www.lidl.de

Private Company
Founded: 1930
Employees: 80,000
Sales: $67.87 billion
NAICS: 551114 Holding Companies; 445110 Grocery
  Stores

∎ ∎ ∎

The Schwarz Group is a German retailing giant that operates discount grocery store and superstores, most notably Lidl and Kaufland, but also Kaufhof, Handelshof, Ruef, and Warenhandels. The stores of the Schwarz Group are located throughout Germany as well as in 22 other European countries. The jewel of the Schwarz Group is the discount grocery store chain Lidl. Lidl stores are small, no-nonsense facilities that stock a limited range of each product, selling primarily their own store brands. The chain has approximately 2,900 stores in Germany and another 4,370 located in Austria, Belgium, Bulgaria, Croatia, the Czech Republic, Denmark, Finland, France, Germany, Greece, Hungary, Ireland, Italy, Luxembourg, the Netherlands, Poland, Portugal, Romania, Slovakia, Slovenia, Spain, Sweden, and the United Kingdom. The Schwarz Group's other

important chain is Kaufland, a group of superstores that also sell a broad selection of groceries and toiletry products, as well as clothing, electronics, and other general merchandise. There are about 750 Kaufland stores, primarily in Germany and the Czech Republic, but also in Poland, Romania, and Bulgaria.

The Schwarz Group is a privately owned company with a complex organizational structure comprised of several hundred corporate entities altogether. Ownership and management power are split between two corporations. The Dieter Schwarz Stiftung gemeinnützige GmbH owns 99.9 percent of the firm's stock but holds no voting rights in the company. The Schwarz Unternehmenstreuhand KG, on the other hand, owns but a 0.01 percent share while controlling all the corporate voting rights. Both the Lidl and Kaufland chains are run as independent corporations within the Schwarz Group, and each of these is in turn divided into a number of legally independent regional organizations. The Schwarz Group also operates a separate company that owns and manages the group's corporate real estate, as well as leasing out property to other businesses. The Schwarz Group is one of the top ten retail corporations in the world.

A GROCERY EMPIRE BEGINS

The earliest incarnation of Schwarz Group dates back to 1930 when Josef Schwarz became a partner in the company Südfrüchte Großhandlung Lidl & Co., a produce distributor in Heilbronn, a midsized city on the Neckar River in southern Germany. When Schwarz joined the firm, it was still a small local undertaking that delivered fruit and vegetables by horse-drawn wagon to local produce stands. However, under Schwarz's management, the company grew into an important produce distributor in the region of Baden-Württemberg.

The company flourished through the 1930s until the difficult days of World War II. It was completely destroyed in December 1944 in a bombing raid that wiped out 82 percent of Heilbronn. After the end of the war, the firm was reestablished in Heilbronn. Josef Schwarz became its sole owner in 1951 and by 1954 Lidl & Co had resumed its normal operations. The company grew as it had in the decade before the war and by 1970 had estimated annual revenues of DEM 100 million.

The year 1972 was significant for two reasons. First, the firm moved its headquarters to the nearby town of Neckarsulm. More fateful for its future, however, was the entry of Josef Schwarz's 32-year-old son, Dieter, into the business. The junior Schwarz had big ideas for his father's company. Impressed by the success of the new discount grocery store Aldi in Germany, Dieter Schwarz wanted to launch his own chain of retail discount supermarkets. His father opposed the idea, at least at first, preferring to limit the company's activities to wholesale distribution.

Dieter Schwarz pressed ahead, however, with his plan. One initial problem was finding a name for his new markets. His own name was never seen as a possibility: Schwarz-Markt in German means "black market." Various legal considerations prevented him from simply taking over the name of his father's company Lidl & Co, but in the summer of 1972, he chanced upon an article in the local newspaper about a retired vocational school teacher named Ludwig Lidl. Schwarz contacted Lidl and bought the rights to his name. It cost Schwarz DEM 1,000, then worth about $300.

FIRST RETAIL MARKET OPENS

Schwarz opened his first Lidl market in 1973 in the town of Ludwigshafen. The direct model for Schwarz's new grocery store was the Aldi chain, Germany's first so-called discount market that began its remarkable growth in the early 1960s. The idea behind the discount grocers was simple: small, spartan stores with a limited selection of products. There was generally only one type of each product to choose from, and that was an inexpensive house brand. The early Lidl stores differed from Aldi only insofar as Lidl's average selection was about twice as large as Aldi's—a typical Lidl carried approximately 1,300 items at as opposed to about 600 at Aldi.

By 1977, the year Schwarz's father passed away at the age of 74, the Lidl chain had expanded to more than 30 stores in Germany, and was on its way to establishing itself as Aldi's main competitor in the German discount grocery market. Lidl not only patterned its business model on Aldi, it was also similar to Aldi in that for the next 35 years it would engage in virtually no corporate communication with the press or public. Lidl's secretiveness about its operations became legendary.

During the next decade the growth of the company, which at that time was named Lidl & Schwarz, was limited to the southwestern areas of the Federal Republic of Germany. By 1980 its annual revenues had reached an estimated DEM 1 billion. Toward the end of the 1980s Lidl made a significant expansion in its main areas of operation with the purchase of 66 Grosso-Magnet stores from the Tengelmann Gruppe, the operators of Plus, another discount grocery chain in Germany. In addition to its discount supermarkets, Lidl & Schwarz had by then also established a network of some 400 superstores in West Germany under various names including Kaufland, Kaufmarkt, and Handelshof. The firm had not begun its real growth however.

EXPANDING BEYOND GERMANY

In 1989 Lidl & Schwarz made its first jump into the foreign market, one of two areas that would fuel the company's remarkable growth in the 1990s. It opened its first stores in France in 1989 and was a success. This came as a surprise to many industry observers who had maintained previously that the French placed too high a value on quality goods and services to be interested in Lidl's no-name bargains. Within five years, however, Lidl had become one of France's top grocery chains. Lidl expanded systematically into other European countries, to Italy in 1991 and to Spain in 1993. The success of its expansion policy was clear.

KEY DATES

■

1930: Josef Schwarz joins Südfrüchte Großhandlung Lidl & Co.

1972: Dieter Schwarz joins Lidl & Co.

1973: A Lidl discount market is opened in Ludwigshafen, Germany.

1984: The first Kaufland superstore opens in Neckarsulm, Germany.

1989: A Lidl market opens in France, opening foreign markets.

1990: The first Kaufland store opens in eastern Germany.

1992: Lidl markets are opened in eastern Germany for the first time.

1996: A DEM 100 million service center is established in Lübbenau, south of Berlin; Hauser Baumarkt reorganizes as Hauser GmbH & Co. KG.

1997: The 100th Kaufland opens in eastern Germany.

1999: Lidl & Schwarz are completely reorganized.

2000: The first Lidl stores open in Ireland.

2001: The Schwarz Group is established as a holding company.

2002: Lidl opens its first Scandinavian stores in Finland.

2003: Eleven Lidl stores are opened in Sweden.

2004: Labor union Ver.di publishes *The Black Book of the Schwarz Retail Company.*

2007: The first Lidl stores are unionized.

Revenues reached DEM 5 billion in 1990. Only one year later they had jumped to DEM 8 billion, and in 1992 to DEM 11 billion.

Foreign expansion was only half of the story, however. In 1990 a huge new market opened in the eastern regions of Germany, the areas of the German Democratic Republic that had been sealed off by the Berlin Wall for more than 25 years. East Germans were craving a selection of western foodstuffs—in particular fruits and vegetables—at prices they could afford, given uncertain economic situation in eastern regions following the fall of the wall. Lidl & Schwarz capitalized immediately on the openness of eastern Germans to discount grocery stores. Starting in 1992, new Lidl stores sprung up like mushrooms in the East.

By 1994, Lidl's savvy was showing in its bottom line. The chain had an estimated DEM 14 billion in revenues. It had become Germany's eighth largest grocery store chain and its 14th largest retail chain. It had DEM 10 billion less in annual revenues than its main competitor Aldi. However, the mid-1990s were a difficult period for German retailers, and like so many other German stores at the time, Aldi's sales had dropped. Lidl's, by contrast, were growing rapidly. The fact that its growth was being powered primarily by expansion in eastern Germany and foreign countries was reflected in a poll taken in January 1994 that showed that only 13 percent of West Germans recognized the Lidl brand. Nonetheless, regardless of its level of brand-name recognition in the old West German states, by the end of 1994 market leader Aldi considered Lidl its primary competitor.

INTERNATIONAL GROWTH CONTINUES

Lidl & Schwarz continued to enter other European countries at a steady pace. In 1994 the first Lidl markets were opened in Britain, and within a year there were 30 stores operating there. A year later it established its first markets in Belgium, the Netherlands, and Portugal, while continuing to spread throughout Northern Italy. In fact, in order to finance the development of foreign markets, Lidl was forced to cut back on the number of new stores it opened in Germany.

Supplying its new foreign stores with product was an often expensive proposition. These stores usually purchased their products from suppliers in based in Germany. Before the introduction of the euro as a general European currency, these suppliers expected to be paid in deutsche marks. The foreign stores, however, were doing business in their own currencies, which, in the case of the British pound, the Italian lira, and the Spanish peseta, for example, were weak against the mark at the time. This led in turn to lower revenues. Similar losses also occurred when percentages of foreign income were transferred from abroad to Lidl & Schwarz accounts in Germany.

Other problems encountered by Lidl during its years of foreign expansion were costly price wars with established foreign market chains, disagreements with unions over Lidl's treatment of workers, and complaints that Lidl was engaging in illegal advertising and pricing practices. By late 1997, Lidl & Schwarz was operating some 1,700 stores throughout Europe with total annual revenues of approximately DEM 22.6 billion. Its employee rolls had grown to some 38,000 from 15,000 in 1990. By then Lidl had overtaken Aldi and had become the undisputed market leader among discount groceries in France, Italy, and Spain.

MILESTONE FOR KAUFLAND STORES

In 1997 Lidl & Schwarz opened its 100th Kaufland store in eastern Germany. The first Kaufland superstore had opened in 1984 near Lidl & Schwarz's headquarters in Neckarsulm. Like Lidl, the Kaufland chain took early advantage of the opening of the market in eastern Germany. In October 1990 a Kaufland opened in Meissen in the eastern German state of Saxony. After that the chain grew rapidly throughout the region. Although the first Kauflands in eastern Germany were frequently nothing more than large tents that were overly hot in the summer and overly cold in the winter months, customers flocked to them. Kaufland buildings were enormous, 4,000 square meters or more in size, and they carried a full range of products, with a heavy emphasis on food and beverages.

Between 1990 and 1997 Lidl & Schwarz opened new Kaufland stores at a rate of one approximately every three weeks. During the same period Kaufland's revenues increased from DEM 0.5 billion to an estimated DEM 4.5 billion. Lidl & Schwarz essentially ignored its 30-year anniversary in 1998, focusing instead on its expansion into two new countries. The first Lidl market opened in Austria in November 1998, with five to ten additional stores planned in the coming year. One month later, in December 1998, 11 Kaufland superstores opened their doors in the Czech Republic.

By the end of the 1990s Dieter Schwarz had quietly crept into the ranks of the world's wealthiest individuals. In 1999 *Forbes* named him the 37th richest person in the world and the richest of all in Germany. This angered Schwarz, who had always guarded his privacy jealously; after all, Aldi cofounder Theo Albrecht had been kidnapped and held for a multimillion-mark ransom in 1971. Schwarz protested to *Forbes,* and he did not appear on subsequent "Richest Man" lists in the magazine.

NEW STRUCTURE FOR OWNERSHIP AND ADMINISTRATION

In 1999 Schwarz decided to end his involvement in the day-to-day operations of Lidl & Schwarz, and the firm underwent a thorough reorganization. The most important step was the nearly complete separation of ownership and management power. The Dieter Schwarz Stiftung gemeinnützige GmbH—the Dieter Schwarz Foundation, Ltd.—took over ownership of 99.9 percent of Lidl & Schwarz but was given no voting rights in the business. A second company, the Schwarz Beteiligungs GmbH—the Schwarz Holding Company Ltd.—held a miniscule 0.1 percent share of the various businesses but had 100 percent of the voting rights.

The Lidl and Kaufland stores were split into two companies independent of each other, both subsidiaries of Schwarz Beteiligungs GmbH. At the same time, the regional Lidls were organized into literally hundreds of smaller companies. One reason behind the complicated new organization, some critics argued, was to block the unionization of the supermarket chain. In 2001 the companies were given the name the Schwarz Group.

TROUBLES IN THE MIDST OF SUCCESS

The year 2002 was known in German retailing as the "crisis year." It was the worst for business since the end of World War II. People still had to eat, though, and the discount grocers benefited from reduced consumer spending in other areas. Lidl had 2002 revenues estimated at EUR 23 billion, a 10 percent jump from the year before. By then the Lidl chain had more than 2,300 stores in Germany and another 2,500 in Britain, France, Spain, Italy, and ten other European nations. In terms of stores, Lidl had become Europe's largest discount store chain, besting its rival, Aldi. Lidl's foreign revenues increased 50 percent in 2002.

The Schwarz Group had its share of difficulties, however, in the early 2000s. German antitrust authorities launched an investigation of alleged predatory pricing by Lidl, an investigation that was dropped after Lidl restored its former prices. Around the same time the Vereinte Dienstleistungsgewerkschaft (Ver.di), a large service workers union, drew public attention to systematic abuses of workers alleged to be taking place at Lidl stores. Ver.di promoted 2002 as its "Lidl Year" and launched a series of programs aimed at unionizing the chain's stores. The Schwarz Group fought the Ver.di effort tooth and nail, using tactics as varied as splitting up regional operations to nullify judicial rulings or simply closing stores where the union had won the right to organize.

By mid-2004 Lidl had moved into Finland with ten stores and into Sweden with 11 more, and it was making plans to enter the Norwegian market. With a total of 6,200 discount markets and superstores, the Schwarz Group had become the second largest of all European grocery retailers, not only discounters. The group's revenues had grown to an estimated EUR 35 billion, and it employed some 80,000 workers. It had passed all other German discounters except for Aldi.

LABOR ISSUES AND NEGATIVE PRESS

However, the good news was followed by bad news. In 2004 the union Ver.di published *The Black Book of the Schwarz Retail Company.* The book, which appeared in both English and German, documented the conditions that Lidl store employees were forced to endure, including long overtime hours without pay, long periods without bathroom breaks, unfounded accusations of theft, and firings without notice. The book called once again for the immediate formation of labor councils at Lidl stores. Toward the end of 2007, Ver.di was finally able to unionize Lidl stores in Hamburg and Stuttgart.

The negative publicity did not hurt Lidl's bottom line. In May 2006 the company announced that revenues had increased an astonishing 76 percent over the previous two years, reaching EUR 44 billion. It was pursuing—albeit not without difficulties—broad expansion in the Netherlands and Ireland. In January 2007 it took its place as one of the top ten retail companies in the world.

Lidl was constantly pushing the boundaries of what typical discount grocery stores in Germany stocked. It was one of the first, for example, to stock fresh meat. In 2005 Lidl stores introduced full sections of personal care items such as cosmetics, shampoo, lotions, and other toiletries. In January 2006 Lidl introduced organic foods—meats, vegetables and fruit—as part of its product line. The Schwarz Group evidently saw great promise in the latter trend, for in August 2007 it attempted to acquire a majority interest in Basic AG, Germany's second largest chain of health food markets.

Reactions against the proposed takeover were profound. Two of Basic's founders, opposed to working with a company that had Lidl's reputation for treating both its suppliers and employees badly, sold all their Basic AG holdings in protest. Basic's customers voiced their "simple disgust," as one German newspaper described it, at the idea of the takeover. Three months later, the Basic board of directors bucked their CFO and voted unanimously to quash his plan to let the Schwarz Group absorb Basic.

MORE GROWTH AND NEW CONTROVERSY

As 2008 began, Lidl and the Schwarz Group had achieved another year of monumental success. Its revenues had shown double digit growth once again, surpassing the previous year by 12 percent, reaching EUR 49 billion. It had passed its arch-competitor Aldi in total stores. Aldi still had more in Germany—4,200 to about 2,900 for Lidl. Worldwide, however, Lidl was operating 7,271 stores, almost 300 more than Aldi. Moreover, the Schwarz Group had 500 Kaufland stores in Germany and eastern Europe. Lidl had achieved this lead despite the fact that Aldi operated 900 stores in the United States, where it had been active for more than 30 years.

Lidl itself had been planning an entry into the U.S. market for a good five years without any visible progress. The Schwarz Group accelerated those plans in 2008 and intended to open the first American Lidl stores by 2012. The chain was also preparing a beachhead in Switzerland, where it planned to open 80 stores in 2009. At the same time, however, in March 2008 the Schwarz Group announced it was abandoning Norway where it had been operating 50 discount grocery stores. The firm cited ongoing problems with local zoning officials.

Lidl was struck with another salvo of bad publicity, possibly the worst to that point, when *Stern,* a national news magazine, revealed that the company had installed secret cameras in some 500 of its stores in Germany to monitor employees. Using the cameras and microphones, a security company hired by the Schwarz Group had kept detailed notes on the personal behavior and conversations of employees, reminding many Germans of the surveillance techniques of the Stasi, the East German secret police, prior to the fall of the Berlin Wall. The Schwarz Group, in one of its rare public statements, claimed that the monitoring had been undertaken only to combat inventory losses due to theft that, the firm said, totaled some EUR 80 million annually. Lidl also responded to the revelations by ending its involvement with the security firms and offering every full-time Lidl employee EUR 300 in compensation.

The following September civil rights officials in several German states announced their intention to seek some EUR 1.5 million in damages from Lidl. If awarded, the 35 regional Lidl organizations would each be forced to pay between EUR 10,000 and EUR 310,000 in damages to employees. That same month, Schwarz Group board chairman Wilfried Oskierski, one of the secretive firm's most powerful insiders, was relieved of all responsibility, reportedly for his role in the surveillance scandal.

Gerald E. Brennan

PRINCIPAL SUBSIDIARIES

Schwarz Unternehmenstreuhand KG; Dieter Schwarz Stiftung gemeinnützige GmbH; Schwarz Beteiligungs GmbH; Lidl Dienstleistung GmbH & Co. KG; Kaufland Dienstleistung GmbH & Co. KG; Kaufland Stiftung & Co. KG; Lidl Stiftung & Co. KG; Schwarz Objekt- Management GmbH & Co. KG; Mitteldeutschen Erfrischungsgetränke; Choc 1 GmbH & Co KG.

PRINCIPAL COMPETITORS

ALDI Group; Edeka Zentrale AG & Co. KG.

FURTHER READING

Boyes, Roger, "Big Brother Supermarket Is Watching You … and You," *Times* (London), March 27, 2008, p. 38.

Creevy, Jennifer, "Lidl Goes a Long Way," *Retail Week,* October 10, 2008.

"Der Geheimnis-Kraemer," *Focus Magazin,* August 23, 2004, pp. 146–52.

Doorley, Tom, "Why I'm Proud to Be a Lidl Man," *Daily Mail,* March 1, 2008, p. 26.

Dougherty, Carter, "In Germany, U.S. Model Is Tough Sell," *International Herald Tribune,* August 5, 2006, p. 11.

Hamann, Andreas, and Gudrun Giese, *The Black Book on the Schwarz Retail Company,* Ver.di Verlag, 2005.

Hanke, Gerd, "Quetscht Studienabsolventen 'wie eine Zitrone aus,'" *Lebensmittel Zeitung,* November 14, 2003, p. 6.

Hielscher, Henryk, "Öko-Branche Lidl steigt bei Bio-Kette Basic aus," *WirtschaftsWoche,* November 9, 2007, http:// www.wiwo.de/unternehmer-maerkte/lidl-steigt-bei-bio-kette-basic-aus-238522/.

Hirn, Wolfgang, Christian Rickens, and Jörn Sucher, "Managerschwund beim Aldi-Jäger," *manager-magazin,* January 25, 2007, http://www.manager-magazin.de/unternehmen/artikel/0,2828,461991,00.html.

Kerbusk, Klaus-Peter, "Der Geheimniskrämer," *Der Spiegel,* August 12, 2002, p. 85.

Kuipers, Pascal, "Kaufland: The Industrialisation of Retailing," *Elsevier Food International,* vol. 5, no. 3, September 2002.

———, "Lidl: Darwinian Discount," *Elsevier Food International,* vol. 7, no. 1, February 2004.

Langer, Karsten, "Aldis Erzfeind," *manager-magazin,* March 2, 2004, http://www.manager-magazin.de/koepfe/unternehmerarchiv/0,2828,288662,00.html.

"Lidl steigt in die Weltliga auf," *Frankfurter Allgemeine Zeitung,* January 22, 2007, p. 18.

"Lidl vor der Inquisition," *Lebensmittel Zeitung,* December 15, 1995, p. 34.

"Mehr als 500 Filialen wurden überwacht," Tagesschau, ARD-TV, May 5, 2008, http://www.tagesschau.de/wirtschaft/lidl14.html.

Petrescu, Sergiu, "Deutsche Discounter im Ausland," *Lebensmittel Zeitung,* August 27, 2004, p. 10.

Riera, Jose, "Lidl Targets Seven Virgin Markets to Outflank Aldi," *Retail Week,* July 23, 2004, p. 6.

Servidyne Inc.

1945 The Exchange, Suite 325
Atlanta, Georgia 30339-2029
U.S.A.
Telephone: (770) 933-4200
Toll Free: (800) 241-8996
Fax: (770) 933-4201
Web site: http://www.servidyne.com

Public Company
Incorporated: 1925 as A.R. Abrams Inc.
Employees: 82
Sales: $19.7 million (2008)
Stock Exchanges: NASDAQ
Ticker Symbol: SERV
NAICS: 233320 Commercial and Institutional Building
Construction; 541330 Engineering Services;
531120 Lessors of Nonresidential Buildings

■ ■ ■

Formerly known as Abrams Industries Inc., Servidyne Inc. offers energy efficiency solutions to owners and operators of buildings. Through its Building Performance Efficiency division, Servidyne provides its customers with solutions designed to reduce energy consumption and cut utility costs, and also offers environmental sustainability and occupant satisfaction programs. The company's customers include owners and operators of corporate, commercial office, hospitality, gaming, retail, light industrial, distribution, healthcare, government, and education buildings and facilities, as well as energy service companies. Servidyne also invests

in and develops commercial real estate. Abrams Industries acquired Servidyne in 2001 and adopted its name five years later.

ALFRED ABRAMS AND SONS

In 1925, World War I veteran Alfred R. Abrams, then 26 years old, started a construction business in West Palm Beach, Florida. It was a pioneering effort in more ways than one, because Florida's boom years had not yet begun. Air conditioning was still relatively new and far from universal, meaning that people were not yet flocking to Miami and Fort Lauderdale, as they would in coming decades. Abrams himself would move his business north 15 years later, to Atlanta.

Not long after Abrams relocated in 1940, the United States entered another world war, and when it was over, his company in 1946 began producing in-store fixtures for retailers. This was the origin of Abrams Industries' manufacturing segment, which became Abrams Fixture Corporation. At that time, however, the overall company was simply A.R. Abrams Inc., a sole proprietorship. In 1960, Albert Abrams incorporated Abrams Industries under Delaware law. That year also saw the beginnings of the company's third segment, real estate.

Alfred Abrams had two sons: Bernard, born in 1925, the year Alfred began his business, and Edward, born in 1927. Like his father, Bernard Abrams entered the military and considered a career in the army, but suffered wounds during the Korean War—in which he served as a captain—that forced him to return to civilian life. Younger son Edward Abrams would later describe his father as "a real martinet" as a corporate leader. The statement, in an *Atlanta Journal and Constitution* article about family-run public companies, referred not to the policies of the elder Abrams with his workforce in general, but rather to his treatment of his sons. Alfred Abrams apparently did not want his boys to grow up thinking that just because they were the boss's sons, they should have it easy.

When Alfred Abrams died in 1979 at the age of 80, his sons had long since taken charge of the company; within just a few years, their sons would also come on board. Thus Abrams Industries, whose stock was traded on NASDAQ, would become both a public and a family-run enterprise.

UPS AND DOWNS

In the mid-1980s, Bernard Abrams served as chairman and chief executive officer of the company, while Edward Abrams served as president. The company had several things going for it, but it faced potential challenges as well. At that time Abrams Industries consisted of seven subsidiaries, including a division specializing in electrical and fire protection contracting. A 1986 profile of the company in the *Atlanta Journal and Constitution* lauded the development of what had grown from a small construction company into a $61.5-million-a-year corporation, but also regarded the firm as on the defensive in the face of declining market share.

At that time a single client, discount retailer Kmart, accounted for more than one-third of Abrams Industries' revenue, and this company's share of Abrams Industries' total business had declined from 44 percent in 1983 to 35 percent in 1985. With such a heavy reliance on a single client, the company's fortunes were bound to rise and fall with the retailer's, and the *Journal and Constitution* reported, "Kmart and other retailers aren't adding stores and fixtures as they used to."

Moreover, the outside responsibilities of Bernard Abrams created another challenge, because they placed a strain on his time and diverted his attention as chairman of the company. Although he had long since left the army, he remained committed to acting on behalf of the military, becoming involved in public work to improve communication between U.S. citizens and their armed forces by working as an aide to the secretary of the Army. These activities and his other civic commitments often divided his attentions, and in 1986 he admitted, "I feel as though I must give more time to the business."

The *Journal and Constitution* article noted that Abrams Industries had "the kind of strategic defense any soldier would write home about," and the military-minded Bernard Abrams spoke of how his experience in the army had taught him to handle "moments of tension." His defensive strategy involved relying on the most successful parts of the company to make up for those that lagged behind, and also required that management stay calm: "If a wall falls down," Bernard said, "we don't panic. We'll just fix the wall."

In fact, while Abrams Industries had experienced slowing in some areas, other segments helped offset losses with larger profits. The electrical and fire protection segment was small, and would eventually be discontinued altogether; production of store fixtures, however, while not the largest area of the company in terms of dollar volume, was nonetheless highly profitable. Contracting and engineering had suffered losses partly because of overbuilding in the multifamily housing market, and real estate had likewise posted losses.

THE THIRD GENERATION OF THE ABRAMS FAMILY

In the 1980s, a third generation of the Abrams family began to move into management positions. Edward's sons Alan and J. Andrew (Andy) and Bernard's son David all joined the family business. Edward told the *Journal and Constitution* in 1989 that he had wanted his sons to join the company for several years: "I thought, wouldn't it be a shame not to give these kids an opportunity to continue?" Bernard said proudly of his son and nephews, "These men know that my brother and I have worked very hard for this business."

All three of the grandsons of Alfred Abrams had extensive educations. Alan R. Abrams, who had studied history at Columbia University and earned an MBA from Atlanta's Emory University, had first gone into investment banking before joining Abrams Industries. Andy Abrams graduated from the University of Notre Dame with a double major in English and electrical engineering, and he too found himself being invited into the family firm. "Dad had never asked me for anything," he told Susan Harte of the *Journal and Constitution,* adding, "so when he did, I listened." His first job with the company was hardly one that put all his education to work: "I can still shape a very nice

KEY DATES

1925: Alfred R. Abrams starts a construction business.
1960: Abrams Industries incorporates.
1996: The company begins restructuring its fixture business in an attempt to shore up profits.
2000: Abrams Fixture Corp. is sold.
2001: Abrams buys Servidyne Systems Inc.
2004: The company exits the construction business.
2006: The company changes its name to Servidyne Inc.

ditch," he recalled of his early employment at an Abrams construction site in Florida. By 1989, he was working as construction coordinator for Abrams Properties. As for David Abrams, he was the only one of the Abrams cousins who had "an underlying assumption that the family business would be a part of my life." Hence his education most closely mirrored the needs of the company: a chemical engineering degree from Princeton and MBA training from Harvard.

By 1996, Alan Abrams and Andy Abrams, who had grown up the least prepared for a career with Abrams, remained with the company. Alan Abrams was serving as president of Abrams Properties Inc. while Andy Abrams was named vice-president of Abrams Fixture Corporation. As for the older generation, they had changed roles: Edward Abrams was chairman of the board and CEO of Abrams Industries Inc., and Bernard Abrams was chairman of the executive committee for Abrams Industries Inc. Seven years had brought a great deal of change, not only in the company's leadership, but throughout Abrams Industries.

CHALLENGES LEAD TO RESTRUCTURING

In the quarter ended July 31, 1990, the company reported net losses of around $300,000 for the company, attributed mainly to Abrams Fixture, the segment that created merchandise displays. According to Bernard Abrams, this disappointing showing owed chiefly to the fact that two large retailers had postponed orders until later in the year.

The poor performance of the manufacturing segment portended future results in that area of the company. Once a highly profitable part of the Abrams operations, by 1996 the subsidiary had definitely fallen on hard times. In response, management decided to

"build our business to our customers," rather than "build our customers to our business," by reengineering the manufacturing segment. Toward that end, leadership decided to redesign Abrams Fixture Corporation from the ground up. Abrams instituted a three-part renovation of the company, which would last into the summer of 1997. As for revenues and profits from the manufacturing segment during this time, profits had dipped in 1993, risen slightly in 1994, and then plummeted in 1995. By 1996, the losses were smaller, and the company anticipated gains from the closing of some facilities.

Real estate was in better shape, partly because the company had redeveloped a Kmart location in Jackson, Michigan, that it had owned since the early 1970s, creating a 105,000-square-foot shopping center with Kroger and Big Lots as its anchor stores. Abrams properties also had activities at a North Fort Myers, Florida, shopping center in which, by adding a large portion in 1996, it held 240,000 square feet of area available for lease. It also had properties in Oakwood and Tifton, Georgia; Englewood, Florida; and other locations. Revenues from real estate were down from a 1994 high, and losses exceeded $1 million on receipts of almost $11.5 million. The company attributed the shortfall to two factors: the loss of rental income during the renovation of the Michigan site and costs of maintaining and re-tenanting that and other locations. Again, the company was optimistic about future returns from existing activities, in this case its addition of new space for lease.

In contrast to the corporate picture a decade earlier, construction was the brightest spot for Abrams by this time. In 1996, the company completed more than 130 projects in some 22 states, mostly for major retailers. Revenues in this area exceeded $108 million, and earnings were nearly $3 million. The company attributed the success of its construction segment to "the untiring effort and dedication of all our people to produce the customer's product in the most efficient manner and in the shortest possible time."

A REMARKABLE TURNAROUND

While dramatic changes had taken place in corporate structure and performance, some aspects of Abrams were much the same as before. Uneven performance of the different subsidiaries remained, although the underperformers had shifted. A high degree of reliance on a few customers still existed, though by this time the emphasis had shifted away from Kmart. In 1996, the company did 48 percent of its business with Atlanta-based Home Depot Inc. and approximately 18 percent in building and development for Baby Superstore.

Alan Abrams, as Abrams Properties president, told the *Atlanta Business Chronicle* in 1997 that the company had sold two Kmart properties in addition to the one in Michigan, the others being in Georgia and Oklahoma. More importantly, the company was adopting a new diversified strategy in its real estate operations. To that end, Alan Abrams and executive vice-president Gerald T. Anderson II had spent a great deal of time on the road, drumming up new business.

For the fourth quarter of its 1997 fiscal year, which ended on April 30, the company had posted profits in all three of its segments. Alan Abrams told the *Business Chronicle:* "It's important for people who follow us to know that we're using the proceeds to invest in a more diversified mix." He added, "We had 22 properties where Kmart was either the lead tenant or single tenant in all but one. We've now sold several of those Kmart properties, and we're trying to broaden the base of our tenants." Among the significant elements in the invigorated real estate strategy, he said, were a new involvement with office and industrial properties as well as a focus on "second-tier" cities such as Chattanooga, Tennessee, and Macon, Georgia.

Gerald Anderson told the *Business Chronicle* that he and Alan Abrams had "lived on airplanes for quite a while" as they went around the country to grow the business and "turn our portfolio." Alan Abrams was cautiously upbeat: "We had a couple of tough years," he said, "but the companies, especially the manufacturing subsidiary, have done a remarkable turnaround."

MOVING INTO THE 21ST CENTURY

Despite management's optimism, it became apparent that Abrams would have to shift its focus in the early years of the new millennium in order to remain afloat. Plans were set in motion to sell its manufacturing operations and in early 2000, the company sold Abrams Fixture Corporation to fixture manufacturer MII Inc. for $2.2 million. Later that year, the company sold its manufacturing facility in Douglas County, Georgia, for approximately $11 million. The company began outsourcing property management in 2001.

By this time, the company's continuing operations included commercial construction and real estate investment. The company purchased Atlanta-based Servidyne Systems Inc. in 2001. The deal gave Abrams a foothold in the energy solutions market, a sector it believed was ripe for future growth. With energy costs rising and a growing focus on environmental concerns, Servidyne provided its customers engineering and management services designed to reduce energy-related costs in buildings and facilities. Servidyne's operations would eventually become the backbone of the company's business.

Meanwhile, revenues in the company's construction business began to decline in 2002. At the same time, the company discovered that several executives were involved in illegal job bidding activities. Michael Merritt, president and CEO of the company's construction arm, resigned as a result of the improprieties. Sales continued to decline and in April 2004, Abrams shuttered its construction activities. At the same time, Abrams sold its shopping center in Englewood, Florida, as well as locations in Davenport, Iowa, and Jackson, Michigan.

The company acquired iTendant Inc., a manufacturer of service and maintenance tracking software, in 2004. Believing that its Servidyne operations were the key to its future success, Abrams continued to focus heavily on energy management solutions. Indeed, the company signaled its shift in focus by changing its name to Servidyne Inc. in July 2006.

Under its new name, the company touted itself as an energy, infrastructure, and productivity management services provider to commercial real estate operators. Servidyne also remained involved in commercial real estate investment and development. During 2008 Servidyne acquired Atlantic Lighting and Supply co. Inc., an energy-efficient lighting products distributor.

Alan R. Abrams had remained chairman, president, and CEO of Servidyne during its transformation. While the company had made significant changes to its operating structure, management claimed its mission remained unchanged—to serve and meet the needs of owners and operators of buildings.

Judson Knight
Updated, Christina M. Stansell

PRINCIPAL SUBSIDIARIES

1945 The Exchange, LLC; Abrams Construction, Inc.; Abrams Power, Inc.; Abrams Properties, Inc.; Abrams-Columbus Limited Partnership; Abrams Orange Park, LLC; AFC Real Estate, Inc.; AI North Fort Myers, LLC; Atlantic Lighting & Supply Co., LLC; Benncoff, LLC; Chipjax, LLC; Merchants Crossing of North Fort Myers, Inc.; Merchants Crossing, Inc.; Newnan Office Plaza, LLC; Servidyne Systems, LLC; Stewartsboro Crossing, LLC; The Wheatstone Energy Group, LLC.

PRINCIPAL DIVISIONS

Building Performance Efficiency; Real Estate.

PRINCIPAL COMPETITORS

Brasfield & Gorrie LLC; Fisher Development Inc.; Paul H. Schwendener, Inc.

FURTHER READING

"Abrams Industries Acquires iTendant Inc.," *Dow Jones News Service,* April 20, 2004.

"Abrams Industries Acquires Servidyne Systems," *Business Wire,* May 10, 2001.

"Abrams Industries Changes Name to Servidyne," *PR Newswire,* July 17, 2006.

"Abrams Industries Closes Abrams Fixture Asset Sale for $2.2 Million," *Dow Jones Business News,* February 8, 2000.

"Abrams Industries Inc.," *Wall Street Journal,* May 31, 2000.

"Abrams Industries Sells Ga. Plant for $11 Million," *Dow Jones News Service,* April 24, 2000.

Burritt, Chris, "Abrams Industries to Report Net Loss for Quarter," *Atlanta Journal and Constitution,* August 22, 1990, p. B8.

Garrett, Montgomery, "Abrams Shakes Up Portfolio, Seeks New Markets," *Atlanta Business Chronicle,* August 4, 1997.

Harte, Susan, "A Relative Question: Nepotism in a Publicly Traded Firm Frowned On, but Could Be Beneficiary," *Atlanta Journal and Constitution,* July 17, 1989, p. C1.

Lawrence, Calvin, "Company Profile: Abrams Industries Inc. Undoubtedly Has Battle Plan for Total Victory," *Atlanta Journal and Constitution,* February 3, 1986, p. C2.

Mallard, W. Morgan, "Abrams Wants Its House a Bit More Orderly," *Atlanta Journal and Constitution,* November 17, 1986, p. E6.

"Servidyne Buys Atlantic Lighting," *Electrical Wholesaling,* July 1, 2008.

Wilbert, Tony, "Unhappy Investor Tells Abrams to Improve," *Atlanta Business Chronicle,* April 25, 1997, p. A10.

Simon & Schuster Inc.

—————————————◼—————————————

1230 Avenue of the Americas
New York, New York 10020
U.S.A.
Telephone: (212) 698-7000
Fax: (212) 632-8090
Web site: http://www.simonsays.com

Wholly Owned Subsidiary of CBS Corporation
Incorporated: 1924
Employees: 1,518
Sales: $671 million (2006 est.)
NAICS: 511130 Book Publishers

■ ■ ■

Simon & Schuster Inc. is the publishing arm of CBS Corporation; it publishes approximately 2,000 titles annually. The company operates seven consumer-focused divisions: Simon & Schuster Adult Publishing Group, Simon & Schuster Children's Publishing, Simon & Schuster Audio, Simon & Schuster Online, Simon & Schuster UK, Simon & Schuster Canada, and Simon & Schuster Australia. Its famous imprints include Simon & Schuster, Scribner, Pocket Books, Fireside, Touchstone, Washington Square Press, Atheneum, MTV Books, and Wall Street Journal Books. The company prints the work of many popular authors of consumer fiction and nonfiction trade books under imprints that include Pocket Books, The Free Press, and Scribner. Simon & Schuster also publishes audio books and e-books, and delivers book content on CD-ROM. The company had won 54 Pulitzer Prizes by 2008 and was

the recipient of numerous National Book Awards and National Book Critics Circle Awards.

CROSSWORD PUZZLE ORIGINS

Richard L. Simon and M. Lincoln Schuster founded the company in January 1924. Their first publication—at the suggestion of Simon's aunt, a crossword puzzle enthusiast—was *The Crossword Puzzle Book,* which came out in April. The book sold more than 100,000 copies, and Simon & Schuster followed it with three other crossword puzzle books in the company's first year. All four books were top nonfiction bestsellers, and by the end of the year Simon & Schuster had sold more than a million of them.

The puzzle books were highly profitable, but the craze eventually waned, and Simon & Schuster had to diversify. Its first few efforts produced moderate successes, including a tennis book by Bill Tilden and an investment guide by Merryle Stanley Rukeyser, and several failures, such as a novel called *Harvey Landrum* and a biography of Joseph Pulitzer. The company's first big success outside of the puzzle books was Will Durant's *The Story of Philosophy,* a bestseller in 1926 and 1927. The book established Simon & Schuster as a serious publishing company and led to Durant's writing, with his wife, Ariel, the multivolume *Story of Civilization* series for Simon & Schuster over the next half-century.

Simon & Schuster quickly developed a reputation as a highly commercial publishing house (one successful project was a compilation of the "Ripley's Believe It or Not" newspaper cartoon features), but at the same time brought out many distinguished works. In its first two decades, Simon & Schuster's output included Leon Trotsky's *History of the Russian Revolution,* Felix Salten's *Bambi,* Rachel Carson's *Under the Sea-Wind,* Wendell Willkie's *One World,* and three volumes of the Durants' *Civilization* series. Simon & Schuster had a Pulitzer Prize winner in 1935, *Now in November* by Josephine Johnson.

Other achievements of the early years were the publication of a collection of George Gershwin's songs, followed by similar compilations of the works of Noel Coward, Cole Porter, Jerome Kern, the team of Richard Rodgers and Lorenz Hart, and Rodgers's later teaming with Oscar Hammerstein II, as well as the Treasury series of oversized gift books, such as 1939's *A Treasury of Art Masterpieces,* followed by similar books on the theater, oratory, and the world's great letters.

ADDING A PARTNER

Aside from the founders, key figures in Simon & Schuster's early years were Leon Shimkin, the company's business manager, and Clifton Fadiman, editor-in-chief. While Fadiman left in the mid-1930s and achieved fame as a book reviewer and radio quiz-show host, Shimkin became an equal partner, financially and operationally. With the founders, he stayed on for many years and was highly influential in the company. In the late 1930s, he brought in two highly successful properties—Dale Carnegie's *How to Win Friends and Influence People* and J. K. Lasser's *Your Income Tax.*

In 1939, Simon, Schuster, and Shimkin put up 49 percent of the financing for Robert F. de Graff, an experienced publisher of hardcover reprints, to start Pocket Books, a line of inexpensive, mass-market paperback reprints. Although paperback books had appeared in the United States as far back as the 1770s, the format's full potential was not realized until the founding of Pocket Books, which was followed by several competitors. Initially priced at 25 cents a copy, Pocket Books became a great success; during World War II,

various wartime agencies shipped 25 million Pocket Books overseas. Shimkin was able to weather wartime paper rationing by taking over the paper quotas of publishing companies that were not able to use their entire allotment.

Five of the initial 11 Pocket Books titles remained in print into the 21st century: William Shakespeare's *Five Great Tragedies,* Pearl S. Buck's *The Good Earth,* James Hilton's *Lost Horizon,* Agatha Christie's *The Murder of Roger Ackroyd,* and Felix Salten's *Bambi.* Eventually, Pocket Books published original titles as well as reprints of hardcover books; its most successful publication was Dr. Benjamin Spock's *Baby and Child Care,* first printed in 1946. Periodically updated, more than 33 million copies of this book had been printed by 1989. Pocket Books was merged into Simon & Schuster in 1966.

In 1942, Simon & Schuster started another line of inexpensive books, Little Golden Books, aimed at children. Full-color, high-quality children's books had not been available at such low prices before—Little Golden Books, like Pocket Books, sold for 25 cents a copy. Simon & Schuster was able to keep costs down by running 50,000 copies per title, a previously unheard of quantity. Simon & Schuster handled editorial, art, and sales functions for the books, and Western Printing and Lithographing Company took care of production and manufacturing. The venture was highly successful; by 1958, more than 400 million Little Golden Books had been sold, and the line had spawned such offshoots as Big Golden Books, Giant Golden Books, the Golden Encyclopedia, and Little Golden Records. Perhaps fearing a shakeout in the expanding children's book industry, or enticed by Western Printing's offer, Simon & Schuster sold its half interest in the venture to Western Printing in 1958.

ACQUISITION AND RETURN

In 1944, Field Enterprises, the Chicago communications company headed by Marshall Field, acquired Simon & Schuster from its principals—Simon, Schuster, and Shimkin—for about $3 million. The principals stayed on with long-term management contracts and operated quite independently of Field Enterprises. In 1957, shortly after Marshall Field's death, the executors of his estate were eager to get out of the book publishing business and sold Simon & Schuster back to the principals for $1 million.

Major titles published by Simon & Schuster in the 1940s and 1950s included William L. Shirer's *The Rise and Fall of the Third Reich,* Evan Hunter's *The Blackboard Jungle,* Meyer Levin's *Compulsion,* Kay Thompson's *Eloise,* Joseph Davies's *Mission to Moscow,* popular authors included Harold Robbins, Jacqueline Susann, and Joseph Heller.

In 1957, Richard Simon, who was in poor health, retired from Simon & Schuster. He died in 1960, at which time Schuster and Shimkin each acquired half of his stock, making them equal partners of the company. When Schuster retired in 1966, he sold his share to Shimkin. Simon & Schuster subsequently went public, with its stock traded on the over-the-counter market and later listed on the American Stock Exchange.

CHANGING LEADERSHIP

In the next few years, Simon & Schuster negotiated with several potential acquirers. In May 1970, the company agreed in principle to be bought by Norton Simon Inc., a diversified company whose interests included magazine publishing. The deal fell apart two months later, however, in part because of the stock market's drop. In November of that year, Kinney National Service Inc. reached an agreement in principle to buy Simon & Schuster, but Shimkin became dissatisfied with the offer during the negotiation process. In 1974, Simon & Schuster agreed to a merger with Harcourt Brace Jovanovich, which had substantial textbook publishing operations but little in trade publishing, which was Simon & Schuster's strength. The deal was called off abruptly later that year. Both parties cited the depressed stock market as a reason, but observers said Shimkin had been offended by certain public statements made by William Jovanovich: "He implied that his firm was taking over Simon & Schuster lock, stock, and barrel, and one got the impression that Leon Shimkin would be fortunate if he got a job in the mailroom," longtime Simon & Schuster executive Peter Schwed later wrote in his book, *Turning the Pages: An Insider's Story of Simon & Schuster, 1924–1984.*

A successful deal came through in 1975, when Gulf+Western Industries purchased Simon & Schuster through a swap of one share of Gulf+Western stock for every ten shares of the publishing company. As a condition of the deal, Richard E. Snyder, who had been executive vice-president of Simon & Schuster, moved up to the presidency. Snyder succeeded Seymour Turk, who had been named president in 1973 when Shimkin relinquished that role. Shimkin remained chairman of Simon & Schuster. Gulf+Western, which also owned Paramount Pictures, changed its name to Paramount Communications in 1989.

AGGRESSIVE EXPANSION

Under Snyder, Simon & Schuster expanded aggressively. It set up a dozen new imprints, or brand names, under

---

KEY DATES

■

1924: Richard L. Simon and M. Lincoln Schuster found the company.

1926: The company has its first big success outside of puzzle books with Will Durant's *The Story of Philosophy.*

1942: Simon & Schuster starts a line of inexpensive books aimed at children, Little Golden Books, with Western Printing.

1944: Field Enterprises acquires Simon & Schuster.

1957: Field enterprises sells Simon & Schuster back to founders Simon, Schuster, and Shimkin; Simon retires.

1958: Simon & Schuster sells its half interest in Little Golden Books to Western Printing.

1966: Pocket Books is merged into Simon & Schuster; Schuster retires and sells his share to Shimkin.

1975: Gulf+Western Industries purchases Simon & Schuster through a stock swap.

1985: Prentice Hall Inc., a major textbook publisher, is merged into Simon & Schuster.

1994: Simon & Schuster Interactive, the company's consumer software publishing unit, is established; Viacom acquires company.

1998: Viacom sells Simon & Schuster's reference and educational divisions to Pearson for $4.6 billion and shifts its focus to consumer books.

2002: Jack Romanos takes over as CEO; Viacom integrates Simon & Schuster into its Viacom Entertainment Group unit.

2005: Viacom splits into two companies, one of which is CBS Corporation, which inherits Simon & Schuster.

2008: Carolyn Reidy becomes the first female CEO of the company.

Mary McCarthy's story collection *The Company She Keeps,* Alexander King's *Mine Enemy Grows Older,* Herman Wouk's first book, *Aurora Dawn,* Laura Z. Hobson's *Gentleman's Agreement,* and Sloan Wilson's *The Man in the Gray Flannel Suit.* Humorous books also were important to the publishing house; these included cartoon collections by Walt Kelly, creator of "Pogo," and Al Capp of "Li'l Abner" fame, as well as verbal humor from James Thurber, P. G. Wodehouse, and S. J. Perelman. Moving into the 1960s, Simon & Schuster's which it published books, and its sales grew impressively, from $44 million at the time of the sale to Gulf+Western to $210 million in 1983. By 1989, revenues were up to $1.3 billion. One of the most financially successful new ventures was a line of romance novels called Silhouette Books. Simon & Schuster launched Silhouette in the early 1980s after it lost the U.S. distribution rights to the Harlequin Romances, published by Harlequin Enterprises Ltd. of Toronto. Silhouette soon rivaled Harlequin in popularity among romance readers, and Harlequin's parent, Torstar Corporation, bought Silhouette from Simon & Schuster for $10 million in 1984.

Simon & Schuster entered the textbook field in 1984 by buying Esquire Inc., which no longer owned *Esquire* magazine, for $170 million. The acquisition nearly doubled the Simon & Schuster staff, to 2,300, and lifted it from 13th to the nation's sixth largest book publisher. Later that year, Gulf+Western bought Prentice Hall Inc., a major textbook publisher, for about $710 million and merged it into Simon & Schuster early in 1985, making Simon & Schuster the nation's largest book publisher. Ginn & Company, another educational publisher, was added into the Simon & Schuster fold in 1982, after being bought by Gulf+Western for $100 million. In 1986, Gulf+Western bought Silver Burdett Company, an elementary textbook publisher, for about $125 million and combined its operations with Ginn. In the increasingly computerized decade of the 1980s, software also became an important business for Simon & Schuster.

With the diversification into textbooks and information services, trade book publishing, which was Simon & Schuster's only business at the time of the sale to Gulf+Western, became only a small part of the business, about 6 percent of sales in 1989. It remained a high-profile aspect of the company, however, which published both fiction and nonfiction books that ranged from highly commercial to highly prestigious efforts. Major titles in the 1970s and 1980s included Bob Woodward and Carl Bernstein's *All the President's Men* and *The Final Days;* Woodward's *Wired* and *VEIL: The Secret Wars of the CIA, 1981–1987;* Jackie Collins's *Hollywood Wives;* Taylor Branch's *Parting the Waters;* and former U.S. President Ronald Reagan's *An American Life.*

GOING ONLINE

In 1994, Viacom bought Gulf+Western. This move allowed Simon & Schuster to launch several new imprints in conjunction with channels owned by Viacom's MTV Networks. Viacom acquired Paramount in 1994, and Jonathan Newcomb replaced Dick Snyder as chairman and CEO. Four years later, Viacom sold Simon & Schuster's reference and educational divisions to Pearson for $4.6 billion and shifted its focus to consumer books. Simon & Schuster also acquired Macmillan Publishing Company in 1994.

During the 1990s, however, the trend in the publishing industry was not in traditional print publishing, but toward electronic publishing, or any computer-related materials. In 1996, President and CEO Jonathan Newcomb stated that the company's goal was to generate half of its revenues from electronic publishing, such as via CD-ROMS, videodisks, and the Internet, by the year 2000. At the time, the portion was 25 percent, but Newcomb set about achieving this goal by creating Corporate Digital Archive (CDA). CDA involved a reorganizing of the publisher's editing, production, and other processes so that everything could be categorized in databases. The archive then allowed material to be recalled and manipulated as desired by any division of the company. The company also launched its web site in 1996.

With all of the editorial content owned by Simon & Schuster, the next step was to translate it into software. In 1997, Simon & Schuster Interactive, the consumer software publishing unit of Simon & Schuster Consumer Group opened in 1994, formed a joint venture with GT Interactive Software Corp. The aim was to develop PC titles derived from the interactive and electronic properties cited in the Consumer Group catalog and market them globally.

In that same year, Simon & Schuster sold part of American Teaching Aids Inc., the unit that published teacher resource materials, to Frank Schaffer Publications. The development of new media for teachers continued, however. Simon & Schuster's Education Group announced the formation of an Internet resource, Edscape (www.edscape.com), a subscription service that delivered interactive curriculum content for teachers of grades kindergarten through 12, as well as online professional development. College-level instructors were included in another venture formed by Prentice Hall and Xilinx, Inc., a supplier of programmable logic solutions. The agreement allowed the two companies to produce the Xilinx Student Edition, the first complete digital design-learning environment for college-level instruction. In 2000, the company became the first major publisher to offer a major book, Stephen King's *Riding the Bullet,* exclusively online. The company launched an e-bookstore selling electronic books for download at its SimonSaysShop.com site in 2001.

NEW LEADERSHIP AND OWNERSHIP IN THE 21ST CENTURY

Newcomb left the company in 2002 to work at an investment firm, and COO and President Jack Romanos took over as CEO. That year, parent Viacom integrated Simon & Schuster into its Viacom Entertainment Group unit. The company also acquired Distican, its Canadian distributor of books and audio products, in 2002. In the years following, Simon & Schuster began several new publishing initiatives. It launched Threshold Editions, which focused on politically conservative books, as well as a Hispanic/Latino line in its new Atria imprint. It entered into a partnership with Beyond Words Publishing, which published works of spiritual and New Age appeal. The company also made two acquisitions: Strebor Books, which focused on the African American marketplace, and Howard Books, a Christian publishing company. Meanwhile, Viacom was undergoing reorganization and split into two companies at the end of 2005: CBS Corporation (which inherited Simon & Schuster) and Viacom. It 2006, Viacom re-branded Simon & Schuster Online as Simon & Schuster Digital in recognition of the unit's increased importance to the publisher's bottom line.

In 2007, Simon & Schuster partnered with Turn-Here to launch Bookvideos.tv, an Internet channel that featured online videos with Simon & Schuster authors and sneak previews of new releases. In so doing, it became the first publisher to systematically employ Internet videos as a means of marketing books and authors. In 2008, Romanos retired, and Carolyn Reidy, former president of the Simon & Schuster Adult Publishing unit, became his replacement.

Under Reidy, the publisher looked increasingly to the Internet as a way to reach readers and to ensure its role as an industry leader. The company's Digital Division, home of SimonSays.com, began to offer reading groups, book clubs, bulletin boards, e-mail updates, on-line chats with authors, and book excerpts to visitors. The weekly SimonSays Podcast featured audio excerpts, author interviews, and other original content. Simon & Schuster started to sell books directly to readers via its web site as a means of achieving more direct contact with consumers. Simon & Schuster Digital also brought the publisher's titles into many different e-book formats. Online or on the page, Simon & Schuster would remain a leader in the publishing industry.

Trudy Ring
Updated, Dorothy Kroll; Carrie Rothburd

PRINCIPAL DIVISIONS

Simon & Schuster Children's Publishing; Simon & Schuster UK Ltd.

PRINCIPAL COMPETITORS

Hachette Book Group USA; Random House Inc.; Houghton Mifflin Harcourt Publishing Company.

FURTHER READING

Korda, Michael, *Another Life: A Memoir of Other People,* New York: Random House, 1999.

McDowell, Edwin, "The Media Business; Is Simon & Schuster Mellowing?" *New York Times,* October 29, 1990.

Schwed, Peter, *Turning the Pages: An Insider's Story of Simon & Schuster, 1924–1984,* New York: Macmillan, 1984.

Shinkle, Kevin, "Simon & Schuster Sale-Bound," *Los Angeles Daily News,* January 15, 1998.

Verity, John W., "A Model Paperless Library," *Business Week,* December 23, 1996, pp. 80–82.

"A Woman in the House," *Crain's New York Business,* October 8, 2007.

Smart Balance, Inc.

115 West Century Road, Suite 260
Paramus, New Jersey 07652-1450
U.S.A.
Telephone: (201) 568-9300
Web site: http://www.boulderspecialtybrands.com

Public Company
Incorporated: 2005 as Boulder Specialty Brands Inc.
Employees: 46
Sales: $175.5 million (2007)
Stock Exchanges: NASDAQ
Ticker Symbol: SMBL
NAICS: 311423 Dried and Dehydrated Food Manufacturing; 523999 Miscellaneous Financial Investment Activities

■ ■ ■

A NASDAQ-listed public company based in Paramus, New Jersey, Smart Balance, Inc., is a marketer of "functional foods," food or food ingredients that have a demonstrated health benefit beyond the traditional nutrients they contain. Buttery spreads, made from a blend of natural oils with no trans fatty acids or hydrogenated oils to provide a more healthful balance between good and bad cholesterol make up the flagship product line carrying the Smart Balance brand. They include light, low-sodium, organic, and omega-3 versions. Other Smart Balance products include cooking oils, sprays, and shortening; Omega Peanut Butter; a light mayonnaise; cheese products; cream cheese; four types of fortified milk; and Smart Balance Popcorn, a

microwavable product that eliminates hydrogenated oil and trans fatty acids.

In addition Smart Balance offers natural and organic products under the Earth Balance label, including buttery spreads, vegan buttery sticks, cream cheese, natural shortening, natural peanut butter, and natural almond butter. Smart Balance and Earth Balance products are available in all 50 states, in grocery, convenience, and mass merchandise stores. The company has enjoyed limited penetration into international markets as well as foodservice and industrial channels. While Smart Balance develops all of its products, manufacturing is done on a contract basis using Smart Balance formulas, with the company providing frequent quality-control checks.

PREDECESSOR COMPANY FOUNDED

The company that would become Smart Balance was founded in Columbus, Ohio, in 1973 as Nutrition Industries Corporation by Robert M. Harris, whose family history led him to become interested in healthful foods. "All the males in my family died of heart disease," he told the *Record* of Bergen County, New Jersey. "My father died at 40, and my two brothers also died young." He relocated the business to Cresskill, New Jersey, in 1980. Initially, Nutrition Industries marketed products under the Weight Watchers label through licenses for such categories as margarine, processed and natural cheeses, mayonnaise, and "spoonable" salad dressing. The company also acquired food brands in need of relaunching, including H-O Oatmeal and other hot cereals, once well known in the New York City area.

The Weight Watchers line, however, was the core business. In 1978, H.J. Heinz Co. acquired Weight Watchers International, and over the next decade launched dozens of frozen and nonfrozen food items under the Weight Watchers label. Although Nutrition Industries did well, growing sales to about $70 million in 1987, Harris grew frustrated with his giant corporate partner. "They restricted new ideas and new products," he explained to the *Record*. "We were a very active, innovative company, but they had to approve of everything we did. So I decided to sell it to them."

After Harris sold the Weight Watchers assets to Heinz in 1988, he used the corporate structure he already had in place to start a new company, Great Foods of America Inc., later renamed GFA Brands Inc. It continued to market H-O hot cereals but also looked to become involved in some of the same product categories as it had with the Weight Watchers licenses. In the summer of 1990, GFA introduced a new light buttery spread under the Heart Beat label, the first product on the market to be free of trans fatty acids. Other Heart Beat products included low-fat cheese, salad dressing, and canola oil. In 1991 the Food and Drug Administration (FDA) cracked down on the labeling of low cholesterol foods and took exception to GFA's use of the word *heart*. GFA suggested "Health Beat" as an alternative, and when that was rejected as well, the company opted for "Smart Beat," establishing the company's use of the word *smart*.

FOCUSING ON HEALTHFUL FATS

The buttery spread that would take the name Smart Balance was not developed by GFA. Rather, the company was approached in 1996 by Brandeis University, whose researchers had developed a low-fat buttery spread using a combination of natural vegetable oils to help people improve their balance of good and bad cholesterol. Rather than being fat-free, like Smart Beat products, Smart Balance offered healthful fats. A Smart Balance spread and cooking oil began test marketing in March 1996. As the products were

systematically rolled out across the country, sales increased to $3 million in 1997.

Interest in the Smart Balance products grew not only because of excellent results in taste tests but also due to increased consumer awareness of the dangers of trans fat, which clogged arteries and increased the possibility of heart disease. In 2002 sales topped $40 million and Smart Balance controlled 3.4 percent of the U.S. margarine market. Not only did the spread product enjoy strong growth, GFA added other Smart Balance products based on the Brandeis formula, including peanut butter, mayonnaise, and popcorn. Just three years later total sales approached $100 million.

Part of the Smart Balance success was due to Harris's ability to pitch the products on radio ads. "I was urged to try it because of the credibility," he told the *Record*. "And it was cheaper. I'm not an announcer, but it seemed to work for us. I know the story and I believe in it." Another boon to business came in January 2005 when the FDA mandated that food labels include the percentage of trans fat they contained and recommended that consumers avoid trans fat as much as possible. Major cities such as New York and Boston then banned restaurants from using trans fats. With success also came imitation and patent infringement. GFA went to court three times to defend its license. In one case, a cookie manufacturer was converted into a Smart Balance licensee, an arrangement that benefited GFA as well as the other company, which avoided both litigation and the problem of reformulating its recipes.

CHANGE IN OWNERSHIP

As he got older Harris planned to turn over control of GFA to his 41-year-old son James, an attorney who served as executive vice-president of the company. To gain some liquidity, in 2004 Harris sold a stake in GFA to TSG Consumer Partners, a private equity firm that focused on consumer products companies, and not only provided infusions of cash but also worked closely with owners and managers to further grow their businesses. After two years allied with TSG, Harris decided in 2006, when sales increased to $137.4 million, to sell GFA to Boulder Specialty Brands, Inc., a new company with no business.

Boulder Specialty Brands was established by Stephen Hughes in 2005. A business school graduate from the University of Chicago, he was a seasoned marketer and administrator with ample experience in the realm of healthful foods. Working for ConAgra, in 1988 he spearheaded the effort to launch the Healthy Choice line of food products, a brand that in just four years reached $1 billion in sales. In 1994 he went to

KEY DATES

1973: Robert M. Harris establishes Nutrition Industries Corporation, markets products under the Weight Watchers label.
1988: Harris sells Weight Watchers line to H.J. Heinz Co.; forms Great Foods of America Inc. (later GFA Brands Inc.).
1996: Test marketing begins on Smart Balance buttery spread.
2005: Stephen Hughes founds Boulder Specialty Brands, Inc.
2007: Boulder Specialty Brands acquires GFA Brands, changes name to Smart Balance, Inc.
2008: Smart Balance milk products introduced.

work for Tropicana Products and led the turnaround of the U.S. business, which doubled sales to $2 billion in four years. Hughes was then named chief executive officer of herbal tea company Celestial Seasonings, a post he held until 2000 when the company was acquired.

Hughes next became CEO of Frontier Natural Products for two years, followed by a stint with Dean Foods' White Wave Foods, where he enjoyed success in building the Silk brand. Hughes's reputation was such that after he left White Wave he was able to incorporate Boulder Specialty Brands in May 2005 and take it public at the end of the year as a special acquisition, "blank check," corporation, or one formed solely for the purpose of acquiring another entity. On the basis of the involvement of Hughes, the company was able to raise $98.4 million.

NEW OWNERS AND NEW NAME

Nine months after the offering, Hughes, his management team, and board of directors settled on GFA Brands, extremely excited about the growth potential of the Smart Balance and Earth Balance brands. Their research indicated that about 95 percent of all grocery stores carried at least one Smart Balance product, and that on average they carried six Smart Balance products. Market research also concluded that this average could be increased to ten products. Boulder Specialty Brands reached an agreement to acquire GFA Brands in September 2006 for $490 million in cash, stock, and debt, and announced that it planned to change the name of Boulder Specialty to Smart Balance, Inc.

The acquisition was finalized in May 2007 and the name change took effect. Harris stayed on during a transition period and for a time remained the Smart Balance pitchman on radio spots. Although corporate headquarters remained in New Jersey, product development was moved to Boulder, Colorado. On the investor front, the company, whose stock had been trading on the over-the-counter basis, secured a listing on the NASDAQ Global Market System in August 2007.

The new owners of the Smart Balance brand were quick to bolster patent vigilance, not only to protect their rights but also to grow sublicensing income. They also wasted little time in building up the marketing effort. In October 2007 the company launched a $40 million television, print, and online advertising campaign targeting younger, healthy lifestyle-oriented consumers. They were very much an untapped source of new sales, given that the typical Smart Balance customer was over 50 years of age. The campaign, which ran into 2008, was also used to launch several new products: four new buttery spreads containing omega-3 fatty acids; milk products without hormones and antibiotics, including 1 percent skim, fat free/lactose free, and chocolate; cream cheese; and butter blend sticks. Management also launched a "Plus Six" initiative to increase the average number of products on grocery shelves closer to the goal of ten.

RISING COSTS AND HIGHER PRICES

With the marketing effort providing help for part of the year, Smart Balance increased sales 27.7 percent to $175.5 million in 2007, spurred by strong consumer demand. Rising costs of raw materials also led to higher prices that helped to inflate revenues. This situation continued in 2008, but as Smart Balance and its competitors were forced to raise prices in February, June, and August due to higher milk and cheese costs, demand softened because many consumers, who also had to contend with a deteriorating economy, began to drop major brands for less-expensive store brands of margarine, milk, and cheese products. Investors took note and began bidding down the price of Smart Balance stock. By August, Smart Balance had lost 30 percent of its value since the beginning of the year.

During the first half of 2008, sales were higher than they had been the prior years, but that was mostly due to forced price increases. More indicative of the company's health was that Smart Balance grew its share in the spreads category for the 26th straight quarter. While conditions were difficult, the company was confident that its long-term prospects were healthy. The sale of Smart Balance and Earth Balance products to younger consumers remained very promising. The company also planned to intensify its efforts to increase the sale of its products to foodservice accounts, including restaurants and college cafeterias. Smart Balance also had negligible international sales, offering another source of new revenues. Moreover, Smart Balance held the rights to the Brandeis brand until 2015, providing plenty of time to prepare for its expiration. According to *Barron's*, "The real end game for Smart Balance might be a takeover by a food giant seeking a fast-growing niche business. Says CEO Hughes: 'That possibility is always out there, but for now we're quite content expanding our niche and creating good-tasting, heart-healthy foods for consumers.'"

Ed Dinger

PRINCIPAL COMPETITORS

Campbell Soup Co.; General Mills Inc.; Sara Lee Corp.

FURTHER READING

Avery, Greg, "A $465 Million Smart Balance Bet," *Boulder (Colo.) Daily Camera,* September 27, 2006.

Broihier, Kitty, "Trans-Free Spreads Score Points for Margarine," *Food Processing,* January 1998, p. 32.

DeMarrais, Kevin G., "Heart of the Matter; Cresskill Firm Takes the Low Cholesterol Road," *Record* (Bergen County, N.J.), October 17, 2004, p. B06.

Facenda, Vanessa L., "Smart Balance Spreading the Word with $40M Push," *Brandweek,* October 8, 2007, p. 9.

Martin, Neil A., "Next Stop: Fat City," *Barron's,* September 17, 2007, p. 28.

Shanley, Will, "Boulder Specialty Brands Buys GFA Brands," *Denver Post,* September 27, 2006.

Solar Turbines Inc.

———————■———————

2200 Pacific Highway
San Diego, California 92101-1745
U.S.A.
Telephone: (619) 544-5000
Toll Free: (800) 416-5024
Fax: (619) 544-5825
Web site: http://mysolar.cat.com

Wholly Owned Subsidiary of Caterpillar Inc.
Incorporated: 1927 as Prudden-San Diego Airplane Company
Employees: 6,000
Sales: $13 billion (2007 est.)
NAICS: 333611 Turbine and Turbine Generator Set Unit Manufacturing; 333912 Air and Gas Compressor Manufacturing

■ ■ ■

Solar Turbines Inc. is a leading producer of midrange industrial gas turbines used in power generation, natural gas compression, and pumping systems. Gas turbines are rotary engines that extract energy from liquid gas through compression, combustion, and expansion processes. Solar Turbines is a wholly owned subsidiary of Caterpillar Inc., a *Fortune* 500 company and the world's largest maker of construction and mining equipment, diesel and natural gas engines, and industrial gas turbines. Solar produces, finances, installs, and services six gas turbine product lines: Saturn, Centaur, Mercury, Taurus, Mars, and Titan. It also produces eight centrifugal gas compressor product families, including

both pipeline and multistage compressors, as well as control systems, gas turbine–powered compressor sets, mechanical drive packages, and generator sets. Based in San Diego, California, Solar has 43 worldwide branches. One of the 50 largest U.S.-based exporters, about 75 percent of Solar products are exported outside the United States, but 80 percent of the company's employees and 85 percent of its physical assets are in the United States.

FROM AIRPLANES TO TURBINES

The origins of Solar Turbines would not have predicted that the company would eventually become a world leader in the global industrial gas turbines and turbomachinery packages industry. The company began by producing not turbines but airplanes. The Prudden-San Diego Airplane Company was founded in 1927, building just three all-metal airplanes before the Great Depression beginning in 1929 flattened demand for its products. During the Depression, the company renamed itself Solar Aircraft Company, apparently referring to San Diego's sunny climate, and switched to making a variety of components for other manufacturers. The company set itself apart by developing techniques for working with high-temperature materials such as stainless steel for airplane engine exhaust manifolds. During World War II, Solar made over 300,000 exhaust manifolds for U.S. defense airplanes.

Solar Aircraft took the first steps toward involvement in the turbine industry during World War II, overseeing the development of high-temperature components for the first jet engines (aircraft gas turbines) in America. However, after the war ended,

COMPANY PERSPECTIVES

Headquartered in San Diego, California, Solar Turbines is a leading provider of industrial gas turbine engines and centrifugal gas compressors used for oil and gas production, crude oil pumping, and gas transmission. Solar is your first choice to provide solutions in power generation for combined heat and power processes at manufacturing facilities, universities, hospitals, and airports. Gas turbines are also ideally suited for mobile and distributed power applications bringing the power closer to the people. Primary uses include electric power generation, oil and natural gas production, and gas transmission. Solar designs and manufactures the most durable, efficient, and reliable energy solutions available for the most demanding applications and locations around the world. Twenty-four hours a day, seven days a week, and in 93 countries, Solar Turbines is supporting customers in a wide variety of industries producing power and products for our world.

Solar Aircraft Company went through another difficult period, as demand fell for products that had been needed during the war. Eventually, the company began producing aircraft and aerospace hardware, including items such as jet engine afterburners and rocket components, keeping itself afloat by also manufacturing a variety of unrelated products: stainless steel caskets, frying pans, bulk milk containers, and redwood furniture.

In the mid-1940s, the company started designing and manufacturing gas turbines. The catalyst was a contract from the U.S. Navy to develop small gas turbines to power portable pump units for fighting ship fires. A second Navy contract enabled the company to manufacture gas turbines to generate shipboard electrical power. A third Navy contract in the late 1950s set the company firmly on the path toward its future, with the development of the Saturn gas turbine, intended to aid in high-speed boat propulsion. The Saturn turbine, which was made available in 1960, would become the world's most widely used industrial gas turbine. Its popularity stemmed from its unusually small and lightweight profile, as well as its reliability and ease of maintenance.

In 1960, International Harvester Company acquired Solar Aircraft. Three years later, Solar Aircraft became a division of International Harvester. Solar Aircraft began building its own line of centrifugal-flow natural gas compressors to match the Saturn engine and provide a user-friendly package, shipping its first compressor to Trunkline Gas in Mississippi in 1961. Ultimately, the line would include 18 models. In the 1960s the company also developed the more powerful Centaur gas turbine, which premiered in 1968. While it pioneered developments in turbines, the company also continued to develop vital components for the aircraft/aerospace industry, including mission-critical fuel lines, communications antennae, nuclear generator thermal radiators for the Saturn/Apollo lunar landings, hot-section components for airline jet engines, and aerodynamic control devices for the F-4 Phantom jet fighter plane.

BUILDING A TURBINE BUSINESS

In 1973, Solar Turbines turned its attention exclusively to industrial gas turbines, turbomachinery systems, and support services. Leaving the aircraft/aerospace industry, the company was able to better focus on producing the largest and most powerful engine to date, the Mars gas turbine, which debuted in 1977. In 1981, the Peoria, Illinois-based Caterpillar Tractor Co. (which later became Caterpillar Inc., the world's leading manufacturer of diesel and natural gas reciprocating engines, construction, and mining equipment) acquired Solar Turbines, which became a wholly owned subsidiary. In 1991, Solar's gas turbine sales reached $700 million according to the January 27, 1992, *San Diego Business Journal.*

After launching its Saturn, Centaur, and Mars turbines, Solar Turbines developed three other turbine families—Taurus, Titan, and Mercury—and variations on its earlier models. The powerful Centaur 50 debuted in 1985, and it would ultimately rank second to the Saturn in total units installed worldwide. The Taurus 70 was introduced in 1993 and the Titan 130 was developed in 1997 for industrial applications. Also in 1997, Solar developed the Mercury 50 turbine generator system in partnership with the U.S. Department of Energy for the Advanced Turbine Systems program, which sought to create turbines that were high-efficiency, low on pollutants, and 10 percent lower in cost than previous models.

The Mercury 50 was fully launched in 2004, after over 48,000 hours of operation. The Taurus 65 premiered in 2004, crafted to meet the need for a more efficient, lower-emission, and higher exhaust temperature product in its size category. The Taurus 65 combined the design of the Centaur 50 and Taurus 60 with the technology of the Taurus 70 and Titan 130,

KEY DATES

1927: Prudden-San Diego Airplane Company is founded to build airplanes.
1960: Saturn turbine launched; International Harvester acquires Solar Aircraft.
1968: Centaur turbine premiers.
1973: Solar Turbines leaves aircraft/aerospace industry to focus exclusively on industrial gas turbines, turbomachinery systems, and support services.
1977: Mars gas turbine debuts.
1981: Caterpillar Tractor Co. acquires Solar Turbines.
1985: Centaur 50 turbine launched.
1992: SoLoNOx pollution prevention technology launched.
1993: Taurus 70 turbine launched.
1995: Company wins California Quality Award.
1998: Company wins Malcolm Baldrige National Quality Award.
2004: Mercury 50 turbine generator system launched; Taurus 65 turbine launched; Titan 130 Mobile Power Unit launched.

and it incorporated Solar's SoLoNOx low-emissions combustion system. Also in 2004, Solar introduced the Titan 130 Mobile Power Unit, responding to the demand for peaking power.

Solar Turbines served two major markets. The first was power generation, where its products aided with co-generation, base-load electricity, dispersed power, combined-cycle, peak shaving, district heating/cooling, and standby power for installations such as industrial/processing facilities, buildings and institutions, and mobile electronic power generation. The second was oil and gas production and transmission, which involved powering compressors, pumps, and generators for the production, processing, and pipeline transmission of natural gas and crude oil. The company's products have been used in sustainable development of oil, natural gas, and power generation projects around the world.

PIONEERING NEW TECHNOLOGIES

Solar Turbines became known for its leadership in pioneering and developing new technologies that responded to industry needs and concerns. For example, in 1987, the company debuted a process whereby high-temperature steel alloys were made into fins, and then wrapped and brazed onto steam generator tubing. The idea of fin-wrapping was not new, but Solar's process was implemented in a more economical and production-oriented manner than ever before, adding about 50 percent more horsepower at no additional fuel cost, according to company representative Jack Oshel, cited in the March 16, 1987, *Metalworking News.*

Solar Turbines was a frequent recipient of contracts and grants from the Department of Energy, geared toward development of innovative technologies that extended the efficiency, safety, or productivity of turbines. In 1986, Solar Turbines was one of four companies selected by the Department of Energy to develop coal turbines for use in the transportation, co-generation, and electric utility markets. The other companies were General Motors, General Electric, and Westinghouse Electric Corp. In 1993, the company was one of four gas-turbine makers, including General Electric Power Generation, Westinghouse Electric Corp., and General Motors Corp.'s Allison Gas Turbine Division, to receive a total of $10.6 million from the Department of Energy for the second phase of the government-funded Advanced Turbine System program's concept development. The program sought to develop more efficient, lower-emission gas turbines.

In 1997, the company was selected by the Department of Energy to develop the world's first industrial gas turbine with ceramic (as opposed to metal) components. While metal components required cooling technologies that would keep temperatures down to acceptable levels, ceramic components would enable higher temperatures, higher thermal efficiency, and lower exhaust emissions of both nitrogen oxide and carbon monoxide. Field testing of ceramic components in the Centaur 50 turbine began in 1997.

In the 1980s and 1990s, regulatory agencies made it clear to gas turbine manufacturers and operators that nitrogen oxide emissions levels would have to be reduced. Solar Turbines was noted for its leadership in pollution prevention, especially through its development of SoLoNOx in 1992, a cost-effective, dry technology that reduced nitrogen oxide emissions, thereby diminishing smog. SoLoNOx produced lower emissions by mixing fuel and air upstream from the primary combustion zone, resulting in lower combustion temperatures. This combustion technology was available for Centaur, Mercury, Taurus, Mars, and Titan turbines. The Taurus 70 was the first engine in the gas turbine industry to feature this pollution prevention technology as a standard feature. By June 2006, over 1,470 gas turbines with SoLoNOx were in use or had been ordered, logging approximately 35 million hours in operation.

In 2001, Solar Turbines took additional steps toward pollution prevention when it joined Catalytica Energy Systems to combine Catalytica's Xonon pollution-preventing combustion technology (eliminating the need for installation of exhaust cleanup systems) with Solar's Taurus 60 gas turbine. The project was funded by a $3 million grant made to Solar by the California Energy Commission.

CHALLENGES AND CONTROVERSIES

Headquartered in San Diego, California, Solar Turbines occupied a prime piece of real estate on Harbor Drive, near the downtown waterfront. As one of the country's largest private employers, in 1992 the company provided work for approximately 3,000 San Diegans at its downtown site and Kearny Mesa neighborhood plant. Faced with rising real estate costs and taxes at its aging plant, Solar Turbines executives notified its landlord, the San Diego Unified Port District, that unless certain concessions were made the company was likely to relocate in order to secure financing for its future development. The company proposed a major redevelopment and environmental cleanup of the Harbor Drive plant—which had become an eyesore—along with lease and rent concessions and a new 1,800-space parking structure. Ultimately, the port granted lease and rent requests but refused to build a new parking garage or provide financial credits for anti-contamination efforts. Solar executives accepted the compromise and the company remained in San Diego.

Adding to the challenges Solar Turbines faced in 1992 was a soured business deal with the U.S. Navy. A decade earlier, the U.S. Navy had agreed to pay the company $55 million to develop Rankine-Cycle Energy Recovery System (RACER), a new alternative to increasingly expensive oil that would extend the cruising range of the Arleigh Burke–class destroyer, funded by Congress. However, while Congress continued to back Solar's RACER equipment, the Navy apparently changed its mind. Navy officials were unhappy about reverting to steam power, and they worried that RACER was noisy enough to call the attention of enemy submarines. Citing the "RACER Strategy" detailed in a Navy memo of 1985, Solar contended that the Navy tried to back out of the deal by forcing Solar to spend to the point of bankruptcy on RACER. Solar sued the Navy in federal claims court, asking for $11 million to compensate it for lost resources spent on RACER for the Navy.

In another controversy, the company's turbines were central to an international smuggling effort in violation of the U.S. trade embargo against Libya in 1994. Seven companies and four individuals were charged with participating in a scheme to smuggle over $3.5 million of Solar Turbines gas turbine generator systems to Libya. Libya had used Solar Turbines products in its oil producing industry before the embargo. The accused parties allegedly diverted turbines through Holland and sold them to Libyans at a dramatically increased price. A Solar spokesperson affirmed in the May 12, 1994, *San Diego Union-Tribune* that the company was a bystander in the case, and that it provided full cooperation and assistance in the investigation.

LEADING THE WAY IN THE 21ST CENTURY

As the 20th century closed, Solar Turbines was the world leader in industrial turbines up to 25,000 horsepower. In 1995, the company won a California Quality Award and was designated as "Best in Class" in large manufacturing. According to the November 23, 1998, *San Diego Business Journal,* sales tripled in the 1990s, and revenues neared $1.3 billion in 1997, with about 75 percent from exports. The company was the world leader in production of industrial turbines in 1998, with approximately 10,000 units operating in 85 countries. It was ranked number 16 on the *Business Journal*'s List of Largest Employees in the county with 6,200 employees, including 3,700 in San Diego. Also in 1998, Solar Turbines became the first San Diego-based company to receive the prestigious Malcolm Baldrige National Quality Award, given annually to three companies that demonstrated superior achievement in quality and business performance.

In the 21st century, the company had truly reached global proportions. By 2008, over 12,000 Solar units were in use in 93 countries, and Solar turbines had been in operation for over one billion hours (equivalent to more than 100,000 years). That year, the company celebrated a milestone when the 5,000th centrifugal gas compressor was shipped from the San Diego plant. Despite a humble start as a Depression-era airplane manufacturer, Solar Turbines had risen to the top of the global industrial turbines industry.

Heidi Feldman

PRINCIPAL COMPETITORS

General Electric Company; Westinghouse Electric Corporation; Siemens Corporation; ABB; Capstone Turbine Corporation.

FURTHER READING

Allen, Mike, "Solar Turbines Receives Malcolm Baldrige Award; Prestigious National Honor Given for Superior Quality and Performance," *San Diego Business Journal,* November 23, 1998, p. 7.

Cary, Peter, "Double Cross: How Not to Do Business," *U.S. News & World Report,* July 13, 1992, p. 29.

"Catalytica and Solar Will Develop Xonon-Equipped Taurus 60 Turbines," *Power Engineering,* November 2001, p. 154.

"Caterpillar Solar Turbines Unit Announces Supply Agreement with ChevronTexaco," *PR Newswire,* January 28, 2003.

"Ceramics Boost Small Gas Turbine Performance," *Modern Power Systems,* May 1994, p. 27.

"Department of Energy Funds Gas Turbine Projects," *Electric Light & Power,* November 1993, p. 24.

"DOE Funding Coal Turbine Research; Costs Shared with 4 Firms," *Oil Daily,* April 29, 1986, p. 5.

Dower, Rick, "Solar, Port Cut Deal to Keep Big Employer Happy—and Local," *San Diego Business Journal,* March 30, 1992, p. 1.

———, "Solar Turbines Says Deal with Port Is Crucial to Its Future Viability Here," *San Diego Business Journal,* January 27, 1992, p. 1.

Fusaro, Dave, "Solar Develops New Way to Wrap, Braze Alloy Fins," *Metalworking News,* March 16, 1987, p. 15.

"Gas Turbine Remote Monitoring and Diagnostics," *Diesel & Gas Turbine Worldwide,* April 2003.

Krueger, Anne, "Four Accused of Helping Libya Get Equipment from Solar Turbines, Inc.," *San Diego Union-Tribune,* May 12, 1994.

Kurz, Rainer, "Industry Benefits from Efficiencies of Modular Gas Compressor Design," *Pipeline & Gas Journal,* October 2004, p. 65.

Mercer, Mike, "Solar's Mercury 50 Commercialized," *Diesel & Gas Turbine Worldwide,* April 2004.

Rawlins, Douglas C., "Solar Opts for Dry, Lean Premixed Low NOx Concept," *Modern Power Systems,* May 1994, p. 79.

Zink, John C., "Gas Turbine Models Proliferate," *Power Engineering,* March 1998, p. 25.

TAME (Transportes Aéreos Militares Ecuatorianos)

Avenida Amrazonas 1354 y Avenida Colón
Quito,
Ecuador
Telephone: (593 2) 396-6300
Fax: (593 2) 396-6377
Web site: http://www.tame.com.ec

State-Owned Company
Founded: 1962
Employees: 970
Sales: $83.91 million (2006 est.)
NAICS: 481111 Scheduled Passenger Air Transportation

■ ■ ■

TAME, the acronym for the last four words of Empresa Estatal de Aviación Transportes Aéreos Militares Ecuatorianos, is Ecuador's national airline. It is owned by the Republic of Ecuador, administered by the nation's air force, and offers commercial passenger, cargo, and mail service, both domestic and international. TAME has administrative autonomy and is responsible for financing its operations from its own resources. However, it cannot act purely as a commercial enterprise, because its commitment to national integration means it is expected to serve remote communities that are not attractive to private airlines. Because of a lack of funds, the airline restricts its international service to a single destination: Cali, Colombia. Within Ecuador, it provides service to nearly a dozen destinations, including two in the Galápagos Islands. TAME carries cargo and mail as well as about a million passengers a year.

SERVICE FIRST, COMMERCE SECOND

Ecuador was served only by foreign airlines until 1946. The first national airline to establish itself firmly was Compañia Ecuatoriana de Aviación, S.A. (Ecuatoriana), founded in 1957. However, this company's finances were shaky, and in 1962 the government stepped in to ensure that service within Ecuador would continue by establishing Transportes Aéreos Militares Ecuatorianos (TAME). In this way it intended to link the most remote population centers in Ecuador to the big cities even though there was no purely commercial rationale to do so.

The fledgling air carrier had a fleet of two air force Douglas DC-3s. They were put into service immediately plying the route between Guayaquil, Ecuador's commercial capital and chief port, and Quito, the political capital, in the Andes Mountains. They also made stops at five cities north and south of Quito.

TAME's mission, its director general, Lt. Col. Carlos Elizalde, told Richard G. O'Lone for *Aviation Week & Space Technology* in 1964, was to "link up distant parts of the territory, off the regular routes, and give air transport to people who otherwise could not afford it." The airline's flights departed and landed at military airfields. TAME charged lower fares than Ecuatoriana and another private carrier but offered fewer amenities.

TAME came under new management in 1964, at which time the three destinations south of Quito were dropped and four in southern Ecuador added, including Cuenca. Three coastal cities in northern Ecuador were also added, and one further inland. Additional Douglas

COMPANY PERSPECTIVES

Our Mission is to provide national and international commercial aviation transport with modern aircraft, ensuring our customers the highest standards of quality, efficiency, and safety.

transport planes were provided for the increased traffic. The airline at that time had been flying about once a month to the Galápagos Islands, and in 1967 it acquired a long range craft, the Douglas DC-6B, for this purpose. At least once-weekly service on this 800-mile route began the next year, when TAME made arrangements with a Quito tourist agency to transport visitors to a floating offshore hotel, from where—in the absence of any hotel facility on the islands—they could continue their journey.

In the fall of 1969 two TAME DC-3s were hijacked by insurgents, and one was flown to Cuba with a number of hostages aboard. One copilot was killed and another wounded during refueling in Colombia. Despite this incident, TAME continued its plan, completed in 1970, to reorganize itself as a mixed enterprise with private participation, although no partner was ever announced and the airline remained under air force administration. By this time, TAME had transferred its operations in Quito and Guayaquil to civil airports. Two Hawker Siddeley HS 748s began service in 1972, allowing the older DC-3s to be relegated to minor routes and cargo runs.

FACING CHALLENGES

After Ecuatoriana suspended operations in 1974 because of financial difficulties, the company was nationalized and attached to the ministry of defense by means of the air force. Its shares of stock and four Lockheed L-188 Electra turbojets were turned over to TAME. Ecuatoriana did not cease to exist, however. After a period of reorganization, it continued to be the nation's long range national flag carrier, offering flights to several destinations in the Americas, including Miami, Mexico City, Lima, and Bogotá, in Boeing 720B jet transports decorated with rainbow-like markings of red, yellow, black, green, and pale, medium, and dark blue. Administered by a former deputy director of TAME, it was profitable by the end of 1975. Within Ecuador, Ecuatoriana flew only between Quito and Guayaquil. TAME continued to be the national airline for domestic

flights, although beginning in 1974 it sometimes undertook charter flights to other countries.

For several years, Ecuatoriana moved from success to success. By 1979 its network of routes took in New York and Los Angeles; Nassau, Bahamas; Panama City; and three South American capitals: Buenos Aires, Caracas, and Santiago. Chicago and San José, Costa Rica, were stops added later. Service to Madrid, Frankfurt, and Paris was within the airline's sights, aboard wide bodied Boeing 707 jets. However, the 1980s was a decade of economic crisis in Latin America, and Ecuatoriana consistently lost money. The company's last operational aircraft was seized by creditors in 1993. Two years later, a Brazilian airline purchased a majority interest in Ecuatoriana but failed to make it profitable and eventually abandoned it.

TAME received its first jet in 1980, when a new Boeing 727 was delivered and placed on the Guayaquil-Quito main line. However, the dangers of flying over some of the highest mountains on earth became only too evident during the early 1980s, a period during which three TAME airliners crashed with all aboard lost. Another crash, in 1988, also left no survivors. There had been earlier crashes in 1971 and 1976 as well, apparently without survivors.

The Ecuadorian airline took a step toward significant international operations in 1992, when it leased two Boeing 727s from Air France in order to fly from Quito and, after stopping in Bogotá, connect with Air France flights departing to Europe from Caracas. Air France flights landing in Caracas from Europe at that time connected to a TAME flight to Bogotá and Quito. TAME for four years was also linked to Lufthansa in Bogotá, and it flew to Santiago and Buenos Aires during 1994–95. Also in 1992, TAME began flying four times a week from Tulcán and Esmeraldas in northern Ecuador to Cali, Colombia. Another Boeing 727 was acquired in 1996, when twice per week service began to Santiago and Panama City, and once a week service to Havana.

The relationship with Air France soured when one of the Boeing jets leased to TAME crashed on departure from Bogotá's international airport in 1998, killing all persons aboard. The craft, bound for Quito, failed to make a right turn and in conditions of poor visibility struck a mountain about 150 feet below its summit three minutes after takeoff. Most of the passengers had arrived at Bogotá on an Air France flight from Paris. It was TAME's 12th crash since 1971. This disaster took place in the midst of criticism in France about leasing, code sharing, and outsourcing agreements with smaller airlines based in countries that might not be meeting international safety standards. A Federal Aviation

KEY DATES

■

1962: Founding of Transportes Aéreos Militares Ecuatorianos (TAME).

1968: TAME is flying at least once a week to Ecuador's remote Galápagos Islands.

1980: The airline takes possession of its first jetliner, a Boeing 727.

1992: TAME begins several years of providing service to several South American capitals.

1998: Crash of a jetliner linked to an Air France route blights TAME's international aspirations.

2005: The airline contracts to purchase four Brazilian jetliners.

2007: TAME is serving about 20,000 passengers a week on 163 flights.

Administration review had concluded that Ecuador did not meet these standards.

TAME IN THE 21ST CENTURY

With the demise in 2000 of a competing private Ecuadorian airline, SAETA Air Ecuador, S.A., TAME increased its share of the domestic market. Later in the year the Ecuadorian government sent to Congress a proposal to privatize the enterprise in collaboration with a strategic partner. TAME was seeking $250 million during the next few years to replace its ten-aircraft fleet. It also wanted to assume SAETA's flights to the United States but as a military-run enterprise could not by law enter the U.S. market. The search for a partner proved fruitless, however.

Disaster again struck TAME in 2002 when all 92 occupants aboard a flight from Quito perished in a crash on the heavily clouded slopes of a Colombian volcano while attempting to land at Tulcán. The flight was intended to continue to Cali after passengers deplaned at Tulcán, near the border with Colombia. Sources indicated that the TAME Boeing 727 probably had no ground-proximity warning system installed and had failed to make a left turn needed to line up with the runway at a critical moment, with the 15,630-foot Cumbal volcano only a few miles to the west.

By 2007 memories of this crash had faded, and an average of 900 passengers were taking the three flights daily linking Quito and Cali by way of Tulcán. Colombians liked the flight because they did not have

to pay a landing fee or a tax on international flights. The same terms applied to the Cali-Esmeraldas-Guayaquil route introduced in 1999 by TAME and promoted as a Pacific Coast tourist destination. A direct three times per week Esmeraldas-Guayaquil route over the Pacific was introduced in 2008.

TAME's flights to destinations farther from Ecuador had come to an end, however, at least for the time being. The airline was serving 13 destinations in Ecuador, including two in the Galápagos Islands. Some 20,000 or so passengers were aboard an average of 163 TAME flights per week in 2007. The airline's mission was the same as it had always been: to connect various local communities in Ecuador and thus to promote national integration, social development, business, tourism, and production. The company had a frequent flyer program and accepted prepaid FlyCards. Its operational revenue came to about $84 million in 2006, and it also received $61.6 million in loans during the year.

The Inter-American Development Bank approved a $62.25 million loan in 2007 so that TAME could pay for four jet planes it had contracted for in 2005 from Empresa Brasilera de Aeronáutica S.A. (Embraer) for $77.6 million. The loan was for a 20-year term with a grace period of one year. By early 2006 TAME had taken delivery of two of the airplanes and had a fleet of ten aircraft.

Although it had two privately owned competitors, TAME seemed likely to remain the principal nationally owned air carrier in Ecuador. It was serving more communities and passengers than the other two airlines. According to the *Lonely Planet* travel guide for Ecuador, TAME and the other two had safety records on a par with most world airlines.

Robert Halasz

PRINCIPAL COMPETITORS

Aerolíneas Galápagos S.A.

FURTHER READING

Brownlow, Cecil, "Ecuatoriana Moves to Recapture Market," *Aviation Week & Space Technology,* January 27, 1975, pp. 32–33.

Croft, John, "Ecuadoran Airline Crash Claims 92" *Aviation Week & Space Technology,* February 4, 2002, pp. 48–49.

Davies, R. E. G., *Airlines of Latin America Since 1919,* Washington, D.C.: Smithsonian Institution Press, 1983, pp. 279–83.

Homewood, Brian, "TAME Seeks Partner in Privatisation Bid," *Airline Business,* September 1, 2000, p. 16.

"Inter-American Development Bank Approves U.S. $62.2 Million to Ecuador for Renewal of Aircraft Fleet," *US Fed News Service,* November 29, 2007.

Lefer, Henry, "New Regime Holds Key to Ecuatoriana's Future," *Transport World,* July 1979, pp. 52–54.

Luna, Matte, "Desde los cielos ecuatorianos, TAME crece," *Visión: La Revista Latinoamericana,* June 1, 1997, p. 34.

O'Lone, Richard G., "Military Controls Ecuador's Civil Aviation," *Aviation Week & Space Technology,* September 14, 1964, pp. 92–93.

"727 Crash Kills 53," *Aviation Week & Space Technology,* April 27, 1998, p. 45.

"TAME, a la conquista del suroccidente columbiano," *Portafolio,* June 22, 2007.

Tastefully Simple Inc.

1920 Turning Leaf Lane SW
Alexandria, Minnesota 56308
U.S.A.
Telephone: (320) 763-0695
Fax: (320) 763-2458
Web site: http://www.tastefullysimple.com

Private Company
Incorporated: 1995
Employees: 300
Sales: $138 million (2007 est.)
NAICS: 445299 All Other Specialty Food Stores

■ ■ ■

Headquartered in Alexandria, Minnesota, Tastefully Simple Inc. is a leading gourmet foods enterprise. The company relies on the direct sales approach, using independent consultants to market easy-to-prepare items such as breads, soups, spices, salsas, dip mixes, oils and dressings, recipe books, and various seasonal items. In addition to selling products to others via the phone or the Internet, consultants rely on in-home "taste-testing parties" to market the company's wares. Consultants earn commissions as high as 36 percent, while people who host parties are rewarded with gourmet food, based on the amount of money their guests spend. Tastefully Simple is a member of the Direct Selling Association, an entity that maintains standards for companies in the burgeoning direct sales industry, which was worth an estimated $32.18 billion around 2005.

ORIGINS

Tastefully Simple was founded by Jill Blashack in Alexandria, Minnesota. A native of Glenwood, Minnesota, Blashack grew up on a dairy farm near Alexandria, earned a two-year degree in sales and marketing from Alexandria Technical College, co-owned a Villard, Minnesota-based restaurant named Jill's Grill with her father John Schmitz, and helped establish a tanning salon named Sun Studio.

Although Blashack established Tastefully Simple in 1995, the company's origins can be traced back a few years earlier, when she was instilled with an entrepreneurial spirit while operating a gift basket business called Care with Flair. After selling that business, Blashack teamed up with friend, hair salon owner, and Minnesota native Joani Nielson to sell a snack called "reindeer chips," which consisted of pretzels coated in chocolate or almond bark.

In 1993 Blashack and Nielson were asked to sell their edible creation at an annual arts and crafts event in Alexandria called the Holiday Crafters Tour. In addition to the reindeer chips, Blashack showcased a few gourmet food items she had included in her gift basket enterprise. Attendees were able to taste such items as her beer bread, honey mustard, and raspberry salsa before committing to a purchase. While reindeer chip sales at the two-day event totaled $200, this paled in comparison to gourmet food sales of $2,500.

Similar results at the 1994 Holiday Crafters Tour convinced the two partners that they had the makings of a successful business approach. However, they were not sure how to execute it on a larger scale. The answer came to Blashack a week after the tour, at 3:00 A.M. Unable to sleep, Blashack read an article in *Entrepreneur* magazine about a business that used home parties to sell home décor items, and saw the model's potential for a food-related business.

After securing a $20,000 Small Business Association loan and raising about $15,000 of private financing, Blashack hit the ground running in June 1995. For the company's first five years, Blashack headed Tastefully Simple Inc., while cofounder Joani Nielson was involved as a silent partner. An inventory associate named Dolly Frost was the company's first actual employee.

FORMATIVE YEARS

In an October 29, 2002, Associated Press release by Deneen Gilmour, Blashack recalled her philosophy at the time the company was established, commenting: "I foresaw us to be like a Mary Kay or Discovery Toys. It was more guts than sense. My market research said if these products sell in rural Minnesota where we tend to be conservative, then they'll sell anywhere in America."

On the strength of seven consultants, Tastefully Simple ended its first year with sales of $100,000. The company focused on food items that were easy to prepare, calling for only one or two extra ingredients. Operations were initially based in a storage shed adjacent to Nielson's home, where a pool table was used for packing purposes. However, growth soon prompted the new business to relocate to a larger, 6,000-square-foot facility in 1998.

Only three years into her new business, Blashack's husband passed away following an illness. In the October 29, 2002, Associated Press release, she recalled this difficult period, commenting: "I used Tastefully Simple as a diversion. After Steve died in 1998 I knew this was my sole income. It had to work. Fear was a motivator. I thought one day at a time, one second at a time. The key to my survival was my group of friends."

Blashack brought her then ten-year-old son, Zach, with her to the office, and moved forward. In 1998,

sales totaled $1.4 million on the strength of 168 independent consultants. The following year, the company's sales mushroomed to $4.25 million through the efforts of 494 consultants in 33 states. By early 2000, Tastefully Simple's consultant base had grown to include 700 representatives in 37 states. That year, Blashack was named Entrepreneur of the Year by Ernst & Young in the Minnesota and Dakota region's Emerging category.

DEVELOPING OPERATIONAL SOPHISTICATION

By the beginning of 2000, construction was under way on a new, 17,000-square-foot facility. Built at a cost of about $1 million, the new building was scheduled to open its doors midway through the year. That year, cofounder Joani Nielson officially joined Tastefully Simple as founding partner and chief operating officer.

In Tastefully Simple's new facility, the pool table upon which Blashack once packed orders was put on display in the warehouse, as a reminder of how things were during the company's early years. The new facility included a lounge called the Squirrel's Nest, with cozy amenities like couches and fireplaces, as well as a kitchen, and computers workers could use to check their e-mail. In addition, the headquarters facility also contained a gift shop and areas where workers could participate in activities such as exercise classes.

Only five months after moving into its new facility, Tastefully Simple outgrew the building and had to add on an additional 2,220 square feet of space for administrative staff. The company expanded its warehouse in 2001 with a 10,000-square-foot addition. With revenues of $28.2 million, Tastefully Simple was named to *Inc.* magazine's list of the nation's fastest-growing private companies in 2001, with a rank of 40. The company's success propelled it to a rank of seven on *Inc.*'s list in 2002.

Expansion unfolded so quickly that Tastefully Simple achieved annual growth of almost 200 percent from 1998 to 2002. This was largely due to the company's independent consultants. During the early years of the new century, new Tastefully Simple consultants invested anywhere from $500 to $1,000 for a start-up inventory, as well as $150 for items related to marketing and training.

In 2002, Tastefully Simple's growth prompted the company to invest in a 20,000-square-foot expansion to its warehouse facility, as well as new information technology resources. Back-office software from Lawson Software was obtained to manage processes such as procurement and inventory control. That year, the

KEY DATES

1995: Jill Blashack establishes Tastefully Simple Inc. with silent partner Joani Nielson.

1999: Sales reach $4.25 million on the strength of 494 consultants in 33 states.

2000: Tastefully Simple moves into a new 17,000-square-foot facility; cofounder Joani Nielson officially joins the company as founding partner and chief operating officer.

2001: Revenues reach $28.2 million, and Tastefully Simple is named to *Inc.* magazine's list of the nation's fastest-growing private companies for the first time.

2005: The company celebrates its tenth anniversary.

2007: Sales reach $138 million, and independent consultants number 23,700.

company had about 10,000 consultants in place, although Tastefully Simple's product line was kept to a manageable 35 items at any given time.

CONTINUED GROWTH

In addition to its massive base of independent consultants, Tastefully Simple had about 275 actual employees by 2002. Although the environment at the company's headquarters was often very fast-paced, workers enjoyed warm, soothing surroundings marked by antique furniture and decorative dessert plates that doubled as nameplates on cubicles and office doors. Tastefully Simple's cofounders each contributed to the company's success in different ways. Blashack, who was a finalist for Ernst & Young's national Entrepreneur of the Year honor in 2003, focused more on public relations and marketing, while Nielson concentrated on operational matters such as finance.

For many of Tastefully Simple's direct sales consultants, being involved in the business was not done solely for monetary reasons. Instead, it provided them with opportunities to try new food items, entertain friends, and meet other people. However, for some it provided a substantial income. For example, in 2003 Kim E. Young of Sinking Spring, Pennsylvania, earned more than $100,000 per year. Serving as a senior team mentor, she was responsible for more than 500 team members in 30 states who generated sales of $3.8 million.

Stories like Young's were becoming more commonplace as the larger direct selling industry caught on.

According to figures from the Direct Selling Industry, in 2003 alone some 13 million people worked in the industry, generating sales of about $29.5 billion. In 2004, Tastefully Simple's sales increased to approximately $120 million, driven by a base of consultants that had grown to include some 20,000 people. That year, a 48,000-square-foot addition was made to Tastefully Simple's headquarters, including an onsite fitness center.

A number of special milestones were reached in 2005. A major one occurred in June, when Tastefully Simple celebrated its tenth anniversary. Hostesses that month were given a chance to obtain the company's range of stoneware for free, and a few earned $2,500 vacations for two or $250 cash prizes.

CHANGING THE BUSINESS MODEL

By this time Tastefully Simple's product range included tasty items such as Cha Cha Cheeseball Mix. The number of employees at the company's 178,000-square-foot headquarters, which was situated on 79 acres of land, numbered 322. Together, they supported 21,240 independent consultants. Around this time, Tastefully Simple made a change to its business model, when it moved away from having its consultants offer all of the company's products available for taste-testing at parties, as well as maintaining inventory to fulfill orders. As the number of products reached the 50-item mark, these were becoming difficult tasks.

Blashack noticed that many consultants were preparing only a few items for tasting, and relying on their sales materials to promote the rest. When she discovered that the revised method did not hamper sales, the company made the transition to the new model. In addition, Tastefully Simple began shipping orders directly to party hostesses, an approach that a growing number of consultants had already adopted.

Several other milestones were reached in 2005. That year, Blashack ranked second in *Fast Company's* list of the nation's "25 Top Women Business Builders." In addition, Tastefully Simple was inducted into the *Inc.* 500 Hall of Fame, and Blashack was named an *Inc.* 500 All-Star. Despite her success, she lived a humble lifestyle and was committed to spending time with her son Zach.

Propelled by the success of popular products such as Bountiful Beer Bread and Perfectly Potato Cheddar Soup, Tastefully Simple contributed to the rise in the larger direct sales industry, which saw its sales increase about 30 percent from 1998 to 2004, reaching nearly $30 billion.

In 2006 Tastefully Simple's sales reached $120 million. The company's growth was a testament to the power of word-of-mouth promotion, considering the enterprise did virtually no traditional advertising. Things also looked brighter for Blashack on the personal front. After persevering through the death of her husband and raising a son by herself, she married a Texas businessman, whom she met on the dating web site eHarmony.com, and changed her last name to Blashack Strahan.

Tastefully Simple's sales reached $138 million in 2007, and the company's base of independent consultants continued to grow, totaling 23,700 late in the year. The changes that Tastefully Simple made to its presentation model, including fewer items required for taste-testing, as well as the way it shipped products, required a major overhaul of accounting, warehousing, and order entry systems. However, the changes were worthwhile because they allowed Tastefully Simple to recruit new consultants more easily.

Other accomplishments in 2007 came when Minnesota Entrepreneurs Inc. named Blashack Strahan as its 2007 Entrepreneur of the Year. That year, she chronicled her accomplishments in a new book titled *Simply Shine.* In 2008 the Center for Values Research ranked Tastefully Simple in the top 5 percent of employers for the fifth straight year. The company remained the nation's leading home taste-testing company. With its burgeoning base of independent consultants, Tastefully Simple seemed well positioned for further success in the 21st century's second decade.

Paul R. Greenland

PRINCIPAL COMPETITORS

Fingerhut Direct Marketing Inc.; Harry & David Holdings Inc.; The Pampered Chef Ltd.

FURTHER READING

Applegate, Jane, "Food-Sales Business Racks up the Dough," *Chicago Sun-Times,* May 11, 1999.

Blanchette, Aimee, "Business People; Today's Spotlight: Jill Blashack Strahan," *Star Tribune,* December 24, 2007.

Gilmour, Deneen, "Women Turn Backyard Operation into Multimillion-Dollar Giant," *Associated Press State & Local Wire,* October 29, 2002.

Sitaramiah, Gita, "For Can-Do CEO, 'It's All Opportunity.' Tastefully Simple Outgrew a Backyard Shed in Alexandria to Become Home-Party Empire," *Saint Paul Pioneer Press,* July 3, 2005.

"Tastefully Simple Celebrates 10th Birthday; Company Continues to Grow in Direct Selling Industry," *PR Newswire,* June 15, 2005.

Youngblood, Dick, "Enjoying the Sweet Taste of Success," *Star Tribune,* February 20, 2000.

———, "Small Business; Getting a Taste of Success," *Star Tribune,* November 14, 2007.

Toyota Motor Corporation

———■———

1, Toyota-cho
Toyota City, Aichi 471-8571
Japan
Telephone: (81 565) 28-2121
Fax: (81 565) 23-5800
Web site: http://www.toyota.co.jp

Public Company
Incorporated: 1937 as Toyota Motor Co., Ltd.
Employees: 300,000
Sales: $262.39 billion (2008)
Stock Exchanges: Tokyo New York
Ticker Symbol: TM
NAICS: 421110 Automobile and Other Motor Vehicle Wholesalers; 332311 Prefabricated Metal Building and Component Manufacturing; 336111 Automobile Manufacturing; 336112 Light Truck and Utility Vehicle Manufacturing; 336120 Heavy Duty Truck Manufacturing; 336211 Motor Vehicle Body Manufacturing; 336312 Gasoline Engine and Engine Parts Manufacturing; 336322 Other Motor Vehicle Electrical and Electronic Equipment Manufacturing; 336330 Motor Vehicle Steering and Suspension Components (Except Spring) Manufacturing; 336340 Motor Vehicle Brake System Manufacturing; 336350 Motor Vehicle Transmission and Power Train Parts Manufacturing; 336399 All Other Motor Vehicle Parts Manufacturing

■ ■ ■

Toyota Motor Corporation is Japan's largest car company and the world's largest as measured by net worth, revenue, and profit. General Motors sold slightly more cars and trucks than Toyota in 2007, leaving that company in the role of number one in terms of vehicles sold. However, Toyota is on track to claim all the measures of global automotive leader by 2009. The company holds about 40 percent of the Japanese auto market, and over 10 percent globally. It operates through 540 subsidiaries and some 226 affiliated companies. Its vehicles are sold in 170 countries and regions worldwide. Toyota maintains 12 automotive plants in Japan and 53 overseas, with many more affiliated manufacturers making parts and components. Its total global production is over nine million vehicles annually. Some leading Toyota car brands include the Lexus, the hybrid gas-electric Prius, and the Corolla. Toyota has long been an innovator in its management and in its production, allowing it to cut costs and extend its worldwide reach. From its roots in wartime Japan, the company has become one of the preeminent global corporations in the 21st century.

PREWAR EMERGENCE OF JAPANESE AUTOMOBILE MANUFACTURING

In 1933 a Japanese man named Kiichiro Toyoda traveled to the United States, where he visited a number of automobile production plants. Upon his return to Japan, the young man established an automobile division within his father's loom factory and in May 1935 produced his first prototype vehicle. General Motors and Ford already were operating assembly plants in Japan, but U.S. preeminence in the worldwide automotive industry did not deter Toyoda.

COMPANY PERSPECTIVES

Guiding Principles: 1) Honor the language and spirit of the law in every nation and undertake open and fair corporate activities to be a good corporate citizen of the world. 2) Respect the culture and customs of every nation and contribute to the economic and social development through corporate activities in the communities. 3) Dedicate ourselves to providing clean and safe products and to enhancing the quality of life everywhere through all our activities. 4) Create and develop advanced technologies and provide outstanding products and services that fulfill the needs of customers worldwide. 5) Foster a corporate culture that enhances individual creativity and teamwork value, while honoring mutual trust and respect between labor and management. 6) Pursue growth in harmony with the global community through innovative management. 7) Work with business partners in research and creation to achieve stable, long-term growth and mutual benefits, while keeping ourselves open to new partnerships.

Since Japan had very few natural resources, the company had every incentive to develop engines and vehicles that were highly fuel efficient. In 1939, the company established a research center to begin work on battery-powered vehicles. This was followed in 1940 by the establishment of the Toyoda Science Research Center (the nucleus of the Toyota Central Research and Development Laboratories, Inc.) and the Toyoda Works (later Aichi Steel Works, Ltd.). The next year Toyoda Machine Works, Ltd., was founded for the production of both machine tools and auto parts.

WARTIME DIFFICULTIES AND POSTWAR CHALLENGES

As Japan became embroiled in World War II, the procurement of basic materials for automobile manufacturing became increasingly difficult. At one point Toyoda was manufacturing trucks with no radiator grills, brakes on only the rear wheels, wooden seats, and a single headlight. Nearing the limits of resource conservation as the course of the war began to cripple Japan's economy, the company started piecing together usable parts from wrecked or worn-out trucks to build "recycled" vehicles.

When the war ended in August 1945 most of Japan's industrial facilities had been wrecked, and the Toyoda (or Toyota as it became known after the war) production plants had suffered extensively. The company had 3,000 employees but no working facilities, and the economic situation in Japan was chaotic. However, the Japanese tradition of dedication and perseverance proved to be Toyota's most powerful tool in the difficult task of reconstruction.

Just as the Japanese motor industry as a whole was beginning to recover, there was mounting concern that American and European auto manufacturers would overwhelm the Japanese market with their economic and technical superiority. Japan's automakers knew that they could no longer count on government protection in the form of high import duties or other barriers as they had before the war.

Since American manufacturers were concentrating their efforts on medium-sized and larger cars, Toyota's executives thought that by focusing on small cars the company could avoid a head-on market confrontation. Kiichiro Toyoda likened the postwar situation in Japan to that in England. "The British motorcar industry," he said, "also faces many difficulties, but its fate will be largely determined by how strongly American automakers feel they should concentrate on small cars." It was January 1947 when Toyota engineers completed their first prototype for a small car. Its chassis was of the backbone type (never used before in Japan), its front suspension relied primarily on coil springs, and its maximum speed was 54 miles per hour. After two years of difficulties the company seemed headed for success.

LABOR CONFLICT

Success would not be accomplished as easily as expected, however. In 1949 Toyota suffered its first and only serious conflict between labor and management. Nearly four years had passed since the end of the war, but Japan's economy was still in poor shape. Goods and materials of all kinds were in short supply, inflation was rampant, and people in the cities were forced to trade their clothing and home furnishings for rice or potatoes to survive.

That year the Japanese government took measures to control runaway inflation. However, these moves drastically reduced consumer purchasing power and worsened the severely depressed domestic automotive market. Japanese auto manufacturers found themselves unable to raise the funds needed to support their recovery efforts. The new governmental policy had discontinued all financing from city banks and the Reconstruction Finance Corporation, and so Toyota struggled.

finally found itself on the verge of bankruptcy.

```
┌─────────────────────────────────────────────┐
│                                             │
│              KEY DATES                      │
│                  ■                          │
│                                             │
│  1918:  Sakichi Toyoda establishes Toyota   │
│         Spinning & Weaving Co., Ltd.        │
│  1933:  Automobile Department is created    │
│         within Toyoda Automatic Loom Works. │
│  1935:  First Model A1 passenger car        │
│         prototype is completed.             │
│  1937:  Toyota Motor Co., Ltd., is formed.  │
│  1950:  Toyota Motor Sales Co., Ltd., is    │
│         established.                        │
│  1956:  Toyota creates the Toyopet dealer   │
│         network.                            │
│  1957:  Toyota Motor Sales, U.S.A., Inc.,   │
│         is formed.                          │
│  1962:  Toyota Motor Thailand Co., Ltd.,    │
│         begins operations.                  │
│  1982:  Toyota Motor Company and Toyota     │
│         Motor Sales merge to form Toyota    │
│         Motor Corporation.                  │
│  1995:  Hiroshi Okuda becomes company       │
│         president.                          │
│  1998:  Toyota acquires majority share in   │
│         Daihatsu Motor Co., Ltd.            │
│  2000:  U.S. launch of the Prius hybrid.    │
│                                             │
└─────────────────────────────────────────────┘
```

Under these conditions the company's financial situation deteriorated rapidly. In some months, for example, the company produced vehicles worth a total of ¥350 million while income from sales reached only ¥250 million. In the absence of credit sources to bridge the imbalance, Toyota soon was facing a severe liquidity crisis.

In large part because of wartime regulations and controls, Toyota had come to place strong emphasis on the production end of the business. So in the early postwar years, not enough attention had been paid to the proper balance between production and sales. The Japanese economy at that time was suffering from a severe depression. Because the Toyota dealers were unable to sell cars in sufficient quantities, these dealers had no choice but to pay Toyota in long-term promissory notes as inventories kept accumulating.

Finally, Toyota was unable to meet its regular payroll. Delayed payments were followed by actual salary reductions and then by plans for large-scale layoffs. Then in April 1949, the Toyota Labor Union went on strike. Negotiations between labor and management dragged on, with the union leaders bitterly opposed to any layoffs. As a result, Toyota was compelled to reduce both production and overhead. Workers staged demonstrations to press their demands. All the while, Toyota kept falling further into debt, until the company

REBUILDING

Production dropped to 992 vehicles in March 1949, to 619 in April, and to 304 in May. Crucial restructuring efforts included a proposal to incorporate Toyota's sales division as a separate company, leading eventually to the formation of Toyota Motor Sales Company Ltd. in April 1950. Toyota Motor Sales Company handled all domestic and worldwide marketing of Toyota's automotive products until July 1982, when it merged with Toyota Motor Company.

In the meantime, discussions between labor and management finally focused on whether to admit failure, declare bankruptcy, and dissolve the company, or to agree on the dismissal of some employees and embark upon a rebuilding program. In the end management and labor agreed to reduce the total workforce from 8,000 to 6,000 employees, primarily by asking for voluntary resignations. At the management level, President Kiichiro Toyoda and all of his executive staff resigned. Kiichiro, Toyota's founder and a pioneer of the Japanese automotive industry, died less than two years later.

Not long after the strike was settled in 1950, two of the company's new executives, Eiji Toyoda (now chairman of Toyota Motor Corporation) and Shoichi Saito (later chairman of Toyota Motor Company), visited the United States. Seeking new ideas for Toyota's anticipated growth, they toured Ford Motor Company's factories and observed the latest automobile production technology. One especially useful idea they brought home from their visit to Ford resulted in Toyota's suggestion system, in which every employee was encouraged to make suggestions for improvements of any kind.

On their return to Japan, however, the two men inaugurated an even more vital policy that remained in force at Toyota through the 1990s: the continuing commitment to invest in only the most modern production facilities as the key to advances in productivity and quality. Toyota moved quickly and aggressively in the 1950s, making capital investments in new equipment for all of the company's production facilities. Not surprisingly, the company began to benefit almost immediately from the increased efficiency.

In addition to improvements in its production facilities, Toyota also worked to develop a more comprehensive line of vehicles to contribute toward the growing motorization of Japanese society. During 1951, for example, Toyota introduced the first four-wheel-drive Land Cruiser. Moreover, as the domestic demand for taxis rapidly increased, production of passenger cars also rose quickly, from 50 units per month to 250 units per month by 1953.

CEMENTING THE DOMESTIC MARKET

In production control, Toyota introduced the "Kanban" (or "synchronized delivery") system during 1954. The idea was derived from the supermarket system, where "consumers" (those in the later production stages) took "products" (parts) from the stock shelves, and the "storekeepers" (those in the earlier production stages) replenished the stock to the degree that it was depleted. The Kanban system became the basis for Toyota's entire production system.

By the early 1950s, just as Toyota had anticipated, the Japanese market was crowded with vehicles from the United States and Europe. It soon became apparent that to be competitive at home and abroad, Toyota would not only have to make additional investments in manufacturing facilities and equipment, but also undertake a major new research and development effort. This was the reasoning behind Toyota's decision in 1958 to build a full-scale research center for the development of new automobiles (which also was to become Japan's first factory devoted entirely to passenger-car production). Toyota also began to offer a more complete line of products. Beginning with the Crown model, introduced in 1955, Toyota quickly expanded its passenger-car line to include the 1,000-cubic-centimeter Corona, then added the Toyo-Ace (Japan's first cab-over truck) and a large-sized diesel truck.

Throughout these years Toyota also was working hard on another important, if less conventional, approach to adapting itself to the rapid motorization of Japan, brought about by a remarkable increase in national income. When, for example, Toyota Motor Sales was capitalized at ¥1 billion, 40 percent of that amount (¥400 million) was immediately invested to establish an automobile driving school in an effort to help citizens acquire driver's licenses. Through this and similar efforts, Toyota made a major contribution to Japan's growing motorization in the years following 1965, a trend that was to lead to a mass domestic market for automobiles.

DRIVE FOR HIGH QUALITY LEADS TO DEMING PRIZE

In 1955, ten years after its defeat in World War II, Japan became a member of the General Agreement on Tariffs and Trade (GATT), but automobiles remained one of Japan's least competitive industries in the international arena. Toyota, foreseeing the coming age of large-scale international trade and capital liberalization in Japan, decided to focus on lowering its production costs and developing even more sophisticated cars, while at the same time attempting to achieve the highest possible level of quality in production.

This was a joint effort conducted with Toyota's many independent parts suppliers and one that proved so successful that ten years later, in 1965, Toyota was awarded the coveted Deming Prize for its quality-control achievements. That was also the year that the Japanese government liberalized imports of foreign passenger cars. Toyota was ready to compete with its overseas competitors, both in price and quality.

In subsequent years Japan's gross national product expanded rapidly, contributing to an impressive growth in auto sales to the Japanese public. The Toyota Corolla, which went on sale in 1966, quickly became Japan's most popular family car and led the market for autos of its compact size. Toyota continued to make major investments in new plants and equipment to prepare for what it believed would be a higher market demand. In 1971 the government removed controls on capital investment. In the wake of this move, several Japanese automakers formed joint ventures or affiliations with U.S. automakers.

INNOVATION IN RESPONSE TO THE OIL CRISIS AND ENVIRONMENTAL CONCERNS

Two years later, the 1973 war in the Middle East erupted and the world's economy was shaken by the first international oil crisis. Japan, wholly dependent upon imports for its oil supply, was especially affected. The rate of inflation increased and demand for automobiles fell drastically. However, in the face of the overall pessimism that gripped the industry and the nation, Toyota's chairman Eiji Toyoda proposed a highly aggressive corporate strategy. His conviction was that the automobile, far from being a "luxury," had become and would remain a necessity for people at all levels of society. As a result, Toyota decided to move forward by expanding the company's operations.

The 1973 oil crisis and its aftermath were valuable lessons for Toyota. The crisis demonstrated the necessity for a flexible production system that could easily be adapted to changes in consumer preferences. For example, Toyota did away with facilities designed exclusively for the production of specific models and shifted instead to general-purpose facilities that could be operated according to changes in market demand for the company's various models.

Environmental concerns also led to new developments. In December 1970 the U.S. Congress passed the Muskie Act, which set limits on automobile engine emissions. In the United States the enforcement of this law was eventually postponed. In Japan, however, even stricter laws were promulgated during the same time with no postponement of enforcement deadlines. When the Muskie Act was first proposed, automakers all over the world were opposed to it. They argued that it would actually prohibit the use of all internal combustion engines currently used, and they requested that the enforcement of the law be postponed until new technology, able to meet the law's requirements, could be developed.

Notwithstanding these developments, Toyota moved forward on its own to develop a new generation of cleaner and more fuel-efficient engines. After studying all the feasible alternatives (including catalytic systems, rarefied combustion, rotary engines, gas turbine, and battery-powered cars) Toyota settled on the catalytic converter as the most flexible and most promising and succeeded in producing automobiles that conformed to the world's toughest emissions-control standards. Meanwhile, imported cars were given a three-year grace period to conform to Japan's strict emissions-control standards.

INTERNATIONAL GROWTH

In 1980 Japan's aggregate automobile production was actually better than that of the United States. In the same year, Toyota ranked second only to General Motors in total number of cars produced. In addition, Toyota made efforts over the years to improve the international cooperation between automakers. For example, it procured parts and materials from overseas manufacturers. Yet Japan's successes in the world auto market nonetheless resulted in the Japanese automobile industry becoming a target of criticism.

Shoichiro Toyoda, president of Toyota during the middle and late 1980s, possessed a solid understanding of American culture. Toyoda reportedly believed that Toyota's future success depended in part on the way it handled public relations with the United States. He perceived the United States to be extremely bitter about losing trade battles with Japanese industry. By means of intense advertising and controlled public relations under Toyoda's direction, Toyota tried to elevate the principle of free competition in the minds of the American people. At the same time, Toyoda carefully committed his company to greater international cooperation in both technological and managerial areas.

In 1984, for example, Toyota entered into a joint manufacturing venture with American giant General Motors called New United Motor Manufacturing, Inc. (NUMMI). This state-of-the-art facility allowed Toyota to begin production in the United States cautiously at a time of increasing protectionism, as well as learn about American labor practices. At the same time, it provided General Motors with insight into Japanese production methods and management styles. The plant was slated to build up to 50,000 vehicles a year. In the fall of 1985, moreover, Toyota announced that it would build an $800,000 production facility near Lexington, Kentucky. The plant, which was expected to begin assembling 200,000 cars per year by 1988, created approximately 3,000 jobs.

By the end of the 1980s, Toyota's position as a powerful, exceptionally well-run car company was nearly unassailable. After a decade of prodigious growth, the company stood atop the Japanese automobile industry and ranked number three worldwide, a position it had held since 1978 and strengthened in the ensuing years. By the beginning of the 1990s, Toyota commanded an overwhelming 43 percent of the Japanese car market, and in the United States it sold, for the first time, more than one million cars and trucks.

Aside from these two mainstay markets, Toyota was solidifying its global operations, particularly in Southeast Asia, and carving new markets in Latin America, where the burgeoning demand for cars promised much growth. Toyota also spearheaded the Japanese automobile industry's foray into the luxury car market, leading the way with its Lexus LS400 luxury sedan, which by the mid-1990s was outselling market veterans BMW, Mercedes-Benz, and Jaguar.

COMPETITION AFTER 1990

Despite these favorable developments, all of which pointed toward further growth and underscored the car company's vitality, Toyota's management continued to strive for improvements. In 1990, for example, when the company was posting enviable financial results and its manufacturing processes provided a model for other companies to follow, Shoichiro Toyoda eliminated two layers of middle management, effected substantial cuts in the company's executive staff, and reorganized Toyota's product development. With the highest operating margin of any carmaker in the world, Toyota was a formidable competitor.

Toyota had little control over external forces, however, and as the 1990s progressed, a global economic downturn brought the prolific growth of Japan's largest car manufacturer to a halt. The recession stifled economic growth throughout the world, while a rising yen made Japanese products relatively more expensive in overseas markets. Toyota's profits declined for four consecutive years between 1991 and 1994, falling to the lowest level in more than a decade.

Midway through Toyota's net income slide, the company gained new leadership when Totsuro Toyoda succeeded his brother in September 1992. Under Totsuro Toyoda's stewardship, a cost-cutting program was enacted that reduced expense account budgets 50 percent, limited travel expenditures, and eliminated white-collar overtime. Toyoda also continued the trend toward moving production to less expensive overseas markets by ordering the construction or expansion of six assembly plants in Great Britain, Pakistan, Thailand, Turkey, the United States, and Japan.

As Toyota's profit decline continued, however, the mounting losses persuaded Toyoda to intensify his cost-cutting measures. Design changes in the company's vehicles coupled with reductions in manufacturing and distribution costs saved Toyota ¥150 billion in 1993, and another ¥100 billion in savings was expected to be realized in 1994. That same year, the fourth consecutive year of negative net income growth, Toyota recorded ¥125.8 billion in consolidated net income, a little more than a quarter of the total posted in 1990, when the company earned ¥441.3 billion.

THE NEW GLOBAL BUSINESS PLAN: 1995 AND BEYOND

When Hiroshi Okuda was promoted to company president in 1995, his chief ambition was to revitalize Toyota's standing in the global marketplace. In June he unveiled Toyota's New Global Business Plan, which placed renewed focus on innovation and international expansion. Okuda's targets were clearly defined. He wanted to raise production to six million vehicles a year; to increase Toyota's international market share to 10 percent; and to increase its share of the domestic market to 40 percent.

He believed the first two goals would be achieved through the construction of new manufacturing plants in foreign markets, along with an increased emphasis on the "localization" of parts production. The purpose of localization was to reduce the time and expense involved with shipping components across great distances, enabling Toyota to increase its overall automobile production and devote greater resources to research and development. By widening the scope of operations in Toyota's overseas locations, Okuda envisioned a more streamlined, cost-effective manufacturing process. Furthermore, the stimulation of local economies was an effective public relations tool, enhancing the value of the Toyota brand name in foreign markets.

Okuda wasted no time putting his vision into practice. In 1995 Toyota announced its intention to set up a manufacturing operation in Indiana, in the hope of becoming a major participant in North America's highly competitive large truck market. In 1997 the company opened new plants in Canada and India, and in December it announced plans to build a second European plant in Valenciennes, France, to begin production of a new line of cars specifically designed for the European consumer. The year 1997 also saw increased production in Toyota's Thailand operations, with a total output of 240,000 vehicles.

In 1998 the company raised its export levels from the Thailand plants to 20,000 units, with most of the vehicles destined for the Australian and New Zealand markets. That same year, the company opened a new operation in Brazil, and in 1999 it began construction of a transmission production plant in the Walbrzych Special Economic Zone in Poland, which would begin exporting the parts to Toyota's manufacturing centers in France, Turkey, and the United Kingdom by 2002.

LATE 20TH-CENTURY DEVELOPMENTS

One of the most promising automobile markets to open up in the late 1990s was in China. By March 1998 Toyota already had stakes in four Chinese parts manufacturing plants, one of them a wholly owned subsidiary. The company took a more significant step in November 1998, when it established the Sichuan Toyota Motor Co., Ltd., Toyota's first vehicle production plant in China. A joint venture with the Sichuan Station Wagon Factory and Toyota Tsusho Corp., the new plant was scheduled to begin manufacturing coaster-class buses by 2001.

Okuda also assumed an aggressive approach to Toyota's role in the domestic market. In late 1996 he made drastic cuts to Toyota's vehicle prices in Japan, a move that incensed the competition. In August 1998 Toyota extended its hold over the domestic market with the purchase of a majority stake in Daihatsu. The company also implemented a number of environmental initiatives during this period, both at home and abroad. In July 1999 it inaugurated an initiative that aimed to eliminate all landfill waste by 2003, and in 2000 it introduced stricter environmental regulations in its U.S. manufacturing plants, which actually went beyond then current Environmental Protection Agency standards.

One of the most radical innovations to arise from Okuda's revolution was the Prius, Toyota's first hybrid car. Launched in October 1997, the Prius combined a highly efficient gas engine with a self-regenerating electric motor, reducing carbon dioxide emissions by half. Although initial estimates showed that production would have to surpass 200,000 vehicles a year for the Prius to turn a profit, by March 1998 demand was surpassing supply, and the future of the eco-car on the domestic market looked promising. Prius finally hit the U.S. and European markets in late 2000, amid increased fuel prices and mounting concerns over global warming.

Although a weakened euro caused Toyota to suffer losses in Europe toward the end of the 1990s, the new operation in France, scheduled to begin production in 2001 at a rate of 150,000 vehicles a year, was expected to reverse this trend. The company also experienced strong sales in the United States and Japan during this time, and in 2000 Toyota's total worldwide production exceeded five million vehicles for the first time ever.

GLOBAL REACH IN THE 21ST CENTURY

By 2003, Toyota had reached its goal of 10 percent of the global automotive market share. Yet the company was unable to rest. It pushed further, setting a new goal of 15 percent of global market share by 2010. This would put it past General Motors as the world's biggest. For Toyota, to surpass the world's leader was attainable. The company found ways to cut its costs and retool its factories for maximum flexibility, and went after increased sales in Europe.

Key to Toyota's continued drive forward was its new "global body line." This was a radical redesign of the company's manufacturing processes so that the company could make multiple car models on a single production line. Often the company could see that it needed to increase production of a certain model as demand peaked. However, retooling a factory so that it could, for example, stop making compact cars and begin making trucks, was expensive and time-consuming. In addition, from a design standpoint it was not always possible if models were of very different dimensions. Beginning in the early 2000s, Toyota installed a new system in its factories that significantly increased each production line's ability to shift to different models.

Toyota's previous manufacturing system used a trio of braces called pallets to hold the roof and sides of the vehicle as the car was welded together. A factory making several different models needed a huge storehouse of pallets. The global body line system vastly simplified the operation by using just one pallet to brace the body. This one was held from the inside rather than the outside, a new approach. Factories using the global body line system could make eight different models as easily as a single model.

The new system cut the amount of capital needed to retool a factory for new production by about 70 percent. It saved space as well. Two lines could be fit into the space formerly devoted to just one. Thus the company reaped magnificent savings while increasing its responsiveness to market shifts.

INCREASING SALES IN EUROPE

Toyota also hoped to build market share in Europe. It had long lagged behind other car companies there, where its designs were perceived as dull. Toyota invested in European production, which lowered its costs in distributing to that region. With a new factory in Valenciennes in 2001 and a joint venture with Peugeot Citroën in 2005, Toyota expected to sell as many cars in Europe as Ford by 2010. It designed with a more European look in mind. Its Yaris model became so popular that the Valenciennes factory had to add a third shift in 2004 to keep up with demand. European market share in 2004 was over 5 percent, and sales rose in double digits in the early 2000s.

Toyota also saw increasing sales in the United States and in China. China allowed plenty of room for growth. The company had gotten into the China market later than General Motors and other competitors. Yet ferocious consumer demand there meant that Toyota could confidently predict 60 percent sales growth in the later years of the first decade of the 2000s. Its Lexus, Camry, and Scion models sold well in the United States, and Toyota had unexpected success with its hybrid gas-electric model, the Prius.

A HIT WITH PRIUS

Toyota had started work on the Prius in the late 1990s. In a profile of the brand, *Fortune* magazine (March 6, 2006) claimed the Prius offered the first "serious alternative to the internal combustion engine since the Stanley Steamer ran out of steam in 1924." The Prius prototypes, however, suffered undignified difficulties. They would not start consistently and could not take cold weather, and the bulky battery ran the danger of catching on fire. When the first models arrived in the United States, testers found they could not fit a baby stroller in the trunk. The cars were noisy, slow to get up to speed, and the savings in gas did not actually make up for the higher sticker price.

After only a year, however, Hollywood celebrities were driving the Prius, proud to make a statement about saving energy. A redesigned model came out in the United States in 2003, and production could not keep up with demand. U.S. sales doubled in 2004 and almost doubled again the next year. Toyota had a significant advantage over all other carmakers. It had a head start on hybrid technology, and it had its enormous and flexible global manufacturing capability to take advantage of the new turn toward radically more fuel-efficient cars. Toyota had always been an industry leader in its ability to contain costs. By the middle of the first decade of the 2000s, the company seemed to have a real leg up on its competitors in many ways.

In 2007 Toyota was ranked the biggest carmaker in the world in terms of its sales and profits. General Motors, however, sold more cars, by approxmately 3,500 units. Toyota's masterful performance nonetheless seemed to leave it poised to sweep the number-one spot very soon.

Much about the auto industry was up in the air in 2008. The global financial market began to shudder as the bursting housing market bubble in the United States sent repercussions around the globe. Uncertainty and volatility in the stock markets left banks unable to issue credit and consumers paralyzed. Toyota's profits dropped almost 30 percent in the quarter ending in June 2008. The company altered its global sales projection downward, and laid off workers in Japan.

Although Toyota's figures were miserable, other automakers were in even worse shape. General Motors and Ford lost a combined $24 billion during the same period. The numbers that came out in October 2008 were even more sobering. Toyota's U.S. sales that month were 23 percent behind October 2007. The U.S. auto industry as a whole saw a slide of 32 percent compared to the previous October. For the year, Toyota predicted its profits would decrease over 73 percent compared to 2007. In November 2008 top leaders of General Motors, Chrysler, and Ford jointly pleaded with the U.S. government for federal loans to avert bankruptcy. With the U.S. automotive industry in crisis, the effects on all other players in the global automotive industry were bound to be far-reaching, whatever happened.

Jeffrey L. Covell
Updated, Stephen Meyer; A. Woodward

PRINCIPAL SUBSIDIARIES

Toyota Motor Engineering and Manufacturing North America, Inc.; Toyota Motor Europe; Daihatsu Motor Co., Ltd. (51%); Toyota Motorsports GmbH; Toyota Technical Center Asia Pacific Thailand Co., Ltd.; Toyota Technical Center Asia Pacific Australia Pty. Ltd.; Toyota Argentina S.A.; Toyota Motor Manufacturing France, S.A.S.; Toyota South Africa Motors, Ltd.

PRINCIPAL COMPETITORS

Ford Motor Company; General Motors Corporation; Honda Motor Co., Ltd.

FURTHER READING

Bremner, Brian, and Chester Dawson, "Can Anything Stop Toyota?" *Business Week,* November 17, 2003, p. 114.

Brown, Stuart F., "Toyota's Global Body Shop," *Fortune,* February 9, 2004, p. 120.

Butler, Steven, "Toyota Puts It on the Line: Stung by Recession, the Auto Maker Embarks on Deep Cost Cutting," *U.S. News and World Report,* August 23, 1993, p. 47.

Edmondson, Gail, with Adeline Bonnet, "Toyota's New Traction in Europe," *Business Week,* June 7, 2004, p. 64.

Higgins, James V., "Toyota Is Ready to Lead a New Japanese Wave," *Detroit News,* August 30, 1995, p. B1.

Kamiya, Shotaro, with Thomas Elliott, *My Life with Toyota,* Toyota City: Toyota Motor Sales Co., 1978.

Kiley, David, "The Toyota Way to No. 1," *Business Week Online,* April 26, 2007.

"No Traffic Ahead for Toyota," *Business Week Online,* February 7, 2006.

Pollack, Andrew, "Toyota Profit Declines for a Fourth Year; Loss Had Been Feared; Future Called Brighter," *New York Times,* August 26, 1994, p. C2.

Rowley, Ian, "Toyota's All-Out Drive to Stay Toyota," *Business Week Online,* November 27, 2007, p. 46.

———, "Toyota's Tough Quarter," *Business Week Online,* August 8, 2008.

Spindle, William, "Toyota Retooled: Profits and Global Output Are Up, and New Models Are on the Way," *Business Week,* April 4, 1994, p. 54.

Sugawara, Sandra, "Toyota Steps on the Gas: A Leaner, Tougher Company Gambles on Global Leadership with New 'Eco-Car,'" *Washington Post,* December 14, 1997, p. H1.

Taylor, Alex, "A Back-to-Basics U-Turn in Japan," *New York Times,* August 26, 1994, p. C1.

Taylor, Alex, III, "The Birth of the Prius," *Fortune,* March 6, 2006, p. 111.

"Toyota Profits Tumble as Yen Soars," *Business Week Online,* November 7, 2008.

Williams, G. Chambers, III, "Electric/Gasoline Car Is on the Road to U.S.," *Fort Worth Star-Telegram,* January 2, 1999, p. 1.

Universal Studios, Inc.

———————■———————

100 Universal City Plaza
Universal City, California 91608-1002
U.S.A.
Telephone: (818) 777-1000
Fax: (818) 866-1402
Web site: http://www.universalstudios.com

Wholly Owned Subsidiary of NBC Universal Inc.
Incorporated: 1912 as Universal Film Manufacturing
   Company
Employees: 15,000
Sales: $2.14 billion (2007 est.)
NAICS: 512120 Motion Picture and Video Distribu-
   tion; 512220 Integrated Record Production/
   Distribution; 513210 Cable Networks; 713110
   Amusement and Theme Parks; 453220 Gift,
   Novelty, and Souvenir Stores

■ ■ ■

Universal Studios is a part of NBC Universal Inc., one
of the world's leading media and entertainment
companies, which was formed in 2004 through the
merger of NBC and Vivendi Universal Entertainment.
The company's Universal Pictures subsidiaries produce
and distribute mainstream movies to a global audience,
while its Focus Features produces smaller-budget films.
Universal Studios also operates theme parks through its
Universal Parks & Resorts unit. Universal Studios Home
Entertainment is in the business of DVD marketing and
distribution. Other business activities involve licensing
for consumer products, such as apparel with movie and
television characters.

EARLY 20TH-CENTURY ORIGINS

Carl Laemmle's entry into the motion picture production began in the industry's infancy. In 1905, while
Laemmle searched for a place to open a clothing store in
Chicago, he stumbled onto a line of people waiting to
see a nickelodeon. Intrigued by the popularity of moving pictures, Laemmle changed careers and opened The
White Front Theater. In one month, Laemmle recouped
his investment and opened a second theater with Robert
Cochrane, a business associate. Laemmle expanded
further with the Laemmle Film Service, which became
the largest movie distributor in the country. By 1909,
Laemmle and Cochrane were grossing $10,000 a week
doing business in the Midwest and in Canada.

Laemmle and Cochrane's production of motion
pictures stemmed from a dispute with the Motion
Picture Patents Company, which had attained
monopolistic power at the time. Finding himself with
no motion pictures to exhibit, due to the rift with the
patent company, Laemmle decided to make movies
himself. The first effort of the Independent Motion
Picture Company (IMP) involved a one-reel film titled
Hiawatha. Eventually, production increased to an average of one film per week. The Universal Film
Manufacturing Company was formed in 1912 when
IMP merged with five other companies; Laemmle
became president and Cochrane vice-president of the
new concern.

Universal offered a variety of motion picture packages that allowed an exhibitor to show a different film every day. The Complete Service Plan, for example, included a two-reel comedy, a serial, and a feature film. In 1913, the company began to offer a regular newsreel titled *The Universal Animated Weekly.* Universal's first full-length feature film, *Traffic in Souls* (1913), grossed $0.5 million; the movie's real significance was in innovative editing and plot lines which gave the impression of simultaneously occurring events, a concept never before conveyed in film.

Universal expanded its movie-making capacity with the opening of Universal City in 1914. Laemmle acquired the 230-acre Taylor Ranch north of the Hollywood Hills for $165,000, envisioning a studio as a city. Laemmle's promotion of the grand opening of Universal City, aimed primarily at theater owners, attracted thousands of people from the general public as well. The promotion stated that everyone should come to see how movies are made "to make the people laugh or cry or sit on the edge of their chairs the world over." The public was so fascinated with film making that Universal City offered organized tours for 25 cents apiece, which included a box lunch, and the company erected bleachers near the sets. About 500 people visited Universal City daily until the advent of sound movies required enclosed stages.

A GROWING INDUSTRY

In 1915, Universal produced over 250 films, primarily two-reel shows and serials, but also feature-length films of over 70 minutes long. The company classified films according to budget and status. A Red Feather film and a Bluebird film received low and midrange budgets, respectively. A Jewel film involved a large budget and prestigious stars of the time, such as Harry Carey, Carmel Myers, and Rudolph Valentino, and directors such as Erich von Stroheim. John Ford helped to define the genre of American westerns in the numerous films he directed after joining Universal in 1914.

Renamed Universal Pictures Corporation in 1922, the company continued to focus on short, low-budget serials, westerns, and melodramas through the 1920s and 1930s while other studios shifted to feature films. The company did produce two feature films in the 1920s, however, which became silent film classics. *The Hunchback of Notre Dame* (1923), starring Lon Chaney and directed by Wallace Worsley, achieved critical acclaim and financial success. *Phantom of the Opera* (1925) starred Chaney as well as a large cast of the studio's popular stars.

Dynamics of the film industry troubled Universal in the mid-1920s; the company did not have the advantage of affiliation with a theater chain where most first-run movies in major cities were shown. Universal contracted with independent theaters that tended to be in rural areas; so movies at this time catered to rural audiences. Universal also accessed European markets where American westerns and action movies found an audience.

When Carl Laemmle Jr. became general manager in charge of production in 1929, Universal adopted a more sophisticated approach. Laemmle Jr. cut the studio's output by 40 percent to allow for longer films of higher quality. His interest in novels led to several prominent productions. Universal received its first award from the Academy of Motion Picture Arts and Sciences, for best picture for the sound motion picture *All Quiet on the Western Front* in 1930. Laemmle Jr. was also the driving force behind the studio's production of *Dracula* (1931), starring Bela Lugosi. In fact, Universal would gain renown for its horror movies, with eight films produced between 1931 to 1935, including *Frankenstein* (1932) and *The Mummy* (1932), both starring Boris Karloff.

Most of the higher-quality films that Laemmle Jr. initiated did not engage the audiences of their day, however, and box-office receipts did not compensate for the high cost of feature film production. When Laemmle Jr.'s production of the Broadway musical *Showboat* went over budget in 1935, his father offered his controlling interest as collateral for over $1 million in debt to fund the project. When the investors called their option in 1936, Standard Capital acquired Laemmle's interest in the company for $4.1 million, ending the Laemmle era at Universal.

CONSOLIDATION UNDER A NEW NAME

Renamed New Universal, the company consolidated its resources by reducing production and closing European operations. In 1936, Universal completed two films begun before the change in ownership: *My Man Godfrey* and *Three Smart Girls* received nine Academy Award

KEY DATES

■

1912: The Universal Film Manufacturing Company is formed when Carl Laemmle's Independent Motion Picture Company merges with five other companies.

1913: *Traffic in Souls,* Universal's first feature-length film, is produced.

1914: The company builds Universal City.

1922: The company is renamed Universal Pictures Corporation.

1930: The studio receives its first Academy Award for Best Picture for *All Quiet on the Western Front.*

1936: Standard Capital acquires Laemmle's interest in the company, which is renamed New Universal.

1946: New Universal merges with International Pictures.

1952: Decca Records acquires Universal.

1958: Decca cuts production and sells Universal City to the Music Corporation of America (MCA).

1962: MCA acquires Decca Records.

1964: MCA renovates Universal City's studio facilities and reinstitutes tours.

1982: Universal City expands to become the largest movie lot in Hollywood.

1988: Universal Studios Florida opens in Orlando.

1990: MCA and Cineplex Odeon Corporation engage in a joint venture to open Universal Studios Florida as a movie-theme entertainment complex; Matsushita Electrical Industrial Company acquires MCA.

1995: Matsushita sells an 80 percent interest in MCA, Universal's parent company, to Seagram Company Ltd.

1996: MCA is renamed Universal Studios; the company opens theme parks in Spain and in China.

1997: Seagram sells most of Universal's television assets to USA Networks.

2000: Vivendi acquires and merges Seagram and French pay television Canal Plus to create Vivendi Universal.

2001: Vivendi acquires USA Networks and forms Vivendi Universal Entertainment.

2004: Vivendi Universal and General Electric's NBC merge to form NBC Universal.

nominations between them. Deanna Durbin, the 15-year-old soprano star of *Three Smart Girls,* became one of the studio's biggest stars, making 21 movies during her 12 years at Universal. In 1938, Durbin received a special Oscar for bringing youthfulness to the silver screen.

With the arrival of two RKO executives at Universal, Nate Blumberg as president and Clifford Work as head of production, the company hoped to entertain the masses on a lower budget. Universal recovered from its losses with the popularity of Durbin's movies as well as the success of *Destry Rides Again* (1939), starring Marlene Dietrich and James Stewart. From a net loss of $1.8 million in 1936, Universal garnered a net profit of $1.5 million in 1939.

The onset of World War II increased public demand for escape through motion pictures. Youth-oriented productions included Sherlock Holmes, Inner Sanctum mysteries, and the Bud Abbott and Lou Costello comedy team, whose debut in *One Night in the Tropics* (1940) featured the famous skit, "Who's on first?" Universal produced monster movies, low-budget westerns, movie sequels, and desert dramas, also know as "sand 'n' sex" movies. War-themed movies included 13 films featuring the popular Andrew Sisters released between 1940 and 1945. Mature movies included the genre of film noir, which had not yet attained its appreciated status. Some of Universal's notable films included *Shadow of a Doubt* (1943), directed by Alfred Hitchcock, *The Suspect* (1944), directed by Robert Siodmark, and *Scarlet Street* (1945) by Fritz Lang. Wartime production peaked in 1945 when Universal averaged one feature-length motion picture per week; between 1940 and 1945 production neared 350 movies.

Universal's 1946 merger with International Pictures stemmed from the desire to improve the quality of motion picture productions. Two new production heads, Leo Spitz and William Goetz, eliminated short serials, "programmer" westerns, and low-budget movies to concentrate on feature-length films. They dropped several stars, but retained Abbott and Costello, Durbin, and Donald O'Connor, star of *Francis the Talking Mule* and its sequels (1955–56).

Universal Pictures made several higher-quality movies, but these did not bring high returns at the box office. One exception, *The Egg and I,* was the top-grossing movie of 1947 at $5.75 million. Operating at a loss in the late 1940s, Universal Pictures exploited the popularity of the low-budget Ma and Pa Kettle movies with ten productions.

MID-CENTURY DEVELOPMENTS AND THE IMPACT OF TELEVISION

Ownership changed again in 1952 when Decca Records acquired controlling interest in Universal Pictures. With Milton Rackmil as president and Ed Muhl as vice-president of production, gross receipts increased $7 million by 1954. Muhl sought lesser-known independent producers to make movies at the studio's facilities. The company succeeded with Albert Zugsmith, known for *The Incredible Shrinking Man* (1954) and *Touch of Evil* (1958), Aaron Rosenberg, who produced *The Glenn Miller Story* (1954), and Robert Arthur, producer of *Operation Petticoat* (1959) which grossed $9.5 million.

Universal's most successful producer at this time was Ross Hunter, the so-called King of the Weepies. Hunter collaborated with director Douglas Sirk on ten films between 1953 and 1959, including romantic dramas, such as the remake of *Imitation of Life* (1959) with Lana Turner. Hunter's production of *Pillow Talk* (1959), starring Rock Hudson and Doris Day, grossed $7.5 million and prompted a surge in the romantic comedy genre. The studio's stars at this time included Audie Murphy, Kirk Douglas, Tony Curtis, Maureen O'Hara, Charlton Heston, and Jane Wyman.

Despite the quality of movies being made, television proved quite a competitor, and movie audiences began staying home. In 1957, Universal leased 550 movies made before 1948 to Screen Gems for airing on television. After profits of $4 million in 1956 and 1957, Universal lost $2 million in 1958, while the motion picture industry experienced a 12 percent decline in ticket sales. As a result, Decca cut production and sold Universal City to the Music Corporation of America (MCA) for $11.25 million.

In 1962, MCA acquired controlling interest in Decca, thus obtaining the Universal studios, which MCA wanted for television production. MCA renovated studio facilities and reinstituted tours of Universal City in 1964. Early movie productions under MCA included Alfred Hitchcock's *The Birds* (1962), which grossed $4.6 million, and *To Kill a Mockingbird* (1962), which won three Academy Awards, including Best Actor for Gregory Peck. Ross Hunter continued to be the company's most successful producer with *Thoroughly Modern Millie* (1968), followed by the all-star blockbuster *Airport* (1970), which grossed $45.3 million.

BLOCKBUSTER YEARS START IN THE SEVENTIES

The year 1973 unfolded as a high-water-mark year for Universal. Richard Zanuck and David Brown's produc-

tion of *The Sting*, starring Robert Redford and Paul Newman, grossed $79 million at the box office and won seven Academy Award nominations, including best picture. In fact, Universal films competed with each other that year for the Oscars, as George Lucas's production of *American Graffiti*, which grossed $56.7 million, received four nominations. Other highly acclaimed and financially successful movies included *The Day of the Jackal* and *High Plains Drifter.* The year was also notable as Lew Wasserman became chairman and CEO of MCA, while Sidney Sheinberg, responsible for bringing Steven Spielberg to Universal, became chief operating officer and president.

Universal made its share of the succession of Hollywood blockbusters. *Jaws* (1975), produced by Zanuck and Brown and directed by Spielberg, drew the largest movie audience to date, grossing $133.4 million, only to be topped by Twentieth Century Fox's *Star Wars* two years later. While Universal suffered huge flops, such as *Gable & Lombard,* the company produced several popular films, such as *Smoky and the Bandit* (1977), *National Lampoon's Animal House* (1978), and *The Blues Brothers* (1980).

AWARD WINNERS IN THE EIGHTIES

During the 1980s Universal released several award-winning movies. *Coal Miner's Daughter* (1980) grossed $38.5 million, and Sissy Spacek won an Oscar for best actress. *On Golden Pond* (1981) grossed $63 million and won three of ten Academy Award nominations, including best actor for Henry Fonda and best actress for Katharine Hepburn. Universal's success peaked with Spielberg's production of *E.T.–The Extra-Terrestrial,* which broke box-office records within three months and grossed $300 million by the end of 1982. Among Universal's 16 Oscar nominations in 1982, *E.T.* won four of eight nominations, while Meryl Streep won best actress for *Sophie's Choice.* Sidney Pollack's production of *Out of Africa* (1985) won seven Academy awards, including best picture and best director for Pollack. Other popular movies included *Back to the Future* (1985), *Dragnet* (1987), *Field of Dreams* (1989), and *Back to the Future II* (1989).

Wasserman's expansion of studio facilities, completed in 1982, included the addition of 220 acres, making Universal City the largest studio lot in Hollywood. New facilities included 36 sound stages, a Technicolor film processing laboratory, and a 14-story administration building. A 200,000-square-foot office complex housed independent producers in "bungalows." When Spielberg started his own production company, Amblin Entertainment, Universal installed him in a bungalow with editing facilities, a screening room, and other facilities not typically provided.

With Tom Pollock as president of Universal Pictures in 1986, the company adopted new procedures to reduce capital outlay. For the production of *Twins* (1986), Universal contracted with the two stars, Arnold Schwarzenegger and Danny DeVito, to accept a smaller salary balanced by a percentage of the gross. The strategy succeeded as *Twins* grossed $57.2 million in domestic distribution in less than a year. Pollock's philosophy involved a mix of A- and B-quality movies to lower production costs. *Fried Green Tomatoes* (1991) proved a sleeper hit among the company's B movies. Pollock also helped Ron Howard and Brian Grazer form Imagine, whose award-winning production *Apollo 13* (1995) grossed $162 million within the first ten weeks.

EXPANSION IN FLORIDA AND NEW OWNERSHIP

In 1988 Universal Studios Florida opened in Orlando for television, motion picture, and commercial advertising production. Two years later, the facility would open for public tours. The movie-theme entertainment complex, a joint venture between MCA and Cineplex Odeon Corporation, included rides and attractions. The backlot and facilities accommodated small film and television projects. Some major motion production also took place there, including Imagine's *Parenthood*.

Long-term agreements were made with Unitel Video's television and mobile production facilities and Century III's all-digital edit bay. Hanna-Barbera Productions opened an animation studio and an attraction based on its popular cartoon characters at Universal Studios Florida, while cable network Nickelodeon produced most of its shows at its facility, including game shows that sought contestants and audience members among studio visitors.

Matsushita Electrical Industrial Company of Japan acquired MCA in November 1990. Matsushita was the largest manufacturer of home electronics in the world under the Panasonic brand and had created the VHS format. During Matsushita's ownership, Universal released *Jurassic Park, Schindler's List,* and *We're Back! A Dinosaur's Story.* The Amblin productions grossed $548.7 million; 60 percent of Universal's movie revenue was derived from three of 18 movies released in 1993.

Conflicts between Matsushita and MCA's executives over strategic expansion hampered the company's tenure of ownership. Moreover, Universal lost its top producer when Spielberg formed a new studio company, DreamWorks SKG. In 1995, Matsushita sold an 80

percent interest in MCA to Seagram Company Ltd. for $5.7 billion. The Seagram board named Frank Biondi as CEO and chairman of MCA, which they renamed Universal Studios, Inc., thus consolidating the various entertainment companies, including the music recording companies, under one name.

Edgar Bronfman Jr., chairman of Seagram, led the company through decisions that the board, Bronfman family members, and many shareholders questioned. Seagram sold 25 percent of its stake in DuPont to acquire MCA which proved to be the first of several controversial decisions. Bronfman acquired Polygram for its profitable music business but was unable to sell the film division in one piece. In September 1997, he merged USA Network with HSN, the parent of the Home Shopping Network. Although Universal still owned 46 percent of USA Network, critics were wary when USA chairman Barry Diller gained control of a business that generated cash for Seagram. Biondi, hired for his strengths in television, resigned as CEO after 18 months at Universal.

INTERNATIONAL BRANDED TELEVISION AND OTHER INDUSTRY CHANGES

The Universal Studios Networks Division was created in August 1997 for the international marketing of branded televisions channels. USA Network licensed Universal's library for domestic use, while Universal distributed internationally. The division successfully launched "13th Street–The Action Suspense Channel" in France, featuring dubbed versions of such American favorites as *Miami Vice, Magnum P.I.,* and similar shows. The station was launched in Spain and Germany in 1998, while some shows aired on USA Network Brazil and USA Network Latin America. Through eight international offices, the division attained program distribution in over 180 countries, including production of local talk shows in England and the Netherlands. Universal eventually integrated Polygram's television division and began productions of domestically syndicated shows, such as *Motown Live* and *Blind Date.* A new version of *The Woody Woodpecker Show* debuted in 1999.

While Bronfman brought a traditional business approach to Hollywood, creativity waned in movie making. Bronfman streamlined management and implemented several cost-saving measures, but Universal's market share for movie tickets declined due to lower production, with only 12 films in 1997. Major failures included *Fear and Loathing in Las Vegas* (1998), which grossed $10 million. Nevertheless, Universal rebounded with the releases of *Patch Adams, Notting*

Hill, and *The Mummy,* which together grossed $790 million globally by mid-August 1999, while a joint release with Miramax, *Shakespeare in Love,* won box-office success and seven Academy Awards. The Universal Pictures division lost $200 million despite revenues of $3.38 billion in 1999, but had high hopes for Imagine's late 2000 release of a feature-length version of *The Grinch Who Stole Christmas,* starring Jim Carrey, which had the potential to become a perennial holiday favorite.

Universal Studios succeeded in other areas. In 1999, *The Mummy* garnered over $1 billion in video and digital video discs (DVD) sales. Universal sought to expand on this success with the release of its horror classics, such as *The Invisible Man* (1933) and Alfred Hitchcock classics on DVD. Universal Music Group carried the company with strong profits. In electronic video games, the company experienced positive returns on the summer 2000 launch of E.T. Interactive.

Universal also sought to improve its profits through theme park expansion. In 1996, Universal City in California introduced Jurassic Park: The Ride, a replication of the theme park in the popular movie. Universal also acquired Port Aventura in Spain, and opened The Universal Experience in Beijing. Universal Studios Florida added the Islands of Adventure theme park, featuring five islands of attractions, one based on the children's literature of Dr. Seuss and another on popular superheroes.

A SUBSIDIARY OF VIVENDI AND GENERAL ELECTRIC IN THE 21ST CENTURY

As the company headed toward the new century, some industry analysts speculated that Seagram might try to sell Universal as the film studios continued to lose money. Seagram head Edgar Bronfman Jr. did sell Universal's television holdings to media magnate Barry Diller. Then, French media company Vivendi stepped in, acquiring both Seagram and the French pay-television service, Canal Plus, and merging the two to create Vivendi Universal in 2000. The following year, Universal Studios Recreation Group, which oversaw all of Universal's theme parks in Hollywood, Japan, Beijing, and Spain, moved to Orlando, Florida, and opened another theme park opened in Osaka, Japan.

In 2002 Vivendi formed Vivendi Universal Entertainment (VUE), from the merger of USA Networks' television and film divisions and Universal Studios. However, Vivendi suffered as part of the worldwide downturn affecting media companies. Burdened with debt, in 2004, it sold 80 percent of VUE, including the studio and theme parks, to General Electric's NBC, which named the company NBC Universal. NBC Universal's television broadcasting and production units became separate units, while its theme parks and film holdings became Universal Studios. Universal Studios sold its theme park in Spain in 2004.

In 2005 Universal entered into one of the largest-scale negotiations in recent Hollywood history when it attempted to purchase DreamWorks. Despite the fact that the negotiation ultimately fell through (Viacom's Paramount Pictures acquired DreamWorks after acquisition talks between GE and DreamWorks stalled), the studio moved on to its most profitable year ever in 2007, with five films that each grossed over $100 million domestically: *Knocked Up, Evan Almighty, I Now Pronounce You Chuck & Larry, American Gangster,* and *The Bourne Ultimatum.* Along with its other entertainment sales, the company set an all-time record for worldwide grosses of $2.13 billion.

Universal Studios also continued its worldwide growth in theme parks after the turn of the century with the planned addition of new parks in Singapore; Seoul, Korea; and Dubai, all to be completed by 2012. The park in Singapore would be bigger than Universal's theme park in Hollywood and comparable to its flagship in Orlando. Even though some industry observers expressed doubts that tightly organized, profit-minded General Electric was a good leader for Universal Studios, the pair seemed to work well.

Mary Tradii
Updated, Carrie Rothburd

PRINCIPAL DIVISIONS

Universal Pictures Distribution; Universal Pictures Home Video; Universal Pictures International Marketing and Distribution; Universal Pictures International Video; Universal Pictures Marketing; Universal Pictures Production; Universal Studios Consumer Products Group; Universal Studios Home Entertainment Family Productions; Universal Studios Home Video; Universal Studios Parks & Resorts; Universal Studios Hollywood; Universal Orlando; Universal Studios Japan.

PRINCIPAL COMPETITORS

CBS Corporation; Time Warner Entertainment Company L.P.; The Walt Disney Company; DreamWorks; Viacom Inc.; Fox Entertainment Group Inc.; Lions Gate Entertainment Corporation; Lucasfilm Ltd.; Metro-Goldwyn-Mayer Inc.; Six Flags Inc.; Sony Pictures Entertainment Inc.

FURTHER READING

Block, Alex Ben, "2008 Leadership Award: Ron Meyer," *Hollywood Reporter,* July 30, 2008.

Cox, Dan, "U Passing the Hat," *Variety,* January 18, 1999, p. 1.

Deckard, Linda, "Universal Hollywood Eyes 5 Mil Attendance," *Amusement Business,* June 21, 1993, p. 3.

Dennis, Laura, "At Universal, Beginning May 24, Dinosaurs Again Will Rule," *Travel Weekly,* February 22, 1996, p. 22.

Dick, Bernard F., *City of Dreams: The Making and Remaking of Universal Pictures,* Lexington: University Press of Kentucky, 1997.

Egan, Jack, "Barry Diller Wheels and Deals," *U.S. News & World Report,* November 3, 1997, p. 62.

Emmons, Natasha. "Universal Studios City Walk Hollywood Set for 93,000 Square-Foot Expansion," *Amusement Business,* December 27, 1999, p. 70.

Fannin, Rebecca, "Putting the Plus in Canal+: Europe's Leading Pay TV Operator Faces Life As Part of the Huge Media Conglomerate Vivendi Universal," *Multichannel News International,* April 1, 2002, p. 15.

Fitzpatrick, Eileen, "Mummy Shoots Universal's Sales over $1 Bil.; Retailers Win with Sight and Sound," *Billboard,* December 25, 1999, p. 63.

Hirschhorn, Clive, *The Universal Story,* New York: Crown Publishers, Inc., 1983.

Kent, Lisa, "Nickelodeon to Produce at Universal Complex in Orlando in 1990," *Back Stage,* June 10, 1988, p. 6.

Littleton, Cynthia, "Diller Redefines USA, Eyes New Day," *Variety,* February 16, 1998, p. 37.

———, "Sale Returns U to Syndie TV Arena," *Variety,* December 14, 1998, p. 149.

Masters, Kim, "Bronfman Stirs Universal: Despite Weak Films and a Rash of Firings, the Young Boss Keeps Insisting that His Studio Will Do Just Fine," *Time,* May 4, 1998, p. 46.

McConnell, Chris, "Century III at Universal Studios," *Broadcasting & Cable,* September 12, 1994, p. 56.

Medina, Hildy, "In Need of a TV Network, Universal Turns to Europe," *Los Angeles Business Journal,* September 15, 1997, p. 13.

Miller, Richard, "Universal Studios and Hanna-Barbera Productions," *Back Stage,* June 10, 1988, p. 6.

Morden, Ethan, *The Hollywood Studios: House Style in the Golden Age of the Movies,* New York: Alfred A. Knopf, 1988.

Moshavi, Sharon D., "AMC Buys Universal Packaging," *Broadcasting,* May 20, 1991, p. 55.

"New Productions at Universal Studios Florida Keep Studios and Backlots at Capacity." *Orlando Business Journal,* December 7, 1990, p. 2A.

Parkes, Christopher, "Entertainments More Bad News to Come from Universal Studios, Company Warns," *Financial Times,* May 7, 1999, p. 30.

"Resignation of Universal Studios Head Spells Trouble for Seagram," *Knight-Ridder/Tribune Business News,* November 20, 1998.

Scally, Robert, "Kmart, Universal: Licensing Classics," *Discount Store News,* November 23, 1998, p. 3.

"Seagram May Sell Universal Studios, Drinks Group Eyes Disposal of Lossmaking Film Unit: The Theme Parks Could Go Separately," *Financial Times,* February 4, 2000, p. 21.

"Seagram: Mr. Bronfman in Tinseltown," *Economist,* November 21, 1998, p. 66.

Thomas, Tony, *The Best of Universal,* New York: Vestal Press, Ltd., 1990.

"Unitel to Open Unit at Florida Universal Studios," *Back Stage,* October 9, 1987, p. 1.

"Universal Studios and Hanna-Barbera Productions," *Back Stage,* June 10, 1988, p. 6.

"Universal Studios Created," *Television Digest,* August 11, 1997, p. 6.

UTG Inc.

───────●───────

5250 South Sixth Street
Springfield, Illinois 62703
U.S.A.
Telephone: (217) 241-6300
Fax: (217) 786-4372
Web site: http://www.utgins.com

Public Company
Incorporated: 1984
Employees: 74
Sales: $38.87 million (2007)
Stock Exchanges: over the counter
Ticker Symbol: UTGN
NAICS: 524113 Direct Life Insurance Carriers

■ ■ ■

UTG Inc. is a Springfield, Illinois-based life insurance holding company. Through its many subsidiaries, the company provides both life insurance and administrative services. UTG has approximately 550,000 customers throughout the United States, and services more than 1,500 insurance plans. In addition to its insurance business, the company provides administrative services to corporate clients and fraternal organizations, such as the Illinois-based Independent Order of Vikings.

FORMATIVE YEARS: 1984–89

UTG's origins can be traced back to December 14, 1984, when Thomas Morrow, Larry Ryherd, and others formed United Trust Inc. (UTI) in Springfield, Illinois.

At that time, the company issued $15 million in stock to approximately 6,300 shareholders throughout Illinois. Developments during the company's early years set the tone for the next several decades, which were marked by a flurry of mergers and acquisitions, as well as the formation of new businesses.

A new life insurance subsidiary named United Trust Assurance Company (UTAC) was established in 1986. In December of that year, UTI asked the Springfield City Council to approve up to $600,000 in revenue bonds, which it wanted to use for the purchase and renovation of property for a new corporate headquarters. At that time, the company was based at Iles Park Place, and it wished to relocate to a location at 725 South Second St.

In January 1987, industrial revenue bonds totaling $541,000 were approved for UTI's headquarters project. Along with this good news, the company revealed plans to expand its payroll after occupying the location. This growth was followed by an uptick in business activity. UTAC began selling life insurance products in 1987, and that same year, UTI formed a new enterprise named United Income Inc. (UII) in Ohio.

Midway through 1989, UTI's UTAC subsidiary acquired Kansas-based Cimarron Life Insurance Co. The deal expanded the parent company's geographic footprint, which included companies based in Illinois, Kansas, Ohio, and Texas. Cimarron was licensed to sell insurance in Colorado, Kansas, Nebraska, North Dakota, Oklahoma, and Texas, and had assets of approximately $6 million. UTI rounded out the 1980s with Chairman and President Larry Ryherd at the helm,

COMPANY PERSPECTIVES

UTG is a solid, secure and growing company providing life insurance and administrative services. The foundation of our business is a commitment to excellence in customer service and ensuring profitability through administrative efficiency.

roughly $1 billion of insurance in force, and about $30 million in assets. For the year ended December 31, 1989, the company recorded earnings of $92,558 on revenues of $7.17 million. This was a significant increase over 1988, when the company registered a $196,859 loss on revenues of $3.48 million.

Growth also continued at UTI's UII business. By July 1989 that operation had raised $6.8 million through a stock sale in Ohio, which had begun in March 1988. The majority of these proceeds were used for the capitalization of Ohio-based United Security Assurance, a new company that planned to commence insurance sales in 1990.

MILESTONES AND
ACQUISITIONS: 1990–92

An important milestone was reached in July 1990, when UTI's stock listed on the NASDAQ under the symbol UTIN. This enabled the company to market its insurance products to a broader audience and grow the number of its shareholders. The following month, UTI reported progress with its UII subsidiary, which had raised about $17.5 million via its public offering.

One of UTI's differentials during the early 1990s was its focus on personal service. This principle benefited the company as it operated during a national economic recession, and at a time when scandals related to the savings and loan industry had made consumers especially cautious about financial matters. Revealing a bit of the company's philosophy in a January 26, 1992, *State Journal-Register* article by Kevin McDermott, UTI President Larry Ryherd said: "Our philosophy is a lot different (from others in the industry). We sit down with customers and use 'personal marketing.'"

UTI kicked off 1992 with news that its Cimarron Life Insurance Co. business planned to acquire Oklahoma-based Home Security Holding Co., a holding company for Home Security Life Insurance Co. The deal increased UTI's assets to approximately $60 million. In February that year UTI was involved in one of the largest insurance deals in Springfield, Illinois, history when it agreed to acquire Springfield-based Commonwealth Industries Corp. for $17.5 million. The transaction caused UTI's assets to swell, reaching $290 million. Specifically, UTI and its UII subsidiary each devoted roughly $10 million to the deal, which led to the formation of a new subsidiary named United Trust Group.

POST-MERGER DEVELOPMENTS

One major benefit of the deal with Commonwealth was the acquisition of real estate, including a 22,000-square-foot operations center in Springfield. UTI made plans to vacate its headquarters on Second Street and relocate to the headquarters formerly occupied by Commonwealth. After insurance regulators and lenders in five states granted approval for the deal, the merger with Commonwealth was completed in June 1992.

Although UTI was growing during difficult economic times, the company's financial security was questioned by some observers during the early 1990s. In November 1992, the *Chicago Tribune* profiled an Insurance Solvency Review report from Standard & Poor's Co. that evaluated the financial status of approximately 3,000 health and property casualty insurance firms nationwide. In Illinois, 17 companies—including UTI—were given a "vulnerable" ranking, indicating that they did not offer policyholders adequate security.

However, by early 1993 UTI was involved in more than just insurance. For example, the company's real estate subsidiary, Beacon Realty, had joined with Universal Guaranty Investment Co. to develop five subdivisions in the Springfield area. Important developments continue to unfold into the mid-1990s. In June 1996, the Philadelphia-based insurance and financial services management firm LaSalle Group agreed to make a $19 million equity investment in both UTI and its UII subsidiary.

By the mid-1990s UTI's assets had grown to $356 million, and the company had roughly 5,700 shareholders. Along with UII, the company had a controlling stake in Abraham Lincoln Insurance Co., Appalachian Life Insurance Co., United Security Assurance Co., and Universal Guaranty Life Insurance Co. Heading into the end of the decade UTI offered its employees a progressive work environment. At the company's headquarters, work stations were organized into clusters to promote teamwork and interaction. UTI allowed staff members to share desks and some were even allowed to relocate to new clusters on a weekly basis—a concept known as "hoteling."

KEY DATES

1984: Thomas Morrow, Larry Ryherd, and others form United Trust Inc. (UTI) in Springfield, Illinois.

1987: UTI establishes United Income Inc. (UII) in Ohio.

1990: UTI's stock lists on the NASDAQ.

1998: Kentucky-based First Southern Funding LLC acquires almost 930,000 shares of UTI's common stock.

1999: UII merges into UTI, resulting in a new entity named United Trust Group Inc.

2005: United Trust Group Inc. reincorporates in Delaware and adopts the abbreviated name UTG.

LATE-DECADE LEADERSHIP CHANGES

Two noteworthy things happened in August 1997. At that time, one of UTI's founding members, Thomas Morrow, announced his retirement from the company. In addition, six of UTI's top managers agreed to invest $2.6 million into the company as part of an effort to prepare it for future acquisition activities. At the time, Larry Ryherd was serving as chairman and CEO of both UTI and UII. A high-level leadership change unfolded in November 1997, at which time James Melville was named UTI's president and chief operating officer. Additionally, George Francis was appointed executive vice-president, chief administrative officer, and secretary for all UTI companies.

In November 1998, Kentucky-based First Southern Funding LLC (FSF) acquired almost 930,000 shares of UTI's common stock. As part of the deal, UTI received nearly $11 million, and some of its shareholders received almost $1 million in cash. This marked the beginning of Jesse T. Correll's involvement with the company. Correll held a majority ownership stake in FSF and the holding company First Southern Bancorp Inc., which owned First Southern National Bank.

The FSF deal, which allowed Correll to become UTG's leading shareholder, benefited UTG in a number of ways. In addition to allowing the company to reduce its debt, UTG put itself in a better position to grow through acquisitions. Additionally, legislation that removed barriers between banks and insurance and insurance companies gave each company an opportunity to cross-sell services to the other's customers.

Key changes were made to UTI's corporate structure in July 1999. At that time the company's UII subsidiary—which in turn owned the United Trust Group Inc. business formed in February 1992—merged into UTI, resulting in a new entity named United Trust Group Inc. (UTG). At this time, the United Trust Group Inc. entity formed in 1992 was dissolved, and the new UTG began trading on the NASDAQ under the symbol UTGIV. Another change followed five months later, when UTG's wholly owned life insurance subsidiary, UG, absorbed its United Security Assurance Co. business, leaving only UG.

GROWING INTO THE NEW MILLENNIUM: 2000–08

UTG began the new millennium on solid footing. Through an intrastate public offering of its securities, the company planned to raise approximately $12 million through 2001. Over the next several years, UTG and its numerous subsidiaries were engaged in a number of deals, some of which fell outside the insurance realm. For example, the company's UG business formed a subsidiary named Hampshire Plaza LLC in September 2001 in order to acquire a 254,000-square-foot office tower in Manchester, New Hampshire, that was connected to a 72,000-square-foot retail plaza and a parking garage.

Midway through 2002, UTG established a business process outsourcing alliance with Fiserv Inc.'s Fiserv Life Insurance Solutions unit. Over the years, UTG had gained experience administering policies for the nearly 40 different companies it had acquired. At the time of its connection with Fiserv Life Insurance Solutions, UTG was administering approximately 500,000 insurance policies. The deal allowed the company to provide similar administrative services to other firms on an outsourced basis. More specifically, UTG would provide these services using a Fiserv software system named ID3.

In November 2003, UTG formed another subsidiary named HP Garage LLC, which acquired a 580-space parking garage, which also was located in New Hampshire. By 2005 UTG also had established a business named North Plaza, which had several real estate holdings in Kentucky, including a shopping center in the town of Somerset and some 14,000 acres of timberland.

Jesse Correll had been named as UTG's chairman and CEO by the middle of the first decade of the 2000s. The company executed a reincorporation merger in July 2005, at which time UTG changed its state of incorporation to Delaware. At this time, United Trust

Group also adopted the abbreviated UTG as its formal name.

UTG and its subsidiaries employed a workforce that included about 55 people in 2006. In December of that year, the company furthered its growth by agreeing to acquire a controlling stake in Acap Corp. Valued at approximately $14.5 million, the deal resulted in the addition of 200,000 additional policies, $160 million in assets, and two new life insurance subsidiaries.

During the later years of the first decade of the 2000s UTG's workforce included nearly 75 people. Chairman and CEO Jesse Correll and the companies under his control remained UTG's largest shareholder. Correll continued to hold a majority stake in Kentucky-based FSF, as well as the financial services holding company First Southern Bancorp Inc., which conducted business via a subsidiary named First Southern National Bank. Either directly or through these companies, Correll's stake in UTG stood at 68 percent in late 2007.

By the latter part of 2008, UTG had grown considerably in size. Its corporate family had grown to include roughly 50 organizations. UTG looked forward to celebrating its 25th anniversary in 2009. Based upon its performance in the last quarter century, the company's prospects for continued growth and development seemed promising.

Paul R. Greenland

PRINCIPAL SUBSIDIARIES

ACAP Corporation; American Capitol Insurance Company; Cumberland Woodlands LLC; Hampshire Plaza Garage LLC; Hampshire Plaza LLC; North Plaza of Somerset; Roosevelt Equity Corporation; Stanford Wilderness Road LLC; Universal Guaranty Life Insurance Company; UTAG Inc.

PRINCIPAL COMPETITORS

Massachusetts Mutual Life Insurance Company; MetLife Inc.; Prudential Financial Inc.

FURTHER READING

Landis, Tim, "Employee Friendly. Designing Offices So They Will Carry the Workload," *State Journal-Register*, February 2, 1997.

McDermott, Kevin, "Experts Say Insurance Companies Won't Have S&L-Style Crisis," *State Journal-Register*, January 26, 1992.

Randle, Wilma, "U.S. Insurers' Financial Health Rises, S&P Says," *Chicago Tribune*, November 19, 1992.

"United Trust Closes Deal on Commonwealth Takeover," *State Journal-Register*, June 17, 1992.

"United Trust Group Teams with Fiserv Life Insurance Solutions to Supply Business Process Outsourcing Services," *Business Wire*, June 10, 2002.

Vinmonopolet A/S

P.O. Box 1944-Vika
Dronning Mauds gate 1
Oslo, N-0125
Norway
Telephone: (47) 22 33 45 60
Fax: (47) 22 01 50 09
Web site: http://www.vinmonopolet.no

State-Owned Company
Incorporated: 1922
Employees: 1,787
Sales: NOK 12.16 billion ($1.79 billion) (2007)
NAICS: 445310 Beer, Wine, and Liquor Stores

■ ■ ■

Vinmonopolet A/S holds the monopoly on retail alcoholic beverages in Norway. A state-owned company, Vinmonopolet plays a central role in the Norwegian government's efforts to limit the consumption of alcohol in the country by reducing access to purchases of wine, spirits, and beer with an alcohol content greater than 4.7 percent. The government further places heavy taxes and tariffs on alcoholic beverages, which raise prices of individual bottles to as much as three times those of other European countries. Vinmonopolet stores, which vary greatly in size according to their location, also have limited business hours. Vinmonopolet's methods appear to be successful, as Norway's average consumption levels remain the lowest in Europe. The largest Vinmonopolet stores carry what the company calls its "full assortment" of 1,440 beverages, representing 690 producers. The

group's smallest shops, called branches, offer only 150 of the most popular drinks. The company's full catalog features more than 10,600 different products, which can be ordered through the company's retail stores and from its web site. Vinmonopolet's retail monopoly gives it control of approximately 85 percent of all legal Norwegian alcoholic beverage sales. Arcus, formerly part of Vinmonopolet, remains its largest supplier. Kai G. Henriksen is the company chief executive officer. In 2007, the company's sales topped NOK 12 billion ($1.7 billion).

TEMPERING THE TWENTIES

Among the many consequences of the Industrial Revolution was a rapid increase in alcohol consumption during the 19th century. The urbanization of the population and the appearance of an urban working class were matched with new large-scale production techniques at the nation's distilleries. The growing availability of alcoholic beverages, especially spirits, led to dramatic increases in their consumption. By the 1840s, the average Norwegian consumed about 13 liters of hard alcohol per adult each year.

The social consequences of excessive alcohol consumption and its impact on the population's health stimulated the rise of a temperance movement in Norway. The idea of limiting access to alcohol became a central feature of the movement. By the early 1870s the first locally licensed shops had begun to appear. The first of these was opened in Kristiansand in 1871. While privately owned, these wine and spirits shops were placed under control of the local authorities, which used the profits from their sales for the public welfare. The limited transportation methods available at the time gave the shops an effective monopoly over spirits sales in their local markets.

In the aftermath of World War I there was a new drive by the temperance movement toward a total prohibition of alcoholic beverages. In 1919, the movement succeeded in bringing the matter to a national referendum. More than 61 percent of the population voted in favor of the prohibition of spirits and fortified wine.

Prohibition was not immediately carried out, however. Norway's reliance on its own exports—particularly dried fish, as well as other goods—as its economic backbone threw a wrench into the temperance movement's works. The economic crisis that swept through Norway and the rest of Europe in 1920 further confronted the country's prohibition movement with economic reality. France, in particular, protested the banning of wine in Norway. While the ban on spirits and fortified wine was implemented in 1921, the wine trade received a different treatment.

In trade negotiations, France pushed for an agreement that would allow wine consumption to continue in Norway. France's importance as a trading partner was evidenced by the Norwegian government's accession to its demands and to the French suggestion that the Norwegian government itself take over control of the country's alcoholic beverage distribution. This led to the creation of a new company, Vinmonopolet, in 1922.

Vinmonopolet then took over monopoly control of the distribution of wine in Norway.

GOVERNMENT CONTROL IN THE THIRTIES

Vinmonopolet at first operated as a private limited company, and began establishing its own network of retail shops across Norway. Vinmonopolet also operated at both the wholesale and production levels, importing bulk wine to be packaged for sale. By 1923, the company's mandate was expanded with the repeal of the ban on fortified wines. Three years later, prohibition was phased out altogether, and Vinmonopolet took over the monopoly for spirits sales as well.

A 1930 scandal over the company's purchasing practices brought Vinmonopolet more closely under the control of the Norwegian government. Vinmonopolet's position as the sole outlet for the import and sale of alcoholic beverages in the country had led to abuses. Following a highly publicized trial the government took steps to limit the ability of individuals to affect Vinmonopolet's procurement policies.

In 1931 the government passed new legislation, called the Vinmonopol Act, which transferred the company to direct government oversight under the Health and Social Affairs ministry. The company's board of directors and managing directorship now became government appointees. At the same time, the government began buying out the company's private shareholders. By 1939 the Norwegian government had succeeded in acquiring 100 percent control of Vinmonopolet.

BREAKING UP IN 1996

Vinmonopolet gradually built up a nationally operating chain of retail shops. The stores, which varied in size according the population of their local markets, maintained highly restrictive business hours, generally closing before other retail stores. Sales were largely carried out over the counter. Indeed, self-service operations were introduced into the chain only in the late 1990s. Through Vinmonopolet, the Norwegian government also placed heavy tax and import duties on alcoholic beverages. As a result, Norwegian drinkers were forced to pay prices as much as three times higher than their counterparts in other European countries.

While Vinmonopolet appeared to have succeeded in limiting alcohol consumption in Norway—into the next century the country's per-capita consumption remained the lowest in Europe—the system nonetheless exposed itself to certain abuses. Cross-border purchases became

KEY DATES

1871: The first locally licensed outlet for alcoholic beverage sales is opened in Kristiansand.

1922: Following the enactment of prohibition laws, the Norwegian government creates a wine import and sales monopoly, Vinmonopolet.

1923: Vinmonopolet takes over monopoly for fortified wine sales.

1927: Vinmonopolet acquires monopoly for spirits sales as well, following the final repeal of prohibition in Norway.

1939: The Norwegian government takes over full control of Vinmonopolet, which is placed under the Ministry of Health and Social Affairs.

1996: Vinmonopolet spins off its production and wholesale arm as Arcus to comply with European Union regulations.

1999: Vinmonopolet begins converting its stores to a self-service format.

2002: Vinmonopolet launches its e-commerce web site.

2007: The company begins testing new small-store Filialer format.

frequent as Norwegian drinkers traveled to Sweden and Denmark both to drink and to buy alcoholic beverages. At the same time, the monopoly had also stimulated the growth of a black market for alcoholic beverages, as well as a growth of the number of clandestine distilleries and the consumption of "moonshine."

This situation became particularly troubling beginning in the early 1980s when Vinmonopolet was confronted with a steady decline in its spirits sales. Tax and price reductions on alcoholic products in Sweden and Denmark starting in the 1990s further stimulated this trend. By the early 2000s Vinmonopolet had suffered a decrease of some 50 percent in the volume of spirits sold through its stores. In 2002 the Norwegian government finally responded with a reduction on the tax on spirits. A second tax reduction carried out in 2003 appeared to have finally reversed the downward trend in Vinmonopolet's spirits sales.

By then, Norway's entry into the European Economic Union had had its own major impact on Vinmonopolet's operations. In 1996, in accordance with European Union (EU) rules, the Norwegian government agreed to a breakup of Vinmonopolet. As part of that

process, the company's production and bottling operations wing, as well as its import and wholesaling business, were spun off into a new company, Arcus. The streamlined Vinmonopolet became wholly focused as a retail operation.

Despite the breakup, Vinmonopolet retained its monopoly status as the sole retailer for alcoholic beverages above 4.7 percent in Norway. A series of legal challenges, including a 1997 lawsuit to break up Vinmonopolet's strong beer monopoly, upheld Vinmonopolet's legality under EU law. Another court case, a challenge to the company's monopoly on table wine sales, was similarly decided in Vinmonopolet's favor. A third unsuccessful challenge lobbied against the company's counterpart in Sweden, where alcohol sales were also controlled by the government, again confirmed the legality of Vinmonopolet's monopoly status into the new century.

RETAIL FOCUS IN THE 21ST CENTURY

Nonetheless, Vinmonopolet recognized the importance of adapting and expanding its retail operations. This effort started in the early 1990s, when the company received permission to adopt longer business hours. In 1999 the company rolled out its first self-service stores. By the later years of the first decade of the 2000s the company had converted the entire retail network to the self-service format.

At the same time, Vinmonopolet vastly increased its portfolio. In the early 1990s the group's catalog of wine and spirit brands had previously been limited to just 500 or so. By 2008 the company's catalog had been radically expanded, numbering more than 10,000 brands. An important step in this direction came with the launch of the group's online shop in 2002.

Vinmonopolet also took steps to expand its retail network. The company lobbied the government for permission to open new shops. The company's primary argument was that increasing the proximity of its shops to consumers would help reduce both the purchase and the consumption of illegal alcoholic beverages, and limit the appeal of cross-border trips made solely for the purpose of consuming and buying alcohol. The government agreed, and Vinmonopolet set out a new expansion plan calling for the operation of at least two Vinmonopolet stores per county. By the end of 2007 the company operated 215 stores.

At the same time the company had begun developing a new small store format, called Filialer, or "branches." Featuring a more limited range of just 150 of the company's best-selling labels, the new format enabled Vinmonopolet to achieve greater proximity to smaller rural markets. Testing of the new store format began in 2007, with an initial evaluation of the format slated for 2009. By then the company expected to have expanded its overall store network to nearly 250 stores.

MONOPOLY CONCERNS

Vinmonopolet came under increasing market pressure in the 1990s, as more Norwegians began to demand a liberalization of the government's alcohol distribution policies. Consumer polls in the early 2000s indicated that as many as two-thirds of the population favored the sale of wine in the country's grocery stores. The sentiment also found favor among a number of the country's political parties as well.

A new scandal also threatened Vinmonopolet's legitimacy in the middle of the first decade of the 2000s. In 2005, 15 of the company's employees were charged with having accepted gifts from one of the company's major wine suppliers. The investigation then focused on then-CEO Knut Groenholt, who, although not implicated in the influence-peddling scandal, was charged with illegally reading employee e-mail. Groenholt was forced to step down. In his place was named Kai Henriksen.

Throughout the decade Vinmonopolet continued in its quest to adapt to the new retail climate. The company continued to loosen its business hours, allow-ing stores to remain open later in some markets. In 2008 the company also announced that it would begin allowing purchases with credit cards, ostensibly as a convenience to foreign tourists. The move was nonetheless criticized by the temperance movement, which remained highly active in Norway. Vinmonopolet continued to play a central role in limiting Norway's access to alcoholic beverages, a role it referred to as its social responsibility in contributing the health and social welfare of the country.

M. L. Cohen

FURTHER READING

Gurubacharya, Binaj, "Norwegian State Liquor Monopoly Names New Head After Scandals, Police Probe," *America's Intelligence Wire,* April 21, 2006.

"Norway Relaxes Sale on Liquor, Allows Use of Credit Card," *Philippines News Agency,* July 21, 2008.

"Norway's Alcohol Monopoly Reports First Sales Increase in Years," *Nordic Business Report,* June 25, 2002.

"Sales up for H1 at Vinmonopolet, June Struggles," *just-drinks. com,* August 1, 2008.

"Vinmonopolet Expansion to Be Delayed?" *Dagens Naeringsliv,* November 25, 2002.

"Vinmonopoly to Launch e-Store in May," *Dagens Naeringsliv,* April 19, 2002.

"Vinmonopolet to Test Self-Service," *Aftenposten,* February 17, 1999, p. 3.

Vizio, Inc.

39 Tesla
Irvine, California 92618
U.S.A.
Telephone: (949) 428-2525
Toll Free: (888) 849-4623
Web site: http://www.vizio.com

Private Company
Incorporated: 2002 as V, Inc.
Employees: 90
Sales: $2.1 billion (2007 est.)
NAICS: 334310 Audio and Video Equipment Manufacturing

■ ■ ■

Vizio, Inc., is a privately owned manufacturer of flat-panel, high-definition televisions (HDTVs), based in Irvine, California. The company has quickly become one of the top-selling HDTV makers in the United States by running an extremely lean organization, with many employees charged with additional duties. Founder William Wang, for example, is both chief executive officer and chief technology officer. Vizio also contracts out manufacturing, relying on high-quality components produced by others but assembled according to the company's designs. A key partner is Taiwan-based contract manufacturer AmTran Technology Co., which holds a stake in Vizio and therefore gives Vizio preferential treatment, such as pressuring component suppliers to make sure what they provide is on time and

of high quality. Additional manufacturing is done in Mexico.

Other tasks, including warehousing and shipping, are outsourced to professional management companies. A close eye is also kept on cash flow, with the focus on just-in-time inventory. The resulting liquid crystal display (LCD) and plasma sets are able to provide the important features consumers want with prices significantly lower than the competition. Another key to success is the retail partners who carry the televisions. Vizio avoids chains that impose high markups in favor of warehouse clubs and other high volume retailers who keep prices down. They include Wal-Mart, Wal-Mart's Sam's Club Division, BJ's Wholesale Club, Costco, Dell, Target, and Sears. Many of the models are carried on an exclusive basis.

EARLY FASCINATION WITH ELECTRONICS

Vizio's founder, William Wang, was born in 1963 in Taiwan, where his father was an executive for a cable and wire manufacturer. The family moved to Hawaii and when he was 14 they relocated to Huntington Beach, California, where he grew up fascinated by electronic gear, an early adapter of beepers and cell phones. After Wang earned an electrical engineering degree at the University of Southern California in 1986, he returned to Taiwan to work for Tatung Co., a maker of computer monitors for IBM. For the next four years he worked in tech support, primarily handling customer calls. Well familiar with the standard IBM monitor, Wang decided that he could build a better product.

Although just 26 years old, he decided to leave Tatung and in 1990 formed a company in the United States called MAG Innovision, backed with $350,000. Of that amount, $150,000 came from his former boss, $150,000 from an Asian shareholder, and the rest from his own savings and money he borrowed from his parents.

Wang's timing proved fortunate. The computer business was enjoying strong growth and MAG Innovision prospered, increasing from a handful of employees to about 400 at the peak. In a matter of just six years, Wang grew sales to $600 million. As he would later do with Vizio, Wang contracted his manufacturing overseas. Later in the 1990s, however, the dynamics of the computer industry changed as PCs became more mainstream and volume production led to falling prices. Instead of being a high-margin industry driven by technology, it became a commodity industry that had to contend with razor-thin margins. Wang's lack of business experience, which had not been a factor during the flush times, became a serious problem. He had not assembled a strong management team and overhead was too high. After massive layoffs did not help, in 1998 Wang sold the business to his manufacturer.

ACCIDENT CHANGES WANG'S LIFE

Wang next tried his hand at several ventures. He started a company called Princeton Graphic Systems, pursued the HDTV business through a research and development unit he set up in Asia, and attempted to make a business out of creating custom-built video panels for slot machines and Internet-enabled HDTVs. These and other ideas did not succeed and by November 2000 Wang found his finances in ruin and his life in shambles. He flew to Taiwan to meet with his creditors to attempt to work out his financial problems. He then flew back to Los Angeles on a Singapore Airlines 747. The captain of the massive jet was told to take off from runway 5-L. By mistake he took runway 5-R, which was under construction. Just as the plane began to lift off, with the nose in the air, it clipped some construction equipment. Fueled up for the transpacific flight, the 747 exploded, the wreckage coming back to earth and skidding down the unfinished runway.

"It was just the front of the plane—the back was gone already," Wang recalled in an *Inc.* interview. "It was like a silent movie. I don't even remember any noise. I assume people were screaming. When the plane stopped moving, I just got out." Other than some carbon monoxide poisoning, Wang was unharmed. Half the flight's passengers and crew, 83 people, perished. During the ordeal, Wang said he thought of two things; the first was his family. "The second thing was that all my headaches were suddenly gone. I was still stuck with all these bad businesses, but I had a better attitude. I mean, at the end of day, we're all going to die, right? So after the plane crash, it took a year or two to clean everything up."

In 2002 Wang noticed an ad for a $10,000 flat-panel TV offered by Philips. He sensed that there must be a market for flat-panel televisions at a price point that was affordable to the average consumer. From his days manufacturing monitors, he knew where in Taiwan to find many of the parts needed to assemble a flat-panel TV, and with a bulk discount he was certain he could produce inexpensive HDTVs. Once again he launched a new business, which he wanted to call "W" after himself. Because the "W" hotel chain had laid claim to the letter, he elected to call the company V, Inc., which was launched in 2002 with $600,000 that Wang raised by mortgaging his house in Newport Beach, California, and borrowing money from family and friends.

His plan to enter the TV market was delayed, however, when the CEO of the Gateway computer company, Ted Waitt, approached him about a job. Gateway had been one of Wang's customers during his days with MAG Innovision, selling the monitors under the Gateway label, and Waitt had been something of a mentor to Wang. Waitt at this time hired Wang to create a television plan for Gateway stores, because in addition to computers, he wanted the stores to carry higher-margin consumer electronics.

V, INC., OFFERS FIRST FLAT-PANEL SETS

Because of the Gateway project, Wang was able to try out some of his ideas for structuring an affordable HDTV company. He helped Gateway introduce a 42-inch plasma TV priced at $2,999, at the time a

KEY DATES

2002: William Wang launches V, Inc.
2003: First flat panels on market.
2004: AmTran invests in company.
2006: AmTran acquires additional 15 percent share of business.
2007: Company name is changed to Vizio, Inc.
2008: Vizio begins selling in Japan.

significant drop in the price for plasma of this size. The set did well for the Gateway stores, but once Gateway decided to eliminate its retail unit, TVs were dropped, since it was difficult to sell televisions without a retail presence where people could determine the picture quality for themselves. Wang then decided the time had come to produce his own flat panels.

With just two employees, Wang made V, Inc., operational in Fountain Valley, California, and in January 2003 introduced his first flat panels, the "V" line of 32-inch, 42-inch, 46-inch, and 50-inch plasma sets, ranging in price from $2,999.99 to $5,999.99. At the same time, the company introduced a DVD player under the Bravo name. Also that month Wang met with Costco executives to pitch his 46-inch plasma set at the price of $3,800, half the going rate. Costco agreed to stock the set in ten warehouses and by March the flat panels did well enough that they were carried by all 320 of the club's warehouses. All told, Wang sold about 2,000 of his sets but they received poor reviews, leading him to focus on improving quality while continuing to lower prices. It was also in March 2003 that the company unveiled a 46-inch plasma sold under the Vizio brand name. For the year, the company generated $18 million in sales and because of its frugalness was able to turn a profit.

In 2004 V Inc. introduced a line of improved Vizio sets, a new Bravo DVD media player, as well as rear projection televisions using digital light processing technology, and a new premium line of flat panels sold under the Velite name for specialty retailers and custom installers. The company was beginning to gain market share, and Wang was looking for further funding to help grow the business. Instead of venture capitalists, he turned to manufacturers who would then have a vested interest in aiding the company's success, in particular AmTran, one of whose founders was a friend of Wang. AmTran agreed to pay $1 million for an 8 percent stake in V, Inc., and began a strategic partnership. Wang was then able to use this manufacturing relationship to

increase the number of HDTV models he could offer and attract additional retail partners, including Wal-Mart's Sam's Club and BJ's Wholesale Club Inc.

FOCUS ON LCD AND PLASMA TECHNOLOGIES

At the start of 2005, V, Inc., introduced its new product slate. Gone were the Velite line, rear projection sets, and Bravo DVD players. The company at this time focused on its Vizio LCD and plasma flat panels. The company was able to grow sales to more than $400 million in 2005, despite scarce marketing support. Moreover, by doing the bulk of its business in warehouse stores, the company did not have the benefit of sales clerks to tout the Vizio products. Instead, the company redesigned their cardboard boxes, essentially turning them into combination sales pieces and billboards suitable for a warehouse setting.

Business continued to soar in 2006 while Vizio's price points steadily declined. The company was able to offer a 42-inch plasma TV for $1,500, a far cry from the more than $2,000 such sets regularly cost. The ties also deepened with AmTran, which acquired another 15 percent of V, Inc., from the company's chief financial officer who decided to return to Taiwan and wanted to sell his shares in the business. When the year came to a close, V, Inc., posted sales of $959 million and net earnings of $31.5 million.

By the start of 2007 the company changed its name to Vizio, Inc., to take advantage of the growing Vizio brand. Later in the year Vizio emerged as the largest flat-panel TV maker in North America, commanding 12 percent of the market, due in large part to the addition of new retailers, including Wal-Mart Stores, Kmart, Circuit City, and Sears. The company also began to invest in growing brand awareness, in the fall signing football player LaDainian Tomlinson to anchor an ad campaign. When the year came to a close, Vizio had more than doubled sales over 2006, reaching $2.1 billion.

Vizio made news in early 2008 at the annual Las Vegas Consumer Electronics Show when its new line of flat panels included a 32-inch plasma TV at a time when no other company offered a plasma television smaller than 42 inches. It was sold on an exclusive basis by Wal-Mart at around $550, considerably less than a Vizio LCD HDTV of the same size. Plasma sets were generally considered to offer the highest picture quality, and unlike LCD sets did not experience blurring during sporting events and fast-action movie sequences; however, they suffered from a reputation for image retention and burn-in (shadow images and uneven pixels), problems that by this time were no longer as serious as they once had been. Later in 2008 Vizio introduced an affordable LCD set with a 120HZ refresh rate and a "Smooth Motion" chip to address the blurring issue for LCD sets.

Vizio had made its mark in the United States, and in 2008 the company began turning its attention to international sales. In August Vizio began offering a 42-inch LCD TV in Costco stores in Japan. Later in the year the company began selling sets in Canada. By 2010 Vizio hoped to be doing business in China and Europe. While Vizio's rise to the top ranks of the flat-panel industry was swift, whether it would be able to maintain a crucial price difference to remain competitive with its much larger rivals remained to be seen.

Ed Dinger

PRINCIPAL COMPETITORS

LG Group; Samsung Electronics Co., Ltd.; Sony Corporation.

FURTHER READING

Chuang, Tamara, "Vizio Sales Strategy Is Highly Defined," *Orange County Register,* October 3, 2006.

Gentile, Gary, "Upstart Maker Tops in Flat-Panel TVs," *Seattle Times,* September 10, 2007, p. E1.

Kessler, Michelle, "Flat-Panel TV World Crowns Unexpected New King," *USA Today,* August 21, 2007, p. 3B.

Lawton, Christopher, Yukari Iwatani Kane, and Jason Dean, "Picture Shift: U.S. Upstart Takes on TV Giants in Price Waw," *Wall Street Journal,* April 15, 2008, p. A1.

Nuttall, Chris, "Vizio Eclipses Bigger Rivals in LCD TV Sales," *Financial Times,* November 23, 2007, p. 20.

Pham, Alex, "Focusing on the Big Picture Gives Vizio Edge in TV Market," *Los Angeles Times,* October 13, 2007.

Tan, Jason, "Big Inroads Made by TV Brand Vizio," *International Herald Tribune,* October 7, 2008, p. 16.

Wang, William, and Mark Lacter, "Talk About New Beginnings: How I Did It," *Inc.,* June 2007, p. 106.

Wang, William, and Ryan McCarthy, "William Wang, Vizio: 'I've Loved Cool Electronics Gear Since I Was a Kid,'" *Inc.,* September 2008, p. 102.

Wärtsilä Corporation

———— ■ ————

PO Box 196, John Stenbergin ranta 2
Helsinki, FI-00531
Finland
Telephone: (358 10) 709 0000
Fax: (358 10) 709 5700
Web site: http://www.wärtsilä.com

Public Company
Incorporated: 1834
Employees: 17,000
Sales: EUR 3.76 billion ($5 billion) (2007)
Stock Exchanges: Nordic Helsinki
Ticker Symbol: WRTAV
NAICS: 333611 Turbine and Turbine Generator Set
Unit Manufacturing; 333618 Other Engine Equipment Manufacturing

■ ■ ■

Wärtsilä Corporation is a global leader in the marine power and power generation sectors. The company, formerly a diversified conglomerate with operations ranging from shipbuilding to tableware and other home furnishings, has been restructured in the 21st century to focus on three core divisions. The company's Ship Power division produces engines, propulsion equipment, power distribution systems, sealing systems and related components, and equipment to the global marine industry. The company claims to have placed its engines and equipment on more than one-third of the total global fleet. The Ship Power division contributed 35 percent to Wärtsilä's total revenues of EUR 3.76 billion ($5 billion) in 2007.

The company's Power Plant division, which accounted for 24 percent of group turnover, is one of the world's leading providers of flexible power plants for niche applications, such as islands and other remote environments. This division is also investing heavily in renewable energy and other environmentally friendly power generation systems. The company's largest division is its Services division, which produced 44 percent of total revenues in 2007. The Services division operates offices, workshops, and other service centers in more than 150 locations in 70 countries worldwide. Wärtsilä is listed on the Nordic Helsinki Stock Exchange and is led by CEO Ole Johansson.

FOUNDED AS A SAWMILL IN 1834

Wärtsilä Corporation originated as a small sawmill placed alongside rapids in Tohmajärvi, Finland, in 1834. By 1851, the site had been expanded to include an iron mill as well. The company, which became known as Wärtsilä in 1898, came to own the rapids outright. With this virtually unlimited resource, the company built its own electrical power plant in 1908. This allowed the company to extend its operations to include a smelter and steel mill.

By 1930, Wärtsilä had launched the production of finished steel products, notably galvanized wire. The company was nonetheless hard hit by the Great Depression, and by 1931 had nearly gone bankrupt. Under the direction of Wilhelm Wahlforss, president of the company since 1926, Wärtsilä soon returned to health.

Part of the group's renewed vitality came from its decision to diversify its operations in the 1930s. Over the next decade, Wärtsilä began to emerge as one of Finland's major conglomerates.

The company added new industrial operations, taking control of Kone-ja Siltarakennus (Machine and Bridge Construction) in 1935. In this way, the company added production of machinery for the paper industry. The purchase also gave the company control of Abloy, later to become the world's largest producer of locks. The Kone-ja Siltarakennus acquisition also gave the company another important operational area, shipbuilding, with two shipyards, Hietalahti in Helsinki and Crichton-Vulcan in Turku. Both shipyards were significant players in Finland's armament buildup in the period between the two world wars. The Crichton-Vulcan yard was dedicated to the construction of Germany's secret submarine fleet during the 1930s.

The larger Wärtsilä group then moved its headquarters to Helsinki. Soon after the Kone-ja Siltarakennus purchase, Wärtsilä expanded its industrial base again, buying new engineering plants in Vaasa and in Pietarsaari, both in 1936. Two years later, the company acquired full control of Kone-ja Siltarakennus, which was then merged into Wärtsilä itself. At that time, the company also bought a iron mill in Taalintehdas. The company then restructured, placing all of its operations under the newly established holding company, Wärtsilä Yhtyma (Wärtsilä Group).

Finland's close relationship with Germany permitted another important extension to Wärtsilä's operations, just prior to the outbreak of World War II. In 1938, the company acquired the license to produce diesel ship engines, in a partnership with Germany's Friedrich Krupp Germaniawerft. The company launched construction of its engine plant in Turku in 1939. The outbreak of World War II, and Finland's war with the Soviet Union, slowed down the group's efforts to launch diesel production. It was only in 1942, after the Soviet retreat from Finland, that the company succeeded in producing its first diesel-powered ship engine. In the

end, the company built only two of the Krupp engines. However, Wärtsilä continued to develop its own engine designs. That activity was to become the company's major focus into the next century.

DIVERSIFICATION AND INTERNATIONAL EXPANSION

The need to redirect its industrial operations to nonmilitary sectors in the postwar period led Wärtsilä to further diversification. The company entered the construction and home furnishings market in 1947, when it took over Arabia AB, a manufacturer of ceramic sanitary ware. The company added glass production three years later, with the takeover of a factory in Nuutajärvi.

Through the 1970s, Wärtsilä invested in expanding its production facilities for its diverse operations. In 1968, for example, the company opened a new factory for its Abloy lock production in Joensuun. Two years later, the group built a new factory for its paper machinery production, in Järvenpää. In 1971, the company opened a new sanitary ware plant in Tammisaari. Wärtsilä's shipbuilding division also benefited from the group's expansion, with the opening of a new shipyard in Perno, Turku. By 1983, the new shipyard had taken over all of the group's shipbuilding operations in Turku.

The company also boosted its engineering component, buying the John Stenberg company and its facilities in 1975. The company transferred its headquarters to a new site, acquired during the Stenberg purchase, in Helsinki in 1978. That year also marked Wärtsilä's first move into the international market, when it acquired a majority stake in NOHAB, a diesel engine manufacturer based in Sweden. The company took full control of NOHAB in 1984. The company's lock business also grew during this period, notably through the acquisition of a factory in Björkboda.

Wärtsilä restructured its diversified businesses into six main divisions in 1979. These included shipbuilding, mechanical engineering, sanitary ware, locks, consumer goods, and diesel engines. Wärtsilä then went public, listing its shares on the Stockholm Exchange in 1983. The following year, the company listed its shares on the London Stock Exchange as well, becoming the first Finnish company to do so.

The public offering led the group to further international expansion. In 1986, the company established operations in the United States, buying the Industrial Systems division of GCA Corporation that year. The company purchased a second factory automation producer that year as well, Finland-based W.

KEY DATES

1834: The company originates as a sawmill in Tohmajärvi, Finland.

1851: The company adds an iron mill to its operations.

1898: The company becomes Wärtsilä, begins steel production and electricity generation.

1935: Wärtsilä moves to Helsinki and acquires Kone-ja Siltarakennus, adding shipyards.

1947: The company enters the construction and home furnishings market.

1983: Wärtsilä goes public with a listing on the Stockholm stock exchange.

1986: Wärtsilä acquires shipbuilding operations of Valmet (later Metso), which is merged into new subsidiary, Wärtsilä Marine.

1989: Wärtsilä Marine goes bankrupt.

1990: Wärtsilä merges with Lohja, creating Metra.

1997: Metra merges its marine engines division with those of Fincantieri, creating Wärtsilä NSD.

2000: Metra completes its restructuring around core marine engines operations, and renames itself Wärtsilä.

2002: Wärtsilä acquires marine propulsion group John Crane Lips.

2005: Wärtsilä acquires DEUTZ AG as part of buildup of its services division.

2008: Wärtsilä continues its acquisition drive with purchase of Vik-Sandvik in Norway.

Rosenlew. Both companies were then placed in a new subsidiary, Wärtsilä Cimtec. Elsewhere, Wärtsilä moved into India, opening a diesel engine factory in Khopoli in 1988.

THE METRA ERA

Into the mid-1980s, Wärtsilä's shipbuilding division suffered from the shift of the industry away from traditional centers in the West to the fast-growing Asian markets. The rising competition forced Wärtsilä to seek a new partner, and in 1986 the company reached an agreement with Finnish rival, the state-owned industrial group Valmet (later Metso). Under the agreement, Wärtsilä transferred its paper machinery production to Valmet, taking a minority stake in Valmet Paper Machines Ltd. Wärtsilä then took over Valmet's shipbuilding division, including the Vuosaari shipyard,

built in 1974. Wärtsilä then merged all of its shipbuilding operations into a new company, Wärtsilä Marine.

Soon after the merger, Wärtsilä shut down the Vuosaari yard, transferring its operations to its own shipyards. However, this effort was not enough to reverse the company's declining profits. By 1989, Wärtsilä Marine had been forced into bankruptcy. The collapse of its shipbuilding operations led Wärtsilä to seek a new partner for survival into the recessionary years of the early 1990s. In 1990, Wärtsilä agreed to merge with another Finnish conglomerate, Lohja. The new company, called Metra, focused especially on the diesel engine and construction materials sectors.

By this time, the company's diesel engine division had been boosted by two important acquisitions. The first was of France's SACM, based in Marseille, acquired in 1989. This purchase added production of high-speed engines to the company's marine engines unit. Next, the company moved into the Netherlands, buying a majority stake in Stock Werkspoor, which produced medium-speed engines.

The creation of Metra led to a new restructuring of the group's holdings. The company exited the paper machinery sector, selling its 35 percent stake in Valmet Paper Machines. The company also sold its power generation plants in the Karelia region, and spun off its steel production holdings into Imatra Steel. The restructuring continued with the disposal of the group's building materials operations in 1994. In that year also the company began its exit from the locks sector, merging its Abloy division with the Lock Division of Sweden's Securitas. By the end of that year, the company's stake in the newly created Assa Abloy had been reduced to less than 50 percent.

The Metra era proved short-lived, however. The movement toward the breakup of Metra began in 1996, when the company reached an agreement to merge its diesel engine operations with those of Italy's Fincantieri. The merger was completed in 1997, creating a new company, Wärtsilä NSD. The new company also held a 40 percent stake in another Italian company, Grandi Motori Trieste, which remained majority controlled by Fincantieri.

The breakup of Metra was initially planned for 1998. Poor economic conditions forced the company to postpone that operation. In 1999, however, the first step was taken with the spinoff of the group's ceramics operations as the publicly listed Sanitec. The company later completed the disposal of all of its shares in that company. Next, the group began selling off its remaining shares in Assa Abloy, a process completed by the early years of the new century.

REFOCUSING IN THE 21ST CENTURY

By 2000, the breakup and reorientation of Metra had been completed. Refocused around its engines division, the company was renamed as Wärtsilä that year. By then, the company had also taken full control of Grandi Motori Trieste, as well its operations in the Netherlands.

For its entry into the new century, Wärtsilä sought to reorganize itself around a core of marine engines and propulsion systems on the one hand, and power generation on the other, as well as building a strong services component for both. The company took a major step toward achieving this goal in 2002 with the acquisition of John Crane-Lips, a specialist in marine propulsion systems. The following year, the company boosted its services division, with the purchase of Caltax Marine Diesel, based in the Netherlands. In that year also the company took its first steps into the Chinese market, launching a propeller manufacturing joint venture. The company increased its Chinese presence again in 2005, with the launch of a wholly owned production subsidiary in Wuxi.

Wärtsilä launched an ambitious expansion program beginning around 2005. Acquisitions formed a major part of the company's growth strategy, starting with DEUTZ AG, a marine engine service specialist acquired in 2005 for EUR 115 million. The company also boosted its ship design capacity, with the purchase of Germany's Schiffko in 2006. The following year, the company completed a string of acquisitions, including Marine Propeller (Pty) Ltd. in South Africa; Senitec AB, in Sweden; McCall Propellers, the marine operations of Railko, and Electrical Power Engineering (Scotland), all in the United Kingdom.

By 2008, Wärtsilä had added several more acquisitions. The group added Maritime Service, in Norway, followed by International Combustion Engineering, in Denmark, and Claus D. Christopher Mess- und Regeltechnik, in Germany. The group also boosted its ship design operations, adding Norway's Vik-Sandvik in 2008. These acquisitions not only helped the group establish itself as a world-leading marine engines and systems producer, but also as a leading power plant player specialized in niche markets, especially remote locations, such as islands, offshore platforms, and extreme environments. At the same time Wärtsilä had become a major services provider to the marine and other markets, with operations spanning more than 70 countries. These included Azerbaijan and Dubai, where the company opened new offices in 2008.

Wärtsilä, which began as a small sawmill, was well positioned as a global player in the new century.

M. L. Cohen

PRINCIPAL SUBSIDIARIES

Deep Sea Seals Ltd. (United Kingdom); Electrical Power Engineering Ltd. (United Kingdom); McCall Propellers Ltd. (United Kingdom); SCHIFFKO GmbH (Germany); Wärtsilä Oy; Wärtsilä (China) Ltd. Hong Kong; Wärtsilä (France) S.A.S.; Wärtsilä (Norway) A/S; Wärtsilä (Sweden) AB; Wärtsilä (Switzerland) Ltd.; Wärtsilä Australia Pty Ltd.; Wärtsilä Biopower Oy; Wärtsilä Canada Inc.; Wärtsilä Danmark A/S (Denmark); Wärtsilä Defence S.A.S. (France); Wärtsilä Deutschland GmbH (Germany); Wärtsilä do Brasil Ltda.; Wärtsilä Engine (Shanghai) Co. Ltd. (China); Wärtsilä Ibérica S.A. (Spain); Wärtsilä India Ltd. (98.2%); Wärtsilä Italia S.p.A. (Italy); Wärtsilä Japan Company Ltd. (99.7%); Wärtsilä Korea Ltd. (South Korea); Wärtsilä Lips Inc. (United States); Wärtsilä Nederland B.V.; Wärtsilä North America, Inc.; Wärtsilä Operations, Inc. (United States); Wärtsilä Propulsion (Wuxi) Co. Ltd. (China); Wärtsilä Propulsion Netherlands B.V.; Wärtsilä Shanghai Services Ltd. (China); Wärtsilä Technology Oy Ab; Wärtsilä UK Ltd.; Wärtsilä Vostok LLC Russia; Wärtsilä-CME Zhenjiang Propeller Co. Ltd. (China; 55%); Whessoe S.A. (France).

PRINCIPAL COMPETITORS

China Aviation Industry Corporation; General Electric Co. Power Systems; Siemens AG; Finmeccanica S.p.A.; Liebherr International AG; MAN AG; Harbin Steam Turbine Factory Company Ltd.; Mitsui Engineering and Shipbuilding Company Ltd.; Fincantieri-Cantieri Navali Italiani S.p.A.

FURTHER READING

Blum, Ernest, "Wärtsilä Shipbuilders Ride the Crest of Booming Cruise Industry," *Travel Weekly*, October 22, 1987, p. 65.

Brown-Humes, Christopher, and John Kipphoff, "Smiths Offloads Marine Unit for Pounds 215m," *Financial Times*, January 31, 2002, p. 26.

Marsh, Peter, "Wärtsilä Tries to Throttle Up Stock Market Performance," *Financial Times*, June 21, 2001, p. 31.

"Wärtsilä Acquires Deutz Engine Service," *Marine Log*, February 2005, p. 44.

"Wärtsilä Acquires Green Tech Firm," *Power Engineering International*, March 2007, p. 14.

"Wärtsilä Corp. Has Completed a Deal to Acquire CGL Industries Ltd.," *Workboat,* December 2002, p. 172.

"Wärtsilä Expands into Biopower," *Modern Power Systems,* December 2001, p. 5.

"Wärtsilä Fuel Cell Prototype Starts Up," *Modern Power Systems,* December 2007, p. 55.

"Wärtsilä Makes Its Mark," *Power Engineering International,* September 2003, p. 69.

"Wärtsilä Opens New Office and Workshop in Baku," *AZR-State Telegraph Agency of the Republic of Azerbaijan,* June 6, 2008.

"Wärtsilä Opens Workshop in Dubai to Serve Gulf," *Power Engineering International,* May 2008, p. 197.

"Wärtsilä Shifts Core Focus," *Power Engineering International,* October 2003, p. 15.

"Wärtsilä to Buy Swedish Dinnerware Firm," *Retailing Home Furnishings,* *October 3, 1983, p. 26.

WAXIE Sanitary Supply

———————■———————

9353 Waxie Way
San Diego, California 92123-1036
U.S.A.
Telephone: (858) 292-8111
Toll Free: (800) 544-8054
Fax: (858) 279-6311
Web site: http://www.waxie.com

Private Company
Incorporated: 1954 as WAXIE's Enterprises Inc.
Employees: 800
Sales: $2.52 billion (2007 est.)
NAICS: 424690 Other Chemical and Allied Products
   Merchant Wholesalers

■ ■ ■

WAXIE Sanitary Supply, a private company, is the largest family-owned distributor of sanitary maintenance supplies in the United States. The company distributes cleaning and maintenance supplies and equipment through the Southwest and Pacific Northwest. While the company does not publicize its annual sales figures, company executives estimate that each year WAXIE provides enough toilet paper to go around the world 54 times; enough paper toilet seat covers for every man, woman, and child in the United States; and ten million pounds of plastic garbage-can liners. The company's Inventory Centers serve Alaska, California, Arizona, Nevada, Utah, Idaho, Oregon, Washington, and Colorado. WAXIE provides over 4,500 items, including chemicals, consumables, equipment, and accessories. Its

customers are found in industries such as healthcare, commercial, foodservice, military, contract cleaners, hospitality, education, industrial, and retail. Some of its prominent clients include the University of California, San Diego; San Diego Gas & Electric; the Jet Propulsion Laboratory in Pasadena, California; and Sharp Memorial Hospital.

A FAMILY BUSINESS

A family business from the start, WAXIE Sanitary Supply is named for its founders, brothers Harry and Morris Wax. Originally from Utah, where they grew up in one of the first rural homes in the area to have running water and electricity, the Wax brothers founded their company after completing military service in the 1940s. Harry Wax worked as a bookkeeper before joining the Navy in 1941. He worked with the Seabees, the Navy's construction force, before he was discharged in San Diego. In 1945, he purchased San Diego Janitor Supply and Chemical Company, a small business that would eventually grow to become WAXIE Sanitary Supply. Sales were $50,000 in the first year of the company's operation, according to the April 30, 1994, *San Diego Union-Tribune.*

A year later, Harry Wax was joined by his brother, Morris, who had been stationed with the U.S. Army tank corps for three years in France and Germany. "The company had very little business," remembered Morris Wax in a company publication, "a handful of employees, and one truck with no low gear and a four-foot truck bed!" Stressing customer service from the start, Morris would often take evening orders at home and go out to

COMPANY PERSPECTIVES

It is the mission of WAXIE Sanitary Supply to be the industry leader in the distribution of quality sanitary and related supplies and equipment to the commercial, industrial, contractor and institutional markets in the areas we serve. We will strive to provide quality and innovative products, value-added services, and systems that contribute toward a better community through effective communication, education, and training for our valued customers and employees. We have a sound set of values on which we base all of our policies and actions: respect, customer service, excellence, growth and possibilities, customers, and people. The most important factors in our success are faith in and obedience to these values.

deliver supplies that same night. The immediate post–World War II period proved difficult for an emerging cleaning supplies company. Paper products were scarce, so the company supplemented its income by selling brooms, mops, floor wax, and cleaning solutions.

The company began a process of steady growth during San Diego's postwar boom. In 1948, having run out of space for its operations, it relocated to a building occupying the entire block of 10th Avenue and B Street in downtown San Diego. In 1954, the company was incorporated with the name WAXIE's Enterprises. By 1957, the company had outgrown its space again, and it moved to a larger 15,000-square-foot facility at 1st and G streets in downtown San Diego. During the 1950s and 1960s, the company operated five delivery trucks, each serving one of five San Diego regions. In 1962, the company expanded its service area to include all of Southern California when it acquired the Kleen-Line Corporation, with warehouses in Santa Ana and San Bernardino.

THE NEXT GENERATION OF THE WAX FAMILY

In 1971, founder Harry Wax's retirement marked the end of an era. Seven years later, Harry Wax died. After Harry Wax's death, leadership of the Wax family business stayed in the family, and the torch was passed to the younger generation. Morris Wax's oldest son, Charles, had started working with the company in the 1960s at the age of 12, sweeping floors and stacking products in the warehouse. In 1973, after graduating

from San Diego State University with a bachelor's degree in accounting, Charles Wax went to work for the company as a full-time employee. By 1986, he had moved up the ranks to become president of the company, overseeing all operations. Charles Wax's brother, David Wax, who also grew up working in the family business, became executive vice-president. In an amicable division of labor, Charles handled administration while David oversaw sales and marketing. In 1995, Charles's 17-year-old daughter, Amy, began working in the company's administrative offices, while Morris Wax remained with the company as chairman of the board.

From the 1970s until the economic recession of the early 1990s, the company grew and expanded at an impressive rate, with an average of 10 percent growth annually. In 1977, the company purchased a new property in San Diego's Kearny Mesa area, and in 1978 the company headquarters relocated to Ruffin Road in that neighborhood. The following year, the company opened new sales offices in Los Angeles and El Centro, California. Moving into the Wax brothers' home turf, WAXIE expanded outside of California to Utah in 1984, when it purchased the Lovinger Company, a sanitary supply distributor based in Salt Lake City. Two years later, the company moved its operations into Phoenix, Arizona, and opened a branch office in Palm Springs, California. Expansion continued with new branches opened in Las Vegas, Nevada, in 1988 and Tucson, Arizona, in 1989.

BECOMING A MAJOR ENTERPRISE

The dawn of the new century saw the company become a major enterprise. In the 1990s, the Kearny Mesa headquarters was transformed when the company purchased an additional 14 acres of land and built the WAXIE Business Park. By 1996, the new headquarters included a 58,000-square-foot addition to the corporate and regional offices plus increased warehouse space, for a total of 110,000 square feet. The striking new headquarters, located at One Waxie Way, featured a white-domed entryway surrounded by glass, leading to a gleaming black granite floor and carpeted mahogany staircase, adjacent to a sparkling clean showroom displaying vacuum cleaners and other cleaning apparatus.

When construction of WAXIE Business Park began in 1994, the company had about 385 employees at 11 branches, with approximately 125 in San Diego. In 1996, WAXIE's employee count had grown to 475, and it distributed about 3,000 products to 20,000 customers in the southwestern United States. In 1997, the company added Northern California to its service area

KEY DATES

1945: Harry Wax purchases San Diego Janitor Supply and Chemical Company.

1946: Morris Wax joins his brother in the business.

1948: Company relocates to larger space at 10th Avenue and B Street in downtown San Diego.

1954: WAXIE's Enterprises is incorporated.

1957: Company moves to larger facility at 1st and G streets in downtown San Diego.

1971: Harry Wax retires.

1978: Company headquarters relocated to Kearny Mesa; Harry Wax dies.

1986: Charles Wax becomes company president; company moves into Phoenix, Arizona, and opens a branch office in Palm Springs, California.

1996: WAXIE Business Park opens 58,000-square-foot addition plus warehouse space.

2006: Company moves into Pacific Northwest, opening facility in Portland, Oregon.

2008: Company acquires Asplund Supply, Inc., with locations in Washington and Alaska.

with a new office in San Francisco. The company continued to grow and expand its service areas through acquisitions, purchasing Airkem Intermountain in 1995 (with Airkem henceforth operating under WAXIE's name); Central Valley Sanitary Supply in Bakersfield, California, in 1997; Midwest Chemical & Supply in Denver, Colorado, in 2007; and Asplund Supply, Inc., in Washington State and Alaska in 2008. Between 1998 and 2003, the company built new facilities in Salt Lake City, Utah; San Francisco, California; and Ontario, California. Between 2000 and 2006, the company expanded to serve new market areas in Denver, Colorado; St. George, Utah; Boise, Idaho; Idaho Falls, Idaho; and Portland, Oregon. The Oregon facility served both northern Oregon and Washington.

Amid such rapid growth and expansion were some difficult times. In 1993, due to the economic recession, the company had what President Charles Wax described in the April 30, 1994, *San Diego Union-Tribune* as its toughest year ever. Still, cutbacks in maintenance enabled the company to end the year with a 5 percent increase in gross sales (compared to 10 percent in all other preceding years). The following year, the company set its sights on growth through its entry into the Mexican market, catalyzed by the North American Free

Trade Agreement (NAFTA). In 1994, former WAXIE Chief Financial Officer Robert Richards was arrested and charged with embezzling over $200,000 from the company. In a statement quoted in the April 9, 1994, *San Diego Union-Tribune*, company President Charles Wax indicated that the amount embezzled was not significant to the company's operations.

COMPANY STRATEGIES FOR SUCCESS

The competitive janitorial and sanitary supply (jan/san) business encompassed hundreds of firms, ranging from very small to very large. In the 1990s, many of these firms, with WAXIE as a prime example, consolidated forces through mergers and acquisitions, with large companies buying smaller ones to diversity their products and enlarge their forces and service areas. At the same time, small "mom and pop" local jan/san businesses continued to serve a niche market, comprised of local customers who preferred the emphasis on customer service provided by smaller operations. According to Roger Claus of Claus Management Associates (cited in the July 2001 *Sanitary Maintenance*), providing excellent customer service enabled larger companies to penetrate that niche market and stand out in the crowd. In the slow economy of the early years of the 21st century, such special efforts determined which of the companies that emerged from the era of consolidation would survive. In fact, the January 1, 2006, *Maintenance Supplies* described the period as a "critical time for traditional jan/san supply houses" that found themselves needing to either make significant changes or close up shop.

In the area of consolidation, WAXIE and its competitors often acquired large numbers of new products for distribution each year, striving to be a kind of "one-stop shop" to meet client demand. For many conglomerates, this meant that salespeople were less knowledgeable about each product, unless the company intervened to provide value-added services such as education and training for its employees and clients. In fact, according to a January 2006 article in *Maintenance Supplies* magazine, some 10 percent of cleaning industry employees were not properly trained; commission rates per sales dollar had decreased 40 percent since the 1980s; and only about one out of 20 U.S. workers were employed by the cleaning supplies distribution industry, with many of the best salespersons finding greener pastures in fields such as consumer electronics. As a result of these issues, between 1990 and 2002 the number of jan/san distributors decreased by 17,400.

EMPHASIS ON VALUE-ADDED SERVICE

WAXIE set itself apart during this difficult time by providing its clients with value-added service. The company researched new products, proper use and storage of cleaning products containing hazardous chemicals, training requirements, and technology, and it passed along its expertise to clients. This enabled clients to save on labor costs, which accounted for approximately 90 percent of total cleaning expenditures. The company offered seminars and training for its customers, and it accommodated clients with bilingual seminars in English-Spanish and English-Russian. Its drivers carried Class B commercial licenses and were trained in proper procedures in case products containing hazardous chemicals should spill. Acknowledging the significant rise in consciousness about the risks of chemical exposure in the 1990s and after, WAXIE also offered a full line of Green brand cleaning products that protected health and did not harm the environment, and it provided training in environmentally safe cleaning and disposal procedures.

This approach paid off with clients such as the University of California, San Diego (UCSD), where WAXIE became the supplier for 75 percent of cleaning supplies and equipment. UCSD spokesperson John Stevenson noted in the August 10, 1996, *San Diego Union-Tribune,* "We've stayed with WAXIE while other vendors have come and gone. What I like about them is the follow-up. They'll come out any time, day and night, to train our people. They're very service-oriented." WAXIE was a lifeline for San Diego's Sea World amusement park when the park ran out of toilet paper on July 4, 1996. Even though WAXIE was not Sea World's primary supplier of paper products, the company delivered the needed goods—on a Saturday—when WAXIE's business operations were closed. In 2005, this emphasis on service earned WAXIE the Network Services Co. "Servicing Agent of the Year" award.

CONTINUED GROWTH AND SUCCESS

The company also invested in client-friendly technology, such as laptops that enabled salespersons to quickly check the status of products ordered; bar coding that helped clients to track their supply stock; and electronic ordering and billing processes. The company emphasized employee training and productivity, offering incentives such as a 401(k) pension program and December bonuses for all nonsales employees based on annual growth to increase the feeling of team participation. WAXIE employees tended to remain with the company;

in 1995, according to Charles Wax, 44 percent of employees had been with the company for at least five years, and 20 employees had been with the company at least 20 years. By the beginning of the 21st century, when the number of qualified sales representatives in the jan/san business was diminishing, WAXIE's clients could be comforted by the longevity and training provided by the company's staff.

WAXIE's employee count grew from three in 1945 to over 800 in 2008. Since its simple beginnings with just one delivery truck, WAXIE Sanitary's fleet had grown to 110 delivery trucks, tractor trailers, and service vehicles. In 2002, to accommodate the increased need for equitable distribution among delivery trucks, as well as the need to occasionally reconfigure deliveries to accommodate special orders, the company began using ArcLogistics Route software at five distribution hubs. In 2008 plans were under way to almost double the size of the company's Salt Lake Valley, Utah, facility with a new 80,000-square-foot facility to accommodate growth in that region.

In the January 1, 2006, *Maintenance Supplies,* James Alexy, president and CEO of Network Services Co., outlined the formula for survival in the difficult world of sanitary supply distribution. Alexy affirmed the critical need for three skills: efficient product buying, efficient selling (including product knowledge, training, and in-stock supplies), and excellent service. With these three areas under its belt, WAXIE seemed secure in its role as a leading family-owned distributor with an extensive service area and inventory list and a rare and valuable emphasis on customer service and training.

Heidi Feldman

PRINCIPAL SUBSIDIARIES

Asplund Supply, Inc.; Kleen-Line Corporation; Midwest Chemical & Supply.

PRINCIPAL COMPETITORS

National Paper & Sanitary Supply Corporation; Perkins Paper.

FURTHER READING

DiPaolo, Richard, "Changing Time: Where Is the Jan/San Industry?" *Maintenance Supplies,* January 1, 2006.

Harman, Liz, "This Is One S.D. Business that Is Really Cleaning Up," *San Diego Business Journal,* September 11, 1995, p. 1.

Ludorf, Carol, "Waxie Sanitary Supply and Vehicle Routing/Scheduling Software," *Transport Technology Today,* February 2002, p. 19.

Novarro, Leonard, "Waxie—Squeaky Clean for 50 Years," *San Diego Union-Tribune,* August 10, 1996, p. C1.

Nowlan, Joe, "More Than Keeping Things Clean: As the Jan-san Industry Has Expanded, So, Too, Has Waxie Sanitary Supply—And They're Always Looking for a Few Good Drivers," *Industrial Distribution,* October 1, 2006.

Rattle, Barbara, "WAXIE Sanitary Supply to Build New Facility in SLC," *Enterprise,* May 12, 2008.

Riggs, Rod, "Waxie Views NAFTA As Source of Growth," *San Diego Union-Tribune,* April 30, 1994, p. C1.

Sanders, Seiche, "Is Bigger Better?" *Sanitary Maintenance,* July 2001, p. 1.

Steinberg, James, "Businessman Morris Wax Dies," *San Diego Union-Tribune,* December 26, 1996, p. B1.

"Waxie Ex-CFO Charged with Embezzlement," *San Diego Union-Tribune,* April 9, 1994, p. C2.

"Waxie Supply Buys Airkem Intermountain," *Deseret News,* August 8, 1995, p. D8.

Weather Central Inc.

401 Charmany Drive, Suite 200
Madison, Wisconsin 53719
U.S.A.
Telephone: (608) 274-5789
Fax: (608) 278-2746
Web site: http://www.weathercentral.tv

Private Company
Incorporated: 1974
Employees: 165
Sales: $62.8 million (2007)
NAICS: 511210 Software Publishers

■ ■ ■

Headquartered in Madison, Wisconsin, Weather Central Inc. helps people on every continent determine whether they will need an umbrella, a sun hat, or snow boots before venturing outdoors. The company is a leading developer of the systems that television stations, newspapers, and web sites use to communicate weather forecasts, as well as news, sports, and traffic information. Weather Central's solutions are capable of delivering information in both standard and high-definition formats.

Weather Central's diverse employee base allows the company to fully understand the varying needs of its customers. The company's staff has experience in a wide range of areas, and includes meteorologists, computer scientists, broadcast consultants, news anchors, reporters, producers, graphic artists, data consultants, and support specialists. Together, they work to understand how

Weather Central's offerings can best meet the needs of each individual customer.

Over more than three decades, Weather Central has pioneered numerous technological advancements within its industry, and claims to hold more than 30 product, technology, and software patents in the United States and other countries.

FORMATIVE YEARS

Weather Central's origins date back to 1974, when the company was established as a forecasting service by meteorologist Terry Kelly. Kelly's passion for the weather began during his childhood, when one of his hobbies was maintaining backyard weather stations.

As a college undergraduate, Kelly studied English, pre-law, and experimental psychology while attending Harvard University. There, he found student employment as a riveter for Lockheed Martin, where he helped build Piper airplanes. Kelly went on to become a licensed pilot, which furthered his fascination with weather-related details such as cloud formation.

Kelly's growing interest in the weather prompted him to leave Harvard for the University of Wisconsin–Madison, where he studied meteorology and graduated in 1971 with a bachelor of science degree. In time, Kelly became an academic researcher at the university's Space Science Center.

At the University of Wisconsin–Madison, Kelly was involved in the development of cutting-edge forecasting tools that involved graphical concepts. With the support of Madison-based University and Industry Research, he established a program to provide experimental information to utilities, vegetable canners and freezers, and ski hills, which relied on frequent weather updates. When his new program met with success, Kelly spun it off as a private company called Weather Central in 1974. That same year, he accepted a position with the Madison-based television station WKOW as its chief meteorologist. Before long Kelly became bored with the traditional tools of the weather trade, which then involved drawing on boards and using magnetic maps.

In 1979 the desire for something new led Kelly and his university colleague Dr. Richard Daly to establish ColorGraphics Weather Systems Inc., a new business within Weather Central that sought to combine television weather forecasts with computer technology. ColorGraphics developed one of the industry's first computerized weather graphics systems, called LiveLine. ColorGraphics' new system was a major breakthrough because it pioneered the delivery of real-time, animated forecasts to viewers via the use of colorized satellite images. In time, LiveLine's capabilities were expanded to include the animated display of jet streams, radar, and more.

By the early 1980s Weather Central and ColorGraphics had become the leading providers of graphical weather systems for the television broadcasting sector, generating millions of dollars and enjoying a 70 percent share of major broadcast markets nationwide.

THE DYNATECH EXPERIENCE

The success of Weather Central and ColorGraphics and doubts about their ability to sustain the business over time prompted Kelly and Daly to sell the companies to Burlington, Massachusetts-based Dynatech Corp. in 1982. Following the deal, Weather Central and ColorGraphics became part of Dynatech's video communica-

tions arm. Formally known as the Display Technologies Group, the business was headed by Kelly, who was named group vice-president.

Kelly did his last weather forecast at WKOW in 1986, and was recognized by the American Meteorological Society in 1990 with an Outstanding Service Award for his contributions to the industry. By 1993 Dynatech's Display Technologies Group was generating approximately $100 million in sales on the strength of approximately 15 different companies in the United States, England, Europe, and Hong Kong. That year, Dynatech decided to sell 30 of the 65 companies it owned, including Weather Central. ColorGraphics, however, was not part of the deal.

In 1994 Kelly led a buyout of Weather Central that included Daly and other management employees. The company, which had been somewhat neglected as part of Dynatech, was again under the leadership of its founders. Kelly and his team—which included Bob Lindmeier, Randy Arb, Ron Schwarz, and John Scaif—also acquired the ArtStar and LiveLine systems. They had their work cut out for them, because Weather Central's market share had declined to less than 10 percent, and the company's workforce totaled roughly 25 people—down from a previous high of 50.

With Kelly at the helm, Weather Central hit the ground running. In 1995 a 3-D version of LiveLine was introduced. Called LiveLine Genesis, the system was followed by enhanced versions called LiveLine Super Genesis and GenesisPlus, which were in place as the company headed into the late 1990s.

FOCUS ON FUN AND QUALITY

By 1998 Weather Central had regained a position of market leadership, serving a customer base that included the Weather Channel, *Good Morning America,* and Major League Baseball's Milwaukee Brewers, as well as approximately 100 television stations. In addition the company marketed weather forecasts to some 60 newspapers—including the *Chicago Tribune, San Francisco Chronicle,* and *New York Daily News*—along with a number of business customers, radio stations, and school districts.

In the May 15, 1998, issue of the *Capital Times,* Kelly provided some insight into the company's success, explaining: "We have a philosophy of having fun, trying to do it with high quality and serving our customers well. We deliberately don't set growth goals. We've found growth kind of naturally comes our way if we do those things right. We're really not fixated on being any size company; we're fixated on being the best in the weather business."

In the spring of 1998, Weather Central introduced LiveLine SuperGenesis HD, the first high-definition television weather system in the world. When high-definition television caught on en masse, the new system was prepared to deliver a whole new weather experience to the public, because it allowed the display of weather satellite imagery that standard televisions were not capable of displaying. LiveLine SuperGenesis HD cost about 50 percent more than the company's standard system, with a price tag in the neighborhood of $200,000 to $300,000. Midway through the year, Weather Central had approximately 60 employees and was operating from a 7,800-square-foot headquarters facility on Madison's Tokay Boulevard, which it was in the process of expanding.

Weather Central celebrated its 25th anniversary in 1999. During the late 1990s, one of the company's core products was a computer modeling program called A.D.O.N.I.S., which had been developed at the University of Wisconsin–Madison. The program served as the foundation for products like A.D.O.N.I.S. FutureCast, a national hourly forecasting service, as well as a version for local forecasting that was dubbed A.D.O.N.I.S. MicroCast.

INTRODUCING NEW ONLINE SERVICES

Weather Central ushered in the new millennium by establishing a new Internet-related business called My-Weather LLC. The enterprise was headed by Chairman Terry Kelly and President and CEO Matt Peterson, and involved the use of A.D.O.N.I.S. MicroCast to deliver personalized forecasts via television station web sites, which users could use to predict weather conditions in specific geographic areas, such as a street or neighborhood. Eventually named Personal MicroCast, the service was useful for a wide range of work, lifestyle, and recreational activities.

In December 2000 MyWeather's success was furthered by a $2.7 million equity investment from Cosmos Broadcasting Corp., which chose the company's technology for use by 15 of its television stations. In early 2001 Mark A. Toney, a 20-year broadcast industry veteran, was hired as MyWeather's senior vice-president for business development and given responsibility for marketing, sales, strategic alliances, and subscriber management. Also in early 2001 MyWeather was included in a Preferred Content Provider program offered by WorldNow, a company that provided online services to approximately 125 local news and information providers throughout the United States.

By the early 2000s, weather graphics systems such as those offered by Weather Central had become commonplace at television stations everywhere. In this climate, industry players were forced to continuously search for new features that television stations could use to gain an edge on their competitors. In mid-2002 Weather Central unveiled SuperGenesis:Live. The new system, which cost about $100,000, allowed meteorologists to draw shapes such as circles or lightning bolts over the top of video, thereby giving them additional storytelling tools.

In 2003 Kelly was a finalist for Ernst & Young's Entrepreneur of the Year award. This recognition was especially meaningful, considering that he had never taken a college-level business course, and that Weather Central had never posted an unprofitable year. From the time that Kelly and his associates reacquired Weather Central, sales had increased to more than $15 million, and the company's workforce had grown to include 100 individuals, of which 45 were meteorologists.

RAPID GROWTH AT MID-DECADE

Midway through 2004, Weather Central acquired the Media Division of Burnsville, Minnesota-based Meteorlogix. The deal allowed Weather Central to expand its product line with media products such as MxWeatherSpan RT, MxWeatherSpan X, MxWeather-Span StormCommander, and Triton i7. In addition, Weather Central also saw its client base increase, via the addition of 115 new cable and broadcast television stations. About 15 Meteorlogix employees were retained, and Weather Central saw its workforce grow to 125 people. Some of the former Meteorlogix workers were based at a divisional location that was maintained in Eagan, Minnesota.

Growth continued at Weather Central through the middle of the first decade of the 2000s. By mid-2005 the company counted some 200 newspapers and 350 U.S. television stations among its customers. In addition, another 100 clients were scattered throughout the world in countries such as Australia, Canada, Egypt, England, Israel, Kuwait, Poland, and Spain. By this time Weather Central's annual revenues exceeded $25 million, and the company employed 165 people.

As of early 2006, the company's MyWeather subsidiary was providing information to more than two million people per day via the Internet. In addition the company served some 500 newspapers and more than 400 broadcast television stations. That year, MyWeather formed a joint venture with Madison, Wisconsin-based TrafficCast Inc. and TrafficCast China and unveiled MobiCast, a new technology that combined the Micro-Cast weather service with real-time traffic information, such as details about road construction, accidents, and predictive travel times. Progress continued in 2007, when Weather Central forged an alliance with Microsoft Corp. that involved the latter company's Virtual Earth software.

By 2008, Weather Central had thousands of systems in place throughout the world. Among these was a new, $35,000 weather alert system called LIVE:Wire HD, which debuted early in the year after a successful beta test at a station in Milwaukee, Wisconsin. In addition the company's 3D:LIVE HD system was being used to provide high-definition newscasts at stations in Texas and Washington. Internationally, 3D:LIVE HD was being used by networks in China, England, Spain, and Mexico.

A new product introduction in 2008 was News-Navigator, which allowed newscasters to pinpoint the precise location of a story on an interactive map. The company's MyWeather subsidiary also unveiled a new application called MyWeather Mobile for the popular Apple iPhone. As Weather Central moved toward the 21st century's second decade, the company appeared to be well positioned for continued growth in the weather graphics industry, which it had pioneered during the 1970s.

Paul R. Greenland

PRINCIPAL SUBSIDIARIES

MyWeather LLC.

PRINCIPAL COMPETITORS

AccuWeather Inc.; Meteorlogix LLC; Weather Metrics Inc.; Weather Watch Inc.; Wsi Corporation.

FURTHER READING

Balousek, Marv, "Weather Central's Purchase Brings New Television Clients; The Madison Company Buys the Media Division of Meteorlogix," *Wisconsin State Journal,* May 26, 2004.

"Drinks With … Terry Kelly," *Wisconsin State Journal,* August 31, 2008.

Gribble, Roger A., "Founder Buys Weather Central; Terry Kelly Leads Purchasing Group," *Wisconsin State Journal,* March 22, 1994.

"Management Buys Weather Central," *Capital Times,* March 22, 1994.

Mill, James Edward, "His Passion Goes Beyond the Weather," *Wisconsin State Journal,* July 31, 2005.

Richgels, Jeff, "Weather Central Springs Back; Forecast Sunny Again for Provider of Graphics Systems," *Capital Times,* May 15, 1998.

Romell, Rick, "Blue Skies for Entrepreneur; Weather Central Finds Success Times 2," *Milwaukee Journal Sentinel,* June 23, 2003.

"Weather Central Launches New Internet Venture to Provide Accurate, Personalized Forecasting; MyWeather LLC Will Partner with Local Television Stations to Build Web Revenue and Enhance Value," *PR Newswire,* June 16, 2000.

Willis Group Holdings Ltd.

———— ■ ————

51 Lime Street
London, EC3M 7DQ
United Kingdom
Telephone: (44 20) 3124-6000
Fax: (44 20) 3124-8223
Web site: http://www.willis.com

Public Company
Incorporated: 1828 as Henry Willis & Co.
Employees: 13,000
Sales: $2.57 billion (2007)
Stock Exchanges: New York
Ticker Symbol: WSH
NAICS: 524210 Insurance Agencies and Brokerages

■ ■ ■

Willis Group Holdings Ltd. offers professional insurance, reinsurance, risk management, financial and human resource consulting, and actuarial services. Its customers include corporations, public entities, and institutions found across the globe. With over 400 offices in 120 countries, the Willis Group is the third largest insurance broker in the world. The company has seen significant changes since being taken private in 1998 in a leverage buyout led by Kohlberg Kravis Roberts & Co. It has adopted its current name, returned to the New York Stock Exchange (NYSE), and purchased Hilb Rogal & Hobbs Company. The October 2008 deal nearly doubled its North American presence and stood as the industry's largest acquisition in over ten years.

ROOTS IN THE INDUSTRIAL AGE

The Willis Group originated in Industrial Era England and grew through a long series of mergers. In the early 19th century, British industrial expertise established that country as the world's leading manufacturer, while the kingdom's merchant fleet continued its long reign over the world's oceans. These factors gave rise to London-based financial and insurance industries that dominated the world market.

One of the founding members of Willis was Henry Willis & Co., formed in 1828. Henry Willis, then 28, oriented his business primarily towards Britain's shipping industry, operating as a broker and an agent for marine hull insurance offered by Lloyd's, then one of the world's leading insurers. The mid-19th century saw the appearance of several other future members of the Willis Group. In 1863, another firm, formed by George Henry Smith, began doing business for Lloyd's. Smith's sons, who changed the family name to its Latin form, Faber, set up their own insurance business in 1886. These three firms would form the core of the first development of what would eventually become Willis.

At the same time, other branches of the future Willis Group had made their appearance. One of these was the merger of two London-based insurers, Galbraith and Henderson, in 1848, which, together with the firm of Fletcher and Welton, would grow into the Stewart Wrightson group of insurers. Another was the formation of C. Wuppesahl & Co. Assekuranzmakler, based in Bremen, Germany. In 1843, Henry Dumas opened the Dumas and Wylie firm, which also brokered for Lloyd's. Another branch was represented by the 1865 founding

COMPANY PERSPECTIVES

As we face the future, we have never been more passionate about our vision to become the best insurance brokerage company in the world. To help us get there, we launched a new brand promise that drives our every action: Willis will always challenge the status quo to create new and better ways to serve our clients' best interests. We are the change-agent that truly partners with clients to advance their performance and change the industry for their benefit. Willis never settles for second best or relies on the old ways of doing things.

of Gibb & MacIntyre, later known as James Gibb & Son and then Bray Gibb.

The 1890s set the scene for the first wave of Willis Group mergers. By then, Willis had begun expanding beyond the United Kingdom, entering especially the Italian market as agents for Italia and Generali. In 1892, Henry Willis & Co. reached an agreement with U.S.-based Johnson & Higgins to broker their marine insurance services through Lloyd's. The growing Willis company soon after merged its business with the Faber family, forming Willis Faber in 1898. Another boost to the company came the following year, when it became an agent for Tokyo Marine & Fire Insurance Company.

FAMILY TREE IN THE 20TH CENTURY

At the dawn of the 20th century, Willis Faber opened a new subsidiary, the Cornhill Insurance Company, and moved to increase its international operations, with agencies in Montreal, Canada, and Hamburg, Germany. The period also saw the appearance of several new Willis branches. Principal among these was brokerage specialist R.A. Corroon & Co. Inc., based in New York, as that city's prominence in the world insurance and financial markets grew alongside the overall developing economic power of the entire United States. Two more London companies made their appearance in the first decade of the 20th century: Matthews Wrightson and Arthur Bray & Son, both to become major components of the Stewart Wrightson Group. Stewart Wrightson would later form one of the three principal components of the Willis Group.

Over the next decades, Willis Faber continued to grow both internally and through acquisitions. The early

1920s were marked by the acquisitions of two British companies, Brodrick, Leitch & Kendall and Henry L. Riseley, enabling Willis Faber to expand its British presence into the cities of Cardiff, Liverpool, Bristol, and Birmingham, while also adding the Riseley subsidiary British & Irish Plate Glass Insurance Company, later known as the Sovereign Insurance Company. Internationally, the company was given the London agency representation for the Caja company in Chile, and for Atlantic Mutual in the United States. Willis Faber also formed a treaty with the newly established Soviet State Insurance Organization. At the end of the decade, Willis Faber became Willis Faber & Dumas Limited, after its merger with Dumas & Wylie in 1928.

This move was matched in the United States when R.A. Corroon—which by then had expanded beyond brokerage to include underwriting services as well—merged with another company to form Corroon & Reynolds. In 1929, Corroon & Reynolds became the first insurance broker to obtain a listing on the NYSE. Corroon became the third primary component of the future Willis Group.

In the 1930s, the final branches of the Willis Group appeared. In 1931, J. H. Miller founded a construction bonds surety agency in California; that company took on the name Miller & Day in the following year. At the end of that decade, Miller & Day expanded to become Miller Day & Ames. That name was simplified to Miller & Ames in 1947.

While Willis Faber, established as a leading London broker, appeared to rest from its line of acquisitions, the other branches of the future Willis Group continued the pattern of mergers. In the mid-1960s, Corroon & Reynolds made the decision to sell its underwriting operations and concentrate on expanding its brokering activities. That move was followed by its consolidation with another prominent New York brokerage house, C.R. Black Jr. Corporation, in 1966, forming the Corroon & Black Corporation. The operations of Miller & Ames were added two years later, as Corroon & Black moved to establish a national position. Corroon & Black would continue to build via acquisitions and mergers throughout the 1970s and 1980s. The most prominent of these came in the 1970s, beginning with the reinsurance business of G.L. Hodgson, based in New York in 1970. In 1976 Corroon & Black doubled in size with its merger with Nashville, Tennessee-based Synercon Corporation, the largest such merger in the U.S.-based brokering sector at that time. By the late 1980s, Corroon & Black would hold the

KEY DATES

1828: Henry Willis & Co. is formed.

1863: George Henry Smith forms a company and begins doing business for Lloyd's.

1886: Smith's sons, who changed the family name to its Latin form, Faber, set up their own insurance business.

1898: Willis merges its business with the Faber family, forming Willis Faber.

1928: The company merges with Dumas & Wylie.

1929: Corroon & Reynolds becomes the first insurance broker to obtain a listing on the New York Stock Exchange.

1966: Corroon & Reynolds merges with C.R. Black Jr. Corp., forming the Corroon & Black Corp.

1990: Willis merges with Corroon & Black, forming the Willis Corroon Group.

1998: The company is taken private in a leveraged buyout led by Kohlberg Kravis Roberts & Co.

1999: The company adopts the name Willis Group.

2001: Willis Group lists on the New York Stock Exchange.

2008: Hilb Rogal & Hobbs Company is acquired.

position as the fifth largest insurance broker in the United States.

In the 1970s, Willis Faber went public with a listing on the London stock exchange. By the end of the decade, Willis Faber had established its headquarters at Ten Trinity Square. Meanwhile, the formation of Stewart Wrightson—through the consolidation of the activities of Matthews Wrightson, Bray Gibb, and Stewart Smith—brought that company to the London stock exchange as well.

JOINING THE BRANCHES

Willis Faber hit the acquisition trail again in the early 1980s, adding U.K.-based companies Carter Wilkes & Fane, a reinsurance specialist based in London, and Yorkshire-based Rattray Daffern. At the same time, Willis Faber underwent a change in strategy. Traditionally, Willis Faber had built its business around a core of agency brokering and reinsurance operations. In the 1980s, the company sought greater independence, especially in terms of revenues, by repositioning itself

further into the direct brokering market. With the shift in focus of the world financial and insurance industries to New York, and the British economic crisis of the 1980s, Willis Faber also recognized the need to establish a presence in the U.S. market.

The merger of Willis Faber with Stewart Wrightson provided the company a strong boost in this direction. Renamed Willis Wrightson, the company became the largest direct broker in the United Kingdom, gave the company a strengthened position among the global reinsurance market, and added a strong entry into the United States. By 1990, the third component was in place: Willis Wrightson merged with Corroon & Black, forming the Willis Corroon Group.

Through the early 1990s, the company worked to restructure its operations, expanding its international presence through the opening of offices worldwide, while building its position throughout Europe with the establishment of a network of subsidiary and related operations. The company's U.S. headquarters was also moved from Corroon & Black's former New York offices to Nashville. Willis Corroon's transition was realized by 1993. The company was then one of the world leaders in risk management and brokering services.

The cost of putting the company's new structure into place—at a time when the worldwide market had gone sour with the extended recession of the first half of the 1990s—cut into the company's profits. The company turned to John Reeve, who became the first company chairman brought in from outside the company. In 1995, the company took steps to reorganize its operations, reforming the company into five primary divisions: U.K. Retail, U.K. Wholesale, International, North American Retail, and Global Specialties. These divisions were later refined into the company's late 1990s structure. The reorganization of the company helped lift profits by 1996.

INCREASED SCOPE

During this time period, Willis Corroon had begun to position itself beyond its traditional insurance brokering core into becoming, as stated in its annual report, "a global knowledge-based professional services firm." Beyond simply offering insurance services, Willis Corroon expanded its definition to include problem-solving and other risk management consulting activities. In the late 1990s, the company also began to concentrate on the rapidly opening European market, with a focus on Germany and France. The company concluded an agreement with Germany's Jaspers Wuppesahl to increase Willis Corroon's position in the German company to 30 percent at the beginning of 1998, and to 44.6 percent by the end of 1998, with an option to build a majority position. In late 1997, the company also enhanced its position in India, with the joint venture Willis Corroon Tower (Private) Ltd., based in Mumbai.

By 1998, Willis Corroon Group plc was situated as a world-leading provider of insurance and reinsurance brokerage services. Willis Corroon operated more than 250 offices in 69 countries around the world and offered an extensive range of insurance products to major corporations and public sector organizations, private and public associations, as well as to individuals. Included among the company's areas of expertise were industries including: environment; construction; healthcare; mergers and acquisitions; leisure; food and drink; and "unusual and niche" fields such as the company's 1998 launch of its Fine Art, Jewellery & Specie division.

During the late 1990s, however, Willis Corroon fell victim to intense competition, which in turn led to falling premium rates, lower commissions, and lackluster profits. The company soon found itself considering its options of remaining intact as a public company, merging with a competitor, or forming a strategic alliance. Kohlberg Kravis Roberts & Co. (KKR), a U.S.-based buyout specialist, stepped in with another offer, one which would take Willis Corroon private.

A consortium under the name Trinity Acquisition PLC was formed in 1998 and included KKR along with Guardian Royal Exchange PLC, Royal & Sun Alliance Insurance Group PLC, Chubb Corp., Hartford Financial Services Group Inc., and Travelers Property Casualty Corp. KKR led the $1.4 billion buyout and secured an 81 percent interest in the company while the group of insurance firms and senior executives of Willis Corroon acquired the remaining shares. A July 1998 *Wall Street Journal* article reported Chairman Reeve's thoughts on the deal: "We welcome this offer, which not only gives value to our shareholders but is also good for our employees, clients and industry." The company adopted the Willis Group name in 1999.

MOVING INTO THE 21ST CENTURY

Willis Group entered the new millennium with a new leader. Well-known U.S. banker Joseph Plumeri was tapped to head the company upon Reeve's retirement in 2000. Plumeri, whose experience included running Citigroup's North American retail banking operations and its Primerica financial services arm, was soon charged with launching Willis Group on the U.S. market. In June 2001, the company made a minority offering on the NYSE. The company gave three reasons for going public: public status gave employees an opportunity to

own shares; trading on the NYSE could retain and lure talent to the company; and the proceeds of the offering could be used to fund future growth.

Accordingly, Willis Group acquired Goldman Insurance Services based in San Francisco, California, and increased its shareholding in Willis Italia during 2001. It then purchased a majority interest in Germany's third largest broker, Jaspers Wuppesahl Industrie Assekuranz GmbH & Co. KG, in 2002. With sales and profits on the rise, the company continued to look for ways to expand its business.

Meanwhile, the company found itself in the middle of a highly publicized legal battle. Real estate tycoon Larry Silverstein, owner of the 99-year lease on the World Trade Center in New York City, was in the process of insuring that property when the buildings were destroyed in the September 11, 2001, terrorist attack. Willis Group was his insurance broker and a document it drafted—known as the "WilProp" form—became a key piece of evidence used in court. The WilProp form, which was given to all 25 insurers of the World Trade Center, interpreted the attacks on the World Trade Center as one occurrence. This meant Silverstein would recoup approximately $3.5 billion from insurers. Silverstein argued that there were actually two attacks, which could mean a payout of up to $7 billion. Not all insurers had finished drafting their contracts when the attacks occurred, leaving room for Silverstein to file suit. The courts eventually awarded Silverstein $4.55 billion in insurance payouts, which would be used to rebuild office space at the World Trade Center location.

During this time the Willis Group remained focused on growth, concentrating especially on the U.S. market. Its strategy became evident when it made a $2.1 billion play for Hilb Rogal & Hobbs Company, a U.S.-based insurance and risk management intermediary. The deal was the largest in the insurance broker industry in nearly a decade and doubled the company's size in North America. The acquisition secured Willis Group's position as the third largest insurance broker in the world and was finalized in October 2008. The North American operations of Willis were renamed Willis HRH shortly thereafter.

The Duke of York was present at the grand opening of Willis Group's new headquarters at 51 Lime Street in London's financial district that year. With some of the highest profit margins in the industry, Plumeri had apparently taken the company in the right direction since assuming his leadership position in 2000. While the integration of its most recent acquisition would no doubt take some time, Plumeri and his management team were confident that Willis Group was on track for success in the years to come.

M. L. Cohen
Updated, Christina M. Stansell

PRINCIPAL SUBSIDIARIES

Willis Group Ltd.; Willis Ltd.; Willis Group Holdings Ltd. (United States); Willis North America Inc. (United States); Alexander Forbes Risk Services Zimbabwe (Pvt) Ltd.; Herzfeld & Levy S.A (Argentina); Kieffer & Asociados S.A (Bolivia); PT Willis Indonesia; Willis A/S (Denmark); Willis AB (Sweden); Willis Australia Ltd.; Willis BA India Private Limited; Willis B.V. (Netherlands); Willis Canada Inc.; Willis China (Hong Kong) Ltd; Willis CIS Insurance Broker LLC (Russia); Willis Corretaje de Reaseguros S.A (Venezuela); Willis Corretores de Seguros Ltda (Brazil); Willis Corretores de Seguros S.A (Portugal); Willis Faber Bahrain WLL; Willis GmbH (Austria); Willis GmbH & Co KG (Germany); Willis Iberia (Spain); Willis Insurance Brokers (B) Sdn Bhd (Brunei Darussalam); Willis Italia S.p.A. (Italy); Willis Japan Ltd.; Willis Korea Ltd.; Willis (Malaysia) Sdn. Bhd.; Willis New Zealand Ltd.; Willis Oy AB (Finland); Willis Polska S.A. (Poland); Willis Pudong Insurance Brokers Ltd. (China); Willis (Singapore) Pte Ltd.; Willis s.r.o. (Czech Republic); Willis Kft (Hungary); Willis (Taiwan) Ltd.; JH Asesores y Corredores de Seguros S.A. (Peru); Rontarca Prima Willis S.A. (Venezuela).

PRINCIPAL COMPETITORS

Aon Corporation; Arthur J. Gallagher & Co.; Marsh & McLennan Companies Inc.

FURTHER READING

Bringardner, John, "The Aftermath of Tragedy; Insurers Battle the Technicalities of the 9/11 Attacks," *Law Technology News,* April 20, 2005.

Goldsmith, Charles, "British Insurer Willis Corroon Agrees to Takeover," *Wall Street Journal,* July 23, 1998.

"Grand Opening: Willis HQ Gets Royal Welcome," *Business Insurance,* July 28, 2008.

Gray, Tony, and Claire Wilkinson, "Agreed Bid for Willis Corroon," *Lloyd's List,* July 23, 1998.

Merced, Michael J. de la, "British Insurer to Acquire Hilb Rogal for $2.1 Billion," *New York Times,* June 9, 2008.

"Merger Between Willis Faber and Corroon and Black Goes Ahead," *Reinsurance,* November 9, 1990.

"Plumeri to Head Willis Group," *Financial Times,* September 26, 2000.

Quinn, James, "Joe Plumeri Chairman and CEO," *Daily Telegraph,* August 18, 2008.

Ruquet, Mark E., "Willis CEO Talks About Bringing 'Aggressive,' Family Touch to Brokerage," *National Underwriter Property & Casualty-Risk & Benefits Management Edition,* July 23, 2001.

Sormani, Angela, "Willis Returns to Public Markets," *Buyouts,* May 7, 2001.

Weber, Joseph, "Insurance Broker Willis to Acquire HRH," *Business Week,* June 9, 2008.

Willow Run Foods, Inc.

1006 U.S. Route 11
Kirkwood, New York 13795
U.S.A.
Telephone: (607) 338-5221
Toll Free: (800) 234-7550
Fax: (607) 798-8281
Web site: http://www.willowrunfoods.com

Employee-Owned Company
Incorporated: 1949 as Willow Run Poultry Farm
Employees: 400
Sales: $600 million (2007 est.)
NAICS: 424410 General Line Grocery Merchant
    Wholesalers

■ ■ ■

Willow Run Foods, Inc., is an employee-owned foodservice company based in Kirkwood, New York, near Binghamton. From a single warehouse, more than 250,000 square feet in size, Willow Run on a contract basis supplies fast-food and casual dining restaurants in 14 northeast and mid-Atlantic states, stretching from Maine as far south as Virginia, and including West Virginia and Ohio. Billing itself as a one-stop shop, the company carries 2,400 items, including baked goods, produce, other food items, beverages, light kitchen equipment, sanitary equipment, and general merchandise. Willow Run is affiliated with the UniPro Foodservice, Inc., purchasing and marketing group, a network of about 300 independent foodservice distribution companies. The customers in Willow Run's book of 1,700 accounts include such major restaurant chains as Arby's, Bob Evans Farms, Boston Market, Carvel Ice Cream, T.G.I. Fridays, Sonic, Popeyes, Quiznos, and Wendy's.

In partnership with Ryder Transportation, the company maintains a fleet of about 90 tractors and more than 110 trailers. The Kirkwood location is ideally suited for servicing the company's sales territories, located close to highways running in all directions. The distribution facility receives deliveries from suppliers starting at 5:00 A.M. each morning while orders are received. At 2:00 P.M. inbound deliveries cease, and outbound deliveries take place for the next 12 hours, leaving three hours to prepare for the next day's activities.

COMPANY BEGINS WITH EGG DELIVERY

Willow Run was established in Vestal, New York, in 1949 by Robert Hanley, a college student at the time. He began earning some extra income when a local chicken farmer hired him to deliver eggs to business customers on his way to class. Those customers asked if the reliable young man could deliver other grocery items as well, and soon Hanley had a thriving sideline. It proved so promising that he never completed his college education. Instead, he quit school, bought a van, and started a distribution company, Willow Run Poultry Farm, in Vestal, specializing in eggs and poultry.

Willow Run in the early decades concentrated on what was known as street business, selling door-to-door to restaurants. In addition to "Mom and Pop" restaurants, the company served bakeries and schools. Starting in the late 1970s convenience stores and small restaurant chains were added as customers as the company began to shift away from street business to a contract business with fast-food restaurant chains. A major step in this direction came around 1981 when the Wendy's restaurant chain became a customer.

By the late 1980s the Hanley family was interested in cashing out. Because of capital gains taxes, the owners decided to begin selling the business to the employees through an employment stock ownership plan (ESOP), which provided tax deferrals. In 1989 Willow Run employees acquired 30 percent of the business. Four years later they gained control of the company through the acquisition of an additional 40 percent. Not only did the ESOP benefit the Hanley family, it provided a major incentive to employees, who then shared in the company's success, receiving stock benefits each year in addition to their salaries. Willow Run's motivated workforce drove the growth of the company in the 1990s and into the new century.

Another major factor in the growth of Willow Run was its longtime chief executive, Terry Wood, who took an unusual path to his position. Born in the Binghamton area, in Cortland, he earned a degree in physical education from the State University of New York, and came to Vestal in 1970 to work as an elementary and high school physical education teacher and to serve as a coach. During his free summer months he began building houses, and in the process developed an interest in business. After eight years of teaching he was offered a sales position with A.O. Smith, an electric motor manufacturer. Earning twice as much as he could from teaching, Wood left the education field for good and devoted himself to business. In 1983 he went to work in sales for Willow Run, and in 1989 became general sales manager, becoming president in 1993 and chief executive officer in 1996.

FOCUSING ON CONTRACT BUSINESS

While Wood played an increasingly important role at Willow Run and the employees attained majority control, the company began focusing all of its attention on the contract business with fast-food restaurants. To better serve them, 10,600 square feet of storage space was added in 1991, bringing the size of the company's combined warehouse operations to 92,000 square feet. Late in the year Willow Run sold its street business and began to focus on the contract business. Annual revenues then grew at a rate of 25 percent. Sales reached $110 million in 1996 and increased to $138 million just two years later. Along the way, to meet the needs of its growing slate of customers, the company expanded its warehouse capacity, and soon found itself working from three separate locations, including the main 80,000-square-foot warehouse in Vestal and a former Grossman's lumber yard.

Before addressing the warehousing problem, Willow Run improved the transportation part of the operation. In 1995 the company fleet consisted of just 15 tractors and 16 trailers. At that point it was turned over to Ryder Transportation as Willow Run sought to focus all of its attention on growing its contract business with large fast-food restaurant accounts. Not only did the company's area of operations increase dramatically throughout the Northeast and the mid-Atlantic region, the delivery window narrowed to about an hour, reducing the margin of error within the fleet. By switching to a full-service lease with Ryder, Willow Run's fleet could be maintained at Ryder's many depots, and replacement vehicles were always available as needed. Willow Run could also adjust the size of its fleet as business dictated without a large outlay of cash. Moreover, Willow Run drivers enjoyed the benefits of well-maintained, quality equipment.

Having a reliable, scalable fleet was clearly helpful, but just as important was the warehouse situation. Especially troublesome was a desperate need for more freezer space. There was no option but to move, and Willow Run fielded offers from two Pennsylvania sites before reaching an agreement to build in nearby Kirkwood, New York, the decision influenced by an incentive package of $450,000 provided by state and local governments. In May 1999 Willow Run opened a new 150,000-square-foot state-of-the-art distribution center and corporate headquarters in Kirkwood, built at a cost of $13 million. It included 55,000 square feet of refrigerated space, as well as an onsite maintenance facility where Ryder could service the Willow Run fleet on a 24-hour, seven-days-a-week basis. The Kirkwood site, 30

KEY DATES

1949: Robert Henley begins egg delivery service.

1981: Wendy's fast-food restaurant chain becomes a customer.

1989: Employees begin acquiring company.

1991: Street business sold.

1993: Employees gain majority control.

1996: Terry Wood named chief executive officer.

1999: Company opens new distribution center and corporate headquarters in Kirkwood, New York.

2001: Expansion to Kirkwood facility completed.

2007: Adjoining land acquired in Kirkwood.

2008: Work begins on new cooler and freezer facility.

acres in size, also offered room for further growth, with capability for the facility to more than triple its size.

WAREHOUSE EXPANSION

Willow Run estimated that it would need to add more warehouse space in 2005, but just two years after the Kirkwood facility opened its doors, the company began making plans to increase the size to accommodate new business. In September 2001 a 65,000-square-foot expansion was completed, doubling the facility's refrigeration storage capacity, including freezer and cooler space as well a refrigerated loading dock. Even as the new space came on line, the warehouse remained under pressure because of Willow Run's growing business, especially with the Wendy's and Arby's restaurant chains, resulting in revenues increasing to $260 million in 2001, a 73 percent increase in three years. Willow Run lost a contract to supply Subway sandwich shops, but more than made up for it with a contract renewal from Arby's, the company's second largest customer after the Wendy's chain. Another expansion project was under way at a cost of $2.3 million. Thus, in the fall of 2002, another 43,000 square feet of space was added, bringing the total size of the Kirkwood facility to 255,000 square feet.

The extra space would quickly be put to use due to a pair of contracts signed in late summer 2002 worth about $550 million over the next five years. One new customer was New World Bagel; another was a national fast-food restaurant chain. As a result of these deals, Willow Run sales jumped to $380 million in 2003, and improved to $461 million in 2004, due in part to a new

five-year, $235 million contract to supply Quiznos Sub franchises in the Northeast. Willow Run then seriously considered expanding beyond Virginia and into the Carolinas. The company looked for a site to open a second distribution center in either Maryland or Virginia, comparable in size to the Kirkwood facility. In the end, however, nothing came of the idea.

NEW CONTRACTS AND NEW EMPLOYEES

Sales leveled off, increasing 4.3 percent to $481 million in 2005, and just 1.9 percent in 2006. Business picked up again in late 2006 when Willow Run reached a five-year, $155 million contract with Bob Evans Farms Inc. to serve 81 of the chain's restaurants along the East Coast from Maine to Virginia. Most of the nearly 600 restaurants in the Bob Evans chain were located close to the interstate highway system, making them ideally situated for Willow Run deliveries. The new business led to a spurt in revenue growth in 2007, as did another major contract. In March 2007 Atlanta-based Supply Management Services signed a new five-year $310 million contract to supply about 300 Popeyes restaurants in the Northeast. Popeyes was hardly a new customer, having worked with Willow Run for two decades, but the new agreement added 167 restaurants to the 130 restaurants previously supplied by Willow Run. As a result of the Bob Evans and Popeyes contracts, Willow Run hired scores of new drivers and other employees and increased revenues 22.4 percent in 2007 to $600 million.

The high cost of fuel was a challenge as Willow Run entered 2008, but as the price of petroleum began to drop in the autumn of that year the problem abated somewhat. More important to Willow Run's long-term success was the winning of more sizable new contracts. At the start of 2008 the company signed a four-year extension with the Arby's restaurant chain to supply about 400 units in the northeastern states after a decade of serving Arby's. In addition, Willow Run signed a five-year agreement with the Sonic drive-in restaurant chain, worth another $300 million, to supply existing Sonic restaurants in the Northeast. Not only was Willow Run pleased to win this new business from a fast-growing restaurant chain, there was a high likelihood that there would be more business to be done in the future. Sonic had no units located in New York State, but there was a good chance that the chain would be entering the territory as it made a broad push in the Northeast. In the Binghamton area alone there was talk of four Sonic restaurants opening in the near future. Hence, there was every reason to believe that the $300 million contract with Sonic was just a portion of the potential business Willow Run could draw from the chain.

To handle its increasing business, Willow Run purchased more land adjoining its Kirkwood facility in 2007, about 20 acres. A year later it began working on a 107,000-square-foot freezer and cooler storage facility at a cost of $13 million. Plans also included a railway site to permit Willow Run to receive rail shipment of products. The company was thus well positioned to attract even more business in the years to come.

Ed Dinger

PRINCIPAL COMPETITORS

MBM Corporation; Maines Paper & Food Service Inc.; DiCarlo Distributors Inc.

FURTHER READING

Knopf, Annemarie, "Willow Run Foods Supplies Fast Food Fast," *CNY Business Journal,* November 9, 2001.

Nguyen, My-Ly, "$235 Million Deal Will Add 25 Jobs," *Binghamton (N.Y.) Press & Sun-Bulletin,* p. 8D.

————, "Willow Run Lands 2 Contracts Worth $680M," *Binghamton (N.Y.) Press & Sun-Bulletin,* January 17, 2008, p. 1A.

————, "Willow Run Plans $13 Million Expansion," *Binghamton (N.Y.) Press & Sun-Bulletin,* October 8, 2008, p. 8A.

Platsky, Jeff, "Willow Run Moves to Kirkwood," *Binghamton (N.Y.) Press & Sun-Bulletin,* May 22, 1999, p. 8B.

Wilberstaff, Tom, "Willow Run Expansion Ahead of Schedule," *Binghamton (N.Y.) Press & Sun-Bulletin,* April 13, 2002, p. 8D.

"Willow Run Foods, Inc.," *FoodService Distributor,* August 1, 1997, p. 30.

ZAKŁADY AZOTOWE "PUŁAWY"
SPÓŁKA AKCYJNA

Zakłady Azotowe Puławy S.A.

Al Tysiaclecia Panstwa Polskiego 13
Puławy, 24-110
Poland
Telephone: (48 081) 565 3000
Fax: (48 081) 565 2856
Web site: http://www.zapulawy.pl

Public Company
Incorporated: 1961
Employees: 3,253
Sales: PLN 2.5 billion ($972.7 million) (2007)
Stock Exchanges: Warsaw
Ticker Symbol: ZAP
NAICS: 325311 Nitrogenous Fertilizer Manufacturing;
    325120 Industrial Gas Manufacturing; 325188 All
    Other Inorganic Chemical Manufacturing

■ ■ ■

Zakłady Azotowe Puławy S.A. (Puławy) is one of Poland's largest chemicals companies and its leading producer of nitrogenous fertilizers. Puławy is also a major global manufacturer of melamine, with an annual production capacity of 92 thousand metric tons per year. With a 10 percent global share, and a 20 percent share of the European melamine market, Puławy is the third largest melamine producer in the world. Founded as part of the industrialization of Poland's agriculture in the early 1960s, Puławy has long since reduced its reliance on nitrogen-based fertilizers by expanding its range of chemicals production. As a result, Puławy operates through two primary divisions. The Agro Products division includes its production of urea and ammonium nitrate, ammonium sulfate, potassium salt, aluminum phosphate, hydrogen and liquid carbon dioxide. The group's Chemicals division includes its production of melamine, caprolactum, hydrogen peroxide, and Ad-Blue, a water-based urea product. The group's products are marketed under the Puławy brand.

In the last half of the first decade of the 2000s, Puławy began taking steps to reduce its reliance on natural gas—the primary source of its nitrogenous fertilizer production. In pursuit of this effort, the company concluded a deal to import liquid ammonia from Russia, and in 2008 reached an agreement with the Bogdanka coal mine to build a coal gasification plant. Puławy is listed on the Warsaw Stock Exchange. The Polish government retains a 50.73 percent stake in the company, but was expected to sell off its holding by 2010. Pawel Jarczewski is the company's president. In 2007, Puławy posted revenues of PLN 2.5 billion ($970 million).

FERTILIZING POLISH FARMLANDS IN THE SIXTIES

Zakłady Azotowe Puławy had its origins in the early 1960s, as the Communist-controlled Polish government led the industrialization of the country's agricultural sector. For much of the 20th century, and into the postwar decades, Poland's farming sector continued to operate along traditional methods. The introduction of tractors and other new machinery, as well as other new farming techniques also brought a need to ensure a growing and steady supply of fertilizers.

COMPANY PERSPECTIVES

We are a company operating in the chemistry sector. By pursuing constant development and improvement, building competitive advantages, increasing effectiveness and perfecting our procedures in the human resources area, as well as shaping the Company's internal and external relations, we work to increase the company value.

The decision to create a new company dedicated to the production of nitrogen-based fertilizers came at the end of 1960, when the Polish government founded Zakłady Azotowe Puławy. The new company was charged with building and operating a nitrogen factory in the town of Puławy, with the initial planning phase launched in 1961. These plans called for the incorporation of technologies acquired under license from Denmark's Haldor Topsoe, for the production of ammonia, and from Toyo Koatsu, of Japan, for the production of urea. Puławy was placed under the oversight of the Ministry of Chemical Industries. Construction of the plant finally began in 1962. The facility's production launch was initially planned for 1965.

By then, Puławy had begun to expand its scope of operations. In 1964 the state-controlled body had already made the decision to add a second fertilizer production facility. For this the company acquired a new license, from the Norwegian company Kaltenbach, for the production of Norway saltpeter. The operation also included the production of nitric acid, based on the Starnicarbon method. The new facility, which began construction in 1965, became known as Puławy II.

In the meantime, start-up at Puławy I had been delayed, and initial production of ammonium did not begin until June 1966. By July of that year, however, Puławy I had become fully operational, launching its first production of crystal urea. Puławy II launched production a year later.

By 1968 the Polish government had begun planning the further expansion of the Puławy-based enterprise, as demand for fertilizers soared. The company saw its mandate extended beyond nitrogen-based fertilizers to include organic compounds as well.

ADDING CHEMICALS IN THE SEVENTIES

Puławy grew rapidly through the end of the 1960s. By the beginning of the next decade the company had added 20 fertilizer production plants, expanding Polish nitrogen-based fertilizer production as a whole by some 300 percent. The company's share of the total national market soon topped 60 percent. By the late 1970s Puławy's share of the urea market in Poland had reached 80 percent.

During this time Puławy had also ventured into a number of new areas. These included liquid carbon dioxide and dry ice production, launched in 1967. By 1970 the company had also added a facility for the production of polyethylene bags.

Soon, however, Puławy also took steps to expand beyond its core fertilizers markets. The company's first venture into the chemicals sector began in 1971, when it received authorization to construct a factory for the production of caprolactum flakes, a primary component of nylon. For this effort, the company acquired a license from Switzerland's Inventa, while also developing its own technologies and working in partnership with the Polish Institute of Industrial Chemistry and with Tarnow, another leading Polish chemicals group. In the early 1970s the new factory expanded the group's range of products to include caprolactum, hydroxylamine sulfite, and ammonia sulfite.

A major milestone in Puławy's development was its decision in the late 1970s to add production of melamine resin. Also known as thermoset plastic, melamine provided an important new outlet for Puławy's urea production, as well as opening up entirely new markets for the company. The company began building its first melamine factory in 1975, based on technologies acquired from two Austrian companies, Voest-Alpine and Chemie Linz. Puławy launched melamine production in 1977.

POST-COMMUNIST RENEWAL IN THE NINETIES

Puławy began to address the disastrous environmental consequences of the Soviet bloc's industrial policies as early as the mid-1980s. In 1985 the company introduced a new environmental protection program, that reached into the turn of the century. The first phase of this program was achieved in 1990, when the company completed construction of a wastewater treatment facility to handle the biological waste produced through its caprolactum operations.

The company also expanded its range of products during this period. In 1990 the company started production of a new fertilizer, RSM. The new product was based on a blend of urea with ammonium nitrate (also known as Norway saltpeter). The company initially targeted production levels of 300 tons per day. Strong

KEY DATES

1961: The Polish government founds Zakłady Azotowe Puławy S.A. (ZAP) to produce fertilizer.
1966: Production begins at ZAP's first site in Puławy.
1971: ZAP enters the nitrogen-based chemicals sector with the construction of a factory producing caprolactum flakes.
1979: ZAP launches production of melamine.
1990: ZAP adds production of hydrogen peroxide.
1993: ZAP is reincorporated as a state-owned joint stock company.
2001: Production begins at Melamine II plant, making ZAP the world's third largest melamine producer.
2004: Completion of ZAP's Melamine III plant raises total production to 92,000 metric tons per year.
2005: ZAP completes its initial public offering on the Warsaw Stock Exchange.
2008: Zap enters alliance with Zakłady Chemiczne Police.

demand, however, particularly from Western Europe, encouraged Puławy to expand its RSM production through the 1990s.

In the meantime the former state-owned company had begun its transformation into a modern European fertilizer and chemicals powerhouse. Privatization of the company began in 1992, when Puławy was reincorporated as a state-owned stock company. While the Polish government was to remain Puławy's majority shareholder into the last half of the first decade of the 2000s, the company adopted a new management strategy.

A major part of this strategy called for the thorough modernization of the company's industrial apparatus. Between 1992 and 1994 the company carried out a series of investments in its infrastructure. In 1994, for example, the company replaced its existing granulates tower with a modern facility. Similarly the company replaced its three urea synthesis plants with a single modern facility capable of producing 1,700 tons per day. These investments enabled the company to raise its urea production to 2,700 tons per day.

Another major investment by the company during this period involved the company's decision to add hydrogen dioxide to its product line. This effort was

launched at the end of 1993, with the launch of construction of its H2O2 plant using technology acquired from Chematur Engineering in Sweden. In the second half of the decade, Puławy again extended its product range. The company began building a sodium perborate factory in 1995. Production of the new compound, primarily used in detergents, started in 1998.

MELAMINE LEADER IN THE 21ST CENTURY

The turn of the 21st century was marked by another significant milestone in Puławy's history. In 1999, the company made the decision to boost its melamine capacity. Construction of a new plant, Melamine II, got underway that year and was completed in 2001. The new plant incorporated technology from Italy's Eurotecnica, with a total capacity of 30,000 tons per year. This doubled Puławy's total melamine production, boosting it into the third-place position among the world's largest melamine producers.

The surge in demand for melamine at the beginning of the 2000s led the company to invest in a further expansion of its melamine capacity. In 2002 the company launched construction of its Melamine III factory, once again in partnership with Eurotecnica. Completed in 2004, the new facility raised Puławy's total production to 92,000 tons per year. In this way the company claimed the position of European leader in the melamine market, with a 20 percent share of the market. At the same time Puławy's share of the total global market reached 10 percent.

Preparations for the next phase of Puławy's privatization were underway. This effort was initially launched in the late 1990s, as the Polish government indicated its intention to privatize several of the country's major industrial groups. An initial public offering for Puławy's shares was accordingly scheduled for 2001.

A general collapse in the global investment market that year forced the government to place Puławy's initial public offering on hold. With a new economic upswing, and the completion of Puławy's melamine capacity expansion, the government once again revived its privatization program a few years later. In 2005 Puławy became a public company, listing nearly 30 percent of its shares on the Warsaw Stock Exchange. The successful offering raised PLN 300 million ($115 million) for the company, which was then placed toward its PLN 700 million ($266 million) investment program.

This investment called for further increases in both melamine and fertilizer production. At the same time the group continued to seek new areas for expansion. In

2006, for example, the company announced its intention to add production of AdBlue, a urea-water suspension used as a fuel component by the diesel motor sector. Production of the new product began by the end of that year.

SEEKING ALTERNATIVE SUPPLIERS FOR RAW MATERIALS

In the later years of the first decade of the 2000s Puławy also took steps to limit its dependence on natural gas, and more specifically on the Polish gas monopoly PGNiG. The company first sought an alternative supplier for its natural gas needs, which reached 850 million cubic meters per year. For this, the company signed a purchasing contract with Emfesz, of Hungary in 2006. Also that year the company signed a contract with Technochimserwis of Russia for the supply of liquid ammonia. This enabled Puławy replace part of its own natural gas-based ammonia production.

This contract was the first step toward the company's goal of purchasing 50 percent of its gas supply from sources other than PGNiG. A new move toward this goal came in 2008, when the company announced a partnership agreement with the Bogdanka coal mine to construct a coal gasification plant. The project was expected to cost up to PLN 1.3 billion ($500 million), with a processing capacity of 1.3 million metric tons of coal per year.

The diversification of Puławy's raw materials sources played a role in the group's further investment efforts. In 2008 the group formed an alliance with one of its Polish rivals, Zakłady Chemiczne Police. The alliance sought to minimize the impact of soaring raw materials costs, while also setting the stage for joint acquisitions in the future.

At the same time, however, Puławy maintained its own independent investment effort. In September 2008 the company announced its plans to add two new production facilities in Starachowice. The new facilities included a 270,000-metric-ton per year urea plant, and a 100,000-metric-ton per year AdBlue factory. The company expected to spend up to $65 million on the new facilities, with construction expected to be completed by 2010.

By then Puławy expected to have completed its privatization, after the Polish government indicated it would dispose of its remaining shares in the company by then. Puławy had grown from a small Soviet-era fertilizer producer to become one of Europe's leading nitrogen-based fertilizer and chemicals companies.

M. L. Cohen

PRINCIPAL SUBSIDIARIES

Baltycka Baza Masowa Sp. z o.o. (50%); CTL KOLZAP Sp. z o.o. (49%); D.W. JAWOR Sp. z o.o. (99.96%); ELZAP Sp. z o.o. (90.69%); MEDICAL Sp. z o.o. (91.41%); Melamina III Sp. z o.o.; Navitrans Sp. z o.o. (26.45%); PROZAP Sp. z o.o. (85.51%); REMZAP Sp. z o.o. (96.54%); STO-ZAP Sp. z o.o. (97.99%).

PRINCIPAL COMPETITORS

Koninklijke DSM N.V.; Equistar Chemicals L.P.; Yara International ASA; Bangladesh Chemical Industries Corp.; Liaocheng Luxi Chemical Group General Corp.; Wesfarmers Ltd.; Arkema S.A.; Bayer CropScience A.G.; Azoty Tarnow S.A.; ZA Kêdzierzyn S.A.

FURTHER READING

Alperowicz, Natasha, "Four Major Producers Could Combine Under Privatization Scheme," *Chemical Week,* June, 9, 1999, p. 20.

"A New Chance for Pulawy," *Warsaw Voice,* March 12, 2006.

O'Driscoll, Cath, "Zapping the Competition," *ECN-European Chemical News,* September 27, 2004, p. 30.

"The Partner in Business: Strategic Location of Zaklady Azotowe 'Pulawy' S.A. (ZAP) and Advanced Technologies Make for Unique Investment Opportunities," *Chemical Week,* May 26, 2004, p. 28.

"Poland's Largest Nitrate Producer ZA Pulawy," *Poland Business News,* April 4, 2006.

"Polish Fertilizer Firms Join Forces," *Chemical Week,* June 2, 2008, p. 9.

"Polish Firm to Build Urea Facility," *Chemical Week,* September 15, 2008, p. 29.

"Pulawy Plans New Plant," *Warsaw Business Journal,* October 21, 2008.

"Pulawy's Second Go," *Business Warsaw Journal,* July 5, 2005.

Robinson, Simon, "Privatisation of Polish Plants Planned," *ECN-European Chemical News,* December 19, 2005, p. 6.

———, "ZAP Exports Hit by Strength of Zloty," *ECN-European Chemical News,* October 31, 2005, p. 10.

Cumulative Index to Companies

American Coin Merchandising, Inc., 28 15–17; 74 13–16 (upd.)

American Colloid Co., 13 32–35 *see* AMCOL International Corp.

American Commercial Lines Inc., 99 31–34

American Cotton Growers Association *see* Plains Cotton Cooperative Association.

American Crystal Sugar Company, 11 13–15; 32 29–33 (upd.)

American Cyanamid, I 300–02; 8 24–26 (upd.)

American Eagle Outfitters, Inc., 24 26–28; 55 21–24 (upd.)

American Ecology Corporation, 77 36–39

American Electric Power Company, V 546–49; 45 17–21 (upd.)

American Express Company, II 395–99; 10 59–64 (upd.); 38 42–48 (upd.)

American Family Corporation, III 187–89 *see also* AFLAC Inc.

American Financial Group Inc., III 190–92; 48 6–10 (upd.)

American Foods Group, 43 23–27

American Furniture Company, Inc., 21 32–34

American General Corporation, III 193–94; 10 65–67 (upd.); 46 20–23 (upd.)

American General Finance Corp., 11 16–17

American Girl, Inc., 69 16–19 (upd)

American Golf Corporation, 45 22–24

American Gramaphone LLC, 52 18–20

American Greetings Corporation, 7 23–25; 22 33–36 (upd.); 59 34–39 (upd.)

American Healthways, Inc., 65 40–42

American Home Mortgage Holdings, Inc., 46 24–26

American Home Products, I 622–24; 10 68–70 (upd.) *see also* Wyeth.

American Homestar Corporation, 18 26–29; 41 17–20 (upd.)

American Institute of Certified Public Accountants (AICPA), 44 27–30

American International Group, Inc., III 195–98; 15 15–19 (upd.); 47 13–19 (upd.)

American Italian Pasta Company, 27 38–40; 76 18–21 (upd.)

American Kennel Club, Inc., 74 17–19

American Lawyer Media Holdings, Inc., 32 34–37

American Library Association, 86 15–19

American Licorice Company, 86 20–23

American Locker Group Incorporated, 34 19–21

American Lung Association, 48 11–14

American Machine and Metals *see* AMETEK, Inc.

American Maize-Products Co., 14 17–20

American Management Association, 76 22–25

American Management Systems, Inc., 11 18–20

American Media, Inc., 27 41–44; 82 10–15 (upd.)

American Medical Association, 39 15–18

American Medical International, Inc., III 73–75

American Medical Response, Inc., 39 19–22

American Metals Corporation *see* Reliance Steel & Aluminum Co.

American Modern Insurance Group *see* The Midland Co.

American Motors Corp., I 135–37 *see also* DaimlerChrysler AG.

América Móvil, S.A. de C.V., 80 5–8

American MSI Corporation *see* Moldflow Corp.

American National Insurance Company, 8 27–29; 27 45–48 (upd.)

American Olean Tile Company *see* Armstrong Holdings, Inc.

American Oriental Bioengineering Inc., 93 45–48

American Pad & Paper Company, 20 18–21

American Pfauter *see* Gleason Corp.

American Pharmaceutical Partners, Inc., 69 20–22

American Pop Corn Company, 59 40–43

American Power Conversion Corporation, 24 29–31; 67 18–20 (upd.)

American Premier Underwriters, Inc., 10 71–74

American President Companies Ltd., 6 353–55 *see also* APL Ltd.

American Printing House for the Blind, 26 13–15

American Re Corporation, 10 75–77; 35 34–37 (upd.)

American Red Cross, 40 26–29

American Reprographics Company, 75 24–26

American Residential Mortgage Corporation, 8 30–31

American Restaurant Partners, L.P., 93 49–52

American Retirement Corporation, 42 9–12 *see also* Brookdale Senior Living.

American Rice, Inc., 33 30–33

American Rug Craftsmen *see* Mohawk Industries, Inc.

American Safety Razor Company, 20 22–24

American Savings Bank *see* Hawaiian Electric Industries, Inc.

American Science & Engineering, Inc., 81 22–25

American Seating Company, 78 7–11

American Skiing Company, 28 18–21

American Society for the Prevention of Cruelty to Animals (ASPCA), 68 19–22

The American Society of Composers, Authors and Publishers (ASCAP), 29 21–24

American Software Inc., 22 214; 25 20–22

American Standard Companies Inc., III 663–65; 30 46–50 (upd.)

American States Water Company, 46 27–30

American Steamship Company *see* GATX.

American Stores Company, II 604–06; 22 37–40 (upd.) *see also* Albertson's, Inc.

American Superconductor Corporation, 97 32–36

American Technical Ceramics Corp., 67 21–23

American Telephone and Telegraph Company *see* AT&T.

American Tobacco Co. *see* B.A.T. Industries PLC.; Fortune Brands, Inc.

American Tourister, Inc., 16 19–21 *see also* Samsonite Corp.

American Tower Corporation, 33 34–38

American Vanguard Corporation, 47 20–22

American Water Works Company, Inc., 6 443–45; 38 49–52 (upd.)

American Woodmark Corporation, 31 13–16

American Yearbook Company *see* Jostens, Inc.

AmeriCares Foundation, Inc., 87 23–28

Amerigon Incorporated, 97 37–40

AMERIGROUP Corporation, 69 23–26

Amerihost Properties, Inc., 30 51–53

AmeriSource Health Corporation, 37 9–11 (upd.)

AmerisourceBergen Corporation, 64 22–28 (upd.)

Ameristar Casinos, Inc., 33 39–42; 69 27–31 (upd.)

Ameritech Corporation, V 265–68; 18 30–34 (upd.) *see also* AT&T Corp.

Ameritrade Holding Corporation, 34 27–30

Ameriwood Industries International Corp., 17 15–17 *see also* Dorel Industries Inc.

Amerock Corporation, 53 37–40

Ameron International Corporation, 67 24–26

Amersham PLC, 50 21–25

Ames Department Stores, Inc., 9 20–22; 30 54–57 (upd.)

AMETEK, Inc., 9 23–25

N.V. Amev, III 199–202 *see also* Fortis, Inc.

Amey Plc, 47 23–25

AMF Bowling, Inc., 40 30–33

Amfac/JMB Hawaii L.L.C., I 417–18; 24 32–35 (upd.)

Amgen, Inc., 10 78–81; 30 58–61 (upd.); 89 51–57 (upd.)

AMI Metals, Inc. *see* Reliance Steel & Aluminum Co.

AMICAS, Inc., 69 32–34

Amkor Technology, Inc., 69 35–37

Ammirati Puris Lintas *see* Interpublic Group of Companies, Inc.

Amnesty International, 50 26–29

The Boston Symphony Orchestra Inc.,
93 95–99

Bou-Matic, 62 42–44

Bourbon *see* Groupe Bourbon S.A.

Bourbon Corporation, 82 49–52

Bouygues S.A., I 562–64; 24 77–80
(upd.); 97 82–87 (upd.)

Bovis *see* Peninsular and Oriental Steam
Navigation Company (Bovis Division)

Bowater PLC, IV 257–59

Bowlin Travel Centers, Inc., 99 71–75

Bowne & Co., Inc., 23 61–64; 79
74–80 (upd.)

Bowthorpe plc, 33 70–72

The Boy Scouts of America, 34 66–69

Boyd Bros. Transportation Inc., 39
64–66

Boyd Coffee Company, 53 73–75

Boyd Gaming Corporation, 43 80–82

The Boyds Collection, Ltd., 29 71–73

Boyne USA Resorts, 71 65–68

Boys & Girls Clubs of America, 69
73–75

Bozell Worldwide Inc., 25 89–91

Bozzuto's, Inc., 13 111–12

BP p.l.c., 45 46–56 (upd.)

BPB plc, 83 46–49

Braathens ASA, 47 60–62

Brach's Confections, Inc., 15 63–65; 74
43–46 (upd.)

Bradford & Bingley PLC, 65 77–80

Bradlees Discount Department Store
Company, 12 48–50

Bradley Air Services Ltd., 56 38–40

Brady Corporation, 78 50–55 (upd.)

Brake Bros plc, 45 57–59

Bramalea Ltd., 9 83–85

Brambles Industries Limited, 42 47–50

Brammer PLC, 77 64–67

The Branch Group, Inc., 72 43–45

BrandPartners Group, Inc., 58 36–38

Brannock Device Company, 48 68–70

Brascan Corporation, 67 71–73

Brasfield & Gorrie LLC, 87 72–75

Brasil Telecom Participações S.A., 57
67–70

Brass Eagle Inc., 34 70–72

Brauerei Beck & Co., 9 86–87; 33
73–76 (upd.)

Braun GmbH, 51 55–58

Brazil Fast Food Corporation, 74 47–49

Brazos Sportswear, Inc., 23 65–67

Breeze-Eastern Corporation, 95 67–70

Bremer Financial Corp., 45 60–63

Brenntag AG, 8 68–69; 23 68–70 (upd.)

Brescia Group *see* Grupo Brescia.

Briazz, Inc., 53 76–79

The Brickman Group, Ltd., 87 76–79

Bricorama S.A., 68 62–64

Bridgeport Machines, Inc., 17 52–54

Bridgestone Corporation, V 234–35; 21
72–75 (upd.); 59 87–92 (upd.)

Bridgford Foods Corporation, 27 71–73

Briggs & Stratton Corporation, 8
70–73; 27 74–78 (upd.)

Brigham Exploration Company, 75
72–74

Brigham's Inc., 72 46–48

Bright Horizons Family Solutions, Inc.,
31 71–73

Brightpoint, Inc., 18 74–77

Brillstein-Grey Entertainment, 80 41–45

The Brink's Company, 58 39–43 (upd.)

Brinker International, Inc., 10 176–78;
38 100–03 (upd.); 75 75–79 (upd.)

BRIO AB, 24 81–83

Brioche Pasquier S.A., 58 44–46

Brioni Roman Style S.p.A., 67 74–76

BRISA Auto-estradas de Portugal S.A.,
64 55–58

Bristol Hotel Company, 23 71–73

Bristol-Myers Squibb Company, III
17–19; 9 88–91 (upd.); 37 41–45
(upd.)

Bristow Helicopters Ltd., 70 26–28

Britannia Soft Drinks Ltd. (Britvic), 71
69–71

Britannica.com *see* Encyclopaedia
Britannica, Inc.

Brite Voice Systems, Inc., 20 75–78

British Aerospace plc, I 50–53; 24
84–90 (upd.)

British Airways plc, I 92–95; 14 70–74
(upd.); 43 83–88 (upd.)

British American Tobacco PLC, 50
116–19 (upd.)

British-Borneo Oil & Gas PLC, 34
73–75

British Broadcasting Corporation Ltd.,
7 52–55; 21 76–79 (upd.); 89
111–17 (upd.)

British Coal Corporation, IV 38–40

British Columbia Telephone Company,
6 309–11

British Energy Plc, 49 65–68 *see also*
British Nuclear Fuels PLC.

The British Film Institute, 80 46–50

British Gas plc, V 559–63 *see also*
Centrica plc.

British Land Plc, 54 38–41

British Midland plc, 38 104–06

The British Museum, 71 72–74

British Nuclear Fuels PLC, 6 451–54

British Oxygen Co *see* BOC Group.

The British Petroleum Company plc, IV
378–80; 7 56–59 (upd.); 21 80–84
(upd.) *see also* BP p.l.c.

British Railways Board, V 421–24

British Sky Broadcasting Group plc, 20
79–81; 60 66–69 (upd.)

British Steel plc, IV 41–43; 19 62–65
(upd.)

British Sugar plc, 84 25–29

British Telecommunications plc, V
279–82; 15 66–70 (upd.) *see also* BT
Group plc.

The British United Provident
Association Limited, 79 81–84

British Vita plc, 9 92–93; 33 77–79
(upd.)

British World Airlines Ltd., 18 78–80

Britvic Soft Drinks Limited *see* Britannia
Soft Drinks Ltd. (Britvic)

Broadcast Music Inc., 23 74–77; 90
74–79 (upd.)

Broadcom Corporation, 34 76–79; 90
80–85 (upd.)

The Broadmoor Hotel, 30 82–85

Broadwing Corporation, 70 29–32

Brobeck, Phleger & Harrison, LLP, 31
74–76

Brockhaus *see* Bibliographisches Institut &
F.A. Brockhaus AG.

Brodart Company, 84 30–33

Broder Bros. Co., 38 107–09

Broderbund Software, Inc., 13 113–16;
29 74–78 (upd.)

Broken Hill Proprietary Company Ltd.,
IV 44–47; 22 103–08 (upd.) *see also*
BHP Billiton.

Bronco Drilling Company, Inc., 89
118–21

Bronner Brothers Inc., 92 29–32

Bronner Display & Sign Advertising,
Inc., 82 53–57

Brookdale Senior Living, 91 69–73

Brooke Group Ltd., 15 71–73 *see also*
Vector Group Ltd.

Brookfield Properties Corporation, 89
122–25

Brooklyn Union Gas, 6 455–57 *see also*
KeySpan Energy Co.

Brooks Brothers Inc., 22 109–12

Brooks Sports Inc., 32 98–101

Brookshire Grocery Company, 16
63–66; 74 50–53 (upd.)

Brookstone, Inc., 18 81–83

Brose Fahrzeugteile GmbH & Company
KG, 84 34–38

Brother Industries, Ltd., 14 75–76

Brother's Brother Foundation, 93
100–04

Brothers Gourmet Coffees, Inc., 20
82–85 *see also* The Procter & Gamble
Co.

Broughton Foods Co., 17 55–57 *see also*
Suiza Foods Corp.

Brouwerijen Alken-Maes N.V., 86 47–51

Brown & Brown, Inc., 41 63–66

Brown & Haley, 23 78–80

Brown & Root, Inc., 13 117–19 *see also*
Kellogg Brown & Root Inc.

Brown & Sharpe Manufacturing Co., 23
81–84

Brown and Williamson Tobacco
Corporation, 14 77–79; 33 80–83
(upd.)

Brown Brothers Harriman & Co., 45
64–67

Brown-Forman Corporation, I 225–27;
10 179–82 (upd.); 38 110–14 (upd.)

Brown Group, Inc., V 351–53; 20
86–89 (upd.) *see also* Brown Shoe
Company, Inc.

Brown Jordan International Inc., 74
54–57 (upd.)

Brown Printing Company, 26 43–45

Brown Shoe Company, Inc., 68 65–69
(upd.)

Browning-Ferris Industries, Inc., V
749–53; 20 90–93 (upd.)

Broyhill Furniture Industries, Inc., 10
183–85

Iowa Telecommunications Services, Inc., 85 187–90

Ipalco Enterprises, Inc., 6 508–09

IPC Magazines Limited, 7 244–47

Ipiranga S.A., 67 216–18

Ipsen International Inc., 72 192–95

Ipsos SA, 48 221–24

IranAir, 81 214–17

Irex Contracting Group, 90 245–48

Irish Distillers Group, 96 203–07

Irish Life & Permanent Plc, 59 245–47

Irkut Corporation, 68 202–04

iRobot Corporation, 83 212-215

Iron Mountain, Inc., 33 212–14

IRSA Inversiones y Representaciones S.A., 63 212–15

Irvin Feld & Kenneth Feld Productions, Inc., 15 237–39 *see also* Feld Entertainment, Inc.

Irwin Financial Corporation, 77 213–16

Irwin Toy Limited, 14 265–67

Isbank *see* Turkiye Is Bankasi A.S.

Iscor Limited, 57 183–86

Isetan Company Limited, V 85–87; 36 289–93 (upd.)

Ishikawajima-Harima Heavy Industries Company, Ltd., III 532–33; 86 211–15 (upd.)

The Island ECN, Inc., 48 225–29

Isle of Capri Casinos, Inc., 41 217–19

Ispat Inland Inc., 30 252–54; 40 267–72 (upd.)

Israel Aircraft Industries Ltd., 69 215–17

Israel Chemicals Ltd., 55 226–29

ISS A/S, 49 221–23

Istituto per la Ricostruzione Industriale S.p.A., I 465–67; 11 203–06 (upd.)

Isuzu Motors, Ltd., 9 293–95; 23 288–91 (upd.); 57 187–91 (upd.)

Itaú *see* Banco Itaú S.A.

ITC Holdings Corp., 75 206–08

Itel Corporation, 9 296–99

Items International Airwalk Inc., 17 259–61

ITM Entreprises SA, 36 294–97

Ito-Yokado Co., Ltd., V 88–89; 42 189–92 (upd.)

ITOCHU Corporation, 32 283–87 (upd.)

Itoh *see* C. Itoh & Co.

Itoham Foods Inc., II 518–19; 61 138–40 (upd.)

Itron, Inc., 64 202–05

ITT Educational Services, Inc., 33 215–17; 76 200–03 (upd.)

ITT Sheraton Corporation, III 98–101 *see also* Starwood Hotels & Resorts Worldwide, Inc.

ITW *see* Illinois Tool Works Inc.

i2 Technologies, Inc., 87 252–257

Ivar's, Inc., 86 216–19

IVAX Corporation, 11 207–09; 55 230–33 (upd.)

IVC Industries, Inc., 45 208–11

iVillage Inc., 46 253–56

Iwerks Entertainment, Inc., 34 228–30

IXC Communications, Inc., 29 250–52

J

J & J Snack Foods Corporation, 24 240–42

J&R Electronics Inc., 26 224–26

J. & W. Seligman & Co. Inc., 61 141–43

J.A. Jones, Inc., 16 284–86

J. Alexander's Corporation, 65 177–79

J.B. Hunt Transport Services Inc., 12 277–79

J. Baker, Inc., 31 270–73

J C Bamford Excavators Ltd., 83 216-222

J. C. Penney Company, Inc., V 90–92; 18 269–73 (upd.); 43 245–50 (upd.); 91 263–72 (upd.)

J. Crew Group, Inc., 12 280–82; 34 231–34 (upd.); 88 203–08

J.D. Edwards & Company, 14 268–70 *see also* Oracle Corp.

J.D. Power and Associates, 32 297–301

J. D'Addario & Company, Inc., 48 230–33

J.F. Shea Co., Inc., 55 234–36

J.H. Findorff and Son, Inc., 60 175–78

J.I. Case Company, 10 377–81 *see also* CNH Global N.V.

J.J. Darboven GmbH & Co. KG, 96 208–12

J.J. Keller & Associates, Inc., 81 2180–21

The J. Jill Group, Inc., 35 239–41; 90 249–53 (upd.)

J.L. Hammett Company, 72 196–99

J Lauritzen A/S, 90 254–57

J. Lohr Winery Corporation, 99 229–232

The J. M. Smucker Company, 11 210–12; 87 258–265 (upd.)

J.M. Voith AG, 33 222–25

J.P. Morgan Chase & Co., II 329–32; 30 261–65 (upd.); 38 253–59 (upd.)

J.R. Simplot Company, 16 287–89; 60 179–82 (upd.)

J Sainsbury plc, II 657–59; 13 282–84 (upd.); 38 260–65 (upd.); 95 212–20 (upd.)

J. W. Pepper and Son Inc., 86 220–23

J. Walter Thompson Co. *see* JWT Group Inc.

Jabil Circuit, Inc., 36 298–301; 88 209–14

Jack Henry and Associates, Inc., 17 262–65; 94 258–63 (upd.)

Jack in the Box Inc., 89 265–71 (upd.)

Jack Morton Worldwide, 88 215–18

Jack Schwartz Shoes, Inc., 18 266–68

Jackpot Enterprises Inc., 21 298–300

Jackson Hewitt, Inc., 48 234–36

Jackson National Life Insurance Company, 8 276–77

Jacmar Companies, 87 266–269

Jaco Electronics, Inc., 30 255–57

Jacob Leinenkugel Brewing Company, 28 209–11

Jacobs Engineering Group Inc., 6 148–50; 26 220–23 (upd.)

Jacobs Suchard (AG), II 520–22 *see also* Kraft Jacobs Suchard AG.

Jacobson Stores Inc., 21 301–03

Jacor Communications, Inc., 23 292–95

Jacques Whitford, 92 184–87

Jacquot *see* Établissements Jacquot and Cie S.A.S.

Jacuzzi Brands Inc., 23 296–98; 76 204–07 (upd.)

JAFCO Co. Ltd., 79 221–24

Jaguar Cars, Ltd., 13 285–87

JAKKS Pacific, Inc., 52 191–94

JAL *see* Japan Airlines Company, Ltd.

Jalate Inc., 25 245–47

Jamba Juice Company, 47 199–202

James Avery Craftsman, Inc., 76 208–10

James Beattie plc, 43 242–44

James Hardie Industries N.V., 56 174–76

James Original Coney Island Inc., 84 197–200

James Purdey & Sons Limited, 87 270–275

James River Corporation of Virginia, IV 289–91 *see also* Fort James Corp.

Jani-King International, Inc., 85 191–94

Janssen Pharmaceutica N.V., 80 164–67

JanSport, Inc., 70 134–36

Janus Capital Group Inc., 57 192–94

Japan Airlines Company, Ltd., I 104–06; 32 288–92 (upd.)

Japan Broadcasting Corporation, 7 248–50

Japan Leasing Corporation, 8 278–80

Japan Pulp and Paper Company Limited, IV 292–93

Japan Tobacco Inc., V 403–04; 46 257–60 (upd.)

Jarden Corporation, 93 255–61 (upd.)

Jardine Cycle & Carriage Ltd., 73 193–95

Jardine Matheson Holdings Limited, I 468–71; 20 309–14 (upd.); 93 262–71 (upd.)

Jarvis plc, 39 237–39

Jason Incorporated, 23 299–301

Jay Jacobs, Inc., 15 243–45

Jayco Inc., 13 288–90

Jays Foods, Inc., 90 258–61

Jazz Basketball Investors, Inc., 55 237–39

Jazzercise, Inc., 45 212–14

JB Oxford Holdings, Inc., 32 293–96

JBS S.A., 100 233–36

JCDecaux S.A., 76 211–13

JD Wetherspoon plc, 30 258–60

JDS Uniphase Corporation, 34 235–37

JE Dunn Construction Group, Inc., 85 195–98

The Jean Coutu Group (PJC) Inc., 46 261–65

Jean-Georges Enterprises L.L.C., 75 209–11

Jeanneau *see* Chantiers Jeanneau S.A.

Jefferies Group, Inc., 25 248–51

Kajima Corporation, I 577–78; 51 177–79 (upd.)

Kal Kan Foods, Inc., 22 298–300

Kaman Corporation, 12 289–92; 42 204–08 (upd.)

Kaman Music Corporation, 68 205–07

Kampgrounds of America, Inc., 33 230–33

Kamps AG, 44 251–54

Kana Software, Inc., 51 180–83

Kanebo, Ltd., 53 187–91

Kanematsu Corporation, IV 442–44; 24 259–62 (upd.)

Kansai Paint Company Ltd., 80 175–78

The Kansai Electric Power Company, Inc., V 645–48; 62 196–200 (upd.)

Kansallis-Osake-Pankki, II 302–03

Kansas City Power & Light Company, 6 510–12 see also Great Plains Energy Inc.

Kansas City Southern Industries, Inc., 6 400–02; 26 233–36 (upd.)

The Kansas City Southern Railway Company, 92 198–202

Kao Corporation, III 38–39; 20 315–17 (upd.); 79 225–30 (upd.)

Kaplan, Inc., 42 209–12; 90 270–75 (upd.)

Kar Nut Products Company, 86 233–36

Karan Co. see Donna Karan Co.

Karl Kani Infinity, Inc., 49 242–45

Karlsberg Brauerei GmbH & Co KG, 41 220–23

Karmann see Wilhelm Karmann GmbH.

Karstadt Aktiengesellschaft, V 100–02; 19 234–37 (upd.)

Karstadt Quelle AG, 57 195–201 (upd.)

Karsten Manufacturing Corporation, 51 184–86

Kash n' Karry Food Stores, Inc., 20 318–20

Kashi Company, 89 282–85

Kasper A.S.L., Ltd., 40 276–79

kate spade LLC, 68 208–11

Katokichi Company Ltd., 82 187–90

Katy Industries Inc., I 472–74; 51 187–90 (upd.)

Katz Communications, Inc., 6 32–34 see also Clear Channel Communications, Inc.

Katz Media Group, Inc., 35 245–48

Kaufhof Warenhaus AG, V 103–05; 23 311–14 (upd.)

Kaufman and Broad Home Corporation, 8 284–86 see also KB Home.

Kaufring AG, 35 249–52

Kawai Musical Instruments Manufacturing Co.,Ltd., 78 189–92

Kawasaki Heavy Industries, Ltd., III 538–40; 63 220–23 (upd.)

Kawasaki Kisen Kaisha, Ltd., V 457–60; 56 177–81 (upd.)

Kawasaki Steel Corporation, IV 124–25

Kay-Bee Toy Stores, 15 252–53 see also KB Toys.

Kaydon Corporation, 18 274–76

KB Home, 45 218–22 (upd.)

KB Toys, Inc., 35 253–55 (upd.); 86 237–42 (upd.)

KC see Kenneth Cole Productions, Inc.

KCPL see Kansas City Power & Light Co.

KCSI see Kansas City Southern Industries, Inc.

KCSR see The Kansas City Southern Railway.

Keane, Inc., 56 182–86

Keebler Foods Company, 36 311–13

Keio Corporation, V 461–62; 96 235–39 (upd.)

The Keith Companies Inc., 54 181–84

Keithley Instruments Inc., 16 299–301

Kelda Group plc, 45 223–26

Kelley Blue Book Company, Inc., 84 218–221

Keller Group PLC, 95 221–24

Kelley Drye & Warren LLP, 40 280–83

Kellogg Brown & Root, Inc., 62 201–05 (upd.)

Kellogg Company, II 523–26; 13 291–94 (upd.); 50 291–96 (upd.)

Kellwood Company, 8 287–89; 85 203–08 (upd.)

Kelly-Moore Paint Company, Inc., 56 187–89

Kelly Services, Inc., 6 35–37; 26 237–40 (upd.)

The Kelly-Springfield Tire Company, 8 290–92

Kelsey-Hayes Group of Companies, 7 258–60; 27 249–52 (upd.)

Kemet Corp., 14 281–83

Kemira Oyj, 70 143–46

Kemper Corporation, III 269–71; 15 254–58 (upd.)

Ken's Foods, Inc., 88 223–26

Kendall International, Inc., 11 219–21 see also Tyco International Ltd.

Kendall-Jackson Winery, Ltd., 28 221–23

Kendle International Inc., 87 276–279

Kenetech Corporation, 11 222–24

Kenexa Corporation, 87 280–284

Kenmore Air Harbor Inc., 65 191–93

Kennametal, Inc., 13 295–97; 68 212–16 (upd.)

Kennecott Corporation, 7 261–64; 27 253–57 (upd.) see also Rio Tinto PLC.

Kennedy-Wilson, Inc., 60 183–85

Kenneth Cole Productions, Inc., 25 256–58

Kensey Nash Corporation, 71 185–87

Kensington Publishing Corporation, 84 222–225

Kent Electronics Corporation, 17 273–76

Kentucky Electric Steel, Inc., 31 286–88

Kentucky Fried Chicken see KFC Corp.

Kentucky Utilities Company, 6 513–15

Kenwood Corporation, 31 289–91

Kenya Airways Limited, 89 286–89

Keolis SA, 51 191–93

Kepco see Korea Electric Power Corporation; Kyushu Electric Power Company Inc.

Keppel Corporation Ltd., 73 201–03

Keramik Holding AG Laufen, 51 194–96

Kerasotes ShowPlace Theaters LLC, 80 179–83

Kerr Group Inc., 24 263–65

Kerr-McGee Corporation, IV 445–47; 22 301–04 (upd.); 68 217–21 (upd.)

Kerry Group plc, 27 258–60; 87 285–291 (upd.)

Kerry Properties Limited, 22 305–08

Kerzner International Limited, 69 222–24 (upd.)

Kesa Electricals plc, 91 285–90

Kesko Ltd (Kesko Oy), 8 293–94; 27 261–63 (upd.)

Ketchum Communications Inc., 6 38–40

Kettle Foods Inc., 48 240–42

Kewaunee Scientific Corporation, 25 259–62

Kewpie Kabushiki Kaisha, 57 202–05

Key Safety Systems, Inc., 63 224–26

Key Tronic Corporation, 14 284–86

KeyCorp, 8 295–97; 92272–81 (upd.)

Keyes Fibre Company, 9 303–05

Keys Fitness Products, LP, 83 231–234

KeySpan Energy Co., 27 264–66

Keystone International, Inc., 11 225–27 see also Tyco International Ltd.

KFC Corporation, 7 265–68; 21 313–17 (upd.); 89 290–96 (upd.)

Kforce Inc., 71 188–90

KGHM Polska Miedz S.A., 98 223–26

KHD Konzern, III 541–44

KI, 57 206–09

Kia Motors Corporation, 12 293–95; 29 264–67 (upd.); 56 173

Kiabi Europe, 66 199–201

Kidde plc, I 475–76; 44 255–59 (upd.)

Kiehl's Since 1851, Inc., 52 209–12

Kikkoman Corporation, 14 287–89; 47 203–06 (upd.)

Kimball International, Inc., 12 296–98; 48 243–47 (upd.)

Kimberly-Clark Corporation, III 40–41; 16 302–05 (upd.); 43 256–60 (upd.)

Kimberly-Clark de México, S.A. de C.V., 54 185–87

Kimco Realty Corporation, 11 228–30

Kinder Morgan, Inc., 45 227–30

KinderCare Learning Centers, Inc., 13 298–300

Kinetic Concepts, Inc., 20 321–23

King & Spalding, 23 315–18

The King Arthur Flour Company, 31 292–95

King Kullen Grocery Co., Inc., 15 259–61

King Nut Company, 74 165–67

King Pharmaceuticals, Inc., 54 188–90

King Ranch, Inc., 14 290–92; 60 186–89 (upd.)

King World Productions, Inc., 9 306–08; 30 269–72 (upd.)

Kingfisher plc, V 106–09; 24 266–71 (upd.); 83 235–242 (upd.)

Kingston Technology Corporation, 20 324–26

Kumon Institute of Education Co., Ltd., 72 211–14
Kuoni Travel Holding Ltd., 40 284–86
Kurzweil Technologies, Inc., 51 200–04
The Kushner-Locke Company, 25 269–71
Kuwait Airways Corporation, 68 226–28
Kuwait Flour Mills & Bakeries Company, 84 232–234
Kuwait Petroleum Corporation, IV 450–52; 55 240–43 (upd.)
Kvaerner ASA, 36 321–23
Kwang Yang Motor Company Ltd., 80 193–96
Kwik-Fit Holdings plc, 54 205–07
Kwik Save Group plc, 11 239–41
Kymmene Corporation, IV 299–303 see also UPM-Kymmene Corp.
Kyocera Corporation, II 50–52; 21 329–32 (upd.); 79 231–36 (upd.)
Kyokuyo Company Ltd., 75 228–30
Kyowa Hakko Kogyo Co., Ltd., III 42–43; 48 248–50 (upd.)
Kyphon Inc., 87 292–295
Kyushu Electric Power Company Inc., V 649–51

L

L. and J.G. Stickley, Inc., 50 303–05
L-3 Communications Holdings, Inc., 48 251–53
L.A. Darling Company, 92 203–06
L.A. Gear, Inc., 8 303–06; 32 313–17 (upd.)
L.A. T Sportswear, Inc., 26 257–59
L.B. Foster Company, 33 255–58
L.D.C. SA, 61 155–57
L.L. Bean, Inc., 10 388–90; 38 280–83 (upd.); 91 307–13 (upd.)
The L.L. Knickerbocker Co., Inc., 25 272–75
L. Luria & Son, Inc., 19 242–44
L. M. Berry and Company, 80 197–200
L.S. Starrett Company, 13 301–03; 64 227–30 (upd.)
La Choy Food Products Inc., 25 276–78
La Madeleine French Bakery & Café, 33 249–51
La Poste, V 270–72; 47 213–16 (upd.)
The La Quinta Companies, 11 242–44; 42 213–16 (upd.)
La Reina Inc., 96 252–55
La Seda de Barcelona S.A., 100 260–63
La Senza Corporation, 66 205–07
La-Z-Boy Incorporated, 14 302–04; 50 309–13 (upd.)
LAB see Lloyd Aéreo Boliviano S.A
LaBarge Inc., 41 224–26
Labatt Brewing Company Limited, I 267–68; 25 279–82 (upd.)
Labeyrie SAS, 80 201–04
LabOne, Inc., 48 254–57
Labor Ready, Inc., 29 273–75; 88 231–36 (upd.)
Laboratoires Arkopharma S.A., 75 231–34

Laboratoires de Biologie Végétale Yves Rocher, 35 262–65
Laboratoires Pierre Fabre S.A., 100 353–57
Laboratory Corporation of America Holdings, 42 217–20 (upd.)
LaBranche & Co. Inc., 37 223–25
LaCie Group S.A., 76 232–34
Lacks Enterprises Inc., 61 158–60
Laclede Steel Company, 15 271–73
LaCrosse Footwear, Inc., 18 298–301; 61 161–65 (upd.)
Ladbroke Group PLC, II 141–42; 21 333–36 (upd.) see also Hilton Group plc.
LADD Furniture, Inc., 12 299–301 see also La-Z-Boy Inc.
Ladish Co., Inc., 30 282–84
Lafarge Cement UK, 54 208–11 (upd.)
Lafarge Coppée S.A., III 703–05
Lafarge Corporation, 28 228–31
Lafuma S.A., 39 248–50
Laidlaw International, Inc., 80 205–08
Laing O'Rourke PLC, 93 282–85 (upd.)
L'Air Liquide SA, I 357–59; 47 217–20 (upd.)
Lakeland Industries, Inc., 45 245–48
Lakes Entertainment, Inc., 51 205–07
Lakeside Foods, Inc., 89 297–301
Lala see Grupo Industrial Lala, S.A. de C.V.
Lam Research Corporation, 11 245–47; 31 299–302 (upd.)
Lam Son Sugar Joint Stock Corporation (Lasuco), 60 195–97
Lamar Advertising Company, 27 278–80; 70 150–53 (upd.)
The Lamaur Corporation, 41 227–29
Lamb Weston, Inc., 23 319–21
Lamborghini see Automobili Lamborghini S.p.A.
Lamonts Apparel, Inc., 15 274–76
The Lamson & Sessions Co., 13 304–06; 61 166–70 (upd.)
Lan Chile S.A., 31 303–06
Lancair International, Inc., 67 224–26
Lancaster Colony Corporation, 8 307–09; 61 171–74 (upd.)
Lance, Inc., 14 305–07; 41 230–33 (upd.)
Lancer Corporation, 21 337–39
Land O'Lakes, Inc., II 535–37; 21 340–43 (upd.); 81 222–27 (upd.)
Land Securities PLC, IV 704–06; 49 246–50 (upd.)
LandAmerica Financial Group, Inc., 85 213–16
Landauer, Inc., 51 208–10
Landec Corporation, 95 235–38
Landmark Communications, Inc., 12 302–05; 55 244–49 (upd.)
Landmark Theatre Corporation, 70 154–56
Landor Associates, 81 228–31
Landry's Restaurants, Inc., 15 277–79; 65 203–07 (upd.)
Lands' End, Inc., 9 314–16; 29 276–79 (upd.); 82 195–200 (upd.)

Landsbanki Islands hf, 81 232–35
Landstar System, Inc., 63 236–38
Lane Bryant, Inc., 64 231–33
The Lane Co., Inc., 12 306–08
Lanier Worldwide, Inc., 75 235–38
Lanoga Corporation, 62 222–24 see also Pro-Build Holdings Inc.
Lapeyre S.A. see Groupe Lapeyre S.A.
Larry Flynt Publishing Inc., 31 307–10
Larry H. Miller Group, 29 280–83
Las Vegas Sands, Inc., 50 306–08
Laserscope, 67 227–29
LaSiDo Inc., 58 209–11
Lason, Inc., 31 311–13
Lassonde Industries Inc., 68 229–31
Lasuco see Lam Son Sugar Joint Stock Corp.
Latécoère S.A., 100 264–68
Latham & Watkins, 33 252–54
Latrobe Brewing Company, 54 212–14
Lattice Semiconductor Corp., 16 315–17
Lauda Air Luftfahrt AG, 48 258–60
Laura Ashley Holdings plc, 13 307–09; 37 226–29 (upd.)
The Laurel Pub Company Limited, 59 255–57
Laurent-Perrier SA, 42 221–23
Laurus N.V., 65 208–11
Lavoro Bank AG see Banca Nazionale del Lavoro SpA.
Lawson Software, 38 284–88
Lawter International Inc., 14 308–10 see also Eastman Chemical Co.
Layne Christensen Company, 19 245–47
Lazard LLC, 38 289–92
Lazare Kaplan International Inc., 21 344–47
Lazio see Società Sportiva Lazio SpA.
Lazy Days RV Center, Inc., 69 228–30
LCA-Vision, Inc, 85 217–20
LCC International, Inc., 84 235–238
LCI International, Inc., 16 318–20 see also Qwest Communications International, Inc.
LDB Corporation, 53 204–06
LDC, 68 232–34
LDC S.A.see L.D.C. S.A.
LDDS-Metro Communications, Inc., 8 310–12 see also MCI WorldCom, Inc.
LDI Ltd., LLC, 76 235–37
Le Bon Marché see The Bon Marché.
Le Chateau Inc., 63 239–41
Le Cordon Bleu S.A., 67 230–32
Le Duff see Groupe Le Duff S.A.
Le Monde S.A., 33 308–10
Léa Nature see Groupe Léa Nature.
Leap Wireless International, Inc., 69 231–33
LeapFrog Enterprises, Inc., 54 215–18
Lear Corporation, 16 321–23; 71 191–95 (upd.)
Lear Siegler Inc., I 481–83
Learjet Inc., 8 313–16; 27 281–85 (upd.)
Learning Care Group, Inc., 76 238–41 (upd.)

Martin Marietta Corporation, I 67–69
see also Lockheed Martin Corp.
MartinLogan, Ltd., 85 248–51
Martini & Rossi SpA, 63 264–66
Martz Group, 56 221–23
Marubeni Corporation, I 492–95; 24
324–27 (upd.)
Maruha Group Inc., 75 250–53 (upd.)
Marui Company Ltd., V 127; 62
243–45 (upd.)
Maruzen Co., Limited, 18 322–24
Marvel Entertainment, Inc., 10 400–02;
78 212–19 (upd.)
Marvin Lumber & Cedar Company, 22
345–47
Mary Kay Inc., 9 330–32; 30 306–09
(upd.); 84 251–256 (upd.)
Maryland & Virginia Milk Producers
Cooperative Association, Inc., 80
240–43
Maryville Data Systems Inc., 96 273–76
Marzotto S.p.A., 20 356–58; 67 246–49
(upd.)
The Maschhoffs, Inc., 82 217–20
Masco Corporation, III 568–71; 20
359–63 (upd.); 39 263–68 (upd.)
Maserati *see* Officine Alfieri Maserati
S.p.A.
Mashantucket Pequot Gaming
Enterprise Inc., 35 282–85
Masland Corporation, 17 303–05 *see
also* Lear Corp.
Masonite International Corporation, 63
267–69
Massachusetts Mutual Life Insurance
Company, III 285–87; 53 210–13
(upd.)
Massey Energy Company, 57 236–38
MasTec, Inc., 55 259–63 (upd.)
Master Lock Company, 45 268–71
MasterBrand Cabinets, Inc., 71 216–18
MasterCard Worldwide, 9 333–35; 96
277–81 (upd.)
MasterCraft Boat Company, Inc., 90
290–93
Matalan PLC, 49 258–60
Match.com, LP, 87 308–311
Material Sciences Corporation, 63
270–73
The MathWorks, Inc., 80 244–47
Matra-Hachette S.A., 15 293–97 (upd.)
see also European Aeronautic Defence
and Space Company EADS N.V.
Matria Healthcare, Inc., 17 306–09
Matrix Essentials Inc., 90 294–97
Matrix Service Company, 65 221–23
Matrixx Initiatives, Inc., 74 177–79
Matsushita Electric Industrial Co., Ltd.,
II 55–56; 64 255–58 (upd.)
Matsushita Electric Works, Ltd., III
710–11; 7 302–03 (upd.)
Matsuzakaya Company Ltd., V 129–31;
64 259–62 (upd.)
Matt Prentice Restaurant Group, 70
173–76
Mattel, Inc., 7 304–07; 25 311–15
(upd.); 61 198–203 (upd.)
Matth. Hohner AG, 53 214–17

Matthews International Corporation, 29
304–06; 77 248–52 (upd.)
Matussière et Forest SA, 58 220–22
Maui Land & Pineapple Company, Inc.,
29 307–09; 100 273–77 (upd.)
Maui Wowi, Inc., 85 252–55
Mauna Loa Macadamia Nut
Corporation, 64 263–65
Maurices Inc., 95 255–58
Maus Frères SA, 48 277–79
Maverick Ranch Association, Inc., 88
253–56
Maverick Tube Corporation, 59 280–83
Max & Erma's Restaurants Inc., 19
258–60; 100 278–82 (upd.)
Maxco Inc., 17 310–11
Maxicare Health Plans, Inc., III 84–86;
25 316–19 (upd.)
The Maxim Group, 25 320–22
Maxim Integrated Products, Inc., 16
358–60
MAXIMUS, Inc., 43 277–80
Maxtor Corporation, 10 403–05 *see also*
Seagate Technology, Inc.
Maxus Energy Corporation, 7 308–10
Maxwell Communication Corporation
plc, IV 641–43; 7 311–13 (upd.)
Maxwell Shoe Company, Inc., 30
310–12 *see also* Jones Apparel Group,
Inc.
MAXXAM Inc., 8 348–50
Maxxim Medical Inc., 12 325–27
The May Department Stores Company,
V 132–35; 19 261–64 (upd.); 46
284–88 (upd.)
May Gurney Integrated Services PLC,
95 259–62
May International *see* George S. May
International Co.
Mayer, Brown, Rowe & Maw, 47
230–32
Mayfield Dairy Farms, Inc., 74 180–82
Mayflower Group Inc., 6 409–11
Mayo Foundation, 9 336–39; 34
265–69 (upd.)
Mayor's Jewelers, Inc., 41 254–57
Maytag Corporation, III 572–73; 22
348–51 (upd.); 82 221–25 (upd.)
Mazda Motor Corporation, 9 340–42;
23 338–41 (upd.); 63 274–79 (upd.)
Mazel Stores, Inc., 29 310–12
Mazzio's Corporation, 76 259–61
MBB *see* Messerschmitt-Bölkow-Blohm.
MBC Holding Company, 40 306–09
MBE *see* Mail Boxes Etc.
MBIA Inc., 73 223–26
MBK Industrie S.A., 94 303–06
MBNA Corporation, 12 328–30; 33
291–94 (upd.)
MC Sporting Goods *see* Michigan
Sporting Goods Distributors Inc.
MCA Inc., II 143–45 *see also* Universal
Studios.
McAfee Inc., 94 307–10
McAlister's Corporation, 66 217–19
McBride plc, 82 226–30
MCC *see* Morris Communications Corp.
McCain Foods Limited, 77 253–56

McCarthy Building Companies, Inc., 48
280–82
McCaw Cellular Communications, Inc.,
6 322–24 *see also* AT&T Wireless
Services, Inc.
McClain Industries, Inc., 51 236–38
The McClatchy Company, 23 342–44;
92 231–35 (upd.)
McCormick & Company, Incorporated,
7 314–16; 27 297–300 (upd.)
McCormick & Schmick's Seafood
Restaurants, Inc., 71 219–21
McCoy Corporation, 58 223–25
McDATA Corporation, 75 254–56
McDermott International, Inc., III
558–60; 37 242–46 (upd.)
McDonald's Corporation, II 646–48; 7
317–19 (upd.); 26 281–85 (upd.); 63
280–86 (upd.)
McDonnell Douglas Corporation, I
70–72; 11 277–80 (upd.) *see also*
Boeing Co.
McGrath RentCorp, 91 326–29
The McGraw-Hill Companies, Inc., IV
634–37; 18 325–30 (upd.); 51
239–44 (upd.)
MCI *see* Melamine Chemicals, Inc.
MCI WorldCom, Inc., V 302–04; 27
301–08 (upd.) *see also* Verizon
Communications Inc.
McIlhenny Company, 20 364–67
McJunkin Corporation, 63 287–89
McKechnie plc, 34 270–72
McKee Foods Corporation, 7 320–21;
27 309–11 (upd.)
McKesson Corporation, I 496–98; 12
331–33 (upd.); 47 233–37 (upd.)
McKinsey & Company, Inc., 9 343–45
McLane Company, Inc., 13 332–34
McLeodUSA Incorporated, 32 327–30
McMenamins Pubs and Breweries, 65
224–26
McMoRan *see* Freeport-McMoRan Copper
& Gold, Inc.
MCN Corporation, 6 519–22
McNaughton Apparel Group, Inc., 92
236–41 (upd.)
McPherson's Ltd., 66 220–22
McQuay International *see* AAF-McQuay
Inc.
MCSi, Inc., 41 258–60
McWane Corporation, 55 264–66
MDC Partners Inc., 63 290–92
MDU Resources Group, Inc., 7 322–25;
42 249–53 (upd.)
The Mead Corporation, IV 310–13; 19
265–69 (upd.) *see also* MeadWestvaco
Corp.
Mead Data Central, Inc., 10 406–08 *see
also* LEXIS-NEXIS Group.
Mead Johnson & Company, 84
257–262
Meade Instruments Corporation, 41
261–64
Meadowcraft, Inc., 29 313–15; 100
283–87 (upd.)
MeadWestvaco Corporation, 76 262–71
(upd.)

Sime Darby Berhad, 14 448–50; 36 433–36 (upd.)

Simmons Company, 47 361–64

Simon & Schuster Inc., IV 671–72; 19 403–05 (upd.); 100 393–97 (upd.)

Simon Property Group Inc., 27 399–402; 84 350–355 (upd.)

Simon Transportation Services Inc., 27 403–06

Simplex Technologies Inc., 21 460–63

Simplicity Manufacturing, Inc., 64 353–56

Simpson Investment Company, 17 438–41

Simpson Thacher & Bartlett, 39 365–68

Simula, Inc., 41 368–70

SINA Corporation, 69 324–27

Sinclair Broadcast Group, Inc., 25 417–19

Sine Qua Non, 99 419–422

Singapore Airlines Limited, 6 117–18; 27 407–09 (upd.); 83 355–359 (upd.)

Singapore Press Holdings Limited, 85 391–95

Singer & Friedlander Group plc, 41 371–73

The Singer Company N.V., 30 417–20 (upd.)

The Singing Machine Company, Inc., 60 277–80

Sir Speedy, Inc., 16 448–50

Sirius Satellite Radio, Inc., 69 328–31

Sirti S.p.A., 76 326–28

Siskin Steel & Supply Company, 70 294–96

Sistema JSFC, 73 303–05

Six Flags, Inc., 17 442–44; 54 333–40 (upd.)

Sixt AG, 39 369–72

SJW Corporation, 70 297–99

SK Group, 88 363–67

Skadden, Arps, Slate, Meagher & Flom, 18 486–88

Skalli Group, 67 349–51

Skandia Insurance Company, Ltd., 50 431–34

Skandinaviska Enskilda Banken AB, II 351–53; 56 326–29 (upd.)

Skanska AB, 38 435–38

Skechers U.S.A. Inc., 31 413–15; 88 368–72 (upd.)

Skeeter Products Inc., 96 391–94

SKF see Aktiebolaget SKF.

Skidmore, Owings & Merrill LLP, 13 475–76; 69 332–35 (upd.)

SkillSoft Public Limited Company, 81 371–74

skinnyCorp, LLC, 97 374–77

Skipton Building Society, 80 344–47

Skis Rossignol S.A., 15 460–62; 43 373–76 (upd.)

Skoda Auto a.s., 39 373–75

Skyline Chili, Inc., 62 325–28

Skyline Corporation, 30 421–23

SkyMall, Inc., 26 439–41

SkyWest, Inc., 25 420–24

Skyy Spirits LLC, 78 348–51

SL Green Realty Corporation, 44 383–85

SL Industries, Inc., 77 383–86

Sleeman Breweries Ltd., 74 305–08

Sleepy's Inc., 32 426–28

SLI, Inc., 48 358–61

Slim-Fast Foods Company, 18 489–91; 66 296–98 (upd.)

Slinky, Inc. see Poof-Slinky, Inc.

SLM Holding Corp., 25 425–28 (upd.)

Slough Estates PLC, IV 722–25; 50 435–40 (upd.)

Small Planet Foods, Inc., 89 410–14

Smart & Final LLC, 16 451–53; 94 392–96 (upd.)

Smart Balance, Inc., 100 398–401

SMART Modular Technologies, Inc., 86 361–64

SmartForce PLC, 43 377–80

Smarties see Ce De Candy Inc.

SMBC see Sumitomo Mitsui Banking Corp.

Smead Manufacturing Co., 17 445–48

SMG see Scottish Media Group.

SMH see Sanders Morris Harris Group Inc.; The Swatch Group SA.

Smith & Hawken, Ltd., 68 343–45

Smith & Nephew plc, 17 449–52; 41 374–78 (upd.)

Smith & Wesson Corp., 30 424–27; 73 306–11 (upd.)

Smith Barney Inc., 15 463–65 see also Citigroup Inc.

Smith Corona Corp., 13 477–80

Smith International, Inc., 15 466–68; 59 376–80 (upd.)

Smith-Midland Corporation, 56 330–32

Smith's Food & Drug Centers, Inc., 8 472–74; 57 324–27 (upd.)

Smithfield Foods, Inc., 7 477–78; 43 381–84 (upd.)

SmithKline Beckman Corporation, I 692–94 see also GlaxoSmithKline plc.

SmithKline Beecham plc, III 65–67; 32 429–34 (upd.) see also GlaxoSmithKline plc.

Smiths Industries PLC, 25 429–31

Smithsonian Institution, 27 410–13

Smithway Motor Xpress Corporation, 39 376–79

Smoby International SA, 56 333–35

Smorgon Steel Group Ltd., 62 329–32

Smucker's see The J.M. Smucker Co.

Smurfit-Stone Container Corporation, 26 442–46 (upd.) ; 83 360-368 (upd.)

Snap-On, Incorporated, 7 479–80; 27 414–16 (upd.)

Snapfish, 83 369–372

Snapple Beverage Corporation, 11 449–51

SNC-Lavalin Group Inc., 72 330–33

SNCF see Société Nationale des Chemins de Fer Français.

SNEA see Société Nationale Elf Aquitaine.

Snecma Group, 46 369–72

Snell & Wilmer L.L.P., 28 425–28

SNET see Southern New England Telecommunications Corp.

Snow Brand Milk Products Company, Ltd., II 574–75; 48 362–65 (upd.)

Soap Opera Magazine see American Media, Inc.

Sobeys Inc., 80 348–51

Socata see EADS SOCATA.

Società Finanziaria Telefonica per Azioni, V 325–27

Società Sportiva Lazio SpA, 44 386–88

Société Air France, 27 417–20 (upd.).

Société BIC S.A., 73 312–15

Société d'Exploitation AOM Air Liberté SA (AirLib), 53 305–07

Societe des Produits Marnier-Lapostolle S.A., 88 373–76

Société du Figaro S.A., 60 281–84

Société du Louvre, 27 421–23

Société Générale, II 354–56; 42 347–51 (upd.)

Société Industrielle Lesaffre, 84 356–359

Société Luxembourgeoise de Navigation Aérienne S.A., 64 357–59

Société Nationale des Chemins de Fer Français, V 512–15; 57 328–32 (upd.)

Société Nationale Elf Aquitaine, IV 544–47; 7 481–85 (upd.)

Société Norbert Dentressangle S.A., 67 352–54

Société Tunisienne de l'Air-Tunisair, 49 371–73

Society Corporation, 9 474–77

Sodexho SA, 29 442–44; 91 433–36 (upd.)

Sodiaal S.A., 19 50; 36 437–39 (upd.)

SODIMA, II 576–77 see also Sodiaal S.A.

Soft Sheen Products, Inc., 31 416–18

Softbank Corporation, 13 481–83; 38 439–44 (upd.); 77 387–95 (upd.)

Sojitz Corporation, 96 395–403 (upd.)

Sol Meliá S.A., 71 337–39

Sola International Inc., 71 340–42

Solar Turbines Inc., 100 402–06

Sole Technology Inc., 93 405–09

Solectron Corporation, 12 450–52; 48 366–70 (upd.)

Solo Serve Corporation, 28 429–31

Solutia Inc., 52 312–15

Solvay & Cie S.A., I 394–96; 21 464–67 (upd.)

Solvay S.A., 61 329–34 (upd.)

Somerfield plc, 47 365–69 (upd.)

Sommer-Allibert S.A., 19 406–09 see also Tarkett Sommer AG.

Sompo Japan Insurance, Inc., 98 359–63 (upd.)

Sonae SGPS, S.A., 97 378–81

Sonat, Inc., 6 577–78 see also El Paso Corp.

Sonatrach, 65 313–17 (upd.)

Sonera Corporation, 50 441–44 see also TeliaSonera AB.

Sonesta International Hotels Corporation, 44 389–91

Sonic Automotive, Inc., 77 396–99

Index to Industries

Accounting

American Institute of Certified Public Accountants (AICPA), 44
Andersen, 29 (upd.); 68 (upd.)
Automatic Data Processing, Inc., III; 9 (upd.); 47 (upd.)
BDO Seidman LLP, 96
BKD LLP, 96
CROSSMARK, 79
Deloitte Touche Tohmatsu International, 9; 29 (upd.)
Ernst & Young, 9; 29 (upd.)
FTI Consulting, Inc., 77
Grant Thornton International, 57
Huron Consulting Group Inc., 87
KPMG International, 33 (upd.)
L.S. Starrett Co., 13
McLane Company, Inc., 13
NCO Group, Inc., 42
Paychex, Inc., 15; 46 (upd.)
PKF International 78
Plante & Moran, LLP, 71
PRG-Schultz International, Inc., 73
PricewaterhouseCoopers, 9; 29 (upd.)
Resources Connection, Inc., 81
Robert Wood Johnson Foundation, 35
RSM McGladrey Business Services Inc., 98
Saffery Champness, 80
Sanders\Wingo, 99
Schenck Business Solutions, 88
StarTek, Inc., 79
Travelzoo Inc., 79

Univision Communications Inc., 24; 83 (upd.)

Advertising & Other Business Services

ABM Industries Incorporated, 25 (upd.)
Abt Associates Inc., 95
AchieveGlobal Inc., 90
Ackerley Communications, Inc., 9
ACNielsen Corporation, 13; 38 (upd.)
Acosta Sales and Marketing Company, Inc., 77
Acsys, Inc., 44
Adecco S.A., 36 (upd.)
Adia S.A., 6
Administaff, Inc., 52
The Advertising Council, Inc., 76
The Advisory Board Company, 80
Advo, Inc., 6; 53 (upd.)
Aegis Group plc, 6
Affiliated Computer Services, Inc., 61
AHL Services, Inc., 27
Allegis Group, Inc., 95
Alloy, Inc., 55
Amdocs Ltd., 47
American Building Maintenance Industries, Inc., 6
American Library Association, 86
The American Society of Composers, Authors and Publishers (ASCAP), 29
Amey Plc, 47
Analysts International Corporation, 36
aQuantive, Inc., 81
The Arbitron Company, 38
Ariba, Inc., 57
Armor Holdings, Inc., 27
Asatsu-DK Inc., 82
Ashtead Group plc, 34

The Associated Press, 13
Avalon Correctional Services, Inc., 75
Bain & Company, 55
Barrett Business Services, Inc., 16
Barton Protective Services Inc., 53
Bates Worldwide, Inc., 14; 33 (upd.)
Bearings, Inc., 13
Berlitz International, Inc., 13
Bernard Hodes Group Inc., 86
Bernstein-Rein, 92
Big Flower Press Holdings, Inc., 21
Billing Concepts, Inc., 26; 72 (upd.)
The BISYS Group, Inc., 73
Boron, LePore & Associates, Inc., 45
The Boston Consulting Group, 58
Bozell Worldwide Inc., 25
BrandPartners Group, Inc., 58
Bright Horizons Family Solutions, Inc., 31
Broadcast Music Inc., 23; 90 (upd.)
Buck Consultants, Inc., 55
Bureau Veritas SA, 55
Burke, Inc., 88
Burns International Services Corporation, 13; 41 (upd.)
Cambridge Technology Partners, Inc., 36
Campbell-Ewald Advertising, 86
Campbell-Mithun-Esty, Inc., 16
Cannon Design, 63
Capita Group PLC, 69
Cardtronics, Inc., 93
Career Education Corporation, 45
Carmichael Lynch Inc., 28
Cash Systems, Inc., 93
Cazenove Group plc, 72
CCC Information Services Group Inc., 74
CDI Corporation, 6; 54 (upd.)
Central Parking Corporation, 18
Century Business Services, Inc., 52
Chancellor Beacon Academies, Inc., 53

Observer AB, 55
OfficeTiger, LLC, 75
The Ogilvy Group, Inc., I
Olsten Corporation, 6; 29 (upd.)
Omnicom Group, I; 22 (upd.); 77 (upd.)
On Assignment, Inc., 20
1-800-FLOWERS, Inc., 26
Opinion Research Corporation, 46
Oracle Corporation, 67 (upd.)
Orbitz, Inc., 61
Outdoor Systems, Inc., 25
Paris Corporation, 22
Paychex, Inc., 15; 46 (upd.)
PDI, Inc., 52
Pegasus Solutions, Inc., 75
Pei Cobb Freed & Partners Architects
    LLP, 57
Penauille Polyservices SA, 49
PFSweb, Inc., 73
Philip Services Corp., 73
Phillips, de Pury & Luxembourg, 49
Pierce Leahy Corporation, 24
Pinkerton's Inc., 9
Plante & Moran, LLP, 71
PMT Services, Inc., 24
Posterscope Worldwide, 70
Priceline.com Incorporated, 57
Publicis Groupe, 19; 77 (upd.)
Publishers Clearing House, 23; 64 (upd.)
Quintiles Transnational Corporation, 68
    (upd.)
Quovadx Inc., 70
Randstad Holding n.v., 16; 43 (upd.)
RedPeg Marketing, 73
RedPrairie Corporation, 74
RemedyTemp, Inc., 20
Rental Service Corporation, 28
Rentokil Initial Plc, 47
Research Triangle Institute, 83
Resources Connection, Inc., 81
Rewards Network Inc., 70 (upd.)
The Richards Group, Inc., 58
Right Management Consultants, Inc., 42
Ritchie Bros. Auctioneers Inc., 41
Robert Half International Inc., 18
Roland Berger & Partner GmbH, 37
Ronco Corporation, 15; 80 (upd.)
Russell Reynolds Associates Inc., 38
Saatchi & Saatchi, I; 42 (upd.)
Sanders\Wingo, 99
Schenck Business Solutions, 88
Securitas AB, 42
ServiceMaster Limited Partnership, 6
Servpro Industries, Inc., 85
Shared Medical Systems Corporation, 14
Sir Speedy, Inc., 16
Skidmore, Owings & Merrill LLP, 13; 69
    (upd.)
SmartForce PLC, 43
SOS Staffing Services, 25
Sotheby's Holdings, Inc., 11; 29 (upd.);
    84 (upd.)
Source Interlink Companies, Inc., 75
Spencer Stuart and Associates, Inc., 14
Spherion Corporation, 52
Steiner Corporation (Alsco), 53
Strayer Education, Inc., 53
Superior Uniform Group, Inc., 30

Sykes Enterprises, Inc., 45
Sylvan Learning Systems, Inc., 35
Synchronoss Technologies, Inc., 95
TA Triumph-Adler AG, 48
Taylor Nelson Sofres plc, 34
TBA Global, LLC, 99
TBWA\Chiat/Day, 6; 43 (upd.)
Thomas Cook Travel Inc., 33 (upd.)
Ticketmaster, 76 (upd.)
Ticketmaster Group, Inc., 13; 37 (upd.)
TMP Worldwide Inc., 30
TNT Post Group N.V., 30
Towers Perrin, 32
Trader Classified Media N.V., 57
Traffix, Inc., 61
Transmedia Network Inc., 20
Treasure Chest Advertising Company, Inc.,
    32
TRM Copy Centers Corporation, 18
True North Communications Inc., 23
24/7 Real Media, Inc., 49
Tyler Corporation, 23
U.S. Office Products Company, 25
Unica Corporation, 77
UniFirst Corporation, 21
United Business Media plc, 52 (upd.)
United News & Media plc, 28 (upd.)
Unitog Co., 19
Valassis Communications, Inc., 37 (upd.);
    76 (upd.)
ValleyCrest Companies, 81 (upd.)
ValueClick, Inc., 49
Vebego International BV, 49
Vedior NV, 35
Vertis Communications, 84
Vertrue Inc., 77
Viad Corp., 73
W.B Doner & Co., 56
The Wackenhut Corporation, 14; 63
    (upd.)
Waggener Edstrom, 42
Warrantech Corporation, 53
WebEx Communications, Inc., 81
Welcome Wagon International Inc., 82
Wells Rich Greene BDDP, 6
Westaff Inc., 33
Whitman Education Group, Inc., 41
Wieden + Kennedy, 75
William Morris Agency, Inc., 23
Williams Scotsman, Inc., 65
Workflow Management, Inc., 65
WPP Group plc, 6; 48 (upd.)
Wunderman, 86
Xerox Corporation, III; 6 (upd.); 26
    (upd.); 69 (upd.)
Young & Rubicam, Inc., I; 22 (upd.); 66
    (upd.)
Zogby International, Inc., 99

Aerospace

A.S. Yakovlev Design Bureau, 15
Aerojet-General Corp., 63
Aeronca Inc., 46
Aerosonic Corporation, 69
The Aerospatiale Group, 7; 21 (upd.)
AeroVironment, Inc., 97
AgustaWestland N.V., 75
Airborne Systems Group, 89

Alliant Techsystems Inc., 30 (upd.)
Antonov Design Bureau, 53
Arianespace S.A., 89
Aviacionny Nauchno-Tehnicheskii
    Komplex im. A.N. Tupoleva, 24
Aviall, Inc., 73
Avions Marcel Dassault-Breguet Aviation,
    I
B/E Aerospace, Inc., 30
Ballistic Recovery Systems, Inc., 87
Banner Aerospace, Inc., 14
BBA Aviation plc, 90
Beech Aircraft Corporation, 8
Bell Helicopter Textron Inc., 46
The Boeing Company, I; 10 (upd.); 32
    (upd.)
Bombardier Inc., 42 (upd.); 87 (upd.)
British Aerospace plc, I; 24 (upd.)
CAE USA Inc., 48
Canadair, Inc., 16
Cessna Aircraft Company, 8
Cirrus Design Corporation, 44
Cobham plc, 30
CPI Aerostructures, Inc., 75
Daimler-Benz Aerospace AG, 16
DeCrane Aircraft Holdings Inc., 36
Derco Holding Ltd., 98
Diehl Stiftung & Co. KG, 79
Ducommun Incorporated, 30
Duncan Aviation, Inc., 94
EADS SOCATA, 54
Eclipse Aviation Corporation, 87
EGL, Inc., 59
Empresa Brasileira de Aeronáutica S.A.
    (Embraer), 36
European Aeronautic Defence and Space
    Company EADS N.V., 52 (upd.)
Fairchild Aircraft, Inc., 9
Fairchild Dornier GmbH, 48 (upd.)
Finmeccanica S.p.A., 84
First Aviation Services Inc., 49
G.I.E. Airbus Industrie, I; 12 (upd.)
General Dynamics Corporation, I; 10
    (upd.); 40 (upd.); 88 (upd.
GKN plc, III; 38 (upd.); 89 (upd.)
Goodrich Corporation, 46 (upd.)
Groupe Dassault Aviation SA, 26 (upd.)
Grumman Corporation, I; 11 (upd.)
Grupo Aeropuerto del Sureste, S.A. de
    C.V., 48
Gulfstream Aerospace Corporation, 7; 28
    (upd.)
HEICO Corporation, 30
International Lease Finance Corporation,
    48
Irkut Corporation, 68
Israel Aircraft Industries Ltd., 69
Kolbenschmidt Pierburg AG, 97
N.V. Koninklijke Nederlandse
    Vliegtuigenfabriek Fokker, I; 28 (upd.)
Kreisler Manufacturing Corporation, 97
Lancair International, Inc., 67
Learjet Inc., 8; 27 (upd.)
Lockheed Martin Corporation, I; 11
    (upd.); 15 (upd.); 89 (upd.)
Loral Space & Communications Ltd., 54
    (upd.)
Magellan Aerospace Corporation, 48

Automotive

Beverages

Mississippi Chemical Corporation, 39
Mitsubishi Chemical Corporation, I; 56 (upd.)
Mitsui Petrochemical Industries, Ltd., 9
Monsanto Company, I; 9 (upd.); 29 (upd.)
Montedison SpA, I
Morton International Inc., I; 9 (upd.); 80 (upd.)
The Mosaic Company, 91
Nagase & Company, Ltd., 8
Nalco Holding Company, I; 12 (upd.); 89 (upd.)
National Distillers and Chemical Corporation, I
National Sanitary Supply Co., 16
National Starch and Chemical Company, 49
NCH Corporation, 8
Nippon Soda Co., Ltd., 85
Nisshin Seifun Group Inc., 66 (upd.)
NL Industries, Inc., 10
Nobel Industries AB, 9
NOF Corporation, 72
Norsk Hydro ASA, 35 (upd.)
North American Galvanizing & Coatings, Inc., 99
Novacor Chemicals Ltd., 12
Nufarm Ltd., 87
NutraSweet Company, 8
Occidental Petroleum Corporation, 71 (upd.)
Olin Corporation, I; 13 (upd.); 78 (upd.)
OM Group, Inc., 17; 78 (upd.)
OMNOVA Solutions Inc., 59
Penford Corporation, 55
Pennwalt Corporation, I
Perstorp AB, I; 51 (upd.)
Petrolite Corporation, 15
Pfizer Inc., 79 (upd.)
Pioneer Hi-Bred International, Inc., 41 (upd.)
PolyOne Corporation, 87 (upd.)
Praxair, Inc., 11
Quaker Chemical Corp., 91
Quantum Chemical Corporation, 8
Reichhold Chemicals, Inc., 10
Renner Herrmann S.A., 79
Rhodia SA, 38
Rhône-Poulenc S.A., I; 10 (upd.)
Robertet SA, 39
Rohm and Haas Company, I; 26 (upd.); 77 (upd.)
Roussel Uclaf, I; 8 (upd.)
RPM International Inc., 8; 36 (upd.); 91 (upd.)
RWE AG, 50 (upd.)
S.C. Johnson & Son, Inc., III; 28 (upd.); 89 (upd.)
The Scotts Company, 22
SCP Pool Corporation, 39
Sequa Corp., 13
Shanghai Petrochemical Co., Ltd., 18
Sigma-Aldrich Corporation, I; 36 (upd.); 93 (upd.)
Solutia Inc., 52
Solvay S.A., I; 21 (upd.); 61 (upd.)
Stepan Company, 30

Sterling Chemicals, Inc., 16; 78 (upd.)
Sumitomo Chemical Company Ltd., I; 98 (upd.)
Takeda Chemical Industries, Ltd., 46 (upd.)
Teknor Apex Company, 97
Terra Industries, Inc., 13
Tessenderlo Group, 76
Teva Pharmaceutical Industries Ltd., 22
Tosoh Corporation, 70
Total Fina Elf S.A., 24 (upd.); 50 (upd.)
Transammonia Group, 95
Ube Industries, Ltd., 38 (upd.)
Union Carbide Corporation, I; 9 (upd.); 74 (upd.)
United Industries Corporation, 68
Univar Corporation, 9
The Valspar Corporation, 32 (upd.); 77 (upd.)
VeraSun Energy Corporation, 87
Vista Chemical Company, I
Witco Corporation, I; 16 (upd.)
Yule Catto & Company plc, 54
WD-40 Company, 87 (upd.)
Zakłady Azotowe Puławy S.A., 100
Zeneca Group PLC, 21

Conglomerates

A.P. Møller - Maersk A/S, 57
ABARTA, Inc., 100
Abengoa S.A., 73
Acciona S.A., 81
Accor SA, 10; 27 (upd.)
Ackermans & van Haaren N.V., 97
Adani Enterprises Ltd., 97
Aditya Birla Group, 79
Administración Nacional de Combustibles, Alcohol y Pórtland, 93
AEG A.G., I
Al Habtoor Group L.L.C., 87
Alcatel Alsthom Compagnie Générale d'Electricité, 9
Alco Standard Corporation, I
Alexander & Baldwin, Inc., 10, 40 (upd.)
Alfa, S.A. de C.V., 19
Alfa Group, 99
Alleghany Corporation, 60 (upd.)
Allied Domecq PLC, 29
Allied-Signal Inc., I
AMFAC Inc., I
The Anschutz Company, 73 (upd.)
The Anschutz Corporation, 36 (upd.)
Antofagasta plc, 65
Apax Partners Worldwide LLP, 89
APi Group, Inc., 64
Aramark Corporation, 13
ARAMARK Corporation, 41
Archer Daniels Midland Company, I; 11 (upd.); 75 (upd.)
Arkansas Best Corporation, 16
Associated British Ports Holdings Plc, 45
BAA plc, 33 (upd.)
Barlow Rand Ltd., I
Barratt Developments plc, 56 (upd.)
Bat Industries PLC, I
Baugur Group hf, 81
BB Holdings Limited, 77
Berjaya Group Bhd., 67

Berkshire Hathaway Inc., III; 18 (upd.); 42 (upd.); 89 (upd.)
Block Communications, Inc., 81
Bond Corporation Holdings Limited, 10
Brascan Corporation, 67
BTR PLC, I
Bunzl plc, 31 (upd.)
Burlington Northern Santa Fe Corporation, 27 (upd.)
Business Post Group plc, 46
C. Itoh & Company Ltd., I
C.I. Traders Limited, 61
Camargo Corrêa S.A., 93
Cargill, Incorporated, II; 13 (upd.); 40 (upd.); 89 (upd.)
CBI Industries, Inc., 7
Charoen Pokphand Group, 62
Chemed Corporation, 13
Chesebrough-Pond's USA, Inc., 8
China Merchants International Holdings Co., Ltd., 52
Cisneros Group of Companies, 54
CITIC Pacific Ltd., 18
CJ Corporation, 62
Colgate-Palmolive Company, 71 (upd.)
Colt Industries Inc., I
Compagnie Financiere Richemont AG, 50
The Connell Company, 29
Conzzeta Holding, 80
Cox Enterprises, Inc., 67 (upd.)
Cristalerias de Chile S.A., 67
CSR Limited, III; 28 (upd.); 85 (upd.)
Daewoo Group, 18 (upd.); 57 (upd.)
Dallah Albaraka Group, 72
De Dietrich & Cie., 31
Deere & Company, 21 (upd.)
Delaware North Companies Inc., 7; 96 (upd.)
Desc, S.A. de C.V., 23
The Dial Corp., 8
Dogan Sirketler Grubu Holding A.S., 83
Dr. August Oetker KG, 51
E.I. du Pont de Nemours and Company, 73 (upd.)
EBSCO Industries, Inc., 40 (upd.)
El Corte Inglés Group, 26 (upd.)
Elders IXL Ltd., I
Empresas Copec S.A., 69
Engelhard Corporation, 21 (upd.); 72 (upd.)
Essar Group Ltd., 79
Farley Northwest Industries, Inc., I
Fimalac S.A., 37
First Pacific Company Limited, 18
Fisher Companies, Inc., 15
Fletcher Challenge Ltd., 19 (upd.)
Florida East Coast Industries, Inc., 59
FMC Corporation, I; 11 (upd.)
Fortune Brands, Inc., 29 (upd.); 68 (upd.)
Fraser & Neave Ltd., 54
Fuqua Industries, Inc., I
General Electric Company, 34 (upd.); 63 (upd.)
Genting Bhd., 65
GIB Group, 26 (upd.)
Gillett Holdings, Inc., 7
The Gillette Company, 68 (upd.)
Granaria Holdings B.V., 66

Construction

Containers

Drugs & Pharmaceuticals

National Patent Development
    Corporation, 13
Natrol, Inc., 49
Natural Alternatives International, Inc., 49
Nektar Therapeutics, 91
Novartis AG, 39 (upd.)
Noven Pharmaceuticals, Inc., 55
Novo Nordisk A/S, I; 61 (upd.)
Obagi Medical Products, Inc., 95
Omnicare, Inc., 49
Omrix Biopharmaceuticals, Inc., 95
Par Pharmaceutical Companies, Inc., 65
PDL BioPharma, 90
Perrigo Company, 59 (upd.)
Pfizer Inc., I; 9 (upd.); 38 (upd.); 79
    (upd.)
Pharmacia & Upjohn Inc., I; 25 (upd.)
Pharmion Corporation, 91
PLIVA d.d., 70
PolyMedica Corporation, 77
POZEN Inc., 81
QLT Inc., 71
The Quigley Corporation, 62
Quintiles Transnational Corporation, 21
R.P. Scherer, I
Ranbaxy Laboratories Ltd., 70
ratiopharm Group, 84
Reckitt Benckiser plc, II; 42 (upd.); 91
    (upd.)
Roberts Pharmaceutical Corporation, 16
Roche Bioscience, 14 (upd.)
Rorer Group, I
Roussel Uclaf, I; 8 (upd.)
Salix Pharmaceuticals, Ltd., 93
Sandoz Ltd., I
Sankyo Company, Ltd., I; 56 (upd.)
The Sanofi-Synthélabo Group, I; 49
    (upd.)
Schering AG, I; 50 (upd.)
Schering-Plough Corporation, I; 14
    (upd.); 49 (upd.); 99 (upd.)
Sepracor Inc., 45
Serono S.A., 47
Shionogi & Co., Ltd., III; 17 (upd.); 98
    (upd.)
Sigma-Aldrich Corporation, I; 36 (upd.);
    93 (upd.)
SmithKline Beecham plc, I; 32 (upd.)
Solvay S.A., 61 (upd.)
Squibb Corporation, I
Sterling Drug, Inc., I
Stiefel Laboratories, Inc., 90
Sun Pharmaceutical Industries Ltd., 57
The Sunrider Corporation, 26
Syntex Corporation, I
Takeda Chemical Industries, Ltd., I
Taro Pharmaceutical Industries Ltd., 65
Teva Pharmaceutical Industries Ltd., 22;
    54 (upd.)
UCB Pharma SA, 98
The Upjohn Company, I; 8 (upd.)
Vertex Pharmaceuticals Incorporated, 83
Virbac Corporation, 74
Vitalink Pharmacy Services, Inc., 15
Warner Chilcott Limited, 85
Warner-Lambert Co., I; 10 (upd.)
Watson Pharmaceuticals Inc., 16; 56
    (upd.)

The Wellcome Foundation Ltd., I
Zentiva N.V./Zentiva, a.s., 99
Zila, Inc., 46

Electrical & Electronics

ABB ASEA Brown Boveri Ltd., II; 22
    (upd.)
ABB Ltd., 65 (upd.)
Acer Incorporated, 16; 73 (upd.)
Acuson Corporation, 10; 36 (upd.)
ADC Telecommunications, Inc., 30 (upd.)
Adtran Inc., 22
Advanced Micro Devices, Inc., 6; 30
    (upd.); 99 (upd.)
Advanced Technology Laboratories, Inc., 9
Agere Systems Inc., 61
Agilent Technologies Inc., 38; 93 (upd.)
Agilysys Inc., 76 (upd.)
Aiwa Co., Ltd., 30
AKG Acoustics GmbH, 62
Akzo Nobel N.V., 13; 41 (upd.)
Alienware Corporation, 81
Alliant Techsystems Inc., 30 (upd.); 77
    (upd.)
AlliedSignal Inc., 22 (upd.)
Alpine Electronics, Inc., 13
Alps Electric Co., Ltd., II
Altera Corporation, 18; 43 (upd.)
Altron Incorporated, 20
Amdahl Corporation, 40 (upd.)
American Power Conversion Corporation,
    24; 67 (upd.)
American Superconductor Corporation,
    97
American Technical Ceramics Corp., 67
Amerigon Incorporated, 97
Amkor Technology, Inc., 69
AMP Incorporated, II; 14 (upd.)
Amphenol Corporation, 40
Amstrad plc, 48 (upd.)
Analog Devices, Inc., 10
Analogic Corporation, 23
Anam Group, 23
Anaren Microwave, Inc., 33
Andrew Corporation, 10; 32 (upd.)
Anixter International Inc., 88
Anritsu Corporation, 68
Apex Digital, Inc., 63
Apple Computer, Inc., 36 (upd.); 77
    (upd.)
Applied Power Inc., 32 (upd.)
Applied Signal Technology, Inc., 87
Argon ST, Inc., 81
Arotech Corporation, 93
ARRIS Group, Inc., 89
Arrow Electronics, Inc., 10; 50 (upd.)
Ascend Communications, Inc., 24
Astronics Corporation, 35
Atari Corporation, 9; 23 (upd.); 66 (upd.)
ATI Technologies Inc., 79
Atmel Corporation, 17
ATMI, Inc., 93
AU Optronics Corporation, 67
Audiovox Corporation, 34; 90 (upd.)
Ault Incorporated, 34
Autodesk, Inc., 10; 89 (upd.)
Avnet Inc., 9
AVX Corporation, 67

Axcelis Technologies, Inc., 95
Axsys Technologies, Inc., 93
Ballard Power Systems Inc., 73
Bang & Olufsen Holding A/S, 37; 86
    (upd.)
Barco NV, 44
Bell Microproducts Inc., 69
Benchmark Electronics, Inc., 40
Bicoastal Corporation, II
Black Box Corporation, 20; 96 (upd.)
Blonder Tongue Laboratories, Inc., 48
Blue Coat Systems, Inc., 83
BMC Industries, Inc., 59 (upd.)
Bogen Communications International,
    Inc., 62
Bose Corporation, 13; 36 (upd.)
Boston Acoustics, Inc., 22
Bowthorpe plc, 33
Braun GmbH, 51
Broadcom Corporation, 34; 90 (upd.)
Bull S.A., 43 (upd.)
Burr-Brown Corporation, 19
BVR Systems (1998) Ltd., 93
C-COR.net Corp., 38
Cabletron Systems, Inc., 10
Cadence Design Systems, Inc., 48 (upd.)
Cambridge SoundWorks, Inc., 48
Canon Inc., 18 (upd.); 79 (upd.)
Carbone Lorraine S.A., 33
Cardtronics, Inc., 93
Carl Zeiss AG, III; 34 (upd.); 91 (upd.)
Cash Systems, Inc., 93
CASIO Computer Co., Ltd., 16 (upd.);
    40 (upd.)
CDW Computer Centers, Inc., 52 (upd.)
Celestica Inc., 80
Checkpoint Systems, Inc., 39
Chi Mei Optoelectronics Corporation, 75
Chubb, PLC, 50
Chunghwa Picture Tubes, Ltd., 75
Cirrus Logic, Inc., 48 (upd.)
Cisco Systems, Inc., 34 (upd.); 77 (upd.)
Citizen Watch Co., Ltd., III; 21 (upd.);
    81 (upd.)
Clarion Company Ltd., 64
Cobham plc, 30
Cobra Electronics Corporation, 14
Coherent, Inc., 31
Cohu, Inc., 32
Color Kinetics Incorporated, 85
Compagnie Générale d'Électricité, II
Concurrent Computer Corporation, 75
Conexant Systems, Inc., 36
Cooper Industries, Inc., II
Cray Inc., 75 (upd.)
Cray Research, Inc., 16 (upd.)
Cree Inc., 53
CTS Corporation, 39
Cubic Corporation, 19; 98 (upd.)
Cypress Semiconductor Corporation, 20;
    48 (upd.)
D&H Distributing Co., 95
D-Link Corporation, 83
Dai Nippon Printing Co., Ltd., 57 (upd.)
Daiichikosho Company Ltd., 86
Daktronics, Inc., 32
Dallas Semiconductor Corporation, 13; 31
    (upd.)

Engineering & Management Services

Entertainment & Leisure

Financial Services: Banks

Financial Services: Excluding Banks

Food Products

Health Care Services

Option Care Inc., 48
Orthodontic Centers of America, Inc., 35
Oxford Health Plans, Inc., 16
PacifiCare Health Systems, Inc., 11
Palomar Medical Technologies, Inc., 22
Pediatric Services of America, Inc., 31
Pediatrix Medical Group, Inc., 61
PHP Healthcare Corporation, 22
PhyCor, Inc., 36
PolyMedica Corporation, 77
Primedex Health Systems, Inc., 25
Providence Health System, 90
The Providence Service Corporation, 64
Psychemedics Corporation, 89
Psychiatric Solutions, Inc., 68
Quest Diagnostics Inc., 26
Radiation Therapy Services, Inc., 85
Ramsay Youth Services, Inc., 41
Renal Care Group, Inc., 72
Res-Care, Inc., 29
Response Oncology, Inc., 27
Rural/Metro Corporation, 28
Sabratek Corporation, 29
St. Jude Medical, Inc., 11; 43 (upd.); 97
    (upd.)
Salick Health Care, Inc., 53
The Scripps Research Institute, 76
Select Medical Corporation, 65
Shriners Hospitals for Children, 69
Sierra Health Services, Inc., 15
Smith & Nephew plc, 41 (upd.)
Special Olympics, Inc., 93
The Sports Club Company, 25
SSL International plc, 49
Stericycle Inc., 33
Sun Healthcare Group Inc., 25
Sunrise Senior Living, Inc., 81
Susan G. Komen Breast Cancer
    Foundation 78
SwedishAmerican Health System, 51
Tenet Healthcare Corporation, 55 (upd.)
Twinlab Corporation, 34
U.S. Healthcare, Inc., 6
U.S. Physical Therapy, Inc., 65
Unison HealthCare Corporation, 25
United HealthCare Corporation, 9
United Nations International Children's
    Emergency Fund (UNICEF), 58
United Way of America, 36
Universal Health Services, Inc., 6
Vanderbilt University Medical Center, 99
Vanguard Health Systems Inc., 70
VCA Antech, Inc., 58
Vencor, Inc., 16
VISX, Incorporated, 30
Vivra, Inc., 18
Volunteers of America, Inc., 66
WellPoint Health Networks Inc., 25
World Vision International, Inc., 93
YWCA of the U.S.A., 45

Hotels

Accor S.A., 69 (upd.)
Amerihost Properties, Inc., 30
Ameristar Casinos, Inc., 69 (upd.)
Archon Corporation, 74 (upd.)
Arena Leisure Plc, 99
Aztar Corporation, 13; 71 (upd.)

Bass PLC, 38 (upd.)
Boca Resorts, Inc., 37
Boyd Gaming Corporation, 43
Boyne USA Resorts, 71
Bristol Hotel Company, 23
The Broadmoor Hotel, 30
Caesars World, Inc., 6
Candlewood Hotel Company, Inc., 41
Carlson Companies, Inc., 6; 22 (upd.); 87
    (upd.)
Castle & Cooke, Inc., 20 (upd.)
Cedar Fair Entertainment Company, 22;
    98 (upd.)
Cendant Corporation, 44 (upd.)
Choice Hotels International, Inc., 14; 83
    (upd.)
Circus Circus Enterprises, Inc., 6
City Developments Limited, 89
Club Mediterranée S.A., 6; 21 (upd.); 91
    (upd.)
Compagnia Italiana dei Jolly Hotels
    S.p.A., 71
Daniel Thwaites Plc, 95
Doubletree Corporation, 21
Extended Stay America, Inc., 41
Fairmont Hotels & Resorts Inc., 69
Fibreboard Corporation, 16
Four Seasons Hotels Inc., 9; 29 (upd.)
Fuller Smith & Turner P.L.C., 38
Gables Residential Trust, 49
Gaylord Entertainment Company, 11; 36
    (upd.)
Global Hyatt Corporation, 75 (upd.)
Granada Group PLC, 24 (upd.)
Grand Casinos, Inc., 20
Grand Hotel Krasnapolsky N.V., 23
Great Wolf Resorts, Inc., 91
Grupo Posadas, S.A. de C.V., 57
Helmsley Enterprises, Inc., 9
Hilton Hotels Corporation, III; 19 (upd.);
    49 (upd.); 62 (upd.)
Holiday Inns, Inc., III
Home Inns & Hotels Management Inc.,
    95
Hospitality Franchise Systems, Inc., 11
Hotel Properties Ltd., 71
Howard Johnson International, Inc., 17;
    72 (upd.)
Hyatt Corporation, III; 16 (upd.)
ILX Resorts Incorporated, 65
Interstate Hotels & Resorts Inc., 58
ITT Sheraton Corporation, III
JD Wetherspoon plc, 30
John Q. Hammons Hotels, Inc., 24
Jumeirah Group, 83
Kerzner International Limited, 69 (upd.)
The La Quinta Companies, 11; 42 (upd.)
Ladbroke Group PLC, 21 (upd.)
Landry's Restaurants, Inc., 65 (upd.)
Las Vegas Sands, Inc., 50
Madden's on Gull Lake, 52
Mandalay Resort Group, 32 (upd.)
Manor Care, Inc., 25 (upd.)
The Marcus Corporation, 21
Marriott International, Inc., III; 21
    (upd.); 83 (upd.)
McMenamins Pubs and Breweries, 65
MGM MIRAGE, 98 (upd.)

Millennium & Copthorne Hotels plc, 71
Mirage Resorts, Incorporated, 6; 28 (upd.)
Monarch Casino & Resort, Inc., 65
Morgans Hotel Group Company, 80
Motel 6, 13; 56 (upd.)
MTR Gaming Group, Inc., 75
MWH Preservation Limited Partnership,
    65
NH Hoteles S.A., 79
Omni Hotels Corp., 12
Paradores de Turismo de Espana S.A., 73
Park Corp., 22
Players International, Inc., 22
Preussag AG, 42 (upd.)
Prime Hospitality Corporation, 52
Promus Companies, Inc., 9
Real Turismo, S.A. de C.V., 50
Red Roof Inns, Inc., 18
Regent Inns plc, 95
Resorts International, Inc., 12
The Ritz-Carlton Hotel Company, L.L.C.,
    9; 29 (upd.); 71 (upd.)
Riviera Holdings Corporation, 75
Sandals Resorts International, 65
Santa Fe Gaming Corporation, 19
The SAS Group, 34 (upd.)
SFI Group plc, 51
Shangri-La Asia Ltd., 71
Showboat, Inc., 19
Sol Meliá S.A., 71
Sonesta International Hotels Corporation,
    44
Starwood Hotels & Resorts Worldwide,
    Inc., 54
Sun International Hotels Limited, 26
Sunburst Hospitality Corporation, 26
Super 8 Motels, Inc., 83
Thistle Hotels PLC, 54
Trusthouse Forte PLC, III
Vail Resorts, Inc., 43 (upd.)
WestCoast Hospitality Corporation, 59
Westin Hotels and Resorts Worldwide, 9;
    29 (upd.)
Whitbread PLC, I; 20 (upd.); 52 (upd.);
    97 (upd.)
Wyndham Worldwide Corporation
    (updates Cendant Corporation), 99
    (upd.)
Young & Co.'s Brewery, P.L.C., 38

Information Technology

A.B. Watley Group Inc., 45
AccuWeather, Inc., 73
Acxiom Corporation, 35
Adaptec, Inc., 31
Adobe Systems Incorporated, 10; 33
    (upd.)
Advanced Micro Devices, Inc., 6; 30
    (upd.); 99 (upd.)
Agence France-Presse, 34
Agilent Technologies Inc., 38; 93 (upd.)
Akamai Technologies, Inc., 71
Aldus Corporation, 10
Allen Systems Group, Inc., 59
AltaVista Company, 43
Altiris, Inc., 65
Amdahl Corporation, III; 14 (upd.); 40
    (upd.)

Legal Services

Manufacturing

ZERO Corporation, 17; 88 (upd.)
ZiLOG, Inc., 72 (upd.)
Zindart Ltd., 60
Zippo Manufacturing Company, 18; 71 (upd.)
Zodiac S.A., 36
Zygo Corporation, 42

Materials

AK Steel Holding Corporation, 19
American Biltrite Inc., 16
American Colloid Co., 13
American Standard Inc., III
Ameriwood Industries International Corp., 17
Anhui Conch Cement Company Limited, 99
Apasco S.A. de C.V., 51
Apogee Enterprises, Inc., 8
Asahi Glass Company, Limited, III
Asbury Carbons, Inc., 68
Bairnco Corporation, 28
Bayou Steel Corporation, 31
Berry Plastics Group Inc., 21; 98 (upd.)
Blessings Corp., 19
Blue Circle Industries PLC, III
Bodycote International PLC, 63
Boral Limited, III
British Vita PLC, 9
Brush Engineered Materials Inc., 67
Bryce Corporation, 100
California Steel Industries, Inc., 67
Callanan Industries, Inc., 60
Cameron & Barkley Company, 28
Carborundum Company, 15
Carl Zeiss AG, III; 34 (upd.); 91 (upd.)
Carlisle Companies Inc., 8; 82 (upd.)
Carter Holt Harvey Ltd., 70
Cementos Argos S.A., 91
Cemex SA de CV, 20
Century Aluminum Company, 52
CertainTeed Corporation, 35
Chargeurs International, 6; 21 (upd.)
Chemfab Corporation, 35
Cimentos de Portugal SGPS S.A. (Cimpor), 76
Cold Spring Granite Company Inc., 16; 67 (upd.)
Columbia Forest Products Inc. 78
Compagnie de Saint-Gobain S.A., III; 16 (upd.)
Cookson Group plc, III; 44 (upd.)
Corning Inc., III; 44 (upd.); 90 (upd.)
CSR Limited, III; 28 (upd.); 85 (upd.)
Dal-Tile International Inc., 22
The David J. Joseph Company, 14; 76 (upd.)
The Dexter Corporation, 12 (upd.)
Dickten Masch Plastics LLC, 90
Dyckerhoff AG, 35
Dynamic Materials Corporation, 81
Dyson Group PLC, 71
ECC Group plc, III
Edw. C. Levy Co., 42
84 Lumber Company, 9; 39 (upd.)
ElkCorp, 52
Empire Resources, Inc., 81

English China Clays Ltd., 15 (upd.); 40 (upd.)
Envirodyne Industries, Inc., 17
Feldmuhle Nobel A.G., III
Fibreboard Corporation, 16
Filtrona plc, 88
Florida Rock Industries, Inc., 46
Foamex International Inc., 17
Formica Corporation, 13
GAF Corporation, 22 (upd.)
The Geon Company, 11
Giant Cement Holding, Inc., 23
Gibraltar Steel Corporation, 37
Granite Rock Company, 26
GreenMan Technologies Inc., 99
Groupe Sidel S.A., 21
Harbison-Walker Refractories Company, 24
Harrisons & Crosfield plc, III
Heidelberger Zement AG, 31
Hexcel Corporation, 28
Holderbank Financière Glaris Ltd., III
Holnam Inc., 39 (upd.)
Holt and Bugbee Company, 66
Homasote Company, 72
Howmet Corp., 12
Huttig Building Products, Inc., 73
Ibstock Brick Ltd., 14; 37 (upd.)
Imerys S.A., 40 (upd.)
Imperial Industries, Inc., 81
Internacional de Ceramica, S.A. de C.V., 53
International Shipbreaking Ltd. L.L.C., 67
Joseph T. Ryerson & Son, Inc., 15
Knauf Gips KG, 100
La Seda de Barcelona S.A., 100
Lafarge Coppée S.A., III
Lafarge Corporation, 28
Lehigh Portland Cement Company, 23
Loma Negra C.I.A.S.A., 95
Lyman-Richey Corporation, 96
Manville Corporation, III; 7 (upd.)
Material Sciences Corporation, 63
Matsushita Electric Works, Ltd., III; 7 (upd.)
McJunkin Corporation, 63
Medusa Corporation, 24
Mitsubishi Materials Corporation, III
Nevamar Company, 82
Nippon Sheet Glass Company, Limited, III
North Pacific Group, Inc., 61
Nuplex Industries Ltd., 92
OmniSource Corporation, 14
Onoda Cement Co., Ltd., III
Otor S.A., 77
Owens-Corning Fiberglass Corporation, III
Pacific Clay Products Inc., 88
Pilkington Group Limited, III; 34 (upd.); 87 (upd.)
Pioneer International Limited, III
PolyOne Corporation, 87 (upd.)
PPG Industries, Inc., III; 22 (upd.); 81 (upd.)
Redland plc, III
Rinker Group Ltd., 65
RMC Group p.l.c., III

Rock of Ages Corporation, 37
Rogers Corporation, 80 (upd.)
Royal Group Technologies Limited, 73
The Rugby Group plc, 31
Scholle Corporation, 96
Schuff Steel Company, 26
Sekisui Chemical Co., Ltd., III; 72 (upd.)
Severstal Joint Stock Company, 65
Shaw Industries, 9
The Sherwin-Williams Company, III; 13 (upd.); 89 (upd.)
The Siam Cement Public Company Limited, 56
SIG plc, 71
Simplex Technologies Inc., 21
Siskin Steel & Supply Company, 70
Solutia Inc., 52
Sommer-Allibert S.A., 19
Southdown, Inc., 14
Spartech Corporation, 19; 76 (upd.)
Ssangyong Cement Industrial Co., Ltd., III; 61 (upd.)
Steel Technologies Inc., 63
Sun Distributors L.P., 12
Symyx Technologies, Inc., 77
Tarmac Limited, III, 28 (upd.); 95 (upd.)
Tilcon-Connecticut Inc., 80
TOTO LTD., III; 28 (upd.)
Toyo Sash Co., Ltd., III
Tuscarora Inc., 29
U.S. Aggregates, Inc., 42
Ube Industries, Ltd., III
United States Steel Corporation, 50 (upd.)
USG Corporation, III; 26 (upd.); 81 (upd.)
Usinas Siderúrgicas de Minas Gerais S.A., 77
Vicat S.A., 70
voestalpine AG, 57 (upd.)
Vulcan Materials Company, 7; 52 (upd.)
Wacker-Chemie GmbH, 35
Walter Industries, Inc., III
Waxman Industries, Inc., 9
Weber et Broutin France, 66
Wienerberger AG, 70
Wolseley plc, 64
ZERO Corporation, 17; 88 (upd.)
Zoltek Companies, Inc., 37

Mining & Metals

A.M. Castle & Co., 25
Acindar Industria Argentina de Aceros S.A., 87
African Rainbow Minerals Ltd., 97
Aggregate Industries plc, 36
Agnico-Eagle Mines Limited, 71
Aktiebolaget SKF, III; 38 (upd.); 89 (upd.)
Alcan Aluminium Limited, IV; 31 (upd.)
Alcoa Inc., 56 (upd.)
Alleghany Corporation, 10
Allegheny Ludlum Corporation, 8
Alliance Resource Partners, L.P., 81
Alrosa Company Ltd., 62
Altos Hornos de México, S.A. de C.V., 42
Aluminum Company of America, IV; 20 (upd.)
AMAX Inc., IV

BP p.l.c., 45 (upd.)
Brigham Exploration Company, 75
The British Petroleum Company plc, IV;
    7 (upd.); 21 (upd.)
British-Borneo Oil & Gas PLC, 34
Broken Hill Proprietary Company Ltd.,
    22 (upd.)
Bronco Drilling Company, Inc., 89
Burlington Resources Inc., 10
Burmah Castrol PLC, IV; 30 (upd.)
Callon Petroleum Company, 47
Caltex Petroleum Corporation, 19
Cano Petroleum Inc., 97
Carrizo Oil & Gas, Inc., 97
ChevronTexaco Corporation, IV; 19
    (upd.); 47 (upd.)
Chiles Offshore Corporation, 9
Cimarex Energy Co., 81
China National Petroleum Corporation,
    46
Chinese Petroleum Corporation, IV; 31
    (upd.)
CITGO Petroleum Corporation, IV; 31
    (upd.)
Clayton Williams Energy, Inc., 87
The Coastal Corporation, IV; 31 (upd.)
Compañia Española de Petróleos S.A.
    (Cepsa), IV; 56 (upd.)
Comstock Resources, Inc., 47
Conoco Inc., IV; 16 (upd.)
ConocoPhillips, 63 (upd.)
CONSOL Energy Inc., 59
Continental Resources, Inc., 89
Cooper Cameron Corporation, 20 (upd.)
Cosmo Oil Co., Ltd., IV; 53 (upd.)
Crown Central Petroleum Corporation, 7
DeepTech International Inc., 21
Den Norse Stats Oljeselskap AS, IV
Denbury Resources, Inc., 67
Deutsche BP Aktiengesellschaft, 7
Devon Energy Corporation, 61
Diamond Shamrock, Inc., IV
Distrigaz S.A., 82
Dril-Quip, Inc., 81
Duvernay Oil Corp., 83
Dyneff S.A., 98
Dynegy Inc., 49 (upd.)
E.On AG, 50 (upd.)
Edge Petroleum Corporation, 67
Egyptian General Petroleum Corporation,
    IV; 51 (upd.)
El Paso Corporation, 66 (upd.)
Elf Aquitaine SA, 21 (upd.)
Empresa Colombiana de Petróleos, IV
Enbridge Inc., 43
Encore Acquisition Company, 73
Energen Corporation, 21; 97 (upd.)
ENI S.p.A., 69 (upd.)
Enron Corporation, 19
ENSCO International Incorporated, 57
Ente Nazionale Idrocarburi, IV
Enterprise Oil PLC, 11; 50 (upd.)
Entreprise Nationale Sonatrach, IV
Equitable Resources, Inc., 54 (upd.)
Ergon, Inc., 95
Exxon Mobil Corporation, IV; 7 (upd.);
    32 (upd.); 67 (upd.)
Ferrellgas Partners, L.P., 35

FINA, Inc., 7
Flying J Inc., 19
Flotek Industries Inc., 93
Forest Oil Corporation, 19; 91 (upd.)
Galp Energia SGPS S.A., 98
OAO Gazprom, 42
General Sekiyu K.K., IV
Giant Industries, Inc., 19; 61 (upd.)
Global Industries, Ltd., 37
Global Marine Inc., 9
GlobalSantaFe Corporation, 48 (upd.)
Grey Wolf, Inc., 43
Halliburton Company, 25 (upd.); 55
    (upd.)
Hanover Compressor Company, 59
Hawkeye Holdings LLC, 89
Helix Energy Solutions Group, Inc., 81
Hellenic Petroleum SA, 64
Helmerich & Payne, Inc., 18
Holly Corporation, 12
Hunt Consolidated, Inc., 7; 27 (upd.)
Hunting plc 78
Hurricane Hydrocarbons Ltd., 54
Husky Energy Inc., 47
Idemitsu Kosan Co., Ltd., 49 (upd.)
Idemitsu Kosan K.K., IV
Imperial Oil Limited, IV; 25 (upd.)
Indian Oil Corporation Ltd., IV; 48
    (upd.); 95 (upd.)
INPEX Holdings Inc., 97
Input/Output, Inc., 73
Iogen Corporation, 81
Ipiranga S.A., 67
Kanematsu Corporation, IV
Kerr-McGee Corporation, IV; 22 (upd.);
    68 (upd.)
Kinder Morgan, Inc., 45
King Ranch, Inc., 14
Koch Industries, Inc., IV; 20 (upd.), 77
    (upd.)
Koppers Industries, Inc., 26 (upd.)
Kuwait Petroleum Corporation, IV; 55
    (upd.)
Libyan National Oil Corporation, IV
The Louisiana Land and Exploration
    Company, 7
OAO LUKOIL, 40
Lyondell Petrochemical Company, IV
MAPCO Inc., IV
Maxus Energy Corporation, 7
McDermott International, Inc., 37 (upd.)
Meteor Industries Inc., 33
Mexichem, S.A.B. de C.V., 99
Mitchell Energy and Development
    Corporation, 7
Mitsubishi Oil Co., Ltd., IV
Mobil Corporation, IV; 7 (upd.); 21
    (upd.)
MOL Rt, 70
Murphy Oil Corporation, 7; 32 (upd.);
    95 (upd.)
Nabors Industries Ltd., 9; 91 (upd.)
National Fuel Gas Company, 6; 95 (upd.)
National Iranian Oil Company, IV; 61
    (upd.)
National Oil Corporation, 66 (upd.)
Neste Oil Corporation, IV; 85 (upd.)
Newfield Exploration Company, 65

Nexen Inc., 79
NGC Corporation, 18
Nigerian National Petroleum Corporation,
    IV; 72 (upd.)
Nippon Oil Corporation, IV; 63 (upd.)
OAO NK YUKOS, 47
Noble Affiliates, Inc., 11
Occidental Petroleum Corporation, IV; 25
    (upd.); 71 (upd.)
Odebrecht S.A., 73
Oil and Natural Gas Corporation Ltd.,
    IV; 90 (upd.)
Oil States International, Inc., 77
OMV AG, IV; 98 (upd.)
Oryx Energy Company, 7
Pacific Ethanol, Inc., 81
Pakistan State Oil Company Ltd., 81
Paramount Resources Ltd., 87
Parker Drilling Company, 28
Patina Oil & Gas Corporation, 24
Patterson-UTI Energy, Inc., 55
Pengrowth Energy Trust, 95
Penn Virginia Corporation, 85
Pennzoil-Quaker State Company, IV; 20
    (upd.); 50 (upd.)
Pertamina, IV; 56 (upd.)
Petro-Canada, IV; 99 (upd.)
Petrobras Energia Participaciones S.A., 72
Petrofac Ltd., 95
PetroFina S.A., IV; 26 (upd.)
Petrohawk Energy Corporation, 79
Petróleo Brasileiro S.A., IV
Petróleos de Portugal S.A., IV
Petróleos de Venezuela S.A., IV; 74 (upd.)
Petróleos del Ecuador, IV
Petróleos Mexicanos, IV; 19 (upd.)
Petroleum Development Oman LLC, IV;
    98 (upd.)
Petroliam Nasional Bhd (Petronas), IV; 56
    (upd.)
Petron Corporation, 58
Phillips Petroleum Company, IV; 40
    (upd.)
Pioneer Natural Resources Company, 59
Pogo Producing Company, 39
Polski Koncern Naftowy ORLEN S.A., 77
Premcor, 37
Pride International Inc. 78
PTT Public Company Ltd., 56
Qatar Petroleum, IV; 98 (upd.)
Quaker State Corporation, 7; 21 (upd.)
Range Resources Corporation, 45
Reliance Industries Ltd., 81
Repsol-YPF S.A., IV; 16 (upd.); 40 (upd.)
Resource America, Inc., 42
Rowan Companies, Inc., 43
Royal Dutch/Shell Group, IV; 49 (upd.)
RPC, Inc., 91
RWE AG, 50 (upd.)
St. Mary Land & Exploration Company,
    63
Santa Fe International Corporation, 38
Santos Ltd., 81
Sasol Limited, IV; 47 (upd.)
Saudi Arabian Oil Company, IV; 17
    (upd.); 50 (upd.)
Schlumberger Limited, 17 (upd.); 59
    (upd.)

Publishing & Printing

Real Estate

Zion's Cooperative Mercantile Institution, 33
Zipcar, Inc., 92
Zones, Inc., 67
Zumiez, Inc., 77

Rubber & Tires

Aeroquip Corporation, 16
Bandag, Inc., 19
The BFGoodrich Company, V
Bridgestone Corporation, V; 21 (upd.); 59 (upd.)
Canadian Tire Corporation, Limited, 71 (upd.)
Carlisle Companies Incorporated, 8
Compagnie Générale des Établissements Michelin, V; 42 (upd.)
Continental AG, V; 56 (upd.)
Continental General Tire Corp., 23
Cooper Tire & Rubber Company, 8; 23 (upd.)
Day International, Inc., 84
Elementis plc, 40 (upd.)
General Tire, Inc., 8
The Goodyear Tire & Rubber Company, V; 20 (upd.); 75 (upd.)
The Kelly-Springfield Tire Company, 8
Les Schwab Tire Centers, 50
Myers Industries, Inc., 19; 96 (upd.)
Pirelli S.p.A., V; 15 (upd.)
Safeskin Corporation, 18
Sumitomo Rubber Industries, Ltd., V
Trelleborg AB, 93
Tillotson Corp., 15
Treadco, Inc., 19
Ube Industries, Ltd., 38 (upd.)
The Yokohama Rubber Company, Limited, V; 19 (upd.); 91 (upd.)

Telecommunications

A.H. Belo Corporation, 30 (upd.)
Abertis Infraestructuras, S.A., 65
Abril S.A., 95
Acme-Cleveland Corp., 13
ADC Telecommunications, Inc., 10; 89 (upd.)
Adelphia Communications Corporation, 17; 52 (upd.)
Adtran Inc., 22
Advanced Fibre Communications, Inc., 63
AEI Music Network Inc., 35
AirTouch Communications, 11
Alaska Communications Systems Group, Inc., 89
Alcatel S.A., 36 (upd.)
Alliance Atlantis Communications Inc., 39
ALLTEL Corporation, 6; 46 (upd.)
América Móvil, S.A. de C.V., 80
American Tower Corporation, 33
Ameritech Corporation, V; 18 (upd.)
Amstrad plc, 48 (upd.)
AO VimpelCom, 48
AOL Time Warner Inc., 57 (upd.)
Arch Wireless, Inc., 39
ARD, 41
ARINC Inc., 98
ARRIS Group, Inc., 89

Ascom AG, 9
Aspect Telecommunications Corporation, 22
Asurion Corporation, 83
AT&T Bell Laboratories, Inc., 13
AT&T Corporation, V; 29 (upd.); 68 (upd.)
AT&T Wireless Services, Inc., 54 (upd.)
BCE Inc., V; 44 (upd.)
Beasley Broadcast Group, Inc., 51
Belgacom, 6
Bell Atlantic Corporation, V; 25 (upd.)
Bell Canada, 6
BellSouth Corporation, V; 29 (upd.)
Belo Corporation, 98 (upd.)
Bertelsmann A.G., IV; 15 (upd.); 43 (upd.); 91 (upd.)
BET Holdings, Inc., 18
Bharti Tele-Ventures Limited, 75
BHC Communications, Inc., 26
Blackfoot Telecommunications Group, 60
Bonneville International Corporation, 29
Bouygues S.A., I; 24 (upd.); 97 (upd.)
Brasil Telecom Participaçoes S.A., 57
Brightpoint, Inc., 18
Brite Voice Systems, Inc., 20
British Broadcasting Corporation Ltd., 7; 21 (upd.); 89 (upd.)
British Columbia Telephone Company, 6
British Telecommunications plc, V; 15 (upd.)
Broadwing Corporation, 70
BT Group plc, 49 (upd.)
C-COR.net Corp., 38
Cable & Wireless HKT, 30 (upd.)
Cable and Wireless plc, V; 25 (upd.)
Cablevision Systems Corporation, 30 (upd.)
CalAmp Corp., 87
The Canadian Broadcasting Corporation (CBC), 37
Canal Plus, 10; 34 (upd.)
CanWest Global Communications Corporation, 35
Capital Radio plc, 35
Carlton Communications PLC, 15; 50 (upd.)
Carolina Telephone and Telegraph Company, 10
The Carphone Warehouse Group PLC, 83
Carrier Access Corporation, 44
CBS Corporation, 28 (upd.)
CBS Television Network, 66 (upd.)
Centel Corporation, 6
Centennial Communications Corporation, 39
Central European Media Enterprises Ltd., 61
Century Communications Corp., 10
Century Telephone Enterprises, Inc., 9; 54 (upd.)
Cesky Telecom, a.s., 64
Chancellor Media Corporation, 24
Channel Four Television Corporation, 93
Charter Communications, Inc., 33
Chello Zone Ltd., 93
China Netcom Group Corporation (Hong Kong) Limited, 73

China Telecom, 50
Chris-Craft Corporation, 9, 31 (upd.); 80 (upd.)
The Christian Broadcasting Network, Inc., 52
Chrysalis Group plc, 40
Chugach Alaska Corporation, 60
CIENA Corporation, 54
Cincinnati Bell, Inc., 6
Citadel Communications Corporation, 35
Citizens Communications Company, 79 (upd.)
Clear Channel Communications, Inc., 23
Clearwire, Inc., 69
Cogent Communications Group, Inc., 55
COLT Telecom Group plc, 41
Comcast Corporation, 24 (upd.)
Comdial Corporation, 21
Commonwealth Telephone Enterprises, Inc., 25
CommScope, Inc., 77
Comsat Corporation, 23
Comtech Telecommunications Corp., 75
Comverse Technology, Inc., 15; 43 (upd.)
Corning Inc., III; 44 (upd.); 90 (upd.)
Corporation for Public Broadcasting, 14; 89 (upd.)
Cox Radio, Inc., 89
Craftmade International, Inc., 44
Cumulus Media Inc., 37
DDI Corporation, 7
Deutsche Telekom AG, V; 48 (upd.)
Dialogic Corporation, 18
Directorate General of Telecommunications, 7
DIRECTV, Inc., 38; 75 (upd.)
Discovery Communications, Inc., 42
Dobson Communications Corporation, 63
DSC Communications Corporation, 12
EchoStar Communications Corporation, 35
ECI Telecom Ltd., 18
Egmont Group, 93
eircom plc, 31 (upd.)
Electric Lightwave, Inc., 37
Electromagnetic Sciences Inc., 21
EMBARQ Corporation, 83
Emmis Communications Corporation, 47
Empresas Públicas de Medellín S.A.E.S.P., 91
Energis plc, 47
Entercom Communications Corporation, 58
Entravision Communications Corporation, 41
Equant N.V., 52
Eschelon Telecom, Inc., 72
ESPN, Inc., 56
Eternal Word Television Network, Inc., 57
EXCEL Communications Inc., 18
Executone Information Systems, Inc., 13
Expand SA, 48
Facebook, Inc., 90
FASTWEB S.p.A., 83
Fisher Communications, Inc., 99
4Kids Entertainment Inc., 59
Fox Family Worldwide, Inc., 24

Textiles & Apparel

Tobacco

Transport Services

Utilities

Waste Services

Geographic Index

Ghana

Greece

Guatemala

Hong Kong

Life Care Centers of America Inc., 76
Life is Good, Inc., 80
Life Technologies, Inc., 17
Life Time Fitness, Inc., 66
LifeCell Corporation, 77
Lifeline Systems, Inc., 53
LifeLock, Inc., 91
LifePoint Hospitals, Inc., 69
Lifetime Brands, Inc., 73 (upd.)
Lifetime Entertainment Services, 51
Lifetime Hoan Corporation, 27
Lifeway Foods, Inc., 65
Ligand Pharmaceuticals Incorporated, 47
Lillian Vernon Corporation, 12; 35 (upd.); 92 (upd.)
Lilly Endowment Inc., 70
The Limited, Inc., V; 20 (upd.)
LIN Broadcasting Corp., 9
Lincare Holdings Inc., 43
Lincoln Center for the Performing Arts, Inc., 69
Lincoln Electric Co., 13
Lincoln National Corporation, III; 25 (upd.)
Lincoln Property Company, 8; 54 (upd.)
Lincoln Snacks Company, 24
Lincoln Telephone & Telegraph Company, 14
Lindal Cedar Homes, Inc., 29
Lindsay Manufacturing Co., 20
Linear Technology Corporation, 16; 99 (upd.)
Linens 'n Things, Inc., 24; 75 (upd.)
Lintas: Worldwide, 14
The Lion Brewery, Inc., 86
Lionel L.L.C., 16; 99 (upd.)
Liqui-Box Corporation, 16
Liquidnet, Inc. 79
Litehouse Inc., 60
Lithia Motors, Inc., 41
Littelfuse, Inc., 26
Little Caesar Enterprises, Inc., 7; 24 (upd.)
Little Tikes Company, 13; 62 (upd.)
Littleton Coin Company Inc., 82
Litton Industries, Inc., I; 11 (upd.)
LIVE Entertainment Inc., 20
Live Nation, Inc., 80 (upd.)
LivePerson, Inc., 91
Liz Claiborne, Inc., 8; 25 (upd.)
LKQ Corporation, 71
Lockheed Martin Corporation, I; 11 (upd.); 15 (upd.); 89 (upd.)
Loctite Corporation, 8; 30 (upd.)
LodgeNet Entertainment Corporation, 28
Loehmann's Inc., 24
Loews Corporation, I; 12 (upd.); 36 (upd.); 93 (upd.)
Logan's Roadhouse, Inc., 29
Logicon Inc., 20
LoJack Corporation, 48
London Fog Industries, Inc., 29
Lone Star Steakhouse & Saloon, Inc., 51
The Long & Foster Companies, Inc., 85
Long Island Bancorp, Inc., 16
Long Island Lighting Company, V
The Long Island Rail Road Company, 68
Long John Silver's, 13; 57 (upd.)

The Longaberger Company, 12; 44 (upd.)
Longs Drug Stores Corporation, V; 25 (upd.); 83 (upd.)
Longview Fibre Company, 8; 37 (upd.)
Loos & Dilworth, Inc., 100
Loral Space & Communications Ltd., 8; 9; 54 (upd.)
Lost Arrow Inc., 22
LOT$OFF Corporation, 24
Lotus Development Corporation, 6; 25 (upd.)
LOUD Technologies, Inc., 95 (upd.)
The Louisiana Land and Exploration Company, 7
Louisiana-Pacific Corporation, IV; 31 (upd.)
Love's Travel Stops & Country Stores, Inc., 71
Lowe's Companies, Inc., V; 21 (upd.); 81 (upd.)
Lowrance Electronics, Inc., 18
LPA Holding Corporation, 81
LSB Industries, Inc., 77
LSI Logic Corporation, 13; 64
The LTV Corporation, I; 24 (upd.)
The Lubrizol Corporation, I; 30 (upd.); 83 (upd.)
Luby's, Inc., 17; 42 (upd.); 99 (upd.)
Lucasfilm Ltd., 12; 50 (upd.)
Lucent Technologies Inc., 34
Lucille Farms, Inc., 45
Lucky Stores, Inc., 27
Lufkin Industries Inc. 78
Luigino's, Inc., 64
Lukens Inc., 14
Lunar Corporation, 29
Lunardi's Super Market, Inc., 99
Lund Food Holdings, Inc., 22
Lund International Holdings, Inc., 40
Lutheran Brotherhood, 31
Lydall, Inc., 64
Lyman-Richey Corporation, 96
Lynch Corporation, 43
Lynden Incorporated, 91
Lyondell Chemical Company, IV; 45 (upd.)
M&F Worldwide Corp., 38
M. Shanken Communications, Inc., 50
M.A. Bruder & Sons, Inc., 56
M.A. Gedney Co., 51
M.A. Hanna Company, 8
M.H. Meyerson & Co., Inc., 46
Mac Frugal's Bargains - Closeouts Inc., 17
Mac-Gray Corporation, 44
MacAndrews & Forbes Holdings Inc., 28; 86 (upd.)
MacDermid Incorporated, 32
Mace Security International, Inc., 57
The Macerich Company, 57
MacGregor Golf Company, 68
Mack Trucks, Inc., I; 22 (upd.); 61 (upd.)
Mack-Cali Realty Corporation, 42
Mackay Envelope Corporation, 45
Mackie Designs Inc., 33
Macklowe Properties, Inc., 95
Macmillan, Inc., 7
MacNeil/Lehrer Productions, 87
The MacNeal-Schwendler Corporation, 25

Macromedia, Inc., 50
Macy's, Inc., 94 (upd.)
Madden's on Gull Lake, 52
Madison Dearborn Partners, LLC, 97
Madison Gas and Electric Company, 39
Madison-Kipp Corporation, 58
Mag Instrument, Inc., 67
MaggieMoo's International, 89
Magma Copper Company, 7
Magma Design Automation Inc. 78
Magma Power Company, 11
MagneTek, Inc., 15; 41 (upd.)
MAI Systems Corporation, 11
Maid-Rite Corporation, 62
Maidenform, Inc., 20; 59 (upd.)
Mail Boxes Etc., 18; 41 (upd.)
Mail-Well, Inc., 28
Make-A-Wish Foundation of America, 97
Maine & Maritimes Corporation, 56
Maine Central Railroad Company, 16
Maines Paper & Food Service Inc., 71
Majesco Entertainment Company, 85
The Major Automotive Companies, Inc., 45
Malcolm Pirnie, Inc., 42
Malden Mills Industries, Inc., 16
Mallinckrodt Group Inc., 19
Malt-O-Meal Company, 22; 63 (upd.)
Management and Training Corporation, 28
Manatron, Inc., 86
Mandalay Resort Group, 32 (upd.)
Manhattan Associates, Inc., 67
Manhattan Group, LLC, 80
Manheim, 88
The Manitowoc Company, Inc., 18; 59 (upd.)
Mannatech Inc., 33
Manning Selvage & Lee (MS&L), 76
MannKind Corporation, 87
Manor Care, Inc., 6; 25 (upd.)
Manpower Inc., 9; 30 (upd.); 73 (upd.)
ManTech International Corporation, 97
Manufactured Home Communities, Inc., 22
Manufacturers Hanover Corporation, II
Manville Corporation, III; 7 (upd.)
MAPCO Inc., IV
MAPICS, Inc., 55
Maple Grove Farms of Vermont, 88
Maples Industries, Inc., 83
Marble Slab Creamery, Inc., 87
March of Dimes, 31
Marchex, Inc., 72
marchFIRST, Inc., 34
Marco Business Products, Inc., 75
Marco's Franchising LLC, 86
The Marcus Corporation, 21
Marie Callender's Restaurant & Bakery, Inc., 28
Marine Products Corporation, 75
MarineMax, Inc., 30
Marion Laboratories, Inc., I
Marisa Christina, Inc., 15
Maritz Inc., 38
Mark IV Industries, Inc., 7; 28 (upd.)
Mark T. Wendell Tea Company, 94
The Mark Travel Corporation, 80